CHINA'S GREAT ECONOMIC TRANSFORMATION

This landmark study provides an integrated analysis of China's unexpected economic boom of the past three decades. The authors combine deep China expertise with broad disciplinary knowledge to explain China's remarkable mixture of high-speed growth and deeply flawed institutions. Their work exposes the mechanisms underpinning the origin and expansion of China's great boom. Penetrating studies track the rise of Chinese capabilities in manufacturing and in research and development. The authors probe both achievements and weaknesses across many sectors, including China's fiscal, legal, and financial institutions. The book shows how an intricate minuet combining China's political system with sectoral development, globalization, resource transfers across geographic and economic space, and partial system reform delivered an astonishing and unprecedented growth spurt. The volume chronicles many shortcomings, but concludes that China's economic expansion is likely to continue during the coming decades.

Loren Brandt is professor of economics at the University of Toronto, where he has been since 1987. Previously, he was at the Hoover Institution. Professor Brandt has published widely on China in leading economic journals and has been involved in extensive household and enterprise survey work in China. He is the author of *Commercialization and Agricultural Development: Central and Eastern China, 1870–1937* and was an area editor for the five-volume *Oxford Dictionary of Economic History*.

Thomas G. Rawski is professor of economics and history and UCIS research professor at the University of Pittsburgh. His work covers many dimensions of China's development and modern economic history, including books on *Economic Growth and Employment in China, China's Transition to Industrialism, Economic Growth in Prewar China, Chinese History in Economic Perspective, Economics and the Historian*, and *China's Rise and the Balance of Influence in Asia*.

China's Great Economic Transformation

Edited by

LOREN BRANDT
University of Toronto

THOMAS G. RAWSKI
University of Pittsburgh

CAMBRIDGE
UNIVERSITY PRESS

CAMBRIDGE UNIVERSITY PRESS
Cambridge, New York, Melbourne, Madrid, Cape Town, Singapore,
São Paulo, Delhi, Dubai, Tokyo

Cambridge University Press
32 Avenue of the Americas, New York, NY 10013-2473, USA

www.cambridge.org
Information on this title: www.cambridge.org/9780521712903

First published 2008
Reprinted 2009

Printed in the United States of America

A catalog record for this publication is available from the British Library.

Library of Congress Cataloging in Publication Data
China's great economic transformation / edited by Loren Brandt, Thomas G. Rawski.
p. cm.
Includes bibliographical references and index.
ISBN 978-0-521-88557-7 (hbk.) – ISBN 978-0-521-71290-3 (pbk.)
1. China – Economic conditions – 1976–2000. 2. China – Economic
conditions – 2000–   I. Brandt, Loren.   II. Rawski, Thomas G., 1943–   III. Title.
HC427.92.C46525   2008
330.951–dc22   2007027966

ISBN 978-0-521-88557-7 Hardback
ISBN 978-0-521-71290-3 Paperback

Contents

Figures

Tables

Contributors

Franklin Allen
University of Pennsylvania

Jere Behrman
University of Pennsylvania

Dwayne Benjamin
University of Toronto

Richard M. Bird
University of Toronto

Loren Brandt
University of Toronto

Lee Branstetter
Carnegie-Mellon University

Kimberly Burnett
University of Hawaii and University of Puget Sound

Fang Cai
Chinese Academy of Social Sciences

Kam Wing Chan
University of Washington

Donald Clarke
George Washington University Law School

John Giles
Michigan State University

Stephan Haggard
University of California – San Diego

Emily Hannum
University of Pennsylvania

J. Vernon Henderson
Brown University

Alan Heston
University of Pennsylvania

Chang-tai Hsieh
University of California – Berkeley

Albert G. Z. Hu
National University of Singapore

Jikun Huang
Chinese Academy of Sciences

Yasheng Huang
Massachusetts Institute of Technology

Gary H. Jefferson
Brandeis University

Nicholas R. Lardy
Peterson Institute for International Economics

Jihong Liu
University of South Carolina

Andrew Mason
University of Hawaii

Peter Murrell
University of Maryland

Barry Naughton
University of California – San Diego

Keijiro Otsuka
Foundation for Advanced Studies on International Development

Albert Park
Oxford University

Dwight H. Perkins
Harvard University

Jun Qian
Boston College

Meijun Qian
National University of Singapore

Thomas G. Rawski
University of Pittsburgh

James Roumasset
University of Hawaii

Scott Rozelle
Stanford University

Terry Sicular
University of Western Ontario

John Sutton
London School of Economics

Jan Svejnar
University of Michigan

Kai Yuen Tsui
Chinese University of Hong Kong

WANG Feng
University of California – Irvine

Hua Wang
World Bank

Meiyan Wang
Chinese Academy of Social Sciences

Sangui Wang
Renmin University

Christine P. W. Wong
Oxford University

Susan Whiting
University of Washington

Yaohui Zhao
Peking University

Xiaodong Zhu
University of Toronto

Acknowledgments

Many people and organizations contributed to advancing this project from our initial conversations to the results that fill the pages of this book. Yingyi Qian, Dwight Perkins, Jan Svejnar, and Arthur Waldron helped us to formulate a cohesive framework and present it in compelling language. Generous financing from the Smith Richardson Foundation, the National Science Foundation, the Chiang Ching-Kuo Foundation for International Scholarly Exchange, the University of Michigan's William Davidson Institute, the University of Toronto's Institute for International Business, and the Beijing Office of the Ford Foundation enabled us to turn dreams into realities. We also received extensive encouragement and assistance from the late Michael Berkowitz and Wendy Dobson at the University of Toronto and from William Brustein, George Klinzing, J. F. Richard, and Bell Yung at the University of Pittsburgh. Rawski's visiting appointment at the Institute for Advanced Study facilitated the completion of this book.

In addition to our large group of energetic and cooperative coauthors, many colleagues put their shoulders to our wheels. Carsten Holz, Eric Jones, Andrew Walder, and Daniel Berkowitz contributed fresh ideas and comments at conferences in Toronto and Pittsburgh. We particularly appreciate the patience and advice of Allan Song at the Smith Richardson Foundation; Alex DeAngelis, Mariann "Sam" Jelinek, and Dan Newlon at the National Science Foundation; and Sarah Cook and Butch Montes at the Ford Foundation. Special thanks to Dianne Dakis, Lauree Graham, Paula Riemer, and Haihui Zhang at the University of Pittsburgh and to Carol Brandt and Evelyn Rawski, who endured seven years of cluttered weekends and one side of endless phone consultations.

Loren Brandt and Thomas G. Rawski
September 2007

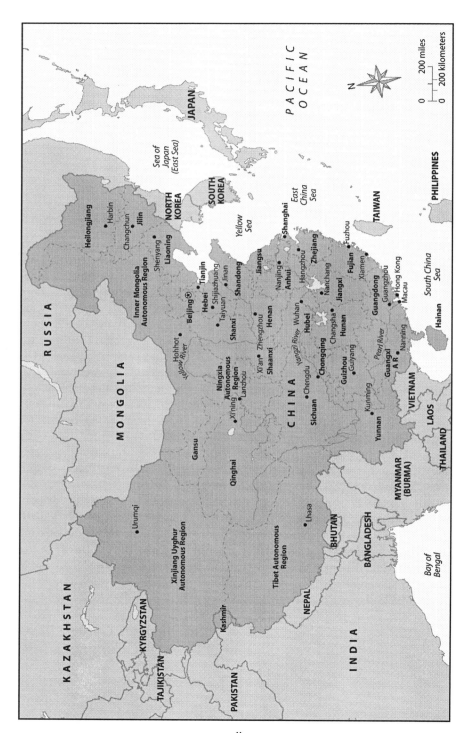

ONE

China's Great Economic Transformation

Loren Brandt and Thomas G. Rawski

In this book, a large and diverse group of researchers pool their knowledge to take the measure of China's massive, protracted, and unexpected economic upsurge, which began in the late 1970s and continues as this is written nearly thirty years later. The magnitude and rapidity of China's recent gains stand out even against the background of stunning growth among China's East Asian neighbors during the late twentieth century.

China's extended boom began at remarkably low levels of income and consumption. Its growth spurt is remarkable for its geographic spread as well as its speed and longevity. While coastal regions have led the upward march of output, exports, and income, China's central and western regions have recorded enormous gains as well.

A brief summary can delineate the magnitude of China's recent economic achievements. One careful review of available data finds that average gross domestic product (GDP) growth increased from approximately 4 percent prior to the reform to 9.5 percent during 1978–2005 (see Chapter 20). Although Young (2003) and others label recent growth as extensive, meaning that the main motive force comes from adding more labor and capital to the production process, the same study finds that productivity improvement accelerated from 0.5 to 3.8 percent per annum after the reform, with productivity change accounting for 40.1 percent of overall GDP growth during 1978–2005, as opposed to 11.4 percent during 1952–1978 and −13.4 percent (i.e., a productivity decline) during 1957–1978 (see Table 20.2).

Tables 1.1 and 1.2 use purchasing-power parity data from the Penn World Tables and the World Bank to compare trends in aggregate and per capita GDP for China and several other nations. Prior to 1978, China's overall output grew somewhat faster than GDP in the United States and India, but lagged dramatically behind Japanese performance. After 1978, rapid expansion in China's relative economic size became the norm, pushing Chinese output from 37.5 percent of Japan's 1978 figure to 219.2 percent of Japan's 2004 GDP, and so on (Table 1.1).

Table 1.2 shows similar trends in per capita GDP. Prior to reform, China recorded slight gains with regard to India and the United States, but lagged far behind Japan

1

Table 1.1. *China's GDP as percent of GDP for other large nations, 1978–2004[a]*

	1952	1978	1990	2000	2004
United States	9.5	13.6	27.9	51.7	64.0
Japan	78.5	38.5	70.5	165.9	219.2
Germany	n.a.	50.8	113.3	244.8	322.1
India	63.9	78.0	122.2	190.6	203.1[b]

[a] Calculated at purchasing-power parity.
[b] Based on data for 2003.
Source: Heston, Summers, and Aten (2006).

Table 1.2. *China's per capita GDP as a percent of figures for other nations, 1952–2005[a,b]*

	1952	1978	1990	2000	2005
United States	2.7	3.2	6.3	11.6	15.7
Japan	11.8	4.6	7.7	16.7	21.3
Korea	25.4[c]	15.0	16.4	25.5	30.1
India	42.6	53.7	90.3	151.4	188.5

[a] Measured at purchasing-power parity.
[b] Annual figure for each comparator nation equals 100.
[c] Figures refer to 1953.
Source: Data for 2005 are World Bank measures in current international dollars; data for earlier years are from Heston, Summers, and Aten (2006).

and Korea. After 1978, the picture changes dramatically, with Chinese per capita income doubling its level relative to that of Korea and achieving even faster growth relative to India, Japan, and the United States.

Rapid advance in output per capita has elevated hundreds of millions from absolute poverty. Ravallion and Chen (2004) report a steep decline in the proportion of rural Chinese mired in absolute poverty: using an early official poverty indicator, the share of impoverished villagers drops from 40.65 percent in 1980 to 10.55 percent in 1990 and 4.75 percent in 2001. A second indicator shows higher proportions living in absolute poverty, but indicates a comparable trend (75.7 percent impoverished in 1980 and 12.49 percent in 2001).

China's economy has abandoned its former isolation in favor of deep engagement with world markets. The trade ratio, which measures the combined value of exports and imports as a share of GDP, jumped from under 10 percent prior to reform to 22.9 percent in 1985, 38.7 percent in 1995, and 63.9 percent in 2005 – a level far higher than comparable figures for any other large and populous nation

(Compendium, 2005, pp. 9, 68; Yearbook, 2006, pp. 57, 733). China has also become a major player in the global market for foreign direct investment, receiving annual inflows in the neighborhood of U.S.$70 billion during 2004–2006 and generating moderate, but rapidly increasing, outflows of direct overseas investment (U.S.$16.1 billion in 2006) (Investment Surges, 2007; UNCTAD, 2007).

China's economic ascent rests on a series of gradual, often discontinuous, and continuing transitions. A massive exodus from the villages has reduced the farm sector's share of overall employment from 69 to 32 percent between 1978 and 2004, while the farm sector's GDP share fell by more than half (see Tables 13.6 and 17.1).

The slow retreat of planning has cumulated into a dominant role for market outcomes. Price determination, formerly concentrated in official hands, now reflects shifts in supply and demand. Data for 2000–2003 indicate an 87 percent share of market pricing (as opposed to prices that are fixed or guided by government) for "means of production"; comparable figures for farm products and consumer goods exceed 90 percent (Li, 2006, pp. 104–106).

Following a quarter century of liberalization, markets for products, labor, and materials are well developed and increasingly competitive. While investment decisions, capital markets, and transfer of ownership rights still bear the imprint of official preferences, the overall impact of market forces continues to deepen.

Despite the dominance of state ownership in finance, telecommunications, steel, petroleum, tobacco, and other important sectors of the economy, private entrepreneurs continue to push into sectors formerly reserved for public enterprise. The Organisation for Economic Co-operation and Development's estimates show the private sector, which scarcely existed at the start of reform, accounting for 59.2 percent of China's gross domestic product for 2003 (OECD, 2005, p. 125).

These momentous shifts, from poverty to growing prosperity, from village to city, from plan to market, from public toward private ownership, and from isolation to global engagement, form the backdrop for this book, which aims to develop an integrated perspective on these remarkable events. In recruiting and guiding our authors, we sought to focus attention on basic questions of long-term significance. How and why did China vault from the moderate growth attained during the plan era (roughly 1952–1978) onto a new path of explosive growth? Once begun, how was the new pace of growth maintained? How did rapid expansion spread across sectors and regions? How did particular sectors and regions contribute to the spurt? How have changing policy structures accelerated or hindered China's economy? What factors constrain China's current and future growth? The chapters that follow address these and many other issues from multiple perspectives. The present essay seeks to establish an analytical framework for examining China's economic evolution since the formation of the People's Republic in 1949.

BACKGROUND: CHINA'S ECONOMY PRIOR TO THE START
OF ECONOMIC REFORM

China's economy experienced modest, but significant, growth in the decades prior to the outbreak of full-scale war with Japan in 1937 (Brandt, 1989; Rawski, 1989). The pattern of pre-World War II economic advance reflected China's openness to international trade and investment. Prewar expansion clustered around two growth poles: the Yangzi Delta area centered on Shanghai, where thriving domestic and foreign private business propelled regional growth; and the northeastern provinces, where infusions of officially directed Japanese capital, technology, and expertise energized an expansion that prefigured the planned economy of the 1950s.

By the 1930s, China had developed a modern sector spanning industry, communications, transportation, banking, and finance, in which domestic ownership predominated. Although this nascent modern sector never surpassed one-tenth of GDP, its rapid development, along with China's growing integration with the international economy, had catalytic effects on agriculture and other sectors that pushed the economy toward modest gains in per capita GDP (Rawski, 1989). Before the collapse of international trade that followed the onset of the Great Depression, China's share of world trade and its own ratio of foreign trade to GDP achieved levels that were not regained for over sixty years (Lardy, 1994). These achievements look even more impressive when viewed in light of the limited capacity of the Chinese state to promote economic development.

Following disruptions arising from an eight-year battle against Japanese invaders, followed by several years of civil strife between Communist and Kuomintang forces, the People's Republic of China, established in October 1949, inherited an economy whose growth potential was obscured by the ravages of war and inflation. Successful application of orthodox macroeconomic policies quelled inflation, restored fiscal balance, revived the money economy, and encouraged a rapid economic revival (Perkins, 1966).

The new regime then moved to create an economic system largely modeled after Soviet experience. Soviet advisers and Soviet-trained specialists worked to establish new institutions organized around annual and five-year plans, extensive state ownership, central control over prices, and material balance plans that issued specific directives governing the allocation of major inputs, products, and financial flows. As in the USSR, the key plan objective was to raise domestic saving, particularly by extracting resources from the rural sector, and to channel these funds toward industrial growth.

China's system was not a carbon copy of the Soviet Union's. Mao Zedong broke new ground by herding Chinese villagers into large-scale collectives known as people's communes in 1958. In addition, management of Chinese industry was significantly less centralized than in the Soviet Union, with substantial authority vested in provincial and local plan bureaucracies (Wong, 1986). Despite these and other differences, the institutions of Chinese planning generated behavior characteristic of what came to be known as "Soviet-type" economies.

During the quarter century prior to the start of economic reform in the late 1970s, China's plan system delivered mixed results (Howe, 1978; Riskin, 1987; Naughton, 1995). Rising rates of saving and investment promoted economic growth, despite short-term disruptions associated with the Great Leap Forward of the late 1950s and the Cultural Revolution of the late 1960s. World Bank estimates covering 1950–1975, a period roughly coterminous with China's plan era, show that China recorded average annual growth of 4.2 percent in per capita GNP, a figure surpassed by only ten of seventy-seven nonindustrialized nations, most of them oil exporters. During these years, China's planned economy outperformed other populous developing nations, including Brazil, Egypt, India, Indonesia, and Mexico, often by substantial margins (Morawetz, 1978, pp. 19–21).

Large-scale technical aid from the socialist bloc helped China to introduce new industries, for example, the manufacture of trucks and equipment for power plants and telecommunications, and to upgrade others. In addition, urgent restructuring efforts necessitated by the downturn following the 1959–1961 famine and simultaneous withdrawal of East Bloc technical aid revealed new technological capabilities on the part of both old and new Chinese firms (Rawski, 1975, 1980).

China's plan system also delivered important gains in the creation of human capital. Mortality, especially among infants and new mothers, declined, and school attendance and educational attainment increased. Census data revealed an increase of slightly more than 50 percent in life expectancy from 42.2 (45.6) years in 1950 to 66.4 (69.4) years in 1982 for males (females). School enrollments increased at all levels; the spread of education reduced the proportion of Chinese aged 16–65, who had not completed primary school from 74 to 40 percent between 1952 and 1978 (see Tables 15.1 and 20.1; see also Chapter 7).

These important achievements coincided with significant failures, most obviously in the area of food supply. The man-made famine of 1959–1961 killed 30–40 million Chinese. Food scarcity did not end in 1961: average rural diets continued to fall short of basic nutrition standards until the start of reform. As a result, food supplies for millions of Chinese villagers were no better in the 1970s than in the 1930s (Lardy, 1983; Bramall, 1989; Rawski, 2006).

Material conditions were better for city dwellers, although they too experienced little improvement in the level of consumption or the variety of (often rationed) commodities after 1957. Urban residents received larger food allotments than villagers. They also benefited from privileged access to government-funded education, health care, housing, and pensions. Substantial differences in income and life chances favoring urban dwellers obliged the regime to curtail migration to the cities by reviving China's traditional system of household registration (*hukou*) and by instituting tight controls over the distribution of food grains, urban housing, and other consumer essentials (see Chapters 18 and 19).

Despite rising output, industry suffered from the inefficiencies associated with Soviet-style central planning: emphasis on quantity at the expense of quality and assortment, focus on investment goods rather than consumer products, neglect of innovation and customer requirements, excessive vertical integration, plan-related seasonal fluctuations in output and investment, and large inventory accumulations (Rawski, 1980).

Underdevelopment of services exacerbated these weaknesses. Neglect of services follows Marxist theory, which omits most tertiary activities from the national accounts. China's intermittent campaigns targeting intellectuals, including a decade-long closure of universities and many other schools during the Cultural Revolution, intensified the relative decline of services. By the end of the plan period, education-linked wage differentials had largely vanished: one study noted that average pay levels in the catering sector exceeded wages in higher education (Hou, 1999, pp. 184–185).

China's isolation from the international economy further enlarged the gap between achievement and potential. The combination of Beijing's autarchic tendencies and a U.S.-led partial trade embargo constricted Chinese participation in global markets (Eckstein, 1966; Lardy, 1994; see Chapter 16). This deprived Chinese producers of valuable information, removed Chinese firms from the discipline and goad of international competition, and skewed domestic output away from the mix associated with comparative advantage. Official efforts to limit domestic as well as international specialization heightened the resulting barriers to the growth of output and productivity (Donnithorne, 1972; Lardy, 1983).

Macroeconomic statistics for 1952–1978 demonstrate the impact of these shortcomings. During this period, China's economy benefited from a wide array of favorable circumstances, including improved technology, rising education levels, low inflation, and, with notable exceptions, domestic political stability. Although each of these factors should contribute to higher productivity, available data show no substantial upward trend for multifactor productivity (meaning output per unit of combined capital and education-enhanced labor) during the plan period (see Table 20.2). In reality, productivity might have declined, which would help to reconcile the failure of rising investment rates during the 1960s and 1970s to accelerate GDP growth (Field, 1983; Ishikawa, 1983).

A quarter century of socialist planning left China's economy riddled with multiple inefficiencies. Market segmentation between the rural and urban sectors, barriers to economic flows across administrative boundaries, and differentials in the marginal productivity of capital and labor between farming and nonagriculture, between private and collective plots, and between producer and consumer manufactures all pointed to large-scale misdirection of resources, a sure sign of static inefficiency. The economy also suffered from wide and persistent gaps between actual and potential output – what economists call "X-inefficiency." Widespread shirking limited productivity in both agriculture and industry.

Planners typically classify outcomes as satisfactory or unsatisfactory. In the absence of special recognition or reward for improvements in quality, variety, cost, or productivity, advances in these areas become uncompensated gifts from producers, who bear the expenses and risks linked to upgrading efforts. Without direct intervention by political leaders ("innovation by order"), innovative effort is shunted aside in favor of pursuing short-term targets for physical output ("fulfilling the plan"). The result is a general failure of dynamic efficiency, as the expansion of society's production frontier lags behind the potential embodied in available knowledge and resources. The consequences are readily visible within individual firms, as when First Auto Works, one of China's premier manufacturers, found its "obsolescence of equipment and models worsening day by day" following "thirty years of standing still" (Li, 1993, p. 83), and also at the macroeconomic level.

We see three underlying sources of productivity stagnation and rampant inefficiency in China's planned economy: noneconomic policy objectives, weak institutions, and poor incentives.

Although China's leaders valued material progress, considerations of national defense and ideology frequently trumped economics during the plan era, with predictably negative effects on output and productivity. Security considerations, for example, dictated the movement of factories from coastal cities to interior regions during the 1950s. Fear of external attack also inspired the "Third Front" policy of the 1960s, which poured massive investments into remote regions (Naughton, 1988). In similar fashion, the pursuit of ideological objectives imposed economic costs, as when schools were closed and urban youths were forced to migrate to rural villages or when small-scale commerce was curtailed to protect citizens from the supposed evils of capitalism's "silver bullets."

The plan system's hostility to entrepreneurship enforces uniformities that inflate firm-level rigidities into economywide excesses. In a market system, if firms cannot obtain repair services in December, entrepreneurs may seek to profit by addressing this gap. But planning earmarks investment funds for specific projects and concentrates research activity in government institutes (which in China often neglected applied studies that could offer immediate support to manufacturing operations), leaving few opportunities for such reactive improvisations. Similar obstacles bedevil innovative efforts within existing enterprises. In the absence of high-level patronage, managers find it difficult to justify the expense, delay, and failure associated with efforts to develop new products and processes.

Weak incentives compound these difficulties. In a market system, individuals and enterprises can expand sales and improve financial outcomes by outdoing rivals in satisfying old and new customers. Under the plan, with both the volume and the direction of sales mandated by official fiat, producers experience neither the opportunity to expand through their own initiative nor the threat of being eclipsed by rival suppliers. As a result, plan systems fail to generate the automatic, decentralized pressure for improvement that suffuses all market systems.

Everyone recognized the death of Mao Zedong in 1976 as a major turning point for the People's Republic. There was wide agreement among China's political elite about the need for economic change, without, as Naughton (see Chapter 4) observes, any clear sense of reform direction. Two economic issues stood behind this consensus. Although China's economy had performed well compared to low-income nations worldwide, China's standing within East Asia was weak. Japan and (South) Korea, societies that many Chinese regard with disdain, had raced far ahead, as had Taiwan and Hong Kong, small entities crowded with refugees from the People's Republic and, in Taiwan's case, led by Chiang Kai-shek's reviled Kuomintang. China's obvious backwardness in its dynamic East Asian neighborhood galled Beijing's elites.

More specifically, the winding down of the Cultural Revolution disruptions failed to resolve chronic food supply problems. During the first half of the 1970s, rising numbers of grain-deficit households, reductions in grain stocks and in cross-provincial shipments, numerous reports of local shortages, and demands that the state return grain procurements to avoid "repeating the error of 1959" – an obvious reference to the Great Leap Forward famine – all point to a system near the brink of a serious food crisis, with no indication of sustained progress (Zhao, 1988, pp. 144–147).

With this background, it is not surprising that the story of China's reforms begins in the farm sector. There was a long history of poor results, with the danger of renewed crisis lurking in the background. The chief mechanism of reform – the restoration of household cultivation – had a proven track record from the 1960s. Protracted policy neglect of the farm sector meant that rural reform would not threaten important political constituencies (Pei, 2006, p. 31; see Chapter 4).

KEY FACTORS IN CHINA'S REFORM SUCCESS

Whatever its merits, China's plan system saddled the economy with costly defects, some inevitable in any plan system, others peculiar to the Chinese variant, that constrained China's economy to a path that delivered modest gains at best and indubitably failed to satisfy Chinese ambitions. In economic terms, Chinese socialism held the economy far below its production frontier while severely restraining the frontier's outward movement. In Japan, a similar knowledge gap combined with a shift from military to civilian production fueled a burst of catch-up growth beginning in the 1950s (Ohkawa and Rosovsky, 1973). China's bleak circumstances of the late 1970s concealed similar possibilities.

In the presence of large gaps between current and potential output, and of neglected opportunities to expand the production frontier, limited reform that even partially ruptures the shackles surrounding incentives, marketing, mobility, competition, price flexibility, and innovation may accelerate growth. Begin with an economy operating well below its potential, partly because its labor force, perceiving that effort hardly affects their incomes, withholds a substantial fraction of its available energy (which itself is reduced by chronic undernutrition). Now restore the link between effort and reward, permit a partial market revival, and open the door to experimentation with international trade and investment. Without the disruptive changes in trade flows and political structures that accompanied early reform efforts in the former Soviet Union and Eastern Europe, such simple initiatives – which approximate the circumstances of China's early reforms – can readily ignite a burst of growth, even if prices, financial institutions, judicial enforcement, policy transparency, corporate governance, and many other features of the economy remain far removed from ideal arrangements.

China's reform experience powerfully confirms the insights of Hollis Chenery, who insisted that pinpointing and then ameliorating key obstacles could accelerate growth in the absence of conditions that are widely seen as essential for development (e.g., Chenery and Strout, 1966; Chenery and Syrquin, 1975). Chinese evidence encourages us to think of a hierarchy of desirable features that support growth or, if absent, hinder it. These growth-enhancing conditions are not equally important. In China, partial measures affecting incentives, prices, mobility, and competition – what we might term "big reforms" – created powerful momentum, which easily dominated the friction and drag arising from a host of "smaller" inefficiencies associated with price distortions, imperfect markets, institutional shortcomings, and other defects that retarded growth and increased its cost but never threatened to stall the ongoing boom.

Early initiatives in the farm sector illustrate the impact of limited reforms affecting incentives and mobility. Household cultivation replaced collective farming, as hundreds of millions voted with their feet to abandon the central feature of the people's communes. The shift to household cultivation meant that farmers could claim the fruits of extra effort for themselves, rather than receiving tiny shares of collective production. The restoration of household farming immediately reinstated the link between effort and reward throughout rural China. The resulting multiplication of work effort resulting from better incentives and, once output expanded, higher energy levels (a factor that figures prominently in historical studies by Nobel Laureate Robert Fogel, 2004) raised farm labor productivity so rapidly that millions of villagers began looking for outside employment. Substantial increases in official purchase prices, especially for grain, added to the rewards from extra effort.

With new incentives spurring work effort, farm output jumped quickly, even though the post-reform rural environment retained important elements of the planned economy. With the state firmly in control of major crop prices, trading networks, and fertilizer supplies, the reformed farm sector actually embodied fewer "free market" characteristics than Chinese agriculture of the early 1950s, not to mention the full market system of the 1920s and 1930s. But despite the rigidities and distortions associated with government control, a "big reform" affecting incentives created sufficient momentum to jump-start China's lethargic rural economy.

The response to early rural reforms quickly spread beyond the farm sector. Rural factories had enjoyed a brief boom during the Great Leap Forward, suffered a considerable retrenchment during the 1960s, and then expanded rapidly during the 1970s. Following the revival of agriculture, rural industry, now fortified by greater access to the cities, rising incomes among potential rural customers, increased supplies of agricultural inputs, and throngs of eager job seekers, bounded ahead with renewed vigor. The resulting shift of employment from farming toward rural industry began the continuing exodus from farming that Brandt, Hsieh, and Zhu identify as an important component of economywide productivity change during the early reform years (see Chapter 17).

Encouraged by the explosive response to partial reform of the rural economy, officials pressed ahead with urban reform efforts focused on improving the performance of state-owned industry. Early urban reforms achieved only limited progress toward their main objective of "enlivening" state-owned enterprises (SOEs). They did, however, contribute to the expansion of rural industry and urban collective enterprises by opening new markets as well as new sources of materials, subcontracting opportunities, and technical expertise.

A unique policy innovation was instrumental in spurring the development of urban and rural collective industry as well as increasing market awareness and efficiency within the state sector (Li, 1997). Rather than eliminate plan allocations at official prices, China's reformers created a dual price system that split transactions for most commodities into plan and market components. Once producers had satisfied plan requirements, they could now distribute after-plan residuals at increasingly flexible prices. This novel initiative thrust market forces into the economic lives of all Chinese households and businesses. Furthermore, this landmark change avoided the economic or political earthquakes associated with privatization (which threatens people's livelihood) or full liberalization of prices (which eliminates long-standing subsidies and undercuts the authority of plan agencies). The arrival of dual pricing instantly recast the plan system as a vast array of taxes and subsidies, recalling Paul Samuelson's observation that the efficiency consequences of pure competition survive the imposition of a lump-sum tax-subsidy regime (Samuelson, 1954; Sicular, 1988).

This novel arrangement reversed two central shortcomings of the plan system: rigid prices and neglect of innovation. Participants in China's economy – including the large SOEs at the core of the plan system – now faced a new world in which market prices governed the outcome of marginal decisions to sell above-plan output or purchase materials and equipment. Despite the continuation of subsidies and price controls, the high market price of coal, for example, signaled the likely future direction of price change and motivated users to plan accordingly.

Dual pricing opened the door to what Naughton (1995) has dubbed "growing out of the plan," in which directing incremental output toward market allocation gradually reduces the importance of the plan sector without a political struggle. As noted earlier, incremental marketization cumulated into a dominant role for market outcomes. It also spurred the expansion of market integration: farm gate prices, for example, now display a high degree of interregional integration (see Chapter 13).

By the turn of the century, notwithstanding significant exceptions associated with the pricing of credit, risk, and foreign exchange, supply and demand had emerged as the main arbiters of prices throughout the Chinese economy.

Expanded, but still incomplete, price flexibility also facilitated the ongoing process of whittling away at barriers to mobility, which had restricted the transfer of labor, capital, commodities, and ideas across administrative boundaries under the plan system. The essays on labor, agriculture, structure, and spatial economy (see Chapters 6, 13, 17, and 19) emphasize the costs associated with these obstacles. The *hukou* system of residential permits offered the largest hindrance to mobility, curtailing productivity-enhancing transfer of workers out of agriculture and stunting the growth of urban service occupations. Additional restrictions arose from campaigns promoting local and regional "self-reliance," which rolled back regional economic specialization, forcing many localities to relive the income-destroying experience of the 1940s by abandoning specialty crops (Shandong peanuts and Guangdong sugar) in favor of low-productivity subsistence farming.

Dual pricing enlarged markets that provided opportunities for entrepreneurs to purchase materials and equipment, manufacture (mostly consumer) products newly in demand or neglected by the plan system, and sell them profitably. The same markets allowed rural migrants to pursue employment opportunities, first in nearby towns and later in distant cities, where they could now use cash to purchase food and other essentials formerly available only to holders of location-specific ration coupons.

Market-oriented price reform and partial removal of restrictions that had prevented households and enterprises from seeking advantage from price gaps and changing prices provided a major impetus for accelerated growth. Although reform did not eliminate price distortions or barriers to the mobility of people and goods, the beneficial consequences of allowing people to respond to price signals were enormous. Villagers needed no precise calculation to see that they could raise their incomes by taking up nonfarm occupations; several hundred million recognized the opportunity and made the choice. Erosion of long-standing prohibitions against development of the tertiary sector produced an explosion of new activity involving restaurants, retail outlets, private schools, and a vast array of other activities. Here again, tens of millions responded to price signals that, however imprecise, indubitably reflected underlying resource scarcities.

As the influence of markets, price flexibility, and mobility expanded within the domestic economy, a separate strand of reform began to move China's isolated system toward greater participation in international trade and investment. During the late 1970s, an abortive plan to expand imports under the short-lived regime of Hua Guofeng revealed huge latent demand for foreign equipment and technology (Riskin, 1987, pp. 259–261). In the ensuing debates, China's leaders agreed to establish four tiny "special economic zones" in the southern provinces of Guangdong and Fujian. Initial operations in these zones seemed directionless and inconsequential, but the arrival of ethnic Chinese entrepreneurs, mostly from Hong

Kong and Taiwan, turned the zones into drivers of regional and eventually national growth.

Beginning in the late 1950s, Taiwan and Hong Kong had emerged as centers for small-scale manufacturing of labor-intensive exports. Rapid expansion raised land and labor costs, leading owners to search for new venues. The opening of south China provided an ideal opportunity for the Hong Kong and Taiwan entrepreneurs; it was also a remarkable stroke of luck for China's nascent reforms. The offshore entrepreneurs uncoupled the pipeline they had established to world markets from their original home bases and reconnected it to China's new export zones.

This novel combination of Chinese venues and low-cost Chinese labor with the market knowledge and entrepreneurial capabilities of overseas Chinese business-men gradually developed into an export bonanza that nudged China toward its current embrace of economic globalization. The unprecedented confluence of ris-ing farm output and rising exports removed long-standing constraints formerly imposed by limited availability of food and foreign exchange.

The limited extent of reform initially restricted the domestic response to grow-ing openness. Large-scale reallocation of cultivated acreage from staple crops to vegetables, horticulture, and other labor-intensive alternatives, for example, came only after the government ended its policy of setting domestic grain prices above world market levels. Even so, the buoyant prosperity of the new zones, particu-larly Shenzhen, prompted cities along the coast and eventually across the nation to clamor for access to the tax, legal, and regulatory concessions that had powered their growth.

The boom in trade and export-related production established a new growth pat-tern that shifted the leading edge of Chinese growth southward. As with California in the United States, novel economic (e.g., mass privatization of collectively owned rural industry) or social (e.g., voluntary rather than compulsory blood donation) behavior often spread across the nation from Guangdong.

China's progression from near-isolation to extensive openness to international trade and investment added a new dimension to economic growth. Access to com-modities, information, and trade opportunities linked to international markets expanded steadily from the tiny initial base as the number of special zones and open cities rose and as the scope of permissible activity stretched to encompass direct foreign investment along with import–export trade. Rapid expansion of overseas study, international travel, and publication of information from abroad (including abundant translations) multiplied the points of contact between the domestic and global economies, as did the easy interchange with overseas Chinese entrepreneurs, tourists, and kinfolk.

Case studies demonstrate the contribution of imported technology, equipment, and expertise to industrial upgrading (see Chapter 15). The emergence of foreign-linked joint ventures, and eventually of wholly owned foreign firms, as major elements of China's economy brought millions of Chinese workers, engineers, and managers into direct contact with the technical standards, engineering processes, and management practices needed to compete in global markets. The expansion of supply networks linked to export production or to foreign-owned businesses connected increasing numbers of purely domestic operators with international standards and practices. Growing foreign presence has consistently strengthened the demand for new reform initiatives, for instance, allowing firms to recruit employees through public advertisements (during the 1980s) or establishing a legal foundation for equipment leasing (during the 1990s).

From an initial position of extreme isolation, China has now attained a degree of openness that is unprecedented among large and populous nations (see Chapter 16; Brandt, Rawski, and Zhu, 2007). With few sectors of the economy effectively shielded from global markets, incumbent suppliers of soybeans, machine tools, retail services, and an endless array of other goods now confront the entry of rival producers from America, Italy, Japan, Bangladesh, or Brazil as well as Jilin, Zhejiang, or Sichuan. The resulting expansion of both dangers and opportunities has delivered enormous benefits. New export industries have raised the productivity and incomes of millions while accelerating the historic shift of labor from the farm sector. Imports have expanded consumer choice, contributed to the development of new industries and the improvement of old sectors, and pushed Chinese suppliers to raise standards and reduce costs. Foreign investment has injected immense flows of technology – for organization, management, and marketing as well as production – into China's economy.

China's reform era coincided with a new stage of globalization powered by rapid reductions in the cost of transport, communication, and information management. As a result, international markets have provided China with opportunities (and also risks) that far exceed those available at the time of Japan's and Korea's big growth spurts. This makes China an important test case for the hotly debated proposition that globalization offers important benefits to poor countries and to low-income groups in these nations. China's experience to date powerfully supports the view of globalization as an engine for growth and prosperity. The open-door policy has tilted China's whole economy toward labor-intensive production, hugely benefiting the mass of Chinese workers whose labor is their chief asset. By rewarding firms that raise quality standards toward global levels and punishing laggards, foreign trade and investment have motivated Chinese firms to abandon long-standing neglect of quality in favor of a broad-based upgrading effort that has enabled a growing array of Chinese products to compete in overseas as well as domestic markets.

Dramatic expansion of incentives, mobility, and markets created unprecedented opportunities for the formation of new enterprises and the expansion of existing firms (including foreign companies) into new markets. The scale of entry is startling: the number of industrial firms rose from 377.3 thousand in 1980 to nearly 8 million in 1990 and 1996; the 2004 economic census, which excluded enterprises with annual sales below RMB5 million, counted 1.33 million manufacturing firms, with Jiangsu and Zhejiang alone reporting more firms than the nationwide total for 1980 (Jefferson and Rawski, 1999, p. 25; Economic Census, 2004, 1, pp. 2, 23);

the number of enterprises in construction jumped from 6,604 to 58,750 between 1980 and 2005, with the latter total excluding subcontractors (Yearbook, 2006, p. 579).

The combination of entry and new flexibility has intensified competition within China's economy. Competition is in many ways the opposite of planning, which attempts to reduce economic uncertainty by pairing suppliers with customers and specifying the nature of future transactions. Under competition, such links arise as unpredictable results of decentralized selection. Unlike the plan system, which promotes uniformity of financial results across enterprises, competition promises widely varying outcomes, with winners receiving fat rewards and losers facing bankruptcy and unemployment. The power of competition arises from the lure of riches and the fear of oblivion, which motivate both prominent and obscure producers to scramble for advantage with a degree of intensity that plan systems rarely match.

Chapters 15, 16, and 19 summarize ongoing debate over the extent of competition and market integration. In our view, reform has pushed China's economy toward extraordinarily high levels of competition. Despite pockets of monopoly and episodic local trade barriers, intense competition now pervades everyday economic life. The auto sector provides a perfect illustration: two decades of competition have sucked a lethargic state-run oligopoly into a whirlwind of rivalries in which upstarts like Chery and Geely wrestle for market share with state-sector heavyweights and global titans. The payoff – rapid expansion of production, quality, variety, and productivity along with galloping price reductions – has injected a dynamic new sector (not just manufacture of vehicles, components, and materials, but also auto dealers, service stations, parking facilities, car racing, publications, motels, tourism, etc.) into China's economy.

Price wars and advertising, two unmistakable signs of competition, have become commonplace. Expenditures on advertising in 2006, estimated at RMB386.6 billion, now match total urban retail sales for 1990 (Advertising, 2006; Yearbook, 2006, p. 678). The decline of former industry leaders like Panda (televisions) and Kelon (home appliances) and the ascent of new pacesetters like Wahaha (beverages), Wanxiang (auto parts), and Haier (home appliances) from obscure beginnings show that competition has added new fluidity to Chinese market structures.

The growth of markets and the expansion of competition, mobility, and price flexibility invite participants to pursue financial gain by capitalizing on market opportunities. The strong response from both households and firms boosted economic performance, demonstrating the vitality of Adam Smith's "invisible hand" argument linking self-interested behavior with social benefits. Government agencies and political leaders also respond to reform-induced economic change, leading to a complex web of interaction between reform initiatives, economic developments, policy responses, and political strategies.

Mass migration now thought to involve 150–200 million persons epitomizes the impact of economic reform on household behavior. The demand for schooling illustrates another dimension of household responsiveness, in this case to the rising wage premium for workers with superior educational attainment (see Chapter 6). China's socialist period witnessed episodic vilification of intellectuals, who were denounced as a "stinking ninth category"; as noted earlier, education-related wage differentials shriveled during the 1960s and 1970s. Once the reform began, households, sensing new economic benefits for educated workers (and also reflecting historic cultural preferences), opted en masse to prolong their children's education despite policy changes that increased the share of costs paid by students and their families (see Chapter 7). Although China's public and private outlays on education may be too small (Heckman, 2005; Fleisher, Hu, and Li, 2006) or inappropriately tilted toward higher education, such marginal distortions represent second-order concerns. The main point is that the price system, however flawed, now provides Chinese households with sufficient information about wages and schooling costs to elicit sensible choices that expand human capital and improve future prospects for individual households and for the entire nation.

After hearing the head of a Shanghai factory explain his work, a visitor asked, "[S]o you just sit there and wait for instructions?" To which the director responded, "[Y]es, that's our job. The upper level issues plans, and we implement them." The manager of another Shanghai plant insisted that he had no information about the unit cost of the sewing machines produced on his assembly line. These episodes, which occurred in 1975 and 1982, would be impossible today, because Chinese firms have evolved from bureaucratic appendages to commercial operators that seek to enlarge strengths, remedy weaknesses, and capitalize on market opportunities.

Two recent developments have strengthened the responsiveness of Chinese firms. One is the growth of R&D spending, which reached 1.4 percent of GDP in 2006, and the shift of R&D activity from government agencies to enterprises, including many outside the state sector (see Chapter 9). The second is the growing influence of foreign firms, which elevates the risks associated with standpat business strategies, but also supports the efforts of domestic firms to generate a dynamic response to intense competition.

The auto sector provides an apt illustration: the rising domestic market shares and export achievements of Chery, Geely, Wanxiang, Fuyao, and other manufacturers of vehicles and components depend on interaction with foreign firms (e.g., for design services) and especially on access to the domestic supply networks established by the foreign partners of China's large-scale auto manufacturers.

The rapidity with which large and small innovations now migrate to China – e-commerce, text messaging, health clubs, organic foods, environmental awareness, flat-screen televisions, and so on – demonstrates the vitality of entrepreneurship in China's business sector. The current rush of international firms to establish China-based research and design facilities can only strengthen China's capacity for decentralized innovation – a hallmark of market systems.

KEY ELEMENTS IN THE POLITICAL ECONOMY OF CHINESE REFORM

We have discussed the key constituents of reform within China's economy, but what of the policy process associated with these extraordinary changes? Despite the authoritarian nature of China's political system, pre-reform policy structures allowed widespread experimentation and regional variation within broad guidelines set by the central leadership. This encouraged local officials to develop strategies whose success might attract high-level attention and also allowed national leaders to "play to the provinces" (Shirk, 1993) by assembling coalitions of like-minded officials to demonstrate the merits of their preferred policy options and to lobby for nationwide implementation of those policies.

This arrangement, under which national policies emphasized broad principles or parameters rather than specific instructions or regulations, continued into the reform period. What changed is the content of the principles articulated at the center, formerly directed toward ideological matters, which now focused increasingly on issues surrounding economic growth.

Looking beyond the principles emanating from the top, we see three additional elements as completing the skeleton of China's reformist political economy. *Decentralization* endows provinces and localities with both the resources and the incentives to experiment with local approaches to specific policies (e.g., rural industrialization) and difficulties (e.g., how to deal with redundant state-sector workers), provided they observe central guidelines. *Competition* within the political system is not new, but now focuses with growing intensity on economic outcomes, which exercise increasing leverage over the career paths of leaders at every level. Continued promotion and recruitment of leaders whose reputation and career prospects rest on past and future economic success has gradually created a large and expanding *coalition among growth-minded, market-oriented individuals and groups* within China's policy elite, whose power and influence help to shift the content of central guidelines in the direction of market outcomes.

Broad Guidelines – What They Can and Cannot Do

Chinese tradition emphasizes government of men (and, beginning in the late twentieth century, some women) rather than laws. There is no Chinese counterpart to the U.S. Federal Register, with its endless minute prescriptions. In the absence of detailed instructions, how do China's top leaders direct the behavior of lower-level governments and individual officials? Functionaries at all levels must study and discuss the speeches and writings of top leaders, which lay out the desired course of public policy and explain what lower levels of officialdom should and should not do. These guidelines become encapsulated in catchy slogans that gain wide currency in official circles and also among the Chinese public. These slogans, and the policy guidelines that inform them, direct the flow of policy implementation at all levels. They tell both leaders and followers what to do and what to avoid.

From the start of China's reform in the late 1970s, these directives increasingly emphasized economic matters. Indeed, China's political economy has come to rest on a grand but unspoken bargain between the Communist Party and the Chinese public, in which the party ensures economic growth and promotes China's global standing in return for public acquiescence to its autocratic rule and anachronistic ideology (Keller and Rawski, 2007). As a result, the articulation and fulfillment of key economic objectives now constitute core ingredients in extending the political legitimacy of the Chinese state. All Chinese officials and citizens learn about these publications, speeches, and slogans, which are not confined to internal government documents or the national press but reverberate at every level of society, where they become benchmarks against which the public can measure the propriety of current or proposed actions. Every Chinese knows Deng Xiaoping's maxim "let some people get rich first." Deng's praise of reform during his southern tour of 1992 was widely seen as a favorable signal for policy innovations, including many that received no specific mention from Mr. Deng. In similar fashion, emphasis on (or omission of) praise for "small and medium enterprises" or "enterprise restructuring" will be interpreted as high-level encouragement of (or caution against) policies favoring private business or accelerated privatization of state enterprises.

Decentralized Experimentation

Twentieth-century experience surely qualifies the Chinese as the world's leading practitioners of economic experimentation. China's reform economy amply displays this penchant for experimentation at every level. We see the national government conducting trials of novel institutions, for example, "special economic zones," while provinces and localities develop their own variations of the household responsibility system, township and village industries, the *xiagang* system of removing redundant workers from the state enterprise payrolls, and so on.

The decentralization of industry, which placed all but the largest enterprises under the control of lower-level governments, and China's fiscal system, which, especially prior to the 1994 fiscal reforms, assigned major revenue streams to provincial and local administrations in both cities and the countryside (see Chapter 12), provided regional and local governments with ample resources with which to pursue such experimentation.

Successful experimentation can raise the visibility (and accelerate the career paths) of local leaders, who might become famous for their role in developing the "Wenzhou model" or the "Sunan model" of development. National leaders regularly conduct inspection tours in search of local experiments that demonstrate the merits of their own preferred policies and also to expand networks of supporters.

Political Competition

Prior to the inception of reform, China developed a tradition of policy entrepreneurship in which local figures compete for high-level attention by demonstrating the beneficial implementation of the principles enshrined in broad central directives. This competition intensified under the reform, with GDP growth, exports, inflow of foreign investment, and other economic criteria replacing ideological benchmarks as the arbiters of success. Thus Li and Zhou (2005) find that promotion prospects for provincial leaders rise, and the likelihood of termination declines as provincial economic performance improves. Whiting (2001) makes similar observations about local officials.

Officials at all levels possess the authority as well as the resources needed to promote local growth. They also have strong incentives to do so, because their career prospects, as well as personal financial opportunities for themselves and their families, friends, and supporters, are closely tied to the economic trajectory of the jurisdictions under their leadership. Rapid local growth pushes local leaders to the head of the queues awaiting recognition, promotion, and bonuses. Growth also expands the pools of public revenue and enterprise profits over which officials exercise varying degrees of control, enlarges business opportunities available to the families and associates of local leaders, and swells the flow of (legal and illicit) rents directed toward official agencies and their managers.

These circumstances have transformed China's local and provincial governments into eager champions of development, each striving to outdo its neighbors and rivals in expanding airports, highways, science parks, and telecommunications and in establishing firm foundations for local "pillar industries." This competition contributes mightily to the persistent "investment hunger" visible in China's economy, as local administrations resist central calls for restraint in enlarging existing facilities and building new ones.

This drive to excel in growthmanship, which has become embedded in government behavior at every level, distinguishes Chinese public administration from the conduct of (especially) local governments in many low-income nations, where local administrations often pay greater attention to supporting local elites or to extracting income from existing economic structures than to promoting growth.

Pro-Growth Coalition

China's reform leaders, like politicians everywhere, endeavor to appoint and promote like-minded successors and subordinates. As Shirk (1993) and others have noted, the reform movement's initial successes acted as a powerful recruiting device, with the lure of rich payoffs adding many influential converts to the cause of reform. As the reform gained momentum, the circulation of elites, including the recruitment or assignment of officials from high growth to less dynamic regions for the express purpose of jump-starting growth, created mentor–student relationships between growth-oriented officials and increased the number of would-be imitators. The widespread practice of sending study teams to absorb the "advanced experiences" of Shenzhen, Hangzhou, and other dynamic localities further expanded the reform constituency among China's policy elites.

Of particular importance is the legacy of the Cultural Revolution, which severely truncated the educational opportunities available to whole cohorts of Chinese. This historical accident created a unique opportunity to advance the reform agenda. When the retirement of Deng Xiaoping and other "revolutionary elders" focused attention on generational change, reformist leaders managed to bypass the customary emphasis on seniority, skipping the "lost generation" of Cultural Revolution victims to promote younger candidates. Widespread replacement of 70-year-old retirees with much younger successors boosted reform advocacy in both government and party. The increasing share of university graduates, including returnees from overseas study and young professionals with close ties to international business, accelerated the development of what became a loose and unorganized but increasingly potent coalition of like-minded officials whose objectives centered on growth-promoting and increasingly market-oriented reforms.

Despite these gains, the evolution of policy toward private business demonstrates the difficulty of translating power and influence into genuine institutional change. Although China's reform quickly removed barriers to the existence of private business, Haggard and Huang (see Chapter 10) observe no steady increase in official encouragement and support for the private sector; indeed, they find that such support actually eroded during the 1990s.

Legal documents confirm the painfully slow expansion of official protection. At the start of reform, private business operated in a legal limbo. Some entrepreneurs disguised their firms as collectives, thus gaining the shelter of a "red hat" that falsely signified public rather than private ownership; others purchased informal protection from powerful individuals or agencies. A succession of amendments to China's 1982 constitution slowly expanded recognition of the nonpublic economy, first as a "complement" to the state sector (1988) and then as an "important component" (1999) of the "socialist market economy" (itself a new term dating from 1993). The "Law on Solely Funded Enterprises," which took effect in 2000, guarantees state protection for the "legitimate property" of such firms, but without using the term "private" or specifying any agency or process to implement this guarantee.

Further constitutional amendments adopted in 2004 breached the former taboo on the term "private" by stating that "citizens' lawful private property is inviolable." The long march toward official recognition of private business came to an end only in 2007 when, following five years of fierce debate, China's legislature enacted a landmark Law on Property Rights which, for the first time, explicitly places privately held assets on an equal footing with state and collective property.

China's treatment of the state-owned sector has followed a comparable path of slow progress cumulating in revolutionary change. In 1978, the state sector accounted for 77.6 percent of industrial production and 51.8 percent of nonfarm employment (Compendium, 2005, p. 48; see Table 17.1). Chen Yun captured the essence of early reform thinking when he likened the economy to a "bird" in a "cage" (meaning the plan) and proposed that expanding the cage would improve the bird's capacity for flight. Chinese economists began to think of shifting state firms toward commercial management, a trend captured by the slogan "separate government from the enterprises" (*zhengqi fenkai*) and by new terminology describing SOEs as "owned" rather than "operated" by the state (*guoyou* vs. *guoying*). Regulations on the state enterprise operation, issued in 1992, invested SOE managers with wide authority (at least in principle) to hire and dismiss workers, set wages, and conduct transactions involving enterprise assets.

Following the adoption of "socialist market economy" as a national objective, Chinese sources began to identify "competitive" industries where the state had no strategic interest, so that market processes could be allowed free rein. As a result, competition has virtually eliminated state ownership from sectors like apparel (see Chapter 15). In line with the slogan "retain the large and release the small" state enterprises (*zhuada fangxiao*), privatization, which had already transferred most rural enterprises from the public sector, expanded to include urban SOEs controlled by provincial and municipal governments. By 2004/2005, the state sector's share in industrial output and nonfarm employment had declined to 15.2 and 13.1 percent; the number of state enterprises in all sectors declined by 177,700 between 2001 and 2004 (State Council Economic Census Group, 2005; Yearbook, 2006, p. 505; see Table 17.1). As reform completes its third decade, we anticipate further privatization, with China's future state sector limited to several dozen large, centrally controlled firms, some with partial foreign (or possibly private domestic) ownership.

CONCLUSION

Starting with the restoration of household agriculture in the late 1970s, China has implemented a long sequence of increasingly coherent, focused, but still partial, gradual, and as yet unfinished economic reforms. Chinese policy has eschewed the "big bang" approach, in part because political realities have repeatedly frustrated ambitious reform proposals (e.g., by Wu Jinglian and Dong Fureng regarding SOE reform during the 1990s; see also Chapters 4 and 10). With hindsight, we also know that China's economy lacked some of the institutional underpinnings essential to the success of sweeping reforms; for example, the undeveloped state of domestic markets for capital and ownership rights might have derailed an early push for privatization.

China's reforms consistently focused on what we have described as "big issues" of incentives, mobility, price flexibility, competition, and openness. China's experience, as well as the record of earlier growth spurts in Japan and Korea, shows that improvements in these areas can power strong economic advance despite the costs and frictions associated with institutional shortcomings, distorted prices, entry barriers, corruption, and other limitations. We attribute China's recent economic gains to the success of reform in activating these key elements in the economy.

The consequences of this partial but effective reform campaign include the following:

- Massive expansion of China's economy, which now trails only the United States in absolute size (measured at purchasing-power parity).
- Universal increases in living standards that have elevated hundreds of millions from absolute poverty.
- A new expansion path on which productivity, innovation, and R&D now contribute substantially to overall growth.
- A major shift from plan to market, which coexists with vigorous government activism of the sort familiar from the high-growth era in Japan and Korea.
- Intense competition in most sectors despite substantial (but shrinking) areas in which official direction remains strong.
- Rapid structural change from rural/agricultural to urban/nonagricultural, from isolation to growing integration with global markets, and from public to mixed (and increasingly, to private) ownership.

In the wake of these remarkable advances, three decades of reform have reshaped China's economy into a hybrid that is increasingly responsive to domestic and international market forces, even though some segments, for example, capital markets and investment spending, reflect the continued legacy of planning. While reform has unleashed enormous growth, its uneven nature has left a penumbra of weakness and imbalance.

Institutional change has lagged behind the growth of material progress from the start. Creative improvisation has repeatedly bridged institutional gaps. Township and village enterprises, odd creatures that combined elements of public and private enterprise, delivered big increases in output, employment, and exports for about 15 years before undergoing rapid privatization during the 1990s. The *xiagang* system of partial layoffs lessened the impact of mass unemployment during the decade spanning the turn of the century.

Heston and Sicular observe that development in China, as in other large nations, creates painful imbalances among regions (see Chapter 2). Such differences may be inevitable, but Chinese policy has surely amplified the coast–interior gap in a number of ways, including uniquely favorable legal and regulatory arrangements for coastal regions already favored by geography and culture as well as slow removal of barriers that limit the flow of benefits to interior regions and their inhabitants.

Focusing on big reforms has left a trail of unfinished business. Although the costs associated with incomplete or delayed reforms pale in comparison with the benefits of unleashing the economic energies of 1.3 billion Chinese, these costs are both real and very large. Some are remnants of the plan era, for example, the underpricing of energy, water, and bank loans, which exacerbates China's environmental and employment problems. Some stem from the reform itself, for instance,

the continuing epidemic of rent seeking and graft. Others, including the consequences linked to weak systems of environmental management, law, public finance,
banking, and investment allocation (see Chapters 8, 10, 11, 12, 14, and 20), reflect
halfway houses that combine inherited political and economic structures with
partial reform efforts.

Such fusion of historic legacies and subsequent reform attempts is nowhere
clearer than in the complex interaction between efforts to energize the state sector and the broader process of national development. Contributions of capital,
technological expertise, and export earnings from the state sector figured prominently in early post-reform economic gains when state firms occupied large segments of China's nonfarm economy. The beneficial legacy of plan-era institutions
devoted to nurturing technology and high-level skills remains visible even today
(see Chapter 15).

Despite these benefits and the rapid decline in the state sector's share in economic activity, it is increasingly evident that state ownership acts as a major
drag on China's economy. Both national and provincial data link state ownership with retarded growth, low capital productivity, slow transfer of labor out of
farming, and many other undesirable phenomena (see Chapter 17). The basic difficulty is that political leverage equips state enterprises with privileged access to
investment funds, which they (on average) deploy unwisely. This inflicts a double
burden on local economies, which suffer from the poor investment choices that
bedevil the state sector and also from the crowding out of more dynamic nonstate
firms.

The conclusion that big reforms involving incentives, mobility, prices, competition, and openness have propelled China's boom in spite of myriad shortcomings
and inefficiencies provides no basis for celebrating defective institutions, policy
failures, or distorted prices. To the contrary, these and other difficulties retard
growth and increase its cost, to the particular disadvantage of tens of millions who,
despite astonishing economic gains at the national level, still languish in poverty
or unemployment. They also threaten the economy's forward momentum and
therefore command the attention of China's policy elite.

China's recent experience confirms our belief that economic outcomes are not
foreordained. Neither domestic nor overseas observers (including the present
authors) anticipated China's great economic transformation of the past three
decades. The success of partial, gradual reform in unleashing China's extended
economic boom does not ensure that similar policies would have comparable effects in different settings. Nor does China's prosperity demonstrate that
"Chinese" policies would have avoided the painful drop in output that accompanied initial reform efforts in the former Soviet Union and Eastern Europe
(see Chapter 3).

Historical legacies and particular circumstances figure prominently in the story
of China's protracted boom. Not every economy can jump-start growth by exploiting a wide gap between current and potential output. Few low-income nations can

equal China's standard of administrative competence. Perhaps none will match the good fortune that endowed China with the extraordinary synergy from the marriage between domestic labor and the capital and knowledge of overseas Chinese entrepreneurs.

The conditions of Chinese "path dependence" were not uniformly favorable. China's reforms had to overcome troublesome legacies of socialism, including considerable erosion of the work ethic, decades of antimarket propaganda, and the "lost generation" whose education disintegrated amid the disturbances of the Cultural Revolution. As a large country, China forfeited the luxury of expanding its role in global trade "under the radar" of intense political scrutiny: many potential partners erected barriers to Chinese exports before agreeing to commence "normal" trade.

The historical experience of Great Britain, Argentina, Brazil, Japan, and, indeed, China itself demonstrate that past success cannot ensure future prosperity. Because bad institutions and poorly conceived policies can result in "growing into trouble" (Doner and Ramsey, 2004), such weaknesses are no mere footnotes to China's remarkable boom, but rather danger signals on the path ahead. China's rickety fiscal system poses a major obstacle to continued growth (see Chapter 12). Continued distortion of capital markets to favor state enterprises undermines efforts to accelerate the painfully slow expansion of employment and raises the likelihood of financial crisis. Insufficient rural education due to a combination of income inequality and fiscal neglect could fuel future problems of structural unemployment.

Despite these and other difficulties, Perkins and Rawski anticipate that China's economy can achieve real GDP growth at average rates of 6–8 percent per annum between 2005 and 2025 (see Chapter 20). Whatever the outcome, China's economic progress since the start of reforms in the late 1970s ensures that the world's appetite for information and analysis about China's economy will continue to grow. Despite limited coverage of monetary policy, transportation, enterprise management, and other important subjects, the essays that follow provide a rich tapestry of information and analysis that expands the foundation on which future research can build.

References

Advertising. 2006. "Review of the Chinese Advertising Market in 2006." Accessed February 23, 2007, from www.pata.org/patasite/fileadmin/news_pata/2007/Nielsen_ad_market_review_06_eng.pdf.

Bramall, Chris. 1989. *Living Standards in Sichuan, 1931–1978.* London: Contemporary China Institute.

Brandt, Loren. 1989. *Commercialization and Agricultural Development: Central and Eastern China, 1870–1937.* Cambridge and New York: Cambridge University Press.

Brandt, Loren, Thomas G. Rawski, and Xiaodong Zhu. 2007. "International Dimensions of China's Long Boom: Trends, Prospects and Implications," in *China and the Balance of*

Influence in Asia. William W. Keller and Thomas G. Rawski, eds. Pittsburgh: University of Pittsburgh Press, pp. 14–46.

Chenery, Hollis B. and Alan M. Strout. 1966. "Foreign Assistance and Economic Development." *American Economic Review*. 56(4), pp. 679–733.

Chenery, Hollis B. and Moshe Syrquin. 1975. *Patterns of Development: 1950–1970*. Oxford: Oxford University Press.

Compendium. 2005. *China Compendium of Statistics 1949–2004*. Beijing: China Statistics Press.

Doner, Richard F. and Ansil Ramsay. 2004. "Growing into Trouble: Institutions and Politics in the Thai Sugar Industry." *Journal of East Asian Studies*. 4, pp. 97–138.

Donnithorne, Audrey. 1972. "China's Cellular Economy: Some Economic Trends Since the Cultural Revolution." *The China Quarterly*. 52, pp. 605–619.

Eckstein, Alexander. 1966. *Communist China's Economic Growth and Foreign Trade: Implications for U.S. Policy*. New York: McGraw-Hill.

Economic Census, 2004. *Zhongguo jingji pucha nianjian 2004* [Yearbook of China's 2004 Economic Census], 4 vols. Beijing: Zhongguo tongji chubanshe.

Field, Robert M. December 1983. "Slow Growth of Labor Productivity in Chinese Industry, 1952–1981." *The China Quarterly*. 96, pp. 641–664.

Fleisher, Belton M., Yifan Hu, and Haizheng Li. 2006. "Economic Transition, Higher Education and Worker Productivity in China." Department of Economics, Ohio State University. Accessed February 28, 2007, from http://www.econ.gatech.edu/research/working-papers/Paper-Fleisher-Hu-Li-03-9-2006-submit.pdf.

Fogel, Robert W. 2004. "Health, Nutrition, and Economic Growth." *Economic Development and Cultural Change*. 52.3, pp. 643–658.

Heckman, James J. 2005. "China's Human Capital Investment." *China Economic Review*. 16.1, pp. 50–70.

Heston, Alan, Robert Summers, and Bettina Aten. September 2006. Penn World Table Version 6.2. Pennsylvania: Center for International Comparisons of Production, Income and Prices, University of Pennsylvania.

Hou Fengyun, 1999. *Zhongguo renli ziben xingcheng ji xianzhuang* [Formation and Present Circumstances of Human Capital in China]. Beijing: Jingji kexue chubanshe.

Howe, Christopher. 1978. *China's Economy: A Basic Guide*. New York: Basic Books.

Investment Surges. 2007. "Chinese Overseas Investment Surges by 32 pc in 2006." 16 January. Accessed June 18, 2007, from http://www.china-embassy.org/eng/xw/t289449.htm.

Ishikawa, Shigeru. June 1983. "China's Economic Growth since 1949 – An Assessment." *The China Quarterly*. 94, pp. 242–281.

Jefferson, Gary H. and Thomas G. Rawski. 1999. "Ownership and Change in Chinese Industry," in *Enterprise Reform in China: Ownership, Transition, and Performance*. Gary H. Jefferson and Inderjit Singh, eds. Oxford and New York: Oxford University Press, pp. 23–42.

Keller, William W. and Thomas G. Rawski. 2007. "China's Peaceful Rise: Roadmap or Fantasy?" in *China's Rise and the Balance of Influence in Asia*. William W. Keller and Thomas G. Rawski, eds. Pittsburgh: University of Pittsburgh Press, pp. 193–207.

Lardy, Nicholas R. 1983. *Agriculture in China's Modern Economic Development*. Cambridge and New York: Cambridge University Press.

Lardy, Nicholas R. 1994. *China in the World Economy*. Washington, DC: Institute for International Economics.

Li Hong, 1993. *Zhongguo qiche gongye jingji fenxi* [Economic Analysis of China's Auto Industry]. Beijing: Zhongguo renmin daxue chubanshe.

Li, Hongbin and Li-An Zhou. 2005. "Political Turnover and Economic Performance: The Incentive Role of Personnel Control in China." *Journal of Public Economics*. 89(9–10), pp. 1743–1762.

Li, Wei. 1997. "The Impact of Economic Reforms on the Performance of Chinese State-Owned Enterprises." *Journal of Political Economy*. 105(5), pp. 1080–1106.

Li, Xiaoxi. 2006. *Assessing the Extent of China's Marketization*. Aldershot: Ashgate.

Morawetz, David. 1978. *Twenty-Five Years of Economic Development, 1950 to 1975*. Baltimore: Johns Hopkins University Press.

Naughton, Barry. 1988. "The Third Front: Defence Industrialization in the Chinese Interior." *The China Quarterly*. 115, pp. 351–386.

Naughton, Barry. 1995. *Growing Out of the Plan: Chinese Economic Reform, 1978–1993*. Cambridge and New York: Cambridge University Press.

OECD. 2005. Organisation for Economic Co-operation and Development. *OECD Economic Surveys: China*. Paris: OECD.

Ohkawa, Kazushi and Henry Rosovsky. 1973. *Japanese Economic Growth: Trend Acceleration in the Twentieth Century*. Stanford: Stanford University Press.

Pei, Minxin. 2006. *China's Trapped Transition: The Limits of Developmental Autocracy*. Cambridge, MA: Harvard University Press.

Perkins, Dwight H. 1966. *Market Control and Planning in Communist China*. Cambridge, MA: Harvard University Press.

Ravallion, Martin and Shaohua Chen. September 2004. "China's (Uneven) Progress Against Poverty." World Bank Policy Research Working Paper 3408. Washington, DC: World Bank.

Rawski, Thomas G. 1975. "The Growth of Producer Industries, 1900–1971," in *China's Modern Economy in Historical Perspective*. Dwight H. Perkins, ed. Stanford: Stanford University Press, pp. 203–234.

Rawski, Thomas G. 1980. *China's Transition to Industrialism: Producer Goods and Economic Development in the Twentieth Century*. Ann Arbor: University of Michigan Press.

Rawski, Thomas G. 1989. *Economic Growth in Prewar China*. Berkeley: University of California Press.

Rawski, Thomas G. 2006. "Social Capabilities and Chinese Economic Growth," in *Social Change in Contemporary China*. Wenfang Tang and Burkart Holzner, eds. Pittsburgh: University of Pittsburgh Press, pp. 89–103.

Riskin, Carl. 1987. *China's Political Economy: The Quest for Development Since 1949*. Oxford: Oxford University Press.

Samuelson, Paul A. 1954. "The Pure Theory of Public Expenditure". *Review of Economics and Statistics*. 37, pp. 350–356.

Shirk, Susan L. 1993. *The Political Logic of Economic Reform in China*. Berkeley: University of California Press.

Sicular, Terry. 1988. "Plan and Market in China's Agricultural Commerce." *Journal of Political Economy*. 96(2), pp. 283–307.

State Council Economic Census Group, 2005. *Diyici quanguo jingji pucha zhuyao shuju gongbao diyihao* [Report #1 of the Main Data from the First National Economic Census]. Issued by the Office of the State Council Leading Small Group for the First National Economic Census and the National Bureau of Statistics. Accessed December 6, 2005, from http://news.xinhuanet.com/fortune/2005–12/06/content_3883969.htm.

UNCTAD. 2007. "Foreign Direct Investment Rose by 34% in 2006." UNCTAD/PRESS/PR/2007/001. Accessed February 28, 2007, from http://www.unctad.org/templates/webflyer.asp?docid = 7993&intItemID = 1528&lang = 1.

Whiting, Susan H. 2001. *Power and Wealth in Rural China: The Political Economy of Institutional Change.* Cambridge and New York: Cambridge University Press.

Wong, Christine. 1986. "Ownership and Control in Chinese Industry," Joint Economic Committee, U.S. Congress. *China's Economy Looks Toward the Year 2000*, vol. 1. Washington, DC: Government Printing Office, pp. 571–603.

Yearbook, 2006. *Zhongguo tongji nianjian 2006* [China Statistical Yearbook 2006]. Beijing: China Statistics Press.

Young, Alwyn. 2003. "Gold into Base Metals: Productivity Growth in the People's Republic of China during the Reform Period." *Journal of Political Economy.* 111(6), pp. 1220–1261.

Zhao Fasheng, ed. 1988. *Dangdai Zhongguo de liangshi gongzuo* [Grain Work in Contemporary China]. Beijing: Zhongguo shehui kexue chubanshe.

TWO

China and Development Economics

Alan Heston and Terry Sicular[1]

We view development economics as a set of empirical generalizations, paradigms, and tools that tell us something about why large differences in productivity and income within and among countries, social groups, and classes seem to persist. How does China fit into the received views of development economics? In answering this question the cup overfloweth with materials, so no attempt is made to be exhaustive. We begin in Part A by using comparative statistics of developing and developed countries to help understand China's present position and its growth experience since 1978. Ensuing sections take up selected topics where development economics and China's development experience intersect. Part B looks at governance issues in a comparative framework, focusing on corruption as a phenomenon that brings together many features of administration that are common across countries. Part C examines the rural sector, focusing on agricultural productivity and land tenure, and Part D reviews the uniquely East Asian phenomenon of rural industrialization. Part E concludes.

CHINA'S COMPARATIVE ECONOMIC PERFORMANCE: A QUANTITATIVE LOOK

How do China's economic performance and structure compare to those of other developing countries? In this section we situate China within the developing world, using comparative measures that are in some cases straightforward and in others somewhat controversial. Jan Svejnar's contribution (see Chapter 3) to this volume contains tables allowing similar comparisons with the transition economies. Variables examined include demographic, environmental, and energy indicators, economic data from national income and product accounts, Gini coefficients and related distributional measures, and selected human capital information.

[1] University of Pennsylvania and University of Western Ontario. The authors thank Loren Brandt and Tom Rawski for useful suggestions on earlier drafts.

For comparison we have chosen three large developing countries, all with populations of over 100 million: India, which is below China's level of gross domestic product (GDP) per capita, and Brazil and Mexico, which are above. Where possible we also make comparisons to the averages for low-, medium-, and high-income countries according to the World Bank income classifications.[2]

In Table 2.1 numbers are expressed in physical units (e.g., energy consumption per capita and population levels), growth rates and ratios, percentages of GDP in national currencies (such as the share of consumption in GDP), changes in labor productivity, and levels of GDP converted at purchasing-power parities. Table 2.1a data are for 2004 and Table 2.1b data for 1980.

The statistics in Table 2.1 indicate that between 1980 and 2004 China has moved from the higher ranks of the low-income group to the middle or even upper echelon of the middle-income group. Certain features of China's economic development, however, do not match those of other countries in these categories. For example, China's population growth rate resembles that in high-income countries, but most other demographic features have been closer to those in upper middle-income countries. With respect to production structure, China appears to be in the lower middle group, though this is mainly due to its unusually large export manufacturing sector. In terms of education, China appears to fall into the middle-income group. China's GDP growth (per capita) and very high savings rate over the whole period are outliers by any typology. More generally, China's economic structure and performance have several distinctive features, including high savings and investment rates, low population growth rates, a somewhat unusual production structure of GDP, and trends in inequality (rising) and poverty (falling) that, while broadly resembling those elsewhere, have been unusual in their extent and speed of change.

Demography

The population totals for China and India dwarf those of all other countries. The population growth rates for China are now estimated at 0.6 percent a year, approaching those of high-income countries. Both China and India have clearly made a demographic transition, though by different routes. For its income level, China is unusual in the speed with which birthrates have declined, as witnessed in comparisons to Brazil and Mexico. India's demographic transition is under way, with an overall growth rate of 1.4 percent. This rate, however, disguises large geographic differences. States like Bihar are well above 2 percent, while Kerala is fast

---

[2] The World Bank defines these income groups on the basis of their Atlas method, which is at exchange rates that are averaged or modified for some countries. In 2001, low income included countries with GDP per capita less than $745; lower-middle income, $2,975; upper-middle income $9,205; and high income above that (World Bank, 2003, p. 243). On this basis, China would be lower-middle income, India, low-income, and Brazil and Mexico, upper-middle income.

Table 2.1a. *Comparative data: China and selected countries (2004, except where noted)*

	China	Brazil	India	Mexico	Low	Middle	High
1. Demographic variables							
(a) Population (millions)	1,296.2	183.9	1,079.7	102.0			
(b) Population growth (annual, %)	0.6	1.4	1.4	1.0	1.8	0.9	0.7
(c) Infant mortality rate (per 1,000 live births)	26.0	31.8	61.6	22.6	79.5	30.9	6.1
(d) Life expectancy at birth (years)	71.4	70.9	63.4	75.1	58.8	70.0	78.7
(e) Males per 100 females, ages 0–4	120 (2000)	104 (2000)	107 (2001)	103 (2003)			
2. Resources, energy, and environment							
(a) Arable land per capita (hectares), 2003	0.111	0.325	0.151	0.245	0.168	0.221	0.366
(b) Energy use per capita (kg oil equivalents), 2003	1,094	1,065	520	1,583	501	1,365	5,410
(c) Energy use per $ PPP GDP (kg oil equivalents per $, current prices), 2003	0.219	0.146	0.191	0.180	0.236	0.234	0.193
3. Economic output measures at PPPs							
(a) PPP GDP per capita (2000 international $)	5,333	7,492	3,180	8,165	2,128	6,176	28,486
(b) Price level (PPP/$ER), United States = 100	26	39	18	72	21	33	97
(c) PPP GDP per capita official growth, annual 1980–2004 (%, at constant national prices)	8.5	0.1	1.8	0.2			
(d) PPP GDP per capita growth, annual 1980–2004 (%, at 2000 international $)	8.2	0.4	3.5	0.5	2.0	4.4	3.0
(e) PPP GDP per worker growth, annual 1980–2004 (%, at 2000 international $)	7.8	0.2	3.4	0.1			
(f) PPP GDP per worker (%, at 2000 international $)	8,889	16,078	7,152	19,098			

(continued)

Table 2.1a (*continued*)

	China	Brazil	India	Mexico	Low	Middle	High
4. *Expenditure distribution (percent of GDP)*							
(a) Final consumption expenditure	54	74	72	80	75	72	80
1. Household final consumption	40	55	61	68	64	58	62 (2003)
2. Government final consumption	14	19	11	12	11	14	18 (2003)
(b) Gross capital formation	43	21	30	22	27	26	20 (2003)
(c) Investment share at PPPs	32	14	12	18			
(d) Gross domestic savings	41	26	28	20	24	28	20 (2003)
(e) Trade exports plus imports	47	29 (2003)	28 (2003)	62			
5. *GDP by production structure (percent of GDP)*							
(a) Primary	13.1	10.4	19.6	3.9	22.1	10.0	2 (2003)
(b) Secondary	46.2	40.0	27.3	26.3	28.1	37.3	26 (2003)
(c) Tertiary	40.7	49.6	53.2	69.8	49.8	52.7	72 (2003)
6. *Distribution, education, and corruption*							
(a) Gini coefficient	0.44–0.47 (2000–2003)	0.59–0.61 (2001)	0.33–0.36 (1999–2000)	0.51–0.56 (2000–2002)			
(b) Poverty headcount at $1/$2 per day (percent of population)	16.6/46.7 (2001)	7.5/21.7 (2003)	36.0/81.3 (2000)	4.5/21.2 (2002)			
(c) Completed education, 2000 (% of population above age 15)							
1. Primary	33.9	62.2	28.2	41.8			
2. Secondary	45.3	14.4	23.8	37.9			
3. Tertiary	2.8	7.5	4.1	10.6			
(d) Average years of schooling, 2000	6.4	4.9	5.1	7.2			
(e) Education expenditures as % of GNI	2.0	4.1	4.0	5.3	3.4	3.6	4.6

(f) Corruption (% of managers ranking corruption as a major business constraint), 2003		27.3	67.2	37.4
(g) Corruption (% of managers lacking confidence in courts to uphold property rights)		17.6	39.6	29.4
(h) Transparency International Corruption score (rank), 2006	3.3 (70)	3.3 (70)	3.3 (70)	3.3 (70)

Notes:

1 Except where noted below, all data are from the World Bank's World Development Indicators 2006 (WDI).

2 Data in row 1c for China, Brazil, India, and Mexico are from the United Nations Social Indicators.

3 Data in row 1e for Brazil, India, and Mexico are from the United Nations Demographic Yearbook (2004; see http://unstats.un.org/unsd/demographic/products/dyb/DYB2004/table07.pdf, accessed February 12, 2007). China's data are from the Chinese 2000 census data, as reported in various sources, including Banister (2004). Banister notes that the ratio from the census data is reasonably close to alternative scholarly estimates of 117–118.

4 Data in rows 3a–b and 3d–f are from Penn World Tables 6.2. These data incorporate recent major revisions in China's national accounts data (see note 5).

5 Data for China in rows 3c–d, 4a–b, and 5a–c are from Yearbook (2006). The data in this yearbook reflect recent major revisions in China's national accounts data based on the 2004 economic census. While these revisions have been subject to criticism (see, e.g., Wu, 2007), they are preferable to the previous numbers and are widely used. Data for China in rows 4d and 6e are not available in the Yearbook (2006), so these are taken from WDI. It is unclear whether these WDI numbers incorporate the recent revisions in China's national accounts.

6 Data for all countries in rows 4c and 4e are from Penn World Tables 6.2.

7 Multiple estimates are available for Gini coefficients, so in row 6a we provide ranges of estimates. In all cases, inequality is measured over per capita income or consumption. Sources and income measures for the Ginis are as follows:

China is disposable income per capita – Chapter 18, this volume; Khan and Riskin (2005); WDI; Gustafsson et al. (2008); WIDER World Income Inequality Database v. 2a (2005), available for download at http://www.wider.unu.edu/wiid/wiid.htm, hereafter WIDER (2005). This is a compilation of data from multiple sources; see WIID (2005) for the original sources.

Brazil is gross income – WIDER (2005); WDI.
India is consumption – WIDER (2005); WDI.
Mexico is disposable income – WIDER (2005); WDI.

8 Data in rows 6c and 6d are from Barro and Lee (2000), available at http://www.cid.harvard.edu/ciddata/ciddata.html, accessed February 11, 2007.

9 Data in row 6e are from the WDI data series "adjusted savings: education expenditure (% GNI)." Note that the number for China may not reflect recent revisions in the national accounts statistics.

10 Data in row 6f are from Transparency International, available at http://www.transparency.org/policy_research/surveys_indices/global/cpi, accessed December 1, 2006.

31

Table 2.1b. *Comparative data: China and selected countries (1980 except where noted)*

	China	Brazil	India	Mexico	Low	Middle	High
1. Demographic variables							
(a) Population (millions)	981.2	121.6	687.3	67.6			
(b) Population growth (annual %)	1.3	2.3	2.3	2.5	2.5	1.7	0.8
(c) Infant mortality rate (per 1,000 live births)	49.0	67.0	113.0	56.0	114.0	60.3	14.0
(d) Life expectancy at birth (years)	66.8	62.6	54.2	66.8	52.5	64.8	73.6
(e) Males per 100 females, ages 0–4	107 (1982)	102	102 (1981)	101			
2. Resources, energy, and environment							
(a) Arable land per capita (hectares)	0.133	0.370	0.237	0.340	0.257	0.199	0.454
(b) Energy use per capita (kg oil equivalents)	610	920	354	1,438	424	1,238	4,612
(c) Energy use per \$ PPP GDP (kg oil equivalents per \$, current prices)	0.799	0.134	0.300	0.183	0.308		0.258
3. Economic output measures at PPPs							
(a) PPP GDP per capita (2000 international \$)	749	6,776	1,348	7,271	1,121	3,262	17,878
(b) Price level (PPP/\$ER), United States = 100	67	54	39	73	23	38	97
(c) PPP GDP per capita growth, annual 1965–1980 (%)	3.1	4.8	1.9	3.1			
(d) PPP GDP per worker growth, annual 1965–1980 (%)	2.8	4.0	2.1	2.5			
(e) PPP GDP per worker (2000 international \$)	1,365	17,285	3,094	22,290			
4. Expenditure distribution (percent of GDP)							
(a) Final consumption expenditure	66	79	84	75	76	60	59
1. Household final consumption	51	70	74	65			
2. Government final consumption	15	9	10	10	11	13	17
(b) Gross capital formation	35	23	19	27	18	28	24.6
(c) Investment share at PPPs	27	24	10	23			
(d) Gross domestic savings	35	21	16	25	13	27	24
(e) Trade (exports plus imports)	13	22	15	28			
5. GDP by production structure (percent of GDP)							
(a) Primary	29.9	11.0	38.9	9.0	36.6	18.0	4.0
(b) Secondary	48.2	43.8	24.5	33.6	24.3	41.1	37.2
(c) Tertiary	21.9	45.2	36.6	57.4	39.1	40.9	58.8

6. Distribution, education, and corruption

(a) Gini coefficient	0.28–0.33 (1980–1985)	0.57–0.60 (1979–83)	0.34 (1983)	0.47–0.51 (1984)		
(b) Poverty headcount at $1/$2 per day (% of population)	63.8/88.1 (1981)	11.8/31.1 (1981)		14.0/39.7 (1984)		
(c) Completed education, population above age 15 (%)						
1. Primary	31.3	59.0	12.6	46.4		
2. Secondary	33.7	9.3	18.5	20.4		
3. Tertiary	0.9	4.3	2.4	5.6		
(d) Average years of schooling	4.8	3.1	3.3	4.8	3.0	3.3
(e) Education expenditures as percentage of GNI	2.1	3.6	2.9	3.0	3.3	5.4

Notes:

[1] Except where noted otherwise, all data are from the World Bank's World Development Indicators 2006 (WDI). Note that the countries classified by the World Bank in the low-, middle-, and high-income country groups, as well as the income cutoffs for the three groups, changed between 1980 and 2004. Importantly, China is included in the low-income group in 1980 and in the middle-income group in 2004, with implications for interpretation of the comparisons.

[2] For row 1e, China's ratio is from the 1982 census data. See Banister (2004). Data in row 1e for Brazil, India, and Mexico are from table 3 of the United Nations Demographic Yearbook (1997) *Historical Supplement* (see http://unstats.un.org/unsd/demographic/products/dyb/DYBHist/HistTab03.pdf, accessed July 27, 2007.).

[3] For 2a, we do not use the WDI number for China's land area per capita because it is improbably smaller than the land per capita given in the same source for China in 2003. Official data for China's cultivated land area were historically understated. The Chinese government carried out a land use survey in 1996 that has served as the basis for revised land area statistics and that gave a total cultivated land area of 130 million hectares in 1996 (see Yearbook, 2006). We use this 1996 figure as the numerator to calculate a rough estimate of cultivated land area per capita for China in 1980. Cultivated land area shrank somewhat between 1980 and 1996, so this number probably understates land area in 1980.

[4] Data for China in rows 4a–b and 5a–c are from Yearbook (2006). The data in this yearbook reflect recent major revisions in China's national accounts data based on the 2004 economic census. While these revisions have been subject to criticism (see, e.g., Wu, 2007), they are preferable to the previous numbers and are widely used. Data for China in rows 4d and 6e are not available in the Yearbook (2006) and so are taken from WDI. It is unclear whether these WDI numbers incorporate the recent revisions in China's national account data.

[5] Data in rows 3a–e, 4c, and 4e for all countries are from Penn World Tables 6.2.

[6] Multiple estimates are available for Gini coefficients, so in row 6a we provide ranges. The estimates underlying these ranges are in WIDER (2005). In all cases, inequality is measured over persons, specifically, disposable income per capita for China and Mexico; gross income per capita for Brazil; and consumption per capita for India.

[7] Data for China in row 6b are from Ravallion and Chen (2004a, table 2; 2004b, table 2). Note that the numbers for 1981 given here are based on what Ravallion and Chen call the "old method," which uses income distribution, while the 2001 numbers in Table 2.1a are based on the "new method," which uses consumption distribution. Numbers based on the new method are not available for years prior to 1990. For the 1990s, however, the two methods give similar poverty levels for China. For 2001, the poverty rates calculated using the old method are 16.5/44.5 and using the new method, 16.6/46.7.

[8] Data in rows 6c and 6d are from Barro and Lee (2000), available at http://www.cid.harvard.edu/ciddata/ciddata.html, accessed February 11, 2007.

approaching 0 percent growth. China also displays considerable geographic variation in population growth among provinces, but the highest rates are only about 1.1 percent (Ningxia, Tibet, and Xinjiang) and the lowest close to zero (Beijing, Liaoning, and Shanghai).[3]

With respect to infant mortality, China is closer to Brazil and Mexico than to India. Again, for both China and India variation across provinces or states is considerable, although in different ranges. The same is true of life expectancy at birth. India in 2002 is about the level of China in 1980, which represents a substantial improvement but leaves some distance to go.

Both China and India are notable for their high male-to-female ratios, a long-standing demographic feature that has become more pronounced in recent years (Table 2.1). Both countries have male-to-female ratios for children aged 0–4 above the world norm of about 1.04. Birth ratios in India of males to females moved from 1.06 to 1.12 between 1990 and 1999 and in China from 1.11 to 1.17 between 1989 and 2000 (Guilmoto and Attane, 2005). Historically, the practice of infanticide, particularly of girls, was common in both countries. Such practices, albeit perhaps in altered form such as sex-selective abortion, are thought to contribute to the high proportion of male children.

China's high ratio of males could also reflect unreported female births, a consequence of penalties for higher-order births under China's relatively strict population planning policies. One should note that a third explanation for the high ratio of males is that hepatitis B, which is endemic in both countries, is correlated with a biased sex ratio at birth. Oster (2005) attributes 75 percent of the missing girls in China and 18 percent in India to hepatitis B. Finally, the sex ratios show a geographic pattern in both countries; in India the highest masculinity ratios are in the most prosperous states of Haryana and Punjab, with lower ratios observed in the East and normal ratios prevalent in the South. In China the high masculinity ratios are in the less prosperous southeast provinces of Guangxi, Yunnan, and Guizhou and lowest in the wealthier coastal areas and large municipalities. Regardless of the reasons, the impact of this high male ratio on both countries' future economic growth and evolution is an open question.

Measurement of GDP: Prices and Other Considerations

Comparisons of, say, investment or education expenditure shares of GDP usually reflect national prices (in either the national currencies or the national currencies converted using an exchange rate). This practice mistakenly assumes that relative prices of these goods are the same in all countries. In fact, systematic differences in price structure are observed for countries at different levels of development, namely, the relative price of investment declines with income per capita and

---

[3] Data are for 2005 (see Yearbook, 2006, p. 100).

the relative price of government goods and services rises. This is one of two main findings of the International Comparison Program (ICP).

The other main finding of the ICP is that the price levels of countries (purchasing-power parity (PPP)/exchange rate (XR)) rise with their level of per capita income. Despite China's minimal participation in the ICP, available estimates from Ren and Chen (1994) and others suggest that this generalization holds for China. China's GDP converted at exchange rates is roughly one-fourth of the GDP converted at PPPs, the latter putting China as the world's second largest economy. As indicated in Table 2.1a, line 3b, China's price level is roughly 26 percent of the United States price level, much lower than Brazil or Mexico, but still above India.

Compared to international prices, this means China is relatively cheap, but some Chinese prices are relatively high and some relatively low. Thus even though China, Brazil, and India export machinery and equipment, the relative price of these items to other goods in GDP is relatively high. This is illustrated in Table 2.1a, lines 4b and 4c, where the 2004 investment ratio for China is 43 percent in national prices and 32 percent in international prices. Brazil and India display a similar pattern, while the opposite is true of high-income countries like Japan, where the investment share in international prices is higher than at national prices.[4]

It should be clear that a great deal of uncertainty surrounds all of the PPP estimates embedded in Table 2.1, including those from the Penn World Tables (PWT), those of the World Bank, which usually present an even lower PPP than PWT, and other higher estimates. The recent Organisation for Economic Co-Operation and Development's Economic Survey of China (OECD, 2005, pp. 70–71) gives a range of estimates of the price level (PPP/XR) of China circa 2000, ranging from 22.1 percent of the U.S. price level (World Bank) to 55.9 percent (Ren, 1997). Quite amazingly, this same publication uses the exchange rate conversion to discuss the size of China in the world economy, likely a political rather than economic decision.[5]

Chinese national income statistics in current and constant prices are also subject to debate that can only be referenced here (see various works by Holz and Maddison, e.g., Holz, 2003, 2006a, 2006b, and Maddison, 1998, 2006). The controversy centers around Angus Maddison's revisions of official statistics, particularly the level estimates for agriculture, services, and manufacturing sectors. Some of the controversy also relates to growth, particularly of services, a controversy that has not been satisfactorily resolved even with the release of a new census of service

---

[4] All data in international prices are derived from Penn World Table 6.2 (PWT.Econ.Upenn.edu).

[5] While the exchange rate is the obvious conversion factor for many purposes, clearly PPP conversions are appropriate for comparing volumes across countries. The OECD Economic Survey of China, however, follows the Chinese position of trying to make its economy look smaller rather than larger and so uses exchange rates. New World Bank PPP estimates forthcoming in 2008 may lower the PPP estimates in Tables 2.1 and 2.2 (see *Economist*, December 1–7, 2007, p. 90).

industries in late 2005. Most observers believe that the new census moves in the right direction by raising the level of service industries in the national accounts revision in 2006, but doubt surrounds the constant price revisions (Wu, 2007), which of course affect the growth rate of the real service share.

A similar veil of doubt surrounds GDP growth rates for China. The official per capita growth rate and that at international prices for China over the period 1980–2004 are 8.5 and 8.2 percent, respectively (Table 2.1a, lines 3c and 3d). Maddison and Wu (2007) have argued that these are overstated and use 6.6 percent, a much lower rate, though still higher than any large country has sustained for such a long period.

The issues raised by the official growth rates are clear when one compares levels of per capita GDP of India with China for 2004 and 1980 in Tables 2.1a and 2.1b. In 2004 China's per capita PPP GDP is 1.68 times that of India, while in 1980 it is 0.56 times that of India. Few would doubt the 2004 estimate and few would accept the 1980 estimate as plausible since most per capita physical output and welfare indicators are at least as high in 1980 for China as for India. Even use of Maddison and Wu's growth rate of 6.6 percent would still give China only 80 percent of the per capita GDP of India in 1980.[6] These issues cannot be resolved here, but they raise important questions about our understanding of China's growth experience.

Growth Rates and Productivity Levels

Even using the conservative estimates of Maddison and Wu, China's per capita growth performance of 6.6 percent per annum is high, exceeding that of the comparator countries and also of all country groups in Table 2.1. Brazil and Mexico compare poorly in part because of the debt overhang of the 1980s, which has been followed by much more rapid growth. In recent years, growth in Brazil and Mexico has been in the range of 8–9 percent, in the same league as that of China, although not sustained for as long a period. Table 2.1b provides growth rates for 1965–1980. China's performance is on a par with Mexico, above India, and below Brazil for per capita GDP and GDP per worker.

Table 2.1a reports GDP per worker at 2000 prices for 1980 and 2004 for the four countries as a rough measure of productivity. The denominator for all countries is the economically active population, which does not reflect employment rates, let

---

[6] There is much evidence that per capita incomes in India and China were very similar circa even 1950 and that China was probably higher in 1978. An early view is that of Eckstein (1977). In the poverty calculations of the World Bank (PovcalNet, 2007), the constant $ mean income in rural China is put at 25.60 in 1980 and in rural India 32.74 in 1983, while urban China is 70.38 in 1981 and urban India 55.02 in 1983. China could not be substantially below India in 1980 according to these estimates from household surveys.

alone hours. Even so, the outcome is so striking that even major adjustments in official figures would likely not change the big picture. Namely, output per worker has tripled in China between 1980 and 2004, and this pace has been maintained to the present. The growth in output per worker in other countries given in Table 2.1 and most of the world is modest by comparison. In Table 2.1 India is the only country that has come close to China's experience, more than doubling its output per worker over the twenty years to 2004.

It is possible that these trends in output per worker reflect China's relatively high rates of investment and increasing amount of capital per worker. This argues for use of total factor productivity (TFP) in making comparisons, rather than output per worker, a partial measure. TFP estimates for China have even more pitfalls than GDP growth estimates, but a review of some recent studies provides at least a rough indication. Overall, estimates of China's TFP growth range from about 1 to 4 percent per year. The higher estimates typically use GDP growth rates that are equal to or close to the official GDP statistics and do not make adjustments for the contribution of human capital and other such factors. Fan, Perkins, and Sabin (1997), for example, using a slightly reduced GDP growth rate, find TFP growth of 4.1 percent from 1979 to 1997. Wang and Yao (2001) calculate the contribution of human capital accumulation at 1.3 percentage points of the growth usually attributed to TFP, and TFP growth net of the contribution of human capital comes down to about 2.3 percent. In this volume, Perkins and Rawski obtain TFP growth of 3.8 percent per year for 1978–2005 net of the contribution of rising education levels (Table 20.2).

Fan, Perkins, and Sabin (1997), Wang and Yao (2001), and Perkins and Rawski (see Chapter 20) use GDP growth rates equal to or close to the official rate of over 9 percent. Use of alternative, lower growth rates would substantially reduce measured TFP growth, because TFP growth is calculated as a residual after subtracting the contributions of various inputs to growth. Thus if China's GDP growth were 6.5 percent as given by PWT rather than 9–10 percent used in these studies, then TFP growth would be only zero or 1 percent per year. Young (2003) uses a GDP growth rate of 6.1 percent and also makes additional adjustments, such as accounting for human capital's contribution. He estimates China's TFP growth at 1.4 percent, which he judges as "moderate but respectable" by international standards.

At worst, then, China has maintained respectable productivity growth; at best, it has had a stellar record. That said, by any estimate the majority of China's growth has been the result of increased use of inputs rather than increased productivity in the use of those inputs. For example, studies that use GDP growth rates of 8 or 9 percent attribute 3–4 percentage points of that growth to TFP increases, leaving 5 percentage points to increased use of inputs. Similarly, studies that that use lower GDP growth rates of 6 percent attribute 1–2 percentage points to TFP growth, again leaving 4–5 percentage points to input increases. Most studies conclude, moreover, that growth in capital inputs has been particularly important in causing growth, followed by growth in labor and human capital.

Savings Rate

Table 2.1 provides a snapshot of China's saving rate that, by any measure, is very high, 35 percent in 1980 and 41 percent in 2004. Aart Kraay (2000) evaluated many features of Chinese savings performance from 1978 to 1995, comparing it with high-performing East Asian economies. China has achieved high savings rates at much lower levels of per capita income, and regardless of income levels only Singapore has reported a higher savings rate during this period. Like other transition economies, the composition of savings has undergone significant change. China has seen a decline in government budgetary savings, but in sharp contrast to other transition economies, China's household savings have increased.

Kraay reviews possible reasons for the very high savings rate in China, including whether China is really an outlier compared to countries at similar levels of development. His analysis is based on the residuals over time from an estimated equation of savings that includes variables like the growth rate, dependency ratio, and income level. China has a positive and large residual of over 10 percent of GDP (reflecting unusually high savings).

What is particularly interesting is the composition of China's savings and the differences between income and consumption versus asset accumulation of households. Public savings declined from 20 percent of GDP in 1978 to become, in some years, negative prior to the fiscal changes of the late 1990s. Household and corporate or enterprise savings rose. Table 2.2 summarizes Kraay's results. National savings greatly exceed what can be accounted for from the various components of savings. Kraay prefers the concept of household savings that is built up from changes in household financial assets plus household fixed investment (Table 2.2, line 3.2) to the household survey concept of income minus consumption expenditures (Table 2.2, line 3.1), which he believes suffers from understatement of income. Using either concept, one finds a very substantial excess of national savings over the sum of different savings components. (Lines 5.1 and 5.2 (Table 2.2) give Kraay's preferred estimates of the residual.)

Kraay notes that one source of the residual is change in stocks (Table 2.2, line 6), which shows up as positive in every year from 1978 to 1995. Most of this inventory investment is by state-owned firms that are thought to maintain and add to inventories on their books whether or not the goods can be sold at these reported values. Even if these inventories were totally written off, though, a substantial residual would remain.

Given the fairly consistent excess of national accounts savings over its major component sources, it appears likely that the data in Table 2.1 overstate the savings rate in China. Kraay's calculations would imply that China's true savings rate is lower, perhaps in the range of 20–30 percent. Even so, it remains high by international standards.

Table 2.2. *Composition of Chinese savings 1978 and 1995, percent of GDP*

Savings components	1978	1995
1. Public savings	20.1	0.5
2. Corporate savings	2.2	7.6
3.1 Household savings income – consumption	7.7	10.6
3.2 Household savings asset accumulation	4.4	20.3
4. National savings	37.8	41.2
5.1 Residual (4–1–2–3.1)	7.8	22.5
5.2 Residual (4–1–2–3.2)	11.0	12.8
6. Change in inventories	8.4	5.3

Source: Kraay (2000), adapted from Table A1.

Structure of GDP

Development is typically associated with a decline in agriculture's relative importance in the economy, the rise of industry initially and then expansion of the service sector. Since 1980 China's structural change has followed aspects of this general pattern. Sectoral shares of GDP are given in lines 5a–c in Tables 2.1a and 2.1b. Note, however, that these shares are in current prices and do not capture changes over time in relative prices of agricultural goods, industrial goods, and services. In fact, relative sectoral prices changed substantially in China after 1980 due in part to the elimination of planned pricing, which undervalued agriculture. Thus the shares shown here overstate agriculture's decline. Fan, Perkins, and Sabin (1997), for example, recalculated agriculture's share for 1980 using 1992 prices, by which year most prices for goods were market based. Using 1992 prices raises agriculture's share from 30 to about 35 percent, while industry's share shrinks from 48 to 40 percent. Even allowing for this price correction, though, agriculture's share has fallen substantially since 1980, and services' share has increased.

A distinctive feature of China's economy in the Maoist era, even after allowing for price distortions, was its anomalously large industrial sector. Due to Maoist policies emphasizing industry, and especially heavy industry, in 1980 China's industrial share was larger than that in most other low-income and even middle- and high-income countries. Maoist policies also discounted the service sector, which in 1980 was noticeably smaller than that in other countries. Despite 24 years of structural change, these anomalies remain in 2004, albeit in somewhat less extreme form. China's production structure, then, remains distinct.

Sectoral reallocation has most certainly been part of China's growth and productivity story and so has trade. During the Maoist era China's economy was autarkic. During the reform era trade policies were greatly liberalized, as were restrictions on capital inflows. The consequences of these reforms are reflected in the remarkable increase in openness as measured by trade's (exports plus imports) share of GDP, shown in Tables 2.1a and 2.1b, lines 4e. Note that these shares are calculated using

PPPs so as to avoid bias due to exchange rate distortions. Between 1980 and 2004 the share of trade in China's GDP nearly tripled, rising from 22 to 65 percent. Compared to other countries, during this period, China was transformed from an economy with a low degree to a high degree of openness. As is discussed in more detail elsewhere in this volume, this transformation has promoted market development, structural change, reallocation of labor into higher-income employment, and overall economic growth. It has also had distributional implications, as access to international markets and capital has been much greater in coastal than inland regions.

Education, Energy, and Resources

The point made earlier about pricing and investment shares also applies to many other aspects of international comparisons, although only education and energy are discussed here.[7] World Bank studies often report that China spends too little on education compared to other countries. Anecdotal evidence that education in rural areas is underfunded is also common.

The most common measure of educational spending is the GDP share of educational expenditures. Clearly, this measure neglects international variations in relative prices: the relative cost of school construction and the salaries of comparable teaching personnel are far lower in China and other developing countries than in the OECD economies. If the PPP for education were used, the share of education in China would be higher than is typically reported in cross-section comparisons.

That said, China's educational spending appears to be low even in comparison to other developing countries where the price structure is similar. Hannum, Behrman, Wang, and Liu (see Chapter 7) report that China spent 2.2 percent of GDP on education in 1998, compared to 3.2 percent for India, 4.9 percent for Brazil, and 2.4 percent for Bangladesh. Indonesia and Pakistan are lower, though, at less than 2 percent. Our data in Table 2.1, line 6e, on education expenditures as a share of gross national income (GNI) from the World Bank's World Development Indicators (WDI) give a similar picture, with China at 2 percent compared to the low-income group average of 3.4 percent and middle-income average of 3.6 percent.

While China's spending levels may be relatively low, evidence on education suggests that the results of that spending have been substantial, especially with respect to primary and secondary education. Educational attainment does, of course, include both pre- and post-reform experiences and so combines different regimes. Based on the average years of schooling measure from Barro and Lee (2000) (see Table 2.1a, line 6d), by 2000 China's population looks well educated

---

[7] Another example is health care. Within the OECD, the United States ranks first in the ratio of health expenditures to GDP in national currencies. But when account is taken of the high price level of health inputs in the United States, a comparison of real quantities puts the United States at the middle of the OECD countries.

in comparison to other countries. With respect to the shares of the over 15 population that have attained different levels of education, China compares especially well for primary and secondary education, but its tertiary attainment rate remains relatively low. For all the countries shown education levels have risen substantially since 1980. China's education improvement is especially evident in the spread of secondary schooling: the share of the adult population with secondary schooling has risen from one-third to nearly one-half.

Energy use provides another example of how pricing can alter international comparisons. Often the ratio of energy consumption per unit of GDP is used in cross-country comparisons to gauge energy efficiency or project future energy use. If GDP is converted at PPPs then the volume of production in each country will be commensurate and a meaningful ratio can be formed. If GDP is converted at exchange rates, however, the resulting comparisons may be very misleading.

Table 2.1 provides the energy intensity of production in terms of kilograms per dollar of GDP converted at PPPs. These numbers show that in 2003 China's energy use was a bit high relative to Brazil, but close to that of India and Mexico and in the same ballpark as the low-income and middle-income group averages. Note further that China has a substantial geographic region with a cold climate requiring use of energy for heating. China, then, does not appear to be particularly inefficient in its energy use compared to other large, developing countries. Consider now what happens if the comparison with Mexico, for example, were done at exchange rates. At PPPs Mexico shows 0.180 kg per dollar of GDP and China 0.219; at exchange rates the numbers would be 0.250 and 0.842, giving a very different impression. If India's number were at exchange rates, its efficiency would be 1.176, reversing its relation with China at PPPs.[8]

As with investment, it is easy to find energy pricing policies that lead to excessive energy use in China and other countries. For example, some states in India provide electricity to users in rural areas free of charge. In view of their levels of development and natural resource endowments, however, it is not plausible that in recent years both these countries use three or four times the energy per unit of GDP as high-income countries, which is the implication of exchange rate conversions. Even at PPPs, however, in 1980 China's energy use was markedly high by international standards. China's energy intensity at that time reflected its unusually large industrial sector with a disproportionate share of heavy industry and also planned prices for energy that were extremely low. China's energy use per $PPP GDP has declined remarkably since 1980. As China's production structure remains skewed

---

[8] Conversion of the PPP energy efficiency measure involves dividing it by the price level expressed as a ratio, for example, for China .219/.23 from table 2.1. The *International Energy Outlook 2005* (U.S. Energy Department, p. 13) began to use PPP conversions this year for its projections of energy consumption. This represented a movement away from the practice of the International Panel on Climate Change that has shown great reluctance to give up the use of exchange rates in forecasting future CO_2 emissions.

toward industry, this decline likely reflects increased efficiency in the use of energy resources due to market and price reforms.

Regarding natural resources, an oft-noted feature of China's economy is its low and declining amount of arable land per capita (Tables 2.1a and 2.1b, lines 2a). China's per capita arable land endowment is lower than that in India, which is also relatively land scarce, not to mention Brazil and Mexico, countries with more abundant land resources but more unequal landholding distributions. The topics of land distribution and land tenure will be taken up later, but here it is worth pointing out that China's experience suggests that land scarcity need not be a barrier to growth. The historical experiences of South Korea and Japan, also extremely land-scarce countries, reinforce this conclusion.

Income Distribution

As with economic growth, the relationship of reforms in China to income distribution has generated a large, often contentious literature. One part of the literature has focused on geographical differences between rural and urban areas and between the coastal provinces, versus the interior provinces, the northeast and the far west. Another strand examines household income distribution. Given China's pre-reform organization, it would be surprising if there were no increase in inequality during the twenty-five years of reforms. The more interesting questions revolve around the extent of the increase in inequality and how it compares to that in other transition and developing economies. In the remainder of this section we first take up regional income differences and then examine household income distribution.

Regional Income Differences

Knotty problems arise when comparing regional differences across countries. Basic regional income data are sometimes obtained by allocation of national totals, or sometimes built up from production, sometimes from expenditure surveys, and sometimes from income estimates. Since income generated in a region is often very different from the incomes accruing to the residents of a region, major data comparison issues result. In addition, the variation in incomes among regions depends upon the number of administrative units into which countries are broken up for statistical purposes. The extremes across China's counties cannot be less than those across provinces, which in turn cannot be less than those across regions. Often the three large cities are excluded as outliers from domestic comparisons within China. The same issue arises elsewhere, for example, Brasilia, India's Delhi State, or the largest city in the world, Mexico City.

A further problem relates to price differences within countries. Even for the United States the consumption price level, when housing services are included, can easily be 50 percent higher in urban areas like San Francisco (127 with U.S. average 100) compared to small urban centers in the South (81) (Aten, 2006). Since similar findings are common in other countries, the implication is that nominal incomes in dollars or yuan are likely to overstate differences between richer and poorer states and provinces. That said, the reported differences in China, even when corrected for price differences, would certainly put China in the group of countries with large regional inequalities. All the countries in Table 2.1 have much smaller regional differences than China.

Similar patterns emerge for urban–rural income differences. Urban–rural income comparisons are usually based on household survey data, and so avoid some of the difficulties mentioned earlier. Another problem emerges, however, due to the existence of large numbers of rural-to-urban migrants. Such migrants are typically not fully captured in household income surveys, and most Chinese studies do not include them at all. A recent study by Sicular et al. (2007), however, provides some estimates that include migrants.

Without migrants, China's urban-to-rural income ratio is now at about 3.3, and with migrants, the ratio declines to about 3.0 (Sicular et al., 2007). Both these ratios are high by international standards. Eastwood and Lipton (2000) give ratios for other Asian countries in the 1990s that lie between 1.3 and 1.8, with the exception of the Philippines at 2.17. Similarly, Knight and Song (1999, p. 338) give urban-to-rural ratios for income and consumption in twelve countries, mostly in Asia but also in the Middle East and Africa. China's ratio exceeds that in all the other countries listed except Zimbabwe and South Africa.

Adjustments for spatial price differences reduce China's urban–rural income gap substantially. Brandt and Holz (2006) give estimates for China of spatial differences in costs of living that imply that prices in urban areas have been 35–40 percent higher than in rural areas in recent years. Once adjusted for spatial price differences, and including migrants, China's urban–rural income gap declines markedly to about 2.1 (Sicular et al., 2007). Even with this adjustment, though, China's urban–rural income gap remains on the high end compared to other countries, particularly since the ratios for other countries mentioned here are not adjusted for spatial price differences.

While geographic differences in incomes are universal, in China these differences seem relatively large. This raises the question of why this is the case, and what can be done about it. China's *hukou* or household registration system and related policies that continue to hinder rural-to-urban movement are the most obvious explanation. Yet, the persistence of urban–rural gaps in other countries suggests that even without such artificial restrictions, migration is unlikely to eliminate the urban–rural income gap or equalize the returns to education and other individual characteristics.

What can governments do about persistent geographic income differences? Government policies to reduce regional differences are typically unsuccessful. It is often noted that the Tennessee Valley Authority in the United States created in the 1930s was associated with improvements in relative incomes in a number of states in the South, though some 40 years later. While TVA may have been a success, it is not clear if it was important in the movement of industries from the Northeast to the

South, or whether the South's lower wages and low rate of unionization would have encouraged this shift anyway. Italy has made much greater efforts to raise provincial incomes in the South beginning in 1950, with no apparent success in 50 years. The same can be said of Northeast Brazil, or the so-called *backward areas* of India. Often regional development policies subsidize capital, whereas the need in most poor regions is to increase employment. Like many other countries, China's low-income regions often have substantial minority populations, which further complicates the political economy of improving conditions. Clearly, China's large-scale infrastructure investment program in the West will be another closely watched attempt to bring about more regional equality in development.

Household Distribution of Income
Economists have long debated the relationship between inequality and growth. The well-known Kuznets (1955) "inverted U" hypothesis that inequality will first rise and then fall as countries develop has been the subject of many theoretical and empirical studies, as yet with no definite outcome. Conclusions depend on the approach and data used, and individual country experiences are quite diverse.

China's recent experience would put it on the upward sloping portion of the Kuznets curve. Over the past two decades China's rapid growth was accompanied by increasing inequality. In the early 1980s China was considered one of the more equal countries in the world, with a Gini coefficient of less than 0.35. By the 2000, after more than a decade of rapid growth, China's Gini had risen to about 0.45. As shown in Table 2.1, this Gini coefficient reflects a level of inequality in the mid to high range compared to our other countries. The Lorenz curves (Figure 2.1) give a similar picture, with China's income distribution resembling those of Mexico and Nigeria.

China's rapid increase in, and relatively high level of, inequality is thought to be a potential source of political and economic instability and has elicited substantial concern both within and outside of the country. Whether those concerns are justi-fied will depend in part on whether inequality remains high and increases further, or whether the sorts of long-term economic forces envisioned by Kuznets cause inequality to stabilize and eventually decline. A look at regional patterns within China hints that such long-term forces may be present. In China's most developed eastern region, inequality initially increased, but then stabilized and now is declin-ing (Gustafsson et al., 2008). The East has consistently been on the forefront of China's economic reforms and development. If other regions follow suit, then the recent rise in inequality need not be a cause for long-run concern.

The Gini coefficients for rural China and India are 36.3 percent (2001) and 28.1 percent (1999), respectively, and for urban areas 33.3 and 35.0 percent. What makes China's overall Gini higher than India's is that average rural income is only 32 percent of urban income, while in India the rural income is 60 percent of urban income (PovcalNet, World Bank). More notably in terms of trends, the Gini coefficient in rural India declines and in urban areas slightly rises over its reform

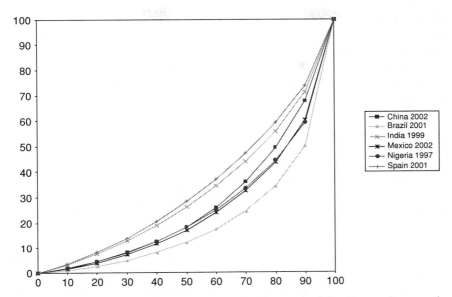

Figure 2.1. Lorenz curves for China and other selected countries (*Note:* Except where noted, the Lorenz curves show the distribution of per capita disposable income. *Source:* China's data are from Gustafsson et al., 2008. Data for other countries are from WIDER, 2005. Brazil's data are per capita gross income, India's per capita consumption, and Nigeria's per capita consumption. For further discussion of inequality data sources, please see Table 2.1a, note 7.)

period. In contrast, in China the rural Gini went from 0.24 to 0.36 and the urban from 0.18 to 0.33, an across-the-board increase in inequality.

While inequality in China has risen, poverty has declined. Although estimates vary, and while progress in poverty reduction has gone through slower and faster phases, all studies concur that China's record in poverty reduction since the start of the reform period has been among the best in the world. As shown in Table 2.1, China's poverty headcount at $1 per day has fallen from 64 to 17 percent between 1981 and 2001; at $2 per day it has fallen from 88 to 47 percent. Ravallion and Chen (2004a, b) report two alternative series of estimates of the poverty headcount ratio using different poverty lines, one of which shows a decline from 23 percent in 1981 to 3 percent in 2001, the other a decline from 53 to 8 percent. The absolute number of people escaping poverty implied by these ratios is staggering, from 200 to over 400 million people.

The following comparison from the World Bank's PovcalNet is also informative. Using the $1 a day poverty line, the percent in poverty in urban China declined from 2.0 percent in 1981 to 0.3 percent in 2001, while in India the decline was from 28.6 percent in 1983 to 19.3 percent in 1999. Poverty rates in urban China have been low throughout and have slowly improved in India. In rural China the 1980 poverty rate was 79.4 percent and in 2001, 26.5 percent. In rural India the rates were 60.2 percent in 1983 and 41.8 percent in 1999. China's progress in reducing rural poverty has been quite impressive (World Bank 2000), while India's progress has been only moderate. The absolute number of rural poor in the two countries remains over half a billion, including more than 200 million in China and more than 300 million in India.

COMPARATIVE ECONOMIC PERFORMANCE: GOVERNANCE ISSUES

The underlying assumption of the New Comparative Economics is that institutions exert a profound influence on economic development. Institutions in this framework include the legal system and its operation, the circumstances that promote corruption and rent-seeking activities, as well as the role that social norms and social capital play in the development process. The New Institutional Economics places emphasis on the conditions of ownership of the means of production and the importance of transactions costs in thwarting/promoting the efficient use of resources. Both these themes have been given an influential spin by De Soto (2000), who has emphasized the dead weight of capital that is not fungible because of the ambiguity of property rights, a theme certainly relevant to China and many other countries.

Prescriptive and Proscriptive Roles of Government

One of the striking findings even for the open economies is that the nature of official interventions is more important than the size of government. Bhagwati (1988) described the distinction as one between *prescriptive* and *proscriptive* governments. Prescriptive governments take an active role, like Japan's Ministry of International Trade and Industry (MITI) in promoting certain industries, but this does not prevent private activity from taking part in other sectors. Proscriptive governments, like Brazil or India, would require permissions and licenses to undertake any activity, with the government acting in a gate-keeper role. While either form of government might command a large share of resources, the proscriptive form by imposing impediments to initiative and creating many opportunities for rent seeking tends to perpetuate itself, with bureaucrats and rent receivers all having a vested interest in retaining the old system.

Viewed in this way, one can see the reform or liberalization efforts in China as taking on many prescriptive features while scrapping some, but hardly all, of the proscriptive features. In this, China has joined many other countries, including Brazil, Egypt, and India, but from a starting point involving much more government control of industrial assets, many more state-owned enterprises, and a much larger cooperative sector.

Trade liberalization is one important reform of Chinese proscriptive policies. In the past twenty-five years China has lowered tariffs to levels comparable to those in the OECD countries (see Chapter 16). The reforms associated with the evolution of Special Economic Zones and joining the WTO have all greatly reduced the potential for rent seeking from external trade barriers. On the domestic front, market reforms have also significantly reduced the potential for rents. In the 1980s China introduced a two-track plan and market system internally, which generated important price differentials and rents. In the 1990s, however, China has largely eliminated the planned track of this system and for goods and services moved almost entirely to markets, in the process removing the potential for rents.

Corruption and Governance

Rose-Ackerman (1999) surveys a wide range of experience and literature on corruption and, following others, distinguishes among three levels of corruption: petty or retail, systemic, and grand corruption. Other definitions are possible, but for present purposes we accept her framework. Petty corruption is not newsworthy but affects everyday life, because transactions or abuse of power often take place in public settings, like hospitals or schools, where admission may require a bribe. Even if the applicant can meet the legal conditions to obtain the needed permit or license, the process itself is not transparent, thus allowing officials too much discretion. Harassment by the police is the common lot of hawkers, street people, and minorities in many developing countries. Regulations, like residential permits in China or the need for a license to sell on the street, provide police and others with the opportunity for extortion.

Petty corruption typically declines as the incomes and salaries of police and other civil service rise. It can also be reduced if truly independent ombudsmen and grievance procedures are established or if a voice for the poor is established by NGOs, other organizations, or the political process. And, as the *king does, so will his subjects*, that is, good governance above the level of those benefiting from petty corruption can rapidly improve the standards of those they supervise.

Systemic corruption tends to be less visible because an agent is typically extorting someone who owns property, like a factory owner routinely making payments to inspectors or householders to meter readers. Sun (2004, p. 78) cites systemic corruption within Shanghai refrigerator plant no. 2, ranging from RMB3,000 to RMB12,000, relatively small amounts. However, much of China's corruption is in more public settings and is often made visible through prosecutions. In the period 1993–1997, Sun (2004, p. 89) lists prosecutions in the RMB100,000 to RMB1 million range for tens of thousands of cases of embezzlement, misappropriations, and bribery. Prosecution for grand corruption at the national level during this period was usually for misappropriation, with five cases in excess of RMB5 million.

The theme of a study by Melanie Manion is that China's approach to fighting corruption harks back to Maoist campaigns of the 1950s, with the same undesirable effects: campaigns are too frequent, do not last long enough to enlist public

Table 2.3. *Correlates of low corruption*

Indicator	Correlation
Central government expenditure as a % of GDP	0.428
Share of SOEs in nonagricultural GDP	−0.299
Share of exports and imports of goods and services in GDP	0.240
Freedom House ranking of economic freedom	0.676
Freedom House ranking of political freedom	0.534
Per capita GDP	0.653

Source: Elliot (1996). Corruption based on index of Transparency International.

confidence, and undermine the growth of long-term institutions of surveillance and enforcement (Manion, 2004, chapter 5).

Correlates of Corruption

A cottage industry of cross-country correlations has reported a number of associations between perceived honesty in government administration and characteristics of economies, some of which are given in Table 2.3 (see also Bardhan, 1997). How does China fit into this literature?

Interestingly, a large share of government in GDP does not necessarily breed corruption, and the share in China is no longer high. It is high in the Scandinavian countries, which rank at the top end of the honesty index. The low Freedom House rankings on economic and political freedoms would also contribute to the high corruption rank for China, though the interpretation of political freedoms here is questionable. State ownership of enterprises does appear to be associated with corruption, a finding that should fit China. The most encouraging finding, however, is that corruption falls with per capita income, and in some cases dramatically over time (as discussed later for the U.S. experience). One reason for this correlation is that salaries of government employees rise with per capita income, and as salaries rise, the potential benefits from petty corruption begin to be outweighed by the costs of losing a job if caught.

Cross-country studies also examine the relationship between corruption and growth in per capita income. Many such studies appear in volumes published or sponsored by major international financial institutions and other groups, a reflection of heightened global concern with corrupt governance (see, e.g., the IMF volume Abed and Gupta, 2002). In general, these studies find that higher economic growth is associated with lower levels of corruption. The negative relationship between growth and corruption is explained as the result of distorted public and private investment and more unequal income distributions.

When countries receive equal weight, the broad relationship between growth and corruption is strongly negative. But a simple plot reveals some very important outliers. Both India and China have growth rates of GDP per capita, well above the OECD average, despite higher levels of corruption. These cases suggest that while corruption may prevent countries from reaching their full potential for economic growth, it does not, in itself, prevent respectable, if not high, levels of growth. They also suggest that the direction of causality between growth and corruption is not clearly understood.

One explanation for the compatibility of growth and corrupt government was offered at a World Bank meeting by an official from Bangladesh, which in 2006 Transparency International puts at 156th and thus among the most corrupt countries in the world. (China, Brazil, India, and Mexico are tied at 70, and the ranking ranges from 1 to 163, with higher numbers being more corrupt; see Table 2.1a). While discussing corruption, the official is alleged to have said he had "never seen a fish grow in clean water." This defense of corruption as a way to achieve second-best outcomes in the face of regulations that thwart getting things done is common and certainly correct. Eliminating laws or administrative mechanisms that create monopolies or undue discretion in granting permits and the like, however, is certainly a better long-run solution than continuing to foster conditions leading to corrupt governance.

Put another way, in the short term, corruption and economic growth may be positively correlated because opportunities for large, irregular gains are part of what drives the rapid disequilibrium growth spurts in early stages of capitalist development, certainly the experience of the United States in the nineteenth century (Glaeser and Goldin, 2006). Only when things slow down and settle into a more equilibrium mode do the legal and regulatory frameworks have a chance to catch up, at which point the possibilities for Schumpeterian entrepreneurship on a large scale are much more restricted. The interesting question, then, is not whether growth is faster or slower with corruption, but how we can explain the emergence of legal, regulatory, and cultural institutions that restrict corruption and bring it under control.

What does this imply about policies to reduce corruption? An interesting example is the striking success of the Independent Commission Against Corruption (ICAC) established in 1974 in Hong Kong (Lee, 1981). One reason why the Hong Kong effort was successful is that it took place concurrently with increases in per capita income and the salaries of government employees. In this regard it follows the conclusions of the studies mentioned earlier.

The Hong Kong case also brings to our attention another ingredient. One lesson of the ICAC is that independence of the commission was a very important ingredient of its success. Moreover, it is much easier for an externally appointed administrator, like the governor of Hong Kong, to grant such independence than it is for an indigenous government; however, it has come to power. India illustrates the difficulty in establishing an independent enforcement body. One of the main criticisms of its anticorruption measures such as establishing ombudsmen, independent auditors, vigilance commissions, and the like is that they have been ineffective because the government has not granted them independence in investigating corrupt practices or disseminating their findings. The ICAC is a model for anticorruption campaigns, but a model that is not necessarily easy to implement and, as Manion suggests, has not been followed in China.

Features of Corrupt Administrations

Monopoly plays a role in determining patterns of corruption in many countries. Local governments are thought to be the most corrupt due to their control over local permits and resources. In federal systems like China, India, and the United States, higher levels of government may institute reforms and regulations to curb local corruption, but their effectiveness is often limited. Goldin and Glaeser emphasize that historically in the United States urban governments have been most corrupt. In China, county and city governments are similarly thought to be main locus of corruption. The mobility of economic resources, however, can contain the ability of local governments to extract rents. In China the reforms have increased mobility of labor and other resources, thus creating an environment where intergovernmental and interagency competition has become important. China has about 3,000 such local governments, which now compete with each other to attract resources and promote local enterprises (Sicular, 1995).

Poorly Defined Property Rights and Corruption

A type of corruption that has received considerable attention in China and other transition economies is the private acquisition or theft of assets for which property rights are poorly defined and weakly enforced. Examples exist in both urban and rural settings. In urban areas questions have arisen over the disposition of the land, buildings, funds, and equipment belonging to state-owned and collective enterprises. In some cases, such assets have simply been stolen. In other cases, assets are sold to company insiders or third parties at suspiciously favorable terms, often with substantial kickbacks to well-placed individuals.

In rural China the major asset is farmland. We discuss property rights in farmland in the following section on land tenure. For present purposes, suffice it to say that in recent years Chinese newspapers have reported numerous cases of peasants protesting the sale of collective farmland out from under them by local cadres and officials. Typically, the peasants receive only a small fraction of the proceeds from such sales, and other parties to the transaction benefit disproportionately.

The emergence of such corruption is directly linked to China's weak system of property rights. Property rights are not clearly defined, and even in cases where the law is clear, the legal system is often unable to enforce property rights effectively. One factor contributing to this situation is the lack of an independent enforcement body, mentioned in the discussion of India earlier. China's judicial system is relatively young, staffed by judges with insufficient qualifications, and unable to operate independently of local governments or the Party (see Chapter 11).

Uncertain title to land or other property is not unique to transition economies. Those living in favelas in Rio, often with magnificent but insecure, views, are easy subjects of extortion and are reluctant to improve their property because of their uncertain tenure.[9] Further, many live on rural and urban property from which they feel secure from eviction but are unable to sell or pledge for loans. These are examples of what De Soto (2000) has described as dead capital, potential venture capital that is immobilized by uncertain property tenure.

In the absence of firm government steps to clarify and enforce property rights, asset-based corruption is probably inevitable. Since the main beneficiaries of such corruption are government officials, movement by the government to carry out reforms in this direction may be unlikely or at least delayed until most of the relevant assets have been claimed or sold off. Despite this problem, China continues to grow, perhaps because the rents obtained through such corruption take the form of income flows that depend on economic growth. Put differently, some forms of rent give bureaucrats an incentive to undermine the reform process, while others do not. The former is consistent with the grabbing-hand scenario described by Frye and Shleifer (1997), and the latter with a guiding-hand scenario described by Che and Qian (1998) and Morduch and Sicular (2000).

Which of these two scenarios applies depends on the particular mechanisms that generate rents from corrupt activities. If rents are derived from quotas, licenses, and monopoly power, then the beneficiaries have an incentive to block reforms that would promote growth by eliminating the institutions that generate such rents. If, however, the rents are derived from control over economic assets, such as land and equipment, then the beneficiaries may have an incentive to support reform policies that promote efficient growth, because such growth can enhance the returns to their illegally acquired assets.

Concluding Governance

Two broad conclusions emerge from this discussion of governance. Problems of governance emerge because an economy is undergoing major economic changes that enable individuals to profit from socially productive ventures as well as purely opportunistic activities that may be in violation of law or simply exploit loopholes

---

[9] A recent study in Buenos Aires (Galiani and Schargrodsky, 2004) illustrates some of these points. It was decided about twenty years ago to provide government compensation to landowners for plots where squatters had settled. Some landowners accepted compensation, while others took it to the slow-moving Argentine courts, thus providing a natural experiment. Those squatters who obtained ownership took the long view, investing more in housing, had smaller families, and the children attained more schooling. Contrary to the De Soto view, there was no difference in types of employment or access to formal credit markets, though credit from families and friends was larger for those squatters who obtained clear title.

in administrative structures. Excesses associated with rapid economic growth in turn generate responses, like public protest or more media coverage leading to at least temporary reductions in the excesses. This can produce the seeming paradox that apparent widespread corruption, while diverting productive potential to nonproductive activities, may be associated with rapid economic growth and with movements to reduce discretion and improve transparency and accountability.

AGRICULTURE AND LAND TENURE

Land Tenure and Development

Development economists have devoted considerable attention to questions related to land distribution and tenure, including returns to scale, forms of tenancy, security of property rights in land, and the equality of landholding distribution. Empirical studies have, for the most part, found either constant or negative returns to scale for all but the smallest farms (see Deininger and Jin, 2003, pp. 4–5, for a summary). With respect to land tenure, owner operation, fixed-rent tenancy, and sharecropping often coexist. Such mixed systems can be efficient in the presence of costs of labor supervision, asymmetric information, and differing efficiencies of potential tenants. Different contractual arrangements can also arise in response to imperfect or incomplete markets, typically for insurance and credit (Deininger and Jin, 2003, p. 5, and Deininger and Feder, 2001, summarize these issues). Definition of property rights to land and the security of land tenure is a third theme in the microeconomic literature on this topic that relates to China's reform experience.[10]

Johnston and Kilby (1975) point out that the skewness and modality of the farm size distribution are key to a country's overall potential for growth and structural change. Relatively equal, unimodal farm size distributions facilitate the development of commodity and factor markets, provide opportunities for the development of skilled labor and entrepreneurship, and allow for broad-based increases in incomes and purchasing power, all of which stimulate the development of nonagricultural sectors. Several studies have examined the relationship between the inequality of initial distribution of landholdings and the aggregate economic growth of countries; all find a negative and significant relationship (Birdsall and Londono, 1997; Deininger and Squire, 1998; Deininger and Olinto, 2000).

Land Tenure in China

China's grand experiments in land reform have naturally drawn the attention of economists interested in land tenure. These experiments have included land redistribution in the late 1940s and early 1950s, the abolition of private land ownership

---

[10] For an extensive discussion of land security and property relations, see Deininger and Feder (2001) and Binswanger, Deininger, and Feder (1995).

and establishment of collective farming under the commune system in the mid- to late 1950s and the shift back from collective to household farming under the household responsibility system (HRS) in the early 1980s. Our discussion will focus on developments since 1980 (for further detail, see Chapter 13 in this volume).

In the early and mid-1980s the HRS was considered a major success. Most observers agree that shifting the locus of decision making to the household overcame incentive and supervision problems associated with China's collective farm system and that the HRS contributed significantly to the rapid growth in rural output and incomes that China enjoyed at that time (McMillan, Whalley, and Zhu, 1989; Lin, 1992; Huang and Rozelle, 1996; see Putterman, 1988, for an alternative viewpoint).

China's agricultural performance, however, has weakened since the mid-1980s. Growth in output and agricultural incomes has slowed, raising concerns about the adequacy of China's food supply, sources of employment for China's large rural labor force, and how to stem the widening rural–urban income gap. In light of these developments, the HRS has come under new scrutiny. Some argue that aspects of the HRS hinder long-term growth.

One relevant issue for China is the question of optimal farm size. The HRS, by shifting the production unit from the collective to individual households, drastically reduced the scale of farm operations in China. Under the HRS, land was initially allocated to households on the basis of household size and composition, creating a pattern of small household farms with limited local variation in farmland per capita. This pattern has, to some extent, been maintained by village reallocations of land among households to promote equity in the face of demographic changes. Small farm sizes have also persisted because, although households have rights to transfer land, the extent of such transfers has remained small, although increasing in recent years (Ho, 2001; Benjamin and Brandt, 2002; Deininger and Jin, 2002; Kung, 2002).

Thus average farm sizes remain small, and the distribution of farm sizes continues to be relatively equal on a land per capita basis, at least locally.[11] China's agricultural census statistics give average size of farm holding of 0.67 hectares. This compares to farm sizes of 1.55 hectares in India, 1.20 in Japan, 2.16 in the Philippines, and 3.36 in Thailand. Furthermore, 98 percent of holdings in China are smaller than 2 hectares.[12]

[11] Benjamin and Brandt (2002, p. 698) find that for a survey of 787 households in two provinces, cultivated land is directly proportional to family size after controlling for village of residence.

[12] See www.fao.org/es/ess/census/default.asp for agricultural census data for different countries, mostly from 1990 to 2000. This source gives China's agricultural census data, which are for 1997 and include information on average farm size and farm size distribution. Note that China's agricultural census data do not seem consistent with data on farm size in other Chinese sources. According to China's National Bureau of Statistics, 2002, average farm size was about 1.2 hectares. This number is based on data from NBS sample surveys of rural households published in the *China Statistical Yearbooks*. (In 2002, the average household size was 4.13 people; average household cultivated land per capita was 2 *mu* or about 0.3 hectares; see

Are concerns about efficiency loss due to small farm size justified? To date, empirical studies for China have generally not found that bigger farms are better. Benjamin and Brandt et al. (2002) find that for a sample of 787 households in two provinces, labor use per unit of land is inversely related to farm size, and output per unit of land is constant across small and large farms. Production function estimates for China typically find roughly constant returns to scale (Wan and Cheng, 2001; Sicular and Zhao, 2004). A large empirical literature on farm size and land productivity in other countries points to the same conclusion (e.g., Bardhan, 1973; Berry and Cline, 1979; Deininger and Jin, 2003, pp. 4–5).

While China appears to resemble other countries, the apparent lack of scale economies may reflect uniquely Chinese circumstances. In China, collectives continue to play a significant role in coordinating agricultural investments, production, and marketing (Vermeer, 1998; Brandt et al., 2002). The presence of bodies that transcend small, individual farms may provide a mechanism for capturing economies of scale. Cooperative production and marketing activities are not unique to China. Operation Flood, a successful dairy marketing system built on village producers' cooperatives in India, illustrates the capacity of collectives to transcend individual farms. These cooperatives procure milk and provide inputs and services to small farmers who produce milk, even those with as few as one or two cows. This program has allowed small-scale production to greatly increase value added, while at the same time lowering prices and improving the quality of milk in urban areas.

Differential access to credit probably does not play as large a role in China as elsewhere, as the formal credit system in rural areas is underdeveloped and informal credit, while increasing in importance, is highly constrained (Findlay et al., 2003). Thus, in China larger farms may not have a substantial advantage over smaller farms in access to or costs of investment funds. This may contribute to the lack of scale economies, in contrast to the situation in other countries, where larger farmers have distinct advantages in access to credit, both in terms of quantity and price.

Related to farm size is the issue of land fragmentation, a common feature of agriculture in many parts of Asia, Europe, and also China. In India in the 1960s, for example, the average size of operational holdings (owned plus leased in minus leased out) was about 2.5 hectares, held in 5.7 fragments averaging 0.45 hectares each. Land consolidation programs have been instituted in most states of India without success, except where the land is very homogeneous and the efficiency gains are clear to all, namely Punjab and Haryana.

In China, land fragmentation has emerged through the process of collective allocation of farmland among households, typically in order to ensure an equitable

---

Yearbook, 2003, pp. 366, 424). Note that the official statistics are thought to understate China's cultivated land area by as much as 50–60 percent (Smil, 1999), but even if adjusted accordingly China's farms remain small by international standards.

distribution of land of different qualities and characteristics among households within the village (Wan and Cheng, 2001). The degree of fragmentation varies considerably among regions but is severe in some areas. In Hubei province, for example, most households operate on eight plots of land, and in some areas the average number of plots reaches 19, with an average size of 0.015 hectare (Wan and Cheng, 2001).

While farmers can and do overcome many of the inefficiencies of very small fragments by sharing assets like tractors, outsourcing ploughing, or buying and selling water, evidence for China suggests that such mechanisms are insufficient to eliminate the inefficiencies that arise from fragmentation. A study by Wan and Cheng (2001), for example, finds that while economies of scale for overall farm size are minimal, output loss due to fragmentation of landholdings is significant and large. They estimate that food grain output would increase by 15 percent if fragmentation were eliminated, with especially large gains in the production of wheat, late rice, and tuber crops.

A further issue raised in the China literature is the definition of property rights to land. China provides an interesting case of a country in transition between communal and private property rights. Farmland in China is still owned communally, but over time reform policies have strengthened the use rights of individual households (Prosterman, Schwarzwalder, and Ye, 2000; Ho, 2001; Cai, 2003; Ho and Lin, 2003). For example, regulations have extended tenure security. Starting in 1984, land contracts were to be fifteen years or longer; in 1993 contracts were extended to thirty years after expiry of the fifteen-year contract; under the revised Land Management Law of 1998, the contract is for thirty years with prohibitions on village reallocation of land among households (Prosterman, Schwarzwalder, and Ye, 2000; Ho and Lin, 2003).

The balance between collective and household rights to land has differed among localities and, within localities, among categories of farmland. Many villages carry out periodic, villagewide reallocations of land among households in contravention of regulations. Because these farmland reallocations are popular among villagers, localities have little incentive to implement the national regulations (Kung, 1995; Kung and Liu, 1997; Kung, 2000; Ho, 2001; Jacoby, Li, and Rozelle, 2002).

Moving toward a system of private property rights has both benefits and costs. One benefit that has received considerable attention in China (and elsewhere) is that by making land tenure more secure, it increases investment and thus long-term agricultural growth. Several studies using the frequency of land reallocations as a measure of insecurity of land tenure find only a small impact of security of land tenure on investment. Works by Brandt et al. (2002) and Jacoby, Li, and Rozelle (2002) compare organic fertilizer use on more secure private plots with that on less secure responsibility plots and by farmers in villages with lower risk of land reallocation with those in villages with higher risk. Organic fertilizer is considered a form of investment as it enhances long-term soil fertility. Another study by Carter and Yao (1999) separates the effects on investment of security of land tenure from those of transfer rights.

Overall, the investment effects of strengthened property rights appear to be relatively small. More secure rights in land may also provide rural households with a form of collateral, and so provide a basis for borrowing and, more generally, rural financial development. Another benefit is to create an instrument for saving to provide for old age. The inability to use land as collateral likely hinders financial development in rural areas (Besley, 1995; Brandt et al., 2002; De Soto, 2000). However, China's Land Law (1998) still prohibits the use of land as collateral, and there is no indication that this policy is likely to change (Prosterman, Schwarzwalder, and Ye, 2000).

These gains from enhancing private property rights must be balanced against the benefits of retaining a communal system. In China periodic land reallocations provide a mechanism by which to maintain relatively equitable access to land. This is particularly important in a context of underdeveloped factor and insurance markets and in the absence of rural social safety nets (Brandt et al., 2002). In areas that have not carried out reallocations, older households that received land on a per capita basis when their children were still at home now enjoy relatively abundant land per capita, while newly established households are land short. Local populations are sensitive to such differences, and this is one reason why land reallocations have remained popular.

RURAL INDUSTRIALIZATION

Economists have long recognized the potential role of rural industry in the development process. Rural industry, because of its geographical location and reliance on labor-intensive technologies, can generate employment for underemployed rural workers, increase rural incomes, promote balanced and equitable growth, and provide an alternative to overurbanization, with its attendant problems of congestion and dislocation (Hayami, 1998; Otsuka, 1998, 2002). Despite these potential benefits, however, relatively few economies have followed a development path in which rural industry has played a significant role. Japan and Taiwan, and now Mainland China, are the best-known cases.

The Role of Rural Industry in China's Development

Rural industry in China is generally equated with township and village enterprises (TVEs). As defined here, China's TVEs are businesses located in townships and villages that are owned collectively or privately, mainly by rural units and individuals. They include collectively owned township and village enterprises, joint venture enterprises with a significant local owner, and household businesses. The pattern of TVE ownership has evolved over time. Initially, collective ownership was dominant, but since the 1990s expansion of private TVEs has been rapid, and many collective TVEs have converted to private ownership.[13] TVEs operate in all sectors but are overwhelmingly in industry, albeit with a significant presence in the service sector.[14]

Published statistics suggest that China's TVE sector has indeed contributed significantly to China's overall growth and has generated both employment and income for the rural population. TVE output has grown noticeably faster than output in other sectors during the reform period and has boosted GDP growth overall. The TVE sector is now a major player in the economy. The share of TVE net value added in China's total GDP has increased from only 6 percent in the early 1980s to more than 30 percent. TVEs are especially important in the secondary sector, where they contribute nearly half of total value added. Employment in the TVE sector has shown similar, rapid growth. Between 1980 and 2002, TVE's share of rural employment rose from 9 to 27 percent.[15]

While we do not have direct information on rural household income from TVEs, data on wage earnings and other nonfarm income provide an indication of the impact of nonagricultural rural development at the household level. In 2002 wage income contributed 34 percent of rural household annual net income, up from about 20 percent in mid-1980s. Net income from nonagricultural household businesses contributed 11 percent of rural household net income, up from 5–7 percent in the mid-1980s. Overall, then income from nonagricultural employment now approaches half of rural household net income.[16] This is about the level achieved in Taiwan by the mid-1970s and in Japan by the mid-1960s (Lane, 1988) (see Tables 2.4 and 2.5).

One reputed benefit of rural industrialization is that it promotes equitable growth. Such has been the case in Taiwan and Japan. Much of the literature on TVE development in China, however, has emphasized its tendency to exacerbate geographical income differences. The distribution of TVEs is highly uneven and heavily concentrated in wealthier eastern and coastal regions (Rozelle, 1994; Yao and Liu, 1998). TVE growth has been fastest in regions that started out with higher initial levels of industrial development (Lin and Yao, 2001; Ito,

---

[13] For discussion of the recent ownership changes in the TVE sector, see Lin and Yao (2001), Park and Shen (2003), Qian (2001), and Sun (2000, 2002). In 1985, collective enterprises contributed 73 percent of value added and 59 percent of employment in the TVE sector. By 2002, collective enterprises contributed only 37 percent of value added and 29 percent of employment in the TVE sector (Yearbook, 2003, pp. 448–449).

[14] In 2002, 77 percent of TVE value added was in the secondary sector, 22 percent in the tertiary sector, and 1 percent in the primary sector (Yearbook, 2003, p. 449). In earlier years, the share of the secondary sector remained at or above this level.

[15] These statistics are calculated from data in the Yearbook (2003). Recent figures are for 2002. The authors acknowledge that the data on China's TVEs are problematic, but they provide a rough indication of the importance of this sector.

[16] These statistics are calculated using the NBS rural household survey data from the Yearbook (2003, p. 367) and various tables in NBS (2002). NBS practices regarding calculation of rural household incomes have changed over time, so numbers from the 1980s are not fully comparable to those for recent years, but the percentages give an approximate indication of trends.

Table 2.4. *Percentages of farm household income from wages and nonagricultural sideline businesses in Taiwan and Japan, 1962–1988*

	Taiwan		Japan	
Year	Wage	Wage + Sideline	Wage	Wage + Sideline
1962	n.a.	n.a.	35.7	45.1
1966	20.1	23.9	41.4	48.4
1970	36.0	38.7	52.8	59.7
1974	37.3	40.8	n.a.	n.a.
1980	52.2	58.4	n.a.	n.a.
1985	n.a.	n.a.	69.5	77.8
1988	n.a.	n.a.	71.9	81.7

Source: Lane (1988, table 9.2).

Table 2.5. *China: percentage of rural household net income from wages and nonagricultural sideline businesses, 1985–2002*

Year	Wage	Wage + Sideline
1985	18.2	26.3
1990	20.2	29.3
1995	22.4	33.1
2000	31.2	46.1
2002	33.9	46.8

Note: Nonagricultural sideline income is calculated as total household net income from household sideline businesses minus net income from agriculture (cultivation, animal husbandry, fishery, and forestry).
Source: NBS (2002, pp. 26–27); Yearbook (2003, p. 367).

2002) and also in regions with higher initial levels of agricultural development (Ravallion, 2002). This is a pattern that is found in other developing countries like India.

TVE development also appears to exacerbate inequality in the distribution of rural household income. Khan and Riskin (2005), for example, find that in 1995 and 2002 wage income contributed 35–40 percent of income inequality and income from household nonfarm businesses an additional 10–20 percent of income inequality among rural households. Together, then, these two forms of nonagricultural income have accounted for well over half of measured inequality among rural households in recent years.

Explaining the Rise of China's Rural Industries

What factors explain the growth of China's rural enterprises, and to what extent are they particular to China? Drawing largely on the experiences of Taiwan and Japan, Otsuka outlines several general factors that are key to the success of rural industrialization (Otsuka, 1998). One factor is the availability of cheap rural labor. Another is decentralization of production through subcontracts with urban enterprises and traders. Subcontracting is important because it provides access to capital funds, technology, and markets, which are often inaccessible to small-scale rural entrepreneurs. Subcontracting requires relatively low transportation and communication costs, which in turn depend on public investments in roads, communications, and other infrastructure. A third factor is the presence of "relational contracting," an idea proposed by Hayami (1998). Otsuka (1998, p. 451) describes relational contracting as "long-term, continuous contract relations that are enforced and maintained by personal ties, mutual trust and community obligations . . . ."

The China literature on rural industrialization outlines the historical and institutional features that contributed to the development of China's TVE sector (see, e.g., Bai, Li, and Wang, 2001; Lin and Yao, 2001). Starting in the 1950s and continuing through the 1970s, China's government promoted the development of collectively owned industrial enterprises run by rural communes and brigades. These enterprises created a base of manufacturing experience and networks in rural areas, thus paving the way for the more recent and rapid rise of TVEs. Several circumstances in the early 1980s further facilitated the initial growth of TVEs. Following substantial agricultural price increases and decollectivization, with its consequent boost to incentives and productivity, in the early 1980s rural household incomes experienced significant growth, while at the same time labor use in agriculture became more efficient. The increase in incomes intensified an already pent-up demand for simple consumer manufactures and also for manufactured farm inputs, which were undersupplied by the existing, mainly state-owned industrial sector. TVEs thus had a ready market.

These historical conditions were complemented by certain institutional factors. Initially, the TVE sector was dominated by collective enterprises that were run by township and village governments. Fiscal reforms during the 1980s gave local governments the scope to develop and rights to retain revenues from such enterprises. The resulting fiscal incentives were reinforced by the natural concern of local governments with growth in local income and employment.

Local governments at the township and village levels were key to the initial success of TVEs. Ownership of the enterprises by the local government provided an incentive for the local government to support and protect, rather than prey on, the enterprises. For these reasons, private entrepreneurs often sought bureaucratic sponsors and registered their businesses as collective firms. This phenomenon was so common that it gave rise to the phrase "wearing the red cap."

Some of these institutional factors have since changed (Bai, Li, and Wang, 2001). The 1994 tax reform reduced the local fiscal incentive for supporting TVEs. With the new formula for tax sharing between the central and local governments, less of the tax revenues from TVEs remain at the local level. Planned allocation has been eliminated and markets are now well developed for most products, diminishing the need for bureaucratic assistance in marketing. Also, the easing of restrictions on labor movement has allowed workers to migrate in search of work, thus easing the pressure on local governments to generate employment locally. Such changes explain in part the recent evolution of TVE ownership structure.

Lessons from the Chinese Experience

China's rural industrialization is fulfilling the roles predicted by development economists. It has contributed to China's overall growth, generated employment and of income for the rural population, and promoted a more equitable distribution income in at least some regards. The factors underlying growth in China's rural industry – abundant cheap labor, relational networks, and the presence of facilitating actors who could provide credit, technological inputs, and marketing – parallel those found in other cases of successful rural development, namely, Japan and Taiwan.

Still, China's experience has in important ways been particular, reflecting the evolution of institutions from the Maoist era and policies specific to the process of economic transition. For these reasons, China does not provide a model that can be easily transferred elsewhere. For the same reasons the role of rural industry in China's future development is unclear. Some have suggested that TVEs benefited from circumstances arising in China's partially reformed economy, such as initial restrictions on migration and fiscal incentives. These circumstances will disappear as China proceeds further toward a well-developed market economy. China's rural industry, then, may eventually decline. Yet even if it does decline, it will likely have had long-term implications for China's path of development. As endogenous growth models demonstrate, where one ends up depends on where one starts and what happens along the way.

CONCLUSIONS

This chapter has examined the post-1978 Chinese economy within the perspective of other developing countries, focusing on both distinctive and common features. We began with a quantitative description of China in comparison to Brazil, India, and Mexico, as well as in comparison to averages for low-, middle-, and high-income countries. Both India and China appear in the upper tier of low-income countries at the start of reforms, with Brazil and Mexico in the middle-income group. In the past twenty-five years India has clearly moved into the middle-income group and China has moved even more rapidly into the upper-middle group along with Brazil and

Mexico. China has performed very well in its overall economic growth, savings, and investment, even allowing for possible overstatement in the official statistics. Not surprisingly, income inequality has increased, but poverty has declined markedly. China has made remarkable progress in reducing birthrates and achieving slower population growth, but with masculinity ratios even higher than those in India. In the area of education, China's record is uneven, with potential negative consequences in the long term.

What are the institutional features that have emerged and influenced China's economic performance? China shares with many developing and transition economies a legacy of governance in which bureaucrats have great discretionary power in decision making. This discretionary power provides opportunities for bribery and corruption. Yet, the experience of China, as well as of Brazil and India, raises questions about the current consensus that corruption represents a major constraint on growth. These three countries, which together account for almost 40 percent of the world's population, have experienced successful growth with relatively high levels of corruption.

The most likely explanation is that in the short term, opportunities for corruption and irregular dealings are closely intertwined with rapid disequilibrium growth. Rapid growth is a messy business, one in which the economy develops more quickly than the social and governance institutions that check irregularities. In the case of China, much corruption has emerged as the result of weak property rights and takes the form of asset grabs. This type of corruption, while questionable from the perspective of equity and justice, can create incentives for growth, as growth generates returns to those improperly acquired assets.

In the longer term, the governance abuses that occur during periods of rapid growth can generate countervailing responses that improve transparency and accountability. For example, as countries become more affluent, the media, now including the Internet, typically becomes more active in reporting corruption and the like. This appears to have been the historical experience in the nineteenth-century United States, and today the potential role of the media is more pronounced as global communications have become much easier. The above notwithstanding, in the long term, economies will be better served by a governance framework that is short on bureaucratic monopoly and discretion and long on transparency and accountability. The tendency of China to wage episodic campaigns against corruption unfortunately tends to undermine the long-term development of watchdog institutions.

China's land tenure reforms are thought to have jump-started China's successful reform process. With the passage of time and slowing growth in agriculture, though, the continuation of collective land ownership with poorly defined property rights may obstruct productivity growth (see Chapters 13 and 18, both in this volume). Privatization is the standard neoclassical prescription. We believe that while China's current land tenure system is in some ways problematic, it has provided important benefits by preserving some degree of equity among households and providing public goods and community-level infrastructure to rural residents. Also, China's relatively unimodal land size distribution, which is closely connected to the land tenure system, has likely had positive implications for macroeconomic growth. Whether these benefits will continue in the future is unclear.

The development of rural industries is another significant feature of the Chinese economy during the reform era. China's township and village industries have been a significant force underlying China's rapid growth during the reform period. They provided large-scale employment opportunities at least into the early 1990s and continue to do so, albeit in altered and increasingly private rather than collective form. It appears that China's experience has parallels in Taiwan and, earlier, in Japan, suggesting an East Asian pattern. The obvious resemblance of labor recruitment patterns in Chinese light-manufacturing enterprises with earlier episodes in Japan (and, for that matter, in Great Britain and New England), for example, heavy use of young females housed in company dormitories, supports this view. In any event, this is an area in which China's experience, while not unique, is nevertheless unusual, because rural industrial development that generates employment and income for rural populations has been noticeably lacking elsewhere in the developing world.

The topics and institutions examined here are not exhaustive, so that our survey unavoidably leaves large gaps. Significant issues that we have neglected, to name a few, include the role of foreign trade and investment, financial institutions, urban-based industrial and ownership reforms, and environmental and public health issues. Fortunately, many of these topics are covered elsewhere in this volume. In addition, China is not standing still, and so the themes covered here, and our approach to them, would likely differ ten years from now.

The issues of property rights, governance, transparency, and income distribution raised in this chapter, however, are not transient but represent central features of the development process that will continue to command the attention of Chinese policymakers and China-oriented research. Our survey illustrates the value of development economics as a useful lens through which to view China's dynamic and turbulent economic evolution. Our observation that many aspects of recent Chinese experience deviate from the standard features of major development paradigms ensures that China will continue to provide constructive challenges for development economics in future decades.

References

Abed, George T. and Sanjeev Gupta, eds. 2002. *Governance, Corruption and Economic Performance.* Washington, DC: International Monetary Fund, xii, 564 pp.

Aten, Bettina. September 2006. "Interarea Price Levels: An Experimental Methodology." *Monthly Labor Review.* 129(9), pp. 47–61.

Bai, Chong-En, David D. Li, and Yijiang Wang. 2001. "Thriving on a Tilted Playing Field: China's Non-State Enterprises in the Reform Era." Working Paper 95. Stanford: Center for Research on Economic Development and Policy Reform, Stanford University.

Banister, Judith. May 2004. "Shortage of Girls in China Today." *Journal of Population Research.* 21(1), pp. 19–45.

Bardhan, Pranab. 1973. "Size, Productivity and Returns to Scale: An Analysis of Farm-level Data in Indian Agriculture." *Journal of Political Economy.* 81(6), pp. 1370–1386.

Bardhan, Pranab. September 1997. "Corruption and Development: A Review of Issues." *Journal of Economic Literature.* 35(3), pp. 1320–1346.

Barro, Robert J. and Jong-Wha Lee. April 2000. "International Data on Educational Attainment: Updates and Implications." Working Paper 42. Cambridge, MA: Harvard Center for International Development.

Benjamin, Dwayne and Loren Brandt. November 2002. "Property Rights, Labor Markets and Efficiency in an Economy in Transition: The Case of Rural China." *Canadian Journal of Economics.* 35(4), pp. 689–716.

Berry, R. Albert and William R. Cline. 1979. *Agrarian Structure and Productivity in Developing Countries.* Baltimore: Johns Hopkins.

Besley, Timothy. 1995. "Property Rights and Investment Incentives: Theory and Evidence from Ghana." *Journal of Political Economy.* 103(5), pp. 903–937.

Bhagwati, Jagdish. 1988. *Protectionism.* Cambridge, MA: MIT Press.

Binswanger, Hans P., Klaus Deininger, and Gershon Feder. 1995. "Power, Distortions, Revolt and Reform in Agricultural Land Relations," Chapter 41 in *Handbook of Development Economics,* vol. 3B. Jere Behrman and T.N. Srinivasan, eds. New York: Elsevier, pp. 2559–2772.

Birdsall, Nancy and Juan-Luis Londono. 1997. "Asset Inequality Matters: An Assessment of the World Bank's Approach to Poverty Reduction." *American Economic Association Papers and Proceedings.* 87(2), pp. 32–37.

Brandt, Loren and Carsten Holz. 2006. "Spatial Price Differences in China: Estimates and Implications." *Economic Development and Cultural Change.* 55(1), pp. 43–86.

Brandt, Loren, Jikun Huang, Guo Li, and Scott Rozelle. January 2002. "Land Rights in Rural China: Facts, Fictions and Issues." *The China Journal.* 47, pp. 67–97.

Cai, Yongshun. September 2003. "Collective Ownership or Cadres' Ownership? The Non-agricultural Use of Farmland in China." *China Quarterly.* 175, pp. 662–680.

Carter, Michael R. and Yang Yao. October 1999. "Specialization without Regret: Transfer Rights, Agricultural Productivity and Investment in an Industrializing Economy." World Bank Policy Research Working Paper 2202. Washington, DC: World Bank.

Che, Jiahua and Yingyi Qian. 1998. "Insecure Property Rights and Government Ownership of Firms." *Quarterly Journal of Economics.* 113(2), pp. 467–496.

De Soto, Hernando. 2000. *The Mystery of Capital: Why Capitalism Triumphs in the West and Fails Everywhere Else.* New York: Basic Books.

Deininger, Klaus and Gershon Feder. 2001. "Land Institutions and Land Markets," Chapter 6 in *Handbook of Agricultural Economics,* vol. 1A. Bruce L. Gardner and Gordon C. Rausser, eds. New York: Elsevier, pp. 287–331.

Deininger, Klaus and Songqing Jin. November 2002. "Land Rental Markets as an Alternative to Government Reallocation? Equity and Efficiency Considerations in the Chinese Land Tenure System." World Bank Policy Research Working Paper 2930. Washington, DC: World Bank.

Deininger, Klaus and Songqing Jin. April 2003. "Land Sales and Rental Markets in Transition: Evidence from Rural Vietnam." World Bank Policy Research Working Paper 3013. Washington, DC: World Bank.

Deininger, Klaus and Pedro Olinto. June 2000. "Asset Distribution, Inequality and Growth." World Bank Policy Research Group Working Paper 2375. Washington, DC: World Bank.

Deininger, Klaus and Lyn Squire. 1998. "New Ways of Looking at Old Issues: Inequality and Growth." *Journal of Development Economics.* 57(2), pp. 257–285.

Eastwood, Robert and Michael Lipton. September 2000. "Rural–Urban Dimensions of Inequality Change." WIDER Working Paper 200. Helsinki: UNU-World Institute for Development Economics Research.

Eckstein, Alexander. 1977. *China's Economic Revolution.* Cambridge and New York: Cambridge University Press.

Elliot, Kimberly Ann, ed. 1996. *Corruption and the Global Economy.* Washington, DC: Institute for International Economics.

Fan, Gang, Dwight H. Perkins, and Lora Sabin. 1997. "People's Republic of China: Economic Performance and Prospects." *Asian Development Review.* 15(2), pp. 43–85.

Findlay, Christopher, Andrew Watson, Enjiang Cheng, and Gang Zhu, eds. 2003. *Rural Financial Markets in China.* Canberra: Asia Pacific Press.

Frye, Timothy and Andrei Shleifer. 1997. "The Invisible Hand and the Grabbing Hand." *American Economic Review.* 87(2), pp. 354–358.

Galiani, Sebastian and Ernesto Schargrodsky. September 28, 2004. "Effects of Land Titling." Paper presented at the Poverty and Applied Micro Seminar, World Bank, Washington, DC.

Glaeser, Edward and Claudia Goldin. 2006. "Corruption and Reform: An Introduction," in *Corruption and Reform: Lessons from America's Economic History.* Edward L. Glaeser and Claudia Goldin, eds. Chicago: University of Chicago Press, pp. 3–22.

Guilmoto, Christophe Z. and Isabelle Attané. 2005. "The Geography of Deteriorating Child Sex Ratio in China and India." XXV *International Population Conference of the International Union for the Scientific Study of Population, Tours, France, July 18–23.*

Gustafsson, Björn, Shi Li, Terry Sicular, and Ximing Yue. 2008. "Income Inequality and Spatial Differences in China 1988, 1995 and 2002," Chapter 2 in Björn Gustafsson. Shi Li and Terry Sicular, eds. *Inequality and Public Policy in China.* Cambridge and New York: Cambridge University Press.

Hayami, Yujiro. 1998. "Toward an Alternative Path of Economic Development: An Introduction," Chapter 1 in *Toward a Rural-Based Development of Commerce and Industry: Selected Experiences from East Asia.* Yujiro Hayami, ed. EDI Learning Series. Washington, DC: World Bank, pp. 1–20.

Ho, Peter. 2001. "Who Owns China's Land? Policies, Property Rights and Deliberate Institutional Ambiguity." *China Quarterly.* 166, pp. 394–421.

Ho, Samuel P.S. and George C.S. Lin. 2003. "Emerging Land Markets in Rural and Urban China: Policies and Practices." *China Quarterly.* 175, pp. 681–707.

Holz, Carsten A. 2003. "Fast, Clear and Accurate: How Reliable Are Chinese Output and Economic Growth Statistics." *China Quarterly.* 173, pp. 122–163.

Holz, Carsten A. 2006a. "China's Reform Period Economic Growth: How Reliable Are Angus Maddison's Estimates?" *Review of Income and Wealth.* 52(1), pp. 85–119.

Holz, Carsten A. 2006b. "China's Reform Period Economic Growth: How Reliable are Angus Maddison's Estimates? Response to Angus Maddison's Reply." *Review of Income and Wealth.* 52(3), pp. 471–475.

Huang, Jikun and Scott Rozelle. 1996. "Technological Change: Rediscovering the Engine of Growth in China's Rural Economy." *Journal of Development Economics.* 49(2), pp. 337–369.

Ito, Junichi. March 2002. "Why Have TVEs Contributed to Interregional Imbalances in China?" EPTD Discussion Paper 91. Washington, DC: International Food Policy Research Institute.

Jacoby, Hanan G., Guo Li, and Scott Rozelle. December 2002. "Hazards of Expropriation: Tenure, Insecurity, and Investment in Rural China." *American Economic Review*. 92(5), pp. 1420–1447.

Johnston, Bruce F. and Peter Kilby. 1975. *Agriculture and Structural Transformation: Economic Strategies in Late-Developing Countries*. New York: Oxford University Press.

Khan, Aziz and Carl Riskin. June 2005. "China's Household Income and Its Distribution, 1995 and 2002." *China Quarterly*. 182, pp. 356–384.

Knight, John and Lina Song. 1999. *The Urban–Rural Divide: Economic Disparities and Interactions in China*. New York: Oxford University Press.

Kraay, Aart. 2000. "Household Saving in China." *World Bank Economic Review*. 14(3), pp. 545–570.

Kung, James Kai-sing. 1995. "Equal Entitlement Versus Tenure Security under a Regime of Collective Property Rights: Peasants' Preference for Institutions in Post-Reform Chinese Agriculture." *Journal of Comparative Economics*. 21, pp. 82–111.

Kung, James Kai-sing. 2000. "Common Property Rights and Land Reallocations in Rural China: Evidence from a Village Survey." *World Development*. 28(4), pp. 701–719.

Kung, James Kai-sing. 2002. "Off-Farm Labor Markets and the Emergence of Land Rental Markets in Rural China." *Journal of Comparative Economics*. 30, pp. 395–414.

Kung, James Kai-sing and Shouying Liu. July 1997. "Farmers' Preferences Regarding Ownership and Land Tenure in Post-Mao China: Unexpected Evidence from Eight Counties." *The China Journal*. 38, pp. 33–63.

Kuznets, Simon. 1955. "Economic Growth and Income Inequality." *American Economic Review*. 45, pp. 1–28.

Lane, David W. 1988. "Political Bases of Rural Industrialization: Korea and Taiwan, China," Chapter 9 in *Toward a Rural-Based Development of Commerce and Industry: Selected Experiences from East Asia*. EDI Learning Series. Yujiro Hayami, ed. Washington, DC: World Bank, pp. 211–240.

Lee, Rance P.L., ed. 1981. *Corruption and Its Control in Hong Kong: Situations Up to the Late Seventies*. Hong Kong: CUHK Press.

Lin, Justin Yifu. 1992. "Rural Reforms and Agricultural Growth in China." *American Economic Review*. 82(1), pp. 34–51.

Lin, Justin Yifu and Yang Yao. 2001. "Chinese Rural Industrialization in the Context of the East Asian Miracle," Chapter 4 in *Rethinking the East Asian Miracle*. Joseph E. Stiglitz and Shahid Yusuf, eds. New York: Oxford University Press, pp. 143–195.

Maddison, Angus. 1998. *Chinese Economic Performance in the Long Run*. Paris: Development Center, OECD.

Maddison, Angus. 2006. "Do Official Statistics Exaggerate China's GDP Growth? A Reply to Carsten Holz." *Review of Income and Wealth*. 52(1), pp. 121–126.

Maddison, Angus and Harry X. Wu. 2007. "China's Economic Performance: How Fast Has GDP Grown; How Big Is It Compared with the USA?" Paper originally presented at World Economic Performance: Past, Present and Future. University of Queensland, Brisbane, Australia.

Manion, Melanie. 2004. *Corruption by Design: Building Clean Government in Mainland China and Hong Kong*. Cambridge, MA: Harvard University Press.

McMillan, John, John Whalley, and Lijing Zhu. 1989. "The Impact of China's Economic Reforms on Agricultural Productivity Growth." *Journal of Political Economy*. 97(4), pp. 781–807.

Morduch, Jonathan and Terry Sicular. 2000. "Politics, Growth and Inequality in Rural China: Does It Pay to Join the Party?" *Journal of Development Economics*. 77(2), pp. 331–356.

NBS [National Bureau of Statistics], 2002. *Zhongguo nongcun zhuhu diaocha nianjian* [China Rural Household Survey Yearbook]. Beijing: China Statistics Press.

Oster, Emily. 2005. "Hepatitis B and the Case of the Missing Women." *Journal of Political Economy.* 113(6), pp. 1163–1216.

Otsuka, Keijiro. 1998. "Rural Industrialization in East Asia," Chapter 14 in *The Institutional Foundations of East Asian Economic Development.* Yujiro Hayami and Masahiko Aoki, eds. New York: St. Martin's Press, pp. 447–475.

Otsuka, Keijiro. 2002. "Poverty Reduction Issues: Village Economy Perspective." *Asian Development Review.* 19(1), pp. 98–116.

OECD. 2005. *China: OECD Economic Surveys.* Paris: OECD.

Park, Albert and Minggao Shen. 2003. "Joint Liability Lending and the Rise and Fall of China's Township and Village Enterprises." *Journal of Development Economics.* 71, pp. 497–531.

Prosterman, Roy, Brian Schwarzwalder, and Jianping Ye. March 2000. "Implementation of 30-Year Land Use Rights for Farmers under China's 1998 Land Management Law: An Analysis and Recommendations Based on a 17 Province Survey." *Rural Development Institute Reports on Foreign Aid and Development*, vol. 105. Seattle, WA: Rural Development Institute.

Putterman, Louis. 1988. "Group Farming and Work Incentives in Collective-Era China." *Modern China.* 14(4), pp. 419–450.

Qian, Yingyi. 2001. "Government Control in Corporate Governance as a Transition Institution: Lessons from China," Chapter 7 in *Rethinking the East Asian Miracle.* Joseph E. Stiglitz and Shahid Yusuf, eds. New York: Oxford University Press, pp. 295–321.

Ravallion, Martin. August 2002. "Externalities to Rural Development: Evidence for China." World Bank Policy Research Working Paper 2879. Washington, DC: World Bank.

Ravallion, Martin and Shaohua Chen. 2004a. "China's (Uneven) Progress Against Poverty." World Bank Policy Research Paper WPS-3408. Washington, DC: World Bank.

Ravallion, Martin and Shaohua Chen. 2004b. "How Have the World's Poorest Fared Since the 1980s?" *World Bank Research Observer.* 19(2), pp. 141–169.

Ren, Ruoen. 1997. *China's Economic Performance in International Perspective.* Paris: OECD.

Ren, Ruoen and Kai Chen. December 1994. "An Expenditure Based Bilateral Comparison of Gross Domestic Product between China and the United States." *The Review of Income and Wealth.* 40(4), pp. 377–394.

Rose-Ackerman, Susan. 1999. *Corruption and Government.* Cambridge and New York: Cambridge University Press.

Rozelle, Scott. December 1994. "Rural Industrialization and Increasing Inequality: Emerging Patterns in China's Reforming Economy." *Journal of Comparative Economics.* 19(3), pp. 362–394.

Sicular, Terry. 1995. "Redefining State, Plan and Market: China's Reforms in Agricultural Commerce." *China Quarterly.* 144, pp. 1020–1064.

Sicular, Terry, Ximing Yue, Bjorn Gustafsson, and Shi Li. 2007. "The Urban-Rural Gap and Income Inequality in China." *Review of Income and Wealth.* 53(1), pp. 93–126.

Sicular, Terry and Yaohui Zhao. 2004. "Earnings and Labor Mobility in Rural China: Implications for China's Accession to the WTO," in *China and the WTO: Accession, Policy Reform and Poverty Reduction Strategies.* Deepak Bhattasali, Shantong Li, and Will Martin, eds. New York: Oxford University Press, pp. 239–260.

Smil, Vaclav. June 1999. "China's Agricultural Land." *China Quarterly.* 158, pp. 414–429.

Sun, Laixiang. 2000. "Anticipatory Ownership Reform Driven by Competition: China's Township-Village and Private Enterprises in the 1990s." *Comparative Economic Studies.* 52(3), pp. 49–75.

Sun, Laixiang. 2002. "Fading Out of Local Government Ownership: Recent Ownership Reform in China's Township and Village Enterprises." *Economic Systems.* 26(3), pp. 249–269.

Sun, Yan. 2004. *Corruption and Market in Contemporary China.* Ithaca: Cornell University Press.

Vermeer, Eduard. 1998. *Cooperative and Collective in China's Rural Development: Between State and Private Interests.* F. Pieke and W.L. Chong, eds. New York: ME Sharpe.

Wan, Guanghua and Enjiang Cheng. February 2001. "Effects of Land Fragmentation and Returns to Scale in the Chinese Farming Sector." *Applied Economics.* 33(2), pp. 183–194.

Wang, Yan and Yudong Yao. 2001. "Sources of China's Economic Growth, 1952–99: Incorporating Human Capital Accumulation." World Bank Policy Research Working Paper 2650. Washington, DC: World Bank.

World Bank. 2000. *China: Overcoming Rural Poverty.* Washington, DC: World Bank East Asia and Pacific Region Rural Development and Natural Resources Unit Report 21105-CHA.

World Bank. 2003. *World Development Report 2003: Sustainable Development in a Dynamic World: Transforming Institutions, Growth and Quality of Life.* New York and Washington, DC: Oxford University Press and World Bank.

WIDER [World Institute for Development Economics Research]. 2005. *World Income Inequality DatabaseV2.0a.* Helsinki: UNU/WIDER. Accessed March 15, 2007, from http://www.wider.unu.edu/wiid/wiid.htm.

Wu, Harry X. September 2007. "The Chinese GDP Growth Rate Puzzle: How Fast Has the Chinese Economy Grown?" *Asian Economic Papers* 6(1), pp. 1–23.

Yao, Shujie and Jirui Liu. November 1998. "Economic Reforms and Regional Segmentation in China." *Regional Studies.* 32(8), pp. 735–746.

Yearbook. NBS [National Bureau of Statistics]. (various years). *China Statistical Yearbook.* Beijing: China Statistics Press.

Young, Alwyn. 2003. "Gold into Base Metals: Productivity Growth in the People's Republic of China during the Reform Period." *Journal of Political Economy.* 111(6), pp. 1120–1261.

THREE

China in Light of the Performance of the Transition[1] Economies

Jan Svejnar

INTRODUCTION

China's post-1978 economic reforms and the post-1989 economic transition in the former Soviet bloc and Yugoslavia provide a unique setting for comparing two paths of transformation of a communist economic system into a market economy. In both cases, the transition followed years of increasingly unsuccessful economic performance. Yet, the transition itself was very different in the two settings. In the case of China, economic growth has from the start exceeded most expectations. In the case of Central and East Europe (CEE) and the Commonwealth of Independent States (CIS), there was a precipitous and unexpected economic decline in the first three to eight years, with impressive growth thereafter. While China adopted a gradual approach and appears to have benefited from sensible policies and relative absence of adverse shocks, the CEE and CIS policymakers underestimated economic problems associated with a rapid transformation and made a number of questionable choices in the first few years of the transition.

In this chapter, I compare China's performance and future challenges with those of the CEE and CIS countries. In presenting data and examples from the CEE and CIS regions, I refer to all twenty-seven transition economies, but I focus primarily on comparing China's experience with that of the five Central European countries (the Czech Republic, Hungary, Poland, Slovakia, and Slovenia), three Baltic countries (Estonia, Latvia, and Lithuania), three Balkan countries (Bulgaria, Croatia, and Romania), and two CIS countries (Russia and Ukraine). The first eleven countries account for most of the CEE region and have a combined population of over 100 million people. Russia (population of 145 million) and Ukraine (population of 47 million) are the two principal economies of the former Soviet Union and now the CIS.

[1] The author thanks Ruchir Aggarwal, Tomislav Ladika, and Brian McCauley for valuable research assistance.

The Soviet-style centrally planned system, adopted to some extent also by China, was relatively well suited to mobilizing resources for expanding existing productive activities, such as during World War II and the postwar reconstruction. The Soviet bloc countries started with an impressive 4.5 percent annual growth rate in per capita gross national product (GNP) during the 1950s, exceeding the 3.7 percent rate of growth of a comparison group of market economies (Gregory and Stuart, 1997).[2] However, the rigidities of the command economy made it much less suitable for invention, innovation, and efficient allocation of resources, resulting in a long-term slowdown in the economies of the entire Soviet bloc since about 1960. While the comparison group of market economies averaged rates of growth of GNP per capita of 4.5 percent in the 1960s, 2.8 percent in the 1970s, and 2.0 percent in the 1980s, the growth of per capita GNP of the Soviet bloc countries is estimated to have fallen to 3.6 percent in the 1960s, 2.8 percent in the 1970s, and 0.8 percent in the 1980s. China followed a somewhat different pattern of growth from that of the Soviet bloc, in that it achieved a relatively fast rate of gross domestic product (GDP) growth (6.5 percent) in the 1952–1957 period, slower growth (2.4 percent) in 1957–1965, but faster growth (4.9 percent) again in the later 1965–1978 period before the major reforms were launched (see Chapter 20). Since starting the reforms, China achieved remarkable long-run rate of growth (9.5 percent during 1978–2005).

The long-term economic slowdown in the Soviet bloc relative to the western economies and the rapid economic growth in China in the late 1970s and 1980s created expectations that after the fall of Soviet and Yugoslav communism, the CEE and CIS economies would generate fast economic growth and gradually catch up with the developed countries.

STRATEGIES FOR TRANSITION

In the early phase, China's policymakers emphasized dual-track reforms that had relatively few visible losers, maintained existing production by permitting only gradual relaxation of central controls in the existing state sector, and allowed the large-scale expansion of township and village enterprises (TVEs) that greatly expanded economic activity (Byrd and Lin, 1990; Qian, Lau, and Roland, 2000; Naughton, 2002). The reform was radical in agriculture, especially in terms of a return to household farming, and it generated unexpectedly fast economic growth there. The gradualist strategy changed somewhat around 1993 as the central government reasserted itself, increased the share of budgetary and extrabudgetary revenues in GDP (Krumm and Wong, 2002), invested more in infrastructure, and

---

[2] In Gregory and Stuart (1997), the Soviet bloc includes all the states of the Soviet Union plus Bulgaria, Czechoslovakia, East Germany, Hungary, Poland, and Romania. The market economies in the sample include Austria, Belgium, Canada, Denmark, France, Greece, India, Italy, Japan, Netherlands, Norway, Spain, Sweden, Turkey, United Kingdom, the United States, and West Germany.

permitted losers to appear, especially in the form of laid-off state-owned enterprise (SOE) workers (Naughton, 2002). This shift also reflected increased competition within the economy and rising influence of market forces.

The policymakers in the former Soviet bloc developed transition strategies that focused on abandoning the centrally planned system and substituting it with a market system in the context of macroeconomic stabilization and microeconomic restructuring, along with institutional and political reforms. While China adopted a relatively gradual and unified overall approach, albeit with much experimentation at the local level, the implementation of transition strategies in CEE and CIS was relatively fast, although it varied across countries in speed and emphasis.

While a major debate took place about the merits of fast or "big bang" reform versus gradual reform, almost all the CEE and CIS governments went ahead rapidly with what I have called Type I reforms (Svejnar, 2002, 2007). These reforms typically focused on macrostabilization, price liberalization, and abandoning central planning. The macroeconomic strategy emphasized restrictive fiscal and monetary policies, income policies (wage controls), and often also a fixed exchange rate. The microstrategy consisted of price liberalization, dismantling the Soviet bloc trading area, the Council for Mutual Economic Assistance (CMEA), opening up to varying degrees to international trade (thus inducing a more efficient allocation of resources based on world prices), reducing direct subsidies to SOEs, and allowing the SOEs to restructure. The strategy also aimed at removing barriers to the creation of new firms and banks, carrying out small-scale privatization, breaking up the "monobank" system, whereby a single state bank system functioned as a country's central bank as well as a nationwide commercial and investment bank, and allowing the creation of new independent banks. Finally, the strategy aimed at developing a social safety net. The Type I reforms proved relatively sustainable.

Significant policy differences ensued in what I call Type II reforms, which involved the privatization of large- and medium-sized SOEs, establishment and enforcement of a market-oriented legal system and accompanying institutions, further in-depth development of a commercial banking sector and the appropriate regulatory infrastructure, labor market regulations, and institutions related to public unemployment and retirement systems. Many CEE and CIS governments carried out these reforms slowly and incompletely, in part because of political resistance and in part because they were more demanding in terms of know-how and logistics.[3]

I will use the key dimensions of the two sets of reforms in the CEE and CIS economies to provide a perspective on China's transformation that is documented in the various chapters of this book.

---

[3] My reading of the Chinese evidence is that China proceeded gradually even with respect to Type I reforms, an aspect that may have helped it avoid the initial depression experienced by the CEE and CIS economies.

Privatization

While China proceeded relatively fast with the introduction of local public owner-ship through TVEs and assigning cultivation rights to individual farm households, it proceeded slowly with privatization. Indeed, significant privatization of TVEs occurred only about fifteen years after their founding, and substantial privatiza-tion of larger firms commenced only about two decades after the start of China's transition. In CEE and CIS, remarkable differences exist across countries in the strategy of privatizing large- and medium-sized firms, but all countries proceeded fast relative to China.

For example, Poland and Slovenia moved most slowly in privatizing SOEs, relying instead on "commercialization" (where firms remained state owned but were run by somewhat independent appointed supervisory boards) and on the creation of new private firms. Yet, they took only ten years to privatize the majority of their industrial firms. Estonia and Hungary proceeded assiduously and surprisingly effectively with privatization of individual SOEs by selling them one by one to outside owners.

This method of privatization was originally viewed by many strategists as being too slow. Yet, it provided much-needed managerial skills and external funds for investment in the privatized firms, it generated government revenue and effective corporate governance, and it turned out to be relatively fast, taking about six to seven years. Russia and Ukraine opted for rapid mass privatization and relied primarily on subsidized management–employee buyouts of firms. This method had the advantage of speed (two to five years), but it led to poor corporate governance in that existing management usually was not able to improve efficiency. The method also did not generate new investment funds and skills, and it provided little revenue for the government.

Finally, countries such as the Czech Republic, Lithuania, and, to a lesser extent, Slovakia carried out voucher privatization, whereby a majority of shares of most firms were distributed to citizens at large. While this approach was fair and one of the best in terms of speed (two to five years), it did not generate new funds for investment, nor did it bring revenue to the government. Instead, it resulted in dispersed ownership of shares and, together with a weak legal framework, poor corporate governance. The poor corporate governance often permitted managers or majority shareholders to appropriate profit or even assets of the firms at the expense of minority shareholders.

Banking System

In the development of a banking system, China first only gradually supplemented the traditional Soviet-style monobank system with new banks and financial insti-tutions. However, in the last ten years, it has permitted the rise of new institutions, mostly on the periphery of the financial sector, and welcomed foreign financial institutions taking minority stakes in virtually all the major core financial institutions (banks, insurance companies, etc.) other than the central bank.

In contrast, virtually all CEE and CIS countries rapidly abolished the monobank system as part of Type I reforms. Some countries, such as Russia, allowed spontaneous growth of new banks from the bottom up, resulting in the creation of hundreds of banks virtually overnight. In CEE, the process was much more government controlled, but even then, dozens of small private banks rapidly emerged in countries like the Czech Republic and Poland. While the banking systems in CEE and CIS differed in various ways, they shared numerous weaknesses. Many of the small banks quickly collapsed. The large banks started the transition with a sizable portfolio of nonperforming enterprise loans and, upon restructuring, they rapidly accumulated new nonperforming loans. The need for repeated bailouts of the large banks led Hungary, the Czech Republic, and Poland to privatize virtually all domestic banks to large western banks in the late 1990s. This was followed by similar privatizations in Slovakia, Bulgaria, Romania, Croatia, and other countries, with the CEE region becoming a laboratory for observing the introduction of a western banking system with few, if any, locally owned banks.

Both China and the CEE and CIS economies have experienced problems associated with soft budget constraints in state-owned banks and failures of new private financial institutions. The CEE countries have opted for a banking system dominated by foreign banks, while China and the CIS have so far given western banks and financial institutions only limited presence.

Labor and Social Institutions

For almost two decades, China maintained much of its original labor and social system that was administered through the SOEs, with urban workers enjoying considerable protection and job security and the rural population receiving only limited social transfers from the central government. The CEE and CIS countries have differed in the nature and speed of the development of labor and social regulations and institutions, but most proceeded relatively fast in comparison to China. By the end of 1991, all the CEE countries developed relatively well-functioning unemployment compensation and social security benefit schemes, with the originally generous benefits becoming somewhat more modest over time (Ham, Svejnar, and Terrell, 1998). In Russia and the other countries of the CIS, the official benefits were low to start with and decreased dramatically in real terms over time – and in the 1990s even the low official benefits were often not paid.

Hence, by proceeding with limited social transfers, China has resembled more the CIS countries than the CEE countries. An important difference is that the population in China is much more rural than that in the CIS, and the benefits provided by the government to the urban Chinese (while small relative to urban incomes) are huge relative to the incomes and benefits available to China's rural residents. The Chinese system hence induces greater urban–rural income inequality.

Legal System and Institutions

China initially maintained and gradually reformed its legal and institutional system as it proceeded with its gradual economic reform. The major systemic transformation in the CEE and CIS countries required completely new laws and institutions; yet, virtually none of these countries succeeded in rapidly developing a legal system and institutions that would be highly conducive to the preservation of private property and the functioning of a market economy, although some countries did better than others. This inability to develop a functioning, market-oriented legal structure has been the Achilles heel of the first decade of transition in the former Soviet bloc countries. Many policymakers underestimated the importance of a well-functioning legal system. In addition, many newly rich individuals contributed to the corruption of public officials and did not want a functioning legal system.

In carrying out the legal and institutional transformations, the more western transition economies benefited from the pre–World War II legacy of a functioning legal system. In the late 1990s and early to mid-2000s, an important impetus for carrying out legal and institutional reforms in the CEE countries was the need to develop a system that conforms to that of the European Union (EU) as a prerequisite for accession to the EU. In China, a major impetus for legal and institutional change was the entry into the World Trade Organization (WTO), a factor that has also been playing a part in Russia. In China as well as the CEE and CIS countries, foreign investment has also contributed to legal and institutional changes as foreign investors press governments to enact legislation creating a more predictable business climate.

In this context, it is useful to consider the implication of the experience of China and the CEE and CIS economies for an important school of thought that attributes the failure of many countries to grow and develop to corruption. Corruption has been present in China throughout the three decades of rapid growth, and it has been an important phenomenon in the former Soviet bloc economies, including Russia, both during the economic decline in the 1990s and the subsequent period of rapid growth. For instance, according to the Transparency International (http://www.transparency.org/publications/annual_report, 2005) annual report, China ranks 85, behind Poland (70), the Czech Republic (47), Lithuania (44), Hungary (40), Slovenia (31), and Lithuania (27), but above Russia (107) and Ukraine (126). Since China has been growing faster than any of the other economies, the record indicates that corruption alone is not an adequate explanatory factor for the presence or absence of economic development and growth.

PERFORMANCE OF CHINA AND THE CEE AND CIS ECONOMIES

China has generally performed very well, although economic performance has varied across provinces and regions. Economic performance has also varied widely across the CEE and CIS countries and over time. The Central European countries of Poland, Slovenia, Hungary, Slovakia, and the Czech Republic initially performed better than the Baltic states of Estonia, Latvia, and Lithuania and the Balkan states of Bulgaria and Romania, which in turn performed better than Russia, Ukraine, and other countries in the CIS. The situation has changed, however, and as I discuss presently, since the late 1990s, the fastest growing economies have been in the Baltic and CIS regions. In what follows, I start with a comparison of macroeconomic indicators and then turn to more microeconomic measures of restructuring and performance.

Gross Domestic Product

Calculating the evolution of GDP is difficult for the early phases of the transition because the communist countries used gross material product, a measure that ignored the production of services. Moreover, the dramatic entry and growth of small firms during the transition was not well captured in the official statistics. Statistical offices and the international organizations have devoted significant resources to estimating GDP for the pretransition years and tracing out GDP accurately thereafter, but the early data obviously have to be interpreted with caution (Ren, 1997; Brada, King, and Kutan, 2000; Filer and Hanousek, 2000, 2002).

With the above caveats in mind, one may carry out a number of comparisons. In 1990, at the start of the transition in CEE and CIS, the sectoral structure China's economy resembled most that of Ukraine and Kazakhstan. In all three economies, agriculture accounted for a bit over 25 percent and industry, including mining and construction, for 41–45 percent of GDP (Russia's shares were 17 and 48 percent, respectively). Since then, China reduced its share of agriculture in the same proportion as Ukraine and some other countries, but it deviated from the other countries in that it increased rather than decreased the share of industry. In particular, between 1990 and 2003, China's share of industry in GDP increased from 41 to 46 percent (Yearbook, 2006, p. 58), while Ukraine's share declined from 45 to 40 percent (EBRD Transition Report, various issues). In general, the CEE and CIS economies moved from agriculture and industry to services, while China moved from agriculture to both industry and services.

In terms of GDP growth, China's performance since 1978 has been unexpectedly strong, while that of the CEE and CIS countries was disappointing to disastrous in the early to mid-1990s and fairly strong thereafter. Figure 3.1 shows indices of GDP growth for selected CEE and CIS economies. Unlike China, which grew fast continuously since the start of the reforms, all the transition economies experienced large declines in output at the start of the transition. The decline varied from 13 to 25 percent in the Central European countries, over 40 percent in the Baltic countries, and as much as 45 percent or more in Russia and almost 65 percent in Ukraine. While the CEE countries reversed the decline after three to four years, in Russia and most of the CIS, no turnaround was visible through most of the 1990s.

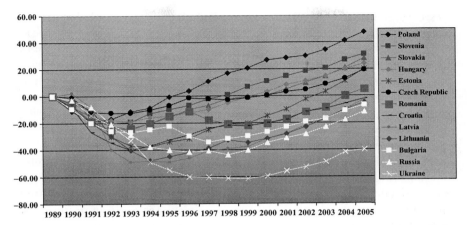

Figure 3.1. Real GDP index (base year 1989) (*Source:* EBRD, various issues; Svejnar, 2007)

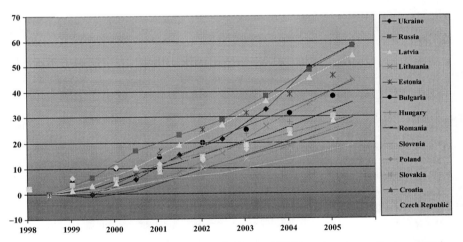

Figure 3.2. Real GDP index (base year 1998) (*Source:* EBRD, various issues; Svejnar, 2007)

Almost all the CEE countries have generated sustained economic growth since the early to mid-1990s and the CIS countries have done so since the late 1990s. In fact, since the late 1990s, the Baltic and CIS countries have grown considerably faster than the countries in Central Europe (Figure 3.2). The engine of growth has shifted east, and the current debate is whether this represents a real sustainable growth or a temporary surge driven in key economies by high natural resource prices.

The strength and persistence of growth in China and the depth and length of the early transition depression in the CEE and CIS countries were both unexpected. A number of explanations have been offered for both. The various chapters in this book present the most recent set of analytical explanations for China. For CEE and

CIS, the arguments for the initial decline (transformation recession), discussed in Roland (2000), include tight macroeconomic policies (Bhaduri, Kaski, and Levcik, 1993; Rosati, 1994); a credit crunch stemming from the reduction of state subsidies to firms and rise in real interest rates (Calvo and Coricelli, 1992); disorganization among suppliers, producers, and consumers associated with the collapse of central planning (Blanchard and Kremer, 1997; Roland and Verdier, 1999); a switch from a controlled to an insufficiently regulated monopolistic structure (Blanchard, 1997; Li, 1999); problems with implementing sectoral shifts in the presence of labor market imperfections (Atkeson and Kehoe, 1996); and the dissolution of the CMEA in 1990. In my view, most of these explanations contain an element of truth, but none is in itself completely convincing. All the CEE and CIS countries have gone through the decline, yet cross-country differences in initial conditions and the nature of reform are substantial enough to make one question the universal applicability of any single explanation. Interestingly, China avoided or delayed all the above phenomena.

Inflation

While China experienced a 15–25 percent annual inflation in the 1993–1995 period, for most of the 1980s, 1990s, and 2000s, it kept inflation below 10 percent. In fact, since 1997, China appears to have achieved considerable price stability. The picture is very different in the CEE and CIS countries. A number of these economies experienced high or hyperinflation as the command system faltered. Poland, Slovenia, Albania, Bulgaria, and Romania all experienced at least one year from 1990 to 1993 when consumer price inflation exceeded 200 percent; Estonia, Latvia, and Lithuania all had one year with inflation around 1,000 percent; and Russia, Ukraine, and Kazakhstan experienced at least one year when inflation was above 2,000 percent. Sometimes these bouts of inflation arose after lifting price controls; in other cases, the inflation grew out of financial sector crises. However, by the late 1990s, policymakers had shown that they could reduce inflation rates with considerable effectiveness.

Table 3.1 shows the rates of inflation for a selected group of transition countries. As may be seen from the table, by the beginning of the 2000s, inflation rates in many transition economies were in single digits. Even countries that experienced very high rates of inflation during the 1990s – Russia, Ukraine, and Bulgaria, for example – had inflation rates in the range of 8–10 percent by 2006.

From the comparative perspective, it is notable that unlike a number of the CEE and CIS economies, China never experienced hyperinflation or major monetary overhang, and hence did not have to impose highly restrictive macroeconomic policies that might choke off its rapid and steady rate of economic growth. It also achieved a rapid rate of growth while for the most part avoiding high rates of inflation.

Table 3.1. *Consumer price inflation*

	1990	1992	1994	1996	1998	2000	2002	2003	2004	2005	2006[a]
Czech Republic	9.7	11.1	9.9	8.8	10.6	4.0	1.8	0.2	2.8	1.9	2.7
Hungary	28.9	23.0	18.8	23.6	14.3	9.8	4.8	4.9	6.7	3.6	2.0
Poland	585.8	43.0	32.2	19.9	11.8	10.1	1.7	0.7	3.5	2.2	1.2
Slovakia	10.8	10.0	13.4	5.8	6.7	12.0	3.3	8.5	7.5	2.7	4.2
Slovenia	549.7	207.3	21.0	9.9	7.9	8.9	7.5	5.6	3.6	2.5	2.5
Estonia	23.1	1,076.0	47.7	23.1	8.1	4.0	3.6	1.3	3.0	4.1	3.4
Latvia	10.8	951.2	35.9	17.6	4.7	2.6	1.9	3.0	6.2	6.7	6.0
Lithuania	8.4	1,020.5	72.1	24.6	5.1	1.0	0.3	−1.2	1.2	2.7	3.0
Bulgaria	26.3	82.0	96.3	123.0	22.2	9.9	5.9	2.3	6.1	5.0	6.5
Croatia	609.5	665.5	975.0	3.5	5.7	6.2	2.2	1.8	2.1	3.3	3.2
Romania	127.9	210.4	136.7	38.8	59.1	45.7	22.5	15.4	11.9	9.0	7.7
Russia	5.6	1,526.0	311.4	47.8	27.6	20.8	15.7	13.7	10.9	12.7	10.5
Ukraine	4.2	1,210.0	891.0	80.0	10.6	28.2	0.8	5.2	9.0	13.5	10.5

[a] Projection.
Source: EBRD Transition Reports, IMF World Economic Outlook; *OECD Economic Outlook*, vol. 72, Economist Intelligence Unit; Svejnar (2007).

Exchange Rates, Current Account, and Exports

During the last three decades, China has increasingly opened up its economy (its trade ratio at 60 percent is higher than that of any large economy), kept a relatively fixed exchange rate, and maintained first balance and then surplus on its current account. Domestic demand has been an important engine of growth, but exports have increasingly provided an outlet for China's production.

Most CEE and CIS economies strongly devalued their currency as a means of ensuring global competitiveness and adopted a fixed exchange rate as part of macroeconomic stabilization. The CEE countries also significantly reoriented their foreign trade away from the old CMEA region and toward market economies – primarily Western Europe. However, with inflation in the 1990s, the fixed exchange rates of many countries became overvalued, leading in some cases to substantial current account deficits. Most countries responded by devaluing their currencies again and adopting flexible exchange rates, although some countries (e.g., Bulgaria, Estonia, and Lithuania) adopted currency boards as a means of long-term economic stabilization. Recently, Slovenia went furthest in fixing its currency to its principal trading partners by joining the Eurozone at the start of 2007. Most of the CEE economies became very open, while the CIS economies have on average remained relatively more closed.

Both China and the large CIS economies have thus remained relatively closed, but China's manufacturing exports and CIS resource exports have been increasingly gaining in importance.

External Debt and Financial Crises

China launched its transformation without foreign debt and gradually became a major creditor to the rest of the world, accumulating sizable foreign exchange reserves. It has also avoided the worst effects of the Asian financial crisis because it was sufficiently insulated from the global financial markets and substituted domestic public investment for falling external demand.

Many, but not all, transition countries started the 1990s with high foreign indebtedness. In Bulgaria, Hungary, and Poland, external debt exceeded 50 percent of GDP in 1990. In Russia, external debt in 1990 was 148 percent of GDP. However, other transition economies, such as Romania, Slovenia, the Czech Republic, and Slovakia, had conservative regimes and foreign debt was less than 20 percent of GDP in 1990.

By the mid-1990s, many of the highly indebted countries reduced their debt/GDP ratio, while a number of the less indebted countries increased theirs. But since about 1996, foreign indebtedness has risen in the relatively more indebted countries and in 1988 Russia defaulted on its sovereign debt. Interestingly, while the Russian financial crisis had a major impact on the CIS countries that still had close trading relations with Russia, it had relatively little impact on the CEE countries, which had already reoriented most of their trade to Western Europe. Hence, both China and the CEE economies managed to avoid the financial crises of the late 1990s, albeit for different reasons.

Budget and Taxes

China has proceeded gradually in reforming its tax system and ensured adequate budgetary revenues from the rapidly growing economy. The seemingly favorable picture may hide significant off-budget expenditures and revenues and potential unfunded future liabilities. However, until now China's fiscal system has not been a major obstacle to rapid growth (see Chapter 12 in this volume).

In contrast, as the transition unfolded, CEE and CIS governments had to develop a number of new fiscal institutions for collecting taxes. This institutional development was one of the hardest Type II reforms to achieve. While tax collection was relatively effective even at the start of the transition in the CEE region, Russia and some other countries of the CIS initially struggled with declines in tax revenues, as many producers avoided paying taxes either by operating through barter or by accumulating tax arrears. The situation was particularly difficult as the governments were facing demands for new public expenditures, including infrastructure and the new social safety net. The relative inability of Russia and other CIS nations to collect taxes was one reason why their social safety nets were from the start weaker than those in CEE.

While Russia and some other CIS economies have successfully reduced tax rates and simplified the tax system dramatically to improve tax collection, many of the

CEE economies have higher tax rates than other countries at a similar level of GDP per capita. Yet, the relatively high ratios of taxes to GDP in these transition economies have not prevented many of their governments from running budget deficits. Russia and other natural resource exporting countries, however, have been running budget surpluses throughout the 2000s.

An especially problematic aspect of the public finances in the CEE economies has been the increasing strain from the pension system. These countries started the transition with publicly funded pensions that covered most of the population, low retirement ages (on average 60 for men and 55 for women), a high and rising ratio of retirees to workers, and high levels of promised benefits relative to recently earned preretirement wages (World Bank, 1994; Svejnar, 1997). Moreover, most of these systems had a perverse redistribution of benefits from lower- to higher-income workers. The systems were largely pay-as-you-go and not sustainable. Several countries, including Hungary, Poland, Latvia, and Kazakhstan, have already moved to raise the retirement age and supplement the public retirement system by a multipillar public/private retirement system with a funded component. Russia and other CIS countries face less of a public sector burden with regard to retirement costs, because the level of government-promised retirement benefits is lower.

As the discussion indicates, the gradual transformation and a rapidly growing economy have enabled China to avoid (at least on surface) the various budgetary problems encountered in the CEE and CIS economies. For different reasons, China and the resource-rich CIS countries (Russia in particular) enjoy a relatively favorable budgetary situation. As mentioned earlier, however, China may face off-budget unfunded liabilities in the future.

Privatization and Creation of New Firms

While experimenting with private ownership, the Chinese authorities decided to delay for over two decades the substantial privatization of SOEs. However, from the early 1980s, they eased access to critical inputs through the dual-track system and permitted a major expansion of the TVEs. The TVEs filled niches, supplied the SOEs, and many eventually started competing head-on with the SOEs. The TVEs generated considerable economic activity and provided industrial and service employment in rural areas. In the last decade, most have turned into private firms and thus constituted a gradual process of de-etatizing China's economy.

The CEE and CIS transition economies proceeded relatively quickly and directly with creating private firms. In the early 1990s, most transition economies privatized small enterprises, primarily through local auctions. The small-scale privatization was instrumental in creating small- and medium-sized enterprises in countries where most firms were, by ideological and practical design, either large or very large. This shift in ownership rapidly increased efficiency and quality of production.

Table 3.2. *Private sector share of GDP (percent)*

	1989	1990	1992	1994	1996	1998	2000	2002	2004	2006
Czech Republic	5	10	30	65	75	75	80	80	80	80
Hungary	5	25	40	55	70	80	80	80	80	80
Poland	30	30	45	55	60	65	70	75	75	75
Slovakia	5	10	30	55	70	75	80	80	80	80
Slovenia	10	15	30	45	55	60	65	65	65	65
Estonia	10	10	25	55	70	70	75	80	80	80
Latvia	10	10	25	40	60	65	65	70	70	70
Lithuania	10	10	20	60	70	70	70	75	75	75
Bulgaria	10	10	25	40	55	65	70	70	75	75
Romania	15	15	25	40	55	60	60	65	70	70
Russia	5	5	25	50	60	70	70	70	70	65
Ukraine	10	10	10	40	50	55	60	65	65	65

Source: EBRD Transition Reports; Svejnar (2007).

Parallel developments were the breakups of SOEs, restructuring of firms and management, and increased competition. Breakups of small, average, and somewhat above-average size appear to have increased efficiency of both the remaining master enterprises and the spun-off units (Lizal, Singer, and Svejnar, 2001). Most of the broken-up firms were subsequently privatized.

A large number of new (mostly small) firms were founded in most transition economies. Like the TVEs, these firms filled niches in demand and started to compete with existing SOEs. Since many of the transition economies became relatively open economies, the new private firms were also competing with imports. The growth of new firms has varied across countries. In general, it proceeded faster and smoother in the CEE countries than in the CIS.

Finally, in most countries, a large part of private assets were generated through large-scale privatization, which differed in its method across countries. What is remarkable, however, is how quickly most countries generated private ownership, irrespective of the particular privatization methods used. In 1989, only Poland and Romania had more than 10 percent of GDP produced by private sector firms, and in most countries private sector share was around 5 percent of GDP (Table 3.2). But these figures increased very quickly. As early as 1994, the private sector accounted for more than 30 percent of GDP in most of the transition economies and represented half or more of GDP in many countries, including Russia. Table 3.2 shows that by 2000, the private sector share of GDP was at or above 60 percent in all the transition economies and in most of them it constituted 70–80 percent. Except for Russia, which has recently backtracked and nationalized some (especially energy) firms, the private sector share has been maintained or has grown steadily since 2000.

The estimated effects of privatization on economic performance have in many respects been disappointing, given the optimistic expectations. At the country level, some of the fastest growing economies (Poland, Slovenia, and also China) have been among the slowest to privatize. At the microlevel, surveys from the late 1990s and early 2000s make assessments that range from finding no systematically significant effect of privatization on performance (Bevan, Estrin, and Schaffer, 1999) to concluding (some cautiously) that privatization improves firm performance (Shirley and Walsh, 2000; Megginson and Netter, 2001; Djankov and Murrell, 2002). Concentrated ownership appears to have a positive effect on performance (Hanousek, Kocenda, and Svejnar, 2007) and the recent survey by Estrin et al. (2007) finds that privatization to foreign owners has by and large increased efficiency and scale of operations, while the effects of privatization to domestic owners have been mostly insignificant. Many of the early microeconometric studies suffer from serious problems: small and unrepresentative samples of firms, misreported or mismeasured data, limited controls for other major shocks that occurred at the same time as privatization, a short period of observations after privatization, and above all, not controlling adequately for selectivity bias. Selectivity bias is likely to be a particularly serious problem since better performing firms tend to be privatized first (Gupta, Ham, and Svejnar, 2000). Thus, comparing the postprivatization performance of privatized firms to the performance of the remaining state-owned firms without controlling for selectivity bias, as many studies do, erroneously attributes some of the superior performance of the privatized firms to privatization.

Studies of China provide a similar, though less bleak, picture (Estrin et al., 2007). For instance, studies of total factor productivity find diverse results, with the effect of nonstate ownership being mostly positive but sometimes statistically insignificant. As in the studies of CEE and CIS, in the studies of China the effect of foreign ownership is more positive than that of other forms of nonstate ownership. In China, a particularly important part has been played by joint ventures whose contribution to industrial output has grown rapidly over time. Together with foreign firms, the joint ventures generate about one-half of China's exports. Overall, the findings of somewhat limited effects of privatization to domestic owners in the transition economies (and to a lesser extent in China) provide sobering evidence since the general expectation was that there would be much improvement in the efficiency of firms as a result of privatization.

Domestic and Foreign Investment

Throughout the 1980s, 1990s, and 2000s, China maintained a high rate of investment. In this sense, China has joined the East Asian tigers. China has also generated a significant inflow of foreign direct investment (FDI) that has had a positive effect on the modernization of China's economy. In recent years, one also observes a reverse flow in the form of Chinese FDI to other countries.

Table 3.3. *FDI net inflows (million U.S.$)*

	1990	1992	1994	1996	1998	2000	2002	2003	2004	2005[a]	2006[b]
Czech Republic	132	983	749	1,276	3,591	4,943	8,276	1,895	3,690	10,135	4,500
Hungary	311	1,471	1,097	2,279	3,065	2,190	2,590	874	3,542	5,353	3,500
Poland	0	284	542	2,741	6,049	9,324	3,901	3,927	12,079	6,716	8,400
Slovakia	24	100	236	199	374	2,058	4,007	549	1,403	1,951	3,400
Slovenia	−2	113	129	167	221	71	1,489	−139	281	−88	88
Estonia	n.a.	80	212	111	574	324	153	763	781	2,250	540
Latvia	n.a.	29	279	379	303	400	374	328	596	497	840
Lithuania	n.a.	8	31	152	921	375	715	142	510	680	803
Bulgaria	4	41	105	138	537	1,003	876	2,070	2,777	2,298	3,000
Croatia	0	13	110	486	835	1,085	591	1,700	871	1,509	2,825
Romania	−18	73	341	415	2,079	1,051	1,080	2,156	6,368	6,587	8,652
Russia	n.a.	1,454	409	1,657	1,492	−463	−72	−1,769	1,662	1,473	2,500
Ukraine	n.a.	170	151	516	747	594	698	1,411	1,711	7,500	4,000

[a] Estimate.
[b] Projection.
Source: EBRD Transition Reports, World Bank Development Indicators; Svejnar (2007).

The Soviet bloc countries and former Yugoslavia, like the East Asian tigers, were known for high rates of investment, often exceeding 30 percent of GDP. Investment rates declined to about 20 percent of GDP in the 1990s in a number of transition economies (EBRD, 1996), although some countries, such as the Czech Republic and Slovakia, maintained relatively high levels of investment throughout. Unfortunately, in the first decade of the transition, much of this investment appears to have been allocated inefficiently by the inexperienced and often politicized or corrupt commercial banks (Lizal and Svejnar, 2002).

As may be seen from Table 3.3, until 1996, Hungary was the only transition economy receiving a significant inflow of FDI. This was in part because early on Hungary created a more hospitable business climate than did other transition countries and also established well-defined rules and regulations for FDI. But starting in 1998, major foreign investments went to the Czech Republic, Poland, Slovakia, and the Baltic countries. Overall, with one-tenth of the population of China, the CEE countries have been receiving roughly one-half of the annual FDI inflows going to China. These sizable FDI inflows have had a major effect on GDP growth and export competitiveness of the CEE countries, with some having foreign-owned firms accounting for two-thirds to three quarters of exports.

Employment Adjustment, Wage Setting, Unemployment, and Income Distribution

China's employment and more generally labor market adjustments have been different from those observed in the CEE and CIS transition economies, although the limited system of social transfers made some features similar to those in the CIS. While the CEE and CIS economies adjusted employment considerably already in the first decade of the transition, China's SOEs started adjusting employment on a major scale only in the second decade of reforms. China's SOEs have hence been adjusting employment but at a slower pace than their counterparts in the CEE and, to a lesser extent, CIS countries. A big employment adjustment occurred in China through the formation of the TVEs, which generated sizable employment for the rural labor force. More recently, China's private firms have been creating employment on a significant scale. Open unemployment is a significant phenomenon in the urban areas but less in the countryside. With declining administrative limitations on migration, Chinese workers move substantially in search of lucrative employment opportunities. Finally, with the rapid economic growth, China's income distribution has become quite unequal, with the Gini coefficient being estimated to be around 50.

In the CEE and CIS economies, SOEs responded to the negative output shock by decreasing employment and/or real wages in the early 1990s (Svejnar, 1999). At one extreme, Hungary experienced a more than 20 percent initial reduction in industrial employment, with real wages rising almost 20 percent. At the other extreme, industrial wages in the Czech Republic declined almost 25 percent, with employment falling less than 10 percent (Basu, Estrin, and Svejnar, 2005). In Russia and the rest of CIS, the adjustment brought a mixture of wage and employment adjustment (Desai and Idson, 2000), and the wage decline was more pronounced than in the CEE region (Boeri and Terrell, 2002). In Central Europe, labor demand elasticities with respect to output and wages rose rapidly to western levels as the transition was launched, indicating that firms started behaving as cost-minimizing entities. Depending on the institutional setting in a given country, the sharp decline in output at the start of the transition was hence absorbed more by employment or wage decreases.

The GDP and employment data suggest that restructuring in the transition economies involved an initial decline in labor productivity, as output fell faster than employment. Productivity has risen since then, however, as output growth has exceeded that of employment. In fact, this recent pattern has given rise to a concern among some analysts and policymakers that the CEE and CIS economies are suffering from "jobless growth."

Unemployment was basically an unknown phenomenon before the transition, but it emerged rapidly in most CEE countries. Within two years after the start of the transition, the unemployment rate rose into double digits in most CEE countries. The high unemployment rates reflected high rates of inflow into unemployment, as firms laid off workers, and relatively low outflow rates, as the unemployed found it hard to find new jobs. The Czech labor market was an ideal model of a transition labor market, characterized by high inflows as well as outflows, with unemployment representing a transitory state between old and new jobs (Ham, Svejnar, and Terrell, 1998, 1999). Unemployment as a serious problem emerged more slowly in the CIS, where firms were somewhat slower in laying off workers and used wage declines and arrears as mechanisms to keep workers with low reservation wages attached to firms.

Over time, the patterns and dynamics of unemployment became more diverse. The Czech Republic was the only Central European country to enter recession in the second half of the 1990s and its unemployment rate correspondingly rose to 8–10 percent. The fast-growing economies of Poland, Hungary, Slovenia, and, to a lesser extent, Slovakia managed to reduce their unemployment rates in the late 1990s. Conversely, the CIS and Baltic countries experienced gradual increases in unemployment as their transition proceeded. By 1997, unemployment rates in Russia and Estonia were near 10 percent. By 1999–2000, the unemployment rate rose again in Bulgaria, the Czech Republic, Poland, Slovakia, and Slovenia, and at present many transition economies have unemployment rates that are at least as high as, and often significantly higher than, those observed in the EU.

While real wages in CEE have increased steadily after their initial decline in the 1989–1991 period, in Russia and a number of other CIS countries, real wages declined until 1993 and stagnated or increased only gradually thereafter (EBRD, 2000). The trajectory of real incomes has thus been different in the more and less advanced transition economies.

Table 3.4. *Income inequality (Gini coefficients)*

	Late 1980s–early 1990s		1990s		Late 1990s–early 2000s	
	Year	Gini	Year	Gini	Year	Gini
Czech Republic	1988	20.0	1992	23.0	1996	25.4
Croatia	1988	28.6	1998	29.7	2001	29.0
Hungary	1987	24.4	1992	26.0	1998	24.4
Poland	1987	25.0	1993	29.8	1998	31.6
Slovakia	1988	19.5	1993	21.5	1996	25.8
Slovenia	1987	19.8	1993	24.1	1998	28.4
Bulgaria	1989	21.7	1993	33.3	2001	31.9
Romania	1989	23.3	1994	28.6	2000	30.3
Russia[a]	1991	26.0	1993	39.8	2000	39.9
Russia[b]	1992	54.3	1994	45.5	1996	51.8
Ukraine	1988	23.3	1996	33.4	1999	29.0

[a] Based on Goskomstat data.
[b] Based on Russian Longitudinal Monitoring Survey.
Source: World Bank Development Indicators; Svejnar (2007).

The reduction in employment in the old SOEs, the rise in unemployment, and the establishment of new firms have brought about considerable destruction and creation of jobs, as well as mobility of labor. Contrary to the main models of the transition process, however, Jurajda and Terrell (2001) show that job creation in new firms has not been necessarily tightly linked to job destruction in the old firms, since many new jobs have been created even in economies that experienced low rates of job destruction. Sabirianova-Peter (2002) provides a related structural insight, namely, that much of the labor mobility in Russia consists of occupational rather than geographic change, with individuals moving from one occupation to another within regions, as jobs in old occupations are destroyed and opportunities in new occupations are created. Compared to the U.S. and China's labor markets, where individuals move geographically, the transition in CEE and CIS has led to more occupational rather than geographic mobility.

Data on the Gini coefficient, measuring the extent of inequality in income distribution, are given in Table 3.4. The communist countries had highly egalitarian income distributions but inequality increased in the CEE and CIS economies during the 1990s and 2000s. Between the late 1980s/early 1990s and the late 1990s/early 2000s, the Gini coefficient rose from 20–25 to 24–32 in Central Europe, from low 20s to low 30s in Bulgaria and Romania, from 23 to 30 in Ukraine, and from 26 to 40 in Russia. Income inequality in the transition economies has hence become comparable to that in advanced capitalist economies and developing countries, such as India. However, the official Russian and Ukrainian data in Table 3.4 probably underestimate the extent of income inequality. In particular, the data from

Table 3.5. *Investor ratings (long-term ratings on foreign currency–denominated sovereign debts)*

As of	1994 November 15	1995 November 15	1996 November 12	1998 November 13	2000 November 1	2001 November 28	2002 November 6	2004 November 11	2005 November 9	2006 November 3
Czech Republic	BBB+	BBB+	A	A–	A–	A–	A–	A–	A–	A–
Hungary	BB+	BB+	BB+	BBB–	BBB+	A–	A–	A–	A–	BBB+
Poland	n.a.	n.a.	BBB–	BBB–	BBB+	BBB+	BBB+	BBB+	BBB+	BBB+
Slovakia	BB–	BB+	BBB–	BBB–	BB+	BBB–	BBB–	BBB+	BBB+	A
Slovenia	n.a.	n.a.	A	A	A	A	A	AA–	AA–	AA
Latvia	n.a.	n.a.	n.a.	BBB	BBB	BBB	BBB+	A–	A–	A–
Lithuania	n.a.	n.a.	n.a.	BBB–	BBB–	BBB–	BBB	A–	A–	A–
Romania	n.a.	n.a.	BB–	B+	B–	B	B+	BB+	BBB–	BBB–
Russia	n.a.	n.a.	BB–	CCC	SD[a]	B	BB–	BB+	BBB–	BBB+
China	BBB	BBB	BBB	BBB+	BBB	BBB	BBB	BBB+	A–	A

[a] SD indicates selective default.

Source: Standard and Poor's Rating Handbook.

the Russian Statistical Office (Goskomstat) are based on contractual wages, but in the 1990s many Russian firms were not fully paying these contractual wages (Desai and Idson, 2000). Inequality calculations based on survey data from the Russian Longitudinal Monitoring Survey of households suggest that income inequality in Russia has reached much higher levels – a Gini coefficient of 52 – resembling the level of inequality found in China and developing economies with relatively inegalitarian distribution of income. It is to be noted that the relatively egalitarian income distribution in the CEE countries has been generated by the social safety nets, which offset the inequality that was brought about by market forces (Garner and Terrell, 1998). In Russia the social safety net was regressive, making the distribution of income more unequal than it would have been without it (Commander, Tolstopiatenko, and Yemtsov, 1999).

Overall, existing studies indicate that income and consumption inequality has increased during the transition and that the increase has been greater in the East and has depended on the relative importance of changes in the distribution of wages, employment, entrepreneurial incomes, and social safety nets. In Russia, in particular, there has been a rapid rise in wage inequality, which has in turn had a strong effect on income inequality dynamics (Mitra and Yemtsov, 2007). The dominant common cause of inequality in all the transition economies appears to be wage decompression, resulting from the attenuation of the centralized wage setting and the high return to skills associated with globalization (Munich, Svejnar, and Terrell, 2005, Mitra and Yemtsov, 2007).

Assessment by the Financial Markets

Except for a short period after the Russian financial crisis, western capital markets have been increasingly positive in their assessment of China, CEE, and CIS. As may be seen from Table 3.5, the transition economies have gradually raised their ratings by international rating agencies such as Standard and Poor's, and the most advanced countries now have ratings that place them among the lower-tier developed countries. Because of its long-term progress and in part because of its formidable foreign exchange reserves, China is now rated A – on par with Slovakia and ahead of all the transition economies except for Slovenia, which has a rating of AA. Country financial ratings hence represent yet another dimension of economic performance where China is a leading transition economy.

CONCLUSION

While China shared many systemic, initial conditions with the transition economies of CEE and the CIS, it had a more agricultural economy and a more stable political–economic system than many CEE and CIS countries. Unlike most of the CEE and CIS countries, China adopted a strategy of gradual economic transformation that maintained the existing system and created new economic activities on top of it.

This enabled China to avoid the transformation depression observed in CEE and CIS and allowed it to generate high rates of economic growth that have now lasted for almost three decades. At the time of this study, the CEE and CIS economies have also completed a decade or more of respectable economic growth, demonstrating that numerous forms of the transition process can generate long-term economic growth. In retrospect, the trade-off for avoiding an initial depression appears to be the willingness to maintain most of the existing economic and political system rather than embarking on a rapid but incomplete economic and political transformation. With a rising economic instability and political pressure, countries such as Poland and the Soviet Union had little choice but to proceed relatively fast. Others, such as East Germany and the former Czechoslovakia, could have retained the centrally planned system, but they abandoned it and communism rapidly for political reasons. Looking forward, the current situation is an optimistic one, with China, CIS, and CEE belonging to the fastest growing regions of the world. It will be interesting to see whether all or only some of these models will turn out to be successful in the long run.

References

Atkeson, Andrew and Patrick J. Kehoe. 1996. "Social Insurance and Transition." *International Economic Review*. 37, pp. 377–402.

Basu, Swati, Saul Estrin, and Jan Svejnar. 2005. "Employment Determination in Enterprises under Communism and in Transition to a Market Economy." *Industrial and Labor Relations Review*. 58(3), pp. 353–369.

Bevan, Alan, Saul Estrin, and Mark Schaffer. January 1999. "Determinants of Enterprise Performance during Transition." Centre for Economic Reform and Transformation (CERT) Working Paper 99/03. Edinburgh: Heriot-Watt University.

Bhaduri, Anirban, K. Kaski, and Frederick Levcik. 1993. "Transition from the Command to the Market System: What Went Wrong and What to Do for Now?" Mimeo, Vienna Institute for Comparative Economic Studies.

Blanchard, Olivier J. 1997. *The Economics of Post-Communist Transition*. Oxford: Clarendon Press.

Blanchard, Olivier and Michael Kremer. 1997. "Disorganization." *Quarterly Journal of Economics*. 112(4), pp. 1091–1126.

Boeri, Tito and Katherine Terrell. 2002. "Institutional Determinants of Labor Reallocation in Transition." *Journal of Economic Perspectives*. 16(1), pp. 51–76.

Brada, Josef C., Arthur E. King, and Ali M. Kutan. 2000. "Inflation Bias and Productivity Shocks in Transition Economies: The Case of the Czech Republic." *Economic Systems*. 24(2), pp. 119–138.

Byrd, William A. and Qingsong Lin. 1990. *China's Rural Industry*. Oxford: World Bank–Oxford University Press.

Calvo, Guillermo A. and Fabrizio Coricelli. 1992. "Capital Market Imperfections and Output Response in Previously Centrally Planned Economies," in *Building Sound Finance in Emerging Market Economies*. G. Caprio, D. Folkerts-Landau, and T. Lane, eds. Washington, DC: IMF.

China Statistical Yearbook. 2006. Beijing: China Statistics Press, Annual.

Commander, Simon, Andrei Tolstopiatenko, and Ruslan Yemtsov. 1999. "Channels of Redistribution: Inequality and Poverty in the Russian Transition." *Economics of Transition.* 7(1), pp. 411–465.

Desai, Padma and Todd Idson. 2000. *Work without Wages: Russia's Nonpayment Crisis.* Cambridge, MA: MIT Press.

Djankov, Simeon and Peter Murrell. 2002. "Enterprise Restructuring in Transition: A Quantitative Survey." *Journal of Economic Literature.* 40(3), pp. 739–792.

EBRD [European Bank for Reconstruction and Development]. Various issues 1996–2006. Transition Reports. London: European Bank for Reconstruction and Development.

Estrin, Saul, Jan Hanousek, Evzen Kocenda, and Jan Svejnar. 2007. "Privatization in Central-East Europe." Working Paper, 30, Ann Arbor, MI: International Policy Center, Gerald R. Ford School of Public Policy, University of Michigan.

Filer, Randall K. and Jan Hanousek. 2000. "Output Changes and Inflationary Bias in Transition." *Economic Systems.* 24(3), pp. 285–294.

Filer, Randall K. and Jan Hanousek. 2002. "Survey-Based Estimates of Biases in Consumer Price Indices during Transition: Evidence from Romania." *Journal of Comparative Economics.* 30(3), pp. 476–487.

Garner, Thesia and Katherine Terrell. 1998. "A Gini Decomposition Analysis of Inequality in the Czech and Slovak Republics during the Transition." *The Economics of Transition.* 6(1), pp. 23–46.

Gregory, Paul and Robert Stuart. 1997. *Comparative Economic Systems,* 6th edn. Boston: Houghton-Mifflin.

Gupta, Nandini, John Ham, and Jan Svejnar. 2000. "Priorities and Sequencing in Privatization: Theory and Evidence from the Czech Republic." Working Paper 323. Ann Arbor, MI: William Davidson Institute, University of Michigan, forthcoming, *European Economic Review.*

Ham, John, Jan Svejnar, and Katherine Terrell. 1998. "Unemployment and the Social Safety Net during Transitions to a Market Economy: Evidence from the Czech and Slovak Republics." *American Economic Review.* 88(5), pp. 1117–1142.

Ham, John, Jan Svejnar, and Katherine Terrell. 1999. "Women's Unemployment during the Transition: Evidence from Czech and Slovak Micro Data." *Economics of Transition.* 7(1), pp. 47–78.

Hanousek, Jan, Evzen Kocenda, and Jan Svejnar. January 2007. "Origin and Concentration: Corporate Ownership, Control and Performance." *Economics of Transition.* 15(1), pp. 1–31.

Jurajda, Stepan and Katherine Terrell. 2001. "Optimal Speed of Transition: Micro Evidence from the Czech Republic and Estonia." Working Paper 355. Ann Arbor, MI: William Davidson Institute, University of Michigan.

Krumm, Kathie and Christine P. Wong, 2002. "China: Fiscal Risks of Contingent Liabilities," in *Government at Risk: Contingent Liabilities and Fiscal Risk.* Hana Polackova Brixi and Alan Schick, eds. Washington DC: World Bank, 2002.

Lizal, Lubomir, Miroslav Singer, and Jan Svejnar. 2001. "Enterprise Break-ups and Performance during the Transition from Plan to Market." *The Review of Economics and Statistics.* 83(1), pp. 92–99.

Lizal, Lubomir and Jan Svejnar. 2002. "Investment, Credit Rationing and the Soft Budget Constraint: Evidence from Czech Panel Data." *The Review of Economics and Statistics.* 84(2), pp. 353–370.

Megginson, William and Jeffrey Netter. June 2001. "From State to Market: A Survey of Empirical Studies on Privatization." *Journal of Economic Literature.* 39(2), pp. 321–390.

Munich, Daniel, Jan Svejnar and Katherine Terrell. February 2005. "Returns to Human Capital under the Communist Wage Grid and During the Transition to a Market Economy." *Review of Economics and Statistics*. 87(1), pp. 100–123.

Mitra, Pradeep and Ruslan Yemtsov. 2007. "Inequality and Growth in Transition: Does China's Rising Inequality Portend Russia's Future?" in *Annual Conference on Development Economics 2007*. Washington, DC: World Bank.

Naughton, Barry. 2002. "Causes and Consequences of Differential Economic Growth of Chinese Provinces," in *China and Its Regions: Economic Growth and Reform in Chinese Provinces*. Mary-Françoise Renard, ed. Cheltenham: Edward Elgar, pp. 57–86.

Qian, Yingyi, Lawrence Lau, and Gerard Roland. 2000. "Reform without Losers: An Interpretation of China's Dual Track Approach to Transition." *Journal of Political Economy*. 108(1), pp. 120–144.

Roland, Gerard. 2000. *Transition and Economics*. Cambridge, MA: MIT Press.

Roland, Gerard and T.Verdier. 1999. "Transition and the Output Fall." *Economics of Transition*. 7(1), pp. 1–28.

Rosati, Dariusz. 1994. "Output Decline during Transition from Plan to Market." *Economics of Transition*. 2(4), pp. 419–442.

Sabirianova-Peter, Klara. 2002. "The Great Human Capital Reallocation: An Empirical Analysis of Occupational Mobility in Transitional Russia." *Journal of Comparative Economics*. 30(1), pp. 191–217.

Shirley, Mary and Patrick Walsh. 2000. "Public versus Private Ownership: The Current State of the Debate." World Bank Working Paper 2420. Washington, DC: World Bank.

Svejnar, Jan. 1997. "Pensions in the Former Soviet Bloc: Problems and Solutions," in *The Coming Global Pension Crisis*. New York: Council on Foreign Relations.

Svejnar, Jan. 1999. "Labor Markets in the Transitional Central and East European Economies," Chapter 42 in *Handbook of Labor Economics*, vol. 3B. Orley Ashenfelter and David Card, eds. Amsterdam: North-Holland.

Svejnar, Jan. 2002. "Transition Economies: Performance and Challenges." *Journal of Economic Perspectives*. 16(1), pp. 3–28.

Svejnar, Jan. 2007. "Strategies for Growth: Central and East Europe," in *The New Economic Geography: Effects and Policy Implications*. Federal Reserve Bank of Kansas City's economic symposium, Jackson Hole, Wyoming, August 24–26, 2006. Kansas City, MO: Federal Reserve Bank of Kansas City, pp. 205–233. Accessed from http://www.kansascityfed.org/PUBLICAT/SYMPOS/2006/sym06prg.htm.

World Bank. 1994. *Averting the Old Age Crisis*. New York: Oxford University Press.

FOUR

A Political Economy of China's Economic Transition

Barry Naughton

China began its transition to a market economy nearly thirty years ago under an authoritarian and hierarchical political system. Today, after market transition has wrought fundamental changes in China's economy and transformed every aspect of China's society, that political system survives, with its basic features intact. Indeed, the two most surprising aspects of China's recent past are the thoroughness of economic change and the durability of the Communist Party (CP)-run political system. During the economic transformation, the CP hierarchy did not sit off to one side, frozen in time while everything else in China changed. Rather, the hierarchical political system shaped the process of market transition, and the political hierarchy itself has been reshaped in response to the forces unleashed by economic transition. The critical economic transition policies were made by national leaders acting in the context of their positions in the authoritarian political system and as a result, many of the basic features of the reform process can be explained by the structure of the political system and the changing needs of politicians within that system.

China's enduring "gradualist" approach to transition obviously suits the needs of its authoritarian leaders. More interesting is that the concrete policy content of China's transition – which differed dramatically in different periods – can also be traced to the changing structure of power and strategic calculations of leaders within the authoritarian system. This chapter explains why reform policies were so different in different periods, focusing on the dramatic change in transition strategy that occurred in the early 1990s. This crucial "transition within the transition" gives insight into the achievements, limitations, and future prospects of reform under authoritarian auspices.

The basic argument is laid out in the first section: for the CP to retain power and survive the economic transition process, it needed to protect and recreate a system of political patronage. This required the regime to meet three challenges: creating new patronage opportunities, tying newly autonomous groups to the existing regime, and increasing rewards for allegiance to the regime during the marketization process. To achieve their objectives, leaders of the regime had to both shape the reform policy package and reshape the rules of the authoritarian hierarchy. The

91

argument is brought into relief most clearly when we contrast two dramatically different periods of reform policymaking. These periods have distinctive political economies and policy outcomes. The second section of the chapter describes the initial period 1978–1993, when power at the top was fragmented, with multiple veto players and cautious, incremental policymaking. In this period, reforms were characterized by decentralization of power and sharing of resources. During the second period, since about 1993, power at the top was much less fragmented, and policymaking became much more decisive and able to impose reform-related costs on specific social groups. In this period, reforms were characterized by recentralization of resources and a tendency toward a more rule-bound and predictable system. The contrast between the sharply different policy outcomes in the two periods shows that economic policy outcomes closely follow changes in the distribution of power. The final section considers the evolution of policy since 2003 and tackles the question of when (and whether) institutions became adequate to support further marketization. The chapter concludes with some speculations about the future relationship between political and economic change in China.

ECONOMIC TRANSITION IN AN AUTHORITARIAN REGIME

The Starting Point: The Command Economy Equilibrium

The highly centralized command economy system had as its counterpart a centralized political system that provided leaders with abundant patronage to distribute to their followers. Two types of patronage goods were most important: physical goods and managerial jobs. Command economies were unique in the extent to which the government directly controlled and distributed physical goods. State-owned enterprises (SOEs) operated in a protected environment limited to government-controlled firms, with government-set prices, walled off from the world economy. As a result, SOEs harvested enormous rents that were then pumped into the government by the fiscal system and used for new investment. State-funded investment projects brought access to scarce materials, and leaders distributed these divisible resources to their clients, providing them with prestige and employment opportunities as well. The second main source of patronage resources were the managerial jobs the CP controlled as part of the *nomenklatura* system, which still exists in today's China. The *nomenklatura* refers to the list of desirable jobs that the CP fills directly: managerial jobs go to CP members and close supporters, and promotion through the hierarchy is a primary instrument through which individual leaders reward their followers and build their support coalitions (Harasymiw, 1969; Voslensky, 1984; Manion, 1985; Burns, 1989, 1994; Heilmann and Kirchberger, 2000). Clients of top leaders are promoted through the hierarchy, step by step, but faster as their patrons can help them. Promotion brings increased perks and income, and the opportunity to bring one's own clients up in the world. Thus, investment projects and promotion opportunities were the key "patronage resources," and the

CP had a monopoly on both. Top leaders had enormous resources available to reward their followers. Even leaving aside the formidable coercive and propaganda apparatus, the system derived significant ability to reproduce itself from its ability to reward supporters. Indeed, Communist systems are arguably hyperstable: up until the point of ultimate collapse, they are far more likely to survive in the face of adverse conditions than are ordinary authoritarian regimes.

This system has no real checks and balances, but some accountability is provided through the actions of leaders checking each other and balancing their subordinates off against each other. Leaders and aspiring leaders compete to promote their own clients to responsible posts and positions that give them a vote in crucial committees and Party Congresses. These meet periodically to relegitimate the system and ratify the leadership. Therefore, leaders' ability to promote their own clients, and block the promotion of their rivals' clients, is crucial to the establishment and consolidation of their power. Party and government positions are interwoven, so that a "dual hierarchy" exists in which the party is charged with overseeing the government.[1] This system was called "reciprocal accountability" by Roeder (1993) and Shirk (1993). Checked only by the modest "reciprocal accountability" among insiders, the system concentrated political power at the top of the hierarchy.

Thus, in normal times, the CP system has been in a political equilibrium. Both resource patronage and promotion opportunities flow down the hierarchy, and in return, allegiance and support for individual leaders flow upward. Urban workers in public firms, and government and military officials, are all fully incorporated within the hierarchical organization. Groups within the system can expect some kind of representation of their interests and attention to their grievances from their patrons, but have no ability to challenge the system. There are no independent economic interest groups or political organizations outside the system, and of course, there was no possibility of regime change through elections. In such a system, change comes primarily from within the system and primarily from top leaders.

When China's leaders made the decision to initiate economic reform in 1978, the top leaders, especially Deng Xiaoping, understood that their system had been profoundly damaged by the final twenty years of Maoism. Not satisfied with preeminent power, Mao Zedong had swept aside the institutions of accountability altogether during the Cultural Revolution. Mao ruled by proclamation and through ad hoc, ever shifting, leadership groups. Maoism produced millions of casualties during the Great Leap Forward and the Cultural Revolution, and seriously undermined the otherwise considerable achievements of Chinese socialism. Amid widespread disillusionment, the political equilibrium was profoundly broken: the normal processes that rewarded officials and workers for compliance with the central government were in disarray, and the exchange of political "goods" was disrupted. The new leaders set out to both bring the economy back to life and

---

[1] At times, additional hierarchies of discipline, military, or public security officials are intertwined with the government and party hierarchies as well.

restore political order. They rehabilitated tens of thousands of purged managers, restoring almost all of them to positions of authority. From the very beginning of the economic reform process, leaders were involved in rebuilding and restructuring the hierarchical system. They sought to promote new groups of followers, to promote their own factions and self-interest but also to restore predictability to the system, and provide for an orderly succession down the road.

Indeed, the first response of China's leaders after Mao's death (1976) had been to fix up the economic system and rehabilitate the CP political equilibrium. They launched a grandiose plan to reignite growth with large-scale imports of western technology while they rebuilt the central planning apparatus. However, this "Great Leap Outward" collapsed in 1978, leaving China's leaders with aggravated crises (in agriculture and the external sector), and a growing recognition that the near collapse of state capacity after ten years of the Cultural Revolution threatened their efforts to stabilize the system. These challenges convinced China's leaders that maintenance of the status quo was simply not an option: over the long term, regime survival and the goals of making China a strong and prosperous country were in jeopardy. They began to contemplate more radical economic policies, even as they struggled to reassemble the traditional political system.

The Political Challenge of Transition

What was the nature of the political risk that China's leaders took in beginning an economic reform process? Economic reforms and market transition were profoundly threatening because they took away the monopoly over the distribution of patronage resources that political elites had enjoyed. The key question facing potential reformers was how much to open up the economic system by lowering entry barriers. In this chapter I use "economic opening" in a specific sense. Economic opening means allowing entry into economic sectors previously monopolized by the state, by businesses that are not subject to direct command and control through the hierarchy. These new firms can come from any source: in China, most important sources included entry by new small-scale private businesses, foreign investors, and, especially, locally owned "township and village enterprises (TVEs)." Economic opening could also come from full or partial privatization of public firms. Economic opening increases the space available for "society" and shrinks the space monopolized by the regime.[2]

Opening the system is dangerous politically. In economic reform, top politicians lose their absolute command over the distribution of benefits and incentives, which begin to be shaped by market forces. Every aspect of the old power equilibrium is

---

[2] Pei (2006) uses the terms "regime" and "society" in ways that at times coincide with my terms "inside the hierarchy" and "outside the hierarchy." I am forced to use the clumsier "hierarchy" term because I need to direct attention to the way incentives and authority relations are altered within the hierarchy as well.

disrupted by the impact of economic reform. Power holders must confront three analytically separate but interrelated challenges: the supply of rents is reduced, the possibilities of autonomy increase, and commitment within the hierarchy declines. First, the supply of traditional patronage resources is reduced because entry creates competition with existing firms, and market forces begin to erode the monopoly profits that government firms earned under the command economy (Naughton, 1992). Opening up the system reduces the monopoly rents available to incumbents; it reduces the volume of resources being pumped into the political leadership class, and it therefore reduces the rewards they can distribute as patronage.

Second, successful entrants create new income streams and accumulate economic and political capital. They thus become new sources of power that are potentially much less beholden to the existing hierarchy. Alternative sources of wealth provide the basis for the growth of organized, autonomous social groups. As standard modernization theory posits (Lipset, 1959; Huntington, 1991), these groups might be able to translate economic resources into political power and influence. The mirror image of this challenge is that economic opening risks offending entrenched interest groups, who may try to block further reforms.

Third, the incentives within the hierarchy become less effective. Under the old system, officials were rewarded with power, prestige, perks, and projects, but not large amounts of money. Since the hierarchy was the only game in town, that was more than sufficient. But economic opening creates new income opportunities that compete with the rewards delivered through the hierarchy. Facing lucrative alternatives, officials may reduce or abandon their commitment to the regime (Nee, 1992; Nee and Lian, 1994). Exit becomes an alternative to compliance, and the regime will reach a crisis if exit becomes a "rush for the door" (Solnick, 1996). Officials can exit by quitting their jobs and starting legitimate business, or by staying on the job while devoting their effort to personal or family enrichment.

Thus, opening the system produces wealth and resilience in the long run, but it reduces the ability of politicians to distribute patronage in the short run. In order for leaders to maintain power during the transition, they must respond to all three of the disruptive changes described earlier. Regime survival demands that leaders nurture new types of patronage resources (to replace the rents eroded by reform), tie newly emerging interest groups to the regime, *and* revitalize incentives within the hierarchy. This is a daunting challenge, and authoritarian leaders feel they have little freedom of maneuver. In fact, Chinese leaders responded to all three challenges, but not all at once. Instead, the government opened up – and eventually withdrew from – different economic sectors at an uneven pace, in a strategy of "disarticulation" (Naughton, 1995) or "selective withdrawal" (Pei, 2006, pp. 31–33). This enabled the regime to build new capabilities and devise adequate solutions for individual sectors on a case-by-case basis. Moreover, as Pei points out, selective opening was used to create new patronage resources. Access to the newly opening "external" sources of income was rationed, and so became a benefit that political leaders provided to their supporters. When it succeeded, this stratagem both renewed the commitment of lower-level officials to the regime *and* reduced the danger of independent groupings of economic power. Contrary to expectations, the Chinese CP has been able to use this approach to rebuild the patronage system and political equilibrium over the course of thirty years of economic reform.

This struggle to maintain regime survival naturally predisposed China's leaders to a strategy of gradualist economic reform, and the economic success of the gradualist reform strategy in turn has been a precondition for the political resilience of the Chinese Communist Party. The gradualist transition provided opportunities for individual leaders to develop coherent political strategies despite the formidable economic changes occurring. At the other end of the spectrum, in Poland and the Czech Republic, the Baltic Republics, and Russia under Yeltsin, "big bang" reforms came only after political regime change and were implemented to consolidate those changes. In that sense, the political calculus behind most big bang reforms was precisely the inverse of that behind gradualism in China. Destruction of the authoritarian hierarchy and the irreversibility of change were seen as important *positive* side effects of big bang reforms. Cautious and gradualist strategies were rejected in part because they involved compromises with CP power holders who democratic reformers feared might claw back political and economic power. Rapid privatization in particular was favored precisely because it created independent sources of political power (Boycko, Shleifer, and Vishny, 1995).[3] Conversely, under gradualism, reversibility was an important positive feature of measures. Reversibility meant that mistakes could be corrected and the overall costs of transition be lowered (Roland, 2000). But, of course, in the face of moderate and gradual reforms, the authoritarian hierarchy was able to reestablish the conditions for its own survival.[4]

---

[3] In fact, the most common early argument against gradualism was simply that it was impossible. Aslund (1992, p. 36) reflected and supported a remarkable consensus argued jointly by all the main international financial organizations when he argued, "Is there a feasible gradual road to a market economy? An international interagency study on the Soviet economy denies it: 'Ideally, a path of gradual reform could be laid out which would minimize economic disturbance and lead to an early harvesting of the fruits of increased economic efficiency. But we know of no such path.' [IMF, IBRD, OECD, EBRD, 1990, p. 2]. As long as nobody has indicated a feasible gradual reform, we can do little but discard it as a nonstarter." Today, the remaining supporters of the big bang approach recognize that Chinese gradualism was indeed feasible, but sometimes still argue that what was possible in China was not possible in Europe. An alternative explanation is much more persuasive, namely, that gradualist transition paths were possible in either environment but that political considerations were more important than economic considerations in determining the transition path adopted.

[4] Gorbachev, at the end of the 1980s, was on the borderline between "gradual" and "big bang" approaches. A product of the apparat himself, Gorbachev tried to completely restructure political power and did away with much of the traditional CP hierarchy. He accumulated enormous personal power and faced few systemic constraints. He tried to create a new political system under the umbrella of his own power, expecting to lead a democratic Russia. However, lacking effective instruments, experience, or clear economic objectives, Gorbachev was unable to shape effective economic policies and adopted sometimes radical but often inconsistent policies. He pushed the economic system toward the precipice of some kind of big bang because he was willing – indeed, eager – to tear down the old political system (Suraska, 1998).

The Chinese leaders' drive for regime survival melded with their strong preference for economic growth as their top domestic priority. Disruption to economic growth was avoided, and individual reforms were often judged in terms of their short-run contribution to growth.[5] As Deng Xiaoping said, "[D]evelopment is the only hard truth." Development meant economic growth, but crucially was seen as including institutional development and strengthening of capabilities. The effort to stabilize the hierarchy and make it more effective was also part of "development." It was as important as economic reform and seen as complementary to it. These motives contributed to China's specific transition path, combining market transition and political authoritarianism.

This chapter is a positive study in political economy, analyzing the incentives faced by incumbent leaders and assessing the resources and constraints that shape their options, not a normative study of the economics of transition. The existing literature on gradualist transition, by contrast, is primarily a normative discussion and policy debate (see Roland, 2000, for an overview). Some of the arguments of this normative discussion are relevant to this positive political economy though: advocates of gradualist economic reform argue that gradual opening lowers the cost of experimenting with reform; it allows the "winners" of reform to be identified, and the discovery of lower-cost mechanisms to compensate smaller groups of "losers," thus enabling winners to mobilize and build constituencies for further reform. In addition, by minimizing losses of economic output caused by the disruption of a "big bang," a gradualist process enables a virtuous circle to take hold. With less disruption of income and more stable expectations about the future, households invest more and take fuller advantage of the opportunities created by economic opening. In turn, increased household saving compensates for the inevitable reduction in government saving that goes along with transition (McMillan and Naughton, 1992). These normative arguments help to explain why economic growth was robust during gradualist transition, and thus why the authoritarian regime was able to develop new patronage resources to shore up its political power. Because gradualist transition was a successful economic strategy, it could support a potentially successful political strategy by China's leaders.

The Initial Steps

The initial steps of economic reform in China were a response to an unusual combination of opportunity and crisis. The top leaders were veteran CP leaders, but

---

[5] It was never conceivable that reformers in China would voluntarily sacrifice economic growth to remake the economic system, whereas in Eastern Europe reformers self-consciously chose this option on many occasions. Eastern European countries had the nearby example of European developed capitalist economic systems and the promise of potential EU membership to anchor expectations of the reform "end point," making it easier to bear larger transition costs up front. China had the example of successful East Asian economies, to be sure, but given its huge size and unique geographical position, there was no conceivable outside model available to anchor expectations of the transitional end point.

also victims of the Cultural Revolution, and after the death of Mao, they could credibly blame most economic problems on the discredited "Gang of Four" and other Cultural Revolution radicals. With all autonomous organizations crushed during the long Maoist ascendance, competition for political power was quite limited, despite a few protests at "Democracy Wall." The result was a diffuse consensus for "reform" broadly held among the public and among a relatively large leadership group with diverse political opinions. At the outset, nobody knew where "reform" would lead, which made it easier to maintain a rough leadership consensus during the first reform steps.

Initially, reform ideas did not extend much beyond "giving farmers a chance to catch their breath" or "expanding enterprise autonomy." Inevitably, initial reforms were "without a blueprint," characterized by experimentation, or "groping for stepping stones to cross the river."[6] However, daunting economic problems in the rural and external sectors prompted three dramatic policy initiatives. First, the poor shape of the rural economy, particularly the stagnation of rural incomes over many decades, drove decision making in the early years. Rural stagnation encouraged the top leadership to transfer incomes (and rents) to rural people whenever possible. Policymakers were willing to contemplate far-reaching changes in agricultural collectives – and ultimately accepted their dissolution – because of their concern about stagnant conditions in agriculture. Grain procurement policy was in crisis, as planners worried that government pressure to sell low-price grain was undermining farmer incentives to produce and might create a drop in output, as had occurred in the Great Leap Forward (Zhao, 1988, pp. 144–168). During 1979, Chen Yun, the key economic policymaker among the veterans, proposed placing agriculture first in the planning process and reducing the economywide investment rate, thereby creating the context for a dramatic shift in resource allocation toward the farm sector.

Second, the regime committed to the first real program of economic opening, which allowed TVEs to enter into new lines of business for the sake of profit. This policy was formalized in a key 1979 document on rural industry that declared that rural enterprises should take over processing of agricultural products and were permitted to engage in almost any income-generating activity (Naughton, 1995, pp. 146–148). These crucial decisions began the process of entry and marketization, and created the context that allowed agricultural reforms to go ahead, later achieving dramatic success.

In the external sector, China faced a serious foreign exchange crisis, as official reserves had dropped to virtually zero. China had little ability to earn foreign exchange, but had recklessly committed billions of dollars worth of foreign exchange to complete plant imports. There were very strong incentives to cast about for new ways to earn foreign exchange, and the third initiative created an

---

[6] This term is frequently attributed to Deng Xiaoping, but was in fact first used by Chen Yun, whose role in the reform is discussed later (Li, 1987; see also Lin, 1989).

opening for foreign trade and investment. Very early in the transition process, foreign businesses were allowed to invest in special economic zones (SEZs) and set up export processing businesses outside the SEZs as well. New central government trade and investment corporations (CITIC and Everbright) and greatly expanded operations of Chinese corporations in Hong Kong created new opportunities for Chinese domestic firms not under the government's direct command.

These initial steps were bold economically, because they represented the first unambiguous breaks with the state monopoly over economic decision making, and the beginning of selective withdrawal. These decisions were driven by economic crisis. Pei (2006, p. 31) points out that "[i]f a regime can choose the sectors to liberalize . . . political logic dictates that it should first liberalize sectors where rents are relatively low and less concentrated." Agriculture fits this logic well: rural areas had much lower income, and also lower power and representation in the Chinese political system. There were no powerful agricultural interest groups in the government, so central leaders were free to recast agricultural policy pragmatically. They worried most about the supply of grain to the cities and were not concerned about surrendering control over revenues in the countryside. Indeed, during the 1980s, an influential maverick think tank in China, the Rural Development Research Center (RDRC) recommended that rural policies of "contracting land to households" should be initiated in poor, backward areas where the government was not procuring grain. Moreover, the RDRC went on to explicitly advocate a broader reform strategy along these lines, of withdrawing selectively from sectors with lower strategic relevance to the national economy (Rural Development Research Group, 1984). TVEs shared the "low-power" characteristics of agriculture: initially small, dispersed, and technologically backward, seemingly little was risked by unleashing these firms.

But the other key early reform sector does not fit this pattern at all. The external sector was potentially the source of large and concentrated rents, the most lucrative of all. Extremely strict monopolization of the external sector is the rule in all command economies. Whoever could exploit the huge price differentials between world and domestic prices could reap quick monopoly rents. Yet, opening went forward in this politically sensitive sector. In practice, the Chinese regime did not have the luxury of choice in determining which sectors to liberalize. Instead, politicians had to trade off costs and benefits in several dimensions in order to decide on selective opening. Was the sector in crisis? Were rents large and concentrated? Could the sector be detached from the central plan without threatening the government's strategic priorities? Would the opening foster autonomous groups that could challenge Communist rule? Foreign businesses were politically nonthreatening (Huang, 2003; Gallagher, 2002). They could be penned up inside special zones and their viability be conditioned on special deals with the elite. Moreover, foreign firms had no standing to claim political rights or voice.

In the beginning, then, reforms started because of crisis in a few sectors where the regime felt it could manage the political challenges involved. The policies did not

threaten significant reductions in the supply of rents to the regime; they strengthened only groups that were politically weak and marginalized in the CP political
system, and it was easy to tie reform-created benefits back into allegiance to the
political hierarchy. The initial opening of the system promised immediate benefits, and the leadership gambled, correctly, that they could manage the political
implications. It is thus relatively easy to see how bold decisions to selectively open
the economic system were made, given the challenges faced by the Chinese leaders
during the crucial turning points of 1978–1980.

But why did reforms persist? The remarkable thing about the Chinese case is
not so much the initial steps, but rather the fact that the leadership allowed the
process to continue, and deepen and broaden, progressively opening the system to
new entrants. As it turned out, the process of opening, once launched, was never
substantially reversed. Yet, the specific configuration of policies was not foreordained by the initial reform commitment and was instead constantly improvised
during reform. Leaders literally made it up as they went along, according to their
interests at the time. As reform unfolded, local innovations, private entrepreneurship, and strategic responses to central government policy all played a crucial role.
Transition overall was an interactive process involving top-down policymaking and
bottom-up response and innovation. Yet, the crucial driver was the willingness of
top leaders to continue moving the process forward, and this is the focus of this
chapter: how did the incentives of top leaders and the structure of power at the top
interact to create a specific reform outcome?

THE FIRST PERIOD OF TRANSITION, 1978 THROUGH 1993

After the beginning in 1978–1980, economic transition maintained a distinctive
character and a consistent pattern through 1993, after which it changed abruptly.

The initial approach of reform – top-down, tentative, and exploratory, with a
focus on a few key sectors – ushered in a remarkably coherent fifteen years of
reform policy. To probe more deeply into the pattern of transition during the
first period, the following discussion proceeds in a top-down sequence of four
descending steps. First, I describe the structure of power at the apex of the political
system. I argue that the structure of power determines the overall policymaking regime, which produces characteristic types of policy outcomes. Within the
framework defined by the policymaking regime, individual political entrepreneurs
create innovative approaches and specific reform initiatives. Finally, these reform
initiatives interact with the economic and institutional environment, and with the
strategic, self-interested responses to these policies, to shape the most important
reform outcomes. In this way, the structure of political power drives the reform
process. In addition, there is a feedback loop from the reform process back to the
system that determines the structure of political power. Politicians are constantly
trying to rebuild the patronage relations in the hierarchy, both to further their
personal careers and to ensure the stability and survival of the system to which

their interests are tied. Indeed, they were mindful of these considerations when they engaged in policy entrepreneurship in the first place. In the final subsection, we examine the way a restructured hierarchical political system emerges from the aggregate of these individual strategies.

The Structure of Power at the Top

From 1978, through the early 1990s, national power in China was fragmented, with numerous "veto players" (Tsebelis, 2002). This may seem a peculiar assertion. The literature on veto players pays attention to the formal structure of institutions, and formally China has a single veto player, the Standing Committee of the Politburo of the Chinese Communist Party. There is no institutionalized system of checks and balances – only the weak "reciprocal accountability" described earlier – and nobody has the authority to veto a Politburo decision. However, under a system of authoritarian rule, power is often personalized and exercised informally. This was particularly true in China in the wake of Mao, and it is essential to look at the informal, as well as the formal, distribution of power at the top of the hierarchy. No clear theory or terminology exists to describe the distribution of power in authoritarian systems, but in China in the 1980s it is relatively easy to identify a dozen or so leaders who had effective veto power over some aspect of economic policy. Moreover, most of the important veto players at the top had extensive patronage networks extending down through the hierarchical system, further complicating policy implementation. This basic structure of power at the top determined much of the trajectory of Chinese economic reforms through the initial fifteen years of reform.

Power at the top was fragmented among a group of "revolutionary elders." Deng Xiaoping was universally recognized as the most important and generally styled as the "paramount" leader. However, there were a large number of important and influential revolutionary elders, who formed a kind of "senate" of influential leaders. The most powerful were sometimes popularly referred to during the 1980s as the "Eight Elders."[7] Alongside these veterans, a handful of younger leaders exercised real power and had been designated as successors by Deng Xiaoping. Most important among the younger group were the Communist First Party Secretary

---

[7] The most common list of the "Eight Elders" (sometimes called the "Eight Immortals") was Deng Xiaoping, Chen Yun, Peng Zhen, Li Xiannian, Wang Zhen, Yang Shangkun, Song Renqiong, and Bo Yibo (see http://en.wikipedia.org/wiki/Eight_Immortals_of_Communist_Party_of_China). The list is not invariant. Some versions put Deng Xiaoping in a separate category and include Deng Yingchao, Zhou Enlai's widow (Chen, 1999, p. 15; cf. MacFarquhar, 1997, p. 331; Baum, 1997) All the Eight Elders were full members of the Twelfth Central Committee Politburo selected in 1982, in which distinguished elders made up twelve out of thirty total members. Another important elder and Twelfth Committee Politburo member, Ye Jianying, died in 1986, but managed to make the province of Guangdong a veto player for several years beyond his death after he established his son, Ye Xuanping, as the power broker in that province (see Gao, 1999).

Hu Yaobang and the Premier Zhao Ziyang. As formal heads of the two most important administrative hierarchies (party and government), Hu and Zhao had their
hands on the levers of power and control of the daily agenda. They had enormous
discretion over whether and how specific directives and policies were carried out.
Despite this power, they were unable to override clearly expressed wishes of the
most important elders. Thus, the power to make or block economic policy was
widely dispersed.

The elders derived power and legitimacy from their personal histories, prestige,
and patronage networks. All the elders had been involved in governing China
since the establishment of the People's Republic in 1949, at the highest levels,
although they were subordinate to Mao Zedong. Their commitment to CP rule
far exceeded their commitment to reform. Ironically, CP veterans were able to
gain legitimacy from both their experience and their status as prominent victims
of Mao. The elders did not get power from their formal institutional position:
rather, institutions were created and adapted to conform to the actual (informal)
structure of power. A Central Advisory Commission was created in 1982 to give
senior leaders a forum to exercise power even after they stepped down from their
formal party and government positions, and similar Advisory Commissions were
set up at provincial and municipal levels.

In economic policy, the most important elders were Chen Yun and Li Xiannian.
These two men had enormous prestige and power. Both men were politically conservative, and neither was committed to economic reform. Yet, during the first two
years of the economic transition process, Chen Yun and Li Xiannian were actually
making economic policy at the national level. Chen Yun personally established
the most important economic policies: shifting priority to agriculture, reducing
investment, liquidating the Great Leap Outward, and explicitly permitting a "market economy" to develop as a supplement to the "planned economy." Chen Yun
was the only elder who could directly compete with Deng Xiaoping in overall influence (Lardy and Lieberthal, 1983; Bachman, 1985; Document Research Room,
2005). Li Xiannian, unlike Chen Yun, had no strong vision or claims of overall
leadership, but he was a consistent hands-on policymaker whose career spanned
both sides of the 1978 watershed. He had major responsibility for the economy as
far back as 1973 and personally made many key economic decisions, including several that were reversed during 1979, when he himself was running the day-to-day
work of government as first deputy premier (MacFarquhar and Schoenhals, 2006,
p. 359). These two individuals had a more direct influence on economic policy
than did Deng Xiaoping. During the 1980s, Premier Zhao Ziyang did gradually
take over control of daily policy formulation, but even then, never completely.

The most important elders were separated by significant ideological distance.
The relationship between Deng Xiaoping and Chen Yun, for example, is usually
characterized as competitive, and they are often portrayed as leaders of a pro-
reform and anti-reform faction, respectively (Lam, 1989). There are elements of
truth in this analysis. Chen Yun was certainly far less committed to reform than

Deng Xiaoping, and he consistently opposed certain reforms (notably, SEZs) and blocked others. But these traditional explanations do not tell the whole story. Deng Xiaoping also had a degree of trust in Chen Yun and other veteran economic policymakers, having worked with them for fifty years. In economic matters, Deng repeatedly deferred to Chen Yun's understanding. Indeed, one of the very few explicit testaments to the power of the elders also gives overt testimony to Chen Yun's expertise in economics: in 1987, at the Thirteenth Party Congress, the elders resigned all of their official Politburo positions. In order to facilitate this formal success, the new younger Politburo Standing Committee pledged to consult with Deng Xiaoping on all important political matters and with Chen Yun on all important economic matters (Baum, 1997). Thus, even when Zhao was actively driving reform policymaking, the power to make crucial economic decisions was dispersed to a number of leaders with divergent viewpoints.[8] Indeed, Zhao quickly lost the confidence of the elders (especially Chen Yun) in his handling of macroeconomic issues, and lost control over macroeconomic policy in 1988. This division set the scene for the bitter split at the time of the Tiananmen Square demonstrations in 1989, after which Zhao lost power completely.

The Overall Policy Regime

What difference did the fragmentation of power in China make? The dispersal of policymaking authority among national leaders with diverse agendas aggregated into a distinctive and enduring overall pattern of economic policy. China's "gradualism" during this first period was characterized by a cautious incrementalism and lack of policy decisiveness that strongly reflected the configuration of power in Beijing. For fifteen years, policy stability was high: policies that departed decisively from the status quo were rare. Once the first key decisions were taken, limited as they were, the overall direction of transition policy was set. Subsequently, it was scarcely altered.

This observation is consistent with an important prediction in the political science literature that relates the pattern of policymaking with the number of veto players in the political system. Tsebelis (2002) predicts that a large number of veto players produce stable and consistent policy, while a small number of veto players produce policy that is less stable, but more flexible and decisive (Cox and

---

[8] Further, Deng Xiaoping, as paramount leader, had a strategy of balancing, both formally and informally. All leaders need to delegate responsibility, but as Deng grew older, he tried to delegate more while also balancing groups off against each other. The most salient part of Deng's "balancing" was setting the younger reformers against the more conservative elders. Deng's political strategy was consistent with the fragmented, multi-veto-player structure of power, and indeed reinforced that structure. The strategy worked fairly well, until Deng Xiaoping lost faith first in Hu Yaobang and then in Zhao Ziyang during 1987–1989. Deng's subsequent shift back to reliance on the elders and their relatively mediocre clients plunged the entire system into disarray.

McCubbins, 2001; MacIntyre, 2003). Both "stability" and "decisiveness" are advantageous in certain situations, and neither is preferable under all circumstances, particularly given that there is a trade-off between them. Policy stability is good when policy is already appropriate, when external challenges are few, and when policymakers seek to delegate authority to administrative and regulatory agencies, such as central banks (cf. Keefer and Stasavage, 2001). Conversely, flexibility and decisiveness are desirable when policy needs to be altered and when changes in external conditions demand rapid response. Multiple veto players in China during the 1980s created a situation in which policy stability was high, creating both benefits and costs.

The initial reform policies – adopted under duress in the late 1970s – actually drove transition through much of the 1980s. This is true in each of the three most important early reform arenas: agriculture, rural enterprises, and opening to foreign trade and investment. The crucial agricultural reform policies that dissolved the collectives were made by indirection, by simply allowing a set of local policy changes to be adopted by a steadily expanding universe of local officials (Unger, 1986). The initial TVE policy of 1979 had implied an opening of the system to competition. The increase in competition, given the absence of privatization, was dependent upon the cumulative entry and expansion of TVEs and private firms. Thus, simply to maintain this policy implied a gradual marketization of the economy. And, in fact, the policy originally set in 1979 survived virtually unchanged until it merged into even more thorough marketization (and privatization) in the late 1990s. The pattern of steady expansion of an existing reform applied to foreign investment as well. Initially, foreign businesses were permitted in four SEZs. In successive waves, the number of "open areas" was increased – to fourteen "open cities," the Yangtze and Pearl River deltas, and successively larger areas – but the essence of the policy was never changed.

The inevitable concomitant of policy stability is a lack of decisiveness. Indeed, through 1993, Chinese policymakers were unable to adopt a reform policy that dramatically broke with the planned economy past, but not from lack of trying. Policymakers repeatedly sought to draw up ambitious reform programs, all of which ultimately came to naught (SRC, 1988). A short list of ambitious packages would include a July 1979 package of industrial and foreign trade reforms, the 1980 package of enterprise reforms, 1984 foreign trade reforms, and the late 1986 program of "integrated" reform. In each case, ambitious goals were simply not enough to compensate for a lack of political muscle to overcome specific entrenched interests. Indeed, in transition policy there are remarkably few milestone events or policy turning points between 1979 and, say, 1993. After reforms were initiated in 1979–1980, the only real turning point came in 1984–1985, as the top leadership agreed to introduce a package of urban reforms in the wake of rural success. Even in this case, the policy package involved some innovative measures, but also much that simply endorsed existing practices that had been informally tolerated, such as the dual-track price system (Fewsmith, 1997). Characteristically, this policy turning point came when Zhao Ziyang carefully crafted and circulated a letter that elicited the acquiescence of the key elders to a few selected measures of enterprise reform (Naughton, 1995, pp. 178–180). Only then was an official reform document promulgated, and later an important Party Congress was convened at the end of 1985. Even in this case, many of the measures formally adopted, such as the *ligaishui* enterprise finance reform, failed in the implementation stage (Shirk, 1993). Indeed, these implementation failures led to subsequent efforts to design a coordinated reform package that also failed: in 1986, after months of study and preparation, Zhao Ziyang listened to the reports of his economic advisers and then abandoned the package, reportedly declaring, "But who will support this program?" Indeed, policy stability and lack of decisiveness even survived the traumatic political breakdown around the June 4, 1989, Tiananmen incident. After June 4, 1989, the reformist Zhao Ziyang lost power to a group of conservative hard-liners. The conservatives declared their intention to roll back key features of reform, including the business freedom enjoyed by TVEs, but their attempted restoration of planning never went anywhere (Naughton, 1995, pp. 274–288; Fewsmith, 1997).

An important reason for the inability to enact dramatic reforms during the 1980s was the fact that each of the important veto players was able to protect specific social groups and block reforms that would have imposed losses on them. Elders prevented radical reforms that would have imposed substantial costs on, for example, workers in SOEs. Bankruptcy and layoffs were scarcely permitted. Policymakers displayed virtually no ability to impose losses on powerful social groups or individuals. This was true not only for large social groups (such as state enterprise workers), but also for agencies and individual politicians who were clients of top leaders. For example, in the 1984 foreign trade reform, import–export companies were instructed to adopt the "agency system" for imports, selling them in the domestic market for the international price plus a markup. However, the minister of foreign trade at that time, Zheng Tuobin, was a client and protégé of top leader, Chen Yun. Zheng simply did not implement the agency system, perhaps because it would have eroded monopoly profits of the trading companies under his purview. There was no way he could be disciplined, given his top-level patronage. Nor was it always conservatives who blocked reforms: in 1985, the People's Bank of China decided to phase out the system of foreign exchange certificates (a higher-value domestic currency acquired by foreigners when they converted foreign exchange) and issued all the necessary documents. At the last minute, the province of Guangdong, home of a lucrative business trading foreign exchange certificates, objected to the policy and it was abandoned: the certificates were phased out only ten years later in 1995. Insider accounts of decision making in the 1980s, appearing much later, strongly support the picture of a highly fragmented and personalized policy process, as well as the continuing influence of the revolutionary elders (Xu Jiatun, 1993; Zhang Liang, 2001; Deng Liqun, 2005).

The lack of decisive policymaking also contributed to macroeconomic instability and, in particular, to inflationary cycles. Policymaking was slow to respond to changes in external conditions, so inflationary pressures repeatedly got out of control (in 1985, 1988, and for the last time, 1992–1993). In each case, policymakers eventually reimposed discipline on the economy, showing that they possessed the tools to discipline local government investment spending once concerns about stability reached a critical point (Huang, 1996). This pattern is consistent with a model of delayed stabilization, in which competing factions struggle over who will pay the ultimate costs (Alesina and Drazen, 1991; Velasco, 1998). As Zhou (1993) notes, if a burst of decentralization destabilized the macroeconomy, conservatives would gain power to slow down the pace of change; conversely, if conservatives threatened to stifle reforms in their quest for stability, reformers would gain power. The result was a pattern of political–economic business cycles, in which policy stance and inflation varied together, but within a reasonably circumscribed scope.

The Pattern of Reform Initiatives

If economic policy had been all stability and no innovation, then China's economic reform would have been smothered in its crib, and there would be no Chinese economic miracle to write about. In fact, though, continuing incremental tinkering with the economic system, combined with the accumulating impact of early choices, kept the marketization process expanding to encompass more of the economy. Economic policymakers, especially Premier Zhao Ziyang, crafted policies that were consistent with both their own political strategies and the overriding political imperative of regime survival. Shirk (1993) described how Zhao Ziyang adopted the strategy of "playing to the provinces," using policy to distribute particularistic benefits to local government interests, which he expected would increase his support in the CP "selectorate." Individual leaders sought to reward supporters and bring new groups into their coalitions; the political strategies they followed aggregated into a predictable and coherent pattern of reform policy (see Naughton, 1995, pp. 201–243; 2007, pp. 90–98).

The key features of the policies that were followed during the 1980s include the following:

– *Particularistic contracting.* "Particularistic contracting" (Shirk, 1993) was the dominant form of reform policymaking. Broad-based tax reforms failed, and individual enterprises instead signed profit contracts, pledging to turn over to the government specified sums of annual revenue. These contracts "grandfathered" in each firm's existing situation, giving that firm incentives to improve profitability from the current achieved level. Particularistic contracting spread to local government fiscal systems, as local governments contracted to turn over specific sums of budgetary revenues to the central government. By the late 1980s, millions of family farms, hundreds of thousands of state enterprises, hundreds of foreign trade corporations, and all thirty of China's provinces had signed contracts with their bureaucratic superiors that fixed the amount of revenue they were to turn over in the coming year.

— *Dual track.* An entire "dual-track" strategy of reform developed, in which firms operated on both a plan and a market track. The dual track can be considered a generalization of particularistic contracting, since each firm had to first fulfill its preexisting plan contracts, which were of course specific to that firm. Above this base, firms were allowed to produce for the market at market prices. This enabled price liberalization, without immediately eliminating the preexisting rents that firms received. Perhaps the most striking innovation of the early period of China's transition was the willingness of top leaders to "freeze" the plan, which greatly strengthened the predictability and improved the incentive properties of "markets on the margin." Only gradually, in this framework, did the economy grow out of the plan (Byrd, 1989; Naughton, 1993).

— *Incentivization.* Throughout the hierarchy, high-powered incentives were introduced. Enterprise managers were allowed by their bureaucratic superiors to keep a large percentage (50 percent or more, often 100 percent) of increased profit beyond the base figure. Within the administrative hierarchy, large cash bonuses "incentivized" government officials (Whiting, 2001; Naughton, 2008). Existing enterprises and nonprofit agencies – even military units – were given substantial leeway to set up income-earning operations or reap rewards by cutting costs on existing operations.

— *Decentralization.* As an inevitable concomitant of the preceding, much decision-making power was remanded to a lower level. Moreover, resources retained at the local level as both budgetary and extrabudgetary funds, increased rapidly. Indeed, the Chinese use the term "decentralization of authority and retention of profits (*fangquan rangli*)" as a shorthand description of this entire period.

Reform Outcomes

These political characteristics gave the 1980s reform process some distinctive economic features. Top leaders would not allow individual reforms that seriously damaged the economic interests of their clients, individuals or social groups. In other words, policy was all "carrot" and no "stick." More radical solutions could never achieve the political momentum necessary to overcome the inertia of the system, which was due to the large number of veto players. Price reforms, which require explicit acknowledgment of winners and losers, were never pushed through. Instead, a dual-track system, which allowed market prices to grow along planned prices, which only gradually erodes the position of incumbents, spread steadily through the economy.

Because of the need to buy off every agency and region, general budgetary revenues eroded and fiscal capabilities declined. Fiscal erosion reflected two simultaneous factors. Lowered entry barriers brought in new firms that steadily competed away the monopoly rents in the old economic system, while the steady decentralization of revenue authority meant the loss of revenues to the formal budget. An index of the process of fiscal erosion is the share of budgetary revenues

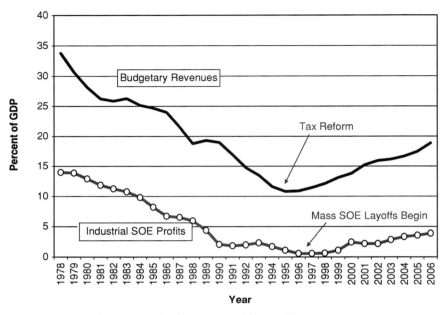

Figure 4.1. Fiscal revenues and industrial SOE profits

in gross domestic product (GDP). As Figure 4.1 shows, budgetary revenues and state industrial enterprise profits began to erode immediately with the beginning of the transition process (see Chapter 12). From 33 percent in 1978, budgetary revenues declined as a share of GDP virtually every year until it hit bottom at 10.8 percent in 1995. Similarly, industrial SOE profits declined from 14.0 to 0.6 percent of GDP between 1978 and 1996. Of course, sustained declines of this magnitude eventually provoked a response. Here, we simply note how strong and sustained the pattern was during the 1980s. Once the system was opened up, steady entry and increased competition steadily eroded the monopoly profits, rents, and revenues that the system used to reproduce itself and reward supporters. The fragmented, multi-veto-gate distribution of power at the top kept China on this track, despite increasing unease about the erosion of central government power.

The 1989 political crisis around the June 4 Tiananmen Square events profoundly shocked the regime and the world. In their wake, Zhao Ziyang and some of his top advisers were purged, the economic leadership was replaced, and the slogans and intentions of top economic policymakers swung nearly 180 degrees. But the overall structure of power continued to be fragmented and the main directions of policy surprisingly stable. In Figure 4.1, we do not see a turning point in 1989–1990 but, rather five or six years later, in 1994–1996.

Along with the decline in fiscal capacity, public goods provision suffered. For more than a decade, China was a chronic underprovider of public goods. Social services such as rural health care and education declined dramatically. Even physical infrastructure investment, which one might expect to be relatively easily provided in such a system, was underprovided. During the 1980s, fixed investment in transport, communications, and electricity averaged less than 4 percent of GDP, below rule-of-thumb benchmarks of 6 percent of GDP for successful growth.

Throughout this period, there were boundaries to reform that were never crossed. Reforms never threatened the job security of urban workers nor did they subject public enterprises to a hard bankruptcy constraint. Rural residents were never allowed to migrate permanently to the city, although the barriers to population movement were lowered slightly. High tariff and nontariff barriers to imported goods were never dismantled. Finally, domestic private business was never given a clearly legitimate position in the economic model. Only very small private businesses were allowed, predominantly the *getihu*, or single-family businesses. To be sure, in many locales individual businesses, especially those well connected, grew substantially larger. But there were only a handful of significant private companies in the whole country. These limitations to the reform process meant that the public enterprises subordinate to the hierarchy remained protected. Lau, Qian, and Roland (2001) labeled this period "reform without losers," because many segments of society became better off, while no obvious sector became worse off. While Lau, Qian, and Roland see this as a characteristic of the gradualist transition strategy, it should in fact be tied more closely to the structure of political power and the types of policies adopted during the 1980s because of that structure. The comparatively privileged position of specific social groups under the socialist system – for example, state enterprise workers – was never seriously challenged during the 1980s.

These limitations on the reform process, along with the dramatic success of early rural reforms, produced an enormous collateral benefit. Early reforms disproportionately benefited individuals in the lower half of China's income distribution, so that inequality in China actually *declined* from the beginning of reform in 1978 through about 1985. Calculations of the Gini coefficient before 1980 are not accurate enough to be meaningful, but in the careful reconstruction of Ravallion and Chen (2004), the national Gini coefficient declined slightly from about 0.31 in 1981 to 0.29 in 1985, making China the most equal large country by a substantial margin. Clearly, that placated opponents and reinforced acceptance of reforms, popularly and among the elite. This was an inadvertent and unanticipated side effect of the pattern of selective withdrawal, in which early benefits of reform and the growth of TVEs were enjoyed by rural residents with low incomes. Opposition to reform was blunted, and support for reform increased, by the growth of the economy and the broad distribution of reform-derived benefits.

Adapting the System: Rebuilding Hierarchy and the Patronage System

While the economic system was undergoing profound changes, politicians were working to shore up their personal positions. The aggregate impact of individual politicians securing their own positions and legacies was the rehabilitation and strengthening of the overall hierarchical system. Politicians confronted the three systemic challenges we described earlier as patronage resources, autonomy, and commitment. Specific strategies to confront these challenges met with varying degrees of success, but the overall effect was to shore up the authoritarian hierarchy. The effort of individual politicians to reward their supporters was hobbled by the decline in traditional monopoly rents. However, politicians were inventive in developing new patronage resources from system reform itself.

With decentralization, national-level politicians granted control over financial resources selectively and successively, creating patronage. But this strategy had an inherent limit, because control, once devolved to the local level, ceased to be an item of patronage for the center. Decentralization must be contingent and reversible if it is to serve as a source of patronage, but contingent and reversible decentralization will not succeed as an economic reform strategy. Politicians found some new sources of rent, the most important of which was the provision of low-interest bank lending for project financing. However, in this first period, bank credit was closely tied to SOEs. As the cushion of monopoly rents shrank, significant numbers of SOEs tipped into the red, and, in an era "without losers," bank credit was inevitably tethered to the need to keep loss-making firms afloat. This kept the reform process moving ahead, but did not provide much new patronage resources to leaders. The squeeze on patronage resources fed the perception that the central government was weak and in crisis by the end of the period.

Politicians were quick to see that selective withdrawal could provide an important source of patronage. Selective access to reform-created income streams gave clients access to lucrative opportunities. The central government, unable to afford budgetary grants, instead granted "flexible policies." At this early stage, the hierarchically planned economy was still large and entrepreneurial opportunities outside the hierarchy were comparatively few, so it was relatively easy to condition access to those opportunities on political status. The process allowed individual leaders to strengthen their personal patronage networks by rewarding clients. Many lucrative new opportunities opened up for central government insiders during the 1980s. SEZs were staffed by the central government; the central government set up independent international "window" corporations, such as CITIC and Everbright; and ministry-run corporations in Hong Kong expanded rapidly: these all provided rich new patronage opportunities. The most extreme examples of selective access were the opportunities provided to family members of the top leaders themselves. By the late 1980s, some two hundred "princelings" (children of top party leaders) were at work in Hong Kong (Xu, 1993, pp. 257–263). Even Deng Xiaoping's son Deng Pufang was a principal in the Hong Kong registered Kanghua Corporation in the 1980s. The children of Wang Zhen (one of the "Eight Elders") were probably the most prolific abusers of selective access, with at least three sons serving as heads of three different government-linked external corporations with operations in Hong Kong and the Shenzhen SEZ.[9] These grants of selective access helped smooth the way politically among the CP elite.

Among ordinary Chinese, the grants of selective access were more routine and institutionalized. Since private businesses did not have a clear grant of legitimacy or protection of property rights, entrepreneurs always had to maintain good relations with government and party officials. Start-up firms with indirect government links played key roles. In the rural TVE sector, many firms were created by private entrepreneurs but struck deals with local officials that allowed them to maintain a façade of collective ownership. More fundamentally, in the absence of personal mobility, entrepreneurs and local officials were thrown together and forced to cooperate if either were to become well off. The resulting system of "local corporatism" tied emerging economic groups to the bottom tier of the hierarchy.[10] Even in cities, many new businesses – such as high-technology start-ups – were created as subsidiaries to existing government enterprises or agencies. With privatization kept off the agenda, the new economic forces created were all dependent on some degree of CP acquiescence for their newfound prosperity.

Strategies to strengthen incentives within the hierarchical system both furthered marketization *and* reinforced allegiance to the regime (Naughton, 2008). These efforts can generally be grouped into two categories. First, the existing hierarchy was "incentivized" through increased monetary payments and more "high-powered" incentives. Second, political career paths were gradually institutionalized, which made career-based incentives more predictable and powerful. Together, these changes linked compensation much more closely to managerial effort and performance, made managers within the hierarchy better off, and strongly reinforced managers' commitment to the regime. It also reinforced managers' sensitivity to specific instructions and patrons within the regime.

---

[9] Indeed, one of Wang Zhen's sons, Wang Jun, is currently the CEO of the largest such international corporation, CITIC. His brother, Wang Zhi, is general manager of Great Wall Computer Company, a joint venture between IBM and the central-government-run Great Wall Company. Wang Bing, the third brother, is head of the Helicopter Company of the Nanhai Offshore Oil Company. All these positions date to the 1980s in one form or another. The establishment of CITIC and Everbright themselves was a reward to two insider/outsiders, Rong Yiren and Wang Guangying, respectively, capitalists who threw in their lot with the Communist regime in the 1950s and as a result suffered during the Cultural Revolution. In compensation, they were given the opportunity to once again accumulate great wealth, with the implicit condition that they provide employment and enrichment opportunities to the sons and daughters of top leaders. The story is a complicated one: there is a great deal of available information, but it is not easily accessible in the English-language literature (see He and Gao, 1992; Xiao, 2000).

[10] The literature on township and village enterprises and local corporatism is large and of very high quality. For a sample, see Chang and Wang (1994), Che and Qian (1998), Weitzmann and Xu (1994), and Oi (1999).

Transition strategy in the first period was tied to this "incentivization." Particularistic contracts were implemented through the hierarchy. Superiors wrote contracts that specified high-powered incentives for their subordinates. The "dual-track" strategy was based on a fixed plan target, negotiated by superiors and subordinates on the basis of past performance. Enterprise managers, for example, tried to please their superiors so that they could ensure a "slack" plan, and superiors converted their ability to grant a slack target into a patronage resource. Managers had more leeway, more resources, and better incentives, but they were still dependent upon a superior in the hierarchy, setting the baseline for their incentive contracts. What Kornai (1987) labeled, the "dual dependence" of the government enterprise – dependent on both the market and the bureaucracy – was perpetuated under the Chinese strategy. The same dynamic was at work wherever particularistic contracts and high-powered incentives were introduced, including central–local fiscal relations and foreign trade companies. Government officials were even rewarded for reform policy entrepreneurship by being designated an "experiment" or a special zone. Inevitably, such experiments received preferential access to various kinds of resources. An expression that described this interaction became popular: "[I]f you're an experiment, you win" (*shei shidian shei deyi*). All these mechanisms provided powerful incentives that rewarded government officials for compliance with the prevailing policy line.

Government officials began to get significant cash bonuses associated with fulfillment of targets and success indicators (Whiting, 2001). Indeed, monetary bonuses spread to nearly every type of government employees, even physicians and teachers. These payments spread because of their incentive properties, but they can also be seen as necessary instruments to reinforce commitment to the regime. As individuals acquired more attractive options outside the system, leaders had to raise the payment for continued commitment. During the first era of reform, a striking group of beneficiaries were the managers of SOEs. They increased their incomes, but even more strikingly increased their autonomy and discretion. After the "factory manager responsibility system" was launched in the mid-1980s, factory managers became much more powerful and influential, as well as better off economically. Yet, managers remained embedded in the hierarchy, and their reward functions were determined primarily by their bureaucratic superiors.

An enormous effort was made to rebuild and regularize the personnel system, recreating and strengthening predictable career incentives within the hierarchy. The rebuilding of the government hierarchy immediately after the Cultural Revolution created many new government jobs. At first, many of these jobs were filled by returned veterans sidelined by the Cultural Revolution. However, the focus quickly shifted to the identification and promotion of capable, relatively educated younger cadres.

Not only did this provide skills and energy the country desperately needed, but it also strengthened the party hierarchy, by making it clear that an orderly promotion path existed. Deng Xiaoping himself took the lead in reestablishing a regular system of promotion and career predictability. Deng was acting in his own interest, to extend his patronage and legacy, but he clearly intended as well to restore the political equilibrium in which patronage and promotion opportunities flow down the hierarchy in predictable patterns, in return for support for leaders running to the top. A key milestone was reached in 1982–1984 when a large group of better educated younger officials was promoted, and a select group among them was fast-tracked for future leadership roles (the third and fourth echelons). This fast-track group included Hu Jintao and many other officials who stepped into the top leadership positions twenty years later, in 2002. The final piece was a regular system of retirement, ending the former system of lifetime tenure. An automatic retirement age was finally decreed in 1988 – automatic, of course, for ordinary officials only, as the top revolutionary elders exempted themselves (Manion, 1992, pp. 20–24).

To be sure, there were more radical proposals for political reform, as for economic reform. Between 1986 and 1988, proposals for deeper political reforms were drafted based on the separation of party and government hierarchies, and the removal of the party from direct management of the economy. Such proposals contributed to the ousting of Hu Yaobang at the beginning of 1987, and yet Zhao Ziyang, in 1988, ordered that party committees in enterprises and government bureaus be dramatically scaled back. Zhao was envisioning a system in which rebuilding the hierarchy would primarily strengthen the government hierarchy, and the party would define a new indirect guidance and supervisory function. These radical initiatives were completely rolled back after the June 4, 1989, Tiananmen incident. What survived, then, was the reinvigoration of the intertwined government and party hierarchies, without their separate features having been distinguished. Instead, both were restructured on the basis of more explicit, predictable, and powerful incentives. With this renewed commitment, the regime survived the shock of Tiananmen.

The basis on which the top leadership was selected changed slowly but steadily. The composition of the top party and government bodies was increasingly determined by regularized promotion procedures. The new process for regulating the succession could become reality only after the elders passed power to the next generation. But it was also clearly understood that a new system of orderly promotion was being created and the system of "reciprocal accountability" being restored. Criteria of promotion were increasingly explicit: education, tenure, and training at a party school. Procedures for promotion were also laid out: nomination, review, and ratification by separate bodies. Of course, these measures were not intended to end political patronage or promotion of favorites, only to subject the process to more predictable rules (Bo, 2004; Li, 2004). These steps laid the foundation for a different kind of politics, but despite this institutionalization and the growing popularity of reform, the regime scarcely expanded its political base. As of the early 1990s, virtually no new constituencies had been brought into the political process.

THE SECOND PHASE OF ECONOMIC REFORM

Through the early 1990s, the Chinese government seemed to be facing a gathering crisis of effectiveness. The debacle at Tiananmen on June 4, 1989, seemed to speak of a government and party in disarray. Persistent policy failures included the inability to implement comprehensive reforms, but also the ineffectual effort to roll back reforms. The persistent failure to stop the decline in budgetary revenues, mirrored by continuing problems to dramatically ease energy and transportation bottlenecks, provided evidence for this decline in effectiveness (Wang, 1995). The perception grew that China might be caught in a reform trap, with the inability to implement decisive policies increasingly attributed to the success of interest groups in blocking needed reforms. Moreover, the declines in budgetary revenue and SOE profit (both shown in Figure 4.1) also implied a drastic decline in the availability of patronage resources. The allocation of investment projects and the supply of jobs depended on budgetary revenues, funded in the past from SOE profits. Eroding SOE profits and budgetary revenues, combined with the limits of decentralization as a strategy for creating patronage, implied that the existing political equilibrium was threatened.

Eventually, China did move away from the policies of "decentralization of power and devolution of resources" that characterized the first fifteen years of reform. As in the late 1970s, gathering crisis propelled drastic action, but the different structure of political power in the 1990s resulted in a qualitatively different response. The ultimate objectives of leaders remained the same: pursue economic opening and consolidate power. However, the overall environment in which decisions were made had changed dramatically. The result was a remarkable burst of decisive reform policymaking that wrenched China out of the preexisting framework of policymaking. Indeed, the entire configuration of reform policies changed dramatically. A whole new pattern of reform emerged after 1993. What was the political economy of this dramatic new turn?

The Structure of Power at the Center

The structure of power at the top of the political hierarchy changed abruptly with the sudden collapse of "elder power" in 1992. Many of the elders were by this time in their late 80s and sidelined by age and infirmity. At the beginning of 1992, the 87-year-old Deng Xiaoping made his famous "Southern tour," in which he emphasized the need to resume economic reforms, and followed up with a final effort to push the enfeebled elders out of the policy arena. The death of Li Xiannian in July was emblematic of the changing order. Chen Yun memorialized their fifty-five years of shared leadership, but then acknowledged that "a lot of effective measures that we used in the past are already inappropriate to the new environment of reform and opening," and essentially relinquished his status as an independent power center (Chen, 1995). Within four months, the institutional incarnation of elder power, the Central Advisory Commission, had been abolished. Within five years, the five most important elders, including Deng Xiaoping, had all passed away.

The passing of the elders led to a reduction in veto players and a relative concentration of power at the top of the hierarchy, opening the door to new policy decisiveness. The spectrum of opinion among the top leadership had already been narrowed by the purge of Zhao Ziyang and his closest advisers. Jiang Zemin, the First Party Secretary appointed in the wake of the Tiananmen Square incidents, consolidated his power and the Politburo Standing Committee became the sole effective veto point in economic policy. Jiang Zemin's power came from his formal position as First Party Secretary. It was the process through which he had been appointed First Secretary – rather than personal charisma or reputation – which provided his legitimacy within the hierarchy. Key decisions were now funneled through the single decision point that was the formal apex of the system, the Politburo Standing Committee chaired by Jiang Zemin. The results were immediately apparent in a new decisiveness and commitment to reform. In September 1992, the Fourteenth Communist Party Congress adopted the goal of a "socialist market economy," the first time that a market economy of any kind had been officially recognized as the end point of transition. A year later, the Third Plenum of the Fourteenth Congress adopted a broad programmatic document that outlined comprehensive reforms with important measures in every major sector. With this document as a road map, many substantial reforms were drafted and implemented within the next eighteen months. Fiscal and tax reform, foreign trade and foreign exchange reform, and banking reform all moved ahead rapidly. Many of the components of this reform program were similar to the abortive reform program of 1986, but this time, all of the main proposals were actually carried out.

The new concentration of power at the top of the hierarchical system did not imply that Jiang Zemin had absolute power. Jiang could not simply ride roughshod over dissenting opinions or strong interest groups. Normal politics continued. Jiang had to make deals and maintain his support coalition, and he gradually consolidated his power and eliminated rivals (Tao, 2001). Jiang fashioned an effective system to exercise power by "balancing" the reformist Zhu Rongji, later premier, against the more conservative Li Peng. In this way, Jiang Zemin retained for himself the final say on the most important issues while also giving significant leeway to Zhu Rongji. Zhu Rongji was admirably suited to the needs of the new political economic configuration: personally self-confident and decisive, Zhu was also strongly committed to many of the objectives of reform. During 2002, power passed to a new leadership group, with Hu Jintao the top CP leader and Wen Jiabao as premier, the head of the government. In terms of personality, these two individuals could hardly have been more different than Jiang Zemin and Zhu Rongji. Moreover, they had very different backgrounds and support coalitions from their predecessors. Nevertheless, the overall structure of power was quite similar. Hu Jintao retained the final word in most matters, but delegated management of the economy to Wen Jiabao, who retained substantial leeway. For all the differences, the system retained the highly concentrated distribution of power established in the early 1990s and remained capable of a type of decisive policymaking that had rarely, if ever, been attained during the 1980s.

The Overall Policy Regime

Beginning in 1993, a series of muscular reform policies were adopted that departed in virtually all respects from the reform policies that characterized the 1980s. The shift in the policy regime follows closely the changes in the structure of political power at the top (Tong, 1999; Zheng, 1999). The specifics of these policies are described in a later section and in other chapters of this volume. Here, we note the key features of the overall policy regime, marking the contrasts with the earlier period.

Under the new decisive policy regime, a succession of milestone reforms were rolled out over the years. The most striking of these were the fiscal, corporate, foreign, and financial reforms that were adopted between 1993 and 1998, in a burst of remarkably decisive and effective reform policymaking transformed every aspect of the Chinese economy. After 1998, the pace of new policy introduction slowed somewhat, but important initiatives have continued. The World Trade Organization (WTO) accession negotiations culminated in late 1999 with dramatic promises of progressive marketization, commitments that required a substantial leadership effort to alter the status quo (Long, 2001; Wang, 2002). A series of major restructurings and recapitalization of the banking system occupied central leaders from 1998 into 2006. Beginning in 2004, major changes in the rural fiscal system laid the groundwork for broader delivery of public services while also making rural local governments more dependent on central budgetary authorities (Wong, 2005; see Chapter 12).

Moreover, all these initiatives have been translated into reality. While implementation has sometimes been uneven, and subject to unforeseen complications and unintended consequences, none has been a dead letter. Thus, the *ability* to implement decisive economic policies has remained part of the Chinese political system consistently since 1993. When policymakers identify a major problem, they are able to mobilize policymaking resources to cope with it. In that sense, the pattern of policy outcomes reflects a qualitative, and ongoing, change in the structure of power that distinguishes the present from the 1980s.

The ability to implement sweeping programs was closely tied to a newfound ability to override specific interest groups. The most striking example came during 1998, when the Chinese People's Liberation Army (PLA) was ordered to divest itself of its economic holdings and get out of business. Many had assumed that the military was such a powerful interest group it could not be touched. The Chinese military has a special independent history and was essential to the survival of the regime on June 4, 1989, at Tiananmen Square; moreover, many of the principals in PLA businesses were sons and daughters of the most senior and highly placed revolutionary elders, including Deng Xiaoping and Wang Zhen. Despite these formidable political assets, over the course of more than two years virtually all military-run businesses were divested. Withdrawal of the PLA was followed by a widespread crackdown on smuggling, which increased China's customs revenues from 31 billion yuan to 224 billion yuan in only two years, between 1998 and 2000.

Yet even more important than the ability to override specific interest groups, no matter how powerful, was a new willingness to pursue reforms that dismantled the privileged status of large segments of society. Most crucially, the hitherto sacrosanct status of urban workers in public enterprises was substantially altered. New policies lowered barriers to migration to the cities and abolished the guaranteed employment of public enterprise workers. SOEs found budget constraints significantly hardened, and barriers against imported goods began to be reduced. Indeed, all the boundaries that had previously limited the reform process were tentatively breached or abolished altogether. With this newfound willingness to address the largest economic distortions, it was inevitable that the period of "reform without losers" would come to an end.

Finally, the new decisiveness was apparent in macroeconomic policy. The delayed responses that had driven China into repeated cycles of inflationary excess shrank substantially. It is true that at the very beginning of the second period in 1993–1994, the resumption of reform momentum set off an inflationary cycle quite similar to those of the earlier period. But subsequently, more vigorous and responsive macroeconomic policymaking resulted in a "soft landing" in 1997–1998 and subsequently in low and stable inflation for the next decade. Comparing the first period with the second period, the average inflation rate dropped from 7.9 to 0.9 percent, and the standard deviation of the quarterly inflation rate dropped from 7.4 percentage points to 1.9 percentage points.[11] The lack of decisiveness that had been so characteristic of Chinese economic policy in the 1980s disappeared almost overnight.

The Pattern of Reform Initiatives: Radical Restructuring and Marketization

Along with the change in the overall policy regime, the specific measures that made up the reform package changed dramatically (Qian and Wu, 2003; Naughton, 2007). The predominant role was played by policies that addressed specific distortions in the economy, imposed a much more comprehensive market discipline, and made the system more rule bound and predictable. Many of these policies are described in more detail in subsequent chapters. The reform package implemented after 1993

---

[11] Based on quarterly consumer price inflation rates from the first quarter of 1983 (when reliable CPI data first become available) through the fourth quarter of 1991, compared with the first quarter of 1997 through the fourth quarter of 2005. In this comparison, the inflationary cycle from the beginning of 1992 until the end of 1996 is not attributed to either period. Note that consumer prices declined for twelve out of thirty-six quarters, explaining why the drop in the average CPI growth rate was so much bigger than the drop in the standard deviation.

was extraordinarily broad, covering virtually every aspect of the economy. During the initial burst of policymaking in 1993–1995, the foundations were laid for change in virtually every area of the economic system. Significantly, implementation of the new wave of reforms began during a period of macroeconomic austerity. National leaders exerted direct political pressure on the banking system to restrain lending, thus hardening the budget constraints of bank branches and indirectly of SOEs as well. These policies created two changes in the external environment that greatly intensified the pressure under which SOEs operated. As the economy slowed, the overall goods market shifted from a state of chronic excess demand to one of temporary excess supply: market competition intensified. At the same time, SOE access to state bank lending was cut back, making it much more difficult for firms to finance chronic losses. SOEs thus simultaneously and suddenly became subject to much stronger capital market discipline and product market discipline.

In four major areas, programmatic laws were passed in 1993–1995 that laid out a new regulatory framework. In each case, the law marked a major reorientation of reform policy as well as an effort to establish a legal charter for future detailed policymaking:

- The Company Law at the end of 1993 created the legal framework for "corporatization" of SOEs. This coincided with the end of the "dual-track" system, which was eliminated at a stroke when planned allocation of materials was abolished at the end of 1993. Corporate restructuring remained gradual, because SOEs reorganized under the new Company Law one by one, as their supervisory organs decided they were ready. However, the intent of the reform was to subject all enterprises to a uniform legal and regulatory framework (see Chapter 11).
- Fiscal reforms, effective January 1, 1994, completely shifted the basis of the tax system, moving to a nearly uniform value-added tax, applied at a uniform rate across ownership categories. Thus, the fiscal reform complemented the Company Law in moving away from an enterprise-specific profit contract and toward a uniform tax system. Moreover, the fiscal reform altered the relationship between central and local governments in parallel fashion. The previous provincial revenue targets were abandoned, and the system began to be transformed into one in which different types of taxes were controlled at different levels. The particularistic bargains that had been struck with each enterprise and local government were thus replaced by a set of rules that, in principle at least, applied equally to all agents. At the same time, the principles of tax assignment substantially increased the central government's share of initial revenue collection. This gave the central government much greater ability to redistribute resources across regions and reinforced the new authoritative stance of central government policymaking (see Chapter 12).
- Foreign exchange reforms, effective January 1, 1994, unified China's dual exchange rate regime at the lower, market currency value and launched a broad liberalization of the trade regime. The reform did away with the division

of foreign exchange into cheaper "within quota" foreign exchange and more expensive market-price foreign exchange, creating a uniform trading system. At the same time, the substantial devaluation implied created the conditions for further liberalization of the trade regime (see Chapter 16).

- Banking system reforms, during 1995, strengthened and clarified the role of the People's Bank of China, giving it a clear mandate to function as a central bank. Reorganization of the commercial banks subjected them to better oversight and hardened their budget constraint. Subsequently, beginning in 1998, the government subjected the financial system to much stronger central control and oversight. Using the disciplinary power inherent in the CP system, the national government overrode the local interests that had established an excessive voice in lending decisions (Heilmann, 2005). The assumption of central control set the stage for the subsequent loan write-offs, injection of capital, and reorganization that put most of the state-owned banks on a (temporarily) sound financial footing after 2005 (see Chapter 14).

In each of these cases, the clear thrust of reforms was to subject different market participants to uniform rules, improve the regulatory framework, and enhance competition. Of course, there were many shortcomings in design and implementation. Attempts to restructure the urban social security system had limited success, and efforts to reform the urban health care system mostly failed. Overall, China is still far from a highly functioning well-regulated market economy. But the direction of reform is strikingly different from that of the 1980s. Even while China retained a general commitment to "gradualism," the specific content of gradualist reforms changed almost completely. From an emphasis on particularistic contracting to ameliorate the existing system, the emphasis shifted to attaining the objective of a well-regulated competitive market.

These reform characteristics continue to the present. In 1998, Zhu Rongji presided over a further wave of administrative reorganization, a reform that abolished most of the economic ministries, reduced in size and consolidated the administration of the planning agencies, and raised the bureaucratic rank of the most important regulatory agencies. China had begun to move toward a regulatory state with a more distant relationship to businesses and some expectation of a level playing field (Yang, 2004; Pearson, 2005). By the late 1990s, as well, China had laid the foundation for its accession to the WTO. The commitment to a rule-based regime tended to lock in reform achievements and had a broad effect on many areas of the economy. While full compliance with WTO remains a work in progress, significant changes have been made.

Reform Outcomes

To a remarkable extent, the reform measures adopted after 1993 produced economic and social outcomes that were the opposite of those observed in the 1980s. Fiscal reforms are an obvious case in point. Relentless fiscal erosion was reversed:

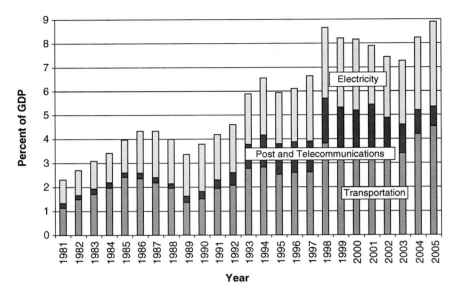

Figure 4.2. Physical infrastructure investment

as shown in Figure 4.1, government budgetary revenue as a share of GDP ended its decade-long slide and began to increase after 1995, adding more than 6 percentage points of GDP over the next ten years. Similarly, fiscal reforms were strongly recentralizing. The central government share of initial revenue collection, which had slipped from 37 percent in 1986 to 28 percent in 1992, jumped to 56 percent in 1994. With central government expenditures stable at around 30 percent of all fiscal outlays, the jump in revenue collection gave the central government control over a substantial volume of revenue transfers to local governments. This fiscal turnaround was followed by improvements in other macroeconomic variables. During the early period, underinvestment in physical infrastructure had been a consistent problem. Figure 4.2 shows that total spending on physical infrastructure increased rapidly after 1993. Infrastructure investment initially jumped to 6 percent of GDP (a "rule-of-thumb" benchmark) and then increased further to an ample 8–9 percent of GDP, where it has remained ever since.

Overall macroeconomic conditions reversed. From a generally inflationary tendency, price trends shifted toward stability, with substantial periods of deflation. The drop in inflation has been discussed earlier, with reference to the quicker and more responsive pattern of macroeconomic policymaking that characterized this period. In addition, greater macroeconomic stability can be plausibly linked to reduced fiscal stress and to the lessening of pressure on banks to loan to distressed SOEs. Central bank credit creation as a share of GDP dropped substantially after 1993. Without the need to cater to myriad specific constituencies, it was far easier to assemble a consistent macroeconomic policy.

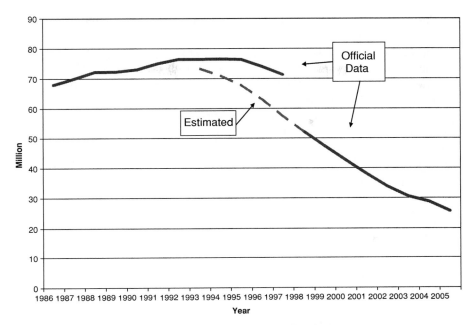

Figure 4.3. Traditional SOE workers

Of all the reform changes after 1993, the most consequential was the turn in policy toward SOEs. After a semblance of macroeconomic stability was established in the mid-1990s, and the bare bones of a social security system created, reformers began to subject SOEs to substantial market discipline. For the first time, significant numbers of SOEs were closed down, and massive numbers of SOE workers were laid off. A relatively privileged and concentrated group – urban SOE workers – bore the brunt of reform-related costs. Although wealthy cities (such as Shanghai) could afford to moderate the costs on SOE workers by extensive retraining and generous early retirement policies, most localities were not able to provide such ample social protection.

As Figure 4.3 shows, the number of state enterprise workers – which had actually increased through the first period of reform – reached a peak of 76 million in 1992–1993. By 2004, the total number of SOE workers had plummeted to only 28 million. Of this dramatic decline in the SOE labor force, more than 30 million were laid off or given early retirement, and 18 million were working in restructured corporations that were no longer considered SOEs but were still controlled by the government. Another 20 million workers in urban collectives also lost their jobs. In addition to these layoffs, many urban workers were made less well off by an intensification of work discipline in newly profit-oriented companies and by gaps in the systems of health insurance that replaced the old public enterprise system. The period of "reform without losers" came to a sudden end after the mid-1990s.

Notwithstanding the costs paid by some social groups, the economy as a whole derived benefit from these more discriminating policies. As policymakers severed the apron strings that tied some of the dependent groups to the state, the burden of subsidizing "losers" was reduced. This, along with the broad-based system of taxation, led to the recovery of the center's revenue-raising capacity. SOEs were pruned back by the elimination of the "zombie firms" that produced no revenues, concentrating production in more efficient firms. The overall profitability of the state sector began to recover (Figure 4.1). Economic growth initially dipped in 1998–1999, as the economy was hit with the massive wave of layoffs and a reduction in export demand in the wake of the Asian Financial Crisis. However, after these shocks were absorbed, growth accelerated after 2000 to a pace slightly faster than the reform-era average.

Adapting the System: Rebuilding Hierarchy and Patronage Resources

National politicians were quick to adapt their strategies to the new era. The challenges politicians faced can again be described as rents, autonomy, and commitment. After restructuring the fiscal system, national leaders were able to rapidly expand the supply of patronage resources. The fiscal system, hitherto the leadership's greatest headache, became once again an excellent source of patronage. Central government budgetary revenues climbed from just under 3 percent of GDP in 1993 to 9 percent in 2005. After funding its own direct outlays, the central government redistributed significant sums among localities. For the first few years of the new fiscal system, most intergovernmental transfers were tied up by the deals the center had to make to win compliance with the new tax system. But as revenues recovered, national leaders were able to direct incremental resources to favored clients. Beginning in 1999, the Western Development Program began to channel fiscal resources to thirteen low-income provinces. After 2003, substantial resources went to the Northeast Revitalization Program, designed to support this lagging (but still relatively developed) region. As in the 1980s, these programs "played to the provinces," by providing targeted benefits to specific regions and local politicians. But unlike the 1980s, these benefits were funded directly from the government budget. Beneficiary regions received roads, bridges, and new productive investments.

Intergovernmental transfers were shaped to fit the needs of patronage distribution, in particular by merging regional policy and social policy. As the central government financial position improved, and China's social needs became more evident with the dissolution of the old urban safety net, China's budgetary authorities began to allocate more resources to social programs. The spending pattern that emerged was of the central government identifying solutions for pressing social needs – for example, underfunded pensions, weak primary education, and nonexistent basic-level health facilities – but only funding them in targeted, usually poorer, provinces in the West or Northeast. Wealthy coastal provinces were expected to fund similar programs from their own budgetary resources. In this manner, the distribution of resources from the center remained ad hoc and susceptible to the intervention of central leaders.

The reliance on the formal budgetary system for patronage resources was extended deeper into the countryside with the abolition of the agricultural tax at the end of 2004 and beginning of 2005 (Lu and Wiemer, 2005). Coming on the heels of a sharp cutback in the extrabudgetary fees and exactions, the end of the agricultural tax left local officials almost completely dependent on upper-level budgetary transfers to fund their local programs. This resource dependency clearly gave top policymakers greater leverage.

Finally, central government patronage was increased by the gradual stabilization of the business system for key monopoly sectors. During the mid-1990s, the central government withdrew from most ordinary competitive sectors, leaving them to local government oversight (as discussed later), and restricted its attention to monopoly sectors. The center developed restructuring plans for key sectors such as energy, telecom, and electricity, which maintained state ownership, but injected moderate competition, typically by creating three or four rival state firms. This system was formalized in 2002, when the central government set up a State Asset Supervision and Administration Commission (SASAC) with responsibility over 199 large central government firms, covering nearly all the monopoly sectors. These firms were well positioned to take advantage of the acceleration of the Chinese economy, and the rise in world energy and materials prices, which occurred after 2003. The firms retained nearly all their profits, which soared to over 3 percent of GDP by 2005. These powerful state-run corporations also became an important source of political patronage. Overall, since the turn of the century, Chinese national leaders have succeeded in recreating a robust stream of patronage resources.

Given that the central government held on to large firms in key financial, strategic and natural monopoly sectors, the overall pattern of only "selective withdrawal" from the economy has continued. However, the terms on which selective opening has been practiced changed dramatically in the second period of reform, with important political consequences. No longer able to restrict economic opening to the politically marginal sectors of rural industry and foreign investment, national leaders threw open most economic sectors, but on terms that gave local political leaders abundant resources and patronage opportunities.

The Chinese economy is now more than ten times as big, as measured by GDP, as it was at the beginning of reform in 1978. Moreover, the sectors already opened had been steadily growing in relative importance, so that access could no longer be restricted without hobbling growth. Finally, the national leadership had to offer something in exchange for the resources it claimed in the recentralization process. To get local government officials to acquiesce in the new fiscal system, which substantially increased the central government's share of the tax take, then Vice Premier Zhu Rongji traveled to many provinces, convincing and cajoling local leaders into accepting the new system. Although Zhu made concessions over details, he was able to tie various aspects of the fiscal system together, exert pressure on the localities, and come up with an overall bargain (Xu, 2001). The central government could not simply override the interests of local government officials – in aggregate, far too large a share of the total CP selectorate – but the outcome demonstrates the newly authoritative style that the political system was capable of generating.

In return for the revenues and authority the center reclaimed, local officials were given much greater freedom to manage their local economies as they saw fit. Central leaders set up a new relationship with local officials, essentially decentralizing to the local government ability to manage the process of selective opening. Local governments were allowed vastly greater sway over their own economic development, their own publicly owned enterprises, and their relations with private and foreign businesses. In this way, the central government relinquished its ownership claim of the tens of thousands of "state-owned" but local government-controlled firms in ordinary competitive sectors. No longer did central and local governments jointly manage most assets. The separation of ownership became a de facto reality during the 1990s and, as mentioned earlier, was formalized in 2002, when central SASAC drew a line between the firms that it directly owned and those owned by local governments. One important result of clarifying local ownership was a wave of privatizations, a trajectory very different from that of the large, centrally controlled firms that stayed predominantly government owned.

Particularly in fast-growing coastal provinces, restructured and new industrial and commercial firms exploded, creating significant resources and wealth. Conversion of state firms into new corporate forms, and frequently into private firms, generated lucrative opportunities for local officials. Local government officials were quick to set up alliances and various forms of partnership with local entrepreneurs. Sometimes favored entrepreneurs were beneficiaries of privatization, and sometimes more complex (and hidden) forms of cooperation were instituted. The process of selective opening became a locally managed one, in which local officials struck bargains with local entrepreneurs. Entrepreneurs were usually more than willing to reach accommodation with local officials (Dickson, 2003). Control of land emerged as a crucial resource under the control of local officials and real estate development became an especially lucrative business for local officials. In essence, local officials were given the freedom to make their own arrangements with emerging businesses, and they formed tight alliances with local business groups. Foreign firms were brought into increasingly wide-ranging and lucrative partnerships with local government. Local patronage complemented the central patronage described earlier.

Central and local were held together, as before, by the *nomenklatura* system. At its bare-bones essentials, the *nomenklatura* system ensured that the heads of provincial and municipal government and party organs were appointed by national leaders. Thus, the center always reserved the right to replace the top officials of any locality and, in practice, frequently rotated the top provincial leaders. The hierarchical system remained firmly in place with respect to the top jobs at the local level. Moreover, the regularization of rules for promotion in that hierarchy now began in earnest, as changes introduced tentatively in the 1980s began to be enforced as norms in the *nomenklatura* system. Rules of promotion in the hierarchy became far more institutionalized than ever before. Mandatory retirement ages, minimum educational standards, and effective term limits had been gradually built into the personnel system during 1980s, and now, with the end of "elder power," they began to apply in earnest (Regulations, 2003; Bo, 2004).

Application of these procedures throughout the *nomenklatura* system resulted in more predictable career paths that served to bind ambitious professionals to the hierarchical system. They also ensured steady turnover and made career mobility and advancement a realistic prospect. Capable individuals, as they moved up, were increasingly rotated among various regional posts, and sometimes through different functional specialties (Li, 2004). The career path of the current (2006) mayor of Beijing, Wang Qishan, while not typical, gives a flavor of the way the system works. Over the past fifteen years, Wang was moved successively into positions as the vice head of the state-run Bank of Construction, the vice governor of Guangdong Province (to clean up financial problems), back to Beijing to serve as the head of the Office of System Reform, then First Communist Party Secretary of Hainan Province, and finally mayor of Beijing. The breadth of Wang's experience is unusual, as is his privileged Party background, but the pattern of rotation through different regional and national jobs is increasingly common. The heads of some of the largest centrally run SOEs now serve in the Communist Party Central Committee. This kind of career path binds the managers of huge and powerful enterprises to the hierarchical system. It also means that the patronage resources of those enterprises are potentially at the service of the hierarchical system.

The increasing predictability and institutionalization does not spell the end of politics or patronage or make it any less necessary for leaders to promote their own factions and followers. It simply means the game is played by different rules, played out over a new terrain with more clearly delineated pathways. Even Jiang Zemin, the top leader, was subject to the new constraints. Deng Xiaoping had insisted that Jiang should step down from his top posts after two full terms and proposed that Hu Jintao should succeed Jiang in 2002. Deng thus used his own prestige to create a new elite consensus about the rules of political succession that constrained the subsequent generation of leaders. Assuming that Hu Jintao steps down at the end of his second term in 2012 and confirms the precedent, regular turnover and predictable career paths will have been established.

The patterns we have traced in this section are consistent. After 1993, the Chinese CP rebuilt a system of patronage politics that breathed new life into its authoritarian hierarchy. The current system bears no relationship to the "separation of party and government" that Zhao Ziyang tried to institute in the 1980s. On the contrary, the CP directly manages key posts and decision-making processes, actively rationalizes its procedures, and tries to improve its capacity as a "governing party." To this end, new sources of patronage resources were developed, new systems of tying outside economic interests to the hierarchy evolved, and the rules that governed the hierarchy itself changed dramatically. One system of authoritarian politics was dismantled, but another was erected in its place.

CONCLUSION: THE POLITICAL ECONOMY OF TWENTY-FIRST
CENTURY CHINA

This chapter has demonstrated that the pattern of "gradualist" economic policymaking in China differed significantly across two periods, and that those differences are closely related to the structure of the authoritarian political system and
the incentives it created. There are virtually no generalizations we can make about
the transition process as a whole: almost every characteristic of the transition process through 1992 has been shown to be inapplicable after 1993. This is not only
true of the economic policy regime, but also true of the practical functioning of the
political system. Although it has remained authoritarian, the actual rules of succession, the sources of power, and the nature of patronage goods have all changed
substantially. Thus, the image of economic change and political immobility that is
sometimes applied to China is quite misleading.

Some studies of the transition process in different formerly socialist countries
have suggested that there is a potential "trap" in the transition process due to
partial and incomplete reforms. Some have argued that the key political obstacle to economic transition comes from the influence of particularistic interest
groups *created in the course of the transition process* (Hellman, 1998; Braguinsky and
Yavlinsky, 2000; Pei, 2006). In this view, selective opening gives precious economic
rents to new interest groups. These groups mobilize to defend the distortions in the
partially reformed economy that are the source of the rents. The defense of these
interests paralyzes the transition process, making it impossible to adopt necessary,
more thorough reforms.

The analysis presented here provides little support for such a view. The "partial
reform trap" approach fails to recognize that the decisiveness of the Chinese government has *increased* during the reform process. Many interest groups have been
created in China during the course of reform, some very powerful. Yet, there is no
evidence of paralysis in economic decision making. Quite the contrary, since 1993,
the government has consistently enacted important reforms once the top leadership has recognized a compelling national interest. The only interest group that
potentially displays the ability to block reform is the regime as a totality, which has
adapted and reformulated itself repeatedly as necessary to protect its own power.
Potentially, this determination could block necessary reforms. But thus far, driven
by a recognition that continuous improvements in the operation of the economy
are essential for long-run political success, political leaders have been willing to
submit to many kinds of external discipline – so long as their ultimate power is
intact.

An example of this comes in the system of managing monopoly sectors. Pei
(2006) points out that a successfully adapting authoritarian regime will end up
controlling those sectors with large, concentrated monopoly rents, which fits the
Chinese case. But Pei goes on to argue that economic stagnation is inherent in this
situation because the "quiet life" and corruption incomes sought by monopolists

will erode those monopoly rents in the long run, and the Chinese experience does not support this argument. Precisely in order to prevent this outcome, China has established a system of oligopolistic competition in key sectors. Two or three large, state-owned firms compete in, for example, the oil or telecom sectors, and that provides enough product market discipline to keep managers on their toes, giving feedback to detect those managers whose performance is unsatisfactory. That system may not be good enough in the *next* phase of development, as the Chinese market economy becomes more sophisticated; but in terms of *today's* economy, the mechanisms are adequate. When analysts invoke economic policy paralysis or broader economic stagnation as a "pitfall" of partial reform, it merely shows that their particular models of gradualism do not fit the Chinese experience.

Yet, if China today is not in a partial reform trap, it is not in a stable long-term equilibrium either. The unexpected vigor and dramatic reinvention of the authoritarian system still leaves China confronting an array of long-run challenges. While the authoritarian system has performed remarkably well in the past twenty-five years, it still relies for its legitimacy on short-run economic performance, which cannot be guaranteed to continue for the foreseeable future. As the economy becomes more sophisticated, it is reasonable to believe that effective functioning of the economy increasingly requires transparency and recourse to impartial independent regulatory authority that the current system is not yet able to provide. More broadly, leaders inevitably seek broader sources of legitimacy, as the initial problems of development and patronage are resolved. There are many long-run questions about the future of Chinese society, the possible sources of political legitimacy, and the potential for democracy that are clearly outside the scope of this chapter.

However, without entering into the broad discussion of democracy and its prospects in China, we can still bring out some of the future implications of the analysis presented here. The specific fashion in which the CP has established a resilient authoritarian system has – partly because of its success – begun to interact with a new set of long-run issues to shape still another phase of economic transition. Driven by complex motives of political competition, drive for legitimacy, need to enhance economic performance, and desire to maintain power, China's leaders have begun to explore new policy areas and start to build new support coalitions.

The easiest way to see this is by contrasting the political strategies of Jiang Zemin and his successor, Hu Jintao. Jiang Zemin was able to consolidate his personal power through skillful political maneuvering, and he built a powerful political coalition. Local government leaders prospered, and Jiang built a strong following, based above all in his native region of Shanghai, but extending across the economically most successful coastal provinces. These local leaders – clear "winners" from the reform process – formed a rough coalition with the technocratic "performance coalition" (the term is due to Shirk) heading central government agencies. With this political alliance, remarkable progress was made in keeping economic transition moving ahead. China thus went from "reform without losers" to a reform run by a coalition of winners in a short time. Indeed, Jiang promulgated a theory, the so-called *Three Represents*, which explicitly stated that the CP should now represent society's advanced material, ideological and cultural forces, that is, the elites and winners in different spheres. As part of this effort, private businesses gained unprecedented voice and recognition. In a well-known July 1, 2001, speech, Jiang proposed inducting entrepreneurs into the CP. This move was followed by a series of regulatory shifts that over the next few years carved out a sphere of legitimate independent operation for private business. Within a few years, the government had gone on record declaring that private businesses were permitted in all sectors that were not explicitly ruled off-limits.

In terms of political reform, however, Jiang's approach was extremely disappointing. There was virtually no opening of the political system. Businesses gained voice, but no power. Consultation increased, but the types of accountability Jiang fostered were within the range of those traditionally adopted in Communist hierarchical systems. Indeed, as argued earlier, the CP hierarchy had become more rule driven, linked by more powerful incentives, and in some ways more insulated from the rest of society. The "Three Represents" did not provide any means for those "advanced forces" to independently influence policy or check the power of the CP. These changes made no difference in the immediate political configuration.

Without political opening, there were few checks on the behavior of officials. Corruption grew worse, at least in the public mind. At the same time, a large group of urban residents now felt themselves to be worse off as a result of economic reforms. The mass layoff of state enterprise workers, as mentioned earlier, created the first large group of reform "losers," who identified themselves as such. Even those workers who remained on the job experienced deteriorating working conditions as their social protections and bargaining power within the enterprise declined. The "iron rice bowl" – the guarantee of employment – was broken, and social insecurity and risk increased substantially. Clearly, these workers were discarded as a CP constituency. At the same time, other groups experienced sustained improvements in income. State workers who kept their jobs enjoyed rapid wage growth, and educated workers everywhere achieved especially rapid gains in income. Overall, economic growth in urban areas accelerated. Rural areas were unable to keep up with such rapid growth, and China began a sustained, rapid increase in household income inequality. From its low point of 0.29 in 1985, China's Gini coefficient soared to 0.45 in 2001 (Ravallion and Chen, 2004; see Chapter 18). With these highly differentiated outcomes, reform led to new social tensions. Jiang Zemin presided over a coalition of winners, but became the target of resentment over corruption, soaring inequality, and lack of accountability. Moreover, Jiang's political theory was frankly elitist, without any actual opening of the political system.

A new administration came to power in the fall of 2002. First Secretary Hu Jintao and Premier Wen, from the first days of their administration, have struck novel themes. Hu and Wen stress themes of equality and social harmony, and populist rhetoric tinges their economic policy proclamations. At first, these thematic differences could be dismissed as mere rhetorical differentiation from the Jiang administration. However, as the Hu–Wen administration has found its feet, actual resource-allocation decisions have increasingly followed this more egalitarian and populist bent. The CP under Jiang and Zhu rebuilt the government's policy effectiveness, and Hu and Wen have now begun to use that government to carry out social policies that go well beyond Jiang and Zhu's initiatives.

Policies of the Hu–Wen administration have become more favorable to farmers, rural-to-urban migrants, and human development. Increased budgetary resources and policymaking attention have gone to pensions, health care, and education. Since the promulgation of the 11th Five-Year Plan in the fall of 2005, environmental issues have taken a position at the front and center of governmental concerns (see Chapter 8).

These important policy shifts should be interpreted from several different perspectives. The new policy package represents a response to widespread criticisms and social tension and an attempt to forestall challenges to the regime. In that sense, it is a response to the failings of the reform process. At the same time, however, the new policy agenda can also be seen as an evolutionary response to past economic gains: as China develops, urbanizes, and achieves higher income status, new issues of economic security, better education, and improved environmental quality naturally take center stage. In this sense, the new policies are a response to the success of economic transition. Finally, the new policies are a response to the specific political trajectory that has shaped economic change: as such they can also be seen as a new effort to distribute patronage in a way that stabilizes the regime – and the power of Hu Jintao and Wen Jiabao – in the face of new political and economic circumstances.

The new populist policies of the Hu–Wen administration bring it into conflict with the beneficiaries of the former Jiang Zemin administration. The local government officials of prosperous coastal provinces were the natural constituency of Jiang's reforms and the government-business groups in coastal China benefited more from Jiang's reforms than any other group. For Hu Jintao, Jiang's beneficiaries constitute the largest political faction interfering with the consolidation of his power inside the CP, and also a sometimes corrupt and privileged interest group. A few high-profile politicians have been accused of crimes of corruption. The most spectacular example was the arrest of the First Party Secretary of Shanghai, Chen Liangyu, in the fall of 2006. National leaders seem to see their future in creating a broader coalition that balances and offsets the interests of the winners of partial reform. Given the formidable resources of the national government – including renewed budgetary and patronage resources, as described earlier – it should be expected that a significant shift in resource allocation will redirect benefits toward weaker and excluded groups. This might even produce a qualitatively different political strategy, though it is impossible to predict. Generally, Hu and Wen have increased their patronage of groups outside the prosperous coastal cities. So far, Hu Jintao and Wen Jiabao's policies have been supportive of continued market transition and have generally been accompanied by noninterference in the economic management of the advanced coastal provinces. Those provinces may not receive much if any of the increased benefits are from central government activity, but they are left alone to prosper (Li, 2007).

The political equilibrium of the Jiang years is also being unsettled in the growth of autonomous private businesses. The selective opening that was a central part of the political strategy of CP leaders in the both 1980s and 1990s has begun to lose some of its political efficacy. Private businesses have begun to grow into a really sizable scale. The legitimation of large-scale private businesses is extremely recent. Such businesses have a very short history, but are growing fast. Local officials had been given wide leeway to develop strategies to harness and coordinate with local business groups, but putting further conditions on their growth is today beyond the power of the central government. It is hard to envisage a viable political strategy for China that does not ultimately include the rapidly emerging business interests that are reshaping the Chinese economy and affecting world markets in sectors ranging from steel to autos to cell phones.

No Chinese political entrepreneur has yet come up with a strategy that harnesses this emerging power. On the contrary, the policies of Hu and Wen, on balance, tend to favor those elements in the economy that are most likely to be part of the old hierarchical system, including government bureaucracies and the CP-dominated labor unions. Policy continues to stress the importance of the authoritarian hierarchy and the need for the CP to improve its capabilities as a "governing party." While Hu Jintao has maneuvered skillfully, it is difficult to see this policy as a long-run stable path toward a more prosperous economy. New economic powers have grown up alongside authoritarian hierarchy, but it is hard to believe that political power will be confined within that hierarchy indefinitely. The failure to broaden constituencies and open the system to new kinds of political influence suggests that further institutional changes will be required before the system can guarantee consistent policy effectiveness.

To date, the survival of the authoritarian hierarchy is perhaps the most distinctive feature of the Chinese transition. We have seen that the structure of power at the top of the hierarchy and the incentives of patrons and agents through the hierarchy determine most of the important features and turning points of the transition process. However, the argument proceeded from the weakly institutionalized Chinese system and a highly contingent and perhaps precarious set of circumstances. Indeed, without an institutionalized system of checks and balances, it is impossible to have complete confidence that *any* set of institutional characteristics will endure. The process is contingent and depends, to an enormous extent, on the flexibility and nimbleness of Chinese leaders. Only time will tell if the Chinese leadership can continue this astonishing high wire act.

References

Alesina, Alberto. and Allen Drazen. 1991. "Why Are Stabilizations Delayed?" *American Economic Review*. 81, pp. 1170–1188.

Aslund, Anders. 1992. *Post-Communist Economic Revolutions: How Big a Bang?* Washington, DC: Center for Strategic and International Studies.

Bachman, David. 1985. *Chen Yun and the Chinese Political System*. Berkeley: Center for Chinese Studies, University of California.

Baum, Richard. 1997. "The Road to Tiananmen: Chinese Politics in the 1980s," in *The Politics of China: Second Edition, The Eras of Mao and Deng*. Roderick MacFarquhar, ed. Cambridge and New York: Cambridge University Press, pp. 340–471.

Bo, Zhiyue. 2004. "The Institutionalization of Elite Management in China," in *Holding China Together: Diversity and National Integration in the Post-Deng Era*. Barry Naughton and Dali Yang, eds. Cambridge and New York: Cambridge University Press, pp. 70–100.

Boycko, Maxim, Andrei Shleifer, and Robert Vishny. 1995. *Privatizing Russia*. Cambridge, MA: MIT Press.

Braguinsky, Serguey and Grigory Yavlinsky. 2000. *Incentives and Institutions: The Transition to a Market Economy in Russia*. Princeton: Princeton University Press.

Burns, John P. 1989. *The Chinese Communist Party's Nomenklatura System: A Documentary Study of Party Control of Leadership Selection, 1979–1984*. Armonk, New York: ME Sharpe.

Burns, John P. 1994. "Strengthening Central CCP Control of Leadership Selection: The 1990 Nomenklatura." *The China Quarterly*. 138, pp. 458–491.

Byrd, William. June 1989. "Plan and Market in the Chinese Economy: A Simple General Equilibrium Model." *Journal of Comparative Economics*. 13, pp. 177–204.

Chang, Chun and Yijiang Wang. 1994. "The Nature of the Township-Village Enterprise." *Journal of Comparative Economics*. 19, pp. 434–452.

Che, Jiahua and Yingyi Qian. May 1998. "Insecure Property Rights and Government Ownership of Firms." *Quarterly Journal of Economics*. 113(2), pp. 467–496.

Chen, An. 1999. *Restructuring Political Power in China: Alliances and Opposition, 1978–1998*. Boulder: Lynne Rienner.

Chen Yun. 1995. "Mourning Comrade Li Xiannian" July 21, 1992, in *Chen Yun Wenxuan* [Selected Works of Chen Yun], vol. 3. Beijing: Renmin, pp. 378–379.

Cox, Gary and Matthew McCubbins. 2001. "The Institutional Determinants of Economic Policy Outcomes," in *Presidents, Parliaments, and Policy*. Stephan Haggard and Matthew McCubbins, eds. Cambridge and New York: Cambridge University Press, pp. 21–63.

Deng Liqun, 2005. *Shierge Chunqiu (1975–1987)* [Record of 12 Years (1975–1987)]. Hong Kong: Bozhi.

Dickson, Bruce J. 2003. *Red Capitalists in China: The Party, Private Entrepreneurs, and Prospects for Political Change*. Cambridge and New York: Cambridge University Press.

Document Research Room, Chinese Communist Party Central Committee [Zhonggong zhongyang wenxian yanjiushi], ed. 2005. *Chen Yun Zhuan* [Biography of Chen Yun]. Beijing: Zhongyang Wenxian.

Fewsmith, Joseph. 1997. "Reaction, Resurgence, and Succession: Chinese Politics Since Tiananmen," in *The Politics of China: Second Edition, The Eras of Mao and Deng*. Roderick MacFarquhar, ed. Cambridge and New York: Cambridge University Press, pp. 472–532.

Gallagher, Mary. April 2002. "'Reform and Openness' Why China's Economic Reforms Have Delayed Democracy." *World Politics*. 54, pp. 338–72.

Gao Xin, 1999. *Xiangfu "Guangdong Bang"* [Taming of the Guangdong Gang]. Hong Kong: Mingjing [Mirror].

Harasymiw, Bohdan. 1969. "*Nomenklatura*: The Soviet Communist Party's Leadership Recruitment System." *Canadian Journal of Political Science.* 2(4), pp. 494–497.

He Bin and Gao Xin, 1992. *Zhongguo Taizidang* [China's Princelings]. Hong Kong: Mirror Books.

Heilmann, Sebastian. March 2005. "Regulatory Innovation by Leninist Means: Communist Party Supervision in China's Financial Industry." *The China Quarterly.* 181, pp. 1–21.

Heilmann, Sebastian and Sarah Kirchberger. 2000. *The Chinese Nomenklatura in Transition: A Study Based on Internal Cadre Statistics of the Central Organization Department of the Chinese Communist Party.* China Analysis No. 1. Germany: Center for East Asian and Pacific Studies, Trier University.

Hellman, Joel S. January 1998. "Winners Take All: The Politics of Partial Reform in Postcommunist Transitions." *World Politics.* 50, pp. 203–234.

Holmstrom, Bengt and Paul Milgrom. January 1991. "Multitask Principal-Agent Analyses: Incentive Contracts, Asset Ownership, and Job Design." *Journal of Law, Economics, and Organization.* 7(Special Issues), pp. 24–52.

Huang, Yasheng. 1996. *Inflation and Investment Controls in China: The Political Economy of Central-Local Relations during the Reform Era.* Cambridge and New York: Cambridge University Press.

Huang, Yasheng. 2003. *Selling China: Foreign Direct Investment during the Reform Era.* Cambridge and New York: Cambridge University Press.

Huntington, Samuel P. 1991. *The Third Wave: Democratization in the Late Twentieth Century.* Norman: University of Okalahoma Press.

IMF, IBRD, OECD, EBRD [International Monetary Fund, International Bank for Reconstruction and Development, Organization for Economic Cooperation and Development, and European Bank for Reconstruction and Development]. December 19, 1990. *The Economy of the USSR.* Washington, DC.

Keefer, Philip and David Stasavage. February 2001. "Bureaucratic Delegation and Political Institutions: When are Independent Central Banks Irrelevant?" World Bank Policy Research Working Paper 2356. Accessed December 28, 2006, from http://ssrn.com/abstract=271251.

Kornai, Janos. 1987. "The Dual Dependence of the State-Owned Firm in Hungary," in *China's Industrial Reform.* Gene Tidrick and Jiyuan Chen, eds. New York: Oxford University Press, pp. 317–338.

Lam, Willy Wo-Lap. 1989. *The Era of Zhao Ziyang: Power Struggle in China, 1986–88.* Hong Kong: AB Books & Stationery.

Lardy, Nicholas and Kenneth Lieberthal. 1983. *Chen Yun's Strategy for China's Development.* Armonk, NY: ME Sharpe.

Lau, Lawrence J., Yingyi Qian, and Gérard Roland. 2001. "Reform without Losers: An Interpretation of China's Dual-Track Approach to Reforms." *Journal of Political Economy.* 108(1), pp. 120–143.

Li, Cheng. 2004. "Political Localism Versus Institutional Restraints: Elite Recruitment in the Jiang Era," in *Holding China Together: Diversity and National Integration in the Post-Deng Era.* Barry Naughton and Dali Yang, eds. Cambridge and New York: Cambridge University Press, pp. 29–69.

Li, Cheng. 2007. "Was the Shanghai Gang Shanghaied? The Fall of Chen Liangyu and the Survival of Jiang Zemin's Faction." *China Leadership Monitor.* 20. Accessed April 7, 2007, from http://media.hoover.org/documents/clm20cl.pdf.

Li Zhining, 1987. *Zhonghua Renmin Gongheguo Jingji Dashidian 1959.10–1987.1* [A Dictionary of Major Economic Events in the PRC, October 1949–January 1987]. Chanchun: Jilin Renmin.

Lin, Cyril. 1989. "Open-Ended Economic Reform in China," in *Remaking the Economic Institutions of Socialism: China and Eastern Europe*. V. Nee and D. Stark, eds. Stanford: Stanford University Press, pp. 95–136.

Lipset, Seymour Martin. March 1959. "Some Social Requisites of Democracy: Economic Development and Political Legitimacy." *The American Political Science Review*. 53(1), pp. 69–105.

Long, Yongtu, 2001. "Long Yongtu tan Zhongguo Rushi: Tanpan shi Jeiyang Wanchengde [Long Yongtu Discusses China's WTO Entry: How the Negotiations Were Accomplished]." Accessed November 14, 2001, from http://news.163.com/editor/011114/011114_306314.html.

Lu, Mai and Calla Wiemer. September 2005. "An End to China's Agriculture Tax." *China: An International Journal*. 3(2), pp. 320–330.

MacFarquhar, Roderick. 1997. "The Succession to Mao and the End of Maoism, 1969–82," in *The Politics of China: Second Edition, The Eras of Mao and Deng*. Roderick MacFarquhar, ed. Cambridge and New York: Cambridge University Press, pp. 248–339.

MacFarquhar, Roderick and Michael Schoenhals. 2006. *Mao's Last Revolution*. Cambridge, MA: Harvard University Press.

MacIntyre, Andrew. 2003. *The Power of Institutions: Political Architecture and Governance*. Ithaca: Cornell University Press.

Manion, Melanie. June 1985. "The Cadre Management System, Post-Mao: The Appointment, Promotion, Transfer and Removal of Party and State Leaders." *China Quarterly*. 102, pp. 203–233.

Manion, Melanie. March 1992. "Politics and Policy in Post-Mao Cadre Retirement." *China Quarterly*. 129, pp. 1–25.

McMillan, John and Barry Naughton. 1992. "How to Reform a Planned Economy: Lessons from China." *Oxford Review of Economic Policy*. 8, pp. 130–143.

Naughton, Barry. January 1992. "Implications of the State Monopoly over Industry and Its Relaxation." *Modern China*. 18(1), pp. 14–41.

Naughton, Barry. 1995. *Growing Out of the Plan: Chinese Economic Reform, 1978–1993*. Cambridge and New York: Cambridge University Press.

Naughton, Barry. 2007. *The Chinese Economy: Transitions and Growth*. Cambridge, MA: MIT Press.

Naughton, Barry. 2008. "Hierarchy and the Market Economy: How Has Political Hierarchy Shaped China's Transition to a Market Economy?" in *Market and Socialism Reconsidered*. Janos Kornai and Yingyi Qian, eds. London: Macmillan, for the International Economic Association.

Nee, Victor. March 1992. "Organizational Dynamics of Market Transition: Hybrid Forms, Property Rights and Mixed Economy in China." *Administrative Science Quarterly*. 37, pp. 1–27.

Nee, Victor and Peng Lian. April 1994. "Sleeping with the Enemy: A Dynamic Model of Declining Political Commitment in State Socialism." *Theory and Society*. 23, pp. 253–296.

Oi, Jean C. 1999. *Rural China Takes Off: The Institutional Foundations of Economic Reform*. Berkeley: University of California Press.

Pearson, Margaret. January 2005. "The Business of Governing Business in China: Institutions and Norms of the Emerging Regulatory State." *World Politics*. 57, pp. 296–322.

Pei, Minxin. 2006. *China's Trapped Transition: The Limits of Developmental Autocracy.* Cambridge, MA: Harvard University Press.

Qian,Yingyi and Jinglian Wu. 2003. "When Will China Complete Its Transition to the Market?" in *How Far Across the River? Chinese Policy Reform at the Millennium.* Nicholas Hope, Dennis Yang, and Mu Yang Li, eds. Stanford: Stanford University Press, 2003.

Ravallion, Martin and Shaohua Chen. September 2004. "China's (Uneven) Progress Against Poverty," World Bank Policy Research Working Paper 3408. Washington, DC: World Bank.

Regulations, 2003. *Dangzheng Ganbu Xuanba Renyong Guiding* [Regulations on Selecting and Appointing Party and Government Cadres]. Beijing: Zhongguo Fazhi.

Roeder, Philip G. 1993. *Red Sunset: The Failure of Soviet Politics.* Princeton, NJ: Princeton University Press.

Roland, Gérard. 2000. *Transition and Economics: Politics, Markets, and Firms.* Cambridge, MA: MIT Press.

Rural Development Research Group. 1984. *Nongcun: Jingji, Shehui* [Countryside: Economy, Society]. Bejing: Zhishi.

Shirk, Susan. 1993. *The Political Logic of Economic Reform in China.* Berkeley: University of California Press.

Solnick, Steven. 1996. "The Breakdown of Hierarchies in the Soviet Union and China: A Neoinstitutional Perspective." *World Politics.* 48(2), pp. 209–238.

SRC [System Reform Commission], 1988. *Zhongguo Jingji Tizhi Gaige Guihua Ji* [Collection of Long-range Plans for China's Economic System Reform]. Zhangjiakou: Zhonggong Zhongyang Dangxiao.

Suraska, Wisla. 1998. *How the Soviet Union Disappeared: An Essay on the Causes of Dissolution.* Durham: Duke University Press.

Tao, Yifeng. 2001. "Reclaiming the Commanding Heights amid Political Succession: The Political Economy of Financial Reform in Post-Deng China." Doctoral dissertation, Columbia University, New York.

Tong Yanqi, August 1999. "The Reform Model of the Post-Deng Era" [in Chinese; review of Zheng Yongnian]. *Ershiyi Shiiji* [Hong Kong: Twenty-First Century]. 54, pp. 131–33.

Tsebelis, George. 2002. *Veto Players: How Political Institutions Work.* New Jersey: Princeton University Press.

Unger, Jonathan. 1986. "The Decollectivization of the Chinese Countryside: A Survey of Twenty-eight Villages." *Pacific Affairs.* 58(4), pp. 585–607.

Velasco, Andrew. 1998. "The Common Property Approach to the Political Economy of Fiscal Policy," in *The Political Economy of Reform.* F. Sturzenegger and M. Tommasi, eds. Cambridge, MA: MIT Press, pp. 165–184.

Voslensky, Michael. 1984. *Nomenklatura: The Soviet Ruling Class.* Garden City, NY: Doubleday.

Wang, Shaoguang. 1995. "The Rise of the Regions: Fiscal Reform and the Decline of Central State Capacity in China," in *The Waning of the Communist State: Economic Origins of Political Decline in China and Hungary.* Andew Walder, ed. Berkeley: University of California Press, pp. 87–114.

Wang, Yong. 2002. "China's Stakes in WTO Accession: The Internal Decision-Making Process," in *China's Accession to the World Trade Organization: National and International Perspectives.* Heike Holbig and Robert Ash, eds. London: RoutledgeCurzon, pp. 82–118.

Weitzmann, Martin L. and Chenggang Xu. 1994. "Chinese Township-Village Enterprises as Vaguely Defined Cooperatives." *Journal of Comparative Economics.* 18, pp. 121–145.

Whiting, Susan H. 2001. *Power and Wealth in Rural China: The Political Economy of Institutional Change.* Cambridge and New York: Cambridge University Press.

Wong, Christine P. W. 2005. "Can China Change Development Paradigm for the 21st Century? Fiscal Policy Options for Hu Jintao and Wen Jiabao after Two Decades of Muddling through." Paper prepared for the Asia Department, Stiftung Wissenschaft und Politik, Berlin, Germany.

Xiao Chong, 2000. *Shangchang Taizidang* [The Princeling Party in Commerce]. Hong Kong: Xiafei'er.

Xu Jiatun, 1993. *Xu Jiatun Xianggang Huiyilu* [Xu Jiatun's Hong Kong Memoir]. Taipei: Lianjing.

Xu Shanda, September 4, 2001. *1994 Nian Zhongguo Caishui Gaige de Shenke Beijing* [The Deep Background of the Tax Reform of 1994]. Zhongguo Hongguan Jingji Xinxiwang.

Yang, Dali. 2004. *Remaking the Chinese Leviathan: Market Transition and the Politics of Governance in China.* Stanford: Stanford University Press.

Zhang Liang, ed. 2001. *Zhongguo 'Liu si' Zhenxiang* [China June Fourth: The True Story]. Hong Kong: Mingjing.

Zhao Fasheng, 1988. *Dangdai Zhongguo de liangshi gongzuo* [Grain Work in Contemporary China]. Beijing: Zhongguo shehui kexue.

Zheng Yongnian, 1999. *Zhu Rongji Xinzheng: Zhongguo Gaige de Xin Moshi* [The New Policies of Zhu Rongji: A New Model of Chinese Reform]. Singapore: Bafang Wenhua Qiye Gongsi.

Zhou, Xiaochuan. 1993. "Privatization versus a Minimum Reform Package." *China Economic Review.* 4(1), pp. 65–74.

FIVE

The Demographic Factor in China's Transition[1]

WANG Feng and Andrew Mason

During the last two and a half decades, China has witnessed demographic change of historic proportions. It has transformed from a "demographic transitional" society, one where reductions in mortality led to rapid population growth and subsequent reductions in fertility led to slower population growth, to a "posttransitional" society, where life expectancy has reached new heights, fertility has declined to below-replacement level, and rapid population aging is on the horizon. In the not-too-distant future – in a matter of a few decades – China's population will start to shrink, an unprecedented demographic turn in its history in the absence of massive wars, epidemics, and famines. In this process, China will also lose its position as the most populous country in the world.

Demographic changes in China are monumental for reasons in addition to the shifts in traditional demographic parameters – mortality, fertility, population growth rate, and age structure. During its economic transitions of the last two and a half decades, China has also seen migration and urbanization processes that are unprecedented in world history for their sheer magnitudes. Population redistribution is inextricably tied to the broad social and economic transitions that China has undergone, and at the same time, it has also shaped important underlying conditions, as opportunities and constraints, for China's economic transition.

At the start of China's economic reform in the late 1970s, the post-Mao Chinese leadership established population control as one of its top policy priorities. Having witnessed rapid population growth during the preceding decades, the leadership believed population control to be a key measure for ensuring growth in per capita income – its new political mandate. Discourse on population control led to the framing of population growth as the root of all evils, shifting public attention to "overpopulation" and away from political and social problems of the late socialist era. This neo-Malthusian perspective (Lee and Wang, 1999) led to the elevation of

[1] The authors thank Robert Retherford, Yong Cai, Fang Cai, Martin K. Whyte, and Kam Wing Chan for helpful suggestions and Maliki, Comfort Sumida, and Turro Wongkaren for their research assistance. Mason's research was supported in part by NIA, R01-AG025488-01.

population control, along with economic reform, as a "basic state policy" and to the implementation of the draconian policy of one child per couple (Wang, 2005).

Two and a half decades later, following China's success in its transition to a market economy and its phenomenal economic growth, public discourse about the adverse development effects of China's large population has faded from view. The discussion, to the extent that it still exists, has shifted to environmental and natural resource issues, subsumed under a new mantle of "sustainable development." The demographic factor, curiously, is virtually being "counted out" insofar as its relationship with economic development is concerned. Despite the change in discourse, economic success, achievement of low fertility, slower population growth, and a rapidly aging population age structure, China's population policy has remained largely intact. The lack of a serious examination of China's demographic realities and its current population policy, just as the lack of a serious debate on China's draconian population-control policy two and a half decades ago, denies the Chinese public and its policymakers the opportunity to understand fully the role demographic factors have played in China's economic transition in the past, and the role it will play in the future.

In this chapter, we focus on three aspects of China's demographic change during its economic reforms of the past quarter century. First, we review and summarize major demographic changes in China during this time period. Second, we consider whether China's economy experienced a "demographic dividend" that complemented other favorable development forces during the past quarter century. We also consider how future economic prospects are likely to be influenced by demographic factors. Third, we identify and highlight a number of the social consequences of China's recent demographic changes.

TWO AND A HALF DECADES OF DEMOGRAPHIC CHANGE

Substantial reductions in death- and birthrates predate the implementation of economic reform programs in the late 1970s.[2] Impressive mortality declines raised life expectancy by more than 50 percent, from the low forties to the high sixties, between 1950 and 1982, the first post-reform year for which data are available (Table 5.1).[3] Under the government's family-planning program that promoted later marriages, fewer births, and longer birth intervals (*wan, xi,* and *shao*), the

---

[2] For a review of demographic changes up to the late 1980s, see Lavely, Lee, and Wang (1990). A more in-depth summary and analysis of the Chinese demographic behaviors can be found in Lee and Wang (1999). Scharping (2003a) provides a comprehensive review and analysis of China's birth-control programs.

[3] No reliable estimates of life expectancy exist for the early 1950s. Available estimates of life expectancy at birth based on census and mortality survey data give 42.2 for males and 45.6 for females for the period of 1953–1964 (Banister and Preston, 1981; Coale, 1984). Mortality estimates based on a retrospective fertility history survey conducted in 1987, consisting of a two-per-thousand sample of China's population, reported life expectancy of 37.9 and 40.0 for the period of 1945–1949 and 46.7 and 49.2 for 1950–1954, for males and females separately

Table 5.1. *Summary demographic indicators, China, 1950–2000*

Indicator	Year 1950	1982	1990	2000
Population size (millions)	551.96	1,016.54	1,143.33	1,265.83
Percent urban	11.18	21.13	26.41	36.22
Birthrate (per thousand)	37.0	22.28	21.06	14.03
Death rate	18.0	6.6	6.67	6.45
Rate of natural increase	19.00	15.68	14.39	7.58
TFR	–	2.9	2.3	1.6*
Mean age at first marriage (F)	–	22.4	22.1	24.15
Life expectancy (M)	42.2	66.43	66.91	71.01
Life expectancy (F)	45.6	69.35	69.99	74.77
Infant mortality rate (M)	145.85	36.47	32.19	20.78
Infant mortality rate (F)	130.18	34.54	36.83	29.15
Mean household size	–	4.41	3.96	3.44

Sources and notes: * indicates authors' estimate. Population size, percent urban, and crude vital rates are from various published official Chinese sources; TFR before 1995 are from *China Population Yearbook* (1995 and 2000; see discussions in the text); marriage age from *China Population Yearbook* (2003); life expectancy under 1950 is for 1953–1964 and is from Coale (1984); infant mortality rates under 1950 are for 1950–1954 and are from Yan and Chen (1993); other mortality numbers are from Li and Sun (2003).

female mean age at first marriage rose from 19.7 to 22.8 during the 1970s. The total fertility rate (TFR) declined from 5.7 births per woman in 1970 to 2.8 births per woman in 1979 (Coale and Chen, 1987).[4] By international standards, China had by and large completed its fertility transition, in the absence of its more recent one-child policy, by the time its economic reforms began at the end of the 1970s.

Such extraordinary demographic accomplishments did not deter the post-Mao Chinese leadership from adopting a population policy that was in sharp contrast to its economic policy. Economic reforms over the last two decades gradually relaxed the state's control and returned the right of decision making to families and individuals. Population policy, on the other hand, further asserted the right of the state to regulate reproductive decision making that previously had been reserved for couples and their families. In 1980, the one-child-per-couple policy was formally announced and promoted nationwide. Popular resistance led to subsequent policy modifications in the 1980s and spared much of rural China from the one-child policy by allowing them a second child (Greenhalgh, 1986). Urban China has been subject to a strict one-child policy for twenty-five years, despite the initial claim that this was to be an emergency measure. Continued state intervention in reproduction,

(Yan and Chen, 1993). These estimates, however, have only limited value, given the nature of the data and the methods by which these estimates were created.

[4] The total fertility rate is the average number of births per woman, given current age-specific birthrates.

in combination with the state's withdrawal from economic and migration control, forms the important institutional background for China's demographic changes of the last two and a half decades.

Institutional Background of Demographic Change

Three sets of institutional changes are crucial to understanding the demographic changes occurring in China since the late 1970s. First, economic and social reforms have shifted the locus of economic decision making from the state to the family and the individual. Second, a strict birth-control policy, with a recent important reorientation of family-planning programs, remains in place. Third, a fundamental shift in migration policy has allowed people to move freely across administrative boundaries.

In sharp contrast to the socialist planned economy era, when much of the cost of childbearing was assumed by either the state or the collective, China's emerging market economy has increasingly placed the financial burden of raising children on the shoulders of the Chinese family. Such changes have profound impacts on behaviors that relate to demographic changes, ranging from health care and mortality, to marriage, fertility, and living arrangements. Dissolution of collective farming in rural China and termination of guaranteed lifetime employment in urban China increased economic risks among adult Chinese and posed serious concerns for parents planning for their children's economic livelihood. Emergence of a labor market that rewards human capital has clearly intensified the desire and competition to provide increased and improved schooling for children. With the end of free education, beyond the government's nine-year compulsory schooling requirement, the cost of education has skyrocketed. Collapse of the rural public health system and abolition of free health care in urban areas have added health care cost as a substantial expenditure borne by Chinese families. Finally, an emerging consumer culture is also encouraging Chinese households to divert expenditures from rearing children to investment in and expenditures on housing, automobile, consumer durables, clothing, and recreational activities (Davis, 2000).

The impact of institutional changes associated with economic reform on demographic behavior is difficult to assess in light of another set of institutional factors: the Chinese government's continued policy and efforts in controlling population growth. Already two and a half decades into its implementation, China has not signaled if and when it would phase out its one-child policy. The most important change in China's birth-control program in the past decade has been improvements in how the program is implemented, not changes to the policy itself. Starting in the mid-1990s, implementation of the birth-control program has shifted from pure reliance on administrative coercion to greater emphasis on service provision (Winkler, 2002; Kaufman, 2003; Merli, Qian, and Smith, 2004). Stringency of the birth-planning policy is revealed by a recent analysis of fertility policies at local levels. By aggregating fertility policies of more than 400 prefectures, the authors report that at the end of the 1990s, the national fertility level as stipulated by local policies should be 1.47, well below the replacement level of 2.1. According to these policies, the majority of Chinese couples, 63.1 percent, could have only one child, 35.6 could have two children, and 1.3 percent could have three children (Wang, 2005; Gu et al. 2007).[5] Moreover, the political pressure generated by a 1991 policy that links birth-control achievement to cadre evaluation has not only encouraged local officials to compete for lower birthrates within their jurisdictions (Greenhalgh, Zhu, and Li, 1994), but also resulted in false statistics that have corrupted the nationwide birth-reporting system (Smith, 1994; Zeng, 1996; Merli, 1998; Merli and Raftery, 2000; Scharping, 2003, 2007).

Chinese demographic behaviors of the last quarter century are further affected by a third important institutional change, the huge increase in domestic labor migration following the government's reversal of its earlier migration-control policy. The massive volume of migrants from the Chinese countryside to cities, and between cities and rural areas, has not only fueled China's economic growth, but also brought a number of far-reaching demographic consequences. The role of migration in demographic processes goes far beyond its simple effect of damping fertility by separating young couples. Young and unmarried women and men often choose better earning opportunities over marriage and having children early in their lives. Migration exposed many to the urban consumer culture and the urban low-fertility environment. At the same time, as often portrayed by the Chinese official media, population migration has made monitoring and controlling births more difficult. Migration opportunities have also resulted in a new household division of labor and new living arrangements at both the origin and the destination.

Major Indicators of Demographic Change

Population Growth and Fertility

Despite the low fertility level already achieved on the eve of China's economic reforms, China experienced a substantial population increase. This increase was due to population momentum resulting from a large number of young people entering the reproductive ages, itself a result of the high fertility and declining mortality of the 1960s and 1970s. Between 1978 and 2000, China's total population rose from less than 1 billion to more than 1.25 billion, a net increase of 31.5 percent. The population added during these two decades, slightly over 300 million, is roughly equal to the increase during the two preceding decades. The rate of population growth during the 1980s and the 1990s, however, was the slowest in the life span of the People's Republic. During the three decades between 1950 and 1980,

---

[5] Couples who could have only one child include those who reside in the one-child policy regions, comprising 35.4 of China's population, and those who reside in 1.5 children policy regions but could have only one child because their first child is a son. More than half of China's population, 53.6 percent, live in regions with a 1.5 children policy, where a couple whose first child is a daughter is allowed to have a second birth (Gu et al., 2007).

the population grew at annual rates of 1.82, 2.26, and 1.73 percent each decade. The growth slowed to 1.46 percent per year in the 1980s and 1.02 percent in the 1990s.[6]

While it can be said with certainty that China's population growth rate has declined to low levels, the exact level of Chinese fertility cannot be stated with the same degree of confidence, primarily due to a virtual collapse of the birth-reporting system in the 1990s. In the 1980s, demographic variables were measured with great detail and accuracy. By the 1990s, few could trust demographic data, particularly fertility data, which were collected and released by government agencies. From the early 1990s, scholars report as many as 30 percent of births were not counted by the family-planning-registration system in selected locales. Problems in birth reporting and registration started to spread to other official demographic data-gathering sources, including the midterm census, annual population surveys, and special fertility surveys. China's 2000 census, while asserting an underreporting rate of only 1.8 percent, itself a sixfold increase from the 1990 census, revealed many apparent anomalies. For instance, the survival ratio between 1990 and 2000 aged 0–4 in 1990 was found to be 1.05 for males and 1.07 for females, suggesting either undercounting of births in the 1990 census or, less likely, double counting in the 2000 census (Li and Sun, 2003, p. 38). In addition, most survival ratios for groups aged 20–29 in 1990 exceed 1.0, an impossible demographic outcome in the absence of flawed data (or significant in-migration). Not long into the 1990s, the two main government agencies responsible for collecting fertility information, the State Family Planning Commission and the National Bureau of Statistics, simply gave up their attempt to provide reliable and detailed information on fertility. Instead, fertility was reported to be "around the replacement level of 2.1 births per woman."

The most recent official report of China's fertility level came with the 2000 population census, but with a number that caused more controversy than comfort. The census reported a TFR of 1.22 for China as a whole. While releasing such a number showed courage and candidness on the part of census personnel, no one in China, including the data collectors, believes it. Such a low number would put Chinese fertility at a level on par with Italy, lower than Japan, and at about a third of the level for less developed countries.[7] This result was both a surprise and an embarrassment, because it came after repeated government appeals to report births accurately in the census and despite promises of not punishing those who disclosed previously unreported births. It also confirmed the long-held suspicion that government-released fertility numbers were no longer to be trusted. In a careful political and demographic analysis of six Chinese sources that release fertility

---

[6] These rates are calculated based on annual population numbers published in official Chinese statistical sources.

[7] China excluded from the group of less developed countries. Data for other countries or region are from the Population Reference Bureau, at http://www.prb.org.

numbers, Scharping (2007) makes a convincing case for confusion and messiness in Chinese fertility statistics.

The demise of the Chinese fertility-data-gathering system and the unbelievably low fertility numbers based on official statistics should not be used to dismiss the possibility of any genuine fertility reduction in recent years. While the Chinese fertility level in the 1980s showed only a modest downward movement in spite of the forceful implementation of the one-child policy (Feeney and Wang, 1993), a number of arguments have been made to suggest that in the 1990s fertility declines were greater. The broad economic changes in the society and a continued stringent population-control policy combined have further affected Chinese young couples' fertility preferences (Merli and Smith, 2002). A direct piece of evidence to such a change is the postponement of marriage and childbearing in recent years. As shown in Table 5.1, the average age at first marriage for females rose by nearly 10 percent in the 1990s, from 22 to 24. Postponement of childbearing due to delayed marriage and further delaying within marriage can result in a substantial reduction in the total fertility level and the number of births (Guo, 2000; Guo and Chen, 2007). Also, while some still believe that current Chinese fertility, at around 1.8 births per woman, remains at a level not far below replacement, others have maintained that this number is simply too high (Zhang and Yuan, 2004; Zhang and Zhao, 2006; Guo and Chen, 2007). Among other reasons, a simple argument is that if the national TFR is indeed at a level of 1.8, it would imply that the 2000 census missed a third of all births nationwide, a possibility not many are willing to accept. Moreover, results from three recent and careful analyses all suggest that the fertility level is around 1.6 children per woman (Cai, forthcoming; Retherford et al., 2005; Zhang and Zhao, 2006).

Mortality and Health

Dissolution of the rural public health care system and reform of the urban public health care system raised concerns at the start of the reform about their potential detrimental effect on Chinese health statuses. Early concerns focused particularly on infant and child health, as immunization and other basic care had previously been delivered largely by the public health care system. Indeed, mortality improvements stalled during the 1980s (Table 5.1). During the 1990s, however, mortality decline continued at a pace similar to that found in other developing countries. Life expectancy increased by about four years for both men and women during the decade. The level of life expectancy in 2000, 71 years for males and almost 75 for females, is well above the average level for less developed countries (61 and 64 in 2003, respectively) and approaching that of developed countries (72 and 79 for males and females, respectively; http://www.prb.org). A major contributor to improvements in life expectancy has been a further reduction in infant mortality.

There are, however, strong reasons to believe that these most recent mortality numbers are too rosy due to underreporting of deaths in the 2000 census (Li and Sun, 2003). Hence, it is difficult to assess the extent to which mortality conditions improved during the 1990s, and it is possible that the gains were more moderate than what is revealed by the 2000 census. Among its many important effects, China's continued one-child policy may have had a negative impact on female infant and child survival, an issue we will return to in a later section of the chapter. An even more difficult issue to assess is the extent to which reform of the health care system accounted for the slower declines in mortality.

Migration and Urbanization

In contrast to fertility and mortality declines that began before China's reforms, increased migration and an accompanying urbanization process are clearly the products of the reform era. This is especially the case for a new category of migrants called the floating population, a unique product of the Chinese political economy system. Constrained by a number of institutional arrangements, ranging from household registration control to the land tenure system, these migrants leave their place of residence for employment elsewhere but do not change their place of household registration or their place of permanent residence. They are therefore migrants who float on the surface of society (Chan and Zhang, 1999; Solinger, 1999; Wang, Zuo, and Ruan, 2002). Over the past two decades, it is the drastic increase of migrants in this category that has accounted for the rapid increase in the overall volume of migrants. At the start of the reforms, the number of Chinese migrants in comparison to its total population was minuscule. Even in 1987, when the Chinese census first included information on migration, only 15.2 million out of over 1 billion, or about 1.5 percent, reported themselves to be migrants away from their place of household registration for more than six months (Chan, 2001, p. 131). By 1990, the size of this population increased to 30 million and by 1995, 56 million. The 2000 census counted 80 million Chinese as members of the floating population. Including migrants who had spent less than six months at their destination would put the estimated number of temporary migrants at 120 million, up from 88.5 million in 1995 (Liang, 2003). Similarly, the annual population sample survey conducted by China's National Bureau of Statistics reports that in 2002, one out of every ten persons was living in a place (town, township, or subdistrict) that was not the location of the person's household registration. In the economically most dynamic regions of China, such as Guangdong, Fujian, Shanghai, and Beijing, 20–30 percent of current residents had household registrations elsewhere.[8] Urban population growth during the 1990s was also one of the most rapid in China's history, with a net gain in the urban population of 157 million. This increase almost equals the sum of the preceding four decades combined. Massive rural–urban migration was the most important force for urbanization, accounting for 60 percent of all urban population growth during the 1990s (Chan and Hu, 2003).[9]

---

[8] Calculated from Yearbook (2003, p. 102).

[9] The remainder of the growth was roughly equally attributed to rural to urban reclassification and urban natural population growth (Chan and Hu, 2003).

Household Type and Living Arrangement

Decreased fertility, increased life expectancy, and increased migration have also contributed to notable changes in the size and composition of Chinese households. In 1982, a history of high fertility, housing shortages, and other conditions led to an average household size of 4.4. By 2000, the average household size had declined to 3.4 (Table 5.1). For urban China, the average household size was barely above 3, reflecting both the rapid decline in fertility over the last two and a half decades and changing preferences in living arrangements.

A major contributing factor to the decline in household size has been an increase in the number of one-couple households, not a reduction in the number of multiple-generation households (those with three generations or more). One-generation households rose from 4.7 percent of all Chinese households in 1982 to 12.7 percent in 2000. As a result of this change, the percentage of households that are one generation (including both one-couple and one-person households) rose from 13.9 in 1982 and 13.5 in 1990 to 22.3 in 2000. While the percentage of three- or more generation households scarcely changed, the share of two-generation households dropped from 66.6 in 1982 to 55.9 in 2000 (Zeng and Wang, 2003). Many of these newly emerged one-generation households are Chinese elderly who live by themselves. In 1982, 10.7 percent of the male elderly population aged 65 and above lived alone, 16.9 percent lived with a spouse only, and 67.9 percent lived with their children. By 2000, these numbers had changed to 8.4, 28.8, and 59.9 percent respectively. Similar changes are also seen for the female elderly population, but with a higher share living alone than males: 13.7 percent in 1982 and 10.7 percent in 2000. In urban China, households with elderly only are more prevalent, with 33.7 percent of the male elderly living with only a spouse in 2000 and only 55.8 percent living with their children (Zeng and Wang, 2003).

IS CHINA'S FERTILITY DECLINE YIELDING DIVIDENDS?

The rationale for China's one-child policy was a neo-Malthusian perspective on the relationship between population and development, a view largely dismissed by mainstream economists. The architects of China's population policy can point, however, to the post-reform economic record as evidence of the success of the policy. This assertion can be questioned on two grounds. The first, discussed earlier, is the extent to which the transition to low fertility was accelerated by the one-child policy. The second, considered in this section, is the extent to which fertility decline, the slowdown in population growth, and changes in age structure contributed to China's economic success.

The demographic transition interacts with a fundamental feature of any economy – its life cycle variation in consumption and production. Humans have an extended period of economic dependency at the beginning of their lives and, in modern industrial societies, at the end. During these ages of dependency or deficit ages, individuals on average consume more than they produce. During the prime working ages or surplus ages, individuals produce more than they consume.

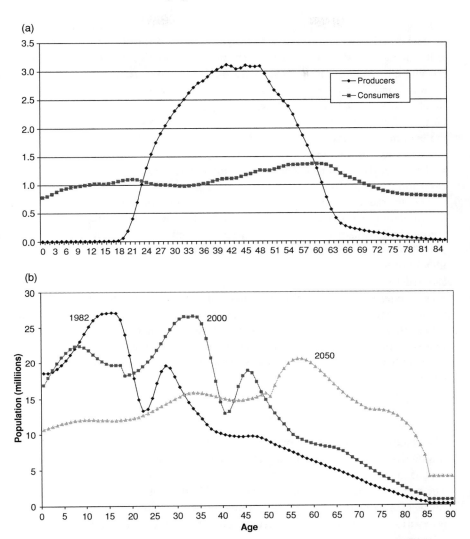

Figure 5.1. (a) Age profiles of consumption and production, urban China, 2000 (*Note:* Profiles normalized to total to one hundred. *Source:* China National Bureau of Statistics, 2000.); (b) Population by age, China, 1982, 2000, and 2050 (*Note:* Population 85 and older uniformly distributed in the 85–90 age groups. See text for sources and methods.)

Detailed information about the life cycle of production and consumption in China is limited. However, the estimated profiles for urban China in 2000 (Figure 5.1a) are similar to those found in other countries.[10]

---

[10] The production and consumption values given in Figure 5.1a are estimated from the 2000 Urban Family Income and Expenditure Survey for China. Both profiles are normalized to aggregate to 100. Details of the estimation procedure are available from the authors.

Unlike many other populations in the world, China's population age profiles contain drastic fluctuations resulting from its unique histories of fertility and mortality change. As shown in Figure 5.1b, in 1982 China's population age profile reveals a clear deficit among those aged around 23, a direct result of the Great Leap Forward famine of 1959–1961. The famine was followed by a baby boom during much of the 1960s, leading to the excess population aged roughly 15–20 in 1982. Fertility decline starting in the early 1970s, meanwhile, resulted in a steady decline in the number of annual births, as shown by the reduction in the number of people from around age 10 and below. These relatively large and small birth cohorts, as well as other fluctuations in the population age structure, are carried over to year 2000 and 2050 (projected).

The divergence between production and consumption interacts with changes in population age structure to generate what is called a demographic dividend (Bloom and Williamson, 1998; Mason, 2001; Bloom et al., 2002) or more recently described as two demographic dividends (Mason and Lee, 2006). The *first* dividend arises because the demographic transition induces changes in population age structure that raise the share of the population concentrated at the productive ages. The *second* dividend arises as individual behavior and public policy respond to anticipated changes in population age structure, for example, increases in the importance of retirement, as discussed in more detail later. An important point that is emphasized later is that the demographic dividends are not independent of the policy environment in which population change is occurring, especially in China.

The First Dividend

The first dividend measures increases in income per capita that occur because the productive population is growing at a faster rate than the total population over part of the demographic transition (for details, see the Appendix to this chapter). The dividend is not always positive, however. As the demographic transition proceeds, growth in the working-age population will be slow relative to the retired population. The effect will be to depress growth in per capita output or per capita consumption.

Analysis that emphasizes only the variation in productivity with age is incomplete. Consumption also varies with age. If the population share of age groups with low productivity and high consumption increases, the aggregate effects are magnified in comparison to the consequences of an increased share for an age group with low productivity and low consumption. Thus, the analysis presented here uses the support ratio – the ratio of the effective number of producers to the effective number of consumers – to quantify the first dividend (Mason and Lee, forthcoming). The support ratio is the ratio of the effective number of workers (weighted by age-specific productivity) to the effective number of consumers (weighted to allow for variation in consumption by age) (Cutler et al.,

1990).[11] Given age profiles of productivity and consumption, output per effective consumer increases at the same rate as the support ratio grows, which depends, in turn, entirely on changes in population age structure.

The magnitude and sign of the first dividend vary substantially over three periods that can be clearly distinguished (Figure 5.2a). From 1982 to 2000, the demographic dividend was especially favorable, as changes in the support ratio had a strong positive effect on output per capita. The support ratio increased by 28 percent or at an average annual rate of 1.3 percent (Figure 5.2a). During the same period, real gross domestic product (GDP) per capita (purchasing-power parity adjusted) grew at an annual rate of 8.4 percent per year (World Bank, 2004). Thus, the first demographic dividend accounted for 15 percent of China's economic growth between 1982 and 2000.

For the most part, the gains from the first demographic dividend have been reaped in China. Between 2000 and 2013, the projected support ratio continues to rise but at a much slower pace. For the entire period the first dividend yields an increase in output per capita of 4.0 percent, an annual growth rate of 0.3 percent. The support ratio reaches a peak in 2013 and then begins a sustained, gradual decline. By 2050, the projected support ratio is only 85 percent of the level reached in 2013. Growth in output per capita is reduced by 0.45 percent per year between 2014 and 2050 as the first demographic dividend unwinds.

Trends in the support ratio combine changes in the effective labor force and the effective number of consumers that are of interest in their own right. These are decomposed in Figure 5.2b. The growth rate in the effective labor force – producers – peaked in the late 1980s and early 1990s at 3 percent per annum. Currently, the rate of growth is about half that at 1.5 percent per annum and declining steadily. Growth will cease altogether by 2020 and turn strongly negative thereafter.

These broad demographic trends conceal important subnational variation. In urban China, where population aging is more rapid, the supply of new labor market entrants from within cities has already started to shrink. In rural China, a more lenient birth-control policy and a later start of fertility decline imply a slower aging process and a stronger labor supply. Thus, better job growth in urban China combined with urban–rural demographic differences will continue to fuel urban–rural migration.

In China – and elsewhere – the first dividend is a persistent but ultimately transitory phenomenon. In China, output per capita is higher by about 10 percent in 2050 than in 1982 due to the first dividend. Were the projection extended further into the future, the net effect would be even smaller. The contribution to annual growth in output per worker during the roughly seven decades tracked is negligible.

---

[11] The effective number of producers is measured using the age profile of productivity shown in Figure 5.1 to weigh the population. The effective number of consumers uses the age profile of consumers. Rural profiles are not available, although we hope to explore this more in the future (see Appendix for details).

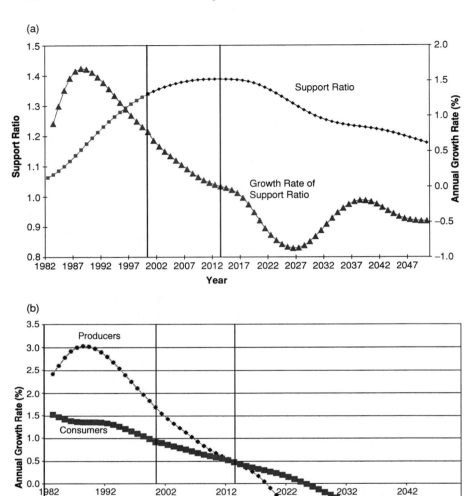

Figure 5.2. (a) Economic support ratio, China, 1982–2050; (b) Effective producers and consumers, annual growth rate, 1982–2050

However, output per capita is substantially elevated over the demographic transition. This is an event of considerable economic significance to those alive during this era. Moreover, the first dividend can have long-lasting effects if it is reinvested in the form of physical capital, human capital, and/or institutional development. This possibility is explored in more detail in the next section.

China's experience is not dissimilar to that of other East Asian economies (Mason and Lee, forthcoming). To compare China's demography with that of others, we

Table 5.2. *Average annual rate of growth in the support ratio (percent), 1982–2050, China and other selected societies*

	1982–2000	2000–2013	2013–2050	1982–2050
China	1.28	0.28	−0.45	0.15
Taiwan	1.07	0.01	−0.60	−0.04
Japan	−0.18	−0.24	−0.60	−0.42
United States	0.44	−0.46	−0.04	0.01
France	0.40	−0.41	−0.17	−0.06

Note: All values calculated using the income and consumption profiles for 1999 urban China.

Source: For China population data, see text; for Taiwan population data, Department of Manpower Planning (personal communication); for Japan, the United States, and France, the United Nations (2003). Single year of age data interpolated using Sprague multipliers.

have constructed the support ratio, using the same productivity and consumption weights employed in the analysis of China, but demographic data for each of the economies shown in Table 5.2. Taiwan's pattern is very similar to China's, although its transition occurred somewhat earlier. Japan also experienced a dividend, but it came much sooner than in other East Asian countries. Throughout the 1982–2050 period, Japan's support ratio is in decline, depressing growth in per capita output by 0.4 percent per annum for the entire period. Many countries in the West also experienced rapid growth in their support ratios primarily because of the baby boom, but many, as illustrated by the experience of France and the United States, are now in a period of decline (Table 5.2).

Population Aging and the Second Dividend

The first dividend quantifies the effects of the support ratio holding output per worker constant. The second dividend arises because changes in age structure influence the processes that lead to the creation of wealth (for details, see the Appendix to this chapter). A possibility – one that has occurred in other East Asian economies – is that population aging will lead to rapid accumulation of capital. If this occurs, the capital intensity of the economy and hence, output per worker will rise. Traditionally, the effect of population on capital deepening is considered in the standard neoclassical model that assumes the saving rate is constant (Solow, 1956). The approach taken here, however, builds on elaborations of the neoclassical model that treat saving and wealth as endogenous (Tobin, 1967; Mason, 1987; Willis, 1988; Lee, 1994).

A second possibility is that population aging will produce a rapid increase in *transfer* wealth rather than capital. This will be the outcome if the consumption needs of retirees are met through familial or state-sponsored transfer programs.

Such programs can effectively redistribute resources across age groups, but they do not create capital and often involve tax policies that undermine work incentives.

With increases in life expectancy, the expected duration of retirement rises. Individuals must accumulate additional wealth or face substantial reductions in standards of living during old age. This wealth can come in several forms, however. One possibility is the accumulation of additional capital. The other is the accumulation of transfer wealth – increases in the obligations of future generations to provide old-age support either through public pension plans or as part of familial support systems. Either form of wealth can meet the retirement needs of a growing elderly population, but increases in capital influence the level of output and economic growth, while increases in transfer wealth do not (Lee, 1994). A third possibility is that neither transfer wealth nor capital is accumulated. In this case, favorable effects on productivity are not achieved and standards of living among the elderly deteriorate.

The analysis presented here relies on a highly stylized model of the economy. Suppose the cross-sectional age profiles of production and consumption – the shape but not the level – are held constant. The profile of production reflects persistent effects of experience and obsolescence. We abstract from changes in labor force behavior, for example, changes in retirement behavior and changes in returns to experience related to increases in educational attainment or other forces. The profile of consumption reflects preferences about own consumption and preferences about the consumption of others, reflecting altruism or political processes.

Under these conditions, changes in China's population age structure lead to a substantial decline in the resources that must be reallocated from working generations to children and a substantial increase in the resources that must be shifted from workers to the elderly. The shift is quite evident in Figure 5.3a–c, which presents the distributions of aggregate consumption and labor income by age for 1982, 2000, and 2050 and the associated age reallocations. These charts are constructed using the profiles and population age distributions shown in Figure 5.1a,b.[12]

Two interage flows, from workers to children and from workers to the elderly, are summarized by the arrows shown in Figure 5.3. The foot of the arrow is located at the mean age of the outflow from workers and the head of the arrow is at the mean age of the inflow to recipients. The width of the arrow is the per capita reallocation. Given golden-rule, steady-state growth, the area of each arrow is equal to aggregate life cycle wealth that must be maintained to support each age reallocation (Lee, 1994; Lee, 2000). In the case of downward flows from older to younger age groups, the life cycle wealth is negative because those who are alive are obligated to make transfers to those who have not yet been born.

---

[12] For a detailed discussion of the theoretical underpinnings of intergenerational transfers, see Lee (1994).

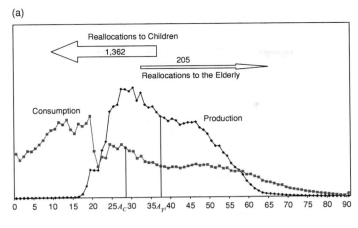

(a)

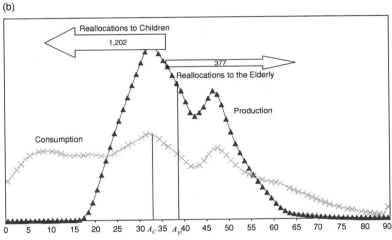

(b)

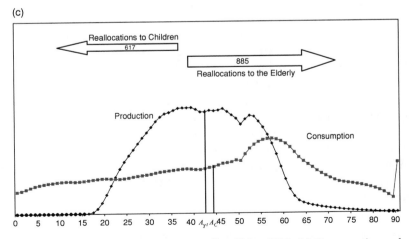

(c)

Figure 5.3. (a) Consumption and income profiles, China, 1982; (b) Consumption and income profiles, China, 2000; (c) Consumption and income profiles, China, 2050

151

Table 5.3. *Mean ages and life cycle wealth variables*

	1982	2000	2050
Mean age of consumption	28.0	32.5	44.4
Mean age of production	37.3	37.8	41.8
Ratio of life cycle wealth to labor income			
TOTAL	−9.2	−5.3	2.6
Support of child dependents	−11.2	−7.8	−4.5
Support of elderly dependents	2.0	2.5	7.1

Note: Calculations use age profiles of household consumption and labor income estimated from the 2000 Urban Income and Expenditure Survey. Estimate of life cycle wealth for the support of child dependents is based on the mean age at childbearing in 2000 from the population projection for China. Life cycle wealth calculations assume golden-rule, steady-state growth.

The effects of age structure on life cycle wealth are quite pronounced (Table 5.3). In 1982, transfers are strongly downward from workers to children, and total life cycle wealth is more than nine times total labor income and negative – dominated by the downward flow to children. As population aging proceeds, flows to children decline and are dominated by flows to the elderly. By 2050, steady-state life cycle wealth will be 2.6 times labor income. Steady-state life cycle wealth required to support consumption by the elderly will rise to 7.1 times labor income. The important implication of Table 5.3 is that population aging in China must lead to rapid growth in the capital stock, to an enormous expansion of public or familial-based transfer programs, or to a significant decline in living standards among the elderly.

The magnitude of the second demographic dividend thus depends on the particular mechanisms used to reallocate resources. Economic reform complicates the picture in China because the institutions and mechanisms used to achieve reallocations are a fundamental features of China's political economy.

Resources can be reallocated from surplus ages to deficit ages in different forms, relying on different institutions (Table 5.4). Three forms are available in complete economies: capital, transfers, and credit. Capital can be accumulated at surplus ages; later, at deficit ages it yields capital income and can be liquidated. An important point to note is that capital can only be used to reallocate resources from younger to older ages. Second, those in deficit ages can rely on current transfers from those in surplus ages. Third, individuals can rely on credit markets. Those at surplus ages can lend to children relying on loan repayments later in life when they are at deficit ages. Credit markets play a small role in interage reallocation systems, however, because of constraints on indebtedness.[13]

---

[13] Credit could play an important role if children financed their own consumption by borrowing from adults with a life cycle surplus. The debt would be repaid when children reached life cycle surplus ages and their creditors reached life cycle deficit ages. When children's consumption is

Table 5.4. *Reallocation system*

	Institution		
Form	Family	Market	State
Capital	Housing Consumer durables Education	Factories Inventories Farms	Public infrastructure State-owned enterprise Funded pension plans
Transfers	Childrearing costs Support of elderly Bequests	Public debt	Public education Public health care Unfunded pension plans
Credit	Familial loans	Consumer credit	Student loans

Source: Adapted from Lee (1994).

In a market economy, three institutions are involved in reallocations. In many societies, the family is the principal institution responsible for reallocating resources across age groups, and in virtually all societies, families dominate reallocations to children. Two other institutions, the market and the state, vary in their importance depending on the economic system. In pre-reform China, market institutions played little or no role and the state played a dominant role. In post-reform China, the emergence of a market economy and the recognition of private property have expanded the mechanisms available for resource reallocations with important economic implications.

Suppose, throughout the entire history under consideration, that the reallocation system for the elderly relied entirely on capital. Prior to reform, this would assume that the state was implicitly funding pensions by investing in state enterprise. After reform, capital accumulation became a combined responsibility of the family, market, and state. Demographic conditions in 1982, under steady-state, golden-rule assumptions, would imply a capital–output ratio of 2.6. Demographic conditions in 2050, again under steady-state, golden-rule assumptions, imply a capital–output ratio of 7.1. Given simple assumptions, an increase in the capital–output ratio of this magnitude would lead to a doubling of output per worker.[14] The impact on the rate of growth of output per worker depends on the time frame over which the capital deepening occurs. Evenly spread over a century,

---

financed through transfers from parents and, to a lesser extent, the state, there is little demand for credit for life cycle purposes.

[14] Given a Cobb–Douglas production function, the relationship between output per worker and the capital–output ratio is

$$\frac{Y}{L} = \left(\frac{K}{Y}\right)^{\frac{\beta}{1-\beta}}.$$

Given an elasticity of output with respect to capital (β) of 0.35, a rise in the capital–output ratio from 2.0 to 7.1 would produce essentially a doubling of output per worker.

output per worker would have to grow at 0.7 percent per year. Spread over fifty years, output per worker would grow at 1.4 percent per year as a result of capital deepening.[15]

These calculations are suggestive and omit many complexities. One is that in pre-reform China a large portion of life cycle wealth, perhaps all, was held as transfer wealth rather than as capital. Life cycle wealth represented the pension obligations or the implicit debt of future generations as embodied in the state and its organs, for example, state-owned enterprises (SOEs). To an unknown extent, economic reform destroyed that life cycle wealth. A continuing issue in China will be through what mechanisms and to what extent life cycle wealth should be replenished. Transfer wealth will necessarily play a major role, because the greatest obligations are to those who are near or who have already reached retirement. For them, accumulating capital is not an option, only transfer wealth. The question then is the extent to which pension obligations are absorbed by the state (taxpayers), shifted to private firms including SOEs that are privatized, or shifted to families.

A second complication for China is separating the transitional issues associated with economic reform from the ongoing issues that arise with population aging. Establishing a large-scale PAYGO pension system would most readily meet the short-term objective of fulfilling obligations to current pensioners. Such a strategy, however, could commit China to a path that foregoes the second demographic dividend.

Direct econometric support for the existence of a second demographic dividend comes in the form of studies of the effect of demographic factors on aggregate saving. Saving rates must rise above their equilibrium level to produce an increase in the capital–output ratio. There is no doubt in East Asia that aggregate saving rates are well above equilibrium, but there are many competing hypotheses about why saving rates are so high in East Asian economies. A number of studies have found evidence to support the view that saving rates have been influenced by changes in age structure (Mason, 1987, 1988; Kelley and Schmidt, 1996; Higgins and Williamson, 1997; Deaton and Paxson, 2000) and life expectancy (Bloom et al., 2003; Kinugasa, 2004). The magnitudes of estimated effects are sensitive to the methods and data employed.

The available evidence supports the conclusion that the demographic transition has led to more rapid growth in output per capita in many East Asian countries where the demographic transition has been especially rapid. China has clearly enjoyed significant gains in output per effective consumer as a result of the first dividend. Whether China will enjoy a second dividend remains to be seen. Demographic change offers an opportunity for significantly more rapid economic growth, but only if the policy environment is supportive.

---

[15] See Lee, Mason, and Miller (2003) for a dynamic simulation analysis of Taiwan. The simulated transition from a low-to-high capital-intensive economy required closer to fifty than to one hundred years.

It would be a serious error, however, to reach any welfare conclusions about demographic change, in general, and fertility decline, in particular. Two reasons for this seem to be of particular importance and warrant emphasis. The first is that capital deepening is achieved by reduced consumption. The resulting growth in output per worker is not a free lunch but comes at the expense of reduced material standards of living among those who are saving at such high levels. The second point is that rapid fertility decline in China may have involved an enormous sacrifice on the part of parents forced to have a single child. We do not know how many children would have been born in the absence of the one-child policy. Nor do we know how to value the costs imposed by the loss of reproductive freedom.

SOCIAL CONSEQUENCES OF DEMOGRAPHIC CHANGE

In addition to the real and potential economic impacts we have examined earlier, demographic changes in China have also resulted in social consequences that will have a broad and lasting impact on Chinese society. In the foregoing paragraphs, we discussed the economic consequences of a rapid aging process in China in terms of capital accumulation and output. The same aging process will also have other economic and social consequences, including rising health care expenditure and the need for family support of the elderly. In the following, we highlight three further social consequences of China's recent demographic change: the rising sex ratio at birth and excess female infant and child mortality, social stratification in marriage, and increasing regional demographic disparities.

Rising Sex Ratio and Female Child Survival

In the past two decades, following China's one-child policy, especially the gender-specific fertility policy that permits rural couples with a firstborn daughter to have a second child, both the sex ratio at birth and the excess female infant mortality shot up (Cai and Lavely, 2003; Zhu and Li, 2003).[16] In 1982, the sex ratio at birth was 108.5, only marginally above the normal range of 104–106. After 1982, it rose sharply, to 114.1 in 1990 and 117.1 in 1995 (Figure 5.4). The most recent census reported a sex ratio at birth of 116.9 in 2000 (not shown in the figure). While some female babies are missing due to either sex-selective abortion or heightened female infant and child mortality, many are simply hidden from government officials and unrecorded in government censuses and surveys. The 2000 census, for instance, revealed more surviving individuals aged 10–14 in 2000 than those counted at ages 0–4 in the 1990 census. It also displays a more balanced sex ratio among the same birth cohorts.

---

[16] A preference for sons will influence the sex ratio at birth to any significant degree only if couples are resorting to sex-selective abortion. The *reported* sex ratio at birth may be influenced by gender-specific infanticide. Thus, the one-child policy affects the sex ratio to the extent that it encourages the use of these mechanisms to achieve the desired sex.

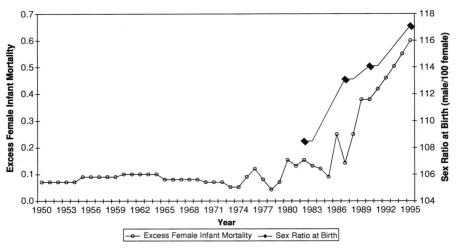

Figure 5.4. Rising sex ratio and excess female infant mortality, China

Underreporting, however, cannot account for all the missing girls and certainly not for most of the sharp increase in excess female infant mortality. It is common to avoid reporting the birth of a female child, but much less common to fake a female infant death. As indicated by the figures given in Table 5.1, while male infant mortality experienced two decades of consecutive decline, roughly 40 percent overall, female infant mortality declined by only about 15 percent, with all the reduction occurring during the 1990s. In 1982, Chinese female infant mortality was lower than that of males, similar to most populations without deliberate practices of gender discrimination against female babies, while in 1990 and 2000, the pattern was reversed.

A declining trend that can be traced to at least the mid-1930s (Coale and Banister, 1994) has been reversed, with excess female mortality at young ages on the rise following the implementation of the one-child policy. As shown in Figure 5.4, excess female infant mortality increased sharply, from around 10 percent in the late 1970s to 60 percent in 1995.[17] Whereas underreporting of female births may inflate the female mortality rate at young ages, it cannot explain all the increase in the ratio between male and female infant mortality, as underreporting exists for both male and female births, though more seriously in the case of females. Moreover, excess female mortality is not confined to the first year of life, but extends to the

---

[17] Female excess infant mortality is calculated as the percentage of observed female infant mortality that is above the expected level. In the absence of deliberate human intervention, male infant mortality is normally higher than the female infant mortality rate, by about 20 percent. The expected level of female infant mortality is calculated by multiplying male infant mortality for the same period by a factor of 0.833.

young ages of 1–4 as well (Choe, Hao, and Wang, 1995; Zhu and Li, 2003).[18] Such an injustice to females so early in life is one of the most glaring forms of social inequality directly resulting from China's birth-control policy.

Social Stratification in Marriage

Demographic abnormalities caused by state policies may combine with other social forces to produce new forms of social inequality, such as increased social stratification in marriage. Public attention has focused on the likely effects of the rising sex ratio on marriage prospects for men. The reality is that poor Chinese men will likely be the only victims of the shortage of women.

In the last two decades, there has been a return of the sharply stratified marriage pattern by social status. Following decades of increasing male marriages, as reflected in a declining proportion of male bachelors at age 40 and the declining significance of social status in the likelihood of marriage (Wang and Tuma, 1993), male marriage once again has become an indicator of social privilege. In the early 1980s, whereas only 0.5 percent of university-educated men were unmarried by age 40, 15.0 percent of illiterate or semiliterate peasants of the same age were still single. In 1990, the share of unmarried bachelors among the rural poor at age 40 rose to 19 percent (Lee and Wang, 1999, pp. 80–81). The most recent census reports that in 2000, nationally only 3.8 percent of males aged 40 were never married. Among those residing in the countryside, and those with the least amount of formal schooling, the percentage was 26.5.[19] At the highest level of educational attainment, college and above, only 1 percent of men were bachelors. Such a social concentration of unmarried males may well worsen as cohorts with increasingly imbalanced sex ratios reach marriage age. In 2000, for instance, among the least educated 30-year-old males, about two in five, 44.8 percent, were still unmarried.

Regional Disparities

Regional demographic differences have become more pronounced in China as economic stratification deepens following the reforms. Differences between urban

---

[18] One encouraging exception to this disturbing reversal of gender patterns is an observed improvement in female adult mortality. Between the ages of 25 and 50, while male mortality rates calculated from the 2000 census are no more than 10–20 percent below that in the 1990 census, female mortality rates are consistently more than 30 percent below the levels a decade ago (Li and Sun, 2003, p. 41; Figure 5.4). Both reduced childbearing and improved maternal health care can be credited for such an improvement.

[19] This and other numbers on marriage are calculated from China's 2000 population census tabulations (Table 5.3, Long Form). The 2000 census used schooling level instead of literacy level as a measure of education for those with below a primary school education. The lowest schooling group here includes those who never attended school or attended only adult schools. Adding primary school educated to this group decreases the percentage to 10.98, a number nearly three times the national average.

and rural areas and between rich and poor provinces portray a demographic profile that resembles the whole world. China's most urbanized provinces have fertility levels that are well below the replacement level and are increasingly relying on a large influx of migrant laborers to sustain their economic growth. These provinces are also years ahead in terms of the health status of their populations, compared with poor provinces.

Estimates of life expectancy based on the 2000 census, for instance, show coexistence of a first and a third world in parts of the same country. In 2000, rural male and female Chinese residents had a life expectancy that was 7.4 and 8.0 percent below city residents (5.6 and 6.3 years, respectively).[20] In 1981, these gaps were at 5.0 and 6.0 percent and in 1989–1990, 3.6 and 5.5 percent.[21] These numbers cannot be interpreted simply as evidence of a growing health gap between urban and rural China because of changes in the urban–rural definition in the data. There is little doubt, however, that a persistent gap has existed.[22] In 2000, just as in 1981 and 1990, life expectancy in China's most urbanized regions, the three centrally controlled coastal municipalities (Shanghai, Beijing, and Tianjin), exceeded those of China's poorest provinces and those with high concentrations of minority populations by more than ten years.

Moreover, as shown by the numbers given in Table 5.5, over a period of nearly twenty years, the mortality gap between these two extreme groups of Chinese provinces has not closed. While the poorest provinces are among those with the largest gains in life expectancy, the richest ones are also in this same group. Although it is more costly and more difficult to reduce mortality at a higher level of life expectancy, the improvement in life expectancy in China's poor provinces is rather modest in comparison with the richer provinces.[23]

In addition, published data on causes of death report that death due to respiratory diseases nearly doubled in rural China between 1980 and 2000, rising from 79 to 142 per 100,000 to become the leading cause of death during the last decade. In urban areas, respiratory disease ranked fourth, after cancer, cerebrovascular, and

[20] Chinese residing in cities (*shi*) had a male life expectancy of 74.95 and a female life expectancy of 79.2. Those residing in the countryside (*xian*), had life expectancies of 69.4 and 72.88 for males and females, respectively (Li and Sun, 2003, p. 43).

[21] In 1981, the city population had life expectancies of 69.08 and 72.74 for males and females, respectively; countryside populations had life expectancies of 65.56 and 68.36, respectively. In 1989–1990, life expectancies for males and females were at 70.1 and 75.05 for the urban population, versus rural life expectancies of 67.6 and 70.9 (China population statistics).

[22] Urban life expectancy numbers in 1981 and 1989–1990 included population residing in towns (*zhen*), whereas the numbers in 2000 included population only in cities, not towns. Populations living in townships, who are not included in the 2000 urban numbers, had slightly lower life expectancies than those in cities (73.18 and 77.68 for males and females in townships, compared with those given in footnote 20).

[23] According to the 2003 World Population Data Sheet published by the Population Reference Bureau (www.prb.org), life expectancy for developed world averaged seventy-six years and for less developed world (excluding China), sixty-three.

Table 5.5. *Mortality change in China's provinces during the reform era*

Province	Life expectancy level Year			Percent of national level Year			Life expectancy index (2000)
	1981	1990	2000	1981	1990	2000	1981 = 100
Shanghai	72.9	74.9	78.1	108	109	109	107
Beijing	72.0	72.9	76.1	106	106	107	106
Tianjin	70.9	72.3	74.9	105	105	105	106
Zhejiang	69.6	71.8	74.7	103	105	105	107
Shandong	70.1	70.6	73.9	104	103	104	105
Jiangsu	69.6	71.4	73.9	103	104	104	106
Liaoning	70.7	70.2	73.3	104	102	103	104
Guangdong	71.3	72.5	73.3	105	106	103	103
Jilin	69.0	68.0	73.1	102	99	102	106
Hainan	–	70.0	72.9	–	102	102	–
Fujian	68.6	68.6	72.6	101	100	102	106
Hebei	70.5	70.4	72.5	104	103	102	103
Heilongjiang	68.3	67.0	72.4	101	98	101	106
Anhui	69.4	69.5	71.9	103	101	101	104
Shanxi	67.8	69.0	71.7	100	101	100	106
Henan	69.8	70.2	71.5	103	102	100	102
Guangxi	70.2	68.7	71.3	104	100	100	102
Sichuan	64.1	66.3	71.2	95	97	100	111
Hubei	65.7	67.3	71.1	97	98	100	108
Hunan	65.6	66.9	70.7	97	98	99	108
Ningxia	65.7	66.9	70.2	97	98	98	107
Shaanxi	65.0	67.4	70.1	96	98	98	108
Inner Mongolia	66.8	65.7	69.9	99	96	98	105
Jiangxi	66.1	66.1	69.0	98	96	97	104
Gansu	65.9	67.2	67.5	97	98	94	102
Qinghai	61.1	60.6	66.0	90	88	92	108
Guizhou	61.6	64.3	66.0	91	94	92	107
Yunnan	61.1	63.5	65.5	90	93	92	107
Xinjiang	60.7	62.6	64.7	90	91	91	107
Tibet	–	59.6	64.4	–	87	90	–
National	67.67	68.55	71.40				106

Source: Life expectancy numbers for 1981 are from Mortality Statistics of CPIRC and for 1990 and 2000 are from Yearbook (2003, p. 117). Chongqing and Hainan provinces are not included due to their recent establishment.

heart diseases. In 2000, the death rate in rural China due to injury, trauma, and toxicosis more than doubled, compared with 1980 figures, and was twice as high than in urban areas (Zhao, 2007). These and other demographic disparities will no doubt further shape China's regional economies and require more interregional links.

CONCLUSION

In many ways, China has always been a demographic early achiever. Its mortality rates declined early and rapidly under a socialist planned economy and public health system. In this regard, China was much more successful than most other countries with similar income levels. China's fertility also declined much faster and earlier in the development process than elsewhere – due partly to a government birth-control program that finds no equal in the extent to which it intruded on the reproductive decisions of couples.

Such a compressed demographic transition positioned China to reap a relatively large demographic dividend at an opportune time. China's first demographic dividend, deriving from fertility decline, materialized at the same time that China underwent its most radical economic transitions and faced the strongest unemployment pressures. The demographic factor was thus favorable in China's economic growth during the last quarter century.

Should one conclude that China's one-child policy was the right course of action? On several counts, the answer is no. First, fertility was declining rapidly even before the one-child policy was implemented; thus, only a small portion of the first dividend can be attributed to the policy per se. Second, more rapid economic growth came with a potentially large and unmeasured cost. Parents were forced to have fewer children than they wanted. There is no reason to suppose that the economic gains outweighed the direct costs on parents who suffered under the one-child policy. Third, analysis that focuses exclusively on the record to date would also be fundamentally flawed, because the economic implications of demographic change will be felt for decades to come.

Being an early achiever brings with it a cost. As we have discussed earlier, as consequences of such a forced demographic transition, China will soon enter a long period of decline in labor supply and face a rapid increase in the elderly population that cannot be reversed easily and quickly. Whereas this aging process may bring with it a second demographic dividend, this favorable outcome depends heavily on the achievement of a suitable institutional environment. State-enforced fertility decline has also resulted in a collapse of the birth statistics collection system, caused a sustained and sharp increase in the sex ratio and in excess female mortality at young ages, and forcefully altered the kinship structure for many Chinese families. These social costs are not only severe but also long lasting.

Moreover, many of the demographic challenges that China faces in the future will vary sharply by region. China's rapid aging process, for example, will not take place evenly across the country, but will vary widely across different locales due to the history of differential birth-control policies. Urban and rural China, as well as China's different regions, vary in almost every demographic aspect: fertility, mortality, age structure, and migration patterns. These demographic differences will play an important role in defining China's future economic and social landscape and will simultaneously increase the need for interregional exchange and interdependence.

APPENDIX: CALCULATING THE DEMOGRAPHIC DIVIDEND

THE FIRST DIVIDEND

Given the age profile of production, an increase in the population concentrated at high-productivity ages must lead to an increase in per capita output. The extent to which the standard of living rises as a consequence may be exaggerated, however, because consumption, and indeed physiological needs, also varies by age.

The effects of age variation in production and consumption are easily incorporated into a simple neoclassical growth model (Cutler et al., 1990; Mason and Lee, forthcoming). Define the effective number of producers as $L(t) = \sum_a w(a) P(a, t)$, where $w(a)$ measures age variation in productivity and $P(a, t)$ is the population of age a in year t. The effective number of consumers is defined in similar fashion as $N(t) = \sum_a c(a) P(a, t)$. Output per effective consumer, $y(t)$, is

$$\frac{Y(t)}{N(t)} = \frac{L(t)}{N(t)} \times \frac{Y(t)}{L(t)} \tag{5.1}$$

or the product of the support ratio (L/N) and output per worker (Y/L).

The rate of growth in output per effective consumer $(\dot{y})$ is equal to the rate of growth of the support ratio (the excess of the rate of growth in the effective labor force over the rate of growth of the effective number of consumers) and the rate of growth of output per effective producer $(\dot{y}^l)$:

$$\dot{y}(t) = \dot{L}(t) - \dot{N}(t) + \dot{y}^l(t). \tag{5.2}$$

The first dividend is captured by changes in the support ratio, that is, the first two right-hand-side terms in equation (5.2).

Computation of the support ratio requires estimates of age-specific productivity and consumption weights. These are estimated for China using the 2000 Urban Survey of Income and Expenditure. The productivity weights are assumed to be proportional to labor income and the consumption weights are assumed to be proportional to estimated consumption.

THE SECOND DIVIDEND

The concept of life cycle wealth and its relationship to population age structure is central to understanding the second demographic dividend. The lifetime budget constraint implies that the current life cycle wealth of an individual, a cohort, or a population must equal the present value of the future stream of consumption less the present value of the future stream of labor income.[24] In the absence of intergenerational transfers (familial support, PAYGO pension systems, bequests, etc.), life cycle wealth consists entirely of capital, that is, real assets held by each individual, a cohort, or the population. Capital represents one form of life cycle wealth.

Transfer systems create another form of life cycle wealth for its participants – transfer wealth, the present value of net lifetime transfers received by an individual, a cohort, or a population. A familiar example of transfer wealth is social security or pension wealth that arises from PAYGO pension programs and consists of the present value of benefits to be received in the future less the present value of taxes to be paid in the future. A less familiar example of transfer wealth arises from childrearing. During childhood, individuals receive transfers directly from parents or indirectly from taxpayers – schooling, for example. When they become adults, individuals make transfers to children, directly to their own children or indirectly to all children in their capacity as taxpayers. Childrearing transfer wealth is the net present value of all transfers associated with childrearing.

Life cycle wealth is closely related to the direction of resource flows. The life cycle wealth associated with upward flows – from younger age groups to older age groups – is positive. Current members of the population can expect to receive more in benefits than they pay in costs in present value terms. This is possible because the current population's wealth includes transfers that will be received from generations that are not yet born. The flip side of transfer wealth is the implicit debt imposed on future generations.

The life cycle wealth associated with downward flows – from older age groups to younger age groups – is negative. Many members of the population have already received benefits but they have not yet incurred the costs associated with downward transfers. A newly married couple, for example, faces childrearing costs but may anticipate few additional transfers from their parents. Hence, their childrearing life cycle wealth is strongly negative.

Changes in age structure have a major influence on aggregate life cycle wealth. As shown earlier, China's young age structure in 1982 must have led to resource flows that were strongly downward. China's projected age structure in 2050 will lead to resource flows that are strongly upward under the assumptions stated earlier. As a result, the changes in age structure will lead to a shift from negative to positive life cycle wealth.

The relationship between life cycle wealth and age structure can be readily summarized given sufficiently strong assumptions. Lee (1994) has shown that given steady-state, golden-rule growth, the ratio of life cycle wealth (W) to labor income (or consumption) is equal to the difference between the mean age of producing and the mean age of consuming ($A_{Y^l} - A_C$):

$$\frac{W}{Y^l} = \frac{W}{C} = A_{Y^l} - A_C, \tag{5.3}$$

---

[24] Any bequests are included in consumption.

where the mean ages of producing and consuming are

$$
A_{Y^l} = \int\limits_0^\omega a N(a) Y^l(a)\mathrm{d}a \Big/ \int\limits_0^\omega N(a) Y^l(a)\mathrm{d}a
$$
$$
A_C = \int\limits_0^\omega a N(a) C(a)\mathrm{d}a \Big/ \int\limits_0^\omega N(a) C(a)\mathrm{d}a.
$$

(5.4)

The mean ages are "dollar-weighted" average ages. The difference between the two measures the lag in years between the age at which a dollar is earned and the age at which it is consumed. The greater this lag, the greater is life cycle wealth. If the population consumes before it produces, on average, its life cycle wealth is negative.

References

Banister, Judith and Samuel H. Preston. 1981. "Mortality in China." *Population and Development Review*. 7(1), pp. 98–110.

Bloom, David E., David Canning, and Jaypee Sevilla. 2002. *The Demographic Dividend: A New Perspective on the Economic Consequences of Population Change*. Santa Monica, CA: RAND.

Bloom, David E., David Canning, and Bryan Graham. 2003. "Longevity and Life-Cycle Savings." *Scandinavian Journal of Economics*. 105(3), pp. 319–338.

Bloom, David E. and Jeffrey G. Williamson. 1998. "Demographic Transitions and Economic Miracles in Emerging Asia." *World Bank Economic Review*. 12(3), pp. 419–456.

Cai,Yong. Forthcoming. "Assessing Fertility Levels in China Using Variable-r Method." *Demography*.

Cai, Yong and William Lavely. 2003. "China's Missing Girls: Numerical Estimates and Effects on Population Growth." *The China Review*. 3, pp. 13–29.

Chan, Kam Wing. 2001. "Recent Migration in China: Patterns, Trends, and Policies." *Asian Perspectives*. 25(4), pp. 127–155.

Chan, Kam Wing and Li Zhang. 1999. "The *Hukou* System and Rural-Urban Migration: Processes and Changes." *The China Quarterly*. 160(1), pp. 818–855.

Chan, Kam Wing and Ying Hu. 2003. "Urbanization in China in the 1990s: New definition, Different Series, and Revised Trends." *The China Review*. 3(2), pp. 49–71.

Choe, Minja K., Hongsheng Hao, and WANG Feng. 1995. "The Effect of Gender and Other Factors on Child Survival in China." *Social Biology*. 42(1–2), pp. 50–64.

Coale, Ansley J. 1984. *Rapid Population Change in China, 1952–1982*. Committee on Population and Demography, Report 27. Washington, DC: National Academy Press.

Coale, Ansley J. and Judith Banister. 1994. "Five Decades of Missing Females in China." *Demography*. 31(3), 459–479.

Coale, Ansley J. and Shengli Chen. 1987. *Basic Data on Fertility in the Provinces of China, 1942–1982*. Honolulu: East–West Population Institute Paper Series.

Cutler, David M., James M. Poterba, Louise M. Sheiner, Lawrence H. Summers. 1990. "An Aging Society: Opportunity or Challenge?" *Brookings Papers on Economic Activity*. (1), pp. 1–56.

Davis, Deborah S. 2000. "A Revolution in Consumption," in *The Consumer Revolution in Urban China.* Deborah S. Davis, ed. Berkeley: University of California Press, pp. 1–22.

Deaton, Angus and Christina H. Paxson. 2000. "Growth, Demographic Structure, and National Saving in Taiwan," in *Population and Economic Change in East Asia, A Supplement to Population and Development Review,* vol. 26. R. Lee and C. Y. C. Chu, eds. New York: Population Council, pp. 141–173.

Feeney, Griffith and WANG Feng. 1993. "Parity Progression and Birth Intervals in China: Policy Initiatives and Demographic Responses." *Population and Development Review.* 19(1), pp. 61–101.

Greenhalgh, Susan. 1986. "Shifts in China's Population Policy, 1984–86: Views from the Central, Provincial, and Local Levels." *Population and Development Review.* 12, pp. 491–515.

Greenhalgh, Susan, Chuzhu Zhu, and Nan Li. 1994. "Restraining Population Growth in Three Chinese Villages, 1988–93." *Population and Development Review.* 20, pp. 365–395.

Gu, Baochang, WANG Feng, Zhigang Guo, and Erli Zhang. 2007. "China's Local and National Fertility Policies at the End of the Twentieth Century." *Population and Development Review* 33(1):129–147.

Guo, Zhigang, 2000. "Cong jinnian lai de shiqi shengyu xingwei kan zhongsheng shengyu shuiping [Examining Life-Time Fertility Level from Period Fertility Behavior of Recent Years]," *Renkou yanjiu* [Population Research]. 24(1), pp. 7–18.

Guo, Zhigang and Wei Chen. 2007. "Below Replacement Fertility in Mainland China," in *Transition and Challenge: China's Population at the Beginning of the 21ˢᵗ Century.* Zhongwei Zhao and Fei Guo, eds. Oxford: Oxford University Press, pp. 54–70.

Higgins, Michael and Jeffrey G. Williamson. 1997. "Age Structure Dynamics in Asia and Dependence on Foreign Capital." *Population and Development Review.* 23(2), pp. 261–293.

Kaufman, Joan. 2003. "Myths and Realities of China's Population Program." *Harvard Asia Quarterly.* 7(1), pp. 21–25.

Kelley, Allen C. and Robert M. Schmidt. 1996. "Saving, Dependency and Development." *Journal of Population Economics.* 9(4), pp. 365–386.

Kinugasa, Tomoko. 2004. "Life Expectancy, Labor Force, and Saving." Ph.D. Dissertation, University of Hawaii, Manoa.

Lavely, William, James Lee, and WANG Feng. November 1990. "Chinese Demography: The State of the Field." *Journal of Asian Studies.* 49.4, pp. 807–834.

Lee, James and WANG Feng. 1999. *One Quarter of Humanity: Malthusian Mythology and Chinese Realities, 1700–2000.* Cambridge, MA: Harvard University Press.

Lee, Ronald D. 1994. "The Formal Demography of Population Aging, Transfers, and the Economic Life Cycle," in *Demography of Aging.* L. G. Martin and S. H. Preston, eds. Washington, DC: National Academy Press, pp. 8–49.

Lee, Ronald D. 2000. "Intergenerational Transfers and the Economic Life Cycle: A Cross-cultural Perspective," in *Sharing the Wealth: Demographic Change and Economic Transfers between Generations.* A. Mason and G. Tapinos, eds. Oxford: Oxford University Press, pp. 17–56.

Lee, Ronald D., Andrew Mason, and Tim Miller. 2003. "From Transfers to Individual Responsibility: Implications for Savings and Capital Accumulation in Taiwan and the United States." *Scandinavian Journal of Economics.* 105(3), pp. 339–357.

Li, Shuzhuo and Fubin Sun. 2003. "Mortality Analysis of China's 2000 Population Census Data: A Preliminary Examination." *The China Review.* 3(2), pp. 31–48.

Liang, Zai. 2003. "Internal Migration in China: Data Sources, Recent Patterns, and a New Research Agenda." Paper presented at the Workshop on Recent Demographic Changes in China, Canberra, Australia.

Mason, Andrew. 1987. "National Saving Rates and Population Growth: A New Model and New Evidence," in *Population Growth and Economic Development: Issues and Evidence*. Social Demography series. D Gale Johnson and Ronald D. Lee, eds. Madison, WI: University of Wisconsin Press, pp. 523–560.

Mason, Andrew. 1988. "Saving, Economic Growth, and Demographic Change." *Population and Development Review*. 14(1), pp. 113–144.

Mason, Andrew. 2001. *Population Change and Economic Development in East Asia: Challenges Met, Opportunities Seized*. Stanford: Stanford University Press.

Mason, Andrew and Ronald Lee. 2006. "Reform and Support Systems for the Elderly in Developing Countries: Capturing the Second Demographic Dividend." *GENUS*. LXII(2): 11–35.

Merli, Giovanna M. 1998. "Underreporting of Births and Deaths in Rural China: Evidence from Field Research in One County of Northern China." *The China Quarterly*. 155, pp. 637–655.

Merli, Giovanna M. and Adrian E. Raftery. 2000. "Are Births Underreported in Rural China? Manipulation of Statistical Records in Response to China's Policies." *Demography*. 37(1), pp. 109–126.

Merli, Giovanna M. and Herbert L. Smith. 2002. "Has the Chinese Family Planning Policy Been Successful in Changing Fertility Preferences?" *Demography*. 39(3), pp. 557–572.

Merli, Giovanna M., Qian Zhenchao, and Herbert L. Smith. 2004. "Adaptation of a Political Bureaucracy to Economic and Institutional Change under Socialism: The Chinese State Family Planning System." *Politics and Society*. 32(2), pp. 231–256.

Retherford, Robert, Minja K. Choe, Jiajian Chen, Xiru Li, and Hongyan Cui. 2005. "Fertility in China: How Much Has It Really Declined?" *Population and Development Review*. 19(1), pp. 57–84.

Scharping, Thomas. 2003. *Birth Control in China 1949–2000, Population Policy and Demographic Development*. London and New York: Routledge Curzon.

Scharping, Thomas. 2007. "The Politics of Numbers: Fertility Statistics in Recent Decades," in *Transition and Challenge: China's Population at the Beginning of the 21ˢᵗ Century*. Zhongwei Zhao and Fei Guo, eds. Oxford: Oxford University Press, pp. 34–53.

Smith, Herbert L. 1994. "Nonreporting of Births or Nonreporting of Pregnancies? Some Evidence from Four Rural Counties in North China." *Demography*. 31(3), pp. 481–486.

Solinger, Dorothy J. 1999. *Contesting Citizenship in Urban China: Peasant Migrants, the State, and the Logic of the Market*. Berkeley: University of California Press.

Solow, Robert M. 1956. "A Contribution to the Theory of Economic Growth." *Quarterly Journal of Economics*. 70(1), pp. 65–94.

Tobin, James. 1967. "Life Cycle Saving and Balanced Economic Growth," in *Ten Economic Studies in the Tradition of Irving Fisher*. William Fellner, ed. New York: Wiley, pp. 231–256.

United Nations, P. D. 2003. *World Population Prospects: The 2002 Revision*. New York: United Nations. Population Division.

WANG Feng. 2005. "Can China Afford to Continue its One-Child Policy?" *Asia Pacific Issues*, vol. 17. Honolulu: East–West Center, pp. 1–12.

WANG Feng and Nancy Tuma. 1993. "Changes in Chinese Marriage Patterns during the Twentieth Century." *Proceedings of the XXIInd General Conference of the IUSSP*. 3, pp. 337–352.

WANG Feng, Xuejin Zuo, and Danching Ruan. 2002. "Rural Migrants in Shanghai: Living under the Shadows of Socialism." *International Migration Review*. 36(2), pp. 520–545.

Willis, Robert J. 1988. "Life Cycles, Institutions and Population Growth: A Theory of the Equilibrium Interest Rate in an Overlapping-Generations Model," in *Economics of Changing Age Distributions in Developed Countries*. R. D. Lee, W. B. Arthur, and G. Rodgers, eds. Oxford: Oxford University Press, pp. 106–138.

Winkler, Edwin A. 2002. "Chinese Reproductive Policy at the Turn of the Millennium: Dynamic Stability." *Population and Development Review*. 28(3), pp. 379–418.

World Bank. 2004. *World Development Indicators 2004*. New York: World Bank.

Yan Rui and Chen Shengli, 1993. "Sishi nianlai Zhongguo renkou fen nianling siwanglu yu shouming de yanjiu [Age-Specific Mortality Rates and Life Expectancy in China in the Last 40 Years]," *Zhongguo shengyu jieyu chouyang diaocha Beijing guoji yantaohui lunwenji* [Proceedings of the International Conference on China's Fertility and Birth Control Sample Survey]. Beijing: Zhongguo renkou chubanshe, pp. 510–529.

Yearbook. 2003. *Zhongguo tongji nianjian* [China Statistical Yearbook]. Beijing: China Statistics Press.

Zeng, Yi. 1996. "Is Fertility in China in 1991–1992 Far below Replacement Level?" *Population Studies*. 50, pp. 27–34.

Zeng, Yi and Zhenglian Wang. 2003. "Dynamics of Family and Elderly Living Arrangements in China: New Lessons Learned from the 2000 Census." *The China Review*. 3(2), pp. 95–119.

Zhang, Guangyu and Zhongwei Zhao. 2006. "Reexamining China's Fertility Puzzle: Data Collection and Quality Over the Last Two Decades," *Population and Development Review* 32(2), pp. 293–321.

Zhang Guangyu and Yuan Xing, 2004. "Dui 1990 niandai chushengloubao he shengyushuiping gujiwenti de sikao" [Some Thoughts on Birth Underreporting and Estimated Fertility Level in the 1990s]," *Renkou yanjiu* [Population Research]. (3), pp. 29–36.

Zhao, Zhongwei. 2007. "Changing Mortality Patterns and Causes of Death," in *Transition and Challenge: China's Population at the Beginning of the 21ˢᵗ Century*. Zhongwei Zhao and Fei Guo, eds. Oxford: Oxford University Press, pp. 160–176.

Zhu Chuzhu and Li Shuzhuo, 2003. "guan ainuhai, baohu nuhai [Love Girls and Protect Girls]," *Renkou yanjiu* [Population Research]. (5), pp. 50–52.

SIX

The Chinese Labor Market in the Reform Era

Fang Cai, Albert Park, and Yaohui Zhao

INTRODUCTION

Since economic reforms began in 1978, the Chinese labor market has undergone a set of remarkable transformations that have dramatically affected the working lives and welfare of China's citizens. Like other rapidly growing developing countries, China has experienced a rapid structural change, featuring a steady flow of labor from agriculture to industry and from rural areas to urban areas. As a transition economy, China has shifted gradually from planned allocation of labor in state-sector jobs to a more open labor market, with increasing numbers of workers employed in the nonstate and private sectors. Table 6.1 summarizes the magnitude of these changes, drawing upon official data. From 1978 to 2005, the share of labor employed primarily in agriculture fell from 71 to 45 percent, the share of labor working in urban areas increased from 24 to 36 percent, and the share of urban labor working in the state-owned or government sectors fell from 78 to 24 percent.

Although the large magnitudes of these changes are impressive, reform of the labor market has been halting, uneven, and difficult, with much additional reform required if China is to complete its transition successfully while maintaining its rapid development trajectory. Many of the challenges of labor market reforms relate to the political difficulty of moving away from a set of institutions and policies that privileged the welfare of urban workers by guaranteeing employment in state enterprises and imposing strict restrictions on population mobility. Relatedly, it has been difficult to establish new institutions to support labor market development, such as portable worker benefits (pensions, health insurance, and housing), reliable social safety net programs, effective enforcement of minimum labor standards, and fair resolution of worker grievances.

In this chapter, we analyze the changes that have occurred in the Chinese labor market over the past three decades. Our focus is to evaluate the extent to which reforms have succeeded in creating a well-functioning market for labor, with a high degree of labor mobility. We focus on labor mobility because it plays a critical role

Table 6.1. *Major trends in Chinese employment, 1978–2005*

Year	Total employment (million)	By sector (%)			By residence (%)		SOE share of urban employment (%)
		Primary	Secondary	Tertiary	Urban	Rural	
1978	404.5	70.5	17.3	12.2	23.7	76.3	78.3
1979	410.2	69.8	17.6	12.6			
1980	423.6	68.7	18.2	13.1	24.8	75.2	76.2
1981	437.3	68.1	18.3	13.6			
1982	453.0	68.1	18.4	13.5			
1983	464.4	67.1	18.7	14.2			
1984	482.0	64.0	18.9	16.1			
1985	498.7	62.4	20.8	16.8	25.7	74.3	70.2
1986	512.8	60.9	21.9	17.2			
1987	527.8	60.0	22.2	17.8			
1988	543.3	59.3	22.4	18.3			
1989	553.3	60.1	21.6	18.3	26.0	74.0	70.2
1990	647.5	60.1	21.4	18.5	26.3	73.7	60.7
1991	654.9	59.7	21.4	18.9	26.7	73.3	61.1
1992	661.5	58.5	21.7	19.8	27.0	73.0	61.0
1993	668.1	56.4	22.4	21.2	27.3	72.7	59.8
1994	674.6	54.3	22.7	23.0	27.7	72.3	60.1
1995	680.7	52.2	23.0	24.8	28.0	72.0	59.1
1996	689.5	50.5	23.5	26.0	28.9	71.1	56.4
1997	698.2	49.9	23.7	26.4	29.8	70.2	53.1
1998	706.4	49.8	23.5	26.7	30.6	69.4	41.9
1999	713.9	50.1	23.0	26.9	31.4	68.6	38.2
2000	720.9	50.0	22.5	27.5	32.1	67.9	35.0
2001	730.3	50.0	22.3	27.7	32.8	67.2	31.9
2002	737.4	50.0	21.4	28.6	33.6	66.4	28.9
2003	744.3	49.1	21.6	29.3	34.4	65.6	26.8
2004	752.0	46.9	22.5	30.6	35.2	64.8	25.3
2005	758.3	44.8	23.8	31.3	36.0	64.0	23.7

Source: Yearbook (various years).

both for economic performance, by improving the efficiency of resource allocation and providing incentives for individuals to invest in human capital and exert work effort, and for distributional outcomes. The labor market, of course, is but one part of a much larger reform challenge. The success of labor market reforms was conditioned by what happened in other reform areas and in turn, had an important influence on other aspects of reform.

The chapter is organized as follows. We begin with an analytical narrative of key reforms and developments in the labor market, starting with a description of the system of labor allocation and wage setting in the pre-reform period, followed by major developments during four subperiods of the reform era. The next two sections analyze trends in and determinants of two key labor market outcomes – employment and wages. We then review the empirical evidence on three dimensions of labor mobility: between rural and urban areas, among regions, and among ownership sectors. Finally, the conclusion summarizes main findings and discusses the key policy challenges that lie ahead.

ECONOMIC REFORM AND THE EVOLUTION OF CHINA'S LABOR MARKET

Antecedents: The Socialist Labor System under Planning

On the eve of socialism, the vast majority of China's population were peasant farmers. Before the anti-Japanese War and subsequent civil war, which disrupted the economy, agriculture was highly commercialized, with markets for key commodities linked tightly both domestically and with the rest of the world (Brandt, 1989; Faure, 1989). Cities served as active centers for trading and manufacturing activity, especially in textiles and clothing. Labor markets appeared to function well, with labor moving relatively freely across regions (Gottschang, 1987; Rawski, 1989).

All that changed with war and the establishment of the People's Republic of China in 1949. China's new socialist leaders emphasized the development of heavy industry (Lin, Cai, and Li, 1996), and the government installed a planning system featuring prices set by the state and administrative allocation of products and inputs, including labor. Urban workers were paid a subsistence wage to support industrialization. The low wage was made possible by low food prices and the direct provision of nonwage benefits (i.e., housing, health care, child care, and pensions) to workers and their families. Work units (*danwei*) organized not just economic, but also political and social dimensions of everyday life, which bound workers to their employers (Walder, 1988). Because all input and output prices, as well as quantities, were determined by planners, the profitability of state enterprises was guaranteed and so did not serve as an indicator of performance.

Managers were deprived of much of their autonomy, including decision-making authority over employment and wage compensation (Lin, Cai, and Li, 1996). The new system centralized labor allocation, ruling out competition for workers. All urban workers were matched to jobs and employers by the Bureau of Labor and Personnel. Once a match was made, there was little possibility for further mobility. Wage reforms in 1956 mandated that wages and other benefits be allocated to workers based on a classification system for occupations, region, industry, ownership (state vs. collective), administrative level (e.g., central and local), and type of workplace (size and technological level) (Bian, 1994; Yueh, 2004). There were eight distinct levels for factory workers and technicians and twenty-four levels for administrative and managerial workers. Thus, under the planning system, wages differed among individuals, but the distribution of wages was compressed and did not directly reward differences in productivity.

In rural areas, collectivization of agriculture was nearly universal by 1956–1957. Rural households were organized into production teams, brigades, and, from 1958, communes, whose leaders distributed incomes based on a highly egalitarian work-point system. Collectives also provided rural public goods and services, such as basic infrastructure and rural health care. The government monopolized the purchase of agricultural products and assigned procurement quotas that required delivery of key commodities for sale to the state at low prices. Staple grains and other necessities were then sold to nonagricultural households at even lower prices, with such sales rationed through the issuance of coupons. Agricultural residents were excluded from this entitlement and others, such as state-provided housing, health care, and pension benefits.

The household registration (*hukou*) system assigned agricultural or nonagricultural status to each person, based primarily on place of birth. In January 1958, the central government issued *Regulations of Hukou Registration*, which required that migration be preapproved by both origin and destination governments and limited temporary stays outside one's place of residence to three months. Especially during the disastrous Great Leap Forward during 1959–1961, the system helped control population movement from rural to urban areas and from smaller to larger cities.

Rural Reforms, 1978–1984

By the late 1970s, it had become clear that the economic planning system had failed to provide adequate effort incentives, leading to low labor productivity, lack of innovation, persistent shortages, and inefficient resource allocation. One of China's earliest and most important economic reforms was the introduction of the household responsibility system (HRS) in agriculture, implemented in rural areas from 1978 to 1983. HRS returned decision-making authority from communes to rural households and made households the residual claimants of profits. Agricultural procurement prices were increased substantially in 1979 and again in 1983. These changes dramatically increased the returns to farm activity and stimulated a large increase in farm productivity. High returns to labor in the nonagricultural sector also motivated farmers to leave agriculture in increasing numbers (Cook, 1999).

However, in the early 1980s, various institutional barriers continued to deter spatial labor mobility, with the government encouraging rural laborers to "leave the land without leaving the village." In 1983, recognizing the need for farmers to find alternative employment and marketing outlets for their output, the government began permitting farmers to engage in long-distance transport and marketing of agricultural products. This was the first time in a generation that Chinese farmers were given the right to conduct business outside their home villages. In 1984, regulations were further relaxed to allow farmers to work freely in nearby towns in collectively owned township and village enterprises (TVEs).

Industrial Reform and the Rise of TVEs, 1985–1992

The period 1985–1992 saw remarkably rapid growth of TVEs in rural areas, reforms to increase the incentives and autonomy of managers of state-owed enterprises in urban areas, and new measures to enable rural labor to work in urban areas on a temporary basis. The dynamism of rural enterprises took Chinese leaders by surprise. After increasing from 28 million in 1978 to 70 million in 1985, employment in TVEs skyrocketed to 123 million by 1993. TVE growth had two important consequences for the labor market. First, it absorbed rural surplus labor and facilitated structural change without a significant increase in migration. Second, because TVEs were less regulated, faced much lower labor costs, and faced harder budget constraints than state-owned enterprises (SOEs), their entry into numerous markets increased competition, which exposed inefficiencies in SOEs and created pressure to reform SOEs.

In urban areas, a number of incremental reforms sought to improve the performance of SOEs. The dual-track pricing system gradually phased out planned prices in favor of market prices, a process largely completed by the late 1980s (Naughton, 1995). In the mid-1990s, an enterprise responsibility system for SOEs was implemented that, following similar principles as the HRS, increased managerial autonomy and improved managerial incentives by allowing enterprises to retain a higher share of profits. In October 1984, the Communist Party passed the "Resolution on Economic Institutional Reform," which changed the total wage quota system, under which planners had fixed each enterprise's total wage bill, to a floating total wage system, in which an enterprise's total wage bill and profit remittances to the government reflected its economic performance in the previous three years (Yueh, 2004). These reforms, implemented in 1985, also permitted profit retention, part of which could go toward worker bonuses. However, government pay scales still largely defined differences in compensation based on pay rank, occupation, region, and type of workplace.[1] Bonus amounts were also regulated, generally set equal to one month's salary in 1986 and one and a half months' salary in 1988. Later in 1992, SOEs were given more autonomy, with wage regulations targeting the total wage bill inclusive of bonuses so that enterprises could set their internal wage structures while at the same time linking the total wage bill more closely with firm performance (Li and Zhao, 2003; Yueh, 2004).

To give managers greater flexibility to adjust employment levels in response to market competition, reforms sought to end the system of permanent employment. In 1986, the State Council issued "Temporary Regulations on the Use of Labor Contracts in State-Run Enterprises" and formally introduced labor contracts to

---

[1] Bian (1994) describes different wage scales for manual workers in enterprises, nonmanual workers in enterprises, manual workers in government or nonprofit agencies, and nonmanual workers in government or nonprofit agencies. For example, the wage scale for manual workers in enterprises consisted of fifteen pay ranks and eleven adjustment levels for different occupations, regions, and types of workplaces.

the labor market (Meng, 2000). Contract workers accounted for 4 percent of total employment in 1985 during the system's experimental stage. This grew to 13 percent in 1990 and 39 percent in 1995. By 1997, one hundred million employees had signed labor contracts with their employers.[2] In practice, the labor contract system was more successful on the hiring side than the firing side. It gave firms the freedom to select and hire suitable workers, but until the late 1990s, the government tightly restricted the dismissal of workers. Enterprises could dismiss no more than 1 percent of their employees each year, were prohibited from dismissing certain types of workers, and were expected to place dismissed workers in new jobs. Nonetheless, the expansion of freedom in hiring increased the competition for productive workers. These changes recognized the need for a more diversified labor-allocation system, featuring "three channels of employment": government direct allocation of labor, spontaneous organization of employment by enterprises, and self-employment under the general guidance of the state plan.

With the removal of food rationing and the growth of nonstate employment, more and more villagers challenged the *hukou* regulations by moving to urban areas. Reforms began to accommodate this spontaneous movement. In 1984, the central government allowed farmers who worked in enterprises or ran their own businesses in small towns to register as "food-self-sufficient households." Such households were recognized as nonagricultural households, but did not receive access to subsidized food and other necessities provided to other urban residents. In 1985, in an effort to improve crime control, the Bureau of Public Security issued regulations requiring migrants to obtain temporary resident permits for stays over three months. In 1988, national identity cards were issued to replace the outdated system of using letters of introduction from origin governments as proof of identity. The identity cards made it easier for migrants to register as temporary residents in cities (deBrauw and Giles, 2006).

By the late 1980s, migrants had formed their own communities in large cities. The growth of migrant populations in cities created tensions with urban residents, leading many city governments to periodically round up migrants and forcibly remove them, especially before national holidays or other politically sensitive occasions. For example, in 1989, the year of the Tiananmen incident, Beijing set a goal of clearing out 200,000 to 250,000 outside workers (Beijing Municipal Bureau of Labor, 1992, p. 58).

Rapid Growth and Marketization, 1993–1996

Following Deng Xiaoping's famous tour to the South in 1992 and the subsequent economic boom, labor demand increased in many cities. Realizing the potential benefits of migrant labor to the urban economy, the attitudes of city governments

---

[2] See Groves et al. (1994) for a description of the increased use of bonuses and contract workers from 1980 to 1990.

toward migrants started to become more flexible. Instead of expelling migrants indiscriminately, city governments enacted rules to regulate the employment of migrant labor. In 1995, the central government required that migrants present four documents (identification card, temporary resident permit, employment certificate issued by the labor bureau in the destination location, and employment card issued by the labor bureau in the home location). Governments could then "regulate" the flow of migrants by setting quotas on employment certificates. Individuals lacking the required documents could be expelled from cities. Some local governments also cashed in on the migration tide by selling urban *hukou* or providing urban *hukou* to migrants who invested a minimum amount of money or purchased commercial housing (i.e., blue-stamp *hukou*).

By the early 1990s, SOE losses had begun to spin out of control (Lardy, 1998). Soft budget constraints and the government's full-employment goals had led to substantial redundant labor in SOEs (Dong and Putterman, 2001, 2003; Li and Xu, 2001). In 1994, the government began a policy of privatizing small and medium SOEs while protecting larger enterprises or "seizing the large and letting go of the small" (*zhuada fangxiao*) (Cao, Qian, and Weingast, 1999). In 1994–1995, the Ministry of Labor issued new rules, allowing listed SOEs to set their own wages as long as wage growth exceeded profit growth but did not exceed labor productivity growth, and encouraged enterprises to consider skills and productivity in addition to occupation and rank in determining wages. These new rules affected about 40,000 SOEs, or about 40 percent of SOEs (Yueh, 2004).

With privatization, some SOEs began to lay off workers, but the process remained limited and tightly controlled. Shanghai implemented a trial subsidy program for laid-off workers as early as 1993. One reason for continued employment rigidity in the state sector at this time was the lack of portable social insurance benefits, especially pensions, and privatized housing. These benefits continued to be provided by employers rather than government, and most cities did not have an effective system in place to honor pension and other obligations if employers became insolvent. The pension reforms in the late 1980s and early 1990s sought to increase pooling of social insurance funds at the municipal and provincial levels, but implementation was slow (Zhao and Xu, 2002). Housing reforms, in which public housing was sold to current occupants at highly subsidized prices, started in some areas as early as 1994 and was completed in most areas by the late 1990s.

In 1994, China passed the Labor Law to take effect on January 1, 1995. The new law established a unified legal framework for labor relations and the safeguarding of workers' rights (Ho, 2006). It built on earlier labor regulations, such as the 1986 regulations on labor contracts, the 1992 Trade Union Law, and the 1993 Regulations on the Handling of Enterprise Labor Disputes. It established equal rights to obtain employment, the right to rest days and holidays, the right to a safe workplace environment, the right to receive social insurance and welfare, the right to bring labor disputes for resolution, the right to a minimum wage, and the right to "equal pay for equal work." It established a maximum eight-hour working day and forty-hour workweek, specified overtime wages, and limited the amount of over-time to three hours per day and thirty-six hours per month. Although implementation has been far from perfect, the law has played an important role in establishing the legal basis for the rights of workers. Significantly, the law also established a framework for equal treatment of workers across ownership sectors. It also permitted no-fault dismissal of workers in response to changing economic conditions, facilitating the process of economic restructuring.

Economic Restructuring and Globalization, 1997 to Present

In 1997, faced with large and unsustainable financial losses of SOEs that threatened the solvency of the banking system and with new social security programs in place, the Chinese government finally moved ahead with aggressive SOE restructuring, marking the end of the "iron rice bowl" of guaranteed employment and benefits for China's urban workers. As part of this initiative, the government established a special one-time urban layoff (*xiagang*) program that provided up to three years of living subsidies (and pension and health care benefits), as well as training and job placement assistance through reemployment centers organized by enterprises.[3] The restructuring led to the layoffs of tens of millions of workers. These changes profoundly affected the functioning of the labor market and the welfare of millions of urban residents. In addition to increased unemployment, there was a sharp reduction in the labor force participation rate (LFPR), especially among older workers. We describe the magnitude of these shocks to employment in detail later in this chapter.

Anticipating the phasing out of the urban layoff program, the government moved to strengthen other social insurance programs. The government standardized its unemployment insurance program in 1999. The program is financed by payroll charges and provides subsidies for up to two years, depending on how long the worker and/or the work unit has participated in the unemployment insurance program. Workers whose three years of *xiagang* subsidies expired became immediately eligible for unemployment benefits. By 1998, most cities also began providing social assistance through the minimum living standard program (MLSP), which provided enough subsidies to households to raise the household's income per capita to a local poverty line designated by each city government. The MLSP was administered by

---

[3] Intended for permanent workers employed before labor contracting began in 1986 or contract workers whose jobs were ended before their contracts expired; the policy provided three years of basic living subsidies, as well as benefits (i.e., health care and pension contributions) based on 60 percent of each worker's final wage. Laid-off workers retained formal ties to their former work units until they found a new job and were expected to register with newly established reemployment centers charged with providing skill training and assistance in searching for new jobs. The *xiagang* subsidies drew upon unemployment insurance funds as well as central and local budgetary expenditures and enterprise contributions, and were intended as a temporary policy to end on January 1, 2001. In practice, many local governments extended benefits to 2003 (Zhang, 2003).

the Ministry of Civil Affairs, but at the start it relied heavily on local financing and was highly decentralized, lacking standardized poverty lines, funding support, administrative apparati, or supervision. Central government financing began in 1999 and expanded significantly in 2001, when expenditures reached 542 million yuan and the number of beneficiaries reached 1.17 million (Zhang, 2003). By 2004, the program was delivering subsidies to 22 million households, or about 6 percent of all urban permanent residents.

To protect vulnerable urban workers from job competition from migrants, some local governments issued discriminatory employment regulations, for example, restricting migrants from working in specific occupations or imposing high fees on migrants entering the city (Cai, Yang, and Wang, 2001). Also, because of the serious underemployment problem in urban areas, small nonstate enterprises and service-sector jobs, which previously received no public support, finally received official encouragement. This promoted greater diversification of China's urban employment structure.

As China entered the new century, migrants had become an integral part of the urban economy. Public support for the gradual dismantling of the *hukou* system reached an unprecedented level. In February 2004, the central government endorsed migration as a key vehicle for increasing the incomes of farmers and demanded the elimination of all fees targeted at migrants as well as equal treatment of migrant children in urban schools. However, implementation of the new measures has been slow and uneven.

By the mid-2000s, China thus had moved in incremental steps to create a functioning labor market, allowing labor to become increasingly mobile and permitting enterprises to give greater weight to market conditions in making decisions about employment and wages. This was not easy, as it necessitated major restructuring of the state sector, the establishment of new social insurance and social assistance programs administered by local governments rather than employers, and a new acceptance of the role of migrant laborers in supporting China's economic development. These changes required a new vision of the role of government in an increasingly market-oriented system. Not surprisingly, in every area of progress, there have also been problems and challenges that have made reforms less than perfect and far from complete.

EMPLOYMENT

The previous narrative describes how many reforms affecting the allocation of and rewards to labor reflected strategic shifts in the government's efforts to promote national economic development while minimizing economic, social, and political disruptions. To maximize efficiency, the nation's labor should be fully utilized and employed in the activities that maximize economic returns based on the principle of comparative advantage. In a market system, achieving such a goal requires incentives that reward workers based on productivity and mobility that allows laborers to move to jobs in which they are most productive. However, for socialist states, creating such a system entails large and politically difficult adjustments of institutions, the structure of economic production, and the distribution of benefits to workers.

In this and the following section, we present empirical evidence on employment and wage outcomes during the reform period and on the basis of these findings, begin to assess the extent to which a true market for labor has emerged in China. In this section, we focus attention on the reasons underlying the emergence of relatively high rates of unemployment since the mid-1990s.

Trends in Unemployment and Labor Force Participation

Prior to the mid-1990s, China's gradualist reform policy emphasized increasing competition between the state and nonstate sectors and strengthening managerial incentives in publicly owned enterprises. Leaders refrained from privatizing enterprises and prohibited managers from firing urban workers. Municipal governments not only protected the jobs of urban local residents but also continued to place new graduates in government or state-sector jobs well into the 1990s even when additional staff or workers were not required. Thus, before the mid-1990s, there was virtually no open unemployment. In this sense, the country was fully employing its labor resources, but incurring large inefficiencies in the allocation of workers to specific activities.[4]

Things changed quite dramatically starting in the mid-1990s, when the Chinese government moved ahead with long-delayed plans to diversify ownership of SOEs and allow inefficient firms to reduce employment or go bankrupt. Aggressive economic restructuring led to the layoffs of at least 10 million workers by 1997 and 27 million workers from 1998 to 2004, mostly from the state sector (Table 6.2). The number of state-sector workers fell from a peak of 113 million in 1995 to 88 million in 1998 and 64 million in 2004 (Table 6.2). There was an even larger percentage reduction in urban collective-sector workers. These adjustments were critical for improving the competitive position of China's publicly owned enterprises.

One result of these downsizing efforts was the emergence of urban unemployment as a policy concern for the first time in the reform era. How high did the unemployment rate rise? Unfortunately, official statistics count as unemployed only those individuals who register for unemployment benefits with local governments and are not based on representative sample surveys. Not surprisingly, the official, or registered, unemployment rate is widely perceived to significantly understate the true unemployment rate. During the second half of the 1990s, the official (registered) unemployment rate ranged between 2.9 and 3.1 percent, before rising in 2001 and 2002 to reach 4.0 percent and peaking at 4.3 percent in 2003 (Table 6.2).

---

[4] Here, we characterize surplus labor in state enterprises and rural areas as part of the inefficiency, although one could also consider it to be underutilization of labor resources.

Table 6.2. *Urban employment indicators, 1998–2004*

Year	Stock of laid-off (xiagang) workers (million)	Of which: laid off in past year (million)	Laid-off (xiagang) SOE workers (million)	Number of SOE workers (million)	Registered unemployed workers (million)	Registered unemployment rate (%)
1997	9.95			107.7	5.77	3.1
1998	8.77	7.39	6.92	88.1	5.71	3.1
1999	9.37	7.82	5.95	83.4	5.75	3.1
2000	9.11	5.12	6.53	78.8	5.95	3.1
2001	7.42	2.83	6.57	74.1	6.81	3.6
2002	6.18	2.11	5.15	69.2	7.70	4.0
2003	4.21	1.28	4.10	66.2	8.00	4.3
2004	2.71	0.49	2.60	64.4	8.27	4.2
TOTAL		27.04	1.53			

Source: Labor Statistical Year Book (1999–2005).

177

These figures overlook millions of workers who were laid off with no expectation of reemployment, who lost jobs but did not register with local governments and who involuntarily retired early, among others (Solinger, 2001).

The lack of reliable and timely unemployment rate estimates consistent with internationally standard definitions is a significant impediment to the design of appropriate macroeconomic and social insurance policies. In Table 6.3, we report the best available evidence on the unemployment rate and the labor force participation rate during China's period of economic restructuring. First, from aggregate statistics based on the government's annual labor force survey (LFS) that includes both urban local residents and migrants, one can calculate the unemployment rate as the difference between the economically active urban population (those aged 16 and older, who are able and desiring to work) and the employed urban population, divided by the economically active urban population.[5] The LFPR is the economically active urban population divided by the total working-age urban population (those aged 16 and older).

In addition, we report independent estimates of the unemployment rate for all workers and urban residents only (excluding migrants) based on surveys of urban workers in five large cities that employ an internationally standard definition of unemployment, with adjustments based on other data to reflect the situation in China as a whole (Giles, Park, and Zhang, 2005). Both measures reveal a steadily rising unemployment rate from 1996 to 2000.[6] The range of estimates over this period increases from 3.9 to 4.5 percent in 1996 to 6.5 to 7.6 percent in 2000 (Table 6.3). After 2000, measures based on the LFSs show a slight decline in the unemployment rate, to 5.8 percent in 2004. One possible reason that the unemployment rate in year 2000 is higher than surrounding years is that aggregate statistics in 2000 were based on census data rather than the annual population and LFS. Consistent with other survey-based estimates (Knight and Xue, 2006), Giles, Park, and Zhang (2005) find that the unemployment rate continued on an upward trajectory after 2000, reaching 7.3 percent in 2002. For urban local residents (excluding migrants), the unemployment rate was higher in all years than for all urban residents, reaching 11.1 percent in 2002 (Giles, Park, and Zhang, 2005). This latter rate may be most salient for policy, because government leaders are most politically concerned about maintaining the welfare of urban local residents and less concerned about the welfare of migrants, who can return home if they are unable to find work.

Recent estimates from the second wave of the China Urban Labor Survey (CULS) in 2005 suggest that the unemployment rate declined from 2002 to 2005, reaching 4.4 percent overall and 6.7 percent for urban local residents in 2005. This suggests that China may have turned the corner in resolving the employment problems of

---

[5] The economically active urban population is calculated as the national economically active population minus the rural labor force.

[6] The only exception is for 1999, when the unemployment rate fell slightly using both measures based on the LFSs.

Table 6.3. *China's labor force participation rate and unemployment rate, 1996–2005*

Year	Unemployment rate – all (AS)	Unemployment rate – all (GPZ)	Unemployment rate – urban residents (GPZ)	Labor force participation rate (AS)
1996	3.9	4.5	6.8	73
1997	4.3	5.0	7.7	72
1998	6.3	5.6	8.5	71
1999	5.9	5.9	9.0	73
2000	7.6	6.5	10.8	66
2001	5.6	7.0	10.8	67
2002	6.1	7.3	11.1	66
2003	6.0			63
2004	5.8			64
2005		4.4	6.7	

AS, from aggregate statistics based on LFS; unemployment rate is the difference between economically active population and employed workers, divided by the economically active population; LFPR is the economically active population divided by the working-age population (above age 16); GPZ, Giles, Park, and Zhang (2005), figures for 2005 are authors' calculations based on second wave of the CULS.

the millions of workers laid off during the process of state-sector restructuring, although it would be a mistake to overlook the plight of discouraged workers who have left the labor force. In some regions of the country, such as the Northeast, employment generation remains a great challenge.

The last column of Table 6.3 reveals a striking decline in LFPR during the second half of the 1990s. The LFPR fell from 73 percent in 1996 to 63 percent in 2003 based on aggregate LFS statistics. Declines were particularly pronounced for women and those near retirement age (Giles, Park, and Cai, 2006a). Many other transition economies also witnessed significant declines in labor force participation. China's LFPR is now more in line with what is typical in other countries. Nonetheless, the magnitude of the fall in LFPR over such a short period is remarkable.

Causes of Unemployment and Slow Job Creation

Due to the dislocation of tens of millions of Chinese workers in the late 1990s, new job creation has emerged as a top policy priority for China's leaders. Until very recently relatively high rates of unemployment, especially of urban local residents, persisted despite continued rapid economic growth. What have been the causes of high unemployment rates in China? Economic restructuring of inefficient SOEs no doubt was the proximate cause of China's employment challenges, just as in other transition economies. Nonetheless, some countries, most notably the Czech Republic, avoided or quickly moderated high unemployment levels during economic transition; such countries often saw sharp real wage declines (Svejnar, 1999). Also, few transition economies enjoyed the sustained rapid economic growth achieved by China, with no significant output fall. In this context, it is meaningful to ask why consistent high rates of growth did not absorb new and dislocated workers more quickly.

One common explanation for high unemployment, especially in Europe, is downward wage or other rigidities associated with labor market institutions, such as unions. In China, however, despite the existence of a model labor union law, in practice labor unions are widely viewed as ineffective in representing the bargaining interests of workers. The legion of potential migrants from rural areas created competition for available jobs, which helped to keep the real wages of unskilled laborers at low levels. The problem in China was not that wages were too high, but rather that many state firms were simply not viable and needed to be shut down or downsized, regardless of whether wages could be adjusted downward. The challenge then has been to create an enabling environment for the creation of new jobs for new and dislocated workers.

It is this latter challenge that China has struggled to meet. Slow job creation can be partly linked to policies in other sectors that were formulated without consideration of their effects on aggregate labor demand. First, industrial development strategy has emphasized the development of heavy, capital-intensive industries, such as automobiles, machinery, and steel that are viewed as keys to modernization, sustained gross domestic product (GDP) growth, and government revenue mobilization. These sectors received preferential access to cheap credit, favorable tax treatment, and supportive public investments. Investments generally did not favor light industries that have the capability to create more employment opportunities. Entry into nonindustrial, labor-intensive sectors such as services was often restricted, limiting their development (Guo, 1999). Especially after 1998 when the government initiated expansionary fiscal and monetary policies, the cost of investment funds for large enterprises became very low. For these reasons, industrial development was very capital intensive (Liu and Cai, 2004).

Large, capital-intensive firms also continued to receive favorable treatment from state-owned commercial banks despite reforms in the banking system (see Chapter 14). Banks had plenty of funds to lend thanks to robust economic growth and large increases in personal savings deposits. Under strong pressure to reduce nonperforming loans, banks perversely had strong incentives to steer funds to large, state-owned enterprises or state-supported projects implicitly backed by the government. State-controlled interest rates were kept at below-market levels, creating incentives for firms to choose capital-intensive technologies. In addition to reducing overall labor demand, if capital is skill biased, it makes unskilled workers relatively worse off. With access to capital tilted toward large state-owned firms, private enterprises, many of which were small and medium in size, found it difficult to obtain loans from state commercial banks and instead turned to alternative financing channels, including foreign direct investment (see Chapter 10). Despite these restrictions, the private sector has accounted for the majority of new job creation since the mid-1990s (Rawski, 2002).

Other underlying forces also have contributed to China's employment challenge by increasing the supply of available workers. As described by Mason and Wang in Chapter 5, demographic changes led China's labor force to grow rapidly by 3 percent per year during the 1980s and early 1990s. Since then, the labor force has increased at a slower rate of about 1.5 percent per year. Only after 2020 is the labor force expected to decline in absolute numbers. For urban labor markets, the large increase in rural migrant labor has been an even more important source of growing labor supply. This, in part, has been due to relaxation of institutional restrictions inhibiting migration, but it also reflects urban biases in public investments and other policies that increase the relative productivity of working in urban versus rural areas. As noted by Huang, Otsuka, and Rozelle in Chapter 13, China's investment in agriculture is small in comparison to other countries at similar levels of development. Through various channels (e.g., taxation, pricing policies, and credit allocation), a large amount of resources have been extracted from the agricultural and rural sectors to support urban industrialization (Cai and Lin, 2003, p. 129).

Employment Adjustments by Enterprises

A few studies have examined firm-level data to analyze whether firms are able to adjust their employment flexibly in response to changing market conditions. Benjamin, Brandt, and Yuen (2003) and Bodmer (2002) use firm-level panel data for 1980–1994 to study the employment decisions of SOEs. They find no evidence that reform of SOEs increased the responsiveness of employment to economic changes before the mid-1990s. Using the same data set, Lee (1999) finds that initial output per worker was positively correlated with changes in employment. He also finds evidence that labor markets for managers and engineers developed more than those for production workers. Dong and Xu (2005) study employment responses of SOEs and other firms, using two firm investment climate surveys covering the periods 1997–2000 and 1999–2002. They find that aggregate SOE employment fell by 9.4 percent in the first period and 5.1 percent in the second and that the elasticities of employment with respect to output and wages were comparable to those found in market economies.

Part of the greater responsiveness of employment to economic conditions may be associated with corporatization of SOEs (usually involving partial privatization). Hu, Opper, and Wang (2006) find that labor retrenchment by corporatized SOEs was more responsive to firm performance than in traditional SOEs and, in contrast to traditional SOEs, was not responsive to political considerations, such as local governments' fiscal position or reemployment conditions. Overall, there appears to have been a marked improvement from the early 1990s to the late 1990s in the ability of firms to adjust their employment levels in response to changing market conditions.

Another way to examine the efficiency of firm employment and wage-setting decisions is to test whether Chinese firms employed too few or too many workers by estimating production functions and comparing wages with marginal products. Unfortunately, such estimates, especially those identified by cross-sectional variation, are often subject to biases due to the endogeneity of input choices and unobserved firm heterogeneity, and so the results should be interpreted cautiously. Dong and Putterman (2001) find that overmanning emerged in SOEs in the early 1990s, which they attribute, among other things, to required wage increases and a lack of authority to adjust employment downward. In separate work, they also argue that in the socialist and early reform periods, SOEs behaved as monopsonies and actually restricted employment, causing marginal products to exceed wages (Dong and Putterman, 2000). Another study suggests that about 20–30 percent of labor in SOEs was redundant by the mid-1990s (Li and Xu, 2001). Although redundant labor was significantly reduced with the massive layoffs that occurred in the late 1990s, Dong and Xu (2005) report that in 2002, one-third of surveyed SOE managers still felt their firms were overstaffed.

The Welfare of Dislocated Workers

Studies have found that shocks to employment associated with restructuring were particularly hard on older workers, women, and the less educated (Appleton et al., 2002; Giles, Park, and Cai, 2006a; Maurer-Fazio, 2007). The massive layoffs created a set of immediate challenges to facilitate the reemployment of dislocated workers. Evidence from the United States and other countries suggests that involuntary unemployment can have scarring effects that have long-lasting consequences on individual earnings and labor force attachment (Kletzer, 1998). The layoffs also created a challenge to government to provide effective safety nets for dislocated workers to prevent poverty and facilitate job search. At the same time, overly generous unemployment benefits could create disincentives to work.

How successful were laid-off workers in finding new jobs? According to the CULS, 34.8 percent of individuals experiencing job separations between January 1996 and November 2001 were employed again within twelve months of leaving their jobs and 44.7 percent were employed again by the end of the period (Giles, Park, and Cai, 2006a). Appleton et al. (2002) found that by the year 2000, 47 percent of retrenched workers in a sample drawn from thirteen Chinese cities had found new jobs. Studies have found that out-of-work duration differed by sex, age, education, and employer ownership type, favoring men, the young, the better educated, and those in the nonstate sector, the same groups less likely to have been exposed to employment shocks in the first place (Appleton et al., 2002; Giles, Park, and Cai, 2006a; Maurer-Fazio, 2007). Giles, Park, and Cai (2006b) estimate the effect of having access to subsidies while controlling for previous job characteristics and find that such access had a large negative effect on the probability of reemployment of men but not of women. Although women did not respond to public subsidies, unlike men their labor supply decisions were influenced by family circumstances.[7] For both men and women, social networks played an important role in finding new jobs.

Is there evidence of scarring? Scarring can be explained by loss of specific human capital, deterioration of human capital when not working, or the lowering of reservation wages as unemployment spells lengthen. According to the CULS, real starting wages in new jobs were slightly higher on average than ending wages of previous jobs and more frequently higher than lower, with the difference between new and old wages being positively associated with younger age and more education (Giles, Park, and Cai, 2006a). However, as seen in Figure 6.1 and as pointed out by Knight and Li (2006), overall real wages grew very rapidly during the late 1990s. Using the same data from thirteen cities as Appleton et al. (2002), Knight and Li (2006) compare wage changes of dislocated workers to those not experiencing unemployment. They estimate that in the late 1990s, unemployment for nineteen months, the mean completed duration of unemployment, reduced earnings by 16 percent.

How well did social safety net programs cushion shocks to employment? Using the CULS data, Giles, Park, and Cai (2006b) find that during the period 1996–2001, fewer than 20 percent of unemployed workers under age 30 had access to public subsidies (including *xiagang* subsidies, unemployment subsidies, and MLSP), and for those aged 30–40, fewer than 30 percent of unemployed men and 25 percent of unemployed women had access to subsidies. For men aged 40–55 and women aged 40–50, coverage was better, with over half of the unemployed receiving subsidies. For those near retirement age, pensions became an important source of support. Overall, public funds supported many older workers who suffered from economic shocks, but many still fell through the cracks. Thus, it is not surprising that analysis of the National Bureau of Statistics (NBS) urban household survey data for 2003 found a strong association between urban poverty and having an unemployed household member (World Bank, forthcoming).

WAGES

Trends in Wages during the Reform Period

We have described how incremental reforms gradually increased the wage-setting autonomy of state enterprises. The continued growth of the nonstate sector, where wages were unregulated, also expanded the market orientation of wage setting, both within nonstate firms and, through competition, within state-owned firms. Figure 6.1 plots mean real wages from 1978 to 2003 based on official data reported

---

[7] Appleton et al. (2002) find that the amount of subsidies did not affect the duration of unemployment. However, the amount of subsidies is likely to be highly correlated with worker productivity because it is calculated on the basis of wages earned before being laid off.

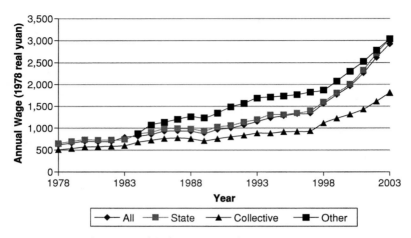

Figure 6.1. China's mean annual wages, 1978–2003

by administrative units.[8] In contrast to most other transition economies, there are no large declines in mean real wages during the reform period. Quite to the contrary, mean real wages rise steadily with only slight hiccups in 1981, 1988, and 1989. Most remarkably, real wages increase at an accelerating rate (14 percent per year) after 1997 when state enterprise restructuring was at its high point.

Even though these increases are probably overstated because administrative reporting misses various types of informal employment that were increasing rapidly in the late 1990s, Figure 6.1 highlights the success of China's economic reforms in delivering amazing welfare gains for the average citizen, with no evidence of widespread wage reductions during the process of adjustment. Continuously rising wages could partly have been led by government policies to significantly increase wages of government and SOE workers. Studies using urban household survey data also confirm the steady increase in real wages. According to NBS urban household surveys in six provinces from different regions, real wages increased steadily from 1988 to 2001, including increases of 9 percent on average from 1997 to 2001 (Zhang et al., 2005, Table 2). Studies describing trends in real urban income per capita also find steady increases with no sharp declines (see Chapter 18; Meng, Gregory, and Wang, 2005).

The NBS urban household survey data from six provinces can also be used to decompose the changes in real wages into cohort, age, and time effects. Following Deaton (1997), we first present age–earnings profiles by birth cohort (Figure 6.2a). For younger cohorts, real wages are higher controlling for age, and age–earnings

---

[8] Nominal average wages are from Yearbook (various years). Real wages are calculated using the urban CPI as a deflator. Wages could be overstated if firms try to underreport profits, but could be understated if firms seek to avoid social insurance contributions for pensions and unemployment insurance.

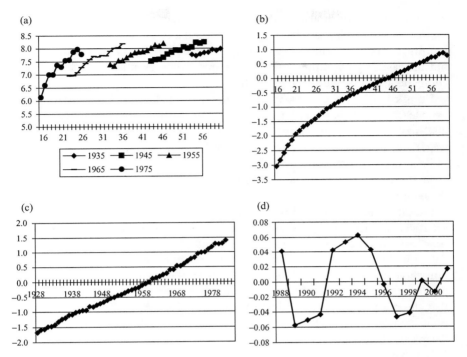

Figure 6.2. Real wages: cohort, age, and time effects. (a) Age-earnings by birth cohort; (b) Age effects; (c) Cohort effects; and (d) Year effects (*Source:* Calculated from the NBS urban household survey data in six provinces over the period 1988–2001.)

profiles are steeper. By regressing real wages on indicator variables for cohort, year, and age, we can decompose the wage differences (Figures 6.2b–d). We find that real wages increase significantly with age, especially at younger ages (Figure 6.2b). Cohort differences are also quite pronounced, and the differences are fairly consistent across time (Figure 6.2c). However, an older person at any given point, on average, has a higher wage because the positive age premium exceeds the negative cohort premium. Finally, time effects are relatively small, but appear to follow the business cycle, with wages falling during periods of retrenchment and tightened control over lending (1989 and 1997) and rising during periods of rapid economic growth (1992–1994 and after 1998).

The Returns to Human Capital

As China moved from a system of government-set wage scales that compressed wage differences to a more open labor market, we would expect the economic returns to human capital to increase and the returns to nonproductive factors to decline. In this section we focus on the returns to education. Following the existing literature, we discuss rural and urban labor markets separately.[9] Reviews of studies estimating the returns to schooling in both rural and urban China find that the returns to schooling remained unusually low in both sectors well into the 1990s, but increased significantly starting in the mid-1990s, eventually reaching levels comparable to other developing countries.

Using rural survey data from six provinces throughout China, deBrauw and Rozelle (2007) estimate that for wage earners, the return to a year of schooling in 2001 was 6.3 percent. Their estimation controls for selection and is based on hourly wage data. Many other estimates rely on annual wages, which deBrauw and Rozelle estimate causes downward bias of about 10 percent in the estimated returns. These estimates are much higher than those from other microstudies for early periods of the reforms.

Education has also been found to strongly predict whether households find jobs off the farm (Zhao, 1997, 1999a,b). The importance of this factor has increased over time (deBrauw et al., 2002; Du, Park, and Wang, 2005). Using rural household panel data from Sichuan, Yang (2004) shows that rural households with more educated household heads are more likely to adjust labor in response to large differentials between the off-farm wage and the shadow wage in agriculture. Some studies find that the most educated individuals in rural areas are more likely to find local, nonfarm jobs rather than migrate (Zhao, 1999a, 1999b; Knight and Song, 2003; Guang and Lu, 2005).

In urban areas, the returns to schooling have risen in recent years to levels that are much higher than in rural areas. Using NBS annual urban household survey data for six provinces, Zhang et al. (2005) report that an additional year of schooling increased annual income by 4.0 percent in 1988 and by 10.2 percent in 2001 (Table 6.4, column 1). By 2003, the returns to a year of schooling reached 11.4 percent in the same six provinces and reached 10.9 percent for the national sample (11.6 percent using hourly earnings; Zhang and Zhao, 2007). Thus, the returns to education by the end of the period were on par or greater than those found in other developing countries for the early 1990s, as summarized by Psacharopoulos (1994). The returns to higher education increased particularly fast. College graduates earned 12.2 percent more than senior high school graduates in 1988, but 37.3 percent more in 2001 (Table 6.2, column 2). The schooling coefficient did not rise in a linear fashion over the period. It rose 0.6 points between 1988 and 1989, stagnated between 1989 and 1992, rose 2.6 points in 1993 and 1994, and stagnated (and even fell slightly) for another three years before rising 3.5 points from 1997 to 2001.

Although the empirical evidence demonstrates convincingly that the returns to education have increased substantially in China during the reform period, especially in the 1990s, we should not automatically attribute all this increase to

---

[9] Because of China's official designations of rural and urban populations, most survey research samples rural and urban households separately, often with different survey instruments.

Table 6.4. *Estimated rates of return to education in urban China, 1988–2001*

Year	Years of schooling	College/above versus high school	Technical school versus high school	High school versus junior high	Junior high versus primary school
1988	4.0	12.2	3.1	11.0	13.9
1989	4.6	14.4	5.8	11.6	17.3
1990	4.7	16.6	9.9	11.5	12.8
1991	4.3	15.9	8.0	9.7	13.4
1992	4.7	20.1	9.2	9.8	10.8
1993	5.2	20.4	7.0	11.5	13.6
1994	7.3	28.7	15.3	14.5	20.2
1995	6.7	24.4	12.0	15.3	18.9
1996	6.8	25.2	10.4	15.6	14.9
1997	6.7	22.3	12.0	17.3	10.9
1998	8.1	32.1	16.5	16.2	12.2
1999	9.9	38.1	17.0	21.0	14.8
2000	10.1	38.7	16.2	20.5	16.4
2001	10.2	37.3	17.8	21.4	13.8

Note: The results are based on a basic Mincerian equation, with gender and regional dummy variables using NBS urban household survey data from six provinces. Regressions are run separately for each year.

Source: Zhang et al. (2005).

labor market reforms. Shifts in the demand for skilled versus unskilled workers, for example, due to skill-biased technical change, could also account for some of the change. However, the timing of the increases coincides with periods of economic liberalization, suggesting that institutional reforms were likely an important part of the story. The returns to schooling increased significantly among all subgroups of the population whether defined by sex, experience, ownership type, sector, or region, suggesting that the changes were deep rooted and not driven by compositional changes in the labor force (Zhang et al., 2005).

Are the estimated private returns to education as high as they should be? Fleisher and Wang (2004) argue that firm wages did not sufficiently reward workers for their skills, by showing that the marginal product of education is much larger than the wage premium paid to more educated workers. However, similar to firm-based estimates of surplus labor, their findings rely on production function estimation that imposes strong identifying assumptions.

Gender–Wage Gap

As in most other countries, men earn more than women in China. This wage gap is related to individual characteristics, such as marital status and education, and job characteristics, such as occupation (Meng and Miller 1995; Hughes and Maurer-Fazio, 2002). In addition, a large share of the gender–wage gap cannot be explained by observable individual or job characteristics, suggesting either discrimination or unobserved productivity differences. Knight and Song (1993), applying the Blinder–Oaxaca decomposition to 1988 urban data from the China Household Income Project (CHIP), find that less than 50 percent of the difference in pay can be explained by observable characteristics.

Given that equality between men and women was stressed during the socialist period, many have expressed concern that market reforms could lead to a return to discriminatory practices against women. Liu, Meng, and Zhang (2000), using two data sets from Shanghai and Jinan in 1995, demonstrate that gender–earnings gaps widen as one moves from the state sector to the collective or private sectors. Using CHIP urban household survey data for 1988 and 1995, Gustafsson and Li (2000) report that the female/male earnings ratio decreased from 84.4 percent in 1988 to 82.5 percent in 1995. They conduct a Blinder–Oaxaca decomposition and conclude that the most important source of the increase in the explained differential is rising returns to education and lower educational attainment of women. A substantial part of the increasing overall earnings gap is attributable to differences in coefficients, which may be due to increased earnings discrimination affecting women and/or lower unobserved productivity among women on average than among men.

Using NBS urban household surveys in six provinces, Zhang et al. (forthcoming) find that the female/male wage ratio declined from 83.5 percent in 1988 to 78.3 percent in 2001. Using the Juhn, Murphy, and Pierce (1993) decomposition technique, they find that the main contributors to this diverging trend were rapid increases in the returns to both observed and unobserved skills that weigh the skill deficit of women more heavily. Women on average also lost in relative terms due to an enlarged gap in unobserved skills or increased discrimination. Although the gender gap in observed skills such as education narrows over time, reducing the gender gap, this effect is not strong enough to offset the forces acting to enlarge the gender–wage gap.

Interfirm Wage Differences

One robust finding in the literature is that differences in wages and benefits in urban enterprises have been increasingly determined by differences in the profitability of employers (Dong, 2005; Knight and Li, 2005). This is very consistent with profit sharing and restrictions on labor mobility (more evidence later), but could also be partly due to other explanations, such as efficiency wage setting (Knight and Li, 2005). Mandated subsidies and other benefits also frequently depend on the financial resources of employers, who bear direct responsibility for part of the expenditure burden.

EMPIRICAL EVIDENCE ON LABOR MOBILITY

In this section, we examine the integration of specific labor market segments. First, we provide direct evidence on the magnitude of labor flows across different markets, which is one indicator of whether markets are integrated. Second, we examine if real wages converge across different markets, although we must be careful to account for possible selection effects, since wage differentials could simply reflect unobserved productivity differences. Third, we look at whether skill premiums, for example, the returns to education, converge across labor markets. Dividing our discussion into three sections, we follow this approach to study separately the extent of labor mobility between rural and urban labor markets, among regions, and across ownership types.

Rural Labor Mobility

In developing countries, faster growth can often be promoted by the rapid shift of labor out of agriculture into other sectors that typically have higher productivity. Rural labor can enter into local, nonfarm employment or migrate to cities. Much attention has been paid to China's large income gap between rural and urban residents and the discriminatory treatment received by rural residents who migrate to urban destinations for work (Solinger, 1999). Following the structure just outlined, in this section we first document the magnitude of labor flows out of agriculture and rural areas and then examine evidence on convergence in the wages and the returns to skill in the urban and rural labor markets.

According to official measures, total rural employment was 306 million in 1978, accounting for 76 percent of the total labor force, and increased to 489–490 million during the period 1995–2002 before declining slightly to reach 485 million in 2005, or 64 percent of the total labor force (Table 6.5). The rapid urbanization of the labor force described earlier was due to both rural–urban migration and the reclassification of rural areas as urban. The rural labor force can be divided into agricultural and nonagricultural workers. As noted in the introduction, the percentage of total labor in China working primarily in agriculture fell rapidly by an average of 0.8 percent per year over the reform period. As a share of rural labor, the agricultural labor share declined from 91 percent in 1979 to 61 percent in 2003. The absolute number of rural workers primarily engaged in agriculture reached its apex in 1990 and has declined ever since (Table 6.5).

The decline in agricultural labor described earlier is likely to understate the amount of labor time that has shifted away from agriculture, since many individuals primarily engaged in agriculture also take on substantial amounts of nonagricultural work. Rawski and Mead (1998) use cost-of-production data on labor use by crop and sown area statistics to estimate the "true" labor time spent in agriculture and suggest that as much as 25 percent of officially recorded agricultural labor

Table 6.5. *Rural employment, 1978–2005*

	Employment (million)				Share of rural employment (%)			
Year	Rural employment	AG	TVEs	Private enterprises	Self-employed	AG	TVEs	Private enterprises	Self-employed
1978	306.4	278.1	28.3			90.8	9.2		
1980	318.4	288.4	30.0			90.6	9.4		
1985	370.7	300.9	69.8			81.2	18.8		
1986	379.9	300.5	79.4			79.1	20.9		
1987	390.0	301.9	88.1			77.4	22.6		
1988	400.7	305.2	95.5			76.2	23.8		
1989	409.4	315.7	93.7			77.1	22.9		
1990	477.1	368.4	92.7	1.1	14.9	77.2	19.4	0.2	3.1
1991	480.3	366.9	96.1	1.2	16.2	76.4	20.0	0.2	3.4
1992	482.9	358.0	106.3	1.3	17.3	74.1	22.0	0.3	3.6
1993	485.5	340.1	123.5	1.9	20.1	70.0	25.4	0.4	4.1
1994	488.0	339.2	120.2	3.2	25.5	69.5	24.6	0.6	5.2
1995	490.3	326.4	128.6	4.7	30.5	66.6	26.2	1.0	6.2
1996	490.3	316.6	135.1	5.5	33.1	64.6	27.6	1.1	6.7
1997	490.4	318.7	130.5	6.0	35.2	65.0	26.6	1.2	7.2
1998	490.2	318.9	125.4	7.4	38.6	65.1	25.6	1.5	7.9
1999	489.8	314.8	127.0	9.7	38.3	64.3	25.9	2.0	7.8
2000	489.3	320.4	128.2	11.4	29.3	65.5	26.2	2.3	6.0
2001	490.9	321.8	130.9	11.9	26.3	65.6	26.7	2.4	5.4
2002	489.6	317.9	132.9	14.1	24.7	64.9	27.1	2.9	5.1
2003	487.9	312.1	135.7	17.5	22.6	64.0	27.8	3.6	4.6
2004	487.2	307.7	138.7	20.2	20.7	63.1	28.5	4.2	4.2
2005	484.9	297.3	142.7	23.7	21.2	61.3	29.4	4.9	4.4

Note: AG refers to agriculture.
Source: Yearbook (various years).

is actually engaged in nonagricultural work. By their calculations, time spent in agriculture began declining after 1980 rather than 1990.

The rural nonagricultural labor force, which should not include permanent migrants to urban areas, increased from 28 million in 1978 to 188 million in 2005. Most of these individuals were employed in rural enterprises, especially TVEs, which are concentrated in coastal provinces. Employment in TVEs reached 135 million in 1996, declined sharply to 125 million in 1998, and grew afterward to reach an all-time high of 143 million in 2005 (Table 6.5). Although official statistics do not fully reflect it, most TVEs were privatized in the mid- to late 1990s. Given their labor-intensive orientation, these privatized firms have the potential to lead the development of China's private sector, although scale economies may encourage them increasingly to relocate to periurban areas. As they continue to grow, such firms will also be likely to employ increasing numbers of migrants from other regions.

Table 6.6. *Rural–urban, urban–urban, rural–rural, and urban–rural migration shares according to the 2000 census*

	Rural–urban	Urban–urban	Rural–rural	Urban–rural
Non-*hukou* migration (%)	49.14	31.12	16.32	3.41
Hukou migration (%)	25.34	48.19	21.93	4.55
All migration (%)	40.84	37.07	18.28	3.81

Note: Migration is defined as moving to one's current township or urban district since 1995 and living in one's current location for more than six months in the last year.

There are numerous estimates of China's "floating population." Solinger (2001) summarizes estimates from Chinese news reports. One reason for differences among these estimates is inconsistency in the definition of migration, which can vary with respect to the geographic scope, the duration of residence outside one's home, and whether the migration was accompanied by a change in *hukou*. The most reliable estimates of migration that facilitate comparisons over time come from government surveys and administrative records.

The 2000 census provides the most authoritative account of recent spatial movement of labor. Table 6.6 summarizes the numbers and percentages of migrants moving from rural to urban, urban to urban, rural to rural, and urban to rural areas. Migrants are defined as those who moved to their current residence location between 1995 and 2000 from outside the township or urban district and who have lived in their current residence for at least six months in the prior year. This is thus a five-year flow measure rather than a stock measure. We distinguish between *hukou* and non-*hukou* migration in Table 6.6. The total number of estimated migrants is 131 million, of which 65.1 percent were non-*hukou* migrants. Rural–urban migration comprised the largest part of the total, accounting for 40.8 percent, or 53.5 million, followed by urban–urban migration, accounting for 37.1 percent (Table 6.6 including migration between districts within cities). About four-fifths of the rural–urban migration was non-*hukou* migration and about two-thirds of the rural–urban migrants migrated for work reasons.

One can also use the 2000 census data to calculate the stock of migrants defined as the share of persons residing in a location for more than six months in the prior year whose *hukou* is from outside the city or county. By this definition, migrants comprised 5.8 percent of China's total population, 12.2 percent of the urban population, and 2.5 percent of the rural population in 2000. In China's cities (excluding townships), migrants accounted for 14.6 percent of the population and 19.6 percent of the employment.

Other estimates of the amount of migration are summarized in Table 6.7. Migration involving changes in *hukou* (official residence location) has remained in the range 16–20 million each year, probably associated mainly with marriages and placement of college graduates from rural areas. Annual non-*hukou* migration is

Table 6.7. *Migration estimates, 1995–2004*

Hukou type	Hukou migrants			Non-*Hukou* migration			
Source	MPS		Census, NBS pop surveys	MOA/MOLSS survey		NBS rural household survey	
Description	Annual flow	Floating pop in cities	Migrants	Rural migrants	Rural migrants	Rural migrants	Rural family migration
Geographic boundary	City or township	City or township	Township or street	Township	Province	Township	Left village
Minimum duration	n.a.	3 days	6 months	1 month	1 month	>0 in past year	n.a.
1995	18.46		49.7				
1996	17.51		60.0				
1997	17.85	37.3	61.8	38.9	14.8		
1998	17.13	40.5	62.4	49.4	18.6		
1999	16.87	40.4	63.7	52.0	21.2		
2000	19.08	44.8	144.4	61.3	28.2		
2001	17.01	55.1		78.5	36.8		
2002	17.22	59.8	108.0	84.0	39.0	81.2	23.5
2003	17.26	69.9	105.9	98.3	40.3	89.6	24.3
2004		78.0	103.0			93.5	24.7

MPS, Ministry of Public Security; MOA, Ministry of Agriculture; MOLSS, Ministry of Labor and Social Security; NBS, National Bureau of Statistics; pop, population.
Source: Chan (2006) reports MPS and census/NBS population survey figures. MOA/MOLSS figures are from Zhang (2005), Liu (2004), MOA (2003), and MOA and MOLSS (1998, 1999). NBS rural household survey results from Rural Household Survey Yearbook (2004, 2005).

much larger. Data from the government's population surveys suggest that the floating population was over 60 million people in the late 1990s (Table 6.7, column 4).

The survey of rural labor conducted by the Ministry of Agriculture (MOA) and the Ministry of Labor and Social Security (MOLSS) annually since 1996 provides the most complete picture of temporary rural migration, recording all those who migrate for at least one month in the past year. As seen in Table 6.7 (column 6), the estimated number of rural migrants increased remarkably from 52.0 million in 1999 to 98.3 million in 2003. Over this period, about 40 percent of migrants went to destinations outside their home province. Since 2002, NBS's annual rural household survey has asked detailed questions about migration, producing estimates of migration very similar to those from the MOA/MOLSS survey (Table 6.7, column 7). Using a village questionnaire, the NBS survey also estimates the amount of family migration (column 8). In 2004, there were 93.5 million individual rural migrants and 24.7 million persons in families that migrated, for a total of 118.2 million rural migrants.

Comparing these numbers to the earlier data on TVE employment, we can see that until the late 1990s, TVEs played a dominant role in absorbing surplus labor from the countryside, but since then migration has become increasingly important. Recent trends indicate that migration is poised to surpass TVEs as the main destination of workers leaving agriculture. (Some migration can also be to work in TVEs in other regions.) Examining retrospective work histories of farm household members interviewed in 2001, deBrauw et al. (2002) find that the share of rural labor working off the farm increased from 15 percent in 1981 to 32 percent in 1995 and 43 percent in 2000. About three-fourths of off-farm workers did not migrate outside the village to work in 1981, but by 2000, nearly equal numbers of workers had migrated or worked locally in self-employment or wage jobs.

Another way to examine the rising importance of nonagricultural work to rural labor is to look at income data from the NBS annual rural household surveys. The share of nonagricultural income in total rural household income increased from 30.6 percent in 1990 to 51.3 percent in 2005 (Yearbook, 2006). Most of the nonagricultural income (75.8 percent in 2005) was from wages. This is a remarkably rapid change in the structure of rural income.

What kind of work do rural migrants do in cities? According to the 2000 census data, in terms of occupations, migrants are most likely to be production or transport workers (51.0 percent) followed by commercial or service workers (36.4 percent; Table 6.8). This is also true for local residents, but the share of white-collar jobs is much higher for local residents (38.8 percent) than for migrants (12.5 percent). Similarly, migrant jobs are concentrated in manufacturing (40.3 percent) and retail and wholesale trade (28.8 percent), while local residents are spread more evenly across sectors and are much more likely to be working in high-skill sectors, such as finance or education.

Has the large flow of labor from rural to urban areas narrowed differences between rural and urban incomes? Figure 6.3 plots the ratio of real rural income per capita and real urban income per capita for the years 1989–2005. We use spatial price indexes from Brandt and Holz (2006) to control for differences in urban and rural prices over time.[10] Although controlling for cost-of-living differences is important for making fair comparisons, Johnson (2001) argues that much of the relative increase in urban versus rural prices is due to relatively faster increases in the quality of urban versus rural consumption.

Figure 6.3 shows a significant increase in rural–urban inequality since the mid-1980s. Rural incomes rose sharply in the early 1980s with introduction of the HRS, reducing the urban–rural gap. The gap narrowed again from 1994 to

---

[10] We use indices for a joint basket of goods common to urban and rural areas. The rural CPI is adjusted to better account for changes in prices (planned vs. market) used to calculate income in different periods.

Table 6.8. *Urban employment of holders of agricultural and nonagricultural Hukou,*
2000 census

	Local residents (%)	Migrants (%)
Occupations		
Government, party, and managers	6.0	2.7
Technical workers	19.8	4.8
Clerical workers	13.0	5.0
Commercial and service workers	24.5	36.4
Production and transport workers	36.7	51.0
Others	0.1	0.1
Sectors		
Mining	2.2	1.0
Manufacturing	31.9	40.3
Utilities	2.5	0.4
Construction	5.6	10.7
Geological survey and water management	0.5	0.1
Transport, storage, post, and communication	7.8	4.2
Retail and wholesale trade	17.8	28.8
Finance and insurance	2.6	0.5
Real estate	1.3	0.8
Social services	7.2	8.5
Health, sports, and social welfare	3.6	1.0
Education, culture, and arts	7.1	1.8
Scientific research and technical service	1.3	0.3
Government, party, and NGOs	7.8	1.2
Others	0.9	0.3

Source: 2000 census data.

1997, when the urban economy slowed following financial retrenchment, while rural incomes grew with rising agricultural prices and yields. China's urban–rural income differences have now reached a historic peak that is considerably greater than when the reforms began in the late 1970s. By 2004, real rural income per capita was only 40 percent of real urban income per capita. The pattern of an increasing rather than decreasing rural–urban income gap during the process of structural change is anomalous when compared to the experience of most other countries.

What can account for the large and rising differences in urban and rural incomes? First, there may be costs to migration, in the form of moving expenses, search (or information) costs, or disutility from leaving one's home and living in a new environment. For the poor, financing constraints may limit migration. Second, policies such as China's *hukou* system may create barriers to labor mobility. Third, the differences could simply reflect productivity differences (e.g., due to human capital differences) of rural and urban workers. Finally, with imperfect mobility, any

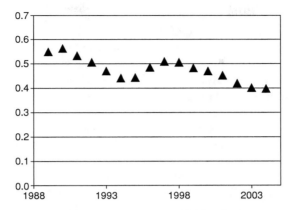

Figure 6.3. Ratio of real rural income per capita to real urban income per capita, 1989–2004 (*Source:* Park, forthcoming. *Notes:* This figure plots the ratio of rural and urban incomes per capita, using urban CPI and adjusted rural CPI for a common bundle of goods in 1990, as calculated by Brandt and Holz, 2006. Rural CPIs are adjusted to better value self-produced goods at market prices. The indices account for the greater cost of living in urban areas, which were 29 percent greater than in rural areas in 2003.)

policy that treats rural and urban areas differently could affect income differences (e.g., differences in capital or infrastructure investment and pricing policies).

Several factors should be taken into account in interpreting trends in reported real rural and urban incomes per capita in China. These statistics are based on separate national sample surveys of urban and rural households conducted each year by the NBS. There are a number of sampling and measurement problems that create potential biases. First, the urban survey excludes residents of townships and suburban districts of province-level cities, likely leading to slight upward bias in urban incomes. Second, migrants living in urban areas were excluded until 2002 and remain severely undersampled; however, Sicular et al. (2006) finds that this does not significantly affect urban–rural differences. Third, the NBS rural household survey includes household members who live away from home for more than six months but whose economic life remains closely tied to the household (e.g., spouses and unmarried children), likely creating upward bias in measured rural income per capita. Fourth, urban incomes may omit nonwage income, such as housing, health care, and pension benefits. Li and Luo (2006) estimate that accounting for such omissions increases urban–rural gaps by as much as one-third. Finally, the definition of urban has changed over time, leading to unknown bias. Regardless of all these concerns, few dispute that differences in urban and rural incomes in China remain substantial and have grown over time despite rapid urbanization.

Rural–urban gaps are substantially smaller in coastal and northeast provinces than in interior provinces. This pattern is consistent with the inverse relationship described earlier between urban–rural gaps and the level of industrialization or economic development. If labor movement out of agriculture into nonagriculture were faster in areas with larger urban–rural gaps, we would expect regional differences in these gaps and in mean income levels to converge over time. However, in China, until the late 1990s, it was still the coastal provinces that witnessed a more rapid flow of labor out of agriculture, an unsustainable pattern once most of the labor in rich provinces has already left agriculture. Income and employment data suggest that in recent years, structural change and labor migration in western provinces have accelerated sharply, providing some hope that regional income differences might begin to narrow (Du, Park, and Wang, 2005).

What, then, are the key factors inhibiting greater rural–urban labor mobility? A large number of studies have estimated models of the determinants of migration decisions using household survey data, providing evidence on which factors may pose barriers to migration. First, education level has become increasingly important over time in positively predicting individual migration (deBrauw et al., 2002; Du, Park, and Wang, 2005). It is common for enterprises to require at least a middle school degree before even considering migrant job applicants. Second, young adults are much more likely to migrate than middle-aged or older workers and are more willing to migrate from their home province; this difference between younger and older workers has increased over time (deBrauw et al., 2002). Third, the relationship between migration probability and the level of household endowments (i.e., poverty) has an inverted-U shape, with both the poorest and richest households less likely to have migrant workers (Du, Park, and Wang, 2005).

Yang (2005), analyzing household panel data from Sichuan from 1986 to 1995, studies the misallocation of labor between farm and nonfarm sectors and finds evidence of underallocation of labor to nonfarm activities. He finds that more educated workers allocate labor more efficiently, so that increasing the highest education level of the household from primary school to middle school increases earnings by 6.1 percent due to better resource-allocation decisions, including 2.3 percent due to allocating more labor to nonagriculture.

The China Rural Poverty Survey conducted in 2000 asked respondents in four poor counties in different western provinces about the extent to which different factors had a significant influence on the migration decision. The responses in order of importance were the following: education level, farm labor requirements, lack of information, financial constraints, child care issues, urban government policies, local government policies, cost of living in urban areas, local income level, *hukou* policy, and quality of life in urban areas (Du, Park, and Wang, 2005). Although responses to such subjective questions should be interpreted cautiously, the results imply that labor supply factors may be more important than labor demand factors and that emphasis on the *hukou* policy as a barrier to migration may be misplaced (even if other urban policies also relate to *hukou* status). The survey also found that most migrants had found jobs before leaving the village (61 percent), consistent with information networks playing an important role in migration decisions.

Reinforcing the importance of information barriers, a number of authors have noted the importance of chain migration patterns in China and other countries. Using village data from eight provinces, Rozelle et al. (1999) find that migration from villages in 1995 is strongly predicted by 1988 migration levels and that an established network in a destination zone leads to new migration of the same magnitude as the existing network size. Giles (2006) also finds that access to village migrant networks significantly increases household incomes and improves the ability of rural households to smooth consumption.

In China, the most often cited reason for large urban–rural differences is the continued enforcement of the *hukou* system, even though rural migration to cities is not officially prohibited. This is because the *hukou* system increases the costs and reduces the potential benefits to migration (Chan and Li, 1999). Until recently, city governments have required migrants to purchase temporary residence permits and pay licensing fees for operating businesses in urban areas. Migrants have been unable to send their children to urban schools unless they pay high additional fees. Rural migrants have lacked access to housing and health care benefits provided to registered urban residents and before grain rationing was phased out in 1993, could not buy grain at subsidized prices. In an effort to protect the jobs of urban residents, especially after economic restructuring led to the layoff of millions of urban workers in the late 1990s, many cities have restricted the job categories in which migrants can legally work. The restricted categories are not always high-skill jobs. For example, rural migrants cannot become taxi drivers or even obtain automobile licenses in urban areas. In addition, as noted earlier, some migrants suffer discrimination and exploitation in the labor market. To the extent that the institutional treatment of migrants as outsiders encourages such behavior, such outcomes represent an important indirect effect of the *hukou* system.

The importance of the *hukou* system in creating the urban–rural divide is often asserted, but empirical evidence quantifying its effect understandably remains elusive. Park, Zhao, and Huang (2006) measure the extent of occupational and sectoral restrictions in urban areas of different provinces by estimating the effect of *hukou* status on occupational choices of nonagricultural workers in multinomial logit models for each province. They find that coastal provinces are much less segmented than central and interior provinces and that the extent of segmentation is positively correlated with the unemployment rate of urban residents and negatively correlated with GDP per capita and the importance of SOEs in industrial output. Rural migrants are less likely to migrate to provinces with higher segmentation indices even after controlling for the level of development.

Irrespective of the extent to which the *hukou* system influences migration, it seems apparent that the importance of the *hukou* system in affecting labor mobility has decreased significantly over time. Gradual development of urban markets for food, housing, and other necessities of life has allowed migrants to meet most of their needs without urban resident status. Recently, new laws have attempted to level the playing field by eliminating fees for temporary urban residence permits and allowing migrants to send their children to urban schools without discrimination. Although successful implementation of these measures has a long way to go, they signal the willingness of government to relax restrictions on migration. In many coastal areas, leaders now perceive *hukou* restrictions as a constraint on economic development because they make it more difficult to attract sufficient migrants to support rapid growth. In the early 2000s, some regions and cities (e.g., Zhejiang and Shijiazhuang) implemented experimental *hukou* reforms, making it easy for rural residents to obtain an urban *hukou*.

There is not much evidence on the extent of discrimination against migrant workers, mainly due to the paucity of high-quality survey data on both migrants and urban residents in common labor markets. Meng and Zhang (2001) find that in Shanghai in the mid-1990s, the hourly wage of rural migrants was half that of urban residents and that only 50 percent of this difference could be explained by observable differences in the personal characteristics of the two groups. Most of the wage differentials were within broadly defined occupation groups rather than due to occupational segregation. Similarly, analysis of the 2005 CULS in five large cities found that 40 percent of wage differences between migrants and local residents could not be explained by differences in observable characteristics, with nearly all of the unexplained difference being within occupations (World Bank, forthcoming). Knight and Song (1999) also find evidence of significantly lower wages for migrants after controlling for differences in observable characteristics. There are also numerous anecdotal accounts of migrants' labor rights being violated (Chan, 2001), suggesting discriminatory behavior by employers. Of course, as is common in such analyses, it is difficult to know what part of the unexplained wage difference is due to discrimination versus differences in unobservable worker characteristics.

Migrants also face other forms of unequal treatment. According to the CULS in four large cities in 2005, 70 percent of migrants with children in school reported facing higher schooling costs because they lacked local *hukou*; they estimated that the costs of schooling would fall by 35 percent if they had local *hukou* (World Bank, forthcoming). Migrants also live in much lower quality housing than local residents, do not have access to urban social assistance programs, and have extremely low social insurance coverage. According to the 2005 CULS in twelve cities, coverage rates for migrants was 8.3 percent for pensions, 6.8 percent for medical insurance, and 4.4 percent for unemployment insurance, compared with 61.7, 52.3, and 18.8 percent for local residents (World Bank, forthcoming).

Interregional Labor Mobility

Because China has such large regional disparities, interprovincial mobility of labor plays an important role in making desirable employment opportunities available to individuals throughout the country, especially rural laborers in interior provinces where poverty is greatest. As seen in Table 6.7, the number of rural laborers migrating to destinations in other provinces exceeded 40 million by 2003. Johnson

Table 6.9. *Regional distribution of migrants*

	All migrants (%)				Interprovincial migrants (%)			
	Origin				Origin			
Destination	East	Central	West	All	East	Central	West	All
East								
1987	91.0	13.6	9.7	40.5	49.7	61.7	44.2	52.0
1990	87.0	18.6	18.1	43.2	56.0	59.0	49.3	54.6
1995	92.6	30.5	22.7	54.1	63.5	71.8	56.5	63.1
2000	95.4	32.0	22.5	54.5	64.4	84.3	68.3	75.0
Central								
1987	5.6	82.7	4.7	30.3	31.3	21.8	21.2	24.6
1990	8.4	75.8	7.5	29.9	28.4	23.5	20.4	24.0
1995	4.1	62.9	4.9	21.6	20.5	12.7	13.4	18.8
2000	2.5	65.1	2.6	22.7	19.7	7.1	7.9	9.8
West								
1987	3.4	3.7	85.6	29.2	18.9	16.6	34.6	23.3
1990	4.6	5.5	74.4	26.9	15.6	17.5	30.3	21.4
1995	3.3	6.6	72.4	24.3	16.1	15.5	30.2	18.1
2000	2.0	3.3	74.9	22.8	15.9	8.6	23.9	15.3

Notes: 1. Migrants in 1987 refer to those who migrated between cities, towns, and counties and stayed at destinations for six months or longer; migrants in 1990 refer to those who migrated between cities and counties and stayed at destinations for one year or longer; migrants in 1995 refer to those who migrated between counties, districts, and counties and stayed at destinations for six months or longer; migrants in 2000 refer to those who migrated between townships, towns (*zhen*), and communities (*jiedao*) and stayed at destinations for six months or longer.

2. Although the statistical criteria of migration timing and space units are different in various years, the results in Table 6.1 can be used as a reference to compare changes in migration directions.

Source: National Bureau of Statistics (1988, 1993, 1997, 2002).

(2003) estimates net interprovincial migration by comparing provincial populations from the 1990 and 2000 population censuses, adjusting for natural population growth rates, and estimates net interprovincial migration over this period to be between 16.3 and 39.7 million. He argues that the implied migration rates are much lower than interregional migration in the United States, especially when the United States had large rural–urban income gaps.

With respect to the regional patterns of interprovincial migration in China, according to population surveys and censuses, the overwhelming trend is for increasing migration to coastal provinces, regardless of origin location (Table 6.9). Table 6.9 also shows that migration to distant regions is least likely for laborers living in the western region, the poorest part of China. This reflects the

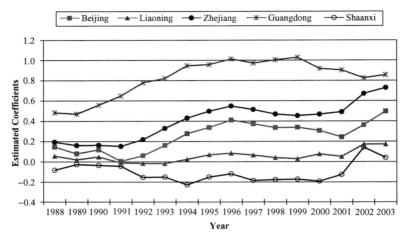

Figure 6.4. Coefficients of provinces (Sichuan, 1988–2003; *Source:* Park et al., 2006)

particular challenges resulting from China's economic geography, in which the poor are located in the landlocked West and most industrial jobs are being created in the eastern coastal regions. Among interprovincial migrants, the percentage going to eastern provinces from western, central, and eastern provinces were 68.3, 84.3, and 64.4 percent in 2000, compared with 44.2, 61.7, and 49.7 percent in 1987 (Table 6.9). One province is a clear outlier in its large population gain during the 1990s – Guangdong (Johnson, 2003). Microeconomic studies of migration also find that rural migrants have become increasingly willing to travel to distant provinces in pursuit of employment opportunities (de Brauw et al., 2002).[11] They also find that migrants predictably respond to wage differentials in choosing destination locations (Zhu, 2002; Lin, Wang, and Zhao, 2004).

Has this responsiveness of labor migration to wage differences led regional wage differences to converge over time? Well-documented evidence of growing regional inequality in per capita GDP and income suggests that this may not be the case (Jian, Sachs, and Warner, 1996; World Bank, 1997). Using urban household survey data for the period 1988–2002, Park et al. (2006) find that in a standard Mincerian wage equation estimation that controls for human capital differences, the coefficients of regional dummy variables became more dispersed in the early 1990s, stabilized in the late 1990s, and began converging in the early 2000s (Figure 6.4). Urban wages in Guangdong remain exceptionally high relative to other provinces, achieving a 100 percent premium over Shaanxi by 2002 despite receiving more migrants than any other province. Cai and Du (2004) conduct annual regressions of provincial manufacturing wages (from administrative reporting) on a set of sector and province dummies, and calculate dispersion measures of the provincial

---

[11] The share of migrants leaving their own province increased from nearly 30 percent to nearly 40 percent from 1990 to 2000.

Table 6.10. *Returns to education by province, 1988–2001*

Year	Beijing	Liaoning	Zhejiang	Guangdong	Shaanxi	Sichuan	Coefficient of variation
1988	2.8	3.8	3.2	3.2	6.3	5.0	0.33
1989	1.6	4.1	3.6	4.7	5.9	5.6	0.37
1990	2.7	4.4	3.0	4.6	6.0	5.8	0.31
1991	2.3	4.5	3.7	3.5	5.3	5.3	0.28
1992	3.4	4.8	3.8	4.0	5.5	5.8	0.21
1993	4.1	5.4	3.8	4.1	6.1	6.6	0.24
1994	5.9	6.8	6.5	6.5	8.7	9.3	0.19
1995	4.9	6.9	4.4	6.5	7.9	8.1	0.24
1996	5.2	6.7	6.1	6.8	7.5	7.4	0.13
1997	4.3	6.9	7.1	7.0	6.4	7.2	0.17
1998	6.1	7.7	7.4	8.6	8.5	8.9	0.13
1999	8.8	10.0	8.4	10.5	10.3	10.3	0.09
2000	9.3	10.7	9.0	9.9	10.1	10.8	0.07
2001	10.5	8.1	10.9	10.5	9.5	12.3	0.14

Source: Zhang et al. (2005).

dummy coefficients. They find that average wage dispersion across provinces declined during the 1990s. Although the two papers disagree on trends in the 1990s and use different samples and data sources, they both conclude that by the end of the period studied, interregional wage differences were converging. Analysis of the 2003 NBS urban household survey data found that after controlling for spatial price differences, coastal wages remain about 20 percent higher than those elsewhere, with differences among noncoastal regions relatively small (World Bank, forthcoming).

Finally, we review mixed evidence on trends in interregional differences in the returns to education over time. Zhang et al. (2005) find strong evidence of convergence in the returns to education over time across provinces. Initially, returns to education were somewhat higher in poorer provinces than in richer provinces, but over time, the returns in rich provinces grew faster and caught up to the returns in poor provinces (Table 6.10). The coefficient of variation in the returns to education fell from a high of 0.37 in 1989 to a low of 0.07 in 2000 (Table 6.10, last column). However, Yang (2005) analyzed the returns to schooling in different cities using urban household survey data from 1988 and 1995 and found that between-city variation in the returns to schooling increased over time.

Overall, the evidence suggests that interregional labor mobility has improved substantially during the reform period, especially since the late 1990s. Importantly, migration is finally beginning to narrow interregional earnings differences, but there appears to be substantial scope for increased migration across regions. Given the higher wages still available on the coast, labor flows to coastal China may continue to increase until migration equalizes wages across regions or capital flows in greater amounts to the interior, a response that to date has not materialized.

Informalization and Job Mobility Across Ownership Sectors

One of the most notable features of the Chinese urban labor market is the categorization of employment by ownership. There were three types of ownerships during the initial phase of the economic reforms: state-owned enterprises (SOEs), urban collective enterprises (UCEs), and individual enterprises. Private enterprises with more than seven workers were nationalized in the 1950s. SOEs are owned by governments at the city/county level and above; UCEs are owned by government units below the city/county levels; individual enterprises are those with seven or fewer employees. Many new forms of ownership emerged as a result of economic reforms. Foreign-invested enterprises, which increased following China's opening to the outside world, include enterprises that are wholly or partially owned by foreign investors. Domestic private enterprises are nonforeign firms that employ more than seven persons. Although the lack of protection for private property limited their growth, their importance grew over the years, and in 1999, they gained recognition in China's constitution. Recent reforms of the state sector created several mixed ownership forms, including cooperative units, joint ownership units, limited liability corporations, and shareholding corporations. One challenge of China's transition process has been to allow workers to move from the state sector to the more dynamic and efficient nonstate sector.

Figure 6.5 presents official data on the share of labor working for employers of different ownership types in urban areas. Until the beginning of the 1990s, the pure state sector (including government) accounted for over 80 percent of urban employment. By 2005, the employment share was below 40 percent. Employment in the SOE sector, which actually grew from 1990 to 1994, then shrunk by an annual average rate of 6.4 percent per year between 1995 and 2000 – a total loss of 31.5 million jobs or 15 percent of the urban labor force.[12] The UCE sector, which began its transformation earlier and had already shed over 10 percent of its 1990 workforce by 1995, shrank by 13.8 percent per year from 1995 to 2000, eliminating another 16.5 million jobs. Meanwhile, employment in mixed enterprises jumped an average of 17.6 percent per year, and employment in the registered (or formal) private sector grew by 10.7 percent per year (Figure 6.5). The fastest growing sector (starting from a very low base) was the informal sector (called "other" in our tables), which grew at 24 percent per year. Note that not all the job losses from the state sector were net job losses to the economy, as some jobs remained when ownership changed.

There is some confusion about what lies behind the dramatic increase in the "other" category of urban employment and to what extent the declining share of

[12] Note that all our SOE employment data include *xiagang* (laid-off) workers until 1997.

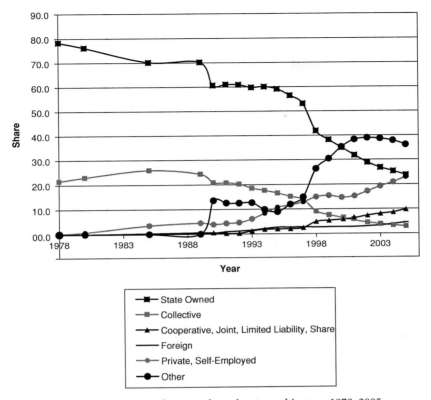

Figure 6.5. Urban employment shares by ownership type, 1978–2005

the state sector seen in official statistics really reflects movement of labor out of the state sector. Because this is a critical issue for understanding labor mobility in China's transitional economy, it is worth examining the data in more detail. Currently, official statistics on employment come from two statistical surveys. One is the Comprehensive Labor Statistics Reporting System (CLSRS), which collects information on urban employment by all independent accounting units. Another is the annual Labor Force Survey (LFS) conducted by NBS using the same sampling frame as the annual Sample Survey of Population Changes. Both surveys in principle cover migrants as well as local residents. The difference between the larger figure for urban employment collected from the LFS and the smaller figure derived from the CLSRS is precisely the "other category" reported in Figure 6.5. Because workers are not reported by their employers, this category by definition includes workers employed informally.

Who are the missing workers? This question is taken up in detail by Cai and Park (2006). The first clue comes from the breakdown of employment according to the LFS (Table 6.11). If one includes agriculture as a type of self-employment, then by 2004, 53 percent of urban employment is in the private sector (48 percent excluding

Table 6.11. *Urban employment by employer type from labor force surveys,*
2001–2004 (percent)

Year	Urban units	TVEs	Agriculture	Private- sector employee	Private employer (*geti*)	Self- employed	Others	TOTAL
2001	49.2	3.7	12.6	12.0	6.1	13.6	2.8	100.0
2002	44.1	3.7	17.2	14.1	6.2	12.8	1.8	100.0
2003	44.0	3.8	15.0	15.5	6.5	13.3	2.0	100.0
2004	40.2	3.7	14.0	18.8	7.1	13.4	2.9	100.0

Source: NBS annual LFS; Labor Statistical Yearbooks (various years).

agriculture from urban employment), compared with just 21 percent in the private sector according to the CLSRS. Thus, many of the missing workers are working in the unregulated private sector. Second, analysis of the 2000 census data finds that there is a correlation of 0.5 between the number of missing workers in a sector and the share of workers who are migrants in that sector, so migrants appear more likely to be "missing." Third, analysis of a 2002 MOL survey in sixty-six cities finds that about 22 percent of those working in the state or government sectors are employed on an informal basis (no labor contract, employed on an hourly basis, etc.). It has been common for laid-off workers to be hired by their former employers or other firms or government agencies on an informal basis. Overall, these results suggest that to a much greater extent than is commonly understood, in recent years, much of the urban labor market has become informal and private in nature.

Next, we look at evidence that workers are mobile between the state and nonstate sector. There is limited direct evidence on the voluntary movement of labor across ownership sectors. In many cases, the changing ownership shares described in Figure 6.5 reflects changing ownership status of firms rather than movement of workers across firms. The CULS finds that from 1996 to 2001, only 26 percent of male job separations and 20 percent of female job separations were voluntary, suggesting that significant barriers remain to labor mobility across jobs (Giles, Park, and Cai, 2006b). Knight and Yueh (2004) study the job mobility of workers in thirteen Chinese cities and find very low mobility overall, with 78 percent of respondents having had only one job and only 6 percent reporting three or more jobs. They do find evidence that mobility is increasing over time.

A second question is whether those separated involuntarily from their previous jobs found new opportunities in the nonstate sector. Using the CULS data, Table 6.12 displays a transition matrix with ownership sector of previous job on the vertical axis and ownership sector of new job on the horizontal axis. Of the 944 workers who left state-sector jobs, 64.5 percent were still out of work in November 2001. Of the 35.5 percent who found new employment, 8.5 percent, or less than one-fourth of reemployed workers, found work in SOEs, 7.0 percent found jobs

Table 6.12. *Mobility across ownership sectors among job changers (January 1996 to November 2001)*

	Number of job separations (percent employed in sector)	New sector (as a percent of separations from previous sector)							Still out of work in November 2001
		Government or party	Wholly SOE	Majority SOE	Collective enterprise	Foreign-invested enterprise	Individual or private enterprise	Other	
Previous sector									
Government or party	68 (30)	26.5	4.4	4.4	10.3	2.9	8.8	1.5	41.2
Wholly SOE	944 (50)	1.8	8.5	1.2	7.0	1.8	14.1	1.2	64.5
Majority SOE	247 (51)	0.8	2.0	11.7	6.9	2.4	14.2	0.4	61.5
Collective enterprise	673 (45)	1.3	1.2	0.4	14.7	1.3	16.9	1.8	62.3
Foreign-invested enterprise	66 (71)	0.0	4.5	0.0	6.1	33.3	16.7	0.0	39.4
Individual or private enterprise	427 (72)	0.9	3.5	0.9	4.7	1.9	41.2	0.9	45.9
Other	45 (34)	0.0	0.0	4.4	4.4	0.0	17.8	20.0	53.3
TOTAL	2,470 (50)	2.0	4.6	2.1	8.7	2.6	19.6	1.5	58.9

Source: Giles, Park, and Cai (2006a).

in collective enterprises, and 14.2 percent of former SOE employees (about 40 percent of the employees who found new jobs) found their new job in the private sector. Similar transitions characterized workers leaving the majority state-owned and collective sectors.

We next examine earnings differentials among ownership sectors. Using household survey data from six provinces in 1996, Zhao (2002) found that given worker characteristics, SOEs paid higher wages than urban collectives, but less than domestic private enterprises and foreign-funded enterprises. But after accounting for employee benefits (pension, health care, and housing), she concluded that state-sector workers earned significantly more than workers in urban collective and domestic private enterprises. Reflecting the legacy of egalitarian compensation in the state sector, unskilled workers in foreign-invested enterprises earned significantly less than those in the state sector, while skilled workers earned more. Shen (2002) analyzes urban household data from five provinces in the late 1990s, and, holding constant individual characteristics (education, work experience, and gender), industries, occupations, and region of residence, found large wage gaps between SOEs and other sectors. The results broadly confirm the patterns in administratively reported wage data (Figure 6.1) as well as Zhao's analysis. UCEs remain the lowest paid sector, and the differences between SOEs and UCEs widened. At the same time, the wage difference between SOEs and mixed ownership forms narrowed, and the wage difference between SOEs and private enterprises remained relatively constant.

Appleton, Song, and Xia (2005) examine four waves of China Household Income Project urban surveys and find that comparing the effects of ownership type in 1999 and 2002 with that in 1988 and 1995, SOE wage premiums held steady relative to collective enterprises, declined relative to private ownership, and fell increasingly behind foreign enterprises. Unfortunately, due to lack of data, these comparisons ignore employee benefits, which during the late 1990s period of restructuring were provided unevenly and incompletely, especially in nonstate enterprises. Cai and Du (2004) find that sectors with a large state-sector share have increasingly higher manufacturing wages relative to other sectors during the 1990s, after controlling for regional wage differences. Overall, there is mixed evidence on the wage premiums enjoyed by SOE workers after the period of economic restructuring, but it does seem evident that SOEs continue to provide better wages and benefits than nonstate enterprises.

Next, we look at changes in the returns to schooling within different ownership sectors, using the annual urban household survey data from 1988 to 2001 (Table 6.13). Because the sample size for the nonpublic sector is very small in the earlier years, rather than running separate sets of regressions, we interact the schooling variable with ownership dummies. We find that the returns to education have been consistently higher for nonpublic enterprises. In contrast, the returns to education within the state sector started low, but rose steadily from 3.0 percent in 1988 to 9.0 percent in 2001. For urban collectives, the rates of return increased

Table 6.13. *Returns to schooling by ownership, 1988–2001*

Year	State sector	Urban collective enterprises	Nonpublic enterprises	Coefficient of variation of returns
1988	3.0	4.2	7.3	0.46
1989	3.7	5.0	9.4	0.50
1990	3.6	4.7	8.0	0.42
1991	3.7	3.4	7.8	0.49
1992	4.1	2.8	9.0	0.62
1993	4.2	3.7	10.6	0.62
1994	5.9	6.1	11.8	0.42
1995	5.5	6.5	9.8	0.31
1996	5.7	5.5	11.0	0.42
1997	5.7	4.8	10.0	0.41
1998	7.0	6.7	11.0	0.29
1999	8.9	8.4	11.3	0.16
2000	8.6	8.7	13.2	0.26
2001	9.0	7.3	10.0	0.16

Note: Returns are percent increase in wage for each additional year of schooling, based on annual OLS regressions of log earnings on years of schooling, potential experience, potential experience squared, a sex dummy variable, provincial dummy variables, dummy variables for ownership groups, and ownership dummies interacted with years of schooling.

Source: Zhang et al. (2005).

from 4.2 percent in 1988 to 8.7 percent in 2000, falling to 7.3 percent in 2001. Thus, the state sector lagged behind the nonstate sector but narrowed the gap over time. The coefficient of variation of the returns to schooling across the three ownership sectors falls from a high of 0.62 in 1992 to just 0.16 in 2001 (Zhang et al., 2005). Dong and Bowles (2002) also find no differences in the returns to education across ownership types when examining 1998 firm survey data from Dalian and Xiamen. These results suggest that competition from nonstate firms prodded SOEs toward reforming their wage setting in ways that increasingly reward productivity differences.

CONCLUSION

Since economic reforms began, China's evolving labor market has played a fundamental role in China's economic development strategy. Socialist commitments to the urban labor force put political constraints on reform, but over time, often with lurches and fits, the labor market continued to develop in step with China's extraordinarily rapid economic ascent. And yet in many respects, reform of the labor market remains incomplete. In nearly all our assessments of the performance of the labor market, we found evidence of rapid change and progress combined with important remaining barriers.

China endured a painful period of economic restructuring in the late 1990s, which led to high rates of unemployment and declines in labor force participation. The good news is that since 2002, the unemployment rate has fallen to much more manageable levels. However, many displaced workers never found new jobs or were forced to accept relatively low wages. New social insurance systems were established, but have incomplete coverage, allowing many dislocated workers and their families to fall through the cracks. Unemployment subsidies may also have created work disincentives for men. Industrial and financial policies have supported capital-intensive industry, reducing the demand for labor, especially low-skilled workers. The ability of firms to adjust employment in response to changes in the economic environment improved significantly in the 1990s, but evidence suggests that many state-sector firms are still overmanned and overall job mobility remains low.

Real wages have increased continuously despite the emergence of unemployment, and wages increasingly reward productivity, as seen in the dramatic increase in the returns to education. At the same time, the gender gap, including the unexplained component, has widened. Moreover, wage liberalization has increased inequality, creating new policy challenges.

Migration flows have increased substantially over time, helping to integrate labor markets in rural and urban areas and across regions. Policy barriers to labor mobility have receded. Increasing migration from poorer western regions has been especially promising, and there is evidence (albeit mixed) that regional earnings disparities are starting to narrow and that the returns to education across regions have converged over time. However, rural–urban income gaps continue to widen; until recently, investment has been slow to flow to poorer, interior regions; and the *hukou* system burdens migrants, who still face unequal treatment that limits their access to jobs, education, adequate housing, social insurance, and social assistance programs in China's cities.

Ownership reform has reduced the share of workers employed in the state sector, and market reforms have given SOEs an increasingly commercial orientation. However, SOEs still provide higher wages and benefits to workers than other types of employers (except foreign enterprises), so that voluntary mobility out of state-sector employment remains low, especially in the lower-skill brackets. At the same time, significant informalization of the urban labor market, characterized by lack of formal labor contracts and few nonwage benefits, has made labor allocation increasingly market oriented but has increased the vulnerability of workers who lack social insurance coverage.

Some of the key challenges that remain include the following: (1) developing an accurate and timely labor statistical information system to report on key indicators, such as unemployment; (2) avoiding industrial, financial, and wage policies which push up the wage/rental ratio; (3) providing an effective safety net for dislocated workers; (4) developing effective social insurance programs that have broad coverage, avoid work disincentives, and create portable benefits; (5) integrating migrants into urban areas by equalizing access to education and gradually extending coverage by social assistance and social insurance programs; and (6) dismantling the *hukou* system.

References

Appleton, Simon, John Knight, Lina Song, and Qingjie Xia. 2002. "Labor Retrenchment in China: Determinants and Consequences." *China Economic Review*. 13, pp. 252–275.

Appleton, Simon, Lina Song, and Qingjie Xia. 2005. "Has China Crossed the River?: The Evolution of Wage Structure in Urban China during Reform and Retrenchment." *Journal of Comparative Economics*. 33, pp. 644–663.

Beijing Municipal Bureau of Labor, 1992. *Laodong zhengce fagui wenjian xuanbian* [Selection of Documents of Labor Policies and Regulations]. Beijing: Beijing laodong baohu ju.

Benjamin, Dwayne, Loren Brandt, and Terence Yuen. 2003. *Employment Dynamics in State Owned Enterprises during Economic Transition*. Unpublished manuscript.

Bian, Yanjie. 1994. *Work and Inequality in Urban China*. Albany: State University of New York Press.

Bodmer, Frank. 2002. "The Effect of Reforms on Employment Flexibility in Chinese SOEs, 1980–94." *Economics of Transition*. 10(3), pp. 637–658.

Brandt, Loren. 1989. *Commercialization and Agricultural Development: Central and Eastern China, 1870–1937*. Cambridge and New York: Cambridge University Press.

Brandt, Loren, and Carsten Holz. 2006. "Spatial Price Differences in China: Estimates and Implications." *Economic Development and Cultural Change*. 55(1), pp. 43–86.

Cai, Fang and Albert Park. 2006. *The Informalization of the Chinese Labor Market*. Unpublished manuscript.

Cai, Fang and Justin Yifu Lin. 2003. *Zhongguo jingji: gaige yu fazhan* [The Chinese Economy: Reform and Development]. Beijing: Zhongguo caizheng jingji chubanshe.

Cai, Fang and Yang Du. 2004. "Labour Market Integration: Evidence from Wage Convergence in Manufacturing," in *China: Is Rapid Growth Sustainable?* Ross Garnaut and Ligang Song, eds. Canberra: Asia Pacific Press, pp. 137–156.

Cai Fang, Du Yang, and Wang Meiyan, 2001. "Household Registration System and Employment Protection," *Jingji yanjiu* [Journal of Economic Research]. 12, pp. 41–50.

Cao, Yuanzheng, Yingyi Qian, and Barry Weingast. 1999. "From Federalism, Chinese Style, to Privatization, Chinese Style." *Economics of Transition*. 7(1), pp. 103–131.

Chan, Anita. 2001. *China's Workers under Assault: Exploitation and Abuse in a Globalizing Economy*. Armonk: ME Sharpe.

Chan, Kam Wing. 2006. "Internal Migration and Rural Migrant Labor: Trends, Geography, and Policies," in *The Labor of Reform in China*. Mary Gallagher, Ching Kwan Lee, and Albert Park, eds. Unpublished manuscript.

Chan, Kam Wing and Li Zhang. 1999. "The *Hukou* System and Rural–Urban Migration in China: Processes and Changes." *The China Quarterly*. 160, pp. 818–855.

China Statistical Yearbook (various years). Beijing: Zhongguo tongji chubanshe.

Cook, Sarah. 1999. "Surplus Labor and Productivity in Chinese Agriculture: Evidence from Household Survey Data." *The Journal of Development Studies*. 35(3), pp. 16–44.

Deaton, Angus. 1997. *The Analysis of Household Surveys: A Microeconomic Approach to Development Policy*. Baltimore: Johns Hopkins University Press.

deBrauw, Alan and John Giles. 2006. "Migrant Opportunity and the Educational Attainment of Youth in Rural China." IZA Discussion Paper 2326.

deBrauw, Alan and Scott Rozelle. 2007. "Returns to Education in Rural China," in *Education and Reform in China*. Emily Hannum and Albert Park, eds. London: Routledge, pp. 207–223.

deBrauw, Alan, Jikun Huang, Scott Rozelle, Linxiu Zhang, and Yigang Zhang. 2002. "The Evolution of China's Rural Labor Markets during the Reforms." *Journal of Comparative Economics*. 30(2), pp. 329–353.

Dong, Xiao-yuan. 2005. "Wage Inequality and between-Firm Wage Dispersion in the 1990s: A Comparison of Rural and Urban Enterprises in China." *Journal of Comparative Economics*. 33, pp. 664–687.

Dong, Xiao-yuan and Paul Bowles. 2002. "Segmentation and Discrimination in China's Emerging Industrial Labor Market." *China Economic Review*. 13, pp. 170–196.

Dong, Xiao-yuan and Louis Putterman. 2000. "Pre-Reform Industry and State Monopsony in China." *Journal of Comparative Economics*. 28, pp. 32–60.

Dong, Xiao-yuan and Louis Putterman. 2001. "The Emergence of Labor Redundancy in China's State Industry: Findings from a 1980–1994 Data Panel." *Comparative Economic Studies*. 43(2), pp. 111–128.

Dong, Xiao-yuan and Louis Putterman. 2003. "Soft Budget Constraints, Social Burdens, and Labor Redundancy in China's State Industry." *Journal of Comparative Economics*. 3(1), pp. 110–133.

Dong, Xiao-yuan and Colin Lixin Xu. 2005. "Labor Restructuring in China's Industrial Sector: Magnitude, Patterns, and Underlying Causes." Unpublished manuscript.

Du, Yang, Albert Park, and Sangui Wang. 2005. "Migration and Rural Poverty in China." *Journal of Comparative Economics*. 33, pp. 688–709.

Faure, David. 1989. *The Rural Economy of Pre-Liberation China: Trade Expansion and Peasant Livelihood in Jiangsu and Guangdong, 1870–1937*. Hong Kong: Hong Kong University Press.

Fleisher, Belton M. and Xiaojun Wang. 2004. "Skill Differentials, Returns to Schooling, and Market Segmentation in a Transition Economy: The Case of Mainland China." *Journal of Development Economics*. 73(1), pp. 315–328.

Giles, John. 2006. "Is Life More Risky in the Open? Household Risk-Coping and the Opening of China's Labor Markets." *Journal of Development Economics*. 81(1), pp. 25–60.

Giles, John, Albert Park, and Fang Cai. 2006a. "How Has Economic Restructuring Affected China's Urban Workers?" *The China Quarterly*. 177, pp. 61–95.

Giles, John, Albert Park, and Fang Cai. 2006b. "Reemployment of Dislocated Workers in Urban China: The Roles of Information and Incentives." *Journal of Comparative Economics*. 34(3), pp. 582–607.

Giles, John, Albert Park, and Juwei Zhang. 2005. "What Is China's True Unemployment Rate?" *China Economic Review*. 16, pp. 149–170.

Gottschang, Thomas. 1987. "Economic Change, Disasters, and Migration: The Historical Case of Manchuria." *Economic Development and Cultural Change*. 35(3), pp. 461–490.

Groves, Theodore, Yongmiao Hong, John McMillan, and Barry Naughton. 1994. "Autonomy and Incentives in Chinese State Enterprises." *Quarterly Journal of Economics*. 109(1), pp. 185–209.

Guang, Lei and Lu Zheng. 2005. "Migration as the Second-Best Option: Local Power and Off-farm Employment." *The China Quarterly*. 181, pp. 22–45.

Guo Kesha, 1999. "Aggregate Demand or Structural Problems? How Distorted Economic Structure Constrains China's Economic Growth," *Jingji yanjiu* [Economic Research]. 9, pp. 15–21.

Gustafsson, Bjorn and Shi Li. 2000. "Economic Transformation and the Gender Earnings Gap in Urban China." *Journal of Population Economics.* 13, pp. 305–329.

Ho, Virginia. 2006. "Labor Law in China's Reform Era: The Evolving Legal Framework for Labor Rights," in *The Labor of Reform in China.* Mary Gallagher, Ching Kwan Lee, and Albert Park, eds. Unpublished edited volume.

Hu, Yifan, Sonja Opper, and Sonia Wong. 2006. "Political Economy of Labor Retrenchment: Evidence Based on China's State-Owned Enterprises." *China Economic Review.* 17, pp. 281–299.

Hughes, James and Margaret Maurer-Fazio. 2002. "Effects of Marriage, Education, and Occupation on the Female/Male Wage Gap in China." *Pacific Economic Review.* 7, pp. 137–156.

Jian, Tianlun, Jeffrey Sachs, and Andrew Warner. 1996. "Trends in Regional Inequality in China." *China Economic Review.* 7(1), pp. 1–21.

Johnson, D. Gale. 2001. *Have the Urban–Rural Disparities Increased Since 1997 in China?* Unpublished manuscript.

Johnson, D. Gale. 2003. "Provincial Migration in China in the 1990s." *China Economic Review.* 14, pp. 22–31.

Juhn, Chinhui, Kevin Murphy, and Brooks Pierce. 1993. "Wage Inequality and the Rise in Returns to Skill." *Journal of Political Economy.* 101(3), pp. 410–442.

Kletzer, Lori. 1998. "Job Displacement." *Journal of Economic Perspectives.* 12(1), pp. 115–136.

Knight, John and Shi Li. 2005. "Wages, Firm Profitability and Labor Market Segmentation in Urban China." *China Economic Review.* 16(3), pp. 205–228.

Knight, John and Shi Li. 2006. "Unemployment Duration and Earnings of Re-Employed Workers in Urban China." *China Economic Review.* 17, pp. 103–119.

Knight, John and Lina Song. 1993. "Why Urban Wages Differ in China." in *The Distribution of Income in China.* Keith Griffin and Renwei Zhao, eds. St. Martin's Press.

Knight, John and Lina Song. 1999. "Employment Constraints and Sub-Optimality in Chinese Enterprises." *Oxford Economic Papers.* 51(2), pp. 284–299.

Knight, John and Lina Song. 2003. "Chinese Peasant Choices: Migration, Rural Industry or Farming." *Oxford Development Studies.* 31, pp. 123–147.

Knight, John and Jinjun Xue. 2006. "How High Is Urban Unemployment in China?" *Journal of Chinese Economic and Business Studies.* 4(2), pp. 91–107.

Knight, John and Linda Yueh. 2004. "Job Mobility of Residents and Migrants in Urban China." *Journal of Comparative Economics.* 32, pp. 637–660.

Labor Statistics Yearbook. Various years. *Zhongguo laodong tongji nianjian* [China Labour Statistical Yearbook]. Beijing: Zhongguo tongji chubanshe.

Lardy, Nicholas. 1998. *China's Unfinished Economic Revolution.* Washington, DC: Brookings Institution.

Lee, Young. 1999. "Wages and Employment in China's SOEs, 1980–1994: Corporatization, Market Development, and Insider Forces." *Journal of Comparative Economics.* 27(4), pp. 702–729.

Li Guo and Colin Lixin Xu, 2001. "State-Owned Enterprises, Labor Redundancy, and Job Creation: The Experience of the Chinese Provinces," *Jingjixue* [China Economic Quarterly]. 1, pp. 97–110.

Li, Shi and Chuliang Luo. 2006. *Re-Estimating the Income Gap between Urban and Rural Households.* Unpublished manuscript.

Li, Shi and Yaohui Zhao. 2003. "The Decline of In-Kind Wage Payments in Urban China." *Journal of Chinese Economics and Business Studies.* 1(2), pp. 245–258.

Lin, Justin, Fang Cai and Zhou Li. 1996. *The China Miracle: Development Strategy and Economic Reform.* Hong Kong: Chinese University of Hong Kong Press.

Lin, Justin, Gewei Wang, and Yaohui Zhao. 2004. "Regional Inequality and Labor Transfers in China." *Economic Development and Cultural Change.* 52(3), pp. 587–603.

Liu Jianjin, 2004. "Rural Labor Employment and Transfer," in *2003–2004 nian Zhongguo jiuye baogao* [China Employment Report 2003–2004]. Rong Mo, ed. Beijing: Zhongguo laodong shehui baozhang chubanshe, pp. 201–222.

Liu, Pak-Wai, Xin Meng, and Junsen Zhang. 2000. "Sectoral Gender Wage Differentials and Discrimination in the Transitional Chinese Economy." *Journal of Population Economics.* 13, pp. 331–352.

Liu Xuejun and Cai Fang., 2004. "Institutional Transition, Technology Choice and Employment." *Zhonguo laodong jingjixue* [China Labor Economics]. 2, pp. 1–24.

Maurer-Fazio, Margaret. 2007. "The Role of Education in Determining Labor Market Outcomes in Urban China," in *Education and Reform in China*. Emily Hannum and Albert Park, eds. London and New York: Routledge, pp. 260–275.

Meng, Xin. 2000. *Labour Market Reform in China.* Cambridge and New York: Cambridge University Press.

Meng, Xin, Robert Gregory, and Youjuan Wang. 2005. "Poverty, Inequality, and Growth in Urban China, 1986–2000." *Journal of Comparative Economics.* 33, pp. 710–729.

Meng, Xin and Paul Miller. 1995. "Occupational Segregation and Its Impact on Gender Wage Discrimination in China's Rural Industrial Sector." *Oxford Economic Papers.* 47, pp. 136–155.

Meng, Xin and Junsen Zhang. 2001. "The Two-Tier Labor Market in Urban China: Occupational Segregation and Wage Differentials between Urban Residents and Rural Migrants in Shanghai." *Journal of Comparative Economics.* 29(3), pp. 485–504.

MOA [Ministry of Agriculture]. 2003. "Analysis of Rural Labor Migration Employment Situation 2003." Production Policy and Rules Department. Internal circulation.

MOA and MOLSS [Ministry of Agriculture and Ministry of Labor and Social Security]. 1998. "China Rural Labor and Migration Situation, 1998." Internal circulation.

MOA and MOLSS [Ministry of Agriculture and Ministry of Labor and Social Security]. 1999. "China Rural Labor and Migration Situation, 1999." Internal circulation.

National Bureau of Statistics. 1988. *Tabulation on the 1987 1 Percent Sampling Population Survey of China.* Beijing: China Statistics Publishing House.

National Bureau of Statistics. 1993. *Tabulation on the 1990 Census of the People's Republic of China.* Beijing: China Statistics Publishing House.

National Bureau of Statistics. 1997. *Tabulation on the 1995 1 Percent Sampling Population Survey of China.* Beijing: China Statistics Publishing House.

National Bureau of Statistics. 2002. *Tabulation on the 2000 Census of the People's Republic of China.* Beijing: China Statistics Publishing House.

Naughton, Barry. 1995. *Growing Out of the Plan.* Cambridge and New York: Cambridge University Press.

Park, Albert. Forthcoming. "Rural–Urban Inequality in China," in Shahid Yusuf and Kaoru Nabeshima, eds. *China Urbanizes.* Washington, DC: World Bank.

Park, Albert, Xiaoqing Song, Junsen Zhang, and Yaohui Zhao. 2006. *Rising Returns to Skill, Labor Market Development, and Rising Wage Inequality in China.* Unpublished manuscript.

Park, Albert, Yaohui Zhao, and Guofang Huang. 2006. *Migrant Workers and Labor Market Segmentation in Urban China.* Unpublished manuscript.

Psacharopoulos, George. 1994. "Returns to Investment in Education: A Global Update." *World Development*. 22, pp. 1325–1344.

Rawski, Thomas G. 1989. *Economic Growth in Prewar China*. Berkeley: University of California Press.

Rawski, Thomas G. 2002. *Recent Developments in China's Labor Economy*. Geneva: Report prepared for International Policy Group, International Labor Office.

Rawski, Thomas G. and Robert W. Mead. 1998. "On the Trail of China's Phantom Farmers." *World Development*. 26(5), pp. 767–781.

Rozelle, Scott, Guo Li, Minggao Shen, Amelia Hughart, and John Giles. 1999. "Leaving China's Farms: Survey Results of New Paths and Remaining Hurdles to Rural Migration." *The China Quarterly*. 158, pp. 367–393.

Rural Household Survey Yearbook. Various years. *Zhongguo nongcun zhuhu diaocha nianjian* [China Yearbook of Rural Household Survey]. Beijing: Zhongguo tongji chubanshe.

Shen, Qi. 2002. "Wage Differentials between State and Non-State Sectors, 1988–1999." MA Thesis, China Center for Economic Research, Peking University.

Sicular, Terry, Ximing Yue, Bjorn Gustafsson, and Shi Li. 2006. "The Urban-Rural Income Gap and Inequality in China." Research Paper 2006/135. Helsinki: United Nations University-World Institute for Development Economics Research.

Solinger, Dorothy. 1999. *Contesting Citizenship in Urban China: Peasant Migrants, the State, and the Logic of the Market*. Berkeley: University of California Press.

Solinger, Dorothy. 2001. "Why We Cannot Count the 'Unemployed.'" *The China Quarterly*. 167, pp. 671–688.

Svejnar, Jan. 1999. "Labor Markets in the Transitional Central and East European Economies," in *Handbook of Labor Economics*, vol. 3. Orley Ashenfelter and David Card, eds. Oxford: Elsevier, pp. 2809–2857.

Walder, Andrew. 1988. *Communist Neo-Traditionalism: Work and Authority in Chinese Industry*. Berkeley: University of California Press.

World Bank. 1997. *China 2020: Sharing Rising Incomes*. Washington, DC: World Bank.

World Bank. Forthcoming. *Rethinking China's Poverty Reduction Agenda: An Assessment of Poverty and Inequality in China*. Washington, DC: World Bank.

Yang, Dennis. 2004. "Education and Allocative Efficiency: Household Income Growth during Rural Reforms in China." *Journal of Development Economics*. 74(1), pp. 137–162.

Yang, Dennis. 2005. "Determinants of Schooling Returns in Transition: Evidence from Chinese Cities." *Journal of Comparative Economics*. 33(2), pp. 244–264.

Yearbook, Annual. *Zhongguo tongji nianjian* [China Statistical Yearbook]. Beijing: China Statistics Press.

Yueh, Linda. 2004. "Wage Reforms in China during the 1990s." *Asian Economic Journal*. 18(2), pp. 149–164.

Zhang Hongyu. 2005. "Research Report on Rural Labor Migration and Employment," in *China's Transitional Labor Market*. Cai Fang, ed. Beijing: Zhongguo renkou chubanshe, pp. 42–54.

Zhang, Junsen, Jun Han, Pak-Wai Liu, and Yaohui Zhao. Forthcoming. "What Has Happened to the Gender Wage Differential in Urban China during 1988–2001?" *Industrial and Labor Relations Review*.

Zhang, Junsen and Yaohui Zhao. 2007. "Rising Returns to Schooling in Urban China," in *Education and Reform in China*. Emily Hannum and Albert Park, eds. London: Routledge, pp. 248–259.

Zhang, Junsen, Yaohui Zhao, Albert Park, and Xiaoqing Song. 2005. "Economic Returns to Schooling in Urban China, 1988 to 2001." *Journal of Comparative Economics*. 33, pp. 730–752.

Zhang, Juwei. 2003. *Urban Xiagang, Unemployment and Social Support Policies: A Literature Review of Labor Market Policies in Transitional China*. Report to the World Bank. Washington, DC: World Bank.

Zhao, Yaohui. 1997. "Labor Migration and Returns to Rural Education in China." *American Journal of Agricultural Economics*. 79, pp. 1278–1287.

Zhao, Yaohui. 1999a. "Leaving the Countryside: Rural-to-Urban Migration Decisions in China." *American Economic Review*. 89(2), pp. 281–286.

Zhao, Yaohui. 1999b. "Migration and Earnings Differences: The Case of Rural China." *Economic Development and Cultural Change*. 47, pp. 767–782.

Zhao, Yaohui. 2002. "Earnings Differentials between State and Non-State Enterprises in Urban China." *Pacific Economic Review*. 7(1), pp. 181–197.

Zhao, Yaohui and Jianguo Xu. 2002. "China's Urban Pension System: Reforms and Problems." *The Cato Journal*. 21(3), pp. 395–414.

Zhu, Nong. 2002. "The Impacts of Income Gaps on Migration Decisions in China." *China Economic Review*. 13, pp. 213–230.

SEVEN

Education in the Reform Era

Emily Hannum, Jere Behrman, Meiyan Wang, and Jihong Liu

INTRODUCTION

Under China's market reforms of the past quarter century, the process of becoming educated has changed in dramatic ways. China's new wealth and new inequalities are part of the story. However, educational opportunities and attainment are also affected by changes in educational policy. Since the end of the Cultural Revolution in the late 1970s, leaders have moved educational policies away from a radical social-ist agenda. Three particularly important changes have occurred. First, reform-era educational policies have sought to improve quality to make schooling better serve the needs of the labor market, stimulate the economy, and promote China's global competitiveness. Second, reform-era educational policies have placed a new prior-ity on efficient use of resources, including private resources, to support education. Third, reform-era educational policies display a new tolerance for disparities within the system in pursuit of quality and efficiency, but this trend has been tempered recently by significant efforts to guarantee basic access and quality in rural areas.

To illustrate these points, this chapter begins by outlining the state of education prior to market transition, under the radical educational policies of the Cultural Revolution. Next, we discuss key reform-era changes in the provision of educa-tion, including educational policy, finance, and quality. Finally, we consider the "outcomes" of these shifts, in the form of indicators of educational attainment, participation, and inequality.

Most of our evidence about school provision and educational finance comes from published governmental data. To investigate participation and attainment, we employ descriptive tables and figures derived from unit-record data from a 0.95 per thousand microsample from the 2000 China population census and the 1989 and 2000 waves of the China Health and Nutrition Survey (CHNS). We also refer to secondary sources that have analyzed census data and population surveys con-ducted through the 1980s and 1990s. We conclude with a discussion of implications of reform-era educational patterns for larger questions of socioeconomic change and inequality.

BACKDROP: EDUCATION DURING THE CULTURAL REVOLUTION

While many of the educational shifts that have accompanied market reforms in China have global parallels, the starting point was unusual. For over a decade prior to market reforms, China lived through the "Great Proletarian Cultural Revolution," a far-reaching and chaotic social movement that brought a radical leftist political agenda to the forefront in politics and education. In 1966, Mao Zedong proclaimed the start of a new educational era in which political recommendation and class background became the primary means of determining progress through the education system (Unger, 1984).

When schools reopened after the initial chaotic years, the ideological agenda of eliminating class differences, whether urban–rural, worker–peasant, or intellectual–manual, dominated the classroom and the curriculum (Thomas, 1986; Sun and Johnson, 1990). Labor and political loyalty were valued over academic achievement, and the link between education and occupational attainment was removed (Unger, 1984). Urban students were sent to the countryside for reeducation (Tsang, 2000).

In higher education, there were dramatic disruptions: a discontinuation of the national examination system for admissions, complete stoppage of admissions of undergraduates for six years and graduate students for twelve years from the start of the Cultural Revolution, admission of peasant and working-class students to "attend, manage, and reform universities," and a 1971 plan to consolidate, close, and reconstruct 106 of 417 institutions of higher education (Tsang, 2000, table 1). The Cultural Revolution is widely viewed as a disaster for higher education in general and for science and technology training in particular (e.g., see Beijing University and Zhongshan University, 2005). Few students traveled abroad during the Cultural Revolution. According to a 1994 report, sending students abroad was halted in the initial chaotic years. Study abroad resumed in 1972, but by 1976, China had sent only 1,629 students to study in forty-nine countries, mainly to study foreign languages (Beijing University and Zhongshan University, 2005, p. 10).

The structure of primary and secondary education was streamlined. Tracking systems were abolished, as were key-point magnet schools, vocational education, and exam-based progressions (Rosen, 1984). The educational system was unified so that, in principle, all students studied the same ten-year curriculum in a 5–3–2 structure (Thogersen, 1990, p. 27). There are few empirical studies of curriculum during the Cultural Revolution, but it was certainly highly ideological. For example, one scholar who studied the contents of primary language textbooks in the early 1970s concluded that "texts devoted their efforts almost exclusively to inculcating in the young in the right political attitudes and outlook, even to the extent of almost excluding the pedagogical function of a language text" (Kwong, 1985, p. 207). Vocational and technical schools were shut down, and, for the first six years, so were secondary teacher training schools (Tsang, 2000).

There is little empirical scholarship on educational finance during the Cultural Revolution. However, evidence from policy documents indicates that much of school finance in China during the Cultural Revolution relied on local community support for *minban*, or people-managed, teachers and schools, which are distinct from *gongban*, or state-managed, teachers and schools. As part of this process, many rural primary teachers were compensated with "work points" instead of salaries and reclassified as rural residents (Tsang, 2000). *Minban* education grew rapidly during the Cultural Revolution, first in the countryside and then in urban areas, as educational authorities ceded authority over state-managed elementary schools to local production teams or brigades, communes, factories, business enterprises, neighborhood revolutionary committees, and so on (Tsang, 2000; Wang, 2002). During this period, *minban* teachers were paid in grain rations and supplementary cash subsidies by work units based on earned work points, while state teachers received government salaries.

Importantly, under this arrangement, it appears that direct costs of schooling were rarely borne by families, even in rural communities. Dongping Han's study of Jimo County in Shandong Province, the single available empirical study of school finance during the Cultural Revolution, showed that virtually every rural child in the county was able to attend primary school at no cost during the latter years of the Cultural Revolution (Han, 2001).

Some of the impacts of the Cultural Revolution on educational inequality have been traced empirically. For example, an essential goal of the Cultural Revolution was to undercut differences between the peasantry and the remainder of the population, and, at least quantitatively, this appears to have happened. While what passed for education during the Cultural Revolution is widely criticized,[1] new policies were effective in promoting educational access among the rural population. For example, the share of teachers and students in rural areas above the elementary level jumped in the 1970s, before declining subsequently (Hannum, 1999a). Before the Cultural Revolution, in the 1960s, there was about one rural junior high school entrant for every four rural primary school graduates. In contrast, this progression ratio was about one to one in cities and towns. Data through the 1970s, during the Cultural Revolution, show that the ratio of rural junior high school entrants to primary school graduates hovered between 0.78 and 0.92. Census data also show dramatic increases in access to education for rural cohorts during the Cultural Revolution.

Similarly, cross-cohort analyses of census and survey data, as well as published statistics from the Ministry of Education, suggest that the Cultural Revolution era saw rapid narrowing of gender gaps in primary and secondary education (Hannum and Xie, 1994; Hannum, 2005). There is no empirical research on ethnic disparities during the Cultural Revolution, although a cohort comparison approach such as

---

[1] See Han (2001) for a dissent from common wisdom on education during the Cultural Revolution.

that used to study gender disparities would be feasible with census data from the post-Cultural Revolution era.

A few studies have addressed socioeconomic disparities in educational attainment during the Cultural Revolution. For data reasons, much of what is available focuses, in one way or another, on urban populations. This limitation is unfortunate, as these studies cannot reveal patterns or trends in disadvantage associated with rural poverty. The rural poor were explicitly targeted by the Cultural Revolution educational agenda and are unlikely to be well represented by the poorer urban residents that the authors of these studies were able to include. In addition, extreme data limitations oblige authors to resort to creative approaches to reconstruct information for the years following the Cultural Revolution.

One key study used national 1982 census data on the nonfarm population of coresident fathers and sons (Deng and Treiman, 1997). Coresidence in the same households allowed an investigation of the association between father's socioeconomic status and son's educational attainment across cohorts that would have moved through the school system at different times. Results showed that the advantage of coming from an educated family or an intelligentsia or cadre family was drastically reduced during the Cultural Revolution, but reappeared soon thereafter.

Another study modeled entry into different levels of schooling using retrospective life-history reports on the timing of educational experiences of a representative survey of residents of twenty cities in 1993–1994 (Zhou, Moen, and Tuma, 1998). Zhou and his colleagues found that coming from an "exploiting-class" or middle-class background had no effect on the probability of entering high school or college during the Cultural Revolution, but significant positive effects in the preceding and subsequent periods. The effects of father's education on entry into these levels of education also varied significantly across historical periods and were stronger in the models for the post-Cultural Revolution period than during the Cultural Revolution.

These studies, using different perspectives, all suggest at least a short-term flattening of rural–urban, gender, and, among more urban populations, socioeconomic disparities in educational access during the Cultural Revolution.[2] These results are consistent with the overarching educational goal of the Cultural Revolution era: to promote a radical socialist agenda of eradicating social differences.

---

[2] See Meng and Gregory (2002) for an opposing view. In a novel approach that employs data from Shanghai, Meng, and Gregory use coefficients from models of tertiary-degree attainment estimated on cohorts not affected by the Cultural Revolution to obtain predicted rates of degree attainment for cohorts that were affected by the Cultural Revolution. They then compare the result to the observed rates of degree attainment for the Cultural Revolution cohorts. The authors conclude that the largest negative impact of the Cultural Revolution was experienced by children with parents of lower educational achievement and lower occupational status.

EDUCATIONAL PROVISION UNDER MARKET REFORMS: POLICIES,
FINANCE, AND QUALITY

Educational Policies

From the late 1970s, a different agenda guided educational policy, as leaders sought to promote market reforms and economic modernization. In March 1978, Deng Xiaoping delivered the opening address at a National Symposium on Science and Technology in Beijing (Beijing University and Zhongshan University, 2005). He reiterated the importance of science and technology for economic modernization and stated that "the basis for training science and technology talent rests in education" (p. 11; see also Shen, 1994).

Policy reforms revolved around perceptions that educational quality was a serious problem at all levels, vocational and technical training was insufficient, and central administration of education was too rigid (Lewin et al., 1994, p. 19). Through reforms, leaders sought to align the educational system with the newly emerging marketization of the economy (Hawkins, 2000).[3] Reforms in the mid-1980s set standards for compulsory education and emphasized linking education to economic reforms, increasing vocational and technical education, decentralizing finance and management, and increasing the number and quality of teachers (Ministry of Education, 1986; Hawkins, 2000).

Many changes occurred in the early reform years. There was an initial attempt to revocationalize education, resumption of the national examination for university entry, decentralization of educational administration and finance, and a greater emphasis on educational quality at all levels and developing key educational institutions at various levels (Tsang, 2000, table 1). Shutdowns of low-quality rural junior secondary schools occurred as part of the upgrade in the early reform years. Higher education, shut down for six years at the start of the Cultural Revolution, was reinvigorated, in recognition of its critical role in supplying the high-level personnel and scientific expertise needed for national development (Tsang, 2000).

Decentralization of administration occurred. While the central government ran and financed certain high-quality institutions of higher education, provincial, county, township, and village governments typically took responsibility for schools at the tertiary, upper secondary, lower secondary, and primary levels (Tsang, 2000, p. 13). In 2001, a county-based financial management system was implemented in which the management of teachers' salaries was shifted from village to county governments, and the central government increased transfer payments for compulsory education in western and central China (Mei and Wang, 2006).

Upgrading of teachers' skills was a priority in the drive to improve the quality of teaching and learning (Ministry of Education, 1993; Shen, 1994). Teaching has

---

[3] Compulsory education was first brought out in the 1985 reforms and passed into law in 1986 (Shen, 1994).

moved away from a focus on egalitarianism and class struggle and back toward more traditional pedagogical goals. For example, Kwong (1985) concludes from her analysis of primary school language texts that the revolutionary ideology present in these materials in the early 1970s had yielded, by the late 1970s, to the pragmatic goal of promoting a solid knowledge base (Kwong, 1985, p. 207).

Most recently, the attention of policy makers has turned to molding the educational system to stimulate critical thinking and creativity perceived to be necessary for the new economy. Learner-centered teaching approaches and the so-called quality education (*suzhi jiaoyu*) reforms are intended to develop the abilities of the whole child and stimulate critical learning (Tsang, 2000). Additional reforms designed to develop locally relevant curricula are also under way.

Finally, while quality rose in importance as a policy priority after the Cultural Revolution, ongoing concerns with inequality in the school system are evident in policy documents and proclamations. Most importantly, although implementation was tied to regional economic development levels, a set of reforms set out in 1985 and codified in 1986 designated nine years of education, six years of primary school and three years of lower secondary school, as compulsory for all children (Ministry of Education, 1986; Hawkins, 2000).

The Education Law of 1995 affirmed a governmental commitment to equality of educational opportunity regardless of nationality, race, sex, occupation, property conditions, or religious belief (Ministry of Education, 1995). The 1999 Action Plan for Revitalizing Education in the twenty-first century confirmed a commitment to implementing compulsory education across the country (Ministry of Education, 1999). A more recent campaign to pour development money into the western interior part of the country, where poverty is concentrated, took education as an important element (State Council, 2000). Most recently, in the early 2000s, significant new policy efforts have emerged to support access to basic education in the countryside. We discuss these initiatives in the conclusion.

Finance

Some of the most important changes in educational opportunity in the reform era can be traced to policies surrounding school finance. Table 7.1 shows that the share of educational outlays in total government expenditures rose from 18.24 percent in 1991 to a peak of 21.06 percent in 1996 and declined to 15.62 percent by 2003. However, total government expenditures themselves rose from just under 16 percent of GDP in 1991 to 21 percent of GDP in 2003. Tsang's research (2000) shows that total educational expenditures increased from 34.63 billion yuan in 1986 to 90.68 billion yuan in 1997 in 1986 constant prices, translating to an average annual growth rate of 9.1 percent for this period (Tsang, 2000, p. 14).

Diversification of finance contributed to the increase in total expenditures on education. Decentralization of educational administration and finance under the 1985 educational reforms was part of a larger reform of public finance dating

Table 7.1. *Indicators of overall government investment
in education, 1991–2003*

Year	Government appropriation for education/total government expenditure	Total government expenditure/gross domestic product
1991	18.24	15.67
1992	19.47	14.05
1993	18.69	13.40
1994	20.28	12.39
1995	20.69	11.67
1996	21.06	11.69
1997	20.17	12.40
1998	18.82	13.78
1999	17.34	16.07
2000	16.13	17.76
2001	16.17	19.42
2002	15.83	20.97
2003	15.62	21.00

Note: Values are in percent.
Source: Our calculations using current yuan; data from National
Bureau of Statistics (various years).

from the end of the 1970s, which sought to mobilize new resources for education (Hawkins, 2000; Tsang, 2000).

The objective of mobilizing new resources appears to have been achieved. Tsang (2000, p. 14) shows that in 1986 constant prices, governmental budgeted funds for education increased from 26.50 billion yuan in 1986 to 48.63 billion yuan in 1997, translating to an average annual real growth rate of 5.7 percent. In the same period, extrabudgetary funds grew much faster, from 8.13 billion yuan in 1986 to 40.25 billion yuan in 1997, translating to an average annual real growth rate of 15.7 percent. Table 7.2 shows selected statistics on educational finance for the years 1991–2004. Consistent with the rising importance of funding outside of the government's control, columns 1 and 2 of Table 7.2 show that the growth rate of total educational funds was higher than the growth rate of government appropriations for education.

Moreover, the share of total education funds coming from government appropriations for education dropped precipitously from 84.46 percent in 1991 to 61.66 percent in 2004. Among the nonbudgetary sources of funds, tuition and fees alone grew from 4.42 percent of educational expenditures in 1991 to 18.59 percent by 2004. Consistent with this picture, data given in Table 7.3 on revenues from tuition and miscellaneous fees by level of school shows dramatic year-on-year increases between 1997 and 2004. These nongovernment resources are important

Table 7.2. *Selected statistics on educational finance, 1991–2004*

Year	Growth rate of spending on education from		Percent of total expenditures on education from					
	All sources (%)	Government appropriation (%)	Government appropriation for education	Budgetary funds	Funds of social organizations and citizens for running schools	Donations and fund-raising for running schools	Tuition and miscellaneous fees	Other educational funds
1991			84.46	62.85		8.59	4.42	2.53
1992	11.41	10.87	84.05	62.13		8.03	5.07	2.85
1993	6.58	3.81	81.87	60.80	0.31	6.62	8.22	2.97
1994	13.15	9.06	78.91	59.38	0.72	6.55	9.87	3.96
1995	7.74	2.63	75.16	54.76	1.08	8.67	10.72	4.37
1996	11.22	9.34	73.89	53.57	1.16	8.33	11.54	5.08
1997	8.87	8.39	73.57	53.63	1.19	6.74	12.88	5.62
1998	17.41	9.99	68.92	53.09	1.63	4.81	12.54	12.10
1999	15.19	14.15	68.29	54.22	1.88	3.76	13.84	12.23
2000	14.45	11.58	66.58	54.19	2.23	2.96	15.45	12.78
2001	19.66	18.47	65.92	55.68	2.76	2.43	16.08	12.81
2002	19.12	15.13	63.71	56.83	3.15	2.32	16.84	13.98
2003	11.95	8.98	62.02	55.63	4.17	1.68	18.06	14.05
2004	12.28	11.63	61.66	55.61	4.80	1.29	18.59	13.65

Source: Our calculations using 1978 constant prices; data from National Bureau of Statistics (various years). Deflator: consumer price index (1978 = 100).

Table 7.3. *Growth rates for tuition and*
miscellaneous fees by school type, 1997–2004

Year	Institutions of higher education	Secondary schools	Primary schools
1997	24.82	24.14	15.22
1998	21.20	15.67	16.01
1999	63.64	24.67	6.91
2000	56.51	28.55	6.63
2001	43.19	28.24	7.11
2002	37.60	24.65	8.73
2003	27.15	18.82	9.72
2004	21.70	12.74	8.71

Source: Our calculations using 1978 constant prices; data
from National Bureau of Statistics (various years). Deflator:
consumer price index (1978 = 100).

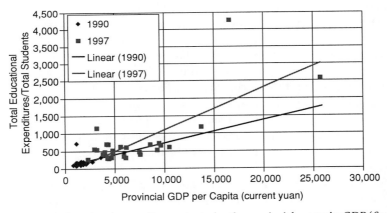

Figure 7.1. Total educational expenditures per student by provincial per capita GDP (*Sources:*
Calculated from International Food Policy Research Institute, n.d., and ACMR, n.d.)

for school functioning: Tsang and Ding (2005, table 6) show that, nationwide, government spending did not cover personnel costs at the primary level and barely covered personnel outlays at the lower secondary level.

While decentralization has successfully mobilized new resources in support of education, it has also enlarged regional disparities in educational investments. As Tsang and Ding (2005) note, in poor rural areas, the capacity to mobilize nongovernmental resources is meager. Figure 7.1 compares total educational expenditures per student with provincial per capita GDP in 1990 and 1997. The dispersion of both variables is greater in 1997 than in 1990. More to the point, the link between the two is stronger, as indicated by the steeper slope of the regression line of expenditure per student on per capita GDP (0.12 vs. 0.07, values not shown) and the higher R-squared value (0.54 vs. 0.29) in the latter year.

Finally, in addition to a rising role of private funding in the state system, the reform era has seen an emergence of private schools, often but not always serving elite populations (Ross and Lin, 2006; Lin, 2007).[4] The 1993 "Outline of Chinese Education Reform and Development" officially adopted a new policy that encouraged the development of schools run by social groups and individual citizens (Tsang, 2000).

Nongovernmental schools have grown rapidly in recent years. Tsang (2000) reports that in 1994, there were an estimated 500 registered nongovernmental schools in urban areas, but the number had reached 4000 by the end of 1997. In 1997, nongovernment schools enrolled 2.55 percent of general secondary enrollment in the Beijing metropolitan area, 3.17 percent in Shanghai, 8.45 percent in Chongqing, and 11.79 percent in Tianjin[5] (Tsang, 2000, table 7). Figures are smaller for primary education.

However, a true sense of the scale of private education is difficult to obtain. Tsang (2000) notes that the wide variety of management and financial arrangements makes many schools difficult to categorize. We can illustrate this complexity with anecdotes from 2005 interviews with students and school personnel in Gansu Province. Schools, particularly those with good reputations, can attract paying students from outside their catchment areas. For example, students in rural Gansu who fail the high school entrance exam often repeat their final lower secondary year at a different school. One private school reported having several state-paid teachers allocated by the local government. Apparently, the local education bureau personnel felt that this arrangement was a better use of resources than building a new government school.

The rising role of private education is not unique to China. In recent decades, many developed and developing countries have undergone efficiency-oriented education reforms, often involving decentralization as well as expansion of private schooling. Sometimes, these reforms have been part of structural adjustment or related policies recommended by international organizations, or as part of a transition strategy for moving from plan to market. With fiscal decentralization, community financing of schooling has often become increasingly important, tightening the links between the regional level of development and the quality of educational services (Bray, 1996).

---

[4] While elite schools have garnered much press, some private schools serve at-risk populations. Examples include: poor rural communities starting their own schools and unregistered schools in cities for migrant children (see Ross and Lin, 2006; Chen and Liang, 2007).

[5] The Tianjin figure refers to both general and vocational secondary schools.

Quality

It is likely that recent changes in educational finance affect the quality of education as well as access to schools. As China progresses in expanding basic education in the more disadvantaged areas, questions of qualitative disparities, which are much harder to assess, become more important. Unfortunately, there are few widely accepted indicators of school quality that can be used to measure quality trends. Often, per-pupil expenditures themselves are used as an indicator of quality, and by this measure, as noted in the preceding section, there is a trend of growth and rising inequality.

Another commonly used dimension of quality is teacher–student ratios or average class size. According to UNESCO estimates, average class size in China was 34.5 for primary level and 56.7 for lower secondary in 2002. The figure for lower secondary schools rose from 51.8 in 1995 due to expanding enrollments (UNESCO, 2005, Annex A4, table 2.9). The lower secondary figure places China at the very top of World Education Indicator participants and Organisation for Economic Cooperation and Development countries. Rising average class size raises concerns about possible declines in quality. However, class size is not a clear indicator of quality, especially if we wish to focus on cross-regional quality variation within China. Good schools and teachers may attract more students, while very resource-poor schools serving sparsely populated communities often have small classes.

A key dimension of educational quality, as conceptualized by reformers, has been the human resources in the schools. An important element of quality-oriented reforms has been efforts to enhance the qualifications of teachers. Table 7.4 shows the educational attainment of teachers in cities, towns, and counties, calculated from a sample from the 2000 census. While sample-size constraints preclude an investigation of disparities across provinces, this data source does permit a look at differences in cities, towns, and rural areas.

At the primary level, fewer than 5 percent of city teachers report qualifications below the senior secondary school level, and nearly 43 percent have some kind of tertiary education. The numbers are somewhat less favorable for townships and strikingly less favorable for county primary school teachers. Among this latter group, about 15 percent had a junior secondary school or lower education and just under 14 percent had some kind of tertiary education. Among secondary school teachers (*zhongxue jiaoshi*) in cities, about 16 percent were themselves trained only to the secondary level, while in towns, the corresponding figure was 22 percent and in counties, 38 percent.[6] These examples suggest a significant degree of disparity in

---

[6] The figures for higher education teachers by location of residence show an expected pattern of higher qualifications for teachers in more urban settings. However, these figures are difficult to interpret, as it seems likely that higher education teachers living in the countryside are not teaching in the countryside. In any case, in higher education, only about 5 percent of city teachers report less than a tertiary-level education, but still under one-fourth of university teachers in cities report graduate education, suggesting substantial room for upgrading. For

Table 7.4. *Educational attainment of teachers by school level and location of teachers' residence*

	Primary or less	Junior secondary school	Senior secondary school	Secondary technical school	Tertiary technical school	Tertiary academic institution	Graduate school	TOTAL
City								
Higher education teacher	0.00	0.76	1.21	3.18	13.77	57.64	23.45	100
Secondary vocational education teacher	0.00	2.45	4.71	11.30	34.09	46.70	0.75	100
Secondary teacher	0.48	1.45	4.78	9.07	42.35	41.04	0.83	100
Primary teacher	0.16	4.08	9.98	43.28	36.76	5.58	0.16	100
Kindergarten teacher	1.89	15.09	17.40	44.03	19.29	2.31	0.00	100
Special education teacher	0.00	0.00	5.56	33.33	55.56	5.56	0.00	100
Other teaching staff	4.17	13.89	22.92	11.11	24.31	22.22	1.39	100
TOTAL	0.53	4.02	7.61	21.87	32.73	29.39	3.85	100
Town								
Higher education teacher	0.00	2.22	0.00	15.56	33.33	46.67	2.22	100
Secondary vocational education teacher	0.00	1.35	5.41	13.51	51.35	28.38	0.00	100
Secondary teacher	0.37	1.71	4.81	15.48	57.53	19.99	0.12	100
Primary teacher	0.47	5.87	9.86	56.65	25.51	1.64	0.00	100
Kindergarten teacher	2.31	20.37	19.91	43.06	14.35	0.00	0.00	100
Special education teacher	0.00	0.00	40.00	40.00	20.00	0.00	0.00	100
Other teaching staff	3.81	19.05	13.33	30.48	23.81	9.52	0.00	100
TOTAL	0.61	4.94	7.91	32.93	41.24	12.27	0.09	100
County								
Higher education teacher	0.00	0.00	0.00	26.32	36.84	31.58	5.26	100
Secondary vocational education teacher	1.41	2.82	9.86	25.35	29.58	30.99	0.00	100
Secondary teacher	0.57	3.27	9.39	24.89	51.71	10.10	0.07	100
Primary teacher	0.77	14.67	19.55	51.16	12.91	0.94	0.00	100
Kindergarten teacher	2.54	34.52	27.41	30.46	5.08	0.00	0.00	100
Special education teacher	0.00	20.00	20.00	20.00	40.00	0.00	0.00	100
Other teaching staff	13.89	19.44	27.78	25.00	13.89	0.00	0.00	100
TOTAL	0.88	12.19	16.98	42.72	23.34	3.86	0.04	100

Source: National Bureau of Statistics (n.d.).

the preparation of teachers, a critical element of school quality, across urban–rural lines. Given the regional dimension to educational investments, it is likely that similar qualitative differences exist between wealthier and poorer areas in China. Unfortunately, outcome-based measures of quality, such as national assessments of student achievement, are not available.

EDUCATIONAL PARTICIPATION AND ATTAINMENT

Past Expansions and the Educational Attainment of the Adult Population

To place comments about education in the reform era in context, it is important to highlight what past educational expansions mean for the current population: there are great variations in educational attainment by age. Figure 7.2 shows selected educational attainment rates in 2000 by 5-year-age cohorts among men and women. At the low end, the figure shows that those without formal education dropped from 51 percent for men and 88 percent for women in the oldest age range of 80 and above to 2 percent for men and 4 percent for women in the youngest 25–29-year age range (Figure 7.2a). Rates of lower secondary and above attainment increased from 12 percent for men and 2 percent for women among the 80+ cohort to 78 percent for men and 68 percent for women in the youngest 25–29-year-old cohort. A break in the expansion appears among the 30–34-year-old cohorts, who were going through the school system in the early transition period, but a resumption of expansion is evident by the youngest adult cohort.

Rates of upper secondary and above attainment, while of course lower, show a similar pattern of dramatic expansion with a temporary break among 30–34-year-olds. For example, about one in one hundred women ages 80 and above report upper secondary educational attainment, compared with about one in five women in the youngest 25–29 age cohort. Tertiary educational attainment rates are much lower, but have also expanded rapidly from 1 percent among the oldest men to 8 percent among the youngest and from zero among the oldest women to 7 percent among the youngest.

Reform Era Changes in the Level and Composition of Enrollment

Next, we turn to indicators of educational participation during the reform era. Figure 7.3 shows gross enrollment ratios (GERs) by level, sex, and year for

tertiary-level teachers in towns and counties, the situation is much worse, with a substantial minority of these teachers (15 percent in towns and 26 percent in counties) reporting a secondary technical education as their highest attainment, and with 5 percent or fewer reporting graduate study.

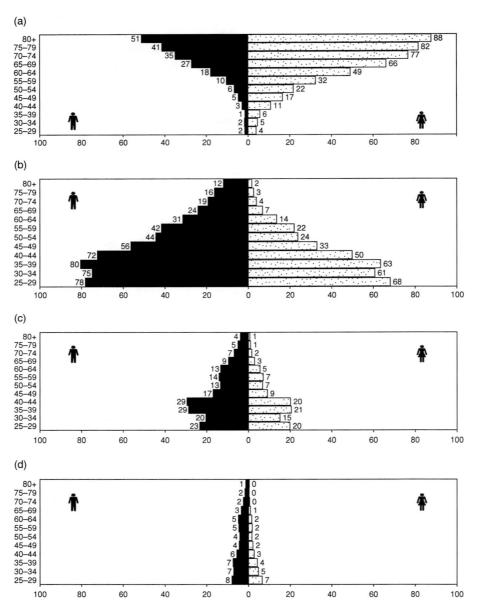

Figure 7.2. Selected educational attainment rates in 2000 by age cohort and gender. (a) Percent no school/literacy classes only by age cohort and gender; (b) Percent lower secondary plus by age cohort and gender; (c) Percent upper secondary or vocational/technical plus by age cohort and gender; (d) Percent tertiary by age cohort and gender (*Source:* National Bureau of Statistics, n.d.)

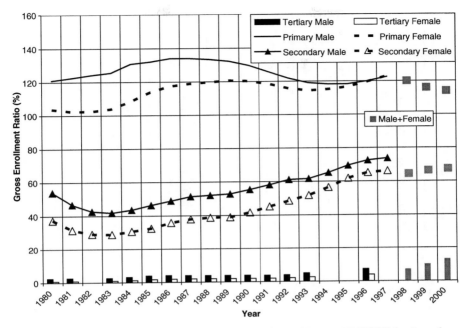

Figure 7.3. Gross enrollment ratios by level, sex, and year (*Sources:* UNESCO Institute for Statistics, 2004; Hannum and Liu, 2005, table 2)

1980–2000.[7] For years marked in gray, we show only total GERs, with no breakdown by sex. Figure 7.3 shows that primary school GERs have been above 100 for males and females since around the start of market reforms, with a gender gap favoring boys in the 1980s basically eliminated by the mid-1990s. The decline in primary school GERs after 1997 probably reflects that fewer students older than the standard

---

[7] China's current levels of enrollment do not stand out relative to those reported by other large countries. Among the nine countries with the largest populations, China is ranked seventh in percentage of GDP spent on education, second in primary GERs, fifth in secondary GERs, and sixth in tertiary GERs (Appendix Table 7.A1). Note that GERs are a very crude indicator of enrollment. GERs are calculated as the total number of students enrolled in a given level of schooling divided by the number of children in the official age range for that level of schooling. The ratios overestimate enrollment rates when, as is the case in many countries, there are enrollees outside of the official age range. Thus, in some cases, declining GERs could be a sign of improved efficiency in the school system. Net enrollment ratios, which count only enrolled children in the specified age range in the numerator, are much preferred but are not widely available over time or across countries, and thus GERs are much more commonly used enrollment indicators. Even net enrollment ratios may be limited indicators of progression toward educational attainment, which is presumably of greater interest than enrollment, because of failure and grade repetition. In Mexico, for example, a recent major reform provides higher scholarships for girls than for boys because in the pre-reform era boys had higher enrollment rates than girls. But in fact in the pre-reform era, girls averaged greater educational attainment than boys, but did not fail and repeat grades as much as boys, so their enrollment rates were lower (Behrman, Sengupta, and Todd, 2005).

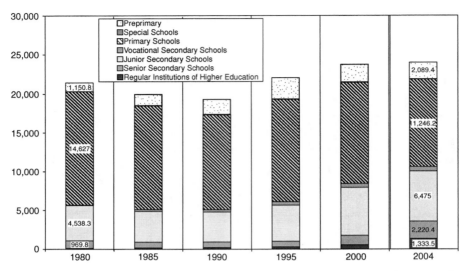

Figure 7.4. School enrollments by level and year (10,000s) (*Source:* National Bureau of Statistics, 2005)

ages were enrolled in primary school and thus may indicate an improvement in the functioning of the system. Secondary school GERs dropped from about 54 for males and 37 for females in 1980 to a low of 42 for males and 29 for females in 1983, before starting a steady climb to 74 percent for males and 66 percent for females in 1997, the last year for which sex-specific numbers are available (so the gender gap declined but did not disappear). Subsequent to 1997, secondary school GERs continued to rise. The temporary downturn at the start of market transition is likely attributable in part to quality-related shutdowns of rural secondary schools. Tertiary school GERs have climbed from 2.5 percent for males and less than 1 percent for females in 1980 to 7.3 percent for males and 3.9 percent for females in 1998. Subsequent figures, not disaggregated by sex, suggest that the rate of growth in tertiary school GERs accelerated in the late 1990s.

As educational provision has expanded, the composition of enrollment has changed. Figure 7.4 shows total enrollments by year and type of school. Proportionally, secondary and tertiary school enrollments have risen over time. Notably, in the most recent years, tertiary school enrollments have expanded dramatically. Enrollments in regular institutions of higher education increased from 1.14 million in 1980 to 5.56 million in 2000 and 13.3 million in 2004.

The compositional changes are clear as well in transition ratios, calculated in Table 7.5 as the number of people starting a higher level of education as a percentage of the number graduating from a lower level of education in the same year. The primary–junior secondary school transition ratio (Table 7.5, column 1) dropped from 76 percent in 1980 to 65 percent in 1984, before rising to a high of

Table 7.5. *Level-to-level transition ratios: new enrollments in A as a percentage of graduates from B, 1980–2000*

A	Junior secondary	General secondary	Technical secondary	Teacher training secondary	Vocational training secondary	General, technical, teacher training or vocational secondary	Regular institutions of higher education	Regular institutions of higher education
B	Primary	Junior secondary	Junior secondary	Junior secondary	Junior secondary	Junior secondary	General secondary	General, technical, teacher training or vocational secondary
Year	1	2	3	4	5	6	7	8
1980	75.5	39.7	2.6	2.2	3.2	47.8	4.6	4.2
1981	68.1	28.4	2.1	1.7	2.3	34.5	5.7	5.0
1982	65.9	27.1	2.3	1.7	4.1	35.2	10.1	8.6
1983	66.5	27.1	3.0	2.0	7.9	39.9	16.6	13.3
1984	65.3	27.6	3.7	2.1	9.9	43.2	25.0	18.6
1985	67.5	25.8	4.5	2.2	11.6	44.1	31.5	22.0
1986	68.8	24.3	4.3	2.1	10.7	41.4	25.5	17.3
1987	68.2	22.8	4.3	2.1	10.1	39.4	25.0	16.3
1988	69.4	21.1	4.7	2.0	10.3	38.2	26.7	17.1
1989	70.5	21.3	4.5	2.0	10.4	38.3	24.5	15.4
1990	73.5	22.5	4.5	2.0	11.1	40.2	26.1	15.7
1991	74.4	22.5	5.1	2.1	12.7	42.3	27.8	15.8
1992	78.2	21.3	5.8	2.2	13.8	43.1	33.3	19.0
1993	80.3	20.1	7.6	2.5	14.2	44.5	39.9	22.7
1994	85.1	21.1	8.1	2.5	15.2	47.0	43.0	23.1
1995	89.3	22.3	8.7	2.5	15.5	49.0	45.9	22.6
1996	91.0	22.1	9.4	2.5	14.8	48.7	47.1	21.6
1997	92.1	22.4	9.0	2.3	14.6	48.2	45.1	20.5
1998	92.6	22.8	8.5	2.0	13.8	47.1	43.1	19.9
1999	92.9	24.9	8.4	1.8	12.2	47.4	60.7	28.0
2000	93.6	29.4	6.9	1.3	11.4	49.0	73.2	35.1

Note: "General secondary" refers to academic senior high schools.
Source: ACMR (n.d.).

231

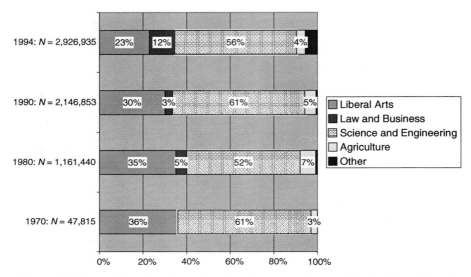

Figure 7.5. Composition of tertiary education, select years (*Source:* Calculated from United Nations Statistics Divisions, 2005. *Note:* Definitions of higher education are not consistent with Chinese sources.)

93.6 percent in 2000. The transition ratio comparing entrants with all forms of senior secondary school to junior secondary school graduates (Table 7.5, column 6) was 48 percent in 1980 and 47–49 percent in the mid-1990s, with some downturns in the intervening years.

Higher educational transitions have also increased notably since the early market-reform period. The ratio of tertiary school entrants to general secondary school graduates, probably the most appropriate ratio for the transition into higher education, shows increases from under 5 percent in 1980 to almost 32 percent in 1985; there was a subsequent downturn and recovery by about 1992, after which the ratio hovered in the mid-40 percent range before jumping to 61–73 percent in 1999 and 2000. If we compare tertiary school entrants to all senior secondary school students, the trend is similar, but the numbers are of course lower, such that by 2000, the ratio reached above one-third. Either comparison suggests dramatic expansion of higher education in the reform period.

The composition by specialization of enrollments in higher education shows both stability and change, in the face of dramatic expansions in numbers. Using UNESCO estimates, Figure 7.5 shows the composition of tertiary education by specialization in 1970, 1980, 1990, and 1994. More than half of students in higher education are in science and engineering. This percentage has remained remarkably stable – between 52 and 61 percent – across the years, despite increases in the size of the student body. After science and engineering, liberal arts is the second most

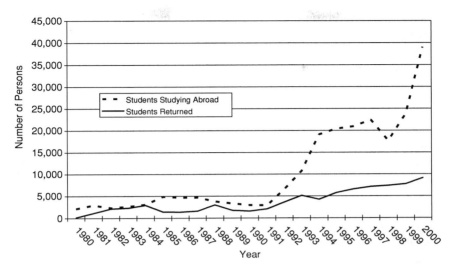

Figure 7.6. Students studying abroad and returned by year (*Source:* ACMR, n.d.)

popular category, though its share is down from over one-third in 1970 to under one-fourth in 1994. A significant new development in higher education is the growth of enrollment in law and business from insignificance in 1970 to 12 percent by 1994. Unfortunately, we have found no comparable figures after 1994.[8]

Overseas study is another element of higher education that has expanded sharply in the reform era. A 1994 report identified overseas study as an important step to scientific modernization, improvement of higher education in China, and international competitiveness (Beijing University and Zhongshan University, 2005). The same source stated that Deng Xiaoping personally made the decision to increase the number of students sent to study abroad for the purpose of learning the advanced science, technology, and culture of the developed Western nations. He issued a directive in 1978 increasing the number of students to be sent abroad (Beijing University and Zhongshan University, 2005). Figure 7.6 shows students studying abroad and students returned by year. The number of students studying abroad increased, though not monotonically, from 2,124 in 1980 to 38,989 in 2000. Returnees are also rising, from 162 in 1980 to 9,121 in 2000.

Enrollment and Attainment Disparities in the Reform Era

Despite rapid expansion of enrollments, changes in financing, coupled with the broader societal trend of rising income inequality, invite consideration of whether

---

[8] More recent tabulations of enrollments in higher education by type are available, but use different categories.

and to what extent historically disadvantaged groups have "caught up." Historically, important disparities in educational enrollment and attainment have been associated with gender, socioeconomic status, location of residence, and ethnicity. Here, we consider inequality with regard to educational attainment and enrollment. We are unable to consider qualitative disparities in schooling.

Gender

Using 2000 census data, Table 7.6 shows the full distribution of educational attainments for 25–34-year-olds, the youngest cohort that could be expected to have completed its formal schooling. While this distribution clearly attests to some continuing lags for women, the gender gap for China as a whole is now moderate. Evidence from a variety of surveys and censuses and from Ministry of Education data, moreover, offers convincing evidence that educational gender gaps have narrowed in recent years (Hannum, 2005; Hannum and Liu, 2005). Figure 7.2 clearly illustrates long-term narrowing of the gender gaps in educational attainment.

Looking at additional measures of educational participation, Tables 7.7 and 7.8 tabulate enrollment and years of schooling among 12–18-year-olds in five provinces in the CHNS by year (1989 vs. 2000) and by sex. Table 7.9 shows results from multivariate analyses of enrollment and years of schooling using the same data.

Consistent with the discussion earlier, Tables 7.7 and 7.8 show substantial improvements in enrollment rates and years of schooling for girls and boys in 2000, compared to 1989. For example, in 1989, 57.6 percent of girls and 61 percent of boys were enrolled; the gender gap was statistically significant (Table 7.7). In the year 2000, corresponding figures were 73.9 percent of girls and 76.4 percent of boys, and this difference was not statistically significant. For years of schooling, the 1989 averages for girls were 6.6 and for boys, 7.0; in the year 2000, the girls' average was 8.2, compared to 8.1 for boys (the difference was not significant) (Table 7.8). A multivariate analysis given in Table 7.9 suggests that, net of other factors thought to matter for schooling, a small female-enrollment disadvantage, but not a years-of-schooling disadvantage, persisted across the years.

Thus, consistent evidence suggests a long-term trend of narrowing gender gaps. Surveys from the 1980s and 1990s found that gender gaps were concentrated in poor households and communities and probably exacerbated by credit constraints (Brown and Park, 2002; Connelly and Zheng, 2003; Hannum, 2003, 2005). Our CHNS data are mixed on this issue. For example, in the year 2000 in Tables 7.7 and 7.8, there is a substantial gender gap in enrollment for children in the poorest quartile of households, among which 56.1 percent of girls and 70.4 percent of boys are enrolled, but the years-of-schooling gap in this subsample is not statistically significant. It could be that in this group, boys are allowed to take longer to finish given levels of schooling, leading to higher enrollment but not substantially higher attainment.

Table 7.6. *Educational attainment of the population ages 25–34 by demographic characteristics, 2000*

	Sample size	Never attended school	Literacy classes only	Primary	Junior secondary school	Senior secondary school	Secondary technical school	Tertiary technical school	Tertiary academic institution	Graduate school
Gender										
Male	113,020	1.2	0.4	22.1	54.7	10.6	3.8	4.9	2.3	0.2
Female	111,048	3.2	1.0	31.6	46.8	7.9	3.9	4.1	1.4	0.1
Ethnicity										
Han	204,904	1.6	0.5	25.7	52.3	9.5	3.8	4.6	1.9	0.2
Minority	19,035	8.5	2.9	38.3	34.5	6.8	4.0	3.4	1.6	0.1
Residence status										
City	56,717	0.8	0.1	10.8	44.8	18.4	7.8	11.0	5.8	0.6
Town	32,778	1.0	0.3	16.4	51.2	14.1	7.3	7.9	2.0	0.0
Village	134,573	3.1	1.0	36.1	53.2	4.2	1.3	0.9	0.2	0.0
Region										
North	25,845	1.1	0.2	18.9	57.0	9.9	4.4	5.3	2.8	0.4
Northeast	19,073	0.9	0.0	21.0	52.2	12.3	4.7	6.2	2.7	0.1
East	64,839	1.4	0.6	26.0	53.7	8.6	3.5	4.3	1.9	0.1
Central south	61,597	0.9	0.2	23.8	55.2	9.9	3.7	4.4	1.6	0.2
Southwest	35,250	5.3	2.0	41.6	37.2	6.0	3.5	3.3	1.1	0.1
Northwest	17,464	6.6	1.7	28.5	41.0	11.4	4.1	5.0	1.7	0.1

Source: National Bureau of Statistics (n.d.).

Table 7.7. *Enrollment rates, youth ages 12–18*

Characteristic	1989				2000			
	N	Male	Female	P-value	N	Male	Female	P-value
TOTAL	1,991	61.0	57.6	0.02	1,479	76.4	73.9	NS
Age								
12–13	522	93.1	92.7	NS	468	96.8	92.2	0.03
14–15	582	77.4	68.9	0.02	442	84.9	82.9	NS
16–17	581	38.3	31.3	NS	358	64.7	57.9	NS
18	306	17.2	16.1	NS	211	34.5	40.0	NS
P-value		0.00	0.00			0.00	0.00	
Urban–rural residence								
Urban	465	68.5	62.6	NS	400	87.4	86.6	NS
Rural	1,525	58.7	53.9	NS	1,079	72.2	69.2	NS
P-value		0.01	0.02			0.00	0.00	
Household head's education								
None	374	51.1	43.6	NS	99	67.8	75.0	NS
Primary	940	58.5	55.2	NS	386	68.9	60.0	NS
Junior high	509	67.9	61.1	NS	611	79.4	74.8	NS
Senior high+	160	74.7	75.4	NS	353	83.2	85.6	NS
P-value		0.00	0.00			0.00	0.00	
Number of consumer items owned by the household								
No report	54	83.3	58.3	0.04	NA			
Lowest quartile	409	54.4	49.7	NS	422	70.4	56.1	0.002
Second quartile	665	56.7	50.2	NS	360	70.9	75.6	NS
Third quartile	588	64.8	60.6	NS	390	77.3	75.4	NS
Highest quartile	275	70.3	67.2	NS	307	91.3	92.4	NS
P-value		0.00	0.00			0.00	0.00	
School-age children in the household								
One	361	44.4	48.7	NS	494	75.9	81.2	NS
Two	480	65.0	54.9	0.004	671	76.9	71.5	NS
Three or more	835	65.5	59.3	NS	314	75.8	69.6	NS
P-value		0.00	NS			NS	0.02	
Province								
Jiangsu	205	62.8	61.3	NS	122	81.7	83.9	NS
Shandong	218	63.1	51.3	NS	179	85.6	76.8	NS
Henan	321	58.7	45.6	0.02	205	74.3	71.9	NS
Hubei	249	67.7	52.8	0.02	259	76.5	72.4	NS
Hunan	249	62.9	66.7	NS	191	80.8	79.3	NS
Guangxi	310	55.9	55.0	NS	286	70.8	76.0	NS
Guizhou	438	59.8	59.8	NS	237	71.7	63.3	NS
P-value		NS	0.01			NS	0.05	
Relationship to household head								
Own child	1858	60.9	55.7	0.02	1,342	76.4	73.1	NS
Others[a]	133	62.9	59.2	NS	134	76.5	80.3	NS
P-value		NS	NS			NS	NS	

[a] Others include grandchildren, siblings, other relatives, and other nonrelatives. (One "spouse" was included in 1989.)

Source: China Health and Nutrition Survey (1989, 2000).

Table 7.8. *Average years of school completed, youth ages 12–18,*
1989 and 2000

Characteristic	1989					2000				
	Male		Female			Male		Female		
	Mean	SD	Mean	SD	*P*-value	Mean	SD	Mean	SD	*P*-value
TOTAL	7.0	2.2	6.6	2.6	0.01	8.1	2.0	8.2	2.1	NS
Age										
12–13	5.4	1.6	5.6	1.7	NS	6.6	1.4	6.6	1.5	NS
14–15	7.1	1.7	6.6	2.5	0.01	8.1	1.4	8.2	1.7	NS
16–17	7.9	2.2	7.6	2.5	NS	9.3	1.7	9.4	1.9	NS
18	7.9	2.5	7.4	3.2	NS	9.6	2.2	9.7	1.9	NS
P-value		0.00		0.00			0.00		0.00	
Urban–rural residence										
Urban	7.9	2.1	8.2	2.1	NS	8.8	2.0	8.7	2.1	NS
Rural	6.7	2.1	6.3	2.5	0.00	7.9	1.9	8.0	2.1	NS
P-value		0.00		0.00			0.00		0.00	
Household head's education										
None	6.5	2.4	6.2	2.9	NS	7.8	2.2	7.8	2.1	NS
Primary	6.8	2.1	6.6	2.4	NS	7.9	2.1	7.8	2.3	NS
Junior high	7.3	2.0	6.9	2.5	NS	8.2	1.9	8.2	1.8	NS
Senior high+	8.3	2.1	8.2	2.3	NS	8.4	1.9	8.8	2.3	NS
P-value		0.00		0.00			0.00		0.00	
Number of consumer items owned by the household										
No report	6.8	2.3	6.4	2.2	NS	NA				
Lowest quartile	6.2	2.2	5.2	2.7	0.00	7.5	1.9	7.4	2.1	NS
Second quartile	6.8	2.0	6.3	2.5	0.00	7.9	2.1	8.0	1.8	NS
Third quartile	7.5	2.0	7.5	2.2	NS	8.4	1.9	8.5	2.0	NS
Highest quartile	8.2	2.1	8.3	2.0	NS	8.9	2.2	9.1	2.2	NS
P-value		0.00		0.00			0.00		0.00	
School-age children in the household										
One	7.8	2.3	7.5	2.7	NS	8.8	2.0	8.8	2.1	NS
Two	7.1	2.1	7.1	2.4	NS	7.9	1.9	8.2	2.1	NS
Three or more	6.6	2.1	6.2	2.6	0.02	7.3	1.7	7.7	1.9	0.05
P-value		0.00		0.00			0.00		0.00	
Province										
Jiangsu	7.8	2.3	7.3	2.8	NS	8.2	2.2	8.6	1.9	NS
Shandong	7.0	2.2	6.4	2.9	NS	8.3	2.1	7.9	1.9	NS
Henan	7.1	1.9	6.8	2.5	NS	8.1	2.1	8.3	1.9	NS
Hubei	7.2	1.9	6.9	2.3	NS	8.1	1.8	8.4	2.2	NS
Hunan	7.2	1.9	7.3	1.8	NS	8.8	2.1	8.7	2.3	NS
Guangxi	7.1	2.3	6.9	2.4	NS	7.9	1.9	8.1	2.1	NS
Guizhou	6.4	2.4	6.1	2.7	NS	7.7	1.8	7.7	2.1	NS
P-value		0.00		0.00			0.00		0.02	
Head										
Own child	7.0	2.2	6.7	2.6	NS	8.1	1.9	8.2	2.1	NS
Others	7.2	1.9	7.2	2.3	NS	7.9	2.4	7.9	2.4	NS
P-value		NS		NS			NS		NS	

Note: *P*-values are results from *t*-tests or ANOVA tests, in the case of characteristics with more than
two categories.
Others include grandchildren, siblings, other relatives, and other nonrelatives. (One "spouse" was
   included in 1989.)
NS, not significant at the 0.05 level.
Source: CHNS (1989, 2000).

Table 7.9. *Logistic regressions of enrollment and linear regressions of years of education, youth ages 12–18, 1989 and 2000*

	Enrollment			Years of education		
	1989	2000	Combined	1989	2000	Combined
Age (years)	−1.452	−0.420	−1.107	3.136	2.793	3.062
	$(2.24)^a$	(0.58)	$(2.29)^a$	$(7.90)^b$	$(8.48)^b$	$(11.39)^b$
Age squared	0.020	−0.010	0.010	−0.090	−0.073	−0.085
	(0.96)	(0.42)	(0.65)	$(6.72)^b$	$(6.57)^b$	$(9.39)^b$
Year indicator (ref: 1989)						
2000			0.853			1.849
			$(2.33)^a$			$(6.95)^b$
Female (ref.: male)	−0.299	−0.260	−0.283	−0.262	0.077	−0.270
	$(2.51)^a$	$(1.66)^c$	$(2.49)^a$	$(2.78)^b$	(0.98)	$(2.85)^b$
Year* female			−0.025			0.356
			(0.13)			$(2.86)^b$
Urban (ref.: rural)	0.458	0.865	0.428	0.795	0.393	0.760
	$(2.48)^a$	$(4.11)^b$	$(2.48)^a$	$(6.15)^b$	$(4.00)^b$	$(6.02)^b$
Year* urban			0.424			−0.386
			(1.60)			$(2.48)^a$
Household head's education (ref.: none)						
Primary	0.329	−0.357	0.333	0.437	0.097	0.473
	$(1.88)^c$	(1.07)	$(1.99)^a$	$(2.75)^b$	(0.43)	$(2.96)^b$
Junior high	0.628	−0.115	0.621	0.722	0.461	0.768
	$(2.95)^b$	(0.34)	$(3.02)^b$	$(4.12)^b$	$(2.03)^a$	$(4.39)^b$
Senior high+	1.132	0.307	1.095	1.089	0.486	1.126
	$(4.04)^b$	(0.84)	$(4.04)^b$	$(5.23)^b$	$(2.06)^a$	$(5.46)^b$
Interaction terms between year and household head's education						
Year* primary			−0.649			−0.466
			$(1.71)^c$			$(1.78)^c$
Year* junior high			−0.683			−0.454
			$(1.73)^c$			$(1.71)^c$
Year* senior high			−0.709			−0.755
			(1.55)			$(2.57)^a$
Number of consumer items owned by the household (ref.: lowest quartile)						
Second quartile	0.104	0.629	0.071	0.551	0.303	0.528
	(0.53)	$(2.89)^b$	(0.38)	$(3.47)^b$	$(2.45)^a$	$(3.33)^b$
Third quartile	0.517	0.685	0.467	1.210	0.554	1.195
	$(2.41)^a$	$(3.15)^b$	$(2.29)^a$	$(7.15)^b$	$(4.60)^b$	$(7.14)^b$
Highest quartile	0.785	1.702	0.698	1.685	1.005	1.648
	$(2.88)^b$	$(5.27)^b$	$(2.67)^b$	$(8.48)^b$	$(7.21)^b$	$(8.51)^b$
Interaction terms between year and number of consumer items owned						
Year* second			0.620			−0.230
			$(2.20)^a$			(1.14)
Year* third			0.336			−0.611
			(1.14)			$(3.00)^b$

(*continued*)

Table 7.9 (*continued*)

	Enrollment			Years of education		
	1989	2000	Combined	1989	2000	Combined
Year* highest			1.208			−0.598
			$(3.10)^c$			$(2.56)^a$
School-age children in the household (ref.: one)						
Two	0.172	−0.271	−0.049	−0.001	−0.180	−0.098
	(1.01)	(1.50)	(0.40)	(0.01)	$(1.81)^c$	(1.17)
Three or more	0.276	−0.216	0.076	−0.405	−0.415	−0.426
	(1.47)	(0.93)	(0.52)	$(2.54)^a$	$(3.16)^b$	$(4.00)^b$
Relationship to household head (ref.: other)						
Own child	0.095	0.319	0.214	0.093	−0.330	−0.063
	(0.36)	(0.98)	(1.07)	(0.53)	$(1.77)^c$	(0.49)
Province (ref: jiangsu)						
Shandong	−0.407	−0.293	−0.318	−0.707	−0.201	−0.496
	(1.50)	(0.80)	(1.52)	$(2.98)^b$	(1.09)	$(3.12)^b$
Henan	−0.378	−0.713	−0.484	−0.284	0.048	−0.167
	$(1.66)^c$	$(2.10)^a$	$(2.66)^b$	(1.43)	(0.27)	(1.19)
Hubei	−0.221	−0.558	−0.320	−0.143	0.079	−0.048
	(0.88)	$(1.69)^c$	$(1.69)^c$	(0.72)	(0.48)	(0.35)
Hunan	0.015	−0.310	−0.084	−0.008	0.089	0.038
	(0.06)	(0.87)	(0.42)	(0.04)	(0.48)	(0.27)
Guangxi	−0.362	−0.765	−0.491	−0.161	−0.338	−0.265
	(1.46)	$(2.35)^a$	$(2.61)^b$	(0.75)	$(1.94)^c$	$(1.82)^c$
Guizhou	−0.049	−0.628	−0.212	−0.547	−0.524	−0.527
	(0.21)	$(1.79)^c$	(1.11)	$(2.65)^b$	$(2.77)^b$	$(3.56)^b$
Constant	17.125	9.838	14.357	−20.540	−17.206	−20.386
	$(3.44)^b$	$(1.77)^c$	$(3.87)^b$	$(7.06)^b$	$(7.06)^b$	$(10.23)^b$
Observations	1929	1446	3375	1924	1429	3353
R-square				0.32	0.47	0.41

Note: Robust z-statistics in parentheses.

[a] $p < 0.05$
[b] $p < 0.01$
[c] $p < 0.1$

Source: CHNS (1989, 2000).

Socioeconomic Status

Socioeconomic status is another important dimension of educational inequality. Indeed, from the broader perspective of the developing world as a whole, gender gaps in educational attainment have declined substantially, but large gaps related to parental family socioeconomic status persist (see Behrman and Sengupta, 2002; NAS–NRC, 2004). Estimates based on data from the late 1980s and early 1990s show significant socioeconomic gaps in enrollment in China (Connelly and Zheng, 2003; Hannum, 2005).

Descriptive results from 12–18-year-old children in five provinces in the CHNS show that both enrollment and years of schooling for children are associated with the household head's education and with the household's quartile standing along a scale measuring ownership of consumer items (see Tables 7.7 and 7.8). For example, on average, the enrollment gap between girls in the lowest and highest quartiles was 17.5 percentage points in 1989 and 36.3 in 2000. The years-of-schooling gap between girls in the wealthiest and poorest quartiles was 3.1 years in 1989 and 1.7 years in 2000.

Multivariate analysis in Table 7.9 shows that the odds ratio of enrollment for being in the highest quartile versus the lowest quartile was 2.19 in 1989 $(\exp[.785] = 2.19)$, but 5.48 in 2000; a test of interaction between year and consumer item quartile suggests that the effect of wealth was stronger in the latter year. In contrast, household head's education was significant in 1989, but not in 2000. For the years-of-schooling outcome, in contrast, findings suggest a diminishing, but still significant, effect of both consumer goods and head's education. Thus, our evidence suggests that wealth continues to confer significant enrollment and years-of-schooling advantages, at least among secondary-aged students.

The educational disadvantages of poor households result most directly from inability to pay school fees. For example, about 49 of 100 of village leaders surveyed in Gansu Province in 2004 cited high costs as a reason for children leaving junior high school (Hannum and Park, 2005). In a 2004 survey of 2,000 13–16-year-olds in rural Gansu, 41 percent of mothers of out-of-school children reported not being able to afford school as a contributor to children's school leaving (Hannum and Park, 2005).

However, advantages to wealthy families may also be realized through a myriad of other supports, such as more favorable home learning environments, better health and nutrition, and fewer poverty-related distractions, such as stress about using scarce household resources, pressure to contribute to household coffers, parental illness, or parental absence due to labor migration (Yu, Kao and Hannum, 2004; Yu and Hannum, 2006; Hannum and Park, 2007).

Geography

Poor households in China are disproportionately situated in contexts that are also disadvantaged,[9] and disparities in participation by location of residence remain prominent. For example, data covering the reform period through 1990 show gaps in access to compulsory education across urban–rural lines that showed no signs of narrowing (Hannum, 1999a). In the 2000 census, among the young adult population, there is still significant variation in the attainment of basic compulsory education along the rural–urban continuum. Table 7.4 shows, for example, that 40 percent of village residents report primary or below education, compared to about 17 percent of town residents and just 12 percent of city residents. These figures

[9] For recent evidence on geography and development in China, see Chapter 19 in this volume.

suggest that schooling attainment through the compulsory levels of education remained a problem in rural areas in the recent past (even though Table 7.4 in a sense overstates the extent to which rural areas lag behind because of post-school-selective migration out of rural areas).

The CHNS provides more recent evidence on urban–rural gaps in educational attainment. Analyses suggest a mixed picture of the trend in disadvantage of rural residents in educational attainment, with the urban advantage in enrollment among 12–18-year-olds persisting between 1989 and 2000, despite some signs of narrowing in the years-of-schooling gap (Table 7.9).

Significant educational disparities appear along other geographic lines. Table 7.6 shows that about 8 percent of young adults in the Northwest and about 7 percent in the Southwest have no formal schooling at all; these figures compare to 2 percent or less for all other regions. At the provincial level, many of the more urbanized and coastal provinces have achieved an important benchmark on the way to universalizing nine years of compulsory education: nearly all primary school graduates go on to secondary school. In contrast, in many of the impoverished western provinces, roughly one in ten primary school graduates fails to continue; in Guizhou, the figure is close to 21 percent and in Tibet, a full 45 percent (Hannum and Wang, 2006, table 1). Perhaps unsurprising in light of disequalizing school-finance trends and rising regional economic inequalities,[10] analyses of the impact of birth province on ultimate educational attainment across cohorts in the 2000 census suggest that educational disadvantage is more geographically concentrated among the most recent cohorts than among earlier cohorts.[11]

Still other evidence highlights the significant impact of local community resources, such as income, on enrollment opportunities, net of a variety of household background characteristics. For example, using data from the 1990 census, Connelly and Zheng (2003) showed that county per capita income was positively correlated with the probability of rural-youth enrollment in primary school, middle school, and secondary school. Similarly, analyses of the rural component of a 1992 national survey of children indicated that junior secondary school provision was linked to village income and that both village income and junior secondary school provision significantly predicted enrollment among 12–14-year-olds, net of household socioeconomic status (Hannum, 2003).

---

[10] Interprovincial income inequality increased markedly from the late 1980s at least through the year 2000, and the urban–rural gap in income and living standards remains large (Carter, 1997; Khan and Riskin, 1998; Zhang and Kanbur, 2003). See Chapter 18 in this volume for recent evidence on income-inequality trends.

[11] Specifically, in a regression of approximate years of schooling calculated from levels of schooling reported in the 2000 census, we found that province of birth explained a larger proportion of variation among the most recent cohorts. We also found that indices of dissimilarity assessing the differences in birth province distributions of those with and without each level of education (primary, lower secondary, upper secondary, and tertiary) showed stable or rising trends across more recent cohorts (Hannum and Wang, 2006).

More recent data suggest that the impact of communities on educational opportunity may be increasing. For example, multivariate analyses of enrollment and grade-for-age attainment using three waves of the CHNS indicated that community per capita income became a significant predictor of educational outcomes in the later years (Adams and Hannum, 2005). On balance, these examples point to a persistent, and perhaps increasing, role of geography as an educational stratifier.

Ethnicity

Tied to, but also distinct from, issues of poverty, rural residence and geography is the problem of educational stratification by ethnicity. As Table 7.4 shows, ethnic minorities as a group are at a substantial educational disadvantage, compared to the ethnic majority Han population. The disparity is most striking at the low end of educational attainment: about one in ten minorities in the young adult population has no formal schooling; this number compares to just 2 percent among the Han. Among the minority young adult population, 50 percent have a primary or lower level of education, compared to 28 percent of the Han population.[12] Interestingly, at the tertiary level, disparities are moderate: about 7 percent of Han and about 5 percent of minorities report some kind of tertiary educational attainment.[13]

At basic levels of education, much of the disadvantage faced by ethnic minorities stems from their disproportionate representation among rural residents, among the poor, and in disadvantaged western provinces (Hannum, 2002).[14] However, ethnicity is also linked to educational decision-making in other ways that cannot be simply reduced to poverty and geography. Minority groups in China are diverse with regard to cultural practices and experiences with the larger Han society (Mackerras, 1994, 1995; see also Harrell, 1995; Gladney, 1996). Ethnic groups may develop varying attitudes toward education, depending on whether they perceive that the school system is compatible with aspects of their own cultures and whether they observe tangible returns to education among members of their own communities (Hansen, 1999; Harrell and Mgebbu, 1999). For example, Hansen's fieldwork (1999) indicates that educational disparities among the Dai, Naxi, Hani, and Jinuo in Yunnan can be traced to ethnic differences in perceptions of the economic benefits of education and the accord or opposition between each group's cultural heritage and the educational system.

---

[12] It is important to acknowledge great variation in educational disparities among China's minority groups, with a few groups, especially those concentrated in the Northeast, showing better educational indicators than the Han Chinese (Hannum, 2002).

[13] The much narrower gap at the high end of the educational distribution may be attributable in part to governmental efforts to cultivate minority cadres and to related special policies designed to bring minorities into higher education.

[14] Minorities' poorer status has been confirmed in recent survey data. Using rural household surveys conducted in nineteen provinces, Gustafsson and Li (2003) estimate that in 1995, minorities had an average income per capita less than two-thirds of that of the majority. As in the case of education, much of the income disadvantage is attributed to minority residence in the poor parts of China.

Little evidence is available on changes in ethnic disparities over time. Comparisons of primary entrance and junior secondary school transition rates in the 1982 and 1990 censuses showed improvements for most ethnic groups at the primary level, but a compensating deterioration for many groups at the junior secondary school transition (Hannum, 2002). Ministry of Education data from 1978 to 1997 show that minorities increased their presence as a proportion of total enrollment at all levels of schooling between 1978 and 1997 (Hannum, 1999b, table 3).[15] Whether ethnic gaps are narrowing or not, the striking ethnic disparities apparent among young adults in the 2000 census suggest the critical importance of ethnicity as a stratifier in China.

DISCUSSION AND CONCLUSIONS

China's population bears the marks of phenomenal educational expansion since 1949. Much of this progress occurred prior to market reforms, without the benefit of rapid economic growth. After some faltering in the early 1980s, the long-standing pattern of expansion has reemerged. The pattern of expansion has been different in the reform period than in the preceding era, as policy makers have sought to mobilize private resources and emphasized links between schooling and economic modernization. Leaders moved away from the radical educational agenda that predated market reforms and toward expanding vocational and higher education.

As a result, China's population is increasingly well educated, and the education system itself is more outward looking and also more diverse in structure, finance, and content than in the past. These changes have facilitated China's expansion into international markets (both trade and foreign investments), with important feedbacks throughout the economy (see Chapter 16). At the same time, greater integration into international markets has raised the returns to education in ways that are likely to increase investments in education but also, at least for the near-term future, enlarge inequalities in education and income.

In terms of educational inequalities, gender disparities appear to be narrowing, suggesting that educational expansion patterns have exerted an equalizing impact on this historically important dimension of social inequality. In contrast, differences in enrollment and attainment by socioeconomic status, location of residence, and ethnicity remained striking at the start of the new century. Most disconcerting are the very noticeable disadvantages for minorities and those residing in China's poor regions.

Moreover, while we can measure disparities in access to the system, we know very little about qualitative disparities and their implications. The available evidence suggests that qualitative disparities are likely increasing, even as the system

---

[15] However, interpretation of this trend is complicated by our inability to obtain figures on the proportion of minorities among the school-age population.

becomes more inclusive. Trends in educational finance raise particular concerns about quality disparities along geographic lines.

Government initiatives in the early 2000s have paid significant attention to problems of educational finance in poor rural areas. For example, in 2005, the national and provincial governments invested RMB7.2 billion in central and western China to expand a policy known as "two frees, one subsidy" (*liang mian yi bu*), which waives fees and provides boarding allowances for poor students during their nine years of compulsory education. Under this program, each beneficiary receives RMB210–320 a year, making school fees and textbooks virtually free; some impoverished students in boarding schools also receive living allowances (Chang, 2006).

In 2006, Premier Wen Jiabao pledged that the government would eliminate all charges on rural students receiving a nine-year compulsory education before the end of 2007 (*People's Daily*, 2006b). An amendment to the compulsory education law, which came into effect September 1, 2006, commits to providing nine years of free compulsory education for both urban and rural children, though tuition charges will not be completely waived for a few years (*People's Daily*, 2006a). Central and local governments will have responsibility for expenditures, and local governments are to include outlays for compulsory education in their budgets (*People's Daily*, 2006a).

The outcome of these initiatives will shape China's future social stratification. As societies develop and schooling expands, educational credentials typically play an increasingly central role in labor and marriage markets.[16] In urban China, the tightening link between education and labor outcomes is clear: returns to education have increased dramatically over the course of the reform era in urban areas (Zhang and Zhao, 2007). In rural areas, recent reviews indicate that access to nonfarm jobs is increasingly based on human capital attributes; the greater the extent of the labor market, the higher the returns on human capital (Nee and Matthews, 1996; de Brauw and Rozelle, 2007).

If educational credentials increasingly matter in the labor market and real opportunities for education are distributed equitably across social groups, this rising role of human capital in the labor market can be equalizing. However, when historically disadvantaged groups have poorer relative access to education, the rising importance of education can serve to reinforce, rather than ameliorate, long-standing inequalities, even when access to education is expanding and even if the labor market operates without discriminating on the basis of group membership.[17] As educational credentials rise in importance in the labor market, groups with the least

---

[16] To the extent that educational homogamy occurs, returns to education may be realized through not only labor-market outcomes for individual graduates, but also labor-market outcomes for their spouses.

[17] For example, in the Xinjiang Uygur Autonomous Region, between the 1982 and 1990 censuses, rising ethnic disparities in occupational status could be explained by rising ethnic differences in education. These educational disparities emerged at a time of dramatic improvements in access to schooling for both minorities and ethnic Chinese (Hannum and Xie, 1998).

Appendix Table 7.A1. *Percent of GDP spent on education and GERs, ten largest countries, 1998–2000*

Country	Population (2004) (millions)	Percent spent on education (1998)		Gross enrollment ratios (2000)		
		GNP/GNI	GDP	Primary	Secondary	Tertiary
China	1299	2.2	2.2	114	68	13
India	1065	3.2	3.2	99	48	11
United States	293	5.0	5.0	100	94	71
Indonesia	238	1.6[a]	1.5[a]	110	57	15
Brazil	184	5.1[b]	4.9[b]	151	105	16
Pakistan	159	1.9	1.8	73	24	–
Russia	144	3.7	3.5	109	92	64
Bangladesh	141	2.3	2.4	99	46	7
Japan	127	3.4	3.5	101	102	48

[a] 2000 data.
[b] 1999 data.
Sources: United States Census Bureau (2004) and UNESCO Institute for Statistics (2004).

(or lowest quality) education today will be tomorrow's poor. For these reasons, the educational inequality documented here – by socioeconomic status, location, and ethnicity – provides a forecast of the economic inequalities of the near future.

References

ACMR [All China Marketing Research Co., Ltd]. n.d. "China Statistical Data Compilation 1949–2000." CD-ROM. Beijing: All China Marketing Research Co., Ltd.

Adams, Jennifer and Emily Hannum. 2005. "Children's Social Welfare in China, 1989–1997: Access to Health Insurance and Education." *China Quarterly.* 181, pp. 100–121.

Behrman, Jere R. and Piyali Sengupta. 2002. "The Returns to Female Schooling Revisited." Philadelphia, PA: University of Pennsylvania, mimeo.

Behrman, Jere R., Piyali Sengupta, and Petra Todd, 2005, "Progressing through PROGRESA: An Impact Assessment of Mexico's School Subsidy Experiment." *Economic Development and Cultural Change.* 54(1), pp. 237–275.

Beijing University School of Education and Zhongshan University Institute of Higher Education. 2005. "Retrospect and Analysis of China's Policies with Regard to Students Sent by the State to Other Countries since 1978." *Chinese Education & Society.* 38, pp. 7–62. Translation of Beijing University School of Education and Zhongshan University Institute of Higher Education. 2004. "1978 Nian yilai woguo gongpai liuxue zhengce de huigu yu fenxi," *Chuguo liuxue gongzuo yanjiu* [Research on Work Concerning Overseas Studies]. 1, pp. 15–38.

Bray, Mark. 1996. *Decentralization of Education: Community Financing.* Washington, DC: World Bank.

Brown, Philip H. and Albert Park. 2002. "Education and Poverty in Rural China." *Economics of Education Review.* 21, pp. 523–541.

Carter, Colin A. 1997. "The Urban–Rural Income Gap in China: Implications for Global Food Market." *American Journal of Agricultural Economics*. 79, pp. 1410–1418.

Chang, Tianle. October 9, 2006. "Rural Education: Subsidies Provide Palliative, But Not Panacea." *China Development Brief*. Accessed July 31, 2007, from http://www.chinadevelopmentbrief.com/node/805.

Chen, Yiu-por and Zai Liang. 2007. "Educational Attainment in Migrant Children: The Forgotten Story of Urbanization in China," in *Education and Reform in China*. Emily Hannum and Albert Park, eds. New York: Routledge, pp. 117–132.

China Health and Nutrition Survey [CHNS]. 1989 and 2000. [Computer Data Files]. Chapel Hill: UNC Carolina Population Center. Accessed July 31, 2007, http://www.cpc.unc.edu/projects/china.

Connelly, Rachel and Zhenzhen Zheng. 2003. "Determinants of Primary and Middle School Enrollment of 10–18 Year Olds in China." *Economics of Education Review*. 22(4), pp. 379–390.

de Brauw, Alan and Scott Rozelle. 2007. "Returns to Education in Rural China," in *Education and Reform in China*. Emily Hannum and Albert Park, eds. New York: Routledge, pp. 207–223.

Deng, Zhong and Donald J. Treiman. 1997. "The Impact of the Cultural Revolution on Trends in Educational Attainment in the People's Republic of China." *American Journal of Sociology*. 103, pp. 391–428.

Gladney, Dru C. 1996. *Muslim Chinese: Ethnic Nationalism in the People's Republic of China*, 2nd ed. Cambridge, MA: Council on East Asian Studies, Harvard University.

Gustafsson, Björn and Shi Li. 2003. "The Ethnic Minority–Majority Income Gap in Rural China during Transition." *Economic Development and Cultural Change*. 51(4), pp. 805–822.

Han, Dongping. 2001. "Impact of the Cultural Revolution on Rural Education and Economic Development: The Case of Jimo County." *Modern China*. 27(1), pp. 59–90.

Hannum, Emily. 1999a. "Political Change and the Urban–Rural Gap in Education in China, 1949–1990." *Comparative Education Review*. 43(2), pp. 193–211.

Hannum, Emily. 1999b. "Poverty and Basic-Level Schooling in the People's Republic of China: Equity Issues in the 1990s." *Prospects: The Quarterly Journal of Comparative Education*. 29(4), pp. 561–577.

Hannum, Emily. 2002. "Educational Stratification by Ethnicity in China: Enrollment and Attainment in the Early Reform Years." *Demography*. 39(1), pp. 95–117.

Hannum, Emily. 2003. "Poverty and Basic Education in Rural China: Communities, Households, and Girls' and Boys' Enrollment." *Comparative Education Review*. 47(2), pp. 141–159.

Hannum, Emily. 2005. "Market Transition, Educational Disparities, and Family Strategies in Rural China: New Evidence on Gender Stratification and Development." *Demography*. 42(2), pp. 275–299.

Hannum, Emily and Jihong Liu. 2005. "Adolescent Transitions to Adulthood in Reform-era China," in *The Changing Transitions to Adulthood in Developing Countries: Selected Studies*. Cynthia Lloyd, Jere Behrman, Nellie Stromquist, and Barney Cohen, eds. Washington, DC: National Academies Press, pp. 270–319.

Hannum, Emily and Albert Park. 2005. *Children's Agency and Educational Inequality in Rural China*. Philadelphia, PA: University of Pennsylvania Population Studies Center, mimeo.

Hannum, Emily and Albert Park. 2007. "Academic Achievement and Engagement in Rural China," in *Education and Reform in China*. Emily Hannum and Albert Park, eds. New York: Routledge, pp. 154–172.

Hannum, Emily and Meiyan Wang. 2006. "Geography and Educational Inequality in China." *China Economic Review*. 17(3), pp. 253–265.

Hannum, Emily and Yu Xie. 1994. "Trends in Educational Gender Inequality in China: 1949–1985." *Research in Social Stratification and Mobility*. 13, pp. 73–98.

Hannum, Emily, and Yu Xie. 1998. "Ethnic Stratification in Northwest China: Occupational Differences between Han Chinese and National Minorities in Xinjiang, 1982–1990." *Demography*. 35(3), pp. 323–333.

Hansen, Mette H. 1999. *Lessons in Being Chinese: Minority Education and Ethnic Identity in Southwest China*. Seattle: University of Washington Press.

Harrell, Stevan, ed. 1995. *Cultural Encounters on China's Ethnic Frontiers*. Seattle: University of Washington Press.

Harrell, Stevan and Ma Erzi (Mgebbu Lunze). 1999. "Folk Theories of Success Where Han Aren't Always the Best," in *China's National Minority Education: Culture, Schooling, and Development*. Gerard Postiglione, ed. New York: Garland Press, pp. 213–241.

Hawkins, John N. 2000. "Centralization, Decentralization, Recentralization: Educational Reform in China." *Journal of Educational Administration*. 38(5), pp. 442–455.

International Food Policy Research Institute. n.d. "China: Government Expenditure, Growth, Poverty, and Infrastructure, 1952–2001." [Computer Data File]. Washington, DC: International Food Policy Research Institute.

Khan, Azizur Rahman and Carl Riskin. 1998. "Income Inequality in China: Composition, Distribution and Growth of Household Income, 1988 to 1995." *The China Quarterly*. 154, pp. 221–253.

Kwong, Julia. 1985. "Changing Political Culture and Changing Curriculum: An Analysis of Language Textbooks in the People's Republic of China." *Comparative Education*. 21, pp. 197–208.

Lewin, Keith, Angela Little, Hui Xu, and Jiwei Zheng. 1994. *Educational Innovation in China: Tracing the Impact of the 1985 Reforms*. Essex, England: Long Group Limited.

Lin, Jing. 2007. "Emergence of Private Schools in China: Context, Characteristics, and Implications," in *Education and Reform in China*. Emily Hannum and Albert Park, eds. New York: Routledge, pp. 44–63.

Mackerras, Colin. 1994. *China's Minorities: Integration and Modernization in the Twentieth Century*. Hong Kong: Oxford University Press.

Mackerras, Colin. 1995. *China's Minority Cultures: Identities and Integration Since 1912*. New York: St. Martin's Press.

Mei, Hong and Xiaolin Wang. 2006. *China's Budget System and the Financing of Education and Health Services for Children*. Beijing: United Nations Children's Fund and Office of the National Working Committee on Children and Women under the State Council.

Meng, Xin and Robert G. Gregory. 2002. "The Impact of Interrupted Education on Subsequent Educational Attainment: A Cost of the Chinese Cultural Revolution." *Economic Development & Cultural Change*. 50, pp. 935–959.

Ministry of Education. 1986. *People's Republic of China Law on Compulsory Education*. Beijing: Ministry of Education.

Ministry of Education. 1993. *People's Republic of China Teacher's Law*. Beijing: Ministry of Education.

Ministry of Education. 1995. *People's Republic of China Education Law*. Beijing: Ministry of Education.

Ministry of Education. 1999. *Action Plan for Revitalizing Education for the 21st Century*. Beijing: Ministry of Education.

NAS–NRC [National Academies of Science–National Research Council]. 2004. *Growing Up Global: Transitions to Adulthood in Developing Countries.* Washington, DC: National Academies Press.

National Bureau of Statistics. 1998–2005. *China Statistics Yearbook.* Beijing: China Statistics Press.

National Bureau of Statistics. n.d. ".95 Per Thousand Micro-sample from the 2000 China Population Census." [Computer Data File]. Beijing: National Bureau of Statistics.

Nee, Victor and Rebecca Matthews. 1996. "Market Transition and Societal Transformation in Reforming State Socialism." *Annual Review of Sociology.* 22, pp. 401–435.

People's Daily. June 30, 2006a. "China Adopts Amendment to Compulsory Education Law." Accessed July 31, 2007, from http://english.people.com.cn/200606/30/eng20060630_278583.html.

People's Daily. March 5, 2006b. China Pledges Elimination of Rural Compulsory Education Charges in Two Years. Accessed July 31, 2007, from http://english.peopledaily.com.cn/200603/05/print20060305_248042.html.

Rosen, Stanley. 1984. "New Directions in Secondary Education," in *Contemporary Chinese Education.* Ruth Hayhoe, ed. Sydney: Croom Helm, pp. 65–92.

Ross, Heidi and Jing Lin. 2006. "Social Capital Formation through Chinese School Communities," in *Children's Lives and Schooling across Societies: Research in the Sociology of Education,* vol. 15. Emily Hannum and Bruce Fuller, eds. Boston: JAI/Elsevier Science, pp. 43–70.

Shen, Anping. 1994. "Teacher Education and National Development in China." *Journal of Education.* 176(2), pp. 57–71.

State Council. October 26, 2000. "Circular of the State Council on Policies and Measures Pertaining to the Development of the Western Region." *The China Economic Information Network.* Accessed July 31, 2007, from http://www1.chinawest.gov.cn/chinese/files/zn/ZC/001.htm.

Sun, Hong and David Johnson. 1990. "From Ti-Yong to Gaige to Democracy and Back Again: Education's Struggle in Communist China," *Contemporary Education.* 61, pp. 209–214.

Thogersen, Stig. 1990. *Secondary Education in China after Mao: Reform and Social Conflict.* Aarhus: Aarhus University Press.

Thomas, R. Murray. August 1986. "Political Rationales, Human Development Theories, and Educational Practice." *Comparative Education Review.* 30, pp. 299–320.

Tsang, Mun C. 2000. "Education and National Development in China Since 1949: Oscillating Policies and Enduring Dilemmas." *China Review-An Interdisciplinary Journal on Greater China,* pp. 579–618. Accessed July 31, 2007, from http://www.tc.columbia.edu/centers/coce/pdf_files/d1.pdf.

Tsang, Mun C. and Yanqing Ding. 2005. "Resource Utilization and Disparities in Compulsory Education in China." *China Review – An Interdisciplinary Journal on Greater China.* 5, pp. 1–31. Accessed July 31, 2007, from http://www.tc.edu/centers/coce/pdf_files/a10.pdf.

UNESCO. 2005. *Education Trends in Perspective: Analysis of the World Education Indicators,* 2005 ed. Paris: UNESCO Publishing.

UNESCO Institute for Statistics. 2004. "Data Centre." [Computer Data File]. Montreal: UNESCO Institute for Statistics. Accessed May 15, 2004, from http://stats.uis.unesco.org. (Revision April 2004.)

United States Census Bureau. 2004. "International Data Base." [Computer Data File]. 2004 Edition. Accessed May 15, 2004, from http://www.census.gov/cgi-bin/ipc/idbagg.

Unger, Jonathan. 1984. "Severing the Links between Education and Careers: The Sobering Experience of China's Urban Schools," in *Education versus Qualifications? A Study of Relationships between Education, Selection for Employment, and the Productivity of Labor.* John Oxenham, ed. Boston: Allen and Unwin, pp. 176–191.

United Nations Statistics Division. 2005. "Tertiary Enrolment Type [25560]." United Nations Common Database (UNCDB). [Computer Data File]. New York: United Nations. Accessed from http://unstats.un.org/unsd/cdb/default.asp.

Wang, Chengzhi. 2002. "Minban Education: The Planned Elimination of the 'People-Managed' Teachers in Reforming China." *International Journal of Educational Development.* 22, pp. 109–129.

Yu, Shengchao and Emily Hannum. 2006. "Poverty, Health and Schooling in China." In *Education, Stratification and Social Change in China.* Gerard A. Postiglione, ed. Armonk, NY: ME Sharpe, pp. 53–74.

Yu, Shengchao, Grace Kao, and Emily Hannum. 2004. "Labor Migration and Its Impact on Children's Schooling in Rural China." Philadelphia, PA: University of Pennsylvania, mimeo.

Zhang, Junsen and Yaohui Zhao. 2007. "Rising Schooling Returns in Urban China," in *Education and Reform in China.* Emily Hannum and Albert Park, eds. New York: Routledge.

Zhang, Xiaobo and Ravi Kanbur. October 2003. "Spatial Inequality in Education and Healthcare in China." Cornell University Department of Applied Economics and Management Working Paper 2003–35. Ithaca: Cornell University.

Zhou, Xueguang, Phyllis Moen, and Nancy B. Tuma. 1998. "Educational Stratification in Urban China: 1949–94." *Sociology of Education.* 71, pp. 199–222.

EIGHT

Environmental Resources and Economic Growth

James Roumasset, Kimberly Burnett, and Hua Wang

INTRODUCTION

This chapter assesses the nature and degree of environmental degradation and resource depletion in China and their relationship to economic activity and environmental policies. We describe regulatory and other policies and consider their political economy determinants. Inasmuch as this objective can only be partially achieved, we hope to contribute to a research agenda for environmental and resource economics in China.

Claims have been made that the damage to China's environment is significant and has had a negative influence on economic growth. Critics argue that uncontrolled waste of resources and environmental degradation have offset much of China's economic growth over the past twenty-five years. Accordingly, a secondary objective of this chapter is to address whether environmentally augmented accounting substantially reduces the magnitude of China's economic gains.

We begin by reviewing evidence on air and water pollution, including environmental Kuznets curves (EKCs) for three major air pollutants, in the section on "Pollution." "Natural Capital" follows with an overview of the country's natural resources, and how their quality and quantity have changed over time. In the section on the "Natural Resources Kuznets Curve," we develop a theory regarding a country's *natural resource Kuznets curve* and apply it to empirical data on the value of China's natural resource degradation over a thirty-year period. To formally address the question of China's growth rate, we extend green accounting theory to facilitate a comparison of conventionally measured net national product (NNP) and *green* NNP (GNNP). The section on "Green Net National Product" provides a discussion of forces that cause GNNP to grow at first more slowly but then faster than NNP. Available estimates of China's GNNP conform to these predictions. An indicator of sustainability similar to genuine saving, termed *genuine capital accumulation* (GKA), is shown to be dramatically increasing in the section on "Genuine Capital Accumulation." The section on "Policy Environment" reviews the current policy environment, emphasizing both accomplishments and shortcomings, and the last section concludes.

POLLUTION

Air Pollution

Currently, the three air pollutants of concern are sulfur dioxide (SO_2) from the burning of coal for power generation; nitrous oxides (NO_x), mainly from motor vehicle emissions; and total suspended particles (TSP) due in part to the growing desertification of the Northwest and energy consumption in the South. Due to China's dependence on coal (68 percent of energy consumption), windblown SO_2 emissions from China may account for more than 13 percent of sulfur deposits in South Korea and up to 50 percent in Japan (Wishnick, 2005). Higher incomes have led to increased car ownership (although this is still less than 2 percent), and motor vehicles account for 45–60 percent of NO_x emissions and 85 percent of CO_2 emissions in cities (Wishnick, 2005). One-third of China's total land area is prone to desertification, including 262 million hectares of pastoral and oasis land in the Xinjiang, Inner Mongolia, Tibet, Gansu, and Qinghai provinces.

Air pollution is a major health issue. Ambient and indoor air pollution has been blamed for the high incidence of premature deaths (World Bank, 1997). Particulate matter with a diameter less than 10 microns (PM-10) is the most damaging air pollutant in terms of health costs. In 2002, China's State Environmental Protection Agency (SEPA) tested the air quality in over 300 cities and found that two-thirds did not meet standards set by the World Health Organization (WHO) for acceptable levels of TSP (Economy, 2004). In 1995, the World Bank estimated that health damages due to air pollution accounted for 7.1 percent of national income (World Bank, 1995). This estimate may be inflated, however, inasmuch as the methodology infers the value of life in China from U.S. estimates, without accounting for the extent of overpopulation (see, e.g., Dasgupta, 1993, 2001).

A recent report from the State Environmental Protection Administration (SEPA, 2004) asserts that either air pollution in major cities has been improving or the speed of deterioration has decreased, with falling emission levels and improved efficiency in plants. Total levels of NO_x, as shown in Figure 8.1, have fallen recently. Statistics show that SO_2 and TSP have been declining in the major cities since the mid-1980s, as shown in Figures 8.2 and 8.3. These figures represent ambient concentrations of the three major pollutants for eleven of China's major cities.[1] With China's rapid development, a natural question arises regarding how these levels have fallen given increased production and economic output over this same

---

[1] The sample cities are as follows: Tianjin, Guangzhou, Beijing, Shanghai, Chengdu, Changchun, Taiyuan, Anshan, Nanchang, Shenzhen, Yinchuan, and Guilin (chosen for their completeness of data).

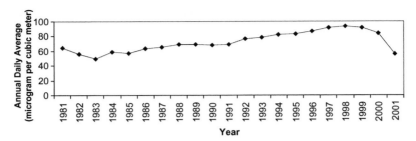

Figure 8.1. Ambient NO_x concentrations in eleven Chinese cities, 1981–2001 (*Note:* The observations are population-weighted averages of data for individual cities.
Source: Ambient concentration data: World Bank's Development Research Group (DRG); population data: http://www.citypopulation.de/China.html.)

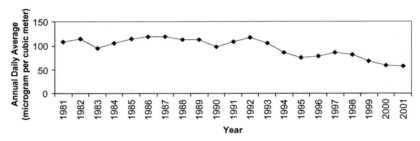

Figure 8.2. Ambient SO_2 concentrations in eleven Chinese cities, 1981–2001

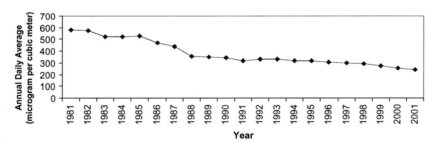

Figure 8.3. Ambient TSP (<40 microns) concentrations in eleven Chinese cities, 1981–2001

period. For example, SEPA asserts that in 2002, national environmental quality was maintained at the level of the previous year, while the national gross domestic product (GDP) grew by 8 percent. Furthermore, SEPA (2004) reports reduced levels of dust and sulfur dioxide, stable water quality, and improved air quality in many cities.

The statistical picture of pollution trends contrasts starkly with bleak qualitative reports by authors, such as Economy (2004). Indeed, the evidence in Dasgupta et al. (2002), Gallagher (2003), and Diesendorf (2003) suggests that

China's environmental regulations are ahead of where European countries were at similar levels of per capita income. What additional data might give a more complete picture of the trends in air pollution? Some areas of possible improvement are discussed later. The first issue pertains to the measurement of TSP and NO_x concentrations. A second issue concerns the decentralization of polluting industries and the lack of solid source–receptor data.

The measurement of TSP concentrations is complicated by its ambiguous components. Since TSP is the general name for particulate matter up to 40 microns in diameter, authorities measure the concentration of TSP per cubic meter of air. Nothing can be deduced about the small versus large particles within this cubic meter. The problem is that the most accurate measure of serious particulate pollution is fine particulate matter, or PM-10. While the United States monitors particulates as small as PM-2.5, PM-10 monitoring data in China are scarce (although daily monitoring of PM-10 has recently begun in some cities). Based on correlations between PM-10 and TSP in other data sets, a World Bank study (2001b) found that PM-10 is the most damaging air pollutant in China in terms of health complications.

The smaller particles are directly emitted from the combustion of fossil fuels and also result from postproduction photochemical reactions. The larger particles are the result of fugitive dust from wind and soil erosion and particles from industrial processes, such as metal and fiber production. So while total TSP emissions appear to be falling, it is unclear how the composition of the fine versus coarse particulates is changing. Concentrations of PM-10 may actually be increasing, even as TSP is decreasing, but this cannot be ascertained without more detailed information on the composition of TSP measurements.

There is a similar problem with the measurement of nitrous oxides. NO_x is measured as any combination of N and O, whether it be NO or NO_2 (as with TSP, authorities have begun measuring NO_2 separately, although not on a large-scale basis across the country). Uncertainty about the composition makes levels of NO_x difficult to compare with NO_2 gas concentrations reported in the United States and is referred to widely in the literature on air pollution epidemiology and health. Researchers have found that NO_2 level averages two-thirds of the NO_x level in China (U.S. Embassy Beijing, 1998).

In recent years, the government has begun to decentralize the polluting industries.[2] But as industry moves out of cities, the pollution data are still largely collected in these cities. It is possible then that total emissions may be increasing, but are more decentralized. Although it appears that urban China has stabilized or reduced ambient concentrations of the three major pollutants, air quality data are generally unavailable outside of major cities. Supplementary data are needed on the level

---

[2] SEPA's Ninth Five-Year Plan includes moving hundreds of polluters out of major industrial areas to curb pollution in those areas. In 2001, around 1 million square meters were cleared in Beijing as a result of relocations and another 6 million square meters are scheduled for clearing between 2001 and 2005. The city of Beijing wishes to move polluters out, making room for industrial marketing, research institutes, and more environment-friendly industries.

Table 8.1. *Regression results*

Per capita emissions	NO_x per capita	SO_2 per capita	TSP per capita
GDP per capita	0.0000387	0.0001089	0.0002378
	(5.77×10^{-6})	(0.0000174)	(0.0000607)
GDP per capita^2	-6.85×10^{-10}	-9.09×10^{-10}	-2.66×10^{-9}
	(8.11×10^{-11})	(2.47×10^{-10})	(8.51×10^{-10})
Year	-0.027 (0.0027)	-0.113 (0.0081)	-0.251 (0.0281)
Constant	0.263	0.089	2.265
R-square	0.17	0.22	0.11
F-value	53.70	74.06	32.75

Note: Standard errors have been given in parentheses.

of pollutants elsewhere, especially in the areas to which polluting industries are dispersing. Additionally, because source–receptor data are unavailable, it is hard to know how pollution created by specific industries affects various areas. Some will end up concentrated within the same city it was produced in; other polluters will have their emissions blown out of the region, with adverse impacts instead affecting downwind areas. It is not clear that current policies take these issues into account.

Although the statistics focus on large cities, the trend toward decentralization does have an important economic justification. Falling emissions in the cities means fewer people may be exposed to the pollution. It follows that decentralization of industry may significantly reduce health damages.

The Environmental Kuznets Curve

The EKC is a stylized fact according to which air pollution first increases and then falls as per capita income rises. The standard explanation is that environmental quality is a luxury good and that political economy forces induce environmental regulation accordingly. The rise and fall of the manufacturing sector relative to the whole economy and the comparative advantage that low-income countries have in the exportation of "dirty goods" are also cited (Grossman and Krueger, 1991; Panayotou, 1993; Lieb, 2002).

Figures 8.1–8.3 depict the population-weighted average ambient concentration levels of NO_x, SO_2, and TSP for eleven cities from 1981 to 2001. The majority of these eleven cities are major population centers. To investigate whether these pollutants followed the stylized EKC shape, we conducted a fixed-effects regression analysis for three pollutants in eighty cities from 1990 to 2001. Results for the three regressions are presented in Table 8.1 and are illustrated in Figures 8.4–8.6. While the order of emissions reaching their turning points in other countries is typically SO_2, TSP, and then NO_x (Brown, 2005), for China we find that the NO_x turns first at

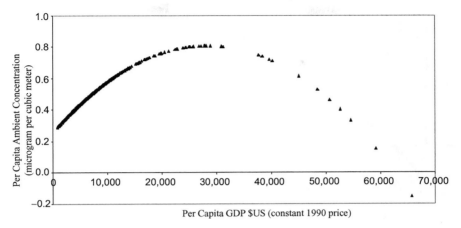

Figure 8.4. EKC for NO_x in eighty cities, 1990–2001

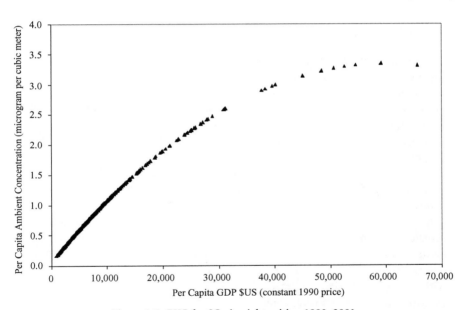

Figure 8.5. EKC for SO_2 in eighty cities, 1990–2001

a per capita income level of around 28,000 yuan (approximately 3,461 U.S. dollars), followed by TSP around 44,000 yuan (approximately 5,440 U.S. dollars), and then finally SO_2, which is just reaching the flat portion of its curve around 58,000 yuan (or approximately 7,171 U.S. dollars). The order of the turning points appears to be reversed from that of Western countries, presumably due to the early fall in NO_x.

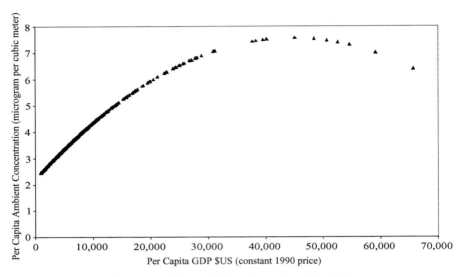

Figure 8.6. EKC for TSP in eighty cities, 1990–2001

The early turning point and the dramatic reduction in emissions of the NO_x EKC (Figure 8.4) may be an accurate portrayal of NO_x in industry, but may misrepresent what is happening to total NO_x, including mobile sources. Given the rapid increase in automobile ownership after our data period (1990–2001), it is quite possible that total NO_x is now increasing. In 2002, automobile purchases increased by 56 percent. In 2003, purchases grew by 75 percent and by another 15 percent in 2004, when the government tightened rules on credit for car purchases.[3] A 25 percent increase in auto sales from 2005 to 2006, with sales reaching 7.22 million units, indicates a strengthening of auto consumer demand despite recent regulatory measures (*China Daily*, 2007). Indeed, a revised EKC for NO_x may eventually show two peaks. This helps to remind us that EKC is a stylized fact, not an economic law, and that the revealed pattern may not always conform to the simple one-turning-point case because of sectoral composition, trade patterns, and other complicating factors.[4]

The EKC for TSP takes the expected shape and the turning point is consistent with other studies. Falling per capita emissions despite rapid growth of heavy industry and manufacturing could reflect that either the country's reforestation efforts are indeed working or there is a problem with seasonal measurement (see section "Soil" for further discussion). There is also the issue of the exact makeup of TSP. While the smaller particles that are more detrimental to human health (less than 10 parts per million) have begun showing up as separate measurements, it is

[3] "Dream Machines." *The Economist.* June 2, 2005, available at http://www.economist.com/ business/displaystory.cfm?story_id=4032842.
[4] The NO_x discussion is suggestive of a "weak EKC hypothesis" according to which emissions increase in the early stages of development and decrease in the latter stages. In intermediate stages of development there may be one or more turning points.

not clear how the total composition has changed over time. Another issue that may be leading to the decrease in reported emissions is that manufacturing activities have, to some extent, moved away from city centers, even though the receptors that monitor pollution have remained relatively fixed. Finally, China appears to be just reaching the flat portion of its EKC for SO_2 emissions.

Auffhammer, Carson, and Garin-Munoz (2004) found that most areas in China are likely approaching the flat portion of the EKC for CO_2; that is, further increases in per capita income will not tend to cause increases in per capita carbon emissions. Using more recent data, however, Auffhammer and Carson (2006) came to a very different conclusion. Utilizing a provincial-level panel data set with 588 observations (thirty provinces from 1985 to 2004), CO_2 emissions are forecast to increase dramatically over the next decade. The authors conclude that China's CO_2 emissions are highly unlikely to peak in the coming decade absent a dramatic change in energy policies and question the stationarity of EKCs in light of structural economic shifts, especially over space.[5] On the other hand, CO_2 may be the exception that proves the EKC rule.

Inasmuch as carbon emissions are a global public good, the effect of rising incomes on the demand for cleaner air would not be expected to appreciably increase regulations aimed at reducing carbon emissions. Another cause of the EKC pattern is that in the course of economic development, the relatively clean service sector grows faster than the manufacturing sector, and emissions eventually decline accordingly. In China's case, however, vigorous relative growth of manufacturing has persisted beyond the typical level of per capita income because of the larger role of exports in China's development. Finally, Auffhammer and Carson proxy CO_2 emissions by waste-gas emissions, which are presumably positively affected by the rapid growth in the stock and use of automobiles.

These observations suggest that China's emission history is mostly consistent with the EKC hypothesis and indicates that total pollution per capita may have stabilized or begun to fall, despite rapidly increasing production. This conclusion is limited by the possibilities of measurement error in NO_x and TSP and by the mitigating effects of decentralization and increased automobile ownership. Nonetheless, it appears that China's regulatory policies have achieved an overall turning point in air pollution, especially in terms of exposure,[6] at a per capita income less than the income level at which European countries reached peak levels of contamination.

Water Pollution

Much less progress has been made with respect to water quality improvements. Water pollution problems are especially severe in the North, particularly in the

---

[5] The authors suggest that the magnitude of the projected increase is several times larger than the recommended carbon reductions induced by the Kyoto Protocol and that China's carbon emissions will surpass U.S. carbon emissions by 2010.

[6] Exposure is a measure of pollution that weighs emissions according to exposed population.

Table 8.2. *Water quality trends in China's rivers, 1997–2003*

	Water class	1997	1998	1999	2000	2001	2002	2003
Total length of rivers evaluated (km)		65,405	109,700	113,600	114,043	121,010	122,602	134,593
	I		5.4	5.5	4.9	5.0	5.6	5.7
	II	32.8	24.4	24.5	24.0	27.6	33.1	30.7
	III	26.3	33.0	32.4	29.8	28.8	26.0	26.2
Percentage in water class	SUBTOTAL ("above standard")	*56.4*	*62.8*	*62.4*	*58.7*	*61.4*	*64.7*	*62.6*
	IV		13.7	12.6	16.1	14.2	12.2	10.9
	V	27.7	6.6	7.8	8.1	7.8	5.6	5.8
	VI+	15.9	16.9	17.2	17.1	16.6	17.5	20.7

Source: World Bank (2001b).

catchments of the Hai and Huang (Yellow) rivers and in the Huai in central China. The last decade has brought improvement to some of the larger rivers even as the total picture continues to deteriorate. It has been said that even if all point sources that empty into these northern rivers complied 100 percent with national discharge standards, the river systems would still be environmentally overloaded. Freshwater lakes and coastal water quality have not improved, and there is evidence that groundwater pollution may be increasing (World Bank, 2001b). The most problematic pollutant is organic material from industrial and domestic sources.

Table 8.2 shows water quality[7] of some major rivers. The rivers evaluated include the southeast, southwest, and northwest systems, including the Songhua, Liao, Hai, Huai, Huang, Changjiang (Yangtze), and Zhu (Pearl) rivers. These rivers drain over 45 percent of total land area and account for more than 54 percent of its freshwater resources. While the total length of the rivers evaluated continues to increase, the percentage "above standard" remains fairly constant, signaling falling water quality in more water bodies.

If we were to separate these percentages for the North and South, the percentage of poor-class water bodies would be significantly higher in the North. The incidence of Class V and worse tends to be about three times higher in the North (World Bank, 2001b). Rapid industrialization of the North, with its accompanying population

---

[7] China's water bodies are divided into five classes according to their utilization and protection status: Class I applies to the water from remote sources and national nature reserves. Class II consists of "protected areas for centralized sources of drinking water, the protected areas for rare fishes, and the spawning fields of fishes and shrimps." Class III applies to the "second class of protected areas for centralized sources of drinking water and protected areas for the common fishes and swimming areas." Class IV covers "the water areas for industrial use and entertainment which is not directly touched by human bodies." Class V applies to "water bodies for agricultural use and landscape requirement" (World Bank, 2001b).

Table 8.3. *Water quality trends in China's lakes, 1998–2005*

	Water class	1998	1999	2000	2001	2002	2003	January 2005
Total number of lakes evaluated		16	24	24	24	24	52	52
Percentage in water class	III or above	37.5	41.7	37.5	41.7	25.0	40.4	40.4
	Partially polluted	25.0	20.8	16.7	8.3	25.0	9.6	9.6
	Severely polluted	37.5	37.5	45.8	50.0	50.0	50.0	50.0

Source: World Bank (2001b).

growth, means that more people are relying on increasingly worse water supplies. The number and probably the proportion of people using the poorer classes of water are likely to be rising. Table 8.3 documents similar trends in the country's lakes.

Class V and worse water continues to be used by households and agriculture, posing dire health risks. SEPA samples do not include smaller rivers, which are said to be in extremely poor shape as a result of the discharge from township and village enterprises (TVEs). Water quality in the Huai River is reportedly getting worse again, despite considerable effort by the government. In Guiyu, in Guangdong Province, levels of lead in the water were 2,400 times higher than WHO drinking guidelines (Economy, 2004).

Furthermore, total wastewater discharge is increasing, particularly in the residential sector. Although increased regulations have ameliorated industrial discharge, the total amount of wastewater is increasing. Confounding the problem is the increasing reality of water shortages. The combination of growing waste discharge (see Figure 8.7) and shrinking water flows exacerbates the already serious water pollution issues. This situation is illustrated in Figure 8.7.

In the absence of comprehensive time-series data, information concerning groundwater quality remains anecdotal. Groundwater usage is poorly controlled. Excessive extraction has become common, particularly in the North. Anecdotal evidence suggests that groundwater quality is deteriorating, especially in near-surface aquifers and the vicinity of major cities (World Bank, 2001b).

NATURAL CAPITAL

Forests

Centuries of population growth have burdened China with a long history of deforestation. In addition, China spent the second half of the twentieth century overexploiting its timber resources and then mandating reforestation/afforestation

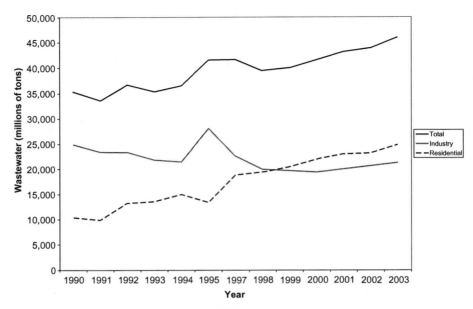

Figure 8.7. Wastewater trends, 1990–2003

(Yearbook, 2005).[8] The forestry management regime is split between the state and the local communities. State management covers only about 20 percent of the total resources, although this segment contains the higher-quality trees. The remaining reserves are collectively managed forests, which are owned by local communities and operated by village leaders.

Government's concern over the high levels of timber cutting was first documented in 1950 when the government issued "Instructions on the Work of National Forestry" to stop the random felling of trees (China Report). Afforestation became a government prerogative the next year, mandated in "Instructions on Strengthening the Leadership for the Work of Forestry" (China Report). Despite the government's efforts, forest cover continued to decrease to 12 percent of China's 96 million square kilometers of land area, as calculated in the Third Forest Census of 1983–1987 (Yearbook). This is approximately 115,250,000 hectares of forestland (Yearbook). Subsequent data show a slight recovery due to increases in both afforestation and reforestation (see Tables 8.4 and 8.5). The proportion of afforestation for the purpose of timber harvest declined dramatically in the late twentieth century, while the lands designated for nature preserves increased substantially.

Data for the volume of timber harvested no longer appear among the industrial indicators in the Yearbook after 1987. This may reflect the government's decision

---

[8] Reforestation is the process of encouraging forest growth in lands that were previously forested, basically replenishing depleted forests. Afforestation is the process of converting previously unforested land into forests, or the process of forest creation.

Table 8.4. *Trends in forest resources, 1981–2004*

Year	Forested area (million hectare)	Forest cover (percent)	Forest volume[a] (billion cubic meter)
1981–1982	119.78	12.50	9.35
1983–1987	115.25	12.00	10.26
1988–1990	124.65	12.98	9.141
1991–1996	128.63	13.40	10.868
1997	133.70	13.92	11.785
1998–2002	158.94	16.55	12.49
2004	174.91	18.22	13.618

[a] Forest Standing Stock.
Source: Yearbook (various years).

Table 8.5. *China's forests: trends in planting, harvesting, and protection, 1952–2004*

Year	Total afforested area (million hectare)	Area afforested for timber (hectare and percent)	Timber production (million cubic meter)	Nature reserves (million hectare)
1952	1.085	0.50, 46.08	12.33	n.a.
1957	4.355	1.73, 39.84	27.87	n.a.
1965	3.426	1.72, 50.41	39.78	n.a.
1978	4.496	3.13, 69.62	51.62	n.a.
1984	8.254	5.06, 61.38	58.00	n.a.
1989	5.0233[a]	n.a.	89.64[b]	22[c]
1993	5.9034[a]	2.504,[a] 42.42	63.92[a]	66.18[d]
1999	4.9007[a]	1.418,[a] 28.93	52.36[a]	88.15
2000	5.105	1.21, 23.86	47.23[a]	98.21
2001	4.953	0.90, 18.28	45.52	129.89
2002	7.7709	0.89, 12.73	44.361	132.95
2003	9.1188	1.17, 12.98	47.58[a]	143.98
2004	5.598	0.87, 15.56	51.97[a]	148.23

[a] Data taken from *Forestry Statistics Yearbook* (various years).
[b] Value calculated based on Timber Industry Production Index found in China Report: Social and Economic Development.
[c] 1988 value.
[d] *Environmental Statistics Yearbook.*
Source: Yearbook (various years).

to scale back the timber industry. The timber harvest peaked volumetrically in the late 1980s and has declined since then.

The reforms of the 1980s included policies to encourage afforestation and limit overharvesting. These policies aimed to change the management practices of state forestry enterprises and also to influence the actions of farmers and forest dwellers.

There is great disagreement about the outcome of these reforms. Some observers cite an 8.5 percent increase in national forest cover between 1980 and 1988 as evidence of success (Yearbook), while others have asserted a negative impact. Rozelle et al. (1998) provide evidence that policy changes in the state sector did stimulate reforesting, but provided few incentives to curtail high rates of harvesting. Indeed, according to Economy (2004), forest resources are characterized by decreasing reserves and illegal logging. In the first years of reform, logging increased by 25 percent, consistent with the volumetric peak in timber harvests late in the 1980s. The country is now the world's second largest consumer of timber.

A U.S. Embassy report identifies deforestation as the root cause of the increased damages caused by the Yangtze River floods in 1998. It reports that forest cover in Sichuan Province decreased from 19 percent in 1950 to a low of 6.5 percent and that the average tree-cutting rate was more than double the natural tree growth rate. The Earth Policy Institute reports that by 1998, the Yangtze River basin had lost 85 percent of its total forest cover (Brown, 1998). Destruction of forests results in water storage losses as well as silting of the riverbeds and lakes. The Ecological Section of the SEPA (reported in the U.S. Embassy document) calculates that removing 70,000 hectares of forest eliminates 1 million cubic meters of natural water storage. In addition, the root systems of trees help anchor the soil, preventing silt from raising the height of the riverbed and, consequently, the heights of the floodwaters. Timber harvest rates dropped significantly following the flood crisis.

In response to this loss of forest cover, the government started the conservation set-aside (or offset) program "Grain for Green" in 1999. Easily one of the largest conservation set-aside programs in the world, its main objective was to increase forest cover on sloped cropland in the upper reaches of the Yangtze and Yellow River basins to prevent soil erosion. When available in their community, households set aside all or parts of certain types of land and plant seedlings to grow trees. In return, the government compensates the participants with grain, cash payments, and free seedlings. By the end of 2002, officials expanded the program to twenty-five (of thirty) provinces. To date, 7 million hectares of cultivated land has been converted to forest and pasture land.[9]

While this afforestation program certainly reduced domestic food production, the land that was removed from tillage was of such low quality (much lower quality than the average land that was opened up during the 1980s and 1990s to compensate for cultivated land lost to urbanization) that the program had only a marginal impact on overall food prices (Rozelle, Uchida, and Xu, 2005). Additionally, afforestation campaigns in general, which have had a long history in the country, are often undertaken with inappropriate technologies and poor oversight.

---

[9] "Impact of WTO Accession on China's Agriculture, Rural Development, and Farmers," by Li Xiande, Institute of Agricultural Economics, Chinese Academy of Agricultural Sciences. May 16, 2006, presentation to World Bank Institute Beijing, available at siteresources.worldbank.org/INTRANETTRADE/Resources/WBI-Training/288464–1152217173757/Session20_LiXiande.pdf

Table 8.6. *Total water resources in China*

Year	Precipitation	Ground water	Surface water	Overlap of ground and surface water	Total water resources
1997	5,816.90	694.20	2,683.50	592.20	2,785.50
1998	6,763.10	940.00	3,272.60	810.90	3,401.70
1999	5,970.20	838.70	2,720.40	739.50	2,819.60
2000	6,009.20	850.20	2,656.20	736.30	2,770.10
2001	5,812.20	839.00	2,593.30	745.50	2,686.80
2002	6,261.00	869.70	2,724.30	768.50	2,825.50

Note: Values are in billion cubic meters.
Source: Ministry of Water Resources, China.

Therefore, despite increased biomass, the value of China's forests may have declined in recent years. Afforestation is taking place on lower-quality land as opposed to natural forest habitats and is further from market centers. As a result, neither the potential biological nor market benefits are being delivered with the optimal effectiveness, for example, regarding the appropriate composition of fast-growing versus high-value trees. Rozelle, Huang, and Benziger (2003) also report evidence that the increase in aggregate forest cover experienced between 1980 and 1993 came at the expense of forest diversity. With natural forests transformed into plantations, the ability to provide environmental services, such as species habitat, has declined. The change in forest structure may also affect the livelihoods of certain populations, as well as contribute to growing desertification and increased sandstorms in the North.[10] Unfortunately, the official statistics do not allow complete verification of these apparent trends. We have data on deforestation and reforestation, but no good indicators of actual stock levels. Furthermore, the total reforestation is not reported, only what is reforested in a given year. And because the age distribution of the timber stock is unknown, it is impossible to estimate the value of this resource. Better reporting would account for the changing *stock* of forest resources, including quality, location, and age distribution.

Water

Rapid economic growth has led to an increased demand for water, increased water pollution, and a change in sources of water pollution. Table 8.6 describes the change in total water resources in China in recent years, and Table 8.7 reports supply and consumption patterns.[11] Although the national supply of freshwater, 2,500 cubic

---

[10] In May 2000, then Premier Zhu Rongji warned that the rapidly advancing desert would necessitate moving the capital from Beijing (Economy, 2004).

[11] Surface water refers to the water volume from rivers, lakes, and glaciers, that is, the surface runoffs of natural rivers, lakes, and so on. Groundwater is the water from precipitation and surface water that seeps into the ground and is potentially available via pumping. The total water resource figure is found by summing the surface water and groundwater and then deducting the overlapping portion.

Table 8.7. *Water supply and consumption in China*

Year	Water supply	Water consumption	Water depletion	Depletion as percentage of consumption
1997	562.30	556.60	317.80	57.10
1998	547.00	543.50	306.20	56.34
1999	561.30	559.10	302.80	54.16
2000	553.10	549.80	301.20	54.78
2001	556.70	556.70	305.20	54.82
2002	549.70	549.70	298.50	54.30

Note: Values are in billion cubic meter.
Source: Ministry of Water Resources, China.

meters per capita, is above the World Bank's definition of a water-scarce country, the geographic distribution of China's water resources is highly uneven. Availability is greatest in the South, where average rainfall is as much as nine times greater than that in the Northwest. The northern rivers have far less assimilative capacity than southern rivers, due to lower flows. Distribution of groundwater resources is also skewed – the South gaining four times more than the North. Most of the water is directed toward agriculture. (Eighty-five percent arable land in the North is irrigated, compared with 10 percent in the United States.)

Access to water resources is increasing due to investments in water resources engineering. As of 2000, 85,000 dams had been constructed with a total storage capacity of 518 billion cubic meters, of which 397 are large sized with a total storage capacity of 326.7 billion cubic meters and 2,634 are medium sized with a total storage capacity of 72.9 billion cubic meters. China's water engineering projects also include 270,000 kilometers of embankments and ninety-eight flood storage or detention zones for the Yangtze, Yellow, and Huai rivers, with a total area of 34,500 square kilometers and a total storage capacity of 100 billion cubic meters (Ministry of Water Resources, 2004).

Rapid economic growth and a growing population have increased demand. Historically, government has met rising demand via dams and other public works that capture a greater percentage of available surface water and increase total water storage. These are increasingly expensive per unit of water made available and their remaining potential is quite limited.

There is evidence of falling water tables, especially in the northern regions. A study conducted in 2001 by the Geological Environmental Monitoring Institute in Beijing reported that in Hebei Province, the average level of the aquifer dropped 2.9 meters in 2000.[12] In some cities around the province, it fell by nearly 6 meters. The water deficit (a summation over time of the extent water supplies falls below average) in the North may now exceed over 40 billion tons per year.

---

[12] http://www.thestudentzone.com/articles/chinawater.html.

The most recent water projections suggest that irrigation use will decline from 73 percent of total consumption to 50 percent in 2050 (World Bank, 2001b). Consumption for industrial and urban purposes, however, is expected to increase substantially. Since both of these forms of consumption lead to emissions of polluted water, it will be increasingly difficult to maintain water quality. The UNDP, UNEP, World Bank, and the World Resources Institute define water scarcity as 1,000 cubic meters per person or less. The water consumed per person (from both surface and groundwater) includes not only what is normally classified as domestic/residential water consumption per capita, but also the individual's share of national water consumed for productive activities – agriculture and industry – and the individual's share of water required for ecosystem needs. Using this definition of water scarcity, the country as a whole will be classified as water scarce by 2010 at the current rate of population growth (Shalizi, 2004).

There is no clear solution to the enormous disparity in water supply between the north and the south of China, nor to the rising overall shortage in per capita supply. Although the country is implementing numerous water storage projects and building channels intended to transport large volumes of water from south to north, the trends of these supply stresses show that they are likely to overwhelm such efforts. In particular, the South to North Transfer Project commenced construction in 2002 and is expected to deliver its first benefits to Beijing residents in 2008. The project consists of three canals covering 1,300 kilometers, transferring water from the lower, middle, and upper reaches of the Yangtze River by channeling it to the Yellow, Huai, and Hai rivers. The Ministry of Water Resources estimates that 94 percent of the volume of the Yangtze River annually flows into the East China Sea. The project is expected to cost 59 billion U.S. dollars and take fifty years to complete (Ministry of Water Resources, 2004). A U.S. Embassy report questions the engineering feasibility of certain aspects of the project, such as crossing the Yellow River, whose bed is rising annually due to siltation. Additional criticisms in the report address the lack of concern for environmental and supply effects to donor regions, especially in drought years, and for the water use rights of downstream localities (U.S. Embassy, 2000).

The severity of China's water problems varies widely across regions, with the greatest difficulties arising in the northwest and north China regions. Gross underpricing of water resources compounds the difficulties arising from rising production, population growth, and urbanization. Inevitably, the potential for successful water management must rest primarily with demand-side conservation.

Soil

Since the 1990s, desertification[13] has become a major land resource concern. Desertification affects some 262 million hectares, giving China the world's highest ratio

---

[13] Desertification has been defined by the United Nations as "land degradation in arid, semi-arid and dry sub-humid areas, resulting from various factors, including climatic variations and human activities."

of actual-to-potential desertification (World Bank, 2001b). The North (including the capital of Beijing) is periodically covered in dust for days at a time, dust that travels as far as Japan, Korea, and the United States. It has been estimated that 5 billion tons of topsoil is lost every year.[14]

A series of government-sponsored policies to increase grain production, partly in response to Lester Brown's *Who Will Feed China* (1994), exacerbated problems in land-use practices. A 1994 policy required that all cropland used for construction be offset by land reclaimed elsewhere. Coastal provinces paid other provinces to plow land to offset losses, and these provinces reclaimed vast tracts of grasslands and continued to plow more land. Overall, the campaign failed to achieve its objectives and created unintended consequences, including the substitution of poor-quality land for good-quality land.

Peter Lindert (2000) examined one aspect of Brown's challenge: can China feed itself? Lindert's analysis suggests that Brown's findings are somewhat exaggerated. Lindert shows econometrically that productivity does not necessarily decline with soil loss. There are a number of additional factors that would prevent loss of productivity despite loss of soil, for example, sufficient soil depth.

This is not to suggest that soil resources are being optimally managed. While on-site damages from lost soil may be low, off-site damages may be considerable, including siltation in irrigation systems, water transport systems, increased water pollution, nearshore effects, and health complications from increased windblown dust. These concerns appear to be more serious than productivity loss. Relatedly, asking whether China can feed itself may be the wrong question. While the country has increased imports, this is a sign of comparative advantage, not necessarily of an inability to be self-sufficient in food.

Energy

China is the world's largest producer and consumer of coal, which dominates domestic energy consumption and constitutes the chief source of air pollution. Rapid economic growth has led to a 5 percent annual increase in energy consumption. It is estimated that to meet projected electricity demands in 2020, China would need an additional 1.2 billion tons of coal per year (*People's Daily*). In its search for alternative sources of power, China has constructed mammoth hydroelectric generating dams, forayed into solar and wind technology, and, in the last two decades, invested significantly in nuclear power production. However, substantial reliance on coal, the source of most sulfur dioxide and soot emissions, continues. In 2000, the per capita stock of domestic reserves was 2.6 tons for petroleum, 1,074 cubic meters for natural gas, and 90 tons for coal. Forty percent of coal consumption is for electricity generation. Much of it is unwashed, perhaps in part because of the water shortages in Northern China.

---

[14] China's Agenda 21, www.acca21.org.cn/english.

Table 8.8. *Coal use, 1990–2003*

	Final consumption			Intermediate consumption		
Year	Residential	Industry	Total	Power generation	Heating	Cooking
1990	16,699.7	35,773.8	60,205.9	27,204.3	2,995.5	10,697.6
1995	13,530.1	46,050.3	66,156.1	44,440.2	5,887.3	18,396.4
2000	7,907.2	34,122.0	46,821.4	55,811.2	8,794.1	16,496.4
2003	8,174.7	35,981.2	49,044.8	81,976.5	10,895.5	23,639.9
2004	8,173.2	46,083.0	59,543.7	91,961.6	11,546.6	25,349.6
2005	8,739.0	48,040.7	62,154.1	103,098.5	13,542.0	31,667.1

Note: Values are in 10,000 tons.
Source: Yearbook (2006, table 7.5).

Table 8.8 summarizes trends in China's consumption of coal. The data show rising coal use as well as important changes in the structure of consumption. Residential consumption declined by 50 percent between 1990 and 2003, reflecting substitution of natural gas and other relatively clean fuels for coal as well as new prohibitions against domestic coal burning in many cities. Final consumption of coal in industry rose and then fell, apparently reflecting widespread substitution of electricity (mainly coal-fired) for direct use of coal to power industrial processes.[15]

At the same time, rising coal production has supported large increases in intermediate usage of coal for producing electricity and for heating and (commercial) cooking, all of which have recorded substantial growth. Coal consumption for power generation alone rose from 272 million tons in 1990 to over 1 billion tons in 2005. In addition, rising coal production has allowed China to become the world's second largest coal exporter after Australia, having jumped from 32 million tons in 1998 to more than 90 million tons of exports in 2001.[16] This figure continued to grow, reaching 94 million tons by 2003, before dropping to 87 and 72 million tons in 2004 and 2005 (Yearbook). Rapid export growth reflects government assistance to state-owned coal mines, export incentives, relatively low cost, proximity to Asian

---

[15] Colleagues suggest several explanations for the decline in industrial coal consumption (Kang Wu of East West Center and Jeff Brown of FACS, personal communication). First, more advanced equipment associated with growing industrialization has called for increased use of electric power. The direct use of coal in the industrial sector has, to a great extent, been replaced by coal-fired power, which is more energy efficient. Second, diesel is often favored over coal for its cleanliness and efficiency. Finally, high hauling charges discourage the transportation of coal and encourage the substitution of electricity and diesel. Moreover, imported equipment may run on diesel only, or on electric power. As a result, between 1995 and 2002, China's use of electric power in the industrial sector increased notably, the use of diesel was higher, while the use of coal declined. Other possibilities for this trend include the relatively longer time it takes to install coal-using capital equipment, increased oil demand due to the rapid increase in China's stock of motor vehicles, and the possible difficulty of rapid increases in coal production or even coal imports.

[16] Source: Geoff Hiscock, CNN Asia Business Editor. Monday, March 10, 2003, at CNN.com.

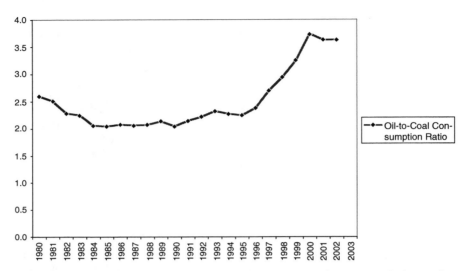

Figure 8.8. Oil-to-coal consumption ratio, 1980–2003 (*Source:* http://www.eia.doe.gov/)

markets, expanded production capacity, and the desire of some Asian coal buyers to diversify their sources of supply.

Available figures also show important changes in the broader structure of energy consumption. Steep increases in the use of oil have led to a rise in the ratio of oil-to-coal use, although very recently, that trend has abated (Figure 8.8). Beginning in 1993, China's trade balance in petroleum turned negative; since then, net imports have risen steeply, reaching 138.84 million tons in 2006. This is a 17 percent increase from imports in 2005; net imports of refined oil were up 38 percent the same year (*China Daily*, 2007). Official forecasts anticipate further growth of petroleum imports, which are expected to reach 60 percent of total consumption by 2020 (www.cei.gov.cn).

China has also increased production of natural gas, which has largely replaced gasoline as the fuel for buses and taxis. In 2005, natural gas accounted for 3.3 percent of China's energy output and 2.9 percent of consumption, both record levels (Yearbook, 2006, p. 261). Plans to construct facilities for large-scale imports of liquid natural gas underscore Beijing's commitment to increase the role of natural gas in China's energy economy.

Another effort in this direction is the use of photovoltaics, especially in remote southern areas. The success of this endeavor would cut down on transmission costs and provide a clean alternative energy source. To tap into the wind resources across the country, the country has invested 3.7 million U.S. dollars a year since 2003.[17]

China has embraced nuclear power as a partial solution to the overwhelming levels of pollution caused by their number one source of electricity: coal burning.

---

[17] www.chinaview.cn, August 11, 2005.

The first nuclear plants in China began producing electricity in 1994, according to the World Nuclear Association (WNA). Three reactors were put into operation that year, one of which is the first to be designed and constructed entirely by Chinese corporations (China National Nuclear Corporation). In 2005, 2.1 percent of China's electricity was provided by nuclear power plants, a total of 52.3 billion kWh (WNA).

Overall, China appears to be taking clean and renewable energy efforts seriously. Taxation is the implementation tool of choice in most cases. The Standing Committee of the National People's Congress and the Ministry of Finance have recommended tax rebates for renewable energy usage, lower taxes on fuel-efficient cars, and relief from value-added taxes on energy-saving business investments, along with additional taxes imposed on nonrenewable energy usage. Other measures include requiring annual reports on energy use and efforts from energy-intensive industries, a focus on "green buildings" in new construction, sustainable transportation, and clean energy production (NDRC, 2004; Winning, 2006). China's 2006 Renewable Energy Law stipulates that renewable energy should account for 10 percent of energy consumption by 2020 (Renewable Energy Access, 2006). Also, the central government has called for a general investment slowdown (Oster, 2006), but this is not particular to more energy intensive industries and seems to be a general effort to check excessive growth.

As with water, underpricing undercuts efforts to reduce resource utilization. The low user cost of coal burning is especially problematic: at its 2005 annual meeting, China's Senior Policy Advisory Council reported actual external costs of SO_2 emissions from coal combustion for thermal power generation of 0.0938 RMB/kWh, a figure ten times the emissions charges for coal combustion, currently set at just 0.0096 RMB/kWh. Such inefficiency clearly provides inadequate incentive for Chinese electricity producers to promote reductions in SO_2 emissions (China Senior Policy Advisory Council Report, 2005).

Other Resources

Fisheries

China is the largest fish producer in the world and has the largest number of fishing boats. Since 1990, fish production has ranked first in the world, reaching around 40 million tons in 1999 and accounting for 30 percent of the world total. Years of overfishing have combined with growing water pollution to erode China's traditional fishery resources.

The expansion of aquaculture has had a profound impact on the structure of the fishery sector. Since 1978, the area of ponds, lakes, reservoirs, and seas used for aquaculture has steadily increased. In 1999, this area reached 7.75 million hectares, a threefold increase from 1978. Total aquaculture production increased from 1.60 million tons in 1978 (27 percent of total fisheries production) to 25.78 million tons (60 percent) in 2000 (Li, 2003). There has also been a notable movement of labor to aquaculture from agriculture/capture fisheries. By 1990, over 2 million people switched to aquaculture from agriculture and other industries. Total fishery (cultivation plus capture) labor in 2000 reached 18.6 million, of which full-time employment in the aquaculture sector amounted to 3.7 million, a sevenfold increase over the 1978 level (Li, 2003). Other important contributions from aquaculture include improvements in fisheries techniques and yields, diversification of farmed species, and diversification in modes of farming.

Minerals

As of early 2003, total mineral reserves included 158 detected minerals, with 10 energy minerals, 54 metal minerals, 91 nonmetal minerals, and 3 liquid–gas minerals.[18] China possesses abundant deposits of metallic minerals, such as iron ore. As of 1996, estimated reserves of iron ore amounted to 46.3 billion tons, which placed China among world leaders in this category, following Russia, Australia, Canada, and Brazil (Liu, 2007). Iron ore is found in most regions of China. The northeast and north China areas have the richest reserves, followed by the southwest. Among China's provinces, Liaoning ranks first in proved reserves, followed by Hebei, Sichuan, Shanxi, Anhui, Yunnan, and Inner Mongolia (Ministry of Land and Resources, People's Republic of China, 2007). Ore quality is generally low, however, with the average grade of China's iron ore at only 37.5 percent (Liu Haoting, from China's *Steel Industry Yearbook*).

While reserves of highly demanded minerals have been depleted, reserves of rare minerals such as tungsten, stibium, and rare earth elements are plentiful. Reserves of manganese, gold, and silver have been increasing steadily since the 1950s. In particular, from 1991 to 1995, total known gold reserves increased by over 300 percent. By the end of 1994, the reserve of rare earth elements[19] was 107.35 billion tons, the most in the world.

Despite the large scale of mineral resources, China's per capita reserves are low and falling. By 2020, dependence on imported crude oil is expected to rise to 60 percent and natural gas to 40 percent. According to projections of future supply and demand, by 2020, domestic resources will fully supply only nine of forty-five varieties. In particular, crude oil, iron ore, copper, and bauxite, items essential to national economic security, are all in long-term deficit. Of 415 large and medium mines nationwide, half experience a crisis of depleted reserves or face closure, while forty-seven mining cities face resource exhaustion (You and Qi, 2004).

As the ratio of income and manufacturing output to domestic mineral resources continues to rise, future growth will require large imports of an expanding array of mineral products. The scale of future imports and the range of minerals needed

[18] *Source:* http://www.mlr.gov.cn/GuotuPortal/appmanager/guotu/index?_nfpb=true&_pageLabel=desktop_index_page_zygk.

[19] There are seventeen rare earth elements: scandium, yttrium, lanthanum, cerium, praseodymium, neodymium, promethium, samarium, europium, gadolinium, terbium, dysprosium, holmium, erbium, thulium, ytterbium, and lutetium.

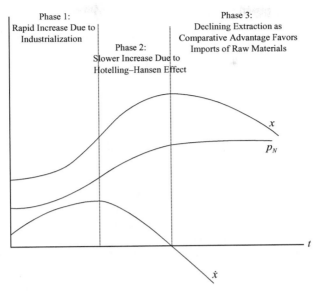

Figure 8.9. Phases of a natural resources Kuznets curve

have propelled Chinese efforts to establish a wide network of trade partners to supply these mineral demands. Declining mineral reserves implies that the country will become increasingly dependent on trade for nonrenewable resources. This dependence may lead China's foreign policy to emphasize cooperative approaches to resolving contentious international issues (Brandt, Rawski, and Zhu, 2007).

NATURAL RESOURCES KUZNETS CURVE

Natural Resources Kuznets Curve Theory

The EKC theory has been well developed in the literature. In this section, we propose a "natural resource Kuznets curve" (NRKC), whereby both resource extraction and the value of this extraction initially increase, reach a peak, and then decrease over time with increased wealth. Figure 8.9 illustrates the idea for a nonrenewable resource, where t is time, p_N represents the shadow price of the resource, x represents extraction of the resource, and the dotted variables represent the associated time derivatives. During early stages of development (phase 1), resource extraction increases as the economy industrializes. Extraction increases at an increasing rate, until rising extraction costs squeeze resource rents (Hotelling–Hansen effect; Hotelling, 1931; Hansen, 1980) causing the rate of extraction to decline, even in the face of rising demand. For a rapidly growing economy such as China, comparative advantage shifts to manufactured goods and away from the production of primary

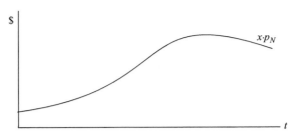

Figure 8.10. Value of resource extraction over time

goods, including energy. Eventually increased demand for energy is sufficiently offset by increased energy imports that the Hotelling–Hansen effect dominates, thus causing extraction to fall, as shown in phase 3.

Based on the path of resource extraction and resource prices shown in Figure 8.9, we lay out the corresponding trend in the total value of resource extraction in Figure 8.10. Initially, the value of resource extraction increases as both price and the extraction rate rise. As the decrease in extraction rate comes to dominate the decelerating increase in resource price, the value of extraction begins to decline. This represents the Kuznets relation for the value of resource extraction.

A similar story can be told for renewable resources. In the initial phase, resources such as forests and fisheries are depleted; later on, in a second phase, the rate of depletion slows. In contrast to nonrenewable resources, renewable resources accumulate (or decline) according to the difference between the stock's natural growth rate and the amount harvested. As a result, the Kuznets peak will arrive sooner than with nonrenewables. In phase 3, total extraction will begin to fall as depreciation approaches zero. As capital accumulation increases the marginal product of renewable resources throughout the economy, and as comparative advantage induces increasing imports of renewable resource products, the domestic stock of renewable resources eventually increases; that is, harvest is less than natural growth plus replanting/restocking. In this phase, the value of net renewable resource depletion becomes negative.

NRKC Empirics

Using data from the World Bank's Adjusted Net Savings Data Center (World Bank, 2001a), we calculate the value of a corresponding natural resource Kuznets curve for forests, minerals, and energy. Data for selected years are presented in Table 8.9. For net forest depletion, rent on depletion was calculated as the rent on that amount of extraction that exceeded the natural increment in wood volume. For mineral and energy depletion, rent was measured as the market value of extracted material minus the average extraction cost. Note that this estimate is a preliminary indicator. Ongoing data collection may make it possible to expand the

Table 8.9. *The value of resource depletion, selected years*
1975–2000

Year	NNP	Net forest depletion	Mineral depletion	Energy depletion
1975	159.07	0.10	1.26	19.62
1980	213.85	0.35	1.83	38.66
1985	289.07	0.85	2.54	40.88
1990	412.76	1.39	3.28	33.58
1995	677.74	1.47	3.24	31.11
2000	1,061.41	0.73	2.65	31.76

Note: Values are in billions of 2004 U.S. dollars; ten-year moving averages are reported, with the exception of 2000, which is a three-year average.

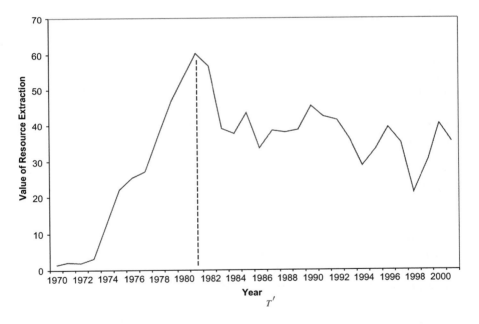

Figure 8.11. Natural resource Kuznets curve: value of resource depletion, 1970–2001 (*Source:* World Bank, 2001a,c, 2004.)

estimate in the future to include other resources, such as soil, water, and marine resources.

We illustrate the NRKC by summing up the values of China's forests, minerals, and energy depletion in Figure 8.11. T' represents the peak of the NRKC for this series. The peak's relationship to the growth rate of a green accounting income measure is examined in the next section.

GREEN NET NATIONAL PRODUCT

GNNP: Theory

A central pillar of the sustainability movement is the call to include environmental accounting in standard measures of economic performance. This increased transparency would, in principle, mitigate the temptation of economic managers and policymakers to increase growth in material consumption at the expense of the environment. Moreover, as Repetto (1989) and others have argued, deducting depreciation of produced capital from NNP but not deducting depreciation of natural capital is inconsistent and debases NNP as a possible indicator of welfare. In addition to deducting the depreciation in natural capital, GNNP treats pollution in a more appropriate fashion. While defensive expenditures to limit pollution are counted as production in current NNP accounting, the correct practice is to deduct both defensive expenditures and pollution, valued at its marginal damage cost. Accordingly, defensive expenditures must be deducted twice from the standard accounts.

The theoretical framework for GNNP requires consideration of three separate categories: nonrenewable resources, renewable resources, and pollution (stock and flow). For distinction, we refer to GNNP as the complete green income measure (subtracting both the depreciation of natural capital and the pollution damages) and GNNP' as excluding adjustments for pollution. For nonrenewable resources in a closed economy, GNNP' grows faster than NNP if and only if $\dot{y} p_N x - y(\dot{p}_N x + p_N \dot{x}) > 0$, where y represents NNP, p_N represents the first-best shadow price of the resource, x represents extraction of the resource, and the dotted variables represent the associated time derivatives.[20] In the early stages of economic growth, both a country's resource extraction rate and the price of the resources are increasing, resulting in GNNP growing more slowly than NNP. (That is, the second term dominates the first.) In later stages, the change in resource extraction decreases due to increased resource scarcity and – in the case of a rapidly growing economy – to the shifting comparative advantage in manufactures relative to resources. Moreover, the Hotelling–Hansen effect causes the rate of the price increase to decline. The two forces combine to make the first term dominate the second (and the second term to eventually become negative). Thus GNNP'(i.e., adjusting for resource depletion but not pollution) will grow faster than NNP, as illustrated in Figure 8.12.

T' in Figure 8.12 corresponds to the peak of the NRKC described in the section on "NRKC Empirics" earlier and represents the point at which GNNP' will begin growing faster than NNP. As suggested by Figure 8.11, China has already passed this peak. With optimal management, stock pollution, for example, coral reef sedimentation, will demonstrate an EKC similar to the NRKC. Adding pollution to GNNP' results in a complete green income measure, GNNP. Growth of GNNP

---

[20] This condition is obtained by taking the time derivative of GNNP.

Table 8.10. *Partial estimate of green net national product,*
selected years 1975–2000

Year	NNP	Net forest depletion	Mineral depletion	Energy depletion	GNNP
1975	159.07	0.10	1.26	19.62	138.08
1980	213.85	0.35	1.83	38.66	173.02
1985	289.07	0.85	2.54	40.88	244.80
1990	412.76	1.39	3.28	33.58	374.50
1995	677.74	1.47	3.24	31.11	641.91
2000	1,061.41	0.73	2.65	31.76	1,026.28

Note: Values are in billions of 2004 U.S. dollars. Ten-year moving averages are reported, with the exception of 2000, which is a three-year average.

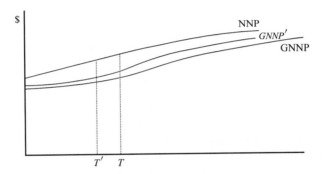

Figure 8.12. Growth of NNP versus GNNP′ and GNNP

will become faster than NNP at point *T*. Because the EKC for China peaks later than the NRKC and because of an additional price effect (pollution is a normal good), *T* is shown as greater than *T*′ .

GNNP: Empirics

In what follows, we provide a partial estimate for GNNP by subtracting three components from NNP: net forest depletion, mineral depletion, and energy depletion.[21] Data are in 2004 U.S. dollars. Table 8.10 provides the value of each component.

Figure 8.13 illustrates the growth of NNP versus our partially corrected measure, denoted PGNNP′. Unlike the theoretical construct, which is based on efficient extraction profiles, the empirical growth rates are more uneven and illustrate

[21] Forest, energy, and mineral depletion data were obtained from the World Bank's "Adjusted Net Savings: Results" spreadsheet, downloaded from www.worldbank.org/environmentaleconomics, December 1, 2004. GNI data from World Bank's World Development Indicators, 2004.

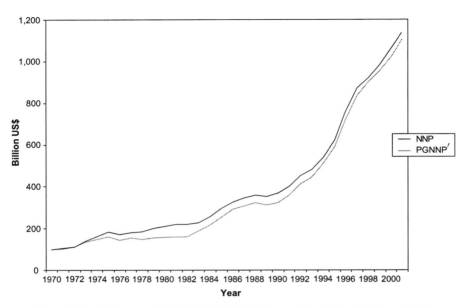

Figure 8.13. NNP versus PGNNP′, 1970–2001 (*Source:* World Bank, 2001a,c, 2004)

the possibility that PGNNP′ can grow slow, faster, and then slower again than NNP in contrast to the theoretical pattern that has only one such switch point.

Nonetheless, the empirical pattern approximates the theoretical one; that is, until the early 1980s, NNP was almost always growing faster than PGNNP′, but starting in 1982, the pattern was reversed with a few exceptions. Note also that the difference between NNP and PGNNP′ is rather small and after the mid-1980s, growth in PGNNP′ is closely approximated by NNP. Overall, the partial evidence given earlier suggests that China has already reached the point in the theoretical depiction where GNNP starts to grow faster than NNP. As data become available on the value of air and water pollution, however, a more comprehensive GNNP may reveal a later turning point at which GNNP begins to grow faster. Inasmuch as the growth rates of the two measures are quite close, however, even a revised estimate would not show GNNP growing appreciably slower than NNP. To the extent that actual pollution and natural resource extraction vary from their optimal quantities, the potential remains for GNNP to grow even faster, as resource and environmental inefficiencies are removed over time.

GNNP accounting is still evolving, as statisticians struggle to design measurement protocols that conform to new theoretical requirements. As a result, we find numerous partial estimates that explore the gap between conventional and green national accounts and obtain differing results (Smil, 1996; Mao et al., 1997; Du, Wang, and Long, 1999; Hou, Qi, and Yu, 1999; Lei, 1999). Most recently, in 2004, SEPA and the National Bureau of Statistics enlisted provincial and local authorities

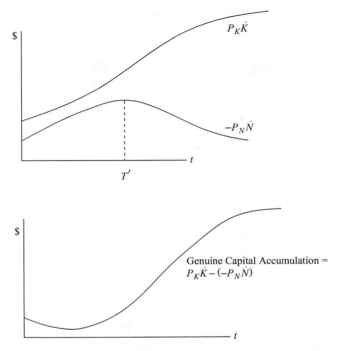

Figure 8.14. Capital, natural capital, and genuine capital accumulation

in an effort to quantify green GDP. The team released the first national green-GDP report in September 2006, estimating total losses for 2005 at 64.5 billion U.S. dollars (Ansfield and Liu, 2007). How much of this difference arises from the comprehensive nature of the 2006 report versus the partial estimates reported earlier (e.g., the 2006 report includes both soil depletion and water pollution) and how much is due to methodological differences is not yet clear. It is possible that the more comprehensive measure would show that sustainable development in China has not yet reached the turning point where GNNP begins to grow faster than NNP.

GENUINE CAPITAL ACCUMULATION

Genuine Capital Accumulation: Theory

Growth theory provides a mechanism to expand national accounting and an indicator of when economies are on an unsustainable development path. The World Bank has dubbed this indicator *adjusted net saving* or *genuine saving* (see, e.g., Hamilton, 2000). Genuine saving measures the rate of saving in an economy after taking into account pollution, depletion of natural resources, and investment in human capital. We illustrate a modified version of this concept in Figure 8.14. Define genuine

Table 8.11. *Genuine capital accumulation, 1990–2001*

Year	Genuine capital accumulation($)
1990	48.6
1991	58.6
1992	69.0
1993	74.5
1994	150.1
1995	160.6
1996	184.1
1997	233.9
1998	248.4
1999	248.6
2000	218.9
2001	254.4

Note: Values are in billion U.S. dollars.

capital accumulation (GKA) as the value of produced capital accumulation, $p_K \dot{K}$, plus natural capital accumulation, $p_N \dot{K}_N$. This is equivalent to capital accumulation minus natural capital depletion. Combining the pattern of produced capital accumulation from neoclassical growth theory with the NRKC discussion in the section on "Natural Resources Kuznets Curve Theory," note that GKA grows faster than produced capital accumulation after T'.

Genuine Capital Accumulation: Empirics

Using the World Bank data from the previous sections, we develop an estimate of China's GKA from 1990 to 2001. As is evident in Table 8.11, GKA has been increasing over time, suggesting that the country's growth is not unsustainable. Figure 8.15 illustrates this acceleration.

POLICY ENVIRONMENT

After ignoring the environmental consequences of economic policy decisions during the period of Mao Zedong's leadership (Shapiro, 2001), China's government became somewhat more vigilant about environmental regulation in the 1990s. The SEPA was established in 1998, and environmental laws and regulations began to appear shortly after its establishment.

Since then, China's environmental policies have evolved largely in response to domestic events (e.g., sandstorms in Beijing, the 1998 Yangtze floods, growing realization of health problems related to air pollution) and to China's growing involvement in international environmental diplomacy (e.g., the ratification of the

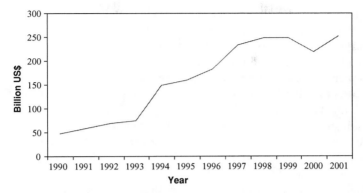

Figure 8.15. Genuine capital accumulation, 1990–2001

Montreal Protocol). Attention has also been increasing due to a domestic environmental movement, including growing environmental concerns among China's urban elites, many of whom are keenly aware that Chinese environmental conditions lag behind the norm for urban areas in more developed nations.

The main regulatory framework to date is command and control, with SEPA issuing regulations, sending inspectors to check on implementation, and imposing fines on violators. These regulations include discharge limits based on both total emissions and ambient concentrations of emissions. New manufacturing enterprises are required to receive certification before production can begin, and time limits are set for compliance on the part of existing enterprises. These regulations are far from consistent across firms, with enforcement typically focusing on large firms and often neglecting small-scale enterprises, especially TVEs located in rural areas. This in part reflects the tendency of officials to overlook pollution from enterprises that support local economies with jobs and tax revenue.

There are significant difficulties with enforcement, due in part to local government incentive structures geared to emphasize growth. Local officials sometimes prevent inspectors from completing their work or pay them to overlook violations. In other instances, local officials evade orders to close down polluting plants. For example, when the three-year "zero-hour operation" to clean up the Huai River targeted small factories along the river beginning in 1998, local officials sought to keep plants running by amalgamating small mills into larger units or by stopping daytime production but operating the plants at night. Similar problems surround efforts to compel factories to add pollution abatement facilities. One-third of such equipment operates only during inspections. One-third sits idle because managers see pollution abatement equipment as imposing excessive costs. Only the remaining third are operating as required by regulation standards (Watson et al., 2000).

Firms may purchase waste treatment equipment in accord with requirements but neglect to install the equipment. A joint effort among Massachusetts Institute of Technology (MIT), Qinghua University, and the Swiss Federal Institutes of

Technology to improve boiler efficiency begun in over 200 sites in Henan, Jiangsu, and Shanxi provinces initially failed, despite developing a number of well-tailored and inexpensive measures for the various boiler sites. The MIT-led team found that the plant directors had no immediate incentive to upgrade the technologies in their plants. The team then researched the linkage between pollution and local health costs to help persuade local officials of the project's importance (Watson et al., 2000). The Watson study also found that perceived additional cost causes many industries to disregard end-of-the-pipe technologies. Even if multinationals provide pollution-control equipment, Chinese firms may fail to respond because the cost of installing and operating these devices is much higher than the financial penalty they might suffer for exceeding pollution limits.

Despite such difficulties, there is evidence that environmental incentive systems have reduced pollution discharge intensities. Analysis of both provincial- and plant-level data on water pollution suggests that discharge intensities are highly responsive to variations in provincial levies (Wang and Wheeler, 2003, 2005). Similarly, Wang (2002) shows that plant-level expenditures on end-of-pipe wastewater treatment are strongly responsive to pollution charges. The pollution charge system has been in place for over twenty years. The main problem is that the charges are too low. If prices were increased, the response would probably deliver a significant reduction in the total quantity of pollution.

However, other command and control regulations such as enforcement and environmental zoning appear to have little impact on abatement expenditures. Inspections, rather than pollution levies, are found to have a significant effect on firm-level environmental compliance (Dasgupta et al., 2001).

In a 2003 empirical study, Wang et al. examine the determinants of environmental enforcement (Wang et al., 2003). The authors analyze the determinants of firms' relative bargaining power with local environmental authorities in connection with the enforcement of pollution charges. Results from the study suggest that private-sector firms have less bargaining power than state-owned enterprises and that firms facing adverse financial situations have more bargaining power and tend to pay relatively smaller pollution charges. The greater the social impact of a firm's emissions, the less bargaining power it has with local environmental authorities.

Further difficulties arise from poor coordination between environmental policies and other official measures that affect the behavior of plant operators and other resource users. In particular, China has been very slow to break out of a long tradition of low pricing for electricity, water, wastewater treatment, and, more recently, gasoline. This encourages excess use of water, coal, and other resources and discourages recycling, all of which may have negative consequences for efforts to reduce effluents and improve ambient air and water quality.

SEPA is pushing to expand public disclosure of environmental performance as a means of directing public attention to severe pollution problems that persist despite the application of traditional regulatory instruments (Wang et al., 2004; Wang and Wu, 2004). Since 1998, SEPA has worked to establish GreenWatch, a public disclosure program for polluters. Adopted from a program in Indonesia, the GreenWatch rates firms' environmental performance from best to worst in five colors – green, blue, yellow, red, and black – and publicizes these ratings through the media. In 2000, pilot programs were implemented in Zhenjiang (Jiangsu) and Hohhot (Inner Mongolia). Reaction to the programs has been positive, leading Jiangsu to expand implementation to the entire province in 2001. SEPA is currently preparing for nationwide implementation of public disclosure.

Experimentation with new economic incentives includes noncompliance fines, consumer subsidies for energy-saving products, discharge permits, sulfur emission fees, and emissions trading. Select provinces and cities allowed trading of sulfur emission rights since 1997. There has also been a concerted effort to decentralize pollution by moving major effluent sources – most notably, Beijing's Capital Steel complex – away from urban centers.

Recent developments in the policy arena include a ban on leaded gasoline, stringent new emission requirements for cars, preparation for Beijing Olympics, escalating attacks on "growth at any cost" and "extensive growth," and strong emphasis by top leaders on "quality" growth and on reducing the social costs of economic development. All of this suggests that environmental issues may begin to get the high-level priority that seems essential to addressing some of the incentive issues and policy conflicts mentioned earlier.

CONCLUSION

Despite disparaging reports, the available figures show that China's growth is sustainable. Nonetheless, opportunities for improving environmental and natural resource management and accounting practices abound. After years of neglect, environmental issues have attracted growing attention within China's economic policy community. Although many regulations have been initiated, numerous opportunities remain for aligning private incentives with the public interest, especially on an ecosystem level.

With respect to air pollution, available statistics suggest that China has passed the flat part of the EKC for two of three major pollutants, consistent with its expected progress at current per capita income. Available measures show some improvement in urban air quality, in part because of decentralization of industry away from the pollution receptors, which remain clustered in the traditional industrial areas. Significant decreases in pollution per unit of output are offset by rapidly increasing industrial production. Despite considerable effort, there has been less success in controlling water pollution.

One might surmise from popular accounts of pollution and resource depletion that GNNP, a more accurate indicator of economic welfare, must lag far behind traditional measures of economic performance, such as NNP. In reality, our partial adjustments suggest that GNNP for most of the last two decades has grown slightly faster than NNP. Even allowing for serious problems of water scarcity and water pollution, the possibility of increased air pollution outside of the urban core, and a devalued forest stock, future efforts to compile more comprehensive environmental accounts are unlikely to show that GNNP is growing noticeably slower than NNP. This is largely because the wedge between the two measures is small and swamped by other components of growth. Nor is China's growth unsustainable. Indeed, its GKA is large and accelerating.

Despite China's impressive record of environmentally adjusted economic growth and GKA, many challenges remain. Among the most serious concerns are increasing water scarcity, especially in urban areas in the North, and the nationwide decline in water quality. In the past, China has successfully increased available water resources by building storage and delivery infrastructure. This strategy is not sustainable, due to the declining natural limits on exploitable water sources and the increasing cost of tapping the limited unexploited sources. Despite these difficulties, abundant opportunities for reducing waste through demand management remain, thus exemplifying the common belief that the Chinese character for crisis embeds the character for opportunity.

Similarly, while China has recorded considerable progress in decentralizing pollution control, substantial opportunities remain. Weaknesses in public administration, for example, have limited the impact of initial forays into emission-permit trading. Any scheme of fines, levies, or permits is only as strong as its implementation. In China today, inspectors are often unable or unwilling to impose effective controls. Measuring the declining quantity and quality of China's water resources remains an important task for future research.

Reforms are also needed to improve environmental accounting. For example, efficient air pollution control requires not only monitoring the quantities and types of emissions but also distinguishing them according to damages by receptor–source. Sampling protocols and indexing of pollution according to health risks are also needed. Similar challenges surround the measurement of natural resource depreciation, especially accounting for the changing composition and value of resource stocks.

References

Ansfield, Jonathan and Melinda Liu. 2007. "Policy: A Scene Set for Change." *Newsweek*. January 15, 2007. Accessed July 30, 2007, from http://www.msnbc.msn.com/id/16500199/site/newsweek/.

Auffhammer, Maximilian and Richard Carson. 2006. "Forecasting the Path of China's CO$_2$ Emissions: Offsetting Kyoto – And Then Some." Working paper. Berkeley: Department of Agricultural and Resource Economics, University of California.

Auffhammer, Maximilian, Richard Carson, and Teresa Garin-Munoz. 2004. "Forecasting China's Carbon Dioxide Emissions: A Provincial Approach." Berkeley: Department of Agricultural and Resource Economics, University of California.

Brandt, Loren, Thomas G. Rawski, and Xiaodong Zhu. 2007. "International Dimensions of China's Long Boom: Trends, Prospects and Implications," in *China and the Balance of Influence in Asia*. William W. Keller and Thomas G. Rawski, eds. Pittsburgh: University of Pittsburgh Press, pp. 14–46.

Brown, Jeremy. April 2005. "Travelling the Environmental Kuznets Curve." *Fraser Forum.* pp. 16–17.

Brown, Lester. 1998. "A Human Hand in the Yangtze Flooding." *International Herald Tribune.* August 17, 1998. Accessed July 26, 2007, from http://www.iht.com/articles/1998/08/17/edbrown.t_0.php.

China Senior Policy Advisory Council Report. 2005. *Tax and Fiscal Policies to Promote Clean Energy Technology Development*, Eighth Senior Policy Advisory Council Meeting, November 18, 2005: The Great Hall of the People, Tiananmen Square, Beijing, People's Republic of China.

"China's Crude Oil Imports Up 14.5%." *China Daily.* January 13–14, 2007. Accessed February 20, 2007, from http://english.peopledaily.com.cn/200701/12/eng20070112_340690.html.

Dasgupta, Partha. 1993. *An Inquiry into Well-Being and Destitution.* Oxford: Clarendon Press.

Dasgupta, Partha. 2001. *Human Well-Being and the Natural Environment.* Oxford: Oxford University Press.

Dasgupta, Susmita, Benoit Laplante, Nlandu Mamingi, and Hua Wang. 2001. "Inspections, Pollution Prices, and Environmental Performance: Evidence from China." *Ecological Economics.* 36(3), pp. 487–498.

Dasgupta, Susmita, Benoit Laplante, Hua Wang, and David Wheeler. 2002. "Confronting the Environmental Kuznets Curve." *Journal of Economic Perspectives.* 16, pp. 147–168.

Diesendorf, Mark. January–March 2003. "Sustainable Development in China." *China Connections*, pp. 18–19.

Du, Donghai, Zhixiong Wang, and Yulin Long. 1999. "A Case of Mineral Resource Accounting of Xinjiang, China," in *Resources Accounting in China.* Allesandro Lanza, ed. Dordrecht: Kluwer Academic Publisher, pp. 117–125.

Economy, Elizabeth. 2004. *The River Runs Black: The Environmental Challenge to China's Future.* Ithaca: Cornell University Press.

Environmental Statistics Yearbook. Annual. *Zhongguo huanjing tongji nianjian* [China Environmental Statistics Yearbook]. Beijing: Zhongguo tongji chubanshe.

Forestry Statistics Yearbook. Annual. *Zhongguo linye nianjian* [China Forestry Yearbook]. Beijing: Zhongguo linye chubanshe.

Gallagher, Kelly. May 2003. "Development of Cleaner Vehicle Technology? Foreign Direct Investment and Technology Transfer from the United States to China." Paper presented at United States Society for Ecological Economics 2nd Biennial Meeting, Saratoga Springs, New York.

Grossman, Gene M. and Alan Krueger. 1991. "Environmental Impact of a North American Free Trade Agreement." Working Paper 3914. Cambridge, MA: National Bureau of Economic Research.

Hamilton, Kirk. 2000. "Genuine Savings as a Sustainability Indicator." Environment Department Paper 77. World Bank Environmental Economics Series. Washington, DC: World Bank.

Hanson, Donald. 1980. "Increasing Extraction Costs and Resource Prices: Some Further Results." *Bell Journal of Economics.* 11(1), pp. 335–342.

Hotelling, Harold. 1931. "The Economics of Exhaustible Resources." *Journal of Political Economy.* 39(2), pp. 137–175.

Hou, Yuanzhao, Wang Qi, and Ling Yu. 1999. "Introduction to Forest Resources Evaluation Study in China," in *Resources Accounting in China.* Alessandro Lanza, ed. pp. 171–180. New York: Springer.

Lei, Ming. 1999. *Green Accounting for Sustainable Development – Integrated Accounting of Natural Resources-Economy-Environment.* Beijing: China's Geography Press.

Li, Sifa. 2003. "Aquaculture Research and its Relation to Development in China," in *Agricultural Development and the Opportunities for Aquatic Resources Research in China.* Malaysia: WorldFish Center, pp. 17–28.

Lieb, Christoph 2002. "The Environmental Kuznets Curve and Satiation: A Simple Static Model." *Environment and Development Economics.* 7, pp. 429–448.

Lindert, Peter H. 2000. *Shifting Ground: The Changing Agricultural Soils of China and Indonesia.* Cambridge, MA: MIT Press.

Liu Haoting. 2007. "Steel Mills Dig in Overseas." *China Daily*, April 27, 2004. Accessed February 20, 2007, from http://www.chinadaily.com.cn/english/doc/2004–04/27/content_326730.htm.

Mao, Yushi, Datong Ning, Guang Xia, Hongchang Wang, and Vaclav Smil. 1997. "An Assessment of the Economic Losses Resulting from Various Forms of Environmental Degradation in China." Occasional Paper of the Project on Environmental Scarcities, State Capacity, and Civil Violence, American Academy of Arts and Sciences and the University of Toronto, Cambridge.

Ministry of Land and Resources, People's Republic of China. Accessed January 16, 2007, from http://www.mlr.gov.cn/pub/mlr/english/default.htm.

Ministry of Water Resources. August 27, 2004. The Ministry of Water Resources of the People's Republic of China (MWR), "North to South Water Transfer Project." Accessed January 16, 2007, from http://www.mwr.gov.cn/english1/20040827/39304.asp.

NDRC [Natural Resource Defense Council]. March 12, 2004. "NDRC's China Clean Energy Project." Accessed September 29, 2006, from http://www.nrdc.org/air/energy/china/default.asp.

Oster, Shai. 2006. "China Steps up Effort to Curb Growth." *Wall Street Journal Online* [Free Preview]. Accessed September 29, 2006, from http://online.wsj.com/public/article/SB115582157779038279-cNfqsjzcEVGjqnIYOdX4wn83u1E_20060824.html?mod=regionallinks.

Panayotou, Theodore. 1993. *Green Markets: The Economics of Sustainable Development.* San Francisco: ICS Press for the International Center for Economic Growth and the Harvard Institute for International Development.

"Problems with Car Boom." *China Daily.* January 13–14, 2007, p. 4.

Renewable Energy Access. 2006. "China Passes Renewable Energy Law." Accessed September 29, 2006, from http://renewableenergyaccess.com/rea/news/story?id=23531.

Repetto, Robert. 1989. *Wasting Assets: Natural Resources in the National Income Accounts.* Washington, DC: World Resources Institute.

Rozelle, Scott, Heidi Albers, Guo Li, and Vincent Benziger. 1998. "Forest Resources under Economic Reform: Response in China's State and Collective Management Regimes." *China Information.*

Rozelle, Scott, Jikun Huang, and Vincent Benziger. 2003. "Forest Exploitation and Protection in Reform China: Assessing the Impact of Policy, Tenure, and Economic Growth," Chapter 6 in *China's Forests: Global Lessons from Market Reforms.* William F. Hyde, Brian Belcher, and Jintao Xu, eds. Washington, DC: Resources for the Future, pp. 109–134.

Rozelle, Scott, Emi Uchida, and Jintao Xu. 2005. "Grain for Green: Cost-Effectiveness and Sustainability of China's Conservation Set-Aside Program." *Land Economics.* 81(2), pp. 247–265.

SEPA. 2004. "Analysis on the State of the Environment in China." Accessed July 30, 2007, from http://www.sepa.gov.cn/english/SOE/analysis/index.htm#pollutant.

Shalizi, Zmarak. 2004. "Water Issues and Options in China (draft)." Prepared for the 11th Five Year Plan of China.

Shapiro, Judith. 2001. *Mao's War Against Nature.* Cambridge and New York: Cambridge University Press.

Smil, Vaclav. 1996. *Environmental Problems in China: Estimates of Economic Costs.* Honolulu, Hawaii: East West Center Press.

U.S. Embassy Beijing. 1998. "PRC Air Pollution: How Bad Is It?" Accessed July 26, 2007, from http://www.usembassy-china.org.cn/sandt/Airq3wb.htm.

US Embassy Beijing. 2000. "The Cost of Environmental Degradation in China." Accessed July 26, 2007, from http://www.usembassy-china.org.cn/sandt/CostofPollution-web.html.

Wang, Hua. 2002. "Pollution Regulation and Abatement Efforts: Evidence from China." *Ecological Economics.* 41(1), pp. 85–94.

Wang, Hua, Jun Bi, David Wheeler, Jinnan Wang, Dong Cao, Genfa Lu, and Yuan Wang. 2004. "Environmental Performance Rating and Disclosure: China's GreenWatch Program." *Journal of Environmental Management.* 71, pp. 123–133.

Wang, Hua, Nlandu Mamingi, Benoit Laplante, and Susmita Dasgupta. 2003. "Incomplete Enforcement of Pollution Regulation: Bargaining Power of Chinese Industries." *Environmental and Resource Economics.* 24, pp. 245–262.

Wang, Hua and David Wheeler. 2003. "Equilibrium Pollution and Economic Development in China." *Environment and Development Economics.* 8, pp. 451–466.

Wang, Hua and David Wheeler. 2005. "Financial Incentives and Endogenous Enforcement in China's Pollution Levy System." *Journal of Environmental Economics and Management.* 49(1), pp. 174–196.

Wang, Hua and Changhua Wu. 2004. *Public Access to Environmental Information in China: Practices and Challenges.* Washington, DC: World Bank Development Research Group.

Watson, Jim, Xue Liu, Geoffrey Oldham, Gordon Mackerron, and Steve Thomas. 2000. "International Perspectives on Clean Coal Technology Transfer to China." Final Report to the Working Group on Trade and the Environment. Sichuan: China Council for International Cooperation on Environment and Development.

Winning, David. 2006. "China Think-Tank Urges Tax Overhaul to Save Energy-Report." *Dow Jones News Wires.* September 19, 2006. Accessed September 29, 2006, from http://www.easybourse.com/Website/dynamic/News.php?NewsID=59052&lang=fra&NewsRubrique=2.

Wishnick, Elizabeth. 2005. "China as a Risk Society," in *East-West Center Seminar*, Honolulu, HI.

World Bank. 1995. *China: Regional Disparities.* Washington, DC: World Bank.

World Bank. 1997. *Clear Water, Blue Skies: China's Environment in the New Century.* Washington, DC: World Bank.

World Bank. 2001a. "Adjusted Net Savings: Results." downloaded from Accessed December 1, 2004, from www.worldbank.org/environmentaleconomics.

World Bank. 2001b. *China: Air, Land, and Water.* Washington, DC: World Bank.

World Bank. 2001c. *World Development Indicators.* Washington, DC: World Bank.

World Bank. 2004. "World Development Indicators." Accessed December 1, 2004, from http://www.worldbank.org/data/.

You, Wan and Jianguo Qi. 2004. "China's Long Term Development Trend and Environmental Economy," *Caimao jingji* [Finance and Trade Economics]. 10, pp. 11–17.

NINE

Science and Technology in China[1]

Albert G. Z. Hu and Gary H. Jefferson

INTRODUCTION

Economists agree that the long-term growth of living standards depends on the capacity of an economy to sustain technological progress, whether by adopting technologies from abroad, through its own technological innovations, or, most likely, through a combination of adoption and innovation. The purpose of this chapter is to describe and analyze China's science and technology (S&T) capabilities and the economic, institutional, and policy context that together are shaping the range and growth of these capabilities. We conduct this analysis against the background of a large and fast-growing literature on the subject.

China's national innovation system is making two transitions – from plan to market as it moves away from a centrally directed innovation system and also from low-income developing country toward Organisation for Economic Co-Operation and Development (OECD) industrialized country status as it intensifies its innovation effort and more effectively deploys the ensuing technological gains.

Many of the impulses and policies of China's current S&T system are legacies of the nation's traditional economy going back to the nineteenth century and before. These include the recognition that access to Western S&T is critical to China's economic modernization and the consequent openness to foreign technology, advisors, and investment, particularly in special zones in the coastal areas. While the socialist era largely insulated China from these overseas influences, save for its

[1] The authors appreciate the helpful comments of John Sutton and other participants in the conference, as well as Loren Brandt and Thomas Rawski, who offered extensive comments on earlier drafts of this chapter while also organizing the program that made this research project possible. In addition, we thank the participants in the conference "China's Economic Transition: Origins, Mechanisms, and Consequences" held on November 5–7, 2004, in Pittsburgh for their wide-ranging and helpful comments. This research was also supported by the National Science Foundation (award no. SES-0519902) and the U.S. Department of Energy's Biological and Environmental Research Program (contract # DE-FG02–00ER63030), which helped finance a substantial portion of the background research work that is included in this chapter.

reliance on technology, advisors, and investment from the Soviet Union during the 1950s, throughout the three decades of that era, China maintained a relatively high level of S&T effort with an eye toward catching up to the West. Even so, with few exceptions, China's overall technology gap with the West grew substantially over this period. The section "China's S&T System in Historical Perspective" focuses on the role of China's traditional and socialist eras in shaping the S&T system of present-day China.

In the section "China's S&T Level in International Context," we situate China within a comparative context that examines levels and trends of S&T activity – both inputs to innovation and S&T outputs. While starting from low levels, China's rate of advance in research and development (R&D) spending in relation to its gross domestic product (GDP) and patenting activity, particularly when we include patents by foreign firms, indicates strikingly rapid progress. Against the backdrop of the S&T takeoffs of the large OECD countries and Asia's newly industrialized countries, we inquire whether China has begun its S&T takeoff. We return to this issue in the section "How Sustainable Is the Growth of China's S&T Activity." The quickening pace of S&T activity in China is not synonymous with a comparable increase in innovation quality. China still lags well behind its OECD counterparts in the proportion of R&D spending that it devotes to basic research and the citations it receives for its scientific publications. The disproportionate emphasis on applied research is reflected in an overwhelming preponderance of utility patents that are typically viewed as proxies for imitation. China remains a substantial distance from the world's innovation frontier.

As a low-income centrally planned economy, government-funded research institutes and state-owned enterprises that responded to innovation directives were at the center of China's pre-reform S&T system. Since the reform, China's S&T system has exhibited a rapid shift in S&T resources to sources of innovation that increasingly lie outside the state sector. This shift, which we examine in the section on "The Shifting Locus of R&D Activity" is visible in the growing portions of R&D spending accounted for by the enterprise sector, particularly the nonstate sector, the restructuring of China's research institutes, and the growing role of universities as a critical locus of research activity. Over these past two decades, the role of the government in promoting and financing technology innovation has changed dramatically.

A central feature of China's economic transformation is the extensive role of the foreign sector. Nowhere has this been more evident than in the numerous vehicles that have developed to facilitate technology transfer – trade, foreign direct investment (FDI), foreign-funded R&D, and markets for the import and sale of foreign technology. Some analysts argue that the research activities of the foreign sector dominate those of the domestic sector, which itself exhibits anemic innovation capabilities. While our perspective grants critical importance to the foreign sector, our view is that rather than through direct spending on R&D, its principal contribution operates through the channel of FDI that creates both competition and technological opportunity that in turn motivates Chinese firms in an effort to survive to spend resources on R&D and innovation. The role of the foreign sector is the subject of the section "Contribution of the Foreign Sector."

The governments of all the large, successful innovation economies in the OECD play an active role in shaping innovation incentives and directing resources to R&D. China follows this pattern, increasingly through indirect channels, but also through direct means in areas that are deemed to be critical to the nation's technological goals. Over these past two decades, the role of the government in promoting and financing technology innovation has changed dramatically. One example of this change is the substantial phase out of direct government subsidies for R&D in the enterprise sector in favor of indirect instruments, such as tax credits. A range of programs that are intended to promote innovative effort and encourage technology transfer are described in the section "Government Policies and Programs in Support of S&T."

Innovation efforts – whether successful or unsuccessful – typically involve the interplay of a complex set of factors and players. As a large, open, technologically ambitious, yet transitioning economy, China's pursuit of technology advance is a particularly vigorous and encompassing undertaking. In the section "Case Studies," we attempt to illustrate the interaction of domestic and foreign and government and private players and resources within an extraordinarily heterogeneous regional, institutional, and technological environment. We illustrate this range of circumstances that shapes technological advance with two industry case studies – the semiconductor industry and the automobile industry.

Because R&D is undertaken to enhance firm performance and innovation, the section on "What Has Been the Impact of R&D on China's Economy?" reviews the literature assessing the impact of R&D on key measures such as productivity, profitability, and patenting. This section also examines the impact of complementary factors, such as educational levels and overseas collaboration, as they enhance R&D returns, the interactions between internal R&D and technology transfer, and the factor bias of R&D, that is, the extent to which R&D used by China's industrial enterprises results in choices of factor intensities that are consistent with China's underlying comparative advantage.

Over the past two decades, in particular since 1995, when China's R&D spending to GDP ratio has risen from 0.6 to 1.4 percent, China has given the unmistakable appearance of a country that is on the path to closing the gap with most of the OECD economies. Indeed, in its current Tenth Five-Year Plan, China's government has set 2015 as the date for the country to achieve the plan's goal of an "innovation economy." Many conditions, including China's openness, size, and emerging S&T class, all suggest that this goal is achievable. And yet, China remains a developing economy with the majority of its population still at or near subsistence living standards. Even if China is on an inexorable road to OECD levels of S&T intensity and achievement, this path may take more years than the leadership would hope. While South Korea required only five years to transition from the levels of R&D

intensity of a developing economy to OECD levels of R&D intensity, the same trajectory required nineteen years for Japan. In the section "How Sustainable Is the Growth of China's S&T Activity," we assess the conditions that seem to be pushing China toward OECD style levels of S&T activity. To do this, we draw on a unique data set that provides detailed information about the production, financial performance, and R&D activity of China's approximately 23,000 large-and medium-size industrial enterprises.[2]

Finally, as suggested at the beginning of this introduction, the topic of S&T activity in China is a fast-changing and growing field. In the final section of this chapter, we draw conclusions from our analysis and also raise questions and speculate on some of the important but still imponderable issues that will determine China's S&T future.

CHINA'S S&T SYSTEM IN HISTORICAL PERSPECTIVE

Patterns of China's current S&T development are in part shaped by China's historical experience – both technological development in the traditional, pre-1949 economy and the S&T system that emerged during the socialist period. We focus on the features of these earlier periods that help us understand the strengths, weaknesses, and institutional and policy orientation of China's now evolving S&T system.

The Pre-1949 Period

Joseph Needham has documented the prodigious scientific achievements of China during ancient and imperial times.[3] While paper, printing, the compass, and gunpowder are celebrated as the four great inventions of ancient China, Chinese inventors also made substantial strides in agricultural technology and astronomy.[4]

A continuing subject of debate among scholars of Chinese history is why China did not develop a scientific revolution and why during the nineteenth century China fell behind Europe. Some contend that China did accomplish its own scientific revolution in the seventeenth century.[5] Others argue that China's political system was hostile to scientific progress, a perspective refuted by Benjamin Elman.[6] More recently, historians have questioned political and cultural explanations and

---

[2] The data, collected annually by China's National Bureau of Statistics, provide detailed data by the ownership and industry classifications that have been formulated by the NBS.

[3] For an excellent overview of Needham's seven volumes of *Science and Civilization in China*, see Goldsmith (2006).

[4] Agricultural innovations include the iron-tipped plow, the moldboard, and the seed drill widely used during the Han dynasty. See Lin (1995) for a description of other early Chinese inventions.

[5] See, notably, Sivin (1982).

[6] See Elman (2005).

have instead focused on economic causes. One intriguing economic explanation, advanced by Elvin (n.d.), is that China's labor abundance caused it to enter a "high-level equilibrium trap" that impeded the mechanical revolution spawned in the West (Elvin, n.d.). According to this interpretation, the nonmechanized processes in agriculture and industry were so well developed and efficient that they outcompeted early mechanized processes, thus making capital investment in mechanization unprofitable. The "trap" presages China's contemporary condition in which the continuing abundance of labor resources shapes the technological choices it faces today, including the tension between exploiting homegrown labor-using technologies and the import of more capital-using, labor-saving technologies employed in the advanced OECD economies.

Lin (1995) offers an alternative interpretation, which is based on his distinction between two modes of innovation: technological inventions that stemmed from the experiences of artisans and farmers that dominated in premodern times and scientific innovations that mainly result from modern experimentation cum science. Lin hypothesizes that China enjoyed a comparative advantage in premodern times, while Europe during the scientific revolution changed to planned experimentation for its scientific advance. China was slow in making the transition, according to Lin, due to the content of China's civil service examinations and criteria for promotion, which distracted the attention of intellectuals away from investing in the human capital necessary for modern scientific research.

Whether Elvin's "high-level equilibrium trap" or Lin's distraction hypothesis explains China's loss of its technological advantage, once lost, China's intelligentsia exhibited a set of distinctive attitudes and strategies that shaped its adoption of Western technologies beginning in the nineteenth century. With China weakened by the demands of the Taiping Rebellion (1850–1864), notable figures in the country's military and scholarly classes formulated the "self-strengthening" (*ziqiang*) movement that advocated making selective use of Western technology. In 1864, patrons of the movement[7] dispatched the first Chinese citizen to have graduated from an American university back to the United States to purchase the equipment needed to establish an arsenal near Shanghai. With the help of Western technicians the arsenal successfully refurbished a foreign steam engine in 1868 and launched the first Chinese steam-powered vessel. Soon thereafter, modeled after the Shanghai arsenal, a second arsenal was built in Fuzhou, and schools were founded, under the direction of foreign advisors, "for the study of mechanical skills and navigation . . . (while) translation projects for technical works were started on an ambitious scale" (Spence, 1991, p. 199).

Later, following the Sino-Japanese War (1894–1895), the Western powers further expanded their economic influence. According to Spence, "Western powers had imposed their presence on China and were now beginning to invest heavily

---

[7] Among the most notable advocates were Zeng Guofan, a Hunanese scholar-general, and Feng Guifen, who wrote most extensively about the ideals of the Self-Strengthening Movement.

in the country, especially in mines, modern communications and heavy industry" (Spence, 1991, p. 224). While embracing the virtues of China's essential philosophical values and traditions, China's intellectuals further recognized the critical role of Western technology, which gave rise to the *ti-yong* movement (combining "essence" and "practical use"). Holding on to the belief that the essence of Chinese civilization would endure, influential elements of China's scholar-official class then believed that China should proceed to quickly adopt all sorts of Western practices to be facilitated by the hiring of Western advisors (Spence, 1991, p. 226).

This ambitious vision of technology transfer was frustrated during the first half of the twentieth century by a succession of weak central governments, the Japanese invasion in the 1930s, and by civil war. Nonetheless, the self-strengthening and *ti-yong* movements represented the underlying intellectual and moral foundations for China's quest for Western technology, investment, and advisors as vehicles for restoring the technological and economic vitality of Chinese society. These early patterns of encounter with Western technology founded on the impulse of China's intelligentsia arguably presaged the current openness to Western technology as represented by China's large and growing trade ratio, robust FDI, active markets in imported foreign technology, and proliferating special economic zones. Furthermore, the potential reasons for China's relative technological decline – its labor abundance and success at localized incremental innovation and imitation – remain central to its model of technological progress today.

The Socialist Era[8]

From the 1950s through the 1970s, despite being a low-income country, China pursued a strategy of high S&T effort. With the Soviet Union as its model during the 1950s, China not only incorporated basic Soviet technologies, but also adopted centralized organizational structure for the entire national system of research and innovation. China mobilized available intellectual resources, particularly for defense purposes, and created elite research institutes, notably in the Chinese Academy of Sciences (CAS). China's rapid progress in nuclear technology, space technology, and genetic engineering in the 1960s and 1970s testifies to the partial success of this system.

Under China's pre-reform innovation system, state patronage shaped the allocation of innovation resources. In lieu of private pecuniary incentives, the government employed official recognition and professional prestige and advancement to motivate research focus in certain limited areas. This system was effective in supporting basic research, where despite low private returns, the social returns and hence the attention and accolades afforded by the government were high. However the components of socialist institutions and policies could not calibrate the complex incentive structure required for a broad-based system of commercial innovation

---

[8] This section borrows from Naughton (2007, chapter 15).

that could effectively respond to the needs of the producer and consumer sectors operating outside the immediate realm of the government's S&T priorities.

While industrial innovation did occur in the enterprise sector, the emphasis on assigning quantitative innovation targets to industrial enterprises, as well as the absence of a price system that reflected underlying scarcities seriously compromised the economic value of the mandated innovations. When Jefferson and Rawski interviewed a senior engineer at the Beijing No. 1 Lathe Factory, who had participated in the factory's technology development program during the 1970s, he explained that the motivation then was solely to fulfill (or exceed) the plan targets, believing that such compliance would enable China to catch up with the West. No serious assessment was made of the economic impact of innovations on productivity or profitability, since no economically meaningful measure of these accounting categories then existed.

When China and the Soviet Union abruptly split in the early 1960s, China was cut off from its technology source at a time when it had no alternative technology partners and very little market access to technology. Thus, China approached a state of technology autarky for a decade from the mid-1960s through the mid-1970s. During this period, China's strategy was to import a handful of factories that embodied specific industrial technologies and then reverse engineer and replicate them domestically. A few key technologies in metallurgy and synthetic fibers were transferred in this way, and incremental improvements were made on some Soviet-legacy technologies, such as electricity generation, where equipment was scaled up to larger more efficient units.[9]

China's inability to achieve more than a modest rise in living standards during the quarter century after 1949 reflects the relative ineffectiveness of the innovation system. Specifically, according to Chow (1985) in 1979, total factor productivity in the agricultural sector was lower than it had been in 1952. Over a similar period, from 1957 to 1978, Chen et al. (1988) report that multifactor productivity in the industrial sector rose at a rate of just 0.4–1.1 percent per annum.[10] While China had made notable advances in a few areas, overall the S&T gap between China and the West grew during the socialist era.

Two legacies of China's socialist-era S&T system stand out. First, the highly centralized system of innovation concentrated China's research capabilities within government institutions, leaving China unable to develop a broad-based set of research capabilities that could sustain the broad-based productivity growth needed to raise living standards. A second legacy was the treatment of invention as a public good. China's socialist system was antithetical to a culture and the requisite institutions (e.g., patent laws, royalties, and courts) necessary for the creation and protection of intellectual property rights. Reliance on state patronage for innovation and the

---

[9] Naughton (2007).

[10] The difference arises from the use of both Cobb Douglas and translog functions, which yielded the lower and higher estimates, respectively.

absence of an intellectual property rights tradition remain as legacies that hinder the creation of a robust national innovation system.

The Reform Period

China's reform of its national innovation system is in key respects similar to the "growing out of the plan" scenario that has characterized much of China's economy since 1979. This is certainly true for the enterprise sector. The most important change in the enterprise sector, arguably, was the entry of new enterprises – joint ventures and wholly owned foreign enterprises, township and village enterprises (TVEs), and other nonstate enterprises – which created severe competition across many industries. The resulting erosion of profit margins motivated many enterprises to search for new process and product innovations needed to enable survival and continuing wage increases.

Nonetheless, while China's enterprises increasingly established their own independent R&D operations, by 1990 the share of the enterprise sector in total national R&D spending still amounted to only about one-half the typical enterprise share in the OECD economies. Furthermore, within the enterprise sector, nearly two-thirds of total enterprise R&D spending was still controlled by state-owned enterprises. At the same time, more than 5,000 research institutes that accounted for one-third of the country's scientists and engineers remained largely under the supervision of one or more government agencies and fundamentally unchanged throughout the 1980s and most of the 1990s.

By 2000, these conditions had either changed dramatically or were on the path toward fundamental change. In 2000, 60 percent of the country's R&D spending was funded and performed by the enterprise sector, comparable to that of most OECD economies. Moreover, with the acceleration of ownership restructuring in the later half of the 1990s, by the year 2000, the majority of enterprise-funded R&D was performed outside the state-owned enterprise sector.

The restructuring of China's more than 5,000 research institutes also became a priority during the late 1990s. Under the reform initiative that began to be implemented in 1999, government research institutes were converted to nongovernment S&T enterprises and nonprofit research institutes. The financially self-sufficient enterprises and institutes were to decide by themselves what direction their research should take and become responsible for whatever profits or losses they incurred. During 1999–2004, through conversion and consolidation the number of government-financed research institutes fell from 5,573 to 3,973.[11]

During the reform era, China at first tried to keep government R&D outlays high. However, with government SOE revenues eroding and the budget's share of GDP declining, the country struggled to sustain R&D spending as a proportion of GDP. In 1987, China invested only about 0.7 percent of GDP in R&D; in 1994, the

[11] Ministry of Science and Technology annual survey of research institutes, 1995–2003.

intensity slipped further to below 0.6 percent. By this time, China was beginning to look like a "normal" low-income country, with R&D outlays at or even below the level that cross-country comparisons adjusted for living standards would indicate. But wanting to drive China's S&T advance, China's policymakers actively sought to raise the ratio of R&D to GDP. After 1996, levels of R&D intensity began a sustained raise; by 2006, the reported R&D ratio rose to 1.4 percent, more than twice its level of 1994 (Wang, 2007).

Beginning in the 1980s and continuing into the 1990s, China's government formulated a series of programs that were designed to establish the central government as a major contributor to basic research while also promoting technology diffusion. More than any other broad government-funded R&D programs, the *863 Program* and *973 Program* focused on enabling China's S&T capabilities to catch up with those of the OECD countries. While these programs largely focus on basic research and frontier technologies, the *Torch Program* supports high-tech industries, and the *Spark Program* focuses on invigorating China's rural economy through the appropriate application of S&T. Since the Torch Program started in 1986, there have been 150,000 technological projects nationwide, covering 90 percent of China's counties.[12] In addition, China's government provides direct R&D grants and tax incentives to industry. Over the past decade the latter have grown to increasingly supplant the former. Finally, in an effort to nurture innovation the Chinese government in 1985 reinstated its patent law, followed in 2001 by its accession to the World Trade Organization (WTO) and signing of the Trade-Related Aspects of Intellectual Property Rights (TRIPS) Agreement. By the early years of the 2000s, China's national innovation system had acquired many of the attributes that might be expected of a large newly industrializing economy.

In the following sections, the discussion primarily focuses on the development of China's S&T system since 2000.

CHINA'S S&T LEVEL IN INTERNATIONAL CONTEXT

To assess China's progress in the arena of S&T, we first compare China's level of S&T activity with the levels of other countries – both OECD countries and other emerging industrial economies. Our comparison focuses on three measures of innovation effort and three measures of S&T achievement. First, we measure the intensity of R&D inputs.

Measures of Innovation Effort

Among the numerous measures of R&D effort, those for which coverage is most comprehensive and consistently reported, are the ratio of R&D expenditure to

---

[12] *People's Daily Online*, October 16, 2006, http://english.people.com.cn/200610/16/eng 20061016_312140.html.

Table 9.1. *Comparative measures of R&D intensity, 1991–2003*

R&D expenditure/ GDP	1991	1995	2000	2003
China	0.74	0.60	1.00	1.23[a]
USA	2.72	2.51	2.76	2.62
Germany	2.52	2.25	2.49	2.50
Japan	2.93	2.89	2.99	3.12[b]
Korea	1.92	2.50	2.65	2.96
Taiwan	–	1.78	2.05	2.16
France	2.37	2.31	2.18	2.20[b]
Italy	1.23	1.00	1.07	–
Brazil	0.46	0.69	1.05	–
India	0.85[b]	0.77[a]	0.86[b]	–

[a] Indicates data for the following year.
[b] Indicates data for the previous year.
Source: NBS/MOST (2004, p. 385).

GDP, the proportion of scientists and engineers in the total population, and the proportion of R&D dedicated to basic research.

R&D Intensity

The data in Table 9.1 show that China's R&D intensity sharply accelerated during 1995–2000 and continued to rise into the current decade. Hovering in the range of 0.60 in 1995, by 2006, China's R&D intensity rose to 1.4 percent. By comparison, the R&D intensity of most OECD economies and Taiwan lay in the range of 2–3 percent.

For China, this level of R&D intensity is high given its living standards. Among the world's low- and low-middle–income countries, China has been the only country whose level of R&D intensity has risen beyond 1 percent.[13] While Brazil, a middle-income economy, exhibits a similar pattern of rising R&D intensity, its level of (exchange-rate-adjusted) per capita income is approximately three times that of China. India's level of R&D intensity remained relatively stable during the decade of the 1990s, hovering in the range of 0.8 percent in 1990, 1996, and 1999.

Figure 9.1 shows the trajectories of R&D intensification across the largest OECD countries, Taiwan, and Singapore, all of which exhibited rapid increases in their ratios of R&D spending as a share of GDP. The figure confirms that China's R&D intensity has risen rapidly from 1996 to the range of 1.2–1.3 percent, having outpaced the rise in R&D intensity of Brazil and India. In the section "How Sustainable Is the Growth of China's S&T Activity," we return to these patterns of R&D takeoff

---

[13] In the data reported in UNDP (2001), China's level is just 0.7 percent. Comparative country data in NBS (2003), however, indicate that by 2002 the R&D intensities of other low-middle–income countries had not exceeded 1 percent.

Table 9.2. *Comparative measures of innovative intensity, 2003*

Country	China	USA	Korea	Canada	Turkey
Scientists and engineers per 10,000 population	10	90	62		10
Basic research (percentage of total R&D)	5.0	18.1	12.6		
R&D funds (percentage of enterprise funded)	60.4	68.9	74.9	53.7	33.4

Source: NBS/MOST (2004, p. 386).

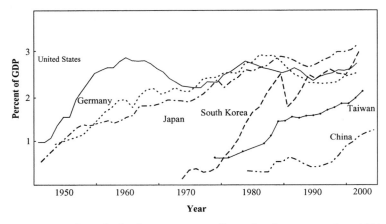

Figure 9.1. Research and development expenditure in five economies, 1950–2004 (*Source:* Gao and Jefferson, forthcoming)

shown in Figure 9.1 and attempt to identify the factors responsible for the acceleration of R&D expenditure in relation to GDP.

Scientists and Engineers

According to *China's Statistical Yearbook on Science and Technology, 2004,* in 1998, China had 12 scientists and engineers per 10,000 population; by 2004, the ratio had risen to 15 (NBS/MOST, 2006, p. 348). As shown in Table 9.2, this ratio is notably less than those of Japan (102), the United States (90), Korea (67), and Italy (29). At 10, only Turkey (data for 2002) lagged behind China (data for 2003) in this measure. Nonetheless, because of its large population, the sheer number of scientists and engineers in China exceeds the numbers for all countries except the United States whose totals China is also likely to surpass soon. In 2003, China graduated 54,557 scientists and engineers with degrees at the master's level or above. In that same year, however, 137,181 students enrolled in science and engineering programs at the master's level and above (NBS, 2004, pp. 20, 22). This increase in matriculating students relative to graduating students underscores the extraordinary growth in Chinese higher education in the fields of science and engineering.

Basic Research

Although the intensity of R&D in China's economy is rising sharply and approaching that of certain OECD counties, the basic research component of these funds is substantially less than that of their OECD counterparts. Table 9.2 shows that in 2004, the share of basic research in total R&D in China stood at 6.0 percent, one quarter to one-third of the proportions reported by the United States, Japan, and Korea. Moreover, over the past decade, this proportion of basic research to total R&D in China has remained relatively constant in the range of 5–6 percent. Given that in relation to the United States China's GDP is approximately one-sixth, its R&D intensity about one-half, and its proportion of basic R&D spending about one-third, China's total spending on basic research is barely 3 percent that of the United States.

Measures of S&T Achievement

We focus on three measures of S&T achievements. These are patents that have been granted by the United States and Chinese patent offices to the residents of China compared with other nations, publications in international scientific journals, and measures of the relative technological sophistication of China's exports.

Patenting

The first R&D output measure that we use is the number of patent applications filed with the Chinese patent office. Figure 9.2 shows a sharp increase in patent applications, particularly domestic patent applications, from the late 1990s. The figure also shows that invention patents, which are required to meet a higher standard of novelty than utility design and applied patents, rose in the domestic and foreign sectors at comparable rates from 1999 to 2006.

Table 9.3 shows a profile of approved patents registered with the U.S. patent office by the residents of different countries. The number of such patents registered by Chinese residents, while significantly less than those of any of the OECD countries and Taiwan, was in 2005 more than India and Brazil while growing faster than any of the countries shown in the list given in Table 9.3. This measure of innovativeness, a measure of the rents that producers can capture from their R&D spending, lags substantially behind measures of S&T effort, namely, R&D spending and the number of scientists and engineers. Whereas China has more scientists and engineers than all countries but the United States, the relative productivity of these technical personnel in producing internationally patentable innovations remains low.

Table 9.3. *Patents granted by the U.S. patent and trademark office, 1991–2003*

Residence of recipient	1991	1995	2000	2003
China	50	62	119	297
USA	51,177	55,739	85,068	87,901
Japan	21,025	21,764	31,295	35,517
Korea	405	1,161	3,314	3,944
Taiwan	906	1,620	4,667	5,298
France	3,030	2,821	3,819	3,869
Italy	1,209	1,078	1,714	1,722
India	22	37	131	341
Brazil	62	63	98	130

Source: http://patft1.uspto.gov/netahtml/PTO/srchnum.htm.

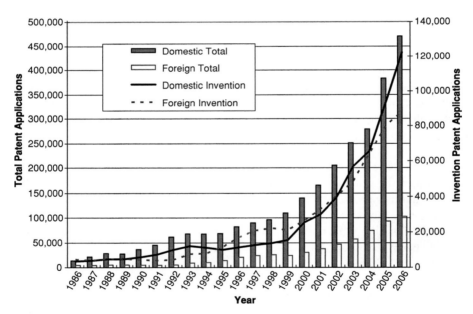

Figure 9.2. Number of patent applications received by China SIPO (*Source:* Hu and Jefferson, 2006)

International Scientific Publications

China's share of international publications rose rapidly during the recent decade, from a rank of seventeenth in 1993 to fifth in 2004 (ISTIC, 2005). In 2003, China accounted for over 5 percent of the world's scientific publications. Papers with authors affiliated with Chinese institutions now account for 10 percent of the

Table 9.4. *High-technology exports as a percent of exports of manufactures, 2002*

Low-middle income (17%)	China	India	Thailand	Brazil
	23	5	31	19
Upper-middle income (21%)	Malaysia	Hungary	Mexico	Argentina
	58	25	84	7
High income (23%)	USA	Japan	Korea	Taiwan
	32	24	32	42

Source: World Bank (2005, pp. 262–263).

literature in materials science and 8 percent in mathematics and physics, while China remains one of the smaller players in the life sciences.[14] In terms of citations received by Chinese publications, China's relative ranking is low, just fourteenth in 2004 (Zhou and Leydesdorff, 2006). Papers in many fields, including physics, chemistry, and geosciences, still have "low average impact factors." Like high-quality patents, China's incidence of scientific publications and citations has yet to measure up to the sheer volume of the country's S&T effort.

Export Quality

Data compiled by the World Bank and reported in Table 9.4 show a steady rise in the proportion of high-tech exports to approximately 23 percent in 2003. The data for other countries, middle-low–income countries like China as well as upper-middle–income and upper-income countries, show that for broad groupings of countries the share of high-tech products in total manufactured exports rises monotonically with income per capita; nevertheless, the specific country data show substantial variation within income groupings. Table 9.4 shows that China (23 percent) compares favorably with India (5 percent), Brazil (19 percent), and Japan (24 percent), but trails the United States (24 percent), Korea (32 percent), Thailand (51 percent), and Mexico (84 percent).

Of greater significance from a dynamic perspective is the rapid growth of the high-tech share of China's exports from about 6 percent in 1990 to 23 percent in 2002. Moreover, while in 1995, foreign-funded enterprises (FFEs) accounted for as much as 80 percent of China's overall exports in such capital- and technology-intensive industries as electronics and electrical appliance, by the year 2000, the share that originated from domestically owned firms rose to about 50 percent (Walsh, 2003, pp. 4–5).

From another perspective, Schott (2004) assesses the relative sophistication of China's exports in terms of the degree of overlap between Chinese exports to the United States and those originating from the OECD countries other than the United States. Table 9.5 shows a rapid rise in the measure of overlap, having grown over

---

[14] *Nature*, vol. 431, p. 116 (September 9, 2004), http://www.nature.com/nature/journal/v431/n7005/full/431116b.html.

Table 9.5. *Percent of China's U.S.-bound exports that
overlap with OECD exports to the United States*[a]

1972	1981	1991	2001
0.09	0.28 (10)	0.55 (4)	0.75 (3)[b]

[a] Manufacturing export similarity indexes with the OECD.
[b] The number in parentheses represents China's rank among all non-
OECD countries, excluding Korea; after Mexico (0.80) and Korea
(0.80).
Source: Schott (2004).

the recent 30 years, from just 9 percent in 1972 to 75 percent in 2001. Moreover, Schott reports that the extent of China's OECD overlap exceeds that of the other Asian economies and Latin America.

Overall, indicators show that China's S&T intensity is rising rapidly.[15] This rising S&T intensity, however, has not yet propelled China into the upper ranks of innovating countries, as measured by basic research and high-quality invention patent production. This relative paucity of basic R&D combined with the rarity of high-quality patents suggests that the vast proportion of China's S&T resources are focusing on technology transfer and process innovation. As suggested by the rising quality of China's exports, this focus seems to be enabling Chinese producers to match the quality and production efficiency of an increasingly large proportion of goods that are found on world export markets.

Regional Distribution of S&T Effort

While the previous discussion treats China as an integrated, homogenous economy, it is clear that China's level of technology development varies strikingly across regions. The eastern provinces dominate the country's R&D spending. Furthermore, within the eastern region, the cities of Beijing and Shanghai and Guangdong and Jiangsu provinces account for two-thirds of the region's R&D spending. Table 9.6 shows that while covering less than 15 percent of China's population and just 30 percent of its GDP in 2002, these four subjurisdictions accounted for 45 percent of the nation's total R&D spending. That is, on a per capita basis, the R&D intensity of these four provinces/metropolitan areas is approximately three times that

---

[15] Some observers question the quality of China's R&D data, such as that shown in Table 9.1. The provision of tax subsidies for R&D spending, for example, may provide an incentive to Chinese firms to overreport their R&D spending. However, at least until recently, the rates of taxation levied on R&D-related investments have been 33 percent for domestic firms and just 17 percent for foreign firms (Walsh, 2003, p. 29), thus providing a countervailing incentive for domestic firms to underreport in relation to foreign firms. It should also be noted that the United States and many European countries, like China, maintain incentives for R&D (see Data Brief, 2001).

Table 9.6. *Regional comparisons of R&D spending, 2002*

	R&D expenditure	Percent of total
TOTAL	128.8	100.0
Central region	20.9	16.2
Western region	17.0	13.2
Eastern region	91.6	71.1
Of which:	–	–
1. Beijing	22.0	17.1
2. Guangdong	15.6	12.2
3. Jiangsu	11.7	9.1
4. Shanghai	11.0	8.7
SUM of (1–4)	60.3	47.1

Note: Values are in billion yuan.
Source: NBS/MOST (2004).

of the remainder of the country. Much of the story of China's R&D intensification is centered on the rapidly rising R&D activity of these four most technologically advanced centers.

For some perspective on the geographic concentration of China's R&D activity, we note that R&D spending in China is more concentrated than that in the United States. While Massachusetts, Michigan, and California, the states with the highest R&D intensity, account for 17.8 percent of the U.S. population, their combined R&D spending amounts to 35.2 percent of total U.S. spending. In China, Beijing, Shanghai, Tianjin, Guangdong, Jiangsu, and Liaoning account for an equivalent 17.8 percent share of China's population, whereas the combined R&D spending of these regions account for 53.6 percent of the national total (Jefferson, 2006).

Several authors have also documented the skewedness of S&T outputs across China's provinces. Research by Wei (2004), Jefferson and Su (2002), and Jefferson and Zhong (2004) shows that the distribution of S&T outputs – patenting and new product development – is highly correlated with the distribution of R&D expenditure across China's regions.

THE SHIFTING LOCUS OF R&D ACTIVITY

As a developing country, China's shift toward the consumption and production of goods and services with comparatively high-technology content is expanding S&T roles for the business sector and research institutes as they seek to exploit the returns provided by the growing demand for new technologies. In the case of China, however, the country is also moving away from central planning, in which the government was the primary source of S&T resources and the majority of the enterprise sector and complex of research institutes were under official supervision. These shifts from low income to the living standards of a newly industrializing

Table 9.7. *Distribution of R&D by performance (financing)*[a]

Year	Enterprise	Research institute	Higher education	Government	Others
1995	≤45.9	42.0	12.1		
2000	60.0	28.8	8.6		2.7
2003	62.4 (60.1)	25.9	10.5	(29.9)	1.1 (10.0)[b]

[a] Values are in percent.
[b] Comprising foreign funds (2.0 percent) and other funds (8.0 percent).
Source: NBS/MOST (2004, p. 7).

country and from central plan to market economy are rapidly altering the loci of R&D activity and the incentive structure of China's innovation system.

The Enterprise Sector

Table 9.7 shows the shift in the sectoral distribution of R&D from 1995 to 2003. While Table 9.7 does not report the enterprise share of R&D spending in 1995, the numbers indicate that in 1995, the enterprise share could not have exceeded 45.9 percent. These numbers point to a dramatic increase in the enterprise share of national R&D spending between 1995 and 2000, which was also a period of rapid restructuring in China's enterprise sector. This rapid rise in the enterprise sector's share of R&D spending is also accompanied by a rapid rise in the proportion of enterprise R&D undertaken by nonstate enterprises. By 2005, among China's industrial large and medium enterprises (LMEs), the nonstate enterprise share of enterprise sector's R&D had risen to 74 percent (NBS/MOST, 2006, pp. 219–220).

Table 9.8 shows the adoption of R&D operations within the industrial LME sector and the intensification of R&D operations among existing R&D performers. We see rising rates of participation in R&D activity by China's industrial LMEs during 1995–2002, when R&D performers as a proportion of all LMEs rose from 20.2 percent to 31.5 percent, a rise of more than one-half. Over the same period, firms that had been R&D performers in 1995 intensified their R&D operations. The proportion of high-performing LMEs with ratios of R&D to sales ratios in excess of 4 percent grew from 6.4 percent to 14.7 percent in 2002. As established R&D performers gain experience and access to foreign technology, rising returns to R&D motivate firms to move more resources into their R&D operations, thereby causing industrial R&D intensity to rise. One conclusion that we draw from Table 9.8 is that the rise in the enterprise sector's share of total R&D spending did not result from a reduction in R&D performance or spending by the other sectors – government, research institutes, or universities – but rather the rapid rise in the enterprise share of R&D spending rose as a result of the rapid increase in the sheer volume of enterprise spending on R&D activity.

Table 9.8. *Distribution of ratio r = 100*R&D/VA among large and medium industrial enterprises, 1995–2002*

Year	0	$0 < r \leq 1$	$1 < r \leq 2$	$2 < r \leq 4$	$4 < r \leq 6$	$6 < r \leq 10$	$r > 10$
1995	79.8	7.2	3.2	3.4	1.4	1.7	3.3
2001	70.9	6.7	4.0	4.8	3.0	3.5	7.1
2002	68.5	7.5	4.3	5.1	3.2	3.9	7.6
Percentage increase, 1995–2002	−14.2	4.2	34.4	50.0	128.6	129.4	130.3

Note: Values in the top three rows represent the share of LMEs that fall within each percentile range of R&D intensity in percent.
Source: NBS-LME data set.

The Research Institutes

In 2002, China reported on the activities of 4,347 research institutes. Of these, 744 were directly supervised by the central government, including the 98 institutes that comprise the CAS. More than one-half of the Chinese government's S&T funding is channeled to the 744 research institutes that it directly supervises (NBS/MOST, 2006, pp. 6, 30).

With 11.6 percent of the R&D budgets of these research institutes dedicated to basic research – compared with 5.0 percent for total R&D spending – we see that China's research institutes are the locus of basic research in China's S&T system, particularly those directly under the control of the central government that account for 96 percent of the basic research in the government research institute sector (NBS/MOST, 2003, p. 31).

Beginning in the late 1990s, China's government initiated a substantial restructuring of its research institutes, involving efforts to place them on an independent financial footing. In 2004, the Ministry of Science and Technology (MOST) reported that 1,214 of the 5,573 government research institutes that were in operation in 1999 had been restructured. Among the restructuring outcomes, conversion to S&T enterprises (*kejixing qiye*) accounted for 90 percent. In addition, 371 institutes were merged, acquired, or liquidated. Most had been incorporated into enterprise groups, while a small number were incorporated into universities.

Jefferson et al. (2006) find significant economies of scale in their sample of research institutes.[16] The finding that a multitude of relatively small research units have the potential to increase efficiency by combining into larger organizations suggests the importance of the government's restructuring program, in which institutes have the authority to negotiate mergers and acquisitions that can result in efficiency-enhancing economies of scope and scale.

---

[16] This finding is consistent with that of Jin et al. (2003), who in their study of forty-six wheat and maize breeding institutes from 1981 to 2000, found robust economics of scale in China's crop breeding research. According to their findings, the current large number of small crop breeding institutes is the main source of inefficiency.

Universities

In 2003, China reported the operation of 1,552 institutes of higher learning, representing about a 50 percent increase from 1995. In the aggregate, higher education accounted for 17.3 percent of the nation's total R&D personnel, somewhat below the 1995 figure of 19.2 percent. Over the same period, the higher-education sector's share of total R&D expenditure fell from 12.1 percent in 1995 to 10.5 percent in 2003. While the sector's share of both total R&D personnel and total R&D spending fell during 1995–2003, its share of basic research rose from 36 percent in 1995 to 37.5 percent in 2003.[17]

Overall, we find in China, particularly during the past decade, the emergence of a more vigorous research establishment – enterprises, independent research organizations, and universities – which are largely self-financed. By 2004, government provided slightly less than 30 percent of total R&D financing, while the contribution of the nongovernmental sector had grown to more than 60 percent.

CONTRIBUTIONS OF THE FOREIGN SECTOR: DIRECT AND INDIRECT

Much of the literature on China's S&T system divides over the importance of the foreign sectors in driving China's technological advance. Some accounts emphasize the contributions of foreign businesses to promoting the expansion of productivity and capabilities among domestic firms (Walsh, 2003; Chapter 15 in this volume). Gilboy (2004) takes a decidedly skeptical view of the capabilities of China's domestic S&T capabilities, characterizing China's domestically owned firms as hampered by

> ... an "industrial strategic culture" that encourages them to seek short-term profits ... (and) forego investment in long-term technology development and diffusion .... Most Chinese industrial firms ... have not increased their commitment to developing new technologies .... R&D expenditure as a percentage of value added at China's industrial firms is only about one percent, seven times less than the average in countries of the OECD (p. 43).

We focus on three dimensions of the role of the foreign sector in driving China's R&D intensification and S&T performance: foreign-funded R&D, FDI, and imported technology.

Role of Foreign-Funded R&D

To test Gilboy's proposition that firms with FDI participation dominate R&D operations in China, we turn to our data set for China's industrial LMEs. According to the LME census data, in 2001 total R&D expenditure within China's domestic industrial LME sector was approximately four times that of the FIE sector, for which we use the definition employed by the National Bureau of Statistics that includes

---

[17] These ratios are calculated from data reported in NBS/MOST (2004, pp. 4, 6, 293).

Table 9.9. *Domestic versus foreign contributions to R&D spending in 2001 (industrial LMEs)*

	Domestic	Foreign and HMT
1995		
Firm count	16,823	1,323
R&D exp (RMB1,000s)	67,130	6,480
R&D/value added (%)	1.11	0.99
2001		
Firm count	14,429	4,360
R&D exp (RMB1,000s)	281,770	53,380
R&D/value added (%)	3.29	2.63
Ratio: 2001:1995		
R&D exp (RMB1,000s)	4.19	8.23
R&D/value added (%)	2.96	2.66

Note: HMT refers to firms with investors from Hong Kong, Macao, and/or Taiwan.

Source: NBS-LME data set (2001).

both foreign firms and firms with investment from Hong Kong, Macao, and Taiwan (HMT). That is, in 2001 domestic firms accounted for 78 cents of every R&D dollar spent by the enterprise sector.[18] Moreover, as shown in Table 9.9, in 2001, while the ratio of R&D to value added in China's domestic LMEs had reached 3.29 percent, for the foreign firms it stood at just 2.63 percent. This finding is broadly consistent with a recent OECD report that states, "[F]oreign firms that invest in China appear to have engaged in only limited levels of R&D activity and their role in the innovation process seems even more limited" (OECD, 2002, p. 267). The imbalance shown in Table 9.9 appears to persist. In 2005, while R&D expenditure as a percentage of *total sales revenue* for China's domestic-funded LMEs stood at 0.8 percent, that for the FFEs and enterprises with funds from Hong Kong, Macao, and Taiwan reported ratios of 0.6 and 0.5 percent, respectively (MOST, 2006, pp. 113, 115). In conclusion, at least in terms of China's surging R&D intensity, during 1995–2005, the direct contribution of China's domestic enterprise sector has outpaced that of the foreign sector.

Role of FDI

China has emerged as the leading recipient of FDI, although on a per capita basis, FDI flows to China are comparable to those of countries in Southeast Asia and

---

[18] Chinese statistics classify firms with full or partial foreign investment as "foreign-invested enterprises." In 2001, domestic owners held 61 percent of the overall equity in such firms. We use this share to assign a proportion of FIE research and development spending to the domestic side of the ledger. The domestic share of China's LME industrial R&D spending then rises to 91 cents on the dollar.

substantially less than that of the United States. FDI is likely to motivate R&D effort through two channels. First, concentrations of FDI create technological opportunities for domestic firms, as they can use research funds to imitate products and processes that enter their geographic and technological space. Furthermore, infusions of FDI create competition; simply to survive, domestic firms are obliged to upgrade technologically, so that their product quality and production efficiency enable them to remain competitive.

To test the hypothesis that industry FDI concentration motivates R&D intensity, Gong and Jefferson (2007) examine the impact of horizontal FDI (i.e., investment in the same three-digit industry group and the same province) on R&D intensity. They find that foreign-funded FDI (excluding that from Hong Kong, Macao, and Taiwan) interacts with domestic in-house R&D to motivate greater levels of R&D intensity.

In their study of the determinants of patent applications filed with China's State Intellectual Property Office (SIPO), Hu and Jefferson (2006) find a surprising result: even after controlling for R&D expenditure and ownership type, concentrations of FDI within the same three-digit standard industrial classification industry group substantially increase the firm's propensity to patent. When they subdivide their sample into domestic and foreign firms, they find that while this result is extremely robust for domestic firms, it is insignificant for patenting by foreign-owned companies. The result seems to indicate that access to enlarged technological opportunity afforded by proximity to kindred FDI substantially expands patenting opportunities for Chinese firms. The robust association between FDI and domestic company patenting may also reveal a pattern of strategic patenting, in which domestic firms use the patenting system to lodge law suits, secure settlements, or simply to force delay to weaken competitor company claims to intellectual property rights. Whether the motivation is to exploit new technological opportunity or to infringe on the intellectual property of competitors, Hu and Jefferson (2006) show that industry FDI is an important driver of domestic firm patenting.

Role of Imported Technology Markets

Again according to Gilboy, "Chinese firms are taking few effective steps to absorb the technology they import and diffuse it throughout the local economy, making it unlikely they will rapidly emerge as global industrial competitors" (2004, p. 38). Once again, the LME data set shows a different picture. In 2001, 1,460 LMEs, over 80 percent domestically owned, recorded purchases of imported technology. Furthermore, the foreign-invested enterprises (FIEs) purchased virtually nothing in China's domestic technology markets. Except for their parent companies from whom they transfer technology, the FIEs are substantially less connected with local technology markets than their domestic counterparts.

Table 9.10 shows the importance of technology purchases in relation to overall S&T spending with China's industrial LMEs. As a proportion of total internal S&T

Table 9.10. *LME spending in technology markets*

	2000	2003	Annual growth (%)
Internal S&T expenditure[a]	82.4	146.8	21.2
Purchase of imported technology	24.5 (29.7%)	40.5 (27.6%)	18.2
Purchase of domestic technology	2.6 (3.2%)	5.4 (3.7%)	27.6

Note: Values are in billion yuan; figure in parentheses is proportion of total internal S&T expenditures.
[a] Internal expenditure refers to intramural outlays or spending within the firm.
Source: NBS-LME data sets for 2000 and 2003.

expenditure (i.e. intramural outlays or spending within the firm), the purchase of imported technology, nearly 30 percent in 2000, stood at 27.6 percent in 2003, having grown at an annual rate of 18.0 percent during 2000–2003. At just 3.7 percent of total internal S&T expenditure in 2003, the purchase of domestic technology played a much smaller role; however, with purchases having doubled over the period 2000–2003, it represents a growing share of total internal S&T spending.

Firms that purchase imported technology invariably support in-house R&D operations. In-house R&D shows strong complementarities with technology imports, enabling domestic firms to capture higher returns to their own R&D spending.[19] Our research also finds that domestic firms that combine in-house R&D with imported technology are more likely to be active exporters.[20] By creating incentives for domestic firms to perform R&D while also enhancing the impact of R&D by combining it with foreign technology transfer, China's fast-growing foreign sector is supporting the growing capabilities of Chinese-owned companies to compete on world markets.

One component of the foreign sector does seem to be contributing substantially to China's R&D effort – that is, majority-owned U.S. affiliates, which in 2000 numbered 458. Such affiliates with major R&D activities include DuPont, Ford, GE, GM, IBM, Intel, Lucent Technologies, Microsoft, and Motorola. According to Moris (2004), during 1997–2000, the R&D/VA ratio of these firms rose from 1.1 percent in 1997 to 9.2 percent in 2000. The level of R&D intensity of these U.S. affiliates of 9.2 percent substantially exceeds the 3.3 percent level of R&D intensity for aggregate U.S. affiliates in all host countries, a measure of the relative draw of China and possibly the impact of the government's "technology for markets" policy. In addition, a number of these foreign affiliates with substantial R&D operations have established R&D alliances with Chinese counterparts. Referencing the Thomas Financial Joint Ventures Alliances database, Moris reports that from 1990 to 2001, U.S. and Chinese-owned companies and other organizations formed

---

[19] Hu, Jefferson, and Qian (2005) show this result within the context of a production function. Fisher-Vanden and Jefferson find this result using a cost function approach.
[20] Fisher-Vanden and Jefferson (2004).

105 new business alliances with large R&D components, substantially more than the 78 alliances that U.S. companies formed with Japanese, German, British, Singapore, and Canadian companies during the same period.

Summarizing, we find that FIEs are not leading the intensification of China's R&D effort. However, the foreign sector does play a key role in motivating rising R&D intensity through at least two indirect channels. One is FDI that motivates domestic R&D spending and patenting; the second is through technology markets that interact with imported R&D to enhance the innovative efficiency in China's domestic enterprise sector. While the R&D affiliates of multinational firms do indeed exhibit high levels of R&D intensity, the total volume of their research activity remains a small percentage of China's total R&D spending.

GOVERNMENT POLICIES AND PROGRAMS IN SUPPORT OF S&T

China's government is committed to advancing China rapidly to the ranks of the world's leading innovators. The Tenth Five-Year Plan sets 2015 as the target for China's emergence as a leading innovation economy. Here, we review the essential government components of China's public S&T system. These include its organization, specific government programs that provide R&D financing, and incentives for private innovation.

Organization

Three key organizations administer most civilian science and engineering research in China, although the Ministries of Defense, Health, and Agriculture, the State Forestry Administration, and other economic agencies also have significant research operations under their direct management. The Ministry of Education oversees and funds all universities in the country.

The MOST provides policy guidance on the S&T system reform agenda and formulates policies on how to strengthen basic and applied research and technology development, especially in the high-tech area. Recently, MOST has focused on S&T development strategies that complement the nation's economic reform and development agenda. The ministry provides funds for S&T programs in both basic and applied research, for instance, the high-technology R&D program commonly referred to as the "973 Program." MOST also collects a range of statistical data relating to China's S&T system and publishes annually *China's Science and Technology Yearbook*, in collaboration with the NBS, and publishes biannually the *China Science and Technology Indicators*, which reviews the state of China's S&T system.

The *National Natural Science Foundation of China* (NSFC) was consciously modeled after the National Science Foundation of the United States, when it was established in 1986 with the mandate to "encourage innovation and to fund excellent and creative research through fair competition on the basis of scientific and democratic principles . . . ." NSFC funds peer-reviewed basic and applied research in the natural sciences, that is, physics, mathematics, and chemical and life sciences. As such, China's NSFC incorporates the functions and resources that in the United States would be assigned to the National Institutes of Health. Within these functional areas, peer review panels recommend awards. Principal grant awardees are Chinese universities and CAS research institutes.[21]

The CAS operates on two levels. Elected academy members have a significant consulting and advisory role. More substantively, however, CAS loosely manages close to 100 independent research institutes, which conduct scientific research in all branches of the natural sciences. Each institute's funding is an amalgam of resources from CAS Headquarters, MOST, and the NSFC. In addition, institutes earn varying amounts of money from owning and operating spin-off enterprises. CAS Headquarters also owns spin-offs. The Chinese Academy of Engineering was formed more recently and is a much smaller organization than CAS, playing only a consulting and advisory role, with no research institutes, graduate school, or research centers, such as those in CAS.

Government Programs

China's government supports two distinct types of programs: those that focus on supporting basic and frontier research and those with a primary objective to promote the diffusion of applied technologies. Table 9.11 summarizes their key features. The programs that focus on basic research include the "Key Projects Program" (*Gongguan*), the "863 Program" (*Baliusan*), and the "973 Program" (*Jiuqisan*). Programs that focus on diffusion include the "Torch Program" (*Huoju*), which focuses on the commercialization and dissemination of new technologies in industry, and the "Spark Program" (*Xinghuo*), which is focused on the development of S&T in rural areas.

Focusing on basic research, the "863" and "973" programs are largely funded by the state and mostly performed by universities and research institutes. We are not aware of any systematic studies in the public domain that evaluate the effectiveness of these programs. Indirect and anecdotal evidence suggests that they have been productive. For example, in 2002 these programs together accounted for 408 invention patents, or 7 percent of all the invention patents granted to domestic inventors in China.

The other three programs – the *Key Projects*, the *Torch*, and the *Spark* programs deal mostly with the "D" or the development and diffusion stage of innovation. The Key Projects Program is a top-down program, with the government acting as

---

[21] Executive Summary of China's Science and Technology System and its Impact on the Research Community, An October 2002 Report from U.S. Embassy Beijing, http://www.usembassy-china.org.cn/sandt/ST-ReportSum.htm.

Table 9.11. *Major national science and technology programs*

Program	Year started	Focus and objective
Key Technologies R&D Program	1982	Aims to solve the key and comprehensive problems concerning national economic and social development; covering agriculture, electronic information, energy resources, transportation, materials, resources exploration, environmental protection, medical and health care, and other fields. Investing the most funds and employing the most personnel, this program was the largest S&T program in China in the twentieth century
National High-Tech R&D Program ("863" Program)	1986	The "863" Program includes twenty themes, such as biotech, space flight, information, laser, automation, energy, and new material. The research agenda of the program is decided by panels of scientists, who are responsible for closely monitoring developments in international scientific research so as to set research goals and programs that warrant government support. Its results are intended to be quickly deployed to industry
National Program on Key Basic Research Projects ("973" Program)	1997	Like "863," "973" focuses on enabling China's S&T capabilities to catch up with those of the OECD countries. However, it intends to focus on those issues that challenge China's economic and social development in the twenty-first century. These include basic research with a multidisciplinary approach in fields such as agriculture, energy, information, environment of resources, population and health, and materials
Torch	1988	Focuses on the commercialization of new technologies, developing high-tech products that meet international technology standards, and establishing high-tech development zones across China, including the nurturing of entrepreneurship through incubators and science parks
Spark	1986	Aims to revitalize the rural economy through S&T and to popularize science in rural areas. As of 2004, there were more than 100,000 scientific and technological demonstration projects being carried out in 85% of rural areas across China

Source: http://www.china.org.cn/english/features/China2004/107131.htm.

an agent between enterprises and research institutes and universities. The *Torch* and *Spark* programs differ from the others in that they combine the "push" of direct government funding with the "pull" of market demand.

For example, an important part of the *Torch Program* is the nationwide establishment of S&T parks to encourage the formation of high-technology start-ups. Instead of grants, government support is limited to preferential tax treatment within the parks. Perhaps in part to compensate for risk taking by the enterprises, the government has allowed for a greater role of nonstate ownership in these parks, which increases the private returns that entrepreneurs can expect to reap from their innovations.

In a similar spirit, the *Spark Program* is intended to reduce barriers to technology diffusion in rural China by setting up over 500 technology "demonstration stations" across the country to educate and train farmers and rural entrepreneurs. With the majority of financing coming from self-raised funds and bank lending, it is the entrepreneurs who decide which technologies to adopt.[22]

Both the Torch and the Spark programs have been successful. Walcott (2003) provides rich institutional details of China's S&T parks established under the Torch Program. Hu (2007)) shows that these technology parks have been growing much faster than the cities that host them. He finds that their superior performance may have been driven more by policy incentives than by agglomeration or localization externalities. In a systematic evaluation of the Spark Program, Du and Xu (1997) document the multidimensional success of the program. For example, they report that in 1995 TVEs included under the Spark Program had an average profit rate of 7.83 percent, much higher than the national average of 3.09 percent. Furthermore, the TVEs set up under the Spark Program had generated on average 139 new jobs. Although program evaluation is a difficult task, the Spark Program did seem to have generated measurable economic benefit.[23]

Incentives for the Enterprise Sector

In China, the central government also stimulates R&D through the provision of grants and tax incentives to the enterprise sector. China's large- and medium-size enterprises, which account for three quarters of China's industrial R&D spending and over one-half of its industrial sales, receive the majority of these R&D grants and tax subsidies. Over the period 1998–2004, R&D grants as a proportion of R&D spending by LMEs fell by two-thirds, while the proportion of tax subsidies rose by approximately 40 percent. These proportional changes suggest two observations. First, government support for R&D in the enterprise sector has shifted from direct grants toward indirect subsidies. Second, the decline in grant support indicates that

---

[22] http://www.chinaconsulatesf.org/eng/kj/kjjh/.
[23] It is unclear that the study takes into account the nonrandomness of participation in the Spark Program. So the evidence presented is only suggestive.

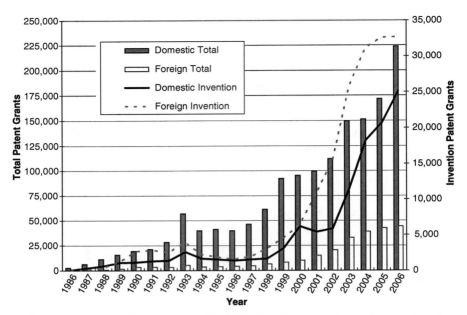

Figure 9.3. Number of patents granted by China SIPO (*Source:* Hu and Jefferson, 2006)

the abrupt increase in the enterprise sector's R&D spending has not been driven by government funding.

In addition, the national *Torch Program* provides a range of public services to high-tech enterprises, notably, in technology development zones, including incubators and educational services. Furthermore, companies that are certified as new/high-tech enterprises become eligible for a range of tax subsidies, including a two-year income tax exemption and lesser continuing tax reductions thereafter.[24]

The Patent System

China's National People's Congress passed China's first patent law in 1984. The substantial revision of the patent law in 1992 expanded in the scope of patent protection. The impact of stronger patent protection is clearly reflected in the annual patent grants plotted in Figure 9.3. The number of patents granted rose sharply in 1993. The temporary fall back in 1994 was followed by the persistent and rapid growth of patenting, particularly during 1997–2002 when total patent grants increased at an average annual rate of 21 percent.

Figure 9.3 also shows that the surge in patenting is driven by "utility" and "design" patents, which represent incremental innovations and receive far weaker legal

---

[24] http://us.tom.com/english/446.htm.

protection than that afforded by "invention" patents.[25] The contrasting perfor-mance of domestic and foreign inventors exhibited in Figure 9.3 further cor-roborates the hypothesis of an increasingly robust patent system. In 2003, over 300,000 patent applications were submitted. This number, however, includes "util-ity model" and design patents, which are relatively modest adaptations of existing technologies. If we limit our scope to the 105,318 applications for new inventions, we find that almost half (48,549) were from foreigners and over half (56,769) were from Chinese citizens. Clearly, the patent system is beginning to play a role in the strategies of foreign companies in China, which increasingly seek to protect intellectual property whatever the source. At the same time, Chinese inventors are finding it worthwhile to begin protecting their own intellectual property.

Technology Standards

China's effort to promote indigenously developed technologies as industry stan-dards has received wide attention.[26] Suttmeier and Yao (2004) interpret these devel-opments through the lens of "neo-techno-nationalism," that is, the pursuit of national interest by establishing national technology standards that give advan-tage to Chinese suppliers. In the face of an avalanche of foreign technologies that result in substantial payments from Chinese (and other) users, a central objective of China's government is to encourage and enable Chinese industry to develop intellectual property that will reverse the flow of rents in favor of Chinese firms. An important part of this strategy is for the government to organize technol-ogy standards, indeed a technology architecture that will provide Chinese inno-vators with an advantageous environment in which to achieve these technology goals.

The greatest attention has been given to the Chinese government's efforts to promote standards for third-generation (3G) mobile telephone technology and the Time Division Synchronous Code Division Multiple Access (TD-SCDMA) standards. China also continues to develop an alternative to the Windows operat-ing system by promoting Linux systems. Finally, the introduction of a new security standard for wireless devices, the WLAN Authentication and Privacy Infrastruc-ture standard (WAPI), has received international attention. In addition, Suttmeier

---

25 Another indication of the low-invention content of Chinese patents is the sharp contrast between invention patents granted to Chinese inventors in China and in the United States shown in Table 9.1. Clearly, the economic value of many Chinese patents seeking protection in the United States is not large enough to compensate for the costs involved in obtaining a U.S. patent.

26 Suttmeier and Yao (2004) provide a list of these standards: Dragon Chip, Enhanced Versatile Disc, AVS (Audio, Video Coding Standard for MPEG), IGRS for communicating among digi-tal devices, IPV6 (a new Internet protocol), RFID (radio frequency identification tagging), TD-SCDMA (Time Division Synchronous Code Division Multiple Access) for third-generation mobile communication technology, and WAPI (Wireless LAN Authentification and Privacy Infrastructure for mobile microprocessors).

and Yao (2004) identify several areas in which efforts are under way to promote standards. These include the following:

- China's own microprocessor (the "Dragon chip");
- China's own successor to DVDs (the "EVD" – Enhanced Versatility Disc) standard;
- A new digital audio standard (AVS – Audio, Video, Coding Standard);
- A Chinese standard (IGRS – Intelligent Grouping and Resources Sharing) for communicating among digital devices;
- A new Internet protocol (IPV6); and
- Radio frequency identification tagging (RFID).

China's focus on promoting technology standards that apply to the information technology industry is not a matter of coincidence. The actual and potential size of the Chinese market for information products raises the stakes for standard setting in China. In such markets, proprietary control of the industry standard can command lucrative rewards. For these reasons, China's recent attempts to influence the standard setting in various sectors of the information technology industry go beyond nationalism or national pride.

Other governments have also intervened in standard setting. For example, in selecting the standard for high-definition television (HDTV), Europe and Japan followed a centralized approach, whereas the United States relied on market forces (Farrell and Shapiro, 1992). In the case of WAPI, China attempted to overturn the industry standard with a technology that was not necessarily superior. This was bound to meet with opposition. But given China's increasingly sophisticated technological capabilities and sustained economic growth, the Chinese government is likely to continue trying to leverage the size and the anticipated growth of the Chinese market to influence technology standard setting to the benefit of Chinese firms.

However, another element of the government's S&T development strategy may work against the process of establishing independent technology standards, that is, the government's emphasis on establishing channels for international cooperation. According to a recent publication of the MOST,[27] China is a member of more than 1,000 international cooperation organizations. China's government has established S&T cooperation ties with 152 counties and regions and signed intergovernmental cooperation accords with 96 countries. Under one of these accords, China and the United States established in 2005 the China-U.S. Nanotechnology Institute, involving collaboration between Zhejiang University and the U.S. California Nano-System Institute. The goal of the accord is to "set a role model for S&T system reform in Zhejiang province . . . and the whole country." As of September 2005, approximately 160 Chinese universities and research institutes had established

---

[27] *China Science and Technology Newsletter*, The Ministry of Science and Technology, People's Republic of China, http://www.most.gov.cn/eng/newsletters/2006/t20060213_28707.html.

S&T collaboration with EU counterparts, involving EU investments of 418 million euros.

Thus, we observe two opposing forces that impinge on the motive for China to set national technology standards: efforts to create a technology framework that will enable Chinese firms to develop new technologies that generate IPR rents formerly ceded to foreign firms along with the desire to maintain an open collaborative technology playing field, so that China can access, adopt, and possibly improve upon the latest technologies, using already-established foreign technology standards.

CASE STUDIES

This section presents case studies that focus on two industries – semiconductors, including elements of the electronics industry, and automobiles, pillar industries that the Chinese government has targeted for rapid development through its industrial and S&T policies. The case studies summarize the state of technology in each industry in relation to the international frontier, the strategic issues for catch-up, and the role of policy in facilitating or hindering technological advance.

Semiconductors

China's emerging semiconductor industry constitutes an important backward linkage to China's electronics industry, which is rapidly growing in both the volume and the range of electronic consumer goods and industrial equipment.

State of the Technology
China's first S&T plan, formulated in 1956, selected electronics technology, including semiconductors, as one of the twelve targeted areas for intensive government support (Yuan et al., 1992). Chinese scientists developed the silicon digital integrated circuit in 1965 – seven years after Robert Noyce and Jack Kilby invented the integrated circuit – placing China within reasonable reach of U.S. leadership in semiconductor technology. However, the disruption caused by the Cultural Revolution and the parallel explosive growth of semiconductor technology left China far behind by the late 1970s. In China's second major S&T planning exercise in 1978, electronic computing was again selected as one of the eight major target areas for state support (Yuan et al., 1992).

A most remarkable example of technological catch-up is the rise of the East Asian semiconductor industry led by Korea and Taiwan (Matthews and Cho, 2000). From 1984 to 2003, the Asia Pacific's share in world semiconductor production, consisting largely of Taiwanese and Korean firms, increased from 6 to 39 percent. During this period, U.S. and Japanese shares declined from 47 and 31 percent to 19 and 23 percent, respectively.[28] Korea is now the world leader in DRAM (dynamic

---

[28] See www.sia-online.org.

random access memory) manufacturing, whereas Taiwan hosts the world's largest semiconductor foundries. Will China be the next to leapfrog to the world's semiconductor technology frontier?

Strategic Issues for Catch-Up

A confluence of events has contributed to the rapid rise of China's semiconductor industry. Industrial and S&T policies have perhaps played the most important role in jump-starting the industry and catapulting it to a fast growth track. Also critical has been the inflow of FDI, particularly Taiwanese investment, which has contributed investment, technology, and human talent. An important although indirect factor has been the rapid growth of China's consumer electronics, computers, and telecommunication equipment industries that has generated insatiable demand for semiconductors.

When China started to rebuild its semiconductor industry in the early to mid-1980s, the industry was in a primitive state and was mainly engaged in producing low-end discrete semiconductors, such as diodes and thyratrons; China possessed neither the capital nor the technology required to develop a modern semiconductor industry. To modernize its semiconductor industry, the Chinese government implemented Project 908. In 1994, Project 908 assisted a state-owned company, Huajing Electronics, acquire 0.9-μm technology from Lucent Technologies. A year later, under Project 909, the Chinese government selected the Japanese firm NEC as the joint-venture partner to build a wafer-processing line in Shanghai that was capable of producing 20,000 8-inch silicon wafers per month. The production line represented a major jump for China's semiconductor technology – from 1–2 μm to 0.35–0.5 μm. A further joint-venture agreement with NEC saw the establishment in June 1998 of the Beijing Huahong NEC IC Design Co. Ltd. that added important design capabilities to China's nascent semiconductor industry.

Establishing semiconductor joint ventures with leading foreign semiconductor firms has been one of China's key industrial development strategies. While in the early stage China insisted on a controlling interest in these joint ventures, more recently, foreign wholly owned semiconductor firms, particularly Taiwanese companies, have built new production facilities. Of the twenty-one semiconductor-manufacturing plants operating as of 2003 or expected to operate in 2004 in China, nine were built after 2001 and four are 100 percent owned by foreign investors (Howell et al., 2003, figure 10). SMIC (Semiconductor Manufacturing International Corp), based in Shanghai and founded by Taiwanese engineers and capital, launched a foundry facility to manufacture wafers using the 0.13-μm technology, thereby placing China among the world's top semiconductor makers (*Reuters News*, September 25, 2004).

Role of Policy

China's ambition to become a leading design and manufacturing base for integrated circuits was articulated in State Council Circular 18 published in June 2000.

The Chinese government proposed a wide variety of policies aimed at attracting foreign investment in the semiconductor sector. Most critical and controversial of the incentives still in effect is the value-added tax (VAT) rebate that applies to semiconductors produced within China. China levies a VAT on imported semi-conductors of 17 percent. But domestic designers and manufacturers receive a tax rebate that reduces the effective VAT rate to 3 percent on devices made and sold in China. Howell et al. (2003) argue that Taiwanese manufacturers are largely attracted to Mainland China by the tax incentive rather than by the manufacturing cost advantage. China has agreed to phase out the tax subsidy in compliance with WTO requirements.[29]

In addition, integrated circuit (IC) manufacturers can receive a five-year corpo-rate income tax holiday. Semiconductor companies set up in high-technology parks also benefit from all the preferential treatment in tax and infrastructure subsidies that these parks offer. In addition to central government policy, local governments, particularly those in Beijing and Shanghai, offered their own "Circular 18" on even more attractive terms. These policies represented a watershed in the develop-ment of China's semiconductor industry. From 2001 to 2003, a total of nineteen Taiwan-invested foundries, including those by the world's top players, UMC and TSMC, were operational, under construction, or being planned on the Mainland, compared to only seven such start-ups in Taiwan during the same period (Howell et al., 2003).

China's semiconductor industry still faces serious challenges in acquiring IC design and overall new product development capabilities. Most of the technologies and equipment are purchased from foreign firms. However, in a highly cyclical world market, China's fast-growing electronics industry creates a stable and robust demand for China's nascent semiconductor industry. Given the rate of capital, technology and human talent inflow, and rapid technological progress, the semi-conductor industry perhaps represents one of China's best hopes of leapfrogging to the world technology frontier.

Automobile Industry

While China built its first automobile plant in 1953, only in recent years has con-sumer demand begun to emerge to support a domestic automotive industry with the potential to operate at with the scale economies needed for efficient automotive production.

State of Technological Development
When China began opening its economy three decades ago, its automotive industry lagged woefully behind that of the world's major automobile producers. China's first automobile plant, First Automotive Works, located at Changchun in Northeastern

---

[29] See www.ecommercetimes.com, September 7, 2004.

China, manufactured the *Jiefang* (Liberation) trucks, using technology transferred from the Soviet Union. Dissatisfaction with the slow progress of China's indigenous automotive industry, which lacked the technological capability to design and manufacture high-quality vehicles, encouraged China's government to open the domestic market to foreign investment while also requiring that foreign companies team up with local companies to make cars.

Representing perhaps the beginning of its modern automobile industry, China's first automobile joint venture, Beijing Jeep Corporation (BJC), was established in 1983 between Beijing Automobile Industry Corporation, owned by the Beijing municipal government, and American Motors Corporation (AMC), which was later acquired by Chrysler, which later merged with Daimler-Benz in 1999. BJC produced two models, BJ212, a technology transferred from the Soviet Union in the 1950s, and Jeep Cherokee XJ. It took Chrysler eighteen years to introduce its second model, the Grand Cherokee, to the joint venture in 2001. When Volkswagen formed the joint venture with Shanghai Automobile Industry Corporation in 1985, it produced a model, Santana, which was no longer produced anywhere else (Gallagher, 2003).

Fast forward to March 2006, when Honda prepared to introduce its latest version of the Civic in China just months after it went on sale in Europe, Japan, and the United States, and Toyota was already assembling its Prius gasoline–electric hybrid car in China, the only country outside Japan where the car is produced. Ford just opened a second production line in China that is almost identical to one of its most advanced factories in southwestern Germany (Bradsher, 2006).

Notwithstanding allegations of intellectual property rights violation, the Chinese indigenous automobile makers have emerged from anonymity and irrelevance to become significant market players. In January 2006, they accounted for 28.7 percent of the domestic Chinese market, followed by Japanese (27.8), European (19 percent), American (14 percent), and Korean brands (10.3 percent). This was the first time Chinese indigenous brands had leapt ahead of foreign brands in China (Bradsher, 2006).

In 2005, China became the world's second largest automobile market after the United States, with sales of 5.92 million units. A development that went relatively uncelebrated occurred in 2005 when China became a net vehicle exporter for the first time, exporting 172,800 units, up 120 percent from a year earlier (*Reuters News*, February 10, 2006), although in dollar terms export volume trailed imports by a ratio of one to three, 1.595 billion and 5.953 billion dollars, respectively.

Strategic Issues for Catch-Up

China's enormous market potential has convinced every major international automobile manufacturer to enter the Chinese market by setting up a joint venture with a local Chinese partner as required by the Chinese government. The early entrants' faith in the Chinese automobile market has paid off with the explosive growth of automobile sales since the beginning of the century. In the process, the Chinese government has leveraged the potential of the Chinese market by extracting technology transfer from foreign investors through the requirements of local content and domestic majority ownership.

In addition, the Chinese government also protected the domestic automobile industry through high tariff and nontariff barriers. These policies have arguably generated mixed or even dubious results and have been inconsistent over time. China's entry into WTO forced the Chinese government to eliminate or significantly curtail its protective policies. Ironically, entry into WTO has not weakened China's automobile industry as many in China had feared. In fact, FDI, technology transfer, and the growth of indigenous Chinese automobile manufacturers all accelerated after China's entry into WTO; the automobile industry grew by 60–70 percent each year from 2001 to 2004. Greater competition in the industry as a result of China's entry into WTO is the most likely explanation. We further examine three of these factors later.

Foreign automobile manufacturers have accelerated entry and investment in China and have transferred ever advanced and new models to the Chinese market. Foreign investment totaled 880 million dollars in the 1980s. However, foreign investment into the automobile and related industries reached 60 billion dollars in the 1990s (Gallagher, 2003), a figure that is likely to have been exceeded during the first five years following China's entry into WTO in 2001.[30]

With surging investment from all major international automobile manufacturers, the Chinese automobile industry is becoming increasingly competitive. The top ten passenger-car manufacturers in China by sales in 2005 are Shanghai-GM, Shanghai-VW, First Auto Works (FAW)-VW, Beijing Hyundai, Guangzhou-Honda, FAW-Xiali, Chery, Dongfeng-Nissan, Geely, and Dongfeng-Citroen. Together they accounted for 73 percent of total car sales (NBS, 2006). Chery and Geely are two indigenous Chinese firms with their own brands. Shanghai-VW for the first time lost its number one spot to Shanghai-GM. While Volkswagen, Shanghai-VW, and FAW-VW had captured 60 percent of the Chinese market in the mid-1990s, as a result of the rapid entry of foreign competitors and technology transfer to domestic manufacturers, notably, Chery and Geely, by 2005 VW's market share had dropped to just 17.3 percent.

The Role of Policy

In 1994, a decade after the first automobile joint venture was established, the Chinese government formulated its explicit industry policy for the automobile sector. The policy has three major components. First, the policy aimed to consolidate the dozens of automobile makers to achieve economies of scale. At the time, no

---

[30] A rough and partial count of foreign investment in the automobile industry includes Volkswagen investing 2 billion dollars in 2002, Ford investing 100 million dollars in 2001, Nissan committed to investing 1 billion dollars in 2002, and Daimler-Chrysler investing 1 billion dollars via Hyundai in 2003, not to mention outlays by GM, Honda, Toyota, Volvo, and many others.

automobile manufacturers were able to reach the minimum efficient scale of 150,000 cars per year for chassis and power train manufacturing. The government was targeting the creation of a "Big Three, Mini Three" mix of automobile manufacturers. Second, tariff barriers were created to protect the domestic automobile manufacturers from foreign import competition. Tariffs in 1994 were 110–150 percent for finished vehicles. There were also import quotas. Lastly, as a way to extract technology transfer, all foreign automobile manufacturers were required to form joint ventures with local partners in which foreign ownership was limited to 50 percent. All these joint ventures were also required to source at least 40 percent of their parts and components locally. The foreign joint ventures were encouraged to set up technical centers to train Chinese engineers, technicians, and workers.

China's first automobile industry policy largely failed to achieve its objectives. At the turn of the century, the automobile industry remained fragmented, causing production to be well below the efficient scale. During the same period, there had been limited technology transfer from foreign automobile makers.[31]

The National Development and Reform Commission issued a new automobile industry policy in 2004.[32] Entry into WTO required China to adopt a number of liberalizing measures with respect to the automobile industry. These include reducing import tariffs for complete vehicles and automobile parts to 25 percent and 10 percent, respectively, by July 1, 2006; gradually phasing out import quotas and licenses by 2005; and eliminating requirements for technology transfer and localization. With the exception of firms operating in the special economic zones, foreign ownership was still limited to 50 percent.[33] Under the new policy, new automobile-manufacturing projects have to make an initial investment of at least 2 billion yuan. The 2004 policy also adopted an explicit objective of encouraging indigenous research and development. Finally, the policy also emphasized the development of a secondhand car market, car financing, and a network of car dealers.

Following China's entry into WTO, growing market competition and declining import restrictions caused automobile prices to fall – the price of a VW Santana fell from 120,000 yuan (14,500 dollars) in 2001 to 80,000 yuan (9,700 dollars) in 2003 (Goldman, 2003) – while also prompting foreign automobile makers to introduce more and newer models to the Chinese market. Greater competition and falling prices have spurred a new wave of foreign investment rather than discouraging it. Instead of stifling the indigenous car-manufacturing industry, China's own automobile manufacturers and their brands have never been stronger;

---

[31] Gallagher documented the failure of foreign manufacturers in transferring current air-pollution-control technology to China.

[32] http://www.china-embassy.org/eng/gyzg/t127767.htm.

[33] Multinationals can still own only half a joint venture. But foreign investors will be allowed to control stakes of more than 50 percent in automobile and motorcycle joint ventures (JVs) with Chinese partners "if their joint ventures are built in China's export processing zones and shoot at overseas markets."

three Chinese automobile makers, Shanghai Automotive Industry Corporation, Chery, and Geely, have announced plans to sell low-cost cars to the U.S. and European markets (*Reuters News*, April 24, 2006).

Problems persist in the industry. The president of China's Chang'an Motors complains that while the Chinese "authorities will encourage the development of low-emission vehicles, such as compact cars our company produces . . . . [M]any cities are implementing discriminatory measures against mini vehicles, prohibiting them from driving on main avenues. That is a problem that the new policy has no means of addressing, and that will require stronger regulations to resolve."[34]

A second issue facing the industry is intellectual property disputes. Japanese motor companies, such as Toyota, Honda, and Nissan, have acted as plaintiffs in intellectual property rights (IPR) lawsuits against China's young automobile makers. A number of Chinese automobile makers – Geely, Chery, Lifan, Shuanghuan, and Great Wall Motors – which have their own brand cars stand accused of copyright infringement, patent right infringement, and unfair competition. Honda has brought two actions against China's largest private motorcycle manufacturer – Chongqing Lifan Industrial Group – in Beijing and Shanghai.

Besides Japanese automobile companies, General Motors (GM) denounced Chery's QQ mini car for copying its own Chevrolet Spark. GM claimed that both the QQ and the Spark are based on the Matiz of South Korea's Daewoo Motor, which has been already acquired by GM. The Spark is produced at GM's joint venture in South China's Guangxi Zhuang Autonomous Region. GM China Group said that it had completed its investigation of Chery's alleged piracy. But Chery Automobile Company announced that Chery itself had developed the QQ mini cars, having already acquired the relevant patent rights. Chery denied violating the IPR rights of other automobile makers. The Ministry of Commerce invited GM representatives and officials from relevant Chinese departments late last year for discussions on how to solve the dispute between GM and Chery. But no result was ever reported.

Among the rising number of IPR lawsuits and disputes between foreign and domestic automobile makers, the only judgment so far was made in November 2003 in the lawsuit put forward by Toyota against Chinese automobile maker Geely for trademark infringement and unfair competition. Geely won the case, which was the first ever foreign-related motor lawsuit after China's entry into the WTO. The Beijing No. 2 Intermediate People's Court rejected Toyota's claim, which sought compensation of 14 million yuan (1.7 million U.S. dollars) from Geely – one of China's major economy car producers based in Zhejiang. Toyota claimed that the logo of Geely is similar to that of Toyota, resulting in trademark infringement and unfair competition. Toyota also charged that Geely advertising intentionally

[34] Yin Jiaxu, president of Chang'an Motor Corporation, China's biggest mini vehicle maker. The firm jointly produces compact cars with Japan's Suzuki Motors, http://www.chinadaily.com. cn/english/doc/2004–06/09/content_337978.htm.

misled consumers by suggesting that Geely had close relations with the Japanese brand. After losing the case, sources within the court said that Toyota accepted the judgment rather than appealing to a higher court.[35] While Chinese automobile companies have yet to lose to a foreign plaintiff in a Chinese court, once China begins exporting its cars to the U.S., EU, and Japanese markets, so that foreign automobile makers acquire standing in their home courts, foreign IPR claims may be more rigorously enforced.

WHAT HAS BEEN THE IMPACT OF R&D ON CHINA'S ECONOMY?

In this section, we present a broader overview of the some of the economic effects of China's growing S&T capabilities. We examine several areas of impact: the returns to R&D, the role of technology transfer and its interaction with internal R&D, the factor bias of R&D in relation to China's comparative advantage, and the role of R&D in promoting product development and exports.

The Returns to R&D

The value of high R&D intensity depends significantly on the returns that R&D investments generate. In Table 9.12, we summarize the results of a number of studies that have investigated the impact of R&D on a range of performance measures. These include cost, productivity, profitability, and new product development. All show robust returns to R&D. We review these studies later.

Hu and Jefferson (2004a)
Using a panel of approximately 1,000 industrial LME enterprises for 1991–1997 from the Beijing region, the authors estimate an R&D expenditure equation, a production function, and a profit function. They find substantial and significant returns to R&D in the cross-section dimension; however, they also find in their sample that the returns to R&D decline substantially over the sample period.

Cheung and Lin (2004)
While the principal purpose of this paper is to estimate the impact of FDI on patent innovation in Chinese industry, the authors also estimate the impact of innovation inputs on domestic patent applications. With either fixed or random effects, the authors find that expansion of either S&T expenditure or S&T personnel results in a significant expansion of patent applications.

Jefferson, Bai, Guan, and Yu (2004)
Using a recursive three-equation system, this paper investigates the determinants of firm-level R&D intensity, the process of knowledge production, and the impact

---

[35] http://www.sipo.gov.cn/sipo_English/gftx_e/IPR%20Special/t20040906_33373.htm.

Table 9.12. *Returns to R&D*

Study	Data	Functional form; estimation method	Key findings
Hu and Jefferson (2004a)		Production function; OLS	A positive elasticity of TFP w.r.t. R&D personnel
Cheung and Lin (2004)	Provincial data		A positive elasticity of patent production w.r.t. S&T personnel
Jefferson et al. (2006)	5,451 LMEs	Production function; instrumental variables (IV)	A positive elasticity of TFP w.r.t. to R&D personnel; variations in the orientation and effectiveness of R&D across ownership types
Jefferson and Zhong (2004)	1,800 surveyed firms in five Chinese cities and Seoul	Production function; OLS	A positive elasticity of TFP w.r.t. R&D personnel; emphasis on the complementarity of a large number of firm-level, S&T network, and public policy variable in enhancing the impact of R&D
Hu, Jefferson, and Qian (2005)		Production function; IV	A positive elasticity of TFP w.r.t. R&D personnel; highly significant interaction terms between R&D and imported technology
Fisher-Vanden and Jefferson (2004)		Cost function; fixed effects	R&D-negative cost elasticity w.r.t. technology development spending; positive cost elasticity w.r.t. imported technology. R&D biased toward saving capital and energy; using labor and materials

of innovation on firm performance. The key statistical relationships are surprisingly robust, including the contributions of R&D expenditure to new product innovation, productivity, and profitability. New product innovation accounts for approximately 12 percent of the total returns to R&D. Returns to industrial R&D in China appear to be at least three to four times the returns to fixed production assets. Across ownership types, the authors find that foreign firms exhibit unusually high returns to R&D in new product development, a result that most probably reflects their access to a wide range of products that are already produced by their parent companies. State-owned enterprises, while extremely inefficient at creating new knowledge, appear to put new knowledge to good advantage. This result may reflect the monopoly power of some SOEs (e.g., in the tobacco industry). In addition, their relative initial inefficiency may allow SOEs to attain large efficiency improvements from small restructuring efforts.

Jefferson and Zhong (2004)

Using a single cross section based on a survey of 1,800 firms distributed over five Chinese cities and Seoul, the authors examine the impact of R&D personnel on firm productivity and profitability. Interacting R&D personnel with a large number of firm- and metropolitan-specific characteristics, the authors identify a substantial list of factors that effectively complement the firms' basic R&D operations: these include the share of foreign ownership, location in an industrial park, proportion of the workforce with foreign experience, the purchase of outside technology, and the receipt of external R&D assistance. The most interesting finding is that among the five Chinese cities, Shanghai enjoys both the most extensive R&D capabilities and the highest returns to R&D. Its R&D capabilities and returns are more similar to those of Seoul than the other Chinese cities. The authors also find that the net returns to R&D personnel in the four Chinese cities exceed the returns to R&D personnel in Seoul.

Hu, Jefferson, and Qian (2005) use a panel of approximately 10,000 industrial LMEs from 1995 to 2001 to estimate the direct and interactive impacts of R&D spending and the purchase of both domestic and imported technology. The paper examines the contributions of each of these avenues, as well as their interactions, to productivity within Chinese industry. At least for the scientific industries, such as chemical, pharmaceutical, machinery, and electronics, in-house R&D significantly enhances productivity. The estimation results show that in-house R&D significantly complements technology transfer – whether of domestic or foreign origin. FDI, which we assume is an important channel of proprietary within-firm technology transfer, does not facilitate the transfer of market-mediated foreign technology.

Fisher-Vanden and Jefferson (2006)

This paper employs a panel of approximately 1,500 energy-intensive industrial LMEs over the period 1997–2001. They use a translog cost function and fixed effects estimator to assess both the neutral and the factor-biased impacts of technology development expenditure on cost. Among the authors' key findings is that in-house R&D exerts a significant neutral cost-reducing effect on production. Additionally, in-house R&D exhibits a robust capital- and energy-saving and labor- and material-using bias. These biases of deliberate technical change are consistent with China's underlying comparative advantage. Fisher-Vanden and Jefferson also find that imported technology tends to *increase* costs. The cost-increasing effect of imported technology reflects the function of this technology, which is to facilitate new product development through the use of relatively capital-intensive production methods.

What have we learned from these studies? We emphasize several findings.

— *R&D has become an important strategic investment.* Using different samples, different modeling methods, and different estimation techniques, these studies consistently show robust returns to R&D. The consistency of these results leads us to conclude that the use of R&D resources is the result of deliberate, strategic intent that typically results in lower costs, improvement in product quality, and higher profits.

— *The returns to R&D depend on complementary factors.* A central lesson from these studies is the importance of a range of complementarities for enhancing the effectiveness of R&D. The measure of innovation potential entails far more than a measure of the volume of R&D spending or R&D personnel. Factors that complement the effectiveness of R&D include the quality of training of R&D personnel and their managers, R&D networks with research institutes, universities, and overseas collaborators, and the institutional context of R&D, including the forms of corporate governance and public policy. By continuing to expand this set of R&D complements, the work by Jefferson and Zhong (2004) shows that China's enterprises and cities can further enhance the quality and intensity of firm-level R&D. Our own work finds that domestic firms that operate in FDI-rich industries tend to increase their R&D intensity more rapidly than other firms.

— *Internal R&D and technology transfer interact and complement each other in important ways.* Multiple sources of technology development operate within China's economy.

  • Hu, Jefferson, and Qian (2005) find strong complementarity of internal R&D and imported technology; this complementarity is stronger for domestic firms than for FIEs.
  • Fisher-Vanden and Jefferson (2004) find that in-house R&D focuses primarily on process innovation; imported R&D focuses more on product innovation.

The Factor Bias of R&D

Gilboy's analysis focuses largely on the role of R&D innovation in supporting China's export sector. Yet, high-tech exports account for barely more than 4 percent of China's total GDP.[36] The story of China's technological transformation is far more subtle than the development and export of high-tech goods.

During the era of central planning, a mantra of China's political leadership was to catch up with the West. One way in which it pursued growth and a rise in living standards was to emphasize capital-intensive growth, which involved the

[36] UNDP, 2000, calculated from the data on p. 199.

establishment of an extensive set of capital-intensive industries, including steel, petrochemicals, heavy machinery, and transportation equipment. An unfortunate result of this capital-intensive pattern of growth was that, in the absence of market signals, the allocation of China's scarce supply of capital was highly wasteful. Moreover, the pursuit of capital-intensive growth that was fundamentally inconsistent with China's underlying comparative advantage in labor, not capital, created further inefficiencies that rendered Chinese industry incapable of competing on world markets.

This pattern of development appears to be changing. Two studies indicate that at least since the mid-1990s, innovation in China has tended to be labor using and capital and energy saving.[37] Enterprises that have spent the most on in-house R&D appear to be concentrating on installing new processes that are relatively intensive in their use of labor. One implication of this emphasis on the development and use of labor-intensive production processes is that China is using its relatively scarce resources – that is, capital and energy – far more efficiently than it would if it were continuing along its capital- and energy-intensive growth path.

That China is now developing and investing in relatively labor-intensive and capital- and energy-saving technologies, with the support of research and development, is an enormous achievement in its quest for economic efficiency and political stability. One consequence of greater efficiency and profitability is that retained earnings, the principal source of firm R&D spending in the OECD economies, are becoming more available to finance China's continuing rise in R&D intensity. At a time when funding for R&D from the Chinese government and banking sectors is in relative decline, growing efficiency and retained earnings are critical to sustaining the growth of China's R&D investments and its technological advance. This fundamental reorientation – Chinese enterprises learning to capitalize on China's comparative advantage – is critical for establishing the foundation of an efficient, sustainable national R&D program while also moving China's economy up the technology ladder to expand its presence on international markets across an increasing variety of goods and services.[38]

HOW SUSTAINABLE IS THE GROWTH OF CHINA'S S&T ACTIVITY?

Has China begun its S&T takeoff? From 0.6 percent in 1996, China's statistics show its R&D intensity accelerating rapidly to 1.4 percent in 2006. At 1.4 percent,

---

[37] Using a translog cost function approach, Fisher-Vanden and Jefferson (2004) find that in-house R&D is labor using and capital and energy savings. Jefferson and Su (2002) find that privatized enterprises invest in labor-using technologies far more than unconverted state-owned enterprises.

[38] A particularly buoyant account of China's move up the technology ladder into foreign export markets is provided by Fishman (2004). A key point in that article is the ability of domestic producers to outcompete foreign-invested enterprises by establishing labor-intensive workshops that produce high-end domestic products and export goods of similar quality at lower cost.

China's R&D intensity is more than one-half that of the United States and substantially greater than what should be expected given the country's level of per capita income.[39] This acceleration raises two questions: what is driving China's R&D intensification? Has China begun its S&T takeoff?

The endogenous growth literature is one useful starting point for understanding the factors that are contributing to the intensification of China's R&D effort. These are the following[40]:

- The rising relative share of R&D spending on products embodying labor-intensive versus technology-intensive intermediate inputs, including capital goods.
- Rising R&D productivity spurred by the growth of complements.
- Scale economies in innovation as expansion of the underlying body of knowledge creates opportunities for new innovation.
- Effective subsidies to R&D.

We focus on the role of each of these four factors:

- *Shifting consumption and production patterns.* As living standards rise, the composition of goods and services shifts from products with low-technology content to goods and services that are more technology intensive. Automobiles substitute for bicycles; consumer electronics become ubiquitous; medical services and the equipment that supports them become more sophisticated. This pattern of technology intensification that accompanies rising living standards parallels Engel's law. As incomes rise, not only is the income elasticity of demand for nonagricultural goods greater than 1, but also goods with low-technology content (e.g., bicycles, handicrafts, and rudimentary medical care) become inferior goods. Conversely, the income elasticity of demand for high-technology goods is high.

Within China, electronics and telecommunications illustrate China's emerging high-tech sectors. Table 9.13, which features three of these industries, shows that, during the latter half of the 1990s, the ratio of R&D spending to value added among large- and medium-sized firms in the electronic and telecommunication sectors accelerated by 250 percent to reach nearly 7.5 percent. The overall impact on Chinese industry of growing R&D intensity was magnified by the doubling of this sector's share in total industry sales over this period. The table also demonstrates the same association between rising R&D intensity and growing market share for China's electrical equipment and machinery industry and the instrumentation sector. While some portion of

---

[39] In 2003, the World Bank defined the category of "lower-middle–income" countries to include those countries with per capita incomes in the range of 745–2,975 dollars. With a reported level of per capita income of 890 dollars in 2002, China lies toward the bottom of this range.

[40] These factors are motivated by Jones (1995) in an endogenous growth model focusing on the determinants of demand for R&D personnel. Gao and Jefferson (forthcoming) apply the factors to China.

Table 9.13. *The role of changing industry composition (LME database)*

Industry	R&D/VA 1995 (%)	R&D/VA 2000 (%)	R&D/VA 2000/1995	Sales share 2000/1995
Electronic and telecommunication equipment	2.97	7.34	2.49	1.91
Electrical equipment and machinery	1.71	4.98	2.91	1.15
Instruments and meters	2.86	4.65	1.63	1.28
Total industry	1.52	1.98	1.29	1.00

Note: VA, value added.
Source: Jefferson, Bai, Guan, and Yu (2006).

Table 9.14. *Comparison of Seoul and five Chinese cities*

City	Composite index of R&D capabilities	Estimated returns to R&D personnel (dollars) (1)	R&D personnel wage (dollars) (2)	Ratio (1:2)
Seoul	31.88	37,639	20,847	1.81
Shanghai	25.15	24,086	5,655	4.26
Guangzhou	6.63	14,984	3,249	4.62
Beijing	0.00	13,479	3,494	3.86
Chengdu	−7.92	9,676	3,102	3.12
Tianjin	−10.26	8,818	1,569	5.62

Source: Jefferson and Zhong (2004, table 9).

this relative growth in the production share of high-tech products is driven by changes in patterns of domestic consumption, the growth of export demand also contributed to rising production of technology-intensive goods.

– *Rising productivity of R&D personnel.* As part of a World Bank study on innovation in East Asian cities, Jefferson and Zhong (2004) compare the R&D capabilities of five Chinese cities – Beijing, Chengdu, Guangzhou, Shanghai, and Tianjin – and Seoul, South Korea. The index of R&D capabilities shown in Table 9.14, based on surveys of 300 firms in each of the six cities, summarizes differences reported by the firms in each of the cities with respect to openness, human capital resources, R&D networking, and institutional quality. The index shows Seoul as the city with the greatest overall R&D capabilities, followed by Shanghai, Guangzhou, Beijing, Chengdu, and Tianjin. The estimates show a robust relationship between the metropolitan indexes of R&D capabilities and returns to R&D.

We conclude that the availability of complements to R&D – graduate training in science and engineering, experience abroad, investment in IT equipment and technology parks, and technology networking – is an important driver of the productivity of R&D personnel. Moreover, in China the rate of increase in these complements is motivating a rapid rise in R&D productivity measured in terms of the marginal revenue product per R&D worker.

– *Rapidly expanding knowledge base rich with new technological opportunity.* In a small closed economy, it is reasonable to expect that rising R&D intensity might encounter diminishing returns to R&D. Without the replenishment of technological opportunity from a large and diversified industrial base or the inflow of new technologies from abroad, innovation possibilities are likely to fade. Among the world's developing economies, China may be unique. The size and openness of China's economy, including the intensity of trade, volume of FDI inflow, and rapidly growing markets in domestic and imported technologies continuously replenish the opportunities for new technological innovation. The impact of China's inflow of FDI on technology development has been documented by Hu and Jefferson (2006), who show the robust impact of FDI on domestic patenting and by Girma, Gong, and Gorg (2005), who show the impact of FDI on the rate of new product innovation. In China, the scale of technology transfer and the opportunity to move up the technology ladder are combining to offset tendencies to diminishing returns to R&D.

– *Subsidies to R&D labor.* Perhaps the finding of greatest interest is the large margin between the cost of R&D personnel and the returns to R&D personnel in Chinese cities compared with international standards, as represented by Seoul. This result suggests that foreign firms can raise their returns to R&D by outsourcing portions of their R&D operations to China rather than Seoul (or other overseas locations).

Specifically, as shown in Table 9.14, we have used the World Bank database to estimate the average returns to R&D personnel in five Chinese cities and also to calculate the average cost of an R&D worker. As shown in Table 9.14, in 2000 an investor in R&D who spent 20,847 U.S. dollars to hire one worker in Seoul could expect a return of 37,639 dollars. In Shanghai, the same amount could hire in nearly four R&D workers who together would generate nearly 100,000 dollars in revenue. Given the rapid increase in the productivity of the R&D sector and the rate of increase in the training of new young S&T graduates, Chinese R&D personnel, at least in the early part of the decade, seem to have offered a bargain. While compensation paid to China's R&D personnel has risen rapidly, it appears that R&D productivity has risen faster.

Why So Early?

We speculate on possible reasons why China displays signs of an apparent S&T takeoff at an unusually low level of per capita income.

High Rates of Literacy

At 16.5 percent, China's adult illiteracy rate in 1999 was approximately twice that of Singapore, similar to those of Brazil (15.1 percent) and Turkey (15.4 percent) with substantially higher incomes, and well below that of India (43.5 percent).[41] Comparatively high rates of literacy in China are likely to enhance the demand for and utilization rate of technology-intensive goods and services, such as telecommunications services, computing, and medical services. The paucity of installed infrastructure for earlier-generation technologies, such as land telephone lines, early vintages of automobile assembly lines, and early computing technologies, both hardware and software, opens the door for the rapid dissemination and adoption of new vintages of technologies. Certain key sectors, such as telecommunications, exhibit a substantial degree of technology leapfrogging.[42]

Market Size

The rise of living standards in some countries leads to more extensive imports of technologically sophisticated electronic and telecommunications equipment and other high-tech goods, including electrical machinery, instrumentation, and automobiles. In China, multinationals are clamoring to set up production for these R&D-intensive industries in proximity to China's burgeoning consumer markets. This commercial desire to produce in proximity to large markets may explain why S&T takeoff has not occurred in certain smaller OECD countries (e.g., Norway, Australia, Belgium, and New Zealand) while, with the exception of Italy, it has occurred in all the largest OECD economies.[43] Through its "markets for technology" strategy, China's government has been able to leverage the size of its markets to push international firms toward accelerating the shift of design, R&D, and component production toward China. Commenting on the decision by Airbus to assemble its A320 plan in China, one analyst was quoted, "Everything else being equal, you would never choose to put a production line in China" (Landler and Bradsher, 2006).

Proximity to Dynamic Economies

Arguably, China's greatest asset in making its transition from plan to market and accessing the capital, technology, and talent needed to move along the trajectory from low- to middle-income economy is its physical and cultural proximity to Hong Kong and Taiwan and to a lesser, but still significant, degree to Korea, Japan, and Southeast Asia. One measure of this importance is that approximately one-half

---

[41] UNDP (2001).

[42] For an account of technology leapfrogging in the Japanese steel industry, see Ruttan (2001, chapter 5).

[43] The desire to serve large and fast-growing consumer markets creates a premium for the establishment of production centers that can benefit from learning by doing and learning by using in proximity to burgeoning demand.

of the accumulated FDI in China has originated with Hong Kong, Taiwan, and Macao. Another is the concentration of FDI in specific regions within China, including Taiwanese investment in Dongguan (Guangdong Province), which has become the primary source of many PC components. Singaporean investment in the Shanghai area and Korean investment in China's northeast region have also spurred technological advance. This proximity has at once served as a channel for technology transfer and access to the human capital that can use it not only within the foreign sector but also within China's domestic sector through joint ventures, licensing, and contracting.

The four factors associated with the endogenous growth process have been central to the intensification of R&D across all countries that have achieved S&T takeoff. But not all emerging economies have experienced S&T takeoff. We suggest that China's high literacy rates, perceived potential, and proximity to dynamic economies have driven China's S&T takeoff along an earlier and steeper trajectory than would have been the case without these particular characteristics. If China follows historical statistical patterns, we should expect the continuation of growth of R&D expenditure to outpace GDP growth until R&D intensity levels out in the 2–3 percent range.

CONCLUSIONS AND DISCUSSION

China has made striking progress over the past 25 years in reforming its S&T system and creating the conditions for successful R&D and sustainable technological development. The locus of R&D and innovation has moved from a system of state patronage to a largely market-driven enterprise system that has absorbed a substantial portion of the country's restructured research institutes and is complemented by a dynamic foreign sector.

The sheer size and geographic diversity of the economy, including the proximity of certain coastal areas to Hong Kong, Taiwan, and OECD trade and FDI flows, have created an unusually high degree of technological diversity within China's borders. This diversity will continue to propel China along multiple technology development tracks entailing a variety of technology outcomes. While several large metropolitan areas, principally along the coast, are developing the capabilities to approach the international technological frontier of certain industries, the country's huge pool of surplus labor will generally move China along the path of a comparatively labor-intensive mode of production and growth. China's accession to the WTO and continuing integration with the world economy is likely to magnify this emphasis on China's comparative advantage in labor-intensive production. The research we review shows that as China moves away from its tradition of central planning with an emphasis on capital-intensive heavy industry, many of its R&D resources are being used to develop ways of adapting and utilizing foreign technologies to a more labor-intensive setting.

The foreign sector is playing a critical role in promoting China's S&T development. Increasingly large numbers of foreign-trained scientists and engineers are returning to China. By expanding technological opportunity, promoting competition, and eroding the rents of established Chinese firms, the flood of FDI is promoting the adoption and intensification of R&D operations in domestic firms. In some industries, such as semiconductors and automobiles, China is rapidly developing its internal R&D capabilities, often in an environment of large inflows of FDI and increasingly competitive international trade, which requires that production, for both domestic and overseas sales, closely approximate established international standards.

China's S&T development and its ongoing economic restructuring are mutually reinforcing. Many of China's high-technology companies grew out of murky ownership and property rights arrangements. Continued reform of the governance of China's enterprise and financial systems is needed to unleash the innovative potential of China's emerging companies. Sustained technological change, in turn, propels rising living standards and the demand for increasing technological content in Chinese-produced goods and services. The demand for technology-intensive production further reinforces the impetus for continued reform and institutional upgrading. For example, the growing demand for goods and services in technology-intensive industries, such as telecommunications, software, and consumer electronics, spawns domestic constituencies that potentially support the effective enforcement of intellectual property rights, which in turn is needed to support new investment, both domestic and foreign, in these sectors.

The current model of technology import and imitation cannot in the long run sustain China's technological advance. As China narrows the gap with the world technology frontier, opportunities for easy gains from imitating will dissipate. To create proprietary cutting-edge technologies, China will need a strong science base that will require more than liberalization and market competition. The Chinese government's continuous and deepened support for basic research and applied research of fundamental significance is needed to create the bedrock of an innovation system that will ensure sustained S&T success in China.

China is facing a golden opportunity to achieve technological catch-up with the West despite its relatively backward condition just 25 years ago. A fast-growing domestic economy, a globalizing world economy that encourages the flow of capital and diffusion of technology, and a rich endowment of human talent are contributing to the prospect of China's S&T takeoff. However, significant barriers stand between China and its goal of becoming a world technology power. If China succeeds in fortifying its market institutions, including reforming its financial system to allow for more private resources to enter risky ventures and promoting the more rigorous enforcement of intellectual property rights, and continues to promote its openness to foreign technology and investment, its economy is likely over the next 10–15 years to emerge as a global technology power.

References

Chen, Kuan, Gary H. Jefferson, Thomas G. Rawski, Hongchang Wang, and Yuxin Zheng. 1988. "Productivity Change in Chinese Industry: 1953–1985." *Journal of Comparative Economics*. 12, pp. 570–591.

Cheung, Kui-yin and Ping Lin. 2004. "Spillover Effects of FDI on Innovation in China: Evidence from the Provincial Data." *China Economic Review*. 15(1), pp. 25–44.

Chow, Gregory, 1985. *The Chinese Economy*. New York: Harper & Row Publishers.

Data Brief. March 23, 2001. "R&D Spending is Highly Concentrated in a Small Number of States." National Science Foundation, Division of Science Resources Studies. Accessed July 31, 2007, from http://www.nsf.gov/statistics/databrf/nsf01320/sdb01320.htm.

Du, Qian and Datu Xu. 1997. *Evaluation Report on the Effects of the Spark Program*. China. Beijing: National Research Center for Science and Technology for Development.

Elman, Benjamin A. 2005. *On Their Own Terms: Science in China, 1550–1900*. Cambridge, MA: Harvard University Press.

Elvin, Mark. n.d. "The High-level Equilibrium Trap." Accessed July 31, 2007, from http://www-personal.umd.umich.edu/~delittle/elvin.pdf.

Farrell, Joseph and Carl Shapiro. 1992. "Standard Setting in High Definition Television," with Joseph Farrell, Brookings Papers on Economic Activity: Microeconomics. Washington, DC: Brookings Institution.

Fishman, Ted C. 2004. "The Chinese Century." *The New York Times Magazine*. July 4, 2004, pp. 24–51.

Fisher-Vanden, Karen and Gary H. Jefferson. 2006. "Technology Diversity and Development: Evidence from China's Industrial Enterprises." Unpublished manuscript.

Gallagher, Kelly Sims. 2003. "Foreign Technology in China's Automobile Industry: Implications for Energy, Economic Development, and Environment." *China Environment Series*, no. 6, pp. 1–18. China Environment Forum. Washington, DC: Woodrow Wilson Center.

Gao, Jian and Gary H. Jefferson. 2007. "Has China Begun its Science and Technology Takeoff?: The Sources of China's R&D Intensification." *Asian and Pacific Business Review*. 13(3), pp. 357–371.

Gilboy, George J. 2004."The Myth Behind China's Miracle." *Foreign Affairs*. July–August 2004, pp. 33–48.

Girma, Sourafel, Yundan Gong, and Holger Gorg. 2005. "Can You Teach Old Dragons New Tricks? FDI and Innovation Activity in Chinese State-Owned Enterprises." Research Paper Series 2005/34. Nottingham: Leverhulme Center, University of Nottingham.

Goldman Sachs. February 21, 2003. "Global Automobiles: The Chinese Auto Industry." Goldman Sachs Global Equity Research. Accessed August 2, 2007, from http://www2.goldmansachs.com/hkchina/insight/research/pdf/chinese_auto_industry.pdf.

Goldsmith, Oliver. June 7, 2006. "Joseph Needham's Contribution to the History of Science and Technology in China." Accessed July 31, 2007, from http://www.unu.edu/unupress/unupbooks/uu01se/uu01se0u.htm.

Gong, Yundan and Gary H. Jefferson, 2007. "Research and Development in Chinese Industry: The Role of FDI in Motivating R&D Intensification (draft manuscript)." Waltham, MA: Brandeis University.

Howell, Thomas, Brent L. Bartlett, William A. Noellert, and Rachel Howe. October 2003. "China's Emerging Semiconductor Industry." Report prepared by Dewey Ballantine LLP for the Semiconductor Industry Association. Accessed August 2, 2007, from http://www.deweyballantine.com/docs/publications/2089.pdf?u=%22China%27s%20 Emerging%20Semiconductor%20Industry%20%2D%2D%20The%20Impact%20of%

20China%27s%20Preferential%20Value%2DAdded%20Tax%20on%20Current%20Investment%20Trends%22.

Hu, Albert G. Z. 2007. "Technology Parks and Regional Economic Growth in China." *Research Policy*. 36(1), pp. 76–87.

Hu, Albert G. Z. and Gary H. Jefferson. 2004a. "Returns to Research and Development in Chinese Industry: Evidence from State-Owned Enterprises in Beijing." *China Economic Review*. 15(1), pp. 86–107.

Hu, Albert G. Z. and Gary H. Jefferson. 2006. "A Great Wall of Patents: What Is Behind China's Recent Patent Explosion?" Accessed August 2, 2007, from http://courses. nus.edu.sg/course/ecshua/Chinapat%20Jan%202006.pdf.

Hu, Albert G. Z., Gary H. Jefferson, and Jinchang Qian. November 2005. "R&D and Technology Transfer: Firm-Level Evidence from Chinese Industry." *Review of Economics and Statistics*. 87(4), pp. 780–786.

ISTIC [Institute of Scientific and Technical Information of China], 2005. *Statistics of Chinese Scientific and Technical Papers 2004* [Zhongguo keji lunwen tongji jieguo 2004]. Beijing: Institute of Scientific and Technical Information of China.

Jefferson, Gary H., Huamao Bai, Xiaojing Guan, and Xiaoyun Yu. 2006. "R and D Performance in Chinese Industry." *Economics of Innovation and New Technology*. 15(4–5), pp. 345–366. Special issue: "On Empirical Studies of Innovation in the Knowledge Driven Economy," Bronwyn H. Hall and Jacques Mairesse, eds. (guest).

Jefferson, Gary H., Bangwen Cheng, Jian Su, Duo Deng, Haoyuan Qin, and Zhaohui Xuan. May 19–21, 2006. "Restructuring China's Research and Development Institutes." Presented at the workshop on Innovation in Greater China, sponsored by the Stanford Project on Regions of Innovation and Entrepreneurship (SPRIE) of Stanford University and the China Institute for Science and Technology Policy (CISTP). Beijing: Tsinghua University.

Jefferson, Gary H. and Jian Su. 2002. "China's Economic Growth: An Investigation into the Process of Endogenous Growth at the Firm Level." Background paper prepared for the World Bank. Washington, DC: World Bank. Paper can be obtained from authors.

Jefferson, Gary H. and Kaifeng Zhong. 2004. "An Investigation of Firm-level R&D Capabilities in Asia," Chapter 10 in *Global Production Networking and Technological Change in East Asia*. Shahid Yusuf, M. Anjum Altaf, and Kaoru Nabeshima, eds. Washington, DC: World Bank–Oxford University Press, pp. 435–480.

Jefferson, Gary H. 2006. "High Tech Regions in China: Pathways to Technology Diffusion or Centers of Increasing Technology Concentration?" Presented at the SPRIE-ITRI workshop on High Tech Regions: Sustainability and Reinvention, November 13–14, 2006.

Jin, Songqing, Scott Rozelle, Julian Alston, and Jikun Huang. November 2003. "Economies of Scale and Scope, and the Economic Efficiency of China's Agricultural Research System." Working Paper 03–003. Davis, California: Department of Agricultural and Resource Economics, University of California.

Jones, Charles. 1995. "R&D-Based Models of Economic Growth." *Journal of Political Economy*. 103, pp. 759–784.

Keller, Wolfgang. 2004. "International Technology Diffusion." *Journal of Economic Literature*. 62(3), pp. 752–782.

Landler, Mark and Keith Bradsher. 2006. "Airbus, China and Quid Pro Quo." *New York Times*. March 15, 2006, p. 4

Lin, Justin Y. F. 1995. "The Needham Puzzle: Why the Industrial Revolution Did Not Originate in China." *Economic Development and Cultural Change.* 43(2), pp. 269–292.

Matthews, John and Dong-Sung Cho. 2000. *Tiger Technology: The Creation of the Semi-Conductor Industry in E. Asia.* Cambridge, UK: Cambridge University Press.

Moris, Francisco. February 2004. "U.S.-China R&D Linkages: Direct Investment and Industrial Alliances in the 1990s." *INFOBRIEF.* NSF 04–306.

Naughton, Barry. 2007. *The Chinese Economy: Transitions and Growth.* Cambridge, MA: MIT Press.

NBS [National Bureau of Statistics]. 2003. *China Statistical Yearbook.* Beijing: China Statistical Publishing House.

NBS [National Bureau of Statistics]. 2004. *China Statistical Yearbook.* Beijing: China Statistical Publishing House.

NBS-LME Data Set. 2001. *Data Set for China's Large and Medium-Size Industrial Enterprises, 1995–2001.* Beijing: National Bureau of Statistics.

NBS [National Bureau of Statistics; Web site]. 2006. "Shichang yingling, jiaoche jiegou zouxiang chengshu [Led by Market, Structure of Passenger Car Market Becomes Mature]," *Zhongguo xinxibao* [China Information Daily]. Accessed February 16, 2006, from http://www.stats.gov.cn/tjfx/ztfx/2005sbnjjsp/t20060216_402305832.htm.

NBS/MOST [National Bureau of Statistics and the Ministry of Science and Technology]. 2003. *China Statistical Yearbook on Science and Technology.* Beijing: China Statistics Press.

NBS/MOST [National Bureau of Statistics and the Ministry of Science and Technology]. 2004. *China Statistical Yearbook on Science and Technology.* Beijing: China Statistics Press.

NBS/MOST [National Bureau of Statistics/Ministry of Science and Technology]. 2006. *China Statistical Yearbook on Science and Technology.* Beijing: China Statistics Press.

OECD [Organization of Economic Cooperation and Development]. 2002. *OECD Science, Technology and Industry Outlook.* Paris: OECD.

Ruttan, Vernon. 2001. *Technology, Growth, and Development: An Induced Innovation Perspective.* New York: Oxford University Press.

Schott, Peter K. 2004. "The Relative Sophistication of Chinese Exports." Presented at the NBER China Workshop, October 1, 2004, Cambridge, MA.

Sivin, Nathan. 1982. "Why the Scientific Revolution Did Not Take Place in China – Or Didn't It?" The Edward H. Hume Lecture, Yale University. *Chinese Science.* 5, pp. 45–66. Reprinted in *Transformation and Tradition in the Sciences.* Everett Mendelsohn, ed. Cambridge and New York: Cambridge University Press, 1984, pp. 531–554.

Spence, Jonathan. 1991. *The Search for Modern China.* New York: W. W. Norton.

Suttmeier, Richard P. and Xiangkui Yao. 2004. "China's Post-WTO Technology Policy: Standards, Software, and the Changing Nature of Techno-Nationalism." Special Report, National Bureau of Asian Research, no. 7, May 2004.

UNDP [United Nations Development Program]. 2001. *Human Development Report 2001: Making New Technologies Work for Human Development.* New York: Oxford University Press.

Walcott, Susan. 2003. *Chinese Science and Technology Industrial Parks.* Burlington, VT: Ashgate.

Walsh, Kate. 2003. *Foreign High-Tech R&D in China: Risks, Rewards, and Implications for US-China Relations.* Washington, DC: Henry L. Stimpson Center.

Wang Shanshan. 2007. "Science Goals Set Out for 2020." *China Daily.* January 30, 2007, p. 1.

Wei Houkai, May 2004. "Woguo diqu gongye jishu quanxinli pingjia [An Evaluation of Our Country's Regional Industrial Technical Innovation Capabilities]," *Zhongguo gongye jingji* [China Industrial Economy]. 194, pp. 15–22.

World Bank, 2005. *World Development Report, 2005: A Better Investment Climate for Everyone.* New York: World Bank–Oxford University Press.

Yuan, Guangzheng, Xiaosu Gao, Qing Xiang, Ye Tian, and Ning Zhang. 1992. *Programs and Plans for the Development of Science and Technology of China.* Beijing: National Defense Industry Press.

Zhou, Ping and Loet Leydesdorff. May 19–21, 2006. "A Comparison between the *China Scientific and Technical Papers Citation Database* and the *Scientific Citations* in terms of journal hierarchies and international-journal citation relations." Presented at the workshop on Innovation in Greater China, sponsored by the Stanford Project on Regions of Innovation and Entrepreneurship (SPRIE) of Stanford University and the China Institute for Science and Technology Policy (CISTP). Beijing: Tsinghua University.

TEN

The Political Economy of Private-Sector Development in China

Stephan Haggard and Yasheng Huang[1]

A central theme in the current literature on the political economy of growth is the relationship between the government and the private sector. Governments that create the appropriate conditions for private risk taking foster capital accumulation, efficient allocation of resources, and sustained growth. Governments that arrogate "too much" economic activity to themselves risk low levels of investment, inefficiencies in the state sector, and defensive private strategies, such as capital flight and nonproductive investments.

There is substantial debate, however, on how to structure business–government relations in an optimal way, or even what dimensions of the relationship might be consequential (Maxfield and Schneider, 1997). One strand of the institutional economics literature emphasizes the importance of the government's role as a protector and enforcer of private property rights (Barzel, 1997, for an overview). Such protections, if credible, provide assurances to private agents that assets and income will not be expropriated and thus incentives for investment. A growing body of empirical literature attempts to document these claims. These studies show the role that property rights protection and other aspects of the institutional setting that support these protections, such as transparency or even democracy, might play in checking the predatory tendencies of the state (Keefer, 2004).

However, a very different body of theoretical and empirical literature identifies the key barrier to growth not in an overbearing state, but in the capture of public institutions by private actors and the introduction of various policy-induced distortions (e.g., Murphey, Schleifer, and Vishny, 1993). This literature on rent seeking suggests that it is the private sector, as well as the state, which must be checked, either through the design of policy (e.g., through liberalization of markets)

[1] In writing this chapter, the authors received extensive and helpful feedback from Barry Naughton, Thomas Rawski, and Loren Brandt. Yasheng Huang thanks Jean Hung at the Universities Service Centre (USC) at the Chinese University and Nancy Hearst at Harvard University for providing assistance in locating the data and documents used in this chapter. The usual caveats apply.

or by various political and institutional mechanisms (e.g., laws on corruption and campaign financing).

These broad themes have been replayed in the literature on East Asia's growth (for an overview, see Haggard, 2004). Neoclassical interpretations of East Asia's growth emphasize the self-restraining characteristics of East Asian governments, such as their relatively small size and extensive incentives for private capital accumulation. Other accounts, however, have noted that "strong" states were an integral component of the East Asian model and that at least one component of this "state strength" was the capacity to check, or in Alice Amsden's felicitous phrase "discipline," the private sector (Amsden, 1989; Haggard, 1990).

China's rapid growth has posed a very similar set of questions, and thus provides an opportunity to place the country in a wider regional context. References to China as another newly industrialized economy (NIE), following a development path similar to those pioneered by South Korea, Taiwan, Hong Kong, and Singapore, are increasingly common. Despite obvious differences, there are at least some superficial similarities, beginning with the growth record itself. China's growth in the 1980s and 1990s rivaled the performance of the East Asian NIEs in the 1960s and 1970s. The Chinese economy also appeared to take off following the adoption of a more open, export-oriented development strategy. Despite its large size, the trade/gross domestic product (GDP) ratio of the country is extraordinarily high. Yet another similarity is political. China's remarkable economic transformation has occurred in an authoritarian political context. As with respect to the NIEs, there have been ongoing debates over whether single-party rule was a necessary condition for such rapid economic transformation.

In this chapter, we address these issues by presenting an empirical examination of the Chinese government's relationship with the private sector. To what extent has the government retained direct control over productive activities rather than delegating them to private actors? To the extent that it has relied on the private sector, how have the respective roles of local and foreign firms changed over time? We offer two major empirical observations, one more controversial and less noted than the other. The first is that despite the well-documented process of economic reform in China, the domestic private sector remains relatively small and subject to a variety of policy and economic constraints. In the early reform period, the role of the private sector underwent a quite substantial change, but this fundamental shift in policy was not sustained. State firms continue to occupy an important role in the Chinese economy, and the growth of mixed property forms that maintain central or local government ownership and control has far outstripped the growth of private firms, narrowly defined.

The second observation is that to the extent that the Chinese government has provided a space for private capital, it has shown a revealed preference for foreign over domestic firms. The rapid growth of foreign investment in the Chinese economy and its overall role in the growth process is well documented, and we therefore spend somewhat less time in documenting it. However, the revealed preference for foreign over domestic private firms is somewhat unusual given that governments more typically demonstrate so-called home-country bias: various restrictions on foreign investment designed to protect domestic firms. This observation raises the intriguing political economy question of why the growth of foreign investment in China has not been matched by an equal expansion of the domestic private sector.

This pattern of growth suggests some striking differences with the growth trajectory of other countries in the region. Except for the case of Singapore, the growth of the "first tier" of the East Asian NIEs – Korea, Taiwan, and Hong Kong – was driven by the development of indigenous private sectors. In the East Asian NIEs, the relationship between the state and the private sector was not always cozy. But in Taiwan and particularly in Korea, the government aggressively promoted the growth of the private sector. In the case of China, however, the image of a reformist government has led analysts to overlook the extent to which the state has imposed substantial constraints on the development of private Chinese firms.

We begin by providing a detailed exposition of the policy environment facing the domestic private sector in China in the 1980s and 1990s. We make a distinction between policies *permitting* the operations of private firms and policies actively *supporting* private-sector growth. China took considerable steps to allow private firms to operate, for example, by providing some property rights security, reducing the ideological stigma associated with the private sector, and thereby granting political legitimacy to its activities. The government has also undertaken at least some privatization. But the government has been much less forthcoming in actively supporting the private sector, particularly through such crucial policies as the investment approval process necessary for firms to enter new activities and the provision of finance. We show that biases in investment and financing have not abated significantly during the reform era since 1978. In fact, some of our measures show that these policy constraints increased sharply in the 1990s when compared to the 1980s.

The second section assesses our findings against the prevailing literature on the Chinese political economy. We focus on two strands of argument in particular. One is the observation that China has considerably liberalized its financial sector in the course of the 1990s. The other is the claim that China's growth, and growth model, resembles that of the other East Asian NIEs. We argue that both of these perspectives require significant qualification.

The conclusion returns in a somewhat more speculative way to some of the political economy questions posed by our empirical analysis. One possible objection to our findings is that they are not particularly surprising. Given that China remains under Communist Party rule, we would expect a certain aversion to the growth of private economic power. State control over the means of production – or at least the "commanding heights" of the economy – has long been a key political pillar of the socialist model. More recently, support for the state sector also reflected internal political pressures to protect declining sectors dominated by state-owned enterprises (SOEs). But this explanation does not account for the apparent change in policy over time, from an initial opening to the private sector to a partial retreat during which some crucial supporting policies have, in fact, become less generous.

We speculate that this change has something to do with the availability of foreign direct investment (FDI). In the early reform period, China lacked credibility with foreign investors. Of necessity, the government relied on reform of the state sector and a larger space for domestic private firms to reinvigorate the economy after the long disruption of the Cultural Revolution. During the 1990s, however, as the reformist turn gained credibility and the government experimented successfully with the special economic zones, foreign interest boomed. The huge inflow of FDI eased capital constraints, offset entrepreneurial shortcomings of the centrally planned economy, and thus reduced the political leadership's need to cater to private-sector concerns. We show that this pattern was very different than the political dynamic in the East Asian NIEs during the 1960s and 1970s, where at least tacit support from the private sector was seen as a prerequisite for successful political rule more generally. We close our chapter by assessing some of the more recent policy changes in China and what they suggest about the possible future of state–private sector relations in the future.

THE POLICY ENVIRONMENT FOR THE PRIVATE SECTOR IN CHINA

Defining China's private sector is not straightforward, in part because the reforms have spawned a variety of hybrid and highly ambiguous ownership forms. The most common measure in the literature is the nonstate sector, which some analysts have equated with the private sector.[2] These nonstate firms include collective enterprises, de jure private firms, shareholding enterprises, domestic joint-ownership firms, and foreign-invested enterprises (FIEs). In some studies, SOEs that have issued shares on stock exchanges are also counted as a part of the nonstate sector.

This definition is very imprecise and has been used in dramatically different ways. When wanting to illustrate the extent of economic reform, as in a study undertaken by a research institute under the State Planning Commission (SPC), the government has equated a term commonly associated with the private sector in China (*minying qiye*, literally translated as "people-run enterprises") with the nonstate sector more generally (Wang, 2002). When seeking to prove that the reforms have not undermined state control, as in a manual prepared by the National Bureau of Statistics (NBS), the government assigns firms typically classified as nonstate, such as collective firms and shareholding firms in which the state maintains a substantial equity interest, to the state sector (National Bureau of Statistics, 1999a).

The two methodologies produce vastly different estimates of the size of the nonstate sector. Under the SPC's definition, the share of the nonstate sector in

---

[2] See Lin et al. (1996) for an earlier usage. More recently, Bai et al. (2003) used the growth of the nonstate sector as a measure of the progress of the reforms.

industrial output (by value) was 68.4 percent in 1997.[3] Under the NBS's definition, the nonstate sector accounted for only 21.2 percent of industrial value added in the same year. Even if we acknowledge the substantial difference between output value and value added, the difference between these two definitions of the nonstate sector is obviously quite large.

For much of the 1990s, equating the nonstate sector with the private sector clearly overstates the size of the private sector. While the revenue rights of many collective firms are private, their control rights are not. This is apparent even to those who rely on the nonstate sector as a measure of private-sector development. Bai et al. (2003, p. 99) acknowledge this point explicitly: "In reality, collective enterprises are under close control of a government. Major investment and employment decisions could not be made without government direction or approval."

The alternative is to rely on a narrower and a more conservative measure of the private sector. These are firms – or households in some of the data series – which are registered as explicitly private in the Chinese system. They are either individual businesses (*getihu*) or privately operated enterprises (*siying qiye*). The distinction between these two types of entities has become more blurred in recent years, but the most important nominal difference has to do with the size of employment. *Getihu*, by tradition, employ eight or fewer outside employees; *siying qiye* employ more than eight employees.

In this chapter, we rely on this narrower definition of the private sector, which we call the de jure private sector. The advantage of this definition is that it is straightforward and unambiguous. The disadvantages are that it is conservative and narrow. Our definition does not include private firms with an ambiguous registration status. These firms are registered as collective firms, such as township and village enterprises (TVEs), rather than as private firms but are, for all practical purposes and from a control perspective, under private control. For example, as is well known to Chinese researchers, many Chinese entrepreneurs have registered their firms under the more politically acceptable category of "collective firms" to alleviate policy constraints associated with purely private status. These so-called red-hat firms enjoy political protection, the ability to enter into businesses otherwise off-limits to de jure private firms, and easier access to credit and financing. Our registration-based definition also does not include those collective firms or SOEs that have been privatized but have retained their previous registration status as either collective firms or SOEs. According to various estimates, the number of "red-hat" firms and privatized firms in the 1990s was substantial.

The omission of the ambiguous private firms from our data is a problem only if our objective is to measure the "true" size of the private sector in the Chinese economy. In this chapter, we sidestep this question; instead, our principal objective is to characterize the policy environment facing the domestic private sector over time. For several reasons, the de jure private sector is in fact a good measure of the policy

---

[3] Table 4.5 in Bai et al. (2003).

environment. First, the focus on the de jure private sector has certain analytical advantages for examining the Chinese reform process. One of the most influential ideas in the comparative study of socialist transitions is that China succeeded by adopting a "gradualist" approach to reform. According to this argument, China purposely encouraged the entry of new private firms rather than undertaking the politically costly and economically uncertain privatization programs characteristic of the transition in Russia and the other former Soviet Republics.[4] A logical upshot is that the policy stance toward these new private-sector entrants – de jure private firms in our terms – should be more supportive over time. We can thus assess the "gradualist" hypothesis by examining how the policy environment facing de jure private firms has (or has not) changed over time.

Our second rationale for focusing on de jure private firms begins with the observation that there are costs as well as benefits associated with an ambiguous ownership status. Some mixed property firms arise precisely because de facto private firms face a variety of regulatory and other barriers, and private entrepreneurs thus register their firms as collectives (so-called red-hat firms) to access markets and financing that are exclusively reserved for state-controlled firms. The resulting distortions introduced by ambiguous ownership rights are well documented, however, and include a variety of transactions costs and the potential for conflicts of interest between the government and private owners. If the business is well run and profitable, government owners and bureaucrats have incentives to seize control of the firm. The Chinese press is full of such horror stories.[5] As a result, managers have incentives to keep finances and operations opaque, often maintaining three sets of books: one for the government, one for the bank, and one for themselves.

The fact that some entrepreneurs are willing to incur these risks suggests that there are offsetting benefits associated with mixed property forms. These benefits include easier access to credit and other policy favors and the political and legal protection required to operate in a biased policy environment (Li, 1996). If the Chinese state has liberalized entry for private-sector firms, reduced policy biases against them, and withdrawn support for the state sector, then all else being equal, the benefits accruing to mixed and ambiguous property forms would also fall. As

---

[4] The idea is that the reforms have apparently improved the welfare of the population across the board, by creating conditions for entrepreneurial growth, while no significant segment of the population suffered an absolute loss. According to a noted formulation, the Chinese reform has been "Pareto optimal" in that it has created winners without creating losers (Lau et al., 2000).

[5] According to one, a private entrepreneur registered his firm as a collective, and in a side – and most likely under-the-table – agreement, he gave 30 percent of the equity stakes to the local government, even though he provided all the equity capital. After paying out all the agreed dividends and taxes, he used a portion of the residual profits to settle a loan, which led to an embezzlement charge. He was sentenced to death by a lower-level court. The case went all the way to the country's Supreme Court and his life was spared only when the State Administration of Industry and Commerce, the branch of government in charge of registering firms, confirmed that the firm was in fact privately owned (Zhang and Ming, 1999).

a result, we would see an increase in the size of the de jure private sector relative to other property forms. A focus on the de jure private sector allows us to test whether this is in fact the case through explicit comparison with other ownership forms.

The output measure commonly used in the literature to define the private sector has another disability: the problem of distinguishing the effects of policy on the growth of this sector from a variety of other firm-level characteristics that might also be at work. Let us explain by an example. Many analysts have used output data as an indicator of the extent of the reforms. Since 1978, the share of the private sector in total output has increased steadily, leading to the widespread perception that the policy environment for the private sector has improved correspondingly. In 1985, de jure private firms accounted for only 1.85 percent of gross industrial output value; in 1997, this ratio rose to 17.9 percent, a dramatic change in only twelve years.[6]

However, this output-based measure of reform incorporates the consequences of two very different effects. One is the "policy effect": the increase in the private-sector share that resulted from a more favorable policy environment toward private activity. But this measure also incorporates what might be called the "efficiency effect." If private firms are more efficient than SOEs – and there is evidence they are – then they generate more value added per unit of input. An increase in the output share of private firms can therefore occur without any improvement in the policy environment as long as there is competition between private firms and SOEs. As an illustration, in 1985, the industrial output of the private sector (by value) was about 2.9 percent of that of the state sector; by 1997, this ratio had risen to 70.2 percent. While the policy environment no doubt improved for the private sector during this period, it would be highly misleading to conclude that the policy environment facing the private and SOE sectors had nearly converged.

In this chapter, we do not use the standard output-based measures of private-sector growth but rely on two measures that more cleanly capture government policies. The first measure consists of a number of indicators about financing constraints from private-sector surveys, one conducted in 1992 and one in 2002. These surveys provide direct evidence on the perceptions of private entrepreneurs about the policy environment. The second measure consists of a number of indicators based on fixed-asset investment data. Fixed-asset investment – whether undertaken by SOEs, mixed forms, or purely private entities – typically involves government approval and thus provides a second way of assessing policy biases.

There are obvious a priori reasons to believe that these two measures should be strongly correlated: firms that report themselves as financially constrained are unlikely to engage in substantial fixed-asset investment. Thus, we would gain confidence in our findings if we found that subjective indicators from surveys and the

---

[6] The ratios are calculated on the basis of the data provided in Table 13.3 in National Bureau of Statistics (1998).

data on investment moved in parallel and told a broadly similar story; we find that this is in fact the case.

Private-Sector Survey Data on Financial Constraints

In one cross-country survey, private firms in China are found to be among the most constrained in the world in terms of their access to capital. Batra et al. (2003) provide survey evidence on over 10,000 firms in eighty-one countries around 2000. The subjective perceptions of Chinese entrepreneurs of the financial constraints they face are quite similar to those prevailing in other transitional economies, such as such as Croatia, the Czech Republic, Romania, and Slovak Republic, or in poor economies, such as Ghana and Ethiopia. Indian entrepreneurs fared far better in this regard than their Chinese counterparts. The same study also shows that Chinese firms relied more substantially on retained earnings and informal finance than firms in India.[7]

The surveys organized by the Chinese government reach similar conclusions. A research report based on a private-sector survey conducted in 2002 concludes as follows[8]:

In the survey, many private firms say that financing is difficult. This is an old problem. Government, banks, firms, All-China Federation of Industry and Commerce have made many efforts but the results are not obvious. We can see from the survey that lending to the private firms is scarce and that informal sources represent a substantial part of a firm's finance.

In this section, we focus on the financing environment facing China's private firms. There are several reasons to focus on the financial nexus. The most obvious is that systems of financial intermediation and firms' access to long-term and working capital are an essential component of the growth process.[9] A focus on finance also gets at important elements of the political economy story we seek to capture.

As elsewhere in Asia, the Chinese government has controlled the bank-dominated financial system (Lardy, 1998). As a result, the allocation of financial resources is a good indicator of the fundamental policy orientation of the state.

To provide more detail on this issue, we focus on the findings from two surveys, one from 1993 and one from 2002.[10] These two surveys were a part of the regular survey efforts organized by the All-China Federation of Industry and Commerce to solicit information and views from the Chinese private sector. Altogether, there have been six such surveys – in 1993, 1995, 1997, 2000, 2002, and 2004; the results from the 1993 and 2002 surveys provide the perspective of a decade and

---

[7] See tables A2.1 and A2.4a (Batra, 2003). It should be pointed out that China fares much better when it comes to labor and licensing regulations.

[8] See the report downloadable from http://www.china.com.cn/chinese/zhuanti/283076.htm.

[9] See the influential papers by King and Levine (1993) and Levine (1997).

[10] The data sets are obtained from the University Service Centre of the Chinese University of Hong Kong. The assistance provided by Jean Hung of USC is deeply appreciated.

are also nationwide in scope.[11] These surveys provide information on (1) firm size, status of development, organization, and operation; (2) management system and decision-making style; (3) socioeconomic background of enterprise owners; (4) social mobility and network of owners; (5) source and composition of employees and employee–employer relations; and (6) incomes, expenditures, and assets of entrepreneurs. Of most interest to us, however, they also provide information on entrepreneurs' views on a range of issues related to government–business relations, the overall business environment, and the availability of financing. Both the 1993 and 2002 surveys contain questions about access to bank credits on the part of the respondent firms. We rely on these questions to assess the financial treatment of the private sector in the 1980s and 1990s.

Both the 1993 and 2002 surveys are nationwide; that is, they covered all the provinces in China. The survey instruments are quite similar, although there are important differences that will be noted later. Both surveys were organized by the Department of the United Front – the branch of the Communist Party in charge of managing relations with the non-Communist components of Chinese society and economy – and the All-China Federation of Industry and Commerce, the organization that represents the private sector. The surveys were designed with input from researchers and academics from the Chinese Academy of Social Sciences, Beijing Academy of Social Sciences, and Renmin University. All the surveyed firms were selected from the registration lists maintained by the local bureaus of industry and commerce. Thus, these firms were explicitly registered as private firms at the time of the survey, which means that they include both private start-ups and enterprises converted from SOEs or collective firms.

One difference is that the 1993 survey is smaller, covering 1,440 firms, whereas the 2002 survey covers 3,258 firms. The second difference is that the 2002 survey apparently is more heavily focused on larger firms than the 1993 survey. In a document reporting on the 2004 survey results, the Chinese researchers revealed that the 2002 survey included many firms that were members of the All-China Federation of Industry and Commerce, which are relatively large, whereas other surveys focused on "ordinary private firms." The survey data bear out this point. In the 1993 survey, there are 568 firms that are classified as *siying qiye*, privately operated firms. This is about 39.5 percent of the full sample. Privately operated firms are usually larger than individual businesses, which employ only up to eight employees. Almost all the firms in the 2002 survey appear to be *sying qiye* rather than individual businesses. Also, the average employment of firms in the 1993 survey appears to be in line with the registration data published by the Chinese government, whereas the 2002 survey indicates a substantially higher level of average firm

[11] There was another private-sector survey in 1991 but that one was limited to what is termed as "individual businesses," that is, small single proprietorships with a few employees. The 1993 and the private-sector surveys thereafter began to focus on larger private firms that have multiple shareholders and a large number of employees. The data from the 2004 survey have not been released, although the Chinese press has made references to its summary findings.

Table 10.1. *Perception of credit bias: 1993 private-sector survey*

Year	(1) Percentage of firms reported receiving formal finance				(2) Percentage of firms reported receiving informal finance			
	(1a) Most important	(1b) Second important	(1c) Third important	(1d) Average	(2a) Most important	(2b) Second important	(2c) Third important	(2d) Average
1980	8.6	23.1	33.3	21.7	17.1	26.9	53.3	32.5
1981	14.8	28.6	71.4	38.3	11.1	33.3	14.3	19.6
1982	3.6	35.3	70.0	36.3	17.9	29.4	10.0	19.1
1983	5.9	29.4	18.4	17.9	20.6	29.4	42.1	30.7
1980–1983 average	**8.2**	**29.1**	**48.3**	**28.5**	**16.7**	**29.8**	**29.9**	**25.5**
1984	15.7	24.1	31.5	23.8	15.7	34.8	32.9	27.8
1985	21.7	23.1	26.2	23.7	18.8	31.7	44.6	31.7
1986	5.6	19.0	34.1	19.6	16.9	42.9	38.6	32.8
1987	18.3	18.9	36.7	24.6	18.3	34.7	40.0	31.0
1988	9.7	24.4	19.7	17.9	21.1	30.3	46.1	32.5
1989	8.0	17.1	31.6	18.9	17.2	38.2	38.0	31.1
1984–1989 average	**13.2**	**21.1**	**30.0**	**21.4**	**18.0**	**35.4**	**40.0**	**31.2**
1990	13.8	17.6	22.8	18.1	22.9	37.6	42.1	34.2
1991	13.6	11.3	18.4	14.4	17.5	41.3	38.8	32.5
1992	8.5	19.6	28.1	18.7	15.5	43.3	36.8	31.9
1990–1992 average	**12.0**	**16.2**	**23.1**	**17.1**	**18.6**	**40.7**	**39.2**	**32.9**

Source: Based on question 22 in the 1993 Private-Sector Survey.

346

employment.[12] In comparing the results from these two surveys, we should bear in mind the differences between these two surveys. We will first report the findings from these two surveys and then discuss some complications related to them.

Table 10.1 presents the findings from the 1993 survey and Table 10.2 presents the findings from the 2002 survey. Both tables present historical data, stretching back to the early 1980s. The 1993 and the 2002 surveys contain retrospective questions about access to bank credit at the time of the founding of the firm and we use these questions as the basis to assess the historical evolution of the financial treatment of private firms. (There are, however, complications related to the retrospective questions and responses, which we will address later.) Question 22 of the 1993 survey asks the respondents to pick up to three sources of their start-up capital and to rank the importance of each source, from most important to second and third most important. Nine choices are offered: (1) inheritance, (2) savings, (3) equity capital from business partners, (4) overseas investments, (5) loans from relatives, (6) loans from banks, (7) loans from credit unions, (8) loans from collective units, and (9) loans from individuals. We classify loans from banks, credit unions, and collective units as formal finance and loans from relatives and individuals as informal finance. Because our primary interest is to understand the financial environment facing private firms and the relationship between the state and the private sector in particular, we mainly focus on external sources of capital and the relative importance of formal and informal external sources of capital. We do not include equity financing in part because of the uncertainty over its classification and also because it is easier to compare credit financing between the 1993 survey and the 2002 survey.

The figures in Table 10.1 are percentage shares of firms that reported receiving formal or informal finance during their start-up year out of the total number of firms that have provided a response; averages for three different periods (1980–1983, 1984–1989, and 1990–1992) are highlighted in bold. There are two very interesting findings. First, the early years of the reforms in the 1980s are by no means a dark era for the de jure private sector, nor is the subsequent period of reform one of improved access to finance. In fact, almost the opposite is the case. While only 8.2 percent of firms reported that formal finance was their most important source of start-up capital during the 1980–1983 period, a very high portion of firms reported formal finance as their second (29.1 percent) or third most important (48.3 percent) source of start-up capital. On average, 28.5 percent of private firms reported receiving formal finance ranked as most important, second most important, or third most important source of their start-up capital during the 1980–1983 period. This is higher than the figure for 1984–1989 (21.4 percent) and

---

[12] According to the government's registration data, in 1993, the average number of employees in a *siying qiye* was 16.62 persons in 1992 and 13.4 persons in 2001. (Notice that the average employment declined.) In the 1993 survey, the average employment was 15 but in the 2002 survey, the average employment was 97 persons.

Table 10.2. *Perceptions of credit bias: 2002 private-sector survey*

	(1) Percentage of firms reported receiving bank loans in the start-up year		(2) Percentage of firms reported receiving informal loans in the start-up year	
	(1a) Privately founded firms	(1b) Privately founded firms in rural areas	(2a) Privately founded firms	(2b) Privately founded firms in rural areas
1984	25.0	36.4	29.2	18.2
1985	26.5	50.0	20.6	33.3
1986	23.3	15.8	27.9	15.8
1987	29.0	38.5	34.2	46.2
1988	27.0	27.8	23.8	16.7
1989	16.2	27.3	23.5	27.3
1984–1989 average	**24.5**	**32.6**	**26.5**	**26.3**
1990	21.3	25.0	27.7	28.1
1991	16.2	16.7	27.0	30.0
1992	23.8	25.0	27.8	22.5
1993	18.8	26.4	34.2	18.9
1994	18.2	27.6	33.2	36.2
1995	19.6	25.7	32.9	29.7
1996	19.1	25.6	31.3	30.8
1997	20.9	29.2	35.6	29.2
1998	22.3	34.3	30.9	31.4
1999	21.8	34.6	34.6	34.6
2000	18.4	28.0	28.6	24.0
2001	15.0	13.8	27.0	41.4
1990–2001 average	**19.6**	**26.0**	**30.9**	**29.7**

Source: Based on question 8 in the 2002 Private-Sector Survey.

1990–1992 (17.1 percent). In 1992, a year widely believed to have ushered in a series of liberalizing reforms, only 18.7 percent of private firms reported receiving formal finance ranked at least as the third most important source of start-up capital. This is substantially lower than 1981 (38.3 percent), 1982 (36.3 percent), 1984 (23.8 percent), 1985 (23.7 percent), and 1987 (24.6 percent).

The second finding follows directly from the first: informal finance increased in relative importance over time. Under column 2d (Table 10.1), the proportion of firms receiving informal finance increased linearly. During the 1980–1983 period, it was 25.5 percent, 31.2 percent during 1984–1989, and then 32.9 percent during 1990–1992. In 1980–1983, the share of firms reporting that they received formal and informal finance was approximately equal. During 1984–1989, 10 percent more firms reported receiving informal finance than formal finance, and this gap grew to be 15 percent in the 1990s.

How should we interpret the increasing reliance on informal finance and the seeming reduction in the role of formal finance? One interpretation is that the emergence of informal finance itself indicates the government's tolerance of a greater play for market forces and private decision making outside of its direct control. This is the framework used by Tsai (2002) to explain the prominence of informal finance in some regions of China. Another way to say this is that formal and informal finances are complements.

But this is not what we observe in the data. In the 1990s, the role of formal finance declined and that of informal finance increased. The changing composition of sources of finance suggests an alternative interpretation that these two sources of finance are substitutes. Although more research would be needed to establish this point empirically, it is likely that private entrepreneurs turned to informal finance as they faced diminishing access to formal finance. The reason is not hard to understand. Informal finance is much more expensive than formal finance. According to one study, the curb market rate in Beijing for small private firms in the late 1990s was as high as 18 percent, compared with 6 percent on the formal loans (Fang, 2005).

The findings based on the 2002 survey show exactly the same trends: the importance of formal finance declined and the importance of informal finance increased. Question 8 in the 2002 survey asks the respondents to check off their sources of start-up capital from the following choices: (1) savings from running small businesses, (2) savings from running small-scale production, (3) donations from friends and relatives, (4) wages, (5) informal loans, (6) bank loans, and (7) inheritance. We adopt a conservative classification scheme and classify bank loans as formal finance and informal loans as informal finance. Table 10.2 reports the percentage of firms that have checked off either formal loans or informal loans as a source of initial capital. Period averages are highlighted in bold. Very few firms in the 2002 survey were founded before 1984 and thus we omitted data on those firms. We report only on those private firms that were founded as such and exclude privatized firms. We do not have information about when these firms were privatized, and therefore cannot know their ownership status when they received formal or informal finance. Moreover, the question contains an important ambiguity in asking for information about the firm during its "start-up stage": we do not know whether respondents interpreted the question to mean the start-up of the original firms or their start-up as privatized firms.

Nonetheless, the results are remarkably similar to the data based on the 1993 survey. The number of firms reporting a reliance on formal finance, at least for the subset of firms founded as private firms, declined over time. During 1984–1989, an average of 24.5 percent of private firms reported receiving formal finance; this ratio declined to 19.6 percent during 1990–2001. For firms founded in 2001, the year touted as a breakthrough for the private sector because of Jiang Zemin's invitation for capitalists to join the Communist Party, only 15 percent of private firms reported receiving formal finance (see Table 10.2, column 1a). In 1984, 25 percent of firms did so and in 1987 as many as 29 percent of firms did so.

Over the same period, the number of firms reporting a reliance on informal finance increased dramatically. For firms founded during 1984–1989, on average, 26.5 percent of firms reported receiving informal finance; for those founded in 1990–2001, 30.9 percent did so. The gap between those reporting a reliance on formal and informal finance increased substantially in the 1990s as well. For firms founded in 1984–1989, the number of firms relying on formal and informal finance during the start-up period was roughly similar. For the firms founded in 1990–2001, 30.9 percent of firms reported receiving informal finance as we have seen, but only 19.6 percent reported receiving formal finance. The 1990s therefore witnessed a decline in the share of private firms able to tap resources through the formal financial sector and a corresponding growth in firms' reliance on the informal sector.

The finding that fewer private firms had access to formal finance in the 1990s than in the 1980s is striking but we should be cautious about how to interpret this finding. In the 1980s, private firms were smaller and it did not take much capital to start up a firm. Moreover, the absolute number of private firms was less and the boom was of more recent origin. In the 1990s, by contrast, the size of the average private firm had almost certainly grown and the number of firms seeking to enter was higher as well. (It should be noted, however, that the individual size of private firms in the 1980s was in fact surprisingly large as compared with that in the 1990s.) As a result, demand for financial resources in the private sector was probably larger. Our finding does not necessarily suggest that there were clear policy reversals in the 1990s. But it does suggest that the formal financial sector lagged in its capacity to supply capital to emerging private firms. As we will see in comparing China with other countries in the region, other Asian governments faced similar circumstances but moved more actively to channel financial resources to the private sector.

We also need to sort out four complications related to our data. One is that the survey questions refer to loans extended during the start-up years of the respondent firms, not during their subsequent operations. It is possible that Chinese banks have reduced their lending to start-up ventures but have stepped up lending to those enterprises already in operation. Chinese banks may have become more risk averse over time and thus increasingly preferred to lend to established firms rather than new entrants. Thus, the dynamic reported in Tables 10.1 and 10.2 may reflect this change in banks' behavior, with no implications for the availability of credit to private firms that are already established.

If loan availability is contingent on the operating history of a firm, then older firms should receive more favorable treatment from the banking system than younger ones. In addition to the questions about whether they received loans during the start-up years, both the 1993 and 2002 surveys also contain questions about whether firms were carrying bank debt at the time of the survey. We use these questions to examine the hypothesis that Chinese banks may have been more willing to lend firms with an operating history in 2002 than they were in 1993.

There is no evidence that operating history mattered more in 2002 than it did in 1993. Of those firms in operation for four years in the 1993 survey (i.e., firms founded since 1989), 35.6 percent reported carrying bank debt at the time of the survey. For the 2002 survey, this number is almost identical, 35.5 percent. In the 1993 survey, 35.1 percent of firms with three years of operation reported carrying bank debt, compared with 34.1 percent in the 2002 survey. For firms with two years in operation, 32.7 percent of them reported carrying bank debt in the 1993 survey as compared with 33.6 percent in the 2002 survey. These simple comparisons do not control for firm-level characteristics, but it is unlikely that firm-level characteristics should affect the results substantially. In fact, given that the 2002 survey sampled the larger firms in the private sector, the finding that the ratio of firms receiving bank loans hardly changed at all between 1993 and 2002 is all the more remarkable.

A second potential objection to the conclusion that the availability of formal finance decreased over time has to do with the combination of liberalizing regulatory changes and the entry of greater numbers of private-sector firms. In the 1980s, one can hypothesize that the regulatory environment was highly restrictive and thus only well-connected private firms could gain access to formal-sector finance. In the liberalized regulatory environment of the 1990s, all sorts of private firms were established. Fewer of them could gain access to formal financing, but this was an artifact of the combination of a more liberal environment and the entry of more firms into the market rather than an indication of any policy change.

We can examine this hypothesis only indirectly because we do not have any direct measures of the number of new entrants, the extent of financial market liberalization, or the extent of political privilege. However, it is safe to assume that private firms located in townships or rural areas should be less politically connected when compared with private firms located in large- and medium-sized cities. The reasoning is that the urban firms are closer to both the decision makers and the banks themselves. Also in the larger urban areas, it is more difficult to gain entry due to the dominance and the incumbency of SOEs as compared with the rural areas. Thus, those private firms that did gain entry can be presumed to be more politically powerful and connected. This political hypothesis predicts that urban private firms would have greater access to finance.

Column 1b of Table 10.2 reports the share of firms located in the rural areas, reporting that they received bank loans during their start-up years. Except for two years, 1986 and 2001, far higher proportions of rural firms received bank loans in the start-up years as compared with the sample as a whole (Table 10.2, column 1a). On average, in both the 1980s and 1990s, 7 percent more rural firms received loans as compared with the sample as a whole. This finding casts at least some doubt on the hypothesis that bank lending to the private sector was driven by the political power of urban private firms. Rather, this finding is consistent with a commonly acknowledged fact about the Chinese reforms that economic liberalization started earlier and went deeper in the rural areas than in the urban areas (Naughton, 1996).

A third objection to our survey evidence has to do with a potential survival bias in the data. Those private firms that were better financed in the 1980s were endogenously more competitive than other firms that were denied financing. Thus, better-financed firms in the early period had a higher probability of making it into the 1993 and 2002 surveys. The higher ratios of firms with bank loans in the 1980s can reflect this survival bias, rather than any underlying changes in the banks' policies or practices.

There are both conceptual and empirical difficulties with this interpretation. At a conceptual level, what is most evident in the data provided in Tables 10.1 and 10.2 is the change in the *composition* of loans rather than the level of lending. In the 1980s, private firms drew more loans from the formal financial sector but less from the informal financial sector. In the 1990s, it was the other way around. If the level of financing, rather than its composition, determined firm competitiveness, there is no reason to believe that private firms with greater access to formal lending in the 1980s should necessarily be more competitive than those with less access to formal lending in the 1990s.

Second, the survival-bias interpretation would predict a linear pattern in the data. Firms that were founded earlier should be better financed. However, while the period-average data in both the 1993 and 2002 surveys do exhibit clean linearity, the annual data within a given period do not. For example, in the 1993 survey, very few firms in the early 1980s ranked formal lending as the most important source of capital. In the second half of the 1980s, the ratios were moving around quite a bit annually rather than constantly declining as the survival-bias view would predict. One way to minimize the survival bias is to examine those years close to the time of the survey. By this indicator, there is no evidence at all that access to credit improved substantially for the de jure private firms in the early 1990s, as reported in the 1993 survey, or in the late 1990s, as reported in the 2002 survey.

Fixed-Asset Investment Indicators[13]

We now turn to our second measure of the policy environment: fixed-asset investments or investments made by firms in new property, plant, and equipment.[14] As

---

[13] The data on fixed-asset investments used in this section come mainly from a series of publications by NBS specifically devoted to covering fixed-asset investment activities. We have checked the data in these specialized publications with those published in the annual Yearbooks. In comparison with the Chinese data on output, Chinese data on fixed-asset investments are remarkably consistent across a number of publications. The data used in the text come from National Bureau of Statistics (1987, 1989, 1991, 1992, 1997a, 1997b, 1999b). The data on some of the latest years are from National Bureau of Statistics (2003).

[14] In the Western accounting system, this is known as investments in property, plants, and equipment (PPE), as distinct from investments in stock or bonds, which denominate existing assets.

compared with similar activities in a market economy and with other economic activities in the Chinese economy, fixed investments are heavily controlled by the government. All investment projects above a fairly low threshold require government scrutiny and approval. For this reason, fixed-asset investment is a superior measure of the policy environment than the output-based measures that are so frequently used.[15]

Table 10.3 provides the ownership breakdown of fixed-asset investment activities from 1980 to 2003 for four types of firms: SOEs, collective firms, "individual economy," which includes households and the de jure private firms in our definition, and firms of other ownership.[16] These four types of firms are exhaustive and mutually exclusive, and thus their totals add up to 100 under column e of Table 10.3.

Despite the widespread impression that China has undertaken substantial economic liberalization, the de jure private sector's share of total fixed-asset investment in the 1990s was actually smaller than it was in the 1980s. In the first six years of the 1980s, between 1980 and 1985, the "individual economy" already accounted for 20.7 percent of total fixed-asset investments. This share climbed slightly in the second half of the 1980s. Between 1986 and 1990, this sector accounted for 21.9 percent of total fixed-asset investment. In contrast, during 1991–1995, the "individual economy" accounted for only 13.2 percent of the total fixed-asset investments, rising only slightly to 13.9 percent during 1996–2000. Panel B of Table 10.3 provides annual data for selected years. In 1993, the "individual economy" accounted for only 11.9 percent of total fixed-asset investments, a drop of a full 10 percent from what was prevailing in the second half of the 1980s (at 21.9 percent). Since 1993, this ratio climbed up slowly to 15 percent in 2002 and then fell back to 14.1 percent

---

[15] There is a great deal of economic evidence that the governmental control of the investment process has remained substantial during the reform era. A telling piece of evidence, as marshaled by Thomas Rawski, is that China's seasonal investment recycles, as recently as the 1999–2001 period, matched almost perfectly those prevailing during the centrally planned era. Since fixed-asset investment is a large component of China's GDP, the fluctuations of investment levels have a substantial impact on GDP. Here, Rawski shows that China's quarterly GDP growth patterns differed substantially from those in South Korea, Taiwan, and Hong Kong, an indication that factors such as weather or traditional Chinese holidays are not the principal determinant of China's GDP's seasonal rhythm. Rawski (2002) quotes from a Chinese economist in his overall assessment of Chinese investment process:

Many basic components of a pure market economy are still in their incipient stage in China, although market-oriented reform started two decades ago. Government-guided investment mechanisms, a state-controlled banking system and dominant state-owned enterprises ... still run in a framework molded primarily on the previous planned economy.

[16] Individual economy refers to what we term as de jure private sector in this chapter. We use private sector rather than private firms for a reason because individual economy also encompasses households, which are, by definition, private. We will come back to the issue of households later on but for now let us focus on the changes in the fixed-asset investments during this period.

Table 10.3. *Ownership composition of fixed-asset investment*[a]

Year	(a) SOEs	(b) Collective firms	(c) Individual economy: urban and rural	(d) Of individual economy: urban only	(e) Other ownership	(f) TOTAL
			Panel (A): Period data			
1980–1985	66.7	12.7	20.7	1.6	0.0[b]	100.0
1986–1990	64.8	13.4	21.9	2.9	0.0[b]	100.0
1991–1995	59.0	16.3	13.2	2.7	11.0	100.0
1996–2000[c]	52.5	15.0	13.9	4.1	18.7	100.0
2001–2003	42.7	14.1	14.4	7.6	28.8	100.0
			Panel (B): Annual data			
1993	61.5	17.9	11.9	2.7	8.8	100.0
1997	52.5	15.4	13.8	3.0	18.3	100.0
2000	50.1	14.6	14.3	5.5	21.0	100.0
2001	47.3	14.2	14.6	6.6	23.9	100.0
2002	43.4	13.8	15.0	7.8	27.9	100.0
2003	39.0	14.4	13.9	8.1	32.7	100.0
2004		14.1	14.2			100.0

[a] Values are in percent.
[b] Constructed to be zero, as this category did not exist prior to the 1991–1995 period.
[c] In 1997, the government made a change in the investment reporting/approval procedure. Beginning in 1997, the investment reporting threshold was revised from 50,000 yuan to 500,000 yuan, but this change only applied to SOEs and urban collective firms. The effect of this change is that the published amount of fixed-asset investment in the state and the urban collective sectors is smaller than the actual amount. For 1996, the government published both the revised and unrevised data. In the unrevised data, the SOEs invested 1,205.6 billion yuan in fixed assets and the collective firms invested 366 billion yuan. In the revised data, the SOEs invested 1,200.6 billion yuan and the collective sector invested 365.2 billion yuan. The difference is about 0.4 and 0.2 percent, respectively.
Sources: Based on various sources on fixed-asset investment compiled by NBS. See the text for a detailed explanation.

in 2004, just one percentage point higher than at the very onset of the reforms in 1980.

Because our measure covers only fixed-asset investment activities in the de jure private sector, we must return to the question of whether this measure is too narrow. In particular, the "other" ownership category exploded from effectively zero in the second half of the 1980s to 11.0 percent in 1991–1995 and then to 18.7 percent during 1996–2000. To what extent are these "other" ownership forms effectively capturing domestic private investment?

Table 10.4 further decomposes firms in the "other" ownership category into four types of firms: (1) joint-ownership firms, (2) shareholding firms, (3) foreign-invested enterprises, and (4) unclassified firms. Shareholding firms and foreign-invested firms dominate this category of firms. During 1996–2000, shareholding

Table 10.4. *Composition of fixed-asset investment by firms in the "other ownership" category*

Year	(a) Joint-ownership firms	(b) Shareholding firms	(c) FIEs	(d) Unclassified category of firms	(e) TOTAL
		Panel (A): Period data			
1996–2000	1.94	42.0	53.2	2.9	100.0
2001–2003	1.11	68.2	29.0	1.8	100.0
		Panel (B): Annual data			
1993	5.1	21.2	71.2	1.9	100.0
1997	2.7	30.4	63.3	3.6	100.0
2000	1.4	58.8	37.8	2.0	100.0
2001	1.1	63.6	33.7	1.6	100.0
2002	1.1	68.7	28.5	1.6	100.0
2003	1.0	70.1	27.0	1.9	100.0

Note: Values are in percent.

Sources: Based on various sources on fixed-asset investment compiled by NBS. See the text for a detailed explanation.

firms accounted for 42 percent of the fixed-asset investments of firms in the other ownership category, and FIEs, another 53.2 percent. Since then, shareholding firms have become dominant, accounting for 70.1 percent in 2003. FIEs accounted for about 27 percent.[17]

To what extent are shareholding firms effective vehicles for private-sector investment activities? At least until the late 1990s, the answer appears to be "not much." Of China's largest shareholding firms, that is, those listed on China's two stock exchanges, only 6.97 percent were private initial public offerings (IPOs) between 1990 and 2003. The rest were SOEs that issued minority shares but in which, managerial control remained very clearly in state hands.[18] Put differently, many shareholding firms in China have private revenue rights, but their control rights still rest with the government and they should properly be considered state firms.

[17] Although there are complications, it is safe to say that FIEs are private firms, although in the foreign sector. This chapter is primarily concerned about the domestic private sector, so we will not discuss FIEs in great detail here, except to make two points here. One is that in the early 1990s, FIEs absolutely dominated the other ownership category of firms. They accounted for 71.2 percent of all the fixed-asset investments by these firms in 1993. Second, this juxtaposition of the seemingly liberal policy toward de jure private but foreign firms and the substantial restrictions on the de jure domestic private firms is a fascinating topic, to which we will return later.

[18] See http://www.baidu.com/s?cl=3&wd=http://news.xinhuanet.com/stock/2004–09/07/content_1952118.htm.

Other researchers have corroborated this finding that listed firms are effectively controlled by the state. According to a detailed study of over 600 firms on the Shanghai and Shenzhen Stock Exchanges in 1995, the three main groups of shareholders – the government, legal persons, and private individual investors – each controlled about 30 percent of outstanding shares. However, Xu and Wang (1997) report that, on average, individual shareholders controlled only 0.3 percent of the board seats of those listed firms, while the government retained 50 percent of the board seats and state-owned institutions controlled the rest.

That said, many of the small shareholding firms – for example, a category known as "shareholding cooperatives" – should properly be classified as private firms. Shareholding cooperatives are converted from TVEs and small SOEs and are typically majority owned by their employees. As such, they should be classified as private firms, but in the fixed-asset investment data they are lumped together with other shareholding firms. Thus, there is no question that our "individual economy" category understates the importance of the private sector in fixed-asset investment. But this bias cannot be very big. As of 2002, the shareholding cooperatives accounted for only 2.89 percent of China's industrial output by value, as compared with 11.7 percent by privately operated enterprises (*siying qiye*).[19] According to a recent study by researchers at the International Finance Corporation, privatization of small SOEs and TVEs became significant only after 1998.

A partial solution to this attribution problem is to compare the *de jure* private sector with the state sector and the collective sector. This approach produces ratios that approximate investment approval odds of the private sector relative to the state sector and the collective – or ambiguously private – sector. A decrease in the ownership biases should be associated with a rising ratio; an increase in the ownership biases should be associated with a declining ratio.

Table 10.5 presents data on fixed-asset investment in the de jure private sector as a ratio of fixed-asset investment in the state sector, collective sector, and firms of other ownership category. Data under columns 1a, 2a, and 3a of Table 10.5 show the same trend as that of Table 10.3. In the 1980s, the fixed-asset investments undertaken by the de jure private sector in both urban and rural areas already amounted to about one-third of fixed-asset investments in the state sector. The ratio of individual economy to SOEs, under column 1a (Table 10.5), was 0.31 in the 1980–1985 period and 0.34 in the 1986–1990 period. But this ratio declined sharply between 1991 and 1995, to only 0.22. Between 1996 and 2000, this ratio rose moderately, to 0.27. Between 2001 and 2003, despite a period of rapid growth and at least the perception of bold economic reforms, the ratio of fixed-asset investment by purely private to state firms managed to recover only to the level prevailing at

---

[19] It should be noted that NBS stopped using "individual economy" for its data series on industrial output, although it is using "individual economy" category for its fixed-asset investment reporting. The 11.7 percent quoted in the text referred only to *siying qiye* and presumably does not include industrial *getihu* (see National Bureau of Statistics, 2003, p. 459).

Table 10.5. *Fixed-asset investment ratios of individual economy to firms of other ownership types*

Year	(1) Individual economy/SOE ratios		(2) Individual economy/collective firm ratio		(3) Individual economy/other ownership ratio	
	(1a) Urban and rural	(1b) Urban only	(2a) Urban and rural	(2b) Urban only (urban collective only)	(3a) Urban and rural	(3b) Urban only
Panel (A): Period data						
1980–1985	0.31	0.024	1.64	0.13 (0.41)	–	–
1986–1990	0.34	0.045	1.64	0.22 (0.51)	–	–
1991–1995	0.22	0.045	0.80	0.16 (0.58)	1.15	0.23
1996–2000	0.27	0.078	0.93	0.27 (1.24)	0.74	0.22
2001–2003	0.34	0.18	1.02	0.54 (2.9)	0.50	0.27
Panel (B): Annual data						
1993	0.19	0.044	0.66	0.15 (0.56)	1.35	0.31
1997	0.26	0.056	0.89	0.19 (0.93)	0.75	0.16
2000	0.29	0.11	0.98	0.38 (1.8)	0.68	0.26
2001	0.31	0.14	1.03	0.47 (2.4)	0.61	0.28
2002	0.35	0.18	1.09	0.57 (3.1)	0.54	0.28
2003	0.36	0.21	0.96	0.56 (3.1)	0.43	0.25
2004						

Sources: Based on various sources on fixed-asset investment compiled by NBS. See the text for a detailed explanation.

the very onset of the reform era. For much of the 1990s, there is no evidence that ownership biases disappeared, as private/state investment approval odds in fact declined.

A comparison between the "individual economy" and the collective sector tells a more dramatic story (Table 10.5, column 2a). Throughout the 1980s, the de jure private sector was responsible for more fixed-asset investment – about 64 percent more – than the collective sector. In the first half of the 1990s, however, the de jure private sector's share contracted substantially relative to the collective sector. By 2000, the private sector achieved parity with the collective sector, as indicated by the ratio around 1 in 2001, 2002, and 2003. But it should be stressed that this is 64 percent less than the level prevailing in the 1980s. Thus even if it is true that much of the collective sector is effectively under private control, it is also the case that the liberalization of the 1990s had a greater impact on the growth of these mixed or ambiguously defined private firms than it did on de jure private firms. The ratios of de jure private sector to other ownership also dropped in the course of the 1990s (Table 10.5, column 3a).

As in other areas of the Chinese economy, there may be substantial differences in the urban and rural areas. This is especially true in the case of private-sector development. In the 1980s, a majority of private entrepreneurs originated from or were based in the rural areas. Almost all the private fixed-asset investments in the 1980s occurred in the countryside. For example in 1982, of 21.1 billion yuan in fixed-asset investments attributed to the so-called individual economy, 19.9 billion yuan, or 94 percent, occurred in the rural area. The massive entry of rural private entrepreneurship was due to a combination of a preexisting market economy in China's countryside even before the reforms and to the deep and substantial liberalization of the agricultural sector.

Both Tables 10.3 and 10.5 present data on fixed-asset investments by the urban de jure private sector. Column d of Table 10.3 presents the percentage shares of fixed-asset investments by private units located in the urban areas only. Columns 1b, 2b, and 3b of Table 10.5 present fixed-asset investment ratios of the urban private sector to those of SOEs, collective firms, and other ownership units, respectively. These data together suggest a fascinating pattern. While the policy treatment of the whole private sector deteriorated in the 1990s compared with the 1980s using this measure, the position of the urban private sector improved in the 1990s, especially in the second half of the decade and even more after 2001. As a percentage share of total fixed-asset investments, the urban private sector was very small in the 1980s, only 1.6 percent for 1980–1985 and 2.9 percent for 1986–1990. The first half of the 1990s witnessed a decline to 2.7 percent but the share rose to 4.1 percent for 1996–2000 and then to 7.6 percent for 2001–2003. Relative to the SOEs and collective sector, the position of the urban private sector shows a considerable improvement if we compare the period since the late 1990s with the 1980s. The first half of the 1990s, again, turned out to be a low point as compared with the second half of the 1980s.

These findings suggest three larger substantive points. One is that the position of the private sector registered a relative decline mainly in China's countryside. Our survey data bear out this point as well. Table 10.2 shows that the financing constraints increased more for the firms located in the countryside than for firms located in the cities. The second point is that it is not clear whether the relative improvement of the position of the private sector in the cities was due to liberalization, more active support measures, or simply benign neglect. However, it is important to underscore the major finding: in 1993, the urban private sector accounted for only 2.7 percent of all fixed-asset investments and after a decade of further reform, this had risen to only 8.1 percent. The third point is that the widespread impression among academic researchers about private-sector growth in the 1990s may have been driven by this boom in the *urban* private sector. But because of the far larger incipient role of the private sector in China's countryside, lags in agricultural reforms in the 1990s – widely acknowledged in China and by Western researchers – had a disproportionately negative effect on China's private sector as a whole.

As with the survey research findings, there are methodological issues with the fixed-asset investment data that should be addressed before drawing any firm conclusions about government policy toward the private sector. One problem with the data on fixed-asset investments attributed to the so-called individual economy is that it incorporates investment activities in the household sector. This presents two problems. One is the apple–orange problem, in which investment activities in the SOEs and collective firms are all in the corporate sector. The other problem is that if the private sector engaged in more housing investments in the 1980s than in the 1990, then the declining share of the private sector in total fixed-asset investments may not indicate a policy change but simply a change in the composition of corporate and household investments.

Unfortunately, we do not have an unambiguous breakdown between fixed-asset investments taking place in the corporate and household sectors. But there are clues. One approach is to calculate the share of the stock of fixed assets held by private firms. This approach will net out household investments from our data. In 2002, the total book value of fixed assets in all industrial firms with sales of at least 5.0 million yuan was 9.4 trillion yuan. If we subtract from this figure the value of fixed assets in (1) the SOEs and state-holding enterprises, (2) collective firms, and (3) FIEs, we arrive at the value of fixed assets in the domestic private sector. This calculation would yield a figure of 704 billion yuan. This is about 7.5 percent of the book value of all industrial fixed assets in China, which is about half of the private sector's share of fixed-asset investment flows during this period. We draw two conclusions. One is that both the flow and stock data are consistent with each other in that the fixed-asset investment activities in the private sector have been very small. Second, household investment activities probably comprise a substantial portion of the fixed-asset investments attributed to the "individual economy" in the Chinese data.

An alternative approach is to rely on the Chinese data that break down investment activities by their uses. One is a distinction between expenditures on "construction and installation" and expenditures on "equipment and machinery." A second is a distinction between production-related and non-production-related investment activities. One should bear in mind some of the problems with these statistical categorizations in interpreting the following findings. Construction and installation includes residential housing but also factory buildings and facilities. Nonproduction-related investment activities refer to construction of facilities that supply social services (such as schools or hospitals). While these facilities themselves reflect investment in social infrastructure and are not production related, it should be kept in mind that the firms that construct these facilities derive income from their construction.

One benefit of this breakdown is that we can construct a set of measures that are based on the same underlying economic activities. Table 10.6 reports on the ratios of investment expenditures on equipment and machinery under

Table 10.6. *Fixed-asset investment in equipment/machinery purchases and production-related purposes: individual economy compared with SOEs and collective firms*

	(a) Equipment and machinery purchases		(b) Production-related fixed-asset investment	
	Relative to SOEs	Relative to the collective firms	Relative to SOEs	Relative to collective firms
Panel (A): Period data				
1980–1985	0.24	1.12	0.13	0.62
1986–1990	0.09	0.34	0.11	0.47
1991–1995	0.055	0.166		
Panel (B): Annual data				
1991			0.10	0.47
1992			0.08	0.27
1996	0.065	0.365		
1997	0.07	0.166		
1998	0.068	0.168		
1999	0.15	0.315		
2000	0.148	0.33		
2001	0.18	0.36		
2002	0.24	0.395		
2003	0.338	0.43		

Sources: Based on various sources on fixed-asset investments compiled by NBS. See the text for a detailed explanation.

column (a) between the de jure private sector and SOEs or collective firms. Table 10.6 also provides data on a similar set of comparisons of production-related investments.

Table 10.6 confirms the findings that we have reported earlier. Expenditures on equipment and machinery by the de jure private sector are a fraction of these expenditures in the state and collective sectors throughout the reform era. Production-related investments in the de jure private sector are also small compared with the state and collective sectors. An additional confirmatory finding is that these ratios declined in the 1990s compared to the 1980s and that they began to rise only modestly in the late 1990s. One difference from the previous finding is that the private sector's share of equipment expenditures and production-related investment declined sooner than overall fixed-asset investments. In the case of expenditures on equipment and machinery, the de jure private sector's share began to decline sharply in the second half of the 1980s relative to the state and collective sectors, rather than in the 1990s. Why this measure declined so much sooner than the other measures is worth exploring further.

DISCUSSION

In the foregoing sections we have tried to track the evolution of the policy environment for private sector in China since the onset of the reforms, using survey and investment data. Although imperfect, these indicators are more accurate measures of policy biases than the standard output measures commonly used in the literature. The findings are robust across different indicators and go against the grain of the standard view of the Chinese reforms as well. The private sector has grown throughout the reform era but its growth has occurred against substantial and even growing financing constraints and apparent limits on the range of its investment activities.

In this section of the chapter, we will first put our findings in the context of existing work on the financing of private-sector development. Some economists believe that the financial constraints we have documented here have been alleviated over time. We revisit some of the themes and findings in that genre of work. We then take up a second line of analysis that seeks to compare China's development path to the growth experience of the other East Asian NIEs. We dispute this characterization and show that profound differences existed between China and the NIEs with respect to the relationship of the state to the domestic private sector.

State and Private Sector in China: Reconciling with Existing Research

There is general agreement among China scholars that the country's financial sector is closely tied to the SOE sector. As a result, it suffers from a number of inefficiencies, manifest in the extraordinarily high level of nonperforming loans even at a time when the economy was growing rapidly. Nonetheless, some have argued that Chinese banks became more market oriented and profit driven in the 1990s and therefore more supportive of the emergent private sector. We first address this seeming discrepancy between our findings and those in the literature, and then will report other research findings that are consistent with what we have found here.

Shen and Park (2001), for example, report that more bank managers ranked profitability as important in 1997 than in a 1994 survey. But this finding per se does not conflict with ours. If licensing policies restrict private firms to low-margin businesses, then TVEs or SOEs would in fact appear more profitable. Shen and Park (2001) also note that the authority to issue new loans became highly centralized in the 1990s. Again, this finding does not conflict with ours, as higher-level government officials often favor SOEs at the expense of private firms.

Another strand of the literature stresses that financing constraints varied considerably across different regions in China, either in the formal financial sector (Brandt and Li, 2003) or in the informal financial sector (Tsai, 2002). Our findings do not confirm or reject this view, but there is no reason why an increase in financing constraints facing private firms over time could not be accompanied by a degree of cross-sectional heterogeneity. However, it is worth noting that if we look beyond three or four liberal provinces, credit availability to the private sector in the 1990s in fact did not vary much across different provinces. In 1999, the short-term bank debt outstanding to the de jure private sector from all financial institutions (including rural credit unions) was 57.9 billion yuan (People's Bank of China, 2000). The top three provinces with the largest credit outstanding to the de jure private sector in 1999 were Zhejiang (11.4 billion yuan), Guangdong (8.4 billion yuan), and Fujian (3.4 billion yuan). *These three provinces accounted for 40.3 percent of the entire short-term bank debt outstanding to the private sector; Zhejiang alone accounted for nearly half of that.* The view that there is considerable regional heterogeneity is true only of a number of provinces.

Other researchers have obtained findings that are quite consistent with our results. International Fund for Agricultural Development (2002) and Nyberg and Rozelle (1999) reported that the state of China's rural finance has deteriorated in the 1990s, which is broadly consistent with our results. China's central banker, Zhou Xiaochuan, was reported to have said that 90 percent of China's nonperforming loans was generated in the 1990s, not in the 1980s.[20] A study by the International Finance Corporation, based on the survey in the late 1990s, shows that newer private firms faced greater financing constraints than older firms (International Finance Corporation, 2000).

There is also research showing considerable financial support for the private sector in the 1980s. Based on an extensive reading of numerous, internal bank documents, Huang (2008) has found instances where heads of Chinese banks, such as those of the Agriculture Bank of China and the Bank of China, issued detailed and specific instructions to branch managers to lend to private businesses as early as 1981 and 1982. A number of Chinese sociologists have reported that banks financed a very high proportion of private firms during their start-up phase in the 1980s, similar to our findings based on the 1993 and 2002 surveys. These findings are based on surveys conducted in the 1980s, which means that they are not based on retrospective evaluations and are not contaminated by issues, such as survival biases. Zhang Houyi and Ming Lizhi (1999) summarized findings from six large-scale surveys – all conducted in 1987. One survey, covering 97 firms in eleven provinces, shows that 40.6 percent of private firms received start-up bank loans. A survey of 281 firms in Hebei reported that 54.8 percent received bank lending; another survey of 56 firms in Hunan reported that 28.5 percent did so. The remaining three surveys reach similar conclusions from other parts of the country: 66.3 percent of 130 firms in Shaanxi received bank loans, one-third of ten firms in Guangdong, and 23.3 percent of 50 firms surveyed in Wenzhou. Even the survey that shows the smallest share of private-sector firms receiving formal-sector financing substantially exceeds the average number of such firms receiving such credit during their start-up phase in the 1990–2001 period, 19.6 percent.

[20] Steinfeld (2002) made this reference.

Comparison with the East Asian NIEs

For some time, it has been common to view East Asia's rapid growth as the result of a common regional model. This perspective on the "East Asian miracle" has been popularized by a series of World Bank publications, in particular.[21] The view that China is the most recent exemplar of this regional pattern is based on a few stylized facts that suggest commonalities with other countries in the region. These include rapid GDP growth, following a period of economic reform; the adoption of an export-oriented growth strategy; and attention to other "fundamentals," such as investment in education and the pursuit of relatively stable macroeconomic policies.

We suggest that there are, however, some quite substantial differences between China and the East Asian NIEs in the growth models they pursued. For the purpose of this chapter, we focus on two closely related differences that are germane to our political economy interests. First, while China's policy stance toward the private sector was at best ambivalent – and remained so throughout the reform era, as we have shown – governments in the rest of East Asia showed much greater political acceptance of the role of the private sector in the economy and society. The main exception to this rule was Singapore. Moreover, many governments not only adopted passive policies that permitted the private sector to emerge and flourish, but also pursued more active forms of support for private-sector development, including the provision of preferential finance.

Second comparison with the rest of the region suggests a hypothesis that we explore in more detail in the conclusion that the Chinese government's posture toward the domestic private sector is related to its stance with respect to foreign capital. In the 1990s while China continued to impose substantial restrictions and constraints on the development of the domestic private sector, it substantially liberalized FDI. Chinese policy appeared to follow the unusual course of favoring foreign private investors over domestic ones. In the rest of the region, one observes a quite different mix, again with the important exception of Singapore. The opening to FDI was cautious and typically contained provisions designed to protect the domestic private sector from head-to-head competition with foreign firms.

The takeoff into sustained growth in the East Asian NIEs was accompanied by a steady increase in the private-sector share of investment and output. SOEs survived well into the 1980s and even 1990s in a number of strategic industries, particularly in intermediate goods (Korea's POSCO) and the nontraded services sector (Singapore's Singtel, state-owned banks in a number of countries). Privatization – the sale of state assets – played some role in the gradual decline in the weight of the SOE sector across the region, but the main reason was the rapid growth of domestic private firms (Helleiner, 1989; Lim and Fong, 1991).

---

[21] World Bank (1993), Stiglitz and Yusuf (2001), and Yusuf and Evenett (2002).

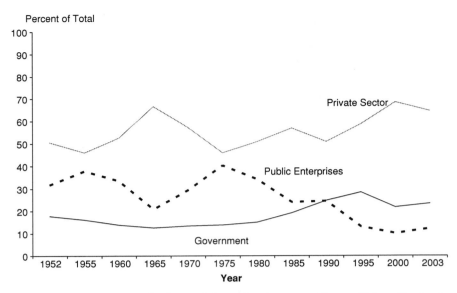

Figure 10.1. Taiwan: gross fixed capital formation, by owner (*Source: Taiwan Databook,* 2004)

This fundamental difference with China can be highlighted by considering briefly the evolution of the government's posture toward the private sector in Korea and Taiwan. We focus on developments through the mid-1980s in particular. The first four decades of postwar development are somewhat comparable in that they encompass periods of fundamental economic reform and also correspond to the period when both countries were under authoritarian rule: a dominant party in Taiwan and an alternation between semidemocratic rule and more overt forms of authoritarianism in Korea. These two cases are frequently juxtaposed on a number of dimensions, including the policy instruments used in supporting domestic firms. But when compared to China, the two countries exhibit important similarities.

Under Kuomintang (KMT) rule, Taiwan inherited a long tradition of direct state involvement in productive activities. In 1952 – the earliest year for which data are available – the government accounted for 17.7 percent of gross domestic capital formation (GDCF) and public enterprises another 31.7 percent; the private sector accounted for the remaining 50.6 percent. By 1965, the private sector accounted for 66.5 percent of GDCF. This was to vacillate somewhat in subsequent years, as Figure 10.1 shows; the government turned to SOEs as an instrument for pushing select heavy industries in the mid-1970s, and the government's direct role in fixed capital formation shows a trend increase after 1980. But unlike in China – where basic investment and financing decisions still fell under government control to a large extent – such barriers to private-sector activity fell steadily throughout the period. If we focus only on the private and SOE sectors, the trends are unmistakable: the SOE role in GDCF shows a steady decline and in the Taiwan case. From 1978 to 1985, the SOE sector accounted for only 7.4 percent of economic activity; for the 1986–1991 period, this falls to 6.4 percent.

A brief comment on the political economy of this process provides a comparative backdrop to developments in China. Differences between statists and those favoring promotion of the domestic private sector were an important undercurrent of economic policy debates throughout the 1950s in Taiwan. As in China, concern about the rise of private economic power was at least one consideration, particularly given the divide between the ruling party that had relocated from the mainland and the indigenous sources of capital (Cheng, 1993). The shift toward a more outward-oriented development strategy in the late 1950s and early 1960s saw a resolution of this debate in favor of support for the growth of the domestic private sector.

The 1960 Statute for the Encouragement of Investment is emblematic of this change. The statute offered tax relief to companies in "pioneering" industries and placed particular emphasis on the promotion of exports. In the early years of industrialization, light industries such as textiles, consumer electronics, and components were favored, but over time, investment in labor-intensive industries was discouraged in favor of more skill- and capital-intensive products.

In a small number of capital-intensive industries where domestic firms were unable or unwilling to shoulder the risk, including steel, upstream petrochemicals, and certain capital goods, the government did revert to the establishment of new SOEs during the 1970s. However, the establishment of this new generation of SOEs was designed in major part to supply inputs to downstream private firms. A similar pattern can be seen in the establishment of research consortia, such as those that have been well documented in the electronics sector, which supported private companies through R&D and were thus complementary to private-sector growth rather than a competitor to it (Kuo, 1995).

The allocation of credit followed a broadly similar path. The state-owned banking system in Taiwan was initially a conduit for financing the SOE sector, and the government never used preferential finance as a tool of private-sector development to the extent that the Korean government did. Private firms therefore had to rely on what we have called informal financial arrangements to a greater extent. But these differences should not be overstated, particularly when we compare the evolution of the financial sector in Taiwan to what has occurred in China. As Kuo, Ranis, and Fei (1981, pp. 80–81) observe, "[I]n the 1960s, as a result of the government policy to encourage private industry, the composition of loans given by all banks was modified to favor private enterprises. The percentage of loans going to private enterprises increased from 24% in 1953 to 77% in 1979."

Government–business relations in Korea appear to follow a somewhat different path. In contrast to the KMT, which was dominated by mainlanders and maintained some political distance from Taiwanese firms, domestic political elites in Korea

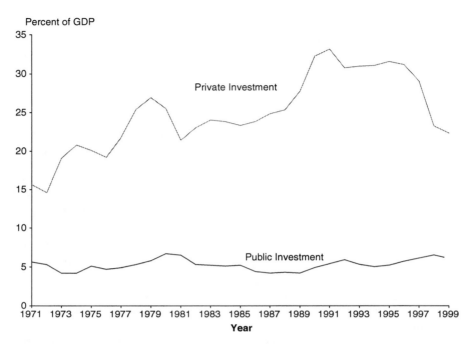

Figure 10.2. Korea: public and private investment (*Source:* Everhart and Sumlinski, 2001)

forged close relationships with existing entrepreneurs. As a result, the support of
the private sector took a more active form. But for our purposes the most important point remains the support extended by the government to the private sector.
Figure 10.2 shows trends in public and private investment over time. The public-
sector share of total GDCF is more constant than that in Taiwan, accounting for
roughly 5 percent of GDP throughout the period. The SOE share of total output
is also more constant than that in Taiwan, accounting for 9.7 percent of economic
activity in 1978–1985 and even rising to 10.3 percent in 1986–1991. But as in
Taiwan, these levels are much lower than those in China. And as in Taiwan, what is
striking is the explosion of private investment, which nearly doubles between 1971
(15.6 percent of GDP) and 1991 (33.1 percent). Comparable historical data on
the share of bank lending to the public and private sector are not available, but in
1990, bank claims on official entities – including local governments, government
investment institutions, and state-owned enterprises – were only 4.5 percent the
size of the claims on the private sector.

   Again, a brief sketch of the political economy of private-sector growth in Korea
helps establish some contrast with China. Privatization of Japanese assets initially
played a more direct role in the growth of the private sector, but trade protection
and preferential contracting relations with favored firms also fueled private-sector
growth in the immediate aftermath of the peninsular war. These networks of rent

seeking were one object of both the 1960 popular uprising against the Syngman Rhee government and the military coup that occurred only a year later. Initially, the military junta considered a strategy that imposed much greater constraints on the private sector. But a combination of pressure from the United States and recognition of the political dependence of the military leaders on private investment pushed in the direction of more symbiotic relationship.

As in Taiwan, the transition to export-led growth was accompanied by a new battery of incentives to private firms. Central to these was the aggressive use of financing as a tool for supporting export-oriented firms and favored sectors (Woo, 1991; Choi, 1993). This financing came directly from state-owned banks and relied to a much greater extent than in Taiwan on foreign borrowing. As in Taiwan, the government was not immune from the use of the SOE as an instrument of policy; the steel and petrochemical sectors are, again, the best-known examples. The government also maintained monopolies of key service sectors such as telecommunications until the 1980s and 1990s. But the dominant force behind Korea's overall and export growth was the rapid expansion of a relatively small number of highly diversified industrial groups, the *chaebol.* This process of concentration reached its apogee during the heavy and chemical industry drive of the late 1970s, when the state-owned banking sector was used most aggressively to push into a variety of new activities, including shipbuilding, chemicals, capital goods, and the electronics sector.

The close nature of business–government relations in Korea can be demonstrated not only by following the changing balance between the public and private sectors or the course of industrial policy, but through a political economy lens as well. As important work by Woo (1991), Kang (2002), and others has shown, the flip side of industrial policy was extensive corruption and the "reverse flow" of rents from the private sector back into the ruling party's campaign financing and other political needs. In Taiwan, the KMT controlled independent sources of funding, through both its own network of quasipublic corporations and its effective control of the state apparatus. Although the government fostered the development of the local private sector, it was not until the onset of political liberalization in the 1980s that KMT (as well as opposition) politicians began to actively court private-sector support and the KMT became a party of business. In Korea, the political relationship between the government and the private sector was more incestuous throughout the postwar period.

In sum, whatever other similarities might be drawn between China and the other newly industrializing countries of East Asia, the relationship between the government and the domestic private sector appears quite different. Not surprisingly, the SOE sector remained a favored instrument of policy for much longer in China. When liberalizing factions of the government did favor privatization and restructuring, they faced a much more entrenched and politically challenging task than was the case in the other NIEs. Governments in both Taiwan and Korea exhibited a strong revealed preference for the development of the domestic private sector, which quickly came to dominate overall economic activity.

Finally, it is worth noting that while government support for the private sector did amount to an effective form of risk sharing and created problems of moral hazard, we do not find evidence of the mixed property forms that became such a dominant feature of Chinese development. Debt financing from state-owned banks in Korea in particular could be seen as a form of "quasiequity" that resulted in bailouts *ex post*. Yet, ownership was private. Indeed, the willingness of the government to extend massive public assistance to these private firms – and their owners – provides even more convincing evidence of the very different political economy of these cases.

CONCLUSION

Let us summarize our empirical findings. First, we have argued that the debate about the development of the private sector in China could benefit from a more narrow focus on what we call the "de jure" private sector: those firms that are actually registered as private entities under Chinese law. This definition is narrow to be sure, but it also has a number of significant advantages over the standard measurements, such as nonstate sector. Second, we have suggested two alternative ways of capturing the policy environment facing the private sector: surveys of private entrepreneurs about their financing constraints and data on fixed-asset investments. These measures, we believe, are superior to the output-based measures common in the literature. Third, using these alternative measures, we have not found evidence to support the standard interpretation of a more-or-less linear evolution in the Chinese government's posture toward the private sector. In fact, there is evidence that those "support" policies – such as financing or granting investment approvals – became less favorable in the 1990s as compared with the 1980s.

An even more difficult question is why this distinctive pattern? It is not enough to simply note that China remains a Communist system antithetical to the private sector. As we have seen, the party made a strategic decision in the early 1980s to liberalize the domestic private sector and orient state-owned banks toward supporting the domestic private businesses, at least on the margin. The puzzle is that this policy course appeared to shift in the 1990s. We close with some broad, tentative, and speculative conjectures about why this occurred.

The first observation is that during the 1990s when the financing constraints on the domestic private sector appeared to have increased, the Chinese government was aggressively courting FDI through policy liberalization and conferrals of tax benefits on foreign firms. There is also evidence – based on survey data – that the policy treatment of foreign firms is substantially more favorable than that of domestic private firms. One hypothesis is that the Chinese leadership might have viewed FDI as a substitute for the domestic private sector. In the 1980s with almost no FDI, the Chinese state had to liberalize the private sector as an alternative to SOEs. In the 1990s, with a huge inflow of FDI this urgency eased considerably.

Probably the most dramatic example of this foreign bias is the policy treatment of domestic entrepreneurs and foreign investors in the wake of the 1989 Tiananmen crackdown. In 1990, the Chinese government stepped up its efforts to attract FDI, by, among other policy measures, dropping the provision in the 1979 Joint Equity Venture Law that required that the chairman of the board of any joint venture be Chinese. The central government designated all of Shanghai a special economic zone. FDI rose from $3.2 billion in 1988 to $3.4 billion in 1989 and to $3.5 billion in 1990.

By contrast, between 1989 and 1991, the conservative post-Tiananmen leadership launched a systematic assault against the domestic private sector. Both the number of individual businesses (*getihu*) and their employment fell dramatically between 1988 and 1991. In 1988, there were 14.5 million registered individual businesses; by 1990, this number was 13.3 million. Private-sector employment fell from 23.1 million to 20.9 million (Zhang and Ming, 1999). Throughout the 1990s, this bias against the domestic private sector persisted in financing policies as well. While the domestic private sector created far more jobs than the foreign sector, bank credits to the foreign sector ranged between two times (in 2002) to ten times (in 1994) those to the domestic private sector.[22]

Our second observation is related to the first. China's restrictive policy stance toward the domestic private sector, combined with a liberal policy toward foreign firms, forms another sharp contrast with Korea and Taiwan. In Taiwan, the opening to FDI was a component of a broader liberalization trend, and it was cautious.[23] Throughout the takeoff period, Taiwan's reliance on FDI was relatively low, as compared with China in the 1990s. As a share of gross capital formation, FDI peaked in the 1960s at around 3 percent. In contrast, in China in the 1990s the ratio was more than 15 percent.

In Korea, FDI policies were even more restrictive. The government showed a stated preference for foreign borrowing, much of which was channeled to building up domestic firms, over foreign direct investment (Haggard, 1990, pp. 197–208). Foreign firms accounted for an extremely small share of domestic capital formation: only 1.6 percent from 1966 to 1972 – the immediate postreform period – and even

---

[22] Huang (2003) explores the issue of FDI and private-sector development in great detail.

[23] The 1960 Statute and its subsequent amendments applied to foreign and domestic firms alike. At least with respect to this statute, Taiwan's regulatory framework was relatively neutral between domestic and foreign business. But the government restricted access to a number of sectors monopolized by the state, such as finance and telecommunications, which were not opened until the 1980s and 1990s and even then only slowly. Foreign investment in manufacturing was courted through the construction of export-processing zones. These zones are often seen as conferring a variety of benefits on foreign enterprises, for example, with respect to taxes or employment practices. But it is also the case that these enclaves can be used to provide protection for domestic firms since they typically require that all output be exported and thus limit foreign firms' access to the lucrative domestic market. Such restrictions were gradually lifted beginning in the 1970s, but only gradually and as we have seen the share of FDI in total capital formation was relatively small.

less than that during the heavy industry drive of the 1970s. These firms were generally confined to export-processing zones, had scant access to the domestic market, and faced a variety of sectoral restrictions well into the 1980s. In the 1980s and 1990s, even after some FDI liberalization, FDI as a share of GDCF was about half that of Taiwan: 1.2 percent during the 1986–1991 period and 1.3 percent during the 1992–1998 period. In fact, this low FDI dependency was found not only in the restrictive environment in Korea and Taiwan, but even in laissez-faire Hong Kong where the FDI/GDCF ratio was never above 6 percent through the 1970s. Only in Singapore, where the government had a similar skepticism toward the private sector, do we see a similar reliance on foreign investment to that seen in China in the 1990s.

Our third observation is that the political economy dynamics differed between China and the East Asian NIEs. Korea and Taiwan operated under authoritarian systems, and Taiwan was ruled by a dominant party that resembled the Chinese Communist Party (CCP) in important respects. But the state never exercised the kind of complete economic as well as political control as the CCP. Initially, Communist strategy provided little if any space for a private sector to operate, and at least until recently, the CCP did not allow independent private-sector organization. Moreover, the absence of even token forms of political competition meant that the CCP did not rely on the private sector for financial contributions and political support, as was the case in Korea in particular.

In contrast, in both Taiwan and Korea, state elites accommodated themselves to a preexisting private sector. In Taiwan, the KMT initially had only weak connections with domestic business, which was dominated by Taiwanese entrepreneurs and firms. Political conservatives saw Taiwan as little more than a staging area for retaking the mainland and were associated with a policy line that favored a large SOE sector and restrictions on the private sector. When it became unambiguously clear in the late 1950s that the KMT would get no American support for its revanchism, the leadership reached out economically, if not politically, and began to provide active support for private-sector development (Gold, 1986; Kuo, 1995). In Korea, the political relationship with the private sector was even closer. Operating in a semicompetitive, if not fully democratic, setting the succession of leaders from Rhee to Park to Chun developed very close political as well as economic relationships with representatives of the private sector as well as individual firms. The private sector not only provided investment and exports in return for incentives of various sorts, but was deeply implicated in financing the more purely political activities of the government. The full extent of this was revealed following the transition to democratic rule, when bribery scandals broke revealing direct presidential control over slush funds emanating from private-sector contributions valued in excess of $500 million (Kim, 2000).

We end our chapter by speculating about future developments. There is increasing evidence that the current Chinese leadership is rethinking its private-sector policies. While the privatization policies became more permissive in the late 1990s under Jiang Zemin and Zhu Rongji, the leadership of Hu Jintao and Wen Jiabao has sought to improve the business environment for the de jure private sector. Their most significant policy measure –and one that clearly distinguishes them from the previous leadership – is that they have given more weight to agricultural reforms. Private entrepreneurship was most vibrant in China's rural areas in the 1980s and a deepening of agricultural reforms would be conducive to further private-sector development.

In March 2004, the Chinese Parliament passed a constitutional amendment that would enhance property rights security for private investors. The leadership also undertook significant regulatory liberalization to effect a more equal treatment between domestic private firms and foreign firms with respect to the sectors in which they can enter and invest. As an explicit acknowledgment that government policies had privileged foreign firms, a State Council directive issued in early 2005 declared that "all the economic sectors open to FDI should be open to domestic private participation." Domestic private firms, for example, are now allowed in energy exploration a right long monopolized by state-owned firms and given to foreign firms since the early 1990s. It is too soon to tell whether these cumulative policies will immediately and substantially improve the business environment for the domestic private sector, and much will depend on political as well as policy developments, but the current direction of policy change is quite clearly in the direction of more state support for China's private businesses.

References

Amsden, Alice. 1989. *Asia's Next Giant: South Korea and Late Industrialization.* New York: Oxford University Press.

Bai, Chong-En, David D. Li, and Yijiang Wang 2003. "Thriving on a Tilted Playing Field," in *How Far Across the Rivers? Chinese Policy Reform at the Millennium.* Nicholas C. Hope, Dennis Tao Yang, and Mu Yang Li, eds. Stanford: Stanford University Press, pp. 97–121.

Barzel, Yoram. 1997. *Economic Analysis of Property Rights.* Cambridge and New York: Cambridge University Press.

Batra, Geeta, Daniel Kaufmann, and Andrew H. W. Stone. 2003. *Investment Climate around the World: Voices of Firms from the World Business Environment Survey.* Washington, DC: World Bank.

Brandt, Loren and Hongbin Li. 2003. "Bank Discrimination in Transition Economies: Incentives, Information or Ideology?" *Journal of Comparative Economics.* 31, pp. 387–413.

Cheng, Tun-jen. 1993. "Guarding the Commanding Heights: The State as Banker in Taiwan," in *The Politics of Finance in Developing Countries.* Stephan Haggard, Lee Chung, and Sylvia Maxfield, eds. Ithaca: Cornell University Press, pp. 55–93.

Choi, Byung-sun. 1993. "Financial Policy and Big Business in Korea: The Perils of Financial Regulation," in *The Politics of Finance in Developing Countries.* Stephan Haggard, Chung H. Lee, and Sylvia Maxfield, eds. Ithaca: Cornell University Press, pp. 23–54.

Everhart, Stephen S. and Mariusz A. Sumlinski. 2001. "Trends in Private Investment in Developing Countries: Statistics for 1970–2000." International Finance Corporation Discussion Paper 44. Washington, DC: World Bank.

Fang, Xinghai. 2005. "Reconstructing the Micro-Foundation of China's Financial Sector," in *Financial Sector Reforms in China.* Yasheng Huang, Anthony Saich, and Edward S. Steinfeld, eds. Cambridge, MA: Harvard University Asia Center.

Gold, Thomas. 1986. *State and Society in the Taiwan Miracle.* Armonk: ME Sharpe.

Haggard, Stephan. 1990. *Pathways from the Periphery: The Politics of Growth in the Newly Industrializing Countries.* Ithaca: Cornell University Press.

Haggard, Stephan. 2004. "Institutions and Growth in East Asia." *Studies in Comparative International Development.* 38(4), pp. 53–81.

Helleiner, Gerald K. 1989. "Transnational Corporations and Direct Foreign Investment," in *Handbook of Development Economics,* vol. 2. Hollis Chenery and T. N. Srinivasan, eds. Amsterdam: North-Holland, pp. 1142–1180.

Huang, Yasheng. 2003. *Selling China: Foreign Direct Investment during the Reform Era.* Cambridge and New York: Cambridge University Press.

Huang, Yasheng. 2008. *Capitalism with Chinese Characteristics.* Cambridge and New York: Cambridge University Press.

International Finance Corporation. 2000. *China's Emerging Private Enterprises: Prospects for the New Century.* Washington, DC: International Finance Corporation.

International Fund for Agricultural Development. 2002. *Rural Financial Services in China.* Rome: International Fund for Agricultural Development.

Kang, David. 2002. *Crony Capitalism: Corruption and Development in South Korea and the Philippines.* Cambridge and New York: Cambridge University Press.

Keefer, Philip. 2004. "A Review of the Political Economy of Governance: From Property Rights to Voice." World Bank Policy Research Working Papers WPS 3315. Washington DC: World Bank.

Kim, Myoung-Soo. January–February 2000. "Causes of Corruption and Irregularities." *Korea Focus.* 8(1). Accessed August 20, 2007, from http://www.koreafocus.or.kr/essays/view.asp?volume_id=5&content_id=976&category=G.

King, Robert and Ross Levine. 1993. "Finance and Growth: Schumpeter Might be Right." *Quarterly Journal of Economics.* 108(3), pp. 713–737.

Kuo, Cheng-tian. 1995. *Global Competitiveness and Industrial Growth in Taiwan and the Philippines.* Pittsburgh: University of Pittsburgh Press.

Kuo, Shirley W. Y., Gustav Ranis, and John C. H. Fei. 1981. *The Taiwan Success Story: Rapid Growth with Improved Distribution in the Republic of China, 1952–1979.* Boulder: Westview Press.

Lardy, Nicholas R. 1998. *China's Unfinished Economic Revolution.* Washington, DC: Brookings Institution.

Lau, Lawrence J., Yingyi Qian, and Gerard Roland. 2000. "Reform without Losers: An Interpretation of China's Dual-Track Approach to Transition." *Journal of Political Economy.* 108, pp. 120–143.

Levine, Ross. 1997. "Financial Development and Economic Growth: Views and Agenda." *Journal of Economic Literature.* 35(2), pp. 688–726.

Li, David. 1996. "Ambiguous Property Rights in Transition Economies." *Journal of Comparative Economics.* 23(1), pp. 1–19.

Lim, Linda Y. C. and Pang Eng Fong. 1991. *Foreign Direct Investment and Industrialization in Malaysia, Singapore, Taiwan and Thailand.* Paris: OECD.

Lin, Justin Yifu, Fang Cai, and Zhou Li. 1996. *The China Miracle: Development Strategy and Economic Reform.* Hong Kong: Chinese University Press.

Maxfield, Sylvia and Ben Ross Schneider, eds. 1997. *Business and the State in Developing Countries.* Ithaca: Cornell University Press.

Murphey, Kevin, Andrei Schleifer, and Robert Vishny. 1993. "Why Is Rent-Seeking So Costly to Growth?" *American Economic Review*. 83(2), pp. 409–414.

National Bureau of Statistics, 1987. *Zhongguo guding zichan touzi tongji ziliao (1950–1985)* [Statistical Materials on Chinese Fixed Asset Investment (1950–1985)]. Beijing: Zhongguo tongji chubanshe.

National Bureau of Statistics, 1989. *Zhongguo guding zichan touzi tongji ziliao (1986–1987)* [Statistical Materials on Fixed-Asset Investment in China (1986–1987)]. Beijing: Zhongguo tongji chubanshe.

National Bureau of Statistics, 1991. *Zhongguo guding zichan touzi tongji ziliao (1988–1989)* [Statistical Materials on Fixed-Asset Investment in China (1988–1989)]. Beijing: Zhongguo tongji chubanshe.

National Bureau of Statistics, 1992. *Zhongguo guding zichan touzi tongji ziliao (1990–1991)* [Statistics on Fixed-Asset Investment in China (1990–1991)]. Beijing: Zhongguo tongji chubanshe.

National Bureau of Statistics, 1997a. *1997 Zhongguo guding zichan touzi tongji* [China Statistical Yearbook on Fixed Asset Investments 1997]. Beijing: Zhongguo tongji chubanshe.

National Bureau of Statistics, 1997b. *Zhongguo guding zichan touzi tongji 1950–1995* [China Statistical Yearbook on Fixed Asset Investments 1950–1985]. Beijing: Zhongguo tongji chubanshe.

National Bureau of Statistics, 1998. *Zhongguo tongji nianjian 1998* [China Statistical Yearbook 1998]. Beijing: Zhongguo tongji chubanshe.

National Bureau of Statistics, 1999a. *Guanyu tongjishang ruhe fanying suoyuzhi jiegou wenti de yanjiu* [Research on Statistical Reporting on Ownership Structures]. Beijing: Zhongguo tongji chubanshe.

National Bureau of Statistics, 1999b. *Zhongguo guding zichan touzi tongji 1999* [China Statistical Yearbook on Fixed Asset Investments 1999]. Beijing: Zhongguo tongji chubanshe.

National Bureau of Statistics. 2003. *China Statistical Yearbook 2003*. Beijing: Zhongguo tongji chubanshe.

Naughton, Barry. 1996. *Growing Out of the Plan: Chinese Economic Reform, 1978–1993*. Cambridge and New York: Cambridge University Press.

Nyberg, Albert and Scott Rozelle. 1999. *Accelerating China's Rural Transformation*. Washington, DC: World Bank.

People's Bank of China, 2000. *Zhongguo jinrong tongji 1997–1999* [Chinese Financial Statistics 1997–1999]. Beijing: Zhongguo jinrong chubanshe.

Rawski, Thomas G. 2002. "Will Investment Behavior Constrain China's Growth?" *China Economic Review*. 13(4), pp. 361–372.

Shen, Minggao and Albert Park. 2001. Decentralization in Financial Institutions: Theory and Evidence from China. Ann Arbor, MI: Department of Economics, University of Michigan.

Steinfeld, Edward S. 2002. *Chinese Enterprise Development and the Challenge of Global Integration*. Cambridge, MA: Department of Political Science, MIT.

Stiglitz, Joseph E. and Shahid Yusuf, eds. 2001. *Rethinking the East Asian Miracle*. New York: Oxford University Press.

Taiwan Databook. 2004. Republic of China Council for Economic Planning and Development. *Taiwan Statistical Data Book 2004*. Taipei: Council for Economic Planning and Development.

Tsai, Kellee S. 2002. *Back Alley Banking: Private Entrepreneurs in China*. Ithaca: Cornell University Press.

Wang Yuanjing, 2002. *Zhongguo minying jingji touzi tizhi yu zhengce huanjing* [The Investment System and the Policy Environment for China's People-Run Economy]. Beijing: Zhongguo jihua chubanshe.

Woo, Jung-en. 1991. *Race to the Swift: State and Finance in Korean Industrialization.* New York: Cornell University Press.

World Bank. 1993. *The East Asian Miracle.* New York: Oxford University Press.

Xu, Xiaonian and Yan Wang. 1997. *Ownership Structure, Corporate Governance, and Corporate Performance.* Washington, DC: World Bank.

Yusuf, Shahid and Simon J. Evenett. 2002. *Can East Asia Compete?* New York: Oxford University Press.

Zhang Houyi and Ming Lizhi, 1999. *Zhongguo siying qiye fazhan baogao (1978–1998)* [Report on Development of China's Private Enterprises (1978–1998)]. Beijing: Shehui kexue wenxian chubanshe.

ELEVEN

The Role of Law in China's Economic Development

Donald Clarke, Peter Murrell, and Susan Whiting[1]

INTRODUCTION

Economic growth requires economic agents to believe that political, social, and economic conditions are such that they can expect a reasonable return from their investments in property and from the agreements they make with others. Where such beliefs exist, they can arise as a result of many different mechanisms. Property owners might view government as constrained by law within a democracy or believe that a particular autocratic government has an interest in not expropriating property. Promisees might have blind trust in their fellow citizens or know that the court system will make appropriate judgments in case of a breach of contract. Therefore, in exploring the determinants of a country's growth performance, it is critical to understand which mechanisms fostered expectations among property owners and among those making agreements.

The emphasis in the recent economics literature, echoed in the pronouncements of the World Bank and similar organizations, is on formal institutions or the rule of law as crucial in fostering the appropriate expectations (Hall and Jones, 1999; Acemoglu, Johnson, and Robinson, 2001; Rodrik, Subramanian, and Trebbi, 2004). Such emphasis follows an important line of thought in institutional economics dating back to Max Weber and carried forth by Douglass North (1990), which we call here the rights hypothesis (Clarke, 2003b). This holds that economic growth requires a legal order offering stable and predictable rights of property and contract. In this chapter we assess the development of the formal legal system in China and analyze its role in the economy, examining the degree to which the rights hypothesis is borne out by China's experience in the post-Mao reform era.

[1] We thank Loren Brandt, Thomas Rawski, and the participants in the Pittsburgh and Toronto workshops on China's Economic Transition for helpful comments and Giulia Cangiano, Janet Xiaohui Hao, Hsu Hsiao-ch'i, Zhou Yang, Lin Ying, and Li Xingxing for research assistance. Whiting's research was funded by the Institute for International Research of Johns Hopkins University and Nanjing University and the Royalty Research Fund of the University of Washington.

The assessment begins in "The Development of Law during the Era of Economic Reform" with an extended analysis of the development of China's legal system in the era of reform. We first characterize the role of law at the beginning of reform, a role that focused on running the state sector rather than on private economic activity. As reforms gradually altered the mix of economic agents within the economy and increased the importance of activities outside the supervision of government administrators, the need arose for a set of rules and institutions that could govern relations between agents who were not under a common superior. The legal system, tentatively and incompletely, began to fill this need. In "The Development of Law during the Era of Economic Reform," we provide a timeline of the changes in the legal system that constituted this process. These changes allowed broader scope for different types of economic agents and different types of economic activities, and provided some support for these activities, stimulating the need for further legal reform. Hence, the relationship between legal and economic development was bidirectional – a coevolutionary process. We close the section with an analysis of the current status of the legal system in the economic sphere and its problems.

Our discussion of the interaction between economic and legal developments sets the stage for an examination of the role of law in three prominent spheres of activity – property rights, agreements to trade goods and services, and corporate governance – in "Are Property Rights Secure? Do They Matter?," "Transactions in Goods and Services," and "Corporate Governance." The questions motivating the discussion in all three areas are whether law plays an important role, how that role has changed over time, and what the current problems are. The conclusions differ across areas. For example, the legal system currently plays a less important role in property rights than in agreements to trade. Indeed, it is impossible to make the case that the legal system has been crucial in protecting property rights. In contrast, in the area of transactions of goods and services, we present new data showing that the legal system is more important than might be assumed, given the enormous emphasis that personal and social relationships have played in the literature discussing markets in China. Nevertheless, one common theme in all areas is that the rights hypothesis, as traditionally interpreted, provides little explanatory power for China.

This conclusion, however, leaves open the question of the source of the expectations of reasonable returns from investments in property and from agreements that are universally assumed to be necessary for the success of a market economy. We address this question in "Are Property Rights Secure? Do They Matter?," "Transactions in Goods and Services," and "Corporate Governance," reflecting on the role of mechanisms other than law that might produce such expectations. There are many possibilities, such as a stable growth-oriented governmental administration, social relationships, a culture of trustworthiness, and so on.[2]

---

[2] See Murrell (2003) for a much fuller cataloging of these mechanisms in transition economies and a discussion of their relevance.

Indeed, one way to view development is as the process of generating functional substitutes for the formal institutions that are the focus of the rights hypothesis.[3] However, information on the relative importance of these substitutes in China is limited, as everywhere. We briefly summarize the information where it exists, focusing on some major examples, such as the role of local government in property rights and the dual-track reforms in transactions. But given the lack of knowledge about the mechanisms driving the expectations that must have underpinned China's growth, a major subject for future research must be the pursuit of more detailed and concrete information on how these expectations were generated.

THE DEVELOPMENT OF LAW DURING THE ERA OF ECONOMIC REFORM

In this section, we chronicle the changes that have taken place in the legal framework in the nearly three decades of economic reform. We document how the role of law shifted over time, beginning as a tool to manage the state sector and then taking on the more recognizable function of providing the rules and processes that govern, however incompletely and imperfectly, the interactions of independent economic agents. This process of change has been gradual, coevolving with economic reforms, and it is very much still in process. Therefore, we also discuss what is missing in the current legal framework.[4]

The Place of Law in the Early Years of Reform

Economic reform in China was marked from the beginning by a recognition that law had a new and important role to play. Yet this role was not at first the one contemplated by those who stress the importance of formal institutions in the process of economic development, which is essentially a claim about how healthy private economic activity is fostered. Early reform policy did not contemplate a major role for the private sector. It was about running the state sector better and therefore was not concerned with what might encourage entrepreneurship.

The early reform-era role for the legal system can perhaps be best understood by seeing what it was intended to replace: the discredited ideological controls of the past and a system of internal bureaucratic communication where the authoritativeness of particular documents was often unclear. The old system was incapable of imposing unity and order upon the processes of government, and so a new system was sought. In particular, a key ambition of those promoting legal reform was to bring regularity to government operations and to policymaking as a cure for the excessive devolution of power from the center and the resultant policy inconsistencies (Clarke, 1992).

---

[3] See, in particular, Qian (2003) on China.
[4] As throughout this chapter, we stick with legal issues directly relevant to economic matters.

In the economic realm, law was intended to be a mechanism for regulating the operation of state-owned enterprises (SOEs), replacing the particularistic bargaining regime of the past with a regime of strict, impersonal, and universalistic rules that would impose discipline on enterprise managers and encourage efficiency. A prime example of this type of mechanism was the Bankruptcy Law (1986), passed in 1986. According to contemporary commentary, "[T]he threat of bankruptcy urges all enterprises and people on and will turn muddleheaded people into shrewd ones and lazy people into diligent ones" (Hu, 1986). Prior to the Bankruptcy Law, however, the state already had the power to close down loss-making enterprises. Thus, this law and similar enactments were as much efforts by the state to effect policy in a new way as they were new policies.

To assess whether law in this sense, as a form of policymaking, could be successful in promoting economic development, or indeed in affecting anyone in any way, requires an understanding of the associated institutions available for making its rules meaningful. To return to the Bankruptcy Law as an example, we must ask whether there were any actors in the system who had both the means to put loss-making SOEs into bankruptcy and the incentives to do so. In fact, creditors who did have incentives to bring court proceedings found that the process remained under the control of the enterprise's administrative superior. Of course, that superior department could choose to put the enterprise through bankruptcy proceedings and close it down, but it could have chosen to do the same thing before the enactment of the Bankruptcy Law.

The Economy and the Law Coevolve

The effects of China's economic reforms gradually made this early approach to law less viable. The movement from planning to the market entails a reduction in the role of the individualized judgments of bureaucrats and an increase in the importance of universally applicable rules. Decentralization reinforces this process. The devolution of effective enterprise ownership and decision-making power to local governments, if it is genuine, necessarily means that the central government can no longer resolve disputes simply by issuing commands. The alternative to specific commands is a set of generally applicable rules. The growth of the private sector has the same consequence. Enterprises outside the bureaucratic system have no common superior; some other body must resolve their disputes with reference to a preexisting body of rules. Of course, decentralization, the market, and a private sector do not make these changes inevitable, but they do create demands that can be addressed by legal reforms.

A sea change in the relationship between the legal and the economic systems did indeed occur. The amount of important economic legislation passed by the National People's Congress (NPC) – the body with (at least theoretically) the authority to pass rules that bind all citizens and governmental actors – has mushroomed. The role of the courts has expanded considerably, and at least in the cities the salaries and benefits enjoyed by judges have been enhanced greatly through court fees.[5] Perhaps most symptomatic of the change in the role of law has been the change in the role of lawyers. In 1983, five years into the reform era, China had only 8,600 full-time lawyers (Chen, 2004). By 2005, that number had increased to well over 100,000,[6] and the year 2004 saw over 40,000 new LL.B. graduates (China School Net, 2005). There is no reason to doubt that this is a supply response to income opportunities, which in turn suggests that what lawyers do has much more value than before. Of course, some of this work may be old-fashioned "fixing." But it is fixing within an increasingly dense web of rules that barely existed at the outset of reform.

Just as Naughton (1995) has characterized the economic reform process as "growing out of the plan," so may the process of legal reform be described as growing out of the system of administrative directives. Unlike in the states of the former Soviet Union and Eastern Europe, in China the planned economy was not suddenly abolished. Within the Chinese state sector, the replacement of administrative directives with legal methods of supervision and control has been very gradual. Even today the senior management of enterprises in which the state has an important stake are selected and vetted through the Communist Party personnel system, with the board of directors merely supplying legitimacy.[7] Yet the operations of state enterprises are increasingly subject to legal instead of administrative regulation. For example, contract disputes with nonstate suppliers and customers cannot be resolved administratively, because there is no common superior.

The great expansion in the number and importance of economic actors that are not core parts of the traditional state system reinforced the process of growing out of the system of administrative directives. Privately owned enterprises have had to rely largely on the legal system for organizational vehicles[8] and remedies for wrongs suffered. Early on, the legal system did not provide much, but over time it became more responsive. For example, article 31 of the 1986 General Principles of Civil Law (GPCL) requires a written agreement for a partnership. However, just one year

---

[5] As of 2004, for example, an experienced senior judge in Shanghai could have annual earnings of 110,000 yuan (Gechlik, 2005).

[6] The exact number depends on whom you count. There were more than 103,000 full-time lawyers in law firms, but another 16,000 working part-time or in government, the military, companies, or legal aid services (Ministry of Justice, 2005).

[7] In November 2004, for example, the Chinese government undertook a remarkable reshuffling of top executives in its majority-owned, but ostensibly independent, telecommunications companies, with the executive vice president of China Mobile becoming the president of China Telecom, the executive vice president of China Telecom becoming the president of China Unicom, and the president of China Unicom becoming the president of China Mobile (*Financial Times*, 2004).

[8] By contrast, state-owned enterprises, for example, existed for decades before the promulgation in 1988 of a law providing for their existence and organization.

after the GPCL came into effect, the Supreme People's Court issued a document allowing courts to treat associations with the characteristics of a partnership as if they were partnerships, even if there was nothing in writing (Supreme People's Court, 1988).

This coevolution of economics and the law is nicely exemplified in the sphere of foreign economic interactions. Although the main motor of change in the Chinese legal system has been domestic developments, the policy of opening up to foreign trade and investment has had an unmistakable impact on both substance and procedure. At the outset of the reform era and for many years afterward, the Chinese government, recognizing that the domestic legal system was in many ways unattractive for foreign investors, attempted to establish a special, separate legal system for foreigners. As reforms in China's domestic economy progressed, however, it became increasingly apparent that the segregated legal system did not make sense over the long term. The effect of unifying the separate legal regimes has generally been to make the regime for Chinese parties look more like the one for foreigners, not the other way around.

A good example of the foreign regime leading the way in substantive law is that of the promise within the 1979 Equity Joint Venture Law that joint ventures would not be nationalized or expropriated and that if expropriated, "appropriate" (*xiangying*) compensation[9] would be paid. To this day, the Chinese legal system does not provide for compensation for lawful takings in general.[10] The desirability of this principle, however, was recognized in March 2004 via an amendment to the constitution, and enabling legislation (constitutional provisions are not self-executing in the Chinese legal system) is expected soon.

The Development of Economic Law: A Timeline

The whole period of economic reform saw a continuing succession of changes in formal law and legal processes, sometimes following economic change and sometimes spurring it. This subsection describes those legal changes. The description is complemented by Table 11.1, which lays out these changes in a schematic chronology.

---

[9] "Appropriate" compensation is a term of art in the international lexicon of governmental expropriations; it is understood to mean something less than the alternative formulation of "prompt, adequate, and effective" compensation, which in turn means the fair market value of the expropriated investment immediately before the expropriation (Jarreau, 2004, pp. 474–475).

[10] The State Compensation Law and other regulations do provide for compensation when government organs cause loss through *unlawful* actions, but do not make the uncompensated taking of assets per se unlawful. Otherwise taxation would be prohibited. Individual regulations may provide for some compensation for specific types of takings – for example, those involving real property.

Table 11.1. *A Timeline of legal developments, 1978–2004*

Periods	Dates	Item	Comment
Pre-1979	*December 1978*	*Third Plenum of Eleventh Central Committee*	*Official jettisoning of class struggle as main task of the Party; adoption of goal of economic reform and development. Reorientation of development strategy to reduce heavy industry investment, shift resources to agriculture and consumption.*
1979–1984		*First stage of economic reform: attempts to rationalize the state sector*	*This phase saw no commitment to markets; it was largely an attempt to make the planning system work better in the end. The individual economic sector (i.e., economic activities by self-employed individual entrepreneurs with fewer than eight employees) was called a necessary "supplement" to the state and collective sectors of the economy. Market activities were ad hoc and provisional. By 1984, the success of agricultural reforms was clear to all, while reforms in the urban state sector were much less successful; SOE behavior remained unchanged.*
	July 1, 1979	Law on Sino-Foreign Equity Joint Ventures passed	This landmark piece of legislation marked the official welcoming of foreign investment to China, as well as a decision to put such policy in the form of an NPC statute. This law is quite short and is more of a general policy statement than a detailed set of rules; it has required considerable supplementation in the ensuing quarter century.
	August 23, 1982	Trademark Law passed	
	December 4, 1982	Constitution passed	This is the initial version of the current constitution. It is a complete reworking of the previous 1978 constitution and is not considered a mere amendment. This constitution declared that the basis of China's economic system was socialist public ownership of the means of production and that the state sector was to be the leading sector in the economy. The individual economy (i.e., very small scale businesses of fewer than eight employees) was declared to be a "complement" to the socialist public economy. Socialist public property was declared sacred and inviolable, but there was no parallel declaration respecting private property.
	December 13, 1981	Economic Contract Law passed	This statute covered contracts between domestic entities other than individuals. It was intended largely to regularize relations between SOEs.

(continued)

381

Table 11.1 (*continued*)

Periods	Dates	Item	Comment
	March 12, 1984	Patent Law passed	
1985–1989		*Second stage of economic reform: the embrace of the market*	*This stage saw the open embrace of markets as a critical component of the economy. It also saw the emergence of the private sector as a supplement to the public sector, with a rise in the number of privately run and "red-hat" enterprises.*
	March 21, 1985	Foreign Economic Contract Law passed	This statute covered contracts between Chinese entities and foreign parties, and was part of the policy of the era that aimed at providing separate legal regimes for foreigners and foreign-related transactions.
	April 12, 1986	Law on Wholly Foreign-Owned Enterprises passed	This statute allowed for the first time an enterprise organized under Chinese law to be wholly owned by one or more foreign investors, with no Chinese equity participation. Only in 2006 did it become possible for a Chinese investor other than a governmental entity to be the sole founding shareholder in a Chinese limited-liability entity; multiple shareholders were required.
	April 12, 1986	General Principles of Civil Law passed	This statute was intended to provide the basic legal principles for the operation of a market economy populated by individual actors making decisions based upon free will. It did not, however, contain detailed rules in important areas, such as contract, tort, and property.
	December 12, 1986	Enterprise Bankruptcy Law passed	This law should really be named the "SOE Closing Law." It was intended not to protect creditors, or even to assist in the reallocation of inefficiently used capital, but to improve SOE performance through the threat of closing. As government departments had already had the power to close an SOE prior to this law, and retained the power to keep money-losing SOEs operating after it, the law has unsurprisingly not had a great effect on the economy. The corporate landscape remains heavily populated with money-losing enterprises, whose assets creditors cannot (or for various reasons connected with the peculiar incentives facing certain types of creditors, will not) seize and sell off under this law.
	October 1987	Thirteenth Congress of CCP recognizes "private economic sector" as necessary supplement to state sector	

Date	Event	Description
August 5, 1987	Provisional Regulations on the Administration of Urban and Township Individual Industrial and Commercial Households passed	These regulations provided some legal form to small sole proprietorships. In addition to stipulating some limitations in the form of needed permits, it also provided some protections.
April 13, 1988	Law on Sino-Foreign Cooperative Joint Ventures passed	This statute allowed for a joint venture with more flexible features that allowed under the Law on Sino-Foreign Equity Joint Ventures.
April 13, 1988	Law on Industrial Enterprises Owned by the Whole People passed	This statute was intended to operate as a formal organizational and regulatory statute governing SOEs. Of course, SOEs had been organized and regulated prior to this statute, so the statute represented less in new substance than it did the idea that SOEs *should* be governed by legislation issuing from the NPC.
April 12, 1988	Constitution amended to acknowledge the private sector as a "complement" to the socialist public economy that is allowed to develop "within the limits prescribed by law"	Somewhat grudging acceptance of role of private sector. Constitutional amendment still stipulates that state exercises "guidance, supervision, and control" over private sector.
April 12, 1988	Constitution amended to allow land leasing	This amendment, in giving legal sanction to the granting and subsequent transfer of long-term leases, was a key step in the commodification of land and allowed governments at various levels to reap significant revenues. At the same time, it made land use more subject to market forces and less subject to bureaucratic priorities.
June 25, 1988	Provisional Regulations on Private Enterprises passed	These regulations, still in effect today although seriously dated, legitimize sole proprietorships, partnerships, and limited liability companies having eight or more employees. However, the regulations allow only a limited class of persons to form such enterprises: farmers, the urban unemployed, retired persons, and so on. The regulations contemplate business formation as a supplementary activity by those not connected to the urban socialist economy, not as a normal part of economic life.
April 4, 1989	Administrative Litigation Law passed	Established principle that government agencies must justify their actions by reference to published laws and regulations. Only the execution of rules, however, and not the rule-making process itself, is covered.
1989–1992	Post-June 4 retrenchment	*This period saw an attempt by the post-Zhao Ziyang leadership to undertake a significant rollback of economic reforms, recentralize, and strengthen planning. This attempt did not last long, however, and momentum for reform had begun to build anew by the end of 1990.*

(continued)

Table 11.1 (*continued*)

Periods	Dates	Item	Comment
	May 19, 1990	Provisional Regulations on the Grant and Transfer of Use Rights in Urban Land passed	These regulations made the commodification of urban land possible. They provide for long-term leases from the state of up to seventy years that may be transferred relatively freely.
	September 7, 1990	Copyright Law passed	
1992–2001		*Economic reform and markets fully embraced once more*	*Beginning of creation of system that explicitly embraces private sector as an important component of the economy; looks to rules-based market system through institutionalization of property rights and markets. Rapid development of private firms, building of market institutions and associated laws.*
	January 1992	Deng Xiaoping's Southern Tour	Gives a decisive push to renewed reform momentum.
	May 15, 1992	Normative opinion on Joint-Stock Companies passed	This document, passed by the State Commission on Reform of the Economic System, served as one half of China's first post-1949 general Company Law, and provided an organizational vehicle for enterprises that wished to restructure and list shares on the stock exchanges. This document was intended largely to facilitate restructuring by existing enterprises, not to facilitate the formation of new enterprises.
	May 15, 1992	Normative opinion on Limited Liability Companies passed	This document, passed by the State Commission on Reform of the Economic System, served as the other half of China's first post-1949 general Company Law, and provided an organizational vehicle for enterprises that wished to restructure into companies with investors holding equity shares, but not to list on the stock exchanges.
	October 1992	Fourteenth Congress of CCP endorses "socialist market economy" as goal of reform	

Date	Event	Description
March 29, 1993	Constitution amended to demote planning and promote the market	The amended article 15 had read, "The state practices economic planning on the basis of socialist public ownership" and referred to the "supplementary role" of the market. The amended article 15 states, "The state practices the socialist market economy." Articles 16 and 17 were also amended to eliminate the duty of SOEs and collective enterprises to fulfill the state plan.
April 22, 1993	Provisional Regulations on the Administration of Issuance and Trading of Stock passed	This State Council regulation was in effect China's first law on securities.
September 2, 1993	Law against Unfair Competition passed	
September 2, 1993	Economic Contract Law amended	The amendment brought contracts signed by individual industrial and commercial households (*getihu*) under its ambit. Contracts signed by individuals in other capacities remained outside, covered by the GPCL. Since *getihu* contracting had been since 1986 covered by the looser GPCL, bringing them under the Contract Law may not have been a liberalization.
December 29, 1993	Company Law passed	This law, effective in 1994, formalized in NPC legislation the limited liability company and the joint stock company previously sanctioned under the 1992 Normative Opinions issued by the State Commission on Reform of the Economic System.
May 12, 1994	Foreign Trade Law passed	Provided default rule that any good was tradable unless regulations provided otherwise. (This default rule did not apply to trade in services.) Prohibited natural persons from engaging in trade. Authorized various restrictions on imports and exports, some GATT compatible and some not. Also provided in principle for antidumping and countervailing duties procedures, but without any details as to procedure.
May 10, 1995	Negotiable Instruments Law passed	This law was intended to make payments by checks and other methods easier. To date, however, checks are not widely used in China. There is no central institution similar to the Federal Reserve Bank that guarantees checks to its member banks. Thus, checks take much longer to clear.

(*continued*)

Table 11.1 (*continued*)

Periods	Dates	Item	Comment
	June 30, 1995	Security Law passed	This law made secured lending possible. There have, however, been a number of problems in implementation.
	February 23, 1997	Partnership Law passed	This law was intended to provide a new organizational vehicle for certain small businesses carried on by a group of individuals.
	March 25, 1997	Antidumping and Antisubsidy Regulations passed	These regulations contained some WTO-incompatible elements and were superseded by later regulations in late 2001, just before China's entry into the WTO.
	September 1997	Fifteenth Congress of CCP recognizes private sector as important component of the economy	
	December 29, 1997	Price Law passed	This law was part of an effort to reform the pricing system. It established the principle that the great majority of prices should be set by the market, that is, decided by producers themselves. However, it still contained provisions designed to prevent prices deemed excessively high or low.
	December 29, 1998	Securities Law passed	Although China had previously had lower-level regulations on securities, this statute finally provided NPC-level rules.
	March 15, 1999	Constitution amended to upgrade role of law	Article 5 supplemented to read, "The People's Republic of China practices ruling the country in accordance with the law and building a socialist rule-of-law state." These words by themselves do not of course mean any change in the role of the legal system. They represent a policy declaration by the government that the legal system is to be given greater weight as a technique of governing.
	March 15, 1999	Constitution amended to sanction larger role for nonpublic sector and nonwage income	Article 6 describes the economic system of the state. Originally mentioning only public ownership, it was amended to acknowledge "diverse sectors" of the economy developing side by side with the publicly owned sector (which was to remain dominant). The amendment also blessed "a variety of modes of distribution" in addition to distribution according to work; this legitimized income such as interest and dividends (which had not been unlawful before, but lacked such high-level sanction). Article 11 amended to call the private, individual, and other nonpublic sectors "major components" of the socialist market economy.

386

March 15, 1999	Contract Law passed	This law replaced three prior laws, thus providing significant unity to the contract law regime. The replaced laws were the Economic Contract Law (covering contracts between domestic businesses, but not individuals), the Foreign Economic Contract Law (covering contracts in which one party was a foreigner), and the Technology Contract Law (covering technology transfers such as licensing).
August 30, 1999	Law on Individual Wholly Owned Enterprises	Provided sounder organizational vehicle for small business. A complement to the Partnership Law, which provided a form for groups. Like the Partnership Law, this law specifies that the investors shall *not* enjoy limited liability.
2000–2001	Passage of several laws and regulations aimed at regularizing the lawmaking procedure itself	Law on Legislation (2000); Regulations on the Procedure for Formulating Administrative Regulations (2001); Regulations on the Procedure for Formulating Departmental Regulations (2001).
April 28, 2001	Trust Law passed	
July 1, 2001	Jiang Zemin announces that private entrepreneurs can become party members	Questionable results. So far entrepreneur members seem to have been Party officials first, who then went into business. As far as is known, there are relatively few entrepreneurs who then become Party members.
November 26, 2001	Antidumping Regulations and Antisubsidy Regulations passed	These regulations were designed to fit WTO requirements.
December 11, 2001	China joins WTO	
August 27, 2003	Administrative Licensing Law passed	Established the principle that licensing of business activities should be justified only by public necessity.
March 14, 2004	Constitution amended to specify that compensation must be paid for expropriation of land and other property; also provides further sanction for nonstate economy	Article 11 was revised yet again to include the term "nonpublicly owned economy" and to provide that the nonstate sector was not only permitted, but encouraged. Further rhetorical protection for private property was provided.

1978–1984

Economic reform and concomitant legal reform began with the watershed Third Plenum of the Eleventh Central Committee of the Communist Party of China, which officially jettisoned class struggle as the main task of the Party and embraced the goal of economic development. The first stage, from late 1978 until about 1984, saw the effort to introduce efficiency-enhancing incentives to the rural sector in the form of the household responsibility system in agriculture and to rationalize the state sector so that planning of industry and commerce could work better. Neither of these changes, however, took the form of laws; the major rural reforms, for example, took the form of a series of Communist Party Central Committee and State Council documents. By contrast, foreign investment was officially sanctioned with the adoption of the Law on Sino-Foreign Equity Joint Ventures in 1979, but the policy behind this law marked only a very modest liberalization. Chinese parties to such joint ventures were contemplated to be SOEs – individuals were not allowed to be parties at all – and the state attempted to keep such joint ventures, and their foreign investors, within a special legal regime that was segregated from the domestic system.

This first stage of reform created a small but significant opening for the non-state sector outside of agriculture. Nonstate enterprises with public investment such as township and village enterprises (TVEs) (formerly commune and brigade enterprises) were successful in the early reform period in part because they were unconstrained by formal plan obligations and yet were partially integrated into the planned economy and had politically acceptable collective status. The State Council issued a major document in 1979 affirming the significance of TVEs and calling for their continued rapid development (State Council, 1979); subsequent documents called for the closer integration of TVEs into the state planning system (CCP Central Committee and State Council, 1984). Although the first draft of the Law on Township and Village Enterprises was circulated in 1984, it was not to be passed by the NPC until 1996 (*Township and Village Enterprise Yearbook*, 1997, p. 87).

In 1981, the State Council established provisions governing private investment in the form of individual household firms (*getihu*) in cities and towns, limiting the number of employees to seven (State Council, 1981). The 1982 Constitution declared that the basis of China's economic system was socialist public ownership of the means of production and that the state sector was to be the leading sector in the economy. The individual economy was declared to be a "complement" to the socialist public economy. Central Party Document No. 1 of 1983 extended the provisions on the individual economy to rural areas (CCP Central Committee, 1983). This was the most legitimation the private sector received at that time. Neither policy nor law provided an organizational vehicle for larger private enterprises. The only way for such enterprises to exist was as "red-hat" enterprises: businesses formally registered as collective instead of private in exchange for a fee paid to the local government for protection against predation and to qualify for various benefits available only to the public sector.

In the pre-reform planned economy, contracts were simply a means of implementing the plan. Beginning in 1979, the State Administration for Industry and Commerce was established and charged with overseeing economic contracts. In the same year, economic divisions were put in place in the court system to hear economic disputes (Ling, 2002). But the system was still state-centered. The People's Republic of China (PRC)'s first contract law, the Economic Contract Law (ECL) of 1981, perpetuated into the reform era the Soviet concept of economic contract – primarily a means of implementing the plan. Its terms applied only to contracts between "legal persons" (i.e., enterprises and organizations) and excluded individuals from its ambit. The intent of the law was that only enterprises "subject to state control could enter into meaningful economic activity" (Potter, 1992, p. 32). There was to be no contract law covering individuals until 1986.

1985–1989
The second stage of reform, from 1985 until 1989, saw the abandonment of the effort to make the planning system work better and marked an open embrace of the principle of market allocation. This was perhaps best symbolized by the adoption in 1986 of the GPCL. The GPCL are modeled on the German Civil Code and contemplate a universe of equal actors, forming and altering legal relationships by acts of free will. This is a very different universe from that of the planned socialist economy (Jones, 1987). The other major legal contribution to marketization lay in the 1988 amendment of the constitution that legitimized land leasing. In giving legal sanction to the granting and subsequent transfer of long-term leases, this amendment was a key step in the commodification of land, making land use more subject to market forces and less subject to bureaucratic priorities.

The status of the private sector was enhanced during this second stage of reform. Whereas the 1982 Constitution had recognized only the individual sector, the Thirteenth Congress of the Chinese Communist Party in 1987 recognized more generally the private sector as a necessary supplement to the state sector. The constitution was amended in 1988 to reflect this change, and the State Council passed the Provisional Regulations on Private Enterprises later the same year. These regulations, still in effect today, legitimize sole proprietorships, partnerships, and limited liability companies having eight or more employees.

However, the embrace of the market was by no means unqualified. In recognizing the private sector, the 1988 amendment to the constitution still placed that sector under the "guidance, supervision, and control" of the state. Under the terms of the Provisional Regulations on Private Enterprises, only a limited class of persons is eligible to form such enterprises: farmers, the urban unemployed, retired persons, and so on.[11] The drafters of the regulations, which are still in effect today, apparently contemplated business formation as a supplementary activity for those unconnected to the urban socialist economy, not as a normal part of economic life. Moreover, a "private enterprise" under the 1988 Provisional Regulations remained the sole organizational vehicle available – to the extent it was available – to privately owned limited liability businesses of any size. Although this period saw a significant rise in the number of private businesses, many still preferred to remain "red-hat" enterprises or to adopt alternative organizational forms, such as shareholding cooperative enterprises (*gufen hezuo qiye*), which afforded collective status (Ministry of Agriculture, 1990).

The focus of government lawmaking still remained on the public sector, with the problems of the private sector deemed not really the concern of a major legislative body such as the NPC but rather a technical issue to be handled by administrators at the State Council. The Law on Industrial Enterprises Owned by the Whole People was passed, providing a statute-based organizational form to SOEs. As SOEs had of course existed prior to the passage of this law, the real change was in implementation of the idea that business organization should be governed by NPC-level statutes. The Enterprise Bankruptcy Law (passed in 1986 but not in effect until 1988) was mostly a procedure for closing down SOEs (as opposed to one for dealing with the effects of insolvency): losses due to bad management, not adverse changes in the market, were to be the basis for closure. In a similar vein, while the basic elements of the legal regime for foreign trade and investment regime were completed in this period, there was no change in the basic principle of keeping foreigners in a separate legal regime. This principle was reflected in the passage of the Foreign Economic Contract Law, the Law on Wholly Foreign-Owned Enterprises, and the Sino-Foreign Cooperative Joint Venture Law.

The period closed with the passage of the Administrative Litigation Law. This law was of great symbolic importance, since it enshrined the principle that the acts of government agencies had to have a legal basis, and that if challenged by citizens aggrieved by a specific administrative act, such agencies would be required to show that legal basis. The law did not, however, cover the rulemaking process itself, which has remained above citizen challenge.

1989–1992

The third period of the reform era was the brief interlude between the June 4, 1989, crackdown and Deng Xiaoping's "Southern Tour" (*nanxun*) in early 1992. This period saw a brief attempt by the leadership under Li Peng to roll back reform, recentralize, and strengthen central planning, but the logic of reform soon reasserted itself. As early as 1990, for example, the Provisional Regulations on the Grant

---

[11] It should be noted that many cities have over the years passed their own regulations on private enterprises that are less restrictive. Such local regulations in practice provide reasonably sufficient security for entrepreneurs despite whatever the national regulations might say.

and Transfer of Use Rights in Urban Land provided concrete procedures for the commodification and leasing of urban land.

1992–present

What might be called the beginning of the fourth and current stage of reform was marked by Deng Xiaoping's famous Southern Tour in January 1992, during which he gave speeches supporting economic reform. The next decade saw a series of measures successively expressing greater acceptance of the market. The Fourteenth Congress of the Chinese Communist Party in 1992 endorsed the "socialist market economy" as the goal of reform, and the constitution was amended in 1993 to replace a reference to "economic planning on the basis of socialist public ownership," with a reference to "the socialist market economy." Here again, law followed rather than led the market. In 1996, the NPC passed the law on TVEs, just as this sector began to face significant competition from private firms.

By 1997, the Communist Party was ready at its fifteenth congress to recognize the private sector as an "important" (not just supplemental) component of the economy; amendments to the constitution in 1999 did the same, pronouncing a blessing on "diverse sectors" of the economy. Another amendment sanctioned "a variety of modes of distribution" in addition to distribution according to work, meaning that interest and dividends were now recognized as fully legitimate. In 2001, Jiang Zemin announced that private entrepreneurs could become Party members. Further constitutional amendments in 2004 provided that the "nonpublicly owned" sector was not only permitted but encouraged, and gave more rhetorical protection to private property.

The same period saw the construction of the legal infrastructure of a rule-based market system, in which distinctions between state and nonstate actors, as well as between Chinese and foreign actors, were gradually eroded. A much fuller range of vehicles for business organization became available to both public and private investors. In 1992, the State Commission on Reform of the Economic System promulgated a proto-Company Law in the form of two "normative opinions" on joint-stock companies and limited liability companies, and these vehicles were formalized in the Company Law passed the following year (Company Law, 1993). While the business vehicles of the Company Law were largely designed for restructuring SOEs, they were also intended to be used by private businesses. Changes in China's foreign investment regime have gradually opened up these business forms to foreign investors, who are no longer confined to joint ventures and wholly foreign-owned enterprises. Regulations on stock issuance and trading were promulgated in 1993, followed by the higher-status Securities Law in 1998. A Partnership Law was also passed in 1997, providing an additional vehicle for small businesses, as did the 1999 Law on Individual Wholly Owned Enterprises, although neither law provided limited liability for investors.

The legal regime governing business organization was substantially revised in the middle of the current decade. Both the Company Law and the Securities Law were substantially revised in October 2005, as were the Partnership Law and the Bankruptcy Law in August 2006.

Several laws governing market behavior were also passed. The Law against Unfair Competition of 1993 was followed in 1997 by the Price Law, which established the principle that the great majority of prices should be set by the market while still containing provisions designed to control prices deemed excessively high or excessively low. The ECL was amended in 1993 to cover almost all domestic contracting parties except individuals. Essentially any properly registered and licensed business entity could now enter into legal contracts. The Economic Contract Law, together with the Foreign Economic Contract Law, was replaced in 1999 by a unified Contract Law, designed to cover contracts by individuals and enterprises alike, regardless of ownership or nationality.

A series of laws and regulations marked China's increasing integration into the world trading system. The Foreign Trade Law of 1994, while specifically prohibiting natural persons from engaging in trade, provided a default rule that any good was tradable unless regulations provided otherwise. It authorized various restrictions on imports and exports, some compatible with the General Agreement on Tariffs and Trade (GATT) and some not. That law also provided in principle for antidumping and countervailing duties procedures, which were given concrete form for the first time in the 1997 Antidumping and Antisubsidy Regulations. These were revised for World Trade Organization (WTO) compatibility and reissued in 2001. China's full engagement with the world trading system was, of course, symbolized by its formal accession to the WTO in December 2001. Although some analysts have viewed WTO accession as the start of a new stage in China's economic reform process, it is better seen less as a driver of further reform than as a manifestation of the stage reached by China's ongoing reform process.

Finally, the current reform era has seen the passage of legislation regularizing the operation of the legal system itself, again with generally market-friendly results. In 1999, the constitution was amended to give formal recognition to the value of the legal system in governance. The years 2000 and 2001 saw the passage of the Law on Legislation and two regulations on the procedure for formulating administrative regulations at various levels of government. In 2003, the Administrative Licensing Law was passed, which established the principle that licensing schemes could be imposed only for reasons of public necessity. As with many other statutes, the principles set out in this law may not be readily enforceable to the benefit of business operators, but they represent a policy orientation and discourse that may be expected to work its way gradually into governmental practice.

The Formal Legal System Today and Its Problems

Enormous changes have occurred in the role envisioned for law in the economy: contrast the measures discussed in the previous paragraphs with the baseline from which the legal system began at the time of the Third Plenum of the Eleventh

Central Committee in 1978. At that time, the NPC and its local counterparts played a very small role in rulemaking. The vast majority of the rules that counted were made by the central Party apparatus or the State Council and its ministries and commissions and were of limited effect outside the bureaucratic reach of the body that promulgated them. Since 1979, a mountain of laws and regulations has been enacted at the central and local levels (Pei, 2001).

In the planned economy, legal institutions were not needed to resolve disputes. The role of the courts in 1978 was largely to carry out sentencing in criminal matters and to handle disputes involving individual citizens in civil matters. Economic change and legislation has vastly expanded the set of activities over which courts have jurisdiction, and as is documented in later sections of the chapter, businesses are going to the courts in increasing numbers.

Despite considerable legislative activity, significant gaps have persisted in China's legal structure governing economic activity. China long lacked a systematic statement of the law of property – that is, the law governing rights of ownership as opposed to rights of contract. Promulgation of such a law was delayed for years because of the sensitive political questions involved; for example, how farmers' rights over "contracted" land should be characterized and what remedies would be available against state infringements of property. This lacuna was filled only in March 2007 with the passage of the Property Law (2007). Another important item of legislation that has been delayed for years is the Antimonopoly Law. At the time of the writing of this chapter, a final version seems close, but the issue of state monopolies has proved difficult to resolve. Finally, and especially significant given the pervasiveness and importance of administrative regulations, which in practice often trump NPC legislation, a law on administrative procedure still seems far away. China currently has a law governing citizen litigation against administrative agencies (the Administrative Litigation Law) that allows challenges for the misapplication of administrative rules. It does not, however, have a law requiring such things as notice to affected parties and hearings when administrative rules are being drafted, and there is no procedure for challenging the rules themselves in court.

Crucially, the system lacks a number of institutional features that could be effective in identifying and reducing the inevitable gaps and ambiguities that occur in any legal system. On the level of substantive law, there is no good system for authoritatively resolving conflicts between different rules. Although both the constitution and the Law on Legislation prescribe a hierarchy, regulations promulgated by lower levels of government seem often in practice to trump theoretically superior regulations promulgated by higher levels. Long-term land leasing, for example, was first permitted under local rules in Shenzhen at a time when it was forbidden by national statute and the constitution.[12] The mechanisms provided by

---

[12] There are many other examples too numerous to mention. In the late 1990s, the State Council issued documents essentially stripping secured creditors of their rights under the Security Law in certain circumstances, despite dubious legal authority to do so in the technical sense (Clarke, 1997). The Seed Law case, discussed elsewhere in this chapter, is another example.

statute for resolving conflicts – a report to the appropriate legislative or government body followed by action by that body – have not worked in practice. The mechanism that would advance legal development best – allowing courts, in specific disputes, to acknowledge the conflict and resolve it one way or the other – is not permitted.[13]

This lacuna is doubly important because of the bewildering array of bodies that have the right or the practical power to make rules of varying degrees of binding effect. The formal lawmaking structure of the Chinese legal system is set forth primarily in the constitution (1982), the Law on Legislation (2000), and the State Council's Regulations on the Procedure for the Enactment of Administrative Regulations (State Council, 2001). The NPC and its Standing Committee stand at the apex of the system. Both have the power to pass statutes (*falü*), which are more authoritative than any kind of rule other than the constitution.[14] The constitution and certain statutes themselves reserve certain exercises of state power (such as the deprivation of personal freedom) to those that are authorized by statute; institutions such as the State Council or local governments, for example, have no formal power in such cases. The State Council may enact what are called "administrative regulations" (*xingzheng fagui*) in furtherance of constitutional and legislative objectives. People's Congresses at the provincial level, as well as in certain large cities, may enact "local regulations" (*difangxing fagui*) to govern local issues. All the preceding enactments have the formal status of law within the Chinese legal system and are, at least in theory, enforceable by courts (Keller, 1994; Peerenboom, 2002; Chen, 2004). Even more problematic are rules enacted by ministries of the State Council and by local governments, generally known as *guizhang* and labeled "tertiary" rules by Keller (1994), which are not generally enforceable by courts[15] but which can substantially alter the rights of individuals and could well be appealed to by one party in private litigation against another (see the discussion later in "Are Property Rights Secure? Do They Matter?").

In all cases, the constitution and relevant statutes are clear that rules of lower status must yield before rules of higher status. The problem is that there is no

---

[13] See the discussion of the Seed Law case elsewhere in this chapter.

[14] In practice, the constitution has marginal status as a strictly *legal* document. Institutions of legal interpretation and enforcement such as courts would not give priority to a constitutional rule over a clearly conflicting statutory rule.

[15] However, in administrative litigation cases courts may "refer" to tertiary rules where they do not clearly conflict with higher-level rules (Administrative Litigation Law, 1989). In Chinese legal discourse, for a court to decide "with reference to" some rule is different from its deciding "according to" some rule; the former rule is thought of as somewhat less authoritative. As a practical matter, the distinction seems to boil down to the court's having more discretion to ignore the former kind of rule. At the same time, however, a court's decision whether to apply a certain rule is supposed itself to be rule based. Here, we can only note, and not solve, this conundrum. For more on the theory and practice of "with reference to," see Wu (2003) and Zou and Zhang (2003).

effective system either for enforcing jurisdictional and subject-matter limitations on any particular body's lawmaking power or for resolving the conflicts that must invariably arise. Various bodies such as the NPC, its Standing Committee, and the State Council may review and invalidate legislation passed by lower-level bodies. To date, however, the NPC Standing Committee is not known to have overturned a single administrative or local regulation (Chen, 2004, p. 114).

The institution that would appear ideally suited to examine conflicting rules and overambitious claims of jurisdiction in concrete situations, the court system, is unsuited for the task. Although Chinese courts are to prefer a higher-level rule over a conflicting lower-level one, they are at the same time prohibited from invalidating legislation. This prohibition is generally (but not unanimously) interpreted to mean that courts must in practice uphold conflicting lower-level rules, at least when they issue from the level of government that controls the court in question. In short, courts must either seek a resolution of the conflict from a higher-level *legislative* body or rule in accordance with the *lower*-level rule. This principle works against unity within the legal system.[16]

An important feature of the Chinese judicial system that works against unity and consistent enforcement is the dependence of courts on local government. The power of appointment and dismissal of a court's leadership rests formally with the People's Congress at the same administrative level; in practice, it is in the hands of the local Communist Party organizational department. Local governments also control court finances, material supplies, and other welfare benefits for court officials and their families. Thus, it is very difficult for courts to go against the wishes of local government even should they wish to do so.[17]

In fact, courts are recognizably the same institution they were at the outset of reform. Courts are a key institution in turning the law into social reality, but they remain weak and have low status in the political system. The general level of legal training of judges remains low, although it is significantly higher than before in

---

[16] In a recent case, a judge in Luoyang in Henan Province, faced with provisions of a regulation passed by the Henan Provincial People's Congress that conflicted with the national Seed Law, ruled the provincial regulation invalid on the grounds that it conflicted with a higher law. The ruling elicited a major controversy, with the Henan People's Congress Standing Committee issuing a notice claiming that the ruling was an "illegal review of the local regulation in nature and encroachment on the functions of the legislative body" (Meng, 2003). Contemporary commentary suggests that the judge might have avoided much of the controversy by simply ruling in accordance with the national Seed Law, while taking no stand on the validity of – indeed, perhaps not even mentioning – the provincial regulation (see Guo, 2003 (overview); He, 2003 (commentary by Beijing University law professor He Weifang); Cai, 2003 (commentary by Beijing University adjunct law professor Cai Dingjian); Han, 2004 (follow-up); Li, 2004 (same)). Indeed, this is exactly what a higher court was subsequently reported to have done (*New York Times*, 2005). But such invalidation by stealth does not contribute to transparency or to a body of practical jurisprudence that would help in resolving future conflicts of law.

[17] Numerous sources discuss this issue. See, for example, Zhang (2003, pp. 80–82) and Peerenboom (2002, pp. 310–312).

large cities (Clarke, 2003a).[18] Very often, other government agencies may ignore courts with impunity, and they remain subject to the general principle that the rank of the chief officer determines the rank of the institution he or she heads. The application of this principle to the court system illustrates vividly the relative importance of the courts in the political structure. Although the president of a court at any given level of government is not technically subordinate to the head of government at the same level and is appointed by the same body as that head, the court president's official rank is typically just below, and not equal to, that of the head of government.

Courts remain not a source of overarching authority, but simply one bureaucracy among many. When the Supreme People's Court issues an instruction to lower courts on matters such as enforcement of judgments where the cooperation of banks is needed, the instruction must be co-signed by the regulator of the banking system (formerly, the People's Bank of China, now the China Banking Regulatory Commission) if it is to have any hope of being effective.[19] Courts have their own particular sphere of competence and jurisdiction, but it cannot be assumed that any particular law contemplates court involvement in case of violation, or that court involvement would be effective even if contemplated.

More broadly, Chinese legislation is often remarkable for its lack of institutional anchoring. Like the policy documents it has come largely to replace, it appears expected to be read as a set of hortatory instructions by those it regulates (and not just their lawyers), and continues, more than a quarter of a century into the reform era, to contain broad statements of policy and legally unenforceable norms. The substantially revised Company Law of 2005, for example, provides more duties for directors and officers than its 1993 predecessor, but little more by way of remedies for shareholders and others injured by a breach of those duties (Company Law, 2005).

The fundamental view of the state and its officials toward the legal system remains much the same as it was: the legal system is a tool of governance and control and is essentially the property of government, not the citizenry. This view is manifested most prominently in the principle that the operation of the legal system should be secret unless (and sometimes even although) specific rules provide otherwise.[20] Its

---

[18] For an argument that in many courts, especially in rural areas, the importance of formal legal training is vastly overestimated, see Su (2000).

[19] For an extreme example of the need for cosignatures, see People's Bank of China, Supreme People's Court, Supreme People's Procuracy, Ministry of Public Security, Ministry of Justice (1980).

[20] There is no principle of open access to court documents. In most courts it would be difficult for a Chinese, and impossible for a foreigner, to arrive unannounced and ask to sit in on a trial in progress. Although company registration records are supposed to be public, in practice the State Administration of Industry and Commerce will permit only licensed lawyers to review them. And law firm personnel seeking clarification of regulatory issues from government departments – attempting to assist their clients in following the law – must pretend to be calling from a regulated firm, as officials seem to view such efforts by law firms as illegitimate attempts to get free information.

institutions remain government-driven, and not citizen-driven or litigant-driven. Whether and to what degree legal institutions will be used to resolve problems is, to a greater degree than in many other jurisdictions, a government decision. Therefore, the system has limited potential for incorporating and making good use of information from diverse sources to identify and resolve problems.

On the rule-making side, legislative and regulatory drafting remains a secretive process. The bureaucracy in charge of drafting any particular piece of legislation may release draft versions to selected audiences for comment if it so chooses, but there is no general obligation to do so. As a result, avoidable problems can continue uncorrected. On the rule-implementation side, the state remains highly nervous about excessive citizen litigation. Thus, many ostensibly mandatory norms in legislation can be enforced only, if at all, through action by the appropriate governmental agency, and do not confer a private right of action. Even in places where a private right of action might seem to be conferred by law, as for example in suits for misleading disclosures under the Securities Law, the state in the form of the Supreme People's Court has stepped in to impose a nonstatutory requirement that all private suits be preceded by an adverse finding against the defendant in administrative or criminal proceedings (Supreme People's Court, 2003).

Lastly, corruption is an endemic problem in the Chinese legal system (Lubman, 1999; Gong, 2004). With the courts viewed as one bureaucracy among many, very much a part of the political system, and subject to the dictates of local authorities, there is little opportunity for judges to implement a set of ethics that stands above those of the society in general. An independent self-governing bar does not exist. As a result, it is commonly assumed that corruption is growing, with media reports reflecting a large variety of criminal violations of judicial ethics (Gong, 2004, p. 34).

Corruption is hardly unknown, however, in many countries that are at China's stage of development, and it is worthwhile reflecting on whether corruption in the legal system is a particular problem in China. The best evidence on this, although subject to many flaws, is from cross-country surveys. The World Business Environment Survey, conducted by the World Bank (n.d.), collected information on more than 10,000 firms in eighty countries during 1999–2000. One question asked, "In resolving business disputes, [do] you believe your country's court system to be honest/uncorrupt?" and allowed respondents to choose on a six-point scale. According to the respondents, China has less legal corruption than countries at similar levels of per capita income. Moreover, comparing data from a variety of surveys, there is no evidence suggesting that China's legal system is particularly corrupt, compared with other Chinese institutions.

The Future

Barring a political earthquake, the process of coevolution described in the preceding sections is likely to continue, with greater space for individual choice and market relationships, as opposed to state prescription. For example, we expect the

Company Law to move in the direction of being largely a set of default rules that parties may modify if they wish – a trend clearly evident in the 2005 revisions – and the Securities Law to increase its emphasis on disclosure instead of attempting to guarantee the investment quality of securities. Legal distinctions between individual and corporate economic actors, as well as between domestic and foreign economic actors, are also likely to decrease. On the institutional front, dramatic developments are unlikely. While the technical quality of legislation is likely to improve, there is little prospect of an early solution to the problem of conflicting laws and regulations. And while the experience of Meiji Japan demonstrates that a competent, professional, and reasonably independent judiciary is not incompatible with a highly authoritarian state (Teters, 1971), it is hard to see such a judiciary emerging in China soon.

Some scholars see in China's entry into the WTO a major spur for further legal development. In our view, however, WTO membership by itself – as distinct from ongoing economic reforms of which WTO accession was a part – will have a relatively modest effect on the domestic legal system. The WTO does not mandate a perfect legal system, or even a basically fair one, outside of a few specific areas. The only WTO agreement that comes close to a general requirement of fairness in the operation of the legal system is the Trade-Related Aspects of Intellectual Property Rights (TRIPS) Agreement. This agreement does indeed set forth a number of requirements for fair judicial proceedings for the protection of intellectual property rights (arts. 41–50). However, it is worth noting that article 41.5 specifically states,

> [T]his Part [III] does not create any obligation to put in place a judicial system for the enforcement of intellectual property rights distinct from that for the enforcement of law in general, nor does it affect the capacity of Members to enforce their law in general.

It is hard to see a strong mandate here for institutional reforms.[21]

Other WTO agreements such as the GATT and the General Agreement on Trade in Services (GATS) also have provisions spelling out transparency requirements, but once again the obligation is limited. Article X of the GATT contains requirements respecting transparency and the impartial administration of law, but these apply only to a limited subset of China's laws: those affecting international trade in goods. Similarly, the corresponding provision of the GATS applies only to scheduled sectors – those that China has agreed to open up at least partially. In short, there is no general obligation under the WTO agreements to have a fair and well-functioning legal system.

---

[21] Moreover, the TRIPS Agreement's obligations apply only to proceedings for the protection of intellectual property rights. These are a small part of the legal system's activity. Indeed, the very fact that the requirements of Part III are specifically listed in the TRIPS Agreement suggests that those requirements do not apply to the other WTO agreements and do not attach to WTO membership generally; they could almost be read as a list of features a country's judicial system does *not* need to have outside the realm of intellectual property.

ARE PROPERTY RIGHTS SECURE? DO THEY MATTER?

The developments in the legal system have been profound. But this is not the same as saying that they can account for the astounding economic growth of the reform era. Therefore, we now return to the basic question with which we opened this chapter: that of the relationship between the legal system and economic performance. At one level, the answer to the question is transparent from the chronology given earlier. China experienced very rapid growth throughout its reform period, but it was only in the 1990s that legal developments began to catch up with changes in the way that the economy was functioning and in the roles that economic agents were defining for themselves. Indeed, "The Development of Law during the Era of Economic Reform" contains more evidence for the proposition that economic change spurred legal change than for the opposite relation.

Certainly, as a careful reading of "The Development of Law during the Era of Economic Reform" makes clear, the Chinese legal system does not provide a secure system of property rights. Secure legal rights cannot exist when there is a bewildering array of bodies that have the right or the practical power to make overlapping rules of varying degrees of binding effect and no authoritative body to resolve conflicts. Indeed, the rules enacted by ministries of the State Council and by local governments, while officially inferior to higher-level rules, can affect "rights" considerably. For example, in the mid-1990s, the State Council enacted regulations that effectively negated creditor rights established by the Security Law, the Bankruptcy Law, and the Civil Procedure Law (Clarke, 1997). Similarly, in 2001, the Beijing municipal government issued regulations on limited partnerships that if effective would reverse rules on liability appearing in central-level statutes such as the General Principles of Civil Law (1986) and the Contract Law (1999).[22] Such examples are inconsistent with the type of property rights envisaged by those who draw a close connection between growth and legal rights.

Nor can rights be said to be secured by law when the legislation in many cases does not say what is to happen if a particular norm is violated. The point is important because it means that the impressive volume of legislation discussed earlier does not necessarily correspond to an increased volume of legal rights, that is, the power of nonstate actors to put the coercive machinery of the state in motion in the service of their interests.[23]

Nor are rights secured by law when the legal system is unable to resolve conflicts between the rights bestowed by different levels and different arms of government. As made clear in "The Development of Law during the Era of Economic Reform,"

---

[22] These were regulations providing governance and liability rules for limited partnerships established in the Zhongguancun area of Beijing (Beijing Municipal People's Congress, 2000; Beijing Municipal Government, 2001).

[23] For example, see the discussion in the section "The Development of Law during the Era of Economic Reform" of the revised Company Law of 2005, which provides few remedies for shareholders injured by a breach of the law by company directors.

the courts are usually beholden to local politicians and have low status in the political system; often other government agencies can ignore them with impunity. The possibility of court involvement cannot be generally assumed when a law is violated, and even if the courts became involved, their effectiveness is highly uncertain. Thus, the courts in China do not play the role, nor do they have the power, that would be consonant with a legal regime that provided secure property rights, and there are no other governmental bodies that seem capable of playing this role.

In sum, the experience of the reform era in China seems to refute the proposition that a necessary condition for growth is that the legal system provide secure property and contract rights. Given the centrality of security of property and contract in current thinking on the determinants of economic growth, the obvious next question to ask is where such security could have come from, if not from the legal system. It could be that although courts and other formal legal institutions do not effectively enforce rights, security of property and contract is provided somewhere else in the system through some other mechanism. In "Transactions in Goods and Services," we consider the many mechanisms for the vindication of claims arising out of contractual relationships both within and beyond the court system – for example, social or business networks. In the remainder of this section, we focus on property. We argue that the political structure itself has served as an alternative to the formal legal system in providing a reasonable degree of security to certain nonstate investors at the local level.

The notion of a political guarantee for property rights rests on an analysis of the interests of local officials who are part of the state administrative hierarchy. The interests guiding the actions of these officials are shaped by the incentives and constraints contained in the institutional environment. Local officials in reform-era China share an interest in promoting economic development. This interest stems from two noteworthy features of the institutional environment. The first is the cadre evaluation system that sets criteria for and monitors the performance of leading officials in the Party and government; these criteria are one important factor shaping officials' opportunities for advancement as well as their remuneration. Several research findings support the view that officials in the state administrative hierarchy seek to maintain their positions of power and advance within the system.[24] The second institutional feature shaping cadres' orientation toward economic development is the fiscal system. The fiscal contracting system in place until 1994 (the *caizheng baoganzhi*) featured high marginal revenue retention rates for local governments that encouraged local officials to promote economic activity within their jurisdictions. The fiscal contracting system was replaced in 1994 by a

[24] There is significant empirical support for this view (see Huang, 1990; Rozelle, 1994; Whiting, 2001). At the same time, however, to the extent that a career in the state apparatus ceases to offer professional rewards in some way commensurate with rewards in the private sector, officials may increasingly give priority to personal goals over officially defined goals.

tax-sharing system (*fen shui zhi*) that centralized control over revenue and increased intergovernmental fiscal transfers but that left local governments without adequate revenue to perform all the functions assigned to them (see Chapter 12).

The cadre evaluation system, which has been refined and developed since the early years of the reform era, sets specific performance criteria (*kaohe zhibiao*) across a range of policy arenas.[25] While criteria vary across jurisdictions, the most heavily weighted performance criteria typically focus on promoting economic growth and particularly since 1994, when the tax assignment system (*fenshuizhi*) was put into place, targets for the collection of particular tax revenues. Other critical targets focus on maintaining public order, which has often interpreted by local officials as a mandate for generating employment opportunities, and on the provision of merit and public goods, such as primary education and basic infrastructure. Targets are often in effect unfunded mandates, a fact that reinforces the incentives contained in the fiscal system to promote the development of revenue sources at the local level.

During the early years of reform, choices of local officials about how to promote economic growth and employment to meet performance criteria and generate revenue were constrained by the nature of available resources and the broader political environment. Under the fiscal contracting system (*caizheng baoganzhi*), local governments were largely dependent on locally generated revenues and sought, other things being equal, to promote public-sector industrial enterprises from which they could more readily extract tax revenue as well as numerous fees and profit remittances, which were retained at the local level (Whiting, 2001). In areas with a significant legacy of state investment, therefore, local officials often sought to develop and protect local public firms – collectively owned TVEs – by channeling loan capital to them via the state-run banking system and refusing to license private firms. In most cases, cadres acting as representatives of local governments effectively exercised property rights over these firms, including the rights to make decisions about operations and personnel, to control residual income, and to dispose of assets. In areas with little legacy of state investment, by contrast, some local officials actively courted private investment, from which they could extract tax and fee revenue, thereby developing an interest in protecting private property rights. Thus, private investors could find certain jurisdictions in which local officials allowed them to gain a foothold in the local economy and exercise effective property rights over their assets, including the rights to make decisions about operations and personnel as well as to control residual income and dispose of assets. This framework explains the emergence and early growth of both the collective and private variants of the TVE sector in the first decade and a half of reform.

Both the local officials who sought to promote private investment and the private investors who sought guarantees of their claims were constrained by the larger

---

[25] See, for example, CCP Central Committee Organization Department (1979). More recently, see State Council (2000).

political environment, which for the first decade or more of reform sought to delegitimize private domestic investment and control foreign investment. However, the success of private and foreign investment in generating employment and, to a lesser extent, fiscal revenue at the local level eventually influenced the trends in national legislation documented in "The Development of Law during the Era of Economic Reform." Once the broader political environment began to tolerate competition from the private sector, nonstate investment began to step beyond its initial foothold.

Given the conclusion that local officials had an interest in providing security for decentralized property rights, one must ask why China's leaders chose to develop a system that created those interests. Certainly, there are many cases of autocratic governments that did not make this choice, but rather used the levers of power for the purposes of predation and corruption. The answer to this question remains largely beyond the scope of this chapter. The fact is that China's leaders did want to pursue economic growth. Given this objective, if a government is not constrained by the legal system, it must find an alternative mechanism for guaranteeing some form of property rights. Che and Qian (1998) interpret local government ownership of TVEs as such a mechanism.[26] In their formal model, the central government finds that surrendering property rights to the local authorities is better than centralizing or privatizing them. Total revenues flowing to the central government can actually increase when the center surrenders its property rights. This can account for the observation that the property rights of local levels of government have been quite robust against possible infringements by superior levels of government.

The argument therefore is that although there was little capability within the legal system for defining and protecting anybody's property rights in the early years of reform, the political–economic equilibrium was such that one set of actors, local government officials, could exercise property rights directly or bestow them on a specific set of investors within their own jurisdictions. This reasoning is consistent with a current trend in the economics literature, which emphasizes that successful developing countries are able to find some way to generate functional substitutes for the formal institutions that receive so much attention in the analysis of developed countries.

While the incentive structure for local officials led them to create various opportunities for investment in rural industry, the same incentive structure had the effect of reducing the security of land tenure for farm households in many locales. As Brandt, Rozelle, and Turner (2004) point out, local officials are responsible for promoting farm output growth and for ensuring the fulfillment of in-kind quotas.

---

[26] Jin and Qian (1998) explore this and other hypotheses on the TVEs in an empirical context. Their results are consistent with the Che-Qian theory, showing TVEs are more common where property rights are less secure and where the local governments provide more services. Their results suggest that private enterprises are more productive than TVEs, where they can function on an equal footing, but were less common because of the disadvantages of private enterprises in the institutional setting of the 1980s and the early 1990s.

These pressures, along with opportunities for rent seeking, have resulted – in certain places – in repeated administrative reallocations, despite government policy that ostensibly guarantees farm households the right to use the land for at least fifteen years. Markets for land rental and farm labor are thin, and therefore, with changes in family structure and outside labor opportunities, a rigid allocation of land to families would lead to accumulating inefficiencies. Village leaders appear to have had efficiency considerations very much in mind when making (the quite frequent) reallocations of land among villagers. Efficiency considerations dominate equity concerns. Political administration of land allocation appears to be a substitute for a well-functioning system of property rights and markets, which at this stage in China is not a viable alternative. This conclusion is consistent with observations made both above and below: that mechanisms existed in China that substituted for the formal market-aiding legal institutions that are the focus of the rights hypothesis.

In sum, our tentative conclusion is that passably secure property rights might have provided a basis for China's economic growth during the first two decades of reform, but the legal system probably had little to do with the creation and enforcement of these rights. The rights were a product of the political–economic equilibrium, in which important ingredients were the central government's transparent desire for a growing economy rather than class struggle, and decentralization, which was a natural product of both China's size and the events in the decades before reform. Our tentative conclusion is the one that is most clearly supported given both current thinking about the relationship between property rights and growth and our analysis of the legal system. However, our analysis is much less applicable to the current decade, where privatization and the continuing growth of the private sector have made the property rights of local governments less relevant. This highlights the importance of continuing research into the basis of the apparent relative security of property in China, which the continuing developments in the legal system cannot fully explain.

TRANSACTIONS IN GOODS AND SERVICES

In discussions of the institutional bases of economic success, it is standard to highlight two fundamental sets of rights, property and contract. One basis for distinguishing between these two is the differing availability of substitutes for the formal or governmental mechanisms that could produce such rights.[27] Effective property rights must reflect governmental behavior in some way: how can one

---

[27] This intuition finds empirical support in a recent paper by Acemoglu and Johnson (2005), who unbundle "institutions" into institutions that support contract rights and institutions that support property rights. Their ultimate finding is that while contracting institutions do affect some things such as the form of financial intermediation, it is property rights institutions that matter for investment and long-run economic growth.

protect one's self informally from a predatory government? However, there are many effective private mechanisms in the realm of contract: informal and social sanctions, trusted middlemen, networks, reputation (in a repeated-game context), and self-enforcement arrangements such as informal collateral. Thus, in examining the mechanisms that support agreements for the exchange of goods and services, the essential task is to understand the contribution of law relative to these substitutes. Moreover, in transition countries in particular, there is one mechanism that is neither informal nor legal: government bureaucracies can play a large role.

Early Reforms: Incremental Liberalization Supporting Exchange Relationships

The first decade of transition in Eastern Europe and the former Soviet Union (EEFSU) followed a very different path from that of China in the ten years after 1978. In EEFSU, the first few years of transition were characterized by the collapse of the old mechanisms of governance, sometimes deliberately aided by destructive reforms. In China, those old mechanisms were kept largely in place at the beginning of reforms, to wither gradually over the following decades, slowly losing their importance as incremental reforms and economic growth removed their domain and their purpose. Matching this contrast between EEFSU and China was a remarkable difference in economic performance: economic collapse in the first years of transition in the former and spectacular growth in the latter.

A leading candidate to explain the early economic collapse in the EEFSU is the rapid erosion in the authority of existing institutions in a time of liberalization (Murrell, 1992; Blanchard and Kremer, 1997). The idea is straightforward: the old system of economic administration enforced contracts, substituting for institutions that take years to develop in market economies.[28] As new users of industrial inputs emerged, the old mechanisms of enforcement lost their power and new institutions were only in their infancy. Moreover, the binding effects on present agreements of old ties and future opportunities were weakened by the uncertainty created by institutional revolution. Existing suppliers were tempted to break agreements, with reverberations throughout the economy.

In contrast, China began with liberalization at the margin in its dual-track system. Therefore, the old mechanisms of enforcement were automatically applied to old relationships, preventing the type of disruption in supplies that appeared across the whole of EEFSU. New relationships could emerge at the margin, but these were not allowed to undermine the existing flows of inputs between supplier and user. Those new relationships could develop incrementally in a relatively stable

---

[28] These were not contracts in the usual way that we understand them in market economies. They were formulated by the administration and the parties had to accept them, for the most part.

economic environment.[29] Each partner could gradually develop knowledge of the other, generating the experience and the information necessary to secure large-scale, long-term cooperation without recourse to formal institutions. By leaving the bureaucratic methods of enforcing agreements in place for the old patterns of input supplies, the dual-track method of incremental liberalization provided a substitute for more standard institutions that support agreements.[30]

Evolution of Contract Law

The first reform-era laws governing contract – the 1981 Economic Contract Law, the 1985 Foreign Economic Contract Law, and the 1987 Technology Contract Law – had significant flaws when evaluated on the basis of standard criteria: does the legislation create a level playing field for all firms, does it enable parties injured by breaches to enforce the rules and receive compensation, and does it allow nonstate actors to put the coercive machinery of the state in motion in service of their legitimate interests? As "The Development of Law during the Era of Economic Reform" demonstrates, these weaknesses were ameliorated in part by the amendment of the ECL in 1993 and the promulgation in 1999 of a new, unified Contract Law, which was much better suited to a market economy characterized by a diversity of ownership forms.[31]

While prior to the early 1990s political and social substitutes for law created openings for both individuals and private enterprises that were not legal persons to enter into agreements, the absence of a basis in law still hindered the development of the nonstate economy during the first decade of reform (Clarke 1992; Whiting 2001). Although the literature provides only anecdotal and case-study evidence, one can surmise that the private sector might have grown more quickly under a more effective contract regime. Legal obstacles in the ECL were evident even in places like Wenzhou, where the private economy enjoyed strong local political support and extensive social networks. According to an official in Yueqing County, Wenzhou, before the amendment to the ECL in 1993, many firms outside of Wenzhou refused to enter into contracts with private enterprises there (Whiting, 2001). Furthermore, private enterprise owners felt they had no recourse when they encountered contract disputes, since courts were unwilling to recognize their claims. Informal solutions to these contracting problems were vulnerable during

[29] Lau, Qian, and Roland (2000) characterize the efficiency and political economy properties of the dual-track system. The argument here depends not on those properties but simply on the fact that the dual-track system maintained existing relationships.

[30] Li (1999) argues that the dual-track system lessened the effects of the market power of existing producers. This even allows us to view the dual-track system as a substitute for antitrust institutions.

[31] In addition, the new law addressed the inconsistencies and overlapping institutions created or codified by the three initial contract laws and the 1986 General Principles of Civil Law (Ling, 2002).

the 1980s to official crackdowns, like the closure of Wenzhou's informal commodities markets by the State Administration of Industry and Commerce, the state agency responsible for administering economic contracts (Whiting, 2001). Thus, under the ECL, private enterprises functioned only within the interstices, often illegal or only quasilegal, of the planned economy (Zhang and Qin, 1989).

Under the unified Contract Law of 1999, by contrast, natural individuals – not just legal persons – can enter into legally enforceable contracts, and oral contracts have been provided with a firmer statutory footing,[32] significantly expanding the scope of contract. The principle of freedom of contract signals a definitive move away from the planned economy.[33] The law limits the scope of contracts to be monitored by administrative organs; for example, the State Administration of Industry and Commerce is now limited to administrative supervision over illegal acts (Ling, 2002).

These changes eroding the distinctions between state and nonstate actors are clearly reflected in a study of contract disputes in one court in Nanjing from 1999 to 2001.[34] In those cases in which the ownership form is reported, private enterprises are the plaintiffs in 34 percent of the cases and mixed public/private firms are the plaintiffs in another 15 percent. Thus, the records show private enterprises entering into legally enforceable contracts and enjoying recourse to the courts – features of the contract regime that were absent through the early 1990s. The records also show how the law served to foster transactions by recognizing oral contracts. In those cases where it is possible to identify the form of the contract, oral contracts are in dispute in 46 percent of cases. Moreover, reliance on oral contracts does not, in and of itself, appear to unduly prejudice the hearing a plaintiff can receive: the court found for the plaintiff and awarded compensation in 55 percent of the cases involving oral contracts.

Making Agreements

Despite these recent developments, it could be that Contract Law and the courts still play a minor role in underpinning exchange agreements. Scholars working in contexts as diverse as American and Chinese business communities have argued that exchange is anchored predominantly by informal social ties, and not by legal rules

---

[32] Before the Contract Law came into effect, there were a number of cases and judicial interpretations indicating that as long as satisfactory evidence is provided showing the existence of a contract, the contract is enforceable despite the lack of a writing (see, e.g., Supreme People's Court, 1988).

[33] As Ling (2002) indicates, the principle put forward in the Contract Law is "voluntariness," but the "substantive rights recognized under the principle of voluntariness are almost identical to those under the conventional notion of freedom of contract."

[34] The research was conducted by Susan Whiting under the auspices of Hopkins-Nanjing Institute for International Research at Nanjing University in the fall of 2002. It reflects a representative sample ($n = 76$) of purchase and sales contract disputes from 1999 to 2001 gathered from one district court in Nanjing, the capital of Jiangsu Province.

and sanctions (Macaulay, 1963; Landa, 1994). Ultimately, however, the relative importance of formal institutions versus their informal substitutes is an empirical question, on which, unfortunately, only scattered evidence exists anywhere (Hendley and Murrell, 2003). In this and the subsequent section, we review that evidence for China, focusing first on the basis of agreements and then on dispute resolution.

The treatment of relational contracting in Chinese societies focuses on the concept of *guanxi*. As Chung and Hamilton (2001) indicate, "Chinese relational rules personalize transactions, making them part of the interpersonal social matrix of daily life" and "thereby increas[e] the calculability of economic outcomes."[35] In the context of the PRC in particular, the discussion of *guanxi* links not only relations among entrepreneurs but also relations between entrepreneurs and government officials. One explanation of the expansion of economic exchange even preceding significant legal change, then, centers on dense interpersonal networks that extend into the government apparatus. Nee and Su (1996) focus on "long-standing social ties based on frequent face-to-face interactions" as an important basis for trust and cooperation between entrepreneurs and the government. They emphasize that "transaction costs are lower in institutional settings where trust and cooperation flow from informal norms and established social relationships."[36]

Interpersonal networks provide information as well as opportunities to impose sanctions that are important to the establishment of trust. In a similar vein, Lin and Chen (1999) emphasize thick relationships based on familial ties. King (1991) finds that "network building is used (consciously or unconsciously) by Chinese adults as a cultural strategy in mobilizing social resources for goal attainment in various spheres of social life. To a significant degree the cultural dynamic of *guanxi* building is a source of vitality in Chinese society." As this statement suggests, the social network explanation of trust in contractual relations is related to accounts of Chinese culture that emphasize the importance of networks of relations (*guanxi*) as a widespread sociocultural phenomenon (Whiting, 1998).

What do available data tell us about the social basis of contractual relations? Zhou et al. (2003) find that firms rely on a range of search channels to identify contractual partners.[37] Social networks (47.1 percent) and open information sources including advertisements, media, and trade information (47.0 percent) predominate, followed by self-initiative. They find that government sources play a minor role, accounting for only 6.6 percent of search. In a study of firms in Shanghai and Nanjing between 2002 and 2004, Whiting (2005) finds that professional ties predominate over social ones: in identifying suppliers, firms rely on business associates

---

[35] Chung and Hamilton (2001) provide a good review of the massive literature on this topic. With respect to the PRC, see especially Yan (1995), Yang (1994), and Guthrie (1999).

[36] It should be noted, however, that there can be costs to relationships based on informal norms and social relationships (McMillan and Woodruff, 1999; Kali, 2001).

[37] This study is based on a convenience (nonrandom) sampling method and includes 620 firms in Beijing and Guangzhou.

(41.4 percent), trade conferences (12.9 percent), advertising (11.4 percent), self-initiative (10 percent), government (8.6 percent), friends (8.6 percent), and trade associations (5.7 percent).[38] In identifying customers, firms report relying upon business associates (42.9 percent), competitors (21.4 percent), trade conferences (18.6 percent), advertising (14.3 percent), trade associations (11.4 percent), self-initiative, (10 percent), government contacts (10 percent), and contacts through friends (10 percent). Thus, social networks are only one of many search channels for contractual partners.

Moreover, despite the role of social networks, formal, written contract provisions have become the norm: more than 75 percent of firms in the study by Zhou et al. (2003) used such provisions to specify volume, quality, price, deadlines, and contractual safeguards. Written contracts appear even more pervasive in other studies. Whiting finds that firms use written contracts with suppliers in 90.5 percent of cases, while they use written contracts with customers in 98.6 percent of cases. Similarly, a World Bank (2001) study also shows that the use of written contracts is the norm, found in 90.1 percent of contracts with clients and 82.2 percent with suppliers. While Zhou et al. (2003) find that "contracts initiated through social networks have a higher probability of having informal provisions," "network ties play a statistically significant but substantively minor role in the choice of contract forms and provisions."

Dispute Resolution

According to data drawn from the World Bank (2001) survey of 1,500 Chinese firms, in 2000, 31.1 percent of firms had at least one major dispute with clients, while 21.9 percent of firms had at least one major dispute with suppliers.[39] Once enterprises encounter disputes, what mechanisms do they rely upon to resolve them? Theorists from Weber to North emphasize the importance of formal, state-sponsored legal institutions. Yet there is a large literature on contractual relations, spanning cases from the United States to Russia, indicating that contract disputes are often resolved without any recourse, explicit or implicit, to the law. This section examines the dispute resolution mechanisms used by Chinese firms and finds that the courts play a moderately important role in their strategies.

---

[38] This study is based on a survey of contracting and dispute resolution practices administered to seventy-six enterprise managers and owners in Shanghai and Nanjing between 2002 and 2004. The firms were identified through the alumni network of the Nanjing University Business School and the clients of the Economic Legal and Social Consultancy Center of the Shanghai Academy of Social Sciences.

[39] The data set was created from a firm-level survey conducted by the World Bank in 2001. The survey covered 1,500 Chinese firms evenly distributed across five big cities – Beijing, Chengdu, Guangzhou, Shanghai, and Tianjin – and from ten sectors, five in manufacturing and five in services.

Negotiation and Mediation

As in all market economies, negotiation directly between the contracting parties is used extensively for resolving contract disputes in China. In the World Bank (2001) survey, 87.1 percent of firms used negotiation in the final resolution of disputes with at least one client, while 93.2 percent used negotiation in the final resolution of disputes with at least one supplier. In Whiting's study (2005) of Shanghai and Nanjing firms, 92.8 percent of firms typically used direct negotiation in the process of resolving disputes. (The corresponding figures for litigation were 38.8 and 29.8 percent and for arbitration 12.1 and 12.5 percent, reflecting the dual reliance on litigation or arbitration in conjunction with direct negotiation.) That study distinguishes direct negotiation from negotiation using a third party; only 11.8 percent of firms typically turned to a third party.

Self-enforcement, in which two parties bargain to attain a long-term cooperative solution based on the anticipated value of future contracts, is an important mechanism in contractual relations with Chinese firms. In Whiting's study (2005), 90.6 percent of firms reported that in the event of a serious dispute, their *guanxi* (here, the long-term reciprocal relations grounded in social ties) with a supplier or contractor would be broken. Furthermore, reputation also functions within business circles to help police contractual relations. In Shanghai and Nanjing, 74.2 percent of firms said that other businesses would learn about any dispute that arose between the firm and one of its suppliers.

In many economies, trade associations provide transactional services, including dispute resolution. Most trade associations in China are set up by government and mainly perform the function of communicating government policy. In Whiting's study (2005), 67.1 percent of respondents were members of trade associations, yet respondents were very dismissive of them, and virtually no one said that they provided information on creditworthiness (4.3 percent) or contributed to dispute resolution (4.3 percent). In the World Bank study (2001), only 54.5 percent of firms were members of a business association. Of those, only 31.6 percent (17.2 percent of the full sample) agreed that the business association performed the function of "accrediting members to suppliers and customers." And of association members, only 19 percent agreed that the business association performed the function of "helping resolve disputes," which can be viewed as a substitute for transaction-cost–reducing institutions. This was much fewer than those agreeing that business associations represented members' views (46 percent) and stabilized competition (29 percent), which are not normally classified as functions in service of the market.

Arbitration

The Arbitration Law, which provided for the establishment of municipal arbitration commissions, went into effect in 1995; before that year, commercial arbitration functions were handled by local branches of the State Administration of Industry and Commerce. In the first five years following passage of the law,

Table 11.2. *Cases accepted by courts of first instance, 1983–2001*

Year	Economic	Civil	Administrative	Criminal
1983	44,080	756,436		
1984	85,796	838,307		
1985	226,695	846,391		
1986	322,153	989,409		299,720
1987	366,456	1,213,219	5,240	289,614
1988	508,965	1,455,130	8,573	313,306
1989	690,765	1,815,385	9,934	392,564
1990	588,143	1,851,897	13,006	459,656
1991	563,260	1,880,635	25,667	427,840
1992	652,150	1,948,786	27,125	422,991
1993	894,410	2,089,257	27,911	403,267
1994	1,053,701	2,383,764	35,083	482,927
1995	1,278,806	2,718,533	52,596	495,741
1996	1,519,793	3,093,995	79,966	618,826
1997	1,483,356	3,277,572	90,557	436,894
1998	1,455,215	3,375,069	98,463	482,164
1999	1,535,613	3,519,244	97,569	540,008
2000	1,297,843	3,412,259	85,760	560,432
2001	1,155,992	3,459,025	100,921	628,996
Average annual growth (%)	18.8	8.3	21.8	4.7

Sources: Judicial Statistics (2000); *Law Yearbook of China* (various years).

all domestic arbitration commissions accepted only 17,000 cases involving 25 billion yuan (He, 2002). This compares with 1,329,020 strictly economic contract disputes involving 413 billion yuan handled by courts in 1998 alone (Table 11.2). The average value of all arbitration cases is higher than that of litigated cases, however – more than 1.5 million yuan on average (1995–2000), compared with 0.3 million yuan in 1998, the last year for which data on value of litigation are available.

Survey data underscore the relative unimportance of arbitration among domestic Chinese enterprises through the first decades of reform. In the World Bank (2001) survey, of the firms having disputes, only 12 percent used arbitration even once and only 2 percent used it to resolve disputes at least half of the time. In Whiting's (2005) Nanjing/Shanghai survey, some respondents had arbitration clauses in their contracts, but only a few used them. In the Shanghai part of the sample, most respondents (domestic firms) had little awareness or understanding of the potential role for arbitration and perceived it as less authoritative than the courts despite the fact that they could apply for enforcement of arbitral decisions by the courts.

Litigation

Between 1983 and 2001, economic disputes accepted by courts of first instance increased at an average annual rate of 18.8 percent, peaking in 1999 (Table 11.2). Put in wider domestic context, civil disputes increased at less than half that rate on average – 8.3 percent per year over the same period – while the number of criminal cases grew only 4.7 percent per year on average (see Table 11.2). Data for administrative cases are available only for the period 1987–2001, and only administrative cases outpaced the growth of economic dispute cases, increasing at an average annual rate of 21.8 percent from a small base. Thus, the courts appear to play an increasingly significant role during the reform period.

Contract dispute litigation in particular, which accounts for the lion's share of all economic dispute cases accepted by the courts, increased at an average annual rate of 20.1 percent between 1983 and 2001 (see Table 11.3). Data on the average value of disputes are available only through 1998: from 1983 to 1998, the total value of disputes grew 40.9 percent per year on average, while the average value of disputes grew at 11.9 percent per year on average. In China, as elsewhere, litigation of contract disputes is rarely the first resort.[40] Nevertheless, in the World Bank (2001) survey of 1,500 firms in the year 2000, 38.8 percent of firms used litigation in the final resolution of disputes with at least one client, while 29.8 percent used litigation in the final resolution of disputes with at least one supplier.

As with litigation of economic disputes more broadly, litigation of contract disputes peaked in 1999 and has declined since. In interpreting the reasons for the peak and subsequent decline, judges in district and intermediate courts in Shanghai identified several factors operating with a lag. These include the changing prevalence of oral contracts, the tightness of macroeconomic policy, the pace of transition from plan to market, and the pace of transformation of SOEs. Oral contracts are more likely to end up in litigation and may have been more prevalent in the mid-1990s, preceding the active promotion of form contracts by industry associations, for example. Tight macroeconomic policies contributed to a high incidence of nonpayment disputes in the 1990s. The transition from plan to market, most notably in terms of the transformation of small- and medium-sized SOEs, generated a transitory wave of disputes. Indeed, anecdotal evidence suggests that nonpayment disputes may move from negotiation to litigation when new owners repudiate debt.

Judgments and Their Enforcement

Three major trends in the national data (1983–2001) on the disposition of economic contract disputes by the court bear on the issue of enforcement of court judgments[41] (see Table 11.4). First, withdrawals of cases by the plaintiffs have

---

[40] Litigation of contract disputes in the United States commonly involves failed businesses, abandoned product lines, very high stakes, or extreme miscalculations (Keating, 1997).

[41] Note that both court-sponsored mediation and court decisions are enforceable decisions.

Table 11.3. *Economic contract disputes handled by courts of first instance,*
1983–2001

Year	Number of cases accepted	Total value of contracts in dispute (billion yuan)	Average value of contracts in dispute (yuan)	Change in average value (percent)	Change in number of cases accepted (percent)
1983	36,274	1.711	51,541		
1984	69,204	1.497	24,443	−52.6	90.8
1985	206,582	8.978	48,611	98.9	198.5
1986	292,599	7.883	28,144	−42.1	41.6
1987	332,496	8.146	24,552	−12.8	13.6
1988	467,872	11.104	25,033	2.0	40.7
1989	634,941	19.351	31,426	25.5	35.7
1990	543,613	17.313	31,277	−0.5	−14.4
1991	516,507	19.879	37,101	18.6	−5.0
1992	598,610	29.703	49,878	34.4	15.9
1993	824,448	63.422	77,834	56.0	37.7
1994	971,432	97.274	100,875	29.6	17.8
1995	1,184,377	148.308	125,865	24.8	21.9
1996	1,404,921	214.064	153,641	22.1	18.6
1997	1,373,355	263.031	192,336	25.2	−2.2
1998	1,329,020	413.432	310,167	61.3	−3.2
1999	1,410,107	n.a.	n.a.	n.a.	6.1
2000	1,184,613	n.a.	n.a.	n.a.	−16.0
2001	1,062,302	n.a.	n.a.	n.a.	−10.3

Notes: As of 1998, statistics on economic contract disputes accepted by the courts include cases involving foreign entities; as of 1988, statistics on cases involving transport of goods were removed from the larger category of economic contract disputes.

Sources: Judicial Statistics (2000), *Law Yearbook of China* (various years).

increased from approximately 8 percent in the mid-1980s to more than 20 percent in 2001. Interviews with lawyers and enterprise managers suggest that the threat of litigation is just another step in the bargaining process; initiating litigation is one strategy to elicit performance from the contractual partner.

Second, a higher percentage of cases nationwide go all the way to judgment than in the past, increasing from roughly 5 percent in the 1980s to more than 40 percent in 2001. Third, and relatedly, the data show declines in the occurrence of court-mediated settlements from roughly 80 percent of the total in the mid-1980s to 30 percent as of 2001. The decline is significant, since official interference has often been reported to occur most frequently during court-sponsored mediation. According to Potter (1992, p. 99), "[T]he dominance of consensual methods of resolution [including court-sponsored mediation] permitted the personal and organizational relationships of the parties to affect the outcome, thus undermining

Table 11.4. *Disposition of economic contract disputes by courts of first instance,*
1983–2001

Year	Mediated by court	Decided by court	Transferred to relevant bureau	Appeal rejected	Withdrawn	Terminated[a]	Other	TOTAL
1983	79.3	5.5	4.2		8.5	2.4		100
1984	80.6	5.6	3.2		8.7	1.9		100
1985	81.8	5.7	3.1		8.5	0.9		100
1986	79.6	7.5	3.9		8.2	0.8		100
1987	77.3	9.5	2.8		9.6	0.8		100
1988	80.2	8.6	1.9	0.0	8.8	0.5		100
1989	76.8	10.5	2.0	0.0	10.2	0.5		100
1990	69.5	14.7	2.1	0.0	13.0	0.7		100
1991	61.6	20.0	2.2	0.0	14.7	1.5		100
1992	61.7	20.8	1.6	0.5	14.8	0.7		100
1993	63.1	19.5	1.5	0.3	14.9	0.6		100
1994	60.0	20.8	1.5	0.3	16.8	0.6		100
1995	57.7	22.1	1.3	0.3	17.9	0.6		100
1996	53.7	25.5	1.3	0.3	18.4	0.8		100
1997	49.9	29.1	1.5	0.4	18.3	0.8		100
1998	43.2	34.6	1.4	0.6	18.8	0.4	1.0	100
1999	41.3	35.5	0.0	0.8	19.3	0.0	3.1	100
2000	34.6	40.3	0.0	1.3	20.7	0.0	3.2	100
2001	30.8	43.8	0.0	1.4	21.3	0.0	2.7	100

Note: Values are in percent.
[a] An economic contract dispute case would be terminated (*zhongjie*) under article 137 of the Civil Procedure Law when one party died leaving no successor or estate to serve respectively as plaintiff or defendant, thus making further prosecution of the suit impossible.
Sources: Judicial Statistics (2000), *Law Yearbook of China* (various years).

contract autonomy." Interviews with lawyers, judges, and enterprise owners and managers in Shanghai and Nanjing confirm this understanding. Court-sponsored mediation involving government officials occurs most commonly when fulfillment of unpaid contractual obligations may result in layoffs or nonpayment of wages by an enterprise in difficulty. In this situation, judges may proactively invite government officials to participate in court-sponsored mediation, pressuring the plaintiff to accept a smaller or delayed settlement to maintain the work force of the defendant.

Enforcement of judgments is a continuing problem, but this is hardly unique to China. In March 2004, Xiao Yang, president of the China's Supreme People's Court, stated in his work report to the NPC that "[t]he difficulty of executing civil and commercial judgments has become a major 'chronic ailment,' often leading to chaos in the enforcement process; there are few solutions to the problem" (China Law and Governance Review, 2004). According to Ge Xingjun, head of the Supreme

People's Court's Judgment Enforcement Division, approximately 60 percent of civil and economic judgments were enforced at the basic-level court, 50 percent at the intermediate-level court, and 40 percent at the provincial high-level court (China Law and Governance Review, 2004).

In general, inadequate data are available to assess the nature of implementation of judgments (Clarke, 1996), but the Nanjing court sample sheds some light. Of the seventy-six cases in the sample, 29 percent were withdrawn by the plaintiff, court-sponsored mediation occurred in 21 percent of the cases, and cases went to judgment in 47 percent of the cases. The latter two types of cases are subject to enforcement by the courts. Of these, in only 3.8 percent of cases were judgments "automatically" implemented. In 52 percent of the cases subject to enforcement, plaintiffs applied for compulsory enforcement and the vast majority of these applications came from cases that went all the way to judgment.[42] Of the twenty-five cases that indicated the results of compulsory enforcement, 55.5 percent were implemented successfully and 18.5 percent failed to be implemented. However, it must be noted that implementation of judgments is a difficult problem in even the most developed countries, and it is not clear that the 55.5 percent figure should be considered low.

Courts are increasingly used because they are seen as authoritative (despite problems with enforcement). According to one private business owner interviewed in Nanjing, "Going to court is not because it's fair but rather because it's authoritative." Strikingly, an intermediate court judge echoed this sentiment: "You need an authoritative person to handle [the dispute], and the resolution of the most authoritative person is the easiest to accept. It's not necessarily the fairest solution, but fairness isn't the standard. The key is whether it solves the problem." Somewhat surprisingly, attitudes of business people toward the legal system as a whole are solidly average: 56.3 percent of respondents in Shanghai and Nanjing rated the legal system as average, while 25.3 percent found it to be low or very low, and 18.3 percent found it to be high or very high. Fewer were positive about trustworthiness in contracting: 42.9 percent of respondents found it to be average, while 53 percent found it to be low or very low, and only 4.1 percent found it to be high or very high. Thus, there does appear to be a need for a neutral, third-party arbiter, yet such services appear to be undersupplied by informal and formal nonstate institutions. The formal legal system clearly plays an important role, albeit an imperfect one.

Summary

At the beginning of the reform era, contracts in China were little different from the orders given to two arms of a bureaucracy by their common superior, and contact law was oriented toward defining the rules relevant for such contracts. But

---

[42] The court records suggest that the minimum fee for court-sponsored implementation was 150 yuan, but for larger awards, more typically approximately 1.25–1.5 percent of the award amount (a fee incurred by the winning side).

with the increasing latitude given to local government enterprises and nonstate economic agents, a host of economic relationships were developed outside this context, supported, by default, by informal arrangements. There followed, probably as a consequence, changes in formal contract law, which by 1999 gave broad range to freedom of contract and provided rules relevant to the vast majority of economic agreements. Twenty-five years after reforms began, courts, despite their many deficiencies, were playing a significant role in dispute resolution. Survey evidence indicates that this role is much greater than would have been imagined, given the emphasis placed in the literature on the pervasive role of *guanxi* in economic life. In the matter of the arrangements used to support agreements, China looks very much like a typical successful developing country, with the legal system playing a significant role, but one whose quantitative significance cannot be judged even in comparative terms because of the lack of systematic data.

CORPORATE GOVERNANCE

The primary function of corporate governance institutions is to reduce the transaction costs inherent in the agency relationship between owners of firms and their managers. The crucially important byproduct of this function is to facilitate the flow of finance, by giving investors confidence of a reasonable return on their investment in firm ownership. These institutions are of limited importance in the case of small- and medium-size private firms, where the transaction costs are reduced by the physical presence of owners exerting personal control. Moreover, as we have argued above, local governments were the effective owners of all but the largest government-owned enterprises (e.g., of "collective" TVEs) during the first two decades of reform. The problem of corporate governance in these cases was solved, to the extent it was solved, because "owners" had the ability to exert direct control.[43] Thus, discussion of corporate governance in China must focus on two types of very large firms: the very large SOEs inherited from the era of planning, which were directly under the supervision of national authorities, and the very large private and semiprivate firms that have become of major importance over the last decade.

The Early Years of Reform: State Ownership and Managerial Incentives

A universal economic problem is the dilution of managerial incentives arising from the separation of ownership and control that is almost inevitable in large economic entities. Reforming socialist economies faced this problem acutely, since SOEs were very large and liberalizing reforms gave managers greater latitude. Most of the transition countries in EEFSU dealt with this problem through rapid privatization,

---

[43] For these firms, the real issue was the incentives of the controlling officials, which space considerations prevent us from considering.

with the hope that corporate owners would quickly exert the pertinent discipline over managers. This worked in some countries, where the institutional support for mechanisms of corporate governance was better developed, but failed elsewhere, particularly in the former Soviet Union (Djankov and Murrell, 2002).

An alternative approach is to give managers of SOEs stronger incentives to pursue efficiency. This is the route that China took in the 1980s. A succession of papers shows that the stronger incentives had significant and positive effects on profitability, total factor productivity, and return on equity (Groves et al., 1995; Li, 1997; Chang, McCall, and Wang, 2003). The performance of the SOEs in China in the 1980s was far superior to that of the SOEs and former SOEs in EEFSU in the 1990s. However, the relatively poorer performance of the Chinese SOEs in the 1990s led to increasing skepticism about the effects of incentives, a change of views that was no doubt helped by the general impression that incentives had done nothing to solve the problems of inefficient SOEs in EEFSU (Qian, 2000).

These observations raise the possibility that improvements in managerial incentives are a substitute for improved corporate governance institutions in some environments but not in others, and might dominate privatization in those contexts. When seeking to reduce the problems arising from the separation of ownership and control in large SOEs, the strengthening of managerial incentives worked in the less liberalized context of the 1980s and early 1990s in China. This was a time when opportunities for asset stripping were much fewer because of tighter controls on the economy. Perhaps the incentives worked in the China of the 1980s exactly because of the unattractiveness of managerial strategies other than placing effort into improving enterprise efficiency. This stood in contrast to the first decade of reform in the Former Soviet Union (FSU) and later times in China, where more freewheeling economic environments opened up greater possibilities for managers to pursue increases in wealth at the expense of efficiency. These observations suggest that slow liberalization and heightened managerial incentives are a substitute for strong mechanisms of corporate governance, at least in addressing problems arising from the separation of ownership and control. Where institutional development is poor, this policy might be superior to one of rapid privatization, suggesting another reason why the first decade of reform in China had much higher growth rates than the first decade in the FSU.

This analysis reinforces the story of coevolution of the economy and the law that we have presented in "The Development of Law during the Era of Economic Reform." The changing rules on SOE incentives improved economic performance, stimulating further decentralization and the growth of the private sector, which lessened governmental control of the economy, making direct incentives less productive, and therefore spurring the need for corporate governance rules pertinent to a highly decentralized economy. We review the status of those new rules in "The Role of Corporate Governance in Facilitating the Flow of Finance," after discussing another temporary, early institutional substitute, anonymous banking.

The Early Years of Reform: Anonymous Banking and the Flow of Finance

The reasoning in the previous subsection is consistent with a current trend in the economics literature, which emphasizes that successful developing countries find some way to generate functional substitutes for the formal institutions that receive so much emphasis in the analysis of developed countries. One function performed by those formal institutions is to protect financial property rights and thus encourage the flow of finance. All developing countries face enormous problems in mobilizing savings to generate the financial resources for investment (Levine, 1997). These problems are especially severe when the accumulation of wealth is ideologically suspect and when a government pressed for revenues is not constrained by law from expropriating property. Yet Chinese growth does not seem to have been overly hampered by this problem.

Bai et al. (2004) argue that the institution of anonymous banking played an important role in solving this problem. They view the government as having the objectives of raising revenue and pursuing an egalitarian tax policy. An ideal policy would be a free market in secure financial assets, accompanied by higher taxes on the deposits of wealthier citizens. But the identification of depositors combined with a lack of trust in government would encourage households and small businesses to retreat from the financial system. This would be accompanied by a reduction in the incentives to accumulate wealth through productive activities and an increase in wasteful forms of wealth holding (e.g., foreign currencies or less productive durables). With anonymous deposits, the wealth of the holder is not observable to the state and the source of funds (perhaps illegal private market activity) is also unobservable. Punitive taxation of the deposits of the wealthier is prevented because the identity of the depositor is not revealed. Tax levels are then constrained by the politics or the ideology of not taxing the poor too heavily.

A corollary of using anonymous banking is that cash transactions have to be allowed because bank transfers identify firms. (Note that cash was not allowed for interfirm transactions in the early years of transition in many parts of the former Soviet Union.) If cash is used on a large scale, the government has poorer information on firms and a reduced ability to expropriate the revenue flows of firms on a selective basis. Thus, by reducing information flows, the practice of anonymous banking, which is inconsistent with notions of best practice institutions, can be understood as a crude substitute for the protection of financial property rights.

In 2000, the rules were changed and identification of the depositor was required on all new deposits. Of the official reasons offered for the change, the only one with real credibility is the desire to use tax instruments to narrow income gaps (Bai et al., 2004). With the successful growth of the private sector, perhaps political objectives have changed. There is now less emphasis on the effects of general distrust in the security of financial assets, compared with concern over the discontent stirred by the large inequalities generated under the market system. Hence, the anonymous banking rules helped to bring about their own demise, by contributing to the development of the freewheeling semicapitalist system of today. But this system, in turn, generates demands for new institutions.

The Role of Corporate Governance in Facilitating the Flow of Finance

This section focuses on the current status of corporate governance institutions pertinent to publicly listed companies, since a major purpose of legal regulation of corporate governance is precisely to make possible the raising of investment funds from the public at large. While the discussion focuses on problems, since China has far to go, it is worth remembering the starting point, since much has changed. In 1978, all large enterprises were in the state sector, run by government-appointed managers, financed from the state budget, and limited to following plan instructions. Then, following a gradual but incomplete devolution of authority from governmental authorities, reforms led to more modern corporate structures, with boards of directors holding at least nominal authority to make major decisions.

Complaints about corporate governance in listed companies generally center around the nonaccountability of managers for actions that damage shareholders as a whole. Such actions can occur in a variety of ways. One is the misuse of information made possible by nontransparency. Despite a series of China Securities Regulatory Commission (CSRC) rules requiring disclosure of a large volume of information about each company's business, accounting problems undermine the completeness and the accuracy of disclosures. In addition, dominant shareholders are able to use their power over the company to conduct transactions favorable to themselves and disadvantageous to the company and its other shareholders. Such transactions can even include blatantly one-sided transactions such as the outright transfer of funds to the dominant shareholder, without any pretense of an economic quid pro quo.[44]

Furthermore, even (and perhaps especially) when company management is not controlled by a dominant shareholder, it can still damage the company through negligence or deliberate misuse of corporate assets. In Chinese listed companies, this is possible less because of collective action problems facing widely dispersed shareholders – shareholding tends to be highly concentrated – than because of inadequate incentives to monitor on the part of officials representing the dominant (state) shareholder. Analysts have even coined a name for this phenomenon: the "absent owner" (*suoyouzhe quewei*).

Management malfeasance can, of course, occur anywhere. But particular forms flourish in China because of the institutional environment in which listed companies operate. In particular, the standard forms of institutional

---

[44] A 2005 CSRC notice required such funds to be returned by the end of 2006, but a supplemental notice issued in November 2006 by the CSRC and several other agencies made it clear that the problem remained unresolved (CSRC et al., 2006).

restraint – monitoring by government agencies, civil litigation by private parties who suffer damage, and various mechanisms based on the market and civil society (including information and monitoring services provided by intermediaries) – all suffer from serious defects.

The CSRC, for example, has very limited formal power other than that of approving share offerings. Its investigative powers are severely circumscribed: it may, for example, question executives of a listed company about a suspicious transaction, but not executives of the company on the other side of the transaction if the second company is not under the CSRC's jurisdiction. While the CSRC has, in the view of some, exceeded its jurisdiction over securities by attempting to regulate internal corporate governance matters such as the number of independent directors, its views on such matters must be issued in the form of "guidance opinions" and suggestions and must be enforced through the CSRC's power – sometimes effective, sometimes not – to withhold various approvals (e.g., for a stock offering) from offenders.

The stock exchanges – essentially branches of the CSRC and not true civil society organizations – offer even less of a deterrent. They do not have the power to set their own standards for listing and delisting (other than of a strictly technical nature); the delisting decision is made by the CSRC under articles 55 and 56 of the Securities Law (2005) (which spell out circumstances such as major violations of law or losses for three consecutive years).

Civil sanctions through private litigation are of little concern to managers. Both the Company Law and the Securities Law are very stingy in their grants of rights to shareholders, and the court system has proved very reluctant to help shareholders vindicate what rights they have. The Supreme People's Court, for example, has issued a regulation to lower courts under which they may not hear any cases involving claims for damages caused by insider trading or market manipulation and may hear cases involving misleading disclosures only when there has been a prior finding of such by an official body such as the CSRC (Chen, 2003; Hutchens, 2003).

Finally, monitoring by nongovernmental intermediaries such as auditing firms and the financial press[45] remains spotty. Favorable press coverage can often be obtained, and unfavorable coverage suppressed, for a price. Journals that do publish unfavorable stories may find themselves subject to libel suits. Recently, however, there are some grounds for thinking that courts may be coming to recognize the countervailing value of vigorous commentary in such matters. The Guangzhou Huaqiao Real Estate Development Company lost a libel case brought against the journal *China Reform* for having reported on asset stripping at the company. The court ruled that journalists enjoy immunity from suit if the news was backed

---

[45] Although China's press of course remains under significant state control, that control is sufficiently decentralized, and the gray areas sufficiently broad, that in this context it makes sense to think at least of the financial press as significantly more "nongovernmental" than, for example, the two stock exchanges.

up by a source that was reasonable and believable, and was not based simply on rumors.[46]

The importance of these problems is less clear. While the Chinese stock market is, at the time of this writing, languishing, corporate governance, while poor today, is arguably better than in the past when the stock market was booming. One possibility is that instead of law driving market development, the market might be driving law. As argued by Chen (2003), recent scandals and the current market doldrums have awakened investors to the need for better regulation of the securities market and corporate governance, and they have begun to press for needed reforms – part of a "first crash then law" pattern observed in several countries by Coffee (2001). But this conclusion might be premature. Not only retail investors but also many government officials remain of the view that the proper function of securities markets is to go up: the CSRC has been criticized for causing markets to fall through overenthusiastic enforcement. Even the CSRC itself is wary of overregulation – not in the sense of making too many rules, but in the sense of enforcing existing rules – for precisely the same reason. Many in the financial services industry argue that a certain amount of willful blindness on the part of regulators is necessary, at least at the current stage, for public confidence to continue because that confidence is driven more by a continually rising market than by knowledge that corporate governance is sound.

Summary and Reflections

In this chapter we have assessed the development of law in China and analyzed its role in the economy, examining the degree to which China's formal legal system offers stable and predictable rights of property and contract. Although the legal system has made great strides since the beginning of reforms and currently has a role of some significance in the economy, it is impossible to make the case that formal legal institutions have contributed in an important way to China's remarkable economic success. If anything, economic success has fostered the development of law, rather than the reverse. This is not to say that expectations of reasonable and predictable returns from property and contract have been absent in China: it is very unlikely that high rates of investment and growth could have occurred unless investors, producers, and traders expected a reasonable return on their efforts. Rather, our conclusion is that the formal legal system did not play a large role in fostering such expectations.

In this chapter we approached the assessment of the role of law by examining the details of legal rules, the structure of the legal system, and case studies of very specific elements of economic activity. We have largely ignored evidence from the many

---

[46] Excerpts from the text of the judgment as well as commentary by prominent attorney Pu Zhiqiang, who appeared for the defendants, can be found at http://www.epochtimes.com/gb/4/10/18/n694419.htm.

countrywide measures of the strength of institutions developed by economists and political scientists. The reason for bypassing this evidence is that we have found that it is at variance with our detailed contextual analysis, in ways that lead us to doubt the validity of the countrywide measures. For example, on one widely used survey, the World Business Environment Survey (2005), company managers were asked, "To what degree do you agree that the legal system will uphold contract and property rights?" The percentage of Chinese respondents answering with agreement (rather than disagreement) was higher than that for the world as a whole, higher than the average for countries in China's income group, and also higher than that for many countries (such as the United States) with legal systems that most commentators would consider stronger than China's.

If one compares these survey results with our discussion in "Are Property Rights Secure? Do They Matter?," "Transactions in Goods and Services," and "Corporate Governance," then it is clear that respondents must have been interpreting the term "legal system" very differently from the way social scientists would.[47] Perhaps their responses were more visceral, suitable for the phrase "political, social, and economic equilibrium" with which we began this chapter. We view it as quite plausible that the equilibrium in China over the last two decades upheld contract and property rights to some reasonable degree. But the legal system was not by any means the central element supporting that equilibrium: the Weber-North rights hypothesis clearly fails in the case of China. This divergence between the role of the legal system and perceived contract and property rights underscores the importance of detailed study of those mechanisms that must have produced the expectations that drove China's growth performance.

Questions on which mechanisms drove expectations must go largely unanswered for lack of data on institutions and institutional substitutes and their effects, a lacuna that is by no means unique to China (Clarke, 2003b; Hendley and Murrell, 2003). Nevertheless, we were able in "Transactions in Goods and Services" to summarize the results of existing papers and new research, suggesting that courts are playing an increasingly significant role in dispute resolution and personal relationships are relatively less important at present. In sections "Are Property Rights Secure? Do They Matter?" and "Transactions in Goods and Services," we presented information suggesting that the presence of institutional substitutes is important: for example, the cadre system gives local officials certain incentives to respect property rights. Large questions remain. Thus, for example, there is no clear picture of the changing relative importance of political relationships and law in fostering property rights. Similarly, there is virtually no information relevant to China on whether gaps in the formal legal system are most crucial for small firms or large ones, for new firms or old ones, in finance or real property.

One can make only broad judgments about where the gaps in the legal system are really critical. One especially damaging lacuna – economically, politically, and

---

[47] We assume for now that they were being candid.

socially – is the absence of an effective system of rural land ownership, where farmers would have robust rights to land that they could then trade. This would mitigate the increasingly (socially and politically) disruptive process of removing farmers from their land for the purposes of redevelopment, without providing adequate compensation.[48] The tradability would allow land to be put to its most remunerative use. It would also allow for efficient combinations of landholdings.

The case of rural land ownership provides one example where limited legal development is genuinely costly and likely to increase in cost. This case exemplifies a more general phenomenon: China's lack of dispute resolution institutions beyond the control of the political powers whose actions they might be asked to overturn. The economic and social cost of not having such institutions is high now and will be much higher in the future. But the solution to this problem lies far outside the legal realm, in the domain of the political system, where economic arguments for profound legal changes are not likely to carry much weight while economic performance remains at the levels experienced in the reform years.

References

Acemoglu, Daron and Simon Johnson. 2005. "Unbundling Institutions." *Journal of Political Economy.* 113(5), pp. 949–995.

Acemoglu, Daron, Simon Johnson, and James Robinson. 2001. "The Colonial Origins of Comparative Development: An Empirical Investigation." *American Economic Review.* 91, pp. 1369–1401.

Administrative Litigation Law, 1989. *Zhonghua renmin gongheguo xingzheng susong fa* [Administrative Litigation Law of the People's Republic of China]. Available at http://www.law-lib.com/law/.

Bai, Chong-En, David D. Li, Yingyi Qian, and Yijiang Wang. 2004. "Commitment, Incentives, and Information: The Case of Anonymous Banking." Mimeo, University of California, Berkeley. Available at http://elsa.berkeley.edu/~yqian/anonymous%20banking.pdf.

Bankruptcy Law, 1986. *Zhonghua renmin gongheguo qiye pochan fa (shixing)* [Enterprise Bankruptcy Law of the People's Republic of China (For Trial Implementation)]. Available at http://www.law-lib.com/law/.

Beijing Municipal Government, 2001. *Youxian hehuo guanli banfa* [Measures for the Administration of Limited Partnerships]. Available at http://www.law-lib.com/law/.

Beijing Municipal People's Congress, 2000. *Zhongguancun keji yuanqu tiaoli* [Regulations on the Zhongguancun Science and Technology Park]. Available at http://www.law-lib.com/law/.

Blanchard, Olivier and Michael Kremer. 1997. "Disorganization." *Quarterly Journal of Economics.* 112(4), pp. 1091–1126.

Brandt, Loren, Scott Rozelle, and Matthew A. Turner. 2004. "Local Government Behavior and Property Rights Formation in Rural China." *Journal of Institutional and Theoretical Economics.* 160(4), pp. 627–662.

---

[48] As the writing of this chapter was being completed, the critical need for some kind of reform in this area was dramatically illustrated when ten to twenty villagers in southern China were reported killed by gunfire from security forces as part of a conflict over land requisitioning (*Washington Post,* 2005).

Cai Dingjian, 2003. "A Call for a System of Constitutional Review," *Nanfang zhoumo* [Nanfang Weekend]. Accessed November 20, 2003, from http://www.nanfangdaily.com. cn/zm/20031120/xw/fz/200311200862.asp.

CCP Central Committee, 1983. "Dangqian nongcun jingji zhengce de ruogan wenti [Several Questions on Current Rural Economic Policy]," January 2, 1983, in *Nongcun shiyong fagui shouce* [Handbook of Practical Rural Laws]. Beijing: Falü chubanshe, 1987, pp. 68–83.

CCP Central Committee Organization Department, 1979. "Notice of Opinions Regarding Implementing the Cadre Evaluation System," in *Renshi gongzuo wenjian xuanbian – ganbu guanli bufen* [Selected Documents on Personnel Work – Cadre Management Section]. Beijing: Laodong renshi chubanshe, 1987, pp. 12–15.

CCP Central Committee and State Council, 1984. "Notice of Transmission of the Ministry of Agriculture, Pasturing, and Fisheries' 'Report on Initiating a New Phase for Commune and Brigade Enterprises'," March 1, 1984, in *Zhongguo xiangzhen qiye nianjian 1978–87* [China Township and Village Enterprise Yearbook 1978–87]. Beijing: Zhongguo nongye chubanshe, 1989, pp. 422–427.

Chang, Chun, Brian McCall, and Yijiang Wang. 2003. "Implications of Managerial Incentives and Ownership for Performance: Evidence from China's Rural Enterprises." *Journal of Comparative Economics*. 31, pp. 414–428.

Che, Jiahua and Yingyi Qian. May 1998. "Insecure Property Rights and Government Ownership of Firms." *Quarterly Journal of Economics*. 113(2), pp. 467–496.

Chen, Albert. 2004. *An Introduction to the Legal System of the People's Republic of China*, 3rd ed. Hong Kong: Butterworths.

Chen, Zhiwu. 2003. "Capital Markets and Legal Development: The China Case." *China Economic Review*. 14, pp. 451–472.

China Law and Governance Review. 2004. "Enforcement of Civil Judgments: Harder Than Reaching the Sky." Accessed August 3, 2007, from http://www.chinareview.info/issue2/pages/legal.htm#1.

China School Net, 2005. "Jiaoyu Bu gongbu jinliangnian benke zhaosheng, biyesheng jiuye qingkuang [Ministry of Education Announces Situation Regarding Student Intake and Employment for Graduates over the Last Two Years]." Accessed May 15, 2005, from http://www.china-school.net/zyxx/2005515115450.htm.

Chung, Wai-keung and Gary H. Hamilton. 2001. "Social Logic as Business Logic: Guanxi, Trustworthiness, and the Embeddedness of Chinese Business Practices," in *The Legal Culture of Global Business Transactions*. Richard Appelbaum, William F. Felstiner, and Volkmar Gessner, eds. Oxford: Hart Publishing, pp. 325–346.

Clarke, Donald. 1992. "Regulation and Its Discontents: Understanding Economic Law in China." *Stanford Journal of International Law*. 28(2), pp. 283–322.

Clarke, Donald. 1996. "Power and Politics in the Chinese Court System: The Execution of Civil Judgments." *Columbia Journal of Asian Law*. 10(1), pp. 1–125.

Clarke, Donald. April 1997. "State Council Notice Nullifies Statutory Rights of Creditors." *East Asian Executive Reports*. 19(4), pp. 9–15.

Clarke, Donald. 2003a. "Empirical Research in Chinese Law," in *Beyond Common Knowledge: Empirical Approaches to the Rule of Law*. Erik Jensen and Thomas Heller, eds. Stanford: Stanford University Press, pp. 164–192.

Clarke, Donald. 2003b. "Economic Development and the Rights Hypothesis: The China Problem." *American Journal of Comparative Law*. 51, pp. 89–111.

Coffee, John C., Jr. 2001. "The Rise of Dispersed Ownership: The Roles of Law and the State in the Separation of Ownership and Control." *Yale Law Journal*. 111, pp. 16–21.

Company Law, 1993. *Zhonghua renmin gongheguo gongsifa* [Company Law of the People's Republic of China]. Adopted December 29, 1993. Available at http://www.law-lib.com/law/.

Company Law, 2005. *Zhonghua renmin gongheguo gongsifa* [Company Law of the People's Republic of China]. Amended October 27, 2005. Available at http://www.law-lib.com/law/.

Constitution, 1982. *Zhonghua renmin gongheguo xianfa* [Constitution of the People's Republic of China]. Available at http://www.law-lib.com/law/.

Contract Law, 1999. *Zhonghua renmin gongheguo hetong fa* [Contract Law of the People's Republic of China]. Available at http://www.law-lib.com/law/.

CSRC [China Securities Regulatory Commission], Ministry of Public Security, People's Bank of China, State Asset Supervision and Administration Commission, General Customs Administration, State Tax Administration, State Administration of Industry and Commerce, China Banking Regulatory Commission, 2006. *Guanyu jinyibu zuohao qingli da gudong zhanyong shangshi gongsi zijin gongzuo de tongzhi* [Notice on Further Doing Well the Work of Clearing Up the Taking over of Listed Company Funds by Large Shareholders]. Adopted November 7, 2006. Available at http://www.law-lib.com/law/.

Djankov, Simeon and Peter Murrell. 2002. "Enterprise Restructuring in Transition: A Quantitative Survey." *Journal of Economic Literature.* 40(3), pp. 739–792.

Financial Times. 2004. "Investor Concern over China Telecoms 'Musical Chairs'." *Financial Times.* November 2, 2004. Internet edition.

Gechlik, Mei Ying. 2005 [year of actual publication: 2006]. "Judicial Reform in China: Lessons from Shanghai." *Journal of Asian Law.* 19, pp. 97–137.

General Principles of Civil Law, 1986. *Zhonghua renmin gongheguo minfa tongze* [General Principles of Civil Law of the People's Republic of China].

Gong, Ting. 2004. "Dependent Judiciary and Unaccountable Judges: Judicial Corruption in Contemporary China." *The China Review.* 4(2), pp. 33–54.

Groves, Theodore, Yongmiao Hong, John McMillan, and Barry Naughton. 1995. "China's Evolving Managerial Labor Market." *Journal of Political Economy.* 103(4), pp. 873–892.

Guo Guosong, 2003. "A Judge Rules Local Legislation Invalid: Violating the Law or Upholding the Law?" *Nanfang Zhoumo* [Southern Weekend]. Accessed November 20, 2003, from http://www.nanfangdaily.com.cn/zm/20031120/xw/fz/200311200861.asp.

Guo, Yingjie. 2003. "Imagining a Confucian Nation: The Search for Roots and the Revival of Confucianism in Post-Tiananmen China." *The Canadian Review of Studies in Nationalism.* 30, pp. 1–14.

Guthrie, Douglas. 1999. *Dragon in a Three-Piece Suit: The Emergence of Capitalism in China.* Princeton: Princeton University Press.

Hall, Robert and Charles Jones. 1999. "Why Do Some Countries Produce So Much More Output Per Worker Than Others?" *The Quarterly Journal of Economics.* 114(1), pp. 83–116.

Han Junjie, 2004. "The Case of Li Huijuan in Henan Makes Waves Again," *Zhongguo Qingnian Bao* [China Youth News]. Accessed February 2, 2004, from http://www.cyol.com/zqb/gb/zqb/2004–02/06/content_813990.htm.

He Bing, 2002. "Reconstructing the Mechanism of Dispute Resolution," *Zhong-Wai Faxue* [Chinese and Foreign Legal Studies (Peking University Law Journal)]. 14(1), p. 28.

He Weifang, 2003. "A Bushel-Basket of Problems," *Nanfang Zhoumo* [Southern Weekend]. Accessed November 20, 2003, from http://www.nanfangdaily.com.cn/zm/20031120/xw/fz/200311200863.asp.

Hendley, Kathryn and Peter Murrell. 2003. "Which Mechanisms Support the Fulfillment of Sales Agreements? Asking Decision-Makers in Firms." *Economics Letters*. January 1, 2003, pp. 49–54.

Hu Ge, 1986. "The Implications of Enforcing the Bankruptcy System," *Guangming Ribao* [Guangming Daily]. July 26, 1986, p. 3.

Huang, Yasheng, 1990. "Web of Interests and Patterns of Behaviour of Chinese Local Economic Bureaucracies and Enterprises During Reforms." *The China Quarterly*. 123, pp. 431–458.

Hutchens, Walter. 2003. "Private Securities Litigation in China: Material Disclosure about China's Legal System?" *University of Pennsylvania Journal of International Economic Law* 24, pp. 599–689.

Jarreau, J. Steven. 2004. "Anatomy of a BIT: The United States-Honduras Bilateral Investment Treaty." *University of Miami Inter-American Law Review*. 35, pp. 429–498.

Jin, Hehui and Yingyi Qian. 1998. "Public vs. Private Ownership of Firms: Evidence from Rural China." *Quarterly Journal of Economics*. 113(3), pp. 773–808.

Jones, William C. 1987. "Some Questions Regarding the Significance of the General Provisions of Civil Law of the People's Republic of China." *Harvard International Law Journal*. 28, pp. 309–331.

Judicial Statistics, 2000. *Quanguo renmin fayuan sifa tongji lishi ziliao huibian 1949–1998 (minshi bufen)* [Collection of Judicial Statistical Historical Material of National People's Court (Civil Law Section), 1949–1998]. Beijing: Renmin fayuan chubanshe.

Kali, Raja. 2001. "Business Networks in Transition Economies: Norms, Contracts, and Legal Institutions," in *Assessing the Value of Law in Transition Economies*. Peter Murrell, ed. Ann Arbor: University of Michigan Press, pp. 211–228.

Keating, Daniel. 1997. "Measuring Sales Law Against Sales Practice: A Reality Check." *The Journal of Law and Commerce*. 17, pp. 99–130.

Keller, Perry. 1994. "Sources of Order in Chinese Law." *American Journal of Comparative Law*. 42(4), pp. 711–759.

King, Ambrose Y.-C. 1991. "Kuan-hsi and Network Building: A Sociological Interpretation." *Daedalus*. 120(2), pp. 63–84.

Landa, Janet Tai. 1994. *Trust, Ethnicity, and Identity: Beyond the New Institutional Economics of Ethnic Trading Networks, Contract Law, and Gift-Exchange*. Ann Arbor: University of Michigan Press.

Lau, Lawrence, Yingyi Qian, and Gérard Roland. 2000. "Reform without Losers: An Interpretation of China's Dual-Track Approach to Transition." *Journal of Political Economy*. 108(1), pp. 120–143.

Law on Legislation. 2000. *Zhonghua renmin gongheguo lifa fa* [Law on Legislation of the People's Republic of China]. Available at http://www.law-lib.com/law/.

Law Yearbook of China, Various years. *Zhongguo falü nianjian* [Law Yearbook of China]. Beijing: Falü nianjian chubanshe. (References are to year of publication; the yearbook for a given year is published in the following year.)

Levine, Ross. 1997. "Financial Development and Economic Growth: Views and Agenda." *Journal of Economic Literature*. 35(2), pp. 688–726.

Li Kejie, 2004. "Conflicts in Law Should Not Be 'Settled Quietly'," *Nanfang dushi bao* [Southern Metropolitan News]. Accessed from February 7, 2004, http://www.nanfangdaily.com.cn/southnews/spqy/zy/200402070066.asp.

Li, Wei. 1997. "The Impact of Economic Reform on the Performance of Chinese State Enterprises, 1980–1989." *Journal of Political Economy*. 105(5), pp. 1080–1106.

Li, Wei. 1999. "A Tale of Two Reforms: The Importance of Initial Market Conditions." *Rand Journal of Economics.* 30(1), pp. 120–136.

Lin, Nan and Chih-Jou Jay Chen. 1999. "Local Elites as Officials and Owners: Shareholding and Property Rights in Daqiuzhuang," in *Property Rights and Economic Reform in China.* Jean C. Oi and Andrew G. Walder, eds. Stanford: Stanford University Press, pp. 145–170.

Ling, Bing. 2002. *Contract Law in China.* Hong Kong: Sweet and Maxwell Asia.

Lubman, Stanley B. 1999. *Bird in a Cage, Legal Reform in China After Mao.* Stanford, CA: Stanford University Press.

Macaulay, Stewart. 1963. "Non-Contractual Relations in Business: A Preliminary Study." *American Sociological Review.* 28(1), pp. 55–67.

McMillan, John and Christopher Woodruff. 1999. "Interfirm Relationships and Informal Credit in Vietnam." *Quarterly Journal of Economics.* 114(4), pp. 1285–1320.

Meng, Yan. 2003. "Judge Sows Seeds of Lawmaking Dispute." *China Daily.* November 24, 2003. Available at http://english.peopledaily.com.cn/200311/24/eng20031124_128871.shtml. Ministry of Agriculture, March 23, 1990. "Nongmin gufen hezuo qiye zanxing guiding" [Provisional Regulations on Rural Shareholding Cooperatives]," February 12, 1990. Available at http://law.lawtime.cn/d596386601480.html.

Ministry of Justice, 2005. "Woguo zhiye lüshi da 11.8 wan ren [China Has as Many as 118,000 Professional Lawyers]." Accessed August 3, 2007, from http://www.lawroad.net/bbs/viewthread.php?tid=2018.

Murrell, Peter. 1992. "Evolution in Economics and in the Economic Reform of the Centrally Planned Economies," in *Emerging Market Economies in Eastern Europe.* Christopher Clague and Gordon Rausser, eds. Cambridge, MA: Basil Blackwell, pp. 35–54.

Murrell, Peter. 2003. "The Relative Levels and the Character of Institutional Development in Transition Economies," in *Political Economy of Transition and Development: Institutions, Politics and Policies.* Nauro Campos and Jan Fidrmuc, eds. Boston/Dordrecht/London: Kluwer Academic Publishers, pp. 41–68.

Naughton, Barry. 1995. *Growing Out of the Plan.* Cambridge and New York: Cambridge University Press.

Nee, Victor and Sijin Su. 1996. "Institutions, Social Ties, and Credible Commitment: Local Corporatism in China," in *Reforming Asian Economies: The Growth of Market Institutions.* John McMillan and Barry Naughton, eds. Ann Arbor: University of Michigan Press, pp. 111–134.

New York Times. 2005. "A Judge Tests China's Courts, Making History." *New York Times,* Internet edition. November 28, 2005.

North, Douglass. 1990. *Institutions, Institutional Change and Economic Performance.* Cambridge and New York: Cambridge University Press.

Peerenboom, Randall. 2002. *China's Long March Toward Rule of Law.* Cambridge and New York: Cambridge University Press.

Pei, Minxin. 2001. "Does Legal Reform Protect Economic Transactions? Commercial Disputes in China," in *Assessing the Value of Law in Transition Economies.* Peter Murrell, ed. Ann Arbor: University of Michigan Press, pp. 180–210.

Potter, Pitman. 1992. *Legitimation and Contract Autonomy in the PRC: The Contract Law of China.* Seattle: University of Washington Press.

Property Law, 2007. *Zhonghua renmin gongheguo wuquan fa* [Property Law of the People's Republic of China]. Available at http://www.law-lib.com/law/.

Qian, Yingyi. 2000. "The Process of China's Market Transition (1978–1998): The Historical, Evolutionary and Comparative Perspectives." *Journal of Institutional and Theoretical Economics.* 156(1), pp. 151–171.

Qian, Yingyi. 2003. "How Reform Worked in China," in *In Search of Prosperity: Analytic Narratives on Economic Growth*. Dani Rodrik, ed. Princeton: Princeton University Press, pp. 297–333.

Rodrik, Dani, Arvind Subramanian, and Francesco Trebbi. 2004. "Institutions Rule: The Primacy of Institutions over Geography and Integration in Economic Development." *Journal of Economic Growth*. 9(2), pp. 131–165.

Rozelle, Scott. 1994. "Rural Industrialization and Increasing Inequality: Emerging Patterns in China's Reforming Economy." *Journal of Comparative Economics*. 19(3), pp. 362–391.

Securities Law, 2005. *Zhonghua renmin gongheguo zhengquan fa* [Securities Law of the People's Republic of China]. Amended October 27, 2005.

State Council, 1979. "Regulations on Several Questions Regarding the Development of Commune and Brigade Enterprises (Provisional Draft)," July 3, 1979, in *Zhongguo xiangzhen qiye nianjian 1978–87* [China Township and Village Enterprise Yearbook 1978–87]. Beijing: Zhongguo nongye chubanshe, 1989, pp. 427–432.

State Council, 1987. "Several Policy Regulations Regarding the Nonagricultural Individual Economy in Cities and Towns," July 7, 1981, in *Nongcun shiyong fagui shouce* [Handbook of Commonly Used Rural Laws and Regulations]. Beijing: Falü chubanshe, pp. 728–731.

State Council, 2000. "Outline on Deepening the Reform of the Cadre Personnel System," *Guowuyuan gongbao* [State Council Bulletin]. 29, pp. 5–11.

State Council, 2001. *Xingzheng fagui zhiding chengxu tiaoli* [Regulations on the Procedure for the Enactment of Administrative Regulations]. Adopted November 16, 2001; effective January 1, 2002.

Su Li [Zhu Suli], 2000. *Song fa xia xiang* [Sending Law to the Countryside]. Beijing: Zhongguo Zheng-Fa Daxue chubanshe.

Supreme People's Court, 1988. *Guanyu guanche zhixing "Zhonghua renmin gongheguo minfa tongze" ruogan wenti de yijian (shixing)* [Opinion on Several Issues Relating to the Implementation of the "General Principles of Civil Law of the People's Republic of China" (for Trial Implementation)]. Adopted January 26, 1988.

Supreme People's Court, 2003. *Guanyu shenli zhengquan shichang yin xujia chenshu yinfa de minshi peichang anjian de ruogan guiding* [Several Provisions on the Adjudication of Civil Suits for Damages Arising Out of False Representations in Securities Markets]. Adopted January 9, 2003.

Teters, Barbara. 1971. "The Otsu Affair: The Formation of Japan's Judicial Conscience," in *Meiji Japan's Centennial: Aspects of Political Thought and Action*. David Wurfel, ed. Lawrence: University Press of Kansas, pp. 36–62.

Township and Village Enterprise Yearbook, 1997. "Zhonghua renmin gonghequo xiangzhen qiye fa chutai guocheng jianshu [A Brief Description of the Making of the Law of the Township and Village Enterprise in China]," in *Zhongguo xiangzhen qiye nianjian* [China Township and Village Enterprise Yearbook]. Beijing: Zhongguo nongye chubanshe, pp. 87–88.

Washington Post. 2005. "Chinese Police Kill Villagers during Two-Day Land Protest." *Washington Post*. December 8, 2005, p. A01.

Whiting, Susan H. 1998. "The Mobilization of Private Investment as a Problem of Trust in Local Governance Structures," in *Trust and Governance*. Valerie Braithwaite and Margaret Levi, eds. New York: Russell Sage Foundation, pp. 167–193.

Whiting, Susan H. 2001. *Power and Wealth in Rural China: The Political Economy of Institutional Change*. Cambridge and New York: Cambridge University Press.

Whiting, Susan H. 2005. *Contracting and Dispute Resolution among Chinese Firms: Law and Its Substitutes*. Washington, DC: University of Washington.

World Bank. 2001. *Competitiveness, Technology and Firm Linkages in Manufacturing Sector, 1998–2000.* WDI ID 0359. Washington, DC: World Bank.

World Bank. n.d. *World Business Environment Survey.* Accessed from http://www.ifc.org/ifcext/economics.nsf/Content/ic-wbes.

Wu Peng. 2003. "A Study of 'with Reference to' in the Context of Administrative Rules," *Shoudu shifan daxue xuebao (shehui kexue ban)* [Journal of the Capital Normal University (Social Sciences)]. 4, pp. 36–41.

Yan, Yun-xiang. 1995. "Everyday Power Relations: Changes in a North China Village," in *The Waning of the Communist State: Economic Origins of Political Decline in China and Hungary.* Andrew G. Walder, ed. Berkeley: University of California Press, pp. 215–238.

Yang, Mayfair M. 1994. *Gifts, Favors and Banquets: The Art of Social Relationship in China.* Ithaca, NY: Cornell University Press.

Zhang Houyi and Qin Shaoyang, 1989. "Present Problems and Solutions in the Development of Million-Asset Private Enterprises," *Jingji tizhi gaige ziliao 39* [Materials on Economic System Reform 39]. Reprinted in *Fuyin baokan ziliao – Jingji tizhi gaige* [Reprinted Periodical Materials – Economic System Reform]. 6, pp. 59–67.

Zhang, Qianfan. 2003. "The People's Court in Transition: The Prospects of the Chinese Judicial Reform." *Journal of Contemporary China.* 12.34. pp. 69–101.

Zhou, Xueguang, Qiang Li, Wei Zhao, and He Cai. 2003. "Embeddedness and Contractual Relationships in China's Transitional Economy." *American Sociological Review.* 68.1, pp. 75–102.

Zou Xiayu and Zhang Qingguo, 2003. "A Tentative Discussion of the Application of Law in Criminal Proceedings through the Form of 'with Reference to'," *Xiandai faxue* [Modern Law Science]. 5, pp. 27–30.

TWELVE

China's Fiscal System: A Work in Progress

Christine P. W. Wong and Richard M. Bird

Public finance matters. It matters for sustained economic growth. It matters for economic stability. It matters for the distribution of income and wealth. It matters for the delivery of such basic services as education and health. It matters for political stability. These statements are as true in China as in any country. What differentiates China from other countries is not that its development is magically unrelated to what its public sector does and how it is financed but rather that the key to its public finance system lies in intergovernmental fiscal relations.

Unless China begins to tackle more systematically the serious problems that have emerged in the finances of its various levels of subnational government, the problems to which the present unsatisfactory system give rise will over time increasingly distort resource allocation, increase distributional tensions, and in all likelihood slow down the impressive recent growth of the Chinese economy.[1] These statements may seem strong but as we show in this chapter, the evidence on hand – although far from fully satisfactory, given the lack of solid and reliable information on the size and nature of China's real fiscal system – is consistent with this pessimistic reading. China's fiscal and – in time – economic future rests, to a greater extent than generally seems to be understood, on the success achieved in strengthening and extending recent ad hoc reforms to key aspects of its fiscal system within a more consistent and purposive framework. No doubt, once fully seized of the problem, China will be able to deal with it as it has with other problems in the past. Nonetheless, it seems clear that the fiscal dimension of China's development needs more attention than it has received to date.

In "The Development of the Fiscal System," we discuss the strongly "path-dependent" nature of China's fiscal development in the reform era. In "Mobilizing Public-Sector Resources," we consider the revenue side of public finance, with

---

[1] For analyses of local government financial problems, see World Bank (2002) and Wong (2005b, 2007). The World Bank (2002) argues that local government financial problems had, by the late 1990s, become an obstacle to implementation of the national development agenda on health and education. Wong (2005b, 2007) emphasizes the adverse distributional consequences of the present intergovernmental fiscal system.

special attention to the unusual extent to which public-sector activities in China are financed "off-budget." In "Spending and Services," we consider more briefly some aspects of budgeting and public expenditure management. In "The Key to the Fiscal Future," we argue that the revenue and expenditure problems cannot be understood or resolved without dealing with the underlying problem of developing a more sustainable fiscal structure of public agencies and subnational governments. In "China in International Perspective," we briefly consider China's fiscal system in international perspective, and the last section concludes.

THE DEVELOPMENT OF THE FISCAL SYSTEM

China's fiscal development in recent years illustrates clearly the importance of "path dependency." How a country's institutions develop depends critically upon where they start. To understand either the present or the future of China's fiscal system, one must first understand where it came from: would-be reformers everywhere have learned that it can be perilous to underestimate the inertia of fiscal institutions. Although China has been collecting taxes for millennia, fortunately to understand the present system we need to consider only the fiscal system that was installed in the 1950s, largely reflecting then-current Soviet practice.

The Starting Point

Under that system, essentially all expenditures were determined at the center. Importantly for future developments, however, responsibilities for day-to-day public administration and social services, such as education (except universities), public safety, health care, social security, housing, and other local/urban services, were all delegated to local governments. Financing for these services was provided by the central government through the revenue-sharing system, under which all revenues belonged to the central government.

At the time revenues came largely from industrial profits and were collected in a highly uneven pattern from different regions and localities. In principle, sharing rates were set annually at levels leaving each local government sufficient resources to finance its (centrally) approved expenditures. In practice, the revenue-sharing system was largely negotiated in nature. More generally, the way in which taxes and prices were intertwined made both the incidence and the effects of the fiscal system nontransparent. Although the implicitly perverse incentive structure of the pre-reform fiscal system was in part held in check by direct controls and in some instances offset by aspects of the financial structure, on the whole it seems clear that it was conducive to neither growth nor equity.[2]

---

[2] For an early assessment, see World Bank (1988); for more general discussion of the structure and effects of Soviet-type fiscal systems, see Wanless (1985).

The Decline of the Budget, 1978–1993

Once the mechanisms of the planned economy – administrative prices, compulsory procurement and planned delivery, and monopoly state ownership of industry – began to be dismantled, the formal revenue system quickly began to erode. The immediate impact of market reform was a rapid and dramatic erosion in the traditional tax base of the planned economy, as SOE profits and revenue collection declined steeply.[3] Central revenues were especially hard-hit because local governments in rich regions often shielded local enterprises from taxation to avoid sharing revenues with central the government.[4]

To some extent, of course, these results were presumably desired: the central government did not want to hasten the collapse of SOEs, nor did local governments wish to hinder the initial expansion in agriculture and the growth of new, small rural industries by imposing heavy tax burdens. In any case, China had no real tax administration in place that could have taxed rural-based growth. No one recognizable as a modern tax official had been needed under the old system, so it is not a surprise that no such officials existed when fiscal reform began at the end of the 1970s. The Chinese tax system rested on the local collection of revenues that were then remitted to the center, and this administrative structure proved vulnerable to erosion as central economic control lessened. Unfortunately, these fundamental administrative problems were not initially understood, and the immediate fiscal reform as part of the "new Chinese system" took the form of a series of changes in tax structure and revenue-sharing arrangements (Wong, 1992, 1993).

With respect to enterprise profits, for example, in 1984, an income tax on SOEs was introduced to replace profit remittances. This reform met with fierce resistance and in 1986 was replaced by a "contract" system, under which enterprises signed multiyear contracts specifying their profit remittances. Faced with a steep fiscal decline and lacking the capacity to monitor tax effort in the provinces, in 1988 the central government introduced a further system of fiscal contracts (the "fiscal responsibility system") with local governments. These contracts stipulated a lump-sum remittance to the center from each province, to increase annually by an agreed rate, with any additional revenues accruing to the province. In return, provinces accepted responsibility for meeting their expenditure requirements from retained revenues. (For the poor provinces, the fiscal contracts froze the annual subsidies they received from the central government in nominal terms at the 1987 level, so their value was quickly eroded during the high inflation in 1988 and 1989). The

---

[3] Of course, this phenomenon occurred to varying extents in all "transitional" economies (see World Bank, 1996a).

[4] For example, under the planned economy Shanghai remitted more than 80 percent of its revenues to the central government. This high "tax" on Shanghai revenues created incentives for collusion between the municipal government and its subordinate enterprises and the potential for informally sharing the "saved revenues" within Shanghai. For analyses of this evolution, see Oksenberg and Tong (1991) and Wong (1991, 1992).

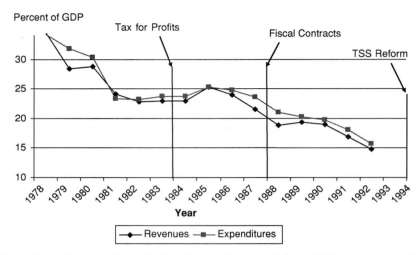

Figure 12.1. The long fiscal decline (*Source:* Calculated from MOF data, adjusted to conventional definitions.)

result was a fundamental change in the fiscal system: by delinking revenue sharing from expenditure needs, fiscal contracts put local governments on a self-financing basis for the first time – a de facto devolution of responsibilities that was later codified in the 1994 Budget Law.

Fiscal contracts did not, however, solve the central government's financial problems, as the ratio of fiscal revenues to gross domestic product (GDP) continued to decline (Figure 12.1) due to continuing problems of SOE profitability and persistent credibility problems of the central government (Wong, Heady, and Woo, 1995). Moreover, as the generous terms of the contracts gave local governments a disproportionate share of new revenues, the central share of revenues fell rapidly, to just over 20 percent in 1993.[5] At the nadir, the central budget allocated only 3 percent of GDP, with seemingly no end to the decline in sight.

Accompanying this decline of the budget, however, "extrabudgetary revenues" grew during the 1980s and 1990s, offsetting the budgetary trend to some extent. It is important to note, however, that the nontax fees and levies and quasifiscal expenditures included under the general rubric of extrabudgetary revenues were even more decentralized than budgetary revenues and were largely outside of the purview of the Ministry of Finance (MOF). Their existence thus did little to offset the erosion of allocative control by the central government. By the early 1990s, the situation for the central government was said to be "desperate," spurring a drastic reform with two paramount objectives – stemming the decline of revenues

---

[5] This was largely because the contracts had failed to anticipate the high inflation rates through the late 1980s and early 1990s, when revenues grew at an annual rate of 12 percent from 1987 to 1993, while remittances grew at low single-digit rates.

Percent of Total

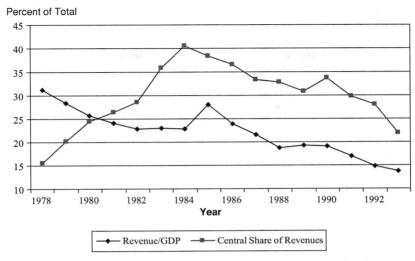

Figure 12.2. The "two ratios" (*Source:* Calculated from MOF data.)

and clawing back a majority share for the central government or "raising the two ratios" (revenue/GDP and central/total revenue) (Figure 12.2).

The 1994 Reform

The major fiscal reform of 1994 aimed to "recentralize" the fiscal system. The fiscal reform package introduced in 1994 actually had three main components: tax sharing, tax modernization, and tax administration (Bahl, 1999). While the tax-sharing system (TSS, *fenshuizhi*) was the most visible and controversial element, the other two were also important changes that have received far less notice.

Tax Modernization

An important component of the 1994 reform was tax modernization, simplifying the tax structure, eliminating distortionary elements, and increasing transparency. The complex multitiered system of turnover taxes borrowed from the Soviet Union was replaced with a value-added tax (VAT), which now applies to all manufacturing, repair, and assembly activities, primarily at a single rate of 17 percent. On eleven products an excise tax (the consumption tax, CT) is applied at differing rates in addition to the VAT: tobacco products, alcohol, and a few luxury consumer goods, such as cosmetics, jewelry, gas and kerosene, and motor vehicles. A business tax is applied to services including banking and insurance, wholesale and retail trade, transfer of real estate and invisible assets, and entertainment, generally at a rate of 5 percent of turnover.

During the 1980s, the multiple-rated turnover taxes had created important distortions, attracting too much investment into some sectors and encouraging vertical integration within enterprises, thus contributing to duplication and convergence in industrial structures across regions. Even after market competition had eroded profit margins, sectors with high product tax rates (up to 60 percent of the price) continued to attract entry. Local governments seeking to maximize revenues would choose to enter sectors where the sum of profits and tax rates was above average, even if profit rates were expected to be low or even negative. This appears to have been the case in industries such as liquor and tobacco. For example, Zhou (2000) reported that even in the late 1990s, thirty of the thirty-one provincial-level units had cigarette-manufacturing plants, even though few provinces grew tobacco. At the firm level, 55 percent of the 178 manufacturers were loss-making on an after-tax basis in 1996. In 1998, although at least four provinces showed negative unit profit rates among cigarette manufacturers in their province, all had positive returns when taxes were included. Differential tax rates thus prolonged local protection of less efficient producers.

The single-rate VAT introduced in 1994 eliminated the undesirable allocative effect of turnover taxes.[6] By taxing only the portion of value added in any enterprise, the VAT also eliminated tax cascading and much of the incentive for vertical integration that had existed under the product taxes (and their predecessors, the industrial–commercial taxes).[7] Since those taxes were paid on gross output value, they had created significant incentives against specialization in the production of intermediate inputs.

The Tax-Sharing System

The TSS fundamentally changed the way revenues are shared between the central and provincial governments by shifting from a negotiated system of general revenue sharing to a mix of tax assignments and tax sharing. Under the TSS, taxes are assigned to central government, local government, or shared (Table 12.1). By assigning the biggest tax, the VAT, as a shared tax and claiming 75 percent of its receipts, the central government reclaimed a majority portion of total revenues.[8] At the same time, however, the TSS essentially swept aside all earlier concerns about the disequalizing effect of the tax assignment, apparently in part at least to win quick agreement from the richer provinces.[9]

---

[6] There had previously been twenty-one rates for the product tax, ranging from 3 to 60 percent, and four business tax rates, ranging from 3 to 15 percent. The reform also unified the turnover tax treatment for domestic and foreign enterprises by eliminating the consolidated industrial and commercial tax (with forty rates ranging from 1.5 to 69.0 percent) previously applied to foreign enterprises, placing them also under the VAT.

[7] Some incentive remained owing to the lack of crediting for capital inputs.

[8] The VAT accounts for nearly half of all tax revenues in China. It is also a reliable tax whose revenues go up with GDP regardless of profitability and is thus less cyclical than income or profit taxes.

[9] See, for example, Zhao (2003), who describes the desperate funding crisis in which the central leadership found that they had also lost control over tax collection at the local levels. In the course of introducing the VAT, for example, Beijing Municipality was found to have underreported 9.8 billion yuan in revenues.

Table 12.1. *Revenue assignments between the central and provincial governments*

I. *Taxes exclusively assigned to the central government*
  1. Excise taxes
  2. Taxes collected from the Ministry of Railroads and from the headquarters of banks and insurance companies
  3. Income taxes, sales taxes, and royalties from offshore oil activities of foreign companies and joint ventures
  4. Energy and transportation fund contribution
  5. Seventy percent of the three sales taxes collected from enterprises owned by the Ministry of Industry, the Ministry of Power, SINOPEC (petrochemicals), and the China nonferrous metals companies.
  6. All customs duty, VAT, and excise taxes on imports
  7. Enterprise income tax collected from banks and other financial institutions

II. *Taxes shared between the central and local governments*
  1. Value-added tax (75 percent central and 25 percent provincial)
  2. Natural resource taxes (coal, gas, oil, and other minerals if the enterprises are fully Chinese owned)
  3. Construction tax on the cost of construction of buildings that are outside the plan and financed from retained earnings
  4. Salt tax
  5. Industrial and commercial tax, and income tax levied on foreign and joint venture enterprises
  6. Security and exchange tax (50 percent central and 50 percent provincial) – added in late 1990s
  7. Income tax of all enterprises – added in 2002
  8. Personal income taxes – added in 2002

III. *Taxes exclusively assigned to local governments*
  1. Business (gross receipts) tax falling on sectors not covered by VAT (transportation and communications, construction, finance and insurance, post and telecommunications, culture and sports, entertainment, hotels and restaurants, and other)
  2. Rural market (stall rental) trading tax
  3. The urban maintenance and construction tax (a surcharge on the tax liability of enterprises for business tax, CT, and VAT)
  4. The urban land-use tax
  5. Vehicle and vessel utilization tax
  6. Thirty percent of the product and VAT revenues collected from enterprises owned by the Ministry of Industry, Ministry of Power, SINOPEC, and the China nonferrous metals companies
  7. Value-added tax on land
  8. Education surtax
  9. Entertainment and slaughter taxes
  10. Property tax
  11. Surtax on collective enterprises
  12. Resources tax
  13. Fixed-asset investment tax (discontinued in 1999)
  14. Fines for delinquent taxes

Source: Adapted from World Bank (2002, table 4.1).

The TSS also cut incentives for local duplication and protectionism by reducing local "ownership" of turnover taxes. Under the previous regime, product tax revenues from local enterprises were pooled with other revenues and shared with the central government. As fiscal decentralization turned over the bulk of marginal revenues to local governments, these product taxes stayed mostly in local coffers. Even though a complicated tax rebate scheme commits the central government to rebating some 30 percent of its new revenues from the VAT and the accompanying excise taxes – the CT – the TSS significantly diluted the linkage between enterprises and local revenues. For the cigarette industry, for example, where the product tax had been 40–66 percent (Ministry of Finance, 1982),[10] it was usually revenue enhancing for local governments to carry loss-making manufacturers. Under the TSS, even though there is a 40 percent excise tax in addition to the VAT, only 25 percent of the VAT accrues to local government, plus 30 percent of any incremental revenues collected by the central government. In a saturated market, if the local cigarette manufacturer is not able to increase sales (on which tax rebates are based), the local government would receive none of the CT revenues and no further rebates on the VAT.

To maintain some incentives for promoting local industry, however, the TSS provided that the enterprise income tax (EIT) would continue to be divided by ownership (or subordination), with central enterprises paying EIT to the central government, provincial enterprises to the provincial government, and so on. Although this meant that local governments still had an incentive to enter industries where profit margins are high, such opportunities were increasingly limited to protected sectors, such as cigarettes, telecommunications, and the automobile industry, where high tariff walls or government controls continued to maintain rents.[11] With only a minor portion of VAT accruing to local coffers, protection of inefficient loss-making enterprises is likely to be more short lived under the TSS. In the cigarette industry, for example, the result over time should be consolidation similar to that occurring earlier in other industries such as breweries and manufacturers of household appliances (see Chapter 15).

Tax Administration

The 1994 reform established a national tax administration in China for the first time. The previous local tax bureaus were split into two distinct offices: a national tax administration responsible for collecting central and shared taxes (the VAT, the CT, and customs duties, as well as the EIT from central enterprises) and a local tax administration responsible for collecting local taxes. By removing central taxes and the VAT from local administration, the reform largely eliminated opportunities for

---

[10] These are embedded (tax-inclusive) rates. Ad valorem rates would be much higher.
[11] Naughton (1992) shows the rapid convergence of profit rates across industries through the 1980s as entry was opened. The exceptions were sectors where government monopolies were retained.

local governments to divert central revenues into local coffers through manipulation of tax assessments. The recovery of revenue collections from the trough of 11 percent of GDP in 1996 to the current level of nearly 20 percent can be attributed primarily to stemming this hemorrhage.

Overview of the Reform

The 1994 reforms, hereafter simply referred to as the TSS, fundamentally changed incentives for local governments. While reducing fiscal incentives for promoting local industry, the TSS also shifted incentives more toward commerce and trade by expanding the business tax on services and assigning it to local governments where it has become an important revenue source that rivals the VAT.

Some distortions remain. For example, sharing revenues of the VAT and the EIT with local governments on a derivation basis (where taxes are collected, such as the headquarters of enterprises) may in the long run hinder the growth of national enterprises and slow down the consolidation process. If an enterprise has production facilities (not independent units) in more than one jurisdiction, the issue of where it pays its VAT and EIT arises. Since these taxes are likely to be paid exclusively in the jurisdiction where the headquarters of the enterprise is located, the result may again be protectionist policies by local jurisdictions attempting to maximize their share of the VAT and EIT, to the detriment of a more efficient allocation of resources. In recent years there have been growing complaints of "tax competition," whereby local governments lure enterprises to move their headquarters with offers to "rebate" a portion of their tax payments.

In addition, by sharing VAT revenues with local governments at a flat rate by origin, the TSS introduced a highly disequalizing feature to revenue sharing, ensuring that revenue-rich regions keep more. Under the TSS, coastal provinces gained revenue shares relative to inland provinces. From 1992 to 1998, the ratio of provincial per capita fiscal expenditures in Shanghai grew from 2.5 to 3.9 times the national average, in Beijing from 2.2 to 2.7, and in Guangdong from 1.1 to 1.4. In contrast, in Henan the ratio fell from 0.44 to 0.42, in Gansu from 0.8 to 0.6, and in Hunan from 0.53 to 0.49 (Ministry of Finance, 2002).

More generally, because the TSS recentralized revenues but left expenditure assignments unchanged, it created a huge fiscal gap for local governments (see Figure 12.3). Unlike the previous regime under which only poor provinces received transfers, under TSS all provincial units including Shanghai and Beijing are now dependent on central transfers to finance expenditures. In aggregate, provinces are now dependent on transfers to finance nearly 50 percent of their expenditures (Figure 12.4). How these transfers are designed thus has a direct impact on distributional outcomes. Despite an initial promise to roll out a formula-based equalization transfer system to counter the regressive effects of the TSS, this was not done. A "transitional intergovernmental transfer" was introduced in 1995 but never accounted for more than 1–2 percent of total transfers through the 1990s. Instead, under the TSS, transfers were dominated by tax rebates that also favor

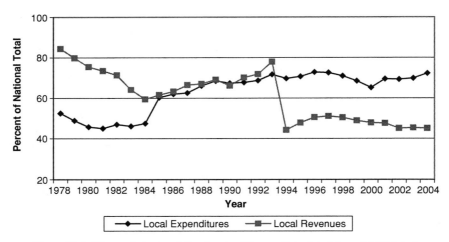

Figure 12.3. The evolving local fiscal status (*Source:* Calculated from MOF data.)

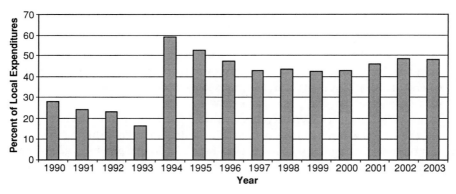

Figure 12.4. Transfers as a share of local expenditures (*Source:* Lou, 2000; Ministry of Finance, *Finance Yearbook of China*, various years.)

the rich, reinforcing the disequalizing character of the TSS itself (see Figures 12.5 and 12.6).

A System in Transition

As this brief account suggests, the most critical fiscal issues in China today essentially arise from the mismatch of expenditures and revenues between levels of government resulting from the 1994 reform and the resulting distortions, as China's various layers of government struggle to find their fiscal feet in this fundamentally distorted structure. Important as it was, the 1994 reform by no means marked the end of the process of fiscal reform, though it may (as Churchill once said) mark the end of the beginning of that process. In recent years, for example, local governments

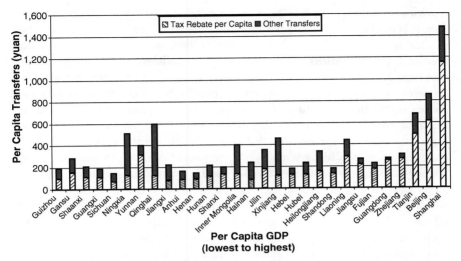

Figure 12.5. Per capita transfers by province (1998) (*Source:* Calculated from provincial final account statistics, Ministry of Finance, *Finance Yearbook of China 1999.*)

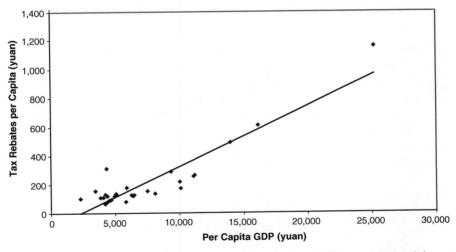

Figure 12.6. The distribution of tax rebates by province (1998) (*Source:* Calculated from provincial final account statistics, Ministry of Finance, *Finance Yearbook of China 1999.*)

have attempted to cope with their increasing fiscal problems by increasing revenues in a variety of legal, quasilegal, and even illegal ways, as we discuss in the next section.

China's current fiscal system is the product of a quarter century of changes, some of them drastic, but it is clearly a system still in transition and remains very much a work in progress. Nonetheless, despite the problems remaining in the fiscal area, it is important to remember two things. First, China has already come far in fiscal terms. The reform era started with a fiscal system that was completely unsuitable for a mixed economy. Over the last two decades, many sensible changes have been introduced in tax policy, tax administration, expenditure management, and even, to a lesser extent, intergovernmental finance. Secondly, as we noted at the beginning, despite getting so many fiscal matters "wrong" China has clearly managed to do incredibly well to date in economic terms. Although in some ways surprising, on closer examination this outcome is by no means inexplicable. To a considerable extent, China has managed to overcome the macroeconomic problems that would otherwise have arisen from its fiscal imbalance through a combination of monetary and financial policy and continued political control from the center. Similarly, despite the relatively chaotic operation of its overwhelmingly important subnational government sector, to date Chinese officials and entrepreneurs have been able to cope amazingly well. They have done so, however, in effect by piling up a series of problems that if not resolved in some more satisfactory fashion than heretofore will, we suggest, increasingly distort and perhaps even eventually halt development.

MOBILIZING PUBLIC-SECTOR RESOURCES

The common view of China's revenue policy over the last two decades is that the government has been fighting a largely losing struggle to maintain its resource base in the face of drastic changes in economic structure. The need for such a "fight" seems obvious, since government revenue as a share of GDP fell drastically from 35 percent in 1980 to 19 percent in 1990 and then still further to a low of 11 percent in 1995–1996 before rising again toward the end of the century. The central government in particular lost out in the earlier years, with its revenues falling to as little as 3 percent of GDP in 1993 and even after the 1994 reform amounting to only 9 percent by 2000.

The Tax System

In many respects China's current tax structure appears as "modern" as that in most countries. Unsurprisingly, however, there is still much room for reform. The VAT, for example, although a major revenue producer, is not really a VAT, because it does not credit capital expenditures and thus penalizes new investment. China's VAT is thus not the destination-based consumption-type tax found in most countries (Ebrill et al., 2001), but rather an origin-based production-type tax that also excludes from the tax base many services which are subject to a separate business tax collected by local governments. This VAT design hampers export competitiveness, penalizes investment, generates distortions through cascading, and creates incentives for local protectionism.

With WTO accession, it has become urgent to reform the VAT to bring it in line with international practice. Shifting to a more normal consumption-type VAT, however, would be expensive. Since investment constitutes 35–40 percent of GDP, exempting investment could cost the government more than one-third of its VAT receipts unless the change is offset either by a rate increase (from the already relatively high 17 percent) or by broadening the base to include services and offsetting the likely effects on local revenues in some way.[12] Currently, reforms are under way to move toward a consumption-type VAT, beginning in the three northeast provinces of Liaoning, Heilongjiang, and Jilin in 2004. Although the reform was to have been rolled out nationwide in 2005, it was postponed, then restarted in 2007 on a limited scale. In the northeast pilot provinces, in order to keep costs under control, tax credits were applied only to selected investments and were also limited to firms that were in business prior to the introduction of the reform.

Similarly, the EIT regime leaves much to be desired. It is marked by tax preferences, with large differences in the treatment of domestic- and foreign-funded businesses that both add to the complexity of the tax system and lead to losses in revenue and unfair competition among enterprises. The present sharing of revenues from both the VAT and the EIT with local governments on a derivation basis is at best a transitional arrangement.[13] For instance, sharing VAT revenues on a derivation basis (where taxes are collected at points such as the headquarters of enterprises) has been a major cause of the increasing disparities in revenue distribution in favor of the richest provinces. Moreover, unfairness has been accentuated because the VAT can be credited and debited in different local jurisdictions. EIT sharing also is suspect: for example, even if an enterprise has production facilities (not independent units) in other jurisdictions, EIT is usually paid exclusively in the jurisdiction where the headquarters of the enterprise are located.[14]

Other aspects of the tax system are also cause for concern. For example, the relatively high taxes imposed on banking deter the development of the financial sector and impose added fiscal costs to saving and investment. More generally, revenues from the formal tax system are relatively low and not very buoyant. In part perhaps reflecting the apparently low level of official concern with emerging interpersonal inequality, little has been done to develop personal income taxes or for that matter the property and land taxes that seem needed to finance China's

[12] The business tax accounted for an average of 24 percent of local "own revenues" before tax rebates in 2000, but was as high as 37 percent in Beijing. For detailed discussion of China's VAT, see Ahmad, Singh, and Lockwood (2004).

[13] Revenue sharing of the VAT and the EIT by the central government with local governments on a derivation basis was a logical move, given the old Soviet system, and many transition economies moving from a Soviet-type tax system took this step. However, it is also a source of unfairness and significant distortions, leading many transition countries to abandon significant parts of this system. Most recently, Russia, Ukraine, and Kazakhstan have discontinued revenue sharing for the VAT and reassigned this tax fully to the central level.

[14] The EIT accounted for an average 13 percent of revenues, but was 20 percent or more for a number of provinces including Beijing, Shanghai, Tianjin, Zhejiang, Jiangsu, and Tibet.

growing urban development in a sustainable fashion (Hong, 2003).[15] There is thus still much that could usefully be done to improve the tax structure.

Equally or more important, tax administration remains weak and there appears to be substantial leakage and much scope for corruption (Li, 1997). These problems seem especially important at the local level, where collection costs are high – estimated at 3–4 percent in the aggregate, and as high as 10 percent or more in some localities.[16] Despite the creation of local tax offices in 1994, no steps have yet been taken to establish an effective local tax administration. Local governments have no tax autonomy: all "local" taxes are assigned, with both rates and bases set by the central government.

Outside the Budget[17]

In China, however, the formal budget is only a part of the fiscal story, and not necessarily the most important part. In addition to the extrabudgetary funds (EBF) that grew so rapidly in the first half of the 1990s, many other implicit and hidden revenues, transfers, and expenditures pervade the system, driven in part by the lack of any good formal local tax bases and facilitated by the continuing obscurity of the line between "government" and "business" at the local level. After prolonged wavering during the 1980s about whether government agencies should be engaged in profit-making activities, tacit permission was given in the early 1990s for these activities to continue (Duckett, 1998). With the TSS recentralization of revenues (raising the central share from 20 to 60 percent) creating a huge fiscal gap for local governments, allowing local governments to tap off-budget revenues was a stop-gap measure to avoid some of the potential adverse effects the TSS reform would otherwise have on economic growth by enabling local governments to secure sufficient finance to carry out their assigned functions.

When Zhu Rongji became premier in March 1998, he announced that fiscal reform would be one of the five areas of reform priority for his administration, and the program to "convert fees into taxes" (*feigaishui*) was the first major effort in fiscal reform. This seemed an appropriate focus because *luanshoufei* (the reckless collection of fees) had become the bane of businesses and citizens alike. This practice also created a serious problem for the central government, as it eroded tax capacity and subverted the whole budgeting process, thereby impeding the government's ability to carry out its core fiscal functions of macromanagement, equalization, and resource allocation.

---

[15] On the greater political than economic importance of such redistributive taxes in emerging democracies, see, for example, Bird (2003) on Latin America. So far, at least, there is little evidence that this has been an important factor in Chinese policy.

[16] These figures are based on fieldwork carried out in 2003–2004.

[17] This section draws heavily from Wong (2001).

A nationwide audit by a blue-ribbon group consisting of the Ministry of Finance, the then State Planning Commission, the State Council Audit Office, the People's Bank of China, and the Ministry of Supervision in mid-1996 found more than 384 billion yuan in "extrabudgetary funds," about 50 percent more than the reported figures and equal to 6 percent of GDP. Given that budgetary revenues were only 11.3 percent of GDP that year, this amounted to more than half of budget revenues and more than one-third of resources available to government. In 1997, the MOF estimated that EBF totaled more than 400 billion yuan. In 1998, estimates of the size of EBF climbed higher still; the MOF used a range of 8–10 percent of GDP,[18] but officials of the State Administration of Taxation (SAT) often cited estimates of 15 percent or more.[19]

As this range of estimates suggests, it is surprisingly difficult to measure the real size of public-sector activities in China. Reporting requirements are much looser for EBF than for budgetary resources. Some EBF consist of incomes and expenditures of extrabudgetary enterprises of government and their agencies, whose interaction with budgetary resources is murky, ill defined, and in flux. These problems are compounded by differing definitions of what is "extrabudgetary" and by the fact that recipients of EBF have no incentive to disclose fully the extent of their receipts and payees are often afraid to report fully the extent of payment. From 1996 onward, still more confusion was sown by the many changes introduced to the reporting of EBF in the budget as well as the reclassification of administrative units under government (see Figure 12.7 and Tables 12.2 and 12.3).

What Are EBF?

A broad definition of EBF is that they constitute all resources managed directly or indirectly by administrative branches of the government outside the normal budgetary process. Since the essence of budgeting is to weigh expenditures against one another, or against increased revenue, from the perspective of public expenditure management the critical distinction between budgetary and extrabudgetary funds is the extent to which the resources are put through the normal budgetary deliberations.[20]

Two common types of EBF are found around the world: (1) special accounts segregated from the budget and intended for carrying out a specific activity or benefiting a specific agency. These accounts are often organized as funds or self-balancing accounting entities. (2) Revenues raised outside the budget framework

---

[18] In a speech at a meeting of finance ministers in Paris in December 1998, Vice Minister Lou Jiwei spoke of government fees and charges that equaled about 10 percent of GDP and were "not entirely under the control of the budget."

[19] This number has been widely cited in the SAT newspaper, *Zhongguo shuiwubao*, and attributed to the highest officials of SAT, including its deputy chief as well as chief economist.

[20] For a discussion of how the management of extrabudgetary funds differs in China from that in OECD countries, see World Bank (2000, chapter 3).

Table 12.2. *Changes in measuring extrabudgetary revenue before and after 1993*

Year	Total EB revenue	Local government EB funds	Administrative unit EB funds	SOE and department EB funds
1990	2,708.64	60.58	576.95	2,071.1
1991	3,243.31	68.77	697.0	2,477.54
1992	3,854.92	90.88	885.45	2,878.59
1993	1,432.54	114.71	1,317.83	–
1994	1,862.53	140.03	1,722.5	–
1995	2,406.5	171.65	2,234.85	–

Note: Values are in 100 million yuan.
Source: Ministry of Finance, *Finance Yearbook of China* (various years).

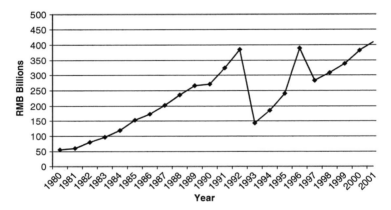

Figure 12.7. Extrabudgetary revenues (billion RMB)
Notes:
- The large decrease in extrabudgetary revenues in 1993 was a result of changes in how extrabudgetary revenues were covered and measured. Specifically, data from 1993 does not include revenues from "state-operated enterprises" and is not comparable to earlier figures (see Table 12.2).
- The large decrease in extrabudgetary revenues in 1997 was accounted for by drops in the revenues of administrative units and local governments. The causes were as follows: removal of business incomes from PSUs from EBF, abolition of many fees under the campaign to stop the "reckless levying of fees," and incorporation of some administrative charges into the budget. The decline would have been even larger except for the inclusion of "revenues from fundraising programs of township governments" in the totals for extrabudgetary revenue (see Table 12.3).
- In 1998, the scope of extrabudgetary revenues was changed again to no longer include "revenue from local governments." However, "revenue of funds" and "other revenue" were added, and "revenues of state-owned enterprises and its governing departments" was also reintroduced into the total extrabudgetary revenues. This involved reclassification of some revenues, such as revenues from sales of land leases, which became "fund revenue" (see Table 12.3).
Source: Yearbook and interviews at MOF.

Table 12.3. *More changes in the measurement of extrabudgetary revenues in 1996 and 1998*

	Total	As percent of GDP	Administrative units	Local governments	Township self-raised funds	Revenue of funds[a]	SOE revenues	Other revenues
1994	186.3	3.9	172.3	14.0				
1995	240.7	4.0	223.5	17.2				
1996	389.3	5.5	339.6	22.5	27.3			
1997	282.6	3.6	241.4	11.6	29.6			
1998	308.2	3.7	198.2		33.7	47.8	5.5	23.0
1999	338.5	3.8	235.4		35.9	39.7	5.0	22.5
2000	382.6	3.9	265.5		40.3	38.4	5.9	32.6
2001	430.0	3.9	309.0		41.0	38.0	6.0	36.0
2002	447.9	3.7	323.8		27.2	37.6	7.2	52.1
2003	456.7	3.4	333.6		29.3	28.7	5.2	59.8

Note: Values are in billion yuan.

[a] Government funds are a new category of created in 1998 to denote selected categories of extrabudgetary revenues that would be reported in the budget reports to the National People's Congress, including social security funds and land revenues – categories that were important to track. This was to have been a first step toward incorporating these funds into budgetary revenues.

Source: Yearbook (various years).

by administrative units as well as off-budget payments by the Treasury, the central bank, or any other organization that has authority over public money. Type 1 EBF are earmarked funds that are protected from annual budgetary deliberations. Type 2 EBF are nonbudgetary revenues of branches of government. Type 1 are thus extrabudgetary by use and Type 2 by source. In most countries EBF tend to be predominantly Type 1. The principal exceptions are former Soviet-type economies, such as China.[21] In the particular case of China, the Budget Law explicitly prohibits the transfer of budgetary revenues to extrabudgetary accounts,[22] so that EBF in China are thus extrabudgetary by both source and use. As discussed later, the primary motivation for the development of EBF in China, especially at the subnational level, has clearly been revenue enhancement rather than earmarking,

The term "extrabudgetary funds" is generally used in China in a narrower sense than the discussion given earlier implies. Following Soviet practice, explicit EBF were first created in the early 1950s as small amounts of funds set aside from centralized management and control.[23] As the concept evolved, however, EBF came to refer to fees and funds that are not taxes or budgetary items but that nonetheless are specifically authorized by some government body.[24] This definition leaves out significant public resources that are neither budgetary nor extrabudgetary in this sense. Such funds are variously called self-raised funds, extraextrabudgetary funds, off-budgetary funds, or extrasystem revenues. One important example is revenue from the sale of land leases: because of the irregular, nonrecurrent nature of such revenue, the MOF agreed that it should not be included in local budgetary revenues to avoid affecting the revenue-sharing base. However, no treatment was clearly specified for such funds. In some localities, such revenues were called extrabudgetary revenue; elsewhere, they were listed as "self-raised funds." It was only in the late 1990s that they began to be treated as "fund revenues" and reported in the budget as a "below-the-line" item. For all these reasons, it is far from simple to tell just what is being counted in references to extrabudgetary resources in China.

The Effects of EBF
In general, both earmarking and EBF tend to increase under conditions of fiscal stress and progressive breakdown of budgetary procedures. Since the passage of Proposition 13 in 1978 severely restricted property tax increases in California,

[21] For a discussion of the situation with respect to EBF in Russia, see World Bank (1996b).
[22] Reported in *Renmin Ribao (People's Daily)*, August 6, 1996.
[23] The earliest examples were the surcharge on the agricultural tax that local governments were permitted to spend without higher-level approval and the surcharge on the wage bill that could be set aside for workers' bonuses, and so on.
[24] While most EBF thus have legal authorization from some level of government or branch, these decrees usually lack specificity and rarely contain detailed criteria for the use of funds. Many are internal documents known only to the relevant authorities.

for example, local governments have resorted to a plethora of user charges to enhance revenues and finance local services. Moreover, tax increases have tended to earmark revenues for specific uses, thus making them extrabudgetary.[25] Similarly, the breakdown of macroeconomic discipline in Argentina during the 1980s led to a proliferation of earmarking: at the peak, more than 30 percent of the budget was locked up in special budgetary accounts.[26] In some ways, China seems to have followed the same path. In the 1990s, a series of laws and decrees carved out pieces of the budget for specific uses: for example, the National Education Law mandated that by 2000, the budget would spend 4 percent of GDP on education, and the Agriculture Law required that budgetary spending on agriculture must grow at a faster rate than budgetary revenues.

However, several features distinguish EBF in China from those in most developing (though not most transitional)[27] economies. One such feature is that the budget is not comprehensive, and government engages in many activities off-budget. Under central planning, allocative decisions by government were only partially reflected in the budget. Administrative prices and the credit plan also played important roles in directing resources to achieve government objectives. As budgetary revenues fell from 35 percent of the GDP to less than 12 percent during the transition, the government understandably depended increasingly on extrabudgetary levers to achieve its policy goals. Throughout much of the 1990s, for example, the government implemented its industrial policy largely through directed lending and financed social expenditures through SOEs. During the 1985–1995 period, quasifiscal spending in the form of directed lending was estimated to have been 6–8 percent of GDP (or half as much as in-budget expenditures). In addition, tax expenditures were another 1–2 percent of GDP (World Bank, 1999).

The sheer size of the EBF sector as well as its composition also distinguishes China. With EBF (excluding extrabudgetary activities and social security) estimated variously at 70–125 percent of the budget (adding together fees and levies equal to 8–10 percent of GDP, quasifiscal spending of 6–8 percent through the banking system, and tax expenditures of another 1–2 percent), China represents an extreme case of dependency on extrabudgetary finance. Importantly, most of these extrabudgetary activities are at the subnational level since subnational governments are responsible for providing significant expenditures, including social safety nets (pensions, unemployment insurance, disability, minimum income support,

[25] A California example is Proposition 99, which imposed a 25-cent per pack tax on cigarettes with revenues earmarked for spending on antismoking propaganda and cancer research.

[26] In Brazil, even without crisis, earmarking at the federal level had, by some measures, grown close to 80 percent of revenues by 2002. For a recent discussion of earmarking in this and other countries, see Bird and Jun (2006).

[27] See, for examples, Wallich (1994), Bird, Ebel, and Wallich (1995), and Bubnova and Way (1998).

etc.) and capital investment (especially the need to replace or refurbish obsolete and poorly maintained infrastructure). In addition, to a considerable extent they have also borne the uncompensated transfers of social expenditures from SOEs – housing, child care, medical care, and sometimes education. How can local governments pay for all this? Even after the 1994 reform, these governments cannot set their tax rates or change the bases of collection; nor can they introduce new taxes. However, they do have ownership over substantial assets, such as land, enterprises, and sometimes natural resources.

In these circumstances, it is not surprising that local governments have responded to fiscal pressures in a variety of ways:

- They have accumulated arrears – wage arrears (to teachers, medical workers, and civil servants) and payments arrears (pensions, unemployment insurance, and debt to suppliers, such as utilities).
- They have borrowed (usually illegally) from SOEs, pension funds, unemployment insurance funds, and banks. Unfortunately, while there is considerable anecdotal evidence about borrowing by local governments in some parts of China, there are no firm numbers on the true extent or precise nature of this phenomenon.[28]
- They have defaulted on obligations to provide social services at adequate levels.
- They have forced enterprises to finance public expenditures – passing on fiscal burdens to the enterprise sector and often via enterprises to the banking sector.
- Most importantly, however, they have focused their efforts on developing EBF. Virtually all levels of government – down to municipal districts and villages – have the capacity to exact payments under various names from local businesses and residents. It is not surprising that most EBF in China are at the subnational level.

Without an effective system of monitoring and control (either by higher-level governments or by an electorate), the extensive decentralized taxing power that exists in reality through the EBF mechanism is obviously prone to abuse. EBF have softened the budget constraint for all levels of government, allowing governments to maintain both bloated workforces and a wide range of activities. The Chinese press cites many instances of excessive spending by local governments – construction of a huge international airport across the border from Hong Kong in Zhuhai, the tens of thousands of "development zones," "tourism spots" and luxury hotels, and, increasingly in the twenty-first century, elaborate plazas and city center shopping malls. Even in poor localities there is a good deal of lavish public spending on banquets and karaoke bars, and so on.

---

[28] Walder (2003) suggests that the mere existence of such borrowing does not imply that subnational governments face a "soft" local budget constraint. On the contrary, he suggests that competition for borrowed funds, driven in part by the ability of local decision makers to reap benefits from such borrowing but checked by continuing party control, is one of the main ways in which "competitive federalism" is at work in China today.

One outcome has been political problems with worsening popular perceptions of government. Converting the present multitude of hidden taxes and transfers to a system of explicit taxes and fees is a necessary but unpopular part of the transition to a market economy. The process has been made even more difficult by the common perception that governments at all levels are abusing their power in imposing fees and levies to enrich themselves.

Local governments and the units (schools, etc.) providing public services at the local level now finance half or more of their expenditures from EBF (Fan, 1998; Wong, 1998; World Bank, 2002). Most of these fees were until recently completely outside the budget. Once a fee was authorized, in most cases local finance departments had no idea how much was collected or what was done with the funds. The 2002 reforms have strengthened attempts to bring extrabudgetary revenues under control, but resistance reportedly remains widespread.

EBF are not all bad, of course. They have provided considerable and arguably desirable autonomy to local governments. At the same time, they have also added considerably to the obscurity and probably also the regressivity of the general public finance scene in China. No one really knows what is going on within the bowels of China's complex and opaque fiscal system.[29] No news is not necessarily good news. In fact, it is decidedly bad news from the perspective of building a more transparent public sector to support China's continuing drive to modernization.

SPENDING AND SERVICES

Getting public money is never easy. Unfortunately, spending it sensibly seems to be equally difficult, or so Chinese experience suggests. Public financial management is weak at all levels of government. It was not until 1999 that any reforms were made in budget preparation, execution, monitoring, and audit, and there is still much to be done in all these areas at the central level of government, let alone at lower levels. Many fundamental problems in financial management remain. For example, since personnel decisions are essentially outside the financial system, significant rigidities and waste are created. The recent reform in rural fees illustrates the problem. The township employees formerly collecting these fees may now be jobless in the sense that they have nothing to do, but they are still there and still have to be paid. Indeed, in many instances they may be paid more now than before in view of the decision to bring township salaries in line with county salaries. Unless changes are made in personnel and financial management systems, increased revenues channeled to townships are thus likely to be eaten up by unproductive salaries.

---

[29] For instance, there is considerable confusion about the real size and nature of the Public Service Units (PSUs) – schools, hospitals, transport systems, and so on – which actually provide services. There is no central data source on the operation and finances of the "public sector" broadly defined: different data are collected by different ministries for different purposes and most of these data are not publicly available in any case.

Budget Reform[30]

Budget reform has lagged in China. Until the end of the century the budgeting process had changed little from the planned economy. As the economy became increasingly decentralized and market oriented, the budget gained importance as the key instrument for resource allocation and macroeconomic management. Its effectiveness as a policy instrument for managing public expenditures, however, was hampered by the increasingly inappropriate budgeting process.[31] The budgeting process was passive and incremental, provided inadequate time for preparation, had little focus on strategic priorities, and was unable to shift expenditures to emerging needs or to track adequately how public funds were spent or even how many people the government employed.

The outcomes of poor budgeting practice are all too evident:

- Spending is poorly matched to policy with the result that inadequate support is provided to priority sectors, while public resources are wasted on sectors that should not be supported by public funds.
- Spending units have too much autonomy due to ineffective oversight and accountability: tasks are not well defined, and no one is really accountable for results.
- The late formulation of the central budget cascades through the intergovernmental system since transfers are determined level by level, and each level has to wait for information from the higher level before it can formulate its own spending and transfer plans. Moreover, since capital subsidies usually have matching provisions, local governments often have to hold large reserves in anticipation.

In addition, the general quality of reporting at subnational levels is poor, financial reports are difficult to compare, and consolidating government financial information is an extremely complex exercise. Audit is particularly poor. Each local government has its own audit bureau that reports to the People's Congress, but as a rule, these bureaus are understaffed and undertrained. Moreover, since they are directly responsible to the government they are auditing, the value of the auditing process is impaired.

Budget reform became a prominent issue in 1999 when, as mentioned earlier, the national auditor-general issued stinging criticisms of the implementation of the 1998 budget and the management of public funds in general. Among the criticisms were:

---

[30] This section draws from World Bank (2000) and Wong (2005a).

[31] See World Bank (2000) for an in-depth analysis of China's public expenditure management system in the late 1990s. The report's analysis remains relevant since many of the problems persist.

- Authorizations releasing funds for spending ministries were not made until well into the fiscal year; indeed, some ministries did not receive their budgets until the fourth quarter. Such delays seriously undermined the significance of the budget.
- Management of government funds was found to be extremely lax. In some instances, funds were diverted to overseas accounts and illegal uses, such as investing in companies and buildings.
- Reporting requirements for EBF were routinely ignored. Indeed, even the MOF itself failed to present final accounts for those EBF that are (paradoxically) included in the budget.
- Uncollected and diverted extrabudgetary fees were rampant. Illegal uses included pension reserves invested in companies or used for speculation in the securities markets.

These concerns led to a comprehensive program of budget reform. The National People's Congress (NPC) directed that immediate changes be made for the next budget cycle, including the introduction of standardized procurement procedures to cut waste and corruption, public disclosure of all intergovernmental transfers by province, and greater consultation with the NPC to participate more actively in the budgeting process.[32] Since 1999, the MOF has introduced new procedures for budget preparation and approval and strengthened budget reporting to the NPC. To adjust to the new budget procedures, the MOF underwent a radical restructuring in 1999 to reorganize its departments. A new budget classification scheme is under preparation and some elements have already been introduced. To improve the accountability of spending units, the MOF began to formulate organizational budgets, shifting from allocation to sectors and functions to allocation to organizations.[33] It also took advantage of this change to require each ministry to show all budgetary, extrabudgetary, and other resources and spending – an important step toward improved accounting and budgeting for EBF. In 2000, the minister of finance announced plans for treasury reform to improve financial management of public funds and introduction of new standards for government procurement.

Despite these useful reforms, however, and progress in a number of related areas – promulgation of a new law on procurement, introduction of organizational budgets to all central government departments, the separation of revenues and expenditures in budgeting for EBF, and rural fee reform (RFR) – the overall pace of change has been slow. This is not surprising: a budget system is a complex set of processes and procedures and of reports and supporting information systems.

---

[32] This last point was a logical extension of the creation of the Budget Committee in early 1999 to replace the more general-purpose Economic and Finance Committee.

[33] In 1999, MOF presented organizational budgets for four ministries to the NPC: Ministry of Education, the Ministry of Science and Technology, the Ministry of Labor and Social Security, and the Ministry of Agriculture. In 2000, this was extended to twenty-six, for approval of the 2001 budget.

Changing the budget system requires a redefinition of all these elements as well as the design and installation of a new and more reliable and comprehensive government financial management information system. Such tasks are detailed and time intensive, requiring large amounts of human and financial resources as well as continuing support from the highest levels of government.

Public Service Delivery

Along with decentralization to local governments, the Chinese fiscal system has also decentralized authority to service delivery units, conferring on these public service units (PSUs) unprecedented and often unwarranted autonomy to expand revenue generation by offering new services. Driven by fiscal pressure, over the last decade or so, the government gradually expanded the autonomy given to such PSUs as schools and hospitals. In effect, the government both invited nongovernment participation in the financing of services that were formerly solely financed by the public sector and also offered marketlike incentives to PSU managers. While rigorous analysis of the outcomes of this policy is not yet possible, what information is available suggests that the outcomes have at best been mixed.

Many PSUs seem to have gone far outside of their core competences and neglected their core tasks in the pursuit of more revenue. Converting "nonproductive" land into commercial ventures has been a particularly favored activity over the past few years.[34] Many examples can be cited – from city parks studded with commercial ventures to produce revenue for the park services department, to universities entering real-estate development ventures and selling or leasing "unneeded" office space or residential apartments. The recent history of the health sector provides one, perhaps extreme, example of commercialization gone astray. Health services have expanded rapidly. At the same time, however, costs have escalated, and access for both the rural population and the urban poor appears to have been reduced. To earn profits to support the operation of health services (and their own salaries), doctors seem to be prescribing both too many drugs and costly diagnostic tests, resulting in expensive and often inappropriate patterns of care. In the absence of effective oversight, and in an environment in which consumers' voices are weak, some PSUs have misused state assets or abused customers, especially in markets characterized by monopolies, imperfect competition, asymmetric information, or external economies.

Although public perception in China appears to be that budgetary support for PSUs, such as schools and hospitals, that provide services has declined, in fact it has been growing in recent years more rapidly than total budgetary expenditures, rising from 23 percent of budgetary appropriations in 2000 to 30 percent by 2002,

---

[34] In addition, a good deal of productive agricultural land near cities is also being converted, often illegally, to such uses (Wu, 2004).

and providing on average a bit less than half the total funding of PSUs, although with wide variations from sector to sector (World Bank, 2005).

Many PSUs also mobilize revenues from a wide variety of other sources, including service revenues, business incomes, remittances from subsidiaries, and, of course, extrabudgetary revenues. Since the definitions of some of these categories are unclear even to those who use them, and many definitions are still evolving – for example, the distinction between service revenues (*shiye shouru*) and business incomes (*jingyingxing shouru*) is frequently blurred – we will simply distinguish between budgetary and nonbudgetary revenues. In reality, even some avowedly nonbudgetary revenues involve implicit transfers from the public sector and hence indirect costs to the budget. For example, monopoly rents may be created by the state and assigned to PSUs in lieu of or as supplements to budgetary appropriations. Thus, a publishing company may be given a monopoly on publishing textbooks, which are very profitable. These monopoly rents show up in the accounts as "business incomes" but are unearned. Another monopoly rent openly used to support the over 500 state-owned presses arises from restrictions on the issuance of ISBN numbers since such a number is in effect a license to publish.[35]

The imputed rental cost attributable to the free use of state assets, such as land and buildings, also constitutes an important public contribution to many PSUs. Strikingly, in recent years it appears that more and more PSUs have been receiving income by conversion of these assets to commercial uses. For example, an art museum recently swapped its site in central Beijing for an annual rental income of RMB15 million, plus an agreement from the renter to build a new campus on the outskirts of the city for the museum's training center. The recent wave of university expansions has been largely financed by land grants, a process that has inadvertently turned some universities into real-estate development companies as they try to monetize these grants through the selling of "excess" residential flats and office space.

Equally obscure is the other side of the ledger, namely, the extent to which what should be budgetary costs are instead borne by PSUs. An important example is pension expenditures. Since most employees of PSUs are included in the traditional pension scheme for civil servants, the contributions to their pensions funded from the budget are counted as budgetary appropriations to the PSU, which of course inflates the true budgetary support of current operations. In some instances, however, such as hospitals, it appears that the appropriations received are insufficient to cover pension costs, so that the PSUs end up in effect being net "taxpayers" with respect to pensions. Sometimes PSUs have also been used to absorb other budgetary "downloads"; for example, when they are required to absorb employees laid off from government and even in some cases graduates who cannot find jobs

---

[35] Under WTO rules the practice of limiting the issuance of ISBN numbers each year is being phased out, beginning in 2004.

elsewhere. Finally, in some instances PSUs have been used to generate profits that are then used to supplement budgetary resources and pay civil servants.

Given the scale of the PSU sector and its important role as both consumer of public resources and provider of public services, public management and budget reform cannot proceed much further without considerable reform in the PSU sector. Given the highly decentralized character of the Chinese fiscal system, this means that a fundamental overhaul of the intergovernmental system is also needed to support such reform.

THE KEY TO THE FISCAL FUTURE: INTERGOVERNMENTAL FINANCE

China's considerable decentralization has sometimes been viewed as largely an incidental fallout of the reform process: certainly, its intergovernmental fiscal system deserves this label. The unsatisfactory state of the intergovernmental finance system is becoming an increasingly important obstacle to development. To date, reforms have invariably been gradualist and incremental, responding to immediate problems with short-term fixes. In some instances, as with the recent rural fee reform, rather than making the serious fiscal adjustments required, government agencies and lower tiers of government have not only been allowed but even encouraged to resort to off-budget means of financing public-sector activities, thus building up more problems for the future.

All this matters because China is, in many ways, one of the most fiscally decentralized countries in the world. Chinese officials of course understand this very well. Unfortunately, despite the central importance of getting intergovernmental finance right in China, the coherence of the intergovernmental fiscal system in China has been steadily chipped away by piecemeal incremental changes over the years. As in the past, future fiscal reforms in China are likely to follow a gradualist path, reacting to crises as they occur. It is not clear, however, that further reactive incremental reform will suffice. Experience in other transitional countries, for example, suggests that gradualism in fiscal matters is sometimes not enough and indeed may sometimes make things worse. Transitional fixes to transitional problems have a way of becoming quasipermanent obstacles to needed long-term institutional change.[36] As Chinese experience shows, partial fixes of complex problems may create new problems requiring new fixes that create new problems, and so on.

Many problems at the top of the national agenda originate in intergovernmental fiscal relations – pension arrears, arrears or defaults on living stipend support for laid-off workers, problems of financing rural basic education, and civil service wage arrears. All are manifestations of the difficulties local governments face in performing their assigned responsibilities. In his report to the NPC in March 2002

---

[36] With respect to taxation, for example, see World Bank (2003) for a recent detailed examination of this process in Ukraine.

noting that many governments at the county and township levels were unable to meet payroll in full for civil servants, Minister of Finance Xiang Huaicheng called for government to "gradually establish a mechanism to ensure normal payment of wages, accelerate changes in the functions of counties and townships . . . and create conditions for fundamentally overcoming financial difficulties in counties and townships."[37] This important task remains to be done.

Under the earlier highly centralized fiscal system, local governments performed delegated functions as agents of the central government in delivering services chosen by the central government, often with norms set by the central government. Revenue assignments were *ex post*, adjusted to finance the delegated functions performed, and highly negotiable. In this system, transfers were necessary only for those provinces that, even after being assigned 100 percent of collected revenues, could not meet expenditure needs. Other local governments were assigned only a small fraction of collected revenues, such as Shanghai.[38]

Growing Fiscal Disparities

During the 1980s, as attention was focused on how to resuscitate revenue collections, reforms to the intergovernmental system were likewise designed to stimulate tax effort by local governments. Virtually no attention was paid to expenditure assignments. Equally little attention was paid to transfers, which were increasingly driven by dwindling central resources (Wong, 1997). By the mid-1990s, the intergovernmental fiscal system had evolved to one in which local governments were saddled with heavy and unsustainable expenditure assignments. Social security and pensions are the responsibility of cities and counties, and education and health care were primarily the responsibilities of city districts and townships until 2001.

These expenditure responsibilities were supported by neither revenue assignments nor an effective system of transfers, leaving many local governments unable to perform their assigned functions. No supporting system was in place to ensure minimum standards of service provision across regions. As economic growth also became more concentrated in coastal regions during the 1990s, income disparities accelerated, and the outcome was a sharp rise in interregional disparities in fiscal spending, accompanied by a gradual deterioration in public services provided in the inland provinces. By the mid-1990s, fiscal problems were very serious in poor regions. According to Heberer (2001), in Yunnan Province on China's southwestern border, 106 of the 127 counties were unable to meet budgeted expenditures in 1995. In neighboring Guizhou (the poorest province in China), many counties could not meet payroll in full. In the Liangshan Yi minority Prefecture in Sichuan Province, this led to the elimination of free medical care and epidemic prevention

---

[37] Reports indicate cumulative arrears of 6.5 billion yuan at the end of year 2001 (Xiang, 2002).
[38] This system was called "highly redistributive" by earlier writers (e.g., Lardy, 1998) and indeed it was in many ways.

programs and free films and cultural activities. Many clinics and health stations closed. Epidemic diseases thought to have been wiped out reappeared. In 1996, only 40 percent of Yi children attended school, a figure that dropped to 10 percent in the poorer villages.

These outcomes are highly regressive, with governments in poor regions providing fewer and lower-quality services and passing along a higher proportion of the costs to their constituents. With local funding problems limiting services, the national government has been unable to deliver on some priority programs, such as universal basic education. For example, China is still years away from providing the nine years of free education to all children targeted for year 2000. In spite of repeated pledges by the State Council to increase investment in human development, budgetary spending on education remained stagnant at about 2.0–2.5 percent of GDP during 1978–1999, half the level called for in the 1985 Education Law, and well below the levels of spending in neighboring East Asian economies. Similarly, in health care, public spending is low, also less than 2 percent of GDP.[39]

Some attempt to reverse this trend of growing inequality began around 1998, when the government began to redirect fiscal resources toward equalization, including the "Go West" development strategy launched in 1999. A major driver of transfer policy in China appears to be a concern for the growing regional disparities that many consider have marred the country's impressive growth performance. As Benjamin et al. (Chapter 18) argue, it may well be that although interregional inequality has indeed grown, so has intraregional inequality, so that the relative importance of the interregional component has not changed. Whether or not one accepts this argument, one may still find the level of interregional inequality "unlovely" and hence worthy of policy correction. While evidence around the world suggests that Heston and Sicular (Chapter 2) are probably correct in arguing that even the best policy can do little to change interregional disparities, countries are of course free to try to do so, as indeed China has been doing for some years through a complex set of intergovernmental transfers.[40]

Five broad types of central transfers are enumerated in Table 12.4. Tax rebates are based on the central government's commitment at the introduction of the TSS reform to return to local governments a share of the growing VAT and excise tax bases. The formula is complex and contested, but returns to each province an additional 30 percent of the incremental central government receipts from VAT and excises derived in the province each year. Quota subsidies are a leftover from the previous revenue-sharing regime, under which provinces that did not collect sufficient revenues to finance their approved expenditures received a subsidy

---

[39] Such spending is highly concentrated in the civil service medical insurance system and in urban hospitals, and little trickles down to the rural sector. World Health Organization (2000) ranked China 144th for the overall performance of the health system out of 191 countries, but 188th in terms of fairness in financial contribution.

[40] Recent useful reviews of transfers may be found in Bahl and Martinez-Vazquez (2006), Zhang and Martinez-Vazquez (2002), and Ahmad, Singh, and Fortuna (2004).

Table 12.4. *Transfers by type*

	1994	1995	1996	1997	1998	1999	2000
1. Tax rebates	179.9	186.7	194.9	201.2	208.3	212.1	220.7
	75.3%	73.7%	72.9%	71.8%	63.4%	53.1%	46.5%
2. Quota	11.4	11.5	11.1	11.2	11.3	11.4	12.0
subsidies	4.8%	4.5%	4.2%	4.0%	3.4%	2.9%	2.5%
3. Transitional		2.1	3.5	5.0	6.1	7.5	8.5
equalization		0.8%	1.3%	1.8%	1.8%	1.9%	1.8%
grants							
4. Earmarked	36.1	34.4	48.9	51.6	59.1	113.9	119.9
grants	15.1%	13.6%	18.3%	18.4%	18.0%	28.5%	25.3%
5. Wage increase						34.3	45.1
transfer						8.4%	9.7%

Note: Values are in billion yuan.
Source: Zhang and Martinez-Vazquez (2002).

each year. These subsidies were frozen in nominal terms around 1987 and set as "quotas."[41]

A few years ago, the MOF began to revise the system of transfers to reduce the dominance of tax rebates and hence increase the amount of regional equalization (see Figure 12.8). An especially important boost was given by a change in 2002 that shifted the EIT and the personal income tax from local taxes to shared taxes. To make this shift more acceptable to local governments, the central government committed itself to retaining only 20 percent of the total receipts from these taxes, its share prior to 2002, and to put all additional receipts into equalization under the "transitional transfer." In 2003 this added about 14 billion yuan to equalization.[42]

The Tenuous Link between Transfers and Services

To some extent, offsetting the government's intention to equalize, however, the continued and accentuated failure of the intergovernmental system has required increasing central government bailouts in response to emerging problems in pension arrears, financing rural basic education, and so on. The costs of such bailouts have risen rapidly since 1998:

---

[41] In addition to fiscal transfers, other policies such as tax incentives and financial subsidies have frequently been employed in the name of regional development in China (Bird and Chen, 1998). The regional development issue, however, is not further discussed here: in any case, as Bird and Smart (2002) note, in principle intergovernmental fiscal transfers have quite distinct objectives from regional development.

[42] Interview with officials at the Ministry of Finance, February 2004. See also Ahmad, Singh, and Fortuna (2004).

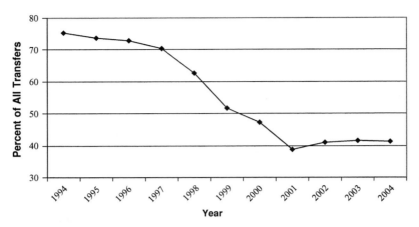

Figure 12.8. The diminished role of tax rebates (*Source:* Calculated from MOF data.)

- Subsidies to local social security schemes rose from zero to RMB10 billion in 2000, 34.9 billion in 2001, 51.2 billion in 2002, and were 111.8 billion in 2003.
- Subsidies for living stipends to laid-off workers from SOEs continue to be substantial, though they are scattered in different categories and difficult to count. (In the 2004, budget pension and living stipends for laid-off workers and their reemployment training came to a total RMB86 billion.)
- Subsidies to local minimum living stipend schemes rose from zero to RMB2.3 billion in 2001 and RMB4.6 billion in the 2002 budget. It doubled again in 2003 to RMB9.2 billion.
- As reform of the civil service has doubled public-sector wages in several rounds since 1999, the central government has been forced to provide "wage adjustment subsidies" to local governments in the poorer regions. This component of transfers has grown to about RMB100 billion yuan by 2003/2004.

An important consequence of this pattern is that increased transfers from the center often do not result in better services at the periphery. Recent experience has taught local governments that the MOF will intervene whenever necessary to preserve social stability and will go to great lengths to prevent wage arrears from getting out of hand. Civil servants are thus in effect "free goods" to local governments. In addition, the nationally unified civil service wage scale translates into salaries that are very high relative to local incomes in poor regions, and this gap has grown even greater, as civil service wages have more than doubled since 1999. This has proved to be an irresistible lure; many local governments added staff during the period when Zhu Rongji was implementing a draconian program at the central government to downsize the civil service. In one extremely poor rural county visited in early 2003, for example, in spite of increased transfers from higher levels, there was no money for nonpersonnel recurrent expenses in any department from schools to agricultural stations essentially because the county had been adding staff at an accelerating rate. The result was that more transfers ended up producing fewer rather than more services to residents.

As these examples indicate, the expenditure side of the intergovernmental fiscal structure is seriously deficient. No effective system of intergovernmental fiscal transfers either supports local governments in carrying out their assigned responsibilities or redresses growing regional disparities. The murkiness of expenditure assignments confuses accountability considerably. When everyone is responsible, no one is responsible. The problems inherent in this murky environment have cascaded down on the lowest level of government in the difficult fiscal circumstances of recent years, as each level has increasingly tried to capture revenues by redefining the "sharing" of revenues in its own favor as much as possible.

Not enough attention appears to have been paid to how fiscal reforms affect local finances and autonomy. The recent experience in the implementation of the rural fee reform (RFR) illustrates how this failure undermined a program that might have provided the first dramatic success and helped build momentum for public finance reform. Rolled out since 2002 for nationwide implementation in three phases, the RFR was intended to reduce the overall burden of taxes and fees in the rural sector and end unreasonable levies by township and village officials. It also aimed to bring into the formal budget many of the extrabudgetary resources that had financed rural government, a laudable measure. It eliminated, in one stroke, all fees levied by the township governments and village associations. The most important of the fees eliminated were the "three levies and five unifieds," which included the rural education surcharges and public reserve funds of village associations that had been key sources of funding for rural education, the militia, subsidies for rural officials, and social relief. Since agricultural taxes have also been abolished in subsequent years, grassroot governments are now virtually completely dependent on central transfers, a situation not conducive to good financial management.

CHINA IN INTERNATIONAL PERSPECTIVE

In this section we stand back from the intricate details of the Chinese fiscal puzzle and take a broader look at China's fiscal development in international perspective.

China is a large, developing, transitional country. Like other large countries, it has had some problems owing to its size and diversity. Like other developing countries, it has at times had difficulty in coping with the pace of change and establishing a sustainable balance between equity and efficiency in the face of severe constraints on administrative capacity. Like other transitional countries, it has found "institution building" in the public sector to be a complex and time-consuming task. As noted earlier, to understand the development of Chinese fiscal policy in the reform period, it is important both to have a clear understanding of the objectives of policy and also to know how fiscal policies worked with (or against) other policies – monetary, exchange rate, regulatory, and so on. Consider, for example, the not-always-clear role played by the fiscal system in relation to changing policies toward (central) SOEs, a matter on which there is considerable controversy (see Chapter 10, this volume). Consider also the more transparent fiscal policy toward foreign direct investment and its less transparent relation to, on one hand, changes in the formal tax system and, on the other hand, financial subsidies (Bird and Chen, 1998). Some changes in fiscal policy appear to have been driven by macroeconomic concerns, some by "control" concerns, and some by the desire to offset or reinforce other policy instruments in achieving particular objectives.

China is particularly unusual in international perspective in the extent to which it assigns heavy responsibilities for the provision of vital social support and nearly all public services to governments at the prefecture, county, and township levels while not adequately supporting these expenditure assignments through either revenue assignments or an intergovernmental transfer system. The assignment of such important and potentially costly services as pensions and unemployment benefits to low levels of the government structure is unusual, and it accounts for the exceptionally high proportion (55 percent) of total budgetary expenditures by these three levels of government. In comparison, for a sample of about 100 countries for which data is available, subnational governments (including states or provinces) account, on average, for only 13 percent of total budgetary expenditures in developing countries and 35 percent in developed countries.[43] In other countries social security is almost always provided by the central government, while "safety net" welfare systems are almost always jointly financed by the national government, in part because their cyclical nature makes them generally inappropriate for local governments. Similarly, the responsibility for basic education and public health is usually shared with provincial and central governments to ensure some minimum provision levels across localities.

Also unusual is that in China, most public goods and services that touch people's lives are delivered by local governments. One result is that many of the problems at the top of the national agenda, such as pension arrears, have at base originated in the financial difficulties local governments face in performing their assigned responsibilities. Local funding problems have also limited the success of priority national programs, such as universal basic education and health.

Even after its substantial recovery since the mid-1990s, the formal revenue system in China remains relatively weak, generating about 18 percent of GDP, only half of which is under the central government's control.[44] At the same time, however, the public sector as a whole raises large amounts of revenues off-budget – perhaps

---

[43] The sample is about 100 countries for which subnational budgetary data are available from IMF, World Bank, OECD, and other sources. We are grateful to Roy Bahl and his associates at Georgia State University for these data.

[44] This compares to central (or federal) revenues of 20 percent of GDP in the United States, 41 percent in France, 19 percent in Thailand and Indonesia, 27 percent in Malaysia, 35 percent in Singapore, and 13 percent in Indonesia in the mid-1990s (Lou, 2000).

more than 20 percent of GDP (if one includes disguised spending through the banks) – although in ways that are often inefficient, inequitable, nontransparent, and distorting.

In all these ways, China does indeed seem different. But in many ways, China's experience can also be readily linked to what has emerged in other countries. With respect to expenditure management, for example, most OECD countries have reformed their systems over the past 20 years, as experience emphasized the critical importance of (1) being clear about who has the authority to make what decisions, (2) matching authority (flexibility) and accountability, and (3) strengthening both the capacity and the willingness to reorder priorities and reallocate resources. These concerns arose owing largely to the rising fiscal imbalances and lagging public-sector performance at the end of the 1970s and early 1980s, which in turn came in part at least from budget processes that were focused on a single year and on inputs rather than results. Detailed line-item budgets and strict central control over expenditures discouraged managers from taking initiatives to achieve better results. These reforms increased budget coverage and moved to a multiyear perspective, enforced spending limits, improved the links between policy priorities and spending, and matched greater managerial autonomy with more accountability for results. China, it seems, may be beginning to follow a similar path.

The experience of other transitional countries also seems relevant to China in many ways, for example, in showing the importance of increasing the realism of the budget by such means as improving budgetary comprehensiveness and transparency, improving the accuracy of revenue estimates, tightening the links between policy priorities and budget allocations during budget formulation, and ensuring the timely flow of budgeted funds to organizations to underpin high-quality service delivery (combined with accountability for their efficiency and effectiveness). Since China has all these problems, it may have something to learn from the extensive (though not always successful) experience elsewhere with budgetary and expenditure management reform.

No doubt, as so often before, in the end there will be a distinct Chinese twist to the ways in which China handles its fiscal problems. Still, no matter what it ends up doing, two general conclusions seem warranted with respect to China's fiscal system. First, while obfuscated by many characteristics of China's institutional structure as well as the rapid and changing pattern of its growth, the basic fiscal problems facing the country do not seem to be all that novel in kind or even in degree. Secondly, something will definitely have to be done on many fiscal fronts, in particular, to disentangle and rationalize the intergovernmental situation if China is to continue to modernize at a rapid pace. At the "micro" as at the "macro" level, the key to future progress in China's fiscal system is to face up to the need to develop a more sustainable system of intergovernmental fiscal relations, an important part of which is to bring into view the enormous range of public-sector activities currently hidden deep in the "off-budget" swamp. As the title of this chapter indicates, China's fiscal system thus continues very much to be "a work in progress."

PUBLIC FINANCE MATTERS

Structural reform of China's public finances and especially of its intergovernmental fiscal system is critical to resolving continuing problems in such core segments of the economy as banking, education, health, and rural development. The centrality of the fiscal system to progress in these areas is not always obvious. On the surface, for example, China's macroeconomic performance looks unproblematic. The record of public investment in growth-supporting infrastructure, such as highways, ports, power plants, and a variety of urban services, has been nothing short of astonishing, and social stability and public safety are high. On the whole, albeit with lags, fiscal policy seems over time to have adapted to reflect both changing links between markets and sectors and changing policy objectives. In all these important respects, the public finance system, though it obviously has some problems, appears to be doing its main job and providing adequate support for government functions.[45]

Far more attention has been paid to the fragility of the financial (banking) sector, for example, than to fiscal problems. In reality, however, many of China's non-performing loans result from the combination of off-loading social expenditures (such as housing, education, health care, and pensions) from the government to SOEs and the accompanying hidden subsidization of SOEs through bank lending. Government-directed bank support of both regional development objectives and commercial investments has recently created yet more nonperforming assets. Such nonperforming loans are in large part simply a way of disguising (larger) government deficits since in the end they essentially represent a transfer of expenditures from the government budget to the banks. Such "financial-sector problems" cannot be fixed until the public sector is reined in and funded on a more disciplined and sustainable basis.

Matters are equally bleak on the revenue side of the budget. The use of state assets by the government and its agencies to raise off-budget revenues is a major source of inefficiencies, distorted incentives, and ultimately loss of state assets. Public finance issues – how the public sector is financed and how public funds are spent – are thus closely interconnected to the very visible problems of both the financial sector and state asset management. Moreover, as the Chinese economy has become more decentralized and market based, the budget has increasingly become the most important instrument available to government to carry out such core functions as maintaining economic growth and stability, allocating resources to achieve national goals, delivering critical public goods, and protecting vulnerable groups in society. The continuing procedural and substantive weaknesses in fiscal policy thus have ramifications for almost every aspect of public policy in China.

---

[45] In contrast, severe economic difficulties have led governments in many other transitional countries (Russia, Hungary, Kazakhstan, etc.) to institute deep reforms that have fundamentally reformed their public finance systems, though often not sufficiently in the view of many observers.

As the Chinese economy comes increasingly to resemble other mixed economies, in which more recognizably "private" agents respond to more distinguishably "public" policies, the key role now played in fiscal policy by discretionary and arbitrary policy adjustments will almost certainly have to decline if growth and well-being are to be sustained. Similarly, as China becomes more integrated into the world economy its tax system too will inevitably tend to converge more toward the norm in certain respects, as indeed WTO accession has already brought to the fore to some extent (Li, 2005). As China's regional and income disparities increase – and they almost certainly will – political necessity will likely lead to more calls for redress, exacerbating the already considerable strain on fiscal resources.

The gradualism that has characterized Chinese fiscal policy to date may still be able to cope with such problems, but it can do so much more effectively if it becomes "gradualism with a purpose" so that incremental reforms move the fiscal system more clearly in the direction of some desired end state. China has in many respects made an excellent start toward solving many of the fiscal problems we discuss in this chapter. Even where it has not done so well, some might argue that "nonoptimal" fiscal policy may to some extent, whether consciously or unintentionally, usefully offset even less optimal policies in other areas (e.g., the financial sector). Up to now, however, China has conspicuously failed to deal systematically with such critical problems of intergovernmental finance as expenditure and revenue assignment, transfer design, subnational borrowing, and, by no means least, the development of an adequate institutional framework within which to develop and adapt such policies. Although partly occluded by continuing party dominance, fiscal errors have accumulated over time to the point where it can be argued that unless China tackles these matters soon, the attempt to build a new economy on the wreck of the old Soviet-type fiscal system may yet come to a grinding halt, pulled down by the morass of ad hoc, piecemeal, and often illicit arrangements that continue to be hastily put into place in attempts to avert imminent fiscal calamity in one or another part of the public sector. While we have no crystal ball that enables us to tell when, or how, the system will change or if the will to change is yet there, some such changes must, we suggest, come soon if China's growth is not to be thrown seriously offtrack.

References

Ahmad, Ehtisham, Raju Singh, and Mario Fortuna. June 2004. "Toward More Effective Redistribution: Reform Options for Intergovernmental Transfers in China." IMF Working Paper WP/04/98. Washington, DC: International Monetary Fund.

Ahmad, Ehtisham, Raju Singh, and Benjamin Lockwood. July 2004. "Taxation Reforms and Changes in Revenue Assignments in China." IMF Working Paper WP/04/125. Washington, DC: International Monetary Fund.

Bahl, Roy W. 1999. *Fiscal Policy in China: Taxation and Inter-Governmental Fiscal Relations.* South San Francisco: The 1990 Institute, University of Michigan Press.

Bahl, Roy W. and Jorge Martinez-Vazquez. 2006. "Fiscal Federalism and Economic Reform in China," in *Federalism and Economic Reform: International Perspectives*. Jessica S. Wallack and T. N. Srinivasan, eds. Cambridge and New York: Cambridge University Press, pp. 249–300.

Bird, Richard M. June 2003. "Taxation in Latin America: Reflections on Sustainability and the Balance between Efficiency and Equity." ITP Paper 0306. Ontario: International Tax Program, Rotman School of Management, University of Toronto.

Bird, Richard M. and Duanjie Chen. 1998. "Intergovernmental Fiscal Relations in China in International Perspective," in *Taxation in Modern China*. Donald J. S. Brean, ed. London and New York: Routledge, pp. 152–186.

Bird, Richard M., Robert D. Ebel, and Christine I. Wallich. 1995. *Decentralization of the Socialist State: Intergovernmental Finance in Transition Economies.* Washington, DC: World Bank.

Bird, Richard M. and Joosung Jun. 2006. "Earmarking in Theory and Korean Practice," in *Excise Taxation in Asia*. Steven L. H. Phua, ed. Singapore: Centre for Commercial Law Studies, Faculty of Law, National University of Singapore, pp. 49–86.

Bird, Richard M. and Michael Smart. 2002. "Intergovernmental Fiscal Transfers: Lessons from International Experience." *World Development*. 30(6), pp. 899–912.

Bubnova, Nina and Lucan Way. 1998. "Trends in Financing Regional Expenditures in Transition Economies, the case of Ukraine." World Bank Discussion Paper 378. Washington, DC: World Bank.

Duckett, Jane. 1998. *The Entrepreneurial State in China: Real Estate and Commerce Departments in Reform Era Tianjin.* London: Routledge.

Ebrill, Liam, Michael Keen, Jean-Paul Bodin, and Victoria Summers. 2001. *The Modern VAT.* Washington, DC: International Monetary Fund.

Fan, Gang. 1998. "Market-Oriented Economic Reform and the Growth of Off-Budget Local Public Finance," in *Taxation in Modern China*. Donald J. S. Brean, ed. London and New York: Routledge, pp. 209–227.

Heberer, Thomas. 2001. "Nationalities Conflict and Ethnicity in the People's Republic of China, with Special Reference to the Yi," in *Perspectives on the Yi of Southwest China*. Stevan Harrell, ed. Berkeley: University of California Press.

Hong, Yu Hung. March 2003. "The Last Straw: Reforming Local Property Taxes in the People's Republic of China." Working Paper, Cambridge, MA: Lincoln Institute for Land Policy.

Lardy, Nicholas. 1998. *China's Unfinished Economic Revolution.* Washington, DC: Brookings Institution.

Li, Jinyan. 1997. "Counteracting Corruption in Tax Administration in Transitional Countries: A Case Study of China." *Bulletin for International Fiscal Documentation*. 44(11), pp. 474–492.

Li, Jinyan. 2005. "Relationship between International Trade Law and National Tax Policy: Case Study of China." *Bulletin for International Fiscal Documentation*. 52(2), pp. 77–86.

Lou Jiwei, ed. 2000. *Fifty Years of Government Financial Statistics in New China*. Beijing: Economic Science Press.

Ministry of Finance, 1982. *Guojia shuishou* [State Taxes]. Beijing: Chinese Finance and Economics Press.

Ministry of Finance. Annual. *Finance Yearbook of China (Zhongguo caizheng nianjian).* Beijing: Ministry of Finance.

Naughton, Barry. 1992. "Implications of the State Monopoly over Industry and Its Relaxation." *Modern China*. 18(1), pp. 14–41.

Oksenberg, Michel and James Tong. March 1991. "The Evolution of Central-Provincial Fiscal Relations in China, 1953–1983: The Formal System." *China Quarterly*. 125, pp. 1–32.

State Administration of Taxation, September 18, 1998. *Zhongguo shuiwubao* [Chinese Tax News]. Beijing: State Administration of Taxation.

Walder, Andrew M. April 2003. "Sociological Dimensions of China's Economic Transition: Organization, Stratification, and Social Mobility." Working Paper. Stanford, CA: Asia/Pacific Research Center, Stanford University. Accessed July 24, 2007, from http://iis-db.stanford.edu/pubs/20208/Walder_Sociological.pdf.

Wallich, Christine, ed. 1994. *Russia and the Challenge of Fiscal Federalism*. Washington, DC: World Bank.

Wanless, P. T. 1985. *Taxation in Centrally Planned Economies*. London and Sydney: Croom Helm.

Wong, Christine. December 1991. "Central-Local Relations in an Era of Fiscal Decline: The Paradox of Fiscal Decentralization in post-Mao China." *China Quarterly*. no. 128, pp. 691–715.

Wong, Christine. April 1992. "Fiscal Reform and Local Industrialization: The Problematic Sequencing of Reform in Post-Mao China." *Modern China*. 18 (2), pp. 197–227.

Wong, Christine. 1993. "Public Finance and Economic Decentralization," in *China's Economic Reform in the 1990s*. Walter Galenson, ed. Ann Arbor, MI: University of Michigan Press, pp. 177–196.

Wong, Christine, ed. 1997. *Financing Local Government in the People's Republic of China*. Hong Kong: Oxford University Press.

Wong, Christine. 1998. "Fiscal Dualism in China: Gradualist Reform and the Growth of Off-Budget Finance," in *Taxation in Modern China*. Donald J. S. Brean, ed. New York and London: Routledge, pp. 187–208.

Wong, Christine. 2001. "Converting Fees into Taxes: Reform of Extrabudgetary Funds and Intergovernmental Fiscal Relations in China," in *Decentralization of the Socialist State: Intergovernmental Finance in Transition Economies*, Chinese edn. Richard Bird, Robert Ebel, and Christine Wallich, eds. Beijing: Central Translation Press, pp. 375–394.

Wong, Christine. 2005a. "Budgeting Issues in China," in *OECD, Governance in China*. Paris: OECD.

Wong, Christine. January 2005b. "Can China Change Development Paradigm for the 21st Century? Fiscal Policy Options for Hu Jintao and Wen Jiabao after Two Decades of Muddling Through." A paper for the Stiftung Wissenschaft und Politik, Berlin, Germany. Accessed on July 31, 2007, from http://www.swp-berlin.org/common/get_document.php?id = 1248&PHPSESSID = 82c3a943f90732e6d4637eb8981c355d.

Wong, Christine. 2007. "Can the Retreat from Equality Be Reversed? An Assessment of Redistributive Fiscal Policies from Deng Xiaoping to Wen Jiabao," in *Paying for Progress in China: Public Finance, Human Welfare and Inequality*. Vivienne Shue and Christine Wong, eds. London, Routledge Press, pp. 12–28.

Wong, Christine, Christopher Heady, and Wing Thye Woo. 1995. *Fiscal Management and Economic Reform in the People's Republic of China*. Hong Kong: Oxford University Press.

World Bank. 1988. *Revenue Mobilization in China*. Washington, DC: World Bank.

World Bank. 1996a. *World Development Report 1996*. Washington, DC: World Bank.

World Bank. 1996b. *Fiscal Management in Russia*. Washington, DC: World Bank.

World Bank. 1999. *China: Weathering the Storm and Learning the Lessons*. Country Economic Memorandum. Washington, DC: World Bank.

World Bank. 2000. *China: Managing Public Expenditures for Better Results*. Washington, DC: World Bank.

World Bank. 2002. *China: National Development and Subnational Finance, a Review of Provincial Expenditures.* Washington, DC: World Bank.

World Bank. 2003. *Ukraine: Tax Policy and Tax Administration.* Report 26221-UA. Washington DC: World Bank.

World Bank. 2005. *China: Deepening Public Service Unit Reform to Improve Service Delivery.* Washington, DC: World Bank.

World Health Organization. 2000. *World Health Report 2000.* Geneva: World Health Organization.

Wu Chong. 2004. "China Takes Firm Stance on Arable Land." *China Daily.* October 29, 2004. Accessed on July 31, 2007, from http://www.chinadaily.com.cn/english/doc/2004-10/29/content_386635.htm

Xiang Huaicheng. 2002. "Report on the Implementation of the Central and Local Budgets for 2001 and on the Draft Central and Local Budgets for 2002." Speech delivered at the fifth session of the ninth NPC, March 6, 2002.

Yearbook, Annual. *Zhongguo tongji nianjian* [China statistics yearbook]. Beijing: Zhongguo tongji chubanshe.

Zhang, Zhihua and Jorge Martinez-Vazquez. 2002. "The System of Equalization Transfers in China." International Studies Program Working Paper. Atlanta, GA: Andrew Young School of Policy Studies, Georgia State University.

Zhao Yining. 2003. "Replaying the Strategic Background to the Tax Sharing System Reform." *Liaowang News Weekly.* September 15, 2003, no. 37.

Zhou, Huizhong. 2000. "Fiscal Decentralization and the Development of the Tobacco Industry in China." *China Economic Review.* 11, pp. 114–133.

THIRTEEN

Agriculture in China's Development

Past Disappointments, Recent Successes, and Future Challenges

Jikun Huang, Keijiro Otsuka, and Scott Rozelle[1]

Economists' views of agricultural and rural development in the modern world have changed dramatically in the past several decades. Traditionally, agriculture was seen as an inferior partner in development. Since the size of the sector falls during development, economists proposed a policy of benign neglect. Why should nations invest in a shrinking sector? Some academics urged policymakers to treat agriculture like a black box from which resources could be costlessly extracted (Lewis, 1954). They recommended directing all investment toward industry and the cities. As a low-productivity sector, agriculture did not deserve attention.

Countries that followed such advice sometimes achieved brief gains, but soon learned that neglect of the farm sector slowed the pace of growth and often led development efforts to fail (Timmer, 1998). Neglect of agriculture excluded a large part of the population from the development process. Without investment in agriculture, it was difficult to redeploy rural resources to support faster-growing segments of the economy. Without rural investment, dualism flourished, and agricultural production often fell, pushing food prices up. Many households fell into isolated subsistence. This undermined the stability that growth requires, causing development to stagnate or even go into reverse.

Many countries encountered these difficulties: Argentina, Mexico, Nigeria, and even to some extent, the former Soviet Union. In contrast, during the last century, nations that grew fast and entered the ranks of developed nations – notably, Japan and South Korea – emphasized heavy investment in agriculture as an integral part of their development strategy.

Today, development economists agree that agriculture and rural development are integral to the process of nation building and sustained development (Johnston and Mellor, 1961; Johnston, 1970). Agriculture plays five important roles in development: (a) supplying high-quality labor to factories, construction sites, and the service sector; (b) producing low-cost food that will keep wages down for

[1] The authors thank Loren Brandt, Thomas Rawski, Dan Rosen, Terry Sicular, Jon Unger, and an anonymous reviewer for comments on this chapter.

industrial workers; (c) producing fiber and other crops that can be inputs to production elsewhere in the economy; (d) supplying exports to earn foreign exchange that can help finance imports of key technology and capital equipment; and (e) raising rural incomes.

In a book assessing the development of China during the People's Republic era, it is of interest to know how well agriculture has performed and the role that it has played in the development process. Has China produced food and other commodities that have contributed to China's growth? Has it been successful in supplying labor to the off-farm sector? How has agriculture contributed to the rise in rural incomes and growth, in general? *In short, one of the overall goals of this chapter is to document the performance of the agricultural sector and use the criteria of Johnston and Mellor to assess how well the agricultural sector has performed.*

This chapter, however, seeks to go further than describing the achievements and shortfalls of China's agricultural economy; we also aim to identify the factors – both domestic policies and economic events as well as foreign initiatives – that have induced the performance that we observe. To create an agricultural economy that can feed the population, supply industry with labor and raw materials, earn foreign exchange, produce income for those who live and work in the sector, and allow them to be a part of the nation's structural transformation requires a combination of massive investments and well-managed policy effort. The process can proceed smoothly only if an environment is created within which producers can generate output efficiently and earn a profit that can contribute to household income. Policies are required to facilitate the development of markets or other effective institutions of exchange. Although the sector is expected to contribute to the nation's development and allow for substantial extractions of labor and other resources, large volumes of investment are also needed. Investments in education, training, health, and social services are needed to increase the productivity of the labor force when they arrive in the factories. Investment is needed in agriculture to improve productivity to keep food prices low, to allow farmers to adopt new technologies and farming practice as markets change, and to raise incomes of those that are still in farming. Investment is needed in technology, land, water, and other key inputs that are in short supply. *In this chapter we seek to point out both policies that have facilitated the performance of the agricultural sector and those that have constrained it.*

Such an ambitious set of objectives, of course, means that our work must also be subject to a set of limitations. The main limitation is in terms of the timing of coverage. While scholars have examined the effect of agriculture during imperial times (Perkins, 1969), the pre-People's Republic era (Brandt, 1989; Rawski, 1989), and the socialist period (Lardy, 1983), there has been less of an effort to comprehensively assess agriculture since the onset of the reforms. However, it is our belief that the reforms can only be truly understood in the context of the period of time from which they came. Therefore, although the focus of the work will be mostly on the reform era, there will be a discussion of the period before transition.

Our central conclusion is that the performance of the agricultural sector differed fundamentally between the pre- and post-reform periods. During the socialist period, while there were some accomplishments – particularly in the areas of agricultural research and development and irrigation to agricultural productivity – agriculture was unable to play many of its roles. Weak incentives, poor property rights, and an absence of markets constrained increases in agricultural output. Although output per person rose slightly, the sector was not even able to provide the nation with 2,300 calories per capita per day (a level near the UN-established minimum) and emergency grain imports almost always were needed to meet food deficits through the 1970s. Cotton and edible oil output also rose, but China's industries were still able to produce to only a level that supplied the population with severely rationed cloth and nongrain food commodities. Planning policies also artificially severed linkages between the rural and urban economies, in essence establishing an agricultural sector with as few points of contact with industry and the entire urban economy as possible. Most damning, incomes per capita were almost the same in the mid-1970s as they were in the mid-1950s. In short, agriculture did not play any of its roles well: it did not (or was not allowed to) supply (a) labor to the nonagricultural sector; (b) sufficient supplies of food to consumers; (c) abundant raw inputs to industry; (d) export to foreign markets; or (e) rising incomes to its own population.

The contrast with the post-reform period could not be more poignant. During the reform-era, agriculture not only increased food output, producing in excess of 3,000 calories per capita per day, but China has also become a net exporter of food. The improved incentives and better property rights that were part of the decollectivization movement led to dramatic increases in productivity. Gradually improving domestic markets and agricultural trade liberalization have induced a fundamental shift in the production orientation of many producers, encouraging higher levels of commercialization and increased specialization into labor-intensive, high-value-added crops that clearly match China's comparative advantage. During this same time, China has become a major importer of land-intensive commodities, such as soybeans, cotton, edible oil, sugar, and hides. Rural industrialization, rural fiscal policies, and general domestic liberalization have also encouraged the creation of strong linkages between the rural and urban economies – through credit markets, markets for commodities and inputs, and especially labor markets. Nearly 250 million rural laborers, almost one in two, are now employed in the off-farm sector; incomes have risen by more than 5 percent per year for over two decades.

The agricultural sector clearly has played a successful role in supplying labor, food, raw materials, exports, and jobs to China's economic miracle. Indeed, the roles in many areas have been played so well that they are no longer needed; China is so rich in foreign exchange that it does not need agriculture for its export earnings. Since the late 1990s, the absolute demand for rice and wheat – the traditional staples that so concerned China's leaders since early imperial times – is actually falling, as consumers with higher incomes, changing preferences, and more market-driven choices are opting to consume more meat, fish, fruits, and vegetables.

The optimism that can be generated by the achievements over the past twenty-five years, however, needs to be tempered by the tremendous challenges that China still faces in trying to build a modern, advanced state. In fact, while we believe that four of the five roles of agriculture (the supply of labor, food, raw materials, and exports) have either already succeeded in meeting their objectives or are no longer relevant, the final role – providing the rural population with the income that it needs to increase the general standard of living of the 800 million people that still live in rural areas – has remained elusive and is far from being realized. Average farm size is smaller now than it was twenty-five years ago. The infrastructure and resource base for agricultural production is fragile in many areas. Further agricultural trade liberalization poses threats to producers in some of China's more vulnerable areas. The rural–urban income gaps continue to widen. There is a core of very poor people who lack the human capital to take advantage of the opportunities available in an economy growing at 10 percent per year. There still are fundamental barriers that discourage permanent migration of individuals and families from rural to urban areas.

Policymakers also face many constraints to their development efforts. Some originate outside the agricultural sector; for example, the legacy of the *hukou* system still raises the cost of permanent migration so high that most rural families cannot even dream of moving to the city. Others are part of the agricultural sector itself. For example, poor land rights may be holding back investment into profitable farming ventures, dampening enthusiasm for farm consolidation and preventing rural households from benefiting from the conversion of low-productivity farm land into high-valued urban uses (which could be used to help families finance their move into a more permanent urban setting).

In summary, the real challenge facing the agricultural sector now is whether it can release large numbers of families to live and work in urban areas (or to become part of an urban landscape that grows up around them), leaving a smaller number of farming families with control of sufficient land and other resources to make a decent living in farming. At the very least, farm incomes need to rise enough to allow families to invest in their children's human capital and their own social capital, and thus raise their capacity to respond to future economic opportunities both within and beyond the farm sector.

To meet our overall goals and show in more detail these findings, we will first briefly recount the performance of the socialist era and then seek to understand the agricultural policies and other economic events that led to these outcomes. In the following section, we have two major tasks: first, we will examine performance during the reform era, and second, we will analyze the importance of the role of policies that have spurred and hindered progress during the 1980s, 1990s, and 2000s. While the reform era, as will be argued, has turned agriculture into a growing sector that contributed to the nation's development, in the final section, we will discuss the limitations of the current set of policies and direction of China's agricultural growth. This will try to help us put into perspective the achievements and failures and inform our appraisal of the state of China's agriculture and its current development path in the light of China's overall economic position.

PRE-REFORM AGRICULTURE: MIXED OUTCOMES AND DISAPPOINTING RESULTS

Socialist policies dominated the 1950s, 1960s, and 1970s in China and had a profound and complicated effect on agriculture. In this section, we first review the performance of the agricultural sector, trying to lay out the successes and failures of the sector. Second, we recount the major policies – inside and outside of agriculture – which we believe are responsible for producing the outcomes that were realized during the socialist period.

Performance during the Socialist Period

The Struggle to Produce Calories
The performance of agriculture in producing food and other raw materials for industry during the socialist period is mixed and, in part, depends on the standard against which the sector's performance is judged. Aggregate trends show that agriculture played an important role in increasing food availability, especially that of staple grains (Table 13.1). Between 1952 and 1978, although total sown area increased by 6.3 percent, grain-sown area was about steady. (It declined by 2.7 percent.) Grain yields, in contrast, increased by 91 percent from 1952 to 1978, an annual growth of 2.8 percent. In the aggregate, China's grain production rose by 86 percent, a rise of 2.5 percent per year. Indeed, the growth rate of grain production outpaced that of the population (1.9 percent), meaning that China's agricultural sector increased per capita calorie availability during the socialist period.

With the rise of sown area, China's producers were able to produce additional amounts of cash crops. For example, the area sown to cotton rose during the socialist era (Table 13.1, columns 4–6). Yields also rose modestly. In total, the areas planted to cash crops increased by 16 percent during the pre-reform period (1952–1978).

While Chinese policy deserves credit for increasing the absolute and per capita levels of food and agricultural raw material availability during a time when many other nations in the world were suffering from falling food production, it is hard to argue that agriculture's performance constituted a transformative force within China's socialist-era economy. Throughout the 1950s, 1960s, and 1970s, China's consumers remained on strictly rationed diets. Coarse grains – maize, sweet potato, millet, and sorghum – made up much of an average citizen's staple food intake. Most consumers were deprived of daily access to cooking oil, sugar, meat, and vegetables for extended periods. Most telling, despite the growth, the average level of consumption in urban areas in the 1970s was still low, only 2,328 calories

Table 13.1. *China's agricultural performance during the Socialist Era, 1950–1978*

	Grain			Cotton			Structure of cropping (grain-sown area/total sown area)
Year	Sown area (million hectares)	Output (million tons)	Yield (ton/ hectare)	Sown area (1,000 hectares)	Output (1,000 tons)	Yield (ton/ hectare)	
1950	114.41	132.13	1.16	3,786	692	0.180	87
1951	117.77	143.72	1.22	5,485	1,031	0.188	87
1952	123.98	163.91	1.32	5,576	1,304	0.233	88
1953	126.64	166.83	1.32	5,180	1,175	0.225	88
1954	128.99	169.51	1.31	5,462	1,065	0.195	87
1955	129.84	183.93	1.42	5,773	1,518	0.263	86
1956	136.34	192.75	1.42	6,256	1,445	0.225	86
1957	133.63	195.05	1.46	5,775	1,640	0.278	85
1958	127.61	197.65	1.55	5,556	1,969	0.353	84
1959	116.02	169.65	1.46	5,512	1,709	0.308	81
1960	122.43	143.85	1.18	5,225	1,063	0.203	81
1961	121.44	136.50	1.13	3,870	748	0.195	85
1962	121.62	154.40	1.27	3,497	702	0.203	87
1963	120.74	165.75	1.37	4,409	1,137	0.255	86
1964	122.10	180.87	1.54	4,935	1,663	0.338	85
1965	119.63	194.53	1.63	5,003	2,098	0.420	83
1966	120.99	214.00	1.77	4,926	2,337	0.473	82
1967	119.23	217.82	1.83	5,098	2,354	0.465	82
1968	116.16	209.06	1.80	4,986	2,354	0.473	83
1969	117.60	210.97	1.79	4,829	2,079	0.428	83
1970	119.27	242.92	2.04	4,997	2,277	0.458	83
1971	120.85	250.14	2.07	4,924	2,105	0.428	83
1972	121.21	240.47	1.98	4,896	1,958	0.398	82
1973	121.16	270.16	2.19	4,942	2,562	0.518	82
1974	120.98	275.28	2.27	5,014	2,461	0.488	81
1975	121.06	284.51	2.35	4,956	2,381	0.480	81
1976	120.74	286.31	2.37	4,929	2,055	0.420	81
1977	120.40	282.73	2.35	4,845	2,049	0.420	81
1978	120.59	304.77	2.53	4,866	2,167	0.443	80

Source: Yearbook (various years).

per capita; dietary intake for the average rural resident was even lower, barely meeting the UN's average minimum requirement of 2,100 daily calories.

The food-production system was so fragile that it was subject to catastrophic failure during the famine of 1959–1961 (Aston et al., 1984). During the three years that followed the failed Great Leap Forward campaign, more than 30 million people starved to death or were not born, most due to malnutrition-related causes. This was by far the worst famine in world history. And, while there were many reasons for

Table 13.2. *China's grain trade, 1970–1980*

Year	Grain Import	Grain Export	Rice Import	Rice Export	Wheat Import	Wheat Export
1970	5.36	2.12	0.04	1.28	5.30	0.00
1971	3.17	2.62	0.13	1.29	3.02	0.00
1972	4.76	2.93	0.20	1.43	4.33	0.00
1973	8.13	3.89	0.07	2.63	6.30	0.00
1974	8.12	3.64	0.12	2.06	5.38	0.00
1975	3.74	2.81	0.07	1.63	3.49	0.00
1976	2.37	1.76	0.29	0.88	2.02	0.00
1977	7.34	1.66	0.13	1.03	6.88	0.00
1978	8.83	1.88	0.17	1.44	7.67	0.00
1979	12.36	1.65	0.12	1.05	8.71	0.00
1980	13.43	1.62	0.15	1.12	10.97	0.00

Note: Values are in million tons.
Source: Yearbook (various years).

the famine, sharp reductions in both agricultural production and food availability were in part to blame (Chang and Wen, 1997).

Food availability, in fact, became such an issue that during the late 1960s and 1970s, China began to turn to international markets to supplement domestic production (Table 13.2). Between 1973 and 1980, China imported on average more than 6 million tons of grain, mostly wheat. During the peak import years, grain accounted for a large percentage (in value terms) of China's imports. At a time when China's planners were trying to jump-start China's industrialization with imported machinery and other technologies, the inability of the agricultural sector to feed China's populace (not to mention providing foreign exchange earnings from exports) severely hindered the nation's development.

In summary, then, the performance of China's agricultural sector was mixed in two dimensions and failed in a third. Total output did rise faster than population. However, the magnitude of the rise was insufficient to supply enough food and raw material for a rapidly growing, modernizing economy. China's population was barely getting enough food and clothing. There was no surplus, no choice, and no extra supply for exports that could earn valuable foreign exchange. In fact, the failure of agriculture to carry out its fundamental role is even clearer in the case of trade. China was forced to spend a large share of its scarce foreign exchange just to be able to supply the minimal diets of the 1970s.

Structural Stagnation

While the story of food availability is mixed, almost everything else about the record of structural change during the first three decades of agricultural development during the People's Republican period is negative. The structure of cropping showed almost no change at all (Table 13.1). In 1952, grain accounted for 88 percent of the sown area; grain was still being cultivated on 83 percent of the nation's sown area in 1970. During the 1970s, there was even less movement (shifting between 80 and 83 percent). Likewise, there was little change in broader structure of the agricultural sector. The value of the cropping sector as a share of total agricultural output value was 83 percent in 1952 and was still 75 percent in 1970. By 1975, the cropping sector's share remained at 73 percent. These figures provide no indication that there was any dynamic moving the agricultural sector in the direction of a new structure oriented toward higher-valued commodities.

Perhaps of greatest importance, income per capita of rural farmers and other metrics of wealth also showed little improvement. Despite the rise in grain output, earnings per capita in the 1970s were almost the same as in the mid-1950s (Lardy, 1983). Housing showed almost no improvement during the 1960s and 1970s (CNBS, 1999). Even by 1978, per capita levels of rural consumption – nearly thirty years after the start of the socialist era – of almost every food in an absolute sense were low, only 1.1 kilograms of edible oil and 6.4 kilograms of meat per year (Huang and Bouis, 2001). The poverty rate was between 30 and 40 percent, depending on the exact definition of poverty.

Finally, the stagnation of income, given (even modestly) rising output, suggests that productivity growth was low. Although data sources do not facilitate rigorous analysis of total factor productivity (TFP), work by Stone and Rozelle (1995) and Wen (1993) finds no evidence of gains in either productivity or allocative efficiency.

This analysis shows that China's agriculture played only a minor transformative role in the nation's development during the socialist era. It was not providing labor to the off-farm sector; it was not generating foreign exchange; it was not creating linkages to the rest of the economy or raising rural incomes. In fact, it was at most playing only minor roles in increasing the availability of food and raw materials for industry. And, as we have seen, it was doing this with a relatively low degree of efficiency and effectiveness.

Socialist Policies and Institutions: The Basis for Agriculture's Poor Performance

The socialist period began much differently in the early 1950s (and, in fact, earlier) than it ended in the late 1970s. Soon after 1949 work groups at the direction of the central and local government orchestrated the largest and one of the most comprehensive land reforms in the history of the world (Perkins, 1994). Taking land mostly from landlords and rich farmers – sometimes by violence and almost never with compensation – land was divided among all of China's rural households. With very few exceptions, every farm household in China was given a plot of land. In some places, land was divided evenly, distributed on the basis of population; in other areas, more complicated criteria were used that essentially left some households with larger landholdings, although these households often had obligations to sell a larger share of their production to the state.

While there is no clear evidence linking the rise of output in the early 1950s to the incentives embodied in the new landholding arrangements, China's socialist leaders quickly moved to implement policies that effectively undercut the newly established system of private land ownership (Lardy, 1983). Soon after the start of the First Five-Year Plan, farmers were organized into cooperatives; the shift to communes, implemented in 1958, eliminated household farming (except on private plots). The shift toward collectivization was gradual, but between 1954 and 1958, farmers in most regions of the country moved from mutual assistance teams/cooperatives to collectives to communes. Some writers claim that, at least initially, farmers and their leaders had some choice about whether to collectivize (Lin, 1998). Our own interviews with village leaders who still remembered the days prior to collectivization have not found a single person who characterizes the collectivization movement as voluntary. Whether or not the decision to pool farm tools and cooperate during planting and harvest was voluntary, it is certain that, once Mao Zedong decided to organize rural China into communes, there was no choice whatsoever.

The main weakness of the communes was the absence of incentives. There were two basic problems. Individual families were not the residual claimants of production; this sapped work effort. To make matters worse, output suffered from concentration of decision making in the hands of collective leaders who often were somewhat removed from day-to-day production and had limited access to information (Putterman, 1993).

Farmers no longer kept the produce from their own lands. Instead, commune members were assigned work points based on particular tasks; these points were converted to grain and cash payouts at the end of each crop year. There is a debate over the extent to which this system motivated farmers to exert effort and pursue production efficiencies (Dong and Dow, 1993; Chang and Wen, 1995; Lin and Yang, 2000). Most scholars believe that free riding and the inability to monitor agricultural labor undermined the rural incentives. The large gap between productivity of private plots and collective fields shows the extent to which farm workers shirked collective duties and diverted inputs onto their own plots (Mead, 2000). The failure to raise productivity during the socialist era almost certainly is due in a large part to the poor incentives that were embodied in the collectivized farming institutions (especially, given the rapid rise of farm output during the first years of reform – see next section).

Pricing and Marketing Agricultural Commodities and Inputs

While the organization of production may have had a major role in the poor performance of the cropping and livestock sectors, socialist-era pricing policy also did little to encourage the efficient production or allocation of goods and services. Prices were fixed by the state (Sicular, 1988b). Between 1962 and 1978, the price of grain remained almost unchanged, being adjusted only three times, rising by a total of less than 20 percent. Input prices played mainly an accounting role, as shortages kept most producers from having access to the quantities that they sought to purchase.

Marketing institutions also did not encourage the development of agriculture; there was little competition and marketing officials did not have an incentive to search out low-cost or quality producers. Prior to the reform period, domestic and international marketing of agricultural products was monopolized by a complex set of government institutions that determined both the producer and consumer prices (Sicular, 1988a, 1988b; Huang and David, 1995). Moreover, production was carried out based on (mostly) planned acreage, target volume, quality, and variety of production. Official plans even stipulated the ratio between home consumption and marketed surplus. Hence, it is easy to see how the nature of marketing institutions also dampened enthusiasm for production and allowed the state to be able to carry out its pricing policy.

Of course, the system also served to indirectly help – at least in the short run – the state's effort at forced industrialization by keeping down the price of staples to allow the state to keep wages low. Except for the amount used for the farm households' home consumption for food, feed, and seeds, almost all production was delivered to the state at low quota prices for specified (compulsory) amounts (Sicular, 1988b). After the early 1960s, the state also procured any surplus production beyond the quota and home consumption at somewhat higher above-quota prices in an effort to provide an incentive to increase the production. The incentives, however, were targeted at collective leaders and not at the farmers on whose effort the harvest depended.

To suppress the demand for agricultural products that were in short supply (and priced low), marketing agencies also exercised tight control over urban food supplies. Staple products were sold by government agencies to urban consumers and rural households in grain-deficit regions at ration prices upon presentation of coupons. These coupons were distributed on a per capita basis, depending on age, type of employment, and other determinants of caloric requirements.

Nonagricultural Policies and Institutions and Agricultural Stagnation
Hukou System. China's approach to planning and its placement of the rural economy into the unplanned sector also had a dramatic effect on the nature of employment and China's structural stagnation (Lyons, 1987). Because China's agricultural sector was so large and undeveloped (and because of the government's pro-urban/industrial policies), leaders decided to make a sharp distinction between urban and rural residents. In return for shipments of fertilizer and small amounts of capital and other inputs, the collectivized agricultural sector was expected to supply food and nonfood commodities to the urban-industrial parts of the economy. The collective agricultural sector was expected to meet all other needs from its own resources.

Farmers were not allowed to freely move out of their collectives. The scope and magnitude of the housing, educational, health, welfare, and other services between rural and urban widened throughout the socialist period. Without a doubt, the *hukou* policies and other restrictions keeping rural people from leaving their villages and restricting opportunities to shift rural production into manufacturing or services artificially limited the pace of structural change during the socialist era and undoubtedly suppressed the growth of incomes and productivity.

Trade Policy. Two key policies also worked against agriculture in the socialist era. First, agricultural trade in the pre-reform era became a tool to supplement the plan (Huang and Chen, 1999; Lardy, 2001). Given the nation's commitment to self-sufficiency in all areas of the economy, imports were limited to procuring products required by state plans – mostly machinery and other investment goods – which could not be manufactured domestically. Almost all trade flowed through eight state-owned trading firms. In the 1970s, the agricultural state trading firm monopolized nearly all food imports and exports. This institutional structure stifled any prospect of specialization in labor-intensive export crops that could be offset by imports of land-intensive staple crops. Agricultural trade was primarily looked upon as a means to generate foreign exchange.

Furthermore, China's overvalued exchange rate was stacked against encouraging agricultural exports (Huang and Chen, 1999). Even under a free-trade regime, imports would have been cheap (hurting agriculture by depressing prices) and exports would have reduced already limited domestic supplies of foodstuffs and other farm products.

Summary: Socialist Agriculture: Disappointing Outcomes, No Transformation

After nearly thirty years under the People's Republic, China's agriculture was in disarray. It was not really playing any of its roles effectively. Although output had risen, this reflected the strategic breakthroughs in agricultural technologies and investment of central and local government funds into water control that was supplemented by involuntary corvee labor by rural conscripts. Productivity and incomes remained stagnant. There was no structural shift toward a more productive, higher-efficiency rural economy. The population was locked into agriculture.

These discouraging results are clearly attributable to the implementation of socialist policies – both inside and outside the agricultural sector. Neither the organization of production nor the systems of pricing and marketing institutions provided suitable incentives. Perhaps the worst feature of these arrangements was the entrapment of Chinese villagers in a system that designated them as second-class citizens and denied them a fair share of investment, services, or opportunities. In short, the agricultural and nonagricultural policy environment undermined every important contribution that agriculture can offer to a dynamic economy.

When analyzed this way, the policy shift under the new government of Deng Xiaoping should come as no surprise. With the economies of East Asia, and especially those of Taiwan, Hong Kong, and Singapore, developing rapidly and providing higher and higher incomes of their citizens, China's leaders felt enormous pressures to reform the policy regime that had pushed them into the productivity trap that characterized the economy in the mid-1970s. Moreover, the rural economy gave leaders the most natural laboratory within which to experiment. Its consistently weak performance invited reform, and its plan-imposed isolation reduced the cost of experimentation; mistakes would have no direct impact on the urban and industrial heartland of Chinese socialism. As a result, the shortcomings of China's socialized agricultural sector encouraged national leaders to choose the rural economy as the starting point for their vaguely defined experiment in reformism.

THE ROLE OF AGRICULTURE IN CHINA'S TRANSITION ERA: RECENT SUCCESSES

This section pursues two main themes. First, we describe the performance of the agricultural sector and its interaction with Chinese growth since the onset of the reform era in the late 1970s. Second, we examine in greater depth the policy initiatives – inside and outside of agriculture – that have helped launch and guide China's agricultural transition. We examine the reform strategy by looking at the rationale, objectives, and implementation for each reform component.

Agriculture in the Transition Era – Performance

In this section we seek to examine the effect of transition-era policies and other events on agriculture's overall performance. We do so by first examining the effects generally. Next, we look at effects on a sector-by-sector basis. In the final section, we review the findings and draw conclusions about the role that agriculture played in China's development during the transition era.

The Revival of Agriculture and Resolution of China's Grain Problem

The ups and downs that characterized the performance of agriculture in the prereform period disappeared after 1978. Once the reform began, every possible metric confirms that China's farm sector surpassed results achieved during the previous three decades by enormous margins. It was only after reform commenced that agriculture finally began to carry out its various roles in the development process. Compared to the early and mid-1970s when the value of gross domestic product (GDP) of agriculture rose by 2.7 percent annually, the annual growth rate more than tripled to 8.2 percent during the initial reform period, 1978–1984 (Table 13.3, row 1). Although annual growth rates have slowed to around 4 percent in real terms during 1985–2000, these are still extraordinarily high rates of sustained agricultural growth.

Table 13.3. *Annual growth of Chinese agriculture by commodity, 1970–2000*

Commodity	Pre-reform period	Reform period		
	1970–1978	1978–1984	1985–1995	1996–2000
Agricultural GDP	4.9	8.8	3.8	4.2
Grain				
Production	2.8	4.7	1.7	0.03
Sown area	0.0	−1.1	−0.1	−0.14
Yield	2.8	5.8	1.8	0.17
Rice				
Production	2.5	4.5	0.6	0.3
Sown area	0.7	−0.6	−0.6	−0.5
Yield	1.8	5.1	1.2	0.8
Wheat				
Production	7.0	8.3	1.9	−0.4
Sown area	1.7	−0.0	0.1	−1.4
Yield	5.2	8.3	1.8	1.0
Maize				
Production	7.4	3.7	4.7	−0.1
Sown area	3.1	−1.6	1.7	0.8
Yield	4.2	5.4	2.9	−0.9
TOTAL (cash crop sown area)	2.4	5.1	2.1	3.5
Cotton				
Production	−0.4	19.3	−0.3	−1.9
Sown area	−0.2	6.7	−0.3	−6.1
Yield	−0.2	11.6	−0.0	4.3
Edible oil crops	2.1	14.9	4.4	5.6
Vegetable area	2.4	5.4	6.8	9.5
Fruit				
Orchards area	8.1	4.5	10.4	1.5
Outputs	6.6	7.2	12.7	8.6
Meat (pork/beef/poultry)	4.4	9.1	8.8	6.5
Fishery	5.0	7.9	13.7	10.2

Notes: Values are in percent. Growth rates are computed using the regression method. Growth rates of individual items and groups of commodities are based on production data; sectoral growth rates refer to value added in real terms.

Source: Yearbook (1980–2001), Agriculture Yearbook (1980–2001).

During the initial stages of reform, all subsectors of agriculture experienced rapid output growth, driven by increases in yields. Between 1978 and 1984, grain production increased by 4.7 percent per year (Table 13.3, rows 2–4). Production rose for each of the major grains – rice, wheat, and maize (Table 13.3, rows 5–13). While sown area did not change, yields for grains, in general, more than doubled between the late part of the pre-reform era and the early reform period (Table 13.3, row 4). During the early reform period, the growth of yields of all major grain crops (Table 13.3, rows 7, 10, 13) exceeded the growth of yields during the early and mid-1970s.

The trend of grain prices demonstrates the success of agriculture in supplying high-quality, inexpensive food. During the reform era, with the exception of price spikes in 1988 and 1995, the real price of rice, wheat, and maize has fallen. When using a regression approach to measure the trends, grain prices have fallen in real terms between 33 percent (maize) and 45 percent (wheat) from the late 1970s to early 2000s. Coupled with rising incomes, falling grain prices have reduced the share of grain in rural households' consumption budgets from nearly 40 percent in the late 1970s to about 14 percent in 2004. In urban areas, grain accounted for more than 20 percent of the total expenditure in the late 1970s, and it has been less than 3 percent since 2003 (Huang, Rozelle, and Wang, 2006).

Beyond Grain: The Transformation of the Agricultural Sector

Far more fundamental than rises in output and yields of the grain sector, China's agricultural economy has steadily transformed itself from a grain-first sector to one that is producing growing amounts of higher-valued cash crops, horticultural goods, and livestock/aquaculture products. Like the grain sector, cash crops in general, and specific crops, such as cotton, edible oils, and vegetables and fruit, also grew rapidly in the early reform period when compared to the 1970s (Table 13.3, rows 14–21). Unlike grain (with the exception of land-intensive staples, such as cotton), the growth of nongrain sector continued throughout the reform era. Hence, in the case of many commodity groups, the high growth rates, which have exceeded those of grains during almost the entire reform era, continue. Clearly, agriculture's contribution now extends far beyond mere subsistence, as it now supplies oilseeds for the edible oil sector, horticultural products for the retail food sector, and cotton for the textile industry.[2]

Some sectors have delivered astonishing growth. For example, between 1990 and 2004 vegetable production has grown so fast that China is adding the equivalent of California's vegetable industry every two years. Orchards now occupy over

---

[2] The fall in cotton production during the later reform period has more to do with pest infestations than with lack of incentives. Since the late 1990s, there has a been a revival of the cotton production, as the advent of insect-resistant, genetically modified cotton has overcome this problem (Huang et al., 2002).

Table 13.4. *Structural change in China's agricultural economy,*
1970–2000

	1970	1980	1985	1990	1995	2000
Share in agricultural output						
Crop	82	76	69	65	58	56
Livestock	14	18	22	26	30	30
Fishery	2	2	3	5	8	11
Forestry	2	4	5	4	3	4

Note: Values are in percent.
Source: Yearbook and Rural Statistics Yearbook (various issues).

5 percent of China's cultivated area, more than double the share in other major agricultural nation.

China is also moving rapidly away from a crop-first agriculture. The rise of livestock and fishery sectors outpaces the cropping sector, in general, and most of the subcategories of cropping (Table 13.3, rows 22–23). Livestock production rose 9.1 percent in the early reform period and has continued to grow at between 6.5 and 8.8 percent since 1985. The fisheries subsector is the fastest growing component of agriculture, rising more than 10 percent per year during the reform era. The rapid and continuous rise in livestock and fisheries has steadily eroded the predominance of cropping (Table 13.4).

Moving Off the Farm
The reform era has brought fundamental, transformative changes not just to agriculture but also to the entire rural economy. While the annual growth of agriculture averaged about 5 percent throughout the entire reform period, the growth rates of the economy as a whole and of the industrial and service sectors were faster (Table 13.5, rows 1–4). In fact, since 1985, the growth of industry and services have been two to three times faster than agriculture. Because of the differences in the sectoral growth rates, agriculture's share of GDP has fallen from 40 percent in 1970 to 16 percent in 2000 (Table 13.6, rows 1–3). Forecasts anticipate that the share of agriculture will fall under 10 percent by 2008. These figures highlight an ironic feature of agricultural development: the more transformative the role that agriculture plays, the faster the pace of development and the corresponding decline in the importance of agriculture.

The shifts in the economy can also be seen in employment (Table 13.6, rows 4–7). Official data show that agriculture employed 81 percent of China's entire labor force in 1970. By 2000, as the industrial and service sectors grew in importance, the share of employment in agriculture fell to below 50 percent; outside estimates indicate a more rapid decline (see Chapter 17). By 1995, more than 150 million rural laborers were working off the farm (Rozelle et al., 1999). By 2000, the number rose to

Table 13.5. *Annual growth of China's economy, 1970–2000*

	Reform period		
	1979–1984	1985–1995	1996–2000
GDP	8.8	9.7	8.2
Agriculture	7.1	4.0	3.4
Industry	8.2	12.8	9.6
Services	11.6	9.7	8.2
Foreign trade	14.3	15.2	9.8
Import	12.7	13.4	9.5
Export	15.9	17.2	10.0
Rural enterprise output	12.3	24.1	14.0
Population	1.40	1.37	0.90
Per capita GDP	7.1	8.3	7.1

Note: Values are in percent. Figure for GDP in 1970–1978 is the growth rate of national income in real terms. Growth rates are computed using the regression method.
Source: Yearbook (various issues).

Table 13.6. *Structural change in China's economy, 1970–2000*

	1970	1980	1985	1990	1995	2000
Share in GDP						
Agriculture	40	30	28	27	20	16
Industry	46	49	43	42	49	51
Services	13	21	29	31	31	33
Share in employment						
Agriculture	81	69	62	60	52	50
Industry	10	18	21	21	23	22.5
Services	9	13	17	19	25	27.5

Note: Values are in percent.
Source: Yearbook and Rural Statistics Yearbook (various issues).

more than 200 million (Rozelle et al., 2000). This evidence of structural economic change – from the perspectives of both output and employment – demonstrates the rural sector's major contribution to the transformation of China's overall economy – from agriculture to industry and from rural to urban (Nyberg and Rozelle, 1999; Rozelle et al., 1999).

Other Changes

Agricultural Trade Liberalization. While much has been made of China's accession to the World Trade Organization (WTO) as a turning point in its relationship with the world, China's open-door policy actually started much earlier (Huang, Rozelle, and Rosegrant, 1999). In the process, China has turned itself from a hermit country into one of the world's great trading nations. Agriculture is a major participant in this transformation. Between 1980 and 2000, the total value of China's agricultural trade grew by about 6 percent annually. Since 2000, it has more than doubled, making China the fourth largest importer of agricultural commodities in the world (Gale, 2006). Furthermore, China's exports of agricultural products have exceeded imports in almost every year since the start of reform (Huang, Rozelle, and Rosegrant, 1999).

Perhaps more remarkable is the shift in the composition of this trade over the past twenty-five years. According to China's customs statistics, the net exports of *land-intensive bulk commodities*, such as grains, oilseeds, and sugar crops, have fallen; at the same time, exports of higher-valued, more *labor-intensive products*, such as horticultural and animal goods (including aquatic products), have risen. In other words, China's exports and imports have shifted in directions that reflect the nation's comparative advantage in labor-intensive products. Disaggregated, crop-specific trade trends show the same sharp shifts (Anderson, Huang, and Ianchovichina, 2004).

The Production and Marketing Environment. After more than twenty-five years of reform, one of the most striking changes concerns the role of government and local leaders in agricultural production and marketing. During the socialist period, commune and brigade officials and bureaucrats in government supply and marketing agencies were deeply involved with all aspects of pre- and postharvest decisions. During the early reform years, there was some change, but intervention into production (e.g., through schemes of unified management) and marketing (e.g., through the grain and cotton procurement systems) continued (Sicular, 1988b, 1995). By 2005, however, the situation had changed dramatically. Indeed, one of the most notable features of China's agricultural economy today (with several exceptions) is the absence of government involvement.

Declining farm size is among the most conspicuous trends in rural production. Between 1980 and 2000, the land controlled by the average farm household has fallen from 0.71 to 0.55 hectare. Moreover, while the rate of growth of production and marketing cooperatives (called Farmer Professional Associations – FPAs) has risen in recent years, few villages and few farmers (percentagewise) belong. According to Shen et al. (2005), only 7 percent of villages have FPAs. And, in the villages that do have FPAs, only about one-third of farmers belong. As a result, in all of China, only about 2 percent of farmers belong to cooperatives. By contrast, other developing nations in East Asia (such as Japan and Korea) and many Western nations (such as the United States and Europe) during their early years attained participation rates approaching 100 percent. From this perspective, the transition to larger, more modern farms has yet to begin. As will be seen, this is likely due to the nature of China's property rights in cultivated land.

Aside from restrictions on land ownership, China today may have one of the least distorted domestic agricultural economies in the world. With the exception of farmers renting village-owned orchards planted in the 1980s and early 1990s, survey responses indicate that 100 percent of farmers make their own planting decisions without compulsion by local officials (Rozelle, Huang, and Sumner, 2006). In a survey of randomly selected households in eight provinces, all farmers reported purchasing chemical fertilizer from private vendors with no intervention by local officials (Zhang, Li, and Rozelle, 2005).

On the procurement side, where government parastatals formerly purchased the output of China's farms, today, a large majority of sales of grains, oilseeds, and fiber crops and literally all sales of horticultural and livestock products flow to small, private traders (Wang et al., 2006a). Indeed, even with the rise of supermarkets and processing firms that are catering to the retail needs of the urban population, a recent survey discovered that almost all purchases of fruit, vegetables, nuts, and livestock products are by the *first buyers*, individual entrepreneurs trading on their own account (Table 13.7). Even by the second link in the marketing chain (*second buyer*), private traders are still handling most of the produce.

The existence of millions of small traders competing with virtually no regulation means that China's markets have become integrated and efficient. Park et al. (2002), Huang, Rozelle, and Chang (2004), and Rozelle and Huang (2004, 2005) find that prices are transmitted across space and over time as efficiently and at levels of integration that meet or exceed those of the United States. Input prices for fertilizer are equally well integrated (Qiao et al., 2003). Indeed, statistical analysis demonstrates that even farmers in remote, poor villages are integrated into national markets (Huang and Rozelle, forthcoming).

Impact of Market Liberalization and Specialization

Although few authors have attempted to quantify the gains from market liberalization, available research shows that farmers have benefited from increased allocative efficiency. For example, deBrauw, Huang, and Rozelle (2004) find a positive effect of increasing marketization on productivity. Lin (1991) and Huang and Rozelle (1996) obtain similar results. In all three papers, the authors conjecture (without an empirical basis) that the gains are due in part to increasing specialization.

To pursue the progress of specialization since the mid-1990s, we conducted a nationally representative survey of 400 communities in 2004. We asked community leaders the following question: Are farmers in your village specializing in any particular crop or livestock commodity? The question related to conditions in 1995 and 2004. If the respondent answered affirmatively, we asked for the commodity in which they were specializing. If the farmers in the community were specializing in a cropping activity, we asked for the area sown to the specialty commodity.

Table 13.7. *Supply and marketing channels for horticultural products in the Greater Beijing area, 2004*

Panel A: First-time buyers (percent)

	Modern supply chains			Traditional supply chains		Other supply chains		
	Supermarkets	Specialized suppliers	Processing firms	Small traders	Farmers sell in local periodic markets	Cooperatives	Consumers direct purchase from farmers	Others[a]
Horticultural crops	0	2	2	79	8	0	7	2
Vegetables	0	3	5	82	5	0	1	3
Fruit	0	1	1	75	11	0	9	3
Nuts	0	6	0	88	3	0	3	0

Panel B: Second-time buyers (percent)

	Modern supply chains			Traditional supply chains		Other supply chains	
	Supermarkets	Specialized suppliers	Processing firms	Small traders	Traders sell to consumers in periodic markets	Cooperatives	Others[b]
Horticultural crops	3	3	10	49	13	0	22
Vegetables	6	0	6	57	11	0	20
Fruit	1	2	9	46	16	0	26
Nuts	3	10	19	50	6	0	12

[a] "Others" (first-time buyers) includes purchases by agents of hotels or restaurants, gifts to other farmers, or procurement by organized groups (such as enterprises for distribution to their workers).
[b] "Others" (second-time buyers) includes sales to other villages and sales to market sites that supply processors and other food firms.
Source: Wang et al. (2006b).

Table 13.8. *Percentage of villages and sown*
area with specialization by region

	Percentage of villages		Percentage of sown area	
	1995	2004	1995	2004
Average	21	30	14	24
Hebei	18	19	20	24
Henan	22	23	4	9
Shanxi	51	74	11	22
Shaanxi	4	5	23	32
Inner Mongolia	9	17	38	40
Liaoning	15	32	13	29

Source: Huang and Rozelle (2005).

The results of our survey show that specialization has indeed expanded in China's agricultural sector. Between 1995 and 2004, the percentage of villages that specialize in an agricultural commodity has increased sharply in every province (Table 13.8, columns 1, 2). On average, throughout our sample from across China, 30 percent of China's villages are specializing in 2004, up from 21 percent in 1995. When examining the composition of the output of villages that are specializing, it is clear that the rise in the demand for horticulture and other specialty products is driving the specialization. In our sample, fully 60 percent of those villages that are specializing are producing fruits (28 percent), vegetables (13 percent), or other cash crops (28 percent – e.g., sugarcane, tobacco, and cotton). Other villages specialize in livestock commodities, oilseed crops, forest products, and other commodities.

Productivity Trends and Rural Incomes
While trends in agricultural productivity may diverge from the path of output, as occurred in the pre-reform period, this has not happened under China's reform. First, as seen in Table 13.2, output per unit of land (or yields) rose sharply. In addition, for the entire reform period, trends in agricultural labor productivity, measured as output per farm worker, parallel those of yield.

Moreover, it is also possible that partial and more complete measures of productivity move in opposite directions (as occurred in the pre-reform period). In reality, most evidence from the literature shows TFP moving in the same direction as the partial measures. Several series of TFP estimates for China's agriculture (McMillan, Walley, and Zhu, 1989; Fan, 1991; Lin, 1992; Wen, 1993; Huang and Rozelle, 1996; Fan, 1997; Jin et al., 2002) uniformly demonstrate that in the first years after reform (1978–1984), comprehensive measures of productivity (either constructed TFP indices or their regression-based equivalents) rose by 5–10 percent per year. Although Wen (1993) worries that TFP growth came to a halt during

Table 13.9. *Rural income per capita in China, 1980–2001 (real terms, 2000 yuan)*

Income group	1980	1985	1990	1995	2000	2001	Annual growth rate, 1980–2001 (%)
Average	711	1,248	1,305	1,702	2,253	2,347	6
Bottom decile (poorest)	312	448	442	493	579	578	3
Top decile (richest)	1,530	2,486	3,253	4,763	6,805	7,159	8

Source: Yearbook (various issues).

1985–1989, Fan (1997) and Jin et al. (2002) demonstrate that during the 1990s, TFP continued to rise at a rate of around 2 percent per year – a substantial advance in international perspective.

With the combined impact of rising productivity, increasing efficiency associated with specialization, production of higher-value crops and livestock, and the expansion of off-farm work, rural incomes have steadily increased during the reform era (Table 13.9). Between 1980 and 2000, average rural per capita incomes have risen (in real terms) from 771 to 2,347 yuan. This remarkable rise (6 percent annually) matches the growth rates experienced in Japan and Korea during their takeoff years. Hence, the amount of media attention given to the rural income problem is surprising. No doubt this reflects the relative advantage of urban incomes, which started from a higher pre-reform base and have risen more rapidly than rural incomes.

The inequality between rural and urban incomes has a parallel within the rural economy: the divergence between incomes of those who entered the reform era with relatively high and relatively low earnings. The growth rate of rural per capita income among those in the richest decile is higher than average, more than 8 percent annually. In contrast, although incomes of those in the lowest decile have risen (at 3 percent annually), the rates of increase are far lower than the richest, meaning in relative terms the poorest of the rural poor are falling behind.

Although rises in income (and income inequality) are closely related to the ability of rural households to gain access to off-farm employment (Riskin and Khan, 2001), agriculture plays a role in mitigating inequality. Two factors are responsible for this: first, agricultural income is distributed more evenly to begin with, and second, the poor are proportionately more involved in agriculture (Rozelle, 1996).

Overall Observation on Agriculture's Performance during the Reform Era

In summary, whereas the socialist era saw little transformation, the transition period has brought dramatic change to China's agricultural sector. Although the sector grew in absolute size, its fall in the importance in the overall economy in terms of both output value and employment reflects the characteristic dynamic of modern growth. The structure of the sector itself is also changing, with farmers diversifying out of coarse grains into fine grains, out of staple grains into higher-valued crops, and out of cropping into livestock and aquaculture. Trade patterns are also shifting toward China's comparative advantage. Although the most dramatic change is visible among the richer households, poorer households also participate in these new developments.

Building the Institutional Base and Policy Strategy of Reform: Enabling Factors

Unlike the transitional economies in Europe, leaders in China did not move to replace the planned economy with liberalized markets in the initial stages of reform (Rozelle and Swinnen, 2004). Policymakers began to shift their focus to market liberalization only in 1985, after decollectivization was complete. Even then, liberalization was start and stop (Sicular, 1995). Lin, Cai, and Li (1996) argue that leaders were mainly afraid of the disruption that would occur if the institutions through which leaders controlled the main goods in the food economy (such as grain, fertilizer, and meat products) were eliminated without the institutions in place that work to support more efficient market exchange. Throughout, leaders were also investing and changing the rules by which domestic producers and consumer interfaced with the external economy.

Price Policy Changes
The administration of prices by the socialist planning apparatus is one of the distinguishing characteristics of pretransition countries. During the socialist period, leaders may have allowed minor items to be traded outside the plan, but for high-priority commodities – which almost always included food and fiber – China's planning ministries allocated goods and services mostly on the basis of quantity-based plans. Prices had little effect on allocation and mostly served accounting functions.

At the start of the reforms, China's leaders had no concrete plan to liberalize markets. They did, however, take steps to change the incentives embodied in the prices that producers received for their marketed surplus. Hence, perhaps one of the least appreciated moves of the early reformers was their bold decision to administratively increase the farmgate prices of major agricultural commodities (Lardy, 1983; Sicular, 1988a). Between 1978 and 1983, in a number of separate actions, planners in China increased the above-quota prices, the payment farmers received for voluntary sales beyond the mandatory deliveries, by 41 percent for grain and by around 50 percent for cash crops (Sicular, 1988a). Official data show that the relative price of grain to fertilizer rose by more than 60 percent during the first three years after reform. This rise in above-quota price represented a higher output price at the margin to farmers. Until 1984, state-run procurement stations regularly purchased all grain sold by farmers at the above-quota price as long as the sellers had fulfilled their mandatory marketing delivery quota that was purchased at a state-set quota price – 50 percent below the above-quota price in the case of rice (Sicular, 1995).

The timing and breadth of the policy changes were of great importance. The first major price rise occurred in 1979, almost at the same time when reformers were deciding to decollectivize. However, given the leadership's decision to gradually implement the household responsibility system (HRS – discussed later), beginning first in the poorest regions, the price increases immediately affected all farmers, both in areas that had been decollectivized and in areas that had not. By 1981, the time of the second major price increase, according to Lin (1992), less than half of China's farmers had dismantled their communes. Hence, as long as there was some, albeit weak, link between the output price and production, the plan-based price rise would have led to increases in China's farm output.

During the early transition era, the state's monopoly agricultural inputs supply corporation maintained its control over the pricing and distribution of farm inputs – especially fertilizer, but also pesticides, diesel fuel, and electricity (Solinger, 1984; Stone, 1988, 1993). Farmers, through their collective leadership, received low-priced fertilizer from the state, but almost all of it was inframarginal. In other words, the government-supplied, subsidized fertilizer was not sufficient to meet the needs of most farmers. Producers in the early reform years typically purchased additional fertilizer from the state at a higher price (Ye and Rozelle, 1994). Hence, unlike other transition and developing countries, at the margin, farmers in China were not able to purchase fertilizer prices at highly subsidized rates. In fact, according to Huang and Chen (1999), during the 1980s the real price of China's fertilizer was above the international price. Although China's leaders administratively raised the price of fertilizer somewhat under rising foreign exchange and budgetary pressures in the mid-1980s, the rise was not large enough to eliminate the positive incentives created by higher output prices (World Bank, 1997).[3]

Empirical studies confirm the strong impact of these price changes on output during the first years of transition (Fan, 1991; Lin, 1992; Huang and Rozelle, 1996; Fan and Pardey, 1997). Lin (1992) finds that 15 percent of output growth during the first six years of reform came from the rise in relative prices. Huang and Rozelle's (1996) decomposition exercise for rice demonstrates that about 10 percent of the increased output between 1978 and 1984 came from the price effects.

Institutional Reforms

China's rural economic reform, first initiated in 1979, was founded on the HRS. The HRS reforms dismantled the communes and contracted agricultural land to households, mostly on the basis of family size and number of people in each household's labor force. Although the control and income rights after HRS belonged to individuals, the ownership of land remained collective.

---

[3] To the extent that access to fertilizer improved during the reform (Stone, 1988), the shadow prices of fertilizer would also have fallen, which would also encourage higher output.

China's land rights are complicated and changing (Brandt et al., 2002). The initial term of the land contracts was stipulated at fifteen years. During this time, while the ownership of the land stayed with the collective, income and control rights were given to farmers. The effects of such a land policy on the equitable distribution of land to farmers and its effect on food security and poverty alleviation have been obvious and well documented.

Although local leaders were supposed to have given farmers land for fifteen years in the early 1980s and thirty years starting in the late 1990s, collective ownership of land has included frequent reallocation of village land. Many people have been concerned that such moves by local leaders could result in insecure tenure and negative effects on investment (Brandt et al., 2002). Many authors have shown, however, that such reallocations have had little effect on either short- or long-run land productivity. Officials remain concerned that collective ownership and weak alienation and transfer rights could affect migration and rural credit (Johnson, 1995). As a result, China passed a new land law, the Rural Land Contract Law, which took effect on March 1, 2003, which seeks to increase security of tenure.

Above all, the government is now searching for a mechanism that permits those who stay in farming to gain access to additional cultivated land to increase their incomes and competitiveness. Even without much legal protection, over the past decade, researchers are increasingly finding that more land in China is rented in and out (Deininger and Jin, 2005). To accelerate this process, the new Rural Land Contract Law further clarifies the rights for transfer and exchange of contracted land. The new legislation also allows family members to inherit the land during the contracted period. The goal of this new set of policies is to encourage farmers to use their land more efficiently and to increase average farm size.

THE EFFECT OF PROPERTY RIGHTS REFORM ON PERFORMANCE

There is little doubt that the changes in incentives resulting from property rights reforms triggered strong growth in both output and productivity. In the most definitive study on the subject, Lin (1992) estimates that China's HRS accounted for 42–46 percent of the total rise in output during the early reform period (1978–1984). Fan (1991) and Huang and Rozelle (1996) find that even after accounting for technological change, institutional change during the late 1970s and early 1980s contributed about 30 percent of output growth.

Empirical researchers also have documented impacts that go beyond output. McMillan, Walley, and Zhu (1989) find that the early reforms in China also raised TFP, accounting for 90 percent of the rise (23 percent) between 1978 and 1984. Jin et al. (2002) show that the reforms had a large effect on productivity, contributing greatly to a rise in TFP that exceeds 7 percent annually. In addition, a number of researchers have suggested that the rising agricultural sector surplus created by HRS triggered subsequent growth dynamics by providing labor for rural industry's takeoff in the mid-1980s (McKinnon, 1993), fueling the nation's overall industrialization drive later in the reforms and creating demand for the products of firms in other parts of the economy (Qian and Xu, 1998).

After the first decade of transition, however, the direct effects of property rights reforms in China were exhausted. deBrauw, Huang, and Rozelle (2004) show how the absence of further property rights reforms accounts for much of the deceleration of cropping output in the late 1990s. This encouraged China's leaders to intensify efforts to increase more traditional investments in the 1990s.

Input Marketing Policies

The reforms in fertilizer, seed, and other input markets followed China's gradualist strategy (Rozelle and Swinnen, 2004). Decollectivization and administrative output price hikes improved incentives to farmers. Leaders who remained responsible for meeting ambitious food-sector goals did little to the rest of the rural economy in the early 1980s, leaving machinery, fertilizer, and the seed systems virtually unchanged and heavily planned. Beginning in the middle 1980s, market liberalization gradually expanded, starting with machinery, pesticides, and plastic film. The meaningful liberalization of strategically important inputs, such as fertilizer, occurred mostly in the early 1990s. The reform of the seed industry did not begin until the late 1990s.

Domestic Output Market Liberalization Policies

In addition to pricing changes and decollectivization, another major task of reform is to create more efficient institutions of exchange. Markets – whether classic competitive ones or some workable substitute – increase efficiency by facilitating transactions among agents to allow specialization and trade and by providing information about the relative scarcity of resources through a pricing mechanism serving both producers and consumers.

To function efficiently, markets require supporting institutions to ensure competition, define and enforce property rights and contracts, ensure access to credit and finance, and provide information (McMillan, 1997). These institutions were almost completely absent in China during the socialist era. Instead, China's central and provincial planning agencies directed production and other economic transactions. Their directives served to enforce contracts involving exchanges among various agents in the chain.

Market liberalization requires the elimination of planning, but the process of shifting from plan to market must be executed in a way that allows continued access to inputs and marketing channels while market-supporting institutions are emerging. In this section we show how China's leaders gradually liberalized markets. We focus, in particular, on three issues: the process of market liberalization, the enforcement of exchange contracts, and how well reformers or some alternative institutions were able to guarantee access to input and output markets during transition.

Unlike reformers in other socialist nations, leaders in China did not dismantle the planned economy in the initial stages of reform (Rozelle, 1996). Sicular (1988a, 1988b, 1995), Perkins (1994), and Lin (1992) all discuss how China's leadership had little intention of letting the market play anything but a minor supplemental guidance role in the early reform period. Major changes to agricultural commerce in the early 1980s almost exclusively centered on increasing the purchase prices of crops (Sicular, 1988a; Watson, 1994). These price increases, however, should *not* be considered as a move to liberalize markets, since planners in the Ministry of Commerce made the changes administratively and the price changes were mostly executed by the national network of grain procurement stations acting under the direction of the State Grain Bureau.

An examination of policies and marketing activity in the early 1980s illustrates the limited extent of changes in the marketing environment before 1985. It is true that reformers did allow farmers increased discretion to produce and market crops in ten planning categories, such as vegetables, fruits, and coarse grains. Moreover, by 1984, the state claimed control only over twelve commodities, including rice, wheat, maize, soybeans, peanuts, rapeseed, and several other cash crops (Sicular, 1988a). While this may seem to represent a significant move toward liberalization, the crops that remained almost entirely under the planning authority of the government still accounted for more than 95 percent of the sown area in 1984. Hence, by state policy and practice, the output and marketing of almost all sown area was still directly influenced by China's planners.

Reforms proceeded with equal caution when reducing restrictions on free market trade. The initial decision to permit the reestablishment of free markets in 1979 allowed farmers to trade only vegetables and a limited number of other crops and livestock products within the boundaries of their own counties. Reformers gradually relaxed these spatial restrictions from 1980 to 1984, but as Sicular (1988a) and Skinner (1985) point out, local rural periodic markets remained the predominant marketing venue during the early 1980s. Farmers did begin to sell their produce in urban settings, but free markets in the cities began to appear only in 1982 and 1983. Throughout this period, private traders were debarred from the marketing of monopolized commodities, which remained under strict control of the state procurement stations.

This review confirms that market liberalization did not begin prior to 1985. Although agricultural commodity markets did emerge during the early 1980s, their number and size made them a small player in China's food economy. In 1984, the state procurement network still purchased more than 95 percent of marketed grain and more than 99 percent of marketed cotton (Sicular, 1995). In all of China's urban areas, there were only 2,000 markets in 1980 and 6,000 in 1984 (deBrauw, Huang, and Rozelle, 2004). In Beijing in the early 1980s, there were only about fifty markets, transacting around 1 million yuan of commerce per market per year. Each market site would have had to serve, on average, about 200,000 Beijing residents, each transacting only 5 yuan of business for the entire year. In other words, it would have been impossible for such a weak marketing infrastructure at that time to meet more than a tiny fraction of the food needs of urban consumers.

After 1985, however, market liberalization began in earnest. Changes to the procurement system, further reductions in restrictions to trading of commodities, moves to commercialize the state grain trading system, and calls for the expansion of market construction in rural and urban areas led to a surge in market-oriented activity (Sicular, 1995). For example, in 1980, there were only 241,000 private and semiprivate trading enterprises registered with the State Markets Bureau; by 1990, there were more than 5.2 million (deBrauw et al., 2002). Between 1980 and 1990, the per capita volume of transactions in Beijing's urban food markets rose almost 200 times. Private traders handled more than 30 percent of China's grain by 1990, and more than half of the rest was bought and sold by commercialized state grain trading companies, many of which had begun to behave as market actors (Rozelle et al., 1999, 2000).

Even after the start of liberalization, the process remained incomplete, and the advance of reform occurred in irregular steps (Sicular, 1995). For example, following the initial commercialization of the grain bureau, rising grain prices led to a temporary halt in the grain reforms as provincial leaders intervened in the flow of grain into and out of their provinces. These controls were relaxed again in the early 1990s, but reappeared in the mid-1990s. Another round of liberalization and retrenchment occurred in the late 1990s.

Despite its start and stop nature, the extension of private trading to include surplus output of all agricultural products (after fulfillment of contractual obligations to the state) began to undermine the foundations of the state marketing system (Rozelle et al., 2000). After record growth in grain production in 1984 and 1985, a second stage of price and market reforms announced in 1985 aimed at radically limiting the scope of government price and market interventions and enlarging the role of market allocation. The intention was to gradually eliminate planned procurement, except for rice, wheat, maize, and cotton. Except for these crops, government commercial departments found themselves obliged to buy and sell at market prices. Even for grain, market incentives began to influence state commercial agencies, as quota volumes dropped and procurement prices increased. The share of compulsory quota procurement in total grain production reached 29 percent in 1984 and then dropped to 18 percent in 1985 and 13 percent in 1990 (Rozelle et al., 2000). At the same time, the share of negotiated procurement at market prices increased from only 3 percent in 1985 to 6 percent in 1985 and 12 percent in 1990.

Technology and Water Infrastructure Development

Agricultural research and plant breeding in China remain almost completely organized by the government. Reflecting the urban bias of food policy, most crop-breeding programs have emphasized fine grains (rice and wheat). For national food security consideration, high yields have been major target of China's research program, except for recent years when quality improvement was introduced into the nation's development plan. Although there have been several private domestic and joint-venture investments into agricultural research and development, policies still discriminate against them.

China's agricultural research system operated effectively prior to the start of reform, but entered the 1980s and 1990s overburdened with poorly trained staff. Extreme decentralization promotes duplication of research effort and discourages investments into basic research. As a consequence, a nationwide reform was launched in the mid-1980s. This initiative sought to increase research productivity by shifting funding from institutional support to competitive grants, supporting research useful for economic development, and encouraging applied research institutes to support themselves by selling the technology they produce.

The outcome of reform in the agricultural technology system is mixed, and its impact on new technological developments and crop productivity is unclear. Empirical evidence demonstrates the declining effectiveness of China's agricultural research (Jin et al., 2002). Our previous work found that while competitive grant programs probably increased the productivity of China's agricultural research system, reliance on commercial revenue to subsidize research and make up for falling budgetary commitments weakened the system.[4] Imperfections in the seed industry may have contributed to the ineffectiveness of research reform measures in crop breeding.

State investment in water control – both irrigation and flood control – swamps the amount invested into agricultural research. As noted earlier, from the 1950s to the 1970s, most of the state's effort was focused on building dams and canal networks, often with the input of corvee labor from farmers. After the 1970s, greater focus was put on increasing the use of China's massive groundwater resources (Wang, Huang, and Rozelle, 2005). By 2005, China had more tubewells than any country, except possibly India. Although, initially, investment was put up by local governments with aid from county and provincial water bureaus, by the 1990s the government was encouraging a huge shift to private ownership of pumps, wells, and other irrigation equipment (Wang et al., 1995; Wang et al., 2006b). At the same time, private water markets (whereby farmers pump water from their own wells and sell it to other farmers in the village) were also encouraged. The main policy initiative after the mid-1990s in the surface-water sector was management reform aimed at raising the efficiency of water use.

Trade Policy
In addition to important changes in foreign exchange policy that steeply depreciated the international value of the *renminbi* and provided traders with greater

---

[4] Findings are based on a series of intensive interviews and survey data gathered from a wide range of agricultural ministry personnel, research administrators, research staff, and others involved in China's agricultural research system.

access to foreign exchange during the 1980s and 1990s, China's international trading system has experienced a number of fundamental reforms (see Chapter 16). Lower tariffs and rising imports and exports of agricultural products began to affect domestic terms of trade in the 1980s. In the initial years, most of the fall in protection came from a reduction in the number of commodities for which export and import activity was controlled by single-desk state traders (Huang and Chen, 1999). Even though decentralization omitted some major products, competition among nonstate foreign trade corporations began to stimulate imports and exports of many specific items (Martin, 2001). In addition, policy shifts in the 1980s and 1990s also changed the behavior of state traders. Leaders allowed the state traders to increase imports in the 1980s and 1990s.

Moves to expand access rights to import and export markets were matched by reductions in border taxes. The simple average of agricultural import tariffs fell from 42.2 percent in 1992 to 23.6 percent in 1998 and 21.0 percent in 2001 (Rosen, Huang, and Rozelle, 2004).

The past twenty years have witnessed an overall decline in agricultural trade distortions (Huang and Rozelle, 2002). This removal of protection has come from changes in the *renminbi* exchange rate, substantial reductions in border taxes, from the decentralization of authority over imports and exports of farm products, and from partial relaxation of licensing procedures that have allowed private firms to replace state traders (e.g., in oil and oilseed imports). Other steps include reductions in the scope of nontariff barriers and changes to quota arrangements (Huang and Chen, 1999). Despite these real and, in some instances, rapid reforms, the conduct of trade for key commodities that leaders consider to be of national strategic importance, such as rice, wheat, and maize, remains subject to substantial official control (Nyberg and Rozelle, 1999).

These extensive changes in China's trade regime mean that while accession to the WTO was a major watershed event that will affect many sectors, in its most basic terms WTO entry represents a continuation of previous trends. Hence, the commitments embodied in China's WTO accession agreement in the agricultural sector – regarding market access, domestic support, and export subsidies – represent exactly what China was doing in the 1990s.

Trade and Poverty. In the same way that the forces of development have generated both progress and problems, the nation's efforts at pushing ambitious agricultural trade liberalization policies have brought both positive and negative consequences (Anderson, Huang, and Ianchovichina, 2004). Research has shown that on average the nation's accession to WTO will help rural residents and improve incomes. In fact, according to Anderson, Huang, and Ianchovichina (2004), China stands to gain more than almost any other country from further trade liberalization, such as proposals being discussed during the Doha round of the WTO negotiations.

Any trade agreement, however, creates both winners and losers. The competitiveness and marketization of China's agricultural economy means that households in most parts of China are fairly well integrated into national markets. As a result, the price effects of trade liberalization will spread rapidly throughout the economy. In general, liberalization will benefit households that produce competitive products and damage the prospects of households involved in the production of items that are not competitive.

Huang et al. (2006a) have studied the effect of WTO and future trade liberalization on China's farmers. They find that the subset of all farmers who suffer from trade liberalization is small. And, it is quite specific. In particular, *poor* maize-, cotton-, and wheat-producing areas in the central and western parts of the nation are the ones that have been hurt. Farmers in most of the rest of China will gain.

Several factors determine the locus of these adverse effects. First, households in these poor areas – due to lower social capital – are less likely to be diversified into the off-farm sector. Thus, while richer households are able to offset the loss from trade liberalization with gains from participation in the off-farm sector, some poorer households are less able to do so (although the rise in migration is making this less of an issue). Second, farmers in poor areas often grow uncompetitive crops – maize, cotton, and wheat. They are less likely to be growing crops in which China has a comparative advantage – horticulture crops and aquaculture products. Finally, because farmers in poorer areas have less physical and human capital than those in richer areas, they often have more difficulty in shifting from those crops that are hurt by trade liberalization into those that benefit.

Concluding Thoughts on China's Transition-Era Agricultural Policies

The scope of China's policy efforts during the transition era is impressive. Policy shifts were made in pricing, the organization of production, marketing, investments, technology, and trade. Although the rate of investment has risen during the reforms, international comparisons suggest that China is still underinvesting in agriculture. Taxes – both those that are explicit and those implicit in pricing and trade policies – have also fallen. Although China certainly has not subsidized the agricultural economy as have neighboring East Asian economies, it appears to be heading in the direction noted by Timmer (1998), in which developing nations at a certain point begin to turn from a period of extraction from agriculture to a period of net investment into the sector.

One of the most important characteristics of agricultural reform in China is the pace of reform. Our analysis is consistent with that of Rozelle (1996), which shows that the sequencing of agricultural reform policies followed the gradualist strategy of China's more general, economywide reforms that McMillan and Naughton (1992) describe. In the initial stages of reform, leaders consciously restricted the promotion of market-based economic activity, allowing at most the exchange of minor products (e.g., minor fruits and vegetables) in sharply circumscribed regions. Not until 1985, after the completion of HRS, did policymakers begin to encourage market activity for more important commodities (e.g., grain), initially within the framework of China's two-tier price system (Sicular, 1988a). Leaders did not commit themselves to more complete market liberalization until the early 1990s, more than a decade after the initiation of HRS. From this description, it is clear that China's reforms fall into two distinct stages: the incentive reforms that dominate the period from 1978 to 1984 and a period of gradual market liberalization that begins in 1985 and extends through the 1990s.

In addition to reforms that directly affected crop selection and the pricing and marketing of farm inputs and outputs, the evolution of Chinese agriculture over the past three decades also reflects the impact of policies directed toward the broader rural economy, including fiscal measures, public administration, and the development of township and village enterprises. In addition, the development of China's agricultural economy was indirectly influenced by urban employment policies, residency restrictions, exchange rate management and other measures that influence relative prices, access to nonfarm employment, and the overall attractiveness of farming relative to other occupations.

In the aggregate, these policies have dramatically altered China's agricultural sector. They have increased food output, lowered prices, and enlarged supplies of nongrain food and materials. The mix of policies – pricing, improved property rights, market liberalization, investment, and trade – has also made producers more efficient, thereby releasing labor to support transformation of the entire national economy. Rapid structural change – including the declining share of grain in cropping, of cropping within agriculture, and of agriculture within China's GDP – demonstrates the scale of agriculture's contribution to the nation's development. These changes have also delivered improved material welfare to rural people (and there have been more than 300–400 million of them) who redirected their work efforts from grain to higher-valued crops, from cropping to livestock or aquaculture, and, most importantly, from rural occupations to off-farm employment.

THE ROLE OF AGRICULTURE IN CHINA'S ONGOING DEVELOPMENT: FUTURE CHALLENGES

Are we too optimistic? Can the development of the agricultural sector really be counted as successful? Critics may accuse us of overemphasizing quantitative performance criteria of growth, structural transformation, and liberalization. This focus puts us at odds with social scientists who focus on rural China's social ills (e.g., Bernstein and Lu, 2000).

Our analysis builds on the assumption that for China to become a modern, wealthy nation, it will have to transform itself from an agriculture-based economy to an industrial/service-based one. To join the ranks of the developed world, China must shift the bulk of the population from rural areas to urban centers. We do not deny that this transformation is wrenching and disruptive of people's lives. We understand the difficulties of migration, the uncertainties of shifting agricultural enterprises, and the risks – and frequent failures – which rural families experience during this transition.

However, in the history of the modern world, all developed countries have traveled similar paths. Our analysis in this chapter is focused primarily on the extent of agriculture's contribution to overall transformation of China's economy. During the socialist era, agriculture's contribution was disappointingly small. The farm sector failed to provide large amounts of inexpensive food for consumers, failed to expand supplies of raw material for industry, failed to enlarge exports, and failed to raise rural incomes. The combined impact of agricultural policies and the broader plan system also prevented the rural economy from supplying labor to industry and minimized linkages could have promoted structural transformation.

In contrast, during the reform era – despite the social costs mentioned earlier – agriculture has provided multiple contributions to development. From the Johnston–Mellor perspective, agriculture has fully satisfied three of its potential responsibilities: food is plentiful, agriculture-based industry enjoys abundant supplies of materials, and China's foreign exchange reserves are the world's largest. Moreover, the cropping sector, in particular, and the agricultural sector, more generally, are being transformed with remarkable speed, as farmers, motivated by strong incentives, respond to market signals by shifting their productive energies toward higher-value commodities that match China's comparative advantage. The linkages between the rural and urban economies are also beginning to strengthen, as more than 200 million people – in more than eight out of ten rural households – have found employment off the farm. The changes reflect the complex and wide-ranging reform policies of the past three decades: the household responsibility system; domestic and international market liberalization; continued investments in water; breakthroughs in agricultural R&D; and the creation of an environment in which farm families – while often still poor – follow market signals that direct them toward higher levels of incomes and assets and growing opportunities to work off the farm.

Despite these advances, China is not yet a developed nation and many of its rural areas remain backward. China has now entered a new stage of agricultural development filled with both opportunity and new, demanding challenges. In this new development phase, policies that aided agricultural development in the past may lose their force or even become counterproductive. Trade policy, in particular, makes China's challenge unique (at least in East Asia), since the rural economy will be forced to develop in a relatively open economic environment.

Unlike the reform era when the main challenges were to provide incentives, allow farmers to make decisions that were more consistent with the economy's resource scarcities, and increase productivity through investments in water control and new technologies, in the future the key tasks will be twofold: first, large numbers of families must permanently settle in the cities, and second, the families that stay behind must modernize their farming operations and do so on substantially larger farms. China's agricultural sector must meet these challenges to complete its contribution to China's economic transformation. Urbanization is essential to improve productivity and provide labor for the increasingly intensive and complex industrial and service sector that is developing in China's coastal and urban areas. Larger farm size is essential to raising the productivity and incomes of those who remain in the farm sector. Higher farm incomes are essential, first, to reduce rural poverty, and, second, to finance investment in the human and physical capital that will enable farm households to modernize agricultural production and prepare for future waves of migration to the cities.

In assessing these challenges, one conspicuous departure from the path taken by China's successful neighbors (e.g., Japan and Korea) is our strong emphasis on the need to enlarge farm size. Elsewhere in East Asia, farm size did not change much during the course of development. Instead, government officials used trade policies to seal off their markets from foreign competition and allow rising domestic demand (aided by policy-provided supports) to bid up agricultural prices. Although such policies are not efficient in pure economic terms, they did serve the purpose of helping to raise rural incomes and inflate the value of rural assets. In contrast, China – due to its WTO commitments – does not have the option of imposing trade restrictions to protect farm incomes. Because the current size of farms, as discussed earlier, is so small, even strong productivity gains from successful agricultural R&D investments will not be sufficient to raise incomes significantly. Higher incomes in Chinese agriculture – incomes that approach the earnings of nonfarm wage workers – can be generated only by increasing farm size and mechanization.

A successful response to these challenges will depend on a number of policies both inside and outside agriculture. The most important support for the continuing shift of rural residents into the cities will be a steady flow of employment opportunities, which ultimately will depend on continued growth. Assuming that China's growth continues at substantial rates, new urban reforms can enhance migration opportunities, especially by eliminating the two-tier system of citizenship embodied in the *hukou* system.

On the rural side, education is the crucial vehicle for enhancing migration opportunities. Despite recent efforts to improve access, rural education remains generally poor in quality, underfunded, and expensive for rural families. We do not believe it is a bad thing that the best educated are first to leave China's villages. Indeed, this is expected, as it reflects the experience of most developing nations. It is because of this pattern that the primary responsibility for funding rural education should rest with the central government. The social return to rural education is very high (Fan, Zhang, and Zhang, 2004). Education also delivers significant private returns not only through higher wages (deBrauw and Rozelle, forthcoming), but also through improved access to off-farm opportunities. Much more is needed in this area and to promote investments in health and child nutrition that also improve human capital.

In a very real sense, policies that help increase farm size and raise incomes will also encourage migration. Migration is always costly; for poor villagers, permanent migration, especially into urban areas where residents already enjoy high average incomes, will be very expensive. Rising incomes will help villagers accumulate savings that can help future migrants pay for housing, health care, education, and living expenses in their new urban homes.

The challenges of increasing farm sizes in China are considerable. Although Deininger and Jin (2005) have shown that the rental transactions are increasingly common, most are still short term and there are many constraints on efforts to amass larger landholdings. Above all, the current system of property rights works against the expansion of farm size (Brandt et al., 2002). Since cultivated land is formally owned by the collective, farm households that want to move to the city cannot sell land to help finance their move. Households that want to expand their landholdings cannot obtain long-term utilization rights; without such rights, their income prospects are insufficient to justify the investments that could make their farm enterprises more productive. Weak property rights also prevent farm households from using land as collateral to finance either farm investment or migration.

So why will China's leaders not consider privatizing land? The most common answer is that land is the rural household's most secure source of insurance. If a member of the household loses a job or if the family business suffers a loss, universal access to land means that each household is at most one season away from providing its own subsistence. If land were privatized, allowing households to sell their lands, any landless household that suffered financial setbacks might become a burden to society or could possibly turn to crime as a source of income. Ravallion and Van der Walle (2003) finds little sign of such consequences following the quasiprivatization of land in Vietnam. In our view, China needs to move toward privatization or at the very least, formal land registration that would give farm households stronger property rights and encourage them to use their land in more productive ways.

The past development of agricultural output and yields may constrain future farm productivity and agricultural incomes because of resource depletion, particularly for water. Huang and Rozelle (2005) show that if farmers lose their ability to irrigate their crop, the cropping income drops significantly. Such hazards, although severe, are limited to a relatively small area. According to Wang et al. (1995), even though nearly 70 percent of farmers in northern China rely on groundwater, less than 10 percent of these farmers (occupying less than 4 percent of China's land area) are in areas that are suffering "serious overdraft" of groundwater. Since water tables have fallen in many other areas, it is evident that China needs to mount a concerted effort to implement coherent groundwater management policies throughout the affected regions. However, our point here is that, despite their severity, water resource problems will not bring China's farm economy to its knees. Blanke et al. (2006) and Huang et al. (2006b) find that water scarcity encourages farmers and local officials to respond by shifting cropping patterns or adopting water-saving technologies.

There may also be other limits to growth, for example, the slowdown of technology-generated TFP and growing conversions of land for housing, roads, and businesses. In China, as in other rapidly developing economies, we must anticipate that urbanization will increase the tensions between agriculture and the nonfarm sector. This calls for better systems of governance that can mediate problems, compensate losers, regulate polluters, and generally implement policies to promote a modern and wealthy agricultural system that can coexist with the large majority of China's population that lives and works off the farm.

References

Agricultural Yearbook. Annual. *Zhongguo nongye nianjian* [China Agricultural Yearbook]. Beijing: Nongye chubanshe.

Anderson, Kym, Jikun Huang, and Elena Ianchovichina. 2004. "Will China's WTO Accession Worsen Farm Household Income?" *China Economic Review*. 15, pp. 443–456.

Aston, Basil, Kenneth Hill, Alan Piazza, and Robin Zeitz. December, 1984. "Famine in China, 1958–1961." *Population and Development Review*. 10, pp. 613–645.

Bernstein, Thomas and Xiaobo Lu. 2000. "Taxation without Representation: Peasants, the Central and the Local States in Reform China." *The China Quarterly*. 163, pp. 742–763.

Blanke, Amelia, Scott Rozelle, Bryan Lohmar, Jinxia Wang, and Jikun Huang. 2006. "*Water Saving Technology and Saving Water in China.*" Working Paper. Beijing: Center for Chinese Agricultural Policy, Institute of Geographical Sciences and Natural Resource Research, Chinese Academy of Sciences.

Brandt, Loren. 1989. *Commercialization and Agricultural Development: Central and Eastern China, 1840–1937*. Cambridge and New York: Cambridge University Press.

Brandt, Loren, Jikun Huang, Guo Li, and Scott Rozelle. 2002. "Land Rights in China: Facts, Fictions, and Issues." *The China Journal*. 47, pp. 67–97.

Chang, Gene and Guangsheng Wen, 1997. "Communal Dining and the Chinese Famine of 1958–61." *Economic Development and Cultural Change*. 15, pp. 1–15.

deBrauw, Alan and Scott Rozelle. Forthcoming. "Reconciling the Returns to Rural Education." *Review of Development Economics*.

deBrauw, Alan, Jikun Huang, and Scott Rozelle. 2004. "The Sequencing of Reforms in China's Agricultural Transition." *Economics of Transition*. 12(3), pp. 427–466.

deBrauw, Alan, Jikun Huang, Scott Rozelle, Linxiu Zhang, and Yigang Zhang. June 2002. "The Evolution of China's Rural Labor Markets during the Reforms." *Journal of Comparative Economics*. 30(2), pp. 329–353.

Deininger, Klaus and Songqing Jin. October 2005. "The Potential of Land Rental Markets in the Process of Economic Development: Evidence from China." *Journal of Development Economics*. 78, pp. 241–270.

Dong, Xiaoyuan and Greg Dow. 1993. "Monitoring Costs in Chinese Agricutural Teams." *Journal of Political Economy*. 101(3), pp. 539–553.

Fan, Shenggen. 1991. "Effects of Technological Change and Institutional Reform on Production Growth in Chinese Agriculture." *American Journal of Agricultural Economics*. 73, pp. 266–275.

Fan Shenggen. June 1997. "Production and Productivity Growth in Chinese Agriculture: New Measurement and Evidence." *Food Policy*. 22, pp. 213–228.

Fan, Shenggen and Phil Pardey. June 1997. "Research Productivity and Output Growth in Chinese Agriculture." *Journal of Development Economics*. 53, pp. 115–137.

Fan, Shenggen, Linxiu Zhang, and Xiaobo Zhang. 2004. "Reforms, Investment, and Poverty in Rural China." *Economic Development and Cultural Change.* 52, pp. 395–421.

Gale, Fred. 2006. *"Food Consumption in China: Feeding the Dragon."* Paper Presented at the 2006 Outlook Conference for US Agriculture, Arlington, VA, February 19, 2006.

Huang, Jikun and Howarth Bouis. 2001. "Structural Changes and Demand for Food in Asia: Empirical Evidence from Taiwan." *Agricultural Economics.* 26, pp. 57–69.

Huang, Jikun and Chunlai Chen. 1999. *Effects of Trade Liberalization on Agriculture in China: Commodity and Local Agricultural Studies.* Bogor, Indonesia: ESCAP CGPRT Centre, United Nations.

Huang, Jikun and Christine David. 1995. "Policy Reform and Agricultural Incentives in China." Working Paper. Beijing: Center for Chinese Agricultural Policy, Institute of Geographical Sciences and Natural Resource Research, Chinese Academy of Sciences.

Huang, Jikun, Carl Pray, Scott Rozelle, and Qinfang Wang. January 2002. "Plant Biotechnology in China." *Science.* 295, pp. 674–677.

Huang, Jikun and Scott Rozelle. 1996. "Technological Change: Rediscovering the Engine of Productivity Growth in China's Agricultural Economy." *Journal of Development Economics.* 49, pp. 337–369.

Huang, Jikun and Scott Rozelle. 2002. "China's Accession to WTO and Likely Shifts in the Agriculture Policy." Working Paper. Beijing: Center for Chinese Agricultural Policy, Institute of Geographical Sciences and Natural Resource Research, Chinese Academy of Sciences.

Huang, Jikun and Scott Rozelle. 2005. "Market Development, Commercialization and Small Farmers in China." Working Paper. Beijing: Center for Chinese Agricultural Policy, Institute of Geographical Sciences and Natural Resource Research, Chinese Academy of Sciences.

Huang, Jikun and Scott Rozelle. Forthcoming. "The Emergence of Agricultural Commodity Markets in China." *China Economic Review.*

Huang, Jikun, Scott Rozelle, and Min Chang. 2004. "The Nature of Distortions to Agricultural Incentives in China and Implications of WTO Accession." *World Bank Economic Review.* 18(1), pp. 59–84.

Huang, Jikun, Scott Rozelle, and Mark Rosegrant. 1999. "China's Food Economy to the 21st Century: Supply, Demand, and Trade." *Economic Development and Cultural Change.* 47, pp. 737–766.

Huang, Jikun, Scott Rozelle, and Honglin Wang. 2006. "Fostering or Stripping Rural China: Modernizing Agriculture and Rural to Urban Capital Flows." *Developing Economies.* 44(1), pp. 1–26.

Huang, Jikun, Jun Yang, Zhigang Xu, and Scott Rozelle. 2006a. "Agricultural Trade Liberalization and Poverty in China." Working Paper. Beijing: Center for Chinese Agricultural Policy, Institute of Geographical Sciences and Natural Resource Research, Chinese Academy of Sciences.

Huang, Qiuqing, Richard Howitt, Scott Rozelle, and Jinxia Wang. 2006b. "Pricing China's Water." Working Paper. Davis, CA: Department of Agricultural and Resource Economics, University of California.

Jin, Songqing, Jikun Huang, Ruifa Hu, and Scott Rozelle. November 2002. "The Creation and Spread of Technology and Total Factor Productivity in China's Agriculture." *American Journal of Agricultural Economics.* 84(4), pp. 916–939.

Johnson, D. Gale April 1995. *"Is Agriculture a Threat to China's Growth?"* Working Paper 95:04. Chicago, IL: Office of Agricultural Economics Research, University of Chicago.

Johnston, Bruce F. 1970. "Agriculture and Structural Transformation in Developing Countries: A Survey of Research." *Journal of Economic Literature*. 8, pp. 101–145.

Johnston, Bruce F. and John W. Mellor. 1961. "The Role of Agriculture in Economic Development." *American Economic Review* 51(4), pp. 566–593.

Lardy, Nicholas R. 2001. *Integrating China into the Global Economy*. Washington, DC: Brookings Institution.

Lardy, Nicholas R. 1983. *Agriculture in China's Modern Economic Development*. Cambridge and New York: Cambridge University Press.

Lewis, W. Arthur. May 1954. "Economic Development with Unlimited Supplies of Labor." *The Manchester School*. 22, pp. 139–191.

Lin, Justin. 1991. "Prohibitions of Factor Market Exchanges and Technological Choice in Chinese Agriculture." *Journal of Development Studies*. 27(4), pp. 1–15.

Lin, Justin. 1992. "Rural Reforms and Agricultural Growth in China." *American Economic Review*. 82, pp. 34–51.

Lin, Justin, Fang Cai, and Zhou Li. 1996. *The China Miracle: Development Strategy and Economic Reform*. Hong Kong: Chinese University Press.

Lin, Justin and Dennis Yang. 2000. "Food Availability, Entitlement and the Chinese Famine of 1959–61." *Economic Journal*. 110, pp. 136–158.

Lyons, Thomas. 1987. *Economic Integration and Planning in Maoist China*. New York: Columbia University Press.

Martin, Will. 2001. "Implications of Reform and WTO Accession for China's Agricultural Policies." *Economics of Transition*. 9(3), pp. 717–742.

McKinnon, Ronald. 1993. *The Order of Economic Liberalization: Financial Control in the Transition to a Market Economy*. Baltimore: Johns Hopkins University Press.

McMillan, John. 1997. "Markets in Transition," in *Advances in Economics and Econometrics: Theory and Applications*, vol. 2. David Kreps and Kenneth F. Wallis, eds. Cambridge and New York: Cambridge University Press, pp. 210–239.

McMillan, John and Barry Naughton. 1992. "How to Reform a Planned Economy: Lessons from China." *Oxford Review of Economic Policy*. 8, pp. 130–143.

McMillan John, John Walley, and Lijing Zhu. 1989. "The Impact of China's Economic Reforms on Agricultural Productivity Growth." *Journal of Political Economy*. 97, pp. 781–807.

Mead, Robert W. 2000. "An Examination of China's Agricultural Reforms: The Importance of Private Plots." *China Economic Review*. 11, pp. 54–78.

MOFTEC [Ministry of Foreign Trade and Economic Cooperation]. 2002. *Foreign Trade and Economic Yearbook of China*. Beijing: China Statistical Press.

Nyberg, Albert and Scott Rozelle. 1999. *Accelerating China's Rural Transformation*. Washington, DC: World Bank.

Park, Albert, Hehui Jin, Scott Rozelle, and Jikun Huang. February 2002. "Market Emergence and Transition: Arbitrage, Transition Costs, and Autarky in China's Grain Market." *American Journal of Agricultural Economics*. 84(1), pp. 67–82.

Perkins, Dwight H. 1969. *Agricultural Development in China, 1368–1968*. Chicago: Aldine Publishing Company.

Perkins, Dwight H. 1994. "Completing China's Move to the Market." *Journal of Economic Perspectives*. 8(2), pp. 23–46.

Putterman, Louis. 1993. *Continuity and Change in China's Rural Development*. New York: Oxford University Press.

Qian, Yingyi and Colin Xu. 1998. "Innovation and Bureaucracy under Soft and Hard Budget Constraints." *Review of Economic Studies*. 65(1), pp. 151–164.

Qiao, Fangbin, Bryan Lohmar, Jikun Huang, Scott Rozelle, and Linxiu Zhang. December 2003. "Producer Benefits from Input Market and Trade Liberalization: The Case of Fertilizer in China." *American Journal of Agricultural Economics.* 85(5), pp. 1223–1227.

Ravallion, Martin and Dominique Van der Walle. 2003. "Land Allocation in Vietnam's Agrarian Transition." Policy Research Working Paper Series 2951. Washington, DC: World Bank.

Rawski, Thomas G. 1989. *Economic Growth in Prewar China.* Berkeley: University of California Press.

Riskin, Carl. and Azizur Khan. 2001. *Inequality and Poverty in China in the Age of Globalization.* New York: Oxford University Press.

Rosen, Daniel, Jikun Huang, and Scott Rozelle. 2004. *Roots of Competitiveness: China's Evolving Agriculture Interests.* Policy Analysis in International Economics, vol. 72. Washington, DC: Institute for International Economics.

Rozelle, Scott. January 1996. "Stagnation without Equity: Changing Patterns of Income and Inequality in China's Post-Reform Rural Economy." *The China Journal.* 35, pp. 63–96.

Rozelle, Scott and Jikun Huang. 2004. "China's Maize Economy: Supply, Demand and Trade." Report for the US Grains Council, Beijing, China.

Rozelle, Scott and Jikun Huang. 2005. "China's Soybean Economy: Supply, Demand and Trade." Report for the American Soybean Association, Beijing, China.

Rozelle, Scott, Jikun Huang, and Daniel Sumner. 2006. "China's Horticulture Economy: Supply, Demand and Trade." Report for the Western Growers American Soybean Association, Beijing, China.

Rozelle, Scott, Guo Li, Minggao Shen, Amelia Hughart, and John Giles. June 1999. "Leaving China's Farms: Survey Results of New Paths and Remaining Hurdles to Rural Migration." *The China Quarterly.* 158, pp. 367–393.

Rozelle, Scott, Albert Park, Jikun Huang, and Hehui Jin. 2000. "Bureaucrat to Entrepreneur: The Changing Role of the State in China's Transitional Commodity Economy." *Economic Development and Cultural Change.* 48(2), pp. 227–252.

Rozelle Scott and Johanne Swinnen. June 2004 "Success and Failure of Reform: Insights from the Transition of Agriculture." *Journal of Economic Literature.* XII, pp. 404–456.

Rural Statistics Yearbook. Annual. *Zhongguo nongcun tongji nianjian* [China Rural Statistics Yearbook]. Beijing: Zhongguo tongji chubanshe.

Shen, Minggao, Linxiu Zhang, Jikun Huang, and Scott Rozelle. 2005. "Farmer's Professional Associations in Rural China: State Dominated or New State-Society Partnerships?" Working Paper. Beijing, China: Center for Chinese Agricultural Policy, Institute of Geographical Sciences and Natural Resource Research, Chinese Academy of Sciences.

Skinner, G. William. 1985. "Rural Marketing in China: Repression and Revival." *The China Quarterly.* 103, pp. 393–413.

Sicular, Terry. 1988a. "Agricultural Planning and Pricing in the Post-Mao Period." *The China Quarterly.* 116, pp. 671–703

Sicular, Terry. 1988b. "Plan and Market in China's Agricultural Commerce." *Journal of Political Economy.* 96(2), pp. 283–307.

Sicular, Terry. 1995, "Redefining State, Plan, and Market: China's Reforms in Agricultural Commerce." *The China Quarterly.* 144, pp. 1020–1046.

Solinger, Dorothy. 1984. *Chinese Business under Socialism.* Berkeley: University of California Press.

Stone, Bruce. December 1988. "Developments in Agricultural Technology." *The China Quarterly.* 116, pp. 767–822.

Stone, Bruce. 1993. "Basic Agricultural Technology under Reform," in *Studies on Contemporary China*. Y. Y. Kueh and Robert F. Ash, eds. Oxford, New York, Toronto, and Melbourne: Oxford University Press–Clarendon Press, pp. 311–359.

Stone, Bruce and Scott Rozelle. August 1995. "Foodcrop Production Variability in China, 1931–1985," in *The School for Oriental and African Studies, Research and Notes Monograph Series*, vol. 9. London: School of Oriental and African Studies.

Timmer, C. Peter. 1998. "The Agricultural Transformation," Chapter 7 in *International Agricultural Development*, 3rd edn. Carl Eicher and John Staatz, eds. Baltimore, MD: John Hopkins University Press, pp. 113–135.

Wang, Honglin, Xiaoxia Dong, Scott Rozelle, Jikun Huang, and Thomas Reardon. 2006a. "Producing and Procuring Horticultural Crops with Chinese Characteristics: A Case Study in the Greater Beijing Area." Working Paper. Beijing, China: Center for Chinese Agricultural Policy, Institute of Geographical Sciences and Natural Resource Research, Chinese Academy of Sciences.

Wang, Jinxia, Jikun Huang, Qiuqiong Huang, and Scott Rozelle. 2006b. "Privatization of Tubewells in North China: Determinants and Impacts on Irrigated Area, Production and the Falling Water Table." *Hydrogeology Journal*. 14, pp. 275–285.

Wang, Jinxia, Jikun Huang and Scott Rozelle. June 2005 "Evolution of Tubewell Ownership and Production in the North China Plain." *Australian Journal of Agricultural and Resource Economics*. 49, pp. 177–195.

Wang, Jinxia, Zhigang Xu, Jikun Huang, and Scott Rozelle. 2005b "Incentives to Water Management Reform: Assessing the Effect on Water Use, Productivity and Poverty in the Yellow River Basin." *Environment and Development Economics*. 10, pp. 769–799.

Watson, Andrew. 1994. "China's Agricultural Reforms: Experiences and Achievements of the Agricultural Sector in the Market Reform Process." Working Paper 94/4. Adelaide, Australia: Chinese Economic Research Unit, University of Adelaide.

Wen, Guangsheng. 1993. "Total Factor Productivity Change in China's Farming Sector: 1952–1989." *Economic Development and Cultural Change*. 42, pp. 1–41.

World Bank. 1997. *Sharing Rising Incomes* Washington, DC: World Bank.

Ye, Qiaolun and Scott Rozelle. May 1994. "Fertilizer Demand in China's Reforming Economy." *Canadian Journal of Agricultural Economics*. 42(2), pp. 191–208.

Yearbook, Annual. *Zhongguo tongji nianjian* [China Statistical Yearbook]. Beijing: China Statistics Press.

Zhang, Linxiu, Qiang Li, and Scott Rozelle. 2005. "Fertilizer Demand in China: What Is Causing Farmers to Use So Much Fertilizer?" Working Paper. Beijing, China: Center for Chinese Agricultural Policy, Institute of Geographical Sciences and Natural Resource Research, Chinese Academy of Sciences.

FOURTEEN

China's Financial System: Past, Present, and Future[1]

Franklin Allen, Jun Qian, and Meijun Qian

INTRODUCTION

We examine the role of China's financial system in supporting the growth of its economy and explore the directions of its future development. Almost every functioning financial system includes financial markets and intermediaries (e.g., a banking sector), but how these two sectors contribute to the entire financial system and economy differs significantly across different countries. Although there is no consensus regarding the prospects for China's future economic growth, a prevailing view on China's financial system speculates that it is one of the weakest links in the economy and it will hamper future economic growth.

A comprehensive examination of all aspects of China's financial system and extensive comparisons with other countries where data are available are provided in this chapter. We also discuss what has worked and what remains to be done within the financial system and examine how further development can better serve the entire economy. Finally, we provide guidelines for future research and policymaking on several important unresolved issues, including how China's financial system should integrate into the world's markets and economy.

We draw four main conclusions about China's financial system and its future development. First, when we examine and compare China's banking system and financial markets with those of both developed and emerging countries, we find

[1] We appreciate suggestions from Loren Brandt and Thomas Rawski (coeditors) and other contributors to the book *China's Great Economic Transformation* that significantly improved the chapter. We also thank Dong Chen, Don Clarke, Ed Kane, Nick Lardy, Anthony Neoh, Katharina Pistor, Phil Strahan, Mengxin Zhao, and seminar/session participants at Baruch College, Columbia Law School, Federal Reserve Bank of San Francisco, UC – Berkeley Law School, Penn Law School, York University, and the 2006 Chinese Finance Association meetings for their comments, Jason Mao, Ying Xia, and Jason Xu for research assistance, and Michael Chui and Richard Herring for providing data on financial intermediaries and bond markets. Financial support from Boston College, the Smith Richardson Foundation, Wharton Financial Institutions Center, and China International Capital Corp, Ltd. (for sponsoring the best paper award at the Chinese Finance Association meetings) is gratefully acknowledged. The authors are responsible for remaining errors.

that China's financial system is currently dominated by a large but underdeveloped banking system. Even with the entrance and growth of many domestic and foreign banks and financial institutions in recent years, China's banking system is still mainly controlled by the four largest state-owned banks with a large amount of nonperforming loans (NPLs). Three of the "big four" banks have recently become publicly listed and traded companies, with the government being the largest shareholder and retaining control. The continuing effort to improve the banking system, in particular, to reduce the amount of NPLs of the major banks to normal levels, is the most important aspect of reforming China's financial system in the short run.

Our second conclusion concerns China's financial markets. Two domestic stock exchanges, the Shanghai Stock Exchange (SHSE) and Shenzhen Stock Exchange (SZSE), were established in 1990. Their scale and importance are not comparable to the banking sector, and they have not been effective in allocating resources in the economy, in that they are highly speculative and driven by insider trading. Going forward, however, financial markets are likely to play an increasingly important role in the economy, and their further development is the most important long-term task for China's financial system. We propose several measures that can increase their size and scope and help to improve the efficiency of the markets.

Third, in a companion paper, Allen, Qian, and Qian (2005b), we find that the most successful part of the financial system, in terms of supporting the growth of the overall economy, is not the banking sector or financial markets, but rather a sector of alternative financing channels, such as informal financial intermediaries, internal financing and trade credits, and coalitions of various forms among firms, investors, and local governments. Many of these financing channels rely on alternative governance mechanisms, such as competition in product and input markets, and trust, reputation, and relationships. Together these mechanisms of financing and governance have supported the growth of a "hybrid sector" of nonstate, nonlisted firms with various types of ownership structures. It is important to point out at the outset that our definition of the hybrid sector is broader than privately or individually owned firms, which are only part of this sector. In particular, firms that are partially owned by *local* governments (e.g., township village enterprises or TVEs) are also included in the hybrid sector. This is for two reasons. First, despite the ownership stake of local governments and the sometimes ambiguous ownership structure and property rights, the operation of these firms resembles more closely that of a for-profit, privately owned firm than that of a state-owned firm. Second, the ownership stake of local governments in many of these firms has been privatized.[2] The growth of the hybrid sector has been much higher than that of

---

[2] The hybrid sector comprises all the firms that are not state owned or publicly listed, and more specifically, it includes the following types of firms: (1) privately owned companies (but *not* publicly listed and traded): controlling owners can be Chinese citizens, investors (or companies) from Taiwan or Hong Kong, or foreign investors (or companies); (2) collectively and jointly owned companies, where joint ownership among local government, communities, employees, and institutions is forged. See Li (1996) and Che and Qian (1998) for arguments

the state sector (state-owned enterprises or SOEs, and all firms where the central government has ultimate control) and the listed sector (publicly listed and traded firms with most of them converted from the state sector) and contributes most of the economic growth. We believe these alternative channels and mechanisms should be encouraged going forward. They can coexist with banks and markets while continuing to fuel the growth of the hybrid sector.

Finally, in our view a significant challenge for China's financial system is to avoid damaging financial crises that can severely disrupt the economy and social stability. China needs to guard against traditional financial crises, including a banking sector crisis stemming from continuing accumulation of NPLs and a sudden drop in banks' profits or a crisis/crash resulting from speculative asset bubbles in the real-estate market. China also needs to guard against new types of financial crises, such as a "twin crisis" (simultaneous foreign exchange and banking/stock market crises) that struck many Asian economies in the late 1990s. The entrance of China into the World Trade Organization (WTO) introduces cheap foreign capital and technology, but large scale and sudden capital flows and foreign speculation increase the likelihood of a twin crisis. At the end of 2006, China's foreign currency reserves surpassed U.S.$1 trillion, the largest in the world. The rapid increase in China's foreign exchange reserves suggests that there is a large amount of speculative money in China in anticipation of a continuing appreciation of the RMB, China's currency, relative to all other major currencies. Depending on how the government and the central bank handle the process of revaluation, there could be a classic currency crisis as the government and central bank try to defend the partial currency peg, which in turn may trigger a banking crisis if there are large withdrawals from banks.

The remaining sections are organized as follows. In "Overview of China's Financial System," we briefly review the history of China's financial system development, present aggregate evidence on China's financial system, and compare them to those of developed and other developing countries. In "The Banking and Intermediation Sector," we examine China's banking system and the problem of NPLs and reforms. In "Financial Markets and Publicly Traded Firms," we examine the growth and irregularities of financial markets and listed firms. In "The Nonstandard Financial Sector and Evidence on Hybrid Sector Firms," we examine the nonstandard financial sector, including alternative financial channels and governance mechanisms. We then examine different types of financial crises and how China's financial system can be better prepared for these crises in the section on "Financial Crises." Finally, "Summary and Concluding Remarks" concludes the chapter. For simplicity, we use the exchange rate of U.S.$1 = RMB8.28 (yuan) for transactions and events occurring before 2005 and U.S.$1 = RMB8 (yuan) for those during and after 2005 throughout the chapter.

on why an ambiguous ownership structure with local governments is more efficient than well-defined private property rights or state ownership in an environment with underdeveloped markets and institutions.

OVERVIEW OF CHINA'S FINANCIAL SYSTEM

In this section we examine China's financial system, focusing on both the banking system and the financial markets, as well as firms' financing channels at the aggregate level, including nonbank and nonmarket channels.

A Brief Review of the History of China's Financial System

China's financial system was well developed before 1949.[3] One key finding in reviewing the history of this period, including the rise of Shanghai as one of the financial centers of Asia during the first half of the twentieth century, is that the development of China's commerce and financial system as a whole was by and large *outside* the formal legal system. For example, despite the entrance of western-style courts in Shanghai and other major coastal cities in early 1900s, most business-related disputes were resolved through mechanisms outside courts, including guilds (merchant coalitions), families, and local notables. In our "Discussion on How the Nonstandard Financial Sector Works" below, we argue that modern equivalents of these dispute mechanisms as well as corporate governance mechanisms are behind the success of hybrid sector firms in the same areas in the 1980s and 1990s.

After the foundation of the People's Republic of China in 1949, all of the pre-1949 capitalist companies and institutions were nationalized by 1950. Between 1950 and 1978, China's financial system consisted of a single bank – the People's Bank of China (PBOC), a central government-owned and controlled bank under the Ministry of Finance, which served as both the central bank and a commercial bank, controlling about 93 percent of the total financial assets of the country and handling almost all financial transactions. With its main role to finance the physical production plans, the PBOC used both a "cash plan" and a "credit plan" to control the cash flows in consumer markets and transfer flows between branches.

The first main structural change began in 1978 and ended in 1984. By the end of 1979, the PBOC departed the ministry and became a separate entity, while three state-owned banks took over some of its commercial banking businesses: The Bank of China[4] (BOC) was given the mandate to specialize in transactions related to foreign trade and investment; the People's Construction Bank of China (CCB), originally formed in 1954, was set up to handle transactions related to fixed investment (especially in manufacturing); the Agriculture Bank of China (ABC) was set up (in 1979) to deal with all banking business in rural areas; and the PBOC

---

[3] We provide more descriptions of the pre-1949 history of China's financial system in a longer version of this chapter (Allen, Qian, and Qian, 2005a). For more anecdotal evidence on the development of China's financial system in the same period, see, for example, Kirby (1995) and Lee (1993).

[4] BOC, among the oldest banks currently in operation, was originally established in 1912 as a private bank and specialized in foreign currency–related transactions.

was formally established as China's central bank and a two-tier banking system was formed. Finally, the fourth state-owned commercial bank, the Industrial and Commercial Bank of China (ICBC) was formed in 1984, and it took over the rest of the commercial transactions of the PBOC.

For most of the 1980s, the development of the financial system can be characterized by the fast growth of financial intermediaries outside of the "big four" banks. Regional banks (partially owned by local governments) were formed in the special economic zones in the coastal areas; in rural areas, a network of Rural Credit Cooperatives (RCCs; similar to credit unions in the United States) was set up under the supervision of the ABC, while Urban Credit Cooperatives (UCCs), counterparts of the RCCs in the urban areas, were also founded. Nonbank financial intermediaries, such as the Trust and Investment Corporations (TICs; operating in selected banking and nonbanking services with restrictions on both deposits and loans), emerged and proliferated in this period.

The most significant event for China's financial system in the 1990s was the inception and growth of China's stock market. Two domestic stock exchanges (SHSE and SZSE) were established in 1990 and grew very fast during most of the 1990s. However, the development of a supportive legal framework and institutions has been lagging behind that of the stock market. On a trial basis, China's first bankruptcy law was passed in 1986 (governing SOEs), but the formal Company Law was not effective until the end of 1999. This version of the Company Law governs all corporations with limited liability, publicly listed and traded companies, and branches or divisions of foreign companies, as well as their organization structure, securities issuance and trading, accounting, bankruptcy, mergers, and acquisitions (for details, see the Web site of China Securities Regulatory Commission, or CSRC, http://www.csrc.gov.cn/). In August 2006, a new bankruptcy law was enacted, and it became effective on June 1, 2007. This new law introduces the role of trustees in the bankruptcy procedure, along with other provisions enhancing creditor rights and facilitating the corporate bankruptcy procedure. We provide a detailed analysis of the status and problems of the stock market in "Financial Markets and Publicly Traded Firms" later.

Following the Asian financial crisis in 1997, financial sector reform has focused on state-owned banks and especially the problem of NPLs. (The China Banking Regulatory Committee was also established to oversee the banking industry.) We will further discuss this issue in the section on "The Banking and Intermediation Sector." China's entry into the WTO in December 2001 marked the beginning of a new era, as we continue to observe increasing competition from foreign financial institutions and more frequent and larger-scale capital flows. While increasingly larger inflows of foreign capital and the presence of foreign institutions will continue to drive further growth of the financial system and economy, larger-scale capital flows can also increase the likelihood of damaging financial crises. We will discuss these issues in the sections on "Financial Markets and Publicly Traded Firms" and "Financial Crises."

A developed financial system is characterized by, among other factors, the important role played by institutional investors. In China, institutional investors began to emerge in the late 1990s, although their scale and significance in the financial system has been limited. The first two mutual funds (Guo Tai and Nan Fang) were established in 1998. There were 268 open-end mutual funds and 58 closed-end funds at the end of 2006 (China Galaxy Securities Co Report), with total net asset value (NAV) reaching 856 billion RMB (or $110 billion), which is small compared to the assets within the banking sector. In 2003, a few qualified foreign institutional investors (QFII) entered the asset management industry, and they have been operating through forming joint ventures with Chinese companies. Endowed with limited capital and problems with the administration of the pension system, pension funds have not played an important role in the stock or bond market.[5] With a fast-aging population and the growth of households' disposable income, further development of a multi-pillar pension system including individual accounts with employees' self-contributed (tax exempt) funds that can be directly invested in the financial markets is important for the development of both the financial system and the fiscal system as well as for social stability. Finally, there is no hedge fund that implements "long-short" strategies at present time, as short selling is prohibited.

Figure 14.1 depicts the current structure of the entire financial system. In what follows we will describe and examine each of the four sectors of the system. In addition to the standard sectors of banking and intermediation and financial markets, we will document the importance of the nonstandard financial sector. Due to space limitation, we do not cover China's "foreign sectors" in this chapter; for discussions on the history and the role of these sectors in supporting the growth of the economy, see, for example, Allen, Qian, and Qian (2005a) and Prasad and Wei (2005) for a review on foreign direct investment (FDI).

Size and Efficiency of the Financial System: Banking and Markets

For a comparison of countries, we follow the law and finance literature and in particular, the sample of countries studied in La Porta et al. (1997a, 1998). Their sample includes forty-nine countries, but China is excluded. In Table 14.1, we compare China's financial system (as of 2002) to those of La Porta et al. sample countries, with some measures for financial systems taken from Levine (2002) and Demirgüç-Kunt and Levine (2001). For definitions of all the variables used in the tables and figures, see Allen, Qian, and Qian (2005a,b).

---

[5] While there is a nationwide, government-run pension system (financed mainly through taxes on employers and employees), the coverage ratio of the pension system varies significantly across regions and is particularly low in rural areas. Moreover, there is a very limited amount of capital in individual accounts and most of the capital has been invested in banks and government projects with low returns. See, for example, Feldstein (1999, 2003) and Feldstein and Liebman (2006) for more details on China's pension system.

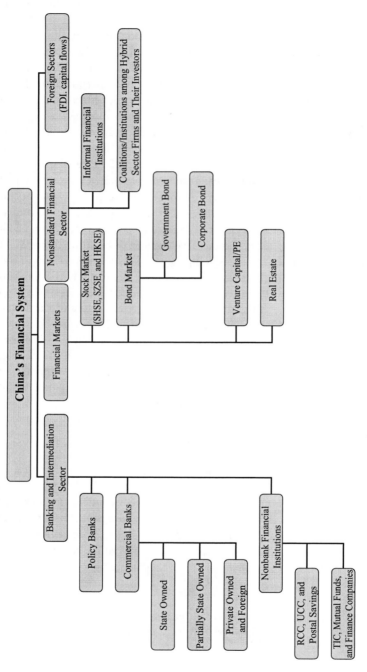

Figure 14.1. Overview of China's financial system

512

Table 14.1. *A comparison of financial systems: bank- versus market-based measures (value-weighted approach)*

Measures		English origin[a]	French origin[a]	German origin[a]	Scandinavian origin[a]	Sample average	China (2002)
Bank and market size	Bank credit/GDP	0.62	0.55	0.99	0.49	0.73	1.11 (0.24)[b]
	Overhead cost/bank total assets	0.04	0.05	0.02	0.03	0.03	0.12
	Market cap/GDP[c]	0.58	0.18	0.55	0.25	0.47	0.32
	Float supply of market cap/GDP[c]	0.31	0.07	0.37	0.08	0.27	0.11
	Structure activity	−0.76	−2.03	−1.14	−1.83	−1.19	−1.07 (0.46)[b]
Structure indices (markets versus banks[d])	Structure size	−0.10	−1.05	−0.77	−0.69	−0.55	−1.24 (0.29)[b]
	Structure efficiency	−4.69	−6.00	−5.17	−6.17	−5.17	−1.48 (−3.07)
	Structure regulatory	7.02	8.21	10.15	7.72	8.95	16.0
Financial development[e] (banking and market sectors combined)	Finance activity	−1.18	−3.38	−0.84	−2.86	−1.58	−0.85 (−2.38)
	Finance size	5.10	4.29	5.22	4.60	4.95	−1.02 (−2.55)[b]
	Finance efficiency	2.18	0.44	2.85	1.04	2.01	−0.60 (1.14)

Notes: All the measures for countries other than China are from Levine (2002); measures on China are calculated using definitions from Levine (2002).

[a] The numerical result for countries of each legal-origin group is calculated based on a value (GDP of each country)-weighted approach.

[b] Numbers in brackets indicate bank credit issued to the hybrid sector of China (instead of total bank credit).

[c] The "floating supply" of the market is a better measure for the size of a stock market (relative to size of the economy) than "market capitalization," because the latter includes nontradable shares, while the former measures the fraction of total market capitalization that is traded in the markets.

[d] Measuring whether a country's financial system is market or bank dominated, the higher the measure, the more the system is dominated by markets (see text for definitions).

[e] These variables measure the entire financial system (banking and market sectors combined), and the higher the measure, the larger or more efficient the financial system is.

Sources: Almanac of China's Finance and Banking (2000–2002), Yearbook (2000–2002).

We first compare the *size* of a country's equity markets and banks relative to that country's gross domestic product (GDP; Table 14.1, first panel). In terms of total market capitalization, China's stock market, 32 percent of its GDP, is smaller than most of the La Porta et al. sample countries with a weighted (by each country's GDP) average of 47 percent of GDP. To measure the actual size of the market, the "floating supply" of the market is a better measure than "market capitalization," because the latter includes nontradable shares, while the former measures the fraction of total market capitalization that is traded in the markets. In this regard, the size of China's stock market (11 percent of GDP) is much smaller than those of La Porta et al. countries (with a weighted average of 27 percent of GDP). By contrast, China's banking system is much more important in terms of size relative to its stock markets, with its ratio of total bank credit to GDP (1.11) higher than even the German-origin countries (with a weighted average of 0.99). However, when we consider bank credit issued (or loans made) to the hybrid sector only, China's ratio drops sharply to 0.24, suggesting that most of the bank credit is issued to companies in the state and listed sectors. Moreover, China's banking system is not efficient: its overhead cost to total assets (0.12) is much higher than the average of French-origin countries (0.05), the next highest group of countries.

Table 14.1, second panel, compares the relative importance of financial markets versus banks ("structure indices"). China has the lowest scores for both "structure activity" (log of the ratio of float supply of market cap/total bank credit) and "structure size" (log of the ratio of market capitalization/total bank credit), suggesting that its banking sector is much larger than its financial markets, and this dominance by the banks over markets is stronger than the average of all La Porta et al. sample countries. In terms of "structure efficiency" (log of product (market capitalization/GDP) × (bank overhead cost/bank total assets)), which denotes the relative efficiency of markets versus banks, China has the highest score, suggesting that its stock markets are actually relatively more efficient than banks compared to other countries. This result is mainly driven by the extremely high (overhead) costs of China's banking system.

We also compare the development of the financial system ("financial development"), including both banks and markets (Table 14.1, last panel). Given that all other countries' measures were based on private bank credit, if we only include China's bank credit made to the *hybrid sector*, we find that China's overall financial market size, in terms of both "finance activity" (log of product of (float supply of market/GDP) × (Private credit/GDP)) and "finance size" (log of product of (market capitalization/GDP) + (private credit/GDP)), is smaller than the La Porta et al. sample average level and is only higher than the French-origin average. In terms of "finance efficiency" (log of (total floating supply/GDP)/overhead cost), China's measure is below all subsamples of La Porta et al. countries. Based on the earlier evidence, we can conclude that China's financial system is dominated by a large, inefficient *banking sector*. Further, relatively little of the lending is to the hybrid sector, which, as we will see in the section on "The Nonstandard Financial Sector and Evidence on Hybrid Sector Firms," is the dynamic part of the economy.

Firms' Financing Channels: Aggregate Evidence

The four most important financing sources for all firms in China, in terms of firms' fixed-asset investments, are (domestic) bank loans, firms' self–fund-raising, the state budget, and FDI. By far the two most important sources of financing channels are self–fund-raising and bank loans. Consistent with previous evidence on China's banking sector, bank loans, including loans from the nonstate banks, provide a large amount of funds to firms and constitute a large fraction of firms' total financing needs.

Self-fund-raising includes proceeds from capital raised from *local* governments (beyond the state budget), communities and other investors, internal financing channels such as retained earnings, and all other funds raised domestically by the firms. Since our current data source does not provide the breakdowns of "self–fund-raising," we can present only the total figures. The size of total self–fund-raising of all firms has been growing at an average annual rate of 17.8 percent over the period of 1994–2006. Total self–fund-raising (for fixed-asset investment) reached $665.5 billion at the end of 2006, compared to a total of $364.8 billion for domestic bank loans for the same year. It is important to point out that equity and bond issuance, which are included in self–fund-raising, apply only to the listed sector and account for a small fraction of this category. Moreover, self–fund-raising is the most important source of financing for many types of firms. For example, individually owned companies (of the hybrid sector), not surprisingly, rely mostly on self–fund-raising (about 90 percent of total financing). Interestingly, even for state- or quasi-state-owned companies, self–fund-raising is also important in that it captures somewhere between 45 and 65 percent of total financing.

The state budget and FDI are the other two important financing sources. As was the case for all socialist countries, China used to rely on a central planning system to allocate the state budget to most of the companies in the country. But the state budget now contributes only 10 percent of *state-owned* companies' total funding. On the other hand, FDI is comparable to the state budget, in terms of both aggregate size and the relative importance in firms' financing. This evidence confirms that China has evolved from a centrally planned, closed economy toward an open-market economy. For example, in terms of the ratio of FDI over GDP, China attracted more FDI than both South Korea and Taiwan during the 1990s.

With knowledge of the four financing channels at the aggregate level, we now focus on different types of firms' financing decisions. The results are presented in Figure 14.2a–c. In all of these figures, each of the four connected lines represents the importance of a particular financing channel over the period of 1994–2002,

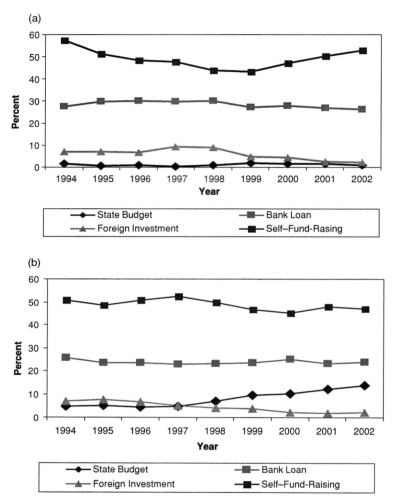

Figure 14.2. (a) Financing sources for the listed sector; (b) financing sources for the state sector; (c) financing sources for the hybrid sector

Figures 14.2a–c examine financing sources (for the investment of fixed assets) of different types of firms in China. In all three figures, each of the four connected lines represents the importance of a particular financing channel over the time period 1994–2002, measured by the percentage of firms' total financing coming from this channel. Figure 14.2a presents financing sources for firms in the listed sector, Figure 14.2b presents results for firms in the state sector, and Figure 14.2c presents results for firms in the hybrid sector. (*continued*)

measured by the percentage of firms' total financing coming from this channel.[6] First, Figure 14.2a (14.2b) illustrates how firms in the listed sector (state sector)

---

[6] After 2002, *Yearbook*, the source of our data, no longer provides the breakdowns of funds by their sources or by firm types, and as a result, the period depicted in all panels of Figure 14.2 is limited to 1994–2002.

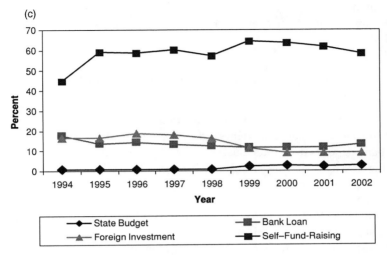

Figure 14.2 (*continued*)

finance their investment for fixed assets. While the listed sector has been growing fast, SOEs are on a downward trend, as privatization of these firms is still in progress. Around 30 percent of publicly traded companies' funding comes from bank loans, and this ratio has been very stable (Figure 14.2a). Around 45 percent of the listed sector's total funding comes from self–fund-raising, including internal financing, and proceeds from equity and bond issuance. Moreover, equity and bond sales, which rely on the use of external markets, constitute only a small fraction of total funds raised in comparison to internal financing and other forms of fund-raising. Combined with the fact that self–fund-raising is also the most important source of financing for the state sector (Figure 14.2b), we can conclude that alternative channels of financing are important even for the state and listed sectors.

Next, we consider how firms in the hybrid sector raise funds (Figure 14.2c). Self–fund-raising here includes all forms of internal finance, capital raised from family and friends of the founders and managers, and funds raised in the form of private equity and loans. Clearly, this category is by far the most important source of financing, accounting for close to 60 percent of total funds raised. Moreover, since firms in this sector operate in an environment with legal and financial mechanisms and regulations that are probably poorer than those available for firms in the state and listed sectors, financing sources may work differently from how they work in the state and listed sectors and in developed countries.

THE BANKING AND INTERMEDIATION SECTOR

In this section we examine the status of China's banking and intermediation sector. After reviewing aggregate evidence on bank deposits and loans, we analyze the problem of NPLs in the banking sector as well as assess solutions to this problem. Finally, we review evidence on the growth of nonstate banks and financial intermediaries.

Aggregate Evidence on Bank Deposits and Loans

As in other Asian countries, China's household savings rates have been high throughout the reform era. Given the growth of the economy, the sharp increase in personal income, and limited investment opportunities, it is not surprising that total bank deposits from individuals have been growing fast since the mid-1980s, with the 2006 figure approaching RMB11 trillion ($1.4 trillion). From Figure 14.3a, residents in metropolitan areas contribute the most to total deposits beginning in the late 1980s (roughly 50 percent), while deposits from enterprises (including firms from all three sectors) provide the second most important source. The role of deposits from government agencies and organizations (including nonprofit and for-profit organizations, not shown in the figure) has steadily decreased over time.

Table 14.2a compares total savings and bank deposits across China, Japan, South Korea, and India during the period 1997–2002. In terms of the ratio of gross domestic savings/gross domestic product ("gross domestic savings," a category in the national accounts, includes more types of savings than bank deposits), China maintains the highest level (an average of 40 percent), while Japan leads the group in terms of total amount. Looking at the breakdown of bank deposits, interest-bearing "savings deposits" are by far the most important form of deposits in China, providing a good source for bank loans and other forms of investment. Figure 14.3b compares total bank credit (over gross national product, GNP) extended to hybrid sector firms in China and privately owned firms (including those publicly listed and traded) in Taiwan and South Korea. For South Korea, we also plot the bank credit ratios during its high economic growth period of the 1970s and 1980s. (Each year appearing on the horizontal axis indicates the period for China, while a particular year *minus* 20 indicates the period for South Korea.) We can see that the scale and growth of China's "hybrid" bank credit during 1997–2006 are far below those (of private bank credit) of Taiwan and South Korea in the same period, but are similar to those of South Korea twenty years ago. Consistent with the aggregate evidence from our "Overview of China's Financial System" earlier and our firm-level evidence later, we find that bank loans were one of the most important financing sources for hybrid sector firms.

Table 14.2b breaks down China's bank loans by maturities, loan purposes, and borrower types. First, along with the growth of the size of loans there has been a shift from short-term to long-term loans (Table 14.2, first two columns). Second, the majority of loans goes to SOEs in manufacturing industries ("industrial loans" and "commercial loans"); further, most of the "infrastructure/construction loans" (a small component of total loans) fund government-sponsored projects, while

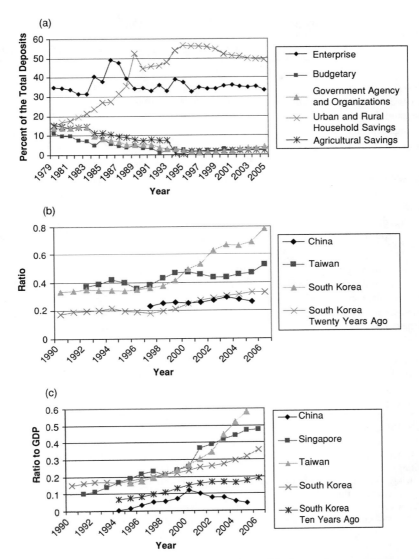

Figure 14.3. (a) Sources for bank deposits in China; (b) Comparing total bank credit; (c) A comparison of assets under management of insurance companies

the size of "agricultural loans" is much smaller. Third, the size of loans made to TVEs, privately and collectively owned firms, and joint ventures (Table 14.2, last three columns), which all belong to the hybrid sector, is also much smaller.[7]

---

[7] Without detailed breakdowns of different types of loans made to different sectors, we cannot estimate the exact share of total loans made to the three sectors.

Table 14.2a. *Comparisons of total savings and deposits*

	1997	1998	1999	2000	2001	2002
China						
Gross domestic saving[a]	373	386	391	421	447	487
Gross domestic saving/GDP (%)	41.5	40.8	39.5	39.0	38.5	39.4
Demand deposits[b]	–	–	60	71	127	109
Savings deposits[c]	–	–	720	777	891	1,050
Time deposits[d]	–	–	114	136	171	199
Japan						
Gross domestic saving[a]	–	–	742	641	577	603
Gross domestic saving/GDP (%)	–	–	14.8	14.3	13.8	13.3
Demand deposits[b]	152	181	220	227	211	259
Savings deposits[c]	105	127	138	117	91	–
Time deposits[d]	2,161	2,540	2,724	2,392	1,821	1,934
South Korea						
Gross domestic saving[a]	108	126	141	135	127	147
Gross domestic saving/GDP (%)	33.7	34.4	33.5	32.6	30.9	29.3
Demand deposits[b]	25	31	37	35	38	47
Savings deposits[c]	48	81	117	123	144	173
Time deposits[d]	33	96	128	163	162	212
India						
Gross domestic saving[a]	90	88	107	105	114	120
Gross domestic saving/GDP (%)	23.1	21.5	24.1	23.4	24.0	24.0
Demand deposits[b]	26	28	29	30	31	35
Time deposits[c]	126	140	158	175	197	231

Note: Values are in billion U.S. dollars.

[a] Gross domestics savings, from the national accounts, is an annual flow measure.

[b] Demand deposits, balance of the accounts can be withdrawn on demand of customers (e.g., check writing).

[c] Savings deposits, interest-bearing accounts that can be withdrawn but not to be used as money (e.g., no check writing).

[d] Time deposits, savings accounts or CD with a fixed term.

Source: The Asian Banker data center (2003, http://www.theasianbanker.com).

According to an International Finance Corporation (affiliated with the World Bank) report (Gregory, Tenev, and Wagle, 2000), which incorporates data published by the PBOC, loans made to privately owned firms (also part of the hybrid sector) from all banks are less than 1 percent of total loans made in 1998, with half of these loans from state-owned banks. Researchers have argued that the imbalance between loans made to the state sector and the hybrid sector reflects the government's policies of wealth transfer from the hybrid sector to the state sector via state-owned banks (e.g., Brandt and Zhu, 2000).

Table 14.2b. *Breakdown of bank loans in China*

Year	Total loans	Short-term loans	Industrial loans	Commercial loans	Infrastructure construction loans	Agricultural loans	Loans to		
							TVEs	Privately owned firms	Joint ventures and cooperative firms
1994	3,997.60	2,694.87	994.83	1,050.98	61.72	114.39	200.24	15.59	79.23
1995	5,054.41	3,337.20	1,177.47	1,283.71	79.93	154.48	251.49	19.62	99.91
1996	6,115.66	4,021.00	1,421.33	1,533.26	97.38	191.91	282.19	27.98	134.63
1997	7,491.41	5,541.83	1,652.66	1,835.66	159.11	331.46	503.58	38.67	189.10
1998	8,652.41	6,061.32	1,782.15	1,975.24	162.87	444.42	558.00	47.16	248.75
1999	9,373.43	6,388.76	1,794.89	1,989.09	147.69	479.24	616.13	57.91	298.58
2000	9,937.11	6,574.81	1,701.93	1,786.85	161.71	488.90	606.08	65.46	304.98
2001	11,231.47	6,732.72	1,863.67	1,856.34	209.96	571.15	641.30	91.80	326.35
2002	13,129.39	7,424.79	2,019.05	1,797.31	274.80	688.46	681.23	105.88	269.74
2003	15,899.62	8,366.12	2,275.60	1,799.44	300.21	841.14	766.16	146.16	256.94
2004	17,819.78	8,684.06	2,389.66	1,707.41	278.01	984.31	806.92	208.16	219.84
2005	30,204.28	8,744.92	2,251.67	1,644.76	298.37	1,152.99	790.18	218.08	197.53

Note: End-of-year figures are in RMB billions.

Source: Statistical Yearbooks of China (1985–2006).

The Problem of NPLs and Possible Solutions

China's banking sector is dominated by large and inefficient state-owned banks, namely, the "big four" banks of ICBC, BOC, CCB, and ABC.[8] The dominance of the big four banks also implies that the degree of competition within the banking sector is extremely low. For example, Demirgüç-Kunt and Levine (2001) compare the five-bank concentration (share of the assets of the five largest banks in total banking assets) and find that China's concentration ratio of 91 percent at the end of 1997 (and for much of 1990s) is one of the highest in the world. However, China's concentration ratio has been falling sharply since 1997 with the entrance of many nonstate banks and intermediaries.

The most glaring problem for China's banking sector, and for the entire financial system in the near future, is the amount of NPLs within state-owned banks and in particular, among the big four banks. Reducing the amount of NPLs to normal levels is the most important task for China's financial system in the short term. The main obstacle when we analyze the severity and possible solutions of the NPLs is the lack of comprehensive and objective data on banks' profitability (aggregate and bank level) and NPLs. The scarcity and deficiency in bank data can be viewed as a strategic disclosure decision of the government, which fuels speculation that the problem of NPLs must be severe. We mainly rely on official sources for our analysis on NPLs, but when examining possible solutions we also speculate based on data from nongovernment sources, including case studies from particular regions or banks. As a result, some of these data and speculations paint a much gloomier picture of the NPLs and China's state-owned banks than the official data suggest. Since without objective and accurate bank-level data we cannot determine the exact amount of NPLs or evaluate the feasibility and effectiveness of different solutions, we present both an optimistic view and a pessimistic view when discussing these issues.

Comparing NPLs

In panel A of Table 14.3a, we compare NPLs in China, the United States, and other major Asian economies during 1998–2006 based on official figures. NPLs are measured by their size (in U.S. dollar billion) and as a percentage of GDPs in the same year (shown in brackets). Measured as the fraction of GDPs, China's NPLs are the highest in the group from 2000 to 2006, as high as 20.0–22.5 percent of GDP (in 2000 and 2001). Notice that the official information on China's NPLs first became available in 1998, but the figures in 1998 and 1999 in Table 14.3a

---

[8] La Porta, Lopez-de-Silanes, and Shleifer (2002) show that the government owns 99.45 percent of the assets of the ten largest commercial banks in China in 1995, one of the highest in their sample of ninety-two countries. Moreover, their result on the negative relationship between government ownership of banks and the growth of a country's economy seems to apply to China's state sector and the banking sector. However, we show that the high government ownership of banks has not prevented the growth of the hybrid sector.

Table 14.3a. *A comparison of nonperforming loans and government debt*

Panel A: Size of NPLs (in billion U.S. dollars and as percentage of GDPs in the same year, in brackets)

Year	China	United States	Japan	South Korea	India	Indonesia	Taiwan
1997	–	66.9 (0.8%)	217.4 (5.1%)	16.2 (3.1%)	12.7 (3.1%)	0.2 (0.1%)	19.6 (6.5%)
1998	20.5 (2.0%)	71.3 (0.8%)	489.7 (12.7%)	23.2 (6.7%)	14.0 (3.2%)	5.5 (5.2%)	21.8 (7.9%)
1999	105.1 (9.7%)	72.2 (0.8%)	547.6 (12.6%)	54.4 (12.2%)	12.9 (2.8%)	3.1 (3.8%)	27.2 (9.1%)
2000	269.3 (22.5%)	90.1 (0.9%)	515.4 (11.1%)	35.5 (6.9%)	13.2 (2.8%)	6.3 (2.7%)	33.2 (10.3%)
2001	265.3 (20.0%)	108.4 (1.1%)	640.1 (15.6%)	12.2 (2.5%)	14.8 (3.0%)	4.3 (1.7%)	37.9 (13.0%)
2002	188.4 (13.0%)	107.8 (1.0%)	552.5 (14.1%)	9.9 (1.8%)	14.6 (2.5%)	3.3 (2.0%)	30.7 (10.4%)
2003	181.2 (11.0%)	95.9 (1.0%)	480.1 (11.3%)	11.7 (1.9%)	14.4 (2.2%)	4.7 (1.5%)	23.1 (7.7%)
2004	207.4 (10.7%)	81.3 (0.9%)	334.8 (7.3%)	10.0 (1.5%)	13.4 (1.7%)	3.8 (2.1%)	16.4 (5.1%)
2005	164.2 (7.3%)	84.6 (0.7%)	183.3 (4.0%)	7.6 (1.0%)	11.8 (1.4%)	6.0 (1.5%)	11.2 (3.2%)
2006 (Q2)	160.3 (6.3%)	88.8 (0.7%)	108.2 (2.4%)	7.4 (0.8%)		7.3 (2.1%)	–

Panel B: Outstanding government debt (billion dollars)

Year	China Outstanding government bonds	United States Total government debt	Japan Total government debt	South Korea Outstanding treasury bonds	India Total public debt	Indonesia Outstanding government bonds	Taiwan Outstanding government bonds
1997	66.5	5,802.8	4,254.0	5.3	–	–	–
1998	93.8	5,788.8	4,858.0	14.4	178.4	–	–
1999	127.3	5,822.7	6,053.1	28.5	260.2	34.1	46.5
2000	165.1	5,612.7	6,209.8	32.7	232.4	45.1	45.5
2001	188.6	5,734.4	6,036.0	39.8	225.4	43.5	58.7
2002	233.5	6,169.4	6,321.3	45.2	250.2	42.1	77.7
2003	273.0	6,789.7	6,852.9	67.9	259.7	48.0	75.7

(continued)

Table 14.3a *(continued)*

Year	Outstanding government bonds	Total government debt	Total government debt	Outstanding treasury bonds	Total public debt	Outstanding government bonds	Outstanding government bonds
2004	311.3	7,335.6	7,446.6	107.0	299.6	44.7	85.2
2005	350.0	7,809.5	8,299.5	165.5	347.1	39.9	–
2006	–	8,289.1	7,880.5	209.1	378.9	44.8	–
Panel C: (NPLs + outstanding government debt)/GDP							
1997	–	0.71 (0.54)	1.05 (0.40)	0.04	–	–	–
1998	0.11 (0.13)	0.67 (0.50)	1.39 (0.63)	0.11	0.46	–	–
1999	0.21 (0.31)	0.64 (0.45)	1.51 (0.64)	0.19	0.62	0.24	0.25
2000	0.36 (0.59)	0.58 (0.40)	1.45 (0.65)	0.13	0.53	0.31	0.24
2001	0.34 (0.54)	0.58 (0.39)	1.63 (0.83)	0.11	0.50	0.30	0.33
2002	0.29 (0.42)	0.60 (0.42)	1.76 (0.90)	0.10	0.54	0.23	0.37
2003	0.28 (0.39)	0.63 (0.45)	1.73 (0.86)	0.13	0.48	0.22	0.33
2004	0.27 (0.38)	0.63 (0.46)	1.70 (0.81)	0.17	0.47	0.19	0.32
2005	0.23 (0.30)	0.63 (0.47)	1.86 (0.84)	0.22	0.47	0.16	–
2006	–	0.63 (0.47)	1.79 (0.89)	0.25	0.46	0.15	–

Notes: This table compares total outstanding NPLs within the banking system, government debt, and the ratio of (NPLs + government debt)/GDP among China, the United States, and other major Asian countries for the period 1997–2006. Panel A presents the size of the NPLs, as measured by U.S. dollar billion and as the percentage of GDPs in the same year. NPLs in the United States measure the outstanding "delinquency loan"; NPLs in Japan measure the "risk management loans" (or loans disclosed under the Financial Reconstructed Law and/or loans subject to self-assessment). In panel B, outstanding government debt is measured at the end of each year; for the United States and Japan, total government debt includes domestic and foreign debt. In panel C, the ratios for China include using the official NPL numbers and using doubled official NPLs (i.e., the ratios in the brackets are (doubled NPLs + government debt)/GDP); the ratios in the brackets for the United States and Japan are (net government debt + NPLs)/GDP, where net government debt is the difference between government borrowing (stock measure) and government lending (flow measure). All figures are converted into U.S. dollars using the average exchange rate within the observation year.

Sources: Statistical Bureau of China, the People's Bank of China, China Banking Regulatory Commission; Board of Governors of the Federal Reserve Bank, Statistical Abstracts of the United States, the Statistical Bureau of Japan; Ministry of Finance, Korea, the Bank of Korea, Korean Statistical Information System; IMF, World Bank; Bank Indonesia; Ministry of Finance, India; National Statistical Bureau of Taiwan.

probably significantly underestimate the actual size of NPLs in those years; this also explains the jump in the size of China's NPLs from 1999 to 2000. The cross-country comparison on NPLs includes the period during which Asian countries recovered from the 1997 financial crisis (e.g., the size of NPLs in South Korea exceeded 12 percent of GDP in 1999, but it was reduced to below 3 percent two years later) and the period during which the Japanese banking system was disturbed by the prolonged NPL problem. (The size of Japan's NPLs is the largest of the group throughout the period except for 2006; the ratio of NPLs over GDP reached 15.6 percent in 2001, but was reduced to below 5 percent by the end of 2005.)[9]

As bad as the numbers in panel A of Table 14.3a appear, they may still significantly underestimate the amount of NPLs within China's banking system according to the pessimistic view. First, the official figures on outstanding NPLs (cumulated within all commercial banks in China) do not include the bad loans that have been transferred from banks to four state-owned asset management companies (AMCs), with the purpose of AMCs liquidating these bad loans. If we add the NPLs held by the four AMCs (book value of RMB866 billion, or $108 billion, shown in the last row of Table 14.3b) in the first quarter of 2006 to the mix of NPLs shown in panel A of Table 14.3a, the total amount of China's NPLs would increase by two-thirds. Second, the classification of NPLs has been problematic in China. The Basle Committee for Bank Supervision classifies a loan as "doubtful" or bad when any *interest* payment is overdue by 180 days or more (in the United States it is 90 days), whereas in China, this step has not typically been taken until the *principal* payment is delayed beyond the loan maturity date or an extended due date and in many cases, until the borrower has declared bankruptcy and/or has gone through liquidation. Qiu, Li, and Cai (2000) estimate that the ratio of loan interest paid to *state-owned* banks over loan interest owed is on average less than 50 percent in 1999, suggesting that the actual ratio of NPLs over total loans made can be higher than 50 percent in 1999. This piece of evidence, along with others, suggests that the amount of NPLs (and as percentage of GDP) could be twice as large as the official figures reported in panel A of Table 14.3a.[10]

Since a large fraction of the NPLs among state-owned banks, and in particular, the big four banks, resulted from poor lending decisions made for SOEs, some of which were due to political or other noneconomic reasons, in our view the government should bear the burden of reducing the NPLs. This view of essentially treating NPLs as a fiscal problem implies that the ultimate source of eliminating NPLs lies

---

[9] With a secondary source from the Asian Banker, we also find that the profitability of China's banking system, measured by the return to equity or assets, is also among the lowest in the same group of countries during 2000–2002.

[10] Consistent with this view, Lardy (1998) argues that, if using international standards on bad loans, the existing NPLs within China's state-owned banks as of the mid-1990s would make these banks' total net worth negative, so that the entire network of state banks would be insolvent.

Table 14.3b. *Liquidation of NPLs by four AMCs*

	Book value of assets (accumulated)	Assets recovered	Cash recovered	Asset recovery rate (%)	Cash recovery rate (%)
			2001		
Hua Rong	23.21	12.54	7.55	54.0	32.5
Great Wall	53.11	6.30	3.69	11.9	6.9
Oriental	18.29	8.51	4.42	46.5	24.2
Xin Da	29.90	22.50	10.49	75.3	35.1
TOTAL	124.51	49.86	26.15	40.0	21.0
			2002		
Hua Rong	32.04	11.43	10.20	35.7	31.8
Great Wall	45.48	7.94	5.47	17.5	12.0
Oriental	22.10	10.60	5.57	47.9	25.2
Xin Da	33.10	17.46	10.51	52.7	31.8
TOTAL	132.73	47.43	31.75	35.7	23.9

	Accumulated disposal	Cash recovered	Disposal ratio (%)	Asset recovery ratio (%)	Cash recovery ratio (%)
			2004		
Hua Rong	209.54	41.34	59.77	25.29	19.73
Great Wall	209.91	21.57	61.91	14.43	10.27
Oriental	104.55	23.29	41.42	29.50	22.27
Xin Da	151.06	50.81	48.90	38.29	33.64
TOTAL	675.06	137.00	53.96	25.48	20.29
			2005		
Hua Rong	243.38	54.39	69.17	26.92	22.35
Great Wall	263.39	27.35	77.88	12.90	10.39
Oriental	131.76	32.01	52.08	28.73	24.30
Xin Da	201.21	62.84	63.82	34.30	31.23
TOTAL	839.75	176.60	66.74	24.58	21.03
			2006 (Q1)		
Hua Rong	246.80	54.66	70.11	26.50	22.15
Great Wall	270.78	27.83	80.11	12.70	10.28
Oriental	141.99	32.81	56.13	27.16	23.11
Xin Da	206.77	65.26	64.69	34.46	31.56
TOTAL	866.34	180.56	68.61	24.20	20.84

Notes: Values are in RMB billion. This table presents results on the liquidation of NPLs by four state-owned AMCs in China during the period 2001 to the first quarter of 2006. These AMCs were set up to specifically deal with NPLs accumulated in the "big four" state-owned banks.

1. Accumulated disposal refers to the accumulated amount of cash and noncash assets recovered as well as loss incurred by the end of the reporting period.
2. Disposal ratio = Accumulated disposal/total NPLs purchased.
3. Asset recovery ratio = Total assets recovered/accumulated disposal.
4. Cash recovery ratio = Cash recovered/accumulated disposal.

Source: Almanac of China's Finance and Banking (2002–2005); the reports of China Banking Regulatory Commission (2004–2006).

in China's overall economic growth.[11] As long as the economy maintains its strong growth momentum so that tax receipts also increase, the government can always assume the remainder of the NPLs without significantly affecting the economy. In this regard, panel B of Table 14.3a compares total outstanding government debt, and panel C presents a comparison of the ratio of (NPLs + government debt)/GDP across countries, with the sum of NPLs and government debt indicating total burden of the government. Depending on data availability, total government debt is measured by either the sum of all types of domestic and foreign debt (the United States, Japan, and India) or the level of outstanding government bonds (all other countries) in a given year.

Unlike the severity of its NPL problem, the Chinese government does not carry a large amount of debt, with total outstanding government bonds growing from only 9 percent of GDP in 1998 to around 16 percent of GDP in 2005. By contrast, countries such as the United States and India have a large amount of government debt, even though their banking sectors are healthy (as measured by low levels of NPLs). Japan is the only country in the group that has large amount of NPLs *and* government debt. When we combine the results from panels A and B (Table 14.3a) and compare total government burden in panel C, we use two sets of ratios for China: the first set of ratios is based on official NPLs numbers presented in panel A, while the second set (presented in brackets) is based on doubling the size of official NPLs. For the United States and Japan, we also present two sets of ratios. In addition to using total outstanding government debt, we also use ratios (in the brackets) based on the sum of *net* government debt and NPLs, where net government debt is the difference between government borrowing (a "stock" measure) and government lending (also a stock measure); not surprisingly, these ratios are much lower than using the gross figures.

From panel C (Table 14.3a), China's total government burden is in the middle of the pack: the ratios of total government burden over GDP (using the official NPL figures) are lower than those in the United States, India, and Japan, are comparable with those in Taiwan, and are higher than those in Indonesia and Korea. China's ratios are much higher if NPL figures are doubled, but total government burden in that case is still comparable with or lower than that of the United States (using gross or net government debt) and much lower than that of Japan. Based on these crude comparisons, it seems that the NPLs will not be a particularly arduous burden for the Chinese government due to its small size of debt, while the same cannot be said for Japan. Caution is again needed for this conclusion: first, new NPLs in China may grow much faster than in other countries, and second, China's currently small government debt may experience a sharp increase in the near future, given the need for higher fiscal spending in areas such as pension plans and other social welfare programs.

---

[11] See, for example, Sachs and Woo (1997, review article), Rawski (2002), and Chapter 20 of this volume for different views on the prospects of long-run economic growth and statistics on growth in China.

Recognizing the importance of reducing NPLs in the big four banks and its responsibility in carrying out this difficult task, the Chinese government has injected foreign currency reserves (mostly in the form of U.S. dollars, T-bills, euros, and yen) into these banks to improve their balance sheets in preparation for going public. This process began at the end of 2003, with the establishment of the Central Huijin Investment Company, through which the PBOC injected U.S.$45 billion of reserves into the BOC and CCB, while ICBC (the largest commercial bank in China and one of the largest in the world in terms of assets) received U.S.$15 billion during the first half of 2005 (e.g., *Financial Times*, January 09, 2004, April 21, 2005; *Asia Wall Street Journal*, January 13, 2004). All three banks have since become publicly listed and traded in either the Hong Kong Stock Exchange (HKSE) and/or the Shanghai Stock Exchange (SHSE). Given that China's total foreign exchange reserve reached U.S.$1.07 trillion at the end of 2006 (*Associated Press*, January 15, 2007), the largest in the world, while the total amount of NPLs is around U.S.$160 billion (using the U.S.$1 = 8 RMB exchange rate) at the end of second quarter in 2006, the foreign reserve itself should be more than enough to remove all the existing NPLs off the books of all the banks in China.

However, the injection plan will not prevent new NPLs from originating in the banking system. In fact, it may create perverse incentives for state-owned banks, in that if these banks (that have received or will receive the cash/assets injection) believe that there will be a "bailout" whenever they run into future financial distress, they lose the incentive to improve efficiency while an incentive to take on risky, negative net present value projects surfaces. This moral hazard problem can thwart the government's efforts in keeping the NPLs in check, while similar problems occurred during and after the government bailout of the Savings and Loan crisis in the United States in 1980s (e.g., Kane, 1989, 2003). Hence, it is important for the government to credibly commit that the injection plan is a one-time measure to boost the capital adequacy of these banks and that there will be no bailout plans in the future, especially after they become listed companies. The second problem arises because the significant increase in foreign reserves is in part due to the presence of large amounts of speculative foreign currencies in anticipation of an RMB appreciation relative to major international currencies. Depending on how the government and the central bank allow the flexible RMB exchange rate mechanism introduced in July 2005 to operate, large movements of the speculative currencies may cause a twin crisis in the currency market and the banking sector. We further discuss this issue in the section on "Financial Crises" later.

Reducing NPLs and Improving the Efficiency of State-Owned Banks

In recent years, the Chinese government has taken active measures to reduce the NPLs and improve the efficiency of the banking sector. First, as mentioned earlier, four state-owned AMCs were formed, with the goal of assuming the NPLs (and offering debt-for-equity swaps to the banks) accumulated in each of the big four banks and liquidating them. The liquidation process includes asset sales, tranching, securitization, and resale of loans to investors.[12] Table 14.3b shows that *cash* recovery on the bad loans processed by the AMCs ranges from 6.9 to 35 percent between 2001 and 2006 (first quarter), while the asset recovery rates are slightly higher. A critical issue that affects the effectiveness of the liquidation process is the relationship among AMCs, banks, and distressed or bankrupt firms. Since both the AMCs and the banks are state owned, it is not likely that the AMCs would force the banks to cut off (credit) ties with defaulted borrowers (SOEs or former SOEs), as a privately owned bank would do. Thus, as the old NPLs are liquidated, new NPLs from the same borrowers continue to surface.

Second, state-owned banks have diversified and improved their loan structure by increasing consumer-related loans while being more active in risk management and monitoring of loans made to SOEs. For example, the ratio of consumer lending to total loans made for the four state-owned banks increased from 1 percent in 1998 to 10 percent in 2002; by the end of 2004, 10 percent of all outstanding bank loans (RMB2 trillion or $250 billion) was extended to consumers. The size of mortgages, now the largest component (almost 90 percent) of consumer credit, grew 100 times between 1997 and 2006, reaching a total of RMB2 trillion ($250 billion) (*Xinhua News*). One problem with the massive expansion of consumer credit is that China lacks a national consumer-credit database to spot overstretching debtors, although a pilot system linking seven cities was set up in late 2004. The deficiency in the knowledge and training of credit risk and diligence of loan officers from state-owned banks is another significant factor in credit expansion, which can lead to high default rates and a large amount of new NPLs if the growth of the economy and personal income slow down. Accompanying the rapidly expanding automobile industry, the other fast-growing category of individual-based loans is automobile loans, most of which are made by state-owned banks. The total balance of all China's individual auto loans rocketed from RMB400 million ($50 million) in 1998 to RMB200 billion ($25 billion) at the end of 2003, and as much as 30 percent of all auto sales were financed by loans during this period (*Financial Times*, May 25, 2005). The growth in both auto sales and loans slowed down significantly since 2004 in part due to the high default rates. Shanghai and Beijing have the largest number of car sales and loans. As many as 50 percent of debtors defaulted on their car loans in these cities. There are examples in which loan applications were approved based solely on applicants' description of their personal income without any auditing (*Barron's*, December 06, 2004). However, the slowdown of the auto loan market was temporary and it quickly resumed its fast pace of growth, in part due to the tremendous potential of the market. In aggregate, auto loans amount to

---

[12] The sale of tranches of securitized NPLs to foreign investors first occurred in 2002. The deal was struck between Huarong, one of the four AMCs, and a consortium of U.S. investment banks led by Morgan Stanley (and including Lehman Brothers and Salomon Smith Barney) and was approved by the Chinese government in early 2003 (*Financial Times*, May, 2003).

10–20 percent of the total amount spent on autos. Most loans mature in three to five years.[13]

The earlier examples on auto loans and consumer credit illustrate the importance of reforming state-owned banks in solving the problems of NPLs and improving the entire banking sector. A central question in reforming the state-owned banks is the ongoing privatization process. There are two imminent issues. First, more competition in the banking and intermediation sector, including the entrance of more nonstate (domestic and foreign) banks and intermediaries, is good for improving the efficiency of both the big four banks and the entire banking sector.[14] Another issue is the government's dual role as regulator and majority owner. These potentially conflicting roles diminish the effectiveness in each of the two roles that the government intends to carry out. In the section on "Financial Markets and Publicly Traded Firms" later, we argue that the nontradable government shares in all listed companies should be gradually sold off to ensure that the privatization process is complete. The same procedure should be applied to the privatization process of state-owned banks. Only after these banks are (majority) owned by nongovernment entities and individuals can they unconditionally implement all profit- and efficiency-enhancing measures. In fact, with a sample of both state- and non-state-owned banks, Berger, Iftekhar, and Zhou (2006) show that the addition of foreign ownership stakes into banks' ownership structure is associated with significant improvement of bank efficiency.

Table 14.3c presents the performance of initial public offerings (IPOs) of three of the big four banks (ABC remains in the state sector) and that of the Bank of Communications (BComm). The most notable case is the IPO of ICBC. Simultaneously carried out in the HKSE and SHSE on October 27, 2006, ICBC raised U.S.$22 billion, making it the largest IPO up to that date in the world. The first day (and first week cumulative) return, measured by the net percentage return of the closing price on the first (fifth) trading day over offer price, was almost 15 percent, suggesting high demand for ICBC's H shares among (foreign) investors. Its current market capitalization ranks ICBC the second largest bank in the world, behind only Citibank, but only 22 percent of the market cap is "free float" or tradable. The largest foreign shareholder is Goldman Sachs, with its 5.8 percent ownership stake negotiated before the IPO. While the IPOs of the other three large banks have not grabbed as much attention, they are also successful in terms of total proceeds raised, and they have all attracted significant foreign ownership at the IPO date. On the other hand (from the *Chinese Banking Regulatory Commission*), Moody's ratings on these publicly listed banks (on both deposits and loans) range from A to Baa

---

[13] A few foreign lenders (e.g., GM and Ford) were approved to enter China's auto loan market by forming joint ventures with Chinese automakers (*Financial Times*, May 27, 2005).

[14] For example, Park, Brandt, and Giles (2003) find that competition among banks and intermediaries leads to better effort of the banks (especially state-owned banks) and better loan decisions in China's rural areas.

Table 14.3c. *Performance of Chinese banks' IPOs*

	ICBC		BOC		CCB	BComm
Listing exchange and currency	HKSE (HK$)	SHSE (RMB)	HKSE (HK$)	SHSE (RMB)	HKSE (HK$)	HKSE (HK$)
IPO date	October 27, 2006	October 27, 2006	June 01, 2006	July 05, 2006	October 27, 2005	June 23, 2005
Offer price (per share)	3.07	3.12	2.95	3.08	2.35	2.5
IPO proceeds (amount; in billions)	124.95	46.64	82.86	20.00	59.94	14.64
First day return (%)	14.66	5.13	14.41	22.73	0.00	13.00
First week return (%)	16.94	4.81	19.49	19.16	−1.06	13.00
Foreign ownership (%)	7.28	–	14.40	–	14.39	18.33

Note: This table presents information on the IPOs of three of the big four banks and that of BComm. ICBC went IPO in both the HKSE (HK dollar) and the SHSE (RMB), while CCB and BComm (Bank of Communications) listed shares only on the HKSE. First day (first week) return is percentage return of closing price of first day (fifth trading day) over offer price. Foreign ownership indicates size of ownership stakes of foreign institutions and investors at the date of IPOs.

Source: IPO prospectuses submitted to SHSE and HKSE.

(highest rating is Aaa), while S&P rates these banks' outstanding bonds between A and BBB (highest rating is AAA).

To summarize, the optimistic view holds that, despite the large amount of existing NPLs, the current reform of state-owned banks and development of the banking sector have already been effective in reducing NPLs, which is why NPLs have been falling in recent years (2000–2006; Table 14.3a, panel A). Given that the economy will probably maintain its current pace of growth, the government can always write off a large fraction of the rest of the NPLs to avert any serious problems for China. However, the pessimistic view believes that NPLs are much bigger than the official statistics suggest to begin with and that a substantial amount of new NPLs will continue to arise within state-owned banks. Moreover, the reform of the banking sector will not be effective, because it will take a long time before the government relinquishes majority control of state-owned banks. During this period, if the growth of the economy significantly slows down, while the accumulation of NPLs continues, the banking sector problems could lead to a financial crisis. This could spill over into other sectors of the economy and cause a slowdown in growth or a recession. In this view, the NPL problem poses a most serious problem to China's continued prosperity.

Growth of Nonstate Financial Intermediaries

The development of both nonstate banks and other (state and nonstate) financial institutions is crucial for China to have a stable and functioning banking system in the future. In addition to boosting the overall efficiency of the banking system and alleviating the problems of NPLs, these financial institutions provide funding to support the growth of the hybrid sector.

First, we examine and compare China's insurance market to other Asian economies (South Korea, Taiwan, and Singapore). In terms of the ratio of total assets managed by insurance companies over GDP (Figure 14.3c), China's insurance market is significantly smaller than that of other economies. At the end of 2006, total assets managed were still less than 10 percent of GDP (while this ratio for the other three economies is over 30 percent). It is clear that the insurance industry is also significantly undersized compared to China's banking industry, and property insurance is particularly underdeveloped due to the fact that the private real-estate market was only recently established. (In the past, most housing was allocated by employers or the government). Despite the fast growth of insurance coverage and premium income, at the end of 2000 only 1.8 percent of the total population was covered by life insurance (resulting in a per capita premium of only RMB127 per year); coverage ratios for property insurance are even lower (*Almanac of China's Finance and Banking*, 2000). The encouraging news is that coverage ratios have been growing steadily at an average annual rate of 6 percent between 1998 and 2005 (*XinHua News*).

Table 14.4a provides a (partial) breakdown of the different types of banks. During the period of 2001–2004, although the big four banks dominate in every aspect of the banking sector, the role of the non–big four banks in the entire banking sector cannot be ignored. As of 2004, other banks and credit cooperatives' total assets comprise close to 50 percent of the big four (the actual fraction is likely to be higher due to incomplete information on all types of deposit-taking institutions); similar comparisons can be made for outstanding loans. In addition, these banks have less NPLs than the big four banks. Table 14.4b provides evidence on the growth of nonbank intermediaries. Overall, the growth of these nonbank intermediaries has been impressive since the late 1990s. In terms of combined total assets held or managed, the size of all the banks and intermediaries outside of the big four banks (Table 14.4b, first column) is about 60 percent of the big four banks at the end of 2004. Among them, "other commercial banks" (many of them are state owned), RCCs, and TICs hold the largest amount of assets; the size of foreign banks and mutual funds (not listed in the table) is minuscule, and these are likely to be the focus of development in the near future.[15] Finally, our coverage of nonbank financial institutions excludes various forms of informal financial intermediaries, some of which are deemed illegal but overall provide important financing to firms in the hybrid sector.

---

[15] Postal savings (deposit-taking institutions affiliated with local post offices) is another form of nonbank intermediation that is not reported in Table 14.4b due to lack of time series data. However, at the end of 1999, total deposits within the postal savings system exceeded RMB380 billion, or 6.4 percent of all deposits in China.

Table 14.4a. *State-owned and private banks in China*

Types of banks	Total assets	Total deposits	Outstanding loans	Profit	NPL rate (%)
		2004			
Big four banks	16,932.1	14,412.3	10,086.1	–	15.57
Other commercial banks	4,697.2	4,059.9	2,885.9	50.7	4.93
1. Joint equity	–	–	–	–	–
2. City commercial banks	1,693.8	1,434.1	904.5	–	11.73
Foreign banks	515.9	126.4	255.8	18.8	1.34
Urban credit cooperatives	171.5	154.9	97.9	–	–
Rural credit cooperatives	3,101.3	2,734.8	1,974.8	9.65	–
		2003			
Big four banks	16,275.1	13,071.9	9,950.1	196.5	19.74
Other commercial banks	3,816.8	3,286.5	2,368.2	–	7.92
1. Joint equity	–	–	–	–	–
2. City commercial banks	1,465.4	1,174.7	774.4	5.4	14.94
Foreign banks	333.1	90.7	147.6	18.1	2.87
Urban credit cooperatives	148.7	127.1	85.6	0.01	–
Rural credit cooperatives	2,674.6	2,376.5	1,775.9	4.4	–
		2002			
Big four banks	14,450.0	11,840.0	8,460.0	71.0	26.1
Other commercial banks	4,160.0	3,390.0	2,290.0	–	–
1. Joint equity	2,990.0	–	–	–	9.5
2. City commercial banks	1,170.0	–	–	–	17.7
Foreign banks	324.2	–	154.0	15.2	–
Urban credit cooperatives	119.0	101.0	66.4	–	–
Rural credit cooperatives	–	1,987.0	1,393.0	–	–
		2001			
Big four banks	13,000.0	10,770.0	7,400.0	23.0	25.37
Other commercial banks	3,259.0	2,530.7	1,649.8	12.9	–
1. Joint equity	2,386.0	1,849.0	1,224.0	10.5	12.94
2. City commercial banks	873.0	681.7	425.8	2.4	–
Foreign banks	373.4	–	153.2	1.7	–
Urban credit cooperatives	128.7	107.1	72.5	2.6	–
Rural credit cooperatives	–	1,729.8	1,197.0	–	–

Note: Vaues are in RMB billion.

Source: Almanac of China's Finance and Banking (2000–2005).

Table 14.4b. *Comparison of assets held by China's financial intermediaries*

Year	State-owned banks	RCCs	UCCs	Insurance companies	TICs	Nondeposit intermediaries	Other commercial banks	Foreign banks
1995	5,373.34	679.10	303.92	–	458.60	48.97	536.91	42.90
1996	6,582.74	870.66	374.78	–	563.70	82.02	769.98	55.30
1997	7,914.41	1,012.20	498.94	–	636.40	100.42	948.61	75.80
1998	8,860.93	1,143.11	560.63	–	802.50	120.97	1,128.18	118.40
1999	9,970.63	1,239.24	630.15	260.41	907.50	137.08	1,376.89	191.40
2000	10,793.73	1,393.06	678.49	337.39	975.90	160.82	1,828.26	379.20
2001	11,188.22	1,610.80	780.02	459.13	1,088.30	223.67	2,255.70	341.80
2002	13,549.60	2,205.21	119.23	649.41	1,544.10	408.10	2,997.72	317.90
2003	16,275.10	2,674.62	148.72	912.28	–	495.58	3,816.80	331.10
2004	16,932.10	3,103.30	171.50	933.41	–	–	4,697.20	515.90

Note: Values are in RMB billion. This table compares *total assets* held by banks and nonbank intermediaries during the period 1995–2004.
Source: Aggregate Statistics from the PBOC (2000–2006).

FINANCIAL MARKETS AND PUBLICLY TRADED FIRMS

In this section, we examine China's financial markets, including both the stock and bond markets, and the recent addition of venture capital and private equity markets. We also compare, at the aggregate level, how firms raise funds in China and in other emerging economies through external markets to determine if China's experience in terms of a firm's fund-raising is unique. We then focus on publicly traded companies and examine their financing and investment decisions. Finally, we discuss how to further develop financial markets as well as improve corporate governance and the performance of listed firms.

Stock Exchanges and Market Inefficiencies

After the inception of China's domestic stock exchanges, the SHSE and SZSE, in 1990, they initially grew quickly. The high growth rates continued in most of the 1990s, and the market reached its peak by the end of 2000. The momentum of the market then reversed during the next five years as it went through a major correction with half of the market capitalization lost. Interestingly, most of the losses were recovered in 2006 and the market reached new heights at the end of 2006. While the rise of the market slowed down during the first half of 2007 as compared to 2006, many observers predict that the bullish market will continue during the second half of 2007 and into 2008. Figure 14.4 compares the performance of some of the major stock exchanges around the world, as measured by the buy-and-hold return in the period 1992–2006 (gross return at the end of 2006 with $1 invested in each of the valued-weighted stock indexes at the end of 1992). While the performance of the value-weighted SHSE index (the calculation for the SZSE is very similar) is better than that of FTSE (London) and the Nikkei Index, whose poor performance was caused by the prolonged recession of the Japanese economy in the 1990s, the SHSE underperforms the S&P 500 and the SBE (India), the best performing market index of the group. Since China's economy was growing at much higher rates than the United States during the period (10.1 percent per annum for China versus 3.0 percent for the United States in real terms), the fact that the SHSE index underperformed the S&P index suggests that listed firms are among the low-quality firms in China.

At the end of 2005, the *combined* total market capitalization of the SHSE and SZSE ranked fifteenth among the largest stock exchanges in the world. However, a significant fraction of all the shares is not traded. The HKSE, where selected firms from Mainland China can now be listed and traded, is ranked tenth in the world by itself. In addition, there are two other markets established to complement the main exchanges. First, a fully electronically operated market ("*Er Ban Shi Chang*" or "second-tier market," similar to the NASDAQ) for small and medium enterprises (SMEs) was opened in June 2004. It was designed to lower the entry barriers for SME firms, especially newly established firms in the high-tech industries. There are currently (by the end of February 2007) 119 firms listed in this market. Second, a

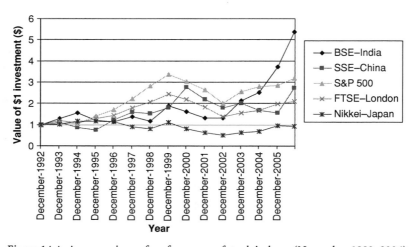

Figure 14.4. A comparison of performance of stock indexes (November 1992–2006)

"third-tier market" ("*San Ban Shi Chang*") was established to deal primarily with delisted firms and other over-the-counter (OTC) transactions. Since 2001, some publicly listed firms on both SHSE and SZSE that do not meet the listing standards have been delisted and the trading of their shares shifted to this market.

China's stock markets are not efficient in that prices and investors' behavior are not necessarily driven by fundamental values of listed firms. For example, Morck, Yeung, and Yu (2000) find that stock prices are more "synchronous" (stock prices move up and down together) in emerging countries, including China, than in developed countries. They attribute this phenomenon to poor minority investor protection and imperfect regulation of markets in emerging markets. With a large data set of individual trading, Feng and Seasholes (2004) find that buy and sell trades are highly correlated (occur at the same time period, such as in the same day) in China, especially among investors who conduct their trades near one of the two stock exchanges or near firms' headquarters.

In addition, there have been numerous lawsuits against insider trading and manipulation. A good case study is the rise and fall of Guangxia Industry Co., Ltd, dubbed as "China's Enron." Located in Ningxia Province, one of the poorest areas of China, Guangxia was listed on the SZSE in 1994 as a manufacturer of floppy disks and related products. After experiencing poor and deteriorating performance in its original line of business and other diversifying new lines of businesses for the first five years, the company reported unprecedented high earnings per share (EPS) at the end of 1999 and claimed that they had mastered the techniques of CO_2 fluid extraction and signed a multiple-year sales contract with a German company. Subsequently, the company's stock price shot up from RMB14 to RMB76 in one year and realized an annual return of 440 percent, highest among all listed companies in either stock exchange in 2000. After an article was published in *Caijing*

Magazine (*Finance and Economics Magazine*, August 3, 2001) that blew the whistle on the "star" company, the Chinese Securities Regulatory Commission (CSRC) launched an investigation and found that the reported earnings as well as many sales records and contracts, including the one with the German company, were fabricated, and in fact the company continued losing money in its businesses. The most damaging fact from this case is that, unlike Enron, Guangxia's managers and other insiders did not use any sophisticated accounting and finance maneuvers to mask their losses (even by China's standards). The company's top executives were criminally charged and its auditors lost their licenses, while shareholders' lawsuits were eventually processed by courts for the first time in the country.

The earlier example also reveals that the inefficiencies in the Chinese stock markets can be attributed to poor and ineffective regulation. The current process of listing companies fosters both a problem of adverse selection among firms seeking an IPO and a moral hazard problem among listed firms. First, even though there is no explicit regulation or law against the listing of firms from the hybrid sector, the going public process strongly favors former SOEs with connections with government officials. For example, until recently each candidate firm must apply and obtain listing quota/permission from the government; all candidate firms must (and still do) disclose financial and accounting information and are subject to a lengthy evaluation process. The process is inefficient due to bureaucracy, fraudulent disclosure, and lack of independent auditing. As a result, most of the listed firms are indeed former SOEs. Second, once listed, managers in firms with severe agency problems do not have an incentive to manage assets to grow, but rather to rely on the external capital markets to raise funds – mainly through mergers and acquisitions (M&As) and seasoned offerings of securities – to pursue private benefits. (For more case studies to illustrate the earlier problems, see Allen, Qian, and Qian, 2005a.)

Overview of Bond Markets

Table 14.5a provides information on China's bond markets. The government bond market had an annual growth rate of 26.9 percent during the period 1990–2005 in terms of newly issued bonds, while total outstanding bonds reached RMB2,877.4 billion (or U.S.$360 billion) at the end of 2005.[16] The second largest component of the bond market is called "policy financial bonds" (total outstanding amount RMB1,781.8 billion, or $223 billion at the end of 2005). These bonds are issued by "policy banks," which operate under the supervision of the Ministry of Finance, and the proceeds of bond issuance are invested in government-run projects and

---

[16] During most of the period 1988–2003, Moody's rated China's government bonds (foreign currency) A2 or A3 (lower than Aa3 and A1, but higher than Baa1; highest rating is Aaa) with a "positive" or "stable" outlook, while the rating on bank deposits (foreign currency ceilings) was Baa, at or above the "investment" grade. These ratings are better than or comparable to Moody's ratings on government bonds from most emerging economies.

Table 14.5a. *China's bond markets: 1990–2005*

Year	Treasury bonds			Policy financial bonds			Corporate bonds		
	Amount issued	Redemption amount	Balance	Amount issued	Redemption amount	Balance	Amounts issued	Redemption amount	Balance
1990	19.72	7.62	89.03	6.44	5.01	8.49	12.4	7.73	19.54
1991	28.13	11.16	106.00	6.69	3.37	11.81	24.9	11.43	33.11
1992	46.08	23.81	128.27	5.50	3.00	14.31	68.37	19.28	82.20
1993	38.13	12.33	154.07	0.00	3.43	10.88	23.58	25.55	80.24
1994	113.76	39.19	228.64	0.00	1.35	9.53	16.18	28.20	68.21
1995	151.09	49.70	330.03	–	–	170.85	30.08	33.63	64.66
1996	184.78	78.66	436.14	105.56	25.45	250.96	26.89	31.78	59.77
1997	241.18	126.43	550.89	143.15	31.23	362.88	25.52	21.98	52.10
1998	380.88	206.09	776.57	195.02	32.04	512.11	15.00	10.53	67.69
1999	401.50	123.87	1,054.20	180.09	47.32	644.75	15.82	5.65	77.86
2000	465.70	152.50	1,367.40	164.50	70.92	738.33	8.30	0.00	86.16
2001	488.40	228.60	1,561.80	259.00	143.88	853.45	14.70	0.00	100.86
2002	593.43	226.12	1,933.60	307.50	155.57	1,005.41	32.50	0.00	133.36
2003	628.01	275.58	2,260.36	456.14	250.53	1,165.00	35.80	0.00	169.16
2004	692.39	374.99	2,577.76	414.80	177.87	1,401.93	32.70	0.00	201.86
2005	704.20	104.55	2,877.40	385.17	205.30	1,781.80	204.65	3.70	401.81
Growth rate (%)	26.90	19.10	26.10	31.40	28.10	42.80	20.40	–4.80	22.30

Note: Amount in RMB billion. This table presents the development of China's bond markets. "Policy Financial Bonds" are issued by "policy banks," which belong to the Ministry of Finance, and the proceeds of bond issuance are invested in government-run projects and industries such as infrastructure construction (similar to municipal bonds in the United States).

Source: Aggregate statistics from the PBOC (2000–2006) and the Statistical Yearbook of China (2000–2006).

538

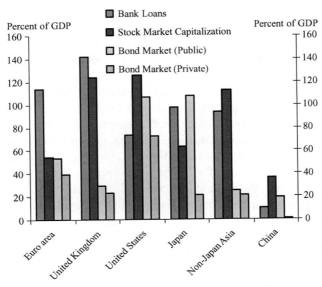

Figure 14.5. A comparison of financial markets in 2003 *Notes*: (a) Bank loans are domestic credit extended to the hybrid sector in China and to the private sector in all other countries. All bank loan data, except Taiwan, are reported in line thirty-two in the International Financial Statistics, September 2003. (b) All outstanding bond data are as of end 2003, except for Japan and Singapore (end 2002 for 2003), Indonesia (end 2000 for 2003), and the Philippines (end 1999 for 2003). (c) Bond figures for Hong Kong, Korea, Malaysia, Taiwan, the United States, the United Kingdom, and Japan are from central banks. Figures for Indonesia and the Philippines are from IFC Emerging Markets Information Centre Database. Figures for Thailand are from Thai Bond Dealing Centre. Figures for Singapore are from estimates based on data from MAS and Thomson Financial. (d) Public sector refers to government bodies and quasigovernment entities; private sector refers to nonpublic sector and includes financial institutions, corporations, and overseas institutions. (e) Bank loans (total amount and percentage of GDP) in the Euro area refer to end 2002 for 2003. (f) Euro area includes Austria, Belgium, Finland, France, Germany, Greece, Ireland, Italy, Netherlands, Portugal, and Spain; non-Japan Asia includes Hong Kong, Korea, Malaysia, Taiwan, Singapore, Indonesia, Philippines, and Thailand.
Sources: Based on figures in Allen, Chui, and Maddaloni, 2004. Direct sources include International Financial Statistics, International Federation of Stock Exchanges, Japan Securities Dealers Association, IFC Bond Database, Thai Bond Dealing Centre, Thomson Financial, CEIC, and various central banks, ECB. *Statistics Yearbook of China*, 2003–2004.

industries, such as infrastructure construction (similar to municipal bonds in the United States). Compared to government-issued bonds, the size of the corporate bond market is minuscule: in terms of the amount of outstanding bonds at the end of 2005, the corporate bond market is less than one-eleventh of the size of the government bond market.

In fact, the underdevelopment of the bond market, especially the corporate bond market, relative to the stock market, is common among Asian countries. In Figure 14.5 we compare different components (bank loans to private sectors or the hybrid sector of China, stock market capitalization, and public/government and private/corporate bond markets; information for all other countries and regions except China is from Allen, Chui, and Maddaloni (2004)) of the financial markets around the world at the end of 2003. First, compared to Europe and the United States, the size of both the government (public) and corporate (private) bond markets is smaller in Asia, excluding Japan (Hong Kong, South Korea, Malaysia, Taiwan, Singapore, Indonesia, Philippines, and Thailand); even in Japan, the size of the corporate bond market is much smaller compared with its government bond market. Second, consistent with previous evidence, the size of all four components of China's financial markets is small relative to that of other regions and countries, including bank loans made to the hybrid sector (private sector) in China (other countries). Moreover, the most underdeveloped component of China's financial markets is the corporate bond market (labeled "private" bond market).

There are a number of reasons for the underdevelopment of bond markets in China and other parts of Asia (see, e.g., Herring and Chatusripitak, 2000). Lack of a sound accounting/auditing system and high-quality bond-rating agencies is an important factor. Given low creditor protection and court inefficiency (in China and most other emerging economies), the recovery rates for bondholders during default are low, which in turn leads to underinvestment in the market (by domestic and foreign investors). Lack of a well-constructed yield curve is another important factor in China. Given the small size of the publicly traded Treasury bond market and lack of historical prices, we can plot only "snapshots" of a partial yield curve (maturities range from one month to one year only) based on pricing data of Treasury bonds in the national interbank market. This is far from the standard yield curve covering interest rates on bond maturities ranging from one month to ten years. The deficiencies in the term structure of interest rates hamper the development of derivatives markets that enable firms and investors to manage risk, as well as the effectiveness of the government's macroeconomic policies. Therefore, it is important that China develop its bond markets in the near future along with its legal system and related institutions.

Fund-Raising through Financial Markets and International Comparison

First, we briefly examine the role of financial markets in helping firms raise funds (Table 14.5b). Both the scale and the relative importance (compared with other channels of financing) of China's financial markets for finance from outside the firm (as of the end of 2002), or external capital as it is called in the literature, are not significant. For example, for the ratio of external capital and GNP, the La Porta et al. (1997a) sample average is 40 percent, compared to China's 16 percent (using only the floating supply part of the stock market, rather than the total market capitalization). For the ratio of total debt (including bank loans and bonds) over GNP, the La Porta et al. sample average is 59 percent, compared to China's 35 percent. However, if we include all debt, including bank loans, issued to all

Table 14.5b. *A comparison of external (outside the firm) capital markets (mean)*

Country	English-origin average	French-origin average	German-origin average	Scandinavian-origin average	La Porta et al. sample average	China (2002)[a]
External capital/GNP	0.6	0.21	0.46	0.3	0.4	**0.49 (0.16)**[a]
Domestic Firms/Pop[b]	35.45	10	16.79	27.26	21.59	**0.93**
IPOs/Population[c]	2.23	0.19	0.12	2.14	1.02	**0.05**
Total Debt/GNP	0.68	0.45	0.97	0.57	0.59	**0.35**
GDP growth (one year)	4.3	3.18	5.29	2.42	3.79	**6.77**
Rule of law[d]	6.46	6.05	8.68	10	6.85	**5**
Antidirector rights[e]	3.39	1.76	2	2.5	2.44	**3**
One share = one vote[f]	0.22	0.24	0.33	0	0.22	**1**
Creditor rights[g]	3.11	1.58	2.33	2	2.3	**2**

Note: This table compares the size of external markets and the strength of investor protection in China versus those in the La Porta et al. (1997a) sample countries, sorted by countries' legal origin. Data for La Porta et al. countries are obtained from La Porta et al. (1997a), while data on China, as of the end of 2002, are obtained from the Almanac of China's Finance and Banking.

[a] The figure in the bracket (0.16) is calculated using the floating supply (or value traded) portion of the total market capitalization to account for external capital.

[b] Listed domestic firms per million population.

[c] Number of IPOs per million population.

[d] Measures strength of tradition of law and order from zero (low) to 10 (high).

[e] Measures the protection of minority shareholder rights from zero (low) to 5 (high).

[f] Dummy variable equals one if each share of common stock carries one vote.

[g] Measures the protection of creditors during reorganization or bankruptcy from zero (low) to 4 (high).

Sources: La Porta et al. (1997a), Almanac of China's Finance and Banking (2003), the 1986 trial version of China's Bankruptcy Law, and the 1999 Company Law.

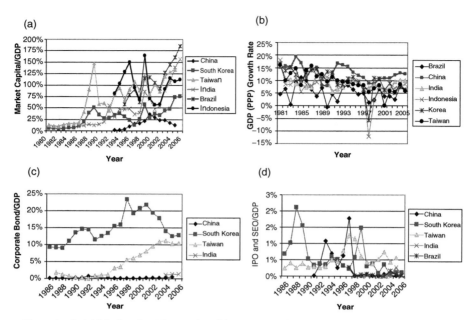

Figure 14.6. (a) Market Cap/GNP ratios; (b) GDP growth rates; (c) Corporate bond market; (d) Equity issuance

Figure 14.6a compares the time series of stock market capitalization/GDP ratios across six emerging economies. Figure 14.6b compares time series of the growth rates of GDP, and the growth area are calculated using PPP-adjusted GDP figures to avoid biases caused by different currency policies. Figure 14.6c presents the time series of the ratios of the amount of corporate bonds outstanding/GNP, while Figure 14.6d presents the time series of IPO and SEO (in a given year)/GDP. The calculations for all the ratios in Figures 14.6a, 14.6c, and 14.6d are based on local currencies of a country in a given year.

sectors including the state sector, this ratio increases to 79 percent, suggesting that the majority of debt does not go through the capital markets, which is consistent with evidence on bank credit.

Next, we compare, at the aggregate level, external financing (i.e., financing from outside the firm) in China and other major emerging economies. We also relate the aggregate financing channels with the growth of the economy during different periods, to determine whether the Chinese experience in financing is unique. First, Figure 14.6a compares the development of stock markets at the aggregate level, while Figure 14.6b compares the growth rates of (purchasing-power parity adjusted) GDP. Both Taiwan and South Korea experienced high GDP growth in the 1970s and early 1980s, while the total market capitalization of their respective stock markets accounted for less than 20 percent of their GNPs during the same period, and the growth of stock markets did not take off until the mid- to late 1980s. Figure 14.6c compares the growth of corporate bond markets: South Korea has the fastest growth path, while in Taiwan and China the corporate bond markets seem to lag the development of stock markets. Finally, Figure 14.6d compares total equity issuance, including initial public offerings (IPOs) and seasoned equity offerings (SEOs). With the exception of South Korea, China seems to be on similar pace in terms of size of equity issuance (as fraction of GNP in a given year) with Taiwan, India, and Brazil.

From the earlier comparisons it is clear that the development of China's external markets relative to its overall economic growth is not dramatically different from other emerging countries. One of the common patterns is that the development of external markets trails that of the growth of the overall economy. During the early stages of economic growth, alternative institutions and mechanisms can support the growth of firms and the overall economy, as is the case for China based on our evidence. Perhaps similar institutions have worked well in other emerging and developed economies as well.

Evidence on the Listed Sector

In this section, we examine publicly listed and traded companies in China. It is worthwhile to first clarify whether firms from the hybrid sector can become listed and publicly traded. Regulations and laws (the 1986 trial version of the Bankruptcy Law and the 1999 version of the Company Law) never prohibit the listing of hybrid sector firms, and selected firms from the hybrid sector enter the listed sector through an IPO or acquiring a listed firm from the inception of SHSE and SZSE. However, the accessibility of equity markets for these firms has been much lower than those for former SOEs in practice due to the enforcement of the listing standards and process. As a result, Allen, Qian, and Qian (2005b) find that 80 percent of their sample of more than 1,100 listed firms is converted from former SOEs. In recent years, the government has attempted to change the composition of listed firms by relaxing regulations toward hybrid sector firms.

Until recently, listed firms in China issued both tradable and nontradable shares (Table 14.6a). The nontradable shares were held either by the government or by other state-owned legal entities (i.e., other listed or nonlisted firms or organizations). Among the tradable shares, Class A and B shares are listed and traded in either the SHSE or the SZSE, while Class A (B) shares are issued to and traded by Chinese investors (foreign investors including those from Taiwan and Hong Kong and QFIIs). While the two share classes issued by the same firm are identical in terms of shareholder rights (e.g., voting and dividend), Class B shares were traded at a significant discount relative to A shares and are traded less frequently than A shares.[17] The "B share discount" has been reduced significantly since the CSRC

---

[17] Explanations of the B share discount include (1) foreign investors facing higher information asymmetry than domestic investors, (2) lower B share prices compensating for the lack of liquidity (due to low trading volume), and (3) the A share premium reflecting a speculative bubble component among domestic investors. See Chan, Menkveld, and Yang (2007) and Mei, Scheinkman, and Xiong (2003) for more details.

Table 14.6a. *Types of common stock issued in China*

Tradable?		Definition
No (private block transfer possible)	**State-owned shares**[a] **(G shares tradable after reform)**	Shares that are controlled by the central government during the process in which firms are converted into a limited liability corporation but before being listed. These shares are either managed and represented by the State-owned Assets Supervision and Administration Commission or held by other state-owned companies. Both types of organizations also appoint board members to firms' boards. After reforms announced in 2005 and implemented in 2006–2007 state shares became G shares and are tradable
	Entrepreneurs' shares	Shares reserved for firms' founders during the same process described earlier; different from shares that founders can purchase and sell in the markets
	Foreign owners	Shares owned by foreign industrial investors during the same process
	Legal entity holders	Shares sold to legal entities (such as other companies, listed or nonlisted) during the same process
	Employee shares	Shares sold to firms' employees during the same process
Yes (newly issued shares)	**A shares**	Shares issued by Chinese companies that are listed and traded in the Shanghai or Shenzhen Stock Exchange; most of these shares are sold to and held by Chinese (citizen) investors
	B shares	Shares issued by Chinese companies that are listed and traded in the Shanghai or Shenzhen Stock Exchange; these shares are sold to and held by foreign investors; starting 2001 Chinese investors can also trade these shares
	H shares	Shares issued by selected Chinese companies listed and traded in the HKSE; these shares can only be traded on the HK Exchange but can be held by anyone

[a] There are subcategories under this definition.

allowed Chinese citizens to trade B shares (with foreign currency accounts) in 2001. In addition, Class H shares, issued by selected "red-chip" Chinese companies, are listed and traded on the HKSE. Finally, there are N shares and S shares for firms listed in the United States and Singapore but operated in China. (We omit discussion of these shares since they are not listed on the domestic exchanges.) After

Table 14.6b. *Tradable versus nontradable shares for China's listed companies*

Year	State/total shares	Nontradable[a]/total shares	Tradable/total shares	A/total shares	A/tradable shares[b]
1992	0.41	0.69	0.31	0.16	0.52
1993	0.49	0.72	0.28	0.16	0.57
1994	0.43	0.67	0.33	0.21	0.64
1995	0.39	0.64	0.36	0.21	0.60
1996	0.35	0.65	0.35	0.22	0.62
1997	0.32	0.65	0.35	0.23	0.66
1998	0.34	0.66	0.34	0.24	0.71
1999	0.36	0.65	0.35	0.26	0.75
2000	0.39	0.64	0.36	0.28	0.80
2001	0.39	0.64	0.36	0.29	0.80
2002	n.a.	0.65	0.35	0.26	0.74
2003	n.a.	0.64	0.35	0.27	0.76
2004	n.a.	0.64	0.36	0.28	0.77
2005	n.a.	0.62	0.38	0.30	0.78
2006 (June)	n.a.	0.57	0.43	0.35	0.81

[a] Nontradable shares include "state owned" and "shares owned by legal entities."
[b] Tradable shares include A, B, and H shares.
Source: China Securities Regulatory Commission Reports (2000–2006) and http://www.csrc.gov.cn.

Table 14.6c. *Ownership and control in the listed firms of China*

Shareholder type	Ownership	Control (board seats)
State	24	21
Legal person	44	48
Employees	2	3
Tradable shares	30	4
TOTAL	100	76

Note: Values are in percent.
Source: Table 4.6, p. 83, "Corporate Governance and Enterprise Reform in China, Building the institutions of Modern Market," 2002, World Bank publication.

the reforms discussed later in the section on "Further Development of Financial Markets," government shares became G shares and are tradable.

Table 14.6b demonstrates that nontradable shares constituted a majority of all shares and most of these shares were held by the state, while the majority of tradable shares were A shares. Table 14.6c provides some evidence on the relation between ownership and control of the board of directors.[18] Consistent with Tables 14.6a and 14.6b and the "one-share, one-vote" scheme adopted by firms in the listed sector, shareholders, including the state and legal person shareholders (which typically own the majority of shares), appoint the board members.

We next describe standard corporate governance mechanisms in the listed sector. First, according to the (2006) Company Law, listed firms in China have a two-tier board structure: the board of directors (five to nineteen members) and the board of supervisors (at least three members), with supervisors ranking above directors. The main duty of the board of supervisors is to monitor firms' operations as well as top managers and directors; it consists of representatives of shareholders and employees, with the rest either officials chosen from government branches or executives from the parent companies; directors and top managers of the firms cannot hold positions as supervisors. The board of directors serves similar duties as its counterparts in the United States, including appointing and firing CEOs. The chairman (one person) and vice chairman (one or two) of the board are elected by all directors (majority votes); with the approval of the board, the CEO and other top managers can become members of the board. The CSRC requires at least one-third (a minimum of two people) of the board to be independent.

Though the Company Law stipulates that board members are elected through shareholder meetings, in practice some directors are nominated and appointed by the firms' parent companies and the nomination process is usually kept secret (as shown in Table 14.6c, in particular for former SOEs). Since not all members of either board are elected by shareholders, a major problem with the board structure is the appointment of and contracting with the CEOs. Fan, Wong, and Zhang (2007) find that almost one-third of their sample of 625 listed companies' CEOs are either current or former government bureaucrats; the performance of these firms is significantly worse than that of other firms without politically connected CEOs. Based on firm-level compensation data (available since 1998 due to disclosure requirements), Fung, Firth, and Rui (2003) and Kato and Long (2004) find that no listed firms grant stock options to CEOs or board members, while the cash-based compensation level for CEOs is much lower than that for their counterparts in developed countries, and the consumption of perks, such as company cars, is prevalent.

Second, the existing ownership structure, characterized by the large amount of nontradable shares including cross holdings of shares among listed companies and institutions, makes it difficult to carry out value-increasing M&As. According to the *China Mergers and Acquisitions Yearbook* (2004), there were 925 M&As, involving listed firms in 2003 totaling U.S.$9.35 billion, only 1.8 percent of the total market

---

[18]   Information provided in Table 14.6c and on corporate governance is based on a survey of 257 SHSE-listed firms conducted in 2000 by Integrity Management Consulting and the Research Center of SHSE, "Corporate Governance and Enterprise Reform in China: Building the Institutions of Modern Market" (Tenev, Zhang, and Brefort, 2002, the World Bank, and Schipani and Liu 2002).

capitalization. In many deals, a hybrid sector firm (nonlisted) acquires a listed firm that is converted from an SOE, but the large amount of nontradable shares held by the state remains intact after the transaction.[19] Such an acquisition can be the means through which low-quality, nonlisted companies bypass listing standards and access financial markets.

Third, an important factor contributing to the occurrence of corporate scandals is the lack of institutional investors (including nondepository financial intermediaries), as they are a very recent addition to the set of financial institutions in China. Professional investors would perhaps not be so easily taken in by simple deceptions. Another factor is that the enforcement of laws is questionable due to the lack of legal professionals and institutions. For example, ineffective bankruptcy implementation makes the threat and penalty for bad firm performance noncredible.[20] As mentioned earlier, the implementation of the new Bankruptcy Law, including the addition of court-appointed trustees to overseeing the bankruptcy procedure, is expected to enhance the protection of creditor rights and expedite the procedure.

Fourth, the government plays the dual roles of regulator and blockholder for many listed firms, including banks and financial services companies. The main role of the CSRC (counterpart of the Securities and Exchange Commission in the United States) is to monitor and regulate stock exchanges and listed companies. The government exercises its shareholder control rights in listed firms through the Assets Supervision and Administration Commission of the State Council or local governments, which hold large fractions of nontradable shares, or other SOEs (with their holdings of nontradable shares). However, since the top officials of the Commission are government officials, it is doubtful that they will pursue their fiduciary role as control shareholders diligently. Moreover, the government's dual roles can lead to conflicting goals (maximizing profits as shareholder versus maximizing social welfare as regulator or social planner) in dealing with listed firms, which in turn weaken its effectiveness in both of its roles.[21] There are cases in which the government, aiming to achieve certain social goals, influenced the markets through

---

[19] If we include the cross-border M&As and transactions between parent companies and subsidiaries, the total amount increases to U.S.$47 billion in 2000, $14 billion in 2001, $29 billion in 2002, and $24 billion in the first three quarters of 2003. Sixty-eight percent of all M&A deals (66 percent in terms of dollar deal amount) are initiated by hybrid sector firms, while former SOEs and foreign firms initiate 29 percent and 3 percent of the rest, respectively (27 percent and 7 percent in deal amount). M&As are most active in coastal regions and in industries such as machinery, information technology, retail, and gas and oil.

[20] Cross-country information on the efficiency of bankruptcy procedures, based on surveys of lawyers and bankruptcy judges around the world, is available from the World Bank (http://rru.worldbank.org/Doingbusiness). Among 108 countries, China's "goals of insolvency" index is equal to the median of the sample.

[21] Gordon and Li (2003) show that the ownership structure (with large state ownership stakes) can be attributed to government collecting monopoly rents from investors and subsidizing listed firms that were formerly SOEs. However, they argue that this behavior is not as efficient as explicit taxes on investors.

state-owned institutional investors (e.g., AMCs) but created unintended adverse effects.

Overall, internal and external governance for the listed sector is weak, and further development of governance mechanisms is one of the main objectives for this sector going forward. In the section on "Further Development of Financial Markets" later we provide some general suggestions. In addition, Allen, Qian, and Qian (2005a) show that the dividend ratio, valuation (Tobin's Q), and post-IPO performance of listed firms in China are much lower or worse compared to similar firms operating in countries with stronger investor protections. In summary, the overall evidence on the comparison of China and other countries' external markets and listed firms is consistent with La Porta et al. (1997a, 1998) predictions: with an underdeveloped legal system and weak investor (both shareholder and creditor) protection, China's small markets for finance from outside the firm and low quality of listed firms come as no surprise.

Private Equity/Venture Capital and the Funding of New Industries

Allen and Gale (1999, 2000a) have suggested that stock-market–based economies, such as the United Kingdom in the nineteenth century and the United States in the twentieth century, have been more successful in developing *new* industries than intermediary-based economies, such as Germany and Japan. They argue that markets are better than banks for funding new industries, because evaluation of these industries based on experience is difficult, and there is wide diversity of opinion. Stock-market–based economies such as the United States and United Kingdom also tend to have well-developed systems for the acquisition and distribution of information, so the cost of information to investors is low. Markets then work well because investors can gather information at low cost and those that anticipate high profits can provide the finance to the firms operating in the new industries.

An important part of this process is the private equity/venture capital sector (see, e.g., Kortum and Lerner, 2000). Venture capitalists are able to raise large amounts of funds in the United States because of the prospect that successful firms will be able to undertake an IPO. With data from twenty-one countries, Jeng and Wells (2000) find that venture capital is less important in other countries, while the existence of an active IPO market is the critical determinant of the importance of venture capital in a country. This is consistent with the finding of Black and Gilson (1998), in a comparison of the United States and Germany, that the primary reason venture capital is relatively successful in the United States is the active IPO market that exists there. Allen, Qian, and Qian (2005a) provide detailed information on the fast-growing private equity/venture capital sector in China.

The reason that China should develop active venture capital and private equity markets is to provide financing for new industries. What is unusual about China (perhaps along with India) is that it currently has the ability to develop both traditional industries, such as manufacturing, and in the near future new, high-tech industries, such as aerospace, computer software, semiconductors, and biogenetics. This is different from the experience of South Korea and Taiwan in the 1970s and that of most other emerging economies in the 1990s, as all these other countries focused on developing manufacturing industries first. In terms of developing traditional industries (e.g., Korea and Taiwan in the 1970s), China has already followed suit in first introducing advanced (relative to domestic companies) but not the most advanced technologies from developed countries and "nationalizing" these technologies within designated companies before moving toward the more advanced technologies. Allen and Gale (1999, 2000a) argue that banks are better than financial markets for funding mature industries because there is wide agreement on how they should be managed, so the delegation of the investment decision to a bank works well. This delegation process, and the economies of scale in information acquisition through delegation, makes bank-based systems more efficient in terms of financing the growth in these industries. Therefore, the banking system can contribute more in supporting the growth and development of these industries than markets.

Further Development of Financial Markets

As we have documented, the financial markets in China do not currently play nearly as important a role as banks. Going forward, if China wishes to develop high-technology industries, as discussed in the section on "Private Equity/Venture Capital and the Funding of New Industries," then it is important that it improves its financial markets. In addition, if it is to enlarge risk management possibilities for its financial institutions and firms, it needs to develop new financial products and markets. Finally, if there is to be an alternative to banks for raising large amounts of capital, then China needs deep and efficient markets.

In recent years, the performance of the stock markets has been volatile. This is somewhat surprising, given the robust performance of the real economy. We attribute this (relatively) poor performance to a number of factors including the following:

1. limited self-regulation and formal regulation,
2. the large overhang of shares owned by government entities,
3. the lack of listed firms originating in the hybrid sector,
4. the lack of trained professionals,
5. the lack of institutional investors, and
6. limited financial markets and products.

It is important that these weaknesses be overcome. However, some of these are problems that must be tackled over the long run. They cannot be solved in a few years. We discuss each in turn.

Improve Regulations

There are two ways in which markets are regulated in practice and each has advantages and disadvantages: first, market forces and self-regulation, and second, government regulation.

A good example of regulation through market forces and self-regulation is provided by the capital markets in the United Kingdom in the nineteenth and early twentieth century (Michie, 1987). The role of government regulation and intervention was minimal. Despite this, the markets did extremely well and London became the financial capital of the world. Many firms and countries from all over the world raised large amounts of funds. Reputation and trust were an important factor in the smooth operation of these markets. For example, in an important paper, Franks, Mayer, and Rossi (2003) compare the early twentieth century capital markets with those in the mid-twentieth century. Despite extensive changes in the laws protecting minority shareholders, there was very little change in the ways in which the market operated. The authors attribute this to the importance of trust.

We later argue that China's hybrid sector is another example of a situation where market forces are effective. Formal regulation and legal protections do not have much impact, and yet financing and governance mechanisms are quite effective. In this case, as we shall see, it appears that competition, as well as reputation and trust, works well.

In contrast, the examples of fraud and other problems of manipulation and the inefficiency of markets pointed to in the section on "Stock Exchanges and Market Inefficiencies" suggest that in China's formal financial markets, these alternative mechanisms do not work well. Although such mechanisms may develop in the long run as in the nineteenth- and early twentieth-century United Kingdom, it seems that in the short run at least it is likely to require formal government regulation of the type developed in the United States in the 1930s and subsequently as a response to the stock market collapse that started in 1929 and the Great Depression. There is evidence from many countries that this type of formal regulation is effective. For example, based on a study of security laws with the focus on the public issuance of new equity in forty-nine countries (China is not included), La Porta, Lopez-de-Silanes, and Shleifer (2006) find that disclosure and liability rules help to promote stock market development.

Sale of Government Shares in Listed Firms

One of the major problems Chinese stock markets has faced in recent years has been caused by the large amount of shares in listed companies owned by the government and government entities shown in Table 14.6b. The Chinese government attempted sales of state shares of selected firms in 1999 and 2001, but halted the process both times after share prices plunged and investors grew panicky about the value of the entire market. This overhang created great uncertainty about the quantity of shares that would come onto the market going forward. This uncertainty was probably in part responsible for the stagnation of share prices between 2002 and 2005 despite the very high levels of growth in the economy.

In 2005 the government announced a new plan of "fully floating" state shares. Under the new plan, the remaining state shares among listed firms are converted to "G" shares. The CSRC outlines the format for compensating existing shareholders and also imposes lockups and restrictions on the amount of G shares that can be sold immediately after they become tradable. The details of the "fully floating plan" for a firm, including the number of G shares to be granted to each Class A shareholder and the time window (e.g., one to three years) for G shares to become fully floating, must be approved by two-thirds of Class A shareholders of the firm.

Three remarks for the sales of state shares are in order. First, the government's commitment to the plan is superior to a series of partially unanticipated trials that are subject to termination if a significantly negative market reaction is observed. Second, while under the current plan the full floating of all G shares may only take a few years (if this is what the majority of shareholders of all firms desire) and hence may trigger some volatility, the plan does compensate Class A shareholders for the negative price impact and allows them to decide on the timing of the floating. Third, there is some uncertainty as to whether firms will sell at the same time or not. If they do sell simultaneously then there may be a lack of overall liquidity and this may induce volatility in the markets. Time will tell the extent to which this will be a problem.

Encourage Listing of Firms from the Hybrid Sector

One of the major problems of the stock exchanges is that most of the firms listed are former SOEs. Relatively few are firms from the more dynamic hybrid sector. A high priority for reform for the markets is changing of listing requirements to make it advantageous for dynamic and successful companies to become listed on the exchanges.

Train More Professionals

This is the most important factor in terms of improving the enforcement of laws and contracts. First, an independent and efficient judicial system requires a sufficient supply of qualified legal professionals. The Ministry of Justice of China states that there are 110,000 lawyers and 9,000 law firms as of 2002, while Orts (2001) estimates that there are 150,000 lawyers in China, roughly the same number of licensed attorneys as in the state of California. Lawyers represent only 10–25 percent of all clients in civil and business cases, and even in criminal prosecutions, lawyers represent defendants in only half of the cases. Among the approximately 5 million business enterprises in China, only 4 percent currently have regular legal advisers. Moreover, only one-fifth of all lawyers in China have law degrees, and even a lower fraction of judges have formally studied law at a university or college. As mentioned before, a similar situation exists for auditors and accounting professionals.

Encourage the Development of Institutional Investors

In most developed stock markets, institutional investors, such as insurance companies, pension funds, mutual funds, and hedge funds, play an important role. They employ well-trained professionals who are able to evaluate companies well. This causes markets to have a higher degree of efficiency than if they are dominated by individual investors. In addition, there can be advantages in terms of corporate governance if institutional investors actively participate in the monitoring of firms' managers and are directly involved in firms' decision-making process as blockholders of stocks. For example, in the United States, pension funds such as CALPERS have become the symbol of shareholder activism that strengthens corporate governance, while in Japan and Germany, financial intermediaries serve similar purposes. For China, an effective way to improve the efficiency of China's stock markets as well as corporate governance of listed firms is to encourage further development of domestic financial intermediaries that can act as institutional investors. With their large-scale capital and expertise in all relevant areas of business, financial intermediaries can provide a level of stability and professionalism that is sorely lacking in China's financial markets.

Currently, institutional investors such as insurance companies, mutual funds and pension funds are relatively small in terms of assets held, given their early stage of development. However, they are expanding dramatically. For example, the sum of all mutual funds' net assets values reached RMB8.6 trillion (or $1.08 trillion) at the end of 2006. One way to further encourage the development of such intermediaries is to give tax advantages to various types of products, such as life insurance and pension-related savings and investments.

Develop More Financial Products and Markets

Another issue is to develop more financial products so that investors can form diversified portfolios with more than just stocks. First, corporate bond markets should be developed, along with better enforcement of bankruptcy laws and bond-rating agencies. Second, more derivative securities such as forwards, futures, and options on commodities (already in place and trading) as well as on other securities should be introduced to the market, so that investors and firms have more tools for risk management. Third, insurance companies should expand their coverage and offer more products in property and auto insurance, as well as life and medical insurance, while other financial services companies should develop the market for asset-backed securities.

THE NONSTANDARD FINANCIAL SECTOR AND EVIDENCE ON HYBRID-SECTOR FIRMS

In this section we study how the nonstandard financial sector helps firms in the hybrid sector to raise funds and to grow from start-ups to successful industry leaders. We also examine the alternative governance mechanisms employed by investors and firms that can substitute for formal corporate governance mechanisms. Due to data limitations, much of this evidence is by necessity anecdotal or by survey.[22]

We first compare the hybrid sector with the state and listed sectors to highlight its importance in the entire economy in "Comparison of Hybrid Sector versus State and Listed Sectors." Second, we consider survey evidence in the section on "Survey Evidence." Finally, our "Discussion on How the Nonstandard Financial Sector Works" considers alternative financing channels and governance mechanisms that support the growth of the hybrid sector.

Comparison of Hybrid Sector versus State and Listed Sectors

Figure 14.7a compares the level and growth of *industrial output* produced in the state and listed sectors combined versus that of the hybrid sector from 1990 to 2004. The output from the hybrid sector has been steadily increasing during this period and exceeded that of the other two sectors in 1998. The total output in 2004 is close to U.S.$1,500 billion for the hybrid sector, while it is around U.S.$800 billion in the state and listed sectors combined.[23] The hybrid sector grew at an annual rate of over 14 percent between 1990 and 2004, while the state and listed sectors combined grew at around 5 percent during the same period.[24] In addition, the growth rates for investment in fixed assets of these sectors are comparable (Yearbook; not reported in this chapter), which implies that the hybrid sector is more productive than the state and listed sectors. In fact, with a large sample of firms with various ownership structures, Liu (2007) finds that the returns to capital are much higher in nonstate sectors than the state sector and that a capital reallocation from state to private sectors will generate more growth in the economy. Fan, Rui, and Zhao (2006) and Li, Yue, and Zhao (2007) find that state-owned firms in China have much easier access to the debt market and accordingly higher leverage than nonstate firms. One reason for the differences is that due to government protection (for economic and social/political reasons), the costs for bankruptcy and financial distress are much

[22] All firms including hybrid sector firms must disclose accounting and financial information to the local Bureau of Commerce and Industry, and most of the reports are audited. However, these data are then aggregated into the Statistical Yearbook without any firm-level publications.

[23] Due to data limitations, our calculations underestimate the output of the state and listed sectors. We use the output produced by SOEs and listed firms in which the state has at least a 50 percent ownership stake as the total output for these sectors, but this calculation excludes output from listed firms that are *not* majority owned by the state; the output for the hybrid sector is the difference between the total output and the total for the other two sectors. However, as mentioned earlier, only around 20 percent of all listed firms do not have the state as the largest owner, and hence the total output of these firms is not likely to change our overall conclusion on the dominance of the hybrid sector over the other two sectors.

[24] There is an ongoing process of privatizing SOEs. Potentially, this may bias the growth rate of the hybrid sector higher, as there are firms shifting from the state sector to the hybrid sector. However, the overwhelming majority of SOEs are transformed into the listed sector (the main channel through which SOEs were partially privatized prior to 2004); thus, this process is unlikely to change the validity of the results stated earlier.

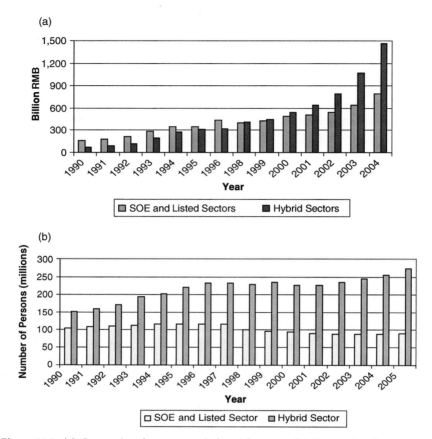

Figure 14.7. (a) Comparing the sectors – industrial output; (b) Comparing the sectors – employment

In Figure 14.7a we plot total "industrial output" for state (SOEs) and listed (publicly listed and traded firms) sectors combined and for the hybrid sector (all the rest of the firms) during 1990–2004. The data source for this table is the Chinese Statistical Yearbook (1998–2006).

In Figure 14.7b we plot total number of workers employed by the state (SOEs) and listed (publicly listed and traded firms) sectors combined and for the hybrid sector (all the rest of the firms) during 1990–2005. The data source for this table is the Chinese Statistical Yearbook (1998–2006).

lower for state-owned firms. These firms also have easier access to bank loans, especially credit extended by state-owned banks.

All of the facts given earlier make the growth of the hybrid sector even more impressive. Not surprisingly, there has been a fundamental change among the state, listed, and hybrid sectors in terms of their contribution to the entire economy: the state sector contributed more than two-thirds of China's GDP in 1980, but in 2004 it contributed less than one-third of the GDP; in 1980, (nonagricultural) privately owned firms, a type of hybrid sector firm, were negligible, but in 2001 they contributed 33 percent of GDP after growing at an average rate of 20 percent during this period (Yearbook, 1998–2002). The trend of the hybrid sector, as given earlier, replacing the state sector will continue in the near future.

Figure 14.7b presents the number and growth of nonagricultural employees in the three sectors. The hybrid sector is a much more important source for employment opportunities than the state and listed sectors. Over the period from 1990 to 2005, the hybrid sector employs an average of over 70 percent of all nonagricultural workers; the TVEs (part of the hybrid sector) have been the most important employers providing (nonagricultural) jobs for residents in the rural areas, while (nonagricultural) privately owned firms employ more than 40 percent of the workforce in the urban areas. Moreover, the number of employees working in the hybrid sector has been growing at 1.5 percent over this period, while the labor force in the state and listed sectors has been shrinking.[25] These patterns are particularly important for China, given its vast population and potential problem of unemployment.

Survey Evidence

Much of the information concerning the hybrid sector comes from surveys. We focus on evidence in Gregory, Tenev, and Wagle (2000), Allen, Qian, and Qian (2005b), and Cull and Xu (2005). The most important findings of these surveys regarding financing channels are the following. First, during the start-up stage, funds from founders' family and friends are an important source of financing. Banks can also play an important role. Second, internal financing, in the form of retained earnings, is also important. During their growth period, financing from private credit agencies (PCAs), instead of banks, as well as trade credits are important channels for firms in Allen, Qian, and Qian's sample. As documented by Tsai (2002), PCAs take on many forms, from shareholding cooperative enterprises run by professional money brokers, lenders, and middlemen to credit associations operated by groups of entrepreneurs (raising money from group members and from outsiders to fund firms; *zijin huzushe*), from pawnshops to underground private money houses.

As far as corporate governance is concerned, when asked about what type of losses concern them the most if the firm failed, every firm's founders/executives (100 percent) included in the Allen, Qian, and Qian study said reputation loss is a major concern, while only 60 percent of them said economic losses are of major concern. Competition also appears to be an important factor ensuring firms are well run.

---

[25] Our calculations of the total number of workers employed by the hybrid sector actually underestimate the actual workforce in the sector, because the Statistics Yearbooks do not provide employment data for all types of firms (by ownership structure) in the hybrid sector.

Cull and Xu (2005) find that firms in most regions and cities rely on courts to resolve less than 10 percent of business-related disputes (the highest percentage is 20 percent), with a higher reliance on courts in coastal and more developed areas. One reason that firms go to courts to resolve a dispute is because the courts are authoritative so that the dispute will be resolved even though the resolution may not be fair (see Chapter 11).

Discussion on How the Nonstandard Financial Sector Works

In this subsection we discuss mechanisms within the nonstandard financial sector in supporting the growth of the hybrid sector. There are two important aspects to alternative financing channels in the hybrid sector. The first is the way in which investment is financed. The second is corporate governance. We consider each in turn.

Once a firm is established and doing well, internal finance can provide the funds necessary for growth. Allen, Qian, and Qian (2005b) find that about 60 percent of the funds raised by the hybrid sector are generated internally. Of course, internal finance is fine once a firm is established, but this raises the issue of how firms in the hybrid sector acquire their "seed" capital, perhaps the most crucial financing during a firm's life cycle. Allen, Qian, and Qian present evidence on the importance of alternative and informal channels, including funds from family and friends and loans from private (unofficial) credit agencies. There is also evidence that financing through illegal channels, such as smuggling, bribery, insider trading and speculation during early stages of the development of financial markets and real-estate markets. Other underground or unofficial businesses also play an important role in the accumulation of seed capital. Although a controversial issue for the government, our view, based on similar episodes in the history of other developing countries, is that depending on the precise nature of the activity and as long as the purpose of money making is to invest in a legitimate company, it may be more productive for the government to provide incentives for investment rather than to expend costs discovering and punishing these activities.

Perhaps the most important corporate governance mechanism is competition in product and input markets, which has worked well in both developed and developing countries (e.g., McMillan 1995, 1997; Allen and Gale, 2000b). What we see from the success of hybrid sector firms in Wenzhou and other surveyed firms recounted in Allen, Qian, and Qian suggests that it is only those firms that have the strongest comparative advantage in an industry (of the area) that survived and thrived. A relevant factor for competition in an industry is entry barriers for new firms, as lower entry barriers foster competition. Djankov et al. (2002) examine entry barriers across eighty-five countries and find that countries with heavier (lighter) regulation of entry have higher government corruption (more democratic and limited governments) and larger unofficial economies. With much lower barriers to entry compared to other countries with similar (low) per capita

GDP, China is once again an "outlier" in the Djankov et al. sample, given that China is one of the least democratic countries and such countries tend to have high barriers to entry. Survey evidence from Allen, Qian, and Qian (2005b) reveals that there exist nonstandard methods to remove entry barriers in China, which can reconcile these seemingly contradictory facts.

Another important mechanism is reputation, trust, and relationships. Greif (1989, 1993) argues that certain traders' organizations in the eleventh century were able to overcome problems of asymmetric information and the lack of legal and contract enforcement mechanisms, because they had developed institutions based on reputation, implicit contractual relations, and coalitions. Certain aspects of the growth of these institutions resemble what worked to promote commerce and the financial system in China prior to 1949 and the operation of the nonstandard financial sector today, in terms of how firms raise funds and contract with investors and business partners. In addition, Greif (1993) and Stulz and Williamson (2003) point out the importance of cultural and religious beliefs for the development of institutions, legal origins, and investor protection.

The factors discussed earlier are of particular relevance and importance to China's development of institutions. Without a dominant religion, one can argue that the most important force in shaping China's social values and institutions is the set of beliefs first developed and formalized by *Kongzi* (Confucius). This set of beliefs clearly defines family and social orders, which are very different from western beliefs on how legal codes should be formulated. Using the World Values Survey conducted in the early 1990s, La Porta et al. (1997b) find that China has one of the highest levels of social trust among a group of forty developed and developing countries.[26] We interpret high social trust in China as being influenced by Confucian beliefs. Throughout this chapter and Allen, Qian, and Qian (2005b) we have presented evidence that reputation and relationships make many financing channels and governance mechanisms work in China's hybrid sector.

There are other effective corporate governance mechanisms. First, Burkart et al. (2003) link the degree of separation of ownership and control to different legal environments and show that *family run* firms will emerge as the dominant form of ownership structure in countries with weak minority shareholder protection, whereas professionally managed firms are the optimal form in countries with strong protection. Survey evidence on the hybrid sector in Allen, Qian, and Qian and empirical results on the listed sector, along with evidence in Claessens, Djankov, and Lang (2000) and Claessens et al. (2002), suggests that family firms are a norm in China and other Asian countries, and these firms have performed well. Second, Allen and Gale (2000a) show that, if cooperation among different suppliers of

---

[26] Interestingly, the same survey, used in La Porta et al. (1997b), finds that Chinese citizens have a low tendency to participate in civil activities. However, our evidence shows that, with effective alternative mechanisms in place, citizens in the developed regions of China have a strong incentive to participate in business/economic activities.

inputs is necessary and all suppliers benefit from the firm doing well, then a good equilibrium with no external governance is possible, as internal, mutual monitoring can ensure the optimal outcome. Allen, Qian, and Qian (2005b) present evidence on the importance of trade credits as a form of financing for firms in the hybrid sector. Cooperation and mutual monitoring can ensure payments (as long as funds are available) among business partners despite the lack of external monitoring and contract enforcement. The importance of trade credits is also found in other emerging economies as well as in developed countries.

It is worth mentioning how entrepreneurs and investors alleviate and overcome problems associated with government corruption. According to proponents of institutional development (e.g., Rajan and Zingales 2003a,b; Acemoglu and Johnson, 2005), poor institutions, weak government, and powerful elites should severely hinder China's long-run economic growth.[27] However, our evidence shows that corruption has not prevented a high rate of growth for China's firms, in particular, firms in the hybrid sector, where legal protection is perhaps weaker and problems of corruption worse, compared to firms in the state and listed sectors. One of the most effective solutions for corruption for firms in this sector is the common goal of sharing high prospective profits, which aligns interests of government officials with those of entrepreneurs and investors. Under this common goal in a multi-period setting, implicit contractual agreements and reputation can act as enforcement mechanisms to ensure that all parties, including government officials, fulfill their roles to make the firm successful. Another potential effective solution for corruption is competition among local governments/bureaucrats from different regions within the same country. Entrepreneurs can move from region to region to find the most supportive government officials for their private firms, which in turn motivates officials to lend "helping hands" rather than "grabbing hands" in the provision of public goods or services (e.g., granting of licenses to start-up firms), or else there will be an outflow of profitable private businesses from the region (Allen and Qian, 2007). This remedy should be typically available in a large country with diverse regions like China.

In addition, the selection and promotion process of government officials also plays a role in curbing the damaging effects of corruption. As Li (1998) points out, starting in the early 1980s, the central government of China implemented a mandatory retirement age for almost all bureaucrats at various levels, which made officials younger and more familiar with capitalist ideas. During the early stages of China's reform, TVEs, in which local governments were partial owners, provided the most important source of growth in the hybrid sector. The enormous success of TVEs and the promotion of the associated officials provided examples and incentives to

---

[27] In a broader context, La Porta et al. (1999) find that governments in countries with French or socialist origins have lower quality (in terms of supporting economic growth) than those with English common laws and richer countries. But clearly China is a counterexample to La Porta et al.'s argument on government.

other officials to follow suit. In addition, one of the key yardsticks in measuring the performance of local officials by the central government is economic growth and the amount of investment from nonlocal sources. These policies encourage interregional competition among officials and induce more government goods and services supplied and higher levels of growth.

FINANCIAL CRISES

Financial crises often accompany the development of a financial system. Conventional wisdom says that financial crises are bad. Often they are very bad, as they disrupt production and lower social welfare as in the Great Depression in the United States. Hoggarth, Reis, and Saporta (2002) carefully measure the costs of a wide range of recent financial crises and find that these costs are on average roughly 15–20 percent of GDP. It is these large costs that make policymakers so averse to financial crises.

It is important to point out, however, that financial crises may be welfare improving for an economy. One possible example is the late nineteenth-century United States, which experienced many crises but at the same time had a high long-run growth rate. In fact, Ranciere, Tornell, and Westermann (2003) report an empirical observation that countries which have experienced occasional crises have grown on average faster than countries without crises. They develop an endogenous growth model and show theoretically that an economy may be able to attain higher growth when firms are encouraged by a limited bailout policy to take more credit risk in the form of currency mismatch, even though the country may experience occasional crises (see Allen and Oura, 2004, for a review of the growth and crises literature and Allen and Gale, 2004a, who show that crises can be optimal).

In this section, we consider financial crises in China. Given China's current situation with limited currency mismatches, any crisis that occurs is likely to be a classic banking, currency, or twin crisis. It is perhaps more likely to be of the damaging type that disrupts the economy and social stability than of the more benign type that aids growth. The desirability of preventing crises thus needs to be taken into account when considering reforms of China's financial system. First, we examine how China can prevent traditional financial crises, including a banking sector crisis and a stock market or real-estate crisis/crash. We then discuss how China should be better prepared for new types of financial crises, such as the "twin crises" (simultaneous foreign exchange and banking/stock market crises) that occurred in many Asian economies in the late 1990s.

Banking Crises and Market Crashes

Among traditional financial crises, banking panics, arising from the banks' lack of liquid assets to meet total withdrawal demands (anticipated and unanticipated), were often particularly disruptive. Over time one of the most important roles of central banks came to be the elimination of banking panics and the maintenance of financial stability. To a large degree, central banks in different countries performed well in this regard in the period following the Second World War. However, in recent years, banking crises are often preceded by abnormal price rises ("bubbles") in the real-estate or stock markets. At some point, the bubble bursts and assets markets collapse. In many cases, banks and other intermediaries are overexposed to the equity and real-estate markets, and following the collapse of asset markets a banking crisis ensues. Allen and Gale (2000c) provide a theory of bubbles and crises based on the existence of an agency problem. Many investors in real-estate and stock markets obtain their investment funds from external sources. If the providers of the funds are unable to observe the characteristics of the investment, and because of the investors' limited liability, there is a classic risk-shifting problem (Jensen and Meckling, 1976). Risk shifting increases the return to risky assets and causes investors to bid up asset prices above their fundamental values. A crucial determinant for asset prices is the amount of credit that is provided for speculative investment. Financial liberalization, by expanding the volume of credit, can interact with the agency problem and lead to a bubble in asset prices.

As discussed earlier in the section on "The Banking and Intermediation Sector," if NPLs continue to accumulate and/or if growth slows significantly then there may be a banking crisis in China. This may involve withdrawal of funds from banks. However, given the government's low level of debt (Table 14.3a), it should be possible for the government to prevent this situation from getting out of control. Since the real-estate markets in Shanghai (largest volume and most developed) and other major cities have already experienced bubbles and crashes (see *China Industry Report*, http://www.cei.gov.cn, and http://house.focus.cn for more details), it is quite possible that similar episodes in the future could cause a banking crisis that will be more damaging to the real economy. With booming real-estate markets, there will be more speculative money poured into properties, with a large amount coming from banks. The agency problem in real-estate lending and investment mentioned earlier worsens this problem. If the real-estate market falls significantly within a short period, defaults on bank loans could be large enough to trigger a banking panic and crisis. This perhaps represents the most serious risk of a financial crisis in China.

Capital Account Liberalization, Currency Float, and Twin Crises

After the collapse of the Bretton Woods system in the early 1970s, a new breed of financial crisis emerged. Lindgren, Garcia, and Saal (1996) found that three quarters of the IMF's member countries suffered some form of banking crisis between 1980 and 1996, and their study did not include the subsequent Asian financial crisis in 1997. In many of these crises, banking panics in the traditional sense were avoided either by central bank intervention or by explicit or implicit government guarantees. But as Kaminsky and Reinhart (1999) find, the advent of financial liberalization in many economies in the 1980s, in which free capital in and out flows and the entrance and competition from foreign investors and financial institutions follow in the home country, has often led to "twin" banking and currency crises. A common precursor to these crises was financial liberalization and significant credit expansion and subsequent stock market crashes and banking crises. In emerging markets, this is often then accompanied by an exchange rate crisis, as governments choose between lowering interest rates to ease the banking crises or raising them to defend the home currencies. Finally, a significant fall in output occurs and the economies enter recessions.

Liberalization of the Capital Account and Financial Sector

Capital account liberation can attract more foreign capital, but large-scale and sudden capital flows and foreign speculation significantly increase the likelihood of a twin crisis. The first key question is when and to what extent should a country open its capital account and financial sector to foreign capital and foreign financial institutions? The prevailing view, expressed by McKinnon (1991), Dornbusch (1998), and Fischer (1998), is that success or failure of this policy hinges on the efficiency of domestic financial institutions and that reforming the financial sector should be a precondition to liberalizing. This view assumes that financial liberalization does not alter the efficiency of domestic financial institutions. But this policy change affects both the supply and the price of capital, two important determinants of lending contracts. With a model of endogenous financial intermediation, Alessandria and Qian (2005) demonstrate that an efficient financial sector prior to liberalization is neither necessary nor sufficient for a successful financial liberalization.

Applying these ideas to China, even though the overall efficiency of China's banking sector (especially state-owned banks) is low compared to international standards, banks can have a stronger incentive to limit the moral hazard concerning borrowers' choices of investment projects through monitoring and designing of loan contracts (e.g., adjusting interest rates and/or maturities) following a capital account liberalization. Therefore, the efficiency of the banking sector improves and the liberalization can generate a large welfare increase, since it leads to both a larger scale of investment *and* a better composition of investment projects. This is more likely to occur with low interest rates in international markets (so that cost of capital for domestic banks is also low). A financial sector liberalization, which allows foreign financial institutions to enter China's lending markets, can further improve welfare, as more competition provides stronger incentives for all banks to further discourage moral hazard in investment. As long as the adverse selection problem (entrance of borrowers with negative-NPV projects in the markets can become worse with more competition in the banking sector) is not severe, financial sector liberalization will further improve welfare. Overall, we conclude that a liberalization of the capital account is likely to be beneficial for China as long as the (post-liberalization) cost of capital for Chinese banks does not rise sharply.

Currency Crisis and Banking Crisis (A Twin Crisis)

A currency crisis that may trigger a banking crisis is a possibility. The rapid increase in foreign exchange reserves in recent years suggests there is a lot of speculative money in China in anticipation of an RMB revaluation. If there is a significant future revaluation or if after some time it becomes clear there will not be one then much of this money may be withdrawn. What happens then will depend on how the government and central bank respond. If they allow the currency to float so they do not use up the exchange reserves, then any fall in the value of the RMB may occur quickly and this may limit further outflows. If they try to limit the exchange rate movement, then there may be a classic currency crisis. This is in turn may trigger a banking crisis if there are large withdrawals from banks as a result. Quickly adopting a full float and avoiding a twin crisis would be preferable.[28]

Financial Contagion

Another phenomenon that has been important in many recent crises (e.g., the 1997 Asian crisis) is that financial crises are contagious. A small shock that initially affects only a particular region or sector can spread by contagion within the banking system or asset markets to the rest of the financial sector and then to the entire economy and possibly other economies. Contagion can occur in a number of ways. In the Chinese context where financial markets are relatively unimportant, it is most likely they will occur from either contractually interconnected financial institutions or large asset price movements that cause spillovers to financial institutions.

Allen and Gale (2000d) focus on the channel of contagion that arises from the overlapping claims that different regions or sectors of the banking system have on one another through interbank markets. When one region suffers a banking crisis, the other regions suffer a loss because their claims on the troubled region fall in value. If this spillover effect is strong enough, it can cause a crisis in the adjacent regions, and a contagion can occur that brings down the entire financial system. Allen and Gale (2004b) show how large price falls can come about as a result of forced liquidations when there is a limited supply of liquidity in the market. Cifuentes, Ferrucci, and Shin (2005) show that contagion is likely to be particularly severe when these two factors interact.

Given China's current financial system, what is the likelihood of financial contagion caused by contractual interlinkages in the interbank market or because of a meltdown in asset prices if there are forced sales? China's interbank market grew very quickly since its inception in 1981; in fact, the growth of this market was so fast, with the participation of many unregulated financial institutions and with large

---

[28] Chang and Velasco (2001) develop a model of twin crises based on the Diamond and Dybvig (1983) model of bank runs. Money enters agents' utility function, and the central bank controls the ratio of currency to consumption. In some regimes, there exists both a "good" equilibrium in which early (late) consumers receive the proceeds from short-term (long-term) assets and a "bad" equilibrium in which everybody believes a crisis will occur and these beliefs are self-fulfilling. If the bad equilibrium occurs, there is a twin crisis.

Table 14.7. *Trading volume of national interbank market*

Maturity	Overnight	7 days	20 days	30 days	60 days	90 days	120 days
2001	103.88	560.69	93.35	35.28	9.40	4.73	0.87
2002	1,059.33	2,086.47	77.69	56.29	13.28	15.45	3.94
2003	641.89	1,456.31	56.60	44.11	10.14	10.18	2.81
2004	641.89	1,456.31	56.60	44.11	10.14	10.18	2.81
2005	223.03	896.26	60.42	29.91	7.51	14.09	1.54
2006 (January–September)	376.51	842.28	30.79	14.29	10.05	2.31	0.90

Note: Values are in RMB billion.
Source: China Interbank Market Annual Reports (1999–2006).

flows of funds through this market to fixed-asset investment, that it exacerbated high inflation in the late 1980s. Since then the government and PBOC increased their regulation by limiting participation of nonbank financial institutions and by imposing restrictions on interest rate movements. In 1996 a nationwide, uniform system of interbank markets was set up. It contains two connected levels: the primary network, which includes the largest PBOC branches, large commercial banks, and a few large nonbank financial institutions, and the secondary network that includes many banks and nonbank institutions and their local branches (see *China Interbank Market Annual Reports* for more details). Table 14.7 documents the growth of the interbank market in recent years: while the trading volume of long maturity contracts (20 days or longer) is low, the volume of short-term contracts (overnight and week long) has been high (reaching RMB1 trillion to 2 trillion, or $125 billion to $250 billion). Therefore, the increasing interlinkages can potentially create a contagion should a crisis develop in one area or sector.

With regard to a meltdown of asset prices, this can happen because of a limited supply of liquidity if there is a rapid liquidation of assets. It seems unlikely that this can occur and cause a serious problem in China's securities markets. A more serious threat is real-estate markets if there are bankruptcies and forced selling. This could potentially interact with bank interlinkages and cause a systemic problem. As mentioned earlier, a crash in real-estate markets is the most likely cause of a financial crisis in China.

SUMMARY AND CONCLUDING REMARKS

One of the most frequently asked questions about China's financial system is whether it will stimulate or hamper economic growth. Our answer to this question, based on examining the history and current status of the financial system and comparing them to those of other countries, is in four parts. First, the large but inefficient banking sector has been the dominant force in the financial system and has played an important role in funding the growth of many types of firms. It is currently plagued by the problem of NPLs, which, if not corrected properly, may cause major economic difficulties. Second, the stock market has been growing fast since 1990 but has played a relatively limited role in supporting the growth of the economy. However, the role of the financial markets is likely to change in the near future and they will play an increasingly important role in the economy.

If we can summarize that the role of the banking sector and financial markets has been that they have done enough *not* to slow down the growth of the economy, our third conclusion is that alternative financing channels have had great success in supporting the growth of the hybrid sector, which contributes most of the economic growth compared to the state and listed sectors. The nonstandard financial sector relies on alternative financing channels including internal finance, and on alternative governance mechanisms, such as those based on trust, reputation, and relationships, and competition to support the growth of the hybrid sector. Going forward, we believe that these alternative financing channels and governance mechanisms should be encouraged rather than replaced. They should be allowed to coexist with the banks and markets and continue to fuel the growth of the hybrid sector.

We conclude by pointing out the most significant challenge for improving China's financial system: economic stability is crucial for the continuing development of the Chinese economy, and the stability of the financial system relates to economic stability in three dimensions. The continuing effort to reduce and eventually bring down NPLs to normal levels is important in avoiding a banking crisis, while the effort to improve the regulatory environment surrounding the financial markets (including governance and accounting standards) can certainly help prevent a stock market crash/crisis. If China opens the capital account, there will be a large inflow of foreign capital, but large-scale capital flows and speculations also bring the risk of a twin crisis (foreign exchange and banking/stock market crisis), which severely damaged emerging economies in Asia in 1997. To guard against such a crisis, policies toward improving the financial system must be made along with supportive fiscal and trade policies.

References

Acemoglu, Daron and Simon Johnson, 2005. "Unbundling Institutions." *Journal of Political Economy*, 113 (5), pp. 949–995.

Alessandria, George and Jun Qian. 2005. "Endogenous Financial Intermediation and Real Effects of Capital Account Liberalization." *Journal of International Economics*. 67, pp. 97–128.

Allen, Franklin, Michael Chui, and Angela Maddaloni. 2004. "Financial Systems in Europe, the USA, and Asia." *Oxford Review of Economic Policy*. 20, pp. 490–508.

Allen, Franklin and Douglas Gale. 1999. "Diversity of Opinion and Financing of New Technologies." *Journal of Financial Intermediation*. 8, pp. 68–89.

Allen, Franklin and Douglas Gale. 2000a. *Comparing Financial Systems*. Cambridge, MA: MIT Press.

Allen, Franklin and Douglas Gale. 2000b. "Corporate Governance and Competition," in *Corporate Governance: Theoretical and Empirical Perspectives*. Xavier Vives, ed. Cambridge and New York: Cambridge University Press, pp. 23–94.

Allen, Franklin and Douglas Gale. 2004a. "Financial Intermediaries and Markets." *Econometrica*. 72, pp. 1023–1061.

Allen, Franklin and Douglas Gale. 2004b. "Financial Fragility, Liquidity and Asset Prices." *Journal of the European Economic Association*. 2, pp. 1015–1048.

Allen, Franklin and Douglas Gale. 2000c. "Bubbles and Crises." *Economic Journal*. 110, pp. 236–255.

Allen, Franklin and Douglas Gale. 2000d. "Financial Contagion." *Journal of Political Economy*. 108, pp. 1–33.

Allen, Franklin and Hiroko Oura. 2004. "Sustained Economic Growth and the Financial System." *Monetary and Economic Studies, Bank of Japan*. 22S-1, pp. 95–119.

Allen, Franklin and Jun Qian. 2007. "*Corruption and Competition.*" Working Paper. Pennsylvania: University of Pennsylvania.

Allen, Franklin, Jun Qian, and Meijun Qian. 2005a. "China's Financial System: Past, Present, and Future." Wharton Financial Institutions Center Working Paper 05–17. Philadelphia, PA: Wharton Financial Institutions Center.

Allen, Franklin, Jun Qian, and Meijun Qian. 2005b. "Law, Finance, and Economic Growth in China." *Journal of Financial Economics*. 77, pp. 57–116.

Berger, Allen, Iftekhar Hasan, and Mingming Zhou. 2006. "Bank Ownership and Efficiency in China: What Will Happen in the World's Largest Nation?" *Journal of Banking and Finance*. Forthcoming.

Black, Bernard S. and Ronald J. Gilson, 1998. "Venture Capital and the Structure of Capital Markets: Bank versus Stock Markets." *Journal of Financial Economics*. 47, pp. 243–277.

Brandt, Loren and Xiaodong Zhu. 2000. "Redistribution in a Decentralized Economy: Growth and Inflation in China under Reform." *Journal of Political Economy*. 108, pp. 422–439.

Burkart, Mike, Fausto Panunzi, and Andrei Shleifer. 2003. "Family Firms." *Journal of Finance*. 58, pp. 2167–2201.

Chan, Kalok, Albert Menkveld, and Zhishu Yang. 2007. "Information Asymmetry and Asset Prices: Evidence from the China Foreign Share Discount." *Journal of Finance*. Forthcoming.

Chang, Roberto and Andres Velasco. 2001. "A Model of Financial Crises in Emerging Markets." *Quarterly Journal of Economics*. 116, pp. 489–518.

Che, Jiahua and Yingyi Qian. 1998. "Insecure Property Rights and Government Ownership of Firms." *Quarterly Journal of Economics*. 113, pp. 467–496.

Cifuentes, Rodrigo, Gianluigi Ferrucci, and Hyun Song Shin. 2005. "Liquidity Risk and Contagion." *Journal of the European Economic Association*. 3, pp. 556–566.

Claessens, Stijn, Simeon Djankov, Joseph Fan, and Larry Lang. 2002. "Expropriation of Minority Shareholders in East Asia." *Journal of Finance*. 57, pp. 2741–2771.

Claessens, Stijn, Simeon Djankov, and Larry Lang. 2000. "The Separation of Ownership and Control in East Asian Corporations." *Journal of Financial Economics*. 58, pp. 81–112.

Cull, Robert and Colin Xu. 2005. "Institutions, Ownership, and Finance: The Determinants of Reinvestments of Profit among Chinese Firms." *Journal of Financial Economics*. 77, pp. 117–146.

Demirgüç-Kunt, Asli and Ross Levine. 2001. *Financial Structure and Economic Growth: Cross-Country Comparisons of Banks, Markets, and Development.* Cambridge, MA: MIT Press.

Diamond, Douglas and Philip Dybvig. 1983. "Bank Runs, Deposit Insurance, and Liquidity." *Journal of Political Economy.* 91, pp. 401–419.

Djankov, Simeon, Rafael La Porta, Florencio Lopez-de-Silanes, and Andrei Shleifer. 2002. "The Regulation of Entry." *Quarterly Journal of Economics.* 117, pp. 1–37.

Dornbusch, Rudiger. 1998. "Capital Controls: An Idea Whose Time is Past." *Princeton Essays in International Finance.* 207, pp. 1–18.

Fan, Joseph, Oliver Rui, and Mengxin Zhao. 2006. "Rent Seeking and Corporate Finance: Evidence from Corruption." Working Paper. Hong Kong: Chinese University of Hong Kong.

Fan, Joseph, T. J. Wong, and Tianyu Zhang. 2007. "Politically-Connected CEOs, Corporate Governance and Post-IPO Performance of China's Partially Privatized Firms." *Journal of Financial Economics.* 84, pp. 330–357.

Feldstein, Martin. 1999. "Social Security Pension Reform in China." *China Economic Review.* 10, pp. 99–107.

Feldstein, Martin. 2003. "Banking, Budgets, and Pensions: Some Priorities for Chinese Policy." Mimeo. Cambridge, MA: Harvard University.

Feldstein, Martin and Jeffrey Liebman. 2006. "Realizing the Potential of China's Social Security Pension System." *China Economic Review.* 17, pp. 1–16.

Feng, Lei and Mark Seasholes. 2004. "Correlated Trading and Location." *Journal of Finance.* 59, pp. 2117–2144.

Fischer, Stanley. 1998. "Capital Account Liberalization and the Role of the IMF." *Princeton Essays on International Finance.* 207, pp. 19–35.

Franks, Julian, Colin Mayer, and Stefano Rossi. 2003. "Ownership: Evolution and Regulation." Working Paper. London: London Business School.

Fung, Peter, Michael Firth, and Oliver Rui. 2003. "Corporate Governance and CEO Compensation in China." Working Paper. Hong Kong: Chinese University of Hong Kong.

Gordon, Roger and Wei Li. 2003. "Government as Discriminating Monopolist in the Financial Market: The Case of China." *Journal of Public Economics.* 87, pp. 283–312.

Gregory, Neil, Stoyan Tenev, and Dileep Wagle. 2000. *China's Emerging Private Enterprises: Prospects for the New Century.* Washington, DC: IFC (World Bank).

Greif, Avner. 1989. "Reputation and Coalitions in Medieval Trade: Evidence on the Maghribi Traders." *Journal of Economic History.* 49, pp. 857–882.

Greif, Avner. 1993. "Contract Enforceability and Economic Institutions in Early Trade: The Maghribi Traders' Coalition." *American Economic Review.* 83, pp. 525–548.

Herring, Richard and N. Chatusripitak, 2000. "The Case of the Missing Market: The Bond Market and Why It Matters for Financial Development." Working Paper. Philadelphia, PA: Wharton Financial Institutions Center.

Hoggarth, Glenn, Ricardo Reis, and Victoria Saporta. 2002. "Costs of Banking System Instability: Some Empirical Evidence." *Journal of Banking and Finance.* 26, pp. 825–855.

Jeng, Leslie A. and Philippe C. Wells. 2000. "The Determinants of Venture Capital Funding: Evidence across Countries." *Journal of Corporate Finance.* 6, pp. 241–289.

Jensen, Michael and William Meckling. 1976. "Theory of the Firm: Managerial Behavior, Agency Costs, and Ownership Structure." *Journal of Financial Economics.* 3, pp. 305–360.

Kaminsky, Graciela and Carmen Reinhart. 1999. "The Twin Crises: The Causes of Banking and Balance-of-Payments Problems." *American Economic Review.* 89, pp. 473–500.

Kane, Edward. 1989. *The S&L Mess: How Did It Happen?* Washington, DC: Urban Institute Press.

Kane, Edward. 2003. "What Economic Principles Should Policymakers in Other Countries Have Learned from the S&L Mess?" *Business Economics.* 38, pp. 21–30.

Kato, Takao and Cheryl Long. 2004. "Executive Compensation and Corporate Governance in China." William Davidson Institute Working Paper 690. Ann Arbor, MI: William Davidson Institute.

Kirby, William. 1995. "China Unincorporated: Company Law and Business Enterprise in Twentieth-Century China." *Journal of Asian Studies.* 54, pp. 43–63.

Kortum, Samuel and Josh Lerner. 2000. "Assessing the Contribution of Venture Capital on Innovation." *RAND Journal of Economics.* 31, pp. 674–692.

La Porta, Rafael, Florencio Lopez-de-Silanes, and Andrei Shleifer. 2002. "Government Ownership of Banks." *Journal of Finance.* 57, pp. 265–302.

La Porta, Rafael, Florencio Lopez-de-Silanes, and Andrei Shleifer. 2006. "What Works in Securities Laws?" *Journal of Finance.* 61, pp. 1–32.

La Porta, Rafael, Florencio Lopez-de-Silanes, Andrei Shleifer, and Robert Vishny. 1997a. "Legal Determinants of External Finance." *Journal of Finance.* 52, pp. 1131–1150.

La Porta, Rafael, Florencio Lopez-de-Silanes, Andrei Shleifer, and Robert Vishny. 1997b. "Trust in Large Organizations." *American Economic Review.* 87, pp. 333–338.

La Porta, Rafael, Florencio Lopez-de-Silanes, Andrei Shleifer, and Robert Vishny. 1998. "Law and Finance." *Journal of Political Economy.* 106, pp. 1113–1155.

La Porta, Rafael, Florencio Lopez-de-Silanes, Andrei Shleifer, and Robert Vishny. 1999. "The Quality of Government." *Journal of Law, Economics, and Organization.* 15, pp. 222–279.

Lardy, Nicholas R. 1998. *China's Unfinished Economic Revolution.* Washington, DC: Brookings Institution Press.

Lee, Tahirih V. 1993. "Risky Business: Courts, Culture, and the Marketplace." *University of Miami Law Review.* 47, pp. 1335–1414.

Levine, Ross. 2002. "Bank-Based or Market-Based Financial Systems: Which Is Better?" *Journal of Financial Intermediation.* 11, pp. 1–30.

Li, David. 1996. "A Theory of Ambiguous Property Rights: The Case of the Chinese Non-State Sector." *Journal of Comparative Economics.* 23, pp. 1–19.

Li, David. 1998. "Changing Incentives of the Chinese Bureaucracy." *American Economic Review.* 88, pp. 393–397.

Li, Kai, Heng Yue, and Longkai Zhao. 2007. "Ownership, Institutions, and Capital Structure: Evidence from Non-Listed Chinese Firms." Working Paper. Vancouver, Canada: University of British Columbia.

Lindgren, Carl-Johan, Gillian Garcia, and Matthew Saal. 1996. *Bank Soundness and Macroeconomic Policy.* Washington, DC: International Monetary Fund.

Liu, Qiao. 2007. "Institutions, Financial Development, and Corporate Investment: Evidence from an Implied Return on Capital in China." Working Paper. Hong Kong: University of Hong Kong.

McKinnon, Ronald. 1991. *The Order of Economic Liberalization.* Baltimore, MD: Johns Hopkins University Press.

McMillan, John. 1995. "China's Nonconformist Reform," in *Economic Transition in Eastern Europe and Russia: Realities of Reform.* Edward Lazear, ed. Stanford: Hoover Institution Press, pp. 419–433.

McMillan, John. 1997. "Markets in Transition," Chapter 6 in *Advances in Economics and Econometrics,* vol. 2. David M. Kreps and Kenneth F. Wallis, eds. Cambridge and New York: Cambridge University Press, pp. 210–239.

Mei, Jianping, Jose Scheinkman, and Wei Xiong. 2003. "Speculative Trading and Stock Prices: An Analysis of Chinese A-B Share Premia." Working Paper. Princeton, NJ: Princeton University.

Michie, Ronald C 1987. *The London and New York Stock Exchanges 1850–1914*. London: Allen & Unwin.

Morck, Randall, Bernard Yeung, and Wayne Yu. 2000. "The Information Content of Stock Markets: Why Do Emerging Markets Have Synchronous Stock Price Movement?" *Journal of Financial Economics*. 58, pp. 215–260.

Orts, Eric. 2001. "The Rule of Law in China." *Vanderbilt Journal of Transitional Law*. 34, pp. 43–115.

Park, Albert, Loren Brandt, and John Giles. 2003. "Competition under Credit Rationing: Theory and Evidence from Rural China." *Journal of Development Economics*. 71, pp. 463–495.

Prasad, Eswar and Shang-jin Wei. 2007. "The Chinese Approach to Capital Flows: Patterns and Possible Explanations," Chapter 9 in *Capital Controls and Capital Flows in Emerging Economies*. Sebastian Edwards, ed. Chicago: University of Chicago Press, pp. 421–480.

Qiu, Yuemin, Bing Li, and Youcai Cai, 2000. "Losses of State-Owned Commercial Banks: Reasons and Policy Response," *Jingji gongzuozhe xuexi ziliao* [Study Materials for Economic Workers], no. 44, pp. 10–16.

Rajan, Raghuram and Luigi Zingales. 2003a. "The Great Reversals: The Politics of Financial Development in the Twentieth Century." *Journal of Financial Economics*. 69, pp. 5–50.

Rajan, Raghuram and Luigi Zingales. 2003b. *Saving Capitalism from Capitalists: Unleashing the Power of Financial Markets to Create Wealth and Spread Opportunity*. New York: Random House.

Ranciere, Romaine, Aaron Tornell, and Frank. Westermann. 2003. "Crises and Growth: A Re-evaluation." NBER Working Paper 10073. Cambridge, MA: NBER.

Rawski, Thomas G. 2002. "Measuring China's Recent GDP Growth: Where Do We Stand?" *China Economic Quarterly*. 2, pp. 3–14.

Sachs, Jeffrey and Wing Thye Woo. 1997. "Understanding China's Economic Performance." NBER Working Paper 5935. Cambridge, MA: NBER.

Schipani, Cindy and Junhai Liu. 2002. "Corporate Governance in China: Then and Now." *Columbia Business Law Review*. 2002, pp. 1–69.

Stulz, Rene and Rohan Williamson. 2003. "Culture, Openness, and Finance." *Journal of Financial Economics*. 70, pp. 261–300.

Tenev, Stoyan, Chunlin Zhang, and Loup Brefort. 2002. *Corporate Governance and Enterprise Reform in China: Building the Institutions of Modern Markets*. Washington, DC: IFC (World Bank).

Tsai, Kellee. 2002. *Back-Alley Banking*. Ithaca, NY: Cornell University Press.

FIFTEEN

China's Industrial Development

Loren Brandt, Thomas G. Rawski, and John Sutton[1]

INTRODUCTION

China's industries have achieved remarkable development since the start of reform in the late 1970s. Although this chapter will outline both the quantitative and institutional dimensions of recent growth, its chief objective is to examine what we see as the central achievement of Chinese industry: the emergence of mechanisms for extending industrial capability, which we measure by the capacity to sell into overseas markets, to a growing array of products and sectors. This accomplishment, which only a few economies – among them Taiwan, South Korea, Israel, India, and Brazil – have matched since the end of World War II, ensures that China's recent boom represents a permanent shift rather than a temporary respite from centuries of poverty.

At the start of reform, Chinese industry had already attained substantial size. Chinese factories and mines employed more workers in 1978 than the combined total of all other third-world nations. Success with nuclear weapons and satellite technology demonstrated new technical strength. Yet, visitors to Chinese factories encountered obsolete and dysfunctional products: vans and transformers that failed to keep out rainwater, sewing machines that leaked oil onto the fabric, power tillers rusting outside a factory that churned out fresh batches of unwanted inventory, and so on.

Three decades of reform have remade Chinese industry along many dimensions. Figure 15.1 displays real value-added growth in China's secondary sector (manufacturing, mining, utilities, and construction) during the first quarter century

[1] The authors gratefully acknowledge financial support from the World Bank, the University of Pittsburgh's Asian Studies Center, and its Hewlett Grant Program, and the Institute for International Business at the University of Toronto, as well as invaluable commentary and assistance from the Chinese Enterprise Confederation, Ling Chen, Xi Chen, Wendy Dobson, Ying Fang, Frank Giarratani, Tingting Huang, Gary Jefferson, Peng Liu, Li Qi, Eric Ramstetter, Xiaoming Shang, Yaojiang Shi, Shinji Tahara, Wei Wang, Yifan Zhang, Yuxin Zheng, and cooperative hosts at several dozen Chinese enterprises.

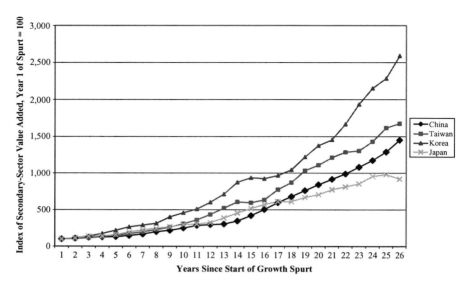

Figure 15.1. Asian growth spurts: real growth of secondary-sector value added over 26 years

of accelerated growth (from 1978) alongside comparable figures for Japan (from 1955), Taiwan (from 1960), and South Korea (from 1965). Results show Chinese growth outpacing Japan's, but lagging behind the smaller East Asian dynamos. Similar figures for labor productivity show Chinese performance surpassing the same East Asian neighbors. Qualitative changes were equally important. Reform has pushed China into global prominence as a leading exporter of manufactures. The composition of manufactured exports, which have come to dominate China's overseas sales, has shifted from textiles, garments, toys, and other labor-intensive products to a more sophisticated mix led by various types of machinery and equipment. Globalization has also thrust China into cross-national networks for production, design, and research in a growing array of industries.

We see the growing impact of market forces, expanded entry, and intense competition as the central impetus, stimulating efforts to expand capabilities and improve performance. Chinese experience shows that despite their undoubted benefits, neither privatization of enterprise ownership nor extensive deregulation, full price flexibility, rule of law, and other widely recommended institutional changes must necessarily precede a broad-gauged advance of manufacturing capabilities.

Although competition provides a universal spur to industrial firms, the process of upgrading differs systematically across sectors. The importance of industry-specific characteristics in shaping the development process leads to the expectation that the evolution of Chinese industry will generally follow patterns established in other nations. Globalization, which multiplies the impact of international market forces on Chinese producers, should accentuate this tendency.

At the same time, China's large size, unusual history, and unique institutional arrangements also shape market structures. Variation across sectors and over time in the degree to which official regulation limits the penetration of foreign- and private-sector competition into sectors initially dominated by state-owned enterprises (SOEs), for example, affects the intensity of competition, the growth and utilization of production capacity, the pace of innovation, and many other aspects of industrial activity. As a result, we expect outcomes that partly conform to international commonalities, but also reflect special features of China's economy.

Chinese industry is a vast subject that no single essay can encompass. In emphasizing the expansion of capabilities, we focus on two central questions. What are the consequences of China's substantial, though incomplete, shift from plan to market? How far has China advanced toward creating a modern, technologically advanced manufacturing sector? To sharpen the focus of our answers, we emphasize specific industries: automobiles, beer, cement, garments, home appliances, machine tools, and steel.

We preface our study with an historical sketch of industrial development under reform and a brief discussion of the extent to which market forces have shaped the evolution of industrial structures in China's transitional economy.

CHINA'S INDUSTRIAL REFORM

Pre-Reform System

At the start of economic reform in the late 1970s, Chinese industry was largely state owned and urban. In 1978, SOEs delivered 78 percent of industrial output and employed 76 percent of all industrial workers; state firms also absorbed 84 percent of increments to industrial fixed assets during 1975–1980 (Fifty Years, 2000, p. 18, 21, 58). The balance of industrial output came from smaller collective firms located in both urban and rural areas, most owned and directed by local governments. The origins of rural collectives date from the Great Leap Forward of the late 1950s. During the 1960s and 1970s, these enterprises grew modestly under China's rural communes and were heavily focused on servicing agriculture (Perkins et al., 1977). Urban collectives concentrated on light industry; rural firms emphasized the manufacture of producer goods that were difficult to obtain under China's pre-reform plan system.

Resource allocation in industry was largely administrative, with prices set to ensure positive cash flows and accounting profits at all but the least efficient final goods producers. Almost all of these profits, in turn, were remitted to fiscal authorities and served as the most important source of government revenue. Unlike the Soviet Union, central planning determined only a modest percentage of resource allocation and investment. Beginning in the 1960s, administrative authority over enterprises, planning and resource allocation increasingly devolved to governments at the provincial level or below. Wong (1986) estimates that by the late 1970s, less than half of industrial output remained under central control.

This decentralization contributed to severe fragmentation at the regional level as local governments deployed significant investment resources in an environment of limited opportunities for trade across administrative boundaries (Lyons, 1987). Donnithorne (1972) coined the term "cellular" to describe the resulting economic structure. As in the USSR, China's plan system emphasized quantity at the expense of assortment, delivery, customer service, and other qualitative dimensions of production. This encouraged firms to pursue vertical integration in order to avoid dependence on unreliable suppliers. Despite its success in expanding industrial production, the pre-reform system's weaknesses, which included limited autonomy for firm managers, strict controls on labor mobility, and weak material incentives, stifled improvements in quality and productivity, which stagnated at low levels throughout the 1960s and 1970s (Rawski, 1975a, 1980; Field, 1983; Ishikawa, 1983; Chen et al., 1988).

Industrial Reform

Beginning in the late 1970s, China embarked on a program of enterprise reform. At the risk of considerable simplification, we may divide industrial reform into two periods. During the first fifteen years, reform efforts focused on expanding the impact of incentives and market forces on the allocation of resource flows. Beginning in the mid-1990s, reform expanded to encompass the restructuring of resource stocks, including large-scale layoffs of redundant state-sector workers and privatization of government-controlled enterprises.

The initial phase of reform in the state sector consisted of two key components: increasing incentives and autonomy at the firm level, and the introduction of a unique system of dual-track pricing that partitioned both inputs and outputs into plan and market segments, with plan quotas transacted at official prices and market exchange relying on flexible prices that increasingly reflected forces of supply and demand (Naughton, 1995; Li, 1997; Lau, Qian, and Roland, 2001). The share of producer goods transacted at market prices rose from zero in 1978 to 13 percent in 1985 and 46 percent in 1991. By 1995, 78 percent of producer goods were transacted at market prices (OECD, 2005, p. 29).

Parallel initiatives allowed the entry of new firms into an increasing number of sectors formerly reserved for state enterprises. The number of industrial enterprises jumped from 936,000 in 1980 to 7.34 million in 1995.[2] Especially prominent in this regard was the emergence of township and village enterprises (TVEs), which were mostly owned and managed by township and village-level governments. These firms could draw on labor released from farming by the introduction of the household responsibility system and inputs now available in the market

---

[2] Fifty Years (2000, p. 16) shows 377,300 firms at and above the township level in 1980, to which we should add 558,700 firms operating at the brigade (*shengchan dui*) level (TVE Yearbook, 1986, p. 12). Data for 1995 are from Industry Census Summary (1996, p. 3).

through the dual-track system. The 1980s witnessed rapid increases in numbers of firms, particularly in rural areas (China Compendium, 2005, p. 48; Bramall, 2007, pp. 52–53). By the late 1980s, township and village-level collectives employed nearly 50 million workers (Bramall, 2007, p. 78).

At the same time, new policies mandating favorable treatment of foreign direct investment (FDI) and a reduction in tariff barriers for these firms contributed to the rapid growth of a foreign enterprise sector, initially in the Special Economic Zones (SEZs) and subsequently, throughout the coastal provinces. As a result, SOEs in many sectors experienced growing competition from both TVEs and foreign-linked firms.

This initial reform stage delivered large increases in output (Figure 15.1), particularly outside the state sector. The share of SOEs in industrial production plunged from 77.6 percent in 1978 to 54.6 percent in 1990 and 34.0 percent in 1995 (Fifty Years, 2000, p. 21). Exports expanded rapidly, with foreign-invested firms and TVEs playing major roles in overseas sales. Productivity outcomes remain controversial, but there is general agreement that improvements in total factor productivity in the state sector were modest at best and tended to trail productivity gains outside the state sector (Jefferson et al., 1999). Within the state sector, growing competition, declining subsidies, and gradual hardening of budget constraints moved enterprises toward market-oriented operations, but the pace of change remained modest and uneven.

Beginning in the mid-1990s, the scope of reform expanded to include major restructuring of inherited stocks of labor and capital. State-sector firms, facing growing financial pressure from new competitors who avoided the redundant labor, cumbersome management structures, and costly fringe benefits inherited from the plan system, slashed tens of millions from their employment rolls. TVE privatization rapidly transferred most rural industries to private ownership (Li and Rozelle, 2004). Amid considerable downsizing of the officially desired scale and scope of state ownership in China's reforming economy, corporatization, privatization, bankruptcy, and both market-based and administratively managed mergers rapidly thinned the ranks of state-owned industrial enterprises, whose numbers dropped by 48.2 percent between 2001 and year-end 2004 (State Council Economic Census Group, 2005; see also Garnaut et al., 2005; Liu and Liu, 2005).

With the exception of employment, which has stagnated or even declined since the mid-1990s as a result of the massive SOE layoffs, overall manufacturing trends remain largely unchanged since 1995, with continued rapid growth of output, product quality, exports, and labor productivity. The character of industrial activity, however, has changed substantially. The past decade has witnessed a steep increase in market-oriented business behavior driven by the rapid expansion of foreign-invested firms, which now employ more workers than the combined total of state and collective enterprises (Yearbook, 2006, p. 505), accelerated growth of domestic private manufacturing, and the increasingly commercial orientation of state-controlled corporate groups, like Baosteel and China Petroleum.

Table 15.1. *Chinese industry in 2002: fifteen sectors receiving largest FDI inflows*

Manufacturing sector	Sector share of industry FDI	Export share of sector output	FIE share of sector exports	Sector share of China's industrial exports
Instruments and meters	10.64	30.45	93.83	13.11
Electronics and telecommunications	7.88	32.16	91.12	19.01
Medical and pharmaceutical	7.03	9.11	56.34	3.42
Transportation equipment	6.50	6.55	64.03	2.78
Nonmetal mineral products	6.14	14.75	76.48	2.74
Ordinary machinery	5.56	18.82	58.13	4.66
Garments	5.07	45.93	61.40	10.63
Beverages	4.30	4.76	58.93	0.48
Textiles	3.52	27.16	50.41	5.54
Paper products	3.37	8.84	77.85	0.86
Electric equipment and machinery	3.35	16.25	81.84	2.79
Food products	3.24	23.26	60.42	2.42
Smelting, rolling of ferrous metals	3.15	7.87	49.13	2.41
Metal products	2.73	19.60	84.80	2.18
Plastics	2.18	17.30	79.19	1.44
Average	4.98	18.85	69.59	4.96
TOTAL(for top fifteen)	74.66			74.47

Note: Values are in percent.
Source: China Industrial Microdata for 2002.
    Coverage includes the entire state sector and other firms with annual sales in excess of RMB5 million (about U.S.$600,000).

Table 15.1 captures the important role of foreign-invested enterprises (FIEs) in Chinese industry as of 2002. At the two-digit level, the ten largest sectoral beneficiaries of FDI absorbed more than 60 percent of accumulated FDI going to industry through 2002. In these sectors, foreign-invested firms recorded nearly half of total industry sales (including exports), exceeding 70 percent in electronics, and instruments and meters, but falling below 30 percent in textiles and nonmetallic mineral products. Although FIEs were also significantly more export oriented than their domestic counterparts, as suggested by their high share of sector exports, two-thirds of their sales went to the domestic market. This considerable presence of foreign-linked enterprises in the domestic marketplace exerted strong pressure on local firms competing in these venues.

The rapid growth of multinational firms' China-based operations, multiplication of cross-national supply networks, and steep expansion of manufactured exports have pulled growing segments of Chinese industry into the global business community. This integration process has stimulated substantial movement in the direction of standard international practices. Many facets of China's industrial system, including supply chain management, accounting practice, demand for MBA training, and industry associations, among others, reflect these new realities. At the same time, we also see the surprisingly persistent legacy of China's quarter century of socialist planning: frequent government intervention in commercial decision making, official control of high-level personnel appointments in state-related enterprises, and SOE dominance among recipients of bank lending (and thus of investment spending) despite the ongoing decline of the state sector's share in manufacturing output.

ROLE OF MARKET FORCES IN CHINA'S REFORMED ECONOMY

We see China's reform as steadily expanding the opportunity for strong firms that raise quality and variety, improve service, and control cost to gain market share at the expense of weaker rivals. This conflicts with the findings of authors who extend Donnithorne's (1972) vision of China as a "cellular economy" with limited interregional links into the reform era (Kumar, 1994; Young, 2000; Poncet, 2002, 2003; Boyreau-Debray and Wei, 2003). These researchers buttress their perspective with information suggesting limited domestic trade expansion, absence of regional specialization, and small cross-provincial flows of commodities and capital.

The basic tenet of the cellular economy perspective is that some combination of official protection and weak physical or institutional infrastructure effectively reserves regional markets for local producers. Favored incumbents sheltering behind strong entry barriers enjoy partial or full immunity from the competitive pressures that underpin our analysis of Chinese market development.

While no one doubts the existence of barriers to domestic trade, abundant evidence confirms the retreat of local protectionism. As a result, domestic trade barriers are no longer a central economic issue in China's economy. As Naughton observes, "[C]haracterizations of Chinese provinces as quasi-autarkic protected economies simply don't fit the facts" (2003, p. 227). Persistent claims of major internal trade barriers appear to arise from calculations based on incomplete transport statistics, excessive aggregation, or both.[3]

Survey analysis shows 70 percent of respondents reporting a weakening of local protectionism over ten years ending about 2003 (Li et al., 2004, p. 89). Travelers

---

[3] Huenemann finds that standard transport data "fail to capture a significant portion of the traffic, and the problem seems to get worse" during the 1990s (2001, p. 372). Rawski and Mead (1998) and Rawski (2005) also discuss the underestimation of transport volumes. Qi (2006) shows that disaggregation undermines the finding of limited capital market integration reported by Boyreau-Debray and Wei (2003).

along China's expanding highway network can observe trucks streaming across wide-open provincial borders. The share of interprovincial flows in railway freight haulage rises in twelve of fourteen years during 1990–2004, with the share of interprovincial shipments growing from 58.1 to 68.4 percent (calculated from data in various issues of Transport Yearbook).

Many phenomena, for instance, the rapid expansion of logistics, branding, and national advertising, contradict the cellular economy perspective. China's press is filled with accounts of cross-regional competition and cross-provincial mergers among makers of appliances, automobiles, beer, machine tools, steel, and many other products. Steinfeld comments that "even the most established firms cope with increasing competition by aggressively discounting and expanding sales volume ... by entering new product areas . . . or . . . by trying to export their way out of trouble," implying the exact opposite of sheltered markets (2004, p. 265). Studies by Bai et al. (2004), Naughton (2003), Park and Du (2003), Qi (2006), and Zhang and Tan (2004) provide additional evidence contradicting the cellular economy perspective.

Notwithstanding the incomplete nature of China's reforms and the well-documented presence of officially directed market segmentation, these observations demonstrate that both individual firms and whole industries typically experience strong influence from fundamental pressures common to all market systems. This perspective, which remains subject to further verification, informs what follows.

ANALYTIC FRAMEWORK

Introduction

How have Chinese market structures evolved? Starting from the late 1970s, liberalization and market expansion arising from the gradual demise of planning, the relaxation of control over international trade and investment, and improvements in transport and communication stimulated entry into formerly closed markets, intensified competition, and deepened market integration.

With market rivalries sharpening and official agencies embarking on a gradual, but accelerating process of reducing subsidies to weak firms, Chinese companies face a steady escalation of financial pressures. The dispersion of outcomes – not just wages, but also investment opportunities, housing, and medical and pension benefits – is increasingly aligned with enterprise financial results. This presages the decline and eventual disappearance of weak firms and the dismissal of redundant workers. Although ongoing subsidies for incumbents, imperfect exit mechanisms and the veneer of prosperity arising from rapid growth slow the process of downward mobility, the basic consequence of economic reform – the idea that participants' economic future depends on the financial outcome of market activity – has gradually come to the fore.

Two main themes are explored in what follows. The first of these relates to the shift toward a market economy that has occurred over the past two decades. Up to the early 1990s, it was widely argued that the shift was limited by geographical segmentation of markets, by political interference, and by the behavior of SOEs. A blow-by-blow listing of barriers to the operation of markets might suggest many impediments of this kind, and yet the cumulative quantitative impact of such barriers would be difficult to assess. In what follows, we take an indirect approach, by looking at the way market structure has evolved in a range of industries of different kinds over the past twenty years. Different industries have different characteristics that affect their mode of evolution in market economies, and by looking across a range of industries of different types we can see whether patterns of development characteristic of market economies have been observed. Clearly, there are two very different situations involved here, since some industries have been long established, while others have essentially grown up from scratch over the twenty-year period. We begin, in the next section with a brief sketch of the different types of industry to be considered, and we then look at the "new" industries before turning to the adjustment paths followed by the "old" industries.

The second theme relates to the question "how far has China come?" How close has its "industrial capability" moved toward that of advanced industrial economies? Before addressing these issues, it is worth pausing to ask what is meant here by "capability."

Some Preliminary Remarks

A firm's *capability* can be defined, for our present purposes, in two steps:

(a) The firm's ("revealed") capability relates to the range of products which it currently produces; specifically, for each (narrowly defined) product line, it refers to (1) the unit variable cost of production expressed as the number of units of materials, and labor input, required per unit of output product, and (2) a measure or index of "perceived" quality defined in terms of buyers' willingness to pay for a unit of the firm's product, as against rival firms' products. (It is worth noting that this index of "perceived quality" can be raised not only by improving the physical attributes of the product, via R&D or otherwise, but also through improvement in reputation, brand image, and so on).

(b) Underlying the firm's revealed capability is the firm's "underlying capability," which consists of the set of elements of "know-how" held collectively by the group of individuals comprising the firm. The importance of this deeper notion of capability lies in the fact that some of these elements of "know-how" will be useful in producing products not currently made by the firm,[4]

---

[4] An early formulation of this idea appears in Rawski (1975b).

and this will enhance the firm's ability to take advantage of new opportunities over time, as shifts occur in the underlying pattern of technology and demand which it faces.

A generic property of the class of models considered here is that competition between firms will generate some "threshold" level of capability below which no firm can survive (in the sense of achieving any positive level of sales revenue at equilibrium). Thus there is a range, or "window," of capability levels at any time, between the current "top" level attained by any firm and this threshold, and any potential entrant must attain a capability that puts it into this window.[5]

It will be useful to begin with a few general remarks about some relevant industry characteristics. Two key characteristics that affect the different patterns of evolution of different industries are as follows:

1. The first factor, labeled $1/\beta$ in Figure 15.2, relates to the process of capability building within the firms. Specifically, β represents the elasticity of the function specifying the level of fixed outlays required to achieve a given level of perceived quality or a given level of productivity (Sutton, 1998, chapter 3). If, for example, an increase in R&D spending leads to a substantial rise in product quality ("product innovation"), or a substantial fall in the unit cost of production ("process innovation"), then $1/\beta$ will be high. In this (narrow) sense, $1/\beta$ measures the "effectiveness of R&D." More generally, the firm may build up its capability using a variety of methods; what is common to all these methods is that they are costly – in all cases, the firm incurs some fixed and sunk cost in equipping individuals with new elements of "know-how," whether these relate to product design, production routines, or other devices that enhance productivity or perceived product quality. Now if we are dealing with a standard commodity product, produced using equipment available for sale on the market, which can be operated effectively by low-skill workers, then the firm's opportunities for raising its level of capability relative to its rivals may be limited, so that $1/\beta$ is low. On the other hand, if the firm can develop, or imitate, new and better routines in its production process, by way of training programs or otherwise, then $1/\beta$ will be correspondingly higher. As we move up vertically in Figure 15.2, we move from commodity-type industries where the relevant technology is largely "embodied" in capital equipment bought in from outside, toward industries in which increasing efforts are devoted to the building up of in-house expertise and know-how.

---

[5] China's pre-reform system, with its weak competition, segmented markets, low incomes, excess demand, and product prices set to allow mediocre firms to cover costs, ensured that most suppliers faced low thresholds and wide sales windows. Customers willingly accepted a wide range of products, including goods with "small defects." In the 1990s, for example, occupants of new housing provided by the Chinese Academy of Social Sciences immediately replaced the (defective) electrical switches installed by the builders.

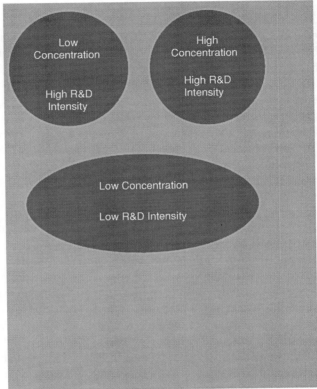

Figure 15.2. Industry characteristics

2. The second factor of interest, labeled σ in Figure 15.2, relates to the relationship between different (firms') products. These relationships arise both on the demand side ("substitutability") and on the supply side ("scope economies"). What σ measures is the extent to which a firm that devotes additional effort to capability building can capture market share from its rivals. The value of σ can be affected, for example, by the cost of transport: in the cement industry, price differences across two different geographical regions may have only a modest impact on the pattern of market shares, in that they may induce switches of consumers only in some intermediate areas more or less equivalent from the rival plants; if this is the case, then σ is low. If, on the other hand, transport costs are low, then small price differences may induce larger shifts in market shares, and σ will be correspondingly higher. More generally, if buyers are insensitive to any differences between the product varieties offered by different producers, so that small price differences have a big impact on market shares, then σ is high.

A second form of linkage arises on the supply side: this linkage operates at the level of the underlying elements of know-how required in the production of rival products ("economies of scope"). Here, if a firm deepens its expertise in the production of one product line, this expertise can place it at an advantage on introducing a second product line, or – if it is already active in the production of that second line – in enhancing its previous level of productivity or quality in that second line.[6] At the opposite extreme, we might imagine the market to include a set of different product types, each based on an entirely different form of technology to the others. A firm investing heavily in its capability may take market share only from those rivals selling the same type of product to its own offering but will not take share from producers in other segments or ("submarkets"). (For a practical illustration of this type of market, see the discussion of the flow meter industry in Sutton, 1998, chapter 5). This again constitutes the kind of linkage that is measured by σ, viz., and increase in a firm's spending on capability building is effective in allowing it to capture a larger share of the market as a whole.

Figure 15.2 shows the pattern of outcomes associated with different combinations of $1/\beta$ and σ; for the underlying analytical arguments, and empirical evidence supporting this summary picture, see Sutton (1998, chapters 3–4). What the figure indicates is as follows: when the effectiveness of capability building is low, then it will be possible to sustain an increasingly fragmented market structure, as the size of the market increases. It is important to note that this outcome does not necessarily emerge; however, the underlying economic mechanisms permit a *wide range* of market structures to be supported.[7]

Now as we move up the vertical axis in Figure 15.2, two alternative patterns emerge, according as σ is low or high. When σ is low, we can once again sustain a fragmented market structure, but now the levels of effort devoted to capability building by firms will be intense, and R&D-to-sales ratios will be high. But as we move across the diagram to the top right-hand corner (high $1/\beta$, high σ), concentration must necessarily be high, *independently of the size of the market*. The key economic mechanism at work here is an "escalation effect": as the market grows, the familiar tendency for new entry to occur, leading to a rise in the number of producers and a fall in concentration, does not operate. Instead, the enhanced profits available to a firm that commands a given share of the larger market induces

---

[6] China's Haier Group, which used its expertise and reputation in refrigerators as a springboard to enter markets for air conditioners and televisions, provides an apt Chinese illustration.

[7] To illustrate this point, consider the case of a large number of cement plants arranged along the coastline from north to south. A fragmented market structure might involve each plant being owned by a different firm; if, however, every second plant is acquired by a single firm, so that each competes only with the same independent local rivals as before, the (price) equilibrium in the market is unaffected, and the new form of market structure is viable and stable, just as was the old "fragmented" structure.

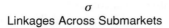

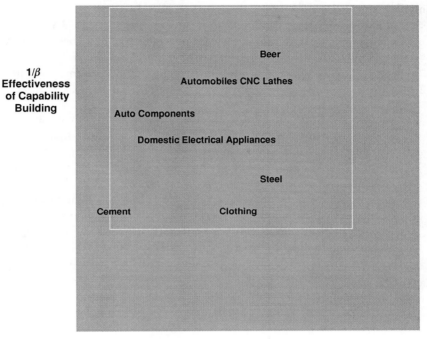

Figure 15.3. Examples of industry characteristics

increased investments in capability building by market leaders. Instead of having more firms, we have an unchanged number of firms, each supporting a correspondingly greater level of R&D spending (or, more generally, spending on "capability building").

It may be useful to note where various industries lie on this figure; this can be done by reference to measurable "industry characteristics" following Sutton (1998; see Figure 15.3)

A comparison of Figures 15.2 and 15.3 allows us to make some preliminary observations as to the way in which market liberalization should be expected to affect the pattern of capability building, and the evolution of concentration, in different Chinese industries.

First, however, a general remark is in order. As noted earlier, the economic mechanisms we are concerned with here operate merely to place a lower limit of the level of market concentration; if, as was the case in Eastern Europe, the preliberalization regime favored the creation and maintenance of highly concentrated industries in which a handful of large SOEs dominated, then the move to a free market environment is consistent with a *fall* in concentration. In the Chinese context, however, the most common starting point featured low concentration because dispersal of manufacturing formed part of China's military strategy and because Chinese economic planners generally ratified the efforts of individual provinces to build "full sets" of industries.[8] Rapid development of rural industry after 1978 accentuated the tendency for market concentration in Chinese industries to fall below the levels typical of similar industries in large market economies.

The impact of liberalization involves three important mechanisms (see Sutton, 2000):

1. As domestic firms come into closer competition with domestically based rivals, or with imports, prices fall, and the least capable firms may no longer be viable.[9] The result is a mixture of exit, and consolidation (aimed at restoring margins), leading concentration to rise. This mechanism operates across all industries, but is relatively weak when σ is low, as in cement.

2. As we move up and across Figure 15.2, toward the top-right corner (high σ, high $1/\beta$), a second mechanism plays an increasingly important role: this involves an escalation of efforts by surviving firms in respect of capability building, leading to higher levels of R&D spending and increased market concentration. This plays a central role in industries such as "Domestic Electrical Appliances," on which we focus in the next section.[10,11]

3. The third mechanism relates to volatility of market shares. As competition intensifies, the market share gap between more capable firms in each market,

---

[8] Printing equipment, a new industry in the 1950s, had spread to twenty-one provinces by 1980 (Machinery, 1983, p. 89). Li Chengrui, a prominent Chinese economist, commented in 1975 that China's regions "all want to speed up production in their own area" and therefore "argue for large state investments in their own provinces" for every sector (Perkins et al., 1977, p. 276).

[9] In China, rising incomes and export expansion tended to raise the lower threshold of sales windows, thus multiplying pressures on low-capability firms.

[10] Mechanisms I and II can be described as follows: as more firms enter the "window," the lower threshold rises. Moreover, the incentives for firms to raise their investments in "capability building" also rise, so that the top of the window (defined by the highest capability attained by any firm) also rises. In other words, the process of entry pushes up the window. While these remarks relate to a single ("closed") economy, the same idea carries over to a multicountry setting: as a new country joins the global market, its firms "enter the window," and the window itself shifts upward, rendering some hitherto viable firms elsewhere nonviable. It is worth noting, finally, that having low wage rates in the "entrant" country reduces the relevant threshold of capability that its firms must attain, but this effect can only partially offset shortenings in quality: even if wage rates become arbitrarily low, the fact that manufacturing firms need some bought-in inputs fixes a lower bound to their marginal costs of production, and this in turn implies that once quality falls below a certain threshold, the firm cannot achieve any positive sales at equilibrium.

[11] How wide, then, is the window? It turns out that it depends not only on the two parameters introduced in Figure 15.2, but also on (a) the nature ("toughness") of price competition in the market, and (b) the range of buyers' "willingness to pay" for quality. In particular, if there are some customers who are indifferent to quality and are concerned only with price, then an arbitrarily large fringe of low-cost, low-quality firms may be viable (see Sutton, 1991, chapter 3 for an example).

and their less capable rivals, widens. Moreover, a firm's current ("revealed") capability is not always mirrored in its underlying ("dynamic") capability, that is, its ability to adjust to shocks in its environment. It follows that shifts in the *ranking* of firms in the market are likely to occur; at its most extreme, this may lead to the displacement of old market leaders by new entrants. Again, this mechanism plays a central role in what follows.

THE NEW INDUSTRIES

China's economic boom has stimulated rapid expansion of many industries, typically in response to a surge in domestic demand arising from increased household incomes. Steven Klepper and several coauthors have discovered a two-stage process that typifies the evolution of firm numbers and industry concentration for new industries in competitive markets (e.g., Klepper and Graddy, 1990; see also Sutton, 1998). At the start, firms rush to participate in the new market, leading to "excess entry." Thereafter, the "escalation" mechanism introduced in the preceding section kicks in: as competition intensifies, successful expansion of capabilities by some firms leads to increased concentration amidst growing production and sales, rising quality thresholds, ongoing product and process innovation, and falling prices. Firms that cannot expand sales sufficiently to support escalating R&D requirements in the face of shrinking profit margins leave the industry, resulting in a "shakeout" that sharply reduces the number of active producers and raises the level of concentration.

This perspective, based on U.S. experience, aptly summarizes the process of market development in new Chinese industries. We focus on household appliances. In 1978, China's production of home appliances was minuscule. Since then, the emergence of new industries has pushed China into the ranks of global leaders in the manufacture of consumer durables. Table 15.2 summarizes physical output trends for several products. Refrigerators illustrate the trend. In 1978, China produced one model and only 29,000 units. Subsequently, annual output jumped to 4.6 million units in 1990, 12.8 million in 2000, and 29.9 million in 2005, with a commensurate expansion in the range of models. Washing machines followed a similar trend, with annual output climbing from 4,000 units in 1978 to 6.6 million in 1990 and 30.4 million by 2005. Production of televisions, air conditioners, and other appliances recorded similarly steep increases.

In the Chinese context, two factors might have modified or offset the anticipated sequence of entry and shakeout. First, government tried to control the evolution of the market (Jiang, 2001, p. 168), but since official intervention favored movement toward structures with modest numbers of large and relatively capable firms (Marukawa, 2001, p. 74), its influence may have complemented natural processes of market evolution. Second, the surge in demand in the 1980s and early 1990s could have been partly met by imports, thus stilling the growth of domestic

Table 15.2. *Chinese production of home
electric appliances*

Year	Color television	Refrigerators	Washing machines	Air conditioners
1978	0.004	0.03	0.0004	0.0002
1985	4.35	1.45	8.87	0.12
1990	10.33	4.63	6.63	0.24
1995	20.58	9.18	9.48	6.82
2000	39.36	12.79	14.43	18.27
2005	82.83	29.87	30.36	67.634
Eight-firm concentration ratios CR 8				
2000	54.1			
2002	47.7	82.0	72.4	35.1

Note: Values are in million units.

Source: Output data from Yearbook (2006, p. 561); concentration ratios calculated from data in *China Markets Yearbook* (2001, 2004) and from China Industrial Microdata for 2002.

production, but strict trade controls limited the share of imports during the 1980s (Marukawa, 2001, p. 61).

As a result, the evolution of China's home appliance sector closely follows Klepper's U.S.-based observations. The number of firms in each industry rose to very high levels during the latter half of the 1980s, but by the late 1990s, the population of appliance makers had begun a steep decline. Washing machine producers, for example, exceeded 180 in 1983, but by 1995, only 30 brands were visible in the market. Eight years later, four dominant Chinese firms shared the much larger domestic market with a comparable number of international manufacturers (Washers, 2003). Refrigerator producers numbered over 200 in 1988; a 2005 report noted "about 40 locally owned household refrigerator and freezer makers in China, down from about 100 in the late 1990s," and predicted that the number would shrink to "fewer than 20" by 2007 (Jiang, 2001; Consolidation, 2005). In color TVs, 87 firms were active in 1990; seven years later, this had fallen to 15.

Although we lack complete data, these shakeouts clearly produced rapid increases in concentration. The four-firm concentration ratio for washing machines jumped from 21 percent in 1982 to 72 percent in 1996; in fridges, it rose from 29 percent in 1988 to 37 percent in 1994; for color TVs, it rose from 43 percent in 1993 to 68 percent by 1998 and over 70 percent in 2005 (Tang and Liu, 2006). Table 15.2 includes additional data.

Despite the general trend toward concentration, the evolution of specific industries displays unexpected twists. The number of competitors in the market for home air conditioners rose during the 1980s, declined during the 1990s, and then witnessed "a dramatic increase" from 2003, when "over 200 brands . . . entered the fray," followed by another steep decline to 69 firms in late 2005, of which 48, each

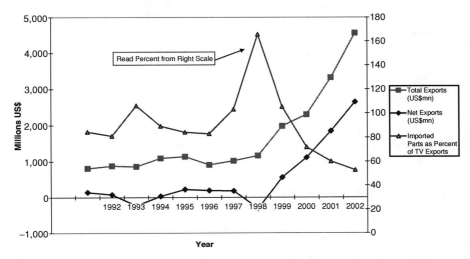

Figure 15.4. China's trade in TVs and components 1992–2003 (U.S.$ million – left scale, and percent)

with market share under 1 percent, seemed destined for a quick exit (Glut, 2005). The balance between foreign and domestic firms is equally unstable. Overseas firms stormed into China's nascent home appliance market in the 1980s, retreated in the face of a powerful domestic response during the 1990s, and then returned in force after 2000, particularly in washing machines, where Toshiba alone held a 20 percent share of the domestic market in 2001, and refrigerators, where local firms face "intense competition from multinationals" (Toshiba, 2001; Consolidation, 2005).

The color television sector illustrates the turbulence surrounding changes in market shares for home appliances and other new sectors. China's color TV industry is a big success. Figure 15.4 shows a classic "product cycle" pattern – initial imports followed by a steep rise in exports and an equally abrupt decline in the ratio of imported components to export sales – that rocketed Chinese producers into a leading position among global exporters of televisions.

The road to success, however, was long and costly. As late as 1990, no province achieved annual output even close to the capacity of plants imported prior to 1985. From the perspective of 1990, China's venture into the manufacture of color televisions appeared to be a costly disaster. The ensuing decade brought a dramatic turnaround as several regions led by Guangdong (home of TCL and Konka) and Sichuan (home of Changhong, the new industry leader) experienced a "takeoff" into mass production and large-scale export. Even then, success left a trail of failed initiatives in regions like Beijing that never attained the production level associated with facilities imported before 1985. With China's top four TV makers holding 30 percent of the global market and 70 percent of domestic sales of color TVs, a Ministry of Commerce researcher summarized the outcome: "many money-loosing [*sic*] or uncompetitive TV makers still exist . . . although some real market players have emerged" (Wang and Dai, 2004; Tang and Liu, 2006).

With firms struggling to master new technologies and stabilize their finances amid fierce competition, rapid shifts in market leadership are commonplace. Nanjing-based Panda was the industry's largest producer in 1993, with a market share of 11 percent. Over the next three years, Panda's position was rapidly eroded by the rise of Sichuan-based Changhong, which had ranked fourth in 1993 with a market share of 4 percent. Panda failed to anticipate Changhong's growing strength and could not match Changhong's big price reduction in 1994. Lower prices sparked a big increase in sales that allowed Changhong to grab sales at Panda's expense. By 1996, Changhong's market share had vaulted to 21 percent, while Panda's had slumped to 5 percent.[12]

Changhong's top ranking was short lived. The new leader faced powerful competition from TCL, which rose from third position in 1996 to supplant Changhong as market leader by 2003. Both TCL and Konka, another strong challenger, established production facilities near Changhong's home base, with the aim of undercutting its former market dominance in western China. In 2004, the collapse of Changhong's partnership with a U.S.-based importer saddled the firm with massive losses. Despite its impressive sales and large annual revenues, Changhong suddenly faced the task of simultaneously rebuilding its finances, maintaining its market share, and integrating new domestic and overseas projects into its operations (Buckley, 2005; Changhong, 2005; Global, 2005).

The cushion of local government financial support (Sugawara, 2005) cannot protect firms like Changhong against market risk. In the television industry, as in many other new sectors (computers, telecommunications equipment, semiconductors, etc.), rapid obsolescence of products, materials, and equipment multiplies the risk of failure. The sudden market shift toward plasma and flat-screen televisions has quickly devalued the supply chains and production experience that China's producers struggled to accumulate over twenty-five years. With their lack of "underlying capability" now frighteningly apparent, Changhong and other big TV makers must scramble to master new technologies, restructure supply chains, and reconfigure manufacturing facilities, incurring huge costs merely to participate in the treacherously shifting market with no promise of success or even survival. Chinese observers are quick to criticize Changhong and other firms that "lack their own core technologies, and compete by making products for overseas brand labels using ruinous price competition to gain market share" (Li, 2003). With flat-screen prices dropping at dizzying rates, Japanese and Korean firms shouldering "the huge upfront costs required to remain . . . major player[s]" and industry executives anticipating that "only three or four TV makers can survive," the impressive achievements of China's television manufacturers cannot conceal the dangers that lie ahead (Flat TV, 2007, p. 7).

---

[12] Data in this paragraph come from interviews and from a variety of published reports.

If the evolution of these "new" industries clearly follows patterns familiar from western economies, what of the older established industries?

ADJUSTING: THE ESTABLISHED INDUSTRIES

Cement. The pressures to adjust in a market environment vary sharply across industries. For the cement industry, even in a free market environment the high level of transport costs segments markets geographically, and the intensity of price competition and the extent of cross hauling across different regions remains low. For Chinese cement makers, adjustment has posed relatively few problems.

Policy decisions and regulations have accentuated the natural tendency for local or regional market segmentation. In Beijing, for example, the BBMG Company is the only large producer. Operating all three large-scale plants in the city area, it supplies one-third of demand, the remainder being filled by forty small "township companies" and by cross hauling from firms in neighboring Hebei Province. Environmental concerns have led the authorities to bar further plant building or expansion in the city area, in spite of the rapid increase in demand. BBMG operates profitably in this setting, and it has focused its strategy on diversification into other types of construction materials. It has several foreign joint-venture partners, in areas ranging from ceramics to chipboard (Interview, August 2, 2004).

A contrasting case is that of the Sunnsy Company in Jinan City (Shandong). A long-established producer, and the largest in its region, it ran at a loss for a decade during the 1980s. The firm launched a "turnaround" strategy in 1990, which focused on expanding its penetration of regional cement markets, first in Shandong and then in neighboring Hebei. By 2004, with annual cement output of 2.5 million tons, or twelve times the level of 1990, Sunnsy had set its sights on extending sales into Beijing's booming construction sector and into nearby Tianjin (Interview, August 3, 2004).

Textiles and Apparel

At the outset of reform, textiles and apparel ranked among China's largest industrial sectors, representing nearly a sixth of the gross value of industrial output. Table 15.3 summarizes the evolution of the textile sector.[13] This sector was also an important source of export earnings, largely from the export of cotton fabric (as opposed to apparel).

---

[13] Chinese data on the textile sector (*fangzhi gongye*) typically include the manufacture of artificial fibers and yarn; production, dyeing, and printing of fabric; and the manufacture of garments, accessories (ribbon, rope, and cord), shoes, hats, and textile machinery. Textile Report (2005, pp. 350–351) provides an English-language list of the major subsectors. Our focus here is on the manufacture of fabrics ("textiles" or "textile industry") and garments. A further complication arises because, starting in 1998, standard data exclude small firms with annual sales below RMB5 million.

Table 15.3. *Overview of China's textile and apparel sector, 1980–2005*

	1980	1985	1990	1995	1997	2000[a]	2005[a]
Number of firms	37,900	46,700	83,800	102,500	79,200	20,926	35,978
Employment (million)	5.02	9.46	12.43	12.43	10.65	8.11	9.78
Gross output value (RMB billion)	88.5	149.2	373.5	839.7	963.2	878.6	1,625.0
Share of aggregate GVIO (%)	17.7	18.0	16.2	12.6	12.9	10.3	6.5
Exports (billion U.S. dollars)	3.6	5.5	12.5	38.0	45.6	49.4	117.5
Share of total exports (%)	19.8	20.2	20.1	25.5	24.9	19.8	15.4
Apparel share in sector exports (%)	37.4	38.7	40.9	63.2	69.7	68.8	62.6
Textile exports as percent of world textile exports	4.6	6.2	7.5	11.7	13.7	14.7	24.1

GVIO, Gross value of industrial output (current prices).

[a] Data for 2000 and 2005 exclude firms with annual sales below RMB5 million.

Sources: For 1980–1995: Shi (2001, p. 67).

For 2000: Firms, output, employment from Industry Yearbook (2001, pp. 48, 49, 53). Export data from Yearbook (2001, pp. 589–590).

For 2005: Textile Report (2005, pp. 3, 4, 360, 364); Yearbook (2006, p. 516).

China share of global textile exports (including clothing) calculated from trade data posted at http://stat.wto.org/StatisticalProgram/WsdbExport.aspx?Language=E, accessed January 24, 2007.

The textile sector experienced rapid growth during the first decade of reform. The number of firms and employees more than doubled between 1980 and 1990 and output quadrupled. Exports rose steeply, with Chinese goods claiming a 7.5 percent share of global textile and apparel exports by 1990. Despite the rapid pace of overall industrial growth, familiar patterns persisted: textiles continued to deliver about one-sixth of all industrial production, exports hovered around one-fifth of total output, and fabrics contributed roughly three-fifths of overall export sales.

Between 1990 and 1997 (note that the coverage of data in Table 15.3 changes after 1997), steep growth of output and exports continued, but familiar patterns began to shift. Both employment and (after 1995) the number of firms began to decline, as did the textile sector's share in overall industrial output. The textile sector's share of China's exports jumped from one-fifth to one quarter, powered mainly by sales of garments, which occupied roughly two-thirds of China's textile exports after 1995.

Underlying these changes was a rapid process of internationalization. Table 15.1 shows that both textiles (i.e., manufacture of fabrics) and garments ranked among the leading recipients of FDI. The establishment of joint-venture firms had a profound effect, particularly in the production of apparel. As noted earlier, rising exports of garments pushed the textile sector's share of China's exports sharply higher, even as textiles began to retreat from its traditional position among China's largest industries.

Table 15.4 draws on results of China's 1995 industrial census to map out the ownership structure of textile and garment manufacturing. Along with internationalization, reflected in the new prominence of joint-venture firms in exports of textiles and especially in the manufacture and export of apparel, the data reveal a substantial shift of market share from the formerly dominant state sector to urban collectives (COEs) and to rural firms (TVEs). The 1995 data essentially partition overall output into four roughly equal segments: SOEs, now confined almost entirely to the (slightly more capital-intensive) manufacture of fabrics; joint ventures, with a heavy emphasis on export-oriented garment manufacture; urban collectives and TVEs, each providing roughly one quarter of China's 1995 output of both textiles and apparel.

Strong outward orientation and the further retreat of the state sector highlight the evolution of China's textile sector after 1995. Table 15.3 documents the continued rapid expansion of output and especially exports through 2005, with overseas sales of garments retaining the lead role established during the early 1990s. State-owned and state-controlled firms accounted for only 8.9 and 6.0 percent of textile-sector gross output value and export earnings in 2005 (Textile Report, 2005, pp. 322–324).

With textiles designated as a "competitive sector," meaning that government maintains a more-or-less "hands-off" policy and allows market outcomes to dictate the rise or fall of individual firms, the state sector's weak productivity and profit performance allowed urban collectives, TVEs, foreign firms, and, most recently, private Chinese operators to add market share at the state sector's expense.

Table 15.4. *China's 1995 output and exports of textiles and apparel, classified by ownership of producers*

Ownership	Textile					Apparel					Totals	
	GVIO	Share of total	Exports	Share of total	Export ratio	GVIO	Share of total	Exports	Share of total	Export ratio	GVIO	Exports
SOE	1,825.2	0.31	508.1	0.31	0.28	102.1	0.05	32.17	0.03	0.31	1,927.34	540.26
JV	824.1	0.14	369.9	0.23	0.45	737.3	0.37	498.8	0.45	0.68	1,561.35	868.72
COE	1,852.2	0.31	388.7	0.24	0.21	631.9	0.31	285.3	0.26	0.45	2,484.10	674.00
TVE	1,382.8	0.23	374.4	0.23	0.27	547.9	0.27	286.4	0.26	0.52	1,930.70	660.80
TOTAL	5,884.3	1.00	1,641.1	1.00	0.28	2,019.2	1.00	1,102.7	1.00	0.55	7,903.49	2,743.78

GVIO, gross value of industrial output; JV, joint ventures (between foreign and Chinese firms); COE, urban collective enterprises; TVE, township and village enterprises.
Note: Values are in RMB billion (current prices); data shown here reflect the "new" definition of gross output value (GVIO).
Source: Publications from 1995 Industrial Census.

The entry and growth of foreign-invested firms, whose activities were heavily tilted toward apparel exports, generated positive spillovers for the whole industry. Foreign-linked firms fostered important backward linkages in the sector for fabric (including dyeing) and accessories, for example, zippers, buttons. Thick new supply chains clustered around export producers, especially in the coastal areas. This facilitated the emergence of vibrant new private firms, which tapped these networks in their quest to meet the demanding quality and delivery requirements of overseas customers and, more recently, domestic buyers.

Branstetter and Lardy (Table 16.1) find that the number of firms authorized to engage in direct overseas sales (as opposed to consigning products to state trading firms) rose from 12 in 1978 to 800 in 1985, 12,000 in 1996, and 31,000 in 2000. The beneficiaries of this liberalization included many producers of textiles and garments. The resulting interaction with overseas customers represents a central element in the growth of private firms in this sector.

The experience of the Nanjing-based Huarui (Ever Glory) Apparel firm, a private company founded in 1993, is illustrative. Ever Glory built its business from the outset on direct links to foreign buyers. Its first major relationship arose from repeated visits to the Shanghai sourcing office of the multinational retailer C&A. Following this success, Huarui focused its efforts on building links to a few large foreign customers. It deliberately pursued sales in Japan, the most demanding market, to force itself to attain high-quality standards, which it then extended to its entire business. Huarui emphasizes close relations with its own suppliers, interacting on a continuing basis with these firms to develop good working relations – a strategy more familiar among the auto industry than among clothing firms (Interview, August 9, 2004).

The recent history of two other firms, Lanyan (Shandong) and Chenfeng (Jiangsu), shows important parallels with Huarui. Both firms acquired direct export rights in the early 1990s and benefited from manufacturing to the demanding standards of overseas customers. Uniquely in the industry, these two firms have become more vertically integrated over time, building on their initial capabilities and reputations. Lanyan's operations started out in the manufacture of denim fabric; by 2004, they had become the world's eleventh largest manufacturer of denim cloth. Building on their capability in denim production, Lanyan has expanded into the export of denim products, for example, blue jeans, to the United States, Japan, and Korea; they provide the fabric, and their customers the designs (Interview, August 4, 2004). Chengfeng, which sells silk apparel to major U.S. customers including Gap, Liz Claiborne, and Jones of New York, has integrated backward into hybrid cocoon production to ensure high-quality standards in their silk fabric. They have diversified into cotton apparel as well (Interview, August 11, 2004).

Adjustment, however, has not been easy for all firms. The combined annual profits of textile SOEs were negative throughout 1993–1999 (Textile Yearbook, 2000, p. 3). As late as 2000, more than 31 percent of all SOEs that remained in the industry were losing money. Between 1999 and 2005, the number of SOEs in the industry declined from 4,247 to 1,480, but the share of loss-making firms remained high – 37.3 percent in 2005.[14] In 2005, value added per worker and value added per yuan of net fixed assets in SOEs were only 60 and 40 percent, respectively, of the industry average, while profits per yuan of assets were only one-sixteenth of the industry average.

The number 12 Textile Factory in Baoji, Shaanxi, which was originally established by the Rong family in 1938 and is now under the direct control of a provincial government corporation, is an intermediate case between the failing SOEs and the firms described earlier. This enterprise has survived in the short run as an efficient exporter of medium-range cotton cloth (360–370 threads per inch), primarily to Japan, South Korea, and Southeast Asia. A distinguishing feature of this firm, however, is the inability or unwillingness of its managers to engage in direct sales to overseas clients. Despite obtaining export rights around 2000, this firm chooses to employ middlemen rather than dealing directly with customers. This likely reflects its limited capabilities in finding customers.[15] Company management has also resisted vertically integrating, or moving into (or overseeing) higher-valued-added stages in the production process, for example, dyeing. With growing pressure from private firms in the coastal areas, and falling cotton cloth prices, this firm's future is less than certain.

Rapidly rising exports are a clear indication of the growing capabilities of firms in this industry. This is nicely reflected in U.S. import data, which show both rising Chinese penetration and a shift into higher-valued-added segments of each submarket. At the four-digit level, average penetration of Chinese products rose from 11.4 percent of U.S. apparel imports in 1987 to 12.6 percent in 1990, 15.7 percent in 1995, and 18.3 percent in 2000. Over the same period, the weighted average ratio of the unit value of imports from China to the unit value of all imports rises from 0.83 in 1987 to 0.91 in 1990, 1.06 in 1995, and 1.28 in 2000.[16] We observe similar, but slightly weaker, behavior in textiles.

Efforts to raise capabilities reflect pressures from domestic as well as overseas customers. The expansion of household incomes and fashion consciousness has

---

[14] The decline in SOE numbers is the result of aggressive government-led restructuring of textile SOEs entailing privatization and bankruptcy, as well as merger and acquisition. Data on SOE numbers and profitability are from Textile Report (2000, p. 236) and Textile Yearbook (2000, p. 130) (for 1999) and from Textile Report (2005, p. 324).

[15] Commissions for intermediaries typically run 1 percent of sales. With 2005 profits averaging 4.0 percent of sales in spinning and weaving and −3.5 percent of sales in Shaanxi's textile sector (Textile Report, 2005, pp. 336, 338, 344, 352), this firm's reliance on intermediaries probably represents a considerable charge against earnings.

[16] Results calculated from UNCOM trade data. Between 2000 and 2004, China's share of U.S. apparel imports increased even further to 26.8 percent, while the ratio of unit values fell to 1.01. The falling ratio of unit values may reflect an increase in lower-quality imports from China following the removal of import quotas that provided incentives for exporting higher-value goods. According to Evans and Harrigan (2004), 74 (57) percent of China's apparel exports to the United States in 1991 (1998) were under binding quotas.

elevated quality requirements in the Chinese market for fabric and garments, which absorbs two-thirds of all sales by textile and apparel firms and one-third of sales for FIEs. At the risk of some simplification, we can divide the domestic market for textiles and garments into two quality segments.[17] Prosperous, fashion-conscious buyers, mainly in urban areas, populate the upper segment, in which rising sales windows reflect growing customer demand for design, quality, and branding. Firms that cannot keep pace with these rising standards find themselves forced to compete in the lower segment, where price remains the primary consideration.

As the upper segment grows in absolute and relative size, domestic firms, some with export experience, are emerging as industry leaders, investing heavily in developing their capabilities and increasingly relying on their own designs and brand names. Firms without export experience, especially those located in the coastal provinces, benefit from China's export success through their ability to tap a well-developed domestic supply chain. Exporters have also become an important conduit for information on international design and fashion trends. These circumstances have created a substantial premium on coastal location: one Shaanxi apparel manufacturer complained of a six-month information lag compared with coastal firms. This disadvantage encouraged them first to procure fabric and accessories from coastal firms and subsequently to abandon manufacturing entirely and focus on design and marketing (Interview, July 21, 2005).

Steel. Table 15.5 summarizes steel industry trends during the past quarter century. After quadrupling physical output during the two decades of reform, China emerged at the turn of the century as the world's largest steel producer, with 2000 production of 128.5 million tons. The following years saw a further steep increase, with crude steel output more than tripling to 418.8 million tons, or one-third of global production, in 2006. Over the same period, the number of firms in the industry more than doubled. In the wake of this massive growth, China's domestic steel market and major steel producers now exert important influence over global steel trends.

Beyond the continuing expansion, China's steel industry presents a complex picture. While market forces continue to gain strength, official influence, both at the national level and below, remains stronger than in many other sectors. China's steelmakers display extreme heterogeneity in terms of scale, productivity, technology, and responsiveness to market forces. Some have achieved rapid progress toward international quality and productivity standards, while others extend the former plan system's legacy of inefficient, tonnage-oriented production.

Industrywide productivity and cost trends demonstrate impressive gains. Despite massive increases in output, sectorwide employment grew by only 32 percent between 1978 and 2005. As a result, output per worker rose more than tenfold from low initial levels (Table 15.5). Trends for basic technical indicators, shown in Figure 15.5, indicate that gradual improvements have cumulated into

---

[17] High-end imports constitute a third market segment, which we omit from this discussion.

Table 15.5. *China steel overview: production, employment, and trade*

Year	Number of firms	Crude steel output (million tons)	Sectoral employment (millions)	Output per man-year (tons)	International trade in finished steel (million tons)			
					Imports		Exports	
					Total	Flat products	Total	Flat products
1978		31.8	2.14	14.9	8.6	4.0	0.3	n.a.
1980	1,332	37.1	2.44	15.2	5.0	1.6	0.5	n.a.
1985	1,318	46.8	2.68	17.5	19.6	5.7	0.2	n.a.
1990	1,589	66.4	3.15	21.1	3.7	1.9	2.1	n.a.
1995	1,639	95.4	3.42	27.9	14.0	6.8	5.9	3.7
2000	2,997	128.5	2.52	51.0	15.6	14.1	5.4	3.5
2001	3,176	151.6	2.32	65.3	17.2	14.9	4.7	1.8
2002	3,333	182.4	2.39	76.2	24.5	21.2	5.4	1.8
2003	4,119	222.3	2.56	86.8	37.2	33.2	7.0	5.2
2004	4,992	282.9	2.61	108.4	29.3	25.1	14.2	5.8
2005	6,604	353.2	2.81	125.7	25.8	22.0	20.5	8.0
2006	6,639	418.8	2.80	149.6	18.5		43.0	

Sources:

Output and trade data for 2006 from Crude Steel (2007); output for prior years from Yearbook (2006, p. 562).
     Number of firms from Steel Yearbook (2005, p. 145; 2003, p. 139); for 2005 and 2006, China Data Online (below).
Employment data for 1980–2000 from Steel Compendium (2003, 1, p. 123).
For 2001: Lee, Ramstetter, and Movshuk (2005, p. 119).
For 2002: Calculated from data in Yearbook (2003, pp. 468, 473).
For 2003 and 2004: From Yearbook (2004, p. 521); Yearbook (2005, p. 491).
For 2005 (December) and 2006 (March) data accessed January 30, 2007, from http://chinadataonline.org/member/hygk/hygkmshow.asp?code=32).
Imports and exports of finished steel for 1978: Yearbook (1989, pp. 378, 381).
     Aggregate data for 1980–2000 from Steel Compendium (2003, 1, pp. 167, 171).
     Aggregate data for 2001–2005 from Yearbook (2004, pp. 664, 667; 2005, pp. 637, 639; 2006, pp. 745, 748).
     Data for flat steel products from Steel Yearbook (1986, p. 529; 1991, p. 304; 1996, p. 103; 2001, pp. 145, 148; 2003, pp. 164, 167; 2005, p. 410); 2005 data from OECD (2006, pp. 9–10).

substantial changes. The adoption of continuous casting, recycling of water, and other improvements has reduced the consumption of energy, electricity, and water per ton of steel.[18]

These results conceal enormous variation. Comparisons involving productivity and material consumption consistently show leading Chinese firms approaching norms for steelmaking in advanced market economies. But wide variation among major Chinese producers, and the steel sector's long "tail" of poorly performing

[18] These indicators represent industrywide consumption divided by steel tonnage rather than direct consumption in steel smelting.

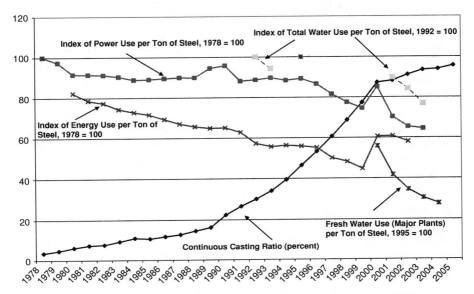

Figure 15.5. Steel sector: technical development indicators, 1978–2005

firms, pushes industrywide averages far below the achievements of Chinese pacesetters.

Workers at Shanghai Baosteel, for example, turned out an average of 588 tons per man-year around 2000, comparable to 1999 productivity of 530–540 tons for French, German, and UK firms.[19] The distance between Baosteel and industrywide domestic labor productivity of 51 tons per man-year in 2000 reflects the extraordinary variation among Chinese steelmakers. Microlevel data for 2005 illustrate this phenomenon: the top 5 percent of all firms recorded revenue per worker more than five times the industrywide average of RMB781,582; the bottom 5 percent of firms achieved revenue per worker less than a tenth of the sector average (Industrial Microdata for 2005).[20]

Information on material inputs reveals a similar picture. Data for 2002 show the best Chinese firms attaining what Chinese industry sources describe as "advanced international levels": 395.35 kg of coal per ton for iron smelting (versus an

[19] See http://www.sas.com/success/shanghaibaosteel.html and http://www.uksteel.org.uk/nw49. htm, both accessed June 8, 2006.

[20] China Industrial Microdata is an annual compilation of enterprise-level data prepared by China's National Bureau of Statistics. Beginning in 1998, these materials are limited to state-owned enterprises and other firms classified as "above designated size" (*guimo yishang*), that is, with annual sales above RMB5 million. In 2005, included firms accounted for 74.1 percent of industrial employment; the same source shows larger values of gross output and "revenue from principal business" (*zhuying yewu shouru*) for the included firms than for the entire industrial sector, indicating some unexplained difference in concept or scope (Yearbook, 2006, pp. 505, 510, 513).

international norm of under 400 kg) and 156 kwh of electricity per ton of electric furnace steel (versus a norm of 350 kwh/ton). The averages for all large and medium enterprises are much higher. Comparisons between "advanced" and "backward" producers indicate huge differences in utilization of energy and water per ton of steel, and also in emissions of SO_2 and dust (Industry Report, 2004, pp. 199–200; 2005, p. 173).

As in textiles and apparel, the Chinese market for steel consists of two broad segments: a highly profitable upper tier that supplies makers of cars, home appliances, and other users whose fortunes increasingly rest on the quality of their products, and a less profitable lower tier, mainly serving construction. When steelmakers' monthly profits hit record levels in December 2004, 949 of 4,947 producers recorded losses. A year later, monthly profits again topped RMB100 billion, but the number of loss makers jumped to 1,731 of 6,649.[21]

Table 15.6, which presents 2005 results for Chinese steelmakers classified by ownership, illuminates this dual structure. The top panel shows that in steel, unlike many other sectors, labor productivity and profitability for state-sector firms compare favorably with industrywide averages. The lower panel, based on the same firm-level data, reveals a dual structure underlying these averages that cuts across ownership lines and across the four major steel subsectors.[22] Altogether, 26 percent of all firms reported making losses in the boom year of 2005, with a slightly higher percentage of both SOEs and FIEs in the red (30.1 and 29.5).

Visits to top-tier steel firms reveal the gradual shift toward emphasis on quality. At Beijing's Capital Steel (*Shougang*):

in the 1980s, there was excess demand, even in the market for low quality steel . . . in 1993, prices for [a superior variety] and for wire rods were the same. There was no reason to produce the higher-valued product. . . . There was no market justification for innovation, so we mostly produced [ordinary] wire rods. . . . Market demand set the tone. . . . When market competition became intense [in the mid- to late 1990s] . . . we were forced to . . . raise product quality (Interview, August 2004).

At Jinan Steel, "Since the 1980s, quality control has become our life. Everything is focused on quality control. . . . In adding a new converter, the #1 emphasis is on the manufacturing process . . . and on quality. . . . This is true not only at our firm – every firm has shifted its basic focus to quality control" (Interview, August 2004).

[21] See http://chinadataonline.org/member/hygk/hygkmshow.asp?code=32, accessed January 30, 2007. This source reports steelmakers' earning monthly profits of RMB104 billion in both December 2004 and December 2005. However the annual profit totals in this source, RMB629 billion for 2004 and 749 billion for 2005, conflict with the smaller profit figure of RMB106.7 billion for 2005 shown in Yearbook (2006, p. 513). Although this conflict raises questions about the monthly figures, the seasonal profit pattern remains credible.

[22] In the lower panel of Table 15.6, we classify 231 firms as "state owned" because "state capital" amounted to 50 percent or more of paid-up capital. The upper panel reflects yearbook data that place the number of state-owned firms at 407 (Yearbook, 2006, p. 520).

Table 15.6. *Ownership structure of China's steel industry in 2005*

| | | Ownership shares in industrywide results | | | | | Indicators of firm size, productivity, and profitability | | | Profit as percent of | | |
| | | | | | | | | | | | | |
Category	Firms	Number of firms	Value added (VA)	Labor (L)	Fixed assets NVFA	Profits Π	Workers per firm	VA/L (RMB1,000s)	NVFA/L (RMB1,000s)	Sales	Total assets	Percent of firms making losses
All Firms[a]	6,649	100	100	100	100	100	422	205.9	238.4	4.8	5.5	26.0
SOE	249	3.7	42.0	38.2	51.7	55.3	4,149	229.1	333.0	6.9	6.3	30.1
FIE	313	4.7	9.7	5.7	8.3	10.3	387	415.1	445.4	4.7	5.9	29.5
Private	3,837	57.7	18.7	25.1	11.1	10.8	183	154.4	104.2	2.6	4.3	25.0
Residual[b]	2,251	33.9	29.6	31.0	28.9	23.6	421	192.2	207.5	3.7	4.8	26.7

Results for firms ranked in descending order of total profit for 2005

Average profit rate (and percentage of loss-making firms)

Ownership		Iron smelting	Steel smelting	Steel rolling	Ferrous alloys	Total
SOE	Profit rate	1.94	6.79	7.16	0.38	6.89
	Percent Π < 0	27.7	30.8	22.1	50.0	30.1
FIE	Profit rate	−1.11	8.33	4.08	2.1	4.68
	Percent Π < 0	35.0	25.0	28.3	43.8	29.5
Private	Profit rate	1.8	2.42	3.2	0.76	2.61
	Percent Π < 0	29.3	30.7	16.4	44.4	25.0
Residual[b]	Profit rate	4.95	2.79	3.86	1.81	3.65
	Percent Π < 0	27.0	25.8	18.3	41.8	26.0
TOTAL	Profit rate	3.12	4.73	5.14	1.24	4.76
	Percent Π < 0	28.6	28.1	17.9	43.5	26.0

Note: Profit rate is the sales-weighted average of profits measured as a percentage of sales revenue.

[a] Excludes nonstate firms with annual sales below RMB5 million.

[b] Residual category includes shareholding and collective enterprises.

Source: Calculated from China Industrial Microdata for 2005.

Interviews illuminate the difficulties associated with upgrading as well as the complex relationships that contribute to success. In China, as elsewhere, the political economy of planning provided weak incentives for innovation, which encouraged firms to focus on quantity rather than quality or cost (Berliner, 1976; Rawski, 1980). Even after reform began to inject market forces into manufacturers' calculations, excess demand stifled incentives to innovate.

Efforts to improve steelmaking facilities are costly, time consuming, and risky. At Capital Steel, improvements to the hot-rolling mill required eight months for "putting the line into operation" (Interview, August 2004). Jiangsu Shagang Group Co. Ltd. imported China's first continuous casting line in 1989 (secondhand equipment from the United Kingdom), but took two years to move the new equipment into production. Shagang officials report that many firms followed their lead, but with mixed results: success at a firm in nearby Jiangyin (Jiangsu) and failure at a Fujian enterprise that installed new equipment but never managed to increase output (Interview, August 2, 2004).

Improvements to production processes and upgrading the mix of products require more than technical skill and management expertise within the enterprise. Extensive cooperation is a key ingredient in building capabilities. In renovating its hot-rolling facilities, Capital Steel relied on SMD Denmark, one of its long-term equipment suppliers.

Shougang's reliance on its equipment suppliers as a channel of capability building is a normal practice in the steel industry. A similar pattern occurred during the 1990s at Jiangsu Shagang, China's thirteenth largest producer. Its upgrading projects during the past decade involved collaborations with equipment suppliers from Switzerland (Concast, in continuous casting), the United States (Morgan, for wire rod rolling), and Germany (Siemens, for control systems).

A particularly deep and continuing involvement began with the installation by Fuchs (Germany) of Shagang's first electric arc furnace (EAF) in 1993–1995.[23] A continuous relationship evolved between the two firms, leading to the installation of two more EAFs, the latest being in 2003. These extended ties between Shagang and Fuchs illustrate a standard pattern of mutually advantageous interactions between equipment suppliers and buyers. When, for example, Shagang's engineers decided to attempt a modification of the process that would allow them to introduce molten iron into the EAF during the course of operation in an energy-efficient way (i.e., without inducing a drop in temperature), they consulted Fuchs, and engineers from the two firms worked together on the project. This led to design modifications on the EAF that were not only of immediate benefit to Shagang, but also of long-term benefit to Fuchs.

While such collaborations with equipment suppliers play a vital role in capability building in the industry, a second channel – of similar importance – involves

---

[23] This was the sixth EAF installed worldwide by Fuchs, and its first in China. It has now installed a total of eleven.

international joint ventures. A notably successful example involves Shagang's link with Posco (Korea) in stainless steel. The partnership was initiated by Posco, which wanted to establish a presence in China, and approached a trading company under the (former) Ministry of Metallurgy, which suggested Shagang as a potential partner. Ownership is 80 percent Posco and 20 percent Shagang, giving Posco a strong incentive to develop the business; investment over the eight-year period has totaled 1 billion U.S. dollars, most associated with the construction of an entire rolling mill and production line. At the time of installation, Posco had thirty personnel on site; this subsequently fell to about eighteen at any time, out of a total plant employment of almost seven hundred. This joint venture has allowed Shagang to broaden its capabilities in a significant way, by establishing itself as one of only three Chinese producers of stainless steel.[24]

Even as steel producers respond to new market conditions with efforts to upgrade facilities and product mix, China's leaders continue to view state ownership and control of leading firms in steel and other key sectors as a central element in their vision of China as a "socialist market economy with Chinese characteristics." Although the scope of these "key sectors" has contracted with the passage of time, governments at all levels include steel among the sectors marked for strong official influence. Following a tradition that dates from the Great Leap Forward of 1958– 1960, steel production is ubiquitous; twenty-seven of China's thirty-one province-level units produced at least 2 million tons of crude steel in 2005 (Yearbook, 2006, p. 562).

Despite the conversion of many firms into shareholding companies, some listed on domestic or overseas stock exchanges, and inroads by private domestic and overseas investors through both entry and expansion, control of China's large steel producers remains concentrated in official hands. According to data compiled by the Iron and Steel Association, the output share of state-sector firms fell from 60 to 52 percent between 1995 and 2005; these figures, which remain far larger than the state sector's overall share in industrial output (see Table 20.8) may overstate the retreat of official influence, which remains strong within the corporate segment of the steel industry (included in the residual category in Table 15.6).[25]

At the national level, official policy, as summarized in a 2005 statement, seeks to nurture a small number of large, Chinese-owned steel producers with world-class technology and global competitive strength. This goal motivates interventions

---

[24] The others are Shanghai Baosteel and Taiyuan Steel.
[25] The difference between the 2005 estimate of 52 percent and the lower figure in Table 15.6 probably reflects differences in the definition of the state sector. In Table 15.6, firms with more than 50 percent of paid-in capital from state funds are classified as SOEs. The higher SOE output share provided by the Iron and Steel Industry Association may include firms in which the state holds a "controlling" ownership share below 50 percent, as well as corporatized firms in which the state or a state institution is the major shareholder.

aimed at consolidating China's steel sector, accelerating the absorption of new technology, channeling resources and opportunities to firms perceived as future industry leaders, promoting consolidation through mergers and acquisitions, and eliminating obsolete production facilities (OECD, 2006).

The multiple interests of provincial and municipal governments as equity holders, development agencies, and tax collectors complicate efforts to restructure China's steel sector. Many provincial and municipal governments see steel as a key element in their own industrial policies. Conflicts among policy objectives at different levels may ensue. With demand booming, many firms (and their official supporters) have opted for expansion rather than risk classification as "small and inefficient" operators that "should be prepared to join large players" (Steel Strategy, 2005). Steel firms are big taxpayers: in 2004, steelmakers paid 79.9 percent of corporate income tax in Hebei and 91.2 percent in Hubei; steel firms provided 70 percent of total municipal revenue in Benxi (Kim, 2006).

This complex web of interests sometimes leads subnational governments to support Beijing's efforts, as when Hebei announces plans "to combine its 202 steel mills into 40 groups . . . over the next five years." Elsewhere, local authorities may contravene national policy, as when Jiangsu officials supported the unauthorized construction of an 8-million-ton steelmaking facility (Gong, 2005b; Xu, 2005).

China's steel industry operates under an unusual mixture of market imperative and official direction. Even as Beijing reiterates its determination to shape the industry's development path, the growing presence of foreign-invested firms, whose small share of industry output rose from 5.5 to 10.1 percent between 1995 and 2005, underlines the expansion of market pressures. China's 2005 decision to ban foreign firms "from becoming majority shareholders in Chinese steelmakers" has not halted the entry of formidable overseas firms into China's steel sector, including POSCO's joint venture with Shagang, Japanese JFE Steel's partnership with Guangzhou Iron & Steel, Mittal's purchase of a 36.7 percent stake in Hunan's Valin Steel Tube in 2005, and Arcelor's 2006 acquisition of a 38.4 percent interest in Shandong's Laiwu Iron & Steel (JFE, 2006; OECD, 2006, p. 22; Yu, 2006).

Recent M&A transactions illustrate the mixture of market forces and official influence surrounding the steel business. Market forces presumably dominate transactions involving international firms. Commercial objectives also motivate some domestic transactions, as with Shanghai Baosteel's purchase of a 5 percent interest in Handan Steel (Hebei), possibly foreshadowing a full takeover, apparently because "Handan Steel shares are undervalued" (Yin, 2006). However, the hand of regulation rests heavily on such efforts. CITIC Pacific Limited, a conglomerate with exquisite political connections, announced the purchase of "a 65 percent stake in Shijiazhuang Iron and Steel Corp, the eighth biggest steel producer in Hebei," in November 2005. Seven months later, the transaction remained in regulatory limbo (Yin and Hui, 2006).

Mergers among steelmakers often reflect bureaucratic choice rather than commercial logic.[26] Reports announcing the 2005 merger between Anshan Iron & Steel Group and Benxi Steel, two of China's top ten steelmakers, originated in Shenyang, the provincial capital, rather than Anshan or Benxi, and included statements by a vice minister of the National Development and Reform Commission (formerly the State Planning Commission) and the vice chairman of the China Iron & Steel Association (the former Ministry of Metallurgy), but no word from leaders of either firm (Wu, 2005b).

With the center's policy efforts at times opposing market forces and on occasion the interests of subnational governments as well, Beijing's goals are not easily attained, especially in the short term. The recent stampede for growth, encouraged by buoyant demand and generous bank lending, has overrun official efforts to restrain capacity expansion and encourage industrywide consolidation. As anticipated by national plans, putative national champions Shanghai Baosteel, Anshan, and Wuhan have expanded through mergers as well as construction. The number of large-scale producers also continues to rise: eight firms produced over 5 million tons in 2002, accounting for 36.7 percent of total output; in 2004, the comparable numbers jumped to fifteen firms and 45.0 percent. But concentration ratios have moved in the opposite direction, with the sales share of the top four firms dropping from 32 to 18.5 percent between 2000 and 2004, and the share of the top ten firms in steel output falling from 48.6 to 39.0 percent between 2000 and 2005 (Industry Report, 2005, pp. 165–166; OECD, 2006, p. 16).

Looking forward, China's steel sector displays an unusual mix of dynamism and drawbacks. Industry leaders have recorded impressive gains in technology, quality, and product mix – all former areas of weakness – while leading a massive expansion of production. Exports of know-how illustrate these growing capabilities. Capital Steel, for example, built wire bar rolling mills in South East Asia in the early 1990s; constructed a blast furnace in India (1997–1998), erected a blast furnace and converter in Zimbabwe (1998), and, more recently, a wide plate rolling mill in Vietnam. In addition, Capital sold an automation system for blast furnace operations, which it had developed in-house to a U.S. buyer during in the early 1990s.

Trends in steel production and trade illustrate the rapid pace of progress. The composition of steel output has gradually shifted from wire rod and other basic construction materials toward sheets, tubes, and strips, which expanded from 30 to 42 percent of finished steel output between 1980 and 2003 (Steel Yearbook, 2004, front matter). Exports, which tilted toward pig iron, semifinished products, and ferrous alloys until 2003–2004, saw a spurt in volume and a rapid shift toward overseas sales of finished products, including flat-rolled steel and hot-rolled coil, bar, and rods (Steel Yearbook, 2005, pp. 166–169).

---

[26] OECD (2006, pp. 17–19) maps out recent mergers involving China's largest steel firms.

The behavior of imports is of particular interest. Even as critics question the ability of domestic producers to provide adequate supplies of "high value-added products, which are insufficient on the domestic market" (OECD, 2006, p. 10), steep reductions in imports decisively rebut concerns over the capacity of China's steelmakers to support domestic makers of cars, appliances, and other steel-using products. Table 15.5 shows an abrupt reversal of what had been a rapid run-up in imports of flat steel, with overseas purchases retreating swiftly from the 2003 peak. For carmakers, "following the expansion of capacity for automotive steel at Baosteel, Wuhan, and Anshan and improvements in assortment and quality, net imports of automotive steel declined by 2.19 million tons, or 40.10% during 2003/2004 . . . with new facilities soon entering production, import dependence should continue to weaken" – a prediction confirmed by subsequent reductions in imports (Steel Yearbook, 2005, p. 122).

Past achievements have created confidence and capabilities that enhance future development prospects. High profits bolster the industry's capacity to finance further improvements. Beneficial contributions from the unusually broad array of supporting institutions inherited from the plan era will continue. This legacy includes universities, research institutes, and design centers focused on metallurgy, domestic engineering firms specializing in steelmaking equipment, professional associations that circulate technical information and provide networks that facilitate recruiting, and the web of contacts radiating from the former Metallurgy Ministry that put Posco executives in touch with Jiangsu Shagang, eventually resulting in a fruitful joint venture.

Along with these advantages, the industry faces two difficulties: overbuilding and excessive official involvement. China's steel industry figures prominently in endless official pronouncements railing against "blind investment," warning of excess capacity for low-end products, and emphasizing the consequent dangers of oversupply, price declines, and losses. In 2004, a Chinese metal consultant warned that the industry was "in dire need of a massive shake-up due to fragmentation." Two years later, the *Wall Street Journal* finds "China Steelmakers Poised for Shake-out" (Gong, 2004; Oster, 2006). But with demand and profits at a cyclical peak, roaring cash flow continues to mask potential weakness.

Although the overhang of excess capacity threatens short-term financial prospects, the current capacity bulge may also represent a prelude to fuller marketization within China's steel sector. Citing work by Zhou Qiren, C. H. Kwan notes that persistent excess capacity "is typically found in industries where the monopoly power of state-owned enterprises is beginning to fade and private enterprises are aggressively trying to enter the market." As private business enlarges its investments, incumbent state-sector rivals "attempt to maintain [market] shares by expanding ... investments" (Kwan, 2006, p. 2). From this perspective, excess capacity signals a possible transition to new circumstances in which commercial results rather than official fiat become the crucial arbiter of corporate success or failure. China's textile sector, in which loud complaints of overbuilding and official efforts to compel the destruction of redundant equipment preceded a major shift toward full marketization in the late 1990s, illustrates the relevance of these observations.[27] If steel, where we see ample evidence of overbuilding as well as official plans "to aggressively cut backward steel production capacity" and "to limit construction of new steel mills," follows a comparable path, the problem of excess capacity may fade from the policy agenda within a few years.

A potentially more serious issue concerns the limited penetration of market forces into the steel industry's core dynamics even after thirty years of reform. In 1997, visitors to Anshan Steel were told that a decision to close a blast furnace required approval from Beijing (Interview, May 1997). While managerial autonomy has surely expanded in the intervening decade, press reports make it abundantly clear that steelmakers, especially the largest firms, confront extensive official supervision.

As noted earlier, mergers among steelmakers often reflect bureaucratic rather than commercial priorities. Official micromanagement pushes firms to scramble for regulatory favors, as when Wuhan Iron & Steel Group purchased a controlling interest in Liuzhou (Guangxi) Iron & Steel Group to "help Wuhan Steel win central government approval to build a 10-million-tonne-a-year steel plant at Fangcheng Port in southern Guangxi province in order to tap demand from local units of carmakers such as Toyota." One informant suggested that this initiative could give Wuhan Steel "a winning edge over [Shanghai] Baosteel," which aspires to expand in the same region (Wuhan, 2005).

As the pace of change in global steel markets accelerates, the delays embedded in official decision making could impose substantial costs. The 2005 policy announcement mentioned earlier was "drafted for more than two years" (Steel Strategy, 2005). While Beijing bureaucrats jousted over the details, their provincial and local counterparts superintended the construction of redundant steelmaking capacity amounting to many millions of tons.

Another shortcoming of the regulatory system is its relentless support of large incumbent firms, which are showered with bank loans, tax breaks, and other benefits, while smaller interlopers, most in the private sector, face a hostile bureaucratic environment. Thus in 2005, the government's effort to "further control steel demand . . . to prevent a resurgence of overheating investment in China's steel sector and excessive steel production" focused on "small steel makers," who "will be prohibited from making goods for overseas clients with imported iron ore, steel scraps, billets, or ingots provided by overseas clients" (Gong, 2005a). Such policies postpone the winnowing of weak firms and consolidation of industry resources in the hands of strong competitors that the regulators hope to stimulate. They also obstruct the development of minimills, which have emerged as efficient competitors in the United States and elsewhere, and could potentially benefit from China's

---

[27] Egan (1999) summarizes the structure and policy environment of China's textile and garment sector as of the late 1990s.

rising supply of domestic scrap. This particular initiative imposed additional costs by restricting the penetration of international standards into the small-scale segment of the industry.

Despite extensive official support, the large steel complexes developed during the plan era have not kept pace. The big centers at Anshan, Wuhan, Baotou, Chongqing, and Beijing show below average increases in value added per worker as well as considerable declines in market share since 1990. New entrants, notably Shanghai-based Baosteel, but also less heralded firms like Jiangsu Shagang, consistently out-perform the older firms that planners include among the proposed centerpieces of future development. In 2005, for example, Jiangsu Shagang reported revenue figures similar to those of Wuhan and Capital Steel despite employing less than 10 thousand workers (versus 56 thousand at Capital and 98 thousand at Wuhan – see Industrial Microdata for 2005). In addition, Shagang requires just less than 300 kwh of power to manufacture 1 ton of steel in its EAFs, nearly 100 kwh less than the current national average of 380–400 kwh. Similar gaps probably exist between traditional industry leaders and aggressive newcomers, including some private firms, in places like Tangshan (Hebei), which is now capable of producing more than 15 million tons per year (Wang and Zhang, 2002).

Given the immense expansion of capacity and production, excess demand for Chinese steel cannot endure for long. Whatever the trigger – global recession, Chinese macroeconomic policy, or a market-induced slowdown in domestic demand growth from the auto or construction sectors – any slackening of demand will unleash market forces with the potential to sweep away whole swathes of today's steelmakers.

But will market forces prevail? If a shakeout and consolidation in China's steel sector were to undercut the commercial viability of familiar industry leaders, would government regulators permit newcomers to overtake, acquire, or even topple firms that have occupied the commanding heights of China's economy for fifty years? The future dynamics of China's steel industry may substantially depend on the extent of official tolerance for the sort of volatility that has roiled China's home appliance and textile sectors during the past fifteen years.

Machine tools. China's machine tool sector, which predates 1949 (Rawski, 1980), occupied a central focus of the pre-reform plan system and was therefore a major recipient of technical support from the USSR and Eastern Europe during the 1950s. China's subsequent isolation from international markets hurt the domes-tic industry, which continued to churn out conventional products, while interna-tional machine-tool makers developed new varieties of computer controlled (CNC) equipment. When Chinese demand shifted toward CNC products in the 1990s, domestic producers found themselves forced to undertake a challenging transfor-mation of their product mix in the face of escalating competition from overseas firms, new China-based joint ventures, and, more recently, wholly owned foreign firms. The transition process continues. To date, China's leading machine-tool firms have established themselves as producers and exporters of basic CNC tools. The challenge is now to reinforce existing strengths, extend capabilities, commercialize the production of increasingly complex products, and address long-standing limitations in quality control and supply chain management.

Published materials provide a quantitative overview of production and demand: results appear in Table 15.7. We focus on "metal-cutting machine tools" (*jinshu qiexiao jichuang*), to which we apply the term "lathes."[28] In the early 1990s, there were more than 800 domestic producers primarily involved in the annual manufacture of 150–200,000 conventional or non-CNC lathes. In addition, China turned out several thousand units of CNC equipment each year, primarily basic (single-spindle, double-axis) CNC lathes produced by SOEs under international licensing agreements or by recently established joint ventures.[29] Output of CNC lathes was highly dispersed, with individual firms producing no more than 125–150 units per year. Imports, amounting to between 5 and 10 thousand units annually during the early 1990s, dominated the domestic market for CNC equipment, especially for sophisticated CNC machines (multiple spindle, multiple axis). At that time, CNC equipment represented between 35 and 40 percent of total domestic expenditure on lathes, while imports, including CNC and non-CNC machines, captured more than half of the entire domestic market.

In China, as elsewhere, machine-tool sales follow the business cycle. During the 1990s, China's machine-tool manufacturers were hurt by falling demand resulting from the implementation of domestic anti-inflation policy in 1993/1994 and from the Asian financial crisis of 1997/1998. The slowdown in aggregate demand concealed a continuing shift of domestic demand toward CNC equipment that accelerated rapidly after 1999, as a new investment boom and widespread industrial upgrading generated a prodigious appetite for machine tools from makers of cars, trucks, machinery, power plant and construction equipment, and defense-related industries (Machine Tool Yearbook, 2005, p. 23). Between 1999 and 2005, domestic consumption of CNC lathes increased more than fivefold from 15,532 to 79,500 units. Over the same period, domestic sales of lathes (CNC and non-CNC) rose from U.S.$2.08 billion to U.S.$10.08 billion, making China the world's largest market for machine tools. Of this, sales of CNC equipment increased from 45 percent to nearly 65 percent of the total.

The experience of Shenyang Machine Tool Limited, China's largest producer of CNC equipment, illustrates both the magnitude of these difficulties and the successful response of some firms.[30] At Shenyang, the years 1994–1998 "were a difficult period," with annual revenue dropping from around RMB1 billion in 1993

[28] In addition to lathes, the machine-tool sector includes machines that grind and shape metals as well as woodworking equipment.
[29] For example, Baoji Machine Tool Works began producing limited quantities (under 150 units per year) of CNC lathes in the mid-1980s under a series of licensing agreements, first with Daewoo (Korea) and subsequently with Daikin (Japan); Beijing #1 Machine Tool started much later under a licensing agreement with Japan's Okuma, their future joint venture partner (Interviews, July 2005).
[30] Material in this paragraph comes from an August 2004 interview and from the 2004 and 2005 editions of the Machine Tool Yearbook.

Table 15.7. *Production, consumption, trade, and pricing of lathes, 1996–2006*

	1996	2000	2001	2002	2003	2004	2005	2006
Number of domestic producers	n.a.	n.a.	382	410	391	388	376	n.a.
Employment	n.a.	208,634	195,900	190,734	177,118	172,932	164,000	n.a.
Physical units								
Production	177,400	176,598	192,109	231,951	306,848	389,284	450,729	n.a.
of which CNC	8,100	14,053	17,521	24,803	36,813	51,861	59,639	n.a.
Consumption	146,790	158,417	190,069	231,501	282,989	311,000	n.a.	n.a.
of which CNC	16,910	23,480	28,535	39,982	52,383	68,155	79,500	n.a.
Imports	52,840	63,444	61,114	75,959	75,338	83,400	75,737	n.a.
of which CNC	10,000	11,155	13,208	18,276	23,320	30,104	30,746	n.a.
Exports	83,450	81,625	63,154	76,409	99,197	143,695	n.a.	n.a.
of which CNC	1,190	1,728	2,007	2,041	2,840	5,478	7,500	n.a.
Value totals (billion U.S. dollars)								
Sales of domestic producers	1.19	1.56	1.88	1.79	2.30	4.15	5.1	7
of which CNC	0.18	0.49	n.a.	n.a.	0.74	1.36	2.18	n.a.
Consumption	2.64	2.57	3.29	3.60	4.89	7.06	10.8	12.9
of which CNC	1.12	1.27	n.a.	n.a.	2.87	n.a.	n.a.	n.a.
Imports	1.48	1.25	1.64	2.08	2.91	4.36	4.63	7.1
of which CNC	0.93	0.81	1.10	1.45	2.18	3.43	3.62	n.a.
Exports	0.21	0.25	0.23	0.26	0.32	0.45	0.66	1.16
of which CNC	0.02	0.03	0.04	0.03	0.06	0.10	0.17	n.a.
Import share in absorption (%)[a]	60.2	48.7	49.8	57.6	59.5	54.1	51.0	54.9
Unit value CNC imports ($U.S.)	93,400	72,972	83,586	79,558	93,396	113,972	117,739	n.a.
Unit value CNC exports ($U.S.)	18,487	19,676	17,838	16,952	19,366	18,985	22,667	n.a.
Ratio of unit values import:export	5.1	3.7	4.7	4.7	4.8	6.0	5.2	n.a.
Unit value of CNC domestic sales by domestic producers	22,927	36,998	n.a.	n.a.	20,208	27,079	38,551	n.a.

Notes: CNC consumption in U.S. dollar terms for 2000 and 2003 calculated from percentage share of total output for 1996, 2002, 2003. CNC Production U.S. dollar terms calculated from other data within the table.

[a] Imports divided by domestic production + imports − exports.

Sources: Machine Tool Yearbook and World Survey (various years), Machine Tool 10 FYP (2006), and Machine Tool Imports (2006).

to RMB500–700 million during 1994–1997, even though "demand for machine tools did not decline." The problem was that "we were producing goods that faced weak demand and not producing the [CNC] goods that were in high demand." Even though the firm began to sell horizontal CNC lathes produced in cooperation with Yamazaki, a Japanese firm, in 1995, revenue remained depressed through 1999. Thereafter, both sales revenue and the share contributed by CNC products began to rise, with revenue doubling between 1999 and 2002 and rising by a further 170 percent to surpass RMB4 billion in 2004. Output of CNC machines topped 3,000 in 2003 and 6,000 in 2004, with revenue from CNC equipment accounting for over half the firm's total sales in both years.

Shenyang's 2005 announcement of a recall on numerical control products sold prior to 2000 underlines the firm's success in improving product quality: "President Chen Huiren said the group would give a thorough check-up, repair and even provide brand-new machine tools for customers who purchased [its] numerical control products up to five years ago . . . [because] the group's products, especially those made before 2000, did have some design and quality problems" (Wu, 2005a).

Shenyang's achievement in expanding both the volume and the quality of CNC products is not unique. Published reports and field visits provide clear evidence of rising capabilities among both foreign-linked and domestic firms. In 2004, fourteen firms produced over 1,000 units of CNC lathes, and six obtained 85 percent or more of sales revenue from CNC products.[31] Domestic products, including equipment from entirely domestic firms, have become highly competitive with Taiwanese and Korean imports at the lower end of the price-quality spectrum. This in turn pushes foreign producers to reduce the cost and price of basic products by expanding domestic manufacturing operations and domestic procurement of components. Thus, the manager of a Taiwan-owned firm located in Hangzhou reports that his CNC products undersell imports by 20 percent, in part because 60 percent of components are sourced domestically (Interview, July 2005).

Although the single-spindle, double-axis machine remains the "bread and butter" of domestic firms, the average "complexity" of the lathes being produced by Chinese firms is rising, with a small number of firms moving slowly into the midrange segment of the market. Simultaneously, we observe an increase in the degree of domestic outsourcing of key components, especially on the part of recently established joint ventures, including spindles, ball-screws, and numerical controls. New opportunities for local sourcing reflect rising capabilities outside the core machine-tool makers. Overseas CNC producers have also begin to outsource the manufacture of key components to these same suppliers.[32]

---

[31] Machine Tool Yearbook (2005, pp. 6, 22). These figures pertain to members of an industry association and may therefore not be comprehensive.

[32] Personal communication from the president of a leading North American machine-tool manufacturer.

The key challenge for firms entering the market for these midrange products is the large variety of models that customers may prefer. Mastering the production of each variety requires time and expense – a start-up investment before sales begin. This initial cost is very large, but declines with the number of models a firm adds to its repertoire. A well-established firm such as Japan's Okuma will have a deep catalog of midrange machines that it can produce on demand. The difficulty facing new entrants is that revenue from early sales will fall far short of production costs, which include large initial investments in learning. This issue is not unique to China: in India, the Ace firm set out to learn how to make midrange machines before they had any customers (Sutton, 2001). The multiplicity of subdivisions within the midrange category of CNC machine tools means that rapid growth of overall demand will not spare new entrants like Ace in India or Shenyang in China from a protracted interval of high start-up costs as they work to penetrate a succession of relatively small submarkets.

Trade data demonstrate that Chinese firms not only survived the sales declines of the 1990s, but have also established a profitable niche in both domestic and international markets for basic CNC lathes. In quantity terms, domestic producers have succeeded in capturing a rising share of the market in the face of steeply rising market volume (Table 15.7). Exports of CNC lathes, which averaged 1,172 units during 1996–2000, rose to 7,500 units in 2005; after hovering around U.S.\$20–25 million for a number of years, export value jumped to U.S.\$100 million in 2004 and U.S.\$170 million in 2005. The rise in the unit values of imported CNC equipment suggests that, with domestic products capturing a larger share of the market for basic products, the quality mix of imports has increasingly shifted toward high-end, specialty products. Exports remain clustered in the lower range of the price-quality spectrum.

In the upgrading process, China's machine-tool producers have benefited from the persistence of a large domestic market for conventional machine tools, which in turn reflects the incomplete penetration of new manufacturing methods and the substantial domestic market for inferior goods. Production of conventional lathes reached a peak of 177 thousand units in 1993, slumped as low as 111 thousand in 1998, recovered to 174 thousand in 2001, and then rose sharply to record levels of 337 and 391 thousand in 2004 and 2005. Continued strong demand for conventional lathes furnishes a financial anchor that allows domestic market leaders to fund their development of commercially viable CNC lathes in the face of tough competition from imports and, more recently, from joint ventures and China-based foreign firms. In India, by contrast, older manufacturers of conventional machine tools disappeared, as local markets were captured by imports and by Ace, a new domestic entrant that successfully marketed basic CNC lathes (Sutton, 2001).

The growing presence of joint-venture or foreign-controlled machine-tool production facilities has figured crucially in the successful transition of Chinese firms into competitive manufacturers of CNC equipment. Initial Chinese efforts to master new varieties of machine tools began with various forms of technical licensing and short-term cooperation. These efforts proved inadequate and soon gave way to new alliances that brought deeper integration between Chinese toolmakers and leading international suppliers, with some of the larger SOEs involved in multiple ventures. This trend has spread to ancillary products, with Harbin no. 1 Tool Corporation joining Germany's PVC in a venture intended to "provide coating service for tool companies in Northeast China" (Li, 2004).

The common element in this new approach is protracted face-to-face interaction between Chinese and foreign personnel. A Chinese leader at a joint venture between Beijing #1 Machine Tool and Okuma (Japan) attributed the need for close cooperation to cultural shortcomings, explaining that "customs and traditions on the Chinese side have resulted in a lower standard of quality – we have a lot to learn from Okuma" (Interview, July 2005).

The same motivation stands behind the newest form of Sino-foreign cooperation, initiatives by Chinese firms to acquire foreign machine-tool makers or to establish overseas facilities. Our Beijing–Okuma informant noted that both approaches seek the same objective: "shortening the time needed to close the technological gap." Thus, Dalian Machine Tool acquired the U.S. firm Ingersoll Production Systems and Crankshaft Equipment, Inc. in 2003 and the German firm F. Zimmerman in 2004. Shenyang Machine Tool purchased Schiess AG of Germany, also in 2004. Shanghai Mingjing Machine Tool purchased Ikegai, Japan's oldest machine toolmaker (Machine Tool Yearbook, 2005, p. 22). In the meantime, Wuxi Kaiyuan Machine Tools Group, a specialized producer of grinding machines, launched UK-based Wuxi Machine Tools (Europe) "to handle technical sales, distribution and support for [its China-made] CNC grinders in this country and continental Europe" as early as 2001 (Chinese Grinder, 2001).

While solidifying their position in basic CNC machines, Chinese firms are pushing to master more difficult segments within this key sector. Industry leaders seek to penetrate markets for more complex and sophisticated equipment than the basic lathes that dominate current CNC output. Joint ventures and wholly owned foreign firms may take the lead in pushing production of more sophisticated products beyond the current experimental stage. The Beijing–Okuma joint venture, for example, has begun batch production of vertical and horizontal CNC machining centers (Interview, July 24, 2005).

The process of upgrading remains challenging. While acknowledging this sector's considerable accomplishments, equipment users and the industry's own trade association are quick to identify multiple difficulties surrounding the manufacture and operation of Chinese machine tools. Problems cluster in three areas:

- Product quality, particularly reliability, durability, and speed (rather than precision). Informants in the shipbuilding industry, for example, report that imported control systems run for 80,000 hours versus 10,000 for domestic products and that the mean time between failures is 800 hours for "advanced international" machine centers versus 600 for domestic equipment (Liu, 2003,

p. 34). High speeds (in excess of 15,000 revolutions per minute) are essential to customers in the top tier of the market, including producers of aircraft, shipbuilding, and military equipment.

- Customer service, including delivery time, which is identified as a "menkan" or threshold that firms must surpass to enter the market, and after-sales service, which receives harsh criticism from many users (Machine Tool Yearbook, 2002, p. 8; Liu, 2003, p. 34).
- Exterior finish and housing, which attract criticism on grounds of appearance and safety (e.g., Zhang, 2004, p. 25).

Quality issues, in turn, reflect difficulties associated with design, manufacturing processes, and procurement. An Anhui maker of farm machinery complains that "domestic makers haven't changed their designs for years," reports differences among machines with identical model numbers and manufacturing dates, and complains of nonuniform parts (Zhang, 2004, p. 25). Another report notes that over 70 percent of CNC machine breakdowns occur in the cutting tool assemblies; within this number, over 70 percent are linked to electronic components. The implication that defective components account for half of all breakdowns for CNC machines focuses attention on limitations among component suppliers, which in turn reflects "the overall development level of Chinese industry" (Liu, 2004, p. 75).

These difficulties raise deeper questions about the organization of China's machine-tool industry, long dominated by large, vertically integrated state-owned firms. The number of firms producing conventional and CNC lathes dropped by more than half between 1993 and 2004 despite considerable entry by private and foreign-invested firms, whose share of machine-tool sales jumped from 20.7 to 38.4 percent during 2001–2005 (Machine Tools 10 FYP, 2006). In 2004 there were still more than 125 firms producing CNC machines, half of which were foreign-linked joint ventures or wholly owned foreign firms. Given the mixed outcome of domestic firms' efforts to meet rising market requirements, it is not surprising to see further consolidation among domestic producers. Recent transactions include Qinquan Machine Tools merging with Shaanxi Machine Tools, The Hangzhou Group's purchase of Changchun #1 Machine Tool, Beijing Electronics Institute Hi-Tech Ltd. taking over Beijing #2 Machine Tool Ltd., and the Shenyang Machine Tool Group's buyout of the Yunnan CY Group and acquisition of a 28 percent stake in Jiaodakun Equipment Technology Ltd. (Machine Tools 10 FYP, 2006).

At present, the balance between market forces and official guidance in determining the path of restructuring for China's machine-tool sector remains unclear. Efforts to develop Shenyang, Dalian, and other traditional industry leaders may reflect technical capabilities that enhance these firms' long-term prospects. Financial data, however, suggest that emphasis on large firms and state ownership may conflict with market imperatives. Table 15.8 provides information for 2005 by ownership type on firm sales, exports, and profitability. Firms with over 50 percent state ownership and former SOEs (and a small number of former COEs) that had

Table 15.8. *Summary information for lathe manufacturers, 2005*

Firm type	Number of firms	Average sales (million RMB)	Exports as percent of output	Profits as percent of sales	Percentage breakdown by ownership		
					Sales	Exports	Profits
SOE	85	142.3	6.31	2.44	26.93	20.66	14.58
FIE	67	73.05	24.93	10.38	10.68	33.58	24.99
Private	222	33.03	12.56	6.65	16.12	24.7	24.27
Other	126	169.74	3.72	3.44	46.27	21.06	36.16
Average		91.27	8.2	4.43	100.0	100.0	100.0

Notes: SOEs are defined to be firms in which 50 percent or more of ownership is by the state; a similar definition applies to FIEs and private firms. "Other" is a residual category consisting largely of corporatized firms with "legal person" or "foreign" shareholders holding majority ownership.
Source: China Industrial Microdata for 2005.

been corporatized were more than two times larger than FIEs and four times larger than private firms. These larger firms, however, lagged significantly in terms of profitability, measured here in terms of profits per unit of sales revenue.[33] Profits for SOEs amounted to only 2.44 percent of sales, compared to 6.65 percent in private firms, and 10.38 percent in FIEs. Forty percent of SOEs operated in the red during 2005. Corporatized former SOEs fared only marginally better, with profits averaging 3.44 percent of sales. Exports present a similar picture, with overseas markets absorbing a much larger share of sales for both FIEs and private producers than for SOEs and other firms.

With this financial background, it is hardly surprising to find critics questioning "the leading role of large and medium SOEs." Skeptical accounts associate state ownership with difficulty in retaining skilled workers as well as "lack of competitiveness, weak sales ability, [and] inability to fully utilize their capacity . . ." (Yang and Yan, 2001, p. 10; Zhang, 2004, p. 27).

The importance of machine tools to China's military industries suggests that the government will insist on a considerable degree of state ownership despite the weaknesses associated with this form of enterprise. The future of China's machine-tool industry rests on the capacity of intense competition, strong innovative efforts, and deepening integration between Chinese and international producers and markets to overcome weaknesses linked to traditions of state ownership and vertical integration.

Beer. Unlike steel, autos, and machine tools, where government retains a prominent role in strategic planning and even day-to-day management, beer is an industry in which domestic and international market forces have supplanted public-sector administrators as the chief determinants of industry output, structure, growth,

---

[33] Profitability estimates based on the rate of return to assets, or profits divided by assets, paint a similar picture.

distribution, investment, and development strategy. Local producers find themselves swept up in a tidal wave of competition, often orchestrated by distant firms, including foreign multinationals, over which their local sponsors and erstwhile protectors have virtually no influence. Competitive pressures have defeated not only local Chinese firms, but also savvy international players, several of whom have sold out to Chinese rivals (Qi, 2001). Recent market dynamics parallel the forces that have determined the beer industry's structure in major market economies, where we see an interplay between the quest for scale economies in production and the establishment of advertising-based national brands (on the United States and Japan, see Sutton, 1991, chapter 14).

Until recently, China's beer market was divided among a very large number of local and regional firms, with only a single nationally recognized brand (Tsingtao). The changing economic environment of the industry has led to a series of moves that set the scene for an escalation of brand advertising that will, in all likelihood, mirror the evolution of concentration in the U.S. market.

Following the reform, rising incomes stimulated a massive expansion of domestic beer consumption. Production jumped from 690,000 tons in 1980 to 22.3 million tons (2000) and 32.73 million tons (2005). The growth rate has declined: physical output grew by 123 percent during 1985/1990 and 127 percent during 1990/1995, but then by 42 percent and 40 percent during 1995/2000 and 2000/2005 (Yearbook, 2006, p. 550). The reason for declining growth is evident: per capita consumption jumped from 0.7 liters in 1981 to 5.4 liters (1990) and 17.6 liters (2000), and is moving toward the global average of 23 liters per year (Yearbook, various issues; Wu, 1999, p. 68).

This stunning growth encouraged international beer majors to jump into the China market. Initial efforts focused on production and marketing of high-priced premium brands yielded poor results, leading several overseas firms to abandon their China ventures, at least temporarily. A second round of initiatives by foreign firms, now aimed at purchasing partial or controlling interests in Chinese breweries and then consolidating operations while maintaining local brand identities, has achieved much better results.

In the meantime, domestic market leaders have worked furiously to expand market share and consolidate control, leading to a blizzard of mergers and buyouts. Tsingtao, China's largest brewery, has led the charge. Backed by tax rebates, low-interest loans, and official encouragement, the Shandong-based firm has acquired "more than 40 breweries . . . since 1997." Tsingtao's initiatives include an alliance with U.S. beer giant Anheuser-Busch, which, according to one Tsingtao executive, will "strengthen our status in the capital market" and, "more importantly . . . sharpen our expertise in business administration and market analysis" (Yatsko, 1996; Wei, 1997; Wang, 2002; Zhou, 2002). The acquisition binge included numerous mergers with firms beyond Tsingtao's Shandong base: new plants include breweries in Xi'an (Shaanxi province) and Yangzhou (Jiangsu). Tsingtao has also built a new plant in Shenzhen (Guangdong) (Yatsko, 1996; Wei, 1997). These

Table 15.9. *The scale of beer producers in China, 1994–2000*

		Number of firms and output share in by firm size						
		1994	1995	1996	1997	1998	1999	2000
Number of firms		655	656	589	550	495	474	495
Average size (1,000 tons)		21.6	25.1	30.6	34.3	40.2	44.3	45.1
Above 200,000 tons	Number	3	7	8	13	18	19	20
	Share (%)	5.4	12.1	14.5	21.4	31.3	35.2	41.8
100,000–200,000 tons	Number	21	23	28	28	26	25	26
	Share (%)	19.9	18.6	21.8	20.9	17.1	17.1	16.7
50,000–100,000 tons	Number	36	44	47	57	60	62	60
	Share (%)	16.6	19.1	18.2	20.1	21.2	21.1	18.9
Below 50,000 tons	Number	595	552	206	452	391	368	389
	Share (%)	58.1	50.2	45.5	37.6	30.4	26.6	22.6

Source: Light Industry Yearbook (1995–2001).

mergers make Tsingtao into a national (rather than regional) market power. Cross-provincial mergers, formerly rare, have become more common in recent years. The underlying difficulties are reflected in a 1996 report that management "expects Beijing to push provincial governments to facilitate Tsingtao's purchase of factories in their region" (Yatsko, 1996).

Efforts by rival domestic firms to expand via mergers, acquisitions, and alliances with overseas firms have resulted in a rapid concentration of ownership and control. China had 800 independent brewers in 1995/1996, a figure that has already fallen to 500. Meanwhile, the top three brewers account for 30 percent of industry sales, while the next three have a combined share of only 10 percent or so. While advertising levels were modest in the 1990s, the leading firms are now moving toward more expensive TV advertising campaigns, and it seems likely that concentration will rise further, as the top three consolidate their positions.

Table 15.9 provides another view of this process: between 1994 and 2000, the output share of large breweries (200,000 annual tons and up) shot up from 5 to 42 percent, while beer from small firms (under 50,000 tons per year) dropped from 58 to 23 percent of national output. Sichuan illustrates the predicament of small breweries and the dominance of large producers. Only two local firms produced over 100,000 tons in 1997. With provincial output rising by 21.5 percent in 1998, the largest firm, Lanjian, broke the 200,000-ton barrier in 1998 and increased production to 467,000 tons in 2000. Lanjian stands out as the province's only strong and viable brewery. Average production for Sichuan's remaining eighteen breweries was less than 50,000 tons in 1998. Small firms producing less than 10,000 tons "basically belong to the ranks of loss-makers." Nationwide, 37 percent of breweries lost money in 1997. In 1998, the proportion of lossmakers jumped to "nearly half" nationally and reached 60 percent in Sichuan (Tao, 2000).

With regional, national, and international giants flexing their economic muscle in China's beer markets, small firms face growing difficulty. They lack distinctive products and unusual packaging (97 percent of Sichuan beer comes in standard bottles). For most small firms, joining forces with a powerful business group offers the only hope of survival. Thus Sichuan's no. 2 firm, the former Mianyang Yatai Brewery, was acquired by the Hong Kong-based Huarun group, which plans to expand production capacity to 500,000 tons.

HOW FAR HAS CHINA COME?

Industrial Structure

Figure 15.6 illustrates changes in eight-firm concentration ratios for 535 four-digit manufacturing sectors between 1993 and 2002. The data show no clear trend either toward or away from concentration within individual sectors: CR8, the eight-firm concentration ratio measuring the share of the top eight firms in sectorwide sales increased in 280 industries and declined in 249. Among sectors in which CR8 changed by more than 10 percentage points, the picture is equally balanced, with 134 industries experiencing CR8 increases of over 10 percentage points and 112 recording similarly large declines. Nor is there any big difference between large and small industries: CR8 rose during 1993–2002 in 48 percent of sectors with above-median 2002 sales 2002 revenues, and in 56 percent of sectors with annual sales below the 2002 median.[34]

This absence of major change in concentration is the resultant of complex forces that include strong pressures for consolidation as well as major opportunities for entry. China's leaders support industrial consolidation because they believe that, in the words of Vice Premier Wu Bangguo, China's future standing "in the international economic order will be to a large extent determined by the position of our nation's large industrial groups" (August 1998 statement quoted in Nolan and Zhang, 2004, p. 234). Many officials welcome a model of national development that assigns a key role to activist government. Impressed by the past successes of Japanese and Korean industrial policy, policymakers announced plans to create "up to fifty giant SOEs" in the wake of China's entry into the World Trade Organization. These firms, situated in sectors like coal, steel, aluminum, shipbuilding, and engineering, qualify for "preferential policies," including "governmental financial support" and preferred access to equity markets. The objective is "to increase competitiveness of Chinese industry in the globalized market" (Fu, 2001; Groups, 2001).

Official statements and initiatives underscore China's continuing policy tilt toward large firms and industrial concentration. Policymakers encourage and often orchestrate mergers that increase the size of leading firms, most visibly in the steel

---

[34] Results based on Industrial Microdata for 2002. We focus on 1993–2002 because the industrial classifications used in Chinese statistics remained virtually unchanged during this period.

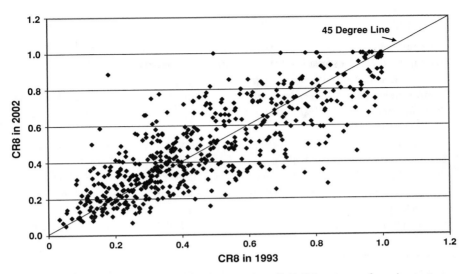

Figure 15.6. Eight-firm concentration ratios for four-digit Chinese manufacturing sectors, 1993 and 2002

sector. Public documents routinely applaud concentration, as when Wu Bolin, director general of the China Machine Tool Association, commented approvingly that "concentration within the machine tool sector rose further . . . with sales of the ten top firms reaching 42.1 percent of total sales revenue, an increase of 10.9 percentage points" (Machine Tool Yearbook, 2005, p. 22).

Mergers and acquisitions, which first appeared during the 1980s, have expanded rapidly, with "2,263 whole or partial acquisitions of China-based companies" valued at more than U.S.$100 billion announced during 2006 (Jefferson and Rawski, 2002; Batson, 2007). These totals include officially orchestrated transactions. But with policy changes reflecting "the government's determination to encourage more acquisitions," so that "market barriers are having less of a drag on M&A activity," commercially inspired restructuring, often involving overseas corporations, occupies a large and growing share of China's market for corporate ownership (Hu, 2006; Zhang, 2006). Overseas acquisitions by Chinese firms have also grown rapidly: transactions in Europe and North America totaled € 4.1 billion in 2005; in 2004, Chinese firms acquired 278 German companies (Pao, Li, and Tian, 2006).

At the same time, China's reform policies have included a succession of official measures that encourage the formation of new enterprises and the entry of existing firms into new markets and new trades. These include allowing TVEs to expand beyond local markets, the opening of China's economy to overseas direct investment, the gradual erosion of restrictions on private domestic firms, steps toward increasing access of small firms to domestic capital markets, and new provisions enabling individuals to form corporations (Jiang, 2006).

Industrial Capability

There are several ways of assessing China's progress in raising industrial capabilities. We can tabulate the spread of key international standards such as the ISO among Chinese firms. Alternatively, we can benchmark performance of Chinese firms against the standards of the advanced industrial economies. Finally, we can examine "revealed performance" by looking at the product mix of Chinese exports and their underlying quality.

The ISO 9000 family, which focuses on systems of quality management, is among the most widely recognized international standards. In 2000 the three standards ISO 9001, 9002, and 9003 were integrated into a single new benchmark, ISO 9001:2000. Achieving ISO qualification provides important advantages for firms that aspire to break into international markets or to supply components or services to multi-national corporations. At the end of 2005, a total of 776,608 firms in 161 countries had attained this standard. Chinese firms have embraced the ISO system with gusto: beginning with a 2001 figure of 7,413, Chinese qualifiers jumped to 143,823, forming the largest national contingent, at the end of 2005. Information about ISO/TS16949:2002, a complementary quality standard for the design, development, production, installation, and servicing of automotive-related products, shows similarly enthusiastic Chinese participation. At the end of 2005, 17,047 firms have achieved this certification (out of an estimated potential market of 30,000), including 2,151 Chinese firms, trailing only the United States (with 3,693 qualifiers) (ISO Survey, 2005).

Turning to benchmarking, we focus in some detail on the auto-components sector, which represents an extreme case in which the incentives to adjust are very high, and the institutional setting facilitates the rapid transfer of know-how. The leading international carmakers have, over the past generation, developed and codified their own working practices in a way that has become remarkably uniform across different countries. In parallel with this, they have forged close relationships with their immediate (i.e., "first-tier") component suppliers. To become a supplier, a firm needs to achieve very high standards of quality and productivity, and liberalization of trade typically leads to the rapid shakeout of all but the most capable suppliers. There are highly effective channels for transferring international best practice. First, carmakers work directly with suppliers, or use a two-way flow of engineering personnel, in order to transfer good practice. Second, suppliers have access to international consulting firms who specialize in the transfer of the appropriate production know-how. As a result, once the main international carmakers establish manufacturing facilities in a particular region, the speed of advance in capability among first-tier suppliers is extremely rapid.

In China's case, when the new wave of carmakers arrived in the 1990s, they faced a government-imposed requirement to source some 70 percent of their components locally (a point to which we return later). The automakers' arrival induced many international first-tier producers to form joint ventures with Chinese suppliers, so

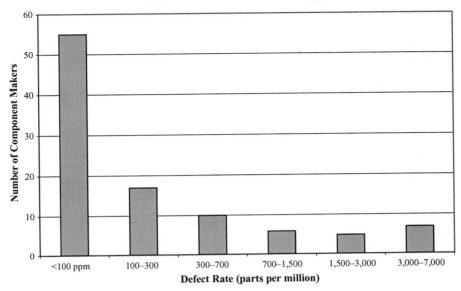

Figure 15.7. Defect rate for component suppliers to a multinational carmaker, 2003 (*Source:* Sutton, 2004, table 2.1)

that the industry's evolution during the 1990s led to a mix of international and domestic Chinese suppliers in the industry's top tier.

A measure of the effectiveness of the transfer of capability in this context is shown in Figure 15.7, where we look at the standard measure of supplier quality (parts per million found defective by the carmaker) for 2003 at one auto assembly plant associated with a multinational carmaker. International best practice currently demands that defect rates for the general run of parts lie below 100 ppm. The observations summarized in Figure 15.7 indicate that new generation automakers in China already enjoy a first-tier supplier base that largely meets this standard.

As we move down the supply chain, however, incentives become weaker. Figure 15.8 shows the profile of a typical first-tier supplier of steering gear, also for 2003. Here, the defect rates for incoming components are very high (and are measured as a percentage, rather than "parts per million"). First-tier suppliers are typically midsize firms, and they are reluctant to invest in training their own suppliers; moreover, they are more willing than are the carmakers to tolerate a higher level of product defects in return for a lower price from their own ("second-tier") suppliers. The result is a much slower rate of capability building, a pattern seen also in the United States, Japan, and Europe, though in the Chinese case the gap between first- and second-tier suppliers is particularly wide.

Subsequent plant visits indicate rapid reduction in defect rates for components delivered to first-tier suppliers. Table 15.10 provides data for 2003 and 2006 from two major first-tier suppliers of braking systems, one in a coastal area and the

Table 15.10. *Defect rates for suppliers to two first-tier manufacturers of braking systems*

Location	Coastal		Interior	
Year	2003	2006	2003	2006
PPM	Percentage of firms	Percentage of firms	Percentage of firms	Percentage of firms
<50	20	60	5	30
50–100	70	30	7	10
100–300	5	5	8	15
300–500	5	5	25	15
500–1,000	0	0	14	10
1,000–2,500	0	0	18	8
2,500–5,000	0	0	8	4
5,000+	0	0	15	8
Average PPM	87.5	67.5	1,967.5	1,070

Source: 2006 interviews.

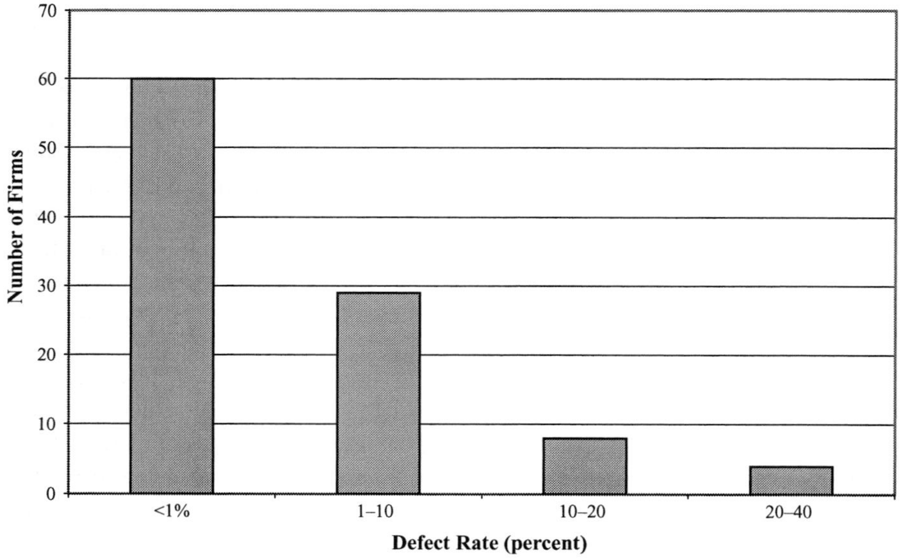

Figure 15.8. Defect rates: component suppliers to a Chinese maker of steering gear, 2003 (*Source:* Sutton, 2004, table 2.6)

other in an interior province. The figures show substantial improvement. For the interior enterprise, the proportion of suppliers meeting the international standard of 100 ppm rose from 12 to 40 percent between 2003 and 2006. For the coastal firm, 90 percent of second-tier suppliers had already attained this international standard by 2003. Similar results appear elsewhere: average defect rates for second-tier suppliers to a large coastal manufacturer of auto exhaust systems (not shown in the table) dropped from 634.5 to 158.5 ppm between 2003 and 2006, with the share of suppliers meeting the 100 ppm norm rising from 28 to 80 percent during the same period.

Benchmarking of quality *and* labor productivity in the assembly of auto seats and exhausts provides additional measures of how far China has progressed (Sutton, 2003, provides more detail). Quality here is captured at two points: final inspection by the supplier, or the "internal" rate, and the "external" rate as assessed by the customer, with the latter typically lower than the former.[35] In the case of seats, in which production processes are very similar across countries, five of the six Chinese firms we surveyed are only slightly below the international standard of one car seat set per man-hour. The sole remaining firm actually exceeds the standard by nearly 50 percent. As for quality, five of the six firms achieved external rates below 100 ppm, with half reporting internal rates well below the international standard of 2,000 ppm. The best Chinese seat manufacturers are producing at or near world-class levels.

The picture for exhaust manufacturers is mixed. The comparison is also more complicated, largely because of differences in product complexity and capital intensity of the production process. Chinese exhaust firms have levels of labor productivity well below the international standard, but they have only been slightly less successful than seat manufacturers in achieving the international external quality standard. Differences in labor productivity partially reflect higher labor intensity of the production process in China, but even the more capital-intensive firms have not achieved significantly higher levels of labor productivity. However, higher capital intensity and, in particular, the use of automated and robotic welders have helped reduce metal scrap rates, a significant component of variable costs, and lowered internal defect rates.

Peter Schott's (2007) detailed examination of Chinese exports to the United States develops important findings from the perspective of "revealed performance." First, Chinese goods have expanded more rapidly across the entire product spectrum of United States imports than exports from other nations. This result holds up controlling for countries' relative endowments. Second, in the 1990s, China's exports sold at a significant discount relative to those from countries with similar income levels and from those from OECD countries. In the 1980s, by contrast, Chinese goods had actually sold at a premium. This behavior does not necessarily signal a decline in the relative quality of China's imports however. In a separate paper,

---

[35] Reworking or scrapping of defective products underlies the lower external rate.

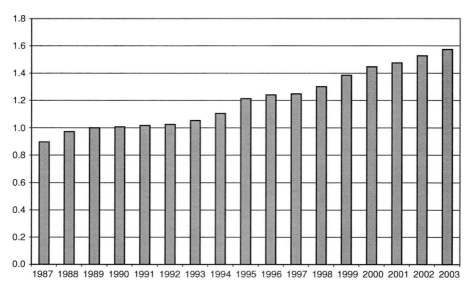

Figure 15.9. R&D intensity of China's exports, 1987–2003 (*Source:* Authors' calculations based on "Annual Line of Business Report 1977" and UNCOM Trade Data.)

Hallak and Schott (2005) find that the decline in relative prices is insufficient to explain China's rapidly rising share of U.S. imports and that the underlying and "unobserved" quality of China's exports must have risen as well. In other words, quality upgrading has been at work.

Our own estimates of the R&D and capital intensity of China's exports point in the same direction. We utilize here the "Annual Line of Business Report for 1977," a unique study that provides ratios for "R&D to Sales" for United States four-digit industries for 1977. We weight each industry's share in China's total exports by the same sector's 1977 R&D intensity (or capital–labor ratio) of that sector in the United States to obtain an estimate of the implicit R&D (capital) content of China's exports that is expressed as a percentage of the U.S. average for 1977. Changes over time will be the product of changes in the composition of China's exports to more or less R&D or capital-intensive sectors.

Figure 15.9 graphs trends in the R&D content of China's exports between 1987 and 2003. In 1987, for example, the average R&D to sales ratio of China's exports was 0.90 percent. This increased only slightly through the early 1990s, but then rose by nearly 50 percent between 1993 and 2003 to 1.6 percent (Figure 15.9).[36] Similar

---

[36] Both Schott's analysis and our own calculations produce results that seem likely to run ahead of the R&D intensity of domestic export production. The shift of assembly work for laptop computers and other products employing sophisticated imported components will lead the measured R&D content of exports to rise more rapidly than the R&D content of value added in domestic export production.

calculations (not shown) indicate that the capital intensity of exports rose sharply between 1987 and 1994, but then leveled off.[37] Clearly, there has been a pronounced shift in China's exports, first to slightly more capital-intensive industry and then to those coming from more knowledge-intensive industry during the last decade, which coincides with the rapid run-up in FDI in China and the growing role of foreign-invested firms. Both of these developments are likely linked to the ongoing quality upgrading of China's exports, as suggested by Hallak and Schott.

CONCLUSIONS

During the past three decades of reform-inspired growth, Chinese industry has delivered increases in output and labor productivity that compare favorably with the achievements of previous East Asian growth spurts. The expansion of quality and variety, features notably lacking under the pre-reform plan system, is equally impressive. Reform-induced growth has stimulated interconnected upward shifts in capability, real wages (see Figure 6.1), and the skill content of output and especially of exports. Changes in costs and capabilities propel a continuing transformation of China's export mix from unskilled labor-intensive (garments, toys, and shoes) to skilled labor-intensive (machinery) and capital-intensive (including high-technology) sectors. This protracted boom has powered China's emergence as a major trading nation, with exponential increases in both exports and imports reflecting the products and requirements of industrial activity.

Our analysis focuses on the process of growth, rather than its quantitative dimensions, and emphasizes the impact of China's sweeping but incomplete shift from plan to market in spurring the transformation of a rising proportion of Chinese manufacturers into dynamic, profit-seeking business entities oriented chiefly to commercial signals rather than official desires.

Marketization, entry, and competition are the key forces underlying China's industrial transformation. Beginning with relaxation of controls over the sales and procurement activities of rural industry in the late 1970s, gradual and incremental steps toward market opening have cumulated into massive change. Reduced tariffs, WTO-linked erosion of import barriers, improvements in domestic transport and communication, and expanded opportunities for foreign and domestic private businesses have created an economy in which wide-open competition is pervasive. New forms of entry – by TVEs, joint ventures linking Chinese and overseas firms, domestic private business, restructured state firms, shareholding companies, wholly owned foreign companies, and, most recently, individually owned corporations – have steadily expanded the scope and intensity of competition in China's

---

[37] We performed similar calculations for China's imports, which are significantly more R&D intensive than its exports, for example, 1.7 versus 0.90 in 1987. Up through 1997, the R&D intensity did not rise, but the ensuing six years showed a marked increase. In 2003, the R&D to sales ratio was 2.6. The capital intensity of China's imports, however, has remained relatively constant, albeit higher than that for exports.

markets for industrial products, materials, components, workers, managers, and ancillary services.

Intense competition and the associated pressure on profitability have pushed growing numbers of firms to focus on raising productivity and upgrading the quality and variety of their products. Rising domestic incomes and increased exposure to international markets, both of which raise the "sales windows" that sellers must occupy to maintain or expand their market positions, have intensified the rush to acquire capabilities and elevated the risks confronting laggards.

Observations from many sectors document robust progress in the capacity to manufacture a growing array of internationally competitive products. At the outset of reform, Chinese firms struggled to produce color TVs from imported production lines. In 2005, four Chinese firms controlled 30 percent of global sales of color TV sets (Tang and Liu, 2006). In 1982, domestic critics asked why vehicle makers were not "putting an end to the history of producing outdated products for decades without a model change" (FBIS 10–15–1982, K21). Today, domestic and global carmakers prepare to ramp up exports of China-made vehicles and parts while showering domestic auto buyers with price reductions and new models amid dizzying gyrations of market shares.

The picture of generalized progress summarized in widespread references to China's emergence as "the world's factory" conceals a plethora of outcomes. The level of manufacturing capability and the timing of advances toward international competitiveness vary widely across sectors, among regions, and, within specific industries, among individual firms. The evolution of individual sectors reflects an array of industry-specific factors as well as economywide trends, such as rising real wages and household incomes, expanding openness to international trade and investment, and the growing ascendancy of market forces. The circumstances that vary across industries, or even within specific sectors, include the legacy of plan-era development, global technology trends, the extent of foreign trade and investment, the nature of industry-specific institutions, and the degree of official involvement in strategic decisions.

Although market economy experience leads us to anticipate a pattern of industrial growth in which bursts of entry give way to periods of consolidation that allow strong firms to accumulate market share by eliminating or absorbing weak rivals, differences in the circumstances confronting various sectors lead to wide variation in the pace and timing of changes in industrial structures. The past fifteen years, for example, witnessed rapid increases in concentration among manufacturers of home appliances and beer, while both cars and steel experienced an upsurge of entry.

Cross-industry variations in the pace and timing of entry and consolidation create a kaleidoscopic outcome. Small firms are rapidly disappearing from some industries (beer and home appliances) but not others (steel). In home appliances, most of the large players are newcomers established during the reform era. In auto manufacture, the present structure encompasses both new (mostly international) and long-established firms. Today's market leaders in steel and machine tools include firms whose national prominence dates from the 1950s.

Official policy is one important determinant of sectoral development. Although the role of market forces has expanded, the impact of government intervention varies dramatically across industries. Officials now accept market outcomes in sectors like beer, textiles, and garments that have little strategic technology and only modest state-sector involvement. But in sectors that are perceived as occupying the "commanding heights" of China's economy, official agencies at the national (and sometimes provincial or even local) level deploy a variety of instruments, including appointments, approvals (*pizhun*), tax holidays, interest-rate forgiveness, and direct intervention to influence major business decisions involving entry, investment, mergers, technology selection, and supply chains. Officials are keenly aware that the lure of access to China's flourishing domestic market enables them to extract concessions from foreign investors – for example, regarding technology transfer or location of R&D activity – that smaller or less dynamic economies could not hope to obtain. Aside from foreign investment, official intervention in negotiations surrounding the price of imported iron ore, efforts to curtail investment in sectors seen as overbuilt, and government direction of mergers and corporate structures in steel, coal, aluminum, tobacco, and machinery, among others, illustrate how official involvement extends beyond the regulatory regime typical of major market economies.

The range of industries subject to intense government management has experienced a slow decline that has cumulated into dramatic change. Marukawa's (2001) study of China's television sector shows how the emergence of a buyer's market following episodes of excess entry can tip particular sectors toward market dominance. Excess supply may force producers into a scramble for markets that sweeps official regulations to the side. It is easy to imagine similar circumstances affecting China's steel and auto sectors, among others, following some future slowdown in demand.

Documentary sources indicate, and field research confirms the key contribution of international links to the advance of manufacturing capabilities. Information showing that foreign-invested firms regularly transact over half of China's exports and imports demonstrates the vital role of direct foreign investment and the associated transfers of technology, production and organizational skills, managerial know-how, and marketing expertise. While access to low-cost labor motivated the initial phase of foreign investment, recent investments increasingly reflect the desire of global businesses to serve China's domestic market, to integrate Chinese operations into transnational production networks, and to tap China's abundant supplies of skilled workers, technicians, and engineers. Foreign-invested firms push both rivals and domestic suppliers toward higher standards. The experience of working with, observing, or competing against foreign firms enhances the knowledge and skill of managers, engineers, researchers, and workers across wide swathes of Chinese industry, raising both current and future productive potential.

Direct foreign investment and exports from foreign-linked firms cluster along China's eastern seaboard. During the past three decades, multiple advantages have permitted the China's coastal provinces to develop ahead of interior regions. In addition to the stimulus arising from deepening links to the global economy, coastal areas draw on their rich heritage of historic involvement in both domestic and overseas commerce. Ironically, China's seaboard now benefits from its limited access to large-scale investments under the pre-reform planned economy. This translates into a relatively small share for the state sector, which reduces legacy costs and enhances policy flexibility in comparison with interior regions burdened with large clusters of SOEs.

The importance of foreign links and the differential advance of coastal areas highlight the limitations of China's industrial boom. Even though China's open trade policy has exposed nearly all sectors of manufacturing to the challenge and discipline of international competition, many enterprises, particularly those located in interior regions, lag far behind domestic and international best practice. Official efforts to shield client firms and their employees from the rigors of market competition, though diminishing, continue to obstruct the process of upgrading by blunting incentives and prolonging the lives of uncompetitive firms. In addition, the gains of high-performance firms cluster within the realm of production; industry has recorded much smaller advances along other segments of the industrial value chain, including R&D, design, product development, branding, and management of supply networks.

Chinese executives, researchers, and policymakers are mobilizing to address these shortcomings. Accelerated privatization of state-owned firms, especially at the local and provincial levels, along with continuing reform of the financial system, promises to extend the reach of market forces. Expanding the development of nonproduction capabilities has become a major focus of industrial strategy. After quoting one specialist's view that "Chinese carmakers are simply cheap assemblers employed by foreign auto manufacturers, which is why they have barely any of their own core technologies," a 2006 report indicates that domestic carmakers "acutely aware of the bind they are in . . . have begun developing their own brands." Thus, Shanghai Automotive Industry Corp, in addition to its partnerships with Volkswagen and General Motors, "plans to spend more than 10 billion yuan (US$1.2 billion) on the development of 30 models by 2010" (Gong, 2006). Accounts of China's television manufacturers tell the same story: steep output increases, advances in low-cost production with no control over core technologies, leading to big investments in new plants and in R&D intended to push Chinese firms into the ranks of advanced international producers (e.g., Tang, 2006).

Ongoing domestic reform facilitates deepening engagement with global markets, and therefore promotes continued upgrading and capability-building among Chinese manufacturers. New legal provisions encourage novel forms of entry on the part of foreign firms, which can now operate fully owned entities without domestic partners and can also acquire ownership stakes in existing Chinese firms (rather than forming joint ventures with specially created subsidiaries of Chinese firms). Increased control over China-based facilities encourages overseas firms to expand the range of technologies and products transferred to their Chinese operations. It also accelerates their participation in China-based research and design activities, a trend already encouraged by the expanding supply of well-trained and modestly priced Chinese university graduates. Erosion of entry restrictions is also visible on the domestic side, as barriers to the creation and expansion of private manufacturing continue to fade and investments across regional boundaries, formerly discouraged by local governments, are now seen as welcome enhancements to capital and employment.

Recent advances in Chinese manufacturing, although costly, uneven, and often foreign led, are noteworthy both for their large scale and for the strong momentum that overwhelmed seemingly powerful obstacles, including intrusive and capricious regulation, extensive corruption, and weak systems of law, management, finance, and corporate governance. Looking forward, we anticipate continued expansion and deepening of manufacturing capabilities in the foreign-linked coastal regions that have dominated China's initial achievements, now bolstered by fresh impetus originating in China-based R&D operations of both multinational and domestic firms, and new streams of upgrading and innovation arising from the expansion of domestic and cross-border mergers and acquisitions, the spread of capabilities across sectors and regions and the overseas expansion of Chinese manufacturers.

Capitalizing on the potential to extend China's manufacturing boom calls for rolling back a variety of constraints. Expertise in supply chain management has emerged as a key determinant of performance in manufacturing. The development of tightly organized and well-managed supply chains contrasts starkly with the extreme vertical integration inherited from China's pre-reform plan system. Figures 15.7 and 15.8, which show wide performance gaps between first- and second-tier suppliers of auto components, illustrate both the achievements and the shortcomings of supply chain management.

Differential development of supply chains contributes to the large and growing gap separating industrial performance in coastal and interior regions. Field research shows that manufacturers in interior regions experience difficulty in securing reliable local suppliers. Managers at a leading maker of auto parts were only able to produce products that were less "quality demanding" in their inland facilities, in part because highly qualified employees refuse assignments in interior locations. They also report that efforts to raise standards encounter broader cultural obstacles at interior plants, even though they regularly use workers from these same provinces to staff their superior coastal plants. Field visits reveal distinct regional differences in business capabilities and entrepreneurial energy, with industrial executives in Shaanxi province, for example, repeatedly commenting on their own firms' poor sales performance and indicating their unwillingness to explore initiatives undertaken elsewhere by "southerners" (*nanfangren* – referring to inhabitants of central and southern coastal regions).

Regional differences are connected to a broader array of shortcomings arising from the plan era. Researchers observe negative links between high shares of state ownership, a common feature of China's interior regions, and a variety of desirable outcomes. State ownership magnifies weak elements in China's political economy: slow exit of faltering firms, ill-considered investment decisions leading to elevated levels of bad debt and financial risk, and limited development of markets for corporate ownership and control.

Broader institutional weaknesses, of which corporate governance, limited contract enforcement, and weak intellectual property rights provide particularly relevant examples, also endanger future growth, especially in sectors that build on the accumulation and exchange of advanced technologies.

The remarkable accomplishments of Chinese industry since the start of reform, together with the confidence and optimism associated with past success, create strong forward momentum. However, Japan's rapid shift from industrial juggernaut to prolonged stagnation, which arose from institutional weaknesses not unlike those that afflict China today, demonstrates that past success cannot ensure future prosperity. China's achievements have initiated a dynamic response from manufacturers above and below China in current world rankings of labor costs and technical sophistication. With global restructuring of entire industrial value chains poised to accelerate, future Chinese growth must depend on ongoing efforts to promote reform, upgrading, and consolidation. Chinese business and government leaders understand that past attainments provide no guarantee of future success. This awareness encourages us to anticipate further rapid development of Chinese manufacturing, with capability building and international competitiveness spreading to a growing array of industries during the coming decades.

References

"Annual Line of Business Report 1977." "Statistical Report of the Bureau of Economics to the U.S. Federal Trade Commission." Typescript dated April 1985 held at Baker Library, Harvard University [call number 9163120].

Bai, Chong-en, Yingjian Du, Zhigang Tao, and Sarah Y. Tong. 2004. "Local Protectionism and Regional Specialization: Evidence from China's Industries." *Journal of International Economics.* 67, pp. 397–417.

Batson, Andrew. 2007. "China's Merger Boom Continues." *Wall Street Journal.* January 12, 2007, p. C5.

Berliner, Joseph S. 1976. *The Innovation Decision in Soviet Industry.* Cambridge, MA: MIT Press.

Boyreau-Debray, Genevieve and Shang-jin Wei. 2003. *Can China Grow Faster? A Diagnosis on the Fragmentation of the Domestic Capital Market 2003.* Accessed October 10, 2003, from http://www.nber.org/~confer/2003/cwgf03/wei.pdf.

Bramall, Chris. 2007. *The Industrialization of Rural China.* Oxford: Oxford University Press.

Buckley, Chris. 2005. "A Legal Battle Exposes Tangled Dealings in China." *New York Times.* January 18, 2005, p. C6.

Changhong. 2005. "Changhong Says May Triple Czech TV Plant Deal." *Reuters.* December 9, 2005. Accessed January 24, 2007, from http://www.appliancedesign.com/CDA/Archives/df014963cea38010VgnVCM100000f932a8c0.

Chen, Kuan, Gary H. Jefferson, Thomas G. Rawski, Hongchang Wang, and Yuxin Zheng. 1988. "Productivity Change in Chinese Industry, 1953–1985." *Journal of Comparative Economics.* 12, pp. 570–591.

China Compendium. 2005. *China Compendium of Statistics 1949–2004.* Beijing: China Statistics Press.

China Data Online. Data for China iron-steel firms. Accessed January 30, 2007, from http://chinadataonline.org/member/hygk/hygkmshow.asp?code=32.

China Markets Yearbook. Annual. Hong Kong: City University of Hong Kong Press.

Chinese Grinder. August 20, 2001. "Chinese Grinder Manufacturer Sets Up in Europe." Accessed January 23, 2005, from http://www.manufacturingtalk.com/phpads/click.php?bannerID=17&UT=1106590113.

Consolidation 2005. "Consolidation among China's Refrigerator Producers to Top 60 Percent." Press release from Global Sources. May 5, 2005. Accessed January 24, 2007, from http://www.corporate.globalsources.com/INFO/PRESS/ARTICLES/MAY0505.HTM.

Crude Steel. 2007. "China's Crude Steel Output up 18.48 Per Cent in 2006." *The Hindu News Update Service.* January 29, 2007. Accessed January 29, 2007, from http://www.hindu.com/thehindu/holnus/006200701291011.htm.

Donnithorne, Audrey. 1972. "China's Cellular Economy: Some Economic Trends since the Cultural Revolution." *China Quarterly.* 52, pp. 605–619.

Egan, Susan Chan. November 1999. "A Complex Connection: China's Government & Garment Industry." *Bobbin.* Accessed January 29, 2007, from http://www.findarticles.com/p/articles/mi_m3638/is_3_41/ai_59481779/pg_3.

Evans, Carolyn L. and James Harrigan. 2004. "Tight Clothing: How the MFA Affects Asian Apparel Exports." NBER Working Papers 10250. Cambridge MA: National Bureau of Economic Research.

FBIS. *Daily Report: People's Republic of China.* Reston, VA: United States Foreign Broadcast Information Service.

Field, Robert M. December 1983. "Slow Growth of Labor Productivity in Chinese Industry, 1952–1981." *China Quarterly.* 96, pp. 641–664.

Fifty Years, 2000. Guojia tongjiju gongye jiaotong tongjisi, compiler, *Zhongguo gongye jiaotong nengyuan 50-nian tongji ziliao huibian, 1949–1999* [50 years of statistics for China's industry, transport and energy]. Beijing: Zhongguo tongji chubanshe.

Flat TV. 2007. ""Battle Heats up over Flat-TV Share. *Nikkei Weekly.* January 15, 2007, p. 1, 7.

Fu Jing. 2001. "Colossal SOEs to Advance WTO Role." *China Daily.* December 8–9, 2001, p. 1.

Garnaut, Ross, Ligang Song, Stoyan Tenev, and Yang Yao. 2005. *China's Ownership Transformation: Process, Outcomes, Prospects.* Washington, DC: International Finance Corporation.

Global. 2005. "Global Business Briefs." *Asian Wall Street Journal.* November 11–13, 2005, p. 12.

Glut. October 26, 2005. "A Glut of Air Conditioners Taking Shape." Accessed January 23, 2006, from www.chinaview.cn.

Gong Zhengzheng. 2004. "Steel Sector to Open up Further." *China Daily.* December 23, 2004, p. 9.

Gong Zhengzheng. 2005a. "Gov't Bans Iron and Steel Processing." *China Daily*. May 12, 2005, p. 9.

Gong Zhengzheng. 2005b. "Hebei Steel Companies to Consolidate." *China Daily*. November 17, 2005, p. 10.

Gong Zhengzheng. 2006. "Own Steam." *China Business Weekly*. April 24–30, 2006, p. 6.

Groups. 2001. "What They Are Saying: Enterprise Groups Needed." *China Daily*. December 10, 2001, p. 4.

Hallak, Juan Carlos and Peter K. Schott. 2005. "Estimating Cross-Country Differences in Product Quality." Unpublished Working Paper. Accessed March 9, 2007, from http://www.som.yale.edu/Faculty/pks4/files/research/papers/hs82.pdf.

Hu Yuanyuan. 2006. "Nation to be Top M&A Destination." *China Daily*. October 21, 2006, p. 10.

Huenemann, Ralph W. 2001. "Are China's Recent Transport Statistics Plausible?" *China Economic Review*. 12.4, pp. 368–372.

Industry Census Summary, 1997. *Zhonghua renmin gongheguo 1995 nian disanci quanguo gongye pucha ziliao huibian* [Compendium of materials from China's 3rd national industrial census in 1995], general volume. Beijing: Zhongguo tongji chubanshe.

Industry Report, 2004. *Zhongguo gongye fazhan baogao 2004* [China industry development report 2004]. Beijing: Jingji guanli chubanshe.

Industry Report, 2005. *Zhongguo gongye fazhan baogao 2005* [China industry development report 2005]. Beijing: Jingji guanli chubanshe.

Industry Yearbook, 2001. *Zhongguo gongye jingji tongji nianjian 2001* [Statistical yearbook of China's industrial economy 2001]. Beijing: Zhongguo tongji chubanshe.

Ishikawa Shigeru. June 1993. "China's Economic Growth since 1949 – An Assessment." *China Quarterly*. 94, pp. 242–281.

ISO Survey. 2005. Accessed February 15, 2007, from http://www.iso.org/iso/en/iso9000-14000/pdf/survey2005.pdf.

Jefferson, Gary H. and Thomas G. Rawski. 2002. "China's Emerging Market for Property Rights: Theoretical and Empirical Perspectives." *Economics of Transition*. 10(3), pp. 585–617.

Jefferson, Gary H., Inderjit Singh, Junling Xing, and Shouqing Zhang. 1999. "China's Industrial Performance: A Review of Recent Findings," in *Enterprise Reform in China: Ownership, Transition, and Performance*. Gary H. Jefferson and Inderjit Singh, eds. Oxford: Oxford University Press, pp. 127–152.

JFE. 2006. "JFE Drops Blast Furnace in China for Rolled Steel Sheets." *Nikkei Weekly*. September 25, 2006, p. 14.

Jiang Wei. 2006. "Single and Available." *China Business Weekly*. February 27–March 5, 2006, p. 5.

Jiang, Xiaojuan. 2001. *China's Industries in Transition: Organizational Change, Efficiency Gains and Growth Dynamics*. Huntington, NY: Nova Science Publishers.

Kim, Dong Ha. May 17, 2006. "M&A in Chinese Steel Industry." Unpublished Report. Beijing: Posco Research Institute (POSRI).

Klepper, Steven and Elizabeth Graddy. 1990. "The Evolution of New Industries and the Determinants of Market Structure." *Rand Journal of Economics*. 21(1), pp. 27–44.

Kumar, Anjali. 1994. *China: Internal Market Development and Regulation*. Washington, DC: World Bank.

Kwan, Chi Hung. June 28, 2006. "Excess Production Capacity is the Result of Not Only Cyclical but Also Structural Factors." Report in series "China in Transition." Accessed January 31, 2007, from http://www.rieti.go.jp/en/china/06062802.html.

Lau, Lawrence J., Yingyi Qian, and Gerard Roland. 2001. "Reform without Losers: An Interpretation of China's Dual-Track Approach to Transition." *Journal of Political Economy.* 108(1), pp. 120–143.

Lee, Hiro, Eric D. Ramstetter, and Oleksandr Movshuk. 2005. "Issues Raised by Restructuring of the Steel Industry in Northeast Asia." *East Asian Economic Perspectives.* 16(2), pp. 117–133.

Li Fangchao. 2004. "Tool Maker in Alliance with PVT." *China Daily.* December 28, 2004, p. 10.

Li Fei, 2003. "How Can the Home Appliance Industry Extricate Itself from Price Wars?" *Jiage lilun yu shijian* [Price theory and practice], no. 11, pp. 55–56.

Li, Hongbin and Scott Rozelle. 2004. "Insider Privatization with a Tail: The Screening Contract and Performance of Privatized Firms in Rural China." *Journal of Development Economics.* 75(1), pp. 1–26.

Li, Shantong, Yongzhi Hou, Yunzhong, Liu, and Bo Chen. 2004. "Survey and Analysis on Local Protection." *China Development Review.* 6(1), pp. 89–93.

Li, Wei. 1997. "The Impact of Economic Reforms on the Performance of Chinese State-Owned Enterprises." *Journal of Political Economy.* 105(5), pp. 1080–1106.

Light Industry Yearbook, Annual. *Zhongguo qinggongye nianjian* [China light industry yearbook]. Beijing: Zhongguo dabaike quanshu chubanshe.

Liu, Guy S. and Xianxuan Liu. 2005. "Research Report on the Survey of SOE's Ownership Transformation and Restructuring in China." Report prepared for World Bank by the Enterprise Research Institute, Development Research Center of the State Council.

Liu Xia, 2004. "Current Situation and Trends of Domestic Accessories for NC Machine Tools," *Zhizao jishu yu jichuang* [Production technology and machine tools], no. 3, pp. 74–75.

Liu Yang, 2003. "Grasp Opportunity, Build Brand Names – Viewing the Market for Chinese-Made CNC Lathes from the Perspective of Shipbuilding," *Shukong jichuang shichang* [CNC machine tool market], no. 10, pp. 33–35.

Lyons, Thomas. 1987. *Economic Integration and Planning in Maoist China.* New York: Columbia University Press.

Machine Tool Imports. 2006. "China's Machine Tool Import Rose in Value and Class in Past Five Years." Accessed October 28, 2006, from http://www.danmex.org/spansk/tekst.php?id=142.

Machine Tool Yearbook, Annual. *Zhongguo jichuang gongju gongye nianjian* [China machine tool and tool industry yearbook]. Beijing: Jixie gongye chubanshe.

Machine Tools 10 FYP. 2006. "Exceptional Development of China's Machine Tool Sector under the 10th Five-Year Plan." Accessed October 28, 2006, from http://www.chinatool.net/news_center/index01.php?id=2591&lx=%B9%FA%C4%DA%D0%D0%D2%B5%B6%AF%CC%AC&bt=%D0%C2%CE%C5%D6%D0%D0%C4.

Machinery, 1983. *Zhongguo jixie gongye de fazhan* [Development of China's machinery industry]. Beijing: Zhongguo nongye jixie chubanshe.

Marukawa Tomoo. 2001. "The Chinese Television Industry: An Example of Gradual Transition," in *China's Industries in Transition: Organizational Change, Efficiency Gains and Growth Dynamics.* Xiaojuan Jiang, ed. Huntington, NY: Nova Science Publishers, pp. 57–82.

Naughton, Barry. 1995. *Growing out of the Plan: Chinese Economic Reform, 1978–1993.* Cambridge and New York: Cambridge University Press.

Naughton, Barry. 2003. "How Much Can Regional Integration Do to Unify China's Market?" in *How Far Across the River? Chinese Policy Reform at the Millennium.* Nicholas C.

Hope, Dennis Tao Yang, and Li Mu Yang, eds. Stanford: Stanford University Press, pp. 204–232.

Nolan, Peter and Jin Zhang. 2004. "The Challenge of Globalization for Large Chinese Firms," in *Transforming China: Globalization, Transition and Development*. Peter Nolan, ed. London: Anthem Press, pp. 233–296.

OECD [Organisation for Economic Co-operation and Development]. 2005. *OECD Economic Surveys: China*. Paris: OECD.

OECD [Organisation for Economic Co-operation and Development]. 2006. "Current Situation of the Chinese Steel Industry." Paper prepared for the Joint India/OECD/IISI Workshop, New Delhi, May 16–17, 2006. Accessed January 31, 2007, from http://steel.nic.in/oecd/DSTI_SU_SC(2006)9_ENG.pdf.

Oster Shai 2006. "China Steelmakers Poised for Shakeout." *Wall Street Journal*. January 17, 2006, p. A15.

Pao Huichun, Li Chao, and Tian Xiaoling, 2006. "Who is Merging with Whom?" *21 shiji jingji baodao* [21st century economic herald], February 20, 2006. Accessed September 10, 2006, from http://www.nanfangdaily.com.cn/jj/20060220/sxygl/200602200089.asp.

Park, Albert and Yang Du. 2003. "Blunting the Razor's Edge: Regional Development in Reform China." Preliminary Draft. University of Michigan.

Perkins, Dwight H., et al. 1977. *Rural Small-Scale Industry in the People's Republic of China*. Berkeley: University of California Press.

Poncet, Sandra. 2005. "A Fragmented China: Measure and Determinants of Chinese Domestic Market Disintegration." *Review of International Economics*. 13(3), pp. 409–430.

Poncet, Sandra. 2003. "Measuring Chinese Domestic and International Integration." *China Economic Review*. 14(1), pp. 1–21.

Qi, Li. 2006. "Capital Flows and Domestic Market Integration in China." Unpublished Paper. Decatur, GA: Agnes Scott College.

Qi. Zhi. 2001. *Beer Market in China 2000*. Accessed May 29, 2003, from http://www.sit.wisc.edu/~cef/beer.html.

Rawski, Thomas G. 1975a. "China's Industrial System," in United States Congress, Joint Economic Committee, *China: A Reassessment of the Economy*. Washington, DC: U.S. Government Printing Office, pp. 175–198.

Rawski, Thomas G. 1975b. "Problems of Technology Absorption in Chinese Industry." *American Economic Review*. 65(2), pp. 383–388.

Rawski, Thomas G. 1980. *China's Transition to Industrialism: Producer Goods and Economic Development in the Twentieth Century*. Ann Arbor, MI: University of Michigan Press.

Rawski, Thomas G. 2005. "SARS and China's Economy," in *SARS in China: Prelude to Pandemic?* Arthur Kleinman and James L. Watson, eds. Stanford: Stanford University Press, pp. 105–121.

Rawski, Thomas G. and Robert W. Mead. 1998. "On the Trail of China's Phantom Farmers." *World Development*. 26(5), pp. 767–781.

Schott, Peter K. 2007. "The Relative Sophistication of Chinese Exports." Accessed March 8, 2007, from http://www.som.yale.edu/Faculty/pks4/files/research/papers/chinex_310.pdf.

Shi Yuzhi, 2001. *WTO yu Zhongguo fangzhi gongye* [WTO and China's textile industry]. Beijing: Zhongguo fangzhi chubanshe.

State Council Economic Census Group, 2005. *Diyici quanguo jingji pucha zhuyao shuju gongbao diyihao* [Report #1 of the main data from the first national economic census]. Issued by the Office of the State Council Leading Small Group for the First National Economic Census and the National Bureau of Statistics. Accessed December 6, 2005, from http://news.xinhuanet.com/fortune/2005–12/06/content_3883969.htm.

Steel Compendium, 2003. *Zhongguo gangtie gongye wushinian shuzi huibian* [Fifty-year compendium of data on China's steel industry], 2 vols. Beijing: Yejin gongye chubanshe.

Steel Strategy. 2005. "Steel Must Fit in with Sustainable Strategy." *China Daily*. July 19, 2005, p. 4.

Steel Yearbook, Annual. *Zhongguo gangtie gongye nianjian* [China steel industry yearbook]. Beijing: Yejin gongye jingji fazhan yanjiu zhongxin.

Steinfeld, Edward S. 2004. *Forging Reform in China: The Fate of State-Owned Industry.* Cambridge and New York: Cambridge University Press.

Sugawara, Toru. 2005. "Props Keep Teetering Firms Upright." *Nikkei Weekly*. October 10, 2005, p. 22.

Sutton, John. 1991. *Sunk Costs and Market Structure: Price Competition, Advertising, and the Evolution of Concentration.* Cambridge, MA: MIT Press.

Sutton, John. 1998. *Technology and Market Structure: Theory and History.* Cambridge, MA: MIT Press.

Sutton, John. 2000. *Rich Trades, Scarce Capabilities: Industrial Development Revisited.* Keynes Lecture. London: British Academy.

Sutton, John. 2001. "The Indian Machine-tool Industry: A Benchmarking Study." Accessed February 12, 2007, from http://personal.lse.ac.uk/sutton/benchmarking_machine_tools.pdf.

Sutton, John. 2003. "The Auto Component Supply Chain in China and India: A Benchmarking Study." Accessed February 12, 2007, from http://personal.lse.ac.uk/sutton/auto_component_sutton.pdf.

Tang Bailu, 2006. "Beijing Dongfang vs. Shanghai Guangdian: Dissolution and Restructuring." *21 shiji jingji baodao* [21st Century Economic Herald], March 6, 2006. Accessed September 10, 2006, from http://www.nanfangdaily.com.cn/jj/20060306/sxygl/200603060105.asp.

Tang Bailu and Liu Yuanzhu, 2006. "With Whom Should the Color TV Manufacturers Link Up?" *21 shiji jingji baodao* [21st Century Economic Herald], March 6, 2006. Accessed September 10, 2006, from http://www.nanfangdaily.com.cn/jj/20060306/sxygl/200603060106.asp.

Tao Xihui, 2000. *Sichuan gongye jingzhengli fenxi* [Analysis of Sichuan industry's competitive strength]. Beijing: Zhongguo jingji chubanshe.

Textile Report, 2000. "Zhongguo fangzhi xiehui, comp," *Zhongguo fangzhi gongye fazhan baogao 2000/2001* [China textile industry development report 2000/2001]. Beijing: Zhongguo fangzhi chubanshe.

Textile Report, 2005. "Zhongguo fangzhi xiehui, comp," *Zhongguo fangzhi gongye fazhan baogao 2005/2006* [China textile industry development report 2005/2006]. Beijing: Zhongguo fangzhi chubanshe.

Textile Yearbook, 2000. *Zhongguo fangzhi gongye nianjian 2000* [China textile industry yearbook 2000]. Beijing: Zhongguo fangzhi chubanshe.

Toshiba. 2001. "Toshiba to Produce Washing Machines in China." *People's Daily English Home Business.* August 6, 2001. Accessed September 9, 2006, from http://english.people.com.cn/200108/06/eng20010806_76639.html.

Transport Yearbook, Annual. *Zhongguo jiaotong nianjian* [China yearbook of transport and communication]. Beijing: Zhongguo jiaotong nianjianshe.

TVE Yearbook, 1986. *Xiangzhen qiye tongji ziliao 1978–1985* [Statistical materials on TVEs 1978–1985]. Beijing: Ministry of Agriculture.

Wang Tianyi and Zhang Jianzhong, 2002. "Analysis of Development Prospects for Tangshan's Iron-Steel Cluster," *Zhongguo gongye jingji* [China industrial economy], no. 9, pp. 32–37.

Wang Yu. 2002. "China's Beer Market." *China Daily Business Weekly*. September 3–9, 2002, p. 8.

Wang Yu and Dai Yan. 2004. "TV Makers Urged to be More Market-Oriented." *China Business Weekly*. April 26–May 4, 2004, p. 1.

Washers, 2003. "Locals Take Tumble in Washer Market." Accessed January 23, 2005, from http://www.chempages.com/html/china/news/display.php?news_id=26032.

Wei Ke. 1997. "Expansion Brewing." *China Daily*. July 15, 1997, p. 5.

Wong, Christine. 1986. "Ownership and Control in Chinese Industry," Joint Economic Committee, U.S. Congress, China's Economy Looks Toward the Year 2000, vol. 1. Washington, DC: Government Printing Office.

World Survey. "World Machine Tool Output & Consumption Survey 2007." Accessed February 14, 2007, from http://www.gardnerweb.com/consump/analysis.htm.

Wu, Yanrui. 1999. *China's Consumer Revolution: The Emerging Patterns of Wealth and Expenditure.* Northampton, MA: Edward Elgar Publishing.

Wu Yong. 2005a. "Machine Tool Firm Recalls Products." Accessed June 11, 2006, from http://www.chinadaily.com.cn/english/doc/2005-08/11/content_467977.htm.

Wu Yong. 2005b. "Merger Set to Create Steel Giant." *China Daily*. August 17, 2005, p. 9.

Wuhan. 2005. "Wuhan Steel for Rival Stake." Accessed June 15, 2005, from http://thestandard.com.hk/news_detail.asp?we_cat=10&art_id=8358&sid=5986316&con_type=1&d_str=20051221.

Xu Shousong, 2005. *Tieben diaocha: yige minjian gangtie wangguo de siwang baogao* [Tieben survey: Report on the death of a private steel empire]. Guangzhou: Nanfang ribao chubanshe.

Yang Wansu and Yan Honghe, 2001. "Analysis of Reasons for the Low Market Share of Ordinary CNC Lathes," *Jixie zhizao yu zidonghua* [Machine manufacture and automation], no. 6, pp. 9–11.

Yatsko, Pamela. October 24, 1996. "Under New Management." *Far Eastern Economic Review*. 159, pp. 68–70.

Yearbook, Annual. *Zhongguo tongji nianjian* [China statistics yearbook]. Beijing: Zhongguo tongji chubanshe.

Yin Ping. 2006. "Baosteel Buys Stake in Handan." *China Daily*. June 2, 2006, p. 9.

Yin Ping and Hui Chinghoo. 2006. "CITIC Pacific Shifts Focus from Aviation to Steel." *China Daily*. June 10–11, 2006, p. 5.

Young, Alwyn. 2000. "The Razor's Edge: Distortions and Incremental Reform in the People's Republic of China." *Quarterly Journal of Economics*. 115, pp. 1091–1136.

Yu Qiao. 2006. "Steel Merger Could Mean More Chinese M&As." *China Daily*. June 27, 2006, p. 6.

Zhang Caiyun, 2004. "Tomorrow Will Be Better: Domestic NC Machine Tools As Seen by Users in the Farm Machinery Industry," *Shukong jichuang shichang* [CNC machine tool market], no. 2, pp. 24–28.

Zhang Ran. 2006. "Draft Rules Aim to Encourage Buyouts." *China Daily*. May 23, 2006, p. 9.

Zhang, Xiaobo, and Kong-Yam Tan. 2004. "Blunt to Sharpened Razor: Incremental Reform and Distortions in the Product and Capital Markets in China." Development Strategy and Governance Group Discussion Paper 13. Washington, DC: International Food Policy Research Institute.

Zhou Kan. 2002. "Beer Giants." *China Daily Business Weekly*. August 20–26, 2002, p. 11.

SIXTEEN

China's Embrace of Globalization

Lee Branstetter and Nicholas Lardy

INTRODUCTION

This chapter summarizes China's progressive opening to foreign trade and investment in the years since 1978. These reforms led China's foreign trade to soar from $21 billion in 1978, when China at best was a marginal player in global trade, to more than $1.1 trillion in 2004, when China became the world's third largest trading economy (National Bureau of Statistics, 2005, p. 161; World Trade Organization, 2005, p. 16). We will briefly review the history of Chinese trade and investment policy from 1978 to 2001 and note the impact of important policy changes on expansion of trade and investment. Because accession to World Trade Organization (WTO) marked an important watershed in the evolution of Chinese policy in this realm, we will also include a discussion of the key features of the agreement under which China joined the WTO and an assessment of the progress China has made to date in implementing its obligations. The WTO accession agreement opens up important components of the service sector of the Chinese economy, and these will receive special emphasis. We will also address the high-profile debate over China's currency regime and discuss the implications of China's expanding trade and foreign investment for the rest of the world.

In providing this overview, we will be emphasizing several themes. First, China achieved a greater degree of openness to foreign trade in manufactures prior to WTO accession than is generally acknowledged, even in much of the best recent scholarship. In fact, the drive to liberalization of trade and foreign direct investment (FDI) regimes seems to have dramatically *accelerated* in the late 1990s.[1] Second, the additional openings mandated under China's WTO accession agreement will likely make China's economy the most open of any large developing country, and, to date, China has made reasonable progress toward meeting her obligations. Third, developments in Chinese trade and investment have generally conformed to

---

[1] This point was stressed in Lardy (2002), and much of the argument presented here is anticipated in that study.

patterns of Chinese comparative advantage, yielding important benefits to China and her trading partners. Fourth, China's current exchange rate regime is no longer compatible with macroeconomic fundamentals. In addition to laying out the key features of this issue, we discuss policy options and steps the government has taken so far. Finally, China's growth as a trading nation has recently reached the point where developments in China have global impact. China's impact is particularly strong in East and Southeast Asia, but the degree to which this impact is on balance a positive one depends on the relative development of the trading partner in question.

THE MOVE TO FREER TRADE PRIOR TO WTO ACCESSION

The Pre-Reform Trade Regime

Up through the 1970s, Chinese trade took place within the context of a planned economy and therefore nearly all trade was subject to very exacting quantitative guidelines. The State Planning Commission's import plan covered more than 90 percent of all imports. The export plan was similarly comprehensive, specifying the physical quantities of more than 3,000 individual commodities. Prior to 1978, a handful of foreign trade corporations owned and controlled by the Ministry of Foreign Trade were responsible for carrying out the import and export plans. In this context, neither exports nor imports were sensitive to exchange rates or relative prices.[2] Furthermore, the composition of Chinese trade had little connection to Chinese comparative advantage, with capital-intensive goods, including refined petroleum products, playing a large role in Chinese exports well into the early 1980s. As a consequence, the volume of Chinese trade, relative to world trade, declined sharply from 1.5 percent in 1953 to 0.6 percent in 1977 (Lardy, 1994, p. 2).

Trade Liberalization

China gradually reformed its trade regime over the 1980s and 1990s. However, progress was neither simple nor straightforward. As the authorities phased out the direct quantitative planning of imports and exports, they began to rely more heavily on a complicated welter of alternative trade policies, including conventional tools such as tariffs and quotas, and less conventional instruments, limiting trading rights and tougher commodity inspection requirements.

The government actually raised import tariffs on most commodities in the early years of the reform period. By 1982, the average statutory tariff rate was a relatively high 56 percent. The government reduced this level to 43 percent in 1985, but then maintained that level throughout the next seven years. Beginning in 1992, however,

---

[2] For more comprehensive examinations of the pre-reform trade regime and early trade and FDI reform, see Lardy (1992, 1994).

Table 16.1. *Growth in companies authorized to conduct foreign trade*

Year	Number of companies
1978	12
1985	800
1986	>1,200
1988	>5,000
1996	12,000
1997	15,000
1998	23,000
1999	29,528
2000	31,000
2001	35,000

Sources: Lardy (1992, p. 39), Zhang (2000, p. 5), Editorial Board of the Almanac of China's Foreign Relations and Trade (1987, p. 48; 1990, p. 38; 1997, p. 50; 1998, p. 48), Ministry of Foreign Trade and Economic Cooperation (1999, p. 192), Chen (2001, p. 4), World Trade Organization (2001, p. 21).

tariff levels fell in a series of adjustments that brought the average tariff level down by two-thirds, to roughly 15 percent on the eve of WTO accession (Lardy, 2002, p. 34). In addition to tariffs, the government restricted trade in a wide range of commodities by quotas and import licenses. This range of commodities actually expanded over the course of the 1980s; by the end of the decade, nearly half of Chinese imports was regulated by licenses or quotas. However, these restrictions were also dramatically cut in the 1990s. The share of imports they regulated fell to about 18 percent by 1992, and by 2001 it had fallen further to about 8.45 percent (Lardy, 2002, p. 39).

Throughout the reform period, the government restricted the right to engage in foreign trade. Nevertheless, there was a rapid and substantial expansion in the number of domestic firms granted trading rights, as shown in Table 16.1. From the initial 12 firms directly controlled by the Ministry of Foreign Trade, this expanded to about 800 firms by 1985. A decade later, the number of trading firms stood at 12,000. By 2001, this has expanded further to 35,000. With such a large number of potential suppliers of trading services, it is likely that the market for such services had become reasonably competitive by the mid-1990s (Lardy, 2002, pp. 40–42).

The Export-Processing Regime

China's openness to imports expanded even faster than the decline in formal barriers might suggest. A major reason has to do with the special privileges extended

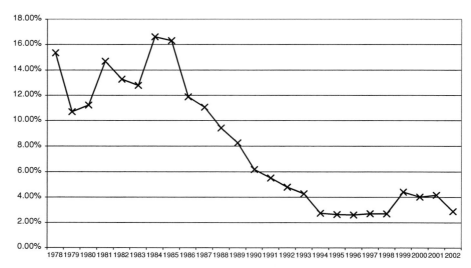

Figure 16.1. Tariff revenues as a fraction of import value, 1978–2002
(*Source: China Statistical Yearbook* 1993, 1998, 2000; Xinhua News Service; *Guoji Shangbao*
(International Business Daily))

to firms involved in export processing, which were set up in 1979. Initially, this legal framework provided various incentives for the processing of raw materials for export and the assembly of imported goods to produce finished goods for export. In 1987, the government expanded these incentives to provide for duty-free import of all raw materials, parts, and components used in the production of goods for export. Also, joint ventures and wholly foreign-owned companies have generally been allowed to import capital goods duty free throughout the reform period. As an increasingly open FDI regime brought in more foreign investment, this allowed a larger and larger fraction of China's imports to escape the formal trade barriers. Finally, in the second half of the 1990s, the Chinese government began to exempt certain categories of domestic firms and other organizations from import duties (Naughton, 1996, p. 307; Lardy, 2002, p. 36).

By the first half of 2000, less than 40 percent of imports were subject to any tariff. Thus, actual tariff revenues have been far lower than the average statutory rates would suggest. As shown in Figure 16.1, tariff revenues as a share of the value of imports peaked in the 1980s at about 16 percent of import values and fell steadily thereafter, reaching a low of about 3 percent by 1994. A substantial portion of this decline reflects the enormous expansion of FDI, the increasing importance of export processing, and the exemption of selected industries and organizations from import tariffs altogether. It also reflects widespread violations of Chinese trade laws (Lardy, 2002, pp. 36–38).

China's Porous Protectionism in the 1990s[3]

In principle, by the mid-1980s, China had two trade regimes – a very open one for foreign firms and domestic enterprises engaged in export processing and a more restrictive trade regime for all other enterprises. Feenstra (1998) called China's trade regime an example of "one country, two systems" and claimed that the maintenance of special privileges for export-processing firms was contrary to both the letter and the spirit of WTO rules.

A dualistic trade regime of this type could, in principle, generate two sets of problems. The first is akin to the problem of "trade diversion" in the economic analysis of customs unions. Domestic Chinese enterprises in some industries might have a comparative advantage at exporting a particular commodity or producing a certain good for the domestic market with imported components. They might nevertheless be supplanted by foreign-invested enterprises (FIEs) due to the FIEs' legislated advantages. In theory, welfare is reduced relative to what would have prevailed under a more even-handed trade regime, even one with a higher level of overall effective protection, because production is undertaken by a set of producers with higher social costs (Naughton, 1996, pp. 298–315). The second potential problem is that a large segment of the Chinese economy could remain effectively protected from foreign competition, but this is masked by the overall trade statistics, which largely reflect the success of the export-processing regime. The notion that large swathes of the Chinese economy were effectively closed off to foreign competition provided the intellectual foundation for the belief that credible implementation of China's WTO commitments would generate destabilizing shocks.

In practice, it is clear that the authorities have never been able to separate China's two trade regimes as completely as the letter of the law would suggest. Substantial quantities of parts and components imported on a duty-free basis have been illegally sold in the domestic market, and there have been substantial illegal sales in the domestic market of goods embodying duty-free imports. In addition to "leakage" into the domestic market of goods imported under the export-processing regime, there has been a significant degree of outright smuggling, much of it via Hong Kong.[4]

Lardy (2002) notes that despite China's virtual ban on imports of U.S. citrus products, U.S. oranges and other fruits were widely available from vendors on street corners in cities throughout China in the 1990s. The value of oranges smuggled into

---

[3] The reference to "porous protectionism" is taken from Kennedy (2004).

[4] China's customs service launched a crackdown in 1998, leading to a large increase in the recorded imports of high-tariff items. The campaign eventually resulted in the arrest of high-level officials and an 80 percent increase in the absolute value of recorded tariff revenue in 1999. In 2000, tariff revenue increased an additional 30 percent, but did not keep pace with the 36 percent increase in import volume recorded in 2000. Tariff revenue as a fraction of import value remains at a very low level. See Lardy (2002, pp. 37–38).

China via Hong Kong annually was a minimum of $43.5 million and more likely several times that amount. Lardy (2002, p. 163) reports that Hong Kong re-exports of cigarettes (another banned item) and 35-mm film to China were $242 million and $159 million in 1998; these numbers were large multiples of the amount of imports from Hong Kong recorded by Chinese trade statistics. Bater (2000) reports that Hong Kong was America's fourth largest market for U.S. pork in 1999, but more than half of that product subsequently made its way into China. Fisman and Wei (2004) conduct an interesting systematic study of the discrepancies between Hong Kong and Mainland Chinese trade statistics, which they term the "evasion gap." Their estimates suggest that an increase in the total import tax rate of 1 percent increases the evasion gap by 3 percent.[5]

"Leakage" of goods and components into the domestic economy via the export-processing regime and outright smuggling increased the de facto level of openness in the economy as a whole. Furthermore, measurable developments in Chinese trade in the latter half of the 1990s suggest some decline in the "dualism" of China's trade regime in these years. Between 1995 and 2000, what the Ministry of Commerce classifies as ordinary imports grew 130 percent, from $43.7 to $100.08 billion. Over the same period, the sum of imports of duty-free parts and components used in processing and the duty-free imports of capital goods of joint-venture firms grew only 37 percent, from $78.33 to $107.32 billion. Growth in ordinary imports has continued to be quite rapid since WTO accession, although it may slow in coming years, as the current investment boom subsides. Growing linkages between firms engaged in export-processing and local firms caused the ratio of value added in export processing to double over the 1990s (Lardy, 2002, pp. 9, 38, 180). This reflected both the displacement of imported parts and components by locally produced parts and rising wages. This suggests that the view of the export sector as an enclave with little connection to the local economy became increasingly out of date by the eve of China's accession to the WTO.

Foreign Exchange Reform and Tax Policy

The expansion of foreign trade was also abetted by changes in foreign exchange and tax policy. Prior to reform, the regime maintained an overvalued exchange rate to subsidize the import of capital goods that could not be produced domestically. Overvaluation led to excess demand for foreign exchange, necessitating an extensive system of rigid exchange controls. Key elements of this control system included a 100 percent foreign exchange surrender requirement for exporters, tight limitations on the rights of individuals to hold foreign currency, and strict controls on the outflow of foreign capital.

---

[5] Hong Kong also plays a complicated role in mediating China's exports to the rest of the world. For an exploration of this and its implications for trade statistics, see Feenstra et al. (1999) and Feenstra and Hanson (2004).

Over the course of the reform period, the government relaxed all of these restrictions. The authorities devalued the official exchange rate in stages, from RMB1.5 to the dollar in 1981 to 8.7 in 1994. Following a modest appreciation, the government effectively fixed the exchange rate at RMB8.3 to the dollar in 1995, a rate that was not changed until the summer of 2005. The International Monetary Fund (IMF) estimates that the Chinese currency lost about 70 percent of its value against the dollar in real terms over the period from 1980 to 1995, substantially enhancing the international competitiveness of China-based export operations.[6] In addition to substantial real devaluation, Chinese exporters were allowed to retain part of their foreign exchange earnings, individuals were allowed to hold foreign exchange, and capital outflow restrictions were relaxed.

Over the course of the reform period, China has come to increasingly rely on indirect taxes to fund government expenditures. The WTO allows the rebate of indirect taxes to exporters, in order to eliminate the disadvantage exporters in such countries face relative to those based in countries that rely on direct taxes on income. The system of indirect taxes in the 1980s was complex and a rebate program for exporters was correspondingly difficult to administer effectively. As the value-added tax (VAT), which had only two basic rates, became more important as a revenue source, the export tax rebate became easier to administer in some respects, but the government still encountered difficulties.

The system was subject to extensive fraud, as firms claimed rebates for goods that were never exported. In addition, the government lacked the revenue to rebate all taxes and fell considerably behind in rebate payments to exporting firms. The central government clamped down on corruption and cut the rebate rates for exporters in 1995 and 1996. The export slowdown experienced in the wake of the Asian financial crisis prompted the government to reverse course, raising the amount of the tax rebated to 100 percent for some commodities and accelerating the actual payment of rebates due. This arguably helped promote the extremely high rates of export growth recorded after the Asian crisis began to abate, but it exacerbated the central government's financial problems.

International versus Intranational Trade

A number of studies have documented the existence and importance of interprovincial protectionism in China (Wederman, 2003). Young (2000, pp. 1091–1135) goes so far as to suggest that China's internal market has become substantially *less* integrated over the reform period, as local governments have sought to shield local producers from competitors based elsewhere in China.[7] This assertion is

---

[6] This change was measured on the basis of the real effective exchange rate, that is, on a trade-weighted basis and adjusted for the rate of inflation in China relative to its major trading partners (IMF, 1996, p. 50).

[7] Branstetter and Feenstra (2002) present estimates of a formal political economy model in which provincial governments are presumed to protect locally based firms from both

undermined by extensive evidence. Naughton (1999) demonstrates that inter-provincial trade flows were quite substantial, even in the early 1990s. The level of interregional trade implied by Naughton's data is hard to reconcile with provincial autarky. Bai et al. (2004), using more recent and more disaggregated data on the province-level industrial composition, find evidence of increasing *specialization* in industrial structure over the course of the 1990s, a direct contradiction of Young's finding. They concede that there is clear evidence of local protectionism, but conclude that it has substantially diminished over time. Huang and Wei (2001) have examined the speed of convergence toward the law of one price for identical products in different cities in China over the 1990s and found that it is comparable to what Parsley and Wei (1996) or O'Connell and Wei (2003) found for the United States. Finally, foreigners who have traveled widely within China in recent years cannot fail to note both the massive program to build major interprovincial highways and the increasing visibility of both foreign and domestic brand names with virtually nationwide distribution and advertising. International integration appears to be proceeding together with intranational integration.

THE OPENING TO FDI PRIOR TO WTO ACCESSION

Liberalization of Foreign Direct Investment

Despite rising interest in FDI in China after the 1972 visit of U.S. president Richard Nixon, a number of severe restrictions on FDI remained in place – including a ban on external financing of FDI projects – such that there was very little inward investment until policies were dramatically changed in 1979. In that year, a new Law on Joint Ventures was passed, providing a basic framework under which foreign firms were allowed to operate. Restrictions on external debt and equity finance were relaxed, and, as has been already indicated, restrictions on foreign trade were reduced. Provincial and local governments were allowed considerable freedom in regulating the joint ventures that were established within their jurisdictions. In the same year, four SEZs were established in which foreign firms were offered preferential tax and administrative treatment and given an unusually free hand in their operations.[8]

These "experiments" in attracting FDI were quite successful. In 1984, the government, in a bid to attract FDI, granted similar exemptions from taxes and administrative procedures to fourteen additional administrative units, mostly municipalities on China's Pacific coast. This granted units, known variously as "opened cities" or "export and technology development zones," the authority to approve FDI projects under $30 million (a threshold later raised to $50 million) at the local level.

---

foreign competition and competitors outside the province. These estimates suggest a substantial decrease in the protectionist tendencies of the government through the mid-1990s.

[8] These SEZs included Shenzhen (across the border from Hong Kong), Zhuhai (across the border from Macau) and Shantou (on the Guangdong coast facing Taiwan), and Xiamen (directly across the Taiwan Straits from Taiwan).

The next major regulatory change in FDI came in 1986, with the implementation of a legal regime change that Feenstra (1998, p. 6) has dubbed the "22 Regulations." These changes represented a major liberalization that applied throughout China. FIEs were made eligible for reduced business income tax rates regardless of location and were given increased managerial autonomy. Tight controls on the remittance of profit in foreign currencies were lifted. Finally, the 22 Regulations designated two categories of foreign investments as being eligible for additional special benefits – "export-oriented" projects (defined as projects exporting 50 percent or more of their production value) and "technologically advanced" projects (defined as projects that upgrade domestic production capacity through the use of "advanced" technology).

The 22 Regulations also set up an approval process for FDI projects that remained in place until WTO accession, albeit with some modification. While the formal regulatory framework implies substantial centralization of power over the approval process and subsequent regulatory oversight of FIEs, there is considerable debate as to how much the central government intervened in the oversight of FIEs after they are established. In practice, there seems to be a considerable degree of de facto local autonomy in regulating FIEs. Investments below a certain threshold size required only local approval, and this lead to the partition of large numbers of FDI projects into subprojects that fell below the threshold, in order to streamline and accelerate the approval and negotiation process.[9]

The Rise, Fall, and Rise of FDI Since 1989

The next major shift in FDI in China marked not so much a regulatory shift as a change in the composition of foreign investors. FDI in China slowed briefly after the Tiananmen incident, but the inflows resumed and quickly grew in the 1990s.[10] Whereas FDI in China in the 1980s had been overwhelmingly dominated by Hong Kong- and Taiwan-based investors seeking to exploit relatively low-cost labor in the special economic zones (SEZs) for export processing, in-flows diversified in the 1990s. Hong Kong- and Taiwan-based investors continued to play an important role, but Japanese, American, and European firms also increased their FDI into China, much of it focused on the domestic market. Figure 16.2 illustrates the growth over time in contracted FDI and actual foreign investment. Figure 16.3 shows variation over time in the number of FDI contracts approved and in the nature of the entity created. Of particular interest is the growth in wholly owned

---

[9] See Rosen (1999, pp. 56–59) for a discussion of the threshold and evidence supporting the view that such partitions took place. Huang (2003, pp. 260–302) regards the small size of many FDI projects in China as a reflection of distortions in the economy.

[10] Barry Naughton (1996, pp. 278–280), among others, suggests that there was a de facto loosening of the official regulations on FDI that allowed multinationals to skirt the official export requirements. Essentially, export requirements were increasingly ignored or the definition of a "technologically advanced" project was broadened to allow even not particularly technology-intensive firms to set up plants to serve the Chinese market.

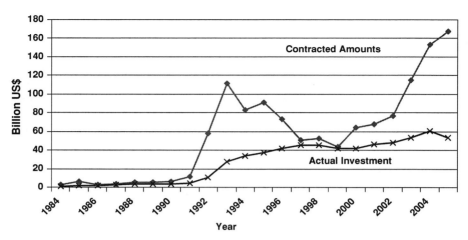

Figure 16.2. Foreign direct investment in China (*Note:* Contracted amounts refers to the total value of the approved investment project, where this total is attributed to the year in which approval is conferred. In practice, of course, these investments are often phased in over a series of years. Actual investment tracks the inflow of FDI on an annual basis. Data are taken from publications of the Ministry of Foreign Trade and Economic Cooperation, which was later incorporated into the Ministry of Commerce.)

foreign enterprises relative to equity joint ventures. Figure 16.4 breaks down growth in actual investment flows by the nationality of the investing country.[11]

As Figure 16.2 shows, contracted FDI peaked in the early 1990s and declined sharply for the rest of the decade.[12] These contracts contained multiyear business plans, so it is not surprising that there is a lag between the approval of a contract and the actual investment associated with it. Nevertheless, the sharp divergence in these two time series hints at some problems that foreign investors, particularly Western firms with little previous experience in China, encountered as they rushed to enter the market in this period.[13] The FDI boom began when China was in the midst of an unsustainable expansion, brought on in part by rapid credit creation.[14]

---

[11] Because of official restrictions on direct Taiwanese investment in the mainland, some Taiwanese FDI gets routed through Hong Kong or through "tax haven" nations, such as the Cayman Islands. Such tax haven jurisdictions are a prominent component of the "other nations" category shown in Figure 16.4.

[12] In 1994, foreign-invested enterprises collectively accounted for about 17 percent of all fixed-asset investment, prompting some scholars such as Huang (2003, pp. 1–62) to refer to the "dependency" of Chinese investment on foreign firms. By 2000, the ratio of FIE investment to total investment had fallen to 10 percent. By 2003, even in the context of a substantial increase in FDI, the share of FIEs in domestic investment had fallen further, to 7 percent.

[13] It is likely that the contracted amounts were subject to some overreporting, as local officials vied to take credit for bringing FDI to their jurisdictions. However, the existence of a likely systematic upward bias in these numbers makes their decline in the mid- to- late 1990s all the more striking.

[14] Debates about the true size of the Chinese economy in the early 1990s suggested that real domestic demand was substantially larger than comparisons at market exchange rates would

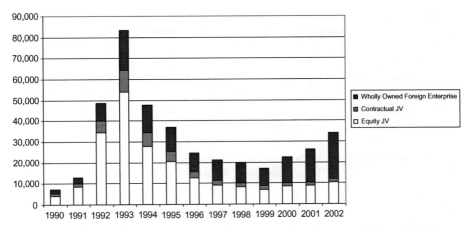

Figure 16.3. Counts of FDI contracts by contractual form (*Source:* Ministry of Foreign Trade and Economic Cooperation, Ministry of Commerce, People's Republic of China)

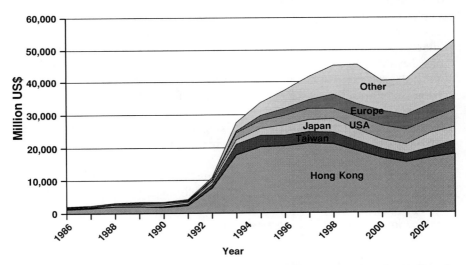

Figure 16.4. Inward FDI in China by source country (*Source:* Ministry of Foreign Trade and Economic Cooperation, Ministry of Commerce, People's Republic of China)

Demand growth was rapidly outstripping supply, leading to a surge in inflation that peaked in 1994, when consumer prices shot up by one-fourth. Zhu Rongji, then serving as vice premier and governor of the central bank, initiated contractionary monetary and fiscal policies that reduced aggregate demand and moderated price

suggest. Some of the adjustment factors then favored have since been rejected as overoptimistic. See Studwell (2002, pp. 158–162) for an account of how this academic debate was presented in the business press. Later research also confirmed that Chinese statistics increasingly overstated the true rate of growth. See Lardy (2002, pp. 11–14).

inflation. By 1996, growth and inflation were down to more sustainable levels. Then the Asian crisis hit, leading to yet slower growth in domestic demand, a dramatic slowdown in export growth, and domestic price *deflation*. The scale and number of FDI projects approved in the early 1990s appear to have been motivated in part by an extrapolation of the (unsustainable) expansion of domestic demand observed in those years. Firms also appear to have been unprepared for the barriers they encountered in attempting to distribute their goods within China.[15] In the context of the domestic demand retrenchment that followed, it is unsurprising that many ventures proved to be spectacularly unprofitable.

The speed with which FDI increased in the early 1990s also generated problems. Western firms, primarily targeting the local market, were hoping to establish dominant market positions in advance of their rivals. However, they were all competing for specialized resources (multilingual Chinese managers, skilled labor, Western-style office space, etc.) whose supply was relatively fixed in the short run. Predictably, costs for these scarce resources rapidly exceeded the projections of some of these firms.[16] Most foreign firms targeting the domestic market were required to form a joint venture with a local Chinese firm, usually a state-owned enterprise (SOE). The supply of well-run, effectively managed SOEs was also quite limited. In their eagerness to set up operations, many firms forged alliances with enterprises that turned out to be far less efficient, amenable to Western direction, or politically connected than they thought. The survey and interview evidence presented by Rosen (1999, pp. 17–83) suggests that many Western investors were unprepared for the cultural clashes, administrative difficulties, and operational inefficiencies created by their "forced marriages" to Chinese SOEs.[17] Figure 16.3 illustrates a sharp downturn in the number of contracts signed and a striking shift toward wholly owned foreign enterprises, as this option became feasible in an expanding number of industries and situations.

The deep disillusionment harbored by some Western expatriates by the end of the 1990s has been vividly captured by Studwell (2002, pp. 137–153). Much of the reporting in the popular press echoed this pessimism, stressing the difficulties multinational firms were having making money in China.

---

[15] Rosen (1999, pp. 159–196) suggests, based on FIE manager interviews, that barriers to distribution arising from the inadequacy of transport infrastructure, institutional constraints preventing FIEs from controlling their own distribution channels, and the control of local governments over the important distribution channels were among the most serious barriers to serving the domestic market in the latter 1990s.

[16] Again, Rosen (1999, pp. 85–115) and Studwell (2002, pp. 115–133) provide evidence of these cost increases. While not solely driven by foreign investors, the commercial real-estate markets in Shanghai and some other major Chinese cities went through a pronounced "boom and bust" in the mid- to- late 1990s.

[17] Some of the operational inefficiencies were related to the "performance requirements" then in place in FIE contracts. Firms were often asked to meet targets for export of final output or localization of parts procurement than ran counter to what profit maximization would dictate. See Rosen (1999, pp. 69–75).

Even as actual FDI levels had begun to fall, reformers in the Chinese government were negotiating terms for WTO accession that dramatically expanded the freedom with which foreign firms could operate in China. Prior to the signing of the agreement, more categories of FIEs were allowed to sidestep joint ventures entirely and set up wholly foreign-owned enterprises. Interference in supply chain management, product development, and operations was scaled back. The final bilateral agreement with the United States, signed in November 1999, signaled a dramatic change in the Chinese operating environment. Contracted FDI increased almost immediately, and levels of actual utilization began to follow suit, as can be seen in Figure 16.2.

A pickup in demand growth also spurred FDI. Chinese export growth rapidly expanded as the regional economy recovered from the effects of the East Asian crisis.[18] While the veracity of the official GDP growth rates in the immediate aftermath of the East Asian crisis have been questioned, even the most pessimistic views suggest that Chinese GDP growth was more resilient than that of other large economies in the region, possibly inducing firms that might have invested elsewhere to focus on China.[19] The austerity regime put in place in the mid-1990s was reversed after the Asian crisis, interest rates were cut several times, lending by state banks was expanded, and the government also sought to use a sizable fiscal stimulus to boost domestic demand.[20] Export growth slowed sharply again in 2001, with the worldwide slowdown generated by the September 11 attacks, but rapidly rebounded in 2002. While difficult to measure with precision, estimates of the profits of foreign enterprises provided in Figure 16.5 appear to be consistent with this pattern, as they declined steadily through 1998 and then rebounded sharply thereafter.[21]

Domestic demand was rapidly expanding again by the end of 2002, as investment spending surged to high levels. Dramatic increases in the availability of consumer credit spurred a sharp rise in purchase of automobiles, apartments, and other "big ticket" items. For firms such as GM, which had rapidly built up technologically advanced production capacity in the mid-to-late 1990s under weak demand

---

[18] Plans to eliminate the duty-free import of capital goods for export processing were abandoned, VAT rebates for exporters were expanded and payments were accelerated, and the government seems to have directed the banking sector to support export growth. See Lardy (2002, p. 18).

[19] Rawski (2001) suggests that growth in 1998 might have been less than one-half of the officially recorded level.

[20] The *Wall Street Journal* reported that American firms had lost money in China in the 1980s, received minimal earnings on their Chinese affiliates throughout much of the 1990s, but earned much higher profits on their China operations beginning in 1999. By 2003, American corporate earnings from China and Hong Kong combined were roughly equal to their earnings from Japan – a much larger economy (see Higgens, 2004).

[21] These estimates aggregate together foreign enterprises primarily engaged in export-processing and foreign enterprises that primarily serve the domestic market. The profitability of the former is generally thought to have been relatively high throughout the period, whereas the profitability of the latter is thought to have fluctuated substantially. ROA is calculated on a pretax basis, using official statistics.

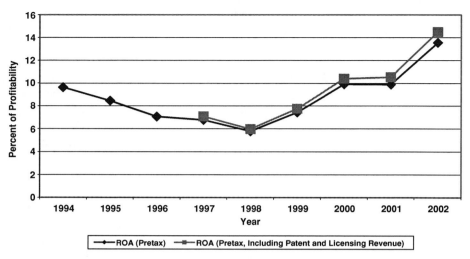

Figure 16.5. Foreign-invested enterprise profitability, 1994–2002 (*Source:* National Bureau of Statistics, China Statistical Yearbook)

conditions, the surge in demand seemed to vindicate their aggressive China expansion strategies.[22]

The impact of more expansionary monetary and fiscal policy on the Chinese economy had been partially offset from 1998 through mid-2001 by a substantial restructuring of state-owned manufacturing enterprises. Most small- and medium-scale state-owned operations were sold off to their managers or to manager and worker investment groups, hundreds of state factories were shut down, and the larger remaining state-owned units began laying off excess workers at an astonishing pace. When the dust settled, the number of workers employed in state-owned manufacturing establishments had fallen by about three quarters, from around 35 million in 1992 to less than 10 million in 2002, with most of the decline occurring in the late 1990s (National Bureau of Statistics, 2004b, p. 134).

Once this period of retrenchment waned, however, the economy began growing at a pace increasingly reminiscent of the boom of the early 1990s. Even the uncertainty created by the outbreak of severe acute respiratory syndrome, a previously unknown and fatal respiratory ailment that rapidly spread throughout East Asia, failed to stall growth momentum in 2003. By late 2003, however, the Chinese government was once again taking steps to try to limit overinvestment and excessive growth, primarily through direct administrative measures rather than higher interest rates or a revalued exchange rate. While these measures appeared to have had some success, the scale of expansion in lending and investment suggested that

[22] Chinese automobile sales grew an average of less than 1 percent per year during the 1998–2001 period. Then they surged 68 percent in 2002 and another 55 percent in 2003. See Ministry of Economy, Trade, and Industry (2003), the National Statistics Bureau Web site, and Wonacott (2004).

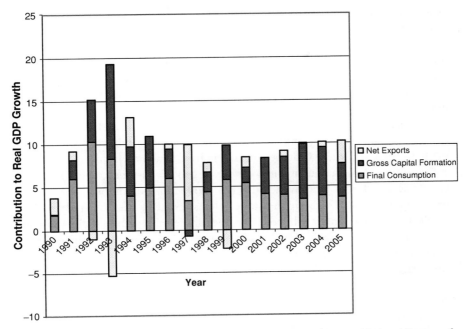

Figure 16.6. The components of real GDP growth, 1990–2005 (*Source:* National Bureau of Statistics, Revised GDP Series, September 2006)

some of the progress made in scaling back nonperforming loans in the late 1990s and early 2000s was likely undone in the investment boom of 2002–2004.[23]

Did Trade and FDI Drive Growth in the 1990s?

The rapid growth of Chinese exports in the decade prior to WTO accession, the relatively large share of GDP the export sector has come to represent, and the persistent and growing trade imbalance with the United States might suggest that net exports, and the FDI that contributed to it, has been an important driving factor in Chinese economic growth in the 1990s. Many accusations of "neomercantilism" on the part of the Chinese government are predicated on this view.

In a narrow growth accounting sense, it is simply not true that net exports have been a consistently important driver of growth in the 1990s, as is illustrated in Figure 16.6, using components of the national income and product accounts taken from the recently revised gross domestic product (GDP) series issued by the National Bureau of Statistics in 2006. Growth in imports has broadly kept pace with growth in exports. In the fifteen years shown in this chart, net exports contributed

---

[23] Similarly pronounced cycles of rapid growth followed by substantial slowdown can be seen in the trade statistics and in measures of domestic investment. For one theory-based analysis of the macroeconomic instability of the reform period, see Brandt and Zhu (2000).

positively to GDP growth in most years and detracted from it in a few years, but with few exceptions, the net impact was modest compared either to capital investment or to private consumption. FDI, much of it export related, has contributed to capital formation, but as we have already noted, that contribution has also been relatively modest, declining from a peak of 17 percent in 1994 to about 7 percent in 2003. Recognition of these facts helps place useful bounds on the degree to which growth in both the 1990s and the early 2000s can be ascribed to trade.[24]

That being said, there is no question that expanding trade and FDI have contributed to Chinese living standards, since the reform period began and particularly in the last decade. Chinese consumers have benefited from price declines and an increase in the quality and variety of goods consumed, and China has been able to alter its pattern of industrial production to conform to its comparative advantage. These are the static gains stressed by classical trade theory. While difficult to quantify with precision, they are certainly substantial. Moreover, these gains are shared with China's trading partners, who have also benefited from cheaper imports, export sales to China, and returns from investment in Chinese enterprises.

China's increasing openness to trade and FDI has also fostered a much greater degree of competition in Chinese product (and, increasingly, service) markets than would have otherwise existed. This has provided a powerful disciplining force constraining the expansion of inefficient enterprises, even when such enterprises received extensive support from other features of the institutional environment, such as the problematic banking system. As foreign producers have been allowed steadily greater freedom to operate in the Chinese market, this competitive pressure has intensified, increasing the likelihood that market share gains are concentrated in the most efficient firms. This, in turn, arguably raises the marginal productivity of capital and labor throughout the economy, although it is clearly difficult to quantify this impact.

China has arguably gained in other dimensions as well, although these benefits are also difficult to quantify. The ability to import technology embodied in capital goods and components has certainly contributed to output expansion. Chinese workers and managers have also benefited from training in foreign technology and management practices. While the Chinese economy as a whole does not appear to exhibit exceptional performance in terms of total factor productivity growth, it is clear that the relative labor productivity of Chinese workers has increased substantially, particularly in the export sector. This has been partially reflected in wage increases and will be eventually reflected in an appreciation of the real exchange rate. Given the level of China's openness to trade, the improvement in

---

[24] Net exports have grown extremely rapidly in the last few years and accounted for about one quarter of total GDP growth in 2005. However, we do not view the trends of the last two years as sustainable in the longer run.

terms of trade that would result from such an appreciation would confer nontrivial welfare effects.[25]

Huang (2003) has suggested that the prominence of FIEs in Chinese production and trade reflects systematic discrimination against indigenous private Chinese firms, making it difficult for them to acquire capital, defend their property rights, and engage in foreign trade. We would not contest the view that the repression of the private sector has generated welfare-reducing distortions, and we agree that misallocation of capital by the Chinese financial system has created serious problems (Lardy, 1998). That being said, we do not regard the prominent position of FIEs as simply reflecting distortions in the Chinese economic system. While it is possible that FIEs would play a less prominent role in a counterfactual world in which these distortions did not exist, we believe that even under these alternative circumstances, foreign investors would find China an attractive place in which to locate export-processing operations. The fundamental attractors of a large, low-cost labor force, relatively good export infrastructure, and the ability to purchase inputs at world prices would still exist under this counterfactual scenario. In addition, China's internal market might, if anything, be even more attractive, and growing even more rapidly, under a counterfactual scenario in which the financial system was not burdened by a large stock of nonperforming loans to SOEs. Despite recent rapid growth in the size, investment, and legal recognition of the private sector in China, FIEs continue to play an important role in mediating China's foreign trade. We expect this to continue, at least in the short-to-medium run.[26]

CHINA'S WTO ACCESSION AGREEMENT AND ITS IMPLEMENTATION

A significant portion of the tariff reduction and other trade liberalization measures that the Chinese government undertook in the 1990s were essentially part of China's WTO accession process. To gain credibility with its negotiating partners that it was seriously committed to opening up its economy, China chose to unilaterally liberalize. Then in its key final bilateral negotiations with the United States

[25] Whalley and Xin (2006) estimate that the expansion of FIEs may have accounted for more than 40 percent of Chinese GDP growth in 2003 and 2004 and that the absence of FDI inflows in those years would have reduced growth by about 3.4 percentage points. They suggest that a slowdown in FDI inflows could cause GDP growth to drop significantly. The growth decomposition on which this calculation is based rests on a number of assumptions that can be called into question. (For example, foreign supplied capital is assumed to be the only nonlabor input to the FIE subeconomy.) We regard Whalley and Xin's calculations as an upper-bound estimate of the impact of FIEs on China in recent years.

[26] Wells (1991) among others has pointed out that while the Asian NIEs were able to expand their exports of labor-intensive manufactures under largely contractual arrangements, the growth of labor-intensive manufacturing exports elsewhere in Asia, such as in the ASEAN countries, has been driven to a much greater extent by FDI. Wells (1991) and the discussion contained therein provide a number of reasons why FDI has been more important in the period since the mid-1980s, even in countries that lacked China's legal and institutional discrimination against private firms.

in 1999 China agreed to additional market opening commitments that were incorporated into China's final WTO accession package. In this process China agreed to a set of conditions that were far more stringent than the terms under which other developing countries had acceded. Indeed, in certain respects China's liberalization commitments exceed those of advanced industrial countries. Why did China's leadership agree to such commitments, given that they were expected to entail substantial short-term adjustment costs?

The most plausible answer to this question was the one given by Premier Zhu Rongji at the time of his visit to the United States in April 1999. On that trip, Premier Zhu, perhaps for the first time, openly expressed the view that China's membership in the WTO was an essential element of his reform strategy. He had come to the view that more competition was an essential source of pressure that would ultimately force SOEs and banks to take additional structural reforms. In his joint press conference with President Clinton he stated, "The competition arising [from WTO membership] will also promote a more rapid and more healthy development of China's national economy" (White House, 1999).

Premier Zhu and most of those around him came to believe that China had no viable alternative to becoming even more deeply involved in the globalizing economy. Long Yongtu, China's chief WTO negotiator, clearly understood that a growing array of goods were being produced in global rather than national production networks. He also had the insight to realize that simply reducing import barriers was insufficient if China wanted to benefit from globalization. Rather, he said, "Countries with planned economies have never been part of economic globalization. China's economy must become a market economy in order to become part of the global economic system, as well as the economic globalization process" (Long, 2000). In short, China's top political leadership made extensive commitments to the WTO in order to advance their domestic reform agenda.

Here, we briefly summarize the most important features of China's WTO accession agreement and note the progress China has made in terms of meeting its commitments. A more thorough treatment of the agreement is available in Lardy (2002). China's commitments regarding its service sector will be examined in the next section.

Trade in Manufactures

China agreed in 1999 to lower its average tariff levels on industrial products to 8.9 percent. Most of these new tariff levels have already been phased in as of the time of this writing in mid-2005, some even well in advance of the timetable required under WTO obligations. Tariffs on some important classes of goods, such as information technology products, have already been cut to zero. Even more significantly, China agreed to eliminate all quotas, licenses, tendering requirements, and other nontariff barriers to imports of manufactured goods by 2005. China has agreed to modify its import registration system to make it consistent with the WTO Agreement on Import Licensing. By and large, these obligations have been met. Recent U.S. criticism has focused on preferential VAT treatment for domestically produced fertilizer and semiconductors, which constituted a de facto import tariff for foreign producers exporting to China. These tax preferences were eliminated for semiconductors in 2004. China eliminated the last import quota, that on automobiles, on January 1, 2005. However, China has the right to maintain indefinitely a fairly high 25 percent import tariff on automobiles. This is expected to limit growth in auto imports.

China will retain the state monopoly on foreign trade for a small number of commodities, which nevertheless includes critical imports, such as crude oil, refined petroleum products, fertilizer, cotton, grain, and vegetable oil, and key exports, such as tea, tungsten, silk, cotton products, and fossil fuels.[27] Outside this narrow set of categories, China promised to abolish by the end of 2004 the designated trading system, by which trade in a broader range of commodities is limited to a small number of trading companies designated by the central government. More generally, China agreed to provide the right to import and export to all firms active in China, foreign and domestic. The USTR (2004, 2005), in its annual reports on foreign barriers to U.S. trade, acknowledged China's progress in meeting these obligations.

Parties opposed to China's WTO accession suggested that China would use discriminatory product standards to keep out imports of industrial products. In December 2001, the Chinese government promulgated a new, compulsory product certification system that required domestic and foreign products in over one hundred product categories to obtain the China Compulsory Certification (CCC) mark. The certification process involves on-site inspection of foreign manufacturing plants, undertaken at producer expense. U.S. firms have complained about the inconsistent and arbitrary enforcement of these rules, which has included the blockage at the border of product samples intended for testing by Chinese government officials. However, there is no evidence that these practices have become a major constraint to trade in the affected categories (USTR, 2004).

FDI in the Manufacturing Sector

The pre-WTO regime regulating FDI contained explicit provisions requiring some FIEs to achieve a certain degree of local content, balance their trade by offsetting imports of components with exports of final products, or meet their foreign exchange requirements through exporting. In addition, FIE approvals were often contingent on technology transfer to domestic partners or the establishment of research centers in China. The WTO Agreement on Trade-Related Investment

---

[27] China is not unique in mandating a state monopoly in trade for a limited range of products, and such practices are not prohibited under the Uruguay Round Agreement.

Measures (TRIMs) explicitly precludes WTO members from imposing restrictions on investment that create trade restrictions or distortions. The measures that are precluded include local content requirements, trade balancing requirements, and foreign exchange balancing requirements. China agreed to fully enforce the provisions of the TRIMs agreement upon accession, and it also agreed not to enforce provisions of existing contracts with foreign firms that are inconsistent with TRIMs. As we have already noted, however, many of these provisions were not strongly enforced even prior to WTO, and the de facto investment regime became steadily more open in the late 1990s.

China agreed in principle to cease the practices of pressuring foreign firms to transfer technology to local partners and to increase the domestic content of automobiles assembled in China. While TRIMs rules out forced technology transfer, there is an extensive set of practices "encouraging" technology transfer that are arguably permissible under TRIMs, and many of these practices appear to persist in China, drawing some criticism from foreign firms and the USTR. State-owned firms are free to "request" technology transfers as part of a sales contract, and international competition among vendors eager to expand in the Chinese market provides these Chinese customers with extensive leverage.[28] The National Development and Reform Commission's new plan for industrial policy in the automobile industry published in May 2004 continues to include provisions that discourage the import of auto parts.[29] This has drawn some criticism from foreign automobile firms.

However, the most serious dispute over "forced technology transfer" since WTO accession was recently resolved on terms favorable to foreign industry. In May 2003, China issued two mandatory standards for encryption over wireless local area networks (WLANs), applicable to domestic and imported equipment containing WLAN (also known as Wi-Fi) technologies. These standards, which were originally scheduled to become fully effective in June 2004, incorporate the WLAN Authentication and Privacy Infrastructure (WAPI) encryption technique for secure communications. This component of the standards differed significantly from the internationally recognized standards that U.S. companies have adopted for global production. China sought to enforce the use of these standards by providing the necessary algorithms only to a limited number of Chinese companies. Accordingly, U.S. and other foreign manufacturers would have to work with and through these companies, some of which were their competitors, and provide them with technical product specifications, if their products were to continue to be sold on the

---

[28] Kranhold (2004) details how GE's power generation business was pressured to transfer sensitive turbine technology in return for contracts with state-owned utilities. The willingness of foreign competitors to transfer technology in return for business was a key factor in GE's decision to do so. No one suggests that this policy is in violation of China's obligations under its WTO accession agreement. Boeing is another U.S. firm that has shown a willingness to voluntarily transfer technology in order to gain a competitive advantage over arch-rival Airbus.

[29] The Chinese government revised the draft plan circulated in 2003 to eliminate a requirement that foreign companies use separate distribution channels for domestic and imported automobiles (USTR, 2005, p. 77).

Chinese market. The U.S. IT industry quickly enlisted top-level government support in opposing this measure, viewing it as a TRIMs-inconsistent attempt to force transfer of sensitive technology to competitors and as a WTO-inconsistent attempt to misuse product standards to restrict trade. After several months of high-level consultation, the Chinese government quietly dropped the proposed mandatory standards (Kennedy, 2004, 2005).

While foreign investors generally have viewed favorably China's implementation of its WTO obligations, an important exception is the area of intellectual property rights. In principle, China is bound under the TRIPs agreement to enact and enforce adequate standards of intellectual property protection. After bilateral negotiations with the United States, China enacted a patent law in 1993, which would seem to be fully in compliance with TRIPs, but lack of enforcement continues to be an issue for foreign firms. While central government officials regularly affirm their commitment to better enforcement, foreign investors claim that local officials take a far more permissive view of patent and trademark infringement.[30]

As part of its pathbreaking commitment to open up the distribution services sector, China also agreed to allow foreign firms much greater control over the advertising, distribution, and after-sales service of their goods, both those produced in China and those imported from outside the country. The increasing participation of foreign distributors in China is expected to improve the efficiency of the sector, ameliorating one of the persistent problems faced by foreign firms seeking to market goods outside the major cities.

Agricultural Trade

China also agreed to significant liberalization of its agricultural markets. China pledged to reduce the average statutory import tariff rate for agricultural products from 21 to 15 percent (Rosen, Rozelle, and Huang, 2004, pp. 8, 41). Prior to WTO accession, China, like many other countries, limited imports of sensitive agricultural commodities with quotas and other nontariff barriers that created effective rates of protection far higher than the 21 percent average statutory rate. Bound by the Agreement on Agriculture in the Uruguay Round, China is required to eliminate nontariff barriers to the import of agricultural products and replace them with tariffs that provide equivalent protection, as part of the goal of making agricultural protectionism more transparent and setting a common basis among countries for negotiating future tariff reductions.

The agreement requires countries to offer minimum "access opportunities" for agricultural commodities subject to tariffication. These take the form of limited levels of imports that are admitted at relatively low tariff rates, with all imports

---

[30] In September 2004, the American Chamber of Commerce in China issued a statement praising the Chinese government for what was viewed as a largely faithful implementation of its WTO obligations. At the same time, the chamber singled out intellectual property rights as a critical exception. See Hutzler and Kyne (2004).

above that level subject to much higher tariff rates. China is noteworthy in terms of the relatively large amount of imports that will be admitted at lower rates and the very low tariff rates being charged on these levels. China agreed to impose tariffs of only 1 percent on "minimum access" levels of imports for wheat, corn, rice, and cotton. The minimum access levels are themselves considerably higher than the actual level of imports of these products in 1998. On the other hand, even when fully phased in, minimum access requirements would be a small share of projected domestic consumption, and China's commitments with regard to rice fall short of the standards specified in the WTO Agricultural Agreement. China's compliance with this agreement remains an area of contention with its trading partners, particularly the U.S. 2002 trade data showed that quota fill-rates for wheat, corn, and cotton were 7.0, 0.1, and 22.0 percent, respectively. However, U.S. agricultural exports to China grew substantially in 2003. U.S. cotton exports increased by 430 percent and soybean exports increased by 218 percent over 2002 levels.[31]

Health standards have been frequently employed as a de facto nontariff barrier to agricultural imports. China agreed to be bound by the WTO Agreement on Sanitary and Phytosanitary standards. Bilateral agreements with the United States prior to WTO accession resulted in the removal of blanket bans on imports of citrus fruit, wheat, U.S. leaf tobacco, and meat from certain U.S. regions that had been justified on the basis of health standards.[32] Since joining the WTO, however, China has issued more than 100 new quality and health standards for foods. U.S. exporters complain that many of these have not been publicly documented with the WTO in detail, as WTO obligations require, and that they are both designed to block imports and applied in ways that discriminate against imports. Phytosanitary barriers continue to block imports of stone fruit, several varieties of apples, pears, fresh potatoes, and processed food products containing certain food additives, according to the USTR.

AQSIQ, the new agency in charge of administering these quality standards, has delisted four U.S. meat-processing plants and continues to hold up imports of citrus products from four counties in the State of Florida. Imports of wheat from the Pacific Northwest, while permitted, are apparently singled out for special treatment by quarantine officials, discouraging imports. U.S. soybean imports were disrupted by the announcement of a ban on imports from four companies trading U.S. soybeans due to detections of *Phytophthora sojae*, which is ubiquitous in China. The suspension of imports was delayed after high-level U.S. government intervention. U.S. exporters are also concerned about new regulations on agricultural biotechnology, testing, and labeling. Transgenic soybean imports have been formally approved, but approval was still pending on six corn varieties as of late 2003.

---

[31] Data are from United States International Trade Commission Database at http://dataweb.usitc.gov.

[32] However, as already noted, there was a substantial amount of smuggling of these "banned" products into China via Hong Kong. The growth in legal exports to China is likely to be partially offset by the decline in exports to Hong Kong.

China also agreed to significant limitations on agricultural subsidies. China has agreed to limit its domestic agricultural subsidies to 8.5 percent of the value of agricultural output and its subsidies of any particular crop to no more than 8.5 percent of the value of that crop. The limit for developing countries under the agricultural agreement is 10 percent. China is forced to include investment subsidies and subsidies for inputs such as fertilizer in calculating total agricultural subsidies, unlike most developing countries. China also agreed to eliminate export subsidies for agricultural products upon accession, something that neither the United States nor the European Union has agreed to do. This was significant given that China employed export subsidies of about $500 million per year in the base period used for negotiation in the Uruguay Round.

A Double Standard for China?

Finally, China accepted an accession protocol that would allow Chinese trading partners to impose restrictions on Chinese exports under conditions that are substantially weaker than those WTO members must ordinarily meet before imposing import restrictions. Restrictions can be imposed solely on Chinese exports, even when exports of the same product from other countries have increased, and they can be maintained without an effective time limit, whereas the WTO Agreement on Safeguards imposes an eight-year time limit. Furthermore, China has accepted limitations on its ability to retaliate that are more stringent than the limitations contained in the Safeguards Agreement. In addition to this transitional arrangement, China has agreed to a special textile safeguard that would allow its trading partners to limit the growth of textile and apparel products to 7.5 percent per year after the phaseout of the WTO Agreement on Textiles and Clothing, the successor agreement to the Multifiber Arrangement negotiated under General Agreement on Tariffs and Trade (GATT). The textile provision will remain in place until 2008.

China has also agreed to accept discriminatory terms in its protocol of accession in antidumping. Under U.S. trade law, China has for many years been treated as a nonmarket economy in antidumping cases. That means that the U.S. Department of Commerce does not compare prices of goods sold in the U.S. market to prices prevailing in China or in third countries, because key inputs may be supplied to Chinese firms at below-market prices. Instead the Department of Commerce calculates "normal value" by soliciting information from Chinese firms on input quantities, using input prices of a third country where input prices are believed to be market determined, and then adding to these direct production cost calculations estimates of "reasonable amounts" for administration, sales, other costs, and a profit margin. Alternatively, the Department of Commerce can simply use as a standard for "normal value" the cost of production in a third country. This creates a double standard that could easily be abused by domestic producers in competition with Chinese exporters. Nevertheless, the Chinese government has allowed the

U.S. and other trading partners to use the "nonmarket economy" methodology in antidumping investigations for up to fifteen years after accession.[33]

WTO Accession: A Watershed, Not a Sea Change

While negotiations over China's WTO entry were ongoing in the late 1990s, a number of studies were conducted, estimating the impact of WTO accession on Chinese trade, employment, and growth. Some predicted that China would incur significant restructuring costs in meeting its WTO commitments.[34] Other studies forecast fairly dramatic increases in imports as import tariffs were reduced. There was a tendency for these studies to overestimate the impact of WTO, because many were based on conditions that existed in the mid-1990s and did not take into account the dramatic acceleration of reform in the years immediately preceding China's WTO entry.

As we have already stressed, China cut tariffs, broadened trading rights, and liberalized its FDI regime even prior to formal WTO accession. The Chinese government also launched a major effort to restructure state-owned manufacturing industries, engineering a dramatic decline in SOE manufacturing employment and an improvement in profitability. Steps were also taken to eliminate or reduce import price differentials prior to WTO accession. The government substantially cut the prices for wheat and corn in 1999, two years before WTO accession, driving prices toward international levels and starting the process of moving farmers out of grain and into less land-intensive crops (Foreign Agricultural Service, 2000; Hoo, 2000; Saywell and Wilhelm, 2000). Steps were also taken to hasten the convergence of prices to world levels for petroleum products, transportation services, wholesale electricity prices, and water and natural gas.[35] Because the structural change and price convergence the WTO-mandated liberalizations would generate were already under way prior to formal accession, the impact of WTO per se has arguably been smaller than some might have predicted.

That being said, the combination of China's pre-WTO and post-WTO reforms is making it arguably the most open large developing economy. By 2005, China's average statutory tariff on industrial products was 8.9 percent. For Argentina, Brazil, India, and Indonesia, the respective percent figures are 30.9, 27.0, 32.4, and

---

[33] Kennedy (2004) studies China's own use of the antidumping law it adopted in 1997, providing statistics and interview-based qualitative evidence on the thirty investigations launched by the middle of 2004. Kennedy finds that foreign respondents won a partial or complete victory in over 40 percent of all concluded AD cases. Kennedy attributes the surprisingly evenhanded application of China's AD law to the interests of import-using industries in maintaining adequate supplies of key inputs.

[34] One study predicted that the opening in agriculture alone would eliminate employment for 8 million wheat farmers, 30 percent of the number engaged in wheat production. Substantial reductions in employment and output were also forecast for natural rubber, plastics, and rolled steel. See Zhang, Zhang, and Wan (1998).

[35] See the discussion of these policy initiatives in Lardy (2002, pp. 26–27).

36.9 (General Agreement on Tariffs and Trade, 1996). China has agreed to bind all tariffs as the new statutory rates are phased in, meaning that it has committed to not raise any existing tariffs on industrial products above existing levels as some are reduced. India, in contrast, has only bound two-thirds of its tariffs (Hufbauer and Rosen, 2000). China's FDI regime is one of the most open and welcoming of any country in the world, and China has made liberalization commitments in all of the service industries covered by the WTO General Agreement on Trade in Services. Only a handful of members come close to meeting this standard. Former U.S. Trade Representative Charlene Barshefsky (1999) described China's commitment to liberalize its distribution system as "broader actually than any World Trade Organization member has made." China has also made relatively strong commitments to liberalize financial and telecommunications services.

This high degree of openness is evidenced by the sharp increase in Chinese imports in recent years, which, in turn, has had an increasingly powerful impact on the East Asian regional economy and, indeed, on the global economy. However, important macroeconomic imbalances, clearly not sustainable in the long run, are also playing an important role in driving this growth. These issues are addressed in the next sections.

CHINA'S LIBERALIZATION IN THE SERVICES SECTOR

China made pathbreaking commitments in its accession to the WTO to open up its service sector to foreign investment and competition. The promised openings were especially significant in distribution, telecommunications, and financial services but commitments were also made in professional, audiovisual, and construction services (Lardy, 2002, pp. 66–75).

Prior to China's entry into the WTO the Chinese government severely restricted the ability of foreign firms to distribute goods in China. They could import inputs, equipment, and other materials directly related to their manufacturing or processing operations. But to import products made outside of China they had to use an agent and generally these goods could not be sold in the same distribution channels these firms used to sell goods they made in China. Thus, for example, it was cumbersome for companies like General Motors or Volkswagen to import and distribute vehicles made outside of China.

Complying with the terms of its entry, China by the end of 2004 had phased out all geographic, ownership, and most other types of restrictions on wholesaling and retailing, as well as related distribution services, such as franchising, commission agents, and repair and maintenance services.[36] As a result, China is "in full compliance with its WTO commitments on trading rights for all Chinese-foreign

---

[36] According to China's distribution commitments, certain product restrictions will not be lifted until the beginning of 2007 and China has denied in perpetuity the right of foreign firms to engage in the wholesale distribution of salt and tobacco or the retail distribution of tobacco products.

joint ventures, wholly foreign-owned enterprises and foreign individuals" (USTR, 2005, p. 75).

China agreed to substantially open its market in banking, insurance, securities, fund management, and other financial services. In banking, many restrictions, such as the number of cities in which foreign banks can operate, were lifted from the beginning of 2005. However, not until five years after accession, at the end of 2006, will Chinese regulators have to offer full national treatment to foreign banks, meaning that any remaining restrictions that apply only to foreign banks must be eliminated. Most importantly, at that time foreign banks will be able to offer domestic currency services to Chinese citizens for the first time.

Liberalization has resulted in a significant increase in foreign bank presence in China. Even prior to China's accession to the WTO foreign banks operated more than 150 branch banks in more than twenty-three cities. They accounted, however, for only 1.5 percent of all bank assets in 2000 (Lardy, 2002, pp. 115–116). From the time China became a member of the WTO to the end of 2004, China authorized an additional thirty-one foreign branch banks to open for business.[37] However, the assets of foreign banks as a share of all financial institutions had increased to only 1.8 percent by year-end 2004.[38] The slow pace of penetration of the market reflects the remaining limitations on the scope of business these banks can conduct and regulatory requirements that increase the cost of providing banking services (USTR, 2005, p. 103).

If foreign banks have made only slow progress in building their businesses through opening branches, they have moved much more rapidly to invest in China's domestic banking institutions. This too got under way prior to China's accession to the WTO but has accelerated since. The Asian Development Bank and the International Finance Corporation (the investment banking arm of the World Bank) paved the way for foreign ownership of Chinese banks by investments that they made as early as 1996 (Lardy, 1998, pp. 67, 167). By 2005 about a dozen foreign banks had taken stakes in various city commercial banks and national shareholding banks. This process was facilitated by China's unilateral decision in late 2003 to increase the limit on the stake that could be held by a single foreign financial institution in a Chinese bank from 15 to 20 percent (Chinese Bank Regulatory Commission, 2003). Even more important, as part of the restructuring and public listing of some of the large state-owned commercial banks, the state sold off strategic stakes to foreign investors in the Construction Bank of China, the Bank of China, and the Industrial and Commercial Bank of China.

By the beginning of 2005, China had swept away geographic restrictions on where foreign insurance companies can do business. In line with its prior commitments,

---

[37] A complete list of all foreign branch banks licensed to operate in China is contained in each issue of *The People's Bank of China Quarterly Statistical Bulletin.*

[38] At year-end 2004 assets of foreign branch banks were RMB516 billion out of financial system total assets of RMB28,205 billion. *People's Bank of China Quarterly Statistical Bulletin,* 2005, 2, pp. 13, 49.

the government has also largely lifted restrictions on the types of products that foreign insurers can provide, allowing these firms to offer property and casualty insurance, health insurance, as well as group policies, pensions, and annuities. However, foreign firms are restricted to operating in joint ventures with Chinese partners with the foreign share limited to 51 percent in a nonlife insurance business and 50 percent in life insurance.[39] Measured by premium income China's overall insurance market is growing rapidly, but the share of the industry controlled by foreign firms remains relatively small at 2–3 percent (USTR, 2005, p. 76).

China's liberalization of its securities and fund management sector is somewhat more restricted than the opening in banking and insurance, since foreign ownership restrictions are somewhat more severe.[40] Moreover, joint-venture securities firms are not allowed to trade in A shares, the largest source of income in the Chinese securities industries. Nonetheless a number of joint-venture securities and fund management firms have been launched. In the fund management business well-known Western firms such as UBS, JP Morgan, Credit Suisse First Boston, Prudential Financial, and Schroder Investment Management have all established joint ventures.

In telecommunications China agreed to ease foreign investment restrictions and, more importantly, agreed to embrace procompetitive principles, such as transparent licensing, cost-based pricing, and the right of interconnection. While China did formally separate the regulatory and operating functions of the Ministry of Information Industry, the successor to the old Ministry of Posts and Telecommunications, and promulgated Regulations on Foreign-Invested Telecommunications Enterprises, which provides the promised regulatory environment for foreign investment in the sector, to date there has been practically no foreign participation in the telecommunications market (USTR, 2005, pp. 110–112).

A number of East Asia's earlier success stories, such as Japan and South Korea, have been characterized as possessing a dual economy (McKinsey & Co, 2000; IMF, 2005). On the one hand, there are export-oriented manufacturing sectors that have been forced to contend with the best competitors in the world for decades. These sectors tend to have productivity levels that compare favorably with those of the United States. On the other hand, the domestically oriented service sectors, in which competition has been muted by government regulations and restrictions on entry, are much less competitive. The low productivity of these sectors drags down living standards for the economy as a whole. China's early opening to FDI in its service sector holds out the possibility that its own service industries will be characterized by a considerably higher level of competition and productivity than was true of Japan or Korea at a similar stage of development. Early inroads by efficient foreign

---

[39] The sole exception is AIG. It received its first license to sell insurance as a wholly foreign-owned company in 1992 and still wholly owns all of its life insurance operations.

[40] Foreign firms are limited to a maximum one-third ownership stake in joint-venture securities businesses. In fund management the foreign share was initially restricted to one-third but this was raised to 49 percent beginning three years after accession in December 2004.

firms could ensure that only efficient domestic firms are able to expand as the market develops. This will prevent the emergence of a dual economy or, at least, will constrain the degree to which it constitutes a drag on living standards going forward.

While we certainly believe the early opening of the service sector will be to China's benefit, the implementation of this opening is an ongoing process, there are important limits to what China has promised in its WTO accession agreement, and the long-run effects are difficult to predict. Large swathes of the service economy (education, health care, and power generation) will remain largely closed to participation by foreign for-profit enterprises, much as they are in many Western countries. Even in the opened sectors, in the short-to-medium run, Western service providers may find it challenging to translate their business models to a Chinese context in which the income level of the population, the economic geography of consumer purchasing power, and the tastes of consumers are likely to be radically different from those found in the providers' home markets. This will be particularly true in financial services, where important features of the regulatory regime, including the closure of the capital account, will starkly limit the potential profitability of foreign firms for the foreseeable future.

Openness to FDI in services in Japan – which has existed in many service sectors for some time – has not yet eliminated the dual economy. Although Japanese income levels are close to American ones, many American firms have struggled to adapt to the different tastes of Japanese consumers, constituting less of a threat to Japanese incumbents than one might have hoped. Barriers to exit for uncompetitive enterprises have also been a factor inhibiting productivity growth in the low-productivity sectors. Some of the barriers – such as government credit subsidies to less efficient firms – are hardly unknown in China. Convergence of the productivity of the Chinese services sector to American levels is likely to take many years.

THE STRUCTURE OF CHINA'S EXPORTS

Does China's rapidly growing trade conform roughly to its comparative advantage or have supporting industrial and other government policies allowed firms to move up the technology ladder much more rapidly than would occur for a market economy with factor endowments similar to China? This question has been posed both by academic economists such as Schott (2006) and Lall and Albaladejo (2004) and by trade and industry associations based in Washington. Schott, for example, finds that over time Chinese exports exhibit rising sophistication relative to countries with similar aggregate endowments and that it exports more products in common with the capital and skill abundant members of the OECD than its peers.[41] Preeg (2004, p. 9), a researcher with the Manufacturers Alliance, charges that China's emergence as a major supplier of information technology,

---

[41] However, Schott (2006) qualifies this finding by documenting a decline in the prices of Chinese exports relative to OECD exports of similar products.

communication, and electronic products is a consequence of policies described as "high-tech mercantilism," which poses a major challenge to U.S. commercial and security interests. Similarly the American Electronics Association (2003) has analyzed China's growing exports of high-tech products and pointed to the threat they represent to U.S. industry.

There is no doubt that the structure of China's exports has changed dramatically over the past two decades. A decade and a half ago China's leading exports were crude oil, refined petroleum products, and apparel. In a seemingly complete transformation, China has emerged in recent years as a major producer and exporter of electronic and information technology products, such as consumer electronics, office equipment and computers, and communications equipment. Globally, it is now the second largest producer of these items, after only the United States. In 2000 China ranked behind Japan, Mexico, and the EU as a supplier of high-tech goods to the United States, but by 2002 it had displaced all three to become the single largest supplier (American Electronics Association, 2003). Does this imply that traditional notions of comparative advantage are useless in thinking about the evolution of China's trade structure?

We strongly disagree, and this point merits a small digression. The "infant industry argument," the classic case for temporary protection of domestic industry in the hopes of fostering economic development, dates at least to Alexander Hamilton (1791) and was endorsed, if cautiously, by some of the great nineteenth-century economists, notably including John Stuart Mill (1848). The international economics literature of the 1980s produced rigorous mathematical models in which temporary protection could, in principle, allow domestic firms to acquire technological capabilities that would have been impossible for them to acquire without government intervention, raising national welfare in the process.[42] Recent work by Brandt, Rawski, and Sutton (Chapter 15), with its strong implicit endorsement of China's protectionist policies in the automobile industry, appeals strongly to these ideas, if not to the formal models themselves.

Yet, it is important to point out that the theorists who launched this intellectual revolution within the discipline of international trade were *not* refuting the principle of comparative advantage. Instead, they were extending it, by allowing the technical capabilities of domestic firms – an attribute that could evolve over time – to influence comparative advantage. While demonstrating the *possibility* that government intervention could lead to gains over time, they remained remarkably unanimous in their skepticism that these gains were very large or that government intervention in practice could actually achieve the gains suggested by theory, and they remained sensitive to the potential costs of these interventions. The notion that the principle of comparative advantage has been rendered obsolete by "dynamic" theories of international trade has been flatly contradicted by the authors of these theories themselves (Krugman, 1994, pp. 245–280).

---

[42] Important contributors to this research stream include, among others, James Brander, William Ethier, Gene Grossman, Elhanan Helpman, Paul Krugman, and Barbara Spencer.

In any case, the critique that Chinese industrial and other policies have allowed China's firms to leapfrog ahead and bend or even suspend the law of comparative advantage falls short on three levels. First, most of the electronic and information technology products, which the Manufacturers Alliance and the American Electronics Association classify as high technology or advanced technology, should not be considered high tech. The single biggest U.S. import product from China in the consumer electronics, office equipment and computers, and communications equipment categories, respectively, is DVD players, notebook computers, and mobile telephones. Each of these is a high-volume, commodity product sold primarily by mass merchandisers of electronic products. For example, in 2003 the United States imported more than 31 million DVD players from China with an average unit cost of under $80, more than 7.5 million notebook computers with an average unit cost of $550 and more than 20 million mobile telephones with an average unit cost of less than $100.[43] The huge volumes and low unit costs of these products undermine the argument that these are high-tech products.

Second, China is able to export huge quantities of electronic and information technology products only because it imports most of the high-value-added parts and components that go into these goods. China, in short, does not in any real sense manufacture these goods. Rather it assembles them from imported parts and components. For example, domestic value-added accounts for only 15 percent of the value of exported electronic and information technology products. All the rest is import content. In short, for many of these products it is doubtful that China is supplying anything but the labor required to produce these goods. China's provision of relatively low-wage "assembly services" is completely consistent with its underlying comparative advantage. Schott's analysis of the growing relative sophistication of China's export bundle does not account for the importance of imported parts and components for a growing share of China's exports. On the other hand, Lall and Albaladejo's analysis of China's competitive threat to East Asian manufactured exports does take into account China's growing import of inputs for export activities. This leads them to the view that even though China is the biggest gainer of market share of exports of high-tech products in the decade to 2000 that there is "complementarity rather than competition between China and its neighbors" in the export of high-tech products.

China's dependence on imported parts and components is reflected in Figure 16.7, showing both China's exports and imports of electronic and information technology products. While China exported $142 billion in electronic and information technology products in 2003, China's imports of these products, overwhelmingly parts and components rather than finished goods, were over $127 billion. In short, China's net exports of electronic and information industry products in 2003 were a relatively small $15 billion.

---

[43] United States International Trade Commission, USITC Interactive Tariff and Trade DataWeb, dataweb.usitc.gov.

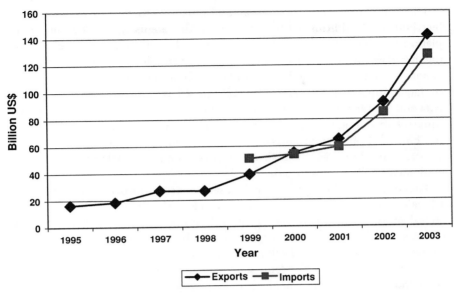

Figure 16.7. Exports and imports of high-tech products (*Sources:* Chinese Ministry of Information Industries, China General Customs Administration)

Imported semiconductors and microprocessors constitute an unusually large share of the imported parts and components that firms in China use in the assembly of electronic and information industry products. Semiconductors and microprocessors are, of course, among the most sophisticated components of electronic and information technology products. China's imports of microprocessors and semiconductors quadrupled from $12 billion in 1999 to over $47 billion in 2003. The entire global market for semiconductors in 2003 was $166 billion, meaning that demand from China alone accounted for more than one quarter of global output. The degree to which China is an assembler of imported parts and components, rather than a true manufacturer of consumer electronic and information technology products, is reflected in the modest volume of China's domestic production of semiconductors and microprocessors compared to the value of its imports of these products. Although domestic semiconductor production is growing rapidly, it is from an extremely small base. In 2003 domestic production was only $4.6 billion, less than one-tenth of the value of imports (Liu, 2004). Investment in domestic production of semiconductors has increased significantly in recent years, which will provide the capacity for a further rapid rise in domestic production. However, given the continued expansion of capacity in China for manufacturing consumer electronics and information technology products, China is likely to remain far and away the world's largest importer of semiconductors and microprocessors for years to come.

Third, most exports of electronic and information products are assembled not by Chinese-owned firms but by foreign firms that are using China as an export platform. Taiwanese firms that have relocated to the mainland dominate the production of electronic and information technology products that are exported from China. The importance foreign firms play in China's emergence, for example, as the largest supplier of computers to the U.S. market, is confirmed by both aggregate data and the ranking of the top 200 export companies compiled by the Chinese Ministry of Commerce. In 2003, for example, foreign firms accounted for 92 percent of China's $41 billion in exports of computers, components, and peripherals and 74 percent of China's $89 billion in exports of electronics and telecommunications equipment (Gilboy, 2004, p. 39).

The dominance of foreign firms in these sectors is confirmed by firm-level data on China's largest exporters. In 2003 Hong Fu Jin Precision Industry, a wholly owned subsidiary of Taiwan's Hon Hai Precision Industry Company (better known by its trade name Foxconn), with exports of $6.4 billion, was China's number one ranked export company for the third successive year. Hon Hai Precision Industry is Taiwan's largest contract electronics manufacturer, churning out videogame consoles, mobile phones, and other electronics products for Sony, Apple, Nokia, and many other brands. Coming in second was Tech Front (Shanghai), a subsidiary of Taiwan's Quanta Computer Inc. the world's largest producer of notebook computers. Quanta is the single largest supplier for Dell Computer Company. Tech Front's exports in 2003 were $5.2 billion. Rounding off the top three exporting firms in China, with exports of $3.1 billion, was Magnificent Brightness, owned by Taiwan's Asutek Computer, another global heavyweight in the production of notebook computers. In all there are 28 Taiwan-owned firms on the list of China's 200 largest exporting firms in 2003. All are electronics manufacturers (China Economic News Service, 2004).

In short, the rapidly changing commodity composition of China's exports does not appear to constitute evidence that Chinese firms are leapfrogging ahead technologically, because these exports are not primarily driven by the expanding "knowledge stock" or innovative capabilities of domestic firms. Indeed, there may be a growing technology gap between foreign firms operating in China and domestic Chinese companies. In part this is because foreign firms in the electronics and information technology space in China are almost entirely wholly foreign-owned companies rather than joint ventures. Wholly foreign-owned firms have strong incentives to protect their technology from competitors, both domestic and foreign, thus limiting the diffusion of technology to indigenous firms. Furthermore, there is evidence suggesting that many indigenous Chinese firms spend little on research and development to develop new technologies on their own (Gilboy, 2004, p. 40). We do not discount the possibility that individual indigenous Chinese firms will, in short order, emerge as important players in technology-intensive industries through the development of proprietary technologies. However, the aggregate transition of the *Chinese economy as a whole* from net importer of technology-intensive goods to net exporter is likely to take many decades.

CHINA'S EXCHANGE RATE REGIME: THE NEED FOR FURTHER CHANGE

Dooley, Folkerts-Landau, and Garber (2003) have argued that China is similar to other Asian countries that have long managed their exchange rates by intervening in foreign exchange markets to limit appreciation of their currencies in order to sustain growth-oriented trade surpluses. Is China's currency undervalued? If so, what is the appropriate Chinese response? What difference would this response make to China's global trade balance?

First, while China's currency is now almost certainly undervalued, it is worth underlining that in contrast with Japan and several other countries in the region, this is a relatively recent phenomenon. Moreover, at least through 2004 part of the very large buildup of foreign exchange reserves in China reflected short-term speculative capital inflows rather than a fundamental disequilibrium.

What is the evidence for the judgment that the currency is undervalued in recent years? Between 1994, when China pegged its currency to the dollar, through 2001 China's current account surplus averaged only 1.8 percent of its GDP. But this number rose to an average of 2.6 percent in 2002–2003, 3.6 percent in 2004, and then 7.2 percent in 2005. And unlike its Southeast Asian neighbors, since the Asian financial crisis China has also had a capital account surplus. This surplus averaged 1.2 percent of GDP in 1999–2001. But it rose to an average of 2.7 percent in 2002–2003 and to 5.7 percent in 2004, before falling to 2.8 percent in 2005 (National Bureau of Statistics, 2003, p. 88; 2004a, p. 86; 2005, p. 89; 2006, pp. 57, 76).[44] It must be noted that while China's nominal exchange rate vis a vis the U.S. dollar was unchanged from 2002 through midsummer of 2005, the trade-weighted value of the renminbi depreciated significantly, even as China's current and capital account surpluses grew. [45]

Although China nominally maintains a relatively closed capital account, prior to 2001 unrecorded capital outflows largely offset these current and capital account surpluses. As a result, China's buildup of foreign exchange reserves was modest by Asian standards. But in 2001 these outflows shrank significantly and in 2002–2004 unrecorded capital inflows soared.[46] To continue to keep the currency pegged at 8.28 yuan to the dollar, in the face of significant surpluses on both the current and capital accounts as well as unrecorded capital inflows, China's authorities since 2001 have had to purchase massive amounts of foreign exchange and reserves have risen accordingly. For example, in 2004 alone reserves increased by $206.7 billion

[44] All of the data on the current and capital account and changes in reserves as a percent of GDP have been calculated on the revised GDP time-series data released by the Chinese Statistical Bureau in January 2006.

[45] This was the inevitable consequence of the depreciation of the dollar on a trade weighted basis over the same period, largely as a result of the appreciation of floating currencies, such as the euro, the pound, and the Canadian and Australian dollars.

[46] Unrecorded capital outflows average $15.1 billion in the three years 1998–2000. In 2001 outflows dropped to $5.9 billion. In 2002 through 2004 unrecorded inflows were $7.8 billion, $18.4 billion, and $27.0 billion, respectively (National Bureau of Statistics 2003, p. 88; 2005, p. 89).

an amount equivalent to 10.7 percent of GDP (National Bureau of Statistics, 2005, p. 89; 2006, p. 57).

The Chinese authorities, through their own actions, have implicitly recognized that the yuan is undervalued. Until July 21, 2005, they chose to try to reduce the pressure on the currency through a series of ad hoc measures, rather than making any change to their exchange rate. Beginning January 1, 2004, for example, the government reduced by an average of 3 percentage points the rate at which it rebates the VAT on products that are exported (USTR, 2004, p. 63). That tends to make Chinese exports more expensive in international markets. But, unlike currency appreciation or revaluation, lowering the rebate rate on the VAT on exports does not lower the price of imports in the domestic market. The authorities also eased the approval process for outward-bound FDI, liberalized the regulations governing outbound Chinese tourism, and allowed one domestic financial institution to issue dollar-denominated debt. In March and August 2004, the relevant regulators announced that the national social security fund and domestic insurance companies could invest in offshore markets. They also approved a qualified domestic institutional investor (QDII) program that allows Chinese financial institutions to invest, on behalf of their clients, in securities traded on foreign markets. Each of these measures increases the demand for or reduces the supply of foreign exchange, thus lessening the buildup in official foreign exchange reserves.

The U.S. policy of encouraging China to liberalize its capital account and adopt a floating exchange rate system, first articulated by Treasury Secretary John Snow in the fall of 2003, is certainly appropriate as a long-term objective. The Chinese authorities over the years have repeatedly expressed the goal of moving toward a convertible currency and a much more flexible exchange rate regime. There is no debate on the long-term desirability of such a policy. A flexible exchange rate regime would not only help to equilibrate China's international accounts but would also give the authorities considerably more ability to use monetary policy to moderate the cyclical character of domestic demand.

In the short and medium run, however, a convertible currency with a floating exchange rate is a risky option for China. At year-end 2005 Chinese households held 14.3 trillion yuan (an amount equal to four-fifths of China's GDP in the same year) in domestic savings deposits. Because the authorized volume of investment in foreign assets under the QDII program is still extremely limited, very few Chinese savers have had an opportunity to diversify the currency composition of their financial savings. Eliminating capital controls could lead to a substantial move into foreign-currency–denominated financial assets, most likely held outside of Chinese banks. Given the well-known weaknesses of China's banks, such a move could precipitate a domestic banking crisis. As a result, the authorities do not anticipate relaxing capital controls on household savings until they have fully addressed the solvency problems of the major state-owned banks. This process is well under way but is likely to take a minimum of two to three years to complete.

If the renminbi continued to be substantially undervalued for two to three more years, there would be substantial adverse effects on China's trading partners and China's central bank would continue to be very constrained in using interest rates as a macroeconomic policy tool. Thus, the preferred approach is to revalue the currency in the short term and only much later, after completing the transformation of the domestic banking system, moving to eliminate capital controls and, at the same time, floating the currency. How large an initial revaluation of the currency is called for? The tentative judgment of Morris Goldstein and Nicholas Lardy in 2003 was that the renminbi was undervalued by an amount in the range of 15–25 percent. They estimated that a revaluation in this range in 2003 would have led to an overall equilibrium in China's balance of payments, thus ending the buildup of foreign exchange reserves. They also argued that at the same time the authorities revalue the currency they should take in two additional steps. First, they should significantly widen the band within which they permit market forces to determine the value of the currency. Second, at the new parity the authorities should peg the Chinese currency to a basket of currencies rather than solely to the U.S. dollar (Goldstein and Lardy, 2003a,b).

The authorities went part way to meeting these objectives in July 2005 when the People's Bank announced a new managed floating exchange rate system that entailed an initial 2.1 percent revaluation of the currency to a new parity of 8.11 to the U.S. dollar; allowing the currency to trade on the foreign exchange market vis a vis the U.S. dollar in a range of plus or minus 0.3 percent on an intraday basis; and a policy of setting the opening price in the market each day at the price prevailing at the previous day's close; and that the currency would not be pegged rigidly to the dollar, but rather with reference to a basket of currencies (People's Bank of China, 2005).

The U.S. Treasury immediately advanced the view that the new system of managed floating would allow the currency to move by the maximum of 0.3 percent per trading day or up to 6 percent per month (Blustein, 2004). This interpretation seemed dubious, however, for two reasons. First, the Chinese authorities have described their exchange rate regime as a managed float since January 1994, so this was not really new. Second, the plus minus 0.3 percent intraday trading range and the provision to open each day's trading at the prior day's closing price had also been a feature of the system since 1994.[47] However, from the middle of 1995 to mid-2005 the nominal exchange rate of the RMB vis a vis the dollar barely moved.

The July 2005 currency reform has not yet ushered in an era in which the value of the renminbi is largely determined by supply and demand in the market, as the language of the announcement by the People's Bank stated. That would have led to significant further appreciation of the currency and over time could have led to

---

[47] Technically, prior to July 21 the opening price each day was to be at the weighted average of prices in trading on the previous day. Since July 21 the opening price is supposed to set at the closing price of trading on the previous day.

greater flexibility in the currency as well, for example, by widening the band around the parity. Both would be highly desirable not only because they would contribute to the reduction of global economic imbalances but also because they would allow the authorities greater flexibility in the use of interest rate policy as a tool of macroeconomic management.

Instead the authorities have continued to intervene massively in the foreign exchange market to limit the pace of appreciation of the RMB. In the twelve-month period from August 2005 through July 2006 the central bank's average monthly purchases of foreign exchange were $18.9 billion, almost unchanged from the $19.0 billion pace in the first six months of 2005, prior to the announcement of the "new" currency regime. As a result, the cumulative additional appreciation of the RMB vis a vis the U.S. dollar in the first year of the new currency regime was a very modest 1.5 percent. The resulting continued undervaluation of the RMB was reflected in a further 36 percent expansion of China's current account surplus in the first half of 2006 compared to the first half of 2005, reaching $91.6 billion, the equivalent of 8 percent of GDP (State Administration of Foreign Exchange, International Income and Expenditure Analysis Small Group, 2006, p. 10). For the full year 2006 China will record the largest current account surplus of any country (Lardy, 2006). As has been pointed out by the IMF (2006, p. 14), "the burden of having to tightly managed the exchange rate in the face of foreign exchange inflows has created a major conflict in monetary policy." Thus it appears that an acceleration of the pace of appreciation of the RMB is desirable, both to improve the authorities' control over monetary policy and to contribute to a reduction in global economic imbalances.

CHINA'S IMPACT ON THE WORLD

Surging import demand generated by the booming Chinese economy in 2003 and 2004 helped power an economic expansion throughout East and Southeast Asia.[48] With China's imports from emerging East Asia rising much faster than its exports to the region, its trade deficit with the rest of East Asia ballooned from $34 billion in 2001 to $47 billion in 2002 to $70 billion in 2003. Growth in exports to China and Hong Kong accounted for 50 percent of overall export growth in Korea and 66 percent of overall export growth in Taiwan. China was even credited with helping revive the long-moribund Japanese economy. In 2003, Japanese exports to China grew over 33 percent in 2003, accounting for nearly 44 percent of total export growth and helping to generate the highest real GDP growth since the mid-1990s (Kwan, 2004; Nihon Keizai Shimbun, 2004b).

While other countries in the region have eyed the rise of China as a trading power somewhat warily, fearing that China's export success and ability to attract FDI

---

[48] The country's imports surged 40 percent in dollar terms in 2003 and were on track for similar growth in 2004 (World Bank, 2004, pp. 17–18).

might be coming at their expense, China was widely seen in 2003 as an increasingly important locomotive of growth in the region. By the fall of 2004, the locus of concern had shifted from fear of an increasingly dynamic Chinese competitor to fear that the Chinese import boom would grind to a halt as government efforts to slow runaway economic growth unintentionally engendered a "hard landing." The tone of popular commentary in the Asian business press had shifted markedly from a depiction of China as a "threat" to praise of a booming Chinese economy as an engine of growth for all of Asia.

On the other hand, in 2004, an election year, China's growing trade surplus with the United States and mounting fears over jobs lost continued to generate political pressure for protection. The Bush Administration had already launched an antidumping investigation against Chinese color TV exporters and levied quotas on textile in late 2003. In late 2004 the U.S. government faced pressure from a coalition of industrial and textile groups seeking to force China to change its exchange rate policy (Schroeder and King, 2004). The bilateral trade deficit with China had displaced the deficit with Japan as America's largest in 2000, and it continued to increase rapidly in absolute value.

However, China's expanding trade surplus with the U.S. largely reflects a real-location of assembly activity from other East Asian countries to China. Much of this assembly is actually undertaken by FIEs from the aforementioned economies, which continue to source components from their home base. As a consequence, China's expanding surplus with the United States, and to a lesser extent, Europe, mirrors its large deficit with the rest of East Asia. China's emerging industrial structure is thus largely complementary with that of the more advanced East Asian countries, and China's continued export expansion represents, for the most part, an opportunity rather than a threat. The implications of China's advance for the less developed ASEAN countries are less unambiguously positive in the short to medium run, a point we shall also discuss.

Figure 16.8, which shows U.S. exports to and imports from China, illustrates the expansion of the U.S. bilateral trade deficit with China. Beginning in 1990, exports of U.S. businesses to China grew more rapidly than to any other large export market (Lardy, 2001). By 2003 U.S. exports to China had increased fivefold to almost $30 billion and China had become the sixth largest foreign market for U.S. goods (Lardy, 2004, p. 27). However, imports grew even more rapidly, so the bilateral trade deficit has continued to widen in absolute terms. Given the rapid growth in this imbalance, it is easy to see how trade with China has become a lightning rod for protectionist interests within the United States.

The relative asymmetry of China's trade flows with the United States is cast into even sharper relief by a comparison with the evolution of the Chinese trade balance with the European Union and Japan, two other major export destinations, as in Figure 16.9. While the bilateral surplus with the EU has expanded in recent years, trade with both economies is substantially more balanced than that of the United States. The United States almost single-handedly accounts for China's modest but robust

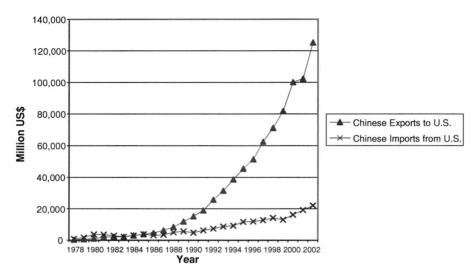

Figure 16.8. U.S.–China bilateral trade imbalance (*Source:* Ministry of Commerce, People's Republic of China)

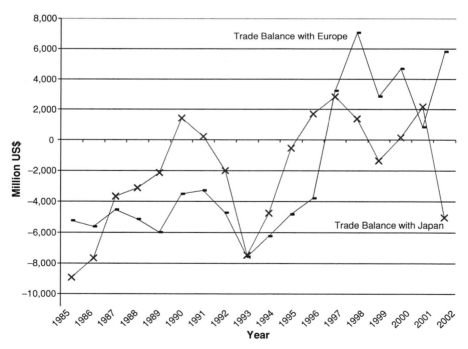

Figure 16.9. Chinese bilateral trade with the EU and Japan (*Source:* Ministry of Commerce, People's Republic of China)

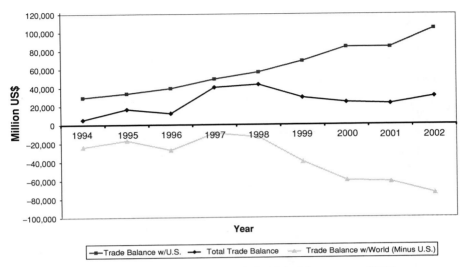

Figure 16.10. China's trade with the United States versus ROW

current account surplus. If one examines China's trade with the rest of the world except the United States, that is a large and growing deficit, as shown in Figure 16.10.

To a great extent, American imports of manufactured goods, especially labor-intensive products, from China have displaced American imports of manufactured goods from other locations in Asia, notably, Hong Kong, Taiwan, and South Korea. As a result the combined shares of the U.S. global trade deficit accounted for by China, Japan, Hong Kong, Taiwan, and South Korea fell from 52.3 percent in 1985 to only 39.4 percent in 2003 (Lardy, 2005, p. 129). The causes of this transformation are rising wages in non-China Asia and China's liberalization of its foreign investment environment. In the 1980s and 1990s, as wages in these countries rose and China liberalized its FDI environment, Asian entrepreneurs moved a growing share of their labor-intensive production to China. Figure 16.4 illustrates the continuing importance of Asian firms in FDI in China. By 2003, China's Asian trading partners collectively accounted for about 70 percent of the cumulative FDI in China. As one can see in the figure, Hong Kong and Taiwan firms have played a conspicuously large role. Unlike U.S. or European firms that tend to invest in China in order to serve the local market, Asian firms tend to use China as an export platform.

They have been quite successful at this. At the end of the 1990s, the two most important categories of goods the United States imported from China were baby carriages, toys, games, and sporting goods and footwear. The rapid growth of U.S. imports in these categories largely reflects the displacement of alternative sources of supply in Asia. Figure 16.11 illustrates this truth for footwear. From 1986 through 1988 almost 60 percent of U.S. footwear imports were from Taiwan and South Korea; China was the source of only 2 percent of U.S. footwear imports. By

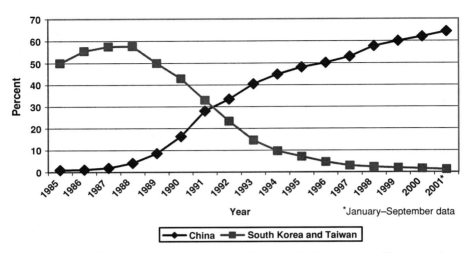

Figure 16.11. Trade displacement in footwear (*Source:* U.S. Department of Commerce)

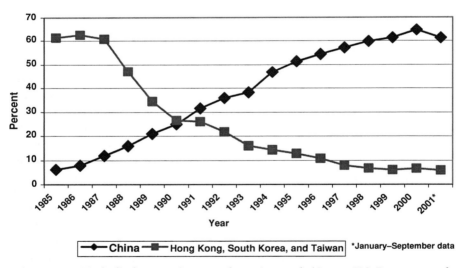

Figure 16.12. Trade displacement in toys and sporting goods (*Source:* U.S. Department of Commerce)

1999, the relative importance of the two sources of supply had reversed completely. Figure 16.12 shows a similar pattern for toys and sporting goods. The degree to which increases in imports from China directly displaced imports from Hong Kong, South Korea, and Taiwan is quite striking.

To say that this production transfer has come at the "expense" of firms or workers in Hong Kong or Taiwan is somewhat misleading. By and large, this transfer of production has not created large losses, either for the investing economies or for their firms.[49] The relationship between these economies and China has been, to a great extent, a complementary one. However, there is also a set of goods in which these countries, as well as Japan and the United States, compete with China. The technological ambitions of the Chinese government, and the desire to expand in sectors such as contract semiconductor manufacturing, suggest that this margin of competition may grow over time.

As we have already indicated, a similar process of "export displacement" is now at work with DVD players, computer peripherals, and laptop computers. In 2002, China became the largest single source of U.S. imports of consumer electronics products and information technology hardware (Lardy, 2004). However, as we have already stressed, much of this export growth is being spearheaded by foreign, particularly, Taiwanese, companies. While these final goods contain high-tech components, Chinese factories specialize in providing relatively low-skill assembly services, importing the more sophisticated components from Taiwan, South Korea, or, significantly, Japan. In 2002, China ran a massive trade deficit of $25 billion in its trade with Taiwan. Two-thirds of these imports are parts and components, subsequently assembled into final goods in factories owned by Taiwanese firms and investors (Lardy, 2004). In 2003, as China ramped up its exports of IT products, imports of electronic components from Japan surged by 60 percent (Nihon Keizai Shimbun, 2004b).

Recent economic analysis based on trade data and the use of simulation models also suggests a complementarity between Chinese growth and the more developed Asian economies. Much of the recent analysis has been undertaken in the context of forecasting the impact of China's WTO accession. Ianchovichina and Walmsley (2005) calibrate and simulate a multicountry, multisector model of international trade, finding that China's WTO access, while improving that country's imports, reduces the exports of Vietnam, the Philippines, Thailand, Indonesia, and Malaysia. On the other hand, Japan and the NIES benefit, mainly due to increased exports to China.[50]

Eichengreen, Rhee, and Tong (2004) undertake a regression study using disaggregated trade data over the 1990–2002 period. They attempt to account for the endogeneity of Chinese exports while allowing for differential effects on different commodity types. They find evidence of a crowding out of exports from Asian

---

[49] In 1981, Hong Kong's manufacturing sector employed more than 900,000 workers in Hong Kong. By 2000, Hong Kong-invested companies employed 5 million workers in China, many in Guangdong Province. In that year, Taiwanese firms employed an estimated 3 million workers on the mainland. See Lardy (2002, pp. 56–57) and Naughton (1998) for a discussion of these issues with particular emphasis on electronics.

[50] An IMF study (2004) uses a computable general equilibrium model to capture the geographical and sectoral structure of trade flows. This analysis finds that Chinese export growth generates small negative effects on the exports and output of all regions, but the impact is stronger on the ASEAN countries than the more developed Asian economies.

countries due to Chinese export growth, but this is largely limited to consumer goods. In contrast, Chinese growth has a strong positive impact on Asian exports of capital goods and equipment to China. On net, the advanced Asian economies benefit from Chinese growth, while the ASEAN countries lose.[51] This finding is consistent with earlier work suggesting China's comparative advantage is similar to that of its ASEAN neighbors.[52] While GDP growth eventually revived in most of Southeast Asia after the financial crises of 1997–1998, the robust inward FDI flows of the precrisis years did not, although real FDI actually increased in China. Complaints among the ASEAN countries that China's success at attracting FDI came at their expense arguably held a grain of truth (World Bank, 2004).

The observation that China's rapid export growth has, to date, largely displaced export-oriented assembly elsewhere might suggest that this process is bound to slow down in the near future. After all, once China accounts for a large majority of global supply within a given category, exports can only grow at something approximating the total growth rate of global demand for the product, and that is likely to be considerably slower than the growth rates China has registered in the recent past. A slowdown in growth of China's exports of footwear and toys and sporting goods is probably not far away. The transfer of production of consumer electronics and IT hardware has proceeded so rapidly that a growth slowdown in this category may not be far off either.

However, China stands ready to benefit more than any other country from the abolition of the WTO Agreement on Textiles and Clothing, the successor to the Multifiber Agreement negotiated under GATT. Under this arrangement, textile and apparel exports from any one country were sharply limited, allowing fledgling apparel industries in nations such as Bangladesh, Saipan, and Mauritius to flourish. This agreement ended on December 31, 2004. Already, major apparel importers in the United States are seeking to consolidate their production operations in a smaller number of low-cost countries. With its low labor costs, relatively high productivity, and excellent infrastructure, China is likely to dramatically increase its share of global apparel exports, at the expense of other producers in Latin America, Africa, South Asia, and Southeast Asia. China currently accounts for only 13.1 percent of American imports of apparel products. If China-based producers were able to collectively achieve, over the next several years, a market share in apparel similar to their current market share in footwear, this would guarantee years of double-digit growth in a very broad category of manufactures.

---

[51] This finding contrasts with the earlier work of Ahearne et al. (2003). Using aggregate trade data, these authors found little evidence of a statistically significant relationship between Chinese exports and the exports of its Asian neighbors, although the estimated coefficients tended to be positive.

[52] A comparison of correlation coefficients on revealed comparative advantage indices in fifty-three labor-intensive products for China and twenty-five other countries suggested significant positive correlations between China and Thailand, Vietnam, and Indonesia. See Boltho et al. (1994).

The expansion of China's role as a mediator of Asian trade with the United States has, up to this point, arguably served the interests of all parties. However, there are also limits to the continued growth of this pattern of trade, at least in the long run. The sustainability of the U.S. current account deficit is being increasingly questioned by policymakers, academics, and financial analysts.[53] U.S. trade with Asia is an important component of this deficit, and Asian central banks, including China's, have played an increasing role in financing it. The currency reform put forward in the previous section is part of an inevitable and essential appreciation of the major Asian currencies (Bergsten, 2004; Mann, 2004). However, the role of Japanese, Taiwanese, Hong Kong, and Korean companies in China's export flow also creates an interesting constellation of interests regarding necessary changes in China's exchange rate regime.

On the one hand, there is a margin along which producers in these countries directly compete.[54] Producers within this zone of competition would tend to support a revaluation of the renminbi.[55] However, as we have already stressed, this zone of competition is limited. There is another large set of producers in these countries that has, and continues to make, large investments in export-oriented production capacity in China. A sufficiently large revaluation of the renminbi could undermine the competitiveness of this capacity and reduce the profits for the foreign investors.

A 2004 survey by the *Nihon Keizai Shimbun* indicated that most large export-oriented Japanese firms do *not* perceive a large renminbi revaluation to be in their interest, precisely because they have already exploited low-cost Chinese production sites as part of their global network (Nihon Keizai Shimbun, 2004a). This sentiment may be broadly shared throughout the developed economies of Asia. The United States has made little headway in its efforts to get other countries in the region to pressure China to revalue its currency. This partly reflects the divided interests of industrial producers in these countries.[56] That division extends to the United States. The National Association of Manufactures did not endorse the filing of a trade complaint by a coalition of U.S., industrial, and agricultural groups accusing China of manipulating its currency (Schroeder and King, 2004). Large-scale U.S.-based retailers, such as Wal-Mart, which sourced 8 percent of its global purchases from China in 2002 and bought an estimated \$15 billion of Chinese merchandise

---

[53] See the special symposium in the 2001 volume of *Brookings Papers on Economic Activity* for a thoughtful exchange on this issue, including Cooper (2001). See also Obstfeld and Rogoff (2000) and Mann (2002, 2004). Stephen Roach, chief economist of Morgan Stanley, has argued in many fora for a "global rebalancing" of demand.

[54] Attempts by China to encourage the development of capital- and technology-intensive industries, such as semiconductor fabrication and telecommunications equipment manufacturing, have received extensive coverage in the popular press. On the former industry, see Dean (2004). On the latter, see Dolven (2004).

[55] In fact, a substantial renminbi revaluation would be a *quid pro quo* for their support of a revaluation of their own currency. See Goldstein and Lardy (2003a).

[56] It also reflects the fact that other countries in the region, including Japan, have massively intervened in foreign exchange markets to prevent revaluation of their own currencies.

in 2003, have a clear incentive in minimizing the dollar-denominated production costs of their goods (Wonacott, 2003). Zhao and Xing (2003a, b) use a formal model of production outsourcing to show how an advanced country can suffer a welfare loss when its currency depreciates against that of a less developed country to which it has outsourced production. The intuition behind this model is clear – cheap imports are good, and making them more expensive lowers welfare and the profits of firms investing in China to serve markets like the United States Unfortunately, the evidence increasingly suggests that the current exchange rate arrangements are no longer consistent with macroeconomic fundamentals.

If not remedied, this could contribute to a real misallocation of resources within China. At the moment, a Chinese producer seeking to serve a customer in California is eligible for an almost complete rebate of the VAT (15 percent), and he or she is able to convert dollars into a domestic currency that could be as much as 25 percent undervalued. This creates a sizable price wedge between an export sale and a domestic sale of the same product to a customer in Xinjiang. A de facto export subsidy of this magnitude, if maintained long enough, could distort the industrial development of the Chinese economy. This is particularly true if we believe that, in at least some product markets, titanic per capita income differences between the export markets and the home market mean that the types of products that could sell well domestically are not necessarily the same types of products that will sell well abroad, and vice versa. Japan, Taiwan, and South Korea also resisted the appreciation of their own currencies. Is it possible that the difficulty these countries have had weaning themselves from export-led growth since the 1980s reflects an overdevelopment of the export sector that was, itself, a function of a long undervalued exchange rate? The longer a currency's undervaluation encourages an overexpansion of the export sector, the greater the power of the lobbying groups that would seek to halt or limit adjustment become, and the more economically costly that adjustment becomes. To the extent that our reading of Asian economic history is correct, we can only hope that it is not repeated.

CONCLUSIONS

China's adoption of one of the developing world's most open trade and FDI regimes stands as one of the most significant accomplishments of the reform era. China achieved a greater degree of openness to foreign trade in manufactures prior to WTO accession than is generally acknowledged, and the drive to liberalization of trade and FDI regimes seems to have dramatically *accelerated* in the late 1990s. The additional openings mandated under China's WTO accession agreement will likely make China's economy the most open of any large developing country, and, to date, China has made reasonable progress toward meeting her obligations. As we have noted, developments in Chinese trade and investment have generally conformed to patterns of Chinese comparative advantage, yielding important benefits to China and her trading partners.

While it would be inaccurate to describe China's growth as export driven, given the limited direct contribution of net exports to overall macroeconomic growth, China's embrace of globalization has increased the degree of competition in her product markets, raised the productivity of factor accumulation, enhanced consumer welfare in China, and benefited consumers around the world. Some of China's key leaders pursued this embrace with a commendable mixture of pragmatism and courage, for which future generations will owe them thanks.

It is difficult to forecast with confidence the full impact of China's opening of its service sector to FDI, in part because there is so little precedent for a developing country to offer such a degree of market access. The possibility of greater participation by the world's leading services firms holds out the promise of preventing the development in China of the kind of dual economy seen in Japan and Korea. The extent to which this promise will be realized remains to be seen, but we anticipate that the Chinese consumer and the overall economy will benefit from this opening, which appears to be taking place in line with China's obligations under its accession agreement.

The one area in which international economic policy has shown less progress in recent years is the currency regime. In all fairness to the Chinese leadership, the undervaluation of the currency emerged only since 2002. However, the costs of delaying significant revaluation of the currency are escalating. And we do not refer here solely to the unprecedented accumulation of foreign exchange reserves or the deterioration of relationships with key trading partners. So long as the currency regime remains little changed, the People's Bank of China will remain acutely constrained in its pursuit of prudent macroeconomic policies to restrain excessive growth. It is also possible – indeed likely – that productive capacity that was built up in some industries in the investment boom that got underway in late 2002 will not be viable at exchange rates closer to long run equilibrium levels. The reforms announced in the summer of 2005 are potentially an important watershed since the longer a significantly undervalued currency is maintained, the greater is the likely extent of resource misallocation.

References

Ahearne, Alan, John Fernald, Prakash Loungani, and John Schindler. 2003. "China and Emerging Asia: Comrades or Competitors?" International Finance Discussion Paper 789, Board of Governors, Federal Reserve System.

American Electronics Association. 2003. *Tech Trade Update 2003*. Washington: American Electronics Association.

Bai Chong-En, Yingjuan Du, Zhigang Tao, and Sarah Tong. 2004. "Local Protectionism and Regional Specialization: Evidence from China's Industries." *Journal of International Economics*. 63(2), pp. 397–418.

Barshefsky, Charlene. 1999. "U.S. Trade Policy in China." Hearings before the Senate Finance Committee on the Status of China's Application to Join the World Trade Organization. Accessed April 13, 1999, from www.fnsg.com.

Bater, Jeffrey. 2000. "Citrus, Wheat Recently Shipped to China." *Dow Jones Newswires.* Accessed April 3, 2000, from http://interactive.wsj.com.

Bergsten, Fred. 2004. "The Risks ahead for the World Economy." *The Economist Online.* September 9, 2004.

Blustein, Paul. 2004. "China's Currency Change May Ultimately Mean Little." *Washington Post.* July 24, 2004.

Boltho, Andrea, Uri Dadush, Dong He, and Shigeru Otsubo. 1994. "China's Emergence: Prospects, Opportunities, and Challenges." Policy Research Working Paper 1339. Washington, DC: World Bank.

Brandt, Loren and Xiaodong Zhu. 2000. "Redistribution in a Decentralized Economy: Growth and Inflation in China under Reform." *Journal of Political Economy.* 108(2), pp. 422–439.

Branstetter, Lee and Robert Feenstra. 2002. "Trade and FDI in China: A Political Economy Approach." *Journal of International Economics.* 58(2), pp. 335–358.

Chen, Yao. 2001. "Trade with Northeast Asia Countries Bounces Back." *China Daily.* June 8, 2001, p. 4.

China Economic News Service. 2004. "Top Three China Exporters All Taiwan Invested." Accessed June 28, 2004, http://news.cens.com.

Chinese Bank Regulatory Commission. 2003. "Measures Governing Investment in Shares of Chinese Financial Institutions by Overseas Financial Institutions," in *Almanac of China's Finance and Banking 2004.* Beijing: China's Banking and Finance Compilation Committee, pp. 322–323.

Cooper, Richard. 2001. "Is the U.S. Current Account Deficit Sustainable? Will It be Sustained?" *Brookings Papers on Economic Activity.* 1, pp. 217–226.

Dean, Jason. 2004. "Long a Low-Tech Power, China Sets Its Sights on Chipmaking." *Wall Street Journal Online.* Accessed February 17, 2004, from http://online.wsj.com/article_print/0,,SB107696027203830630,00.html.

Dolven, Ben. 2004. "China's Telecom Vendors Are Thriving Abroad." *Wall Street Journal Online.* February 19, 2004.

Dooley, Michael P., David Folkerts-Landau, and Peter Garber. 2003. "An Essay on the Revived Bretton Woods System." National Bureau of Economic Research, Working Paper 9971. Cambridge, MA: National Bureau of Economic Research.

Editorial Board of the Almanac of China's Foreign Economic Relations and Trade. 1987. *Almanac of China"s Foreign Economic Relations and Trade 1987.* Hong Kong: China Resources Advertising Co, Ltd.

Editorial Board of the Almanac of China's Foreign Economic Relations and Trade. 1990. *Almanac of China's Foreign Economic Relations and Trade 1990.* Beijing: Finance and Economics Publishing House.

Editorial Board of the Almanac of China's Foreign Economic Relations and Trade. 1997. *Almanac of China's Foreign Economic Relations and Trade 1997/98.* Beijing: Finance and Economics Publishing House.

Editorial Board of the Almanac of China's Foreign Economic Relations and Trade. 1998. *Almanac of China's Foreign Economics Relations and Trade 1998/99.* Beijing: China Economics Publishing House.

Eichengreen, Barry, Yeongseop Rhee, and Hui Tong. 2004. "The Impact of China on the Exports of Other Asian Countries." NBER Working Paper 10768. Cambridge, MA: National Bureau of Economic Research.

Feenstra, Robert. 1998. "One Country, Two Systems: Implications of WTO Entry for China." Working Paper. Berkeley, CA: U.C.-Davis, Department of Economics.

Feenstra, Robert, Wen Hai, Wing Thye Woo, and Shunli Yao. 1999. "Discrepancies in International Data: An Application to China-Hong Kong Entrepot Trade." *American Economic Review*. 89, pp. 338–343.

Feenstra, Robert and Gordon Hanson. 2004. "Intermediaries in Entrepot Trade: Hong Kong Re-Exports of Chinese Goods." *Journal of Economics and Management Strategy*. 13(1), pp. 3–35.

Fisman, Raymond and Shang-Jin Wei. 2004. "Tax Rates and Tax Evasion: Evidence from Missing Imports in China." *Journal of Political Economy*. 112(2), pp. 471–496.

Foreign Agricultural Service, U.S. Department of Agriculture, 2000. *People's Republic of China: Grain and Feed Annual Report 2000*. GAIN Report CH0009.

General Agreement on Tariffs and Trade. 1996. *The Results of the Uruguay Round of Multilateral Trade Negotiations: Market Access for Goods and Services*. Geneva: General Agreement on Tariffs and Trade.

Gilboy, George J. 2004. "The Myth behind China's Miracle." *Foreign Affairs*. 83.4, pp. 33–48.

Goldstein, Morris and Nicholas Lardy. 2003a. "A Modest Proposal for China's Renminbi." *Financial Times*. August 26, 2003.

Goldstein, Morris and Nicholas Lardy. 2003b. "Two-Stage Currency Reform for China." *Asian Wall Street Journal*. September 12, 2003.

Hamilton, Alexander. 1791. "Report on Manufactures," reproduced in *Papers on Public Credit, Commerce, and Finance by Alexander Hamilton*. S. McKee, ed. New York: Columbia University Press.

Higgens, Andrew. 2004. "As China Surges, It Also Proves a Buttress to American Strength." *Wall Street Journal Online*. January 30, 2004.

Hoo, Stephanie, 2000. "China's Wheat Farmers Already Shifting Crop Mix Pre-WTO." *Dow Jones Newswires*. June 16, 2000.

Huang, Li and Shang-Jin Wei. 2001. "One China, Many Kingdoms? Understanding Local Protection Using Individual Price Data." Unpublished Working Paper.

Huang, Yasheng. 2003. *Selling China: Foreign Direct Investment during the Reform Era*. Cambridge and New York: Cambridge University Press.

Hufbauer, Gary and Daniel Rosen. 2000. "American Access to China's Market: The Congressional Vote on PNTR." International Economic Policy Briefs, 00–3. Accessed May 1, 2000, from www.iie.com.

Hultzer, Charles and Phelim Kyne. 2004. "U.S. Businesses Urge China to Rein in Piracy." *Wall Street Journal Online*. September 17, 2004.

Ianchovichina, Elena and Terrie Walmsley. 2005. "Impact of China's Accession on East Asia." *Contemporary Economic Policy*. 23, pp. 261–277.

IMF [International Monetary Fund]. May 1996. *People's Republic of China – Recent Economic Developments*. IMF Staff Country Report 96/40. Washington, DC: IMF.

IMF [International Monetary Fund]. April 2004. "China's Emergence and Its Impact on the Global Economy." *World Economic Outlook*. pp. 82–202.

IMF [International Monetary Fund]. 2005. Republic of Korea: 2004 Article IV Consultation – Staff Report. Washington, DC: Publication Services, International Monetary Fund.

IMF [International Monetary Fund]. October 2006. People's Republic of China: 2006 Article IV Consultation – Staff Report. Accessed October 20, 2006, from www.imf.org/external/pubs/ft/scr2006/cr06494.pdf.

Kennedy, Scott. 2004. "Holey Protectionism!" *China Economic Quarterly*. Q3 2004, pp. 24–28.

Kennedy, Scott. 2005. "China's Porous Protectionism: The Changing Political Economy of Trade Policy." *Political Science Quarterly*. 120, pp. 1–30.

Kranhold, Kathryn. 2004. "China's Price for Market Entry: Give Us Your Technology, Too." *Wall Street Journal Online.* February 26, 2004.

Krugman, Paul. 1994. *Peddling Prosperity: Economic Sense and Nonsense in the Age of Diminished Expectations.* New York: W.W. Norton.

Kwan, Chi Hung. 2004. "China Surpasses Japan to Become World's Third Largest Trading Nation." RIETI Research Paper. Accessed from http://www.rieti.go.jp/users/china-tr/jp/ssqs/040323ssqs.htm.

Lall, Sanjaya and Manuel Albaladejo. 2004. "China's Competitive Performance: A Threat to East Asian Manufactured Exports." *World Development.* 32(9), pp. 1441–1466.

Lardy, Nicholas. 1992. *Foreign Trade and Economic Reform in China, 1978–1990.* Cambridge and New York: Cambridge University Press.

Lardy, Nicholas. 1994. *China in the World Economy.* Washington, DC: Institute for International Economics.

Lardy, Nicholas. 1998. *China's Unfinished Economic Revolution.* Washington, DC: Brookings Institution.

Lardy, Nicholas. 2001. "Issues in China's WTO Accession." Hearing Before the U.S.-China Security Review Commission. May 9, 2001.

Lardy, Nicholas. 2002. *Integrating China into the Global Economy.* Washington, DC: Brookings Institution.

Lardy, Nicholas. 2004. "The Economic Dimension of the U.S.–China Relationship," in *U.S.–China Relations and China's Integration with the World.* Washington: The Aspen Institute, pp. 27–31.

Lardy, Nicholas. 2005. "China: The Great New Economic Challenge?" in *The United States and the World Economy: Foreign Economic Policy for the Next Decade.* C. Fred Bergsten, ed. Washington, DC: Institute for International Economics, pp. 121–141.

Lardy, Nicholas. October 2006. "China: Toward a Consumption-Driven Growth Path." Institute for International Economics Policy Brief PB06–6. Washington, DC: Institute for International Economics.

Liu, Baijia. 2004. "Semiconductor Sector Shakeup." *China Daily.* September 8, 2004, p. 11.

Long, Yongtu. 2000. "PRC Trade Official Long Yongtu on China, Economic Globalization, WTO Entry." *People's Daily.* July 10, 2000. Accessed July 13, 2000, from http://english.peopledaily.com.cn/english/200007/10print200000710_45125.html accessed July 13, 2000.

Mann, Catherine. 2002. "Perspectives on the U.S. Current Account and Sustainability." *Journal of Economic Perspectives.* 16(3), pp. 131–152.

Mann, Catherine. 2004. "Managing Exchange Rates: Achievement of Global Rebalancing or Evidence of Global Co-Dependency." *Business Economics.* July 2004, pp. 20–29.

McKinsey & Co Global Institute. 2000. "Why the Japanese Economy Is Not Growing." Special Report. Washington, DC: McKinsey & Company.

Mill, John Stuart. 1848. "Principles of Political Economy," in *Collected Works of John Stuart Mill,* vol. III. J.M. Robson, ed. Toronto: University of Toronto Press.

Ministry of Economy, Trade, and Industry. 2003. *Trade and Commerce White Paper* (in Japanese). Tokyo: Economy and Industry Survey Group.

Ministry of Foreign Trade and Economic Cooperation, 1999. *Zhongguo Duiwai Jingji Maoyi Baipishu 1999* [China's White Paper on Foreign Trade and Economic Cooperation 1999]. Beijing: Ministry of Foreign Trade and Economic Cooperation.

National Bureau of Statistics. 2003. *China Statistical Abstract 2003.* Beijing: China Statistics Press.

National Bureau of Statistics. 2004a. *China Statistical Abstract 2004*. Beijing: China Statistics Press.

National Bureau of Statistics. 2004b. *China Statistical Yearbook 2004*. Beijing: China Statistics Press.

National Bureau of Statistics. 2005. *China Statistical Abstract 2005*. Beijing: China Statistics Press.

National Bureau of Statistics. 2006. *China Statistical Yearbook 2006*. Beijing: China Statistics Press.

Naughton, Barry. 1996. "China's Emergence and Prospects as a Trading Nation." *Brookings Papers on Economic Activity*. 2, pp. 273–343.

Naughton, Barry, ed. 1998. *The China Circle: Economics and Technology in the PRC, Taiwan, and Hong Kong*. Washington, DC: Brookings Institution.

Naughton, Barry. 1999. "How Much Can Regional Integration Do to Unify China's Markets?" Working Paper. San Diego, CA: University of California.

Nihon Keizai Shimbun. 2004a. "Japanese Firms Committed to China." January 20, 2004.

Nihon Keizai Shimbun. 2004b. "Trade Surplus Surpasses 10 Trillion Yen." Evening Edition, January 22, 2004.

Obtsfeld, Maurice and Kenneth Rogoff. 2000. "Perspectives on OECD Economic Integration: Implications for U.S. Current Account Adjustment." *Global Economic Integration: Opportunities and Challenges*, Annual Monetary Policy Symposium. Kansas City: Federal Reserve Bank of Kansas City.

O'Connell, Paul and Shang-Jin Wei. 2002. "The Bigger They Are, the Harder They Fall: Retail Price Differences Across U.S. Cities." *Journal of International Economics*. 56, pp. 21–54.

Parsley, David and Shang-Jin Wei. 1996. "Convergence to the Law of One Price without Trade Barriers or Currency Fluctuations?" *Quarterly Journal of Economics*. 447, pp. 1211–1236.

People's Bank of China. 2005. "Public Announcement of the People's Bank of China on Reforming the RMB Exchange Rate Regime." Accessed July 21, 2005, from www.pbc.gov.cn.

Preeg, Ernest. H. March 2004. *The Threatened U.S. Competitive Lead in Advanced Technology Products (ATP)*. Washington, DC: Manufacturers Alliance/MAPI.

Rawski, Thomas G. 2001. "What's Happening to Chinese GDP Statistics?" *China Economic Review*. 12(4), pp. 347–354.

Rosen, Daniel. 1999. *Behind the Open Door: Foreign Enterprises in the Chinese Marketplace*. Washington, DC: Institute for International Economics.

Rosen, Daniel, Scott Rozelle, and Jikun Huang. July 2004. *Roots of Competitiveness: China's Evolving Agriculture Interests*. Washington, DC: Institute for International Economics.

Saywell, Trish and Kathy Wilhelm. June 29, 2000. "Seeds of Change." *Far Eastern Economic Review*. pp. 44–46.

Schott, Peter K. 2006. "The Relative Sophistication of Chinese Exports." NBER Working Paper 12173. Cambridge, MA: National Bureau of Economic Research.

Schroeder, Michael and Neil King. 2004. "Coalition to Press White House to Fight China's Trade Practices." *Wall Street Journal Online*. September 9, 2004.

State Administration of Foreign Exchange, International Income and Expenditure Analysis Small Group. 2006. Report on China's International Balance of Payments in the First Half of 2006. Accessed October 6, 2006, from www.safe.gov.cn.

Studwell, Joseph. 2002. *The China Dream: The Quest for the Last Great Untapped Market on Earth*. New York: Atlantic Monthly Press.

USTR [United States Trade Representative]. 2004. *National Trade Estimate Report on Foreign Trade Barriers*. Washington, DC: United States Trade Representative.

USTR [United States Trade Representative]. 2005. *National Trade Estimate Report on Foreign Trade Barriers*. Washington, DC: United States Trade Representative.

Wedeman, Andrew Hall. 2003. *From Mao to Market: Rent Seeking, Local Protectionism, and Marketization in China*. Cambridge and New York: Cambridge University Press.

Wells, Louis. 1991. "Mobile Exporters: New Foreign Investors in East Asia," in *Foreign Direct Investment*. K. Froot, ed. Chicago: NBER and University of Chicago Press.

Whalley, John and Xian Xin. 2006. "China's FDI and Non-FDI Economies and the Sustainability of Future High Chinese Growth." NBER Working Paper 12249. Cambridge, MA: National Bureau of Economic Research.

White House. 1999. Office of the Press Secretary, "Joint Press Conference of the President and Premier Zhu Rongji of the People's Republic of China." April 8, 1999.

Wonacott, Peter. 2003. "Behind China's Export Boom, A Heated Battle Among Factories." *Wall Street Journal Online*. November 13, 2003.

Wonacott, Peter. 2004. "A Fear Amid China's Car Boom." *Wall Street Journal Online*. February 2, 2004.

World Bank. 2004. *East Asia and Pacific Regional Overview*. Washington, DC: World Bank.

World Trade Organization. July 10, 2001. "Draft Report of the Working Party on the Accession of China to the WTO, rev. 7." Geneva. Accessed July 16, 2001, from www.insidetrade.com.

World Trade Organization. 2005. "Developing Countries' Goods Trade Share Surges to 50-year Peak." Press Release/401, April 14.

Young, Alwyn. 2000. "The Razor's Edge: Distortions and Incremental Reform in the People's Republic of China." *Quarterly Journal of Economics*. 115(4), pp. 1091–1036.

Zhang, Yansheng, Zhongxin Wan and Shuguang Zhang. 1998. *Measuring the Costs of Protection in China*. Washington, DC: Institute for International Economics.

Zhang, Yan. 2000. "Access to Trade Rights Expands." *China Daily*. February 23, 2000, p. 5.

Zhao, Lex and Yuqing Xing. 2003a. "Global Outsourcing and Currency Devaluation." Hokkaido University Working Paper. Hokkaidō, Japan: Hokkaido University.

Zhao, Lex and Yuqing Xing. 2003b. "Reverse Imports, Foreign Direct Investment, and Exchange Rates." Hokkaido University Working Paper. Hokkaidō, Japan: Hokkaido University.

SEVENTEEN

Growth and Structural Transformation in China

Loren Brandt, Chang-tai Hsieh, and Xiaodong Zhu

INTRODUCTION

Between 1978 and 2004 China's real GDP per capita grew at a rate of 8.16 percent per year. Some of this growth can be attributed to increases in labor force participation.[1] On a per worker basis, GDP still increased at a real rate of 6.96 percent, implying a doubling of aggregate labor productivity every ten years and a quadrupling every twenty years. This impressive growth performance accompanied two important structural transformations.

The first, a fundamental feature of the economic development process, entailed large-scale reallocation of labor from agriculture to manufacturing and services, which pushed agriculture's share of total employment from 69 to 32 percent between 1978 and 2004. The second, unique to the transition process in former socialist economies, involves the reallocation of labor and other resources from state-owned enterprises (SOEs) to enterprises outside the state sector: over the same period, the state sector's share of nonagricultural employment fell from 52 percent to only 13 percent.

The primary objective of this chapter is to quantify the contributions of these two transformations and of productivity growth within each sector to China's overall growth and to systematically examine the forces driving each of these momentous changes. As will quickly become evident, this approach delivers a substantial payoff in the form of unexpected outcomes and a new perspective on the interaction among structural change, transition from socialism, and productivity growth during the course of China's long boom.

The first surprise comes from information on the annual growth of real output per worker during 1978–2004. Our data show that labor productivity in China's nonagricultural sector grew only 4.65 percent per annum compared to 6.75 percent in agriculture and 6.96 percent in the aggregate. The distinctly superior growth of

---

[1] Between 1978 and 2004, labor force participation rates, defined here as the ratio of the total number of individuals working to the total population, increased from 48.7 to 57.9 percent. This increase largely reflected changes in the demographic composition of the population.

farm labor productivity suggests that agriculture may have played a significant role in China's growth. Indeed, Young (2003) observes, "Despite the popular academic emphasis on industry and exports, a deeper understanding of the success of the world's most rapidly growing economies may lie in the most fundamental of development topics: agriculture, land and the peasant."

Agriculture contributed to Chinese growth both directly, through rapid expansion of productivity, and indirectly, through the release of labor into the nonagricultural sector. China's economic reform followed nearly two decades of urban-oriented policies that concentrated investment in urban industry, tied rural households to the land, and generated a 6:1 gap in output per worker between the nonagricultural and the farm sector. With 70 percent of the labor force in agriculture in 1978, we can see the potential for cross-sector labor reallocation to accelerate aggregate growth.[2]

To understand China's immense post-1978 economic gains, we must also examine the other important structural transformation: the reallocation of labor and other resources from the state-owned nonagricultural sector to the nonstate sector.[3] In principle, the two transformations, from agriculture to nonagriculture and from state to nonstate within nonagriculture,[4] may be linked, for example, through the effect of the state sector's initial size and subsequent growth on relative productivity between agriculture and nonagriculture.

At the outset of reform, the state sector dominated nonagricultural activity, accounting for 80 percent of urban employment, 76 percent of industrial output, and nearly two-thirds of construction output in 1978. The balance of ownership is crucial because labor productivity growth in the nonstate sector ran far ahead of state-sector achievements. Furthermore, the growth of output per worker in the state sector relied heavily on capital accumulation – largely financed through loans from China's state-dominated banking system – implying an even larger shortfall in the growth of total factor productivity (TFP) within the state sector.[5]

---

[2] Hayashi and Prescott (2006) argue that this transfer played an important role in the post–World War II growth acceleration of one of China's Asian neighbors, Japan.

[3] We should be clear at the outset that "nonstate" activity includes but is not limited to the private sector. Through the first decade and a half of the reform, the nonstate sector consisted mainly of urban collectives and mostly of collective township and village enterprises. Over time, through relaxation of restrictions on ownership, privatization of both collectively owned and state-owned firms, foreign direct investment, and so on, private ownership has come to occupy an increasingly prominent position within the nonstate sector.

[4] In what follows, we employ the terms "state" and "nonstate" to indicate the decomposition of the nonagricultural sector along ownership lines. This allows us to avoid clumsy terminology, such as "nonstate nonagricultural sector." Our discussion ignores China's state farms, which are too small to influence the outcome of this analysis.

[5] We define TFP growth to be the increase in output that cannot be attributed to increases in factor use, namely, labor and capital. In our empirical work, TFP also includes the contribution of increases due to the accumulation of human capital. In ongoing work, we examine human capital separately.

Our effort to disentangle these complexities focuses on a series of specific questions. With respect to agriculture, we want to know the following:

- How important was increased agricultural productivity to aggregate output growth?
- How much of the growth in aggregate output per worker can be attributed to the reallocation of labor from agriculture to nonagriculture?
- What factors were most important in determining the speed with which labor was transferred out of agriculture?

Outside agriculture we are motivated by a related set of issues:

- How much did productivity change in the nonstate sector contribute to overall growth?
- What is the role of capital accumulation in the growth of the nonagricultural sector?
- What is the contribution of the reallocation of labor and capital from the state to nonstate sectors?

We address these questions first through the use of simple growth accounting. However, unraveling the complex interactions among capital accumulation, sectoral productivity change, and the reallocation of labor and capital reallocation across sectors requires a more complex analysis than conventional growth accounting can offer. To address these issues more fully, we have pursued the following research agenda:

1. Compile time series of key variables, including output, employment, capital stock, and, for the nonfarm sector, nominal and total labor compensation, over the period 1978–2004 for three segments of the economy – agriculture, state sector, and nonstate sector both nationally and for ten provinces.[6]
2. Develop a dynamic three-sector model that encompasses key features of China's economic evolution, particularly the TFP differences across sectors and the shift of resources from farming and the state sector.
3. Use aggregate data to calibrate the model, which allows us to verify the broad consistency between the model's performance (i.e., predicted outcomes) and actual developments.
4. Use the calibrated model to conduct a series of counterfactual experiments intended to estimate the contributions of specific elements to overall growth. For example, the difference between observed aggregate growth and aggregate growth in a censored version of the model in which the growth of agricultural TFP is arbitrarily fixed at zero provides an estimate of the contribution of increased TFP in agriculture to aggregate growth.

---

[6] The provinces include Shanxi, Jilin, Jiangsu, Zhejiang, Anhui, Henan, Hunan, Guangdong, Sichuan (and Chongqing), and Gansu.

5. Use the provincial data for further experimentation that confirms the initial results.

We leave the details of our dynamic three-sector model to Appendix B, in which we show that the model is able to replicate the broad features of China's economic development during the years 1978–2004. This structural model, while unavoidably complex, allows us to pursue issues that lie beyond the reach of conventional growth accounting and other forms of decomposition; our results also reveal the capacity of these simpler methods to produce erroneous results. Our analysis suggests that the traditional structural transformation, that is, from agriculture to nonagriculture, plays a smaller role than Young (and we) anticipated. Far more important is productivity growth in the nonstate sector and the transfer of labor from the state to the nonstate sectors.

Indeed, neglect of the important heterogeneity within the nonagricultural sector cutting across ownership lines bypasses what our analysis highlights as perhaps the most important determinant of China's rapid growth: TFP growth in the nonstate sector. Careful attention to the separate trajectory of the state and nonstate sectors also directs our attention to other processes such as those described in the chapters on industrial development (see Chapter 15) and on China's participation in the international economy (see Chapter 16) that contributed to productivity growth outside agriculture. Finally, our analysis suggests that cross-provincial differences in the state sector's initial position significantly influenced provincial growth trajectories.

By way of summary, we list our major findings as follows:

1. Productivity growth in agriculture and the relaxation of restrictions on rural labor mobility and use were the two most important factors driving the transfer of labor out of agriculture.
2. Although productivity growth in agriculture was important to the reallocation of labor from agriculture to nonagriculture, it contributed only modestly to aggregate labor productivity growth.[7] Between 1978 and 2004, agriculture's direct contribution to annual output growth was 0.43 percentage points. The reallocation of labor from low-productivity agriculture to higher-productivity activities in nonagriculture was the source of 1.02 percentage points, implying a total contribution of 1.45 percentage points, or 20.83 percent of total growth.
3. Reductions in barriers to labor reallocation, including those between agriculture and nonagriculture and between state and nonstate, were important for both structural transformations. However, it is only the relaxation of the latter set of distortions that had significant effects on growth. The total contribution of barrier reductions to growth is 2.29 percentage points, or close

---

[7] TFP in agriculture, however, contributed significantly more to growth in welfare than it did to output growth. We discuss this briefly in footnote 28 in section "Growth Accounting."

to one-third. Out of this 2.29 percentage point contribution, the reduction in labor market barriers between the state and nonstate sector accounts for 1.77 percentage points, while the reduction in barriers between agriculture and nonagriculture accounts for only 0.52 percentage points.

4. TFP growth in the nonstate sector, which attained an average annual rate of 4.33 percent during 1978–2004, is the most important source of growth between 1978 and 2004. It contributed to 2.83 percentage points, or 40 percent of the overall growth. Looking at the nonagricultural sector in the aggregate conceals this important feature of the growth process. This impressive growth coincided with near-tenfold employment growth in the nonstate sector, from 48.9 million in 1978 to 446 million in 2004.

5. The state sector emerges as a major impediment to growth. With low-TFP growth averaging only a third of that in the nonstate sector, the state sector maintained a substantial position in China's economy only as the beneficiary of large-scale capital-market distortions. The resulting misallocation of capital favoring the state sector at the expense of more productive non-state outlets slowed the pace of growth, resource transfer, and productivity change. Reforms in the 1990s that reduced both the size of the state sector and the wage premiums enjoyed by its employees contributed significantly to the growth of aggregate labor productivity.

6. Cross-provincial data confirm the significant negative impact of the state sector on growth. Provinces with larger state sectors (measured by the state employment share) in 1978 experienced a slower pace of structural transformation and had a larger percentage of investment going to the state sector during the period. As a result, both the aggregate and nonagricultural labor productivity growth rates were lower in these provinces.

The rest of the chapter is organized as follows. "Some Basic Facts" lays out a set of first-order facts relating to China's economic transformation between 1978 and 2004. "A Simple Decomposition Exercise" presents the results of a simple growth accounting decomposition of the sort commonly used to look at the returns to reallocation of labor across sectors. Drawing on a model laid out in Appendix B, "A Heuristic Model of Structural Transformation and Growth" sketches out the potential forces driving the reallocation of labor out of agriculture, followed in "Accounting for Labor Reallocation from Agriculture to Nonagriculture" by an accounting of the contribution of each of these factors. "Growth Accounting," in turn, undertakes a similar accounting of the contribution of resource reallocation, capital accumulation, and productivity growth to China's rapid expansion. All of the analysis through the section on "Growth Accounting" is at the national level. In the section on "Regional Variations," we look to provincial-level data and differences in their growth trajectories for footprints of the causal factors we identified at the aggregate level. Finally, the last section concludes.

SOME BASIC FACTS

We begin by documenting a number of first-order facts relating to sector-level growth, the structure of employment, and the behavior of TFP. These observations will serve as the basis for our quantitative analysis. Sector-level time-series data on nominal and real GDP, employment, wages, investment, and the real capital stock are critical here. There are important issues surrounding the construction of each of these series, especially employment levels in the agricultural and nonagricultural sectors and price deflators linking nominal and real GDP. We leave most of this discussion to a separate data appendix and limit the present discussion to highlighting key facts.[8]

Employment and Employment Share by Sectors

We start with employment because it provides the basis for constructing estimates of labor productivity. China's National Bureau of Statistics (NBS) provides an estimate of total employment and a breakdown by sector: primary, secondary (manufacturing plus construction, mining, and utilities), and tertiary (services). Between 1978 and 2004, the NBS measure of total employment increased from 401.52 million to 752.00 million. The NBS data also show a decline in the percentage of the labor force in the primary sector from 70.5 percent in 1978 to 50.1 percent in 2000, and then to 46.9 percent in 2004.

We find two difficulties with the official data. There is a major discontinuity in the employment data beginning in 1990. This "break" reflects a major upward adjustment to the NBS employment series based on new information from China's population censuses of 1990 and 2000.[9] These adjustments did not extend to years before 1990, leading to a big jump in the NBS employment measure during 1989–1990.

A second issue concerns the possibility that NBS data underestimate the rate of decline in the primary-sector labor force (Chen, 1992; Rawski and Mead, 1998). Critics point to several potential sources of this bias: the exclusion of employment in private and cooperative enterprises owned by households prior to 1984 (Wong, 1988, p. 14), incomplete tabulation of self-employment and part-time work outside agriculture by individuals who derived the bulk of their incomes from farming, and erroneous inclusion of out-migrants in the farm labor force.

Following Holz (2006), we use information from the 1982 Census to adjust the pre-1990 data on total employment in a way analogous to the adjustments made for 1990 and after. We also construct an alternative estimate of "primary"

---

[8] This appendix can be accessed at http://www.economics.utoronto.ca/brandt/China's Great Economic Transformation/Chapter 17/Data Appendix.

[9] Following the revisions, for example, total employment in 1990 increased from 567.40 million to 647.49 million, or an increase of 14.1 percent. In percentage terms, the adjustment in each of the three sectors, primary, secondary, and tertiary, was comparable.

sector employment by utilizing detailed labor supply data for rural households disaggregated by activity collected by the Research Centre for Rural Economy as part of their annual rural household survey.[10]

Table 17.1 lays out our revised estimates of total employment and employment disaggregated between the primary and nonprimary sectors. For the nonprimary sector, we also report employment in the state and nonstate sectors. At the beginning of the reforms, total employment was 468 million, with nearly 70 percent in agriculture. The state sector occupied over half of all employment outside the primary sector in 1978. The remainder of the nonagricultural workforce was divided among urban collective enterprises and rural firms operated by rural townships and villages (commune and brigade level enterprises).

Between 1978 and 2004, total employment grew at an annual rate of 1.82 percent, reaching a terminal figure of 752 million (Table 17.1). Important changes in the composition of employment accompanied this growth. First, primary-sector employment declined by nearly 100 million, and its share of total employment dropped by more than half, from 69.3 to 31.8 percent.[11] Over the same period, employment outside agriculture increased at an annual rate of nearly 5 percent, rising from 144 million to 513 million, with its share in the total expanding from 30.7 to 68.2 percent.

Within the nonagricultural sector, employment in the state sector increased by more than 50 percent, from 74.5 million to 112.6 million workers, between 1978 and 1995, before dropping sharply. By 2004, reflecting a combination of massive layoffs and major restructuring in the state sector, including privatization of many small- and medium-sized firms, employment fell to 67.1 million, occupying only 13.1 percent of nonagricultural employment in 2004. At the same time, employment in China's nonstate sector jumped from 69.5 million to 446.0 million between 1978 and 2004, an increase of 640 percent.

Labor Productivity Levels and Growth by Sectors and Periods

We combine data on output and employment to derive time series for aggregate and sectoral labor productivity in terms of 1978 prices. Results appear in Figure 17.1. Our estimates of real output begin with the most recent revision of the standard NBS data on nominal GDP at the aggregate and sectoral levels. We apply a new set of sector-level price deflators that imply slightly higher (lower) inflation in the secondary and tertiary (primary) sectors than the implicit price indicators

---

[10] By agreement with Research Center on the Rural Economy, we have data for the ten provinces identified in footnote 6.

[11] By way of comparison, our revised estimates actually show a smaller reduction than alternative estimates by Rawski and Mead (1998), using a different methodology. Their estimates, which terminate in 1993, imply a drop of a third in the absolute number working in agriculture, and a reduction in the share of the labor force in primary-sector activity from 70 to 35 percent between 1979 and 1988, before a slight rise the next few years.

Table 17.1. *Revised employment data: 1978–2004*

Year	Total employment (millions)	Primary sector Total (millions)	Primary sector Percentage of total	Nonprimary sector Total (millions)	Nonprimary sector State-owned units (SOU) (millions)	Nonprimary sector Non-SOU (millions)
1978	468.43	324.45	69.26	143.98	74.51	69.47
1979	479.67	314.16	65.50	165.51	76.93	88.58
1980	493.97	305.93	61.93	188.04	80.19	107.85
1981	510.39	298.90	58.56	211.49	83.72	127.77
1982	526.18	291.38	55.38	234.80	86.30	148.50
1983	541.17	283.38	52.36	257.79	87.71	170.08
1984	558.10	276.34	49.51	281.76	86.37	195.39
1985	575.51	269.46	46.82	306.05	89.90	216.15
1986	591.51	277.04	46.84	314.47	93.33	221.14
1987	607.44	277.26	45.64	330.18	96.54	233.64
1988	622.40	282.32	45.36	340.08	99.84	240.24
1989	635.61	299.13	47.06	336.48	101.08	235.40
1990	647.49	301.07	46.50	346.42	103.46	242.96
1991	654.91	300.44	45.88	354.47	106.64	247.83
1992	661.52	299.43	45.26	362.09	108.89	253.20
1993	668.08	292.19	43.74	375.89	109.20	266.69
1994	674.55	281.55	41.74	393.00	112.14	280.86
1995	680.65	277.59	40.78	403.06	112.61	290.45
1996	689.50	268.27	38.91	421.23	112.44	308.79
1997	698.20	267.34	38.29	430.86	110.44	320.42
1998	706.37	266.25	37.69	440.12	90.58	349.54
1999	713.94	259.91	36.41	454.03	85.72	368.31
2000	720.85	254.46	35.30	466.39	81.02	385.37
2001	730.25	255.02	34.92	475.23	76.40	398.83
2002	737.40	250.40	33.96	487.00	71.63	415.37
2003	744.32	243.96	32.78	500.36	68.76	431.60
2004	752.00	238.88	31.77	513.12	67.10	446.02

embedded in the NBS data. As a result, our measure of real GDP growth is roughly 1 percentage point below the official figure for the entire period 1978–2004.

At the beginning of the reform, real labor productivity in the nonagricultural sector was nearly six times higher than that in agriculture (RMB18,000 per man-year vs. RMB3,100 per man-year). This "gap" gradually declined by nearly half as a result of differential growth in labor productivity favoring agriculture. Between 1978 and 2004, average labor productivity in agriculture increased at an annual rate of 6.76 percent compared to only 4.65 percent for the nonprimary sector. Most of this partial convergence occurred very early in the reform process. We attribute this to the large "one-time" gains in agricultural output that followed the introduction of the household responsibility system, the early reform of marketing and pricing,

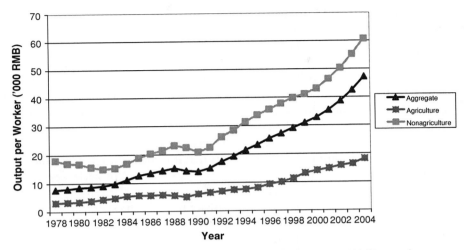

Figure 17.1. Real labor productivity, 1978–2004 (RMB1,000) (See text.)

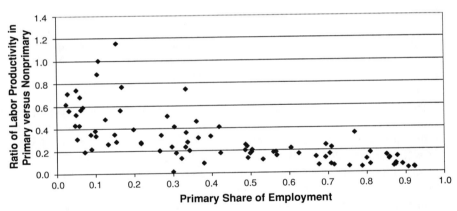

Figure 17.2. Relative labor productivity versus primary share of employment, eighty-five countries

and the ensuing exodus of labor out of agriculture (see McMillan, Whalley and Zhu, 1989; Lin, 1992; see Chapter 13).

Figure 17.2 helps put China's 1978 intersectoral productivity gap into comparative perspective by graphing the ratio of primary-sector to nonprimary-sector labor productivity (vertical axis) against the primary sector's employment share (horizontal axis) for a cross section of eighty-five countries that spans all regions and levels of development. The data are for 1985 for all countries except China, for which we use 1978 data.

Many empirical studies document the universal decline in agriculture's share of employment (and also GDP) as per capita incomes rise. Thus, in Figure 17.2, observations associated with high-income nations congregate near the vertical axis (because they have low shares of primary-sector employment), with China among the low-income nations on the right-hand segment of the graph. Figure 17.2 shows that the ratio of primary to nonprimary labor productivity rises substantially as we move from right to left, that is, from lower to higher levels of per capita income. China, with its gap of 1:6 between agricultural and nonagricultural productivity, does not stand out among low-income countries with most of their labor force employed in the farm sector. This leads us to conclude that, despite the unusual features of China's rural organization in 1978, China was not alone among low-income nations in suffering institutional constraints that impeded efficient allocation of resources across sectors. Indeed, Figure 17.2 suggests that such obstacles appear to be endemic among low-income countries.[12]

What about differences in labor productivity between the state and nonstate sectors? While the NBS data decompose industrial output and value added into state and nonstate components, they provide no similar breakdown for the entire secondary and tertiary sectors. This forces us to rely on wage data for the state and nonstate sectors to approximate such a division for the entire nonagricultural economy.

To do this, we assume that wages are proportional to average value products and that labor shares in the two sectors are the same. Information on wages in the state and nonstate sector, the latter including urban collective, foreign-owned, private, and township and village enterprises (TVEs), suggest that wages outside the state sector were between 60 and 70 percent of state-sector wages between 1978 and 1995, rose to nearly 85 percent by 2000, and then fell slightly thereafter.

These data conceal an important complication: they include only cash compensation and neglect the value of subsidies and in-kind wages enjoyed by workers in the state sector, the largest component of which was probably housing. Rawski (1982), Bannister (2005), and Benjamin et al. (see Chapter 18) offer estimates of the magnitude of these benefits for various years. There is a clear consensus that the relative importance of such noncash benefits has declined markedly over time, with estimates suggesting that they have fallen from rough equality with cash wages in the late 1970s, to half of cash wages by the early 1990s, to perhaps a quarter of cash wages today. These figures imply that total compensation in the nonstate sector almost doubled relative to compensation in the state sector between 1978 and 2004. Although these estimates of overall compensation are unavoidably crude, we note that the implied doubling of relative earnings paid to nonstate workers parallels our estimates of relative labor productivity between state and nonstate industry, which make up the bulk of the secondary sector.[13]

---

[12] See Restuccia, Yang, and Zhu (forthcoming) for a cross-country quantitative analysis of these obstacles to labor reallocation.

[13] In 2004, for example, GDP in industry was equal to 86.6 percent of GDP produced in the secondary sector, which is made up of industry, mining, utilities, and construction (see *Zhongguo tongji nianjian*, 2005, p. 51).

Investment and Capital Accumulation by Sectors

Capital accumulation surely contributed to the rapid growth of labor productivity. Fixed investment increased from 23 percent of GDP in 1978 to 45 percent in 2004. As a result, the capital–labor ratio in the economy grew from RMB14,000 in 1978 to RMB59,000 in 2004. However, fixed investment and the increase in the capital–labor ratio were not uniform across sectors. Between 1978 and 2004, the average annual growth rate of the capital–labor ratio amounted to 5.13, 2.51, and 6.43 percent for the agricultural, nonstate, and state sectors, respectively. For agriculture, the rapid rise in the ratio is partly due to falling employment. The rapid growth of the capital–labor ratio in the state sector, however, is largely a product of huge infusions of investment arising from sizable credit market distortions designed to channel funds to state-sector investment projects.

China's financial system has played an important role in intermediating the economy's growing pool of savings. The annual flow of new savings directed to firms, enterprises, and government through either banks or emerging bond and equity markets has averaged more than 20 percent of GDP since the mid-1980s. China's financial system, however, remains strongly oriented toward serving state-sector firms, which receive the largest portion of these funds (Lardy, 1998; Brandt and Zhu, 2000). Even with recent banking reforms and significant downsizing of the state enterprise sector, more than 60 percent of all new loans were directed to state-owned or state-controlled firms between 1998 and 2003 (Brandt and Zhu, 2007). This is only marginally lower than estimates for earlier years. In addition, funds raised through initial public offerings continue to flow primarily to state-controlled firms.

By contrast, nonstate-sector firms, especially domestically owned enterprises (rather than either joint ventures or wholly owned subsidiaries), have often experienced significant difficulty in raising funds. Discrimination against small- and medium-size private firms has been well documented (see Chapter 14; Brandt and Li, 2003). This bias in the financial system helps explain why investment in the state sector has consistently hovered in the vicinity of 17 percent of GDP despite the state sector's rapidly declining contribution to aggregate GDP and employment.

TFP Levels and Growth by Sectors

The presence of substantial differences in the capital–labor ratio across sectors makes labor productivity a potentially misleading measure of production efficiency. For example, output per worker in the state sector has consistently been higher than labor productivity in the nonstate sector, but this may reflect the state sector's easy access to capital and higher capital–output ratio rather than any superior effectiveness of resource utilization. To measure differences in production efficiency across sectors, we need to control for differences in

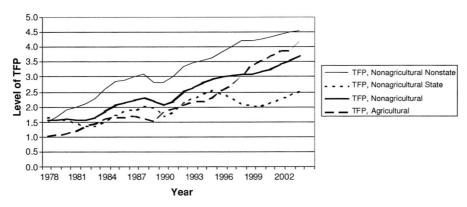

Figure 17.3. Sector TFP, 1978–2004 (see text)

the capital–labor ratio. We do this by estimating the TFP levels for each sector.[14]

Figure 17.3 plots the TFP levels for each of the three sectors. There has been significant growth of TFP in the agricultural and the nonstate nonagricultural sector, which increased at annual rates of 5.38 and 4.33 percent, respectively. By comparison, TFP growth in the state sector has been relatively sluggish, increasing only at the rate of 1.66 percent per annum. In terms of levels, in 1978 TFP in the nonstate nonagricultural sector was nearly the same as that in the state sector. Due to the more rapid growth in the nonstate sector, TFP levels diverge over time so that by 2004 the level of TFP in the nonagricultural sector was 80 percent higher than that in the state sector. This huge gap in TFP levels supports the claim that high rates of capital accumulation in the state sector have been instrumental to maintaining high levels of output per worker.

Labor Market Barriers

There are many institutional and policy constraints that restrict movement of labor from agriculture. Although difficult to measure directly, they generally have the effect of depressing the returns to labor in agriculture relative to those in nonagriculture. Thus, the gap in returns to labor between agriculture and nonagriculture can be used as an implicit measure of the barriers to labor reallocation between the two sectors. We do not have direct data on the average returns to labor in the agricultural and nonagricultural sectors. However, we do have data on the average value product of labor (or nominal output per worker) for the two sectors. Under the assumption that labor shares of income are the same in the two sectors, the gap in the average value product of labor equals the gap in average returns to labor and therefore can be used as a measure of labor market barriers.

---

[14] We discuss briefly the calculation of TFP in Appendix A.

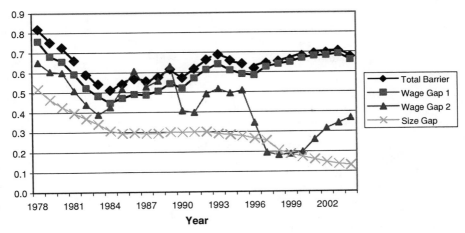

Figure 17.4. Labor market barriers (see text and Appendix B)

Figure 17.4 plots this measure of labor market barriers. Between 1978 and 1984, the gap in average returns to labor between agriculture and nonagriculture declined sharply, from 82 to 51 percent. Subsequently, the gap widened and in 2004, was equal to 68 percent. The gap in average returns to labor can be further decomposed into three sources: the wage gap between the agricultural and the nonstate nonagricultural sector (wage gap 1), the gap in wages between the nonstate and the state sector or the state sector's wage premium (wage gap 2), and the size of the state sector measured by the share of the state sector's share of nonagricultural employment (size gap). Figure 17.4 also plots these three components of barriers separately. While the first component behaves very similarly to the overall gap, the second and the third component decline steadily over time.

A SIMPLE DECOMPOSITION EXERCISE

Differences in the levels and rates of growth of labor productivity between sectors (see the section on "Labor Productivity Levels and Growth by Sectors and Periods") suggest that labor reallocation contributed to aggregate labor productivity growth. Many authors have investigated such possibilities using simple decompositions that begin by noting that aggregate labor productivity can be expressed as the weighted average of productivities in the two sectors:

$$y_t = y_{at}l_{at} + y_{nt}(1 - l_{at})$$

Here, y_t, y_{at}, and y_{nt} are labor productivities in the aggregate, agriculture, and nonagriculture, respectively, in year t, and l_{at} is agriculture's share of total employment in year t. Aggregate labor productivity growth, then, can be expressed as follows:

$$\mathrm{d}\ln y_t = [(y_{at}l_{at})/y_t]\mathrm{d}\ln y_{at} + [(y_{nt}(1 - l_{at})/y_t]\mathrm{d}\ln y_{nt} + [(y_{nt} - y_{at})/y_t]\mathrm{d}\,l_{at},$$

Table 17.2. *Growth rates of output per worker by sector*

	1978–2004	1978–1988	1988–2004
Aggregate	6.96	6.74	7.09
Agriculture	6.76	5.70	7.43
Nonagriculture	4.65	2.47	6.02
State owned	4.87	3.30	5.86
Nonstate owned	5.59	3.89	6.67
Simple growth decomposition: contribution of each source to growth			
Aggregate	100.00	100.00	100.00
Output per worker in agriculture	27.30	23.80	19.40
Output per worker in nonagriculture	48.10	26.40	69.20
Reallocation	24.60	49.90	11.40

Source: See text.

where d denotes the rate of change and ln represents logs. We decompose aggregate labor productivity growth into three sources: labor productivity growth in both sectors and labor reallocation. In the absence of labor movement between the two sectors, that is, with $dl_{at} = 0$, the growth rate of aggregate labor productivity simply equals the weighted average of the growth rates of labor productivity in the two sectors, with the weights equal to the respective GDP shares of the two sectors.

Table 17.2 uses this popular approach to decompose aggregate labor productivity growth into these three components.[15] For the entire period, growth in output per worker in agriculture and nonagriculture contributed 27.3 and 48.1 percent, respectively, to total labor productivity growth. Although output per worker in agriculture actually grew more rapidly during reform, its contribution to overall growth was dampened by the primary sector's relatively small size – slightly more than a quarter of GDP at the beginning of reform. These estimates imply that about a quarter of the growth in labor productivity, that is, $100 - 27.3 - 48.1$, can be attributed to the reallocation of labor from agriculture to nonagriculture. Recall that over this period, the share of labor in the primary sector fell by more than half, from roughly 70 percent in 1978 to 32 percent in 2004.

Decompositions for the two subperiods, 1978–1988 and 1988–2004, reveal that the contribution of labor reallocation from agriculture to nonagriculture to overall growth occurred mainly near the start of China's reform process. During the first decade of reform, the transfer of labor to the higher-productivity nonagricultural

[15] See, for example, OECD (2005, p. 32), which performs similar calculations in the context of a three-sector model for 1983–2003. They find that a fifth or so of the overall growth was due to sectoral reallocations of labor and suggest that the contribution could have been even larger in light of differences in the marginal (as opposed to average) products of labor.

sector was the source of almost half (49.9 percent) of all growth, with productivity growth in the two sectors contributing equally to the remaining half. This behavior is in line with the timing of the reduction in agriculture's share of employment, a significant portion of which occurs very early in the reforms. By comparison, reallocation contributed only 11.4 percent to the growth since 1988. For the period since 1988, growth of labor productivity outside agriculture provides the largest contribution to overall GDP growth.

These simple decompositions tell us that reallocation across sectors is positively associated with growth, but we expect that the estimated magnitude of the reallocation effect resulting from this analysis is likely to be biased. There are two primary reasons for believing that this is the case.[16] First, the reallocation of labor may be a result of the growth in TFP in the two sectors. If that is the case, the decomposition may overestimate the role of the reallocation and underestimate the role of labor productivity growth within sectors.[17] Second, labor productivity growth within each of the two sectors will depend on labor reallocation. Because of diminishing returns, all else equal, the gap in productivities between the two sectors will narrow, as labor is reallocated from agriculture to nonagriculture. Simple decompositions ignore all these potentially important considerations surrounding intersectoral productivity and labor flows. They provide no more than an upper bound for the actual contribution of labor reallocation out of agriculture to overall growth during China's reform period.

To convincingly analyze the impact of labor reallocation on economic growth, we need a structural model that explicitly captures all the interactions between labor productivity and labor flows.[18]

A HEURISTIC MODEL OF STRUCTURAL TRANSFORMATION AND GROWTH

We begin by sketching a simple heuristic model of the traditional structural transformation that moves resources out of agriculture. Appendix B provides a more

[16]   There is also a third potential bias. The decompositions implicitly assume that the "gaps" in average and marginal productivities of labor between sectors are the same. The returns to reallocation depend on differences in marginal productivity; however, the decompositions are based on information on averages. If the underlying production technology is Cobb–Douglas and labor shares in the two sectors are the same, the ratio of average and marginal productivity between sectors will be the same, but this does not hold true for other functional forms. It is an empirical matter as to how sensitive the returns to reallocation are to alternative assumptions about the underlying technology. Based on sensitivity analysis we carried out, this is not an important consideration here.

[17]   This bias generally exists in standard growth accounting in which the contribution of capital accumulation is overestimated and that of TFP is underestimated.

[18]   The problems of using these simple decomposition methods are also revealed in trying to estimate the returns to reallocation of labor between the state and nonstate sectors. At the beginning of reform, average labor productivity in the state sector was actually higher than that in the nonstate. This would imply negative returns to the reallocation. However, differences in TFP between the two sectors offset this.

formal treatment. In this section, we focus on the forces potentially driving the shift of labor out of agriculture. Subsequently, we disentangle the contribution of the reallocation, productivity growth, and capital formation to overall growth.

A Simple Two-Sector Model

Consider a simple two-sector, two-good economy, with three factors of production: labor, capital, and land. Food is produced in the agricultural sector and manufactured goods and services outside. Land is a "fixed" factor that is important for agriculture but less important elsewhere. In a frictionless world, resources flow to their highest valued uses, and returns are equalized on the margins.

Here, we focus on two important qualifications to this ideal outcome. Since land is a fixed factor, there are diminishing returns to labor in agriculture. This means that removing labor from agriculture increases the marginal productivity of the remaining farmworkers, which makes it unlikely that all workers will leave agriculture. Furthermore, since the two sectors produce different outputs, unless the demand for agricultural output vanishes, some resources must remain in agriculture to satisfy this demand, even if TFP in agriculture is very low.[19]

Previous studies of structural transformation during the development process identify four factors that may drive the reallocation of resources toward the nonagricultural sector: (1) increases in agricultural productivity that relax a subsistence food consumption constraint, (2) faster TFP growth in agriculture than in nonagriculture, (3) a reduction in barriers to labor mobility between sectors, and (4) increases in capital formation. We examine each in turn and then discuss their potential relevance in the Chinese context.

Subsistence Food Consumption Constraint and the Rise of Agricultural Productivity

Engel's law reminds us of a universal tendency for the proportion of income that is spent on food to decline as incomes rise. This means that the income elasticity of food demand is less than 1. A simple way to capture this relationship is to assume that each individual must consume a minimum amount of food. When income is low, expenditure is concentrated on satisfying this subsistence requirement, so that the share of food in total expenditure is high. As income rises, more income becomes available for consumption of other goods, and the share of food expenditure declines. The implication of this minimum food consumption constraint is that when agricultural labor productivity is low (and assuming a closed economy), a large amount of labor is needed in agricultural production to satisfy the subsistence food consumption demands. As agricultural productivity improves,

---

[19] For reasons explained later, we implicitly assume that the economy remains closed to international trade.

less labor will be needed for this purpose, thereby allowing the share of labor in agriculture to decline.[20]

Relative Productivity Growth in Agriculture

In a small open economy, world markets determine the relative price of the two goods. Since production levels in a small economy will not affect these prices, higher relative productivity growth in agriculture means higher returns to labor in agriculture and will attract more labor into farming. This "small economy" result is clearly inconsistent with the development experience of large advanced countries, such as the United States, in which differential productivity growth favoring agriculture has coincided with large outflows of labor from the farm sector, evidently because large increases in farm output exerted downward pressure on agricultural prices. As a result, most studies of structural transformation concentrate on closed economy models.

We follow this standard and confine ourselves to a no-trade, closed economy model.[21] This approach fits particularly well with the initial fifteen years of China's transition experience, when global market forces still played only a modest role in determining the domestic terms of exchange between farm and nonfarm products.

In a closed economy with no possibility for labor to move between sectors, faster productivity growth in agriculture has two effects: supply grows faster in that sector, which causes the relative price of agricultural goods to decline, and the decline in relative price will act to increase relative demand for agricultural goods.

If we now permit labor to move freely between sectors, the net effect of accelerated agricultural productivity growth on labor allocation depends on the elasticity of substitution between the two goods. If the elasticity of substitution between agricultural and nonagricultural goods is less than 1, the increase in the demand for agricultural goods will be less than the increase in supply. This will depress prices and wages in the farm sector and encourage labor to shift to the nonfarm sector. If the elasticity of substitution is greater than 1, the logic is reversed, so that labor will flow into, rather than out of, the farm sector. Finally, if the elasticity of substitution equals 1, the relative supply of and demand for agricultural goods increase at the

---

[20] The importance of this subsistence food consumption constraint was pointed out long ago by T.W. Schultz as *the food problem* and is an integral part of more recent models of structural transformation. See, for example, Caselli and Coleman (2001), Kongsamut, Rebelo, and Xie (2001), Hansen and Prescott (2002), Gollin, Parente and Rogerson (2003), Restuccia, Yang, and Zhu (forthcoming), Yang and Zhu (2004), Duarte and Restuccia (2006), and Hayashi and Prescott (2006).

[21] Clearly, food is not completely nontradable. The source of the inconsistency between the implications of the open economy model and the experience of countries such as the United States is beyond the scope of our chapter. As a matter of fact, food imports into China have been a relatively small percentage of domestic agricultural output.

same rate and there will be no reallocation due to the relative productivity growth in agriculture.[22]

Reduction in Labor Market Barriers and Distortions

Barriers and distortions in various forms tend to keep farmers from leaving the land. These may include restrictions on labor mobility or on the kinds of activities that are open to rural labor. Low levels of human capital in the primary sector may also constrain movement into the nonagricultural sector. An important effect of these barriers is to suppress the wages (or the marginal product of labor of households farming their own land) received by workers in agriculture and drive a wedge between the returns earned by laborers working in the two sectors. Thus, the gap in wages between agriculture and nonagriculture is an implicit indicator of the severity of barriers to labor mobility. A reduction in barriers will lead to a reduction in the share of employment in agriculture and convergence of wages in the two sectors.[23]

Increases in the Investment Rate

Capital formation is frequently ignored in this context, but deserves attention as a potentially important influence on the pace and extent of labor reallocation across sectors. Because capital is produced in the nonagricultural sector, an increase in the rate of fixed investment leads to an increase in the demand for nonagricultural goods, which raises the share of employment in the nonagricultural sector.

Driving Forces in the Chinese Context

Which of these forces seem likely to figure prominently in the analysis of Chinese labor mobility? Our analysis of aggregate data suggests that the elasticity of substitution between farm products and nonagricultural goods is close to unity, so we expect that labor allocation is unaffected by changes in relative prices and, therefore, by shifts in relative productivity growth. We therefore focus on the remaining items: subsistence food constraints, labor market barriers, and increases in the rate of fixed capital formation.

Binding Subsistence Constraints at the Beginning of Reform

In 1977, per capita grain availability in China was slightly more than 190 kilograms per capita. Piazza (1983) estimates that total per capita nutrient availability

---

[22] Ngai and Pissaridis (2007) have emphasized this source of labor reallocation. In the U.S. data, the relative productivity in agriculture has increased, while agriculture's share of labor has declined, which suggests that the elasticity of substitution is less than 1. Quantitatively, however, it is not clear how important this effect is in accounting for the labor reallocation.

[23] Recent studies that emphasize the importance of labor market barriers in labor allocation include Caselli and Coleman (2001), Restuccia, Yang, and Zhu (forthcoming), and Hayashi and Prescott (2006).

was 2,247 calories, 95 percent of which was from cereals and vegetables. Piazza places protein availability at 30.6 grams per day. These figures are 4.1 and 23.4 percent above estimated "safe" limits of energy and protein intake, with the margin on total energy intake especially low. These nationwide estimates ignore differences in per capita consumption between urban and rural China. They also ignore regional differences. Additional information on the rural–urban diet gap and the size of urban and rural populations implies that rural calorie adequacy in 1977 was 4 percent below safe levels. In fact, rural calorie consumption was below adequacy levels every year between 1959 and 1977 (Rawski, 2002), and during this period it was lower than consumption levels in the 1930s.

With nearly 70 percent of the labor force in agriculture, labor force participation rates just slightly below 50 percent in the late 1970s, and negative net exports, these levels of consumption, which Riskin (1987, p. 263) terms "spartan," clearly indicate the low level of labor productivity in pre-reform Chinese agriculture. On average, each farmworker produced enough food to support only 2.67 individuals, or even fewer if we convert the population into adult equivalents. Inadequate nutrition and low productivity that trapped most of the workforce in farming highlight the enormous costs of the weak incentives associated with collectivized agriculture, restrictions on rural marketing, unfavorable terms of trade for agriculture, and policies mandating local self-sufficiency in grain. These costs swamped any benefits from ongoing technological progress in agriculture (see Chapter 13 in this volume; Lardy, 1983). Without significant increases in agricultural productivity (or relaxation of constraints on food imports), low farm productivity forced most workers to cluster in the agricultural sector, imposing a low ceiling on the size of China's nonagricultural labor force and population. Indeed, between 1962 and 1977, the percentage of the Chinese population living in the cities failed to grow, holding steady at slightly more than 17 percent.

Barriers

Barriers impeding the movement of labor from agriculture were a pervasive feature of the China's pre-reform economy. These restraints helped to sustain higher returns to labor outside of agriculture. Prior to reform, tight restrictions limited the entry of rural workers into nonagricultural activities; their primary intent was to prevent the diversion of labor from collective agriculture (Lardy, 1983). Additional restrictions limited the sectors open to enterprises run by rural communes and production brigades. In principle, these enterprises were to serve agriculture and infrastructure investment (mainly, water-control projects) in their home localities. These limits were embedded in a broader system that severely isolated the countryside from the cities.

The early rural reforms began to relax some of these constraints on both households and enterprises. Self-employment in transport, crafts, and miscellaneous commercial activity, previously forbidden, expanded rapidly after 1978 (Riskin, 1987). Reforms allowed "specialized households" to enter a host of nonagricultural activities under the principle of "*litu bulixiang*" (leave the land but not the township). At the same time, Central Committee pronouncements on rural development strategy in 1978 and 1984 encouraged fresh expansion of rural industry (Chen et. al., 1994). A relaxation of restrictions of state procurement of agricultural goods, for example, allowed rural factories to enter the business of processing farm products, formerly reserved for urban firms (Naughton, 1992).

More generally, the 1984 introduction of the dual-track pricing system for industrial goods allowed rural enterprises to gain access to key intermediate goods, raw materials, and goods. The share of all producer (agricultural) goods transacted through the market rose from 0 (6) percent in 1978 to 46 (58) percent in 1991. By 1993, these percentages increased to 86 and 83 percent, respectively.[24] The new availability of subcontracting relationships with urban state enterprises facilitated rapid expansion of rural enterprises, which also benefited from unprecedented opportunities to enter into markets not served by SOEs. Key emerging sectors among rural industry included building materials, machinery and metal fabrication, and textiles and apparel (Byrd and Gelb, 1990).

Despite these improvements, which particularly facilitated resource mobility within individual townships (formerly communes), long-standing barriers to mobility continued to obstruct the access of rural households to potential opportunities outside their home townships and contributed to gaps in nonagricultural wages between a burgeoning TVE sector and wages paid in urban-based SOEs. The *hukou* system continued to serve as a de facto internal passport system (Chan, forthcoming). It imposed control on the ability of individuals and households to move between cities, but especially between rural and urban areas, by severely limiting access to housing, education, and other important social services for migrants. These restrictions, combined with preferential government policies supporting workers in the state sector, helped to sustain a gap in wages between the state and nonstate sectors.

A number of forces, however, helped to facilitate more informal labor flows. In the mid-1980s, for example, localities began to issue migration employment registration cards, which facilitated and probably lowered the costs of obtaining administrative permission for out-migration. Beginning in the late 1990s, smaller cities and towns began to facilitate permanent settlement by individuals and households arriving from rural villages.

Efforts to measure the volume of migration must contend with alternative definitions based on final destination, duration, as well as the presence or absence of change in *hukou* status (Chan, forthcoming). *Hukou* migration (i.e., the migrant is officially registered as a resident of the destination community), which can include rural–urban, rural–rural, urban–rural, as well as urban–urban, measured as a flow, has remained relatively constant in the last twenty to twenty-five years at slightly less than 20 million per year. Informal migration is much harder to measure. There

---

[24] See OECD (2005, p. 29).

are estimates based on a number of alternative definitions typically tied to lengths of stay, for example, three days versus six months. This migration includes rural–urban, as well as the other three kinds of migration.

Despite these complications, which interject significant uncertainty into our estimates, we observe several noteworthy trends. The period from the early 1980s to mid-1990s witnessed a significant increase in informal migration, followed by a leveling off in the last half of the 1990s and a further increase after 2000.[25] The rural–urban migration flow totals as much as 100 million. The proportion of migrants moving across county and provincial boundaries has risen during the past decade, creating a very different picture from earlier periods, in which migrants typically moved to cities within their home county or province (see de Brauw et al., 2002; Chan, forthcoming). Coastal provinces, especially Guangdong, have become the largest recipients of these long-distance migratory flows, with the largest labor flows originating in the central provinces (see Chapter 19, Figure 19.3, showing the thirty largest migratory flows).

Investment Rates

Between 1978 and 2004 fixed investment as a percentage of GDP increased from 23 to 45 percent. With most capital goods produced domestically, this rise in the investment rate increases the demand for labor in manufacturing and therefore contributes to the rise of nonagriculture's share of total employment.

ACCOUNTING FOR LABOR REALLOCATION FROM AGRICULTURE TO NONAGRICULTURE

We now evaluate the quantitative importance of the three factors underpinning the shift of labor out of agriculture: TFP growth in agriculture, a reduction in labor market barriers/distortions, and increases in the rate of fixed investment. To do this, we begin with our calibrated dynamic model that, as explained in Appendix B, produces results that closely track the historical statistics of labor reallocation. We then conduct a series of counterfactual exercises, each of which removes one of the factors driving labor reallocation. In each case, the difference between observed labor reallocation and the (smaller) result arising from the corresponding counterfactual trial becomes our measure of that particular factor's contribution to observed reallocation of labor.[26] Table 17.3 summarizes the results of these calculations. Figure 17.5 provides additional detail by tracking the trajectory for the share of labor in agriculture under the alternative scenarios.

[25] The tightening restrictions in the late 1990s appear related to a slowdown in growth accompanying the Asian Financial Crisis and accelerated SOE layoffs. Beijing is a good example of these kinds of policies, as are a number of northeastern cities (Chan, forthcoming).

[26] Since the three factors influence the labor reallocation nonlinearly, their effect on reallocation may not be independent of each other. Thus, the contributions of the three factors do not necessarily add up to the actual total reallocation.

Table 17.3. *Driving forces of labor reallocation*

	Labor reallocation reduction of share in agriculture (L_a/L)	
	1978–2004	1978–1988
Data	38	24
Benchmark model	38	28
Counterfactuals:		
No TFP growth in agriculture	10	13
No reduction in barriers	25	10
No reduction in agricultural nonstate barriers	30	13
No reduction in state employment share	35	26
No reduction in state wage premium	37	27
No TFP growth in NSOEs	38	28
No TFP growth in SOEs	38	28
No reallocation between agriculture and nonagriculture	0	0
No reallocation at all	0	0
No increase in saving rate	30	24

Source: See text. Values are in percent.

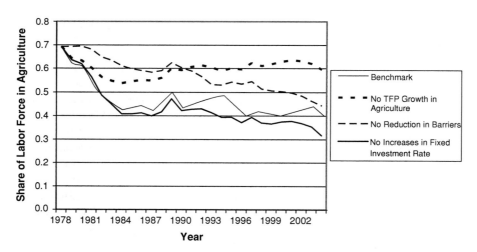

Figure 17.5. Driving forces of labor reallocation (see text)

TFP Growth in Agriculture

Our historic data show that agriculture's share of total employment fell from 69.3 percent in 1978 to 31.8 percent in 2004, a reduction of nearly 38 percentage points. How much of this decline can we attribute to rising agricultural TFP and its role in relaxing a binding subsistence food constraint? To estimate this magnitude, we conduct a trial of our model with the added specification of no change in agricultural TFP throughout 1978–2004. Under the assumption of zero TFP growth in agriculture, the farm sector's terminal employment share in 2004 stands at 59 percent, only 10 percentage points below the 1978 figure. We conclude that growth of TFP in agriculture was responsible for a reduction of 28 (38 − 10) percentage points in agriculture's overall employment share between 1978 and 2004. This implies that by relaxing a binding food constraint facing the economy, TFP growth in agriculture allowed slightly more than a quarter of China's entire labor force to leave the land in search of nonfarm employment. This result pinpoints improvements in agricultural productivity as the most important driver of the transfer of labor out of agriculture. Our calculations attribute 100 × 28/38 or 73.6 percent of the historic decline in agriculture's labor force share during 1978–2004 to the growth of TFP in agriculture.

Reduction in Labor Market Barriers

Our second-trial calculation begins with the assumption that barriers to labor mobility remained at their original 1978 level throughout the period of analysis. When we run a version of our model that eliminates the relaxation of restrictions on nonfarm employment opportunities for rural workers, the terminal employment share of agriculture in 2004 comes to 44 percent (as opposed to the actual share of 31 percent). These results allow us to attribute roughly one-third (13/38) of the total reduction in agriculture's employment share to the relaxation of barriers to the mobility of rural labor.

Most of this contribution occurred fairly early in the reform process. Between 1978 and 1988, agriculture's actual employment share decreased from 69 to 45 percent. In our simulation that excludes the effects of reduced barriers in facilitating movement of labor off the land, the 1988 share would have been 59 percent, or nearly a third higher. This implies that the reduction in barriers was the source of more than half (14/24) of the total reduction in agriculture's employment share during the first ten years of reform. By comparison, TFP growth in agriculture contributed 11 percent of the 24 percent total reduction in agriculture's labor share during the same decade.

As we discussed in the section "Driving Forces in the Chinese Context," these barriers limited the ability of rural labor to enter a host of "local" nonagricultural activities, for example, family run business, TVEs, and so on, as well as restricting movement from village to city and between the state and nonstate components of the nonfarm sector. In our modeling and empirical work, we capture these barriers through three components: the wage premium enjoyed by workers in the state sector, the size of the state sector (as measured by its share of nonagricultural employment), and the wage gap between agriculture and the nonstate sector.

The results of multiple simulations with our dynamic model show that reduction in the last component of these barriers, the wage gap between farmwork and nonfarm employment outside the state sector, provided the largest spur to the reallocation between agriculture and nonagriculture. The impact of the other two components on the speed of the transfer of labor out of agriculture is relatively small. This highlights the important role that relaxation on restrictions on household nonagricultural activity, entry by township and village-level firms, and so on, had in increasing *local* nonagricultural opportunities for rural labor, as opposed to those that could be accessed only through migration to the cities and whose growth was impeded by preferential policies favoring state-sector workers.

Increases in the Rate of Fixed Investment

Like other East Asian economies at comparable development stages, China's ratio of fixed investment to GDP increased significantly between 1978 and 2004. In 1978, the fixed investment rate was a modest 23 percent. By 2004, it has almost doubled to 44 percent. This rise in investment raised the demand for capital goods, which come mostly from the nonagricultural sector. (The actual share of imports is surprisingly small.) As a result, rising investment rates increased the nonagricultural sector's share of total employment. As before, we can estimate the magnitude of this effect using a version of our dynamic model, in which the ratio of investment to GDP is arbitrarily fixed at 23 percent throughout the period 1978–2004. The outcome shows that with no rise in the investment rate, agriculture's employment share in 2004 would have been modestly higher, namely, 39 percent compared to the 31 percent we observe in the data.

In summary, three factors, TFP growth in agriculture, a reduction in labor market barriers, and the increase in the investment rate, have contributed to the reallocation of labor from agriculture to nonagriculture. If we focus on the entire post-1978 period, the TFP growth in agriculture is clearly the most important factor. In absolute terms, its contribution was more than two times larger than that arising from the reduction in barriers, and three and a half times larger than the increase in investment proportions. However, during the critical first decade of reforms, the reduction in local barriers to labor mobility played the largest role.

GROWTH ACCOUNTING

Growth accounting is a popular form of analysis that seeks to attribute changes in output or productivity to particular "sources of growth." The objective is to decompose the overall outcome into a series of "contributions." Here, we use our three-sector framework, which includes the agricultural, the state, and nonstate sectors, to investigate changes in nationwide or aggregate labor productivity growth, which can come from three sources[27]:

- TFP growth within each of the three sectors,
- capital accumulation, and
- intersectoral reallocation of labor and capital from low-TFP sectors to high-TFP sectors.

---

[27] Because we are analyzing contributions to labor productivity (output per worker), there is no need to account separately for the growth of the labor force.

The first two are standard items that are emphasized in many studies of growth accounting. In the Chinese case, the presence of substantial structural transformation and the large cross-sector differences in TFP demands careful attention to the third possible source of aggregate growth in labor productivity: more efficient allocation of labor and capital across sectors, agriculture versus nonagriculture, and state versus nonstate. In particular, we will investigate the extent to which reductions in barriers have contributed to more efficient resource allocation across sectors and, therefore, to economywide increases in aggregate TFP in the economy and in output per worker. As we have emphasized throughout, we must consider two types of barriers: obstacles to reallocation of resources between agriculture and nonagriculture and also within nonagriculture, between the state and the nonstate sectors.

From a growth perspective, it is important to see how the latter barriers may impact the economy. As market competition intensified, many (but by no means all) state enterprises emerged as weak players. In a pure market system, competition would force the exit of such firms through bankruptcy, closure, or acquisition by stronger rivals. Rather than allowing market forces to inflict such outcomes on SOEs, the Chinese government first offered cash subsidies to troubled state enterprises and then used its control over the state-dominated banking system to direct "soft" loans to such firms ("soft" meaning that the borrowers would not qualify for such loans under normal commercial criteria). These credit flows allowed SOE beneficiaries to sustain employment and wages at levels higher than firm-level productivity and profitability would have independently supported.

This arrangement links labor market distortions (SOEs employ more workers and maintain higher wage scales than would occur under normal market conditions) to distortions in the credit market (the state sector receives more loans – leaving fewer loans available to other sectors – than would occur under normal market conditions). Without government support via the banks, wages, employment, and the number of firms in the state sector would all have declined. Directing credit to floundering SOEs affected the economy's overall rate of growth in two important ways. Favoritism toward weak SOEs in the allocation of capital denied capital to stronger firms that could have put the funds to better use, resulting in a reduction of overall growth. Furthermore, this reduction in growth lowered the supply of saving available to fund future investments, inflicting damage on future as well as current growth prospects.

Once again, we construct specially modified versions of our dynamic model to simulate the quantitative contribution of each of these factors: as before, we estimate the contribution of each prospective source of growth by eliminating its influence from the model and then comparing the resulting outcome with the actual historical series. For example, to investigate how much TFP growth in the agricultural sector contributed to overall growth, we conduct a counterfactual experiment that imposes constant agricultural TFP throughout 1978–2004 and then let our model determine the path and rate of growth of aggregate labor productivity. We then take the difference between this hypothetical growth rate

Table 17.4. *Historical and counterfactual estimates of average annual labor productivity growth*

	Labor productivity growth				
	Agriculture	NSOEs	SOEs	Nonagriculture	Aggregate
Data and counterfactuals for 1978–2004					
Historical data	6.76	5.59	4.87	4.65	6.96
Benchmark model	6.77	5.48	4.76	4.54	6.84
Counterfactuals:					
No TFP growth in agriculture	−0.62	6.50	5.78	5.57	5.51
No reduction in barriers	6.12	2.49	2.49	2.49	4.67
No reduction in agricultural nonstate barriers	6.38	5.37	4.65	4.44	6.44
No reduction in state employment share	6.62	3.41	2.69	2.97	5.42
No reduction in state wage premium	6.73	4.83	4.83	4.03	6.37
No TFP growth in NSOEs	6.77	n.a.	0.96	0.96	4.13
No TFP growth in SOEs	6.77	3.98	3.26	3.04	5.57
No reallocation between agriculture and nonagriculture	5.27	7.12	6.40	6.19	5.94
No reallocation at all	5.27	4.92	4.20	4.48	4.72
No increase in saving rate	5.70	4.52	3.80	3.58	5.70
Labor productivity growth					
Data and counterfactuals for 1978–1988					
Historical data	5.52	3.89	3.30	2.29	6.56
Benchmark model	6.13	3.21	2.62	1.81	6.62
Counterfactuals:					
No TFP growth in agriculture	−0.35	4.72	4.14	3.33	4.99
No reduction in barriers	4.39	0.16	0.16	0.16	2.97
No reduction in agricultural nonstate barriers	4.64	3.82	3.23	2.43	5.11
No reduction in state employment share	5.90	−0.24	−0.83	−0.61	4.42
No reduction in state wage premium	6.07	2.97	2.97	1.81	6.57
No TFP growth in NSOEs	6.13	n.a.	−3.22	−3.22	2.88
No reallocation between two sectors	3.58	6.82	6.24	5.43	5.93
No reallocation at all	3.58	3.08	2.49	2.71	2.97
No increase in saving rate	5.93	2.86	2.28	1.47	5.93

Note: Values are in percent.

Source: See text.

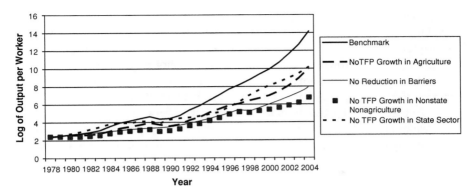

Figure 17.6. Sources of growth (see text)

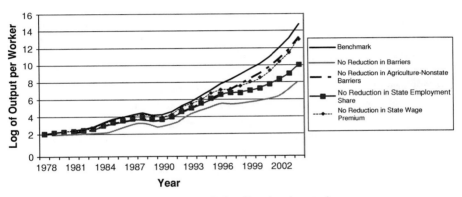

Figure 17.7. Role of barriers (see text)

and the actual rate as our estimate of the contribution of the change in agricultural TFP to overall growth. Table 17.4 provides the results from these counterfactuals. Figures 17.6 and 17.7 add further detail by showing graphic representations of the trajectory of the most important counterfactuals over the entire period of analysis.

TFP Growth in Agriculture

We are interested in the effect of agricultural TFP growth on output per worker both in agriculture and in the entire economy. In agriculture, where land is essentially fixed and the quantity of capital remains modest, the impact of TFP growth on labor productivity in agriculture is enormous: without it, labor productivity in agriculture would have actually declined at an annual rate of -0.62 percent, compared to the 6.76 percent annual growth that we observe in the data. TFP growth in farming also contributed to the reallocation of labor out of agriculture.

However, the total contribution of TFP growth in agriculture to aggregate labor productivity – including the direct effect through labor productivity growth within agriculture and indirect effect through reallocation of labor – is relatively modest. Assuming no TFP growth in agriculture, aggregate labor productivity would have still grown at a robust rate of 5.51, implying that the contribution of TFP growth in agriculture is about 1.45 percentage points, that is, 6.96–5.51, or slightly more than 20 percent of the growth in labor productivity between 1978 and 2004. An important reason for this modest contribution is that agriculture's share of GDP was already below 30 percent in 1978. By 2004, it fell to half of this. As a result, growth in that sector exercised only weak influence on the path of economywide labor productivity.[28]

TFP Growth in the Nonstate Sector

Employment in the nonstate sector grew by nearly 400 million, and its share of total employment jumped from 14.8 to 59.3 percent between 1978 and 2004. Despite this rapid increase, labor productivity grew at an impressive 5.48 percent annual rate. Because the nonstate sector has limited access to capital, labor productivity and TFP, which shows annual growth of 4.33 percent during 1978–2004, are closely linked. We conduct two counterfactual exercises to help quantify the importance of TFP growth in the nonstate sector to aggregate output growth.

First, suppose that there had been no TFP growth in the nonstate sector, but that employment in the sector had experienced the same growth as we observe in the data. In this case, the rapid increase in employment would drive labor productivity growth rates below zero for both the nonstate sector and the nonagricultural sector as a whole. It also implies a much lower aggregate labor productivity growth rate of 2.91 percent.

Alternatively, Figure 17.3 shows that at the beginning of the reform, the level of TFP in the nonstate sector was slightly lower than that in the state sector. Without

---

[28] There is an important caveat to our analysis here: aggregate labor productivity growth does not necessarily capture the true improvement in average living standards or welfare. Given the importance of subsistence demand for the agricultural good, growth of agricultural output has a much larger impact on the household's welfare. Without TFP growth in agriculture, the relative price of food would have increased dramatically, significantly increasing the cost of living and, as a result, households' welfare would have grown much slower. The aggregate labor productivity that we calculated is based on a measure of real GDP that uses the initial relative price as the weight for agriculture and therefore does not capture this price and welfare effect. A better measure would be GDP measured using a chain-weighted index, which captures the change in relative prices. The GDP growth rate measured this way is 6.77 percent per annum, only modestly less than the 6.96 percent per annum obtained using fixed weights. The actual growth rate is not affected much by the difference in the method of aggregation, because the relative price of agricultural goods has not changed much during the period. For the counterfactual, however, there is a large difference. When measured using the chain-weighted index rather than the fixed-weight index, the growth rate of aggregate GDP per worker is 3.95 percent. In other words, TFP growth has been the source of 2.82 percentage points of the growth in average living standard, or 40.5 percent of the total growth.

the TFP growth in the nonstate sector, an efficiency-enhancing growth path would channel all workers moving out of agriculture into the state sector. This would have reduced the nonagricultural sector's labor productivity growth rate to only 0.96 percent and aggregate labor productivity growth to 4.13 percent. In other words, without a nonstate sector with rapidly rising TFP to absorb the growth of nonagricultural employment, the annual growth of aggregate labor productivity in the economy would have been cut by 2.83 percentage points, or 40 percent.

TFP Growth in the State Sector

Consistent with extensive empirical work on the experience in industry (Groves, Hong, McMillan, and Naughton, 1994; Jefferson and Rawski, 1994), we find only modest growth of TFP in the state sector. Although it is significantly lower than that in the nonstate sector, this growth in TFP is moderately important. If TFP in the state sector had not grown, the drag of the state sector on overall growth would have been even larger, as state enterprises would have absorbed an even larger portion of China's capital formation to maintain their employment and wage premiums. Overall, stagnation of state-sector TFP would have reduced nonagricultural labor productivity growth to 3.04 percent and pushed aggregate labor productivity growth down to 5.57 percent, a reduction of roughly one-sixth.

The Role of Capital Accumulation and Increases in the Rate of Fixed Investment
As a result of the reallocation of labor from agriculture to nonagriculture and general increases in total employment, employment in the nonagricultural sector grew rapidly. Although the investment rate has generally moved upward, the increased rate of capital accumulation did not catch up with the rapid employment growth in the nonagricultural sector until the last ten years or so. Before 1995, the capital–labor ratio in the nonfarm sector actually remained below its 1978 level, as nonfarm employment grew faster than the corresponding capital stock. So, capital accumulation played a relatively minor role in the first sixteen years. In the last decade, however, the rate of investment increased dramatically, which led to a doubling in the capital–labor ratio in the nonagricultural sector.

To quantify the impact of this increase in the capital–labor ratio arising from an increase of the rate of investment, we conduct a counterfactual experiment that assumes that investment remained at 23 percent of GDP throughout the twenty-six–year period. For the first fifteen years, the growth rate in labor productivity would have been lowered slightly, falling from 5.97 to 5.21 percent. In the last ten years, however, the growth rate would have been reduced significantly from 7.84 to 6.18 percent.

The Reallocation of Labor from Agriculture to Nonagriculture
As we have seen, three factors influenced the reallocation of labor from agriculture: TFP growth in agriculture, a reduction in labor market barriers and distortions,

and increases in investment. In addition to promoting labor reallocation, each of these factors also has a direct effect on growth. To isolate the pure impact of labor reallocation from agriculture to nonagriculture, we design a counterfactual exercise with the following characteristics: we retain the historical measures of investment rates and of TFP in all sectors. We also retain historic measures of two components of the barriers to labor mobility: the intersector wage differentials and the division of nonfarm employment between state and nonstate enterprises. Recognizing that higher wages in the nonagricultural sector will limit the demand for labor, we raise these wages to a level that pushes the absorption of village migrants into nonagricultural employment to zero. This arrangement simulates the consequences of eliminating the reallocation of labor between agriculture and nonagriculture. Note that this component of the barrier affects growth only through its impact on labor reallocation and has no other direct effect. So the reduction in growth that results can be viewed as the contribution of labor reallocation between agriculture and nonagriculture.

In this counterfactual exercise, the growth rate of agricultural labor productivity falls to 5.27 percent compared to 6.76 percent, leaving agriculture to absorb more labor under conditions of sharply diminishing returns (i.e., adding more workers to the farm sector depresses labor productivity). The absence of labor inflows from the farm sector would actually increase the growth rate of labor productivity in the nonagricultural sector from 4.54 to 6.19 percent. There is a third effect related to the elimination of labor reallocation: economywide average labor productivity is now lower because a larger percentage of employment is allocated to the sector with lower productivity.

Taking these three effects into account, eliminating the transfer of labor across sectors would reduce the annual growth rate of aggregate labor productivity from 6.96 to 5.94 percent, a modest reduction of 1.02 percentage points per year. So, this experiment with our dynamic model shows that the reallocation of labor from agriculture to nonagriculture had three impacts on growth: higher labor productivity growth in agriculture, lower labor productivity growth in nonagriculture, and more efficient labor allocation across sectors. Overall, they translate into an increase of 1.02 percentage points in the growth rate of aggregate labor productivity.

The contribution of labor reallocation to growth obtained from counterfactual simulations based on our dynamic three-sector model is significantly less than the estimate from the "naïve" simple decomposition we carried out earlier. The difference points to the shortcomings of the simple decomposition approach and the need to consider both the role of TFP growth and the general equilibrium effects. The difference is even larger for the first ten years of the reform, when nearly half of the transfer occurred. Our counterfactual simulations suggest that contribution of labor reallocation to overall labor productivity growth is 1.63 percentage points, while the simple decomposition implies a contribution that is two times as large, 3.36 percentage points.

The Reallocation of Labor from the State to the Nonstate Sector

To quantify the contribution of the second structural transformation, that is, the reallocation of labor from the state to the nonstate sector, we do a counterfactual simulation that is identical to the one we described earlier, but with one difference: we let the state sector's share of nonagricultural employment to remain at its 1978 level. Thus, in this simulation, employment in all three sectors grows at the same rate and there is no labor reallocation across sectors. In other words, this is a counterfactual simulation under the assumption that there is no structural transformation. Under this scenario, growth of aggregate labor productivity falls to 4.72 percent a year, or 2.24 percentage points lower than the 6.96 percent growth rate observed in the data. Recall that the first structural transformation, namely, the reallocation of labor from agriculture to nonagriculture, contributed 1.02 percentage points to growth. Thus, this counterfactual simulation implies that the contribution of the second structural transformation is 1.22 percentage points (2.24 − 1.02). Combined, the two structural transformations are responsible for close to one-third of overall growth (2.24 out 6.96).

Reduction in Barriers to Intersectoral Resource Mobility

Systematic barriers to the intersectoral movement of labor and capital constitute an important aspect of China's economic structure during the reform era. There are three components of barriers that we can measure either explicitly or implicitly: the wedge in wages between the agricultural and the nonstate sectors, the state sector's wage premium, and the state sector's share of nonagricultural employment. We examine the impact of each of these three components separately later.

The Wedge between Agricultural and Nonstate Nonagricultural Wages. This component of the barriers affects growth through labor reallocation between the agricultural and the nonstate sector. Much of this reallocation is associated with the growth of TVEs and nonagricultural sidelines in the countryside. If the gap in wages had remained at the same level as in 1978, agriculture's share of total employment would have fallen by 30 percentage points (from 69 to 39 percent) rather than 38 percentage points. The growth impact of this reduction in labor reallocation, however, is fairly small: with the wage gap held constant at the 1978 level, labor productivity growth in the agricultural and nonagricultural sectors would be 6.38 percent and 4.44 percent, respectively, during 1978–2004. The aggregate labor productivity growth rate would be 6.44 percent, only one-half percent lower than the actual growth rate.

The Reduction in the State Sector's Wage Premium. Within the nonfarm sector, state-sector workers receive higher wages than workers outside the state sector; as shown earlier in Figure 17.4, this premium declined. Without this reduction in the wage premium paid to state-sector workers, more capital would have been needed to support the state sector, implying even less capital for the nonstate sector. However, the quantitative effect is not large. A counterfactual experiment in which the wage premium paid to state-sector workers remains fixed at the 1978 level throughout the entire period of analysis would reduce the rate of labor productivity growth in nonagriculture from 4.54 to 4.03 percent and the aggregate labor productivity growth rate from 6.96 to 6.37 percent.

The Reduction in the State Sector's Share of Nonagricultural Employment. Because of the low TFP levels in the state sector, maintaining a large share of employment in the sector becomes very costly. The state sector requires a large injection of capital into its inefficient operations to raise the marginal productivity of labor sufficiently to support the high wages paid to state-sector workers. The higher the state sector's employment share, the more capital it absorbs and the less capital is available for the much more efficient nonstate sector. As a result, raising the share of state-sector employment reduces the growth of the nonagricultural sector. Furthermore, slower growth in the nonagricultural sector would also decrease the growth of aggregate income, thereby reducing the future rate of capital accumulation and economywide growth. Quantitatively, the reduction in the state sector's share of nonagricultural employment is significant. If the share had remained constant, the overall growth rate would have fallen from 6.96 to 5.42 percent.

REGIONAL VARIATIONS

Between 1978 and 2004, we observe significant differences across provinces in the growth rates of labor productivity. Our analysis in the section "Growth Accounting" highlights the important role at the national level played by the relaxation of barriers that allowed labor and other resources to move more freely from the state to the nonstate sector. In this environment of gradual reduction in mobility barriers, differences in the size of the state sector exert direct and indirect effects on the trajectory of provincial economies. In the following discussion, we use detailed time-series data on ten provinces to demonstrate the important contribution of these differences to the heterogeneity of province-level economic performance since 1978.

In Figure 17.8, we graph the relationship between the size of the state sector at the beginning of the reform and the rate of growth of provincial aggregate labor productivity between 1978 and 2004. The size of the state sector here is captured by its share of nonagricultural employment. For consistency reasons, we limit ourselves to the ten provinces for which we have alternative data on the size of the labor force in agriculture (see the section "Some Basic Facts"). The provinces are highly representative geographically. The mean rate of growth of provincial aggregate labor productivity over the twenty-six–year period was 6.86 percent, but the difference in the rate of growth between the fastest and slowest growing provinces was on the order of 2:1. We observe a similar spread with respect to the

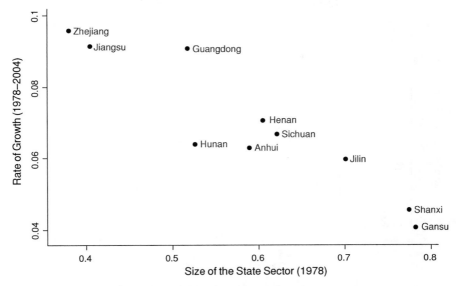

Figure 17.8. Growth of labor productivity versus size of the state sector

size of the state sector in 1978. The relationship between the rate of growth and the initial size of the state sector is clearly negative.

In our modeling and empirical work, the size of the state sector affects growth directly through its influence on credit allocation. Because of the lower rate of growth of TFP in the state sector, higher rates of capital accumulation are required to maintain a commitment to jobs and higher wages in the sector. Since the late 1970s, China's financial institutions have been the primary conduit through which needed funds reach the state sector. Applying the same logic across provinces, and assuming persistence in the size of the state sector (which the data justify), we expect the initial size of the state sector to be positively associated with the severity of the distortions in credit allocation and fixed investment over the entire period.

Figure 17.9, which shows the relationship between the size of the state sector in 1978 and the share of fixed investment going to the state sector between 1978 and 1994, is highly suggestive: the relationship is clearly positive. Over this sixteen-year period, provinces that began the reforms with larger state sectors directed a much higher percentage of fixed investment to the state sector than provinces that began with smaller state sectors. The simple ordinary least squares regression shows that a 10 percentage point increase in the initial share of the state sector is associated with a nearly equal (9.3 percentage point) increase in the share of fixed capital going to the sector over this sixteen-year period. The same relationship holds true over the entire period 1978–2004, although in 2004 the link between the state sector's initial size and the subsequent investment share is weaker (see Figure 17.10).

Distortions in credit allocation provide a direct link between the size of the state sector and the growth in the nonagricultural sector (see Figure 17.11). In all

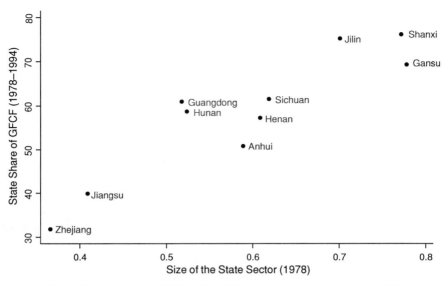

Figure 17.9. State share GFCF, 1978–1994 vs. size of the state sector in 1978

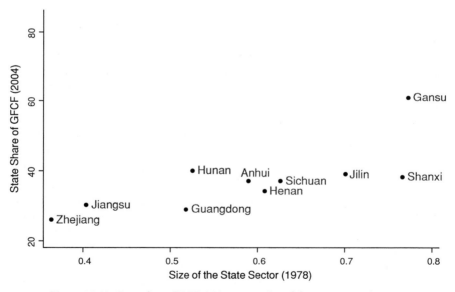

Figure 17.10. State share GFCF, 2004 versus size of the state sector in 2004

likelihood, the effect of the state sector was much more pervasive and operated through more channels than those specified in our modeling. For example, our 1997 interviews with local officials in Jilin and Jiangsu confirm the expectation that provinces with larger state sectors may have acted to protect state-sector interests, by emphasizing restrictive policies that limited nonstate firms in areas such as rights

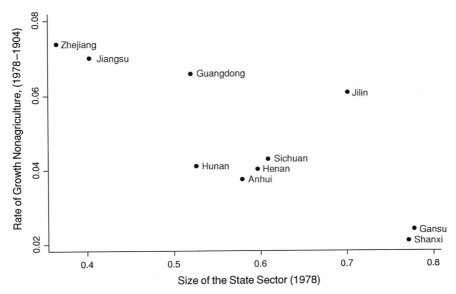

Figure 17.11. Nonagricultural growth versus size of state sector

of entry and access to land, raw materials, and intermediate goods. Such behavior could have reduced TFP growth in the nonstate sector, thus reinforcing the negative relationship between the size of the state sector and the growth in aggregate labor productivity. Weaker competition from local nonstate firms or higher barriers on goods from other provinces may have similarly reduced TFP in state firms.

Efforts to protect the state sector appear to have limited inflows of foreign investment. Working with provincial data, both Branstetter and Feenstra (2002) and Amiti and Jovorcik (2005) find a negative correlation between the level of foreign direct investment and the size of the state sector, which they attribute to local protectionist policies in support of state firms.

The same provincial data confirm our expectation that provinces with relatively large state sectors at the start of reform are likely to experience relatively slow growth of labor productivity in agriculture as well as relatively slow reallocation of labor between agriculture and nonagriculture. Higher initial barriers to mobility in provinces with larger state sectors would clearly slow the pace of labor transfer. Although we lack detailed information on the intensity of migration restrictions in different areas during the late 1970s, we do know that later in the reform process, municipalities and provinces with large state sectors (e.g., Beijing, Liaoning, and Jilin) imposed tighter restrictions on urban opportunities for migrant labor than other regions. Figures 17.12 and 17.13 graph the relationship between the initial size of the state sector and the rate of growth of labor productivity in agriculture (Figure 17.12) and the speed of transfer of labor out of agriculture (Figure 17.13). Both relationships are strongly negative, which helps to identify the

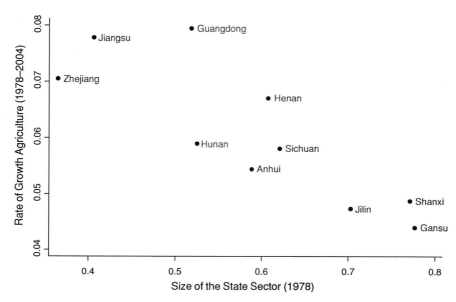

Figure 17.12. Agricultural growth versus size of state sector

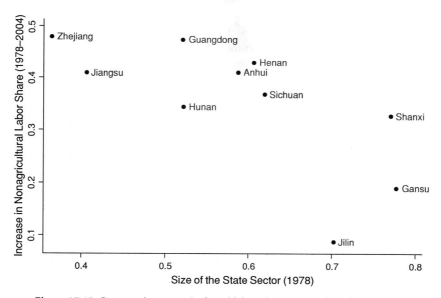

Figure 17.13. Increase in nonagricultural labor share versus size of state sector

state sector as a drag on growth through its influence on local political economy and policymaking.

China may have succeeded in "growing out of the plan" by the end of 1980s (Naughton, 1995), but the process of growing out of the state sector has proved much harder. Even as its share of output and employment declines, the legacy of the state sector survives through the continuation of its preferential access to credit flows. The failure of China's reform to resize the state sector's investment share has delayed the process of institutional reform, retarded investment efficiency and structural change, and lowered the growth of output, employment, and productivity in the nonstate sector and in the economy as a whole. More generally, the size of the state sector mattered for the entire trajectory of economic and institutional reform at the provincial level.

Discussions of regional development often emphasize the "natural" advantages that the coastal provinces enjoyed during China's economic reform. Without denying these circumstances, we would emphasize that the coastal provinces also benefited from the limited expansion of state-sector activity prior to 1978. Guangdong, Fujian, Shandong, and Zhejiang ranked eleventh, fourteenth, seventeenth, and twenty-third in terms of per capita GDP in 1978. Jiangsu ranked a much more respectable sixth. In 2004, these five provinces were ranked fourth to eighth, behind only the three provincial-level municipalities of Shanghai, Beijing, and Tianjin in GDP per capita.

Whereas the weak pre-reform development of the state sector seems to have accelerated reform-era progress in China's coastal regions, the huge levels of investment related to the development of the Third Front in the 1960s and 1970s strengthened the state sector in interior provinces, which influenced, in turn, resource allocation, policy, and growth since 1978. Unfortunately, recent central government initiatives to develop the same western region under the slogan *Xibu dakaifa* may be doing the same through funneling massive investments through the same state institutions.

CONCLUSION

The last three decades, GDP per worker in China has grown at about 7 percent a year. A number of alternative approaches have been taken to explain this achievement, for example, provincial growth regressions that follow in the tradition of cross-country investigations. While studies along these lines, for example, Jian, Sachs, and Warner (1996) and Tao and Zou (1998), are helpful in identifying the factors that are significantly correlated with growth, they are not able to provide quantitative measures of the importance of the contributing factors.

An alternative and complementary method to growth regression is growth accounting, which quantitatively decomposes the overall growth into various sources. A standard growth accounting decomposes the aggregate GDP growth into three sources: capital accumulation, employment growth, and TFP growth. One limitation of this method is that many potential sources of growth are lumped into TFP growth, which then becomes a black box. This includes both intra- and intersectoral improvements in resource allocation, as well as other sources of productivity growth within individual sectors.

In this chapter, we try to go one step deeper than the standard growth accounting by examining the impact of within-sector productivity growth and cross-sector allocations on the overall growth. Admittedly, we are not the first to try to examine the sectoral contributions to overall growth. OECD (2005) and Bosworth and Collins (2007), for example, have also attempted to quantify the contributions of sectoral growth and reallocation across sectors to overall growth. However, these studies use a simple decomposition method that does not take into account the interactions between sectoral productivity growth and reallocations. Our analysis in this chapter goes beyond the simple decomposition by using a three-sector structural model that explicitly takes into account the interactions. Using the three-sector structural model to do growth accounting, we are able to identify and quantify some important sectoral factors that are crucial to China's growth, which we summarize as follows:

1. During the last three decades, China's nonstate nonagricultural sector has been the key driver of economic growth. Underlying this important contribution has been the rapid TFP growth in the sector. Looking at the nonagricultural sector as a whole tends to conceal this important source of growth.
2. At the beginning of the reforms, China's economy suffered under the weight of huge sectoral distortions and barriers that prevented the flow of resources into this emerging dynamic sector. China's reforms have been extremely important in reducing these barriers and thus allowing resources to flow into the sector that experienced the highest TFP growth.
3. Barriers to labor mobility both from agriculture to nonagriculture and from state to nonstate sectors have declined. While the reduction in both types of barriers has contributed to overall growth, it is the reduction of barriers to labor mobility from state to nonstate that has been a more important source of growth.
4. Despite reductions, barriers persist in credit and labor markets, especially in the credit market. Substantial potential gains remain from reducing credit market distortions.

In future work, we intend to build on this framework. Human capital accumulation, for example, needs to be explicitly included in the analysis. The analysis carried out at the national level can also be extended more rigorously to the provincial level. Finally, our analysis highlights the returns to future research into the sources of TFP growth within both agriculture and the nonstate nonagricultural sectors. Moreover, our findings regarding the importance of intersectoral reallocation to aggregate productivity suggest that intrasectoral reallocation may be important to sectoral TFP as well.

References

Amiti, Mary and Beata Smarzynska Javorcik. 2005. "Trade Costs and Location of Foreign Firms in China." World Bank Policy Research Working Paper 3564. Washington, DC: World Bank.

Bannister, Judith. 2005. "Manufacturing Earnings and Compensation in China." *Monthly Labor Review*. 128, pp. 22–40.

Bosworth, Barry and Susan M. Collins. 2007. "Accounting for Growth: Comparing China and India." NBER Working Paper 12943. Cambridge MA: National Bureau of Economic Research.

Brandt, Loren and Hongbin Li. 2003. "Bank Discrimination in China: Ideology, Information or Incentives." *Journal of Comparative Economics*. 31(3), pp. 387–413.

Brandt, Loren and Xiaodong Zhu. 2000. "Redistribution in a Decentralizing Economy: Growth and Inflation in China under Reform." *Journal of Political Economy*. 108(2), pp. 422–439.

Brandt, Loren and Xiaodong Zhu. 2007. "China's Banking Sector and Economic Growth," in *Chinese Financial Transitions at a Crossroads*. Charles Calomiris, ed. New York: Columbia University Press, pp. 86–136.

Branstetter, Lee G. and Robert C. Feenstra. 2002. "Trade and Foreign Investment in China: A Political Economy Approach." *Journal of International Economics*. 58(2), pp. 335–358.

Byrd, William and Alan Gelb. 1990. "Township, Village and Private Industry in China's Economic Reform." World Bank Policy Research and External Affairs Working Paper 406. Washington, DC: World Bank.

Caselli, Francesco and John Coleman. 2001. "The US Structural Transformation and Regional Convergence: A Reinterpretation." *Journal of Political Economy*. 109(3), pp. 584–616.

Chan, Kam Wing. Forthcoming. "Internal Migration and Rural Migrant Labor: Trends, Geography and Policies," in *The Labor of Reform in China*. Mary Gallagher, Ching Kwan Lee, and Albert Park, eds. New York: Routledge.

Chen Xikang, 1992. *Zhongguo chengxiang jingji touru zhanyong chanchu fenxi* [Input-output analysis for China's urban and rural economy]. Bejing: Science Publishing.

Chen, Chunlai, Christopher Findlay, Andrew Watson and Xiaohe Xhang. 1994 "Rural Enterprise Growth in a Partially Reformed Chinese Economy," in *Rural Enterprises in China*. New York: St. Martin's Press.

de Brauw, Alan, Jikun Huang, Scott Rozelle, Linxiu Zhang, and Yigang Zhang. 2002. "The Evolution of China's Rural Labor Market during Reforms." *Journal of Comparative Economics*. 30(2), pp. 329–353.

Duarte, Magarida and Diego Restuccia. 2006. "The Role of Structural Transformation in Aggregate Productivity." University of Toronto Working Paper. Ontario, Canada: University of Toronto.

Gollin, Douglas, Stephen Parente, and Richard Rogerson. 2003. "Structural Transformation and Cross-Country Income Differences." University of Illinois Working Paper. Chicago, IL: University of Illinois.

Groves, Theodore, Yongmiao Hong, John McMillan, and Barry Naughton. 1994. "Autonomy and Incentives in Chinese State Enterprises." *Quarterly Journal of Economics*. 109, pp. 183–209.

Hansen, Gary and Edward Prescott. 2002. "Malthus to Solow." *American Economic Review*. 92(4), pp. 1205–1217.

Hayashi, Fumio and Edward Prescott. 2006. "The Depressing Effect of Agricultural Institutions on the Prewar Japanese Economy." Arizona State University Working Paper. Tempe, AZ: Arizona State University.

Holz, Carsten. 2006. "Measuring Chinese Productivity Growth, 1952–2005." Mimeo. Hong Kong: Hong Kong University of Science and Technology.

Jefferson, Gary H. and Thomas G. Rawski. 1994. "Enterprise Reform in Chinese Industry." *Journal of Economic Perspectives*. 8(2), pp. 47–70.

Jian, Tianlun, Jeffrey D. Sachs, and Andrew M. Warner. 1996. "Trends in Regional Inequality in China." *China Economic Review*. 7(1), pp. 1–21.

Kongsamut, Piyabha, Sergio Rebelo, and Danyang Xie. 2001. "Beyond Balanced Growth." *Review of Economic Studies*. 68, pp. 869–882.

Lardy, Nicholas. 1983. *Agriculture in China's Modern Economic Development*. Cambridge and New York: Cambridge University Press.

Lardy, Nicholas. 1998. *China's Unfinished Economic Revolution*. Washington, DC: Brookings Institution.

Lin, Justin. 1992. "Rural Reforms and Agricultural Growth in China." *American Economic Review*. 82(1), pp. 34–51.

McMillan, John, John Whalley, and Lijing Zhu. 1989. "The Impact of China's Economic Reforms on Agricultural Productivity Growth." *Journal of Political Economy*. 94(4), pp. 781–807.

Naughton, Barry. 1992. "Implications of the State Monopoly over Industry and Its Relaxation." *Modern China*. 18(1), pp. 14–41.

Naughton, Barry. 1995. *Growing Out of the Plan: Chinese Economic Reform 1978–1993*. Cambridge and New York: Cambridge University Press.

Ngai, Rachel L. and Christopher Pissaridis. 2007. "Structural Change in a Multi-Sector Model of Growth." *American Economic Review*. 97(1), pp. 429–443.

OECD [Organisation for Economic Co-operation and Development]. 2005. *Economic Surveys: China*. Paris: OECD.

Piazza, Alan. 1983. "Trends in Food and Nutrient Availability in China, 1950–1981." World Bank Staff Working Papers 607. Washington, DC: World Bank.

Rawski, Thomas G. 1982. "The Simple Arithmetic of Chinese Income Distribution." *Keizai Kenkyu*. 33(1), pp. 12–26.

Rawski, Thomas G. 2002. "Poverty Alleviation in Rural China: Scale and Significance." Incomplete draft.

Rawski, Thomas G. and Robert W. Mead. 1998. "In Search of China's Phantom Farmers." *World Development*. 26.5, pp. 767–781.

Restuccia, Diego, Dennis Tao Yang, and Xiaodong Zhu. Forthcoming. "Agriculture and Aggregate Productivity: A Quantitative Cross-Country Analysis." *Journal of Monetary Economics*.

Riskin, Carl. 1987. *China's Political Economy: The Quest for Economic Development Since 1949*. New York: Oxford University Press.

Tao, Zhang and Hengfu Zou. 1998. "Fiscal Decentralization, Public Spending and Economic Growth in China." *Journal of Public Economics*, 67. pp. 221–240.

Wong, Christine. January 1988. "Interpreting Rural Industrial Growth in the Post-Mao Period." *Modern China*. 14(1), pp. 3–30.

Yang, Dennis Tao and Xiaodong Zhu. 2004. "Modernization of Agriculture and Long-Term Growth." University of Toronto Working Paper. Ontario, Canada: University of Toronto.

Young, Alwyn. 2003. "From Gold to Base Metals: Productivity Growth in the People's Republic of China during the Reform Era." *Journal of Political Economy*. 111(6), pp. 1120–1161.

APPENDIX A: ESTIMATING TFP FOR THE THREE SECTORS

We assume Cobb–Douglas production technologies in all three sectors (agricultural, nonstate nonagricultural, and state sectors). Under this assumption, the TFP in sector i (i = a – agriculture, ns – nonstate nonagriculture, and s – state) can be calculated using the following formula:

$$\text{TFP}_i = \frac{Y_i}{L_i^{\alpha} K_i^{\beta_i}}.$$

Here, Y_i is sector i's GDP, L_i employment, and K_i capital stock, respectively. α and β are labor and capital shares in sector i.

The NBS data report GDPs for the agricultural and nonagricultural sectors, but do not provide a separate breakdown of nonagricultural GDP into the state and nonstate sectors. To generate GDPs for the state and nonstate sectors, we use information on relative wages between the two sectors. Let y_n be the aggregate output per worker in the nonagricultural sector, and y_{ns} and y_s be the output per worker in the nonstate and state sectors, respectively. Then, we have

$$y_n = y_{ns}(1 - \varphi_s) + y_s \varphi_s = y_{ns}[1 - \varphi_s + (y_s/y_{ns})\varphi_s].$$

Here φ_s is the state sector's share of nonagricultural employment. Under the assumption that both sectors use Cobb–Douglas technology with the same factor shares, the ratio of wages in the two sectors equals the ratio of average labor productivities in the two sectors; that is, $y_s/y_{ns} = w_s/w_{ns}$. So, given data on the aggregate labor productivities in the nonagricultural sector, the relative wages between the state and the nonstate sectors and the state sector's shares of nonagricultural employment, we can use the equation given earlier to back out the average labor productivities in the nonstate sector. The state sector's average labor productivities can then be calculated by multiplying the relative wages to the average productivities in the nonstate sector. Finally, GDPs in the state and nonstate sectors are obtained by simply multiplying average labor productivities by employment in the respective sectors.

On the basis of the national income accounts for China and the national input–output tables constructed by the NBS, the labor share in nonagriculture has remained roughly 0.5. These accounts put the labor share α for the entire economy at 0.58–0.60, which implies a share for agriculture of nearly 0.7. Moreover, the falling contribution of agriculture in GDP since 1978 means that the share of labor in agriculture has been rising over time. The high and rising share of labor in agriculture is inconsistent with estimates made on the basis of household data, which suggest a labor share in the vicinity of 0.50. For both sectors, then, we assume that the labor share has been roughly constant, around 0.50. Under the assumption of constant returns to scale, the capital share β is simply one minus the labor share, or 0.5 percent.

In agricultural production, land is a major component of the capital stock. We treat the land as a fixed factor and estimate the value of land as the present discounted value of current and future rental incomes from land.

Note that when we calculate TFPs we do not control for the levels of human capital. Thus, the TFP differences over time and across sectors may also reflect differences in human capital.

APPENDIX B: FULL MODEL

For our quantitative exercises, we consider a three-sector model: agriculture, non-state nonagriculture, and state nonagriculture.

> *Technology.* We assume that all three sectors employ Cobb–Douglas production technologies. Land, physical capital, and labor are the three production inputs. For simplicity, we assume that land is used only in agriculture and physical capital is used only in nonagriculture. We keep the labor share at 0.5 in all sectors. Enterprise-level data suggest that the parameter values in the nonstate and state sectors are the same. For agriculture, since we abstract from physical capital here, the land share in the model is 0.5.
>
> *Preferences.* The household's demand for agricultural and nonagricultural goods is given by a simple Stone–Geary utility function:

$$U(c_{at}, c_{nt}) = a \log(c_{at} - \bar{a}) + (1 - a)\log(c_{nt}).$$

> Here c_{it} is household's consumption of good i ($i = a, n$), $\bar{a}$ is the subsistence demand for the agricultural good, and a is the weight on the agricultural good. Without the subsistence demand $\bar{a}$, households would allocate their expenditures to the two consumption goods according to the preference weights, a and $1 - a$. For $\bar{a} > 0$, however, the agriculture good's expenditure share is greater than a and declines with income.
>
> *Frictions in labor market.* Let w_{it} be the wage in sector i. We assume that

$$w_{at} = (1 - \mu_t)w_{nst},$$
$$w_{st} = (1 + \xi_t)w_{nst}.$$

> Here, μ_t is a wedge between wages in the agricultural sector and the nonstate nonagricultural sector. The existence of this wedge may be due to barriers to labor mobility between the two sectors. ξ_t is the wage premium that the state sector enjoys over the nonstate sector. Let $\varphi_{st} = L_{st}/L_{nt}$ be the state sector's share of nonagricultural employment, which we assume is an exogenous variable that is set by the government.

The average wage in the nonagricultural sector is given by

$$w_{nt} = w_{st}\varphi_{st} + w_{nt}(1 - \varphi_{st}) = (1 + \xi_t\varphi_t)w_{nst}.$$

Using the fact that $w_{at} = (1 - \mu_t)w_{nst}$, we have

$$w_{at} = \frac{1 - \mu_t}{1 + \xi_t\varphi_t}w_{nt},$$

or

$$w_{at} = (1 - \theta_t)w_{nt},$$

where

$$\theta_t = \frac{1 - \mu_t}{1 + \xi_t\varphi_t}.$$

θ_t is a measure of the barriers to labor mobility between agriculture and nonagriculture and is made up of three components: (1) the labor mobility barrier between agriculture and nonstate nonagriculture, μ_t; (2) the state sector's wage premium over the nonstate sector, ξ_t; and (3) the state sector's share of nonagricultural employment, φ_{st}.

We have direct measures of θ_t and φ_t in the data, but no direct measures of μ_t. However, the values of μ_t can be inferred from the last equation. Figure 17.4 shows the evolution of θ_t, μ_t, ξ_t, and φ_t.

Model Implied Employment Share in Agriculture

Given TFP and barriers, in equilibrium agriculture's share of employment is given by the solution to the following equation:

$$l_{at} = \frac{(1 - a)(1 - \theta_t)}{1 - \theta_t + a(1 - i_t)\theta_t} \frac{\bar{c}}{\tilde{A}_{at}} l_{at}^{1-a} + \frac{a(1 - i_t)}{1 - \theta_t + a(1 - i_t)\theta_t}.$$

Here i_t is the investment rate (fixed investment–output ratio) in the economy and

$$\tilde{A}_{at} = A_{at}(Z/L_t)^{1-\alpha}.$$

A_{at} is the TFP in agriculture, Z is the total amount of land, and L_t is total employment in the economy.

The predicted share of the labor force in agriculture is independent of the relative prices. It is a function of productivity in agriculture $\tilde{A}_{at}$, the wedge in wages between the two sectors θ_t, and the investment rate i_t.

Figure 17.3 shows the rise of agricultural TFP. The change in the barriers to labor reallocation is captured by Figure 17.4. The barriers declined sharply in the early years, but reversed trend and increased in the later years. One explanation is that the early decline is mainly a result of the relaxation of restrictions on rural households from engaging in nonagricultural activities; during that period, most of the reallocation is rural to rural (from farm to TVEs) and *within* townships and

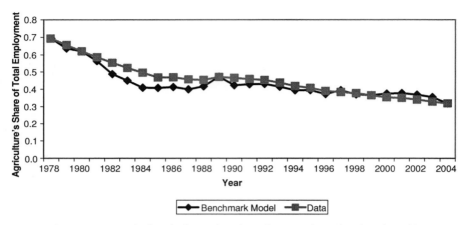

Figure 17B.1. Agriculture's share of total employment (actual vs. benchmark)

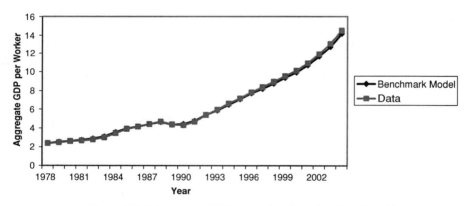

Figure 17B.2. Aggregate GDP per worker (actual vs. benchmark)

counties. In the later years, rural–urban migration becomes a more important way of reallocation and restrictions on migration become binding constraints. Human capital may also figure in.

Accumulation and Allocation of Capital

We take the fixed investment rate as exogenous. The allocation of capital between the state and the nonstate sector is determined by the employment share and wage premium of the state sector. Given the TFP differences between the state and the nonstate sectors, the larger the employment share and the higher the wage premium, the larger the portion of total capital that will be allocated to the state sector.

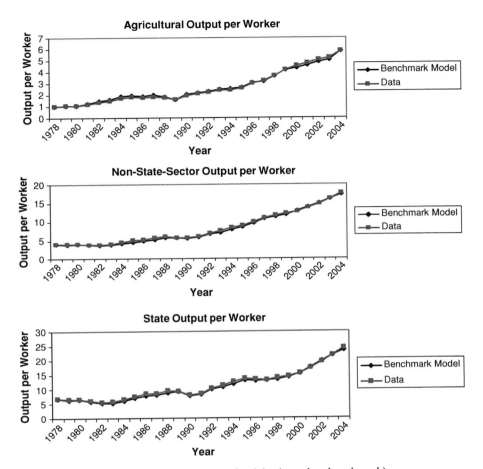

Figure 17B.3. Labor productivity (actual vs. benchmark)

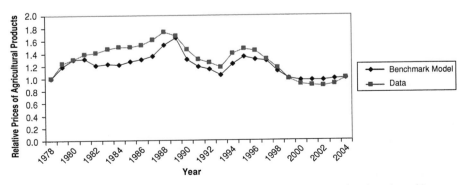

Figure 17B.4. Relative prices of agricultural products (actual vs. benchmark)

Calibration

For our quantitative exercises, we need to choose the values for the parameters in the model. As explained in Appendix A, for production technologies, we let the labor share be 0.5 in all three sectors. There are two parameters in the utility function: the weight on the agricultural good, a, and the subsistence consumption of agricultural good, $\bar{a}$. Both of these parameters have a direct influence on labor allocation between agriculture and nonagriculture. Parameter a determines the agricultural good's expenditure share in the long run and therefore influences the long-run employment share of agriculture. The parameter $\bar{a}$ determines how much labor is needed in agriculture in the short run to satisfy the subsistence food constraint. We choose the values of these two parameters so that the model's predicted share for agricultural employment in 1978 and 2004 match the data exactly. The weight a is equal to 0.235, and $\bar{a}$ is equal to 0.42, which implies that minimum consumption was equal to 42 percent of output per worker in agriculture. Alternatively, each worker in agriculture was producing food to support roughly two and a half individuals.

Given the calibrated parameters and the variables that we take as exogenous, that is, TFPs in the three sectors, the gap in wages between the three sectors, the investment rate, and the relative price of capital, we can calculate the model-implied values for the following variables:

- employment shares of agriculture,
- labor productivities in the three sectors, nonagriculture, and the aggregate, and
- relative price of agriculture to nonagriculture.

In Figures 17B.1 through Figure 17B.4 we compare the model-implied values for agriculture's share of employment, aggregate labor productivity, sector-level labor productivity, and relative prices with the actual data. In general, the model-implied values match the data reasonably well. Thus, the model can be used as a basis for our counterfactual quantitative exercises.

EIGHTEEN

Income Inequality during China's Economic Transition

Dwayne Benjamin, Loren Brandt, John Giles, and Sangui Wang

INTRODUCTION

The primary motivation for China's economic reforms was to increase economic growth and raise living standards after nearly twenty years of stagnation. Given the move to more market-based income determination, the reforms had the potential to conflict with inherited egalitarian-motivated socialist institutions and rhetoric. To what extent have the reforms led to widening inequality? Who have been the winners and losers? Have the reductions in poverty that accompanied growth been sufficient to alleviate concerns over inequality? Do increases in inequality threaten the long-run sustainability of the reforms? Are there identifiable patterns in the evolution of the income distribution that suggest potential policy responses?

The objective of this chapter is to document the evolution of inequality, and the income distribution more generally, during the reform period and where possible to draw conclusions concerning the role that transition has played in increasing inequality. The centerpiece of our chapter is the assembly of three cross-section data sets that allow a relatively consistent calculation of inequality from the mid-1980s onward. It turns out that establishing "first-order" facts about Chinese inequality is quite difficult and that conclusions hinge on mundane (but important) issues of measurement and data quality. In this regard, it is unfortunate that much of the household-level survey data collected annually by China's National Bureau of Statistics (NBS) remains outside the public domain.

Several of our conclusions line up with the existing literature on inequality in China. Overall inequality has unambiguously risen in China, ever since 1987, the first year for which we have data and several years after the reforms began. This increase in inequality is common to both urban and rural China, though as far as we can tell, the increase is higher in urban China. Most of our evidence also suggests that the "official" estimates of inequality are probably too low, with the true Gini probably in the 0.40–0.50 range for both urban and rural areas. The overall (combined urban–rural) Gini probably exceeds 0.50, which is comparable to levels observed in South America.

In urban China, absolute living standards have risen so much that even with rising inequality, "poverty" (or more accurately, "low income"), measured by any plausible benchmark, has virtually disappeared. In rural China, significant gains in income growth during the late 1970s and early 1980s resulting from the introduction of the household responsibility system (HRS) pulled tens of millions out of poverty. Further reductions occurred through the early to mid-1990s, but there was deterioration in the last half of the 1990s, that may have reversed in only the last year or two. There remain reasons for concern, at least as far as our data show: for a significant number of rural households, incomes have remained flat or fallen for a decade or more, and the very poor may be worse off.

In a number of key respects, however, our findings are at odds with some of the conventional wisdom. Overall, geography, as captured by the province or village/city one lives in, plays a much less important role than one might expect: at least half, and perhaps as much as two-thirds, of estimated inequality is driven by income differences between "neighbors" as opposed to income differences based on location (city or village). The role of provincial differences is even smaller.

The same is true for urban–rural differences. Although urban incomes may be on average two-thirds to three quarters higher than rural incomes, these differences are the source of a relatively small proportion of overall inequality in China. More generally, great care must be taken when interpreting "urban–rural" income gaps, especially using official (NBS) data: the accelerating reclassification of rural areas as urban tends to exaggerate rural–urban income differences, as fast-growing rural areas are relabeled as urban. Moreover, significant differences in the cost of living between urban and rural dampen the raw income differentials.

There does, however, appear to be a significant difference in the inequality (and income growth) dynamics between interior and coastal provinces. Inequality increased more rapidly in the interior provinces, a product of a more rapid increase in rural income inequality and a widening urban–rural income differential. As suggested by related research on growth and structural transformation by Brandt, Hsieh, and Zhu (Chapter 17, this volume), some of this can be linked to the more significant legacy of the state sector in the interior provinces and urban bias. In the more dynamic coastal provinces, more rapid job growth in the non-state sector helped reduce urban–rural differentials by fostering more rapid rural income growth and simultaneously helped to limit increases in rural inequality.

Our findings regarding the role of geography and urban–rural differences suggest that we need to focus more attention on the institutions influencing the distribution of endowments, including both human and physical capital, the allocation of factors of production, and factor returns. In the countryside, most of the level and growth of inequality is due to unequal access to nonfarm family business income. In the cities, the decline in subsidies and unequal wage incomes are playing an increasing role in raising inequality. Increasing returns to higher education are very important in explaining growing dispersion of wage earnings. Our results from both urban and rural samples thus underscore the important role likely to be played by education in determining the future evolution of the income distribution, even though the exact channels may be different in cities and the countryside.

Finally, notable by its absence in much of the discussion, is the current role played by a social safety net in providing a floor on incomes, and thus some limit on inequality. In the cities, while they may be in their infancy or underdevelopment, China has yet to develop the array of social policies with the breadth and level of other transition economies. In rural areas the primary safety net has been the egalitarian land allocation mechanism, which effectively guarantees land to all rural households. As it turns out, the income associated with the farm income generated by this land is not enough to buffer households from poverty, at least when crop prices are low. None of this diminishes the otherwise significant contribution that market reforms have made to raise overall living standards.

Our chapter is divided into five sections. In the next section ("Background and Conceptual Issues"), we provide background discussion concerning the measurement of inequality. It is important to draw linkages between the distribution of welfare – which is what we are really interested in – and the summary statistics of the income distribution (like the Gini coefficient). We also briefly outline the factors that we expect would contribute to changing inequality through the reform period. In the section on "Data," we sketch the three data sets that we use. One of the features of research in income inequality in China is the absence of a common publicly available, nationally representative data set. Our study, like most others, uses data sets that are highly informative on trends in income distribution, but the limitations (e.g., coverage) and definitions need close attention. Our main empirical results are presented in sections on "The Mean and Dispersion of Income over Time," "The Role of Geography," and "The Composition of Income." Throughout we provide separate evidence for urban and rural China, beginning with a discussion of the main trends in living standards in the section on "The Mean and Dispersion of Income over Time." "The Role of Geography" focuses on spatial issues: how important are divergent incomes across provinces for driving rising inequality? "The Composition of Income" takes a closer look at the changing structure of income, providing the greatest potential linkage with the factors that may be "causing" the increase in inequality, though attribution of any changes to a particular causal factor is almost impossible, given the scope of change in China over this period.

BACKGROUND AND CONCEPTUAL ISSUES

Summarizing the Income Distribution

How much better off is the Chinese population in the year 2000 compared with 1980, after twenty years of reform? Clearly, the answer will vary along many socioeconomic dimensions. Our objective is to find a few numbers to summarize more than 1 billion potential answers. There are well-developed tools for aggregating the outcomes of a billion people into single indexes that permit comparison of social welfare, or well-being, over time.[1] Social welfare functions provide an abstract way to rank different sets of economic outcomes. Consider a billion people, each of whom has a level of "well-being" represented by his or her utility function, $u_i(c_{it})$, which assigns a level of utility to the consumption of goods and services in period t, c_{it}. A social welfare function could then aggregate, assigning a single value to the resulting distribution of happiness in the population. Ignoring possible differences in utility functions across individuals, social welfare will depend on the underlying distribution of consumption:

$$w_t = W(c_{1t}, c_{2t}, \ldots, c_{Nt}).$$

The evaluation exercise would thus entail collecting data on the distribution of consumption across the N people living in China in 1980, calculating social welfare (w) and then comparing this to social welfare in 2000, based on the distribution of consumption in 2000. The answer would clearly depend on our social welfare function. For example, we might evaluate welfare by the overall size of the pie, in which case social welfare would depend on the sum of consumption across individuals or average consumption. Alternatively, we might care about only the poorest individual, and our welfare measure would depend only on the lowest level of consumption in each year.

While the answer to the "big question" thus depends on the nature of the social welfare function, a major input into evaluating the change in welfare will be the empirical distribution of consumption, or living standards. In principle, the focus of research should thus be a presentation of summary statistics concerning the distribution of consumption. However, we also wish to learn something about how economic reforms and the evolution of institutions are linked to living standards. For this reason, while we report salient statistics concerning consumption, we focus on income instead. Does it matter? In a simple world with no saving or borrowing, consumption would equal income, and choosing between income and consumption would come down to advantages of measurement and survey design.

Since both saving and borrowing are important, using either measure to study inequality has both advantages and drawbacks (see Deaton, 1997, for a detailed discussion). Consumption would probably be the preferred measure, as it is most closely linked to economic well-being and tends to be better measured. However, we are more interested in how the income distribution has evolved, since income ultimately "drives" consumption, and it is the structure of income that we expect to be most directly affected by the economic reforms. In any event, while there are important conceptual issues thus associated with the movement from "welfare" at its most abstract to the distribution of income, for any practical purpose, the

---

[1] See Deaton (1997) for a summary of the various conceptual issues and detailed references, concerning the measurement of social welfare, inequality, and poverty.

distribution of income will be a key input in the determination of the distribution of welfare.

Papers on income distribution in China, including this survey, present a series of summary statistics of the income distribution, usually focusing on means and various indices of inequality. Any inequality index, like the Gini coefficient, entails a significant distillation of potential information to a single number. Setting aside all of the data and sampling issues, it is worth reminding ourselves of the limitations associated with summarizing 1 billion people's economic outcomes by any single number, let alone explaining why that number has changed over time.

At a point in time, every man, woman, and child in China will earn y_{it}, from which they can support their consumption of goods and services. While we care about individual welfare (and income), we will assume that the relevant unit of analysis for economic decision making and welfare determination is the household and that individual welfare is thus a function of household per capita income. We thus wish to summarize the evolution of the distribution of household per capita income, y_{ht}:

$$g_t(y_{1t}, y_{2t}, \ldots, y_{Nt}).$$

While we will show estimates of the entire distribution, g_t, more commonly we (like other researchers) will present only a few salient summary statistics. Mean income, $\bar{y}_{ht}$, provides an estimate of the expected income level for a randomly selected household in year t and allows us to track average living standards. There are several ways to summarize the degree to which improvements in living standards are being shared. One way would be to choose a common benchmark and see how many households had incomes rise above this benchmark. A poverty line could be one such benchmark. We could then compare the probability of being poor in 1980–2000. While useful, such a measure focuses only on the poor, telling us nothing about the nonpoor, whether they be rich or almost poor. If average incomes are rising, and inequality is constant, we would expect poverty to fall. But poverty could easily fall while income inequality is rising, as long as average income levels are rising enough. For this reason we also want to summarize inequality. Our most common measure, reflecting the existing literature, is the Gini coefficient. The Gini depends on the expected absolute difference in incomes between two randomly selected Chinese residents: $|y_{it} - y_{jt}|$, and thus captures one dimension of dispersion of incomes. Understanding the evolution of mean per capita income and the Gini, with an occasional look at poverty, will thus provide most of the first-order statistics necessary to evaluate the distribution of living standards during China's reforms.

Explaining the Rise in Inequality

It should come as no surprise that inequality rose as China moved from an ostensibly egalitarian socialist economy to a more market-oriented one. What is striking is how high inequality has become. Why did this happen? Are there any reasons to believe that the trends will abate? It is almost impossible to provide precise, confident answers to those questions. However, we can identify a variety of factors associated with the rise in inequality, as well as describe many of the institutional changes that may be related. Understanding the distribution of income (or its changes) requires an understanding of the determinants of household income for everyone in the country. While this is a tall order, we can begin with a highly stylized expositional model of income determination at a point in time.

Suppose that a household's income can be written as the sum of income attributed to its various productive characteristics:

$$y_h = \sum_{j=1}^{K} w_{jh} x_{jh},$$

where x_{jh} is a household productive characteristic, like the level of education of the father, the time available to work of the mother, or the amount of land it has. The value, or "price," of this factor is given by w_{jh} and determines how much income is generated by the father's education, the mother's work time, and household's land. These prices depend on a host of other variables, some of which will vary across households and others which may be similar for households in the same village or city.

Between 1980 and 2000, we expect household income to change. It may change along with household endowments of productive factors, for example, because of rising education levels. However, the main changes probably occur in factor prices, or the returns to productive characteristics. Economic reforms were designed to change institutions that determined factor prices, and there is thus a mapping between institutional evolution, factor prices, and the increase in income inequality. We now briefly sketch the most important institutional and economic changes that we expect would lead to rising inequality.

Inequality on the Eve of Reform

The evolution of inequality over the course of China's economic reform cannot be analyzed without some sense of the inequality at the baseline "before" reform. We are however severely constrained in this exercise by data limitations: most data were collected after the reforms were well under way. However, we can sketch a picture of inequality and its likely sources in urban and rural areas separately, and overall. From there we can speculate as to how reforms would lead to a different distribution of income.

Prior to reform, nearly 80 percent of China's population lived in rural areas and was primarily involved in agriculture. Land was collectively farmed, with income supplemented in some periods by income from small private plots.[2] Income from collective farming was allocated at the level of the production team (twenty-five to thirty households) on the basis of both household need and accumulated work points, with the weight between "distribution on the basis of need" and "basis of labor" differing across localities and shifting over time. Overall, differences within localities between households were probably relatively small and largely associated with differences among households in dependency ratios, that is, the ratio of the number of individuals that worked to total household size. A host of services (health, education, and welfare) were also collectively provided, which was probably equalizing. In the language of "prices" and "productive endowments," income (and a household's standard of living) was less sensitive to productivity than would likely be the case after the reforms were started.

But there was no perfect equality in rural China. There were differences across localities and regions reflecting differences in endowments and natural conditions. These differences were also exacerbated by policies of local grain self-sufficiency, which helped limit redistribution across regions. Vermeer (1982) suggests that income differences (of the portion that was collectively distributed) between richest and poorest communes (townships) may have been as high as 6:1. There was also considerable poverty in rural areas, with as many as a quarter or more of the rural population living below, an admittedly low, government-defined poverty line prior to reform (1977 or so). There was a significant geographic component to this poverty as well, with the majority of the poor located in the provinces situated in China's western region, running from Gansu and Ningxia, through Sichuan and to the southwestern provinces of Yunnan and Guizhou.

Incomes in urban areas consisted largely of wage earnings, and a host of subsidies and entitlements that were publicly financed but allocated by work units. Almost everyone worked in state-owned enterprises (SOEs), characterized by a compressed wage distribution, relatively weak material incentives, and low returns to human capital. Differences in the standard of living between households in the same city were further limited by the rationing of many consumer goods, for example, grain and housing, on the basis of need. Regional wage and income differences in the cities were reportedly modest and may have reflected differences in the cost of living; for example, the cost of living was reportedly higher in Shanghai. Like the countryside, some of the largest differences between households were probably related to differences across households in their demographic composition and dependency ratios. Party members, who made up 5 percent or so of the population, may have also been entitled to preferential access to scarce goods and resources.

There was however a sizable urban–rural income gap that was enforced through strict restrictions on migration from the countryside. Through the last half of the 1960s and 1970s, the urban population did not grow much in absolute terms. Factoring in the value of a host of subsidies, Rawski (1982) suggests that on the

---

[2] Very little information exists on differences between or within localities on income earned by households from their private plots.

eve of economic reform, average differences between the city and the countryside were on the order of 5:1 or 6:1, or twice that calculated excluding the subsidies. The gap with respect to rationed commodities was much smaller (Lardy, 1984), and a significant portion of the gap may have taken the form of higher urban savings.

In summary, our impression of inequality before reforms is of relatively low inequality within villages and cities, a stronger regional dimension to inequality in rural areas, and a pronounced urban–rural gap.

Transition versus Development

While we can notionally decompose the change in income distribution to changes in the distribution of productive factors and their rewards, it is also important to recognize that there are two broad, somewhat distinct, sources of these changes: transition and development. As detailed earlier, prior to reform, prices, including wages, and resource allocation were primarily administratively determined. Household income was determined by a set of "local" socialist institutions that mapped a household's endowment, largely consisting of labor or human capital, into income. These same institutions affected the ownership, distribution, and accumulation of other forms of capital by households, such as land or physical capital.

Transition as a process entails moving to market determination of the valuation of productive endowments and incomes. In a perfectly competitive world, incomes would be a simple product of a household's endowments and the market-determined returns to these factors. The introduction of the market affects the returns and rewards to the factors of production, for example, entrepreneurial ability and human capital. It also affects the distribution and accumulation of these same factors, though this process would take longer. Even in a stagnant, stationary world, we would expect a change in factor prices moving from a socialist to market-oriented economy.

Overlaid with transition – and through no coincidence – China experienced economic development at the same time. The process of economic development and growth will also affect the returns to and distribution of factors of production in a way that matters for income distribution. For example, development may alter the relative returns of labor and capital or increase the returns to human capital and other kinds of skills.

This discussion highlights the importance of distinguishing a "transition" effect from a development, or growth effect, at least conceptually.[3] In actuality, it is impossible to separate these effects. However, we can use the distinction as an organizing principle for highlighting the factors we believe have been at play in three primary dimensions. These relate to the urban and rural sectors separately, and finally, to urban–rural income differences.

---

[3] Also see the (slightly) more detailed discussion in Benjamin and Brandt (1999).

Urban Inequality

The evolution of income inequality in Chinese cities would have likely mirrored the experience in Eastern European transition economies. First, liberalization in the labor market – even within the state sector – would have led to greater wage inequality. More successful enterprises could pass profits to workers through bonuses and higher base wages, so that wage inequality would rise across industrial sectors and across firms. Second, food and housing subsidies were slashed in the early 1990s. These important forms of in-kind income were likely very equally distributed, especially compared to the straight wages that (in principle) replaced them. Third, restructuring of SOEs and the end of the "iron rice bowl" in the latter half of the 1990s led to significant layoffs, unemployment, and at least short-term inequality of access to jobs.

On top of these more transition-oriented changes, urban China was considerably affected by the development of a vibrant private industrial and service sector, with wage and employment determination entirely outside the old socialist labor bureaus. As in any globalized developing economy experiencing significant technological change, we might expect dramatic changes in the returns to human capital and skill, which would transmit to higher inequality of earnings and income.

Rural Inequality

The HRS immediately permitted households to retain a greater share of the returns to their own labor and entrepreneurial talent in managing their farms. Liberalization with respect to farm sidelines and the establishment of family run businesses provided another avenue for households to potentially earn more than their neighbors. At the same time, villages retained the ownership of land, which was allocated to households on a fairly egalitarian basis. This limited the extent of local inequality from farm incomes. The establishment of township and village enterprises, and the development of off-farm opportunities more generally, would likely have also provided households a way to earn a living off the farm, potentially generating greater differences in incomes across villages. While it was difficult to move from the country to the city, it was easier to move shorter distances within the countryside. These opportunities for limited migration would also have significantly changed the structure of income for households. It is difficult to predict whether this would increase income inequality, as it would depend on whether these opportunities were available throughout the income distribution.

Alongside the transition from collectivized agriculture, households in rural China also faced increasing integration with the broader Chinese economy, as well as international markets. For farmers, this generated changing terms of trade between agricultural and nonagricultural goods. Over the period of reform, especially in the latter half of the 1990s, agricultural prices declined significantly, lowering the floor provided by crop incomes and potentially leading to a rise of inequality. As in the cities, industrialization and development would also have provided rising returns to human capital and skill, leading to higher income inequality.

To the extent this development was uneven across provinces, it might also lead to widening income gaps across regions.

Urban–Rural Gap

What would we expect to happen to the ratio of urban to rural incomes? From a pure transition perspective, we might expect the gap to narrow. First, the declining support of the state sector and the end of urban food subsidies would potentially reduce the heavy urban bias of government expenditure. However, these changes may have happened too slowly to matter before 2000. Through most of this period there also remained considerable restrictions on migration through the *hukou* system. While these restrictions ended recently, the constraints on mobility would have reduced the convergence of rural–urban incomes. To a limited extent, however, improvements in product and factor market linkages should have served to reduce the urban–rural gap. In the end, the evolution of the rural–urban gap depends on the relative growth rates, or development, of industrial and service sectors. To the extent that such development was concentrated in cities – possibly because of preexisting or continuing advantages of infrastructure, like schools and roads – we would expect average incomes of urban residents to grow faster than those of rural residents. And given that factor mobility remains imperfect, the urban–rural income gap could easily rise through the reform period.

In summary, there are several potential reasons why we would expect the overall level of income inequality in China to increase both within the urban and rural sectors and possibly, between the urban and rural sectors.

DATA

The Data Sources

Access to well-designed, nationally representative household survey, data is essential to measuring changes in the level and distribution of economic welfare. Lacking a comprehensive data source, our analysis draws heavily on three household-level data sets. For the urban areas, we obtained the NBS urban household surveys for a subsample of provinces including Jilin, Henan, Shaanxi, Sichuan, Hubei, Shandong, Shanghai, and Guangdong. This survey has income and consumption measures with relatively comparable definitions for all years. We use the "income" and "consumption" variables defined by the NBS and incorporated into these household microdata. These data are not without serious shortcomings. On the income side, the implicit value of subsidies associated with, for example, food coupons, is missing. These were especially important through the 1980s, but were eliminated in the early 1990s. On the consumption side, the data do not provide an easy way to measure the value of services from consumption durables, notably housing. One other issue worth noting is that the urban data are sampled on the basis of urban household registration. This means that rural-registered migrants living in the cities are not enumerated, a feature that may have significant consequences for interpretation of urban incomes and inequality.

Our primary rural data come from a series of annual household surveys conducted by the Survey Department of the Research Center on the Rural Economy (RCRE) in Beijing. We use household-level surveys covering over 100 villages in nine provinces, including Jilin, Shanxi, Henan, Hunan, Anhui, Jiangsu, Guangdong, Sichuan, and Gansu. The survey spans the period 1986–2002 and includes between 7,000 and 8,000 households per year. The RCRE originally was intended as a longitudinal survey, following the same households over time. While there is a household-level panel dimension to our sample, we observe considerable attrition of households, especially after years when there was no survey. The RCRE was unable to conduct the survey in 1992 and 1994 because of funding difficulties. Households lost through attrition were replaced on the basis of random sampling.

The RCRE survey collected detailed household-level information on incomes and expenditures, education, labor supply, asset ownership, landholdings, savings, formal and informal access to credit, and remittances. That said, the construction of consistent income and consumption measures is quite tricky, especially in calculating self-supplied consumption and the implicit flow of consumption from housing and other durables. Of particular importance for our purposes, especially investigating the role of geographic factors for inequality, we are able to track a panel of villages, even where there has been household attrition. This allows us to maintain geographic comparability over the complete period.

The China Health and Nutrition Study (CHNS) data uniquely allow us to pool urban and rural households. This survey covers the provinces of Liaoning, Heilongjiang, Henan, Hubei, Hunan, Shandong, Jiangsu, Guangxi, and Guizhou for five years: 1989, 1991, 1993, 1997, and 2000. Because of some noncomparability issues with the 1989 survey, we use only the 1991, 1993, 1997, and 2000 data. The CHNS survey is more intensive than either the NBS or RCRE surveys. The survey provides better coverage of urban subsidies, and we believe that some sources of income – especially from nonfarm self-employment – are better measured than in the other surveys. Certainly, there is more detail that can be exploited to explore the robustness of conclusions to definitions of "income." The CHNS does not have consumption or expenditure data, however. One especially important feature of the CHNS is that it (essentially) follows a panel of cities and villages across the survey years. We are also able to evaluate the sensitivity of urban–rural differences to the definition of "urban." This is potentially very important when interpreting "urban and rural" results based on NBS data, where fast-growing and industrializing rural areas are reclassified as urban over the transition period.

Issues Common to All Data Sets

There are a number of important measurement issues that need to be discussed when looking at any series of inequality measures. The estimated level of inequality can be sensitive to the definitions of income and consumption, even from perfectly implemented and comparable household surveys. Since surveys are neither perfectly implemented nor perfectly comparable, it becomes even more important to clarify the definition and measurement of income and consumption. Even a simple question of how to turn household income into per capita measures can be problematic: who is a household member? In the Chinese context, should the member be defined on the basis of registration status? Or, like the World Bank Living Standard Measurement Surveys, on the basis of economic attachment to the household? Should adjustments be made for the age composition of the household; that is, should we convert household members into adult equivalents?

In the numbers that follow, we use the "best" available measure from each survey. For urban households in the NBS survey, income is defined as income earned from all enumerated sources, and household size is based on registration. For the rural RCRE households, we calculate income from all sources, including the implied market value of home-produced grain. Measurement of farm incomes in China can be highly sensitive to a battery of assumptions concerning valuation, and we discuss these issues more thoroughly elsewhere (Benjamin, Brandt, and Giles, 2005). These measurement issues become especially important when comparing RCRE-based results to those from the NBS, such as those reported by Ravallion and Chen (2004). Household membership in the RCRE is also based on registration. For the CHNS, we construct incomes along similar lines to the respective urban and rural surveys. For urban households in the CHNS we are also able to "value" the implicit rents associated with access to food and housing at below-market prices. With the CHNS, however, household membership is defined more on the basis of economic attachment (residency) than registration. Household members other than the head who work and live outside much of the year may not be included (though their remittances would be).

In principle, households included in these surveys form a representative cross section of the population. If not, the researcher must know the sampling weights for purposes of making inferences about the population. In the case of the surveys carried out by both the NBS and the RCRE, there is reason to believe that a disproportionate number of households at both ends of the income distribution, that is, the very rich and the very poor, are being excluded. In part, this reflects the survey protocol's requirement that households maintain diaries of their income and expenditures. This makes participation by illiterate households difficult and elevates the costs associated with record keeping for rich households. Truncation of this sort likely leads to an underestimate of income inequality and poverty.[4]

A final issue worth mentioning concerns the conversion of nominal values into constant-dollar (yuan) prices. We use the official provincial consumer price indices

---

[4] Benjamin, Brandt, and Giles (2005) document this in the case of a comparison of estimates of rural inequality using the RCRE data and several other surveys in which household selection was known to be random.

(CPIs) to convert all nominal values into 1990 yuan.[5] To make welfare comparisons across heterogeneous provinces, it may also be advantageous to control for differences in the cost of living. We accomplish this by using spatial price deflators documented in Brandt and Holz (2006). These deflators allow us to adjust for cross-sectional differences in urban and rural prices across provinces and between rural and urban areas. In general, we expect incomes and price levels to be positively correlated. In urban areas, for example, the cost of the same basket of goods is more than 50 percent higher in Guangdong than it is in Sichuan. Failure to control for these differences can lead to an overestimate of inequality and the contribution of key sources, for example, interprovincial or urban–rural differences.

THE MEAN AND DISPERSION OF INCOME OVER TIME

In this section we document the first-order results concerning the level and distribution of income in China: what were the trends in inequality over the transition period? In both urban and rural China, mean incomes rose significantly over the reform period, as did income inequality. Later on, we provide details on how the benefits of reform were shared.

Urban

Table 18.1 reports the key summary statistics of the evolution of the income distribution for four years: 1987, 1991, 1995, and 2001. To place these numbers in a broader temporal context, we plot the mean and Gini coefficients for all the years for which we have data in Figures 18.1 and 18.2. The NBS-based urban results are in the top panel of Table 18.1. Mean per capita household income grew from 1,533 yuan in 1987 to more than double at 3,411 yuan in 2001, reflecting steady growth of 5.7 percent per year, as illustrated in the top panel of Figure 18.1. For comparison, Table 18.2 provides similar numbers based on the CHNS, with urban results in the top panel. Even though the underlying provinces, sampling frame, and income definitions are different, the urban CHNS paints a similar picture to the NBS. Mean incomes grew from 1,484 yuan in 1991 to 2,532 yuan in 2000. While the level of income is about 20 percent below the NBS, the implied growth rate (over the shorter period) is basically the same, at 5.9 percent per year. In Figure 18.1a, we see that the CHNS observations plot a lower, but parallel, growth path to the NBS observations. Both data sets thus confirm a remarkable improvement in average living standards.

How was this growth shared? In the next rows we provide a variety of inequality measures. Table 18.1 shows significant increases in urban inequality, as captured by NBS. The Gini coefficient increases by almost two-thirds from 0.22 to 0.34 over

---

[5] To help the reader put these real figures into current nominal estimates, the CPI roughly doubled between 1990 and 2003.

Table 18.1. *The distribution of household per capita income selected years urban and rural separately*

	1987	1991	1995	2001
Urban (NBS)				
Mean income	1,533	1,742	2,385	3,411
Gini	0.22	0.25	0.30	0.34
Gini (spatially deflated)	0.20	0.22	0.28	0.33
Theil	0.08	0.10	0.16	0.20
Atkinson (0.5)	0.04	0.05	0.07	0.10
Atkinson (1.0)	0.08	0.10	0.14	0.18
Atkinson (2.0)	0.15	0.18	0.25	0.31
90/10	2.64	2.97	3.90	4.77
Below 0.5 × 1987 median	0.04	0.05	0.02	0.01
Consumption-based measures:				
Mean per capita consumption	1,346	1,491	1,994	2,702
Gini	0.24	0.27	0.32	0.35
Rural (RCRE)				
Mean income	920	877	1,225	1,244
Gini	0.32	0.33	0.33	0.37
Gini (spatially deflated)	0.29	0.30	0.30	0.34
Theil	0.19	0.22	0.21	0.27
Atkinson (0.5)	0.08	0.09	0.09	0.12
Atkinson (1.0)	0.16	0.17	0.17	0.21
Atkinson (2.0)	0.28	0.32	0.33	0.43
90/10	4.06	3.98	3.93	4.99
Below 0.5 × 1987 median	0.16	0.19	0.07	0.11
Consumption-based measures:				
Mean per capita consumption	652	635	864	826
Gini	0.25	0.27	0.27	0.33

Notes: 1. All calculations are based on real per capita income, expressed in constant 1990 yuan.
2. The "spatially deflated" Gini calculation is based on further adjustments for geographic differences in cost of living, as described in Brandt and Holz (2006).
3. "90/10" is the ratio of the ninetieth to the tenth percentiles of the income distribution.
4. "Below 0.5 × 1987 median" is the proportion of individuals with per capita incomes below a constant benchmark, namely, one-half the median 1987 per capita income.

this fourteen-year period. As shown in Figure 18.2, the increase in inequality has been quite steady over this period, with no evidence of a slowing trend. Accounting for differences in the cost of living across cities does little to change this picture. The spatially deflated Gini is slightly smaller, but shows similar growth between 1987 and 2001 (0.20–0.33). Other common measures of dispersion confirm that the inequality results are not specific to the Gini. Whichever parameter of inequality aversion is selected, the Atkinson index shows a pronounced increase of inequality. The 90/10 ratio also rises by nearly 80 percent from 2.64 to 4.77: by 2001, the "rich"

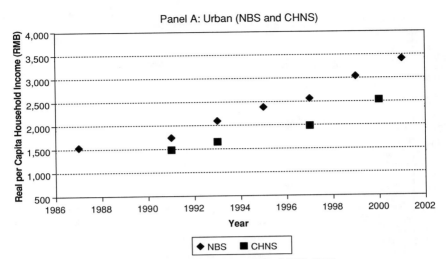

Panel A: Urban (NBS and CHNS)

Implied Annual Growth Rate (NBS): 5.7%
Implied Annual Growth Rate (CHNS): 5.9%

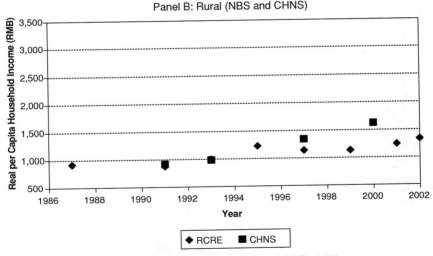

Panel B: Rural (NBS and CHNS)

Implied Annual Growth Rate (RCRE): 2.0%
Implied Annual Growth Rate (CHNS): 6.3%

Figure 18.1. The evolution of mean per capita household income, selected years (*Notes:* (1) All calculations based on real per capita income, expressed in constant 1990 yuan. (2) The "Implied Growth Rate" is the average annual continuously compounded growth rate between the beginning and the end of the sample period. For urban NBS, the end points are 1987 and 2001; for rural RCRE, the end points are 1987 and 2002; and for the CHNS, the end points are 1991 and 2000. (3) See Tables 18.1 and 18.2 for further details.)

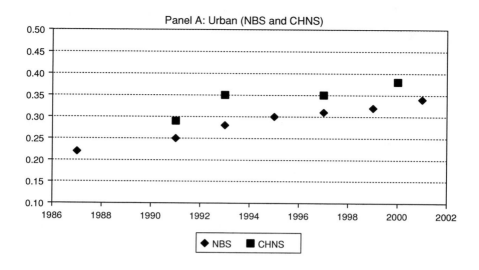

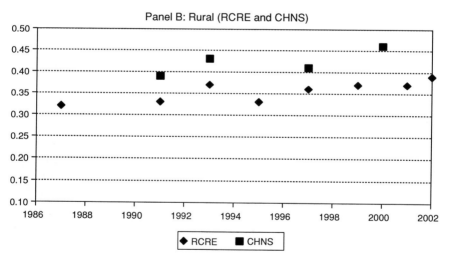

Figure 18.2. The evolution of inequality (the Gini coefficient), selected years (*Notes:* (1) All calculations are based on real per capita household income, expressed in constant 1990 yuan. (2) See notes to Tables 18.1 and 18.2 for further details.)

earn almost five times the poor, as compared to less than three times as much in 1987. The robustness of our conclusions to the index of inequality comes as no surprise once we plot the corresponding Lorenz curves for urban incomes in Figure 18.3. Each curve shows the fraction of the total income accounted for by the "poorest" households. For any cumulative population's share of the "poorest" individuals (e.g., the poorest 40 percent), we see that their cumulative share of

Table 18.2. *The distribution of household per capita income selected years, CHNS urban and rural separately*

	1991	1993	1997	2000
Urban				
Mean income	1,484	1,651	1,982	2,532
Gini	0.29	0.35	0.35	0.38
Theil	0.14	0.20	0.21	0.25
Atkinson (0.5)	0.07	0.10	0.11	0.13
Atkinson (1.0)	0.15	0.22	0.23	0.27
Atkinson (2.0)	0.40	0.50	0.59	0.62
90/10	4.40	6.50	6.32	8.24
Below 0.5 × 1991 median	0.16	0.17	0.14	0.11
Rural				
Mean income	917	984	1,344	1,623
Gini	0.39	0.43	0.41	0.46
Theil	0.26	0.32	0.28	0.36
Atkinson (0.5)	0.13	0.15	0.14	0.18
Atkinson (1.0)	0.25	0.31	0.28	0.36
Atkinson (2.0)	0.31	0.68	0.66	0.77
90/10	7.25	8.78	8.76	11.65
Below 0.5 × 1991 median	0.21	0.22	0.13	0.13

Notes: 1. All calculations are based on real per capita income, expressed in constant 1990 yuan.

2. "90/10" is the ratio of the ninetieth to the tenth percentiles of the income distribution.

3. "Below 0.5 × 1991 median" is the proportion of individuals with per capita incomes below a constant benchmark, namely, one-half the median 1991 per capita income.

income is lower for each passing year: the rich keep getting a bigger slice. These Lorenz curves thus show a clear ordering of the income distributions as far as inequality is concerned: each subsequent reported year lies outside the previous one. So no matter what inequality index is selected, 2001 will show a higher level of inequality than 1995 or 1987.

How representative is our NBS subsample of provinces? NBS-reported inequality figures for 1986–2000 using their entire urban sample show a rise in the Gini from 020 to 0.32.[6] To help put the rise in inequality after 1987 in perspective, the full NBS sample shows an increase in inequality from 0.16 to 0.20 between 1978 and 1986. Clearly, urban inequality has risen since the beginning of economic reforms. Turning to our comparison with the CHNS in Table 18.2 (and Figure 18.2), we see that the CHNS estimates consistently imply higher levels of inequality than the NBS (0.38 for the CHNS in 2000 vs. 0.34 for the NBS in 2001, for example), but a similar increase (in absolute terms) over years in common between the two surveys. Estimates from the China Income Project for 1988 and 1995, which avoid a number

[6] See Meng, Gregory, and Wang (2004) and Ravallion and Chen (2004).

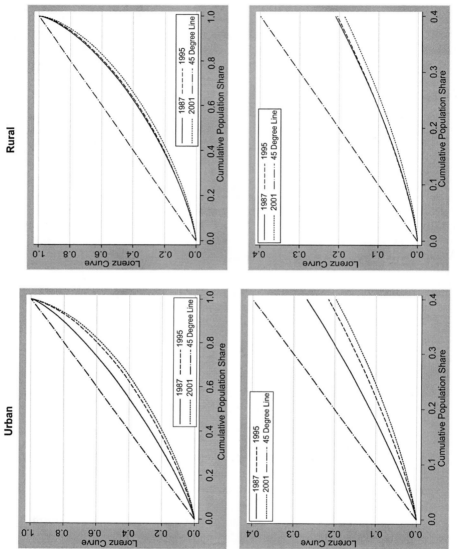

Figure 18.3. Lorenz curves, urban and rural incomes (*Notes*: The Lorenz curves are based on the urban (NBS) and rural (RCRE) data described in Table 18.1. All calculations are based on spatially undeflated, constant 1990 yuan.)

of important weaknesses in the NBS household survey, also reveal significantly higher levels of inequality, but show a similar increase over this seven-year period.[7]

To gauge trends in urban poverty, our final distributional measure is the proportion of households whose income falls below one-half the 1987 median income for urban residents. This line is fixed through time, providing a benchmark of how many households are raised out of "poverty" if the poverty line were set at 50 percent of 1987 median income. For 1987, we see a very low proportion of "poor" households defined in this fashion, with only 4 percent of households with low income. This proportion declines to only 1 percent by 2001. In Figure 18.4 we plot the cumulative distribution functions (CDFs) for household income. The horizontal axis shows the level of real income, while the vertical axis shows the proportion of individuals in households with an income level below that on the horizontal axis. Thus, for any "poverty line" we can estimate the proportion of poor households. For example, if the "poverty line" was a very high 2,000 yuan (higher than mean incomes in 1987), we would see that fewer than 40 percent had incomes below this level in 2001, compared to over 80 percent in 1987. The bottom panel (Figure 18.4) focuses on the bottom part of the distribution, where we can select more reasonable poverty lines. Half the 1987 median per capita income level is approximately 700 yuan. Significantly fewer than 5 percent of individuals had incomes below this level in any of the years, and we can see the fraction steadily declining in each year (as shown in Table 18.1). Higher poverty lines would show similar progress over time.

This finding can be compared with more thorough examinations of urban poverty trends by Meng, Gregory, and Wang (2004) and Ravallion and Chen (2004), which use the entire NBS sample for the period 1986–2000 and calculate poverty lines using alternative procedures.[8] The estimates of Meng, Gregory, and Wang show an uneven rise in the percentage living under poverty from 2 percent to about 5 percent in 1993, which then declines slowly through 2000. Ravallion and Chen's estimates also show a downward trend, but slightly more volatility. Despite some differences, there is general agreement on the relatively low levels of urban poverty in China based on the NBS estimates.

In the final rows of the urban panel of Table 18.1, we report the consumption-based mean levels of income and corresponding Gini coefficients. The consumption-based measures mirror the income-based ones. For urban China, it thus appears that while income inequality has increased significantly, increases in incomes have been large enough and spread throughout the income

---

[7] See Khan and Riskin (1998, 1999), for example.
[8] Ravallion and Chen (2004), for example, use the "official" poverty line of 300 yuan per person per year (in 1990 prices), as well as a more recently constructed poverty line based on updated minimum consumption bundles: 850 yuan for rural and 1,200 yuan for urban (in per capita terms). Meng, Gregory, and Wang (2004) also choose poverty lines based on minimum consumption bundles, as opposed to our more arbitrary – but still constant – half the 1987 median income.

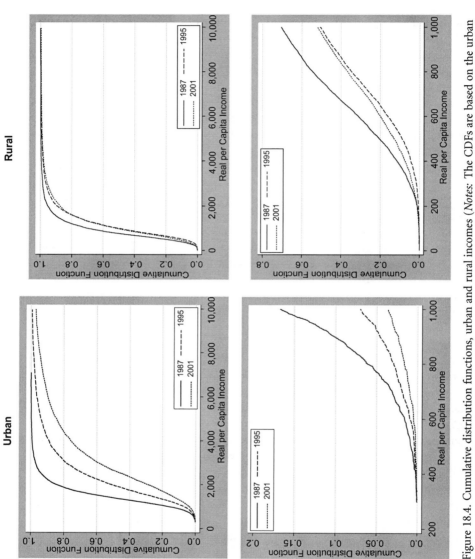

Figure 18.4. Cumulative distribution functions, urban and rural incomes (*Notes*: The CDFs are based on the urban (NBS) and rural (RCRE) data described in Table 18.1. All calculations are based on spatially undeflated, constant 1990 yuan.)

748

distribution, so that almost all urban residents are better off in 2001 than at the beginning of reforms.

Rural

Turning to rural results, we report the distributional characteristics in the bottom panels of Tables 18.1 and 18.2 and Figures 18.1 and 18.2. The rural picture is muddier than the urban one, with conflicting evidence from different data sets. In Table 18.1 we report the RCRE-based results. These show unambiguous improvements in average living standards, with mean incomes rising from 920 yuan in 1987 to 1,244 in 2001, an increase by about one-third. As shown in Figure 18.1, this corresponds to an annualized growth rate of only 2.0 percent. This is lower than most other data sets, including the CHNS, reported in Table 18.2. For the CHNS, income levels are approximately the same as the RCRE at the beginning of the sample, but diverge by 2000: the CHNS-based growth rate is similar to urban areas, at 6.3 percent. Benjamin, Brandt, and Giles (2005) provide a detailed discussion and reconciliation of why the RCRE growth rate differs from the NBS growth rate, explaining how differences in survey design and interpretation – especially the valuation of agricultural output – lead to discrepancies. Concerning the gap between the CHNS and RCRE, it is noteworthy that most of the difference arises only after the mid-1990s and is largely attributable to differences between the RCRE and CHNS surveys in the rate of growth of farm income. Some of this may reflect the kinds of villages that were selected, with more "suburban" villages possibly included in the CHNS, as well in how farm output is being valued. The CHNS villages may have had more acreage in vegetables and other cash crops, and been less exposed to a sharp drop in grain prices that occurred after 1995.

In the next rows we document the evolution of various measures of inequality. Our estimates reveal that inequality is slightly higher in rural than in urban areas, but that rural inequality experienced slightly smaller increases over time. As in our examination of urban inequality, spatially deflating incomes reduces overall inequality, but hardly changes the trend. The CHNS data suggest higher inequality than do the RCRE data (0.46 in 2000 vs. 0.37 in 2001 and 0.39 in 2002, for example), but imply a similar absolute increase over the years in common between the two surveys. A comparison with NBS-based rural inequality estimates (Ravallion and Chen, 2004) shows similar trends, but systematically higher levels of inequality in our two surveys. Using the NBS estimates to extrapolate would also put the Gini coefficient for rural inequality in 1980 in the vicinity of 0.30.

As illustrated in Figure 18.2, much of the increase in rural inequality in the two rural data sets occurs in the late 1980s to early 1990s and then resumes in the late 1990s, with inequality actually falling in between. An important reason for this is the behavior of farm prices. Between 1993 and 1995, farm procurement prices doubled in nominal terms and rose by 50 percent relative to the rural CPI. This disproportionately benefited low-income rural households for whom farming was an important source of income and helped to offset the inequality arising from the rapid growth of nonagricultural incomes. Without this increase in farm prices, we would have observed a more sustained increase in rural inequality. There was a reversal of fortune for the poorest households in the last half of the 1990s, which can be linked to falling farm prices and the behavior of farm incomes. Farm prices and incomes did not begin to recover until 2002–2003.

In Tables 18.1 and 18.2 we report rural inequality for different inequality indices. As for urban areas, all the indices show rising inequality, so our conclusions are not specific to the Gini coefficient. The Lorenz curves in Figure 18.2 also unambiguously show higher inequality in 2001 than in 1987. However, there is a less clear ranking of 1987 and 1995, as the Lorenz curves cross, and essentially lie on top of each other over much of the distribution. In principle, this means that inequality comparisons between 1987 and 1995 may be sensitive to the choice of inequality index. Indeed in Table 18.1, 1995 is ranked more unequal than 1987 for all indices, except the 90/10 ratio.

A crucial question for welfare analysis is thus whether the increase in mean incomes was high enough to offset the increased dispersion of incomes. While the rich got unambiguously richer, what happened to the poor? At the bottom of Table 18.1 we report the percentage of households below the 1987 median. These estimates show uneven progress, with a rise in the late 1980s followed by a sharp drop through the mid-1990s, but then an increase through the end of the decade. By 2001, only 11 percent of households had incomes below one-half the 1987 median income, compared to 16 percent in 1987. Given the perception of rapid growth in the countryside, this modest decline in "poverty" seems disappointing. The stagnation in this dimension is a feature of the late 1990s. Figure 18.4 shows the CDFs for rural areas for three selected years. Lower CDFs correspond to "better" income distributions, with fewer individuals having incomes below any given level. The 1987 CDF is clearly highest over most levels of income. As seen in the bottom panel (Figure 18.4), however, the CDFs for all three years are indistinguishable below incomes of 200 yuan. There are similar – very small – percentages of individuals with incomes this low. The income distribution has thus generally improved since 1987. The outcome is less clear when we compare 1995 and 2001. The top panel (Figure 18.4) shows that the CDFs for 1995 and 2001 cross below incomes of 2,000 yuan. For incomes below 1,000 yuan per year, the 1995 CDF is lower than that for 2001. Thus, even for a very high "poverty line" or benchmark, the 1995 income distribution dominates the 2001 distribution. The increase in inequality over the 1990s thus has the poor getting poorer, with a decline in absolute living standards. These results are not simply an artifact of the RCRE. The CHNS-based numbers in Table 18.2 confirm the stagnation of incomes of the rural poor since 1997.

It would be a mistake, however, to conclude that economic reforms have entirely missed the rural poor. Part of the problem stems from our use of the RCRE data that begin only in 1986 and fail to capture the enormous gains in reducing poverty in the late 1970s and early 1980s, following the introduction of the HRS and rural reform. Subject to limitations in the NBS data, especially for the pre-1984 period, Ravallion and Chen's (2004) estimates show the percentage of rural residents living under poverty fell from 76 percent in 1980 to 22 percent by 1987. Most of the gains made by the poor thus occurred before the first observation of our RCRE sample. With 60 percent of China's population still classified as rural, these estimates also highlight that much of China's poverty remains in the countryside. And the clear stagnation of rural incomes, especially for those in the bottom half of the distribution, suggests little positive news about short-run prospects for rural poverty alleviation.

In the final two rows of the rural panel of Table 18.1, we report the consumption-based means and Gini coefficients, to explore sensitivity of our results focusing on income. While a significant part of the consumption is measured independently of income, for the rural data both income and consumption contain a common component of self-consumed home production. Still, it is reassuring that the consumption-based measures show the same trends as the income-based measures. For rural China, unlike in the cities, it thus appears that increases in inequality do offset the otherwise rosy picture painted by rising mean incomes, at least for those at the bottom of the income distribution.

THE ROLE OF "GEOGRAPHY"

The role of widening regional income differences and their contribution to increasing inequality is a common theme in the literature on inequality in China.[9] Rising disparities between localities, especially provinces (inland vs. coastal, for example) are often seen as the most important sources of the rising income differences we just documented, as some provinces are better situated to take advantage of market liberalization and reforms related to foreign trade and investment. In rural areas, spatial differences may reflect differences in per capita land endowments, access to urban markets, and initial conditions at the time of the reform (e.g., the level of development of commune- and brigade-run enterprises). With the erosion of restrictions on migration enforced by China's residential registration (*hukou*) system and the opening of markets for migrant labor, however, we might expect some degree of regional convergence, and a decline in the "contribution" of region to overall inequality. Our samples, which include the rapidly growing coastal provinces of Guangdong and Jiangsu and slower-growing interior provinces of Sichuan and Gansu, seem reasonably well suited for examining these differences and their trends, as well as for understanding the role of geography in affecting income inequality more generally.

[9] Kanbur and Zhang (1999) provide an excellent overview of the literature on regional inequality, highlighting inland versus coastal and urban versus rural dimensions. See also Gustafsson and Li (2002).

Spatial Income Decompositions

There are a number of approaches to decomposing inequality across regions. Unfortunately, the Gini coefficient is not readily (or neatly) decomposed. Instead, a simple strategy entails decomposing the variance of log income (itself an inequality index) by estimating the following regression:

$$\ln y_i = D'_L \gamma + u_i,$$

where D_L is a vector of dummy variables, indicating the location of individual i. The R-squared from this regression indicates the proportion of the variation (or variance) of $\ln y_i$ that is explained by the location dummies. The remainder is the (within-location) residual variance of log income and a measure of the degree to which household income is not explained by the average income of neighboring households.[10] We carry out this exercise separately for urban and rural households.

Table 18.3 reports the results of the spatial decomposition using each of our data sets. We define location at two levels of aggregation: the city (or village) and province. We estimate the regression given earlier separately for urban and rural samples, with province- and city (or village)-level dummies. We also distinguish between spatially deflated and undeflated household income, as variations in the cost of living reduce spatial income differences.[11]

The first row (Table 18.3) shows results for urban China and the fraction of household income differences that can be explained by province. In 1987, mean differences in provincial income explained only 26 percent of the variation in household income. The majority of inequality was thus due to differences of income among households in the same province. Note that this does not mean that the effect of location is inconsequential: the R-squared from this regression is higher than most human capital earnings functions. Province of residence thus explains as much of the variation of income as does age, education, and other individual characteristics for individual earnings.[12] The point we wish to emphasize, however, is that the majority of income inequality cannot be explained by location. This means that a focus on geography as the key driver of rising inequality is misplaced.

---

[10] For comparability, we also decomposed the Theil index (which is neatly decomposable) and found similar results.

[11] For our extracts of the urban NBS data, the city indicator is available only after 1993.

[12] Consider another "benchmark" for a high or low contribution of geography in a spatial decomposition. We replicated this procedure using a Canadian household survey (the 1996 Family Expenditure Survey). Even though there are significant differences in provincial incomes (e.g., household per capita income is about 15 percent higher in Ontario than in Quebec, the two most populous provinces), "province" explains only 1.5 percent of the variation in log per capita household incomes in Canada: within-province income inequality is 98.5 percent of Canadian income inequality. While low in an absolute sense, the contribution of space to income inequality is thus much higher in China than in Canada, and probably most other developed countries.

Table 18.3. *Spatial variation of incomes, selected years
urban and rural separately various data sets*

	1987	1991	1995	2001
Urban (NBS)				
Province	0.26	0.30	0.37	0.28
City			0.48	0.39
Province (spatially deflated)	0.17	0.17	0.29	0.13
City (spatially deflated)			0.34	0.27
Rural (RCRE)				
Province	0.24	0.22	0.18	0.19
Village	0.50	0.47	0.41	0.43
Province (spatially deflated)	0.13	0.11	0.09	0.11
Village (spatially deflated)	0.43	0.39	0.35	0.33
CHNS-based				
	1991	1993	1997	2000
Urban (CHNS)				
Province	0.04	0.05	0.06	0.02
City	0.29	0.29	0.25	0.13
Rural (CHNS)				
Province	0.06	0.06	0.06	0.05
Village	0.24	0.30	0.22	0.21

Notes: 1. This table reports the proportion of total variation of log per capita income explained by a set of location indicators. This is calculated as the R-squared from a regression of "ln y" on a set of dummy variables for province, city, or cluster, depending on the level of spatial analysis. 2. The "spatially deflated" series refers to incomes adjusted for provincial differences in the cost of living, as calculated by Brandt and Holz (2006).

Local institutions, and differences in the characteristics of, or opportunities for, people living in the same community, are more important.

Continuing through the first row of Table 18.3, our estimates suggest an increase in the role of province up through the mid-1990s, followed by a decline. The sharp increase in the first half of the 1990s may be linked to the elimination of numerous subsidies enjoyed by households, which were less than fully compensated in some provinces by an increase in cash wages (Meng, Gregory, and Wang, 2004).[13] Unexpectedly, the massive layoffs in the SOEs, which began in the mid-1990s and had a significant regional component, did not result in an increase in the role of

[13] An alternative possibility is that the NBS data do not fully capture differences across provinces in earlier years in these subsidies, which would have led to an underestimate in the role of province in the decompositions.

spatial differences through 2001. Less surprising, spatially deflating the data lowers the contribution of "location," but the trend is otherwise very similar. Overall, a quarter to a third of urban inequality can be linked to the province in which a household is located, with a slightly higher percentage (40–50 percent) attributable to the city. In the bottom panel (Table 18.3), we report results from the CHNS data. In the CHNS, city and especially province play a less prominent role than in the NBS sample, with the role of city declining over time.

Turning to the rural sector, aside from a slight increase in the early 1990s, the RCRE data imply a fairly steady decline in the role of location in overall inequality. Spatially deflating has an effect similar to what we observe in the urban data and lowers the role of location considerably. By 2001, both the RCRE and CHNS data suggest that province of residence explains only about 10 percent, and village between 30 and 40 percent, of rural inequality. Most of the inequality in China is *within* the villages and cities in which Chinese households live and work.

Urban and Rural Inequality

So far we have looked at rural and urban inequality in isolation. Yet, one important dimension of rising inequality may be a widening gap between urban and rural incomes. Certainly, these income differences have figured prominently in the literature. Lacking access to the NBS rural household survey data, the CHNS is the only data set that allows us to explore "overall inequality," pooling urban and rural samples. The CHNS thus permits a formal decomposition of spatial inequality that includes allowance for provincial or urban–rural income gaps.

We report summary statistics for the pooled urban and rural sample in Table 18.4. Between 1991 and 2000, real per capita income (in 1990 prices) rose from RMB1,121 to RMB1,912, which implies an annual increase of slightly less than 6 percent per annum. Perhaps surprisingly, pooling the urban and rural samples leads to an overall level of inequality no higher than the rural sample alone. By all measures, inequality increased considerably, with the Gini coefficient increasing from 0.37 to 0.44 and the 90/10 ratio rising from 6.93 in 1991 to 11.04 in 2000. The absolute increase in (and level of) inequality is the same as estimated for the rural sector alone, but slightly smaller than the increase occurring in the urban sector. The behavior of the Gini coefficient for this subsample of provinces is actually identical to that calculated by Ravallion and Chen (2004), using the entire NBS sample, so it is unlikely that this conclusion is an artifact of the CHNS.

In the bottom half of Table 18.4 we report the results for spatial decompositions that provide estimates of the contribution of location and urban–rural differences to overall inequality. The role of province and city (village) in overall inequality is similar to our estimates for the urban and rural sectors separately using the CHNS. By the end of the period we are analyzing, the city or village that a household lives in only explains about a sixth of the inequality, and province only 5 percent.

Table 18.4. *Inequality for combined urban and rural samples CHNS data*

	1991	1993	1997	2000
Pooled distributional characteristics				
Mean per capita income	1,121	1,194	1,560	1,912
Gini coefficient	0.37	0.42	0.40	0.44
Atkinson (0.5)	0.12	0.15	0.13	0.17
Atkinson (1.0)	0.24	0.30	0.27	0.34
Atkinson (2.0)	0.51	0.67	0.66	0.76
90/10 ratio	6.93	8.82	8.49	11.04
Spatial decompositions				
Province only	0.05	0.04	0.05	0.06
Province plus urban–rural (interactions)	0.17	0.14	0.12	0.14
City or village (cluster)	0.31	0.36	0.28	0.17

Notes: 1. This table reports mean incomes and inequality measures for a combined sample of urban and rural households, where adjustment has been made for spatial differences in the cost of living, including urban–rural differences in prices (from Brandt and Holz, 2006).
2. All figures are reported based on spatially deflated, constant 1990 yuan.
3. The spatial decompositions are the same as described in Tables 18.8 and 18.9.
4. "Province plus urban–rural" means province interacted with a rural–urban indicator (which does not permit spatial differences within the urban or rural sectors within a province).

Controlling for the role of provincial differences in mean incomes, we also look at the contribution of urban–rural income differences to overall inequality: how much do mean differences of income between urban and rural households contribute to overall inequality? We do this by including in the spatial decomposition regression province dummies, an urban indicator, and interactions between the province and urban dummies. The interactions allow the urban–rural gap to vary across provinces. To help in the interpretation, the average urban–rural income gap in the CHNS sample (implied in Table 18.2) is 1.6. Combined, province plus the urban–rural distinction explain only about 15 percent of total inequality, or an increase of almost 10 percentage points over that explained by province alone. The contribution of these two geographic dimensions to total inequality is also relatively constant over the period. Our estimates imply that an average urban–rural income gap of 1.6 is actually responsible for only a small part of the inequality in incomes. These results once again point to the significant contribution of differences within urban areas and the countryside to current inequality in China.

Table 18.5. *The sensitivity of urban–rural distinctions to the definition of "rural"*
mean per capita incomes and growth, CHNS

	1991	1993	1997	2000	Growth
Fixed definition of rural					
Rural mean income	917	984	1,343	1,623	0.063
Urban mean income	1,484	1,651	1,982	2,532	0.059
Urban/rural ratio	1.62	1.68	1.48	1.56	
Evolving definition of rural					
Rural mean income	772	766	1,042	1,108	0.040
Urban mean income	1,391	1,474	1,798	2,106	0.046
Urban/rural ratio	1.80	1.92	1.73	1.90	

Notes: 1. This table shows mean per capita incomes expressed in constant 1990 yuan, for two types of rural definition.
2. The first definition of urban–rural is based on the CHNS sampling definition, where "rural" includes "purely" rural and "suburban" households, approximately corresponding to rural-registered households. This definition is fixed for the entire period, so that a 1991 rural household (cluster) remains rural in 2000.
3. The second definition is based on economic structure and evolves with economic development. Clusters are defined as rural if 50 percent or more of households earn 50 percent or more of their income from farming (i.e., most of the households are farmers). This definition is recalculated each survey, so clusters can evolve from rural to urban classification.
4. "Growth" is defined as the implied annual compounded rate from 1991 through 2000.

This result is counter to conventional wisdom that rural areas are being left behind. Interpreting the behavior of urban–rural income differences can be tricky however, largely because of their sensitivity to the definition of "rural." Many publicly reported urban–rural gaps – especially trends – may be a statistical artifact and driven by systematic selection of poorer areas as "rural." This is especially important in the Chinese context because the NBS-based urban–rural comparisons allow for rural areas to be reclassified as urban. If a rural area develops enough, it is "promoted" to urban status. While this makes sense at a point in time, it destroys comparability with the past. By construction, the urban-defined population is in the faster-developing areas, even if growth is concentrated in areas previously defined as "rural." This serves to select the remaining rural sample from the less dynamic areas. Since the late 1970s, the share of the Chinese population that is urban has roughly doubled, a major portion of which is the result of reclassifying rural areas to urban. We use the CHNS to illustrate these points in Table 18.5, comparing the levels and growth rates of incomes in rural and urban areas across alternative definitions of urban and rural.

The first definition holds constant a location's rural status throughout the period. We use the CHNS designation of "rural" plus "suburban" clusters to construct our first rural indicator. This approximately corresponds to a definition based on household registration; that is, in 1990 households in these clusters had rural registration. One important feature of this definition is that the rural–urban status is held constant through 2000. So, even if a rural area completely paves over its farms and industrializes, it will remain "rural." This definition allows rural areas to develop and stay "rural." The second definition is based on economic structure and is malleable over time. We define localities as rural if most of the households are farmers. Specifically, a locality is rural if 50 percent (or more) of the households earn 50 percent or more of their income from farming. A village that industrializes between 1991 and 2000 will thus switch its classification from rural to urban. This is not exactly the same as what the NBS does, but it mimics similar reclassification procedures.

Several findings emerge. First, the urban–rural gap is higher with the second definition, being close to two-to-one. This is not surprising, as the "urban" clusters are positively selected on the basis of having more developed nonagricultural income sources. The ratio for our first definition is around 1.5. Second, with definition one, the urban gap is generally (and slowly) falling (though there are big year effects that cloud the trend). Again, definition one allows "successful," fast-growing rural clusters to retain "rural" status. Systematic reclassification hides the actual convergence that may be occurring between town and country. And third, the growth rates are higher for both urban and rural under definition one. The "rural" growth rate is less than two-thirds as high under definition two, as "successful" villages are systematically dropped. The urban growth rate is also lower under the second definition (0.046 vs. 0.059). This may seem puzzling, except that the relatively rural, formerly "rural" clusters are poorer than the originally urban clusters. The newly "promoted" urban clusters continuously lower the average "urban" income. In summary, people living in rural areas are keeping up with those living cities, though they undoubtedly remain poorer.

INEQUALITY DYNAMICS: INTERIOR VERSUS COAST

Regional differences play a relatively small role in the overall changes in inequality. This does not preclude the possibility of differences in the dynamics of inequality between regions that may be important in their own right and possibly linked to the growth process. Geography may matter in more complicated ways than generating differences in mean incomes. The focus on coastal versus inland economic outcomes may be justified, though for more subtle reasons. In Table 18.6, we provide summary data on incomes, inequality, and the results of a spatial decomposition for the coastal and interior regions separately using the CHNS for the 1990s. Coastal here includes the provinces of Liaoning, Shandong, Jiangsu, and Guangxi, while interior includes Heilongjiang, Hubei, Henan, Hunan, and Guizhou. In 1991, mean incomes in the coastal provinces were only modestly higher than those in the interior, with both urban and rural incomes in the coastal areas higher than their counterparts in the interior. Over the decade, the difference in average incomes between the two regions widened considerably, with mean income in the coastal

Table 18.6. *Combined urban and rural inequality exploring the interaction with geography (inland vs. coastal provinces) (CHNS)*

	1991	1993	1997	2000
	Distributional characteristics			
Coastal regions				
Mean per capita income (combined)	1,167	1,316	1,746	2,215
Mean, urban separately	1,580	1,792	2,153	2,725
Mean, rural separately	991	1,150	1,620	2,065
Gini coefficient (combined)	0.35	0.39	0.37	0.39
Gini, urban separately	0.26	0.34	0.35	0.37
Gini, rural separately	0.38	0.40	0.38	0.39
Interior regions				
Mean per capita income (combined)	1,078	1,086	1,433	1,652
Mean, urban separately	1,352	1,473	1,862	2,338
Mean, rural separately	858	850	1,152	1,265
Gini coefficient (combined)	0.39	0.45	0.41	0.48
Gini, urban separately	0.31	0.37	0.35	0.39
Gini, rural separately	0.40	0.45	0.42	0.49
	Spatial decompositions			
Coastal regions				
Province	0.04	0.01	0.02	0.02
Province plus urban–rural	0.14	0.10	0.06	0.06
City/village	0.46	0.43	0.29	0.24
Interior regions				
Province	0.04	0.04	0.03	0.02
Province plus urban–rural	0.15	0.13	0.10	0.13
City/village	0.35	0.33	0.26	0.30

Notes: 1. This table reports mean incomes and inequality measures for a combined sample of urban and rural households, where adjustment has been made for spatial differences in the cost of living, including urban–rural differences in prices (from Brandt and Holz, 2006).

2. All figures are reported based on the spatially deflated, constant 1990 yuan.

3. The spatial decompositions are the same as described in Tables 18.8 and 18.9. "Province plus urban–rural" means province interacted with a rural–urban indicator (which does not permit spatial differences within the urban or rural sectors within a province).

provinces 2,215 yuan by 2000 compared with 1,652 in the interior, or a difference of a third.

Much of the increase in the gap, however, appears to be the result of a growing difference in incomes between *rural* households in the coastal and interior provinces. By 2000, rural incomes in the coastal provinces are nearly 50 percent higher than those in the interior. For urban areas, however, differences in the rate of income growth between the two regions remain modest, with the ratio of mean or median urban incomes in the two regions staying more or less constant. The failure of incomes in the interior to keep up with coastal areas appears to be a rural phenomenon.

Differences in the behavior of inequality in the two regions are equally telling. Not only is the level of inequality higher in the interior, but the increase through the 1990s is greater as well. In the coastal provinces, inequality increases from 0.35 to 0.39, with the increase occurring largely in the early 1990s. In the interior, it increases from 0.39 to 0.48. The significantly larger increase in the interior can be attributed to two key factors; first, the more rapid increase in inequality in rural areas in the interior compared to the coastal provinces and second, a widening rural–urban income gap in the interior compared to the coastal areas. In the interior, rural inequality increases from 0.40 to 0.49, but in the coastal provinces, inequality remains more or less the same (just under 0.40). In the interior, the rural–urban gap widens from 1.58 to 1.85, while in the coastal provinces it falls from 1.60 to 1.32. Partially offsetting some of this is the more rapid increase in urban inequality in the coastal provinces.

Several of these same trends are also mirrored in mean provincial urban and rural household incomes reported by the NBS, and provided in Table 18.7. We attribute to everyone living in urban (rural) areas in a province the same mean per capita income and use the urban–rural spatial deflators and population weights to construct a mean provincial income. We then use the NBS data and our constructed estimates to look at inequality in mean provincial urban and rural incomes within the two regions separately, the differences in urban–rural incomes, as well as inequality in mean provincial incomes in the two regions. This simulation exercise sets inequality to zero within the urban and rural sectors of each province. Significantly, the pooled Gini is both higher and rises more rapidly in the interior than in the coastal provinces. The primary source of the difference in the behavior between the two regions is the failure of rural incomes in the interior to grow as rapidly as the urban incomes. While the NBS data may suffer from some of the reclassification bias discussed earlier, we observe the same phenomenon in the CHNS (in Table 18.6).

How might we explain these differences in the behavior of the inequality between the two regions? There is a potential link with the analysis by Brandt, Hsieh, and Zhu (Chapter 17, this volume) on growth and structural transformation and the influence of the size of the state sector on the transfer of labor out of the countryside. At the outset of the reforms, the role of the state sector was significantly more important in the interior than in the coastal provinces. Some of this reflected the policy of the Third Front and a redirection of much of China's industrial investment to the interior in the 1960s and 1970s. With reform, the growth of the nonstate sector in the interior provinces has been much slower, as more resources went to support a larger population tied to the urban state sector. This has handicapped the growth in rural incomes through the demand for labor in a host of secondary

Table 18.7. *Spatial income differences across regions*

Year	Mean income			Gini coefficients		
	Rural	Urban	Ratio	Rural	Urban	Combined
Inland provinces						
1985	744	1,225	1.65	0.092	0.087	0.147
1988	743	1,357	1.82	0.092	0.083	0.169
1991	741	1,519	2.05	0.081	0.090	0.197
1994	833	1,911	2.29	0.107	0.103	0.235
1997	1,102	2,122	1.92	0.087	0.111	0.202
2000	1,222	2,672	2.19	0.085	0.109	0.234
Coastal provinces						
1985	857	1,295	1.51	0.065	0.087	0.128
1988	953	1,499	1.57	0.059	0.110	0.151
1991	993	1,717	1.73	0.054	0.099	0.164
1994	1,206	2,268	1.88	0.095	0.114	0.196
1997	1,647	2,566	1.56	0.082	0.100	0.153
2000	1,852	3,140	1.70	0.087	0.102	0.175

Notes: 1. This table shows the "simulated" pooled Gini coefficient for inland and coastal China, in which each rural (urban) individual in a province is assigned the mean per capita rural (urban) income for that province. This effectively sets within-province inequality to zero for urban and rural China, respectively.
2. The urban and rural Gini coefficients are based on spatially deflated per capita incomes, accounting for cross-province price differences, while the pooled Gini also spatially deflates with account for different prices in urban and rural areas.
3. For reference, we also show the ratio of urban to rural spatially deflated mean incomes.
Source: Authors' calculations using NBS yearbooks.

and tertiary industries outside the state sector in both urban and rural regions.[14] As we shall see, the most significant source of growth for rural households has been in nonagricultural activity, especially off-farm wages and family businesses. Although migration to coastal provinces has relaxed some of these constraints, it can be argued that expansion in these opportunities has been more seriously constrained, as more resources have been tied up in the interior provinces in supporting an inefficient state sector. In contrast, growth of the nonstate sector in the more dynamic coastal provinces has helped to keep the urban–rural income gap from rising; it has also provided a wide array of rural opportunities that has prevented a sharp deterioration in rural inequality of the sort observed in the interior.

So geography does matter. However, the story of rising inequality in China is not dominated by divergence of incomes between rich and poor provinces. Economic opportunity clearly varies across regions, and this undoubtedly affects

[14] They find at the provincial level that the reallocation of labor from agriculture to nonagriculture is inversely related to the size of the state sector at the time of the reform.

the development of rural areas. However, a considerable amount of inequality exists and has been rising, within each of China's regions, however we define them.

THE COMPOSITION OF INCOME

If two households were selected at random from the same village (or city) in 1980, and then again in 2000, we have seen that the expected absolute difference in their incomes has unambiguously risen. Why? Addressing this question requires a careful analysis of the evolution of institutions that map household endowments into family income and is a significant research enterprise in itself. Our more limited objective here is to sketch some of the correlates of the within-village or city inequality, particularly those related to the composition of household income. We also present some explorations of other potential correlates of widening income differences between households.

Studying the composition of income provides a direct estimate of the changing economic structure. For example, how important is nonfarm self-employment to rising rural incomes and to what extent is unequal access to such opportunities a driving force in rising inequality? In cities, has self-employment also grown, especially with SOE reform? We report the results of two exercises that summarize the changing composition of income. The first is a straightforward decomposition of mean incomes. Household i's income, y_i, is the sum of its income from K various sources, y_{ik} (some of which may be zero):

$$y_i = \sum_{k=1}^{K} y_{ik}.$$

Mean household income is thus given by

$$\bar{y} = \sum_{k=1}^{K} \bar{y}_k.$$

A 1 percent increase in mean income from source k will increase mean household income by

$$w_k = \bar{y}_k / \bar{y},$$

the average share of income source k in total income. Our first exercise thus reports the changing composition of the levels of income.

The second exercise reports the decomposition of income inequality. What fraction of income inequality can be attributed to inequality of income source k? Our key tool for this analysis is the decomposition proposed by Shorrocks (1982, 1983). The Shorrocks decomposition for a particular source of income k yields s_k, defined by

$$I(y) = \sum_{k=1}^{K} s_k I(y_k).$$

For any income source k, s_k is the proportion of the Gini (or any other inequality index, $I(y)$) "caused" by inequality in the distribution of y_k. Obviously, increases in the inequality of any given income source will lead to an increase in overall income inequality. The Shorrocks decomposition, s_k, differs from the share of the income source w_k, because it accounts for the correlation between the income source and the total income. Certain income sources tend to be earned by the rich or poor. An increase in the inequality of income earned by the rich will increase inequality by even more than its share in total income if the spread in income leads to more of that income going to the rich. Similarly, an increase in inequality of income earned by the poor could, in principle, reduce overall inequality if it increased the relative incomes of the poor. This would lead to a negative s_k, which almost never happens. For our purposes, we view w_k as a reasonable benchmark for s_k. When $s_k > w_k$, then inequality of income source k contributes more to inequality than it does to mean income, which we denote as a disproportionate effect on inequality. In other words, if income from family businesses comprises 10 percent of average income, but inequality of family business income contributes 20 percent of inequality, we will conclude that family business income has a disproportionate effect on inequality.

Urban Incomes

Table 18.8 provides a summary of the structure of urban incomes, as well as the Shorrocks decomposition, using the NBS data. We show results from the beginning and end of our sample to illustrate trends in the composition of income. In 1987, wages comprised 86 percent of income and were by far the most important component of urban incomes. However, as recorded by the NBS, wages do not appear to include many of the subsidies that urban residents received, including access to goods and services at below-market prices, as well as the value of the in-kind component of incomes. These were especially important in the 1980s and then declined sharply in the early 1990s. The NBS numbers thus probably understate the importance of having a wage job.

The Shorrocks decomposition for 1987 shows that while comprising 86 percent of total income, inequality of wage income explained only 66 percent of the total income inequality. While higher wage inequality obviously increases overall inequality, the increase is lower than its share of total income. In 1987, wages were thus relatively equalizing (compared to other sources of income). By comparison, when we move to 2001, we observe a small decline of about 10 percent in the percentage of households with wage income, and an even larger decline in the percentage of income coming from wages, to 68 percent. This is partially offset by modest increases in the share of income from self-employment (still very small in the NBS data) and pensions. By 2001, more than a third of all urban households report pension income, with pensions the source of nearly 20 percent of all income. The notable change in the Shorrocks decomposition is that while wage earnings are now a smaller share of total income than in 1987, they now account for an even larger share of income inequality. Understanding urban inequality, and the rise in

Table 18.8. *Composition of income and inequality decompositions by source sample "end points" urban and rural separately*

	Urban (NBS)					
	1987			2001		
	$p > 0$	Share	Shorrocks	$p > 0$	Share	Shorrocks
Wage income	0.98	0.86	0.66	0.87	0.68	0.72
Family business	0.02	0.01	0.03	0.15	0.05	0.01
Pensions	0.20	0.07	0.12	0.33	0.15	0.11
Family transfers	0.34	0.02	0.10	0.35	0.02	0.03
Other	0.96	0.03	0.09	0.67	0.07	0.13

	Urban (CHNS)					
	1991			2000		
	$p > 0$	Share	Shorrocks	$p > 0$	Share	Shorrocks
Wage income	0.77	0.46	0.32	0.64	0.52	0.46
Family business	0.15	0.07	0.35	0.17	0.10	0.37
Subsidies	0.95	0.28	0.19	0.59	0.07	0.02
Farming	0.18	0.07	0.00	0.06	0.02	0.01
Other	0.55	0.13	0.15	0.65	0.28	0.15
(of which is pensions)	0.30	0.09		0.35	0.17	

	Rural (RCRE)					
	1987			2001		
	$p > 0$	Share	Shorrocks	$p > 0$	Share	Shorrocks
Wage income	0.71	0.25	0.37	0.71	0.42	0.44
Family business	0.62	0.16	0.34	0.47	0.20	0.29
Agricultural income	0.98	0.40	0.13	0.92	0.21	0.06
Agricultural sidelines	0.96	0.13	0.07	0.73	0.10	0.18
Family transfers	0.52	0.05	0.08	0.46	0.05	0.03
Government transfers	0.65	0.01	0.00	0.71	0.01	0.00
Other	0.14	0.01	0.01	0.09	0.01	0.01

Notes: 1. This table reports the composition of income and the associated Shorrocks decompositions for urban and rural per capita household income.
2. "$p > 0$" is the proportion of households (individuals) reporting positive (nonzero) income from the given source.
3. The "share" is the proportion (share) of total income earned in the specified category.
4. The Shorrocks decompositions report the proportion of total inequality that can be attributed to inequality of that particular income source.

urban inequality, thus demands an understanding of changes in the labor market and the determination of individual earnings.

Given the potentially important role of food subsidies, and also the possible underestimation of family business income in the NBS data, we repeat the exercise using the CHNS data. The income categories will not be identical, but broad and rough comparisons are still helpful. The CHNS data provide a much better picture than do the NBS data of the role of subsidies, including access to major consumer goods (primarily food) and housing at below-market prices, childcare, and so on. These subsidies were typically allocated in a fairly egalitarian way to urban residents, often through employers, and in 1991, represented a full quarter of average household income. Between 1991 and 2000, they declined in absolute terms by more than half and by a factor of four when measured as a proportion of income.[15]

The Shorrocks decompositions confirm that these subsidies contributed very little to overall urban inequality and were relatively equalizing. Their decline almost certainly helped contributed to growing inequality. The CHNS data show a smaller share of urban income coming from wages, though some of this may reflect the aggregation of subsidies into the NBS wage income. That said, wage income is still the most important source of income and the largest contributor to urban income inequality. One further striking feature of the CHNS, in contrast to the NBS data, is the importance of income from family businesses. The estimated share of income from self-employment is higher in the CHNS (10 percent vs. 5 percent), while in 2000 it contributes to over one-third of overall inequality. This helps account for the higher level of urban inequality in the CHNS and underscores the limitations of NBS survey data in collecting income on family enterprises.

But earnings inequality is still the main story in cities. It is important, however, to note that there are several potentially important dimensions to wage earnings. As explained in detail by Cai, Park, and Zhao (Chapter 6), urban labor markets underwent considerable change, even over the most recent fifteen years of reform (since 1990). Enterprise reform, especially in SOEs, may have contributed to widening differentials in wage rates across firms and individuals. Workers lucky enough to work in successful enterprises would see their wages grow faster than those in poorly performing firms.[16] Private-sector firms would be more likely to pay on the basis of individual productivity, generating further inequality of wages. With the increase in the layoffs from the state sector beginning in the mid-1990s, and with over 40 million now laid off in industry alone, we might expect some of the growing dispersion in incomes to be coming from a shift into the lower-paying self-employment or perhaps early retirement for some individuals and households. In short, some of the rising inequality of wage earnings may have arisen as some people's wage earnings fell to zero (Meng, 2004). Even among those households with working members in the wage sector, an increase in wage earnings inequality could be coming from growing differences in either time worked (days, months, or weeks) or wage rates per unit of time.

[15] The decline in these subsidies was precipitated by fiscal problems of the central government. By the early 1990s, urban subsidies reportedly represented a quarter of all central government expenditure.

[16] Yuen (2000) confirms that the tighter connection between SOE performance and worker wages led to greater dispersion in wages.

Table 18.9. *The distribution of wage earnings urban, CHNS*

	1991	1993	1997	2000
All households				
Gini	0.49	0.56	0.57	0.67
Theil E	0.46	0.61	0.64	0.91
Coefficient of variation	0.94	1.25	1.26	1.72
Households with positive earnings				
Proportion of all households	0.75	0.72	0.66	0.58
Gini	0.32	0.39	0.36	0.42
Theil E	0.17	0.28	0.23	0.36
Coefficient of variation	0.65	0.92	0.81	1.13

Decomposition of variance of log earnings: hours versus "wages" (among those with positive earnings)

	Var	%	Var	%	Var	%	Var	%
Var (log wage earnings)	0.416	100	0.569	100	0.457	100	0.663	100
Var (log months worked)	0.221	53.1	0.253	44.5	0.18	39.4	0.233	35.1
Var (log monthly wage)	0.163	39.2	0.297	52.2	0.261	57.1	0.365	55.1
Covariance (hours, wages)	0.032	7.7	0.016	2.8	0.016	3.5	0.065	9.8

Notes: 1. This table uses the CHNS data to describe inequality of wage income in urban areas.
2. All nominal figures are expressed in constant 1990 yuan.
3. The top two panels report various measures of wage–income (earnings) inequality, including or excluding households with "zeroes" (unconditional, or conditional, on positive earnings).
4. The bottom panel reports the total variance of log earnings, decomposed into constituent log months worked and log average monthly wages, as well as the covariance between log months worked and log monthly wages ("Covariance (hours, wages)").
5. The decomposition is expressed in levels, as well as the percentage of total variation explained "%."

In Table 18.9 and Figure 18.5 we use the CHNS urban data to look at this dimension of urban inequality more carefully and evaluate the relative contribution of "wages" versus "hours" to overall earnings inequality. The top half of Table 18.9 provides measures of the inequality of wage earnings, first over all households, and then over only those reporting positive wage earnings. For all urban households, the Gini coefficient for earnings rose from 0.49 to 0.67, an increase of almost 50 percent. Some of this increase was driven by the growing number of households without any wage earnings. In the second panel (Table 18.9), we see that the proportion of households with positive wage earnings fell from 75 percent in 1991 to 58 percent in 2000. This significant drop probably reflects the layoffs associated with SOE restructuring, and may be a transitory outcome, as opposed to a long-run trend.

Figure 18.5 expands on these proportions, plotting the wage–employment rates by age category, for men and women separately. To what extent is the decline in wage employment (and thus wage income) concentrated among certain cohorts, especially the elderly? We observe significant reductions in wage employment for all

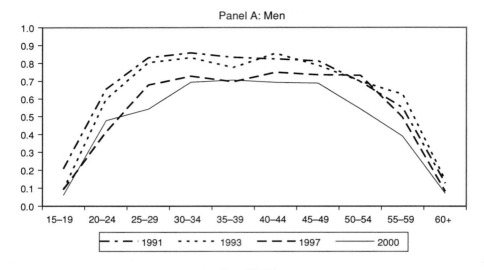

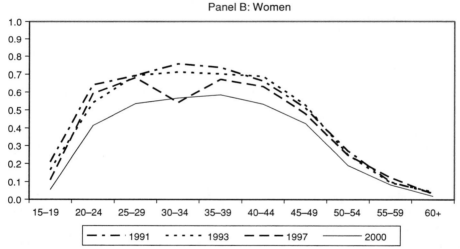

Figure 18.5. Wage–employment by age and sex, urban (*Source:* Authors' calculations based on the CHNS.)

age groups beginning in the mid-1990s. The decline is especially severe at the tails of the age distribution (20–30, 50+) for men and (20–40) for prime-age women; both outcomes appear related to labor market and SOE reform. It turns out that these declines are paralleled by similar reductions in labor force participation rates (in all types of work), so that the percentage of individuals that work in wage employment (among those working) actually remains fairly constant over time. What is most striking, nonetheless, from Figure 18.5, is the huge drop in access to wage jobs for the youngest cohorts. While the elderly clearly have plenty to be concerned about, it is poor job prospects for 20–30-year-olds that may have the most adverse long-run welfare consequences.

Returning to Table 18.9, continuing in the second panel, we see that earnings inequality still rose among those with positive earnings, with the Gini rising from 0.32 to 0.42. How much of this rise is due to quantity worked, as opposed to the returns? In the bottom part of Table 18.9, we provide a simple decomposition of the log of wage earnings for those households with positive wage earnings into constituent log months worked and log monthly wages, as well as the covariance between the two. We express the results in levels, as well as the percentage of the total variation explained.[17] Over the entire period, the variance of the log of wage earnings for those households with wage earnings increased by more than 50 percent. In 1991, 53.1 percent of the variance can be attributed to the variance in the log of months worked, with the variance in the monthly wage explaining 39.2 percent. Over the ten-year period between 1991 and 2000, there is not much of a change in the dispersion of months worked; however, there is a more than doubling in the variance of the log monthly wage. Indeed, most of the increase that we observe in the dispersion of average annual wage earnings can be attributed to an increase in the dispersion of average monthly "wages." As important as access to jobs may be in generating rising inequality, rising wage inequality among those working the same number of months is also an important element of the story.

As documented by Cai, Park, and Zhao (Chapter 6), one likely source of the increase in wage inequality is the increase in the rate of return to human capital. Park et al. (2005) also show that no matter how you partition workers into groups (e.g., high and low educated, old or young), wage dispersion has also increased dramatically. This residual inequality – while poorly understood – is assigned to "unobserved skill." It is not surprising that the returns to unobserved productivity should rise through the reforms. From a policy perspective, however, the returns to schooling are more interesting. Over the 1990s, the average rate of return to an additional year of education increased from 4 percent to more than 10 percent. The increase in return was also not realized uniformly over years of educational attainment; in other words, the percentage increase in wage earnings resulting from an additional year of school was not the same for someone with a middle school degree (nine years) and a high school degree (twelve years). In fact, it appears that a significant amount of the increase was realized by those with university degrees, as wage earnings of university graduates increased significantly relative to holders of high school degrees.

If the distribution of education (or human capital) was immutable, then rising returns to schooling might lead to ever-widening income gaps. As documented by Behrman et al. (Chapter 7), however, educational attainment is rising quickly.

---

[17] We carried out the same exercise using days rather than months and obtained very similar results.

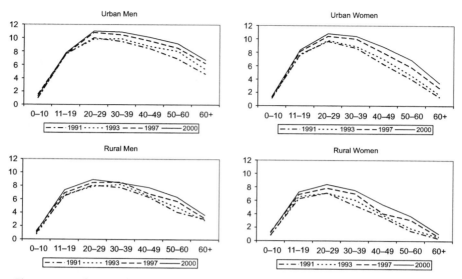

Figure 18.6. Education by age, sex, and year (urban and rural, separately) (*Source:* Authors' calculations based on the CHNS.)

In Figure 18.6 we use the CHNS to plot the age–education profiles for men and women in urban (and rural) China. Two important patterns are confirmed. First is the clear increase in educational attainment for both men and women, *across* the age distribution. It is not only the young benefiting from increased investments in schooling. Subsequent cohorts of prime and middle-aged individuals are also showing the fruits of investments in education made prior to reforms. Second, while men's schooling attainment remains higher than women's, especially for older cohorts, the improvement in schooling levels has been greatest for women. From the perspective of predicting trends in future inequality, a key determinant will be whether the increasing supply of educated workers is enough to offset the increasing demand for educated workers. If it is not, we can expect to see further rising returns to schooling and widening income inequality. If supply increases fast enough, we might instead see an attenuation of the growth in wage inequality, as is believed to have happened in other Asian economies (Birdsall, Ross, and Sabot, 1995).

In our final exploration of urban income inequality, we examine the role of age – or cohort – in rising inequality. To what extent is there an age dimension to urban poverty? For example, are the elderly being left behind? In Figure 18.7 we plot log household per capita income by age group by year, using the CHNS. The plotted lines mirror the means shown in Table 18.2, with significant growth in average incomes between 1991 and 2001. Until age 60, incomes seem to rise with age. Clearly, however, the incomes of those 60 and older are lower than those of younger cohorts, and the gap has been persistent over time. That said, the per capita incomes of the elderly have been improving like everyone else's, so while

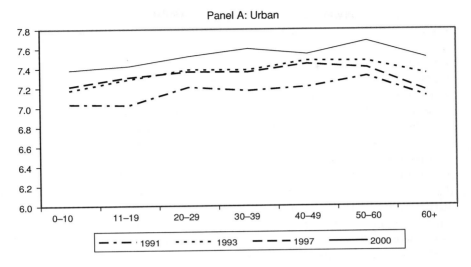

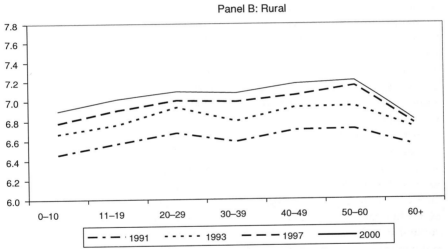

Figure 18.7. Log per capita household income by age (*Source:* Authors' calculations based on the CHNS.)

they may not be as rich as those who are presumably still working, the elderly in China's cities appear to be sharing in the general improvements of living standards.

Rural Incomes

If labor markets lie at the heart of rising urban inequality, what are the most important factors behind the slower changing but higher level of inequality in rural areas? Previous studies have emphasized the role of nonfarm income in contributing to rising rural inequality, especially departing from the relatively equal world of farm incomes derived from an egalitarian land distribution.[18] The bottom panel of Table 18.8 provides data for the composition of rural incomes for 1987 and 2001, using the RCRE data. For 1987, income from farming, including both cropping and agricultural sideline activity (animal husbandry, forestry, and fishery), was the source of more than half of all income. With nearly all rural households receiving allocations of land, nearly all households participated in farming and farm sidelines. Grain alone contributed 30 percent of total household income. Family business, mostly in commerce and services, comprised 16 percent of income, while wage income was the second largest overall component, at 25 percent. Most wage income in the 1980s was earned locally, within the village or township, with more than two-thirds of all households reporting income from wages.

This structure of income changed dramatically by the end of the period, with much of this occurring in the late 1990s. Especially noteworthy is the sharp drop in the percentage of income coming from agriculture, mostly crop income. A significant portion of the decline can be linked to the sharp drop in farm prices beginning in the mid-1990s. As of 2001, agriculture and agricultural sidelines combine for only 31 percent of total household income. We also see an increase in the relative importance of income from family businesses, which rose from 16 to 20 percent as a share of total income. But the largest improvements in family income came from wage earnings, especially wages earned by temporary migrants.[19] Locally earned wages have become less important in both relative and absolute terms, while employment opportunities outside the village and accessed through migration have become a more important source of labor earnings.

Turning to the Shorrocks decompositions for 1987, we find that agricultural income, while disequalizing, contributed *much* less to overall inequality than its share of total income (13 percent vs. approximately 40 percent).[20] The same applied to agricultural sidelines, so that combining all agriculture-related earnings, only 20 percent of total inequality was attributed to inequality of agricultural income, even while this source accounted for 53 percent of total income. For 2001, agricultural income excluding sidelines was almost irrelevant to inequality: while it still comprised 21 percent of income, it accounted for only 6 percent of overall inequality. It was very hard to get rich farming. This reflected the low crop prices already mentioned, as well as constraints on farm size implicit in the administrative allocation of land.

---

[18] See Benjamin et al. (2002) for a survey of these studies, for example, Hare (1994).

[19] The wage earnings of temporary migrants include household members resident in the village, but who commute outside the village to work and return on weekends, as well as wage earnings brought home by locally registered household members who work outside the village for a substantial portion of the year. The RCRE survey does not permit a further disaggregation.

[20] Elsewhere (Benjamin, Brandt, and Giles, 2005) we have carried out the same decompositions controlling for location, which rarely matters. This indicates that composition of income matters within villages much the same way as across villages.

Table 18.10. *The distribution of farm land
inequality and spatial variation rural,
RCRE*

	1987	1991	1995	2002
Land inequality				
Gini	0.37	0.37	0.39	0.48
90/10 ratio	5.43	5.94	7.50	25.60
Spatial variation				
Province	0.34	0.35	0.32	0.31
Village	0.73	0.71	0.62	0.70

Notes: 1. Land is defined as total per capita land managed by the household. This includes village-allocated land, plus land contracted in, less land contracted out.
2. Spatial variation is the proportion of total variation of log per capita land explained by a set of location indicators. This is calculated as the *R*-squared from a regression of "ln per capita land" on a set of dummy variables for province or village, depending on the level of spatial analysis.

We explore the land distribution more specifically in Table 18.10. Here, we report the Gini coefficient, as well as the 90/10 ratio for per capita managed land. Land inequality did grow from 1987 to 2002, but it remains quite low by developing country standards. The Gini in 2002 was 0.48. Note that unlike incomes, however, much of this inequality reflects differences in farm size across space: 70 percent of the variation in farm size is explained by village dummies and over 30 percent by province. Even across space, land area is a poor measure of the land endowment, given the usual negative correlation between land quality and farm size. For example, in some areas land can be multiple cropped (farmed more than once a year). Farm sizes also tend to be smaller in these areas, so "farm size" understates a household's "land capacity." The spatial decomposition based on cultivated area alone will thus exaggerate differences in land across space. Still, there is only limited (but nonzero) effective land inequality within villages. That largely explains why farm income contributes so little to overall inequality: farm income is quite equally distributed. It is worth noting, however, that equality of farm income, even as a consequence of the egalitarian land policy, does not imply that the land distribution policy is necessarily good for overall income inequality. More inequality of farm income might actually reduce overall income inequality. While not quite negative, the Shorrocks decomposition is close to zero. Especially if low-income households have poor nonfarm alternatives, it would be to their advantage to specialize in farming, thus leading to more inequality of farm income (and less total inequality). And unequal access to nonfarm opportunities matters more than ever.

In 2001, agricultural sidelines (like raising livestock or aquaculture) explain 18 percent of inequality, higher than the 10 percent of income they represent. Wage income, however, was the single largest contributor to overall inequality, with forty-four of overall inequality explained by inequality of wage earnings. This is only slightly larger than the now substantial 42 percent wage share of total income. Within the wage category, local wages were relatively disequalizing, while wages from employment outside the village were relatively equalizing. Nonfarm family businesses contributed most to inequality compared to their share of income (29 percent compared with about 20 percent).

Taken together, these decompositions highlight two important sources of inequality, especially when we compare 2001 to 1987. First is the sharp decline in the share of the relatively equalizing income from farming. Second is the relative increase in disequalizing income from nonfarm family businesses, and the failure of nonfarm labor markets to provide enough income opportunities for low-income households to offset the decline of agricultural income.[21] Past emphasis on the role of nonfarm income as a source of inequality was only partially correct. Increasing agricultural incomes – at least in an equalizing way – are unlikely to improve over-all income distribution, if for no other reason than agricultural incomes are only weakly associated with overall income, and they are also very low.

These results also underscore the important potential role of education in affect-ing the future trajectory of inequality. Higher levels of education facilitate success in family businesses and in local and migration-based labor markets. In the short run, as in urban areas, there may be "excess returns" for those with more education, helping generate more inequality. In fact, as discussed by Benjamin et al. (2002), excess returns to education may be higher in remote areas with poorly developed markets. This is also potentially reflected in our previous contrast between the more remote inland versus coastal regions. Inequality of education, poorly devel-oped off-farm opportunities, and low returns to farming do not bode well for the future. What is happening to the distribution of schooling?

Returning to Figure 18.6, we array the average years of schooling by age, sex, and year for rural areas (using the CHNS). As we saw for city dwellers, there have been steady improvements in the level of education, reflected in all age categories. Most remarkable here are the relatively large gains made by women, significantly closing the gap with men, especially for the younger cohorts. The level of education is still lower, however, than in cities. To the extent that rural areas need economic development as much as the cities, it will be important that the urban–rural gap in schooling narrows over time.

Finally, in Figure 18.7 we explore the age dimension of the income distribution. The general shape of the rural age–income profiles is similar to the urban sample:

---

[21] Benjamin, Brandt, and Giles (2005) show that agricultural incomes declined over the late 1990s. In real household per capita terms, farm income fell by almost a full third between 1987 and 1999. Several years later, agricultural incomes began a slow recovery.

per capita income rises with age until age 60 and then falls. Furthermore, the profiles have been moving upward over time, reflecting general improvements in living standards. The most striking difference between the rural and urban pictures concerns the relative position of the elderly. In the countryside, the economic improvements experienced by the elderly (those over 60) are much smaller than for other age groups. The rural elderly are falling behind.

INTERIM CONCLUSIONS AND THEMES FOR FUTURE STUDY

Over the course of two and half decades of reform, China experienced a significant increase in inequality that is likely underestimated by the data we use. These increases are observed within both the urban and rural populations. In rural areas, this increase is tied to the disequalizing role of some forms of nonagricultural income, and laggard growth of farming income, especially beginning in the mid-1990s. In urban areas, on the other hand, a decline in the role of subsidies and entitlements, increasing wage inequality related to labor market and enterprise reform, and the effect of restructuring of SOEs on some cohorts and households through layoffs have all played a part in widening the income distribution. Corruption may have also played a role in distribution of wealth and welfare, but this is much more difficult to measure. Regional (spatial) differences, although certainly present, are much less important than commonly believed for both urban and rural populations, as well as urban and rural combined. The same is true for differences between China's urban and rural areas.

This increase in inequality, however, must be seen in the context of rapidly rising incomes and improvements in welfare that literally pulled hundreds of millions out of poverty, especially in agriculture. Prior to the onset of reforms, urban poverty was already very low, largely because of the severe urban bias in Chinese policy and the fairly egalitarian distribution of incomes in the cities. Despite rising inequality in China's cities, urban poverty has declined still further during the reform era. Poverty does persist however – probably on the order of 10 percent of the Chinese population or in excess of 120 million – and is largely a rural phenomenon. There is a need for more research in estimating and identifying the poor in both urban and rural areas. Probably the most obvious and feasible policy recommendation is to facilitate this research by improving access to nationally representative household survey data, as well as the implementation of household surveys designed to better measure income.

Other areas of public policy need to take account of rising inequality. A recurring theme in our research, as well as other chapters in this volume, is the important role played by education in both urban and rural areas. Probably, no other single factor will exert greater influence over the distribution of benefits from future growth. In addition, China will have to adopt and implement more features of a "social safety net," as even universal education will not be enough to generate a "poverty-free" income distribution. In the countryside, equally distributed land is unlikely to do the job, especially if returns to agriculture remain low. And finally, like most other countries, China will need to adopt a redistributive taxation system, to support the social safety net, to finance public goods, and to allow the broader society to share in the obvious wealth being generated by the top part of the income distribution. Even with a richer understanding of the characteristics of the income distribution, the design and implementation of these and related types of policies will provide a challenging agenda for future research.

References

Benjamin, Dwayne and Loren Brandt. 1999. "Markets and Inequality in Rural China: Parallels with the Past." *American Economic Review.* 89(2), pp. 292–295.

Benjamin, Dwayne, Loren Brandt, and John Giles. 2005. "The Evolution of Income Inequality in Rural China." *Economic Development and Cultural Change.* 53(4), pp. 769–824.

Benjamin, Dwayne, Loren Brandt, Paul Glewwe, and Guo Li. 2002. "Markets, Human Capital, and Inequality: Evidence from China," in *Inequality Around the World.* Richard Freeman ed. London: Palgrave, pp. 87–127.

Birdsall, Nancy, David Ross, and Richard Sabot. 1995. "Inequality and Growth Reconsidered." *World Bank Economic Review.* 9(3), pp. 477–508.

Brandt, Loren and Carsten Holz. 2006. "Spatial Price Differences in China: Estimates and Implications." *Economic Development and Cultural Change.* 55(1), pp. 43–86.

Deaton, Angus. 1997. *The Analysis of Household Surveys: A Microeconometric Approach to Development Policy.* Baltimore and London: Johns Hopkins University Press for the World Bank.

Gustafsson, Bjorn and Shi Li. 2002. "Income Inequality within and across Counties in Rural China 1988 and 1995." *Journal of Development Economics.* 69, pp. 179–204.

Hare, Denise. 1994. "Rural Nonagricultural Activities and Their Impact on the Distribution of Income: Evidence from Farm Households in Southern China." *China Economic Review.* 5(1), pp. 59–82.

Kanbur, Ravi and Xiaobo Zhang. 1999. "Which Regional Inequality? The Evolution of Rural–Urban and Inland–Coastal Inequality in China, 1988 to 1995." *Journal of Comparative Economics.* 27(4), pp. 686–701.

Khan, Azizur Rahman and Carl Riskin. 1998. "Income and Inequality in China: Composition, Distribution and Growth of Household Income, 1988 to 1995." *China Quarterly.* 154, pp. 221–253.

Khan, Azizur Rahman and Carl Riskin. 1999. "Income Distribution in Urban China during the Period of Economic Reform and Globalization." *American Economic Review.* 89(2), pp. 296–300.

Lardy, Nicholas. 1984. "Consumption and Living Standards in China, 1978–83." *China Quarterly.* 100, pp. 849–865.

Meng, Xin. 2004. "Economic Restructuring and Income Inequality in Urban China." *Review of Income and Wealth.* 50(3), pp. 357–379.

Meng, Xin, Robert Gregory, and Youjuan Wang. 2005. "Poverty, Inequality, and Growth in Urban China, 1986–2000." *Journal of Comparative Economics.* 33(4), pp. 710–729.

Park, Albert, Xiaoqing Song, Junsen Zhang, and Yaohui Zhao. 2005. "Economic Returns to Schooling in Urban China, 1988 to 2001." *Journal of Comparative Economics.* 33(4), pp. 730–752.

Ravallion, Martin and Shaohua Chen. 2006. "China's (Uneven) Progress Against Poverty." *Journal of Development Economics.* 82(1), pp. 1–42.

Rawski, Thomas G. 1982. "The Simple Arithmetic of Chinese Income Distribution." *Keizai Kenkyu.* 33(1), pp. 12–26.

Shorrocks, Anthony F. 1982. "Decomposition by Factor Components." *Econometrica.* 50(1), pp. 193–211.

Shorrocks, Anthony F. 1983. "The Impact of Income Components on the Distribution of Family Incomes." *Quarterly Journal of Economics.* 98(2), pp. 311–326.

Vermeer, Eduard B. 1982. "Income Differentials in Rural China." *China Quarterly.* 89, pp. 1–33.

Yuen, Terence. 2000. *Employment and Wage Dynamics: Estimating the Impact of Labour Market Institutions.* Unpublished Dissertation. Toronto: University of Toronto.

NINETEEN

Spatial Dimensions of Chinese Economic Development

Kam Wing Chan, J. Vernon Henderson, and Kai Yuen Tsui[1]

INTRODUCTION

The spatial arrangement of population and economic activities is an important and complex dimension of Chinese economic development. Yet it is understudied, with Yuan-li Wu's (1967) classic work, *The Spatial Economy of Communist China*, standing as the last comprehensive analysis, which is now seriously outdated. This present chapter is not intended to be its update. Instead, we aim at a more modest goal: to examine two key aspects of changes the Chinese spatial economy has undergone in the past half century, with a focus on the last ten or fifteen years. These two changes are (a) the extensive urbanization that has occurred since the early 1980s, involving migration from rural areas to traditional cities and industrialization of the rural sector with growth of many townships into urban centers and expansion of existing cities and (b) the changing spatial inequalities across provinces, resulting from allocation of state investment and budgetary resources, distribution of foreign direct investment (FDI), and other pertinent factors. It is hoped that this chapter will help the reader to understand the enormous changes in the spatial configurations of the Chinese economy, how they are shaped by the institutional landscape and policies, and how they have impinged on economic development.

As a prelude to our subsequent discussion, it is useful at the outset to briefly highlight some critical economic thinking on the importance of the spatial dimension in the process of development.

Urbanization

Economic development and technological change induced by human capital accumulation and technology transfer from abroad lead to urbanization, a shift from

[1] We thank Thomas Rawski and Loren Brandt for their detailed comments and suggestions. We also gratefully acknowledge many useful comments made by the reviewers and participants at the China Economic Transition conferences in Pittsburgh in 2004 and Toronto in 2002.

labor- and land-intensive agricultural production into urban industrial production. Analyses dating back to Marshall (1890) show that urban industrial production is subject to localized external economies of scale such as information spillovers and labor market externalities. It is also subject to the new economic geography's virtuous circle of agglomeration benefits – pecuniary externalities from consumers and producers being able to buy locally produced goods in close spatial proximity with low or negligible shipping costs.

Urbanization changes a country's entire spatial scale. While rural production may be carried out in farms spread across the national landscape serviced by small agricultural towns and market centers, in an urban hierarchy, production takes place in large, densely populated cities, often clustered near coastal areas. At the top of the hierarchy will be mega-cities that are centers of commerce, finance, and business services,[2] which house 10–15 million people in metro areas with high and complex planning and urban infrastructure needs. Urbanization requires developing countries to uproot most of their traditional rural population, invest heavily in urban infrastructure, develop institutions that permit cities to finance those investments, and extend the rule of law and other formal market institutions to replace the social mechanisms of traditional rural societies that are not workable in the anonymity of urban exchange.

Regional Development

Underlying mainstream spatial economic analyses is the assumption of a market economy with free flows of goods and factors that respond to economic incentives, though subject to such constraints as transportation and mobility costs. Market forces shape the structural transformation of the economy as well as the agglomeration or dispersal of economic activities. For example, the new economic geography focuses on the role of regional development and a core–periphery (coastal–hinterland) structure. In these models, transport costs among regions are the key driving force. When transport costs are very high, hinterland regions have protected markets for industrial urban products. As transport costs fall, a core–periphery structure may develop where all industry locates in the core to exploit (pecuniary) agglomeration economies. If transport costs get low enough (diminishing the impact of pecuniary externalities, which measure the benefits of consuming as much as possible in one place to conserve on transport costs) and/or migration is costly, then there may be core–periphery reversal, with industry again

---

[2] Business services in the United States of America include advertising, services to dwellings and other buildings, personnel supply services, management, consulting, and public relations, detective and protective services, and computer and data-processing services. In China until recently such services were reported under "social services" and included public facilities, tourism, recreation, computer services, and information and consultancy (including advertising).

decentralizing to the hinterlands. This type of story has applicability to the current Chinese situation.

However fundamental these market forces may be, economists have come to realize that the actual path of a nation's spatial development is often dependent on and sometimes locked in by its past history and institutions. In this regard, China is no exception. In particular, the Maoist development strategy in the three decades before the reform era imprinted China's spatial economic structure with features that differ from market economies at similar levels of economic development, notwithstanding the subsequent effect of market reforms that have unleashed the forces delineated in standard spatial models. In what follows, we try to make sense of China's spatial development by examining the interactions between China's political economy and market forces.

We begin by describing how history and political institutions have shaped China's spatial development. With this background in mind, the chapter focuses on spatial development of cities and provinces. The section "Urbanization and Growth" provides a broad picture of the configuration of China's urbanization process and the salient features distinguishing it from those of other market economies. Forces shaping provincial economic growth and interprovincial disparities are the subject of the section on "Provinces." The concluding section summarizes the major findings and points to topics in need of further research.

BACKGROUND

Political Economy of Spatial Units

Of the various criteria for drawing spatial boundaries in China, ranging from Skinner's (1985) "macroregions" to geographers' "natural regions," administrative geography plays a critical role in shaping many aspects of economic and social development. Beginning with the first emperor of China who united the nation, how jurisdictional boundaries should be drawn and how to design the administrative hierarchy to solidify China's polity is a perennial theme in Chinese statecraft. In today's China, the system of administrative jurisdictions has evolved into a five-tier hierarchy, consisting of the central government, province-level units, prefecture-level units, county-level units, and towns and townships. The changes in the numbers of these administrative jurisdictions at the county level and above are summarized in Table 19.1. The higher up the administrative hierarchy, the higher is the administrative rank. The rank not only reflects political/administrative power but also has significance in the fiscal system (Wong, 1997; Chan, Tsui, and Yu, 2003).

In the subsequent discussion, we essentially focus on two types of spatial administrative units: the province-level unit and the city. Provinces and cities, for which systematic social and economic data are more readily available, are the major subnational players in China's politics and economics. Cities can be found at the

Table 19.1. *Number of administrative units, cities, and towns in mainland China, selected years*

Year	All administrative units			Cities and towns				
	Province-level units	Prefecture-level units	County-level units[a]	Province-level cities	Prefecture-level cities	County-level cities	All cities	Towns
1955	28	288	2,785	3	83	78	164	4,487
1960	28	244	2,105	2	88	109	199	4,429[b]
1970	29	291	2,583	3	79	95	177	n.a.
1978	29	310	2,653	3	98	92	193	2,173
1982	29	323	2,766	3	112	130	245	2,664
1990	30	336	2,833	3	185	279	467	12,084
1995	30	334	2,849	3	210	427	640	17,300
2000	31	333	2,861	4	259	400	663	20,312
2004	31	333	2,862	4	283	374	661	19,883
2005	31	333	2,862	4	283	374	661	19,522

[a] Including urban districts (*shixiaqu*).
[b] 1961.
Sources: Ministry of Civil Affairs, Planning and Finance Department (1993, 2003, 2004) and Chen and Chen (2003).

provincial, prefectural, and county levels. At times, we also use the broader regional classification of the "East" (or "coastal"), "Central" and "West," as has been used in the standard literature on China. Of course, there are many important and interesting spatial aspects of economic development that can be chronicled and analyzed at other levels (such as counties and towns), but limitations of space leave us no choice but to treat them only in passing.

Relevant to the spatial dimension of economic development are a number of salient features of the evolving system of administrative jurisdictions:

Centralization versus Decentralization
In theory, China is a unitary state with a hierarchy of governments. There is much controversy over the degree of political centralization in different epochs, including the People's Republic (see, e.g., Donnithorne, 1972, 1976; Lardy, 1975, 1976, 1978; Eckstein, 1975; Wong, 1991, 1995, 1997, 2005; Huang, 1995, 2001; Montinola, Qian, and Weingast, 1995; Qian and Weingast, 1997). Centralization can be quite difficult to measure. Many studies focus on the sharing of the fiscal pie. On this score, China may be the most decentralized country in the world by expenditure shares (Wong, 2005). There is, however, another more subtle and less palpable dimension of control: the appointment and dismissal of cadres in subordinate governments that are tightly controlled by the Communist Party (Tsui and Wang, 2002).

When the Communists came to power, China was at a low level of economic development with poor transport infrastructure. The task of micromanaging a vast and heterogeneous country from the center in the same fashion as the Soviet Union was monumental. Even if the center had the power to mobilize strategic resources in time of perceived crises, it would have been overwhelmed by most of the day-to-day planning and running of the whole economy from the top. Common sense and principal-agent models suggest that pure coercion and centralization of power may not be the best way to motivate subordinates, especially in a vast country like China, with local cadres having substantial advantages in obtaining local information. The result was pressure to delegate everyday planning and management to the provincial and subprovincial levels. There were three episodes of decentralization (in the late 1950s, early 1970s, and early 1980s) in the last five decades, delegating the management of local affairs to subnational governments.

The period of the Great Leap Forward ushered in the first wave of decentralization, which was quickly reversed with the collapse of the economy in the early 1960. In the 1970s, Lardy (1975, 1976, 1978) and Donnithorne (1976) debated the nature and extent of administrative decentralization during the pre-reform period.[3] The third wave of decentralization, often referred to as "meals from separate stoves" (*fenzao chifan*), has been unfolding in the reform era with revenue-sharing rules laid down by fiscal contracts between successive tiers of governments (see Chapter 12 in this volume). Up to 1993, Wong (2005) characterizes fiscal reform as "decentralization by default rather than by design," with increasingly larger shares of fiscal revenues accruing to local governments under the generous terms of the fiscal contracts. Some have gone so far as to argue that China has become a de facto federalist state, for example, Montinola, Qian, and Weingast (1995) and Qian and Weingast (1997), though Tsui and Wang (2002) present a more nuanced story of vertical control and question how far China has really moved down the road of decentralization.

Central–local relations are often thought to be critical to determining resource mobilization capabilities of upper-level governments. The alleged swings between centrifugal and centripetal administrative tendencies potentially have important implications for the spatial allocation of resources, economic structures of local jurisdictions, regional specialization, and spatial inequalities.

Administrative Boundaries as Political Barriers

The system of jurisdictions has erected administrative barriers that impede the free flow of goods and factors of production. The architecture of the hierarchical administrative system is per se not congenial to horizontal cooperation. With local governments answerable to upper-tier governments and not subordinate to neighboring jurisdictions, frequent interjurisdictional conflicts often have to be resolved

---

[3] After a trip to China in the mid-1970s, Eckstein (1975) was under the impression that China was more centralized than was suggested by Donnithorne.

by upper-level governments, an adjudication process that may be time consuming and costly. When local implementation of mandates from above becomes a performance indicator for evaluating local cadres, the pursuit of local interests produces local protectionism as well as costly duplication.[4] Such considerations stimulate ongoing debate on the extent of fragmentation within China's economy (see, among others, Donnithorne, 1972; Lyons, 1987; Young, 2000; Naughton, 2003; Poncet, 2003; Bai et al., 2004; Boyreau-Debray and Wei, 2004). The political barriers are further reinforced by such institutions as the household registration system (see later) that has restricted interjurisdictional factor mobility since the early 1960s.

Administrative Rank and Political Power

Implicit in the administrative system is a hierarchical distribution of powers. With industrialization forming the core of China's development strategy since the 1950s, urban jurisdictions have enjoyed higher administrative ranks, enhancing China's persistent urban bias. In this connection, China's urban system is illustrative. All Chinese cities have administrative ranks, indicating their status in China's unitary political/administrative system. Formally, from high to low, there are three levels: provincial, prefectural, and county. In practice, there are five.[5] Local jurisdictions have incentives to climb up the administrative ladder, fueling the proliferation of urban designations and "upgrades," resulting in the rapid increase in the number of especially prefecture-level and county-level cities since the early 1980s (Chung and Lam, 2005; see also Table 19.1). In the last few years, the decrease in the number of county-level cities is a result of the rapid increase in the number of upgrades to prefecture-level as well as annexation of county-level cities by some prefecture-level cities.

Continuity, Reform, and Spatial Economic Development

Paving the way for our subsequent discussion, we review some of the spatial economic issues entailed by this administrative hierarchy. Unlike Russia, China's transition to a market economy is not a clean break from the past. China's pre-reform political institutions have remained essentially intact and have left their marks on the functioning of the economy. As suggested earlier, these political institutions have engendered an incentive system for local cadres whose responses in turn shape the spatial configuration of the economy.

---

[4] The rivalry among cities in the Pearl River Delta (PRD) is a case in point, where channels of horizontal cooperation are weak and disputes often have to be resolved by the center. The construction of several large international airports (in Guangzhou, Shenzhen, and Zhuhai) in the delta is an oft-cited example of duplication due to interjurisdictional rivalry. The same may be found in the Changjiang Delta.

[5] These five levels are (1) province-level cities, (2) deputy-provincial, (3) provincial capitals (excluding those already in level 2 above), (4) prefecture-level cities (excluding those already in levels 2 and 3), and (5) county-level cities.

Spatial Fragmentation, Regional Specialization, Comparative Advantage, and Agglomeration

The vicissitudes of Chinese political economy have impinged on regional special-ization and the formation of an integrated economy. After coming to power in 1949, the Communist regime was obsessed with rapid industrialization. With the state budget financing the preponderant share of investment, planning bolstered the center's resource mobilization capability throughout the pre-reform era (see Lardy, 1975, 1978; Naughton, 2002). The designers of China's big push in the 1950s viewed the concentration of industries in the coastal provinces as an unfortunate legacy of the Nationalist regime and past imperialism. They also saw a more spa-tially dispersed industrial structure as a way to reduce the gap between coastal and inland provinces. Mao Zedong saw the division of resources between coast and interior as one of China's "ten cardinal relations." Military threats from the Soviet Union and the United States of America also contributed to Chinese spatial plan-ning, particularly in connection with the Third Front Campaign, which ploughed investment funds into certain inland provinces between the mid-1960s and the early 1970s (Naughton, 1988).

Rather than regional specialization, a more spatially dispersed industrial struc-ture gradually emerged with a discernible decline in the eastern provinces' share of the secondary sector in the 1960s, as shown later in Figure 19.4. Planners' prefer-ences, especially those of provincial planners, rather than comparative advantage and agglomeration economies, determined allocations. For the pre-reform period as a whole, the "price scissors" problem (discussed later), the uncertainties of securing production inputs from other administrative units, and the difficulty of horizontal coordination mentioned earlier set off a process of "suboptimization" at the local level. Local units pursued local self-sufficiency and induced "backward specialization" (Lyons, 1987). That along with dismal (road) transport resulted in a fragmented economy, a lack of interprovincial trade in final goods, and a cen-ter that had weak economic control. Furthermore, the outbreak of the Cultural Revolution ushered in a ten-year period (1966–1976) of political turmoil that fur-ther hampered efforts to promote economic integration and further obstructed regional specialization.

As a result, China entered the reform era with an economic structure notably lacking in industrial specialization and agglomeration. Declining interprovincial trade in farm products reflected the same weakness within the agricultural sector (Lardy, 1983). It is tempting to think that the reforms of the last twenty-five years have ushered in a host of forces that may potentially enhance efficiency in the spatial allocation of resources: a gradual retreat from central planning, a relative decline in state investment, a bigger role for market forces, and a third wave of fiscal decentralization (*fenzao chifan*). But has reform really helped enhance efficient spatial resource allocation? The answer is far from certain.

Reform has phased out policies of local and national self-reliance and enor-mously increased the role of market forces in the allocation of resources. There is no lack of anecdotes and evidence demonstrating that spatial economic restructuring is taking place, exploiting comparative advantages and agglomeration economies. The experiences of the Pearl River Delta (PRD) and the Yangzi (Changjiang) Delta are illustrative. Focus on heavy industry led China's planners to neglect Guangdong during the Maoist era. Reform has changed Guangdong's fate, pushing this southern province "one step ahead" of China in reform and opening up to the outside world (Vogel, 1989). The share of Guangdong's secondary output in the national total has exhibited a sustained upward trend in the reform era, not least due to the flood of offshore investment exploiting its cheap land and labor boosted by its proximity to Hong Kong. The PRD in Guangdong has fast become "the world's factory," thanks to the influx of FDI and a relaxed *hukou* (household registration) system luring millions of migrants to toil in factories in the delta. The PRD is not alone. A similar hub of industrial agglomeration has also emerged in the Yangzi Delta with Shanghai as its focal point.

Despite these promising developments, the inherited administrative system remains intact, though perhaps in somewhat modified form (Huang, 1995, 2001). Incentives inimical to horizontal coordination continue to shape the behavior of cadres who retain substantial control over local economies. Their mandates have become increasingly oriented toward the paramount goal of promoting local economic development. This encourages officials at all levels to promote local industries, which offer additional benefits in the form of new tax flows for local public coffers (Wong, 1992; Whiting, 2001). Endless anecdotes confirm that interjurisdictional rivalry for economic supremacy breeds local protectionism and blocks interjurisdictional flows of goods and factors.

The path of regional specialization depends on the relative potency of these opposing forces. There is no consensus on the outcome (see, e.g., Wang and Li, 2000; Young, 2000; Poncet, 2003; Naughton, 2003; Bai et al., 2004; Boyreau-Debray and Wei, 2004). In an influential paper, Young (2000) contends that decentralization in the reform era breeds local protectionism, which impedes efficient spatial allocation of goods and factors. He concludes that "twenty years of economic reform . . . resulted in a fragmented internal market with fiefdoms controlled by local officials whose economic and political ties to protected industry resemble those of the Latin American economies of past decades" (Young, 2000, p. 1128). While supported by Poncet (2003), Young's findings did not remain unchallenged (see Chapters 15 and 16 in this volume). Naughton (2003) arrived at a different picture using interprovincial trade data. Fujita and Hu (2001) have argued that industrial agglomeration in the coastal region has become stronger in the reform era, no least due to exports and FDI. Bai et al. (2004) resorting to less aggregate data, come to a more nuanced conclusion that is not entirely consistent with Young's.

Spatial Fragmentation through Another Lens: Urban–Rural Dichotomy

China's urban–rural fault line offers another perspective on spatial fragmentation. Traditionally, urban jurisdictions, as the locus for priority industrialization, belonged to the orbit of planning. In its almost single-minded pursuit of industrialization, pre-reform development strategy in China included a broad array of policies favoring cities and urban residents: the "price scissors," which tilted terms of trade against farmers; the household registration system; and unified procurement and distribution of grains. These arrangements erected "invisible walls" that reinforced rural–urban segmentation (Chan, 1994). The household registration system restricted formal and informal rural–urban migration. Interprovincial migration was limited to participants in state programs (Third Front industrialization and frontier development programs in the 1950s and 1960s).

The urban-based industrialization strategy left its imprint on China's economic structure at the dawn of the reform era. One result was relatively low urbanization level compared to China's industrialization level. Furthermore, without migration as a force to equalize income, urban–rural disparities remained large. Official income data in Table 19.2 show that in 1978, urban income was two and a half times that of rural income. Other more comprehensive measures of "real incomes" show that the urban/rural ratio may have been as much as three or even six to one in 1976 (see Chan, 1994, p. 68). The administrative hierarchy also increased disparities between large cities and small cities due to their administrative ranks.

Restriction of Factor Mobility Across Locales

Administrative borders continue to limit factor mobility. In the Maoist era, capital was subject to various kinds of plan allocations and assignments. As shown in Table 19.14, state appropriations formed the largest share of basic construction investment in the pre-reform era. State investment funds were allocated in accordance with priorities set forth by the plans. Reform has witnessed a sustained decline in the share of state budgetary investment to be replaced by new channels of investment financing. China's increasing openness has attracted a considerable influx of FDI, the spatial distribution of which is largely driven by efficiency considerations.

The effects of other nonstate sources of investment financing, viz., bank loans and self-raised funds, are however not all that certain. The policy of converting state appropriations to bank lending (*bogaidai*) promulgated in the early 1980s was intended to increase efficiency in the use of capital. However, local branches of Chinese state banks were often captured by local governments. The allocation of bank loans was thus not entirely a result of market forces. Decentralization in the reform era has resulted in an explosion of self-raised funds controlled by local governments. Together with profits of local enterprises and administrative units, these funds are channeled through off-budget fiscal accounts into investment projects that fuel local economic development. Self-raised funds, whose distribution is skewed in favor of richer regions, also serve to promote local investment.

In sum, reform has opened up new channels for investment financing, some reflecting market forces, while others remain under the control of local jurisdictions. This is perhaps why Boyreau-Debray and Wei (2004) have found that China's capital market remains weakly integrated by international standards.

Table 19.2. *Rural–urban income disparities*

Year	Rural	Urban	Ratio (urban = 100)
1978	134	343	38.9
1980	186	436	42.6
1985	359	551	65.2
1989	408	627	65.2
1990	416	680	61.1
1991	424	729	58.1
1992	449	800	56.2
1993	463	876	52.9
1994	487	951	51.2
1995	513	997	51.4
1996	559	1,036	53.9
1997	584	1,071	54.6
1998	609	1,133	53.8
1999	633	1,238	51.1
2000	646	1,318	49.0
2001	673	1,430	47.1
2002	705	1,621	43.5
2003	736	1,767	41.6
2004	786	1,903	41.3

Notes: Rural income refers to "per capita annual net income"; urban income refers to "per capita annual disposable income." Urban subsidies and nonmonetary incomes are not included.
Source: NBS (2005).

During the plan era, population was held in place by the *hukou* system, established during the 1950s,[6] which acted as an internal passport arrangement regulating mobility and granting people citizenship in the locality (village, town, and city) in which, traditionally, their mother was a citizen. Except for government-sponsored resettlement programs, permanent changes in residence were rarely allowed during the 1960s and 1970s. Severe restrictions were placed on "upward" migrations (from rural to urban, and up the urban (administrative) hierarchy). This immobility of factors contributed to regional imbalances.

Decollectivization of agriculture, *hukou* reforms, and relaxation of migration controls since the early 1980s, especially in the late 1990s, have resulted in large-scale, mostly "temporary" migration. The stock of non-*hukou* migrants (mostly low-skilled labor) has currently reached a high level of about 150 million (NBS, 2006). For university graduates, there are now rudimentary regional, if not national, labor markets. But still, many impediments to migration remain.

[6] For details about the *hukou* system, see Chan and Zhang (1999) and Wang (2005).

Spatial Disparities

Spatial disparities, like spatial units, can be studied at different levels depending on the purpose and the availability of data. Rural–urban differences and inter-provincial variation are two of the most important aspects underlying the spatial structure and dynamics of the Chinese political economy.[7] As pointed out before, the subject of centralization versus decentralization figures prominently in the discussion of spatial disparities. A recurrent theme in debates over decentralization is the extent to which the pull and push of centrifugal and centripetal administrative forces influenced spatial disparities. Lardy (1975, 1976, 1978) argued that central planning empowered the pre-reform state to mobilize and redistribute resources from the coastal to the inland provinces, thereby reducing regional inequality. Donnithorne (1972), however, portrayed China as a "cellular economy" in which decentralization and the call for self-reliance diluted the effort of the center to reduce regional disparities.

More recently, Naughton (2002) argued that interprovincial inequality is shaped by a "redistributive system" through "the mechanism of industrial investment." Opposing forces affecting spatial inequalities have been at work. Redistributive state investment has declined, but the liberalization of the farm sector in the early 1980s benefited the poorer provinces (which are more agricultural), thereby reducing rural–urban disparities (see Table 19.2). Interregional migration may also improve the relative standing of poorer provinces and rural households (Chan and Wang, 2004; Ma et al., 2004).

Other reforms, however, may have boosted economic efficiency while increasing regional disparities. New patterns of resource allocation reflecting market forces – for example, foreign investment and deployment of off-budget funds – may offer disproportionate benefits to the rich coastal provinces.

With this background, we now turn to our two main topics: urbanization and cities, and regional inequality.

URBANIZATION AND GROWTH

After two decades of relatively limited urbanization and strict control of migration despite high rates of industrialization in the 1960s and 1970s, the last twenty-five years saw a significant change, with high rates of urban growth caused by rural–urban migration and the physical expansion of existing urban centers.

Patterns of Urban Population Growth

One cannot reasonably delineate the contours of China's urbanization without first clarifying the meaning of the term "urban." The definition of urban in China is

---

[7] Again, space does not allow us to delve into other valid issues of disparities, including those within the urban sector, within the rural sector, and within provinces. See, however, Chapter 18 in this volume.

complex, with multiple sources of confusion and difficulties.[8] Urban administrative areas (UAA; city districts, *shiqu*), which are the basis for counting urban population, often include large stretches of farmland and sizable rural populations, thus inflating the urban population figures. At the same time, the *hukou* system treats migrants who may have lived and worked in cities for years as outsiders who are excluded from the annual official population tabulations, thereby undercounting the city population. To compound the difficulties, the rapidity of "urban development" in the last two decades necessitates fairly frequent urban reclassifications and adjustments of urban designation criteria. This makes comparisons of urban growth rates or other urban economic data extremely difficult over time. These complexities also demand great care in using and interpreting Chinese urban statistics.

The current official definition in use by the National Bureau of Statistics (NBS) comes from the 2000 population census, which introduced new criteria for defining urban areas and hence urban populations. Specialists regard these definitions and population figures as reasonably reflective of China's urbanization level (see Chan and Hu, 2003; Zhou and Ma, 2003). Based on presumably comparable data using this definition, the 2005 1 percent national population survey indicates that in November 2005, China's urban population had reached 562 million, or 43 percent of the national total (NBS, 2006). China continues to be the country with the largest urban population in the world.

National Trends Since 1949

The overall national trends of urban growth and urbanization in the second half of the twentieth century are shown in Table 19.3. During this half century, the share of urban population increased from 10.6 percent in 1949 to 43 percent in 2005 (NBS, 2006). The average annual urban growth rate for the second half of the twentieth century, at 4.1 percent, is high and comparable to that of other developing countries, though industrialization in China was faster than in other developing countries (Chan, 1994). A closer look at Table 19.3 shows very rapid urban population growth in the 1950s, fueled by both high rates of natural increase and high net rural–urban migration rates. The 1960s and most of the 1970s were a period of very limited urban growth and urbanization. The reform era since 1978 has shown consistently high rates of urban growth, mainly generated by net rural–urban migration (including urban reclassification). According to the estimates by Chan and Hu (2003), the total net rural–urban migration in the decade of the 1990s is 125.5 million, which is only slightly below the aggregate of the same net migration (134.4 million) for the preceding four decades (1950–1990).

Figure 19.1 draws on a set of reconstructed urban population estimates prepared by Chan and Hu (2003) to show the trends in the 1990s.[9] The annual urban growth

---

[8] See the voluminous literature on this, notably, Chan (1994), Chan and Hu (2003), and Zhou and Ma (2003).

[9] There are serious problems in the annual urban population series published by the NBS, see Chan and Hu (2003).

Table 19.3. *Components of urban growth in China, 1950–2000*

Period	Number of years covered	Average annual urban growth		Average annual change in urban percentage	Components of urban growth*			
		Size (millions)	Percentage		Natural increase		Net in-migration	
					Average annual size		Average annual size	
					Millions	Percentage	Millions	Percentage
1950–1957	8	5.6	7.2	0.59	2.26	40	3.35	60
1958–1960	3	10.4	9.1	1.45	1.91	18	8.50	82
1961–1965	5	−2.6	−2.1	−0.63	2.99	n.a.	−5.62	n.a.
1966–1977	12	3.0	2.0	−0.04	2.09	69	0.93	31
1978–1982	5	9.0	4.8	0.66	2.01	22	6.69	78
1983–1990	8	10.9	4.3	0.66	2.85	26	8.04	74
1991–2000	10	15.7	4.2	1.00	3.16	20	12.55	80
2001–2005	5	20.6	4.1	1.35	2.52	12	18.11	88
1950–2000	51	7.87	4.1	0.50	2.52	33	5.27	67

Note: *Including urban classification

Sources: Urban population figures for 1950–1990 are from Chan (1994, p. 36). Those for 1991–2000 are from Chan and Hu (2003), and 2001–2005 are preliminary estimates based on the assumption of an average annual urban rate of natural increase of 0.5 percent. For technical details, see Chan and Hu (2003, table 2).

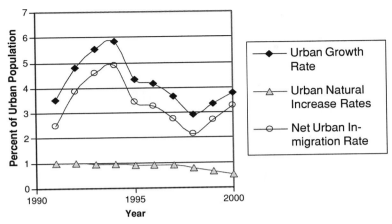

Figure 19.1. Annual urban growth and migration rates, 1990–2000 (*Source:* Based on Chan and Hu, 2003)

rates were at a high level in the early 1990s, attributable to the fervent development momentum generated by Deng Xiaoping's famous tour of south China in 1992. Urban growth slowed in 1995–1998, reflecting an economic downturn. The state-owned enterprise reforms and the increasing pressures of urban unemployment also led to more stringent measures against migration of rural workers to major cities. Since 1999, however, another round of *hukou* reforms and relaxation of the migration restrictions, combined with a recovering economy, seem to have promoted an upswing in urban growth. Based on the latest NBS figures, the average annual urban growth rate between 2000 and 2005 is about 4 percent, the same as the average of the 1990s (Table 19.3).

Population Growth of Cities in the 1990s

In the 1990s, the Chinese urban system expanded quite significantly by adding about 200 new cities and 8,228 towns in net terms (Table 19.1; Chan and Hu, 2003). In 2005, China had 661 cities and 19,522 towns. The newly designated urban centers were important contributors to urbanization in that decade. The other dimension of urbanization was the population growth of the cities and towns that already existed in 1990. The censuses of 1990 and 2000 provide useful population data[10] of individual cities based on the UAA and allow a comparison of the growth rates for population of cities existent in those two years.[11] Table 19.4 summarizes the

[10] The census population numbers are based on "resident population," which includes population without local *hukou* registration but staying in the locale for more than one year (1990 Census) or six months (2000 Census).

[11] In China, the UAA refers to the "city districts" or *shiqu* for prefecture-level cities and above and the entire administrative area for county-level cities. The UAA may not be static over time, as the city grows (most of the cases in this rapidly urbanizing nation) and expands its UAA (by

Table 19.4. *Average annual growth rates of cities,*
1990–2000

	Number	Median	Unweighted mean
All cities	414	1.8	3.0
(A) By city size in 1990			
Superlarge	7	5.7	6.1
Extralarge	79	1.4	2.2
Large	135	1.1	1.7
Medium	149	2.2	3.5
Small	44	4.4	6.1
(B) By city size in 2000			
Superlarge	16	4.6	6.6
Extralarge	98	1.8	3.7
Large	163	1.5	2.3
Medium	114	1.8	2.4
Small	23	3.8	5.1
(C) By administrative rank in 2000			
1. Provincial	4	5.2	6.2
2. Deputy-provincial	15	3.9	5.7
3. Provincial capital	17	4.2	4.2
4. Prefectural	194	2.3	3.6
5. County	184	1.0	1.9

Note: Values are in percent.
Sources: Computed from Chinese census data of 1990 and 2000. See explanations in the text.

average population growth rates based on a sample of 414 city populations of 1990 and 2000.[12]

Largely following the standard classification used in China, Table 19.4 groups the cities by size: superlarge (2 million and above), extralarge (1–2 million), large (0.5–1.0 million), medium (0.2–0.5 million), and small (below 0.2 million).[13] The smallest and the largest cities have the highest median or mean growth rates,

annexing the nearby areas). This of course complicates meaningful comparisons of "urban" areas and population over time. Moreover, there are many cities in China where annexations reflect government administrative arrangements rather than genuine urbanization or urban expansion, creating "overbounded" cities.

[12] 432 cities existed in both 1990 and 2000. The final sample excludes 18 cities with an annual rate of decrease more than 10 percent between 1990 and 2000 and one city with a highly unusual growth rate. A great majority of these cases experienced extraordinarily large reclassification of the UAA.

[13] To avoid confusion, the term "big city" is used in this section to refer to cities of considerable population size while restricting the word "large" to the specific categories of city size, as defined in this section.

Table 19.5. *High population growth cities: top twenty "million cities" with the highest population growth rates in 1990–2000*

City	Administrative rank in 2000	City population size (1,000)		Average annual growth rate (%)
		1990	2000	
Dongguan	4	1,736.9	6,445.8	14.0
Chongqing	1	3,122.7	9,691.9	12.0
Guangzhou	2	3,918.0	8,524.8	8.1
Wuhan	1	3,832.5	8,312.7	8.1
Zhongshan	4	1,227.5	2,363.3	6.8
Kunming	3	1,612.0	3,035.4	6.5
Shanghai	1	8,205.6	14,348.5	5.7
Hangzhou	2	1,476.2	2,451.3	5.2
Changsha	3	1,329.0	2,122.9	4.8
Beijing	1	7,362.4	11,509.6	4.6
Xi'an	2	2,872.5	4,481.5	4.5
Nanning	3	1,159.1	1,766.7	4.3
Fuzhou	3	1,395.7	2,124.4	4.3
Urumqi	3	1,160.8	1,753.3	4.2
Hefei	3	1,099.5	1,659.1	4.2
Jilin	4	1,320.2	1,953.1	4.0
Zhengzhou	3	1,752.4	2,589.4	4.0
Changchun	2	2,192.3	3,225.6	3.9
Chengdu	2	2,954.9	4,333.5	3.9
Nanchang	3	1,262.0	1,844.3	3.9

Notes: "Million cities" are those with at least 1 million population in the 1990 Census. For administrative ranks: (1) province-level cities, (2) deputy-provincial, (3) provincial capitals (excluding those already in level 2 above), (4) prefecture-level (excluding those already in levels 2 and 3) cities, and (5) county-level cities.
Source: Chinese census data of 1990 and 2000.

followed by the medium cities, extralarge cities, and large cities. The growth pattern by size is clearly bipolar.

Recalling our previous discussion on China's administrative hierarchy, there is an almost perfect rank correlation between the administrative rank and growth rate. The higher the rank, the faster is the population growth rate of cities (Table 19.4, panel C). The higher growth rates of the biggest cities reflect the extraordinary growth rates of many cities at the highest administrative ranks and the export-processing centers on the coast during that decade. Table 19.5 shows the twenty cities with the highest growth rates among cities with at least 1 million residents (based on 1990 population data, $N = 93$). These twenty cities include four province-level cities, five deputy-provincial cities, and eight cities with only provincial capital rank. This shows the continuing dominance of the cities of higher administrative ranks in the urban hierarchy and urban growth. Two of only three

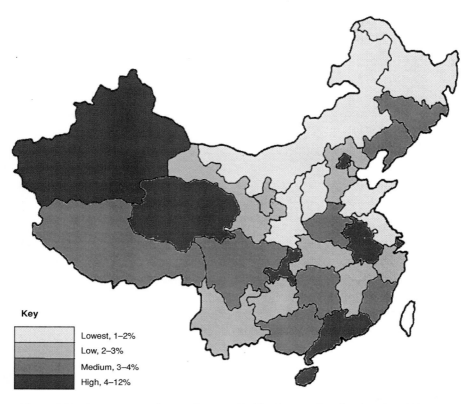

Key

Lowest, 1–2%
Low, 2–3%
Medium, 3–4%
High, 4–12%

Figure 19.2. Average annual growth rate of cities by province-level unit, 1990–2000 (*Source:* Computed from Chinese census data, 1990 and 2000 based on a sample of 418 cities (see explanations of the data in the text).)

cities in Table 19.5 that are below the provincial capital rank are major export-processing centers (Dongguan and Zhongshan, both in Guangdong). If one adds other cities in the PRD region, such as Shenzhen (23 percent average annual growth) and Zhuhai (9.7 percent), it is clear that the export-processing centers represent another major locus of rapid urban growth.

Figure 19.2 shows the average annual population growth rate for the sample cities by province-level unit. The three "hot spots," Guangdong, Beijing, and Shanghai, are (expectedly) in the high growth group, as are Chongqing, Xinjiang, Qinghai, Hainan, and Anhui. Interestingly, the lowest growth group is basically in the "north" and "northeast" quadrants, probably related to the industrial retrenchment in those regions during the 1990s.

The trend in the 1990s is that big cities, especially those at the highest administrative ranks (provincial capital and above) grew quite fast. This is partly a function of the Chinese political-administrative system and policies that favor higher-ranked cities in terms of fiscal resources, FDI policy, and transportation facilities, and partly due to the growth of the tertiary sector (particularly finance and business services), which tend to locate in major cities and administrative centers (Chan, Tsui, and Yu, 2003; Au and Henderson, 2004). It is almost certain that these high rates of urban population growth in big cities were generated by very high volumes of net in-migration (as in Dongguan and Shenzhen) and extensive annexation of surrounding counties (as in Wuhan, Beijing, and Shanghai). Some of these expanding big cities, along with other nearby cities, are developing into large urban regions, with populations ranging from 25–40 millions. One such region is the PRD. Well connected with Hong Kong and Macau, the region already has a combined total population of about 30 millions (Gu, Yu, and Chan, 2002).

However, as pointed out earlier, urban growth in the 1990s was not simply concentrated on the large cities. Instead, there is significant growth of cities in the size category under 200,000 ("small cities"). Some of this growth, especially in the coastal region, reflects the impact of export-processing jobs generated by foreign investment. Other small cities expanded because of domestic imperatives (administration, tourism, and commerce). Many of them were close to major metropolises and benefited from the spillover of industrial development from the bigger cities.

As mentioned earlier, there was voluminous internal migration in the 1990s, mostly in the form of so-called *temporary migration*.[14] Rural–urban migration was the largest type of internal migration, mostly of peasants to cities. Two-thirds of such migrants remain within their home provinces and about one-third leave the province (Chan, 2001). Table 19.6 uses information from two large national samples to tabulate the regional distribution of the cross-provincial stock of rural migrant labor. The number of migrants crossing provincial boundaries increased during 1993–1998. The predominant movement is from the periphery (central and western regions) toward the core (eastern region). This pattern intensified during the second half of the 1990s. In 1998, for example, 87 and 79 percent of rural migrant workers moving across provinces from the central and western regions, respectively, were found in the eastern region. These percentages are significantly higher than in 1993 (especially for migrants from the western region). Data from the 2000 population census also show interprovincial migration increasing between 1990–1995 and 1995–2000, with a significant concentration of interprovincial migrants arriving in a single province, Guangdong (Figure 19.3). For example, of the thirty largest interprovincial streams, eleven went to Guangdong, including the top six flows. These numbers contrast to only seven out of thirty, and only the top three in the 1990–1995 period (Chan, 2001).

---

[14] "Temporary migration" (also called "non-*hukou* migration") refers to migration without official approval for permanent migration. In other words, temporary migrants are not eligible for many state-provided welfare and social services for urban residents and not eligible for certain types of jobs (see Chan, 1994, 2001).

Table 19.6. *Percentage of rural migrant labor population from a different province,*
1993 and 1998

	Origins			
	East	Central	West	All regions
1993 (total stock = 28.9 million)				
Regional share	29.9	45.6	24.5	100
Destinations				
East	71.4	79.2	52.2	70.3
Central	21.8	18.9	9.4	17.4
West	6.8	1.9	38.4	12.3
TOTAL	100	100	100	100
1998 (total stock = 37.8 million)				
Regional share	11.0	55.0	34.0	100
Destinations				
East	72.7	87.3	79.4	83.0
Central	18.2	9.1	5.9	9.0
West	9.1	3.6	14.7	8.0
TOTAL	100	100	100	100

Notes: Rural migrant labor refers to rural laborers who had moved outside their home townships for work in the year under study.
Regional classification:
East = Liaoning, Beijing, Tianjin, Hebei, Shandong, Jiangsu, Shanghai, Zhejiang, Fujian, Guangdong, Guangxi, and Hainan.
Central = Heilongjiang, Jilin, Neimenggu, Shanxi, Henan, Anhui, Hubei, Hunan, and Jiangxi.
West = Xinjiang, Qinghai, Gansu, Ningxia, Shaanxi, Sichuan, Guizhou, Yunnan, and Tibet.
Source: Chan (2001).

Economic Structure of the Urban Sector

In this section we explore the economic structure of the urban sector, examining data for 2001 and 1996–2001 covering about 385 county-level cities and 255 higher-level cities. The data are from the City Statistical Yearbook of China (NBS, various years); some of the same data are available online through the University of Michigan (http://chinadataonline.org/). These city data are based on the UAA concept, including information on GDP by three sectors, FDI, capital stock (of independent accounting units), and some information on local public services. The city population counted is mainly the population with local *hukou*, plus some registered migrants. There is a drawback to use of data based on the *China City Statistical Yearbooks*: they exclude recent unregistered migrants and may undercount longer-term migrants. Because this source undercounts the city population, it may bias estimates of per capita magnitudes by different types of cities.[15]

---

[15] For an examination of the different city population series and implications, see Chan and Bennett (2004).

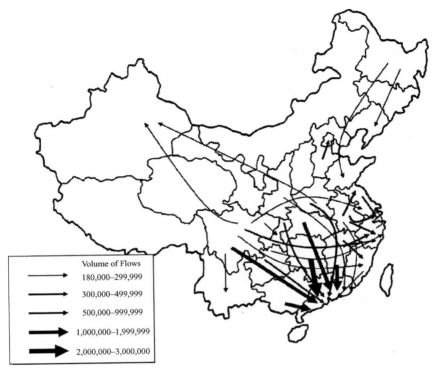

Figure 19.3. The thirty largest interprovincial migration streams, 1995–2000 (*Source:* Based on data from SC and NBS, 2002)

Table 19.7 gives the basic picture of conditions at different levels of the urban hierarchy in 2001. In Table 19.7 we group province-level cities, provincial capitals for which we have data, prefecture-level cities, and county-level cities. The table shows that the administrative hierarchy is also an economic one. Higher-order cities are bigger in population and richer on average in terms of GDP per capita. GDP per capita in provincial capitals is 50 percent higher than that in other prefecture-level cities and 120 percent higher than in county-level cities.[16] Although populations in bigger cities may be relatively undercounted, potentially leaving their GDP per capita figures overstated, their outputs may also be relatively undercounted, especially in the booming, more informal personal service sector. In part higher-order cities are richer because they are recipients of much more FDI and investment per capita. Investment per capita and FDI per capita are four to six times greater in province-level cities and provincial capitals than in county-level cities, helping fuel 2.5-fold GDP per capita differentials. We note this as a prelude to our subsequent

---

[16] Regression analysis suggests that the lower income in county-level cities is almost unrelated to their higher shares of primary-sector activity.

Table 19.7. *City hierarchy, averages in 2001*

City type	Number of cities in data set	Population (1,000s)	GDP per capita (yuan)	Ratio: manu-facturing to service GDP shares	FDI 1999–2001 per capita (dollars)	Investment 1999–2001, per capita (yuan)	GDP share of each city type[a]
Province-level city	4	9,779	24,450	0.91	623	21,300	0.133
Provincial capital	26	2,606	21,163	1.49	335	19,900	0.203
Prefecture-level city (not provincial capital)	224	836	14,619	1.44	287	12,200	0.346
County-level city	385	660	9,506	1.37	99	4,400	0.318

[a] Based on population-weighted averages of GDP per capita by city type (not shown).

Source: Henderson (2005).

Table 19.8. *Growth in the hierarchy over five years, 1996–2001*

City type	Population	GDP per capita	Ratio: manufacturing to service GDP shares
Province-level cities and provincial capitals	0.215	0.392	−0.150
Other prefecture-level cities	0.103	0.340	−0.121
County-level cities	0.0497	0.329	−0.135

Source: Henderson (2005). Average of individual city growth rates for the same set of cities in 1996 and 2001.

argument that while county-level cities and ordinary prefecture-level cities have lower income per capita, this does not mean that they are inherently less productive than province-level cities and capitals. Rather as we will argue, they suffer from policy disadvantages.

The last column of Table 19.7 shows the share of cities at each level of the hierarchy in total GDP produced by all cities. Province-level cities, as well as provincial capitals with their higher GDP per capita, produce disproportionate shares, reflecting their high levels of investment and human capital. Even so, the bulk of city-sector GDP – over 65 percent – is produced in ordinary prefecture- and county-level cities. China's growth is critically dependent on the successful development of these cities.

In Table 19.8, we explore a few basic changes in the urban system from 1996 to 2001. Consistent with Table 19.4 of the prior section, despite the differences in population source numbers, Table 19.8 suggests that population growth is much higher in prefecture-level cities than in county-level cities and that it is strongly focused on provincial capitals and province-level cities. Column 2 in Table 19.8 shows that growth in GDP per capita is only modestly higher in bigger cities, compared to smaller ones, a precursor to our subsequent argument that there is little difference, ceteris paribus, in productivity growth rates across the urban hierarchy. In Table 19.8, the manufacturing/service ratio is falling in all cities, especially the bigger ones, as expected. This reflects the rapid growth of service-sector activity and the departure of industry from the biggest cities. For these cities a key issue is what is happening to the absolute level of manufacturing activity. Since 1997 it has been impossible to get accurate employment figures by cities, except for province-level cities. The data for province-level cities suggest large absolute declines in manufacturing employment, which we analyze later, as these cities transform into service-oriented centers. This transformation was also enhanced by a deliberate policy to reduce state-sector–manufacturing workers in unprofitable ventures.

China's Degree of Urban Concentration

Later on, we will argue that many Chinese cities are undersized. Here we show that, correspondingly, urban concentration is relatively low, compared to most countries and that even the bigger Chinese cities are small by world standards. For example, based on the UAA concept, which already overcounts the true city population of individual cities, the population of China's biggest urban/metro area, Shanghai, was slightly over 14 million in 2000, which places it well below the world's ten largest urban/metro areas. More critically, the 2000 Census figures show that China has only 16 urban areas (UAA) with populations over 3 million, while another 162 or so cities have populations from 1–3 million – a ratio of 0.098, compared to worldwide ratio for the same size categories of 0.27 (based on UN data, see Henderson and Wang, 2007). To give a more common frame of reference for comparisons concerning the degree of urban concentration overall in China, we examine spatial Gini coefficients.

For 1,657 metro areas with populations over 200,000 in 2000 for the world, the spatial Gini is 0.56.[17] The Gini is the usual one: it ranks cities from smallest to largest and plots the Lorenz curve of their accumulated share of total population for the sample (world cities in this case). The Gini is the share of area below the 45 degree line that lies between the 45 degree line and the Lorenz curve. China's Gini is 0.39 in 2000 (based on census data, UAA concept), far below the world norm, and compares to 0.65, 0.65, 0.61, 0.60, 0.60, 0.60, 0.59, 0.58, 0.56, 0.54, and 0.52 for other large countries, respectively, for Brazil, Japan, Indonesia, United Kingdom, Mexico, Nigeria, France, India, Germany, United States of America, and Spain. Only former Soviet Bloc countries have similarly low Gini coefficients: Russia with 0.45 and Ukraine with 0.40. One plausible explanation is that low urban concentration is an artifact of central planning and political control in former Soviet Bloc countries and China. Regardless, we believe this low urban concentration in China reflects insufficient spatial agglomeration throughout the country, in both the urban and rural sectors.

Some Key Features

Industrialization Strategy and Underurbanization

In the pre-reform era, China pursued a development strategy that put emphasis on industry at the expense of agriculture and gave priority to investment over consumption. As part of this strategy, urbanization was limited to only a low level in the 1960s and 1970s. The huge rural–urban disparities also necessitated restricting migration to cities. This was achieved through a series of instruments,

---

[17] Calculated from a world city data set prepared by Rupa Ranganathan, Wang Hyoung, and J. V. Henderson, for 1960–2000.

such as residence control by the *hukou* system. As a consequence, while China had high industrial growth rates in 1950–1980, the rate of urban growth was comparatively low. Relative to China's industrialization level, the urbanization level (the urban percentage) was also low by world standards, leading to a phenomenon of "underurbanization" (Chan, 1994). Since the late 1970s, there have been higher growth rates of the urban population. A significant part of the urban population growth is in the form of rural–urban migrants who lack formal *hukou* registration status at their destination (the "non-*hukou* migration").

Migration Restrictions, Spatial Inequality, and Underagglomeration

The relaxation of restrictions on migration in China varies regionally and the *hukou* system continues as a long-term impediment to truly free migration. Despite considerable in-migration to the cities, in-migrants or temporary urban residents have limited access to housing, schooling for children, health care, and other social welfare benefits. There are also interregional differences in culture and spoken language, discrimination against "peasants," lack of legal rights for migrants *and* their children born or living in cities, and isolation of migrants in dormitories and urban villages, making assimilation more difficult.

The *hukou* system that restricts migration was used to implement urbanization policy formulated in the early 1980s in the Fifth and Sixth Five-Year Plans. That policy relaxed some *hukou* restrictions to allow smaller cities and towns absorb rural out-migration while strictly limiting the population growth of bigger cities. The outcome is reflected in the rapid growth in number of county-level cities in the early 1990s. Policy on urbanization was augmented by strong support of rural industrialization to keep people "in the village," even if they "leave the land." Rural industrialization was initially successful because the town and village enterprise (TVE) sector operated with better management and incentive systems than state-owned industry. But rural industry was always strongly undercapitalized, meaning the rate of return on capital in the rural industrial sector exceeded that in the urban state-owned sector by 25 percent or so in the mid-1990s (Jefferson and Singh, 1999; Au and Henderson, 2006a). It has also been disadvantaged by an initial lack of access to FDI, poor transport access to markets, and severe underagglomeration, as we will discuss later.

China has enormous income inequality, much of which occurs across geographic units rather than within localities (see Chapter 18 in this volume). We see huge differences in GDP per capita between the bigger cities and county-level cities (Table 19.7) and further huge gaps between cities and rural areas (Table 19.2). China's income Gini of 0.42 in 1995 far exceeds comparable figures for South Asian countries, such as India, Bangladesh, and Pakistan[18] (with Ginis around 0.3), not to mention highly equal countries, such as Japan and Korea. With rapid economic growth and people in lagging regions held in place by the *hukou* system, real income differences across geographic units have increased dramatically since

---

[18] From World Development Indicators, 1998, World Bank.

1978 (Lin, Cai, and Li, 1996), looking at both rural versus urban, as in Table 19.2, and coastal versus western or central regions later in this chapter.

These differences across geographic units have enormous implications for efficiency as well as equity. To see this, we look first at prefecture-level cities, then county-level cities, and finally the rural sector.

Underagglomeration in Prefecture-Level Cities

As noted earlier, migration restrictions limit the ability of people to move from low-productivity locations to high-productivity areas and more generally limit the ability of the population to agglomerate at different points in space. Urban production can deliver localized external economies of scale, but only if people can migrate to form high-density urban agglomerations. Have China's migration restrictions allowed sufficient leeway for the population to agglomerate in cities, or even in rural areas to fully exploit potential scale externalities?

To examine this issue, we report estimates of urban productivity relationships, which show how output per worker varies with city size and which allow calculation of efficient sizes for Chinese cities, as well as potential welfare losses from insufficient agglomeration. Using data for 1996 and 1997, Au and Henderson (2006a) estimate city production functions for 212 cities at or above the prefecture level. Output is represented by value added (VA) per worker in the nonagricultural sector of the UAA. Determinants include the ratio of capital stock to labor, the share of accumulated FDI in capital stock, distance to the coast, education, and scale measures. These city-level figures on GDP, investment, and other economic data are considered to be reliable up through 1997 and consistent in collection and accounting methods across cities. Interestingly, on an international level, China appears to be the only country with GDP numbers at the equivalent of a UAA level. These Chinese data provide a unique opportunity to test basic theories concerning agglomeration into cities and aspects of urban systems.

In examining productivity of cities, there are two key aspects to a conceptual framework. Following traditional systems of cities analysis (see Duranton and Puga, 2004, for a handbook treatment of the subject), real output per worker is postulated to be an inverted U-shaped function of local scale, as measured by nonagricultural employment. At low levels of employment, there are the high-scale economies noted earlier from clustering firms together because of information sharing and spillovers across firms and exploitation of pecuniary economies in reducing the cost of shipping intermediate inputs among firms and to consumers. However, there are limitations on city size: as a city grows, at some point these economies may dissipate as commuting costs, congestion, and other urban diseconomies escalate and the extent of a city's market becomes stretched, causing real output per worker to peak and then decline with further increases in city size.

The second aspect of the analysis is that cities inhabit an economic "hierarchy" in which cities specialize in different products and activities. There are many types of cities in any country; each has a different efficient size. In general, in countries well on the path to being fully urbanized, the ratio of manufacturing to service activity declines as city scale rises, or as cities move up the hierarchy. In Table 19.7 we saw that province-level cities had distinctly lower manufacturing/service ratios than other cities, but for the rest the pattern is unclear as cities' industrial structures are all shifting away from manufacturing, as we saw in Table 19.8. Nevertheless in China even in 1997 there is a significant negative correlation between city population size and the manufacturing/service ratio.

To capture this aspect of the hierarchy, Au and Henderson (2006a,b) postulate that the inverted U-shape shifts to the right as the manufacturing/service ratio drops.[19] As motivation, Au and Henderson (2006b) specify a model in which the manufacturing/service ratio represents a structural parameter, where services are an input into manufacturing production. Production that is more intensive in service inputs is viewed as more "sophisticated," in the sense that such producers buy (and the cities they are in supply) a greater variety of specialized service inputs in local markets and that variety is specified to enhance production efficiency as in the new economic geography (see Overman, Redding, and Venables, 2003).

Au and Henderson (2006a) estimate how productivity changes with city employ-ment, controlling for industrial composition, investment, FDI, market potential of the city, access to coastal markets, and the like, using instrumental variable tech-niques and obtaining robust, fairly precise results. Controls on local infrastructure such as roads per unit land area have no significant effect.

China's neat, (almost) "natural" experiment in switching from a planned to market economy gives rise to strong instruments in estimation that help with the identification of causal effects, as distinguished from correlations.[20] For basic urban meta-production function, or productivity equations, Au and Henderson identify the inverted-U of real output per worker against the number of workers in a city. Real output per worker is simply GDP per worker; there is no information with

---

[19] They estimate a relationship for city i, where

$$\ln(\mathrm{VA}_i/L_i) = \beta X_i + \alpha_1 L_i + \alpha_2 L_i^2 + \alpha_3 L_i \mathrm{MS}_i$$

In the equation, X_i are controls on technology, capital–labor ratio, access, and the like. VA_i is value added; L_i is total (nonagricultural) employment, and MS_i is the manufacturing/service VA ratio (secondary-to-tertiary sector VA). In the equation, output per worker peaks where

$$\overset{*}{L_i} = \frac{\alpha_1 + \alpha_3 \mathrm{MS}_i}{-2\alpha_2},$$

where $\alpha_2 < 0$, $\alpha_1 > 0$, $\alpha_1 + \alpha_3 \mathrm{MS}_i > 0$, and $\alpha_3 < 0$. The last reflects the economic hierarchy idea: bigger cities are more service oriented, so $\overset{*}{L_i}$ declines as MS_i rises.

[20] Urban allocations leading up to 1990 are based primarily on planning decisions rather than local market conditions (at least those conditions that enter the error terms in 1997 productivity equations). By 1996/1997, there are significant market reforms moving decision making in urban areas to be more market based. Historical variables are strong instruments due to accumulation processes in capital and labor migration markets and they are uncorrelated with market-related error terms in current productivity equations.

Table 19.9. *Efficient city sizes*

A. City employment (1,000s) at peak of value added per worker								
Ratio: manufacturing/services	0.6	0.8	1.0	1.2	1.4	1.6	1.8	2.0
Efficient size, $\overset{*}{L}$	2,730	2,380	2,030	1,670	1,320	970	620	270
95% confidence interval								
– Lower bound	1,880	1,680	1,420	1,090	670	180		
– Upper bound	3,590	3,080	2,630	2,260	1,980	1,760	1,580	1,430

B. Gain from moving to efficient size, $\overset{*}{L}$				
Gap between current size and peak (percent)	50	40	30	20
Percent gain in VA per worker	35	20	9.5	4.1

which to examine differences in purchasing-power parity. However, across cities at and above the prefectural level in 1997, given the way in which housing markets operated and housing was priced and given the small size of the service sector, we expect such differences were small.

As noted earlier, this inverted-U shifts with city production composition or the manufacturing/service ratio. Panel A in Table 19.9 shows relevant manufacturing/service ratios, the peak points, $\overset{*}{L}$, or city employment levels where VA per workers is maximized and the 95 percent confidence interval for peak scale, $\overset{*}{L}$, is interpreted as the most efficient size for any individual city. Note that the measure of scale is in thousands of *workers*, not population. For example, in the column for a manufacturing/service ratio of 1.2, the peak of the inverted-U occurs within the 95 percent confidence interval of 1,090,000–2,260,000 nonagricultural workers in the city, with the point estimates suggesting a peak at 1,670,000 workers.

Based on the estimates in panel A, Table 19.9, Au and Henderson (2006a) calculate the efficient sizes and 95 percent confidence intervals for the entire sample. They find that most Chinese cities (85 percent) lie to the left of their peak points, with 43 percent falling below the 95 percent confidence interval on peak size; that is, 43 percent of cities are significantly undersized.

Panel B in Table 19.9 shows the percentage gain in VA per worker that might result from increasing the numbers of workers to the level associated with the peak value of real output per worker. These partial equilibrium calculations assume no change in each city's capital/labor ratio or market potential. Au and Henderson (2006b) find similar orders of magnitude, holding each city's cost of capital fixed. In either case, the data for 1997 show that migration restrictions associated with the *hukou* system left China's cities considerably below their optimum economic scale, and therefore imposed high economic losses. The magnitude of such losses is substantial: moving a city that is 50 percent below the efficient size to its best size increases output per worker by 35 percent.[21]

Despite the economic cost associated with China's undersized cities, restricted migration and slower population growth of cities than we observe in other developing countries may have some advantages. Chinese cities have had an orderly development of internal transport systems and relatively little proliferation of slums or shantytowns, although recent migrants have been increasingly located in very low quality housing in rural districts on the urban fringe. Accelerated migration would have allowed fuller exploitation of agglomeration economies and thus greater growth in GDP per capita.

Moreover, looking to the future, for larger cities, the extent to which they are relatively undersized and agglomeration economies underexploited could increase, despite relaxation of many migration restrictions. Technological change in urban production, as is ongoing in China at a high level, increases efficient city size (Black and Henderson, 2003), as do improvements in land-use patterns and in the organization of land markets. As noted earlier, as bigger cities become more oriented toward business service, their efficient sizes should increase, since we believe business services experience higher degrees of scale externalities than manufacturing. Finally, the tendency for manufacturing sectors that remain in the bigger cities to become more specialized in higher-tech, high-value–added activities (see later) may also accentuate the current benefits of agglomeration.

Underagglomeration in County-Level Cities and Rural Areas

For traditional county-level cities that existed in 1990, Au and Henderson (2006a) are unable to quantify an inverted-U, instead they find unbounded scale effects (for these smaller city sizes). More recent work by Henderson (2005) uses less reliable population data to measure city size, since overall employment figures are not available after 1997. The 2001 population data suggest bounded scale effects with an inverted-U for county-level cities, but at very large sizes. For the rural sector, Au and Henderson (2006a) look at both overall township productivity and productivity in the (TVE) sector across provinces. They analyze productivity over a three-year period, instrumenting with historical variables. For TVEs, they also find that local scale economies are unbounded and very large; a 10 percent increase in local scale increases VA by worker by 3 percent. This is the same order of magnitude found by Jefferson and Singh (1999) in terms of the effect of increases in TVE scale, using firm-level data. These numbers suggest that TVEs are underagglomerated and that there are high costs to the continued spatial dispersion of TVEs.

---

[21] While urban population may be undercounted, that does not affect the force of these results. They build on employment data, where undercounting based on migration issues was less problematic in 1997. At that time, urban unemployment and underemployment rates of older workers in SOEs were undercounted, meaning our employment numbers could even be too high.

The conclusion is that overall and at every level there is underagglomeration of population in China. These statements are based on specific econometric evidence on China, in a context where there is no evidence on the subject for cities in other countries, in part because generally other countries do not collect GDP data at the level of the urban area. But the conclusion is also supported by the notion already discussed that China has a very low degree of spatial concentration across cities, compared to the rest of the world. It seems that the *hukou* system has imposed productivity losses and raised income inequality, because populations in low-productivity locations are restricted in their ability to move to high-productivity locations and exploit fully the basic agglomeration economies inherent in urbanization.

Industrial Composition of Cities
In a typical development context, early industrialization occurs initially in the largest cities that have good public infrastructure and access to international markets. As these largest cities grow and the country develops, standardized manufacturing activity typically leaves the largest cities, moving first to nearby satellite cities, as with Korea in the 1970s and Indonesia and Thailand starting at different points in the 1980s. Next, as national infrastructure improves and development progresses, manufacturers start to move to more rural destinations with even cheaper labor and land costs (e.g., Korea from the early 1980s on), so that in a developed country like the United States of America, the rural sector has a much higher relative share of manufacturing than even small metro areas. This progression of manufacturing sites is part of a process of "functional specialization" (Duranton and Puga, 2002), whereby firms decentralize production activities but maintain headquarters and administrative functions in large metro areas for purposes of marketing and outsourcing of business and financial services.

From this perspective, China is unusual in two respects. First, the urbanization policy of the 1980s emphasized early industrialization in rural areas and small cities as well as in large urban centers. So China already has a rural and small city industrial base, which at least until the mid-1990s was outcompeting the urban state-owned sector. Second, China started the 1990s with an anemic business service sector, which is now growing rapidly. This rapid growth means bigger cities will continue to move increasingly into services. Thus as suggested earlier, as the service sector swells nationally with a big city focus, now is the time for the rural and small city industrial base to modernize, as it absorbs manufacturing industries that are decentralizing from larger cities.

This increasing concentration of manufacturing employment in small- and medium-size cities is not unrelated to their desired role in absorbing large portions of the surplus population in agriculture. Increased *relative* industrialization of smaller cities could coincide with what is reasonable in terms of deflecting migrants away from bigger cities. But decentralization of industry and population are two different things. Korea's move of manufacturing to smaller towns and rural areas occurred in the face of population losses in those areas. As noted earlier, the growing service orientation of larger cities may further increase their optimum size.

The successful transformation of bigger cities into service centers and the modernization of manufacturing in smaller cities involve a variety of policy issues and suggest we should look in more detail at changing industrial composition. We start by looking at big cites and then turn to a discussion of small- and medium-size cities.

Larger Cities

The ongoing transformation of China's larger cities involves two components. First is suburbanization and exurban development, with manufacturing decentralizing away from the urban core. So for example from 1990 to 1997, the urban area's share of Beijing's manufacturing total fell from 82 to 69 percent, with similar declines for provincial capitals, such as Chengdu and Changsha. Government policy in some coastal regions has encouraged this process by situating industrial parks and developing transport corridors in exurban areas.

Growth of services is the second aspect of the transformation in China's largest cities. We look at the regional breakdown for key components of services and other industries in Table 19.10, for 1997–2002. We also break out what happens to Beijing and Shanghai. These province-level cities are the only ones for which we can get a reasonably accurate picture of employment breakdown across economic sectors, an issue we turn to momentarily. The table shows the absolute decline in manufacturing employment throughout China and the slow growth of the "trade" (e.g., retail and wholesale) sector. This contrasts with the relatively rapid growth of the financial sector and "social" services (see footnote 2), which contain the business service sector. Growth of financial and business services is greatest in Beijing and Shanghai, the natural locations for such services.

Table 19.11 explores aspects of the absolute and relative decline in manufacturing employment in the big three province-level cities, for 1990–2000. Despite the employment declines, real VA per worker in manufacturing for these three cities has risen much more rapidly than the national average. It appears that their more sophisticated labor forces and better access to capital markets and FDI have allowed these three large centers to move in the direction of high VA per worker activities in manufacturing, with low-productivity operations decentralizing to other cities. Unfortunately, we do not have the detailed industry data to confirm this conjecture. While some detailed data exist on employment in a "two-digit" breakdown of manufacturing, comparisons are difficult, since industry definitions and categories changed between 1990 and 2000.

Finally, there is the issue of how the overall composition of output *within* these big cities is changing. We know they are moving out of primary- and secondary-sector activities into tertiary activities, but are they becoming more or less diverse? Removal of planning structures that encouraged every city to produce everything now permits them to become more specialized, shedding unprofitable activities

Table 19.10. *Sectoral and regional employment: level, share, and growth, 1997–2002*

	Employment level or share in 2002				Annual growth of employment 1997–2002 (percent)			
	Manufacturing	Trade	Finance	Social services	Manufacturing	Trade	Finance	Social services
National employment (10,000s)	8,307	4,969	340	1,094	−2.9	0.7	2.0	6.2
Regional employment shares and growth rates								
Coast	60%	50%	51%	57%	−1.6	2.1	3.2	8.5
Center	28%	32%	32%	27%	−4.7	−2.2	0.3	0.5
West	13%	17%	18%	17%	−4.2	2.6	1.7	9.9
Major cities: level and growth of employment								
Beijing (10,000s)	152	120	8.2	109.6	−2.3	8.5	1.8	15.0
Shanghai (10,000s)	269	116	12.6	60	−3.1	1.5	15.0	9.3

Source: Yearbooks.

Table 19.11. *Changes in employment*
composition in province-level cities

	1993	2001
Manufacturing employment (1,000s) [share of total employment]		
Beijing	1,930 [29%]	1,520 [19%]
Tianjin	1,920 [40%]	1,210 [30%]
Shanghai	3,710 [50%]	2,690 [36%]
Real VA per worker in, manufacturing (RMB 10,000, 1993 prices)		
Beijing	1.52	3.78
Tianjin	1.10	4.95
Shanghai	1.72	5.67
HHI : Raw		
Beijing	0.11	0.10
Tianjin	0.14	0.079
Shanghai	0.26	0.037
HHI: Normalized		
Beijing	0.016	0.024
Tianjin	0.015	0.034
Shanghai	0.040	0.030

Source: Yearbooks.

and specializing to better exploit within-industry scale economies. But the market role of large cities is also to be somewhat diverse – to provide a rich variety of business- and service-sector activities. Moreover as development proceeds, larger cities increasingly move into production of business and financial services and out of manufacturing. As we will see, the forces of increasing specialization with removal of planning strictures and increasing diversification into the service sector are both at work in the largest cities.

Table 19.11 shows the changing sectoral structure of employment in China's three big province-level cities. The third panel of numbers in Table 19.11 shows a raw Hirschman-Herfindahl (HHI)-type index, the sum of squared shares of thirteen non-primary-sector activities in total nonprimary-sector employment in each city. A low index indicates that shares are spread more evenly across the thirteen sectors, while a higher number indicates they are more concentrated. These figures show a sharp *decline* of the raw HHI in all three cities, as employment spreads out of manufacturing into the eleven service subsectors. This reflects the diversification role of large cities.

The last panel in the table gives a normalized HHI. For each sector we calculate its share in local employment and subtract its share in national employment before squaring, and then for each city we sum across sectors.[22] This HHI indicates the extent to which city's employment patterns deviate from the nationwide norm. In all cities this normalized HHI *rose* between 1990 and 2000. This suggests that freedom from the constraints of planning has allowed these cities to become more specialized, or less like the nation in aggregate.

The policy issues that arise for these largest cities are not strictly spatial in nature. Their successful transformation requires efficient operation of the service sector. Allen, Qian, and Qian (Chapter 14 in this volume) and Clarke, Murrell, and Whiting (Chapter 11 in this volume) discuss well-known difficulties surrounding state-owned financial institutions and China's legal system. Perhaps less well known are issues of regulation in advertising and other business services. Private-sector advertising has flourished, even though it competes with state-owned newspapers, as regulation has focused primarily on supervision of advertising content.

There are many related issues, including, for example, problems surrounding software development and restrictions on internet access. Without delving into detail, we emphasize the importance of the rule of law as a foundation for functional specialization and elaborate corporate structures. The key point is that the full-fledged development of large cities in China, which face worldwide competition in business services, remains hampered by restrictions on the expansion of many service activities. China's competitiveness in modern manufacturing is similarly hampered by restrictions that inhibit functional specialization across cities and limit the ability of standardized manufacturing to decentralize to lower-wage, lower-cost, specialized manufacturing centers away from their administrative or headquarters centers.

Smaller Cities and Towns

Henderson (2005) finds that smaller cities, including those at the county level, are "inherently" as productive as higher-order cities and have similar rates of total factor productivity (TFP) growth. Similar "inherent" productivity means that current differences in income levels and growth rates between larger and smaller cities can be explained by observables, such as differences in capital investment and FDI. But while these smaller cities are potentially as productive as higher-order cities, they suffer from policy biases. Successful industrialization of smaller cities and towns, including even satellite towns, will require a number of policy and institutional changes. We list several key areas in which reform would help to equalize the competition for resources between smaller and larger cities.

(a) Firms in smaller cities suffer unambiguously from restricted access to capital markets, compared to prefecture- and above-level cities. That alone hinders

---

[22] For s_{ij} the share of industry i in city j employment and s_i the share of industry i in national employment, then

$$\text{HHI}_{\text{raw}} = \sum_i s_{ij}^2 \text{ and HHI}_{\text{norm}} = \sum_i (s_{ij} - s_i)^2.$$

their development and retards the role they could play in the economic transformation of China. The consequences of restricted access to capital are explored in Jefferson and Singh (1999).

(b) Smaller cities are fiscally disadvantaged because Chinese fiscal arrangements provide them with smaller tax bases than those available to bigger cities, or because (1) Chinese tax codes impose higher corporate income taxes on establishments located in smaller centers and (2) local officials have fewer opportunities to provide businesses with tax incentives/holidays than officials in large cities.

(c) Compared with large urban areas, smaller cities may have less ability to engage in land development, to expand into contiguous rural areas or to relocate TVEs into clusters that can capture local scale externalities. For example, in the late 1990s, even in developed coastal provinces such as Jiangsu and Zhejiang, 75 percent of TVEs were still located in their natural villages. It is difficult to transfer TVE ownership or location, to arrange for township residents to sell their "shares" in local TVEs to facilitate liquidation or relocation, or for TVE employees to shift their residence to other towns. This inability to cluster limits the competitiveness of TVE and obstructs the ability of small- and medium-size cities to further industrialize and modernize.

(d) The *hukou* policy also hurts the economic prospects of smaller cities. College admissions discriminate against applicants with rural *hukou*, who face higher admission standards than urban youths. College graduates often transfer their *hukou* registration to higher-level centers. The result is a gradual drift of talent, including skilled workers, away from smaller towns and cities (Wang and Chan, 2005). Moreover smaller cities, with fewer tax resources and restricted opportunities to hire good teachers, have less ability to, say, offer good senior middle schooling. This issue of what public services can be offered and can be financed, of course, goes beyond schooling.

(e) Smaller cities also suffer from China's traditional underinvestment in roads. To give some perspective, on a world scale, China has operated with an anemic road system. Its ratios of national roads to land, roads to population, or paved roads to land or to population in 1995 were very low by international standards. For example, according to the *International Road Federation World Road Statistics*, China's 1995 ratio of roads to population was 1.2 versus 2.1 for India, 1.5 for Pakistan, 1.9 for Indonesia, or 2.7 for Mexico. Half of these roads are paved in India but only 15 percent in China. The perception is that county-level cities and smaller cities have poor access to local as well as national markets. Consequently, small- and medium-size cities are very dependent on access to bigger cities for successful development.

Table 19.12 illustrates the key role of access to large urban centers for the development of county-level cities. Cities within 2-hour drive (75 miles) of a provincial

Table 19.12. *County-level cities and access to provincial capitals or province-level cities in 2001*

Distance to nearest provincial city/capital (miles)	Number of cities	Population (1,000s)	GDP per capita (yuan)	FDI per capita, 1999–2001 (US $)	Ratio: GDP in manufacturing to services	Growth rate: GDP per capita, 1996–2001	Growth rate: population, 1996–2001	Growth rate: manufacturing/service (GDP) ratio, 1996–2001
0–75	145	718	11,049	125	1.47	0.369	0.0278	−0.168
75–150	128	687	8,628	82	1.32	0.315	0.0284	−0.174
>150	91	581	8,590	82	1.09	0.325	0.0548	−0.114

Source: Henderson (2005). From China City Statistical Yearbooks.

capital or province-level city are bigger, have much higher GDP per capita, much more FDI, and much more manufacturing than cities farther away. And they have faster growth in GDP per capita. The only dimension on which remote cities gain is population growth. For county-level cities near big cities, the "problem" is that the rural populations near them and their own citizens find it relatively easier to migrate to the nearby major metro center. Cities that are far from such centers experience faster population growth, because nearby rural populations are more likely to choose them as migration targets. But smaller- and medium-size cites near major metro centers benefit from higher industrial activity, presumably some portion of it outsourcing parts and component production by industrial firms in the nearby major metro areas.

PROVINCES

As of 2000, China had twenty-seven provinces and four province-level cities (Beijing, Tianjin, Shanghai, and Chongqing). Provincial boundaries have remained relatively stable since the mid-1960s, in contrast to a rapid surge in the number of cities. The figures in Table 19.13 highlight the differences between the poorer inland and richer coastal provinces. Partitioning China into the eastern, central, and western regions, GDP per capita in 2000 decreases from east to west.[23] Not surprisingly, close to 60 percent of the secondary and tertiary output comes from the eastern provinces, which also account for half of the cities' population (see Table 19.13). At the provincial level, salient features induced by the rural–urban dichotomy are translated into differences and disparities between the inland and coastal provinces.

In recent years, much attention has been focused on the allegedly widening gap between the inland and coastal provinces (e.g., Lyons, 1991; Tsui, 1991, 1996; Jian, Sachs, and Warner, 1996; Raiser, 1998; Lin, Cai, and Li, 1999; Wang and Hu, 1999; Fujita and Hu, 2001; Naughton, 2002; Bhalla, Yao, and Zhang, 2003; Lin and Cai, 2003).[24] To examine the trend in interprovincial inequality, we resort to the population-weighted version of the logarithm mean deviation inequality measures (or Theil's entropy measure).[25] Figure 19.5 reports the findings in Tsui

---

[23] Population figures used to derive provincial GDP per capita are from the 2000 Census.

[24] Interprovincial inequality captures only part of China's overall income inequality (see Chapter 18 in this volume). However, the issue of interprovincial inequality is important in China's political economy insofar as it is an important consideration in the formation of national policies, such as the Western Development Campaign and the design of central–local fiscal systems.

[25] The formula for this inequality index is $I(\mathbf{y}) = \sum_{m=1}^{M} f_m \ln(\bar{y}/y_m)$, $\bar{y} = \sum_{m=1}^{M} f_m y_m$, where M is the number of provinces, y_m is the GDP per capita of the mth province, $\mathbf{y} = (y_1, \ldots, y_M)$, and f_m is the population share of the mth province. In 2006, the NBS publicly released a set of revised national income statistics based on the *Census of the National Economy* (*quanguo jinji pucha*) for the period 1993–2004. Comparing the new with the original statistics shows that the size of the tertiary sector was significantly underestimated (NBS, National Income Account Department, 2006). Insofar as tertiary sectors in richer provinces grow faster, our trends for interprovincial inequality based on the original data may have underestimated the extent of inequality.

Table 19.13. *Major provincial indicators, 2000*

	Population (millions) (census)	GDP per capita (yuan)	GDP RMB 100 million	Sectoral share (percentage of province's GDP)			Percentage of national population		
				Primary	Secondary	Tertiary	City population	Town population	County population
Beijing	13.57	18,268	2,478.76	3.63	38.06	58.31	3.25	0.62	0.39
Tianjin	9.85	16,645	1,639.36	4.49	50.03	45.48	1.82	1.07	0.35
Hebei	66.68	7,631	5,088.96	16.2	50.3	33.49	3.93	3.65	6.27
Shanxi	32.47	5,062	1,643.81	10.94	50.35	38.71	2.46	2.55	2.68
Inner Mongolia	23.32	6,007	1,401.01	25.04	39.71	35.26	1.94	2.58	1.71
Liaoning	41.82	11,163	4,669.06	10.78	50.21	39.01	6.31	2.72	2.41
Jilin	26.80	6,795	1,821.19	21.89	43.94	34.16	3.16	2.44	1.72
Heilongjiang	36.24	8,977	3,253.00	10.97	57.44	31.58	4.35	3.58	2.24
Shanghai	16.41	27,738	4,551.15	1.83	47.54	50.63	4.35	1.06	0.24
Jiangsu	73.04	11,750	8,582.73	12.01	51.68	36.3	6.47	7.18	5.38
Zhejiang	45.93	13,142	6,036.34	11	52.74	36.26	4.48	5.57	3.01
Anhui	59.00	5,150	3,038.24	24.1	42.67	33.23	2.88	4.41	5.52
Fujian	34.10	11,496	3,920.07	16.34	43.65	40.01	2.67	3.9	2.52
Jiangxi	40.40	4,958	2,003.07	24.22	34.98	40.8	1.89	3.41	3.73
Shandong	89.97	9,495	8,542.44	14.85	49.69	35.46	7.55	7.37	7.1
Henan	91.24	5,631	5,137.66	22.61	46.98	30.41	4.72	4.56	8.91
Hubei	59.51	7,186	4,276.32	15.49	49.66	34.85	5.67	4.52	4.52

Hunan	63.27	5,835	3,691.88	21.26	39.6	39.14	3.59	4.15	5.85
Guangdong	85.23	11,337	9,662.23	10.35	50.39	39.26	10.34	10.33	4.82
Guangxi	43.85	4,675	2,050.14	26.28	36.49	37.24	2.12	3.7	4.02
Hainan	7.56	6,859	518.48	37.91	19.76	42.33	0.58	0.84	0.57
Chongqing	30.51	5,209	1,589.34	17.81	41.37	40.82	2.25	2.11	2.6
Sichuan	82.35	4,870	4,010.25	23.58	42.4	34.02	4.17	6.08	7.66
Guizhou	35.25	2,819	993.53	27.28	39.04	33.69	1.49	2.46	3.42
Yunnan	42.36	4,615	1,955.09	22.31	43.13	34.56	1.59	3.16	4.14
Xizang	2.62	4,489	117.46	30.92	23.17	45.91	0.07	0.17	0.27
Shaanxi	35.37	4,696	1,660.92	16.81	44.07	39.13	2.36	2.69	3.06
Gansu	25.12	3,914	983.36	19.66	44.73	35.6	1.35	1.25	2.44
Qinghai	4.82	5,465	263.59	14.62	43.25	42.13	0.34	0.34	0.42
Ningxia	5.49	4,841	265.57	17.3	45.2	37.5	0.41	0.35	0.47
Xinjiang	18.46	7,391	1,364.36	21.12	43.01	35.87	1.46	1.19	1.56
Regional share (percent)									
East	38.96		57.29	42.95	59.8	59.97	51.73	44.3	33.06
Central	34.79		27.02	34.44	26.32	24.89	30.65	32.2	36.88
West	26.25		15.69	22.61	13.88	15.15	17.62	23.49	30.06

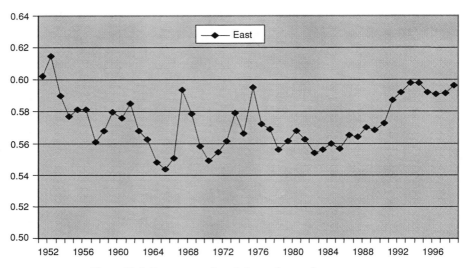

Figure 19.4. Eastern provinces' share of secondary sector output

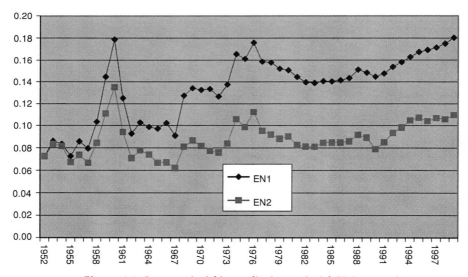

Figure 19.5. Interprovincial inequality in provincial GDP per capita

(forthcoming). One of the two trends in interprovincial inequality, EN1, is based
on official data; EN2 is the result using a different set of provincial GDP deflators
and adjusted population data.[26]

---

[26] Unlike previous studies that rarely try to address the concerns with the underestimation of inflation using official GDP deflators and the distortion of population figures due to interprovincial

The absolute magnitude of EN1 is much larger. Rather than a simple monotonic trajectory, the trends oscillate. Although their overall patterns of oscillation share certain salient features, the two trajectories diverge in some subperiods. Except for the anomalous years of the Great Leap Forward, EN1 seems to be increasing prior to 1968, while EN2 edges downward. For the period between 1968 and 1977, both trajectories oscillate upward. The dawn of the reform era sets off a conspicuous decline in interprovincial inequality up the end of the 1980s for both EN1 and EN2. From then onward, the two trends initially crawl upward to be followed by sharp increases in the first half of the 1990s. The two trends have diverged since the mid-1995. EN1 using official data continues to climb upward and EN2 based on adjusted data instead remains stable.

What are the forces driving the changes in interprovincial inequality? Previous studies have invariably tried to tie the changes in inequality loosely to different forces induced by policy zigzags both before and after 1978. Prior studies emphasize two sets of factors driving interprovincial inequality (see, e.g., Donnithorne, 1972, 1976; Lardy, 1975, 1978; Naughton, 2002). The first affects provincial economic growth through changing spatial allocation of factor inputs induced by shifts in regional development strategies. A second set of factors may be thought of as changes impinging on the overall efficiency or TFP of the provinces. In what follows, we explore how these two sets of factors affect interprovincial inequality over the period 1965–1999. As a prerequisite, we introduce an analytical framework to help disentangle interprovincial inequality into the contributions of these factors.

Forces Shaping Interprovincial Inequality

In the last four decades, China's development strategies have been important in shaping regional development through their effects on the spatial allocation of factor inputs as well as their effects on production efficiency, ultimately impinging on interprovincial inequalities. To capture their effects within a coherent framework, it is convenient to think in terms of provincial production functions whereby economic growth is driven by the growth in physical capital stock (K), quality-adjusted labor (H), and TFP.[27] As already discussed in the section "Continuity, Reform, and Spatial Economic Development," communist rule has witnessed shifts in regional development policy. Specifically, the pre-reform spatial development strategy pursued political and egalitarian goals, often at the expense of comparative advantage and regional specialization, while reforms since 1978 have left the provinces with more room to follow development paths more consistent with their factor

migration in the reform era, EN2 is based on a set of provincial GDP deflators resulting from first deflating the expenditure components of GDP using their corresponding price indices as suggested by Keidel (2001). The estimates for provincial population for the reform period are extrapolated using census data. For details, see Tsui (2007).

[27] Specifically, the production function may be expressed as $Y_m = A_m F_m(K_m, H_m)$. See Tsui (2007) for more detail.

endowments. These policy shifts induced changes in the spatial allocation of factor inputs such as K and H as well as TFP, ultimately impinging on provincial economic growth and changes in interprovincial inequality.

With this logic in mind, *changes* in interprovincial inequality, denoted $dI(y)/dt$, may be conceptually thought of as the sum of the contributions of the differential growth in factor inputs, TFP, and population:

$$dI(y)/dt = CA + CK + CH + C\Pi \tag{19.1}$$

where the first three terms on the right-hand side are the contributions of TFP, capital, and labor; the last term $C\Pi$ is the contribution of changes in sizes and shares of provincial populations. In what follows, we focus on the first three terms for the period 1965–1999.

Making use of this organizing framework, we explore later the trends with respect to CA, CK, and CH by setting them against the backdrop of the prevailing policy environment. Tsui (forthcoming) first estimates an aggregate production function using pooled provincial data and then the estimated parameters are plugged into the expressions on the right-hand side of equation (19.1) to arrive at the contributions.[28] For the sake of clearer exposition, these terms are transformed into their cumulative counterparts:

$$CCA_t = \sum_{\tau=1965}^{t} CA_\tau, \qquad CCK_t = \sum_{\tau=1965}^{t} CK_\tau,$$
$$CCH_t = \sum_{\tau=1965}^{t} CH_\tau, \qquad t = 1965, \dots, 1999 \tag{19.2}$$

because it is easier visually to separate longer-term trends from short-term volatility. Thus, each of the cumulative contributions, *ceteris paribus*, gauges the extent to which that specific factor pushes interprovincial inequality toward levels that are above or below its 1964 level. The results for the period 1965–1999 from Tsui (forthcoming) are summarized in Figure 19.6 and discussed later.

Spatial Allocation of Factor Inputs

In this section, we explore how different policy regimes in the Maoist and subsequently the reform era impinged on the spatial allocation of physical and human investments, that is, CCK and CCH, and thus ultimately on interprovincial inequality.

---

[28] In Tsui (2007), the estimation is based on adjusted data used to arrive at EN2, given earlier. An aggregate production function with a log-linear specification is estimated by pooling all provincial data for the period 1965–1999. Other than factor inputs, a dummy for the most chaotic years of the Cultural Revolution and a time trend for the reform era are also included. A first-difference version of the log-linear specification for the aggregate production function is estimated to avoid possible spurious correlation induced by nonstationarity as well as problems created by unobserved fixed effects. Given the not-too-long time series for the provinces, one advantage of pooling is a gain in the degrees of freedom. The problem is that pooling assumes that the coefficients for capital and labor are stable across provinces.

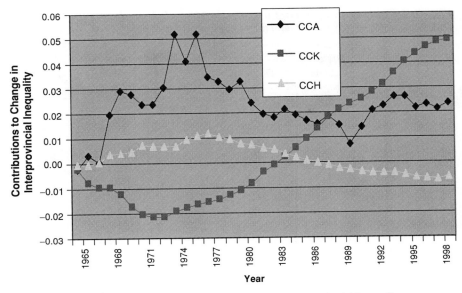

Figure 19.6. Contributions to changes in interprovincial inequality

As already discussed in the section on "Continuity, Reform, and Spatial Economic Development," the spatial allocation of resources shaped by regional policies has attracted vigorous scholarly debate, with Lardy (1975, 1976, 1978) and others insisting that central planning empowered the Chinese state to mobilize and redistribute resources, thereby reducing regional inequality, while Donnithorne and others portray a more decentralized China resulting in a "cellular economy" stemming from the policy of self-reliance. Following Donnithorne's argument to its logical conclusion, interprovincial inequality might have gone up in the pre-reform era. However, scarcity of data in the 1970s prevented commentators at that time from putting their views to the litmus test. In the reform era, new sources of investment funds have emerged. Table 19.14 summarizes the composition of aggregate fixed-asset investment (*quanshehui guding zichan touzi*). Naughton (2003) argues that there has been a retreat from redistributive investment by the state in the reform era. Indeed, as shown in Table 19.14, the share of state budgetary investment (*guojia touzi*) in investment financing has declined, with state funds increasingly replaced by domestic loans (*guonei daikuan*), foreign funds (*liyong waizi*), and self-raised funds plus other investment (*zichou ji qita touzi*).[29]

To what extent did these changes in the sources of investment financing impact interprovincial inequality? One way of answering this question is to resort to the

---

[29] We cannot find separate time series for self-raised funds and other investments.

Table 19.14 *Aggregate fixed-asset investment (quanshehui guding zichan touzi) by sources of funds*

	State appropriations	Domestic loans	Foreign investment	Self-raised funds and other investment
1981	22.7	14.3	4.9	58.1
1982	23.8	12.3	4.7	59.3
1983	23.0	14.1	3.9	59.1
1984	16.0	20.1	3.6	60.3
1985	14.6	21.1	4.4	59.9
1986	13.1	23.0	4.8	59.1
1987	9.3	21.0	5.9	63.8
1988	8.3	17.3	6.6	67.8
1989	8.7	19.6	6.3	65.4
1990	6.8	23.5	5.7	64.0
1991	4.3	27.4	5.8	62.5
1992	3.7	23.5	7.3	65.5
1993	3.0	22.4	9.9	64.7
1994	3.0	20.5	11.2	65.3
1995	2.7	19.5	11.7	66.0
1996	2.7	19.6	11.8	66.0
1997	2.8	18.9	10.6	67.7
1998	4.2	19.3	9.1	67.4
1999	6.2	19.2	6.7	67.8
2000	6.4	20.3	5.1	68.2

Note: Values are in percent.
Source: NBS, Department of Fixed-Asset Investment (2002).

contribution of capital, CCK, in equation (19.1) given earlier.[30] CCK from Tsui (2007) is reported in Figure 19.6, which also presents other contributions for ease of comparison.[31] With regard to CCK, the vertical axis measures the extent to which spatial differences in the growth in physical capital cumulatively push interprovincial inequality above/below its 1964 level (recall eqs. (19.1) and (19.2)), holding all other contributions unchanged. Up to the early 1970s, CCK assumes negative values, indicating the extent to which the changing spatial distribution

[30] Provincial capital stocks in Tsui (forthcoming) are derived using the perpetual inventory approach; that is, $K_m = (1 - d)K_{m,-1} + FA_m$, where K_{m-1} is last year's capital stock, d is the rate of depreciation, and FA_m is gross fixed capital formation (*guding ziben xingcheng zonge*) from the national accounts. Gross fixed capital formation includes in theory all sources of investments and not just basic construction investment (*jiben jianshe touzi*).

[31] CCK, CCH, and CCA in Figure 19.6 are derived using equations (19.1) and (19.2). Together with CCΠ, they add up, to $\sum_{\tau=1}^{t} dI(\mathbf{y})/dt$ and *not* $I(\mathbf{y})$ itself. In principle, the three components may be stacked in a diagram depicting their contributions. However, with the contributions assuming negative values for some years, such a presentation of the figures does not give a clear picture of the trajectory of each contribution.

of capital pushes *ceteris paribus* interprovincial inequality below its 1964 level. This finding nicely captures the effect of the Third Front Campaign, which was behind a surge in investment funds in the inland provinces. However, as shown in Figure 19.6, this trend is reversed in the early 1970s. The Third Front Campaign did not have a lasting effect on interprovincial disparity, confirming Naughton's observation. Redistributive investments were scaled down even before 1978.

In the post-Mao era, CCK continues its increasing trend, meaning that cross-provincial differences in the allocation of investment funds push in the direction of increased interprovincial income inequality. The sustained increase in CCK since the mid-1970s is, as shown in Tsui (2007), attributable to faster growth in capital stocks of the coastal provinces, so much so that, by the 1990s, the increase in CCK is almost entirely driven by the widening of the gap between the eastern and inland provinces.[32] It is tempting to speculate that the trajectory of the contribution by capital (CCK) may be linked to the changing composition in investment funds described earlier. For example, the spatial distribution of foreign investment was and still is highly skewed in favor of such coastal provinces as Guangdong. Self-raised funds *plus* other investment in Table 19.14 also experienced rapid growth in the first two decades of reform, with its share increasing from 58 percent in 1981 to 68 percent 2000. Without additional data, it will be difficult to determine how the different sources of funds have impinged on regional inequality.

So far, we have focused on investments in physical assets, but the spatial distribution of human investments as measured by CCH may potentially be important in shaping interprovincial inequality. In terms of the conceptual framework discussed earlier, human investments increase the provincial stock of quality-adjusted labor H, thereby boosting provincial output. The spread of basic education to less developed provinces, which dates to pre-reform efforts to eradicate illiteracy, is often hailed as an important achievement. International comparisons of literacy rates and life expectancy suggest that China excels in human development (Bramall, 2000). The spatial allocation of budgetary resources for the provision of public goods is critical to the spread of basic education. In the pre-reform era, there seems to be a substantial increase in enrollment and a drastic drop in adult illiteracy initially in richer and subsequently in poorer provinces. Some have argued that human capital accumulation in the Maoist period has provided a solid foundation for the subsequent economic takeoff (Bramall, 2000). Analogous to the spatial distribution of physical investments, the pre-reform era witnessed a rapid spread of basic education to poor provinces.

---

[32] Not reported here, Tsui (2007) has further decomposed CCK into a between-region (BCCK) and within-region components (WCCK); that is, CCK = BCCK + WCCK. Roughly speaking, BBK analytically captures the contribution of K due to the changing gaps between the eastern, central, and western regions while ignoring the changing gaps with respect to provinces within each region. WCCK captures only the contribution with respect to gaps between provinces within each region.

Tsui (2007) has derived the contribution of human capital to interprovincial inequality, CCH (recall eq. (19.2)), and his findings appear in Figure 19.6. An upward trend is discernible up to the mid-1970s and is followed by a downward trajectory. The initial cumulative increase in CCH may be due to the initial highly unequal distribution of human capital. But, with the spread of education since the 1950s and with more graduates from poor provinces gradually entering the labor force, education has reduced inequality. The value of CCH turns negative in 1988, meaning that the inequality-reducing effect of CCH completely offsets its cumulative contribution to increased cross-provincial inequality in the earlier period.

Our discussion has focused on the contributions of capital and labor adjusted for educational attainment without touching the impact of factor mobility on interprovincial inequality. In theory, interregional factor mobility may reduce spatial inequality. However, there is much debate on the extent to which integrated factor markets have emerged in China (see the previous sections on "Political Economy of Spatial Units" and "Continuity, Reform, and Spatial Economic Development"). One should be careful not to infer from the above empirical results the effect of interprovincial factor mobility on inequality, not least because the contributions are induced by each province's *own* accumulation of capital, both physical and human, *as well as* interprovincial factor mobility.

Total Factor Productivity, Comparative Advantage, Regional Specialization, and Agglomeration Economies

In this section, we focus on the contribution of TFP to interprovincial inequality, that is, CCA in equation (19.2). In this connection, roughly three phases are discernible. As shown in Figure 19.6, a shift toward increasing inequality in the pre-reform era up to the mid-1970s gives way to a decreasing contribution to inequality during the 1980s. A reversal since the early 1990s makes up the third phase. Insofar as provincial TFP growth is a residual after deducting the contribution of factor inputs, the usual caveats apply to its interpretation. TFP growth reflects a smorgasbord of factors that may have affected the overall efficiency of provincial economies. In the absence of sufficient data to further decompose the contribution of TFP into its constituent factors, the following discussion is no more than exploratory, leaving much room to further investigate such issues as the effect of changing economic structure, the decline of the state sector, and so on, on interprovincial inequality. Keeping this caveat in mind, what follows focuses on how the evolution of regional development strategy may help explain the oscillation in provincial efficiency and thus regional inequality.

It is widely agreed that pre-reform regional policies disregarded comparative advantage and regional specialization (see, e.g., Donnithorne, 1972; Lardy, 1983; Lyons, 1987), with detrimental effects on the overall efficiency of the provincial economies. In terms of our framework, the distortionary effects of these policies might have worked through the growth in provincial TFP to shape interprovincial inequality. The cumulative contribution of TFP, that is, CCA, helps capture such efficiency-sapping effects on inequality. As shown in Figure 19.6, there is an increase in CCA up to the mid-1970s, more than offsetting the contemporaneous decrease in CCK, largely accounting for the *increase* in overall interprovincial inequality in the period up to the early 1970s.

While inefficient pre-reform policies might have deleterious effects on all provinces, both rich and poor, the upward trajectory of CCA up to the mid-1970s suggests that efficiency-distorting policies apparently hit the poorer provinces harder. Initiatives such as the "grain-first" policy carefully documented in Lardy (1983) lend credence to this interpretation; poor regions such as those in the northwest were particularly hard-hit by this policy, which forced them to abandon crops in which they held a comparative advantage in favor of growing grains to ensure local self-sufficiency. The grain-first policy reduced the growth in TFP especially among poor provinces that had comparative advantages in nongrain crops (Lardy, 1983, pp. 180–183).

The next phase of the evolution in CCA coincides with the policy reversal marking the first ten years of economic reforms. CCA in Figure 19.6 switches course and starts to decline in the late 1970s, with this trend continuing to the end of the 1980s. This finding is consistent with the potential effects of policy shifts and the reversal of inefficient pre-reform policies. One example is the revoking of the pre-reform policy of local grain sufficiency alluded to earlier. Also, rural reforms such as the household responsibility system boosted incentives and thus productivity, particularly among poorer provinces.

On the industrial front, reduced emphasis on heavy industries left more room for such provinces as Guangdong, Fujian, and Zhejiang to develop labor-intensive industries commensurate with their factor endowments, thereby boosting overall productivity and setting the stage for their emergence as global manufacturing hubs. While these provinces have become rich after three decades of sustained economic growth, they were poor at the dawn of the reform era not least because pre-reform development strategies had prevented them from exploiting their comparative advantages. Thus, the decrease in CCA, particularly in the first half of the 1980s, is not just due to the narrowing of the coastal–inland gap, but is to a greater measure induced by significant productivity gains of some coastal provinces catching up with and even outstripping their richer coastal neighbors.[33]

Combining the effects of all the changes discussed earlier, the decline in CCA in the first half of the 1980s is so large that it overwhelms the inequality-increasing contribution of capital, resulting in a decline in overall interprovincial inequality.

---

[33] Tsui (2007) partitions China into the eastern, central, and western regions. CCA is then further decomposed into within-region and between-region contributions of TFP. While both of these two subcomponents exhibit downward trends in the first phase of economic reforms, the magnitude of the decline for WCCA is conspicuously more important. The sharp decline in WCCA corresponds to the poorer coastal provinces, such as Guangdong, Fujian, and Zhejiang, catching up with other richer eastern provinces.

With the effects induced by the first wave of rural reforms petering out and the mitigation of the pre-reform distortionary policies, the contribution of TFP enters a third phase toward the end of the 1980s. The rise of TVEs helped fuel the rural economy in the second half of the 1980s, though the benefits this time by and large accrued to coastal provinces (Lin and Cai, 2003). Also, with the focus of institutional reform switching to the urban sector, the richer and more industrialized provinces stood to gain from new waves of reforms. Quickly climbing up the ladder of opulence in the first phase of reforms, such provinces as Guangdong, Fujian, and Zhejiang continued to press ahead, this time widening their gaps with their inland neighbors. As the concentration of labor-intensive industries transformed the Pearl River Delta and the Changjiang Delta into global manufacturing hubs, the resulting economies of agglomeration probably provided a further stimulus to productivity of the richer provinces in the 1990s (Fujita and Hu, 2001). The increase in CCA in the 1990s, implying that TFP has grown faster in richer provinces, is consistent with such a development.

These findings have interesting implications for ongoing debates about China's regional development strategy. In recent years, there are repeated calls for the Chinese government to direct more fiscal resources to the inland provinces. However, past experiences such as the Third Front Campaign point to the danger that redistributive investment may lead to losses in efficiency. Indeed, as discussed earlier, the egalitarian strategy prevailing in the pre-reform era seems to coincide with an increase in the contribution of TFP growth to interprovincial inequality that more than offsets the decrease arising from the more equal distribution of capital. The result is that the overall trend in interprovincial inequality ratchets upward between the mid-1960s and mid-1970s, even though there was a surge in investments in inland provinces. The opposite is true in the reform era up to the end of the 1980s, even though the retreat from central planning in the reform era is often thought to have aggravated inequality.

CONCLUDING REMARKS

This chapter began with a review of the forces that shaped China's spatial development in the pre-reform era. At the dawn of the reform era, China inherited a spatial configuration that was characterized, *inter alia*, by an extremely dispersed industrial structure, underagglomeration of cities, slow pace of urbanization, low level of regional specialization, and low factor mobility, hindering the formation of a national market. Our main analysis emphasizes development during the past fifteen years, with a particular focus on urbanization, regional development, and inequality. The influence of the pre-reform legacies remains quite significant in the spatial development in the current reform era.

The study of urbanization in the reform era continues to be beset by definitional difficulties and comparability problems. Nonetheless, it is quite certain that urban population growth rate was high in the last two decades of the twentieth century, attributable mainly to net migration and physical expansion of the urban areas. Based on the UAA concept, we examined the growth rates of a sample of 414 cities in the 1990s. The trend shows that big cities, especially those with administrative ranks at or above the provincial capital grew at a higher rate in the 1990s. Large export-processing cities also expanded at a higher rate. There was voluminous internal migration in the reform era, including significant rural–urban and interprovincial migration involving peasant labor. The dominant tendency of interprovincial migration in the 1990s was from the inland provinces toward the coast, especially to the three "hot spots" of economic attraction – the PRD, the Shanghai region, and Beijing region. The trend became even more pronounced in the second half of the 1990s, as Guangdong served as the premier destination for migrants from other provinces.

In terms of economic structure, Chinese cities display two key features. First, China is going through the stage of "functional specialization" whereby manufacturing production decentralizes from the largest cities, while headquarters and business and finance and service activity concentrate there. Not only do cities in China below the top thirty produce the bulk of urban GDP, they produce a significant portion of manufacturing output. Yet, traditionally, policy in China governing the allocation of domestic and FDI has been biased toward the largest cities, even though returns on investment in those cities are lower than those in other locations. Continued successful decentralization of industry from the largest cities and their suburban areas to medium-size cities would be helped by further reform of capital markets.

The second key feature is that urbanization policy, reinforced by the *hukou* system, has limited migration from rural to urban areas. China is still somewhat underurbanized and its urbanization has very low spatial concentration. Overall, there is a lack of spatial agglomeration in China, in both larger cities and even at the village level, which limits the scale benefits of agglomeration and hence productivity overall. As migration restrictions are loosened, more competitive locations will experience accelerated growth and less competitive ones will face population drains.

The trend in interprovincial inequality is a subject that has attracted much attention ever since Lardy and Donnithorne debated this issue in the 1970s. Many commentators have focused on the changing spatial allocation of investment funds as a factor driving the change in regional disparity. Important though investment allocation may be, we must remember that China's regional development policies in different periods determined the extent to which the spatial allocation of resources could exploit comparative advantage, regional specialization, and agglomeration economies, thereby affecting the overall efficiency of provincial economies. In this connection, recent findings in Tsui (forthcoming) show that spatially differential growth in TFP exerted as large an impact on interprovincial inequality during 1965–1999 as the allocation of investment funds.

Furthermore, the contributions of TFP growth and investment to interprovincial inequality did not necessarily move in the same direction. Indeed, interprovincial inequality increased in the pre-reform period (between the mid-1960s and the early 1970s) because the inequality-increasing effect of TFP growth more than offset the equalizing contribution of physical investment. As explained earlier, the policy environment in the pre-reform era might have resulted in slower growth in TFP among poorer provinces. With the unwinding of those inefficient policies, the opposite seems to be true in the reform period up to the late 1980s.

Our findings on the contribution of TFP growth to interprovincial inequality highlight the possibility that regional development policies may either obstruct or enhance the exploitation of regional comparative advantage and agglomeration economies. These policies influence the progress of national market integration, which in turn critically affects the efficiency of resource allocation. Even after three decades of market reform, China is still plagued by the problem of local protectionism. Not only does local protectionism breed inefficiency when factors cannot flow freely across jurisdictions, it may possibly slow down regional income convergence. Similar concerns surround the Western Development Program, through which China's central government seeks to narrow the gap between the coastal and western provinces. But as the outcome of the Third Front Campaign demonstrated, simply ploughing physical resources into less developed provinces does not necessarily reduce regional disparity. What seems equally important is the promotion and crafting of institutions that are more congenial to the emergence of a national market and efficient resource allocation.

From the broad picture painted earlier, we have identified a number of salient features that have distinguished China's path of spatial development from those of market economies. If efficient resource allocation capitalizing on comparative advantage and agglomeration economies is the hallmark of an ideal market economy, China's spatial development in the first two decades of Communist rule was palpably shaped by the visible hand of central planning that fell short of exploiting those advantages. Although reform has pulled China out of the planning straitjacket and gradually unleashed the genie of the market, it is interesting to note that China's political institutions, albeit changing slowly, have by and large remained intact, thereby preserving some key structures that have continued to shape the spatial configuration of resource allocation. Among them is the administrative hierarchy of jurisdictions whose boundaries are often "invisible walls" that inhibit national economic integration. Whether market forces will gain the upper hand and China will converge to the spatial configuration of a "normal country" will in the final analysis depend on how those institutions evolve.

This chapter is far from a comprehensive survey of China's spatial development. Conspicuously missing is a discussion of the spatial issues involving such subprovincial jurisdictions as counties that roughly make up China's rural sector. Nor have we been able to delve into the issue of transportation on China's spatial development. Those are among the important topics that deserve future attention.

References

Au, Chun-Chung and J. Vernon Henderson. 2006a. "How Migration Restrictions Limit Agglomeration and Productivity in China." *Journal of Development Economics*. 2006, 80, pp. 350–388.

Au, Chun-Chung and J. Vernon Henderson. 2006b. "Are Chinese Cities Too Small?" *Review of Economic Studies*. 73, pp. 549–576.

Bai Chong-En, Yingjuan Du, Zhigang Tao, and Sarah Y. Tong. 2004. "Local Protectionism and Regional Specialization: Evidence from China's Industries." *Journal of International Economics*. 63.2, pp. 397–417.

Bhalla, Ajit S., Shujie Yao, and Zongyi Zhang. 2003. "Causes of Inequalities in China, 1952 to 1999." *Journal of International Development*. 15(8), pp. 939–995.

Black, Duncan and J. Vernon Henderson. 2003. "Urban Evolution in the USA." *Journal of Economic Geography*. 3, pp. 343–372.

Boyreau-Debray, Genevieve and Shang-jin Wei. 2004. "Can China Grow Faster? A Diagnosis on the Fragmentation of the Domestic Capital Market." IMF Working Paper 04/76. Washington, DC: International Monetary Fund.

Bramall, Chris. 2000. *Sources of Chinese Economic Growth 1978–1996*. Oxford: Oxford University Press.

Chan, Kam Wing. 1994. *Cities with Invisible Walls: Reinterpreting Urbanization in Post-1949 China*. Hong Kong: Oxford University Press.

Chan, Kam Wing. 2001. "Recent Migration in China: Patterns, Trends, and Policies." *Asian Perspectives*. 25.4, pp. 127–155.

Chan, Kam Wing and Antonia Bennett. 2004. "Which City in China Has the Highest per Capita GDP? A Study of Chinese City Population Numbers and Implications for Research." Paper presented at the Annual Meeting of the Association of American Geographers, Philadelphia, PA, March 18, 2004.

Chan, Kam Wing and Ying Hu. 2003. "Urbanization in China in the 1990s: New Definition, Different Series, and Revised Trends." *The China Review*. 3(2), pp. 49–71.

Chan, Kam Wing and Li Zhang. 1999. "The *Hukou* System and Rural–Urban Migration: Processes and Changes." *The China Quarterly*. 160, pp. 818–855.

Chan, Kam Wing, Kai Yuen Tsui, and Qing Yu. 2003. "Understanding China's Spatial Administrative System and Changes: An Exploration." Paper presented at International Conference on Globalization, the State, and Urban Transformation in China, Hong Kong Baptist University, Hong Kong, December 15–17, 2003.

Chan Kam Wing and Man Wang. 2004. "Remapping Regional Economic Disparities in China in the 1990s." Paper presented at Universities Service Center for China Studies, Chinese University of Hong Kong, Hong Kong, December 16, 2004.

Chen Chao and Chen Hongling, 2003. *Zhonghua renmin gongheguo xingzhengqu yange dituji (1949–1999)* [Atlas of changes of administrative regions in the People's Republic of China (1949–1999)]. Beijing: Zhongguo ditu chubanshe.

Chung, Jao Ho and Tao-chiu Lam. 2003. "China's 'City System' in Flux: Explaining Post-Mao Administrative Changes." *The China Quarterly*. 180, pp. 945–964.

Donnithorne, Audrey. 1972. "China's Cellular Economy: Some Economic Trends since the Cultural Revolution." *The China Quarterly*. 52, pp. 605–619.

Donnithorne, Audrey. 1976. "Comment." *The China Quarterly*. 66, pp. 328–340.

Duranton, Gilles and Diego Puga. 2004. "Micro-foundations of Urban Agglomeration Economies," in *Handbook of Regional and Urban Economics* vol. 4. J. V. Henderson and J-F Thisse, eds. Amsterdam, The Netherlands: Elsevier, pp. 2063–2117.

Eckstein, Alexander. 1975. *China's Economic Development: Interplay of Security and Ideology.* Cambridge and New York: Cambridge University Press.

Fujita, Masahisa and Daping Hu. 2001. "Regional Disparity in China 1985–1994: The Effects of Globalization and Economic Liberalization." *The Annals of Regional Science* 35, pp. 3–37.

Gu Chaolin, Yu Taofang, and Chan Kam Wing. 2002. "Extended Metropolitan Regions: New Feature of Chinese Metropolitan Development in the Age of Globalization (in Chinese)." *The Planner.* 18(2), pp. 16–20.

Henderson, J. Vernon 2005. "Medium Size City Growth in China," in *Brookings-Wharton Papers on Urban Affairs.* W. G. Gale and J. Rothenberg-Pack, eds. Washington, DC: Brookings Institution, pp. 263–295.

Henderson, J. Vernon and Hyoung-Gun Wang. 2007. "Urbanization and City Growth: The Role of Institutions." *Regional Science and Urban Economics.* 37, 283–313.

Huang, Yasheng. 1995. "Administrative Monitoring in China." *The China Quarterly.* 143, pp. 828–842.

Huang, Yasheng. January–February 2001. "Political Institutions and Fiscal Reforms in China." *Problems of Post-Communism.* 48, pp. 16–26.

Jefferson, Gary H. and Inderjit Singh. 1999. *Enterprise Reform in China: Ownership, Transition and Performance.* Oxford and New York: Oxford University Press.

Jian, Tianlun, Jeffrey D. Sachs, and Andrew M. Warner. 1996. "Trends in Regional Inequality in China." *China Economic Review.* 7(1), pp. 1–21.

Keidel, Albert. 2001. "China's GDP Expenditure Accounts." *China Economic Review.* 12(4), 355–367.

Lardy, Nicholas R. 1975. "Centralization and Decentralization in China's Fiscal Management." *The China Quarterly.* 61, pp. 25–60.

Lardy, Nicholas R. 1976. "Replies." *The China Quarterly.* 66, pp. 340–354.

Lardy, Nicholas R. 1978. *Economic Growth and Distribution in China.* Cambridge and New York: Cambridge University Press.

Lardy, Nicholas R. 1983. *Agriculture in China's Modern Economic Development.* Cambridge and New York: Cambridge University Press.

Lin, Justin Y., Fang Cai, and Zhou Li. 1996. *The China Miracle: Development Strategy and Economic Growth.* Hong Kong: Hong Kong Center for Economic Research, Chinese University Press.

Lin Yifu and Cai Fang, 2003. *Zhongguo jingji: gaige yu fazhan* [Chinese economy: Reform and development]. Beijing: Zhongguo caizheng jingji chubanshe.

Lin Yifu, Cai Fang, and Li Zhou, 1999. "Zhongguo jingji zhuanxingqi de diqu chayi fenxi [Analysis of China's regional inequality in the period of transition]," *Jingji yanjiu* [Economic research], no. 6, pp. 3–10.

Lyons, Thomas P. 1987. *Economic Integration and Planning in Maoist China.* New York: Columbia University Press.

Lyons, Thomas P. 1991. "Interprovincial Disparities in China: Output and Consumption." *Economic Development and Cultural Change.* 39, pp. 471–506.

Ma Zhongdong, Zhang Weimin, Liang Zai, and Cui Hongyan, 2004. "Laodongli liudong: Zhongguo nongcun shouru zengzhang de xin yinshu [Labor mobility: A new factor behind China's rural income growth]," *Renkou yanjiu* [Population research], no. 28.3, pp. 2–10.

Marshall, Alfred. 1890. *Principles of Economics.* London: MacMillan.

Ministry of Civil Affairs, Finance and Departmental Affairs Department, 2003–2004. *Zhongguo minzheng tongji nianjian* [Chinese civil affairs statistics]. Beijing: Zhongguo tongji chubanshe.

Ministry of Civil Affairs, Planning and Finance Department, ed. 1993. *Minzheng tongji lishi ziliao huibian* [A compendium of historical statistics on civil affairs 1949–1992]. Beijing: Minzhengbu jihua caiwusi.

Montinola, Gabriella, Yingyi Qian, and Barry R. Weingast. 1995. "Federalism, Chinese Style: The Political Basis for Economic Success in China." *World Politics*. 48(1), pp. 50–81.

NBS [National Bureau of Statistics], 2005. *Zhongguo tongji nianjian 2005* [Statistical Yearbook of China 2005]. Beijing: Zhongguo tongji chubanshe.

NBS [National Bureau of Statistics]. 2006(a). "Report of Major Figures from 2005 1% Sample Population Survey." Accessed March 16, 2006, from www.gov.cn/gzdt/2006–03/16/context_228740.htm.

NBS [National Bureau of Statistics]. Various Years. *China City Statistical Yearbook*. Beijing: Zhongguo tongji chubanshe.

NBS [National Bureau of Statistics], Department of Fixed Asset Investment, 2002. *Zhongguo guding zichan touzi tongji shudian 2000* [Statistical Compendium of Chinese Fixed Asset Investment]. Beijing: Zhongguo tongji chubanshe.

NBS [National Bureau of Statistics], National Income Account Department, 2006. "Jingji pucha hou Zhongguo GDP shuju jiedu zhiyi: GDP zongliang, zengzhang shudu ji renjun GDP [An explanation of the GDP data after the survey of the national economy: Total GDP, growth and GDP per capita]." Accessed October 30, from 2006 http://www.stats.gov.cn.

Naughton, Barry. 1988. "The Third Front: Defence Industrialization in the Chinese Interior." *The China Quarterly*. 115, pp. 351–386.

Naughton, Barry. 2002. "Provincial Economic Growth in China: Causes and Consequences of Regional Differentiation," in *China and Its Regions: Economic Growth and Reform in Chinese Provinces*. Mary-Françoise Renard, ed. Cheltenham, UK, and Northampton, MA: E. Elgar, pp. 57–86.

Naughton, Barry. 2003. "How Much Can Regional Integration Do to Unify China's Market?" in *How Far Across the River? Chinese Policy Reform at the Millennium*. Nicholas C. Hope, Dennis Tao Yang, and Li MuYang, eds. Stanford, CA: Stanford University Press, pp. 204–232.

Overman, Henry, Stephen. Redding, and Anthony Venables. 2003. "The Economic Geography of Trade, Production and Income: A Survey of the Empirics," in *Handbook of International Trade*. James Harrigan and Kwan Choi, eds. Oxford: Blackwell.

Poncet, Sandra. 2003. "Measuring Chinese Domestic and International Integration." *China Economic Review*. 14, pp. 1–21.

Qian, Yingyi and Barry Weingast. 1997. "Federalism as a Commitment to Preserving Market Incentives." *Journal of Economic Perspectives*. 11, pp. 83–92.

Raiser, Martin. 1998. "Subsidizing Inequality: Economic Reforms, Fiscal Transfers and Convergence Across Chinese Provinces." *The Journal of Development Studies*. 34(3), pp. 1–26.

SC and NBS [State Council and National Bureau of Statistics], 2002. *Zhongguo 2000 nian renkou pucha ziliao* [Tabulation on the 2000 population census of the People's Republic of China], vol. 3. Beijing: Zhongguo tongji chubanshe.

Skinner, G. William. 1985. "Presidential Address: The Structure of Chinese History." *Journal of Asian Studies*. 44.2, pp. 271–310.

Tsui, Kai Yuen. 1991. "China's Regional Inequality, 1952–85." *Journal of Comparative Economics*. 15, pp. 1–21.

Tsui, Kai Yuen. 1996. "Economic Reform and Interprovincial Inequalities in China." *Journal of Development Economics*. 50(2), pp. 353–368.

Tsui, Kai Yuen. 2007. "Forces Shaping China's Interprovincial Inequality." *Review of Income and Wealth*. 53(1), pp. 60–92.

Vogel, Ezra F. 1989. *One Step Ahead in China: Guangdong under Reform.* Cambridge, MA: Harvard University Press.

Wang, Enru and Kam Wing Chan, 2005. "The Tilting Scoreline: Geographic Inequalities in Admissions to Universities in China," in *Zhuanxing zhong de Zhongguo laodongli shichang* [Labor market in China's transition]. Cai Fang and Zhang Zhanxin, eds. Beijing: China Population Publishing House, pp. 237–266.

Wang, Fei-ling. 2005. *Organizing Through Division and Exclusion: China's Hukou System.* Stanford: Stanford University Press.

Wang Mengkui and Li Shantong, 2000. *Deng zhu Zhongguo diqu shehui jingji fazhan bupingheng wenti yanjiu* [Research on China's uneven socio-economic development]. Beijing: Shangwu yinshuguan.

Wang, Shaoguang and Angang Hu. 1999. *The Political Economy of Uneven Development: The Case of China.* Armonk: ME Sharpe.

Whiting, Susan. 2001. *Power and Wealth in Rural China.* Cambridge and New York: Cambridge University Press.

Wong, Christine. 1991. "Central–Local Relations in an Era of Fiscal Decline: The Paradox of Fiscal Decentralization in Post-Mao China." *The China Quarterly.* 128, pp. 691–715.

Wong, Christine. 1992. "Fiscal Reform and Local Industrialization: The Problematic Sequencing of Reform in Post-Mao China." *Modern China.* 18, pp. 197–227.

Wong, Christine, ed. 1997. *Financing Local Government in the People's Republic of China.* Oxford: Oxford University Press.

Wong, Christine. January 2005. "Can China Change Development Paradigm for the 21st Century? Fiscal Policy Options for Hu Jintao and Wen Jiaobao after Two Decades of Muddling Through." Research Unit Asia, Stiftung Wissenschaft und Politik, German Institute for International and Security Affairs Working Paper FG 7.

Wu, Yuan-li. 1967. *The Spatial Economy of Communist China.* New York: Praeger Publishers.

Young, Alwyn. 2000. "The Razor's Edge: Distortions and Incremental Reform in the People's Republic of China." *Quarterly Journal of Economics.* 115.4, pp. 1091–1135.

Zhou, Yixing and Laurence J. C. Ma. 2003. "China's Urbanization Levels: Reconstructing a Baseline from the Fifth Population Census." *The China Quarterly.* 173, pp. 176–196.

TWENTY

Forecasting China's Economic Growth to 2025

Dwight H. Perkins and Thomas G. Rawski[1]

Why attempt to forecast China's economic growth? Most importantly, the impact of China on the rest of the world and on the standard of living of its own people depends mainly on whether the nation continues to double the size of its gross domestic product (GDP) every seven to ten years or whether that growth slows markedly or even halts. China already influences the world economy through its booming exports, its demand for natural resources, its influence on global warming, and much else. A GDP four times the current level will multiply China's worldwide impact.

But there is another reason why forecasting Chinese growth is desirable in a volume dedicated to understanding China's present and past economic performance. The ability to forecast is one important test of whether the analysis has gotten the story right. There are many ways to forecast the future, some of which, like simple projections of recent trends, tell us little about the present and not much about the future.

But analytical forecasts based on a model that attempts to sort out the main influences that are likely to shape that future can deepen our understanding of the mechanisms driving Chinese growth. Even if the forecasts are a bit off the mark or downright wrong, a good model allows analysts to review a forecast's strengths and limitations and to identify specific shortcomings that contributed to the gap between predictions and ultimate outcomes. Put differently, the effort to forecast necessitates explicit judgments about which economic forces matter and which do not. If the forecast turns out to be wrong, future analysts and readers are in a position to understand why the forecast was wrong and what changes could have improved it.

[1] The authors gratefully acknowledge research assistance from Yifan Zhang, Tingting Huang, Ying Fang, and Zixia Sheng. Judith Banister, Loren Brandt, Nicholas Lardy, and Carsten Holz stand out among many colleagues who have provided valuable information and advice. The usual caveat applies.

The forecasting model used in this chapter is extremely simple. We start with the supply side growth accounting equation. We use data from the past half century to determine how much of GDP growth can be attributed to larger inputs of capital, human capital, and labor and how much is due to a rise in total factor productivity (TFP) or output per unit of these inputs. This approach has an important advantage in that it is possible to make informed quantitative judgments about the likely growth of labor, capital, and education over the next two decades.

The primary reason for starting with the growth accounting equation, however, is that it provides a basis for separating out the contribution of TFP and capital to China's economic growth. If rapid growth arises primarily from high rates of capital formation, then the forecasting agenda boils down to determining whether high rates of investment will continue. This in turn depends on whether personal savings of the Chinese population will remain high, whether Chinese corporations continue to be an independent source of high savings, and whether the Chinese government will run large fiscal surpluses or large fiscal deficits.

If growth is driven instead by TFP, the considerations critical to any long-term forecast are very different. Rising rates of savings and investment may contribute little to growth. What matters is whether investments deliver high rates of return. But what contributes to a high rate of return? Can a country achieve a high rate of return with a weak financial system? Was China's growth during the 1980s and 1990s the result of reforms that created a one-time rise in the level of TFP? Or, have these reforms created conditions that will promote sustained TFP growth over the coming decades?

The sources of TFP growth are inherently difficult to quantify. Determining the impact of financial reform or greater outward orientation is more complex than measuring an increase in the size of the labor force or in the number of college graduates. Still, we have far more knowledge than existed several decades ago about what kinds of reforms promote accelerated growth. In East Asia, in particular, we have the experience of South Korean and Taiwanese economic reforms in the 1960s through the 1980s and of Vietnamese reforms in the 1990s. We also have the econometric estimates of the "new growth economics" that give us some guidance as to what works and what does not in the relationship between policy, institutional reform, and growth.

There is a fundamental difference between forecasting growth over a twenty-year period, which is the focus of this essay, and short-run predictions targeting the next year or two. Because short-term outcomes depend on a host of economic variables and can be strongly influenced by external shocks, short-run forecasting requires a model that captures how the many different sources of change in the economy impact overall performance. The model thus will depend on a large number of equations. Given that we have few estimates of such equations in the Chinese context, short-term forecasts call for a wide variety of assumptions about the parameters of such equations. Such assumptions invariably involve high error margins. Utilizing short-term models to project longer-term growth is particularly dangerous because rapid shifts in economic structure – such as changes in income distribution or in the relative size of the state and private sectors – seem likely to shift the underlying structure embedded in short-term forecasting models.[2]

Long-term growth, by contrast, is largely independent of sudden shocks or short-term changes in consumption behavior. It is mainly driven by the growth rate of productivity, which in turn is heavily influenced by research and development expenditures, the availability of capital to turn the discoveries of research and development (R&D) into final demand products, and the growth of the labor force.

Long-term growth in developing countries is both a bit simpler and a bit more complicated. It is simpler because efforts to develop and commercialize new technologies typically contribute little to economic growth in poor nations. China may be an exception as the scale of domestic R&D spending increases (see Chapter 9 in this volume) and as multinational firms transfer a growing array of research activity to the People's Republic. Productivity growth in developing countries, however, depends mainly on how fast these countries can adapt the technology and management practices of higher-income economies to their particular situations.

Because developing countries are not, for the most part, in the business of pushing out the frontiers of knowledge, they can avoid the dead ends that technological leaders inevitably encounter. Developing nations may also benefit from opportunities to avoid expensive and time-consuming investments, for example, by building cell-phone networks rather than connecting telephone wires to customers' homes or shops. These advantages give developing countries the potential to grow much faster than high-income nations, at least for a time.

A half century of international development experience demonstrates that low-income nations can capture this unique opportunity for accelerated growth only if they orient their economic systems to take full advantage of being followers. Since we know something about the structures that generate productivity growth, we can compare what China has accomplished in this regard with what has worked elsewhere. Comparisons of this sort do not lead to precise quantitative estimates of the contribution of reform to growth, but they do provide a benchmark for comparing Chinese economic institutions and policies with circumstances in countries that have succeeded in building extended periods of high-speed growth into their economies.

STRUCTURE OF THIS CHAPTER

We begin by measuring the supply side sources of growth between 1952 and 2005 with as much rigor as is possible given the limitations of Chinese data. Making

---

[2] While these more elaborate models are an unreliable basis for forecasting long-term GDP growth, they can be very useful in sorting out the impact of various levels of growth on sector demand and much else.

the measurements is a straightforward if time-consuming task. Interpreting the results is quite another matter. Most analysts select a time period, compile the data, determine whether the contribution to growth of capital is greater than that of TFP or vice versa, and leave it at that. In our view, this approach is inadequate because it fails to examine the dynamic interaction between productivity and accumulation. In China and other nations that experience major economic or institutional reforms, the growth of capital is itself in part the result of acceleration in TFP growth. We see China's recent development as first and foremost a story about productivity growth supported by the growth of factor inputs, notably, capital. From this perspective, China's ability to sustain high rates of GDP growth in the future will depend critically on the capacity to generate continuing growth in TFP.

TFP growth, however, is far from the whole story of either China's past or its future. The next section of this chapter, therefore, looks at the likely future growth of factor inputs. Will the savings rate remain high and will high savings continue to be translated into high rates of investment and capital stock growth? We can be reasonably precise about labor force growth, but considerably less precise about what share of that labor force will end up in high-productivity industrial and service-sector employment as contrasted to low-productivity agriculture or failing state enterprises.

The analysis of Chinese productivity dynamics will begin with a brief review of what our growth accounting equation and our knowledge of Chinese reforms since 1978 can tell us about what drove productivity growth over the past quarter century. Many of the reforms that led to high productivity growth in the past, however, are not likely to continue to provide a comparable stimulus to growth in the future.

The effort to understand where future reforms might impact productivity growth is unavoidably speculative. It begins with a brief look at cross-country econometric growth equations to see what guidance they give us about China's likely growth path over the next two decades. We then focus on key economic institutions, policies, and social issues that are likely to affect future growth.

Finally, we will turn from our supply side approach to look briefly at demand-side issues. Foremost among these is the question of whether and for how long China can continue to expand the share of domestic output exported to its trading partners. If demand-side limits oblige China to rein in export growth, which seems inevitable, will the domestic market suffice to push the economy ahead without losing momentum?

This chapter cannot encompass the multiple forces that could shape China's GDP growth over the coming two decades. We concentrate on economic factors and make only passing reference to political events that could fundamentally alter the country's growth prospects. Will rising incomes and education lead to pressure for fundamental political change, for example, and might the ensuing political changes result in protracted instability? Will war in the Taiwan Straits upset China's growing economic integration with the rest of the world?

Nor can we explore the implications of the GDP growth rates that we project for agriculture and other economic sectors, for China's environment, or for energy demand. Answering those kinds of questions is a very different kind of exercise involving other kinds of models and analysis.

MEASURING SUPPLY SIDE SOURCES OF GROWTH

To measure the sources of growth from the supply side during 1952–2005, we begin with a conventional production function,

$$Y = f(K, H, t), \tag{20.1}$$

where "Y" is GDP, "K" is the stock of fixed capital, "H" is the education-enhanced labor force, which is measured in a way that includes the increase in quality of labor due to the rise in human capital, and "t" represents shifts over time in the production function or changes in the productivity of the factor inputs. To get this equation into a measurable form, we differentiate with respect to t and rearrange terms to arrive at the following standard growth accounting equation,

$$g_y = s_k^* g_k + s_l^* g_h + a, \tag{20.2}$$

where "g_y" is the growth rate of GDP, "g_k" is the growth rate of the capital stock, "g_h" is the growth rate of the education-enhanced labor force, and "a" is the increase in TFP. The parameters "s_k" and "s_l" are, in the calculation we shall make, the shares of capital and labor in total national income. To construct the equation in this way, one must assume constant returns to scale. We could avoid this assumption by estimating "s_k" and "s_l" directly, but we do not believe that currently available Chinese aggregate data can support reliable econometric estimates of these parameters.[3]

The main challenge in estimating the sources of growth for China during 1952–2005 is to obtain reliable time series for the key variables. Any large, low-income nation faces unavoidable obstacles to the accumulation of comprehensive and accurate statistical information. In China, the use of Soviet-inspired accounting methods, the subsequent shift to conventional national accounts, and episodes of widespread data manipulation add to the difficulties surrounding national economic statistics. As a result, the data that we use to measure output, capital, labor, and schooling are beset by issues of reliability as well as a variety of conceptual or theoretical problems. We defer detailed discussion of these issues to an appendix.[4] Here, we summarize the choices we have made in assembling key statistics and

[3] We ignore the numerous controversies surrounding this widely utilized method of analysis. Our calculations follow Robert Solow's (1957) original exposition of this approach to measuring the sources of growth.

[4] The appendix, which describes the sources and methods used to obtain data for our calculations and analysis, is posted at http://post.economics.harvard.edu/faculty/perkins/papers.html.

briefly explain how our data series differ from standard official statistics and from estimates by other researchers.

Official measurements of the level and growth of China's total output have attracted a steady stream of criticism from Chinese and international analysts who argue that distortions inherent in the methods of compiling official data may lead to an overstatement of output growth.[5] There is evidence, for example, that output data for township and village enterprises may mix current and constant prices, imparting an upward bias to growth measures for inflationary years during the early and mid-1990s.

The disruption of regular economic reporting during the Great Leap Forward (1958–1960) and the early years of the Cultural Revolution calls for the application of large error margins for data in those years. More recently, some analysts have argued that political pressures may have elevated China's official growth rates in the aftermath of the Asian financial crisis of 1997–1998.[6]

Although most studies emphasize possible overstatement of Chinese growth, there is good reason to suspect substantial downward bias in official growth measures. Despite multiple adjustments, the complete elimination of long-standing undermeasurement of China's service sector may require further revision. The coincidence of rapid output growth, rising product quality, and falling prices visible in many manufacturing sectors (e.g., autos, home appliances, and electronics) raises the possibility that quality adjustments could produce sharp increases in measured output growth.[7] Work by Klein and others indicates that international pricing conventions such as those currently used by China underestimate quality improvements and hence overstate price increases used to deflate data in current prices.[8]

Despite these strictures, some of which we regard as well founded, we regard standard official data, including revisions announced by China's National Bureau of Statistics (NBS) during 2005–2006, as the best available benchmark for appraising the long-term evolution of China's economy.[9] We therefore take the most recent

---

[5] Perkins (1980) and Ren (1997, chapter 2) review early controversies. Recent contributions include Maddison (1998), Meng and Wang (2000), Young (2003), and Holz (2003, 2006).

[6] Rawski (2001); Lardy (2002) provides an opposing view.

[7] Following adjustments for quality change to price indexes, "the real growth rates for both semiconductor output and intermediate inputs were revised up substantially" in the United States national accounts (Grimm, 1998).

[8] Lawrence Klein and his coauthors, for example, use a technique developed for a related purpose during the Second World War to show that the official Chinese price indexes tend to overstate the increase in price (Klein, Gao, and Tao, 2005). Reiitsu Kojima (2002) anticipated some of the revisions undertaken by the NBS, with analysis showing that underreporting of the service sector remained even after attempts were made to better account for output in this sector.

[9] As we were preparing this chapter, China's NBS revised its GDP estimates from 2004 back to 1993, mainly by increasing the size and share of the services sector. This service-sector adjustment accounted for 93 percent (or RMB2.1 trillion) of the total upward adjustment in GDP of RMB2.34 trillion in 2004 (Xu, 2005, p. 1). These adjustments respond to

NBS measures of nominal and real output and growth as the starting point for studying the sources of growth in China's economy. We do, however, make one important adjustment to official growth measures in order to remove distortions arising from the peculiar structure of relative prices during China's socialist plan period. Following Soviet example, China's government assigned high values to industrial goods and set low prices for agricultural and resource products soon after the 1949 creation of the People's Republic. This price arrangement generated monopoly profits for industry, which provided the main source of government revenue, typically exceeding 20 percent of GDP.

These arrangements, while intended to create a mechanism for financing government investments under successive five-year plans, had an accidental effect on GDP growth. With industry growing more rapidly than agriculture, the use of official prices that artificially exaggerated the relative price of fast-growing manufactures distorts both the overall growth rate of GDP and the GDP share of investment spending (much of which goes to purchase equipment and other overpriced manufactures).

Meaningful analysis of the sources of growth requires that we remove the effect of these price distortions. As Branstetter and Lardy explain in their contribution to this volume (Chapter 16), the dismantling of trade restrictions during the 1990s initiated a broad convergence of Chinese commodity prices to international norms. This steep reduction in domestic distortions allows us to use prices of the year 2000 to recalculate both the GDP and the capital series.

Recalculating Chinese GDP item by item in 2000 prices is well beyond our capacity and would be a major task even for China's NBS. To obtain a long-term measure of Chinese growth that avoids the biases inherent in domestic prices during the plan era, we combine official time series for real value-added in the primary, secondary, and tertiary sectors with nominal sectoral output for 2000 to form a new series of aggregate output valued in 2000 prices for the entire period 1952–2005.

The resulting GDP series provides the output data used in our decomposition of growth into input and productivity components. This procedure does not eliminate all price distortion in the GDP growth estimates: official regulation, for example, continues to hold domestic energy prices below world market levels. However this revision does eliminate the implausibly high relative prices for manufactures that we see as the most important source of distortion in China's official GDP statistics.

Our approach to the measurement of inputs focuses on the available supply of capital and labor. We seek to measure the stock of fixed assets and the non-student population between the ages of 16 and 65. These input measures make no adjustment for changes in utilization rates, unemployment levels, or the standard retirement age. Our series of annual TFP observations simply record trends in output value per combined unit of capital and labor. The results incorporate

---

well-known gaps in official data (see Keidel, 1992). The revisions considerably alter the share of the various producing sectors in GDP, but do not substantially affect the shares of consumption, investment, and net exports on the expenditure side of China's national accounts.

the combined impact of changes in output per unit of employed resources and variations in the utilization of both capital and labor.

Chinese capital stock data are built up by adding new investment valued at current prices to the undeflated sum of past investments, with or without deductions for depreciation, major repairs, and scrap. The resulting figures combine amounts valued in prices of many years and are therefore unsuitable for productivity analysis. Beginning with Chen et al. (1988), analysts routinely apply the perpetual inventory method to build capital stock estimates from standard data on annual investment outlays.

We adopt the same approach, but apply a new deflator for fixed investment that uses the shares of construction and equipment in investment spending to combine separate indexes of construction costs and equipment prices. The new deflator parallels the NBS index of investment costs for 1992–2005; however, it improves on the crude improvisations that various researchers have used to estimate trends in investment costs prior to 1992.

The perpetual inventory method also requires information about depreciation rates and about the initial stock of fixed assets. Available data indicate that until very recently, depreciation rates used by Chinese accountants reflected the physical rather than the economic service lives of buildings and equipment (Gao, 1985, pp. 70–71; Yearbook, 1994, p. 29). We derive capital stock measures using two depreciation rates: 9.6 percent, a figure derived by Zhang, Wu, and Zhang (2004, p. 39) from an earlier study of service lives and an alternate rate of 7 percent to facilitate sensitivity analysis.

We actually have a figure for the national total of fixed assets in 1952, the initial year of our study. Since this figure is known to be incomplete (Ishikawa, 1965, pp. 109–110), we assume that the initial value of the fixed capital stock in 1952 is either the same as 1952 GDP (a 1:1 capital output ratio) or is double the size of 1952 GDP (a 2:1 capital output ratio). Which initial capital stock assumption is used has little influence on the growth rate of the capital stock in the post-1978 reform period, but a major influence on the capital stock growth rate in the 1950s and, to a lesser degree, the 1960s.

We measure annual labor input as the nonstudent working-age population, meaning persons aged 16–65. We decompose the annual labor totals into five categories based on educational attainment: no diploma (L_1), primary school (L_2), junior high school (*chuzhong* (L_3)), high school (L_4), and college (L_5).[10] Standard Chinese sources provide these data only in connection with the population censuses of 1982, 1990, and 2000. Interpolation between the census results is not feasible because of major inconsistencies in the education component of successive census compilations.

---

[10] We group graduates of specialized (*zhongdeng zhuanye xuexiao*) and vocational (*zhiye zhongxue*) secondary schools together with recipients of regular high school (*gaozhong*) diplomas.

Table 20.1. *Nonstudent working-age population, 1952–2005 headcount, educational attainment, education-enhanced total*

Year	Headcount, L (age 16–65)	Percentage of workers in each education category					Ratio H/L
		No diploma	Primary	Junior high	Senior high	Tertiary	
1952	313,346,294	73.9	19.6	4.8	1.4	0.4	0.90
1965	372,783,230	56.8	30.2	9.2	3.0	0.8	0.98
1978	506,667,822	39.6	33.4	20.6	5.7	0.7	1.07
1990	722,042,872	27.6	33.5	25.8	12.1	1.0	1.18
2000	808,414,668	18.5	34.4	30.6	14.7	1.8	1.26
2005	849,636,604	15.1	32.8	33.6	15.7	2.7	1.31
Mincer weights from 2000 wage data		0.818	1	1.346	2.010	3.277	

Source: Appendix. Working-age population includes ages 16–65.

Results from the 1990 census show substantially higher education levels than what we derive by combining the 1982 census outcome with subsequent graduation figures. The 2000 census also reveals a wider expansion of educational attainment than what is implied by the 1990 census findings and subsequent graduation rates. These inconsistencies arise from two factors: China's expanding array of nontraditional training programs and a thriving trade in forged credentials. In addition, official labor totals appear to incorporate definitional changes that introduce an enormous jump in the employed population between 1989 and 1990.[11]

Faced with these difficulties involving both numbers of workers and the growth of educational attainment, we have chosen to construct new time-series measures of the working-age population and the dispersion of education. We begin with the 1982 census totals and use information on births, age-specific mortality rates and annual numbers of graduates to obtain totals for earlier and subsequent years. The appendix explains the details of this procedure.

In addition to deriving time-series estimates of China's nonstudent working-age population, we use information about education-linked wage differentials in 2000 shown in Table 20.1 to construct a new measure of "education-enhanced" labor. We assume that wage differentials reflect differences in productivity. The analysis of wage data, for example, shows that junior high school graduates earned 34.6 percent more on average than primary graduates with similar demographic characteristics in 2000. We attribute this difference to education-linked productivity variation

[11] The reported level of year-end employment (*congye renyuan*) rises by 54.6 million during 1985–1989 and by 40.38 million during 1990–1995, but jumps by 85.8 million during the single year of 1989–1990 (Labor Yearbook, 2001, p. 9).

and record each junior high graduate as equivalent to 1.346 primary graduates in tabulating the education-enhanced work force H.[12] In formal terms,

$$L = L_1 + L_2 + L_3 + L_4 + L_5 \tag{20.3}$$

$$H = w_1 L_1 + w_2 L_2 + w_3 L_3 + w_4 L_4 + w_5 L_5 \tag{20.4}$$

In equation (20.4), the w coefficients are the "Mincer coefficients" or education-linked wage differentials shown in Table 20.1, with w_2, the coefficient for primary graduates, set equal to unity.

Table 20.1 summarizes the outcome of our labor analysis. Our measure of working-age nonstudents aged 16–65, denoted by L, has grown substantially, but at declining rates. The new labor force series L eliminates the implausible bulge in the official totals for 1989–1990. Our measure of the working-age nonstudent population L grows at an annual rate of 2.52 percent during 1978–1995 and rises by 2.09 percent in 1989–1990 in comparison with officially measured employment, which rises at an average rate of 3.15 percent during 1978–1995 and by an implausible 17.03 percent during 1989–1990.

The ratio H/L measures the average educational attainment of the working-age population included in the headcount total L. The initial 1952 figure of 0.90 indicates that the average educational level of Chinese workers was below the primary school level. The ratio H/L attained a value of close to 1.0 (actually 0.98) in 1965, indicating that the average worker at that time still had only a primary school level of education. By 2005, H/L had increased to 1.31, nearly equivalent to the junior high school level (for which the same ratio would equal 1.346). By recognizing only the diplomas issued by traditional educational institutions, our calculation understates the growth of human capital since the reform period began because we ignore the impact of nontraditional training programs, some of which no doubt increased the subsequent productivity of the trainees.[13]

Although we expect that education is negatively related to mortality, our calculations apply age-specific mortality rates without regard to educational attainment level, adding a further downward bias to our estimates of human capital growth. We conclude that our estimates understate the growth of human capital. We believe that the extent of this bias remains modest.[14]

---

[12] The wage differentials in Table 20.1 are based on analysis of rural wages by deBrauw and Rozelle (2004) and of urban wages by Junsen Zhang et al. (2005). Alan deBrauw, Xiaoqing Song, and Yaohui Zhao generously provided unpublished data and answers to many questions.

[13] Many did not increase trainee productivity. Hsi-sheng Ch'i, for example, finds that efforts to expand training programs outside the regular school system "greatly increased the number of cadres with impressive academic degrees or certificates without meaningful improvement of their educational levels" (1991, p. 107).

[14] An alternate measure of education-enhanced human capital incorporating the education stock reported in the 1990 and 2000 population censuses exceeds the measure shown in Table 20.1 by 4.7 percent in 1990, 11.1 percent in 2001, and 7.4 percent in 2005. Insertion of the new index in our TFP calculations reduces the estimated rate of annual TFP growth during 1982–2005 by 0.1–0.2 percentage points, raises the share of GDP growth attributable to labor and human

Table 20.2. *Average annual growth of GDP, fixed capital, labor, and TFP, with contributions to TFP growth, 1952–2005*

| | | Average growth of inputs | | | | Percentage shares of GDP growth attributable to | | |
| | | | Labor input | | | | Education-enhanced labor | |
Period	GDP	Fixed capital K	Raw labor L	Education enhanced H	Average TFP growth	K	H	TFP
1952–2005	7.0	7.7	1.9	2.6	2.1	47.7	21.4	30.9
1952–1978	4.4	5.8	1.9	2.5	0.5	56.3	32.7	11.0
1952–1957	6.5	1.9	1.2	1.7	4.7	12.7	14.9	72.4
1957–1978	3.9	6.7	2.0	2.7	−0.5	73.7	39.7	−13.4
1957–1965	2.4	5.2	1.5	2.1	−1.0	93.1	49.5	−42.6
1965–1978	4.9	7.7	2.4	3.1	−0.2	67.7	36.7	−4.4
1978–2005	9.5	9.6	1.9	2.7	3.8	43.7	16.2	40.1
1978–1985	9.7	9.2	3.4	4.5	3.2	40.6	26.6	32.8
1985–1990	7.7	6.9	2.5	2.9	3.1	38.8	21.5	39.7
1990–1995	11.7	9.1	1.4	1.9	6.7	33.3	9.5	57.3
1995–2000	8.6	10.5	0.9	1.6	3.2	52.7	10.5	36.8
2000–2005	9.5	12.6	1.0	1.8	3.1	57.1	10.6	32.3

Notes: Values are in percent; calculations assume that 1952 capital stock is two times that year's GDP; assumed depreciation rate is 9.6 percent.
Source: Appendix.

THE HISTORICAL GROWTH ACCOUNTING RESULTS

The results of our efforts to estimate the sources of Chinese GDP growth during 1952–2005 appear in Table 20.2 and Figure 20.1. The results from our reconstructed input and output series broadly resemble the findings of previous studies built on simpler methods.[15] Careful analysis of the new results, however, clarifies the dynamics of China's post-reform growth spurt.

Beginning with the period that covers the first Chinese five-year plan (1953–1957), GDP grew rapidly, in large part due to an increase in TFP, which accounts for nearly three-quarters of measured GDP growth. Our estimate of GDP growth in this period (6.5 percent) is well below the official Chinese figure (9.2 percent), but close to the T.C. Liu–K.C. Yeh reconstruction of official estimates made years ago, using prices from 1933, when China approximated a fully open market system.[16] This

---

capital from 12.5 to 14.4 percent, and reduces the share attributable to productivity growth from 45–46 percent to 43–44 percent. We are grateful to Albert Park for recommending this sensitivity analysis.

[15] See Kraay (1996) and Wang and Yao (2001), among others.

[16] Liu and Yeh, it should be noted, made estimates of GDP growth for this period, using the underlying official data but adjusting for the distortions in the 1952 prices and that is the figure that we use here. They also had an estimate, and it was the one that they preferred,

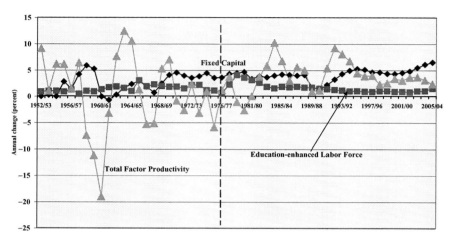

Figure 20.1. Sources of annual GDP growth, 1952–2005: annual change in fixed capital, education-enhanced labor, and TFP

agreement between our estimate of GDP growth and the Liu–Yeh result based on 1933 prices enhances our confidence that the 2000 prices underlying our data more closely approximate the relative scarcities of industrial and agricultural products during the 1950s than do the official prices of the time.

Since the assumption about the initial 1952 level of capital stock heavily influences the capital stock growth rate in this early period, the appendix provides alternative calculations, using different assumptions about the initial capital stock. A high initial capital stock estimate for 1952 lowers the contribution of capital and raises the impact of TFP in accounting for GDP growth, and vice versa. Only a detailed analysis of China's capital stock in the early 1950s, building on the work of Shigeru Ishikawa (1960, 1965), can determine which of these estimates best reflects the reality in China at that time. The calculations presented here report only the results based on assuming that the initial capital stock was twice GDP in 1952, with a depreciation rate of 9.6 percent per year.[17]

---

which made adjustments in the underlying data series that brought down the rate of growth of GDP in the 1953–1957 period in 1933 prices to 4.6 percent. These small differences are now mainly of historical interest, although they led to heated debate at the time. Liu and Yeh (1965, p. 120) and elsewhere. Liu and Yeh do not actually calculate the reconstructed Chinese GDP growth rate in 1933 prices, but a rough estimate can be obtained from the difference between their adjusted estimate and the reconstructed estimate in 1952 prices.

[17] The lower initial capital stock figure (equal to GDP in 1952) produces implausibly low TFP growth in the first five-year plan period when recovery from wartime disruption should have, and in the estimates in the table, did enable substantial improvements in productivity. A lower depreciation rate (we also used 7 percent in our complete calculations in the appendix) has much less influence on the estimates.

China achieved impressive growth of TFP during the first five-year plan period despite undertaking the collectivization of agriculture (1955–1956) and the state takeover of virtually all industry. Offsetting the disruptive impact of these political movements was in part the high rate of capital formation that had risen from very low levels prior to 1949 when total investment probably did little more than cover depreciation if that. Productivity growth mainly reflected continued recovery from the long-term impact of the war with Japan (1937–1945) and the final phase of China's civil war (1945–1949) between the Kuomintang and the victorious Communists.

Recovery from war typically unleashes a quick productivity surge due to the reactivation of capital and labor idled by military strife and the associated chaos. Under these circumstances, simple measures such as restoring electricity and reopening transport routes can deliver major jumps in output. In China, the new government's swift restoration of monetary stability following a decade-long hyperinflation provided a further push toward higher productivity by stimulating the resumption of cultivation and trade in cotton and other commercial farm products (Perkins, 1966).

From 1958 to the eve of the reform period that officially began in December 1978, China's growth slowed markedly. The average GDP growth rate in year 2000 prices fell to 2.41 percent from 1957 through 1965 and then rose to 4.87 percent from 1965 through 1978, producing an average growth rate over the entire period of 3.92 percent (as contrasted to an official growth rate mainly in 1957 prices of 5.4 percent for the whole period[18]).

It would have been remarkable if China had actually maintained a growth rate of over 5 percent a year between 1957 and 1978. This period began with the Great Leap Forward (1958–1960) that left much of industry in shambles and caused a steep decline in agricultural output that led directly or indirectly to excess deaths amounting to tens of millions in the resulting famine of 1959–1961. Compounding these punishing reversals, the Soviet Union withdrew its technical assistance in 1960. Together with China's prohibition of foreign direct investment, political hostility from the far left toward foreign technology in general, and the U.S.-led trade embargo, China effectively was left on its own with only the most limited access to far superior technologies available in the outside world. Despite some modifications in the early 1970s, China's costly economic isolation hardly changed until after the death of Mao Zedong in 1976.

Finally, there was the Great Proletarian Cultural Revolution that reached a peak of disruption in 1967–1968, but which continued to paralyze economic decision making throughout its formal existence from 1966 to 1976. As the data in Table 20.2 indicate, the disruption to the economy caused by the Cultural Revolution, while considerable, was substantially less than what occurred during the Great Leap Forward.

[18]   National Bureau of Statistics (1999, p. 4).

Given this long and formidable list of setbacks, the real question about the 1958–1978 period is how GDP grew at all. The answer is that the growth was primarily made possible by high and rising rates of capital accumulation, which replaced productivity enhancement as the dominant contributor to GDP growth (see Table 20.2 and Figure 20.1). The share of gross investment in GDP (measured in current prices) rose from 17.5 percent in 1957 to 29.5 percent in 1978. Data in Table 20.2 show that capital formation dominated the growth picture during the two decades following 1957, accounting for 93 percent of GDP growth during 1957–1965 and 68 percent of GDP expansion during 1965–1978. TFP, not surprisingly, declined, making a sharply negative contribution to overall growth during the years that encompassed the Great Leap Forward.

The growth that did occur in this period did not provide much help to China's population, which grew at an annual rate of 1.9 percent during 1957–1978 in spite of the famine in 1959–1961. If we subtract capital formation from output growth, we find that real per capita consumption during 1957–1978 rose slightly more than 2 percent per year in 2000 prices.[19] Most of that increase occurred in the urban areas or was eaten up by government consumption. As a result, our calculations confirm work by Lardy (1984), Bramall (1989), and others indicating that China's rural majority experienced little or no improvement in living standards during the two decades prior to the start of economic reforms.

The dramatic change after 1978 is the story that is most relevant to our interest in the future performance of China's economy. Instead of the trendless swings in annual TFP changes typical of 1952–1978, the data underlying Figure 20.1 show annual TFP turning upward in 1976–1978, dipping briefly in 1978/1980, and then rising in each year beginning with 1981/1982. Following negligible growth averaging 0.5 per year during the 1952–1978 plan era, including an actual decline during 1957–1978 (Table 20.2), TFP grows at an annual rate of 3.8 percent during 1978–2005 and accounts for 40 percent of overall growth during this interval of nearly three decades. The size and persistence of this productivity surge is unprecedented in Chinese history. Although TFP growth did average 4.7 percent during 1952–1957, this spurt covered only five years and, as noted earlier, is partly attributable to recovery from the ravages of war and hyperinflation.

The rise in the contribution of capital did not occur independently of the rise in productivity. The rate of capital accumulation in China did not rise after 1978 as a result of efforts by government and the private sector to shift a higher share of resources away from consumption and toward investment. The rate of capital accumulation in current prices as a share of GDP actually declined slightly in the early 1980s and again in the late 1980s before rising again later on (Figure 20.2).

---

[19] This is a rough estimate obtained by subtracting gross fixed capital formation in 2000 prices in 1957 and 1978 from GDP in 2000 prices for those same years. The resulting figure for "consumption" thus includes government consumption and changes in net exports as well as household consumption.

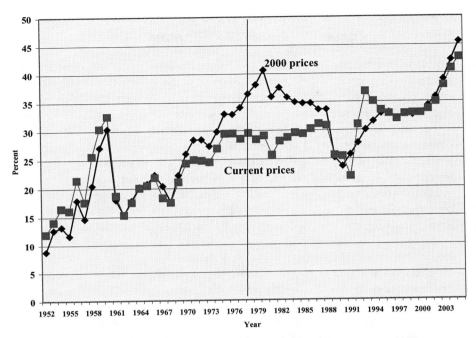

Figure 20.2. China: fixed capital formation proportions, 1952–2005

The higher growth rate of the capital stock (and hence of the contribution of capital to growth) resulted from the same savings and investment effort being applied to a higher growth rate of GDP. Thus, it was the jump in productivity growth leading to a higher GDP growth rate that made possible the greater contribution of capital. Put differently, the story of the 1979–2005 period in China is a story of reforms generating high TFP growth that in turn led to a higher level of capital formation growth than would otherwise have been the case.

This pattern recalls the experience of Japan during its twenty-year growth spurt from the early 1950s. Calculations by Denison and Chung (covering 1953–1971) and by Shinohara (covering 1960–1970), for example, show that TFP accounted for just over half of Japan's 9 plus percent rate of GDP growth in this period.[20] The GDP share of gross fixed capital formation averaged 20.1 percent in the early 1950s, then rose to 24.5 percent in the latter half of the 1950s, and finally to over 30 percent of GDP during the 1960s,[21] where it remained throughout the 1970s even though the Japanese GDP growth rate slowed markedly. Thus in Japan, as in China, it was TFP growth that drove accelerated growth of GDP, leading to a rise in the rate of capital formation. In Japan in the 1970s and into the 1980s, it was a

---

[20] Both results reproduced in Ito (1992, pp. 48–49).
[21] These figures are from Ohkawa and Rosovsky (1973), but Ito (1992) shows an even more dramatic rise in the capital formation rate.

· deceleration in TFP, not a decline in the rate of gross fixed capital formation that accounted for most of the initial slowdown in growth in that period.

The Chinese and Japanese data on the contribution of TFP to GDP growth are similar to the data for South Korea and Taiwan. Reform in all four cases led to a jump in productivity that in turn led to a rise in the growth rate of the capital stock. This close connection between reforms that led to high TFP followed by high growth and hence higher rates of growth of capital has been missed in some earlier studies because of the way the data were presented. There were two major economic reform periods in both South Korea and Taiwan, the turn outward to promote manufactured exports in the early 1960s and the major effort at economic liberalization (reduction in the role of government in limitations on imports and much else) beginning in the mid- to late 1980s. In both reform periods in both countries, the growth accounting data indicate that there was a burst in TFP followed by a rising rate of growth of the capital stock (Perkins and Sabin, 2001).

The picture for China as shown in the yearly growth accounting data in Figure 20.1 is most like the story for South Korea and Taiwan. The pace of institutional reform in China in qualitative terms breaks down into four major periods. The first period, 1979–1984, was the period of the opening up of foreign trade, the return to household agriculture, and the freeing up of rural and many consumer markets. The second period of reform followed closely on the first in 1985 through 1988 and involved the freeing up of industrial inputs for sale on the open market that led in turn to the boom in township and village enterprises that sustained high growth until the hiatus in June 1989 and conservative backlash to reform in the latter part of that year and in 1990. The third phase of reform came after Deng Xiaoping's trip to China's south in 1992 and his call for more not less reform. The fourth phase of fundamental institutional and policy changes came in the mid- to late 1990s with the rapid rise in foreign direct investment, China's decision to do whatever was necessary to join the World Trade Organization (WTO), and the government's disguised but clear decision to reduce sharply its role in the ownership and control of the industrial sector.

The primary question addressed in this essay, however, is not about the past, but about whether China's high growth will continue into the future. Will China continue to enjoy major spurts in TFP followed by accelerated growth in the capital stock or will a new pattern of capital and TFP growth emerge, perhaps one that is still robust but perhaps less volatile than in the past? Previous interludes of reform and accelerated TFP growth were a product of the return of household farming, the shift from plan to market, the removal of most restrictions on domestic and international trade, and other fundamental changes that accompany the transition from a central planning to a market economy. That transition, while not complete, has moved China far toward the market economy end of the economic systems spectrum. Future reforms of this sort will not have the same impact as the freeing up of industrial inputs for sale on the market or the large increase in foreign direct investment. Future agricultural reforms in particular are not likely to have much of an impact on GDP growth, because that sector now accounts for less than

15 percent of GDP. The shift of labor out of agriculture and into industry and services will continue to be important, but only so long as the secondary and tertiary sectors create new jobs.

Thus, future productivity and GDP growth in China over the coming two decades depends primarily on what happens to growth in output and productivity in industry and services. One suspects that these new sources of reform and productivity growth in industry and services are likely to come in a continuing stream of important but smaller and less volatile steps that raise efficiency and upgrade technology year after year. What some of those changes might be is the subject of the discussion that follows. We begin, however, with a discussion of some of the future sources of growth that are a bit easier to predict than the pace of innovation and productivity growth.

CHINA'S GROWTH PROSPECTS

Will the Savings and Investment Rate Remain High?

Even if productivity is the main driving force behind high GDP growth, sustained growth at the levels attained during the past quarter century will require the continued expansion of China's stock of fixed capital at something approximating the 9 percent annual growth that has prevailed since the reform period began. This is because it is difficult to conceive of sustained productivity growth in the absence of the large investments needed to introduce new technologies. In a market system, it is equally improbable to expect investment to remain at high levels if productivity is not growing rapidly. Productivity growth is a central component in the large number of profitable investment opportunities needed to keep investors willing to invest.

In China, the continuing role of official actors in investment choice complicates the relation between growth of investment and productivity. Because of China's consistent record of poor investment decisions, a subject to which we shall return, a decline in the expenditure share devoted to fixed investment could improve the quality of project selection and execution and contribute to a higher rate of TFP growth.

Even though China has become a magnet for overseas investment, annual increments to the capital stock come mostly from domestic sources of investment, which in turn are largely financed by domestic savings.[22] Assuming robust investment opportunities, it is therefore the level of domestic savings over the coming two decades that will largely determine the pace of investment in China and the growth rate of the capital stock.

---

[22] Working with data from a cross section of nations, Feldstein (1983) observed a strong correlation between domestic saving and domestic investment. Jiang (2006) finds that foreign direct investment represents only a small fraction of China's overall capital formation, demonstrating that recent Chinese experience conforms to the same pattern.

Savings in China come from three sources: household saving that accounts for a little over half of total savings, enterprise saving that accounts for roughly one-third of the total, and government saving that has averaged around 15 percent of the total since the 1990s (Yu, 2005). Among these three components, only the household segment is amenable to systematic analysis and forecasting.

Chinese households have recorded high savings levels throughout the reform era. In recent years, both rural and urban households save roughly one-quarter of disposable income, with household savings amounting to about one-sixth of GDP (Kuijs, 2006). There are several reasons for high household savings during the past two decades, not all of which will continue with the same force into the future. One current motivation is to accumulate funds that can be used to purchase expensive durable goods including, for a small but growing part of the population, automobiles. The recent privatization of urban housing has provided an even greater reason for urban households to save. These motivations for saving will continue, but their impact could decline over the coming decades if financial institutions continue to expand the availability of home mortgages, auto loans, and other forms of consumer credit. Since slow growth of aggregate demand has prompted Beijing to strenuous efforts to raise consumer spending during the past decade, policy restrictions are unlikely to slow the expansion of consumer loans and mortgages.

The main motivation for high household savings in China, however, is to save for retirement and to meet the rapidly rising costs of health care and education. None of these factors acted as important determinants of household saving during the plan era. Urban workers expected to receive generous pensions provided by their work units. Rural households were unable to accumulate substantial savings; their retirement incomes depended on whatever reserves their collective farms could accumulate and whatever income their children could share with them. Access to education and medical care was largely determined by nonmonetary considerations.

China's reforms changed all this. Mass layoffs and privatization introduced new uncertainty into urban pension arrangements, while the demise of collectives eliminated the collective reserves on which elderly villagers had depended. Ability to pay became increasingly prominent in the allocation of education and especially health care. Following these changes, multiple studies have shown that Chinese household behavior now fits the life cycle model of savings behavior that economists routinely apply to market economies.[23] This approach postulates an inverse relationship between dependency and savings: children and retirees consume more than they earn, while adults in the prime working ages accumulate savings to benefit their children and finance their own retirement.

China's government lacks the financial resources to establish a public retirement or social security system that will provide ample pension income to more than a

---

[23] Kraay (2000), Modigliani and Cao (2004), and Yu (2005).

Table 20.3. *Population and dependency ratio, 1990–2045*

Year	Population (millions)	Percentage share			
		Working age 16–65		Dependents	
		Work force includes working-age students?			
		Yes	No	Yes	No
1990	1,130	65.4	64.1	34.6	35.9
2000	1,263	66.7	64.5	33.3	35.5
2005	1,308	68.8	65.3	31.2	34.7
2015	1,390	70.6	66.4	29.4	33.6
2025	1,457	67.9	63.4	32.1	36.6
2035	1,489	64.1		35.9	
2045	1,497	61.4		38.6	

Notes: Dependents are defined as persons aged under 16 and over 65. We assume that high school and college students are of working age.

Source: Data for 1990 from official census results for that year. Numbers of high school and college students are from Appendix. Other data are from China population projections posted at http://genderstats.worldbank.org/hnpstats/dp.asp, accessed November 12, 2006.

small segment of the population.[24] This circumstance is unlikely to change dramatically during the next two decades. This means that most households must depend primarily on their own resources for retirement income. The same story applies to health care: most Chinese must expect to pay the bulk of their medical expenses. Given these realities, what then does the life cycle savings model tell us about the likely level of household savings over the next decade or two?

Table 20.3 provides data and projections for China's population and divides the demographic total into two categories: working-age persons (between 16 and 65 years of age) and dependents. One immediate observation from these data is that the dependency ratio, meaning the share of persons above or below working age, is very low.

China's low dependency ratio follows from recent demographic history. The one-child-family policy instituted in the early 1970s led to a marked decline in the number and proportion of young people, and the earlier baby boom that began in the 1950s is only now beginning to approach retirement age (see Chapter 5).

---

[24] The Chinese government is actively discussing and experimenting with a national pension system, and one will no doubt be in place sometime in the next decade or two, the time frame with which we are concerned. That said, however, the resources needed to finance this system will remain meager over this period and pensions, other than for a relatively narrow elite, are likely to remain a small part of what most families will depend on in their retirement years.

Although the age structure of China's population ensures rapid future increases in the proportion of retirees (Howe and Jackson, 2004), the projections in Table 20.3 show the dependency ratio declining to 2015, whether or not working-age high school and college students are counted as dependents. Although the dependency ratio begins a steep ascent of about 3 percentage points per decade from 2015, it is only after 2025 that this ratio climbs above the low figures observed during 1990– 2005. The predictions of the life cycle model, which associates low dependency with robust household savings, therefore indicate that household saving in China is likely to remain high throughout the two decades to 2025.

It is difficult to say much about the future savings of business and government, the other major sources of domestic saving in China. Prior to the reform period, the primary source of saving was enterprise profit that was generated by monopoly pricing of consumer manufactures. The state collected these profits in the form of turnover and profit taxes and used the revenues to fund virtually all investment other than that done by the rural communes. Under the reform, the expansion of entry and price flexibility eliminated this system. Enterprise profits fell sharply (see Figure 4.1) and then recovered to some extent. Industrial profits remain highly concentrated. In 2003 just five sectors (out of a total of 39) accounted for half of all industrial profits; in 2005, the same five sectors – oil and gas, ferrous metallurgy, electric power, electronics, and transport equipment, earned 42 percent of total industrial profits.[25] Although we may speculate that concentration of profits is conducive to high savings, any detailed forecast of business savings requires predictions about profit trends in these and the other thirty-four industrial sectors, as well as commerce, finance, construction, transport, communications, and other branches of economic activity, a task far beyond our competence. In thinking about the future, all we can say is that we see no reason to expect enterprise profits and savings to fall substantially as a share of GDP. If investment opportunities remain robust, enterprises will make substantial profits and will plow a large portion of those profits back into investment.

Forecasting the level of government savings mainly involves reaching a judgment about the likely path of government revenue and, more importantly, how that revenue will be used. The recent shift in government policy toward greater efforts to ameliorate the distributional consequences of rapid growth could boost subsidies for the poor and other welfare expenditures at the expense of government savings. We think it more likely that increased effort to reduce poverty is likely to concentrate on raising investment in education and rural infrastructure rather than subsidizing consumption. Our best guess is that government will continue as a substantial contributor to domestic saving.

In summary, therefore, there is every reason to believe that China's rate of saving and investment will remain high for the next two decades. Inadequate saving is unlikely to constrain China's economic growth between now and 2025.

---

[25] Yearbook (2004, pp. 520–521); Yearbook (2006, pp. 506–507). These data exclude enterprises outside the state sector with annual sales under RMB5 million.

Table 20.4. *Projections of working-age nonstudent population ages 16–65: size and composition, 2005–2025*

Year	Labor force and graduates (millions)			Educational composition of nonstudent workforce (percent)					Ratio H/L
	Working-age nonstudents, L	Annual graduates		No diploma	Primary	Junior high	Senior high	Tertiary	
		Senior high	Tertiary						
2005	849.6	8.3	3.1	15.1	32.8	33.6	15.7	2.7	1.31
2010	885.3	9.9	5.0	11.6	29.3	36.6	17.8	4.7	1.39
2015	913.4	12.8	5.0	9.5	25.3	37.8	20.2	7.2	1.48
2020	903.6	11.5	6.9	7.4	21.9	38.2	21.7	10.8	1.58
2025	885.6	12.8	6.6	5.7	19.4	37.0	23.2	14.7	1.69

Notes: H/L is the ratio of education-enhanced workforce (H) to the actual workforce headcount (L). Values of 1 (respectively 1.35, 2.01, and 3.28) indicate that the average worker has earned a diploma at the primary (respectively junior high, senior high, tertiary) level.
Source: Appendix.

Future Growth of the Labor Force and Human Capital

Since infants born in 2005 will enter the work force in 2021, forecasting China's working-age population to 2025 is not difficult. To accomplish this, we assume that the annual number of births remains constant during 2005–2009 and apply age-specific mortality rates for 2005 to the ensuing two decades. Results appear in Table 20.4. They show that China's workforce, which we define to include nonstudents aged 16–65, will continue to grow slowly until about 2015, and then begin to decline, resulting in a terminal 2025 figure that matches the projected total for 2010.

Our focus, however, is not on total numbers, but rather on the portion of the labor force that is employed outside agriculture and particularly on the changing educational attainments of Chinese workers. We consider these issues in turn.

The growth accounting results summarized in Table 20.2 indicate that a rising workforce has contributed 1 percentage point and often more, to overall growth ever since the 1950s. Should we be concerned that the stagnation and, after 2015, decline in numbers might detract from future growth? We think not, and for two reasons.

To begin, China's long history of labor market segmentation, which dates to the 1950s, institutionalized a large productivity gap between urban and rural workers (see Chapters 6, 17, and 19). Survey data for 2000, for example, show that wages of urban primary school graduates were more than double the earnings of rural workers with similar educational qualifications.[26] Assuming that this wage gap

---

[26] Based on urban and rural survey results underlying Zhang et al. (2005) and deBrauw and Rozelle (2004). As explained in the chapter on labor (see Chapter 6), adjusting for differences

reflects differences in the marginal labor productivity of rural and urban workers, we may anticipate that the transfer of workers from rural to urban occupations, which accounted for a substantial share of output growth during 1978–2005 (see Chapter 17), will continue to spur future growth. The presence of urban scale economies (see Table 19.9) means that shifting workers from rural to urban occupations can increase the productivity of existing urban workers as well as that of the migrants themselves.

Economists analyze rural–urban migration from the perspective of the Harris–Todaro model, which assumes that migration is an increasing function of the gap between urban and rural incomes and of the migrants' probability of obtaining urban employment. The migration of villagers to China's cities and towns, which Chinese sources describe as a "tide of workers" (*mingongchao*), is already the largest in human history.

Government initiatives to remove barriers limiting migration – for example, by abolishing the administrative distinction between "urban" and "rural" residents, allowing trade unions to assist migrants' efforts to claim unpaid wages, and providing medical benefits for migrant workers – promise to improve pay and working conditions, which should increase the flow of migrants (Zheng, Wu, and Guo, 2005; Chen, 2006; Zhu, 2006).

China's recent declining rate of job creation obliges us to hesitate before concluding that the continued transfer of large numbers of workers from rural to urban occupations seems likely to offset the drag on the economy arising from the near-term slow labor force growth and eventual decline in the overall labor force. Employment growth in China's secondary and tertiary sectors dropped sharply during the past decade. One study found that annual creation of formal employment during 1995–2004 was no more than half as much as during 1990–1995 (Rawski, 2006a).

Slow employment growth is partly due to restrictions on the inflow of rural migrants, however. The main difficulty is an array of policies, including official support for capital-intensive projects and sectors, low interest rates for favored borrowers, and policy discrimination against private business, which have the effect of tilting investment spending in directions that limit employment growth (Chapter 6, section on "Causes of Unemployment and Slow Job Creation"). These policies, each with its own rationale, are "formulated without consideration of their effects on aggregate employment" (see Chapter 6) and have the unintended consequence of restricting the growth of employment.

Given the importance that China's present administration has placed on efforts to accelerate the growth of employment, we anticipate that, despite the legacy of migration restrictions and of policies and institutional arrangements that constrain job creation, continued migration out of China's countryside will deliver sufficient

---

in urban and rural prices would reduce this wage differential; adjusting for differential nonwage benefits, however, would push in the opposite direction.

productivity increases to offset the negative impact of slow growth and eventual shrinkage of the labor force on overall economic expansion. In terms of our growth accounting equation, this productivity boost shows up in TFP because lack of sufficient data makes it difficult to separate the labor force in our equation into its rural and urban components.

How does the addition of human capital change this picture? Over the next two decades, growing numbers of high school and college graduates will reshape China's labor force. Our projections assume that the expansion of Chinese high school and college enrollments during 2005–2025 will parallel Japanese enrollment patterns during the two decades from 1955, when Japan's share of agriculture in its national labor force approximated China's 2005 share. The details are left to the appendix, but we assume that the proportion of high school (*gaozhong*) graduates among successive cohorts of 18-year-olds will rise from the 2005 figure of 42 percent to 82 percent by 2005 and that the proportion of successive cohorts earning tertiary diplomas will rise from 16.0 to 44.5 percent between 2005 and 2025.

Our labor force projections, summarized in Table 20.4, show that junior high school graduates will continue to constitute the largest segment of Chinese workers, accounting for a steady proportion slightly above one-third of the total. But the distribution of educational attainment among the remainder of the workforce will shift dramatically between 2005 and 2025, with the share of high school and college graduates doubling from 18.4 to 37.9 percent, while the proportion with primary school diplomas or less drops from nearly half to only one-fourth.

As more students earn higher-level diplomas, their subsequent contribution to GDP will rise. Our projections show the annual numbers of high school and university graduates rising from 11.4 million in 2005 to 17.8 million in 2015 and 19.4 million in 2025, with new university graduates exceeding 6 million in both 2020 and 2025 (Table 20.4).

Table 20.5, which summarizes the results of our projections, shows that, under plausible assumptions about demographic and educational change, the education-enhanced workforce will continue to contribute positively to overall growth between 2005 and 2025 even as the number of workers reaches a peak and begins to decline. This is because the anticipated productivity benefits from the continuing spread of education outweigh the slow growth and subsequent decline in the actual number of working age adults.

Future Growth of Total Factor Productivity

As the earlier discussion indicates, it is possible to base forecasts of trends in factor inputs at least in part on solid information about demographics, school enrollment, savings potential, and investment behavior. No comparably solid foundation exists for estimates of the likely future path of TFP. Since TFP growth accounted for two-fifths of China's overall GDP increase between 1978 and 2005, this poses a major

Table 20.5. *Productivity consequences of input projections and 6 or 9 percent growth, 2005–2025*

| Period | Annual GDP growth (percent) | Average growth of inputs (percent) | | | | Annual growth of GDP (percent) | | | TFP share of GDP growth (percent) |
| | | Fixed capital (K) | Labor input | | Average TFP growth (percent) | Attributable to | | | |
			Raw labor (L)	Education enhanced labor (H)		Fixed capital (K)	Education enhanced labor (H)	TFP growth	
				Version 1					
2005–2015	9.0	9.8	0.7	2.0	3.6	4.2	1.1	3.6	40.4
2015–2025	9.0	8.2	-0.3	1.0	4.9	3.5	0.6	4.9	54.4
2005–2025	9.0	9.0	0.2	1.5	4.3	3.9	0.8	4.3	47.4
1978–2025	9.3	9.4	1.2	2.2	4.0	4.0	1.2	4.0	43.1
1952–2025	7.5	8.1	1.4	2.3	2.7	3.5	1.3	2.7	36.3
				Version 2					
2005–2015	9.0	9.0	0.7	2.0	4.0	3.9	1.1	4.0	44.5
2015–2025	9.0	6.6	-0.3	1.0	5.6	2.8	0.6	5.6	62.4
2005–2025	9.0	7.8	0.2	1.5	4.8	3.3	0.8	4.8	53.4
1978–2025	9.3	8.8	1.2	2.2	4.2	3.8	1.2	4.2	45.6
1952–2025	7.5	7.7	1.4	2.3	2.9	3.3	1.3	2.9	38.3

	Version 3								
2005–2015	6.0	8.1	0.7	2.0	1.4	3.5	1.1	1.4	23.1
2015–2025	6.0	5.6	-0.3	1.0	3.0	2.4	0.6	3.0	50.7
2015–2025	6.0	6.8	0.2	1.5	2.2	2.9	0.8	2.2	37.0
1978–2025	8.0	8.4	1.2	2.2	3.1	3.6	1.2	3.1	39.1
1952–2025	6.7	7.5	1.4	2.3	2.2	3.2	1.3	2.2	32.4
	Version 4								
2005–2015	6.0	7.3	0.7	2.0	1.7	3.1	1.1	1.7	28.7
2015–2025	6.0	4.0	-0.3	1.0	3.7	1.7	0.6	3.7	61.7
2005–2025	6.0	5.7	0.2	1.5	2.7	2.4	0.8	2.7	45.4
1978–2025	8.0	7.9	1.2	2.2	3.3	3.4	1.2	3.3	41.8
1952–2025	6.7	7.1	1.4	2.3	2.3	3.1	1.3	2.3	34.5

Memo item: average TFP growth 1978–2005: 3.8 percent (Table 20.2).

Notes: Versions 1 and 2 assume 9 percent GDP growth; versions 3 and 4 assume 6 percent growth. The ratio of fixed capital formation to GDP declines linearly from the 2005 figure of 42.3 percent to a terminal 2005 level of 35 percent (versions 1 and 3) or 25 percent (versions 2 and 4).

Source: Appendix.

difficulty for our effort to derive a reasonable forecast for economic performance over the coming decades. In order to create the firmest possible foundation for our predictions, we adopt the following step-by-step approach:

- Use our projections of capital and labor input to examine the productivity implications of assumed 6 and 9 percent annual GDP growth during 2005–2025.
- Review the findings of cross-national studies of economic growth for possible relevance to China's economic future.
- Examine the likely future productivity impact – both positive and negative – of specific dimensions of China's economy: further market-oriented reform, research and development, the financial and legal systems, and health and environmental degradation.
- Supplement our discussion of these supply side issues with a brief excursion into the implications of China's expenditure accounts for future growth prospects.

We then conclude by reviewing China's prospects for sustained productivity growth.

Productivity Implications of Expected Growth of Capital, Labor, and Education

We begin with a series of calculations that investigate the productivity implications of combining specific assumptions about the growth of GDP and fixed capital with the labor force projections summarized in Table 20.4. Table 20.5 presents both assumptions and results.

To make the calculations underlying Table 20.5, we assumed annual GDP growth of 9 percent (versions 1 and 2) or 6 percent (versions 3 and 4) throughout 2005–2025. These are not predictions, but simply the starting point for our analysis. We project fixed capital using the perpetual inventory method with annual depreciation of 9.6 percent. Our capital stock projections assume that the GDP share of fixed investment declines linearly from the 2005 figure of 42.3 percent to a terminal 2025 level of 35 percent (versions 1 and 3) or 25 percent (versions 2 and 4).

Together with our projected labor force outcome (Table 20.4), these assumptions produce four growth scenarios, corresponding to various combinations of assumed growth rates (9 or 6 percent) and capital formation paths (fixed investment shrinking to 35 or 25 percent of GDP).

The first thing to note about these projections is that, despite the anticipated expansion of education, the contribution of labor and human capital to projected growth during 2005–2025 is only 0.8 percent annually, well below the 1.5 percent figure derived for 1978–2005 in Table 20.2. Excluding rural–urban migration that shows up in TFP in our calculations, without the increase in high school and university enrollments, the contribution of labor and human capital growth over the coming two decades would be close to zero.

A second observation is that under widely varying assumptions about the growth of GDP and investment, the average annual contribution of fixed capital to overall GDP growth during 2005–2025 varies only between 2.4 and 3.9 percent. Put differently, if China has to rely entirely on inputs of labor (including education) and fixed capital for growth over the next two decades, the nation's GDP growth rate cannot exceed 4.7 percent per year – a figure that is only half the 9.5 percent rate attained during 1978–2005 (Table 20.2).

The central issue in forecasting China's future rate of growth, therefore, involves projecting the likely rate of growth of TFP. That will be the focus of the discussion that follows. One conclusion emerges from these projections alone. To sustain a growth rate of 9 percent per year for another two decades, China would have to push the annual growth of TFP growth above 4 percent – higher than the 3.8 percent growth attained during 1978–2005 and far above the 3.1–3.2 percent rate recorded during 1995–2005. We think such an increase in TFP growth is unlikely. Nor do we think that China can substitute a rapidly rising (as contrasted to our assumption of a falling) rate of capital formation to fill this gap. Our initial conclusion, therefore, is that China's GDP is not likely to grow by 9 percent a year for the coming two decades. Simply maintaining the TFP growth rates of the recent past will be an enormous challenge, and, as is evident from the four different projections in Table 20.5, those rates will produce a GDP growth rate in the range of 6 to well under 9 percent a year.

When the projections for the two decades (2006–2015 and 2016–2025) are separated out, it is clear that China will have much more difficulty achieving a rate of growth above 6 percent in the second of these two decades. All of these projections, the reader should recall, assume that China's economy enjoys a peaceful environment both externally and internally. Assuming a peaceful environment, our belief is that Chinese GDP will grow at a rate of from 6 to 8 percent per year for the next decade and that sometime in the second decade, the economy will slow to a rate of GDP growth that could be as low as 5 percent or as high as 7 percent per year. In the second decade the rate of growth will depend not only on the level of TFP achieved, but also on the rate of growth in the first decade. A slower rate of growth in the first decade will make possible a somewhat higher growth rate in the second.[27]

Would this level of economic performance for China be unprecedented or is there experience elsewhere that would lend credence to these forecasts? An approach that provides some guidance as to how long China can sustain high growth is one that

---

[27] This statement is based on the view that a slower rate of growth will leave more early stage economic reforms and structural changes for the second decade (slower rural–urban migration in the first decade followed by faster migration than would otherwise be the case in the second decade, for example) hence making possible somewhat faster growth.

Table 20.6. *Increase of per capita GDP before and after growth deceleration in three East Asian economies*

Economy	Per capita GDP			Average annual growth of GDP per capita			
	Slowdown begins	When slowdown begins calculated using		Before slowdown		After slowdown	
		PPP (dollars)	Exchange rate GDP (dollars)	Period	Growth rate	Period	Growth rate
Japan	1971	13,800	16,500	1960–1970	10.5	1971–1979	5.2
Taiwan	1990	13,370	10,880	1980–1989	8.1	1990–1999	6.3
Korea	1992	13,370	8,810	1982–1991	9.1	1992–2005	5.3

Notes: U.S. dollars at 2005 prices and percent per year; PPP per capita GDP figures in current prices were converted to 2005 prices using the GDP deflator for the United States, the main source of international prices used in making the PPP calculations.

Sources: World Bank (1981, p. 137), Heston, Summers, and Aten (1982), Directorate General of Budget, Accounting and Statistics (2005, p. 153), Bank of Korea (2006, pp. 162–163).

looks at other nations with similar economies that earlier experienced a sustained (several decades or more) rate of GDP growth comparable to that achieved by China over the past twenty-seven years. There are many economies that have achieved high growth rates for a decade or less starting at low levels of per capita income and a few that have grown at 7–9 percent per year for longer, but only three can be said to have economies similar to that of China.[28] Those three are Japan, the Republic of Korea, and Taiwan. In all three of the economies, growth proceeded for either two decades (Japan) or three decades (Korea and Taiwan) at rates that averaged more than 8 percent per year. But all three eventually slowed down never to grow at rates that high again. In Japan this accelerated growth began in the 1950s when full recovery from World War II was achieved and continued until 1971 when the growth rate dropped precipitously never to recover to "miracle" levels. In South Korea and Taiwan the slowdown was not quite so sudden or sharp, but was pronounced nonetheless and began in 1990 for Taiwan and 1992 for Korea.

As the data in Table 20.6 indicate, this slowdown came at a similar level of per capita income, remarkably similar when GDP per capita is calculated in purchasing-power parity (PPP) terms and converted into prices of a comparable year (2005 prices in the case of this table). When these three economies' per capita GDP

---

[28] A number of oil-rich countries and even a small country with diamonds (Botswana) have managed to grow rapidly for sustained periods. There are also the city states of Hong Kong and Singapore. But none of these countries is both large in terms of population, possesses at the start a large and poor agricultural sector, and has built its economic growth on manufacturing.

passed U.S.$13,000 in PPP terms, the GDP growth rate in the years that followed dropped and did not recover to the levels of the previous decades for even one year. According to the World Bank (World Bank, 2007, p. 288), Chinese PPP GDP per capita in 2005 was $6,600 and the Penn World Tables figure for 2004 updated to 2005 would be about $6,300. Because China does not participate in the United Nations project that calculates PPP GDP figures, these Chinese estimates are subject to more than the usual margin for error. Nevertheless, given that China's GDP per capita in U.S. dollars using the official exchange rate was U.S.$1,717, given that the Chinese currency is widely accepted to be significantly undervalued, and given that developing countries at this level of income typically have a PPP GDP per capita that is two or three times their per capita GDP calculated using the official exchange rate, these Penn and World Bank estimates are plausible.

If one accepts the Chinese estimates of PPP per capita GDP and our GDP growth rate forecasts of 6–8 percent or something over 5.4–7.4 percent per capita per year,[29] then China would reach the slowdown point within ten years (at 7 percent) or 14 years (at just over 5 percent per year). Thus, these international comparisons reinforce our view that China should be able to achieve 6–8 percent GDP growth for another decade (if reforms proceed at a determined pace) but it will be unprecedented for the growth rate to proceed at that pace for another full decade.

Being unprecedented does not mean it cannot happen, but we have no basis for believing that China will outdo the performance of Japan, South Korea, or Taiwan. This international comparison, therefore, reinforces what we have said based on our growth accounting estimates. Given a continued effort comparable to that achieved by Japan, South Korea, and Taiwan, China's economy has the potential to grow at a high rate, as high as 8 percent, for another decade and perhaps a bit longer. But when China's GDP reaches PPP $13,000 (in 2005 prices) a decade or a bit more from now, it is likely that the GDP growth rate will begin to decline on a sustained basis. Whether it will come down sharply, as in the case of Japan, or more gradually as in the case of South Korea, remains an open question.

None of these projections will be realized, however, unless China is able to maintain a high rate of growth of TFP. What kind of evidence can we bring to bear on the question of whether Chinese TFP over the coming two decades will continue at its recent pace or whether it will begin to slow down or even disappear altogether? Our approach to this question is first to look at what we can learn from the various econometric efforts that use an array of variables to study the determinants of economic growth in large numbers of nations. We will concentrate on those variables that might have something to do with TFP. Second, we will then turn to a brief review of well-known sources of inefficiency in specific Chinese sectors and institutions, inefficiency whose elimination could help sustain TFP growth. Some of these latter issues are also discussed at greater length in other chapters in this volume.

---

[29] These per capita figures assume a population growth rate that continues at the current rate of 0.6 percent per year.

Econometric Estimates of the Sources of Growth

A number of researchers have used data from many economies to conduct statistical studies that attempt to pinpoint factors that can be associated with higher or lower rates of long-term growth. The resulting econometric growth equations are not ideal for our purposes, because they typically relate various explanatory variables to the growth rate of GDP rather than to the growth rate of TFP. Furthermore, these equations do not include a variable for capital formation, because the level of capital formation is endogenous and hence the estimates of its relationship to growth will be biased when estimated econometrically. Thus, the explanatory variables used could work as much through capital as through TFP to raise the growth rate of GDP. Variables such as the working population and the total population, for example, are an indirect way of measuring the dependency ratio and hence the likely level of savings and investment.

Despite these difficulties, econometric studies of growth do provide plausible links to productivity growth. Comparing these links with Chinese circumstances reinforces the perception of China as an economy with strong growth prospects.

Jeffrey Sachs and Andrew Warner find a strong positive association between economic openness and growth (Sachs and Warner, 1995). Openness is clearly tied more closely to productivity than to capital formation. In Chapter 16 on China's international economic relations, Branstetter and Lardy show that the dramatic opening of China's economy predates Beijing's 2001 entry into the WTO. Looking ahead, both domestic policy (e.g., the "Go Global" (*zou chuqu*) program that promotes overseas investments by Chinese firms) and China's WTO obligations, which call for further liberalization of trade in services as well as commodities, point to future increases in China's participation in many forms of cross-national exchange.

China earns high marks for openness in terms of the specific criteria employed by Sachs and Warner. In their analysis, "open" economies have tariff rates below 40 percent (China's weighted average tariff rate was 12 percent in 2001), subject no more than 40 percent of imports to quotas and licensing (China applied such measures to only 21.6 percent of imports in 2001),[30] maintain moderate export taxes (China has few taxes on exports), and keep the black market premium for foreign exchange below 20 percent (with China's *renminbi* widely seen as undervalued, there is no black market premium).

Sachs and Warner also find links between geography and growth. Specifically, their work associates slow growth with states that are landlocked, have short coastlines, and/or are located in the tropics. China avoids each of these potential obstacles. The reasons underlying the superior economic performance of nations located outside the tropics and endowed with long coastlines are not entirely clear. Chinese experience suggests that the negative impact of isolation has more to do with the attitudes of people and their governments than with physical limitations. Many

---

[30] These tariff data are from Bhattasali, Li, and Martin (2005, pp. 214–215).

chapters in this volume, particularly the studies of trade, industry, and science, demonstrate that China's dramatic shift from isolation (imposed by politics rather than geography) to growing openness contributed to the economic boom of the last three decades.

Development economists find a negative association between large resource exports and growth, apparently because of management difficulties associated with dominant natural resource exports whose revenues experience wide price fluctuations. From this perspective, China's growth prospects benefit from its growing dependence on imports rather than exports of crude oil, iron ore, and a variety of other resource products: one study finds that "by 2020, China's domestic resources will fully supply only 9 of 45 mineral varieties" (You and Qi, 2004, p. 13).

Robert Barro finds that high levels of government consumption (as a share of GDP) tend to retard economic growth (Barro, 1997). Collection of taxes to fund public consumption, including excessive levels of subsidies and welfare outlays, could divert funds from investment. As Wong and Bird note in Chapter 12 on the fiscal system, China's formal tax system "remains weak," with budgetary revenue and extrabudgetary funds each amounting to roughly 20 percent of GDP. Despite recent increases in defense budgets, China's public spending avoids excessive consumption outlays, perhaps because, as Wong and Bird emphasize, responsibility for most social expenditures rests with poorly funded local administrations. Data for 2005 show that the combined budgetary expenditures of central and local governments amounted to 18.5 percent of GDP, of which roughly one-third may be classified as investment related.[31]

Most cross-national studies include a variable for education. Because growth promotes school enrollment, so that the causation between education and growth runs in both directions, analysts typically make use of education levels at the start of the period being considered. China's 2000 census found that the average adult had received 8.28 years of education or 2.28 years of secondary schooling (Census Research, 2005, p. 1649). The China Health and Nutrition Survey reports a 75 percent secondary school enrollment rate in 2000 among youths aged 12–18, much higher than the 53 percent sample average among ninety-eight countries in Barro's cross-national study (see Table 7.7; Barro, 1991, p. 438). At the beginning of the twenty-first century, China had a high level of schooling given its per capita income. With educational attainments expected to rise further, these growth equations lead us to anticipate that high and growing levels of educational attainment should add momentum to future Chinese growth.

Alesina and others find that cross-national data reveal a positive link between political stability and economic growth (Alesina and Perotti, 1994; Alesina et al., 1996). Chinese experience confirms this observation. Political turmoil slowed

---

[31] Yearbook (2006, pp. 57, 286). Investment-related spending includes outlays on capital construction, innovation, science and technology promotion, prospecting, and operating funds for education, science, and health.

Table 20.7. *China's prognosis for variables included in cross-national growth studies*

Variable (expected correlation with growth)	Chinese prognosis
Openness to trade (+) and foreign investment (+)	Exceptional
Geography (+)	Favorable – long coastline
Tropical location (−)	Favorable – outside tropics
Rich resource endowment (−)	Good (China lacks resources)
Government consumption as share of GDP (−)	Good (Ratio is moderate)
Education/human capital (+)	Good to excellent
Political stability (+)	Good (late 1970s–present)
Quality of institutions	
Law/property rights (+)	Fair
Corruption (−)	Poor/Fair
Administrative competence (+)	Good, perhaps excellent
Growth-oriented policy environment (+)	Excellent
Democratic institutions (+)	Poor

China's economy at many points during the century prior to the establishment of the People's Republic of China in 1949 and again during the chaos of the Great Leap Forward and the Cultural Revolution (1958–1976).

During the reform era, China's economy has clearly benefited from a combination of relative political stability (notwithstanding the uncertainty surrounding the Tiananmen incident of June 1989) and policy focus on economic growth. While this chapter avoids engaging with political issues, we see the continued presence of a stable, growth-oriented political environment as an essential support for the continuation of sustained productivity growth.

Table 20.7 summarizes our reading of China's current position with respect to variables commonly employed in cross-national regression studies intended to pinpoint the determinants of economic growth. In general, these observations show that China is well situated to continue the strong economic performance of the recent past.

Cross-national growth studies typically also include dummy variables for different regions of the world; the estimated coefficient for East Asia is invariably positive, meaning that, after controlling for the other explanatory variables, East Asian performance turns out to be unexpectedly strong. Exceptional growth in East Asia during the 1960s and 1970s provided important motivation for China's reform effort: "no sooner had the Chinese opened their eyes to the outside world after the Cultural Revolution than they exclaimed how far China had lagged behind" (Hua, Zhang and Luo, 1993, p. 27).[32] Now, such studies identify China itself as exceptional in the same fashion: Bekaert, Harvey, and Lundblad find that "standard growth

---

[32] See also Shirk (1993, p. 35) and Lin, Cai, and Li (2003, p. 140).

regressions substantially under-predict . . . Chinese growth. . . . China is a huge outlier with the bulk of its past growth unaccounted for by the standard variables" (2006, pp. 22, 34).

Table 20.7 points to institutions as the single area in which Chinese circumstances fail to provide the conditions that cross-national studies associate with rapid economic growth. To examine the adequacy of Chinese institutions and policies to support sustained growth of productivity over the coming decades, one must get beyond these econometric estimates and focus on the specific situations facing China along a number of dimensions. To do that, we draw in part on a few general trends in the development of market-related institutions in China and in part on studies by others of such growth-related issues as the cost of dealing with environmental problems.

Can Chinese Institutions Support Continued Rapid Growth?

The Role of the State

Although the experiences of Singapore and a few enterprises in Korea (POSCO), the United States (Tennessee Valley Authority), and elsewhere demonstrate that state ownership and management can coexist with economic success, recent Chinese experience supports the view that a higher degree of state involvement in ownership and direct management of economic activity is likely to reduce the future increase of TFP. Chapter 17 in this volume and many other studies associate state intervention and especially public ownership with low growth of output, employment, and productivity, slow progress toward the transfer of labor out of farming and other aspects of structural change, low investment returns, and large seasonal fluctuations in economic activity.

At the outset of China's reforms in 1978, the state controlled virtually all aspects of the economy. Markets governed only the allocation of a few consumer goods and rural sidelines, and even then, prices were set by the state. Private activity was essentially limited to the household plots of farm families, which occupied about 5 percent of China's cultivated acreage.

Since that time, a long sequence of reforms has pushed market forces to the fore in determining the prices of virtually all goods and most services. Among factors of production, wages and urban land prices have moved into the market orbit, while official preferences still exert strong control over the price of capital and especially the price of foreign exchange (see Chapters 14 and 16 in this volume).

Ownership of resources has experienced substantial, though less dramatic, change. Early reform initiatives included the dismantling of collective farms and the restoration of family farming, which effectively privatized farm equipment and livestock, while ownership of land (including mineral deposits) remained in the hands of the state.

Ownership in the secondary and tertiary sectors is more complex, but the trend toward private control is clear (Garnaut et al., 2005). Virtually all retail commerce and much wholesale commerce are in private hands. Even nominally state-owned

Table 20.8. *Changing ownership structure for Chinese industrial output, 1980–2005*[a]

Year		State ownership[b]	Shareholding and limited liability corporations	Collective	Foreign invested[c]	Domestic private
1980		80.78	n.a.	18.51	0.01	0.00
1985		73.12	n.a.	25.48	0.43	0.01
1990		54.60	n.a.	35.62	1.88	5.39
1995		38.50	4.06	37.10	15.85	3.40
2000		34.92	12.52	17.07	26.07	4.46
2005	Output share	15.06	25.73	4.42	30.20	22.36
	Profit share	5.1	33.4	3.8	29.1	18.5
	ROA	3.3	6.4	6.3	6.4	6.7

n.a., category for which no data is provided; ROA, annual pretax profits as percent of total assets.

Notes: Omission of minor categories causes annual shares to sum to less than 100 percent. 1980 and 1985 data limited to "independent accounting units."

1995 data exclude private, individual, and village-level firms with sales below RMB1 million.

2000 and 2005 data exclude nonstate firms with sales below RMB5 million.

[a] Percentage shares of gross output at current prices.

[b] Data for 2000 and 2005 include corporations with 100 percent state ownership.

[c] Includes firms with partial or full ownership by overseas Chinese and non-Chinese interests.

Sources: For 1980 and 1985, Industrial Census (1985, 3, pp. 88–89); for 1990, Industrial Yearbook (1991, p. 3); for 1995, Industrial Census (1995, General volume, p. 6); for 2000 and 2005, Yearbook (2001, p. 401; 2006, p. 505).

department stores mainly rent space to individual traders. Although the state has maintained its control over the finance and utility sectors, as well as railway, airline, and telecommunications networks, privatization has begun to infiltrate these activities, although its extent remains modest.

Industry provides a well-documented illustration of the shift away from state control. Table 20.8 tracks the output shares of different ownership forms between 1980 and 2005. Despite shifts in category definitions and in the scope of industrial output, the trend toward private ownership is evident. The output share of state-owned enterprises plunges from 81 percent in 1980 to 15 percent in 2005.

Even if we assume effective state control of all corporations, the combined share of state-owned and corporate firms in 2005, at 41 percent, is only half the size of the 1980 starting point. While state influence permeates the operations of many corporations, the assumption of across-the-board state control is excessive: China's 2004 economic census found that the sources of capital for shareholding entities included a state share of 52 percent, but for limited liability corporations, the state's capital share (36.2 percent) was considerably less than the share of private Chinese stakeholders (47.2 percent) (State Council Economic Census Group, 2005, table 8).

Even when state ownership is substantial, industrial companies show a growing tendency to pursue commercial interests, as when petroleum refiners, squeezed between rising costs for imported crude oil and controlled domestic prices of gasoline, reduced their production and domestic sales of gasoline, thus creating regional gasoline shortages in order to draw attention to the negative impact of price controls on their finances.[33]

Equally impressive is the growing scale of privately controlled industrial activity. The 2005 data in Table 20.8 show 52 percent of industrial output coming from domestic private firms and from firms with partial or full foreign (including Overseas Chinese) ownership. With the 2004 Economic Census listing the combined share of private and foreign capital as 97.8 percent for domestic private firms, 85.9 percent for firms with investment from Hong Kong, Macao, or Taiwan, and 88.1 percent for firms with other foreign ownership, these enterprises surely fall into the category of private ownership despite pockets of official influence (State Council Economic Census Group, 2005, table 8).

Recent developments demonstrate a continuing shift away from state ownership. The 2004 Economic Census reported that the number of state enterprises in the entire economy dropped by 177,700, while the number of collectives fell by 402,000 between 2001 and 2004, indicating declines of over 45 percent in each of the two most prominent forms of public ownership. At the same time, the entry of 658,000 private enterprises employing eight or more persons pushed the balance of ownership further away from the public sector (State Council Economic Census Group, 2005).

We anticipate further declines both in the number of state firms, especially at the provincial and local levels, and in the state sector's output share. In addition, the proliferation of public offerings and the conversion of nontradable corporate shares held by state-sector entities into tradable shares will further dilute public ownership of corporate firms.

As the share of public ownership shrinks, the issue of state intervention in the operation of the economy, rather than direct state ownership, comes to the fore. The chapters in this volume identify many areas of China's economy in which official intervention is no more intrusive than in many leading market economies. The planning, financing, and implementation of capital formation, which absorbs over 40 percent of aggregate expenditure, represents the biggest exception to this observation. The institutions surrounding investment behavior pose a considerable threat to China's forward momentum. At the same time, weaknesses in these institutions create opportunities for improvements that can stimulate future productivity growth.

The disproportionate role of the state sector in investment spending is widely understood. Despite their declining output share and consistently low profitability (Table 20.8), state-owned units absorbed one-third of investment funds in 2005 (Yearbook, 2006, p. 187). As Allen, Qian, and Qian point out in Chapter 14, bank

---

[33] "As the pump prices were not rising as fast as global crude markets, so firms responded by cutting down on domestic supplies while boosting exports" (Zhan, 2006b).

Table 20.9. *Completed investment in fixed assets: monthly share of annual total*

	1975	1990	2000	2002	2003	2004	2005
January/February	6.4	3.4	3.9	4.3	4.5	5.6	5.6
March	5.1	4.9	5.3	5.6	6.0	6.4	6.4
April	6.0	5.2	5.7	6.5	6.5	6.8	6.6
May	7.2	6.2	6.7	7.5	7.8	7.5	7.6
June	9.1	8.6	9.5	9.8	10.5	10.9	11.0
July	7.4	7.5	7.6	8.2	8.6	9.0	8.9
August	7.3	7.2	7.5	8.3	8.5	8.6	8.7
September	8.9	8.7	9.4	9.9	9.7	10.0	10.1
October	8.0	8.7	9.1	9.4	9.3	9.4	9.4
November	9.8	9.5	10.3	9.9	9.7	9.8	9.9
December	24.8	30.1	25.0	20.7	18.8	15.9	15.8
Q1&Q2	33.8	28.3	31.1	33.7	35.3	37.3	37.2
Q4	42.6	48.3	44.4	39.9	37.8	35.1	35.1

Note: Values are in percent.

Sources: Fixed Asset Yearbook (1997, p. 77), *China Monthly Economic Indicators* (2001, 1, p. 36; 2003, 2, p. 32; 2003, 12, p. 32; various issues for 2004–2005), *China Monthly Statistics* (various issues, 2005–2006), http://www.stats.gov.cn/was40/detail (accessed March 25, 2004).

loans, share offerings, and bond issues flow mainly to state-controlled entities. The unfortunate consequences of extensive official involvement in investment decisions are well documented. Even after twenty-five years of reform, Table 20.9 shows that investment spending displays Soviet-style seasonality, with low activity during the first quarter, minipeaks in June and September, and a fourth-quarter rush. Chinese sources provide a flood of anecdotes chronicling poor investment decisions. Zhang Hanya, secretary general of the China Investment Association, reports a failure rate of 42 percent for medium- and large-scale projects during the Eighth Five-Year Plan period (1991–1995) (Gao, Shi, and Zhou, 2004). Failed investment efforts often arise because "local governments and officials . . . invest in 'image projects' . . . to enhance their performance record" (GDP, 2004).

Recent studies deploy firm-level industrial data to explore the macroeconomic consequences of China's largely unreformed investment system. Using data from more than 100,000 enterprises, Hsieh and Klenow (2006) find that equalizing the marginal product of labor and capital across enterprises within specific four-digit industries could raise output by approximately 100 percent.

Dollar and Wei (2006) employ a smaller data set, but focus precisely on the link between ownership and returns to capital. Preliminary results show that "the average return to capital is more than 50 percent higher for private firms [and also for foreign-invested enterprises] than for wholly state-owned firms. . . . [These results] suggest that state-ownership is systematically associated with lower returns to capital."

It is evident that reductions in state ownership and official intervention in the economy, particularly in the realm of investment decisions, have the potential to propel substantial productivity gains over the coming decades. The benefits of an improved investment mechanism extend far beyond reducing the number of failed projects and the scale of bad debt. Policies that channel investment funds to state-sector projects and artificially reduce interest rates to improve the profitability of state-sector borrowers are largely responsible for the slow pace of job creation visible since 1995 (Rawski, 2006a).[34]

Despite these difficulties, important steps have moved China's economy toward greater commercialization of investment, by which we mean a structure in which decisions governing investment outlays rest primarily in the hands of decision makers whose choices reflect the costs and likely returns to alternative allocations of funds. Substantial privatization has placed increasing shares of assets and profits under the control of profit-seeking entrepreneurs and managers. Removing restrictions on the sale of formerly nontradable corporate shares, while still incomplete, represents another important advance. Ongoing expansion of the market for corporate ownership rights is also highly significant. Business mergers and acquisitions, which increasingly cut across sector, provincial, and national boundaries, can activate assets formerly trapped in low-yielding circumstances.

The emerging agenda for China's State Asset Supervision and Administration Commission (SASAC), established in 2003, represents another significant development. SASAC's objective is to represent the state's interest as the owner and investor in over 150 centrally controlled state enterprises, including China's large "petroleum, petrochemical, electricity, automobile, and telecom enterprises, as well as those that evolved from the old military industry ministries, Chinese government conglomerates based in Hong Kong, the big state-trading and import-export companies, specialized construction companies and research institutes, and quite a few high-tech enterprises including Great Wall Computer and Alcatel Shanghai Bell" (Naughton, 2003, p. 3). Provincial and local commissions will perform similar functions at lower levels of government. This initiative may eliminate long-standing difficulties arising from the absence of any effective agent to implement ownership of state enterprises by "all the people." SASAC, which "formulates its agenda in terms that a Wall Street investment banker would understand," aspires to collect dividends from profitable state enterprises, channel these funds into a capital management budget, and gradually shift the management of state ownership

---

[34] A government economist finds that, on average, investment outlays per new job amount to RMB220,000 in large enterprises, RMB120,000 in medium-sized firms, but only RMB80,000 at small companies (SMEs), so that "promoting SMEs will be more cost effective in job creation" (Zhao, 2002).

interests into the hands of public companies operated by investment specialists (Naughton, 2005, p. 7; 2006).

Recent initiatives at both the central and local levels illustrate the potential productivity benefits of implementing these ambitious plans. In addition to managing the government's interest in centrally controlled state firms, the national SASAC has systematized procedures for management buyouts at provincial and local state enterprises, enhanced the marketability of shares in state firms, expanded listings of state-controlled enterprises, announced plans to accelerate bankruptcies, and supported M&A activity involving centrally controlled firms in the energy and electronics sectors, among others (Li, 2005; Naughton, 2005, 2006; Wang Ying, 2005,2006a, b). At the local level, Shenyang's municipal SASAC "plans to sell a 49 per cent stake in China's top machine tool manufacturer, Shenyang Machine Tool Group " . . . to diversify the company's ownership and improve its competitiveness" (Wu, 2006).

Reforming the Financial Sector

Along with the actions of SASAC and other official agencies, the progress of reform efforts in China's financial and legal systems is likely to exert a powerful influence on the outcome of efforts to improve the quality of day-to-day economic decision making.

We see three levels at which fundamental change in China's financial sector can improve the prospects for sustained productivity growth: cleaning up bank balance sheets, promoting entry and reform to increase the range and quality of financial services offered to Chinese firms and households, and removing politics from the allocation of financial resources.

Chapter 14 by Allen, Qian, and Qian chronicles the recent decline in the share of nonperforming loans in the banking system. Whatever the exact level of bad loans, preventing the future accumulation of nonperforming debt is a key reform objective. Japan's recent experience illustrates the danger associated with high levels of bad loans. Japan's floundering banks sought to protect their weak balance sheets by propping up heavily indebted clients with additional loans while denying credit to potentially dynamic start-up companies. The result was a decade and a half of near stagnation for Japan's economy. With state firms, including many weaklings, absorbing huge amounts of capital and private companies pushed to the margins of the formal financial system (see Chapter 14 in this volume), China's economy could drift into comparable difficulties. To avoid such dangers, China needs to commercialize its financial markets by dismantling long-standing arrangements that favor state firms with preferential access to bank loans and preferential opportunities to tap domestic and international stock and bond markets. The productivity and employment benefits associated with these reforms (and the cost of inaction) will increase as the economy becomes more complex.

Improving the scope and quality of financial services by expanding entry and upgrading existing institutions can provide important support for raising productivity growth during the coming decades. Two key measures have opened the door to long-term development of China's weak financial sector. China's entry into the WTO included a promise to offer national treatment to foreign banks, investment firms, and insurance companies. China's subsequent decision to sell equity stakes in key financial institutions to international firms ensures the implementation of this promise by installing global leaders of international finance within the core of China's financial sector. By selling equity stakes in China's largest banks and insurance companies, China's leaders have implicitly acknowledged both the central importance of commercializing the financial sector and the inadequacy of their own prior reform efforts.

The injection of global financial heavyweights and offshore reporting requirements into key banks and insurance firms should increase pressures to control the fraud and embezzlement that have plagued China's financial sector. Even more important than curbing criminality is the effort to install business rather than politics as the foundation for allocating funds. This will entail rolling back long-standing arrangements under which offices of the Communist Party selected the officers of financial institutions, government quota systems controlled access to stock market listings, "high-risk financial projects ... ended up getting bank loans, usually under orders from government departments," and local bank offices, "with little choice, frequently ignored routine risk calculations and limits on the size of loans ... at the behest of party and government officials" (Sender, 2004; Gao, 2005).

Past efforts to improve China's financial system "have done enough *not* to slow down the growth of the economy" (see Chapter 14, "Summary and Concluding Remarks"). Looking forward, this minimal standard is unlikely to suffice. China's financial system falls far short of arrangements that can offer positive support to (rather than merely permitting) sustained growth of output and TFP.

Recent changes have pushed China's financial system in the right direction. The weak starting point provides ample opportunities for productivity-enhancing improvements in performance. To underwrite continued growth and productivity increase, China needs to raise its financial sector to the level currently operating in Korea and Taiwan. This is not a high standard. Achievement of this outcome – or better yet, one that matches the considerably more effective financial mechanisms currently operating in Hong Kong and Singapore – depends most of all on China's success in wringing politics out of lending and investment decisions.

Strengthening the Legal System

Chapter 11 on law recounts many flaws in China's legal, judicial, and enforcement regimes. The question of how China's economy developed so fast in the face of these weaknesses remains open. Perhaps economists overstate the importance of having governments enforce property rights and uphold contract provisions. Perhaps flaws in China's legal system are less costly than they appear from outside. Perhaps, as both the law and finance papers suggest, Chinese participants have developed alternative mechanisms that partially replace what theorists regard as essential institutional arrangements. The extensive participation of China-based firms in cross-national networks of manufacturing, finance, research, and design demonstrates that, whatever its shortcomings, China's legal system has not decisively blocked national development to date, nor has it prevented Chinese firms from joining in increasingly complex webs of global transactions. At the same time, we cannot doubt that weaknesses of the legal system, beginning with such elementary matters as employers (including government-run firms) refusing to pay wages or electricity purchase agreements being "scrapped because local governments felt that the original contracts were too expensive," impose very large costs on China's economy (Xie, 2005; Defaulting, 2006).

Two areas, intellectual property rights (IPR) and disposition of business property, stand out as particularly important for China's long-term growth prospects. Although the active involvement of official agencies makes the extent of Chinese technological piracy quite unusual,[35] developing nations, including the United States, have typically ignored IPR enforcement at early stages of their growth. The reason is obvious: for nations with little in the way of intellectual property, the benefits of piracy outweigh the cost to domestic innovators.

The rapid expansion of domestic R&D spending described in Chapter 9 on science and technology, together with China's growing success in attracting R&D operations from foreign companies, means that the value of domestic intellectual property, and therefore the potential cost of weak IPR protection, has entered a steep upward trajectory. As more and more Chinese firms join the "battle against pirates and counterfeiters" and Chinese innovators focus on "strengthening . . . defenses . . . [against] other enterprises . . . copying . . . technology . . . without paying any royalties," the future course of public policy seems clear (Liu Weiling, 2005a,b).

Rapid intensification of official efforts to curb IPR violations appears to have begun. Official regulations have outlawed the installation of pirated software in government offices and, most recently, in newly manufactured computers (Poon, 2006). IPR enforcement is emerging as a new dimension of competition among localities. Beijing's municipal government has ordered enterprises to use authentic computer software and plans to establish a hotline to receive IPR complaints, while Guangdong plans to "redouble efforts to improve the system for technological innovations while improving measures to protect intellectual property rights" (Guan, 2006; Zhan, 2006a). Initial results impress often critical foreign media,

---

[35] During the late 1980s, for example, one of the authors encountered a pirated version of an American company's virus-detection software distributed by China's Ministry of Public Security.

which note that "China Moves From Piracy to Patents" and that "China Makes Genuine Progress Against Sellers of Fakes" (Ortolani, 2005; Dickie and Minder, 2006).

The disposition of assets for firms undergoing bankruptcy or restructuring is equally important, especially because these categories encompass large numbers of firms and large amounts of assets. The emergence of national and regional SASAC agendas for the management of state-owned assets represents an important advance, as does the expansion of mergers and acquisitions based on commercial criteria rather than official decisions. Despite these gains, the commercialization of firms now trapped in bureaucratically controlled enterprise groups (*jituan*) holds the prospect of considerable gains in productivity.[36]

It is too early to tell whether China's new bankruptcy law, which took effect in June 2007, will establish a system in which legal precepts rather than official preferences govern the timing of bankruptcy declarations and the disposition of assets held by bankrupt firms. In North America and the European Union, these decisions are made by the firms involved subject to rules set down by the legislature and enforced by an independent and competent judicial system or by independent regulatory bodies. In China, as in much of East and Southeast Asia, these decisions are often made by the executive branch of the government. The courts lack the independence, competence, and authority to determine and enforce the resolution of issues surrounding bankruptcies, mergers, or acquisitions.

The central point here is that the absence of competent and effective judicial or regulatory processes pushes such decisions into the hands of government or party administrators in spite of the high costs associated with official intervention in business decisions. As Perkins (2004) argues, efforts to establish an independent judiciary as the chief arbiter of issues surrounding the disposition of business property will hasten the improvement of corporate governance and the protection of minority shareholder interests, both of which can contribute to future productivity growth.

DO SOCIAL ISSUES POSE MAJOR OBSTACLES TO CHINA'S DEVELOPMENT?

In addition to possible political instability, numerous observers suggest that social issues could pose major obstructions to China's future growth (e.g., Wolf et al., 2003; Pei, 2006). We focus successively on public health and environment.

---

[36] A 2005 visit to a Chinese firm listed on the Hong Kong stock exchange revealed a passive operation completely dependent on instructions from group headquarters. This firm had no discretion over the selection of component suppliers or the disposition of its output. Despite rapidly eroding demand for its main product, the company was not permitted to develop a substitute, because the group headquarters had assigned that task to another enterprise (Interview, July 2005).

Public Health

The SARS scare of 2002–2003 and the longer-term issues surrounding AIDS/HIV have drawn international attention to the limitations of China's public health system. Despite many shortcomings, China's response to both SARS and AIDS/HIV suggests that health authorities have sufficient administrative and financial resources to prevent threats to public health from inflicting severe damage on China's economic prospects.

In the case of SARS, crude but effective official and community action rapidly defused a potentially dangerous situation by curtailing interaction between suspected disease carriers and the general public. Following the collapse of initial efforts to deny the spread of this disease, the official response shifted to "massive, swift, and concentrated action from the center. Strong quarantine measures were introduced, and SARS 'bounties' were paid to help in contact and case finding. The Health Minister was sacked and epidemic monitoring systems tightened up" (Ma et al., 2006, p. 289). Economic damage, though substantial, was confined to the first half of 2003, after which rapid growth resumed (Rawski, 2005).

The official Chinese response to HIV/AIDS followed the same sequence of denial followed by strong action to limit the spread of disease. Recent policy measures include steeply rising appropriations for combating HIV/AIDS; efforts to expand the availability and reduce the cost of medications; investigation and regulation of blood collection networks; imposition of compulsory premarital health checks in Yunnan, the province most seriously affected; and limited offers of free testing and treatment (Ma, 2005; Wu and Sullivan, 2005; Ma et al., 2006; Yunnan, 2006; Zhang, 2006).

Specialists agree that this disease could spread to as many as "10 million infected over the next decade *in the absence of effective measures*" (Ma et al., 2006, p. 289; italics in original). They also report that in 2002 "the Chinese government succeeded in reducing the cost of annual antiretroviral treatment . . . to US$4000–5000 . . . with significant price reductions . . . since 2003" (Ma et al., 2006, p. 293).

We can crudely reckon the direct cost of treating HIV/AIDS under worst-case assumptions: 10 million HIV/AIDS victims with the government bearing the full annual treatment costs of U.S.$5,000 per person. At RMB7.5 per dollar, the annual cost becomes RMB375 billion. Although spending of this magnitude would impose substantial pressure on official budgets, China's government, which increased its revenues by RMB525 billion during 2004–2005 alone, is fully capable of mobilizing funds on this scale without major economic disruption.

We conclude that public health issues, barring some worldwide health catastrophe on the model of the 1918 pandemic or worse, are unlikely to impose major obstacles to the growth of China's economy during the coming decades.

Environment

Environmental issues are widely seen as possible barriers to future growth. The questions that matter for our forecast of the future are whether cleaning up the undoubtedly widespread environmental degradation will cost so much that it will cut significantly into investment in new production or whether that degradation will reduce the health of the labor force enough to materially influence the labor force's contribution to growth. We focus on issues surrounding air quality and water supply.

Focusing on urban air quality, Roumasset, Burnett, and Wang find declining levels of particulates and sulfur dioxide and conclude that "the statistical picture of pollution trends contrasts starkly with bleak qualitative reports" (see Chapter 8). Rawski and Sheng (2008) provide evidence that concentrations of dust and soot outside major cities reached a peak around 2000 and subsequently began to decline, suggesting a general trend toward improved air quality.

International comparison of trends in urban concentrations of particulates and sulfur dioxide can provide historical perspective on Chinese air quality. Figure 20.3 compares trends in concentrations of sulfur dioxide in major Chinese cities with circumstances in the United States, Japan, and Korea. The average for Chinese major cities consistently falls below the readings for Tokyo in 1968, for Seoul in 1990, and in recent years, for New York in 1972. The Chinese average for 1984 matches the 1984 reading for Pittsburgh, which was named "America's most livable city" in the following year. Even the worst of major Chinese cities now reports lower concentrations of SO_2 than Tokyo in 1965 or Seoul in 1990. These observations demonstrate that air quality in major Chinese cities, although well below current standards in today's rich nations, can hardly pose unprecedented hazards to human health or economic growth.

Cross-national data for total suspended particulates (TSP) reinforce the observation that the magnitude of Chinese urban air pollution is not unusual. Figure 20.4 plots primary-sector labor force shares for China, Japan, and Korea against urban TSP concentration for Tokyo, Kitakyushu, and Seoul and compares these observations with the arithmetic average of readings for approximately thirty major Chinese cities. The share of the primary sector (mainly agriculture) in the national labor force is a standard development indicator that declines with rising levels of per capita income.

Each series shows a declining trend in atmospheric concentration of particulates. In Japan, the decline begins when the primary-sector labor force share stands in the range of 20–30 percent. In Korea, the decline starts with primary labor share in the 25 percent range. In China, by contrast, ambient concentrations of TSP begin their downward march much earlier in the development process, when the share of primary-sector workers in the national labor force is approximately

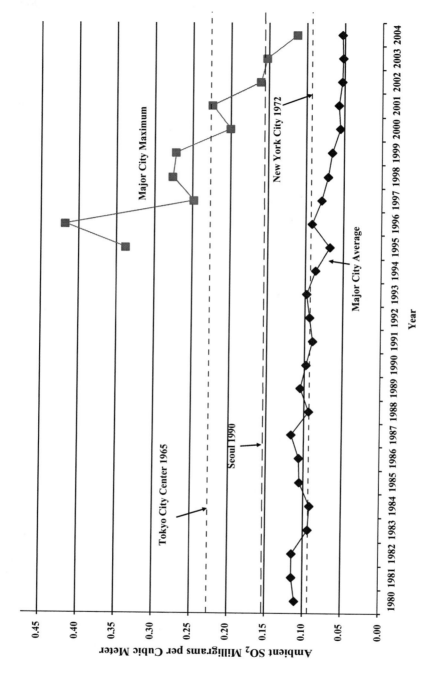

Figure 20.3. China: SO$_2$ levels in major urban areas, 1980–2004, with international comparisons (*Source:* Rawski, 2006b)

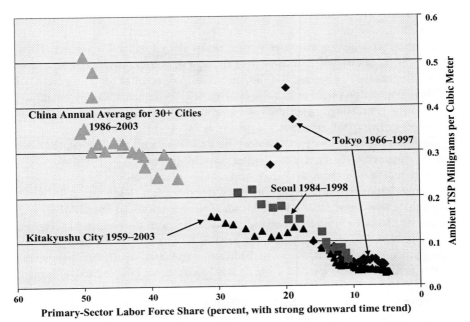

Figure 20.4. Primary labor force share versus urban TSP concentration (*Source:* Rawski, 2006b)

50 percent.[37] These data indicate that the spread of new technologies and especially of awareness about the damaging effects of pollution have prompted China to move toward abatement of urban air pollution at an earlier stage of the development process than occurred in Japan or Korea.

While air quality appears to be improving, China's greatest difficulties with water lie in the future. Elizabeth Economy notes that "[f]or many regions in China, diminishing water supplies pose today's greatest social, economic, and political challenges . . . the Ministry of Water Resources predicts a 'serious water crisis' in 2030, when . . . China's per capita water resources are estimated to decline to the World Bank's scarcity level" of 2,000 cubic meters per capita per year from the 2005 level of roughly 2,150 (Economy, 2004, pp. 67–68; Yearbook, 2006, p. 412). With water tables falling, 400 of 660 cities reporting water shortages, and over 100, including the capital, reporting "very severe" supply problems, it is evident that current arrangements are not sustainable (Water, 2005).

China's water resources are unevenly distributed, with available supplies concentrated in the south, while northern regions cope with extreme supply limitations. One study indicates that 1993 levels of per capita water resources are at 225–356

[37] The Chinese data on primary-sector labor force share in Figure 20.4 come from Chapter 17. Use of official Chinese labor data, which appear to overstate the share of primary sector workers, would accentuate the observations in the text.

cubic meters per person for North China's major river basins (Wolf et al., 2003, p. 78). Although these figures may be too low, data for 2005 show ten province-level units with per capita water resources less than 1,000 cubic meters. These water-short regions, which include the two most populous provinces, Henan and Shandong, as well as Beijing, Tianjin, and Shanghai, account for 34.8 percent of China's population (Yearbook, 2006, pp. 101, 412). With urbanization and industrialization generating higher levels of waterborne effluents, the water-short areas confront growing difficulty with the quality as well as the quantity of water.

Statistics on water usage show a steep tilt toward agriculture. In 2004, the farm sector absorbed 65 percent of total water consumption.[38]

Price increases, structural change, and regulatory controls can help save water. Nationwide data show the average price of water rising from RMB1.63 to RMB3.61 per cubic meter between 1993 and 2001 for agricultural use and from RMB8.2–8.7 to RMB22.8–24 for household and industrial use between 1994 and 2001 (Liu Wei, 2005, p. 217). In Beijing, "the current price is 3.7 yuan . . . more than 30 times the price in 1991" (Xin, 2006). With the Minister of Water Resources insisting that water prices "must be used as a major way" to promote efficient usage, further increases seem inevitable.

Water usage declined from 537 to 465 tons per RMB10,000 of GDP between 2002 and 2003, but these figures are "about four times the global average" (Zhao, 2004; Liang, 2005). This decline may persist as development shifts output and employment toward services and away from farming and water-intensive manufacturing industries. Policymakers have also imposed "Norms of Water Intake" to "mandate rational and efficient use of water" in seven water-intensive industries (Zhao, 2004).

Each of these measures promises important benefits. However, the dominant share of agriculture in water consumption and the difficulty of collecting water fees from farm operators[39] mean that an effective response to growing water shortages will almost certainly include substantial reductions in farmland and agricultural employment, particularly in North China. Compulsory shrinkage of farm activity has also begun: Chicheng county, Hebei, which "provides almost half the water for Miyun Reservoir" in nearby Beijing, shifted cultivated acreage from rice to corn and "dropped sheep grazing . . . to . . . only a quarter" of the 2001 figure "in a bid to provide abundant water resources for Beijing" (Yang, 2006).

In environmental matters, as in the health sector, cost is not a major issue. News that anticipated costs for the initial phase of "China's massive south-north

---

[38] Li (2006). Wolf (2003, p. 78) cites data showing that agriculture absorbed 77–78 percent of overall water consumption in 1993.

[39] Liu Wei cites a 2002 report from the Ministry of Water Resources, noting that "in the past three years," presumably referring to 1999–2001, "50 of 100 water authorities collected at least 75% of fees imposed on agricultural water users, 30 attained a collection rate of 50–75 percent, and 20 collected less than half of the user fees. Among urban units, the collection rate exceeds 90 percent" (2005, p. 220).

Table 20.10. *Investment in prevention and remediation of environmental pollution, 1991–2005*

	1991	1995	2000	2005
Environmental investment	17.0	30.7	101.5	238.8
As percent of GDP	0.84	0.68	1.13	1.30
As percent of annual investment	3.09	1.88	3.08	2.69

Note: Values are in billion current yuan and percent; annual GDP and investment are in current prices.
Sources: Data for 1991 and 1994 from Vermeer (1998, p. 956). Data for 2000 and 2005 from Yearbook (2004, p. 454; 2006, pp. 189, 444).

water diversion scheme" would rise "by around 80 per cent . . . to a total 225 billion yuan," with "the entire project . . . expected to cost 500 billion yuan . . . before 2050" appeared as a routine announcement that reflected no sign of alarm (Diversion, 2006). A figure of 500 billion yuan spread out over one decade would amount to roughly 0.4 percent of average annual gross capital formation each year and spread over two decades would be less than 0.2 percent of gross capital formation each year.[40]

Table 20.10 shows that annual investment in remediation and prevention of pollution, which does not include expenditures on water diversion projects, has jumped from under 1 percent of GDP in the early and mid-1990s to 1.1–1.3 percent in 2004–2005, figures that approach comparable totals for the United States, Japan, and Germany around 1990, when annual spending on environmental protection and pollution control ranged from 1.3 to 1.8 percent of GDP (O'Connor, 1994, pp. 177–178). For China, these outlays amount to no more than 3 percent of annual investment spending. Although these are sizable figures, high levels of current and projected future saving and investment mean that China's economy can easily support a much larger burden of expenditure on environmental remediation without endangering its prospects for rapid growth of output and productivity.

What of the possible impact of global warming on China's development prospects? When and if global warming leads to a major rise in the sea level, China, along with many other nations, will face large expenditures to move people out of flooded areas, notably in the lower reaches of the Yangzi River, or to build dikes to protect low-lying coastal cities. Of greater relevance to the next two decades, the challenge for China, and for other nations, is to restrict CO_2 emissions so that the worst effects of global warming do not occur. Success in this regard will

[40] Chinese gross capital formation in 2005 was 7,956 billion yuan. If it grew at 7 percent a year for two decades, it would reach over 30,000 billion yuan in 2025. Gross capital formation throughout the period would average around 16,000 billion yuan per year. Five hundred billion yuan spread over ten years would be 50 billion per year and over twenty years 25 billion yuan per year.

eliminate the need for remedial investments to control coastal flooding. Efforts to limit CO_2 emissions mainly involve improving the efficiency of energy use, an area in which China lags far behind international best practice. Japan's successful efforts to raise energy efficiency did not damage its economic prospects. We see no reason to expect similar conservation efforts to undermine Chinese economic growth.

We conclude that issues surrounding public health and environment, while confronting China's policymakers with a broad array of complex and difficult problems, seem unlikely to pose fundamental obstacles leading to downward revision of China's prospects for economic growth between now and 2025.

The Demand Side of the Sources of Growth

Most of the discussion in this chapter has approached the question of future growth from the supply side of the issue. But there are also elements on the demand side that will determine whether or not China will be able to sustain rapid growth over the next one to two decades. The contributions of the main expenditure categories to annual growth in China since 1979 are presented in Figures 20.5 and 20.6. There are two trends worthy of note in these figures. The first is that household consumption as a share of GDP declined steadily over time and came to just under 40 percent GDP in 2004 and 2005. The change in household consumption as a share of the change in GDP also fluctuated around a declining trend line and fell to a very small level below 30 percent of the increment to GDP in the years after 2001. The change in government consumption as a share of the change in GDP fluctuated year to year as well, peaking in the late 1990s when, as discussed earlier in this chapter, the Chinese government pump primed in an effort to keep the financial crisis of those years from depressing the growth rate of GDP.

The most notable trend in these charts, however, is that the annual change in exports accounted for a rising share of incremental expenditure on GDP and in the years 2003–2005 accounted for over half of that change in GDP. Put differently, without the extraordinarily rapid growth of exports in recent years, China very likely would have experienced a shortage of aggregate demand, and, unless the government had taken steps to prime the pump as in 1997–1999, the growth rate of GDP would have fallen markedly because of inadequate aggregate demand.

This contribution of the annual rise in exports to GDP was achieved thanks to a growth rate of exports over the past decade that averaged 17.7 percent per year (2005/1995) and averaged 29.9 percent per year over the last five years (2005/2000). There is a large import component to these exports, so the net impact on aggregate demand is moderated, but the point remains – Chinese growth in recent years has been highly dependent on an unusually high export growth rate.

It is highly unlikely that an export rate of growth of this magnitude can be sustained for even one more decade let alone two decades. Exports in 2005 reached U.S.$762 billion. At a growth rate of 15 percent per year, lower than the average of the past ten years, exports in 2015 would reach U.S.$3 trillion and would by then

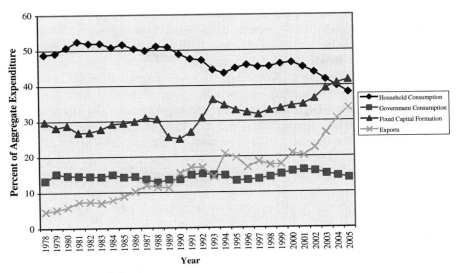

Figure 20.5. Principal components of GDP expenditure, 1978–2005

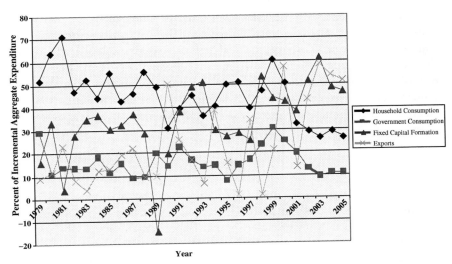

Figure 20.6. Principal components of incremental expenditure on GDP, 1978/1979–2004/2005

be growing at U.S.$450 billion per year. China's factories could probably produce this many toys, shoes, textiles, computers, cars, and television sets per year, but where would they find the markets for these goods? And if they could find the markets, would the importing countries tolerate for long the rapid adjustment that accommodating this massive import surge would require? This seems highly unlikely.

If China needs to sustain high export growth rates for exports to continue to be a main source of growth in GDP from the demand side, how high would that export growth rate have to be? If one assumes that GDP continues to grow at 9 percent a year over the next decade (or in current prices 12 percent per year with inflation at 3 percent annually), then a growth rate of exports (in current prices) at 12 percent a year would produce an annual increment to aggregate demand equal to around a quarter of Chinese GDP in the year 2014.[41] An export growth rate of 7 percent a year (in current prices), in contrast, would contribute only about one-tenth of the increment to GDP in the year 2014. For exports to be a major element in sustaining aggregate demand, therefore, they will have to grow at something like 9 percent per year in real terms or 12 percent annually in nominal terms. Total exports at that rate would reach nearly U.S.$2 trillion by the year 2015, for an average annual increase of more than U.S.$200 billion. Achieving even this lower figure will be a major challenge.

China, therefore, is probably going to have to find a way to stimulate domestic demand as the export share of increments to aggregate demand declines. How it achieves this shift inward in demand, however, could have a major impact on whether the country will be able to sustain a high GDP rate of growth over the next one to two decades. If demand has to be supported as it was in 1997–1999 by government running a fiscal deficit in order to fund expanded government consumption plus state investment in road and airport construction across the country, sustained productivity growth at high rates seems unlikely. High productivity growth is more likely to come from a higher growth rate (and a higher share of GDP) of consumer spending that in turn stimulates a higher or at least high growth rate in private investment. This chapter is not the place to outline the policies required to stimulate this increase in consumer demand, but it is an achievable goal.

CONCLUSION

Our objective in this chapter has been to forecast the broad outlines of Chinese economic growth to the year 2025. The central ingredients in our forecast are analyses of the likely path of factor inputs (labor, human capital, and physical capital) and, of most importance, TFP.

We began by reviewing the performance of China's economy between 1952 and 2005. During China's plan era (roughly, 1952–1978), GDP growth was sustained almost entirely by increases in capital and labor inputs with TFP actually at negative levels during the two decades 1957–1978. Beginning in the late 1970s, China's turn to economic reform brought dramatic change, with productivity emerging as a key driver of accelerated growth, both directly and, through its stimulus to the

---

[41] These calculations used the recently revised GDP figure for 2004 of RMB15,988 billion yuan (National Bureau of Statistics, 2005b).

acceleration of capital formation, indirectly. TFP recorded average annual growth of 3.8 percent between 1978 and 2005, with the pace slackening somewhat during the final decade.

We then used straightforward and, we believe, uncontroversial assumptions to project the growth of fixed capital, labor, and education to 2025. These projections show that the growth of labor, capital, and education alone can propel China's GDP growth at a maximum rate of less than 5 percent during 2005–2025, well below the average rate of 9.5 percent recorded during 1978–2005.

We then focus on productivity, beginning with the TFP implications underlying assumed annual GDP growth of 6 or 9 percent between 2005 and 2025. Because the productivity expansion required to support 9 percent annual growth seems unrealistically high (it is higher than what was achieved during 1978–2005), we focus on the likelihood that China can attain sufficient TFP growth to drive the economy forward at an average annual rate in the neighborhood of 6–8 percent during the two decades ending in 2025. That range does seem feasible over the next decade to 2015, but the upper end of this range appears to be unrealistically high for the entirety of the second decade from 2016 to 2025.

There are two reasons for our conclusion that the likely range of growth rates in this second decade falls between 5 and 7 percent per year. First, the rate of TFP required to sustain a growth rate of 8 percent is higher than the TFP rate sustained by China during 1978–2005 and much higher than TFP growth during 1995–2005. Second, the three economies that in earlier times were most like China's economy today (Japan, South Korea, and Taiwan) each sustained a growth rate for several decades similar to that achieved by China from 1979 through 2005, but each saw the rate of GDP growth rate fall sharply when per capita GDP rose above $13,000 measured in 2005 prices, using the PPP method. China's current per capita GDP in PPP terms is roughly $6,600 and, at a per capita growth rate of 6–7 percent a year, will surpass $13,000 in ten to twelve years.

These projections assume that China continues to enjoy a stable domestic and international political environment over these next two decades. But even if the political environment is stable, growth rates in the 6–8 percent range in 2006–2015 and in the 5–7 percent range in 2016–2025 are not a sure thing. These rates, even the lower end of the ranges, assume that China will continue to pursue economic reform and will maintain a high rate of savings and investment throughout these two decades. That China will sustain a high rate of investment or capital formation will not be seen as controversial by most economists who study the Chinese economy. Our belief that Chinese TFP will continue to grow at a high rate is likely to be more controversial.

In addition to dividing the sources of growth between factor inputs and TFP, one can also look at future growth prospects in terms of moving to the production possibility frontier and moving that frontier outward. Capital formation moves the frontier outward by expanding old industries and starting new ones. R&D expenditures also move the frontier outward and protection of IPRs is one way of ensuring that innovators have the incentive to develop new products and new ways of producing old products. Protecting IPRs in turn requires a legal system that is equitable, efficient, and can enforce its judgments – conditions that do not exist today. As we have shown above, however, China is clearly taking strides to raise R&D, protect IPRs, and strengthen the legal system, but there is a long way for China to travel before it has a system that compares in these areas with the more advanced industrial and postindustrial economies. Having a long way to go means that the expansion outward of the production frontier would slow in the absence of vigorous pursuit of reform in these areas, but it also means that the frontier will keep moving outward if China continues to strengthen its R&D together with steady improvement in the incentives for innovation and the capacity of the legal system to enforce those incentives.

Many of China's potential sources for continued productivity growth come not from moving the production frontier outward, but through moving toward the existing frontier from its current position that is well inside that frontier. Certain reforms discussed in this chapter and in other chapters in this book will play a central role in this regard. The two that we have emphasized in this chapter are the reform of ownership and finance.

China's productivity prospects will benefit from further reforms aimed at getting the state out of direct ownership and management of industrial and service sector enterprises. State ownership and management is clearly associated with lower rates of return than private ownership and management. China has made a great deal of progress in this regard, but, as in other areas, there is still a long way to go. Furthermore, even where private ownership and management exist, state administrative intervention remains necessary to manage efficiently such critical areas as bankruptcy and mergers and acquisitions. Reducing state administrative intervention, however, requires finding a substitute for administrative regulation in these and other areas, and that brings us back to the need to create and strengthen an independent, fair, and technically competent legal or regulatory system.

Moving toward the frontier depends critically on improving China's financial system. The waste connected with a system of investment allocation that is heavily influenced by politics and rent seeking is enormous. Again China has made progress in this area, but decisions particularly by the state owned banking system are still heavily influenced by politicians.

Other areas discussed briefly in this chapter that involve approaching the frontier include reallocation of labor from low-productivity activities in the rural areas to much more productive work in industry and urban services. We have also looked briefly at the challenge China faces in shifting a larger portion of aggregate demand from dependence on exports to a greater dependence on domestic demand.

Finally, in this chapter, we have looked at shocks to the economic system that could derail economic growth. A period of political instability is in this regard probably the greatest danger to China's continued growth, but the conditions that could bring this about are outside the scope of this book. We do, however, consider other potential shocks to the system, such as a major health crisis prompted by a pandemic, such as what might occur with SARS or H5N1 Avian Flu or if HIV/AIDS becomes more prevalent in the population. Some have suggested that China's current environmental situation could be a shock to the system that derails growth, but to do so the cost of cleaning up the environment would have to cut deeply into total capital formation and in China, as we have shown, this is unlikely to be the case. Even the severe water problems of North China and the cost of transferring large amounts of water from the Yangzi River north are well within China's financial capacity.

Our overall belief, therefore, is that China's economy will continue along a path of rapid growth over the next two decades. Our forecast envisions annual growth averaging 6–8 percent in real terms. While considerably below the 9.5 percent real growth recorded during 1978–2005, two decades of expansion at rates between 6 and 8 percent will deliver large increases in the absolute and relative scale of China's economy and in the standard of living available to China's nearly 1.5 billion citizens.

References

Alesina, Alberto, Sule Ozler, Nouriel Roubini, and Phillip Swagel. June 1996. "Political Instability and Economic Growth." *Journal of Economic Growth.* 1(2), pp. 189–211.

Alesina, Alberto and Roberto Perotti. 1994. "The Political Economy of Growth: A Review of the Recent Literature." *The World Bank Economic Review.* 8(3), pp. 351–371.

Bank of Korea. 2006. *Economic Statistics Yearbook 2006.* Seoul: Bank of Korea.

Barro, Robert J. May 1991. "Economic Growth in a Cross Section of Countries." *Quarterly Journal of Economics.* CVI(2), pp. 407–443.

Barro, Robert J. 1997. *Determinants of Economic Growth: A Cross-Country Empirical Study.* Cambridge, MA: MIT Press.

Bekaert, Gert, Campbell R. Harvey, and Christian Lundblad. 2006. "Financial Openness and the Chinese Growth Experience." Paper presented to the NBER China Working Group Meeting, Cambridge, MA, October 13, 2006.

Bhattasali, Deepak, Shantong Li, and Will Martin. 2005. *China and the WTO: Accession, Policy Reform, and Poverty Reduction Strategies.* Oxford: Oxford University Press and World Bank.

Bramall, Chris. 1989. *Living Standards in Sichuan, 1931–1978.* London: Contemporary China Institute, School of Oriental and African Studies, University of London.

Census, 1990. *Zhongguo 1990 nian renkou pucha ziliao* [Materials from China's *1990 Population Census*]. Beijing: Zhonguo tongji chubanshe.

Census Research, 2005. State Council Population Census Management Office and National Bureau of Statistics, Division of Population and Social Science and Technology Statistics, eds. *2000-nian renkou pucha guojiaji zhongdian keti yanjiu baogao* [Research Report on National-Level Key Topics From the 2000 Population Census]. Beijing: Zhongguo tongji chubanshe.

Chen, Hong. 2006. "Medical Insurance Regulation Benefits Migrant Workers." *China Daily.* May 16, 2006, p. 3.

Chen, Kuan, Gary H. Jefferson, Thomas G. Rawski, Hongchang Wang, and Yuxin Zheng. 1988. "New Estimates of Fixed Investment and Capital Stock for Chinese State Industry." *China Quarterly.* 114, pp. 243–266.

Ch'i, Hsi-sheng. 1991. *Politics of Disillusionment: The Chinese Communist Party under Deng Xiaoping, 1978–89*. Armonk, New York and London: M. E. Sharpe.

China Monthly Economic Indicators. Beijing.

China Monthly Statistics. Beijing.

deBrauw, Alan and Scott Rozelle. March 12, 2004. "Reconciling the Returns to Education in Rural China." Unpublished paper.

Defaulting. 2006. "No More Wage Defaulting." *China Daily*, October 27, 2006, p. 4.

Dickie, Mure and Raphael Minder. 2006. "China Makes Genuine Progress against Sellers of Fakes." *Financial Times*. January 17, 2006, p. 6.

Directorate General of Budget, Accounting and Statistics. 2005. *Statistical Yearbook of the Republic of China 2004*. Taipei: Directorate General of Budget, Accounting and Statistics.

Diversion. 2006. "Water Diversion Project Bill Sees 80% Rise." Accessed December 30, 2006, from www.chinaview.cn.

Dollar, David and Shang-Jin Wei. 2006. "Das (Wasted) Kapital: Firm Ownership and Investment Efficiency in China," in NBER China Workshop, Cambridge, MA.

Economy, Elizabeth. 2004. *The River Runs Black: The Environmental Challenge to China's Future*. Ithaca: Cornell University Press.

Feldstein, Martin. 1983, "Domestic Saving and International Capital Movements in the Long Run and the Short Run." *European Economic Review*. 21, pp. 129–151.

Fixed Asset Yearbook, 1997. *Zhongguo guding zichan touzi tongji nianjian 1950–1995* [China Yearbook of Fixed Asset Investment 1950–1995]. Beijing: Zhongguo tongji chubanshe.

Gao Mu, Shi Xisheng, and Zhou Xing. July 27, 2004. "Zhang Hanya: touzi tizhigaige hexin jiushi fangquan," *Jingji cankaobao* [Economic reference news]. Accessed October 8, 2004, from jjckb.xinhuanet.com/www/Article/200472794126-1.shtml.

Gao, Peirong, 1985. *Gongye qiye guding zichan guanli* [Fixed Asset Management for Industrial Enterprises]. Taiyuan: Shanxi renmin chubanshe.

Gao, Shangquan. 2005. "Shifting the Government's Role." *China Daily*. February 11, 2005, p. 6.

Garnaut, Ross, Ligang Song, Stoyan Tenev, and Yang Yao. 2005. *China's Ownership Transformation: Process, Outcomes, Prospects*. Washington, DC: International Finance Corporation.

GDP. 2004. "GDP Not the Only Goal." *China Daily*. February 17, 2004, p. 6.

Grimm, Bruce T. February 1998. "Price Indexes for Selected Semiconductors, 1974–96." *Survey of Current Business*. Accessed February 18, 2007, from http://bea.gov/bea/an/0298od/maintext.htm.

Guan Xiaofeng. 2006. "Beijing Issues IPR Policies for Companies." *China Daily*. April 14, 2006, p. 3.

Heston, Alan, Robert Summers, and Bettina Aten. October 1982. *Penn World Table Version 6.1*. Philadelphia, PA: Center for International Comparisons at the University of Pennsylvania (CICUP).

Holz, Carsten. 2003. "'Fast, Clear and Accurate:' How Reliable Are Chinese Output and Economic Growth Statistics?" *China Quarterly*. 173, pp. 122–163.

Holz, Carsten. March 2006. "China's Reform Period Economic Growth: How Reliable Are Angus Maddison's Estimates?" *Review of Income and Wealth*. 52(1), pp. 85–119.

Howe, Neil and Richard Jackson. 2004. *The Graying of China*. Washington, DC: Center for Strategic and International Studies.

Hsieh, Chang-Tai and Peter J. Klenow. 2006. "Misallocation and Manufacturing TFP in China and India," in NBER China Workshop, Cambridge, MA, October 2006.

Hua, Sheng, Xuejun Zhang, and Hsiao-peng Luo. 1993. *China: From Revolution to Reform.* Houndmills, Basingstoke, Hampshire, England: Macmillan.

Industry Census, 1985. *Zhonghua renmin gongheguo 1985 nian gongye pucha ziliao* [Materials on China's third industrial census in 1985], vol. 3. Beijing: Zhongguo Tongji chubanshe.

Industry Census, 1995. *Zhonghua renmin gongheguo 1995 nian disanci quanguo gongye pucha ziliao hubian* [Compendium of materials from China's 3rd national industrial census in 1995], general volume. Beijing: Zhongguo tongji chubanshe.

Industry Yearbook, 2001. *Zhongguo gongye jingji tongji nianjian 2001* [China Industrial Economy Statistics Yearbook 2001]. Beijing: Zhongguo tongji chubanshe.

Ishikawa, Shigeru, 1960. *Chûgoku ni okeru shihon chikuseki kikô* [China's mechanism of capital accumulation]. Tokyo: Iwanami Shoten.

Ishikawa, Shigeru. 1965. *National Income and Capital Formation in Mainland China; An Examination of Official Statistics.* Tokyo: Institute of Asian Economic Affairs.

Ito, Takatoshi. 1992. *The Japanese Economy.* Cambridge, MA: MIT Press.

Jiang, Wei. 2006. "M&As Emerge as Key Drawcard for Foreign Investment." *China Daily.* September 9–10, 2006, p. 5.

Keidel, Albert. 1992. *How Badly Do China's National Accounts Underestimate China's GNP?* Washington, DC: Rock Creek Research Inc E-8042.

Klein, Lawrence R., Huiqing, Gao and Liping Tao. 2005. "Estimation of China's Inflation Rate." Draft Paper 2005.

Kojima, Reiitsu. 2002. "On the Reliability of China's Economic Statistics with Special Reference to GDP." *The Journal of Econometric Study of Northeast Asia.* 4(1), pp. 15–30.

Kraay, Aart. 1996. "A Resilient Residual: Accounting for China's Growth Performance in Light of the Asian Miracle." Washington, DC: World Bank Policy Research Department.

Kraay, Aart. September 2000. "Household Savings in China." *World Bank Economic Review.* 14.3, pp. 545–570.

Kuijs, Louis. 2006. "How Will China's Saving-Investment Balance Evolve?" World Bank China Office Research Working Paper 5. Washington, DC: World Bank.

Lardy, Nicholas R. 2002. "Evaluating Economic Indicators in Post-WTO China." *Issues & Studies.* 38(4)–39(1), pp. 249–268.

Lardy, Nicholas R. 1984. "Consumption and Living Standards in China, 1978–83." *China Quarterly.* 100, pp. 849–865.

Li Weitao. 2005. "Electronics Giants May Soon Merge." *China Daily.* July 26, 2005, p. 9.

Li, Zijun. 2006. "China Issues New Regulation on Water Management, Sets Fees for Usage." Accessed January 9, 2007, from www.worldwatch.org/node/3892.

Liang Chao. 2005. "Water-Saving More Urgent Than Ever." *China Daily.* May 6, 2005, p. 2.

Lin, Justin Yifu, Fang Cai, and Zhou Li. 2003. *The China Miracle: Development Strategy and Economic Reform*, revised edn. Hong Kong: Chinese University Press.

Liu, Ta-chung and K. C. Yeh. 1965. *The Economy of the Chinese Mainland: National Income and Economic Development, 1933–1959.* Princeton, NJ: Princeton University Press.

Liu Wei, 2005. *Zhongguo shui zhidu de jingjixue fenxi* [Economic analysis of China's water system]. Shanghai: Shanghai renmin chubanshe.

Liu Weiling. 2005a. "Bad Medicine." *China Business Weekly.* November 7–13, 2005. p. 9.

Liu Weiling. 2005b. "Prince of Patents." *China Business Weekly.* October 31–November 6, 2005, p. 9.

Ma Lie. 2005. "Shaanxi Offers Free AIDS Treatment." *China Daily.* July, 15, 2005, p. 3.

Ma, Shao-jun, Sheila Hillier, Kong-lai Zhang, Jay J. Shen, Fan Lu, Min Liu, and Cheng-Gang Jin. 2006. "People's Republic of China," in *The HIV Pandemic: Local and Global*

Implications. E. J. Beck, N. Mays, A. W. Whiteside, J. M. Zunega, and L.-M. Holland, eds. New York and Oxford: Oxford University Press, pp. 282–299.

Maddison, Angus. 1998. *Chinese Economic Performance in the Long Run.* Paris: Development Centre of the Organisation for Economic Co-operation and Development.

Meng Lian and Wang Xiaolu, 2000. "Dui Zhongguo jingji zengzhang tongji shuju kexindu de guji [An evaluation of the reliability of China's statistics on economic growth]," *Jingji yanjiu* [Economic research]. no. 10, pp. 3–13.

Modigliani, Franco and Shi Larry Cao. March 2004, "The Chinese Saving Puzzle and the Life-Cycle Hypothesis." *Journal of Economic Literature.* XLII, pp. 145–170.

National Bureau of Statistics. 1999. *Comprehensive Statistical Data and Materials on 50 Years of New China.* Beijing: China Statistics Press.

National Bureau of Statistics. 2005b. "Key Achievements If the First National Economic Census with New Changes of China's GDP Aggregates and Its Structure." Press Release, Beijing, December 20, 2005.

Naughton, Barry. 2003. "The State Asset Commission: A Powerful New Government Body." *China Leadership Monitor* no. 8, 2003. Accessed. December 5, 2006, from http://www.hoover.org/publications/clm/issues/2904721.html.

Naughton, Barry. 2005. "SASAC Rising." *China Leadership Monitor.* no. 14, 2005. Accessed December 6, 2006, from http://www.hoover.org/publications/clm/issues/2903741.html.

Naughton, Barry. 2006. "Claiming Profit for the State: SASAC and the Capital Management Budget." *China Leadership Monitor.* no. 18, 2006. Accessed December 6, 2006, from http://www.hoover.org/publications/clm/issues/3294311.html.

O'Connor, David and Organisation for Economic Co-operation and Development Centre. 1994. *Managing the Environment with Rapid Industrialisation: Lessons from the East Asian Experience, Development Centre Studies.* Paris: OECD.

Ohkawa, Kazushi and Henry Rosovsky. 1973. *Japanese Economic Growth: Trend Acceleration in the Twentieth Century.* Stanford: Stanford University Press.

Ortolain, Alex. 2005. "China Moves from Piracy to Patents." *Wall Street Journal.* April 7, 2005, p. B4.

Pei Minxin. 2006. *China's Trapped Transition: The Limits of Developmental Autocracy.* Cambridge, MA: Harvard University Press.

Perkins, Dwight H. 1966. *Market Control and Planning in Communist China.* Cambridge, MA: Harvard University Press.

Perkins, Dwight H. 1980. "Issues in the Estimation of China's National Product," in *Quantitative Measures of China's Economic Output.* Alexander Eckstein, ed. Ann Arbor, MI: University of Michigan Press, pp. 246–273.

Perkins, Dwight H. 2004. "Corporate Governance, Industrial Policy, and the Rule of Law," in *Global Change and East Asia Policy Initiatives.* Shahid Yusuf, M. Anjum Altaf, and Kaoru Nabeshima, eds. Oxford: Oxford University Press and World Bank, pp. 293–336.

Perkins, Dwight H. and Lora Sabin. 2001. "Productivity and Structural Change," in *Industrialization and the State: The Changing Role of the Taiwan Government in the Economy, 1945–1998.* Li-min Hsueh, Chen-kuo Hsu, and Dwight H. Perkins, eds. Cambridge, MA: Harvard Institute for International Development, pp. 151–174.

Poon, Terence. 2006. "China Requires Legal Operating Software in PCs." *Wall Street Journal.* p. B3.

Rawski, Thomas G. 2001. "What's Happening to China's GDP Statistics?" *China Economic Review.* 12.4, pp. 347–354.

Rawski, Thomas G. 2005. "SARS and China's Economy," in *SARS in China: Prelude to Pandemic?* Arthur Kleinman and James L. Watson, eds. Stanford: Stanford University Press, pp. 105–121.

Rawski, Thomas G. 2006a. "Recent Developments in China's Labor Economy," in *Restructuring China*. Tomoyuki Kojima and Katsuji Nakagane, eds. Tokyo: Toyo Bunko, pp. 16–47.

Rawski, Thomas G. June 25, 2006b. "Urban Air Quality in China: Historical and Comparative Perspectives." Unpublished draft. Forthcoming in a volume edited by Nazrul Islam.

Rawski, Thomas G. and Zixia Sheng. 2008. "Overall Trends in China's Air Quality." Unpublished manuscript.

Ren, Ruoen. 1997. *China's Economic Performance in an International Perspective*. Paris: OECD.

Sachs, Jeffrey D. and Andrew Warner. 1995. "Economic Reform and the Process of Global Integration." *Brookings Papers on Economic Activity*. 1, pp. 1–118.

Sender, Henny. 2004. "Chinese Banks Slowly Learn to Walk on Own." *Wall Street Journal.* July 9, 2004, p. C1, C4.

Shirk, Susan L. 1993. *The Political Logic of Economic Reform in China*, California Series on Social Choice and Political Economy; 24. Berkeley: University of California Press.

Solow, Robert M. 1957. "Technical Change and the Aggregate Production Function." *Review of Economics and Statistics*. 39(3), pp. 312–320.

State Council Economic Census Group, 2005. *Diyici quanguo jingji pucha zhuyao shuju gongbao diyihao* [Report #1 of the Main Data from the First National Economic Census]. Issued by the Office of the State Council Leading Small Group for the First National Economic Census and the National Bureau of Statistics. Accessed December 6, 2005, from http://news.xinhuanet.com/fortune/2005-12/06/content_3883969.htm

Vermeer, Eduard B. December 1998. "Industrial Pollution in China and Remedial Policies." *The China Quarterly*. 156, pp. 952–985. Special issue: China's Environment.

Wang, Yan and Yudong Yao. 2001. "Sources of China's Economic Growth, 1952–99: Incorporating Human Capital." World Bank Policy Research Working Paper 2650. Washington, DC: World Bank.

Wang Ying. 2005. "Coal Giant Bids for Chemical Co." *China Daily*. July 1, 2005, p. 11.

Wang Ying. 2006a. "Power Companies Build Portfolios." *China Daily*. September 28, 2006, p. 11.

Wang Ying. 2006b. "Sinopec 'Buys Out Subsidiaries'." *China Daily*. February 9, 2006, p. 5.

Water 2005. "New Concept Wanted to Solve Water Shortage." *China Daily*. May 11, 2005, p. 4.

Wolf, Charles, Jr., K. C. Yeh, Benjamin Zycher, Nicholas Eberstadt, and Lee Sung-Ho. 2003. *Fault Lines in China's Economic Terrain*. Santa Monica, CA: RAND.

World Bank. 1981. *World Development Report 1981: National and International Adjustment*. Washington, DC: World Bank.

World Bank. 2007. *World Development Report 2007: Development and the Next Generation*. Washington, DC:

Wu Yong. 2006. "Engineering Firm Seeks Investors." *China Daily*. November 28, 2006, p. 10.

Wu, Zunyou and Sheena Sullivan. 2005. "China," in *Fighting a Rising Tide: The Response to AIDS in East Asia*. T. Yamamoto and S. Itoh, eds. Tokyo: Japan Center for International Exchange, pp. 76–95.

Xie Ye. 2005. "Foreign Firms Quit Power Sector." *China Daily*. January 20, 2005, p. 11.

Xin Dingding. 2006. "Water Conservation Helps Stop Money Going Down the Drain." *China Daily*. September 12, 2006, p. 1.

Xu Dashan. 2005. "Revised GDP for 2004 up by 16.8%." *China Daily*. December 21, 2005, p. 1.

Yang Cheng. 2006. "Storing More Water." *China Business Weekly*. September 4–10, 2006, p. 8.

Yearbook, Annual. *Zhongguo tongji nianjian* [China Statistical Yearbook].Beijing: China Statistics Press.

You Wan and Qi Jianguo, 2004. "China's Long Term Development Trend and Environmental Economy," *Caimao jingji* [Finance and trade economics]. 10, pp. 11–17.

Young, Alwyn. December 2003. "Gold into Base Metals: Productivity Growth in the People's Republic of China during the Reform Period." *Journal of Political Economy*.111, pp. 1220–1261.

Yu, Yongding. 2005. "China's Rise, Twin Surplus, and the Change of China's Development Strategy." Preliminary draft. Institute of World Economics and Politics, Chinese Academy of Social Sciences.

Yunnan. December 2, 2006. "China's Worst AIDS-hit Province Orders Compulsory Pre-Marital HIV Tests." *People's Daily Online*. Accessed December 8, 2006, from english.people.com.cn/200612/02(print20061202_327576.html.

Zhan Lisheng. 2006a. "Guangdong Vows to Encourage Self-Innovation." *China Daily*. February 28, 2006, p. 3.

Zhan Lisheng. 2006b. "No Reason to Panic over Lack of Oil in Guangdong." *China Daily*. April 29–30, 2006, p. 2.

Zhang Feng. 2006. "HIV/AIDS Cases Grow 30% in China." *China Daily 22 November*. Accessed December 8, 2006, from http://www.chinadaily.com.cn/china/2006-11/22/content_739378.htm.

Zhang Jun, Wu Guiying, and Zhang Jipeng. 2004. "Estimates of Tangible Capital Stock for China's Provinces, 1952—2000," *Jingji yanjiu* [Economics Research], no. 10, pp. 35–44.

Zhang, Junsen, Yaohui Zhao, Albert Park, and Xiaoqing Song. 2005. "Economic Returns to Schooling in Urban China, 1988 to 2001." *Journal of Comparative Economics*. 33, pp. 688–709.

Zhao Huanxin. 2004. "Nation Forms Quota Rules to Conserve Water Supply." *China Daily*. October 16–17, 2004, p. 2.

Zhao Xiao. 2002. "Unemployment Aid Needed." *China Daily*. October 31, 2002, p. 4.

Zheng, Caixiong, Yong Wu, and Nei Guo. 2005. "Rural Dwellers to be Granted Urban Rights." *China Daily*. November 2, 2005, p. 3.

Zhu Zhe. 2006. "Unions Help Migrant Workers Win Back Wages." *China Daily*. January 6, 2006, p. 2.

Index